Beneath the Mask

An Introduction to Theories of Personality

Seventh Edition

Beneath the Mask
An Introduction to Theories of Personality

Seventh Edition

Christopher F. Monte
Manhattanville College

Robert N. Sollod
Cleveland State University

WILEY

Sr. Acquisitions Editor   *Tim Vertovec*
Marketing Manager   *Kevin Molloy*
Production Editor   *Barbara Russiello*
Senior Designer   *Kevin Murphy*
Illustration Editor   *Anna Melhorn*
Photo Editor   *Sara Wight*
Cover Design   *Kevin Murphy*
Cover Photo   *Werner Forman Archive*

Cover: Lele mask from Kasai region, Zaire, 20th century

This book was set in 10/12 Times Roman by Matrix Publishing and printed and bound by Hamilton Printing Company. The cover was printed by Lehigh Press.

This book is printed on acid free paper. ∞

Library of Congress Cataloging-in-Publication Data

Monte, Christopher F.
    Beneath the mask : an introduction to theories of personality / Chritopher F. Monte, Robert N. Sollod.—7th ed.
        p. cm.
    Includes bibliographical references and indexes.
    ISBN 0-471-26398-2 (alk. paper)
    1. Personality—Philosophy.   I. Sollod, Robert N.   II. Title.

BF698 .M64 2002
155.2—dc21   2002191098

Printed in the United States of America

10 9 8 7 6 5 4 3

Only connect
E. M. Forster, *Howard's End*

I have striven
Not to ridicule,
Not to decry,
Nor to scorn
Human actions,
But to understand them.
Baruch Spinoza

Dedicated to

My cousin, Marilyn L. Colson,
For her love, example, and unflagging encouragement.

My parents, Bernard and Edith,
For their love, protection, and guidance.

And to
Learning without egotism.

RNS

About the Authors

Christopher F. Monte, Ph.D., died in December 1998. He had long been a Professor of Psychology at Manhattanville College in Purchase, New York. Dr. Monte was known for his thorough and thoughtful scholarship, which is well represented in *Beneath the Mask*. His other books include *Psychology's Scientific Endeavor, Still Life: Clinical Portraits in Psychopathology* and *Merlin: The Sorcerer's Guide to Survival in College.*

Dr. Monte received master degrees from Fairfield University in Counseling and the New School in Psychology, and his Doctorate in Clinical Psychology from St. John's University. Dr. Monte was selected to write the section on "Theories of Personality" for the American Psychological Association's *Encyclopedia of American Psychology,* which was published posthumously in 2000.

Robert N. Sollod, Ph.D., is a Professor of Psychology at Cleveland State University. He received his B.A. in Social Relations from Harvard University, an M.A. from Duquesne University in their psychology program emphasizing existential phenomenology, and a Ph.D. in Clinical Psychology from Teachers College, Columbia University. Dr. Sollod has studied with and interviewed many of the leading personality theorists about whom he has written in *Beneath the Mask* and elsewhere. Prior to moving to Ohio, Dr. Sollod taught at New York University and Yeshiva University.

Teaching at the college and graduate level, Dr. Sollod has been involved in wide-ranging scholarly activities and has maintained a professional practice since 1974. Areas in which he has published include the origins of personality theories and psychotherapeutic approaches, psychotherapy integration, spirituality and psychotherapy, religion and higher education. He contributed the section on "Religious Experience: Religious and Spiritual Practices" in the American Psychological Association's *Encyclopedia of American Psychology.* He is a longtime member of the Society for the Exploration of Psychotherapy Integration (SEPI).

Preface

Human nature has long been a matter of curiosity and great interest. People have always wanted to be able to understand and predict the behavior of others. The award-winning biologist and Pulitzer prize-wining writer Edward O. Wilson coined the term *biophilia*, to indicate the human love for and fascination with the life around us. How much greater is our caring for and interest in other people and their lives.

Until the 1900s, accumulating and conveying the understanding of human nature was left to philosophers, writers, and historians. Educated people tried to fathom human nature not only through personal experience but also by studying Plutarch, Plato, Baruch Spinoza, and Arthur Schopenhauer, reading William Shakespeare and Charles Dickens, and studying the lives of historical figures. Such knowledge, for all its depth and comprehensiveness, did not provide any type of systematic or testable way of looking at human nature.

With the advent of modern psychology, new ways of trying to understand human nature came to center stage. The great personality theories we are studying here are the results of the endeavor in the past century to discover and formulate new *understandings* of personality. These "grand theories" represent humanity's relatively recent flowering of inquiry into personality and human nature. They provide fascinating insights that have affected the ways in which we experience life as well as our thinking and our behavior.

ABOUT *BENEATH THE MASK*

Theories of personality are psychological models of human nature that, with surprising frequency, reflect the nature of their creators. *Beneath the Mask* presents classical theories of human nature, much as each theorist might if the theorist were to teach his or her ideas to people encountering them for the first time. Prominence is given to the theorist's progression of ideas, for often the sequence of the theorist's thinking and the changes embodied in the stream of ideas over time are more engaging and valuable than the final product. We intend to make it possible for the reader to go directly from an account of a theory in *Beneath the Mask* to the theorist's own works without the disorientation that comes from learning ideas in predigested textbook form.

A sympathetic approach to theories of personality is not new. What makes the seven editions of *Beneath the Mask* unique is this continuing emphasis on presenting the ideas of personality theorists *developmentally*. A developmental account of a personality theory necessarily incorporates the *personal origins of ideas* to illuminate the links between the psychology of each theorist and that theorist's own psychology of persons.

To be complete and consistent, a developmental approach to theories of personality requires some exploration of how the personal histories, conflicts, and intentions of the theorist entered that thinker's portrait of people. *Beneath the Mask* has emphasized the importance of understanding these personal sources from its first edition. Experience in the classroom with this approach is that it not only leads to a fuller understanding of the theories, but that it makes them memorable by scaling them to human proportions. Put another way, *Beneath the Mask* demonstrates how the thinking that led to the major theories is nested in the life experience of the theorists within the context of the surrounding culture. In many cases, we find that the theories represent creative solutions to problems experienced by the theorist.

One consequence of a developmental approach for teaching about theories of personality is that the efficiency of reducing complex theories to concise summaries of a few basic principles is lost. Gained is the more time-consuming, but also more interesting and exciting task of following the theorist's creative process, with many of its false starts puzzling personal questions and, one hopes, eventual solutions. There is an important advantage in this approach. Observing the thinking processes of idea-makers is an apprenticeship in cognition: Sometimes totally unaware that they are doing so, readers find themselves inductively reasoning to the solution of a problem as the theorist that they are reading about has done, or they deduce questions, see anomalies, or discover exceptions to a new theory in the way that a previously studied theorist might have done. Attention to thinking about psychological issues, along with its errors and sequential changes, teaches psychological thinking.

THE SEVENTH EDITION: A NOTE FROM THE CO-AUTHOR

Christopher Monte's death before the sixth edition was published created a vacuum that I have done my best to fill. I had been teaching a Theories of Personality course for almost three decades, much of that time using earlier editions of this text. I have long been devoted to the developmental approach of which Christopher Monte was so fond. This edition, I trust, preserves the best qualities of scholarship and erudition of Christopher Monte and, at the same time represents some new points of view, necessary updates, and other additions and changes made in the spirit of the earlier editions of *Beneath the Mask*.

NEW IN THE SEVENTH EDITION

Beneath the Mask, Seventh Edition, is a major revision. It reflects many of the current developments and emphases in psychological thought and the contribution of Edward O. Wilson.

The order of the chapters has been changed to emphasize chronology to a greater degree. For example, the chapters on Sigmund Freud and psychoanalysis are followed by ones on Alfred Adler and Carl Jung, rather than, as in previous editions, by the chapter on Anna Freud.

In order to keep the text timely and in response to readers' and reviewers' suggestions, some material has been removed. The chapter on Ronald Laing has been removed in this edition, and the material on existential phenomenology from that chapter has been placed in the chapter on Rollo May. Sections on the work of Robert White, Heinz Hartmann, and Erich Fromm have also been removed from the current edition. The material from the previous edition's Chapter 16, on John B. Watson, B. F. Skinner, Neal Miller, John Dollard, and Albert Bandura, has been expanded into two chapters: Chapter 14 in this edition is devoted to Watson and Skinner, and Chapter 16 explores the works of Dollard and Miller and Bandura. This was carried out to emphasize the cognitive aspects of the theorists in Chapter 16, rather than including them with two radical behaviorists.

PEDAGOGICAL CHANGES

- Glossaries of terms and concepts have been included for each chapter. These should facilitate reviewing the important concepts that are covered. Glossary terms are indicated in boldface type in the text. Please note that we define terms as used by the theorist or theorists emphasized in each chapter.

- The dates and places of the major theorists' births and deaths are listed at the beginning of each chapter.
- We have included "Only Connect" boxes in most chapters. These boxes point out connections between the ideas of one theorist and other ideas, usually of other theorists.
- The "For Further Reading" sections have been updated.

SPECIFIC CHANGES BY CHAPTER

Chapter 1 has been rewritten with a number of new emphases, one on how the student might best approach the subject of personality theory. We encourage a dialogue between students and the material concerning each of the theorists. Another emphasis is on the historical importance of the term *persona,* which alludes both to the mask which hides each of us as well as the person hidden beneath the mask. We consider the origins of the field of personality theory in the early twentieth century and the activity of Gordon Allport in helping to found this field of scholarly inquiry. In addition, we emphasize the many criteria that may be applied in evaluating personality theories. We removed the section on psychopathology, which is more appropriate to an abnormal psychology course. Material on the "Big Five" has been moved to Chapter 17.

Throughout *Beneath the Mask,* we have tried to encourage readers to see connections between human experience (including their own) and the theories about which they are reading. The approach in Chapter 1 and in the book as a whole is one that welcomes readers to explore with us various dimensions of human experience as unfolded in the lives and the thinking of the major personality theorists.

Chapter 2 includes an increased emphasis on Fraülein Bertha Pappenheim as a patient who contributed to psychoanalytic technique and as a prominent and fascinating person in her own right. In keeping with current scholarship, a more reserved view of Jeffrey Masson's critique of Sigmund Freud is presented.

In Chapter 3, some of the less relevant material on Sigmund Freud's neuropsychological model and on his concept of ontogeny recapitulating phylogeny has been omitted.

Changes to Chapter 4 include a broadened view of Carl Jung with reference to contemporary culture as well as some attention to controversies concerning his life. New material has been added concerning Jung's complex and ambivalent relationship with Freud. Connections between Jung's ideas and those of evolutionary psychology (Chapter 18) are indicated.

Chapter 5 (previously Chapter 8) includes a somewhat greater emphasis on Alfred Adler's humanistic optimism and the relevance of his thinking for contemporary problems. A brief discussion on the flexible application of his birth order hypothesis is included.

Chapter 6 (previously part of Chapter 4) more fully emphasizes Anna Freud's and Margaret Mahler's contributions to psychology. Anna Freud's nurturing approach in reaching out to children who survived concentration camps is highlighted. Her impact on the field of psychological assessment and on the legal system's greater accommodation of the needs of children is also emphasized.

Chapter 7 (previously Chapter 5) now includes some further critical comments relating to the theorists featured within—Melanie Klein, D. W. Winnicott, and Heinz Kohut.

Chapter 8 (previously Chapter 6) on Erik Erikson, includes a consideration of gerotranscendence, a possible ninth stage to be added to his eight stages of human development. His early research on play has been omitted. The chapter contains greater emphasis on the importance of identity in his life and in his theorizing—as well as some comments regarding a more flexible application of his theories.

Chapter 9 now has a greater emphasis on Harry Stack Sullivan's compassionate caring that, as much as his theoretical formulations, may have accounted for his therapeutic successes. The account of his death has been changed to more accurately reflect the surrounding circumstances.

Chapter 10 (previously part of Chapter 13) on the contributions of Karen Horney further emphasizes the importance of her viewpoint as a woman and indicates the relation between her ideas and those of Carl Rogers and Alfred Adler.

Chapter 11 (previously Chapter 14) on Gordon Allport, adds original material on Allport's life and development of his theories. The connection of his thinking with later cognitive theorists is indicated.

Chapter 12 (previously Chapter 11) on Rollo May's approach now includes concepts from phenomenology as well as the existential tradition. May is portrayed as an *existential phenomenologist* rather than as a pure existentialist.

Chapter 13 (previously Chapter 15) includes new material on Abraham Maslow's life, and a more complete understanding of some intellectual and philosophical roots of Carl Rogers' thinking. What some consider the fourth force, transpersonal psychology, is briefly introduced. Additional critical views of Maslow's approach are presented for the first time in order to achieve greater balance.

Chapter 14 (previously part of Chapter 16) on radical behaviorism has been modified only slightly. The strong criticism of John B. Watson, based on his personal flaws and scandals, has been toned down. The section on preparedness has been moved to Chapter 18.

Chapter 15 (previously Chapter 12) on George Kelly includes more about the impact of American culture on his inventive approach and also further material on the connection of his work with other theories and some recent developments in personal construct psychology.

In Chapter 16 (previously part of Chapter 16), the section on Albert Bandura emphasizes his contributions as a social cognitive theorist and includes original material on his life history and the development of his theories. Professor Bandura was kind enough to provide new material through correspondence with the author.

Chapter 17 on Hans Eysenck includes new material on his early life and iconoclastic personality as well as additional material on his many later contributions. Material on the "Big Five" theory in personality, based on factor analysis, has been added to this chapter.

Chapter 18 is a new chapter devoted to evolutionary psychology that explores the development of the major concepts of this theory. The chapter focuses, in particular, on Edward O. Wilson's life and thinking as well as the contributions of other important theorists. An effort is made to explain basic concepts of this theory so that the reader will have an understanding of how evolutionary psychologists actually approach questions about human behavior.

Chapter 19 remains largely the same, with a greater emphasis on the theorists as individuals who creatively formulated issues with which they were familiar and who developed solutions to them. A brief discussion of the theorists' creative roles within their cultural and social-historical contexts is included in the present edition.

A suggestion for students and professors: *Beneath the Mask: An Introduction to Theories of Personality* is a text rich in material. A good deal of this material is biographical and concerns details and important incidents in the theorists' lives. Much of this material can be read in a relaxed manner, as if it were a novel or short story, rather than a textbook every sentence of which has to be studied and memorized. It is suggested that professors encourage students to *absorb*, think about, and discuss the material related to the life history of the theorists and *study, learn* and *dialogue* with the important concepts, theories, and findings of each theory. We have included glossaries of important terms and concepts to assist in such learning. Attempts to study the life history material in a too-detailed way or to attempt to memorize it can result in frustration and the retention of relatively unimportant details, often at the expense of learning central concepts. The biographical material, when read with interest and curiosity, can lead to deeper understanding and greater retention of conceptual material.

Thanks to all those who helped with this edition. Included are Robert Denton, Barbara Durfey, Adriana Faur, Patrick McElfresh, Craig Madden, Irene Mathews, Brad Potthoff, Diane Rethinger, Rosalind Sackoff, and Rebecca Smolak. Susan Pantle further developed the *Instructor's Manual* and *Test Bank*. I have learned much over the years from many of my undergraduate and graduate students. Also members of my department and university offered support, information, feedback, and encouragement.

Quite a few people offered often extensive critical reviews and frank suggestions, many of which I accepted. Some also freely provided resource and autobiographical material. These included Albert Bandura of Stanford University, Cheryl Bluestone of Queensboro Community College, S. R. Coleman of Cleveland State University, Peter Ebersole of California State University-Fullerton, Kevin Keating of Broward Community College, Alan Lipman of Georgetown University, Donald McBurney of the University of Pittsburgh, Kathy Horton of Harvard University, Christine Osgood of Bethel College, Jackson Rainer of Gardner-Webb University, Paul Vitz and David Wolitzky of New York University, and Edward O. Wilson of Harvard University.

The team at John Wiley & Sons excelled in their activities. Tim Vertovec, senior acquisitions editor, encouraged me in the preparation of the manuscript. His editorial assistant Kristen Babroski handled the review process and attended to many details. Thanks to Kevin Murphy who prepared the design of the text and cover. Thanks to Sara Wight for all her enthusiastic help in securing the photos I requested, even as pages were coming in, and always putting in the effort to find something even better. Thanks to Joan Petrokofsky for her help in the beginning, especially for finding the mask used on the cover. Anna Melhorn has made sure that all of the art has found its way into this seventh edition. Kevin Molloy, marketing manager, is thanked for his attention to making sure this book finds its best position in the market. Kathy Drasky has copyedited and proofed this book, trying to make it as readable as possible. Kevin Mulrooney has toiled on the indexes, and helped catch final corrections. And Barbara Russiello has gracefully taken this book from manuscript through bound book with all parts almost magically falling into place.

WEBSITE

A website www.wiley.com/college/monte accompanies the present text. It consists of a Student Companion site and Instructor Companion site. The student site contains relevant links and other resource material. The instructor site contains the *Instructor's Manual* and the *Test Bank*.

Readers may contact me at my e-mail address:

r.sollod@csuohio.edu

My mailing address is:
Robert N. Sollod
Department of Psychology
Cleveland State University
2121 Euclid Avenue
Cleveland, OH 44115

Contents

Beneath the Mask

An Introduction to Theories of Personality

Seventh Edition

Chapter 1

Basic Issues and
Varieties of Theory

*It will happen for a time, that the pupil will find his intellectual power has grown by
the study of his master's mind. But in all unbalanced minds, the classification is
idolized, passes for the end, and not for a speedily exhaustible means, so that the walls
of the system blend to their eye in the remote horizon with the walls of the universe.*

Ralph Waldo Emerson

*And so these men of Indostan
Disputed loud and long,
Each in his own opinion
Exceeding swift and strong,
Though each was partly in the right,
And all were in the wrong!*

John Godfrey Saxe

A USEFUL METAPHOR: THE MASK AND THE PERSON BENEATH

"The terms **personality** in English, *personalité* in French, and *personlichkeit* in German closely resemble the *personalitas* of medieval Latin. In classical Latin *persona* alone was used. All scholars agree that this word originally meant mask." These words were written by the American psychologist, Gordon Allport (1961, p. 25).

Allport further traced the meaning of the term **persona** to an even earlier phrase in Latin: *per sonare,* meaning "to sound through." The phrase "per sonare" or, literally, "to make sound through" referred to the mouthpiece of the theatrical mask through which an actor's voice was projected. Subsequent meanings as cited by Allport demonstrate that the meaning of the term *persona* slowly evolved to a more abstract designation indicating the appearance—the mask—and referring *also* to the person beneath it (Allport, 1961). The **mask metaphor** frequently occurs in personality theories and is a major theme in this text.

Allport has noted the difference between his approach to personality and that of Freud:

> Freud used the word *character,* not *personality.* . . . And most Europeans prefer the word *character* (derived from the Greek word, meaning an "engraving" or "imprinting," therefore something inner, permanent, and inborn). In contrast, Americans have preferred the word *personality*, which . . . derives from persona or mask. Thus, the typical American approach placed relatively more emphasis on social interaction, appearance, and contact to the world, while European characterology stresses more the inner engraving, the fatalistic "stamp." Freud, therefore, says character's guidelines are set by the age or three or five as the case may be. There is, in any case a different feeling in the two terms, *character* and *personality.* (Allport, 1962, p. 1)

Gordon Allport as a Personality Theory Pioneer

Allport was one of the founders of academic personality theory. He drew together the various scraps of research in the then, nonexistent field, did his graduate dissertation on the topic, and developed the first college course taught on the subject of personality. Most courses on personality theory are descendants of his course, which he taught with a great sense of mission from the 1930s through the 1960s at Harvard University.

In 1962, Allport recounted the courage and emerging sense of self-direction necessary for him as a young graduate student to pursue the field of personality as a subject for his dissertation:

> . . . each graduate student was allowed to say in two or three minutes what he was working on for his Ph.D. thesis. It came around to my turn and I said I was trying to make an experimental study of the traits of the human personality. Titchener [a leading experimental psychologist] glared at me. . . . [t]he silence seemed like an hour but probably it was a minute. . . . It was a cruel cut for a young graduate student! (Allport, 1962, p. 3)

Allport continued that his more supportive mentor, who had seen the event, later took him aside and said,

> "Oh, you *don't* care what Titchener thinks." And it suddenly occurred to me I didn't care— it was irrelevant. I think that event probably was a benign trauma because over the succeeding years, I have not cared what my colleagues thought and that's been fortunate. I have definitely been a maverick, a minority deviant in modern psychology. But, I couldn't care less. It doesn't trouble me and I think this early experience has something to do with it. (Allport, 1962, p. 3)

BEGINNING THE STUDY OF PERSONALITY

I remember that, as an undergraduate science major taking a personality psychology course[1] for the first time, I thought it would be a course about only the superficial, surface aspect of people. One of my quickly corrected misconceptions was that it would be a course about popularity, charisma, or personal attractiveness. Some people, I thought, had a "lot of personality" and others did not. I wondered if it was plausible to teach a whole course around this subject.

When I first entered the course, I found that the professor often spoke about the surface of a person—the observable behaviors. It turned out that only some of these behaviors had to do with popularity. I shortly discovered that the personality course also looked beneath the surface to probe the depths and wellsprings of human nature. At times, it went far beneath the surface—*beneath the mask.*

And the adventure I began then in learning to look beneath the surface, to understand or "stand under" the surface, has continued throughout my life and in my work. This adventure has enriched my life and the lives of many other students of personality. Christopher Monte was certainly fascinated and gained much insight over the years by endeavoring to understand the topic of personality and to explore in some depth the personalities of the theorists themselves.

One concept that intrigued me even as a science major entering a personality course was that the human personality is a fundamental unit and level of organization. Knowing a lot about atoms and molecules did not seem to lead directly to much knowledge about personality. Furthermore, personality seemed to be a vital level to study as it seemed to be midway between the microscopic on one hand and the great dimensions of culture, society, and history on the other. In addition, persons are sentient and conscious beings. I did not think it possible to attribute these qualities to molecules, to nations, or to galaxies.

Around this time I discovered the philosophy of personalism, which recognized the inherent value and dignity of the human person. It questioned any type of subordination of the individual to political or economic structures or even to cultural trends. Some spiritual teachings indicated that saving the life of a person was equivalent to rescuing a whole world from destruction. At any rate, personality seemed a topic well worthy of study—even to my mind so steeped in a scientific subculture.

In addition, there was the sense of mystery and unknowability about personality. *How many people fully understand themselves? How many of us can describe our own personalities accurately?* Most of us are, at best, knowledgeable about a few other people and ourselves. New acquaintances may appear mysterious and unpredictable to us until we construct a theory that is more or less adequate to explain and predict their behavior. I was hoping that the Theories of Personality course might provide tools for me to gain greater insight into the people around me, and into myself as well.

As you encounter the theories in this text, it will be interesting to notice if and how the person–mask dichotomy is handled. A theorist may be concerned with peripheral variables that are easily observable—mask, or with central variables that touch upon the very core—the inner person. Some psychologists see no reason to look for "an inner person" when overt behavior is adequate for scientific study or prediction and control of specific behaviors. These psychologists think that theories of personality should attend only to observable behavior with no inferences or assumptions about an inner core of experience.

---

[1] Professor Gordon Allport taught this course.

And a few theorists avoid the distinction between the outer and inner aspects of the psyche altogether.

Those theorists who tried to integrate the inner and outer perspectives hoped personality psychology would be able to reconstruct the whole person and weld together the elements of person and mask into a unified framework. Sigmund Freud emphasized the distinction between the surface and what was beneath it and included aspects of both in his model of the psyche. Carl Gustav Jung considered the persona to be the image presented to others, the social role, as contrasted with the sum total of the person's conscious and unconscious psychic life. He viewed it as one part of a more inclusive whole, which he termed the *psyche*.

ONE TRUTH OR MANY PERSPECTIVES?

When you start to explore the different theories of personality, you will discover many ways of looking at and making sense of personality. The theories are different in their assumptions, the data or evidence they consider, and their conclusions. Some seem diametrically opposed. It is helpful to realize that, if all psychologists agreed on only one way of looking at personality, then there would be no need for a text about "theories" of personality. We could proceed with a single theory that is accepted by all. There is, particularly in academic settings, a tendency for some specialists to advocate a single theory. Perhaps you have had a professor who is such an adherent. Advocating a single theory is useful for focus and for networking, but the subject of personality is so complex that it is difficult to imagine how one single theory would suffice to explain all that we need to know about human behavior.

A Latin phrase is relevant: *Cave hominem unius libri.* Translated literally, it means "Beware the man of one book." It means that people who have a single slant or perspective do not have a balanced or reliable view. This is true of psychology. The well-educated psychologist has a broad background and is familiar with many views and theories—even though he or she may prefer a specific approach. Every theory has some strengths and some weaknesses, and we should be honest enough, even when we prefer a given approach, to be aware of its shortcomings.

Another concept that may be helpful to students of personality is the limitation of **reductionism,** or what could be more colloquially termed "nothing-but-ism." A biologist, who may believe that the cell is the building block of life, may conclude that life is nothing but the behavior of cells. A Freudian may notice nothing but psychodynamics. A behaviorist who has studied patterns of reinforcement and extinction, may conclude that behavior is nothing but those patterns. A cognitive theorist may conclude that personality is nothing but the result of cognitive structures or schemas.

Some personality theorists themselves were passionately involved in trying to prove or argue that their theories were true and that others were false. Some of the theorists were inspired by the idea that their predecessors' ideas—particularly in the case of Freud—were in some way limited or wrong. Allport, for example, is known to have repeated the quote that, as far as the unconscious was concerned, "Freud went down deeper, stayed longer and came up dirtier than anyone else." Freud, for his part, pushed Alfred Adler out of being the editor of a psychoanalytic journal. He wrote, "I have finally got rid of Adler. . . . The damage is not great" (Freud, in Freud & Jung, 1974, p. 376). Jung reported hearing an explosion when he was in a room with Freud. He later curiously explained that he thought this explosion was caused by his irritation with Freud's reluctance to accept his ideas concerning the paranormal (Jung, 1961, p. 155).

Such feuding seems silly and unprofessional, but we need to acknowledge that the great personality theorists were, as we shall see in this text, visionaries and people of ideas. Sigmund Freud wanted people to acknowledge and understand that their real motives were often not as lofty and idealistic as they thought—to acknowledge that they were often hypocrites regarding sex and aggression. He wanted humankind to be elevated by a small group of psychoanalyzed people with a greater degree of self-knowledge and rationality than the common person. Gordon Allport was concerned about the loss of individuality that was accompanying the rise of psychological science. Carl Jung had a deep commitment to understanding the spiritual dimension of human existence, and Carl Rogers wanted psychologists and people in general to agree with him that personal freedom is a fundamental goal. The descriptions and theories of personality by these individuals are not mere neutral descriptions. Their visions of what life is and what life should be are as distinctive and different as the visions of artists such as a Vincent Van Gogh, Norman Rockwell, or Thomas Eakins.

Students of personality thus have a problem. How can we come to grips with various theories with differing concepts—each proclaiming itself to be uniquely true? One answer comes from the philosophy of **pluralism**—the notion that there are many realities and that more than one perspective may be correct. Regarding the theories of Freud and Rogers, for example, it could be that their life experiences and thinking revealed to each of them a different aspect of personality. A phenomenological psychologist would say that each was attuned, or open, to different realities.

It is an intellectual and emotional challenge for both the beginning and advanced student of personality theory to understand the differences between the theorists without siding immediately with one or a few and against the others. Cognitive developmental theorists would see the steps in addressing this challenge as first one of seeing some value in all theories, and then finally siding with a specific theory to which one may become committed (Perry, 1970). This process is parallel on a higher level to the ability to take different visual perspectives—to imagine, for example, what a group of objects might look like when seen from the side or from the back, and then choosing a preferred perspective.

The theorists themselves occasionally tried to understand why they disagreed with their colleagues. Jung was perplexed by the differences between Freud and those around him, including Adler and Jung himself. He said that he developed the theory of psychological types to explain these huge differences. In other words, their conceptions of personality were different because they were temperamentally different.

In this text, we point out that these theorists had different life experiences—especially different childhood experiences. They spent their formative years under a variety of historical, social, and cultural influences, took different paths in life, and had different values. We will see how many theories of personality arose as a creative response on the part of a theorist to the difficult circumstances and challenges of his or her life. Furthermore, each of their life histories occurred within a specific context. In brief, we find that each of the major personality theorists was aware of different aspects of experience and of personality.

What approach do we take in presenting most of the actual theories of personality in this text? We follow the history of each theory's development and demonstrate its progression through the "changes of mind" that its creator may have experienced. We seek to illuminate each theorist's own struggle to understand human nature.

PERSONALITY THEORIES: CREATIVE SOLUTIONS TO PERSONAL PROBLEMS

One question often arises when students think about a career in psychology or in one of the other mental health professions: If I have difficult psychological problems, does this necessarily make me less qualified to help others? The answer provided by the lives of some of the major personality theorists is that your problems may provide a source of understanding and of personal growth. Alfred Adler developed a theory that one's approach to life was a creative response to feelings of weakness and helplessness as a child. Many of our theorists had troubled lives. Having problems, however, is neither a necessary nor sufficient background for a person to become a creative theorist. Problems often have the silver lining of drawing a person's attention to the realm of personality and to the necessity of developing self-knowledge and the knowledge of others. This is true of many people who intend to make helping others psychologically a career focus. Once a person's attention is focused on their problems, they should work toward a successful resolution of them.

A theory of personality and of psychotherapy is often a theorist's means of passing on his or her personal approach or solution to life's difficulties to others. For example, we will find in the case of Sigmund Freud an intense and unwavering introspection, with Carl Jung an ability to merge visions and fantastic inner experiences, with Carl Rogers a focus on an optimistic approach to the challenges of the present, and with Erik Erikson an attempt creatively to develop a unique identity. We take the position in this book that we want to understand the personality theories deeply and unforgettably by trying to understand something about the lives of the theorists and how and why they developed the theories for which they are known.

This approach has the advantage that we will see some theories in terms of the life experiences of the personality theorists and in the social-historical contexts from which the theories emerged. It will become clear, for example, how Freud's theory was a response to many of the difficulties of his own life as well as a response to upper-middle-class European morality at the end of the nineteenth century. Decades later, Carl Rogers' more optimistic theory of personality was deeply connected to and reflective of his own approach to life and affected by trends in American culture and society in the middle of the twentieth century.

Henri Ellenberger (1970) has advanced the notion that a wide range of influential psychological theories have their origins in what he termed the creative illnesses of their creators. A creative illness, or a psychological malady deeply intertwined with a creative process and perhaps contributing to it, can take a variety of forms, ranging in intensity from mild anxiety through neurotic maladjustment to psychotic separations from reality (Ellenberger, 1970, p. 447). The dominating preoccupation is absorption with some intellectual-creative problem involving attempts to make social reality intelligible. The stricken, creatively ill persons become intensely preoccupied with a search for the truth; they become absorbed with self, suffering intense feelings of isolation until, suddenly, the suffering ends abruptly. The termination period is often marked by feelings of exhilaration: "The subject emerges from his ordeal with a permanent transformation in his personality and the conviction that he has discovered a great truth or a new spiritual world" (Ellenberger, 1970, p. 48). Ellenberger regards such major figures as Sigmund Freud and Carl Jung as illustrative cases. He believes they had each resolved their creative illness through the creation of a generalized theory of human nature.

Ellenberger's concept of creative illness is a valuable one. Dramatic and acute personal disturbances are involved in the origination of many theories. In addition to Sigmund Freud and Carl Jung, the clearest cases for creative illness in the theorists we review in *Beneath the Mask* can be made for Alfred Adler, Erik Erikson, and Rollo May. There is less certainty regarding Karen Horney, Carl Rogers, and the behaviorist, B.F. Skinner. In the chapters devoted to each of these theorists, we consider a possible creative illness as the source of their creativity. In other instances, such as that of social learning theory, there is no evidence for the validity of the creative illness hypothesis.

WHAT ABOUT ABNORMAL PSYCHOLOGY?

Most personality theory textbooks do not focus on the specific topic of abnormal psychology. That is another discipline and is centered on the causes, descriptions, diagnoses, and treatments of pathological conditions. Such a project is outside the scope of this text. Much of the formal field of abnormal psychology falls within the medical model of mental disorder. Yet, there is a good deal of overlap between the two fields even though their emphases are very different. In the present text, we will thus consider how each theorist approaches—if at all—the question of psychopathology within each chapter.

From their onset, many theories of personality were constructed with close attention to the abnormal. Psychopathology was seen as an extreme example. By deciphering what had gone wrong in atypical cases, principles could be derived that would explain the typical. With some exceptions, theorists peered into the depths of their own and others' psychopathology to construct their vision of general personality functioning. Sigmund Freud began the trend as early as 1895 with his first model of personality that he described as a "general psychology" with equal importance for normal and abnormal functioning (Freud, 1895, pp. 283–284). But, in truth, his neurologically based theory of personality was derived largely from the treatment of hysterical conversion and other "neurotic" disorders.

Other personality theories had little basis in psychopathology and were based on studying normal or exceptionally healthy or creative people. Gordon Allport's trait theory and Abraham Maslow's concept of self-actualization are two such theories, as is George Kelly's idea that each person is a theory-builder, which is an example of a theory having to do with normal, active coping. Maslow's study of "self-actualization" is parallel to medicine's consideration of "wellness" as more than the simple absence of disease.

It is important to consider that our points of view and values are sometimes involved in the judgment of what is pathological and what is not. One example is that in totalitarian societies with great pressure for conformity, holding certain political opinions may be taken as evidence of psychopathology. In the 1980s, to take a much-noted example, many Soviet dissidents were hospitalized with the diagnosis of "creeping schizophrenia." This diagnosis was based largely on their opinions, social activism, and, in some cases, a judgment reinforced by their belief in God. One of the authors of the present book was acquainted with a street person hospitalized in one of our local medical centers. The street person viewed his mania as a valuable mental state. As expected, he quit taking his medications after discharge. Many children who are currently diagnosed with attention deficit and hyperactivity might have not been so diagnosed only a few years ago. We might ask whether more children are now suffering from this condition or whether our criteria have changed as a result of different expectations. A person with a pattern of changing jobs and partners may be viewed as self-actualizing, narcissistic, or unstable depending on one's perspective. There are many reasons to believe that diagnostic criteria are highly context-dependent.

In addition, as we explore the different personality theories, we will find different explanations for pathology, such as inadequate defenses (Freud), blockage of personal growth (Rogers), faulty conditioning (Skinner), responses to hypercompetitive upbringing (Horney), or lack of balance in psychological development (Jung).

For example, let us examine the case of a college student who is experiencing depression. He is showing the signs of clinical depression and may receive a corresponding diagnosis. Different theories of personality would often lead to varying ways of conceptualizing and understanding the phenomenon of depression. A Freudian psychoanalyst may suspect that the depression is caused by vulnerabilities stemming from the person's childhood experiences. But a Jungian or a practitioner informed by the theories of Erik Erikson may see the depression in terms of having unfulfilled potential for adventure or for involved and caring behavior. Adlerians might see it as resulting from a lifestyle of avoiding challenges, and psychologists in the tradition of Karen Horney might analyze it as a reaction to unloving parenting involving an emphasis on hypercompetitive behavior. A behaviorist may see the depression as a response to a reduced amount of positive reinforcement in this student's environment. A cognitive theorist might consider the depression a consequence of the student's negative views or self-talk. And a psychopharmacologically-oriented practitioner may view the depression in terms of serotonin depletion. These varying explanations have different implications for our attitude toward, and treatment of, depression. What is confusing is that these explanations are not necessarily mutually exclusive.

Psychology does not have as many elaborately defined categories for normal or healthy behavior as for the pathological. This gap reflects a century of emphasizing disorders and deficiencies. In the study of personality we want to try to understand and use theories that explain not only pathological behavior but also normal, healthy, creative, inspiring, achieving, or courageous behavior. The millennial positive psychology movement, which addresses the question of optimal psychological functioning, is currently a very active area of psychological research and theorizing. Some personality theories welcome the study of the whole range of human behavior—from the difficult-to-understand mutterings of people in the dreariest mental hospitals to the daily life of the so-called average person to the achievements of the greatest scientists and artists. Many theories may focus only on health or illness, but it is possible for theoreticians to cover the whole gamut.

EVALUATING THE THEORIES:
PERSONOLOGY OR PERSONALITY THEORY?

One issue in the field of personality is the distinction between personologists and other investigators of personality. Personologists have had distinctively different research traditions and conceptual strategies from that of psychologists who have traditionally been known as personality theorists. Henry A. Murray, an early pioneer of **personology,** defined the concept this way:

> The branch of psychology that principally concerns itself with the study of human lives and the factors that influence their course, which investigates individual differences and types of personality, may be termed "personology" instead of "the psychology of personality". . . . (1938, p. 4)

As Robert White, one of Murray's students and himself an eminent **personologist** explained, Henry Murray came from a tradition of medical research where multiple sources of information, detailed diagnostic interviews, and complete histories were routine procedure. What was not routine was Murray's incorporation of these detailed, clinical methods into personality psychology. At Harvard, in the 1930s, Murray set up a Diagnostic Council of clinical psychologists and graduate students in clinical psychology. Members of the council included students and faculty who would later go on to shape the field of personality, among them Gordon Allport, Erik Erikson, Robert White, and Murray himself. The goal was to examine in detail individual life histories using every method they could devise or borrow: experimentation, observation, interviewing, personality testing, life history analysis, and direct contact of every member of the council with every subject in the research program. The work led eventually to Murray (1938) and his collaborators' classic book *Explorations in Personality*. As White has pointed out, there has been a dearth of efforts in psychology to study the individual personality in all of its complexity and richness (see Sanford, 1985). We prefer sometimes to give two personality tests to a group of people and simply correlate the results as if that were somehow indicative of this intricate and elaborate system called personality.

> Of course there are many elaborations upon this design, introducing experimental situations, different treatments, and highly sophisticated statistical procedures. But none of these entail any real personal contact with the subjects or any attempt to think of them as more than momentarily living people. For some time I have described this type of research as *studying personality without actually looking at it.* (White, 1981, p. 15; italics in original)

Most of the theories we examine have a long historical development. And some of the theories reflect, sometimes to a surprising degree, the richness of the human personality in the tradition of personology. But something is lost for what is gained in detail and complexity. As we shall see, many of the theories are more literary and less scientific than we would like. Striking a balance between study of the individual and obtaining generalizable results is a very difficult art.

Impact of Culture and Society

Students of personality are becoming increasingly aware of the influence of culture and society on the makeup of personality. The study of *multicultural dimensions* of personality is only at its beginning, and we have only a beginning understanding of how personality may differ across cultures. It appears quite likely that certain givens in our Western psychological view, such as the existence of an "identity crisis," are far from universal. One European scholar, J.H. Van Den Berg (1961), argued that the assumption of a fixed human nature was not well taken. Many areas we considered to be part of human nature, he asserted, were actually culturally determined. For example, the stage of adolescence might be viewed as a historical development or invention. Teenagers in the 1800s were considered capable of doing adult work and starting their own families. They did not go through the modern experience of adolescence, which includes a major emphasis on identity issues. Furthermore, the sheltered innocence and naïveté taken as a hallmark of childhood in the 1950s is no longer the case. Many of the theories of personality we are considering do not take into account the makeup of the culture or of the society in which they were formed, even though it is evident that cultural factors had a strong influence on the theories.

Some theorists have taken the position that there are numerous commonalities through time and cross-culturally. These theorists draw from various sources. Carl Jung looked at many cultures to find similar themes. Behaviorists sometimes focus on similarities between humans, all primates and, at times, among all vertebrates. **Evolutionary psychologists** (Chapter 18), making new and, at times, controversial contributions to personality theory, see human behavior in light of underlying commonalities that have come to exist through evolutionary processes.

So, in some way, it appears that both those who argue for the variability of human behavior and the constancy of human nature have some convincing arguments and much evidence on their side. One possible answer is to see the possibility of constancy of human nature and, at the same time, differences and changes that are occurring. Behaviorists understand that conditioning is a given for everyone, but the specific behaviors that might be learned are infinitely variable. In Freud's theory, for example, the formation of a superego is a developmental given, but the contents of a person's superego vary according to upbringing. A person brought up as a pirate, for example, would not consider looting and pillaging particularly guilt provoking.

It is thus possible for personality to be seen as having structural or relatively unchangeable elements as well as content—elements that change. For each theory that we will examine, we may inquire how much the theory sees human nature as immutable and how much it views personality as a protean phenomenon—able to take on many forms. Often this fixed-flexible dimension is seen as a polarity, but, as indicated, some theories represent both fixed and changeable aspects to personality.

The same holds true for the apparent nature-nurture dichotomy. Regardless of how extreme an advocate of nature or nurture we might be, we have to admit the vital importance of the other side. Theories emphasizing the importance of the family environment nevertheless take for granted certain aspects of genetics and the physical environment. Those emphasizing the importance of biological variation assume that the environment is within certain limits. So, we may consider within each theoretical framework the relative impact of nature and nurture. One way of classifying theories is to consider to what extent they emphasize either nature or nurture. We may consider what aspects of nature or nurture are emphasized.

Sometimes personality theories contain within themselves contradictory elements or paradoxes that make evaluating and classifying them quite difficult. This is particularly true of theories that involve psychotherapy. That aspect of the theory used to describe the patient or client is often different from the implicit or explicit view that the theory has of the therapist. For example, psychoanalytic theory views people as largely reactive and driven by unconscious dynamics. However, it is precisely the trained psychoanalyst who has transcended this condition. Rogers' therapist is a person who has learned to be focused on the "other," whereas the Rogerian client is focused on his or her own feelings.

EVALUATING PERSONALITY THEORIES

To evaluate a theory of personality is not simple, and the job demands complex tools. There are so many dimensions on which to compare and to rate theories of personality that the task can be daunting. For someone coming to the field for the first time, the wealth of qualities that can be assessed may obstruct the opportunity of discovering common elements or important strengths and weaknesses.

THREE MAJOR TOOLS:
REFUTABILITY, AGENCY, AND IDIOGRAPHIC FOCUS

Our strategy is to emphasize, in our presentation, three fundamental dimensions to evaluate the theories in this book. At the end of each chapter, you will find an evaluation section in which we discuss the theory at hand in terms of three qualities that give substantial information about the theory's empirical usefulness, validity, and model of human nature. The three qualities we will emphasize as tools of analysis are:

1. **Refutability:** Does a theory state what it would take to prove itself wrong? Scientific theories are refutable or testable, and unscientific ones are not. In general, refutability assures some measurable degree of accuracy, usefulness, and predictive power. The most refutable theories are sometimes less helpful in understanding the complexities of individual experience and behavior. Some aspects of a theory may be testable while others are not.

2. **Active** or **passive human agency:** Does the theory picture people as passive receptacles of reality? Or are they active agents who shape their own inner and outer realities? Does a theory embody a combination of both views?

   3. Idiographic or **nomothetic focus:** Does the theory emphasize the uniqueness or pattern of particular qualities that an individual embodies? Or does it instead explore the general universal aspects of human behavior? Does a theory embody some interactive combination of idiographic and nomothetic focus?

Tool One: Refutability

Refutability (testability) relates to whether there is an empirical basis to the theory and to whether a given theory of personality leads to any specific predictions about behavior. Prediction and control are the usual criteria for scientific theories. A theory may be plausible and have internal consistency and a good deal of comprehensiveness and yet not be helpful in predicting and controlling behavior.

All theories of personality must rely at some point on observed behavior. Each approach begins with observable behavior, albeit to a different degree. Unconscious states, for example, are not directly observable in themselves. Yet even an orthodox Freudian analyst must pay attention to how people actually behave as the result of these underlying states. In the end, whether the theorist postulates an unconscious conflict, frustration of a biological drive, arousal of a brain mechanism, or the reinforcing effects of social approval, he or she must rely on overt behavior to construct and to test the theory.

According to Karl Popper (1959, 1963) a theory must state not only what people are expected to do, but also what, according to its own logic, they should be expected not to do. In effect, the scientific theory must state what observations it would take to disprove it. If such disconfirming observations can be made, the theory is refuted. This criterion of refutability guarantees that scientific theories will be stated in empirical, testable terms. The "good" theory specifies what it takes to falsify itself. The "poor" theory not only fails to specify falsification procedures, but it may be so vaguely stated that it can be compatible with any and all observations.

There is a difference between a theory having the desirable property of refutability and the actual refutation of the theory. A theory that is not refutable cannot be proven either right *or* wrong, whereas a theory that has been refuted is considered disproved. When a philosopher of science says that a theory is refutable, there is no implication that the theory has been or will be refuted. The only necessary quality of a refutable theory is that it be potentially refutable, that is, testable.

Theories that survive the challenge of careful tests increase our confidence in the theory as a useful summarizer of myriad facts and a reliable predictor of new ones. The strongest test of a theory, in fact the strongest test of any kind of explanation, is its power to predict what will happen next. Nothing is so definitive as when someone gives an explanation of something and predicts on the basis of that explanation what will happen. For example, my auto mechanic once said that my car's chronic stalling was due to a clogged fuel filter. He pulled the filter (it was fairly dirty) and replaced it with a clean one. The fee of $50 was well worth it. I paid for the mechanic's predictive knowledge (as well as a little for the filter), and that knowledge was tested and valuable.

Sometimes, a theory is stated in a way that allows for predictions to be made, yet any outcome could be interpreted as compatible with the theory. Let's imagine a different scenario: Suppose the mechanic said, "It's just a minor carburetor adjustment," and then adjusted a screw on the car's engine. This seems to have *no effect,* and I return again and again to the mechanic, who adjusts and readjusts the screw. Eventually the car stops stalling. Is it because one of the many turns of the screw "fixed" the problem? Is there, rather, an alternative explanation, such as the clogged fuel filter passed through some of its dirt? I'll never know. I have *no real* basis on which to decide.

We must point out that refutability is by no means the absolute standard of evaluating personality theories. The restriction of personality theories to observable, refutable (testable) phenomena often removes the flavor, the fullness of explanation that is intuitively and aesthetically satisfying. No theory, in the present state of the art—certainly none of the so-called grand theories from psychology's history—can both comprehensively and refutably account for the wholeness, for the uniqueness, for the universality of human propensities, foibles, drives, abilities, and desires. The person represented in a scientifically testable way is not the real person demanded by common sense and by personologists.

Tool Two: Active or Passive Human Agency

Buss (1978) contends that each major psychological tradition attempts to solve this fundamental scientific puzzle: Does the theory have a view of active human agency or one of passive human agency? Does the person construct reality, or does reality construct the person? Put another way, each school, depending on the history to which it is reacting, asserts either that human beings are active, creative, relatively free constructors of their lives, or that people are passive, uninventive, determined receptacles of reality. In essence, each theory asserts that people are subjects or objects (Buss, 1978, p. 60; Fischer, 1977). Many theories, we will find, combine the two views, even while emphasizing one or the other. This is logical as people may be viewed as both subjects and objects, active creators and passive recipients of stimulation.

Tool Three: Idiographic or Nomothetic Focus

Gordon Allport (1937) introduced into psychology a basic distinction and a fundamental dilemma with which philosophers had struggled for decades. He borrowed the terms *idiographic* and *nomothetic* from the philosopher Wilhelm Windelband (1894) to describe the apparent conflict between two basic interests of the psychologist. As a scientist, the psychologist is interested in obtaining data and results that apply to specific groupings of people or generally to all people. Concerns such as these that focus on generalizability or even universality are called nomothetic.

Consider the viewpoint of the **personologist.** He or she is interested in the individual human being. The personologist is concerned with the special combination of life history factors that contribute to the actions and thoughts of the person under investigation. The clinician who works on behalf of a client has the same concern: how best to understand the client by gathering and analyzing the client's particular diagnostic information, the special or unique personality facts, and the most relevant life events. The clinician proceeds to use this understanding therapeutically for this particular client. Such a clinician's concerns for the individual or for the unique case are termed idiographic. The same thing holds for the psychologist helping to choose a chief executive officer for a large firm. He or she wants to help discover if one particular individual is suited for the role. Intelligence agency psychologists work under a cover of secrecy to understand the personalities and to predict the behaviors of powerful foreign leaders. They rely on life history data, analysis of expressive behaviors, content analyses, and the accounts of many people familiar with the subject. Very little of this work ever sees the light of day.

In many cases, the idiographic and the nomothetic can be complementary, so that information derived from the study of one person may very well have aspects that are shared by other, similar people. Conversely, nomothetic "laws" that purport to be universal may be found to apply to a particular individual in a particular way. There remains a continuing divergence between the idiographic and the nomothetic interests of psychologists. A variety of "solutions" have been proposed. These include appreciating both the nomothetic and idiographic elements in a given theory or integrating them in an interactive way. The psychotherapy integration movement has been active in considering the possibility of actually integrating theories that are generally viewed as incompatible. The classic and contemporary theories that we consider fall at various points between the two extremes.

Allport (1961, 1968) later changed the idea of an *idiographic approach* to that of a **morphogenic approach** to emphasize that uniqueness sometimes results from the individual pattern of general traits that an individual embodies rather than from strictly and absolutely unique qualities. The morphogenic concept is somewhere between a nomothetic approach and the idea of a totally individualized focus on the individual.

ADDITIONAL DIMENSIONS OF PERSONALITY THEORIES

We have already explored some questions that may be asked of any theory of personality. We will be specifically using the three tools of analysis discussed previously: **active** or **passive human agency, refutability, idiographic** or **nomothetic focus.** These questions, as we have seen, need not always be answered yes or no. Many "in-betweens" are known and some theories contain contradictory elements. Honest and informed scholars may arrive at different answers regarding these questions.

In this text, there is enough information for students to make some informed responses regarding additional dimensions of personality theories. (You may arrive at different conclusions than we do regarding human agency, refutability, and idiographic or nomothetic focus.) We encourage students of personality theory to think about these questions and engage in an active dialogue with the text, with other students, and with the professor in regard to the theory you are studying.

Some additional considerations:

- Does the theory stem from the theorist's effort to make sense of her or his own life experience?

- Does the theory seem culturally embedded or is it generally applicable? A more refined version of this question is, "What aspects of a given theory are culturally embedded and which are more universal?"

- How does the theorist's experience as a person of male or female gender affect the theory? To what extent does the theory lead to understanding the role of women at different times in Western culture?

- To what extent is the theory derived from study of pathology, the "normal" person, or of the exceptional individual? A related question is to what extent the theory attempts to explain pathological, normal, or exceptional behavior? Does the theory have a comprehensive view, one that includes psychopathology, normal behavior, and exceptional behavior, or does it focus only on one area?

- Does the theory help us to understand a person? Does the theory help us fathom what a person is thinking and feeling and what his or her underlying goals and motives are? Does it lead to an understanding of how a person is experiencing reality?

- A somewhat different emphasis is the traditional nature-nurture question. Although we take the position that both are necessary factors, it is interesting to see how much weight each theory gives to each side of this debate. Does it recognize an interaction between nature and nurture?

- What, if any, life events have led the theorists themselves to view people as shaped by external forces and inner urges? What life events have led them to interpret people as largely or potentially independent steersmen of reality?

- Does the personality theory include a theory of development? What ages are covered as significant in the process? Is a stage theory included within the theory?

- A historically interesting question is to categorize the theory in one of three ways: (a) directly in the line of Freudian thinking (e.g., Anna Freud's theory), (b) a response against major dimensions of Freudian thinking (e.g., Adler's or Jung's theory), or (c) entirely removed from the Freudian tradition (e.g., radical behaviorism).

- Is there a form of psychotherapy associated with the theory? If so, has the theory led to the development of a psychotherapeutic tradition, with associated institutes, organizations, journals, etc.?

- Evaluate each theory in terms of its values: Does it promote individuality, altruism, religiosity, or communal spirit? Does it seem more consistent with a liberal, conservative, socialistic, or other political philosophy?

- Is the theorist European or American? How does their relation to European or American culture and history influence the personality theory?

- What is the approach of each theory toward spirituality and religion? Does it consider these areas at all? If so, indicate how much, and whether in a positive, neutral, or negative way.

- To what extent does the theorist's religious background and identification have an impact on the theory? What, if any, appears to be the impact?

- Does the theory focus on overt behavior, thinking, emotions, or on the individual's experience of reality?

- A more personal question: To what extent does a given theory overlap or help you understand your own life experience or the experience of those you know? Does it help you understand contemporary or historical personalities or even fictional characters?

We encourage you to add additional questions of your own to consider.

AN INTRODUCTION
TO CONVENTIONAL THEORETICAL CATEGORIES

We would like briefly to introduce some of the categories of personality theories. Note that the categories we mention are not ironclad. Scholars may differ regarding the categorization of a theory. Some theories may be legitimately categorized into more than one category or not fall into already demarcated categories. Personality theory based on evolutionary psychology, which will be introduced in Chapter 18, does not fit into earlier categories.

Let us take a look at the major theorists covered and how we have labeled their approaches:

Sigmund Freud	**Psychoanalytic theory**
Carl Gustav Jung	**Analytical psychology**
Alfred Adler	**Individual psychology**
Anna Freud	**Psychoanalytic ego psychology**
Margaret Mahler	**Psychoanalytic ego psychology**

Melanie Klein	**Object relations theory**
D.W. Winnicott	**Object relations theory**
Heinz Kohut	**Object relations theory**
Erik Erikson	**Psychoanalytic ego psychology**
Harry Stack Sullivan	**Interpersonal theory**
Karen Horney	**Social psychoanalytic psychology**
Gordon Allport	**Humanistic trait and self theory**
Rollo May	**Existential phenomenology**
Carl Rogers	**Humanistic and self-actualization theory**
Abraham Maslow	**Humanistic and self-actualization theory**
John B. Watson	**Radical behaviorism**
B.F. Skinner	**Radical behaviorism**
George Kelly	**Personal construct theory**
Neal Miller and John Dollard	**Psychodynamic social learning theory**
Albert Bandura	**Social cognitive theory**
Hans Eysenck	**Biologically-based typology of personality**
Edward O. Wilson	**Evolutionary psychology**

When we go through the list, we find that many problems emerge with some of the conventional category systems. Just as an example, it is interesting to note that Anna Freud is more closely identified with ego psychology than with psychoanalysis, but she was a direct and loyal disciple of her father and an analyst herself. We have thus placed her work under the label of *psychoanalytic ego psychology,* but this omits mention of her great contributions to the area of child therapy.

What about Jung's approach? Some place him in the psychoanalytic camp, but, even though he shared many approaches with Freud, his theory and psychotherapeutic approach differed considerably. The same can be said of Adler, who disagreed with Freud most vehemently on many topics, debated Freud, and formed his own training institutes. What about Allport, whose trait theory contains largely unacknowledged cognitive components? As we continue, we find a plethora of inadequacies with the standard category systems. Perhaps this is due to the fact that the theorists were very creative and that each had something unique to contribute to our understanding of personality. They are hard to label.

So we are reluctant to adhere strictly to the more conventional categorizing system in this edition of *Beneath the Mask.* We will evaluate each theory on its own and in relation to other theories. We encourage the student of personality to discover additional connections that we have not indicated.

SOME WELCOMING WORDS

We are pleased to welcome you to the study of personality, the study of personality theories, and an introduction to the theorists themselves. We trust that this text will lead to a deep understanding of the topic that will stay with you. By knowing about the biographical and cultural framework in which the theories were developed as well as the thinking that went into developing the theories, we hope that you will develop a deeper than average understanding of the major personality theories. We hope that you will be able, perhaps tentatively at first, to see how these theories may help you understand your own life experience a bit better. We trust that you will become able to see your life and the lives of others from different perspectives. For some students, such understanding has led to considerable insight and personal growth. We hope it brings you the sense of satisfaction that comes from understanding life a little better.

FOR FURTHER READING

We will recommend specific readings for each of the theorists discussed in this book at the end of each chapter. However, some secondary sources on the various theoretical orientations may be helpful at the beginning of your study.

An informative and concise summary by Christopher Monte on the topic of theories of personality was published posthumously in the year 2000 in the American Psychological Association's *Encyclopedia of Psychology* by the Oxford University Press. Monte's entry is in Volume 7 on pages 128–133.

The collection of chapters in Raymond Corsini and Danny Wedding's (Eds.) *Current Psychotherapies* (Itasca, IL: Peacock, 1995) surveys the therapeutic applications of many of the theories covered here. A specialist in the particular theoretical orientation wrote each of these chapters. Richard I. Evans

filmed and taped interviews with the "greats" of psychology for years. Included in the series are conversations with Ernest Jones, Carl Rogers, Neal Miller, Albert Bandura, R.D. Laing, Erik Erikson, B.F. Skinner, Gordon Allport, Erich Fromm, and Carl Jung. Condensed versions of all these interviews were published in a single paperback, *The Making of Psychology,* edited by R.I. Evans (New York: Knopf, 1976), and each is well worth scrutiny.

Reference to the personal sources of a theorist's ideas is provided by Henri Ellenberger in his *The Discovery of the Unconscious* (New York: Basic Books, 1981). Robert Stolorow and George Atwood's *Faces in a Cloud* (New York: Aronson, 1979) treat a variety of personality theories lucidly and often in terms of their relation to the theorists' life histories.

GLOSSARY

Active human agency: The concept that a person is actively in charge of his/her behaviors, thoughts, and feelings. In this view, the individual shapes his or her own inner and outer realities.

Analytical psychology: A term reserved for Jungian theoretical and psychotherapeutic approaches.

Construct theory: George Kelly's approach, which focuses on what people think about the world and how they anticipate future goals and events. This view embodies an active agency model of human nature.

Evolutionary psychology: An approach to theory and research that considers psychological phenomena from the point of view of their evolutionary adaptive significance.

Existential phenomenological theory: An approach to psychology that emphasizes the importance of individual choice and responsibility (existential emphasis) and a focus on human experience prior to any interpretation (phenomenological emphasis).

Humanistic and self-actualization theory: An approach to psychology that asserts that people are motivated by a desire to grow and reach their full potential. It focuses on the private world of experience and personal meaning. This theory assumes a largely active agency model of human behavior.

Humanistic trait and self theory: Gordon Allport's approach, one that combines humanistic insights regarding growth and human agency with the concept of traits.

Idiographic focus: An approach concerned with identifying the unique combination of traits and other characteristics that best accounts for the personality of a single individual. It is an indepth analysis of one individual and the dimensions relevant to that person's personality.

Individual psychology: The term for Adlerian approaches, which emphasize the goals, plans, and values of individuals. This theory is definitely an active agency model of personality.

Interpersonal theory: The term for Harry Stack Sullivan's approach to theory and psychotherapy, one that emphasizes the relevance of early infantile and childhood interpersonal experiences for adult behavior.

Mask metaphor: The dichotomy between appearance (the mask) and the actor (inner person). It deals with an important distinction between superficial and fundamental characteristics.

Morphogenic approach: An approach that classifies people according to the patterns of traits they display. It is midway between an idiographic and a nomothetic approach.

Nomothetic focus: An approach that seeks to establish general laws of human functioning, that is, to understand the behavior and experience of people in general or groups of people.

Object relations: An approach, exemplified by Melanie Klein, D. W. Winnicott, and Heinz Kohut, that focuses on the nature and quality of how the person structures and deals with interpersonal relations, or what they term "object relations."

Passive human agency: The individual is seen as a passive recipient of environmental forces or inner urges. The person is viewed as shaped by inner or outer forces beyond his or her control.

Persona: (literally "sound through") A Latin word that refers to a theatrical mask worn by Roman actors in Greek dramas. Those actors wore a mask to project a role or false appearance.

Personality: A pattern of relatively permanent traits, dispositions, or propensities that lend consistency to a person's behavior and thought processes.

Personologist: A psychologist who is concerned with the life history, the coherent stream of feelings, events, traits, and situations that characterize individual personalities.

Personology: The branch of psychology that principally concerns itself with the study of individual human lives.

Pluralism: A philosophical approach that takes into account the validity of many different points of view and theoretical explanations.

Psychoanalytic ego psychology: An approach to personality that focuses on the ego and its activities and development vis-à-vis external reality and, to a lesser extent, on the ego's relation to instinctual drives. This approach is typified by the work of Anna Freud, Margaret Mahler, and Erik Erikson.

Psychoanalytic social psychology: An approach, exemplified by Karen Horney's theory in this text, that widens psychoanalytic insights to include consideration of interpersonal and socially relevant factors.

Psychoanalytic theory: The Freudian approach to psychological theory, research, and treatment. It asserts that irrational and unconscious psychological forces govern much behavior. This theory embodies a largely passive agency model of human behavior.

Radical behaviorism: This approach to psychology asserts that behavior, with the exception of simple reflexes, is learned and conditioned by environmental circumstances. Rewards and punishments, and other environmental forces shape and condition the individual's responses. This theory embodies a largely passive agency model of human behavior.

Reductionism: Theoretical approaches that attempt to explain all human behavior according to a single theory.

Refutability: The idea that a theory is formulated in such a way that leads to tests either supporting or contradicting its tenets. Refutability leads to a measurable degree of accuracy and predictive power.

Social cognitive theory: Albert Bandura's approach, one that focuses on the determining factor of what people think and choose in the context of an interpersonal world. This theory embodies a largely active agency model of human behavior.

Social learning theory: Neal Miller and John Dollard's integrative approach in which behavioral principles are used to explain complex phenomena, such as repression, which was uncovered by the psychoanalytic approach.

Chapter 2

Sigmund Freud

Psychoanalysis:
The Clinical Evidence

Go, now, and do heart-work
On all the images imprisoned within you,
For you overpower them,
But you know them not.

Ranier Maria Rilke, "Turning Point"

A man on horseback rode through a town at breakneck speed.
A passer-by saw him and called out,
"Where are you going in such a hurry?"
He answered, "I don't know. Ask the horse!"

Anonymous

Sigmund Freud Born: 1856 Freiberg, Moravia, Austro-Hungarian
                                Empire
               Died: 1939 London, England

About Freud's Clinical Psychoanalysis

Freud's theory is the result of one person's quest to understand the conflict between human passion and reason. It was Freud's lifework to explore the convoluted ways that irrationality clashes against rationality.

In this chapter, the central concepts to be distilled from the many changes Freud's ideas underwent are:

1. Many disorders previously considered to be physical in origin are really psychological in origin. They are determined by the experiences and/or the needs and desires of people.

2. *The mind is compartmentalized. Part of the mind is unconscious and often, outside of the person's awareness, determines behavior.*

3. *Neurotic symptoms both partly express and partly shield hidden impulses or taboo memories.*

4. *Just as experience may lead to symptoms, so psychoanalysis, a verbal form of therapy, may lead to their resolution.*

5. *A process involving successive psychosexual stages characterizes normal human development; regression or fixation may occur in instances of psychopathology.*

Freud's classic theory remains a powerful influence on other theorists and clinicians. Even many of those who do not think they are following in his footsteps nonetheless agree with many of his ideas and continue many of his practices.

THE HYSTERICAL NEUROSIS OF BERTHA PAPPENHEIM

It was 1882 in Vienna, the capital of the Austro-Hungarian Empire. Writhing in her bed with labor pangs and evidencing most of the usual signs of advanced pregnancy, 23-year-old Bertha Pappenheim bore no child in her womb. A two-year-long series of bizarre physical and mental symptoms was climaxing now with a frightening and painfully unsettling outcome: **pseudocyesis,** or false pregnancy. This symptom would lead to the termination of an intimate and lengthy doctor–patient relationship between this neurotic upper-class lady and a prominent Viennese physician, Dr. Josef Breuer.

Breuer's work with this patient would eventually lead to a theory of hysterical nervous disorder, a method of psychological treatment, and the germ of a comprehensive theory of personality and psychotherapy that would have a major impact on our thinking about human nature.

Fraülein Bertha Pappenheim, who was to be called "Anna O" in later writings by Breuer and Freud, (Jones, 1953, p. 223n.), was a charming, attractive, intelligent, and witty young woman who had developed a series of disorders. (The name *Anna O* stood for the *alpha* and *omega* of neurosis, or as an author might write today, "Neurosis from *A* to *Z*.") These included paralysis of limbs and disturbed vision—each without apparent organic cause. At one point, she seemed to have a dual personality. Her symptoms seemed to emerge after the onset of her father's long, terminal illness. Though many physicians were consulted, no physical basis had been found for her bewildering maladies. Breuer diagnosed Bertha's collection of symptoms as **hysterical neurosis.** Although recognized from antiquity, the causes of this disorder had thus far not been accurately understood.

The affliction received its name from the ancient Greek word *hysteria,* meaning uterus. It was the opinion of the Greeks that hysteria was "for women only" because the disease was thought to be the result of a wandering womb. By its travels to various parts of the body, the errant womb caused the symptoms of temporary paralysis of limbs or the dysfunction of sense organs. Josef Breuer did not hold such archaic and unscientific views about the nature of hysteria. But he still did not have an adequate explanation for Bertha Pappenheim's symptoms.

She had two markedly different ways of behaving. Breuer described Bertha as follows:

Two entirely distinct states of consciousness were present, which alternated very frequently and without warning and which became more and more differentiated in the course of the illness. In one of these states she recognized her surroundings; she was melancholy and anxious, but relatively normal. In the other state she hallucinated and was "naughty"—that is to say, she was abusive, used to throw the cushions at people, so far as the contractures [in her limbs] at various times allowed, tore buttons off her bedclothes and linen with those of her fingers which she could move, and so on. . . . There were extremely rapid changes of mood leading to excessive but quite temporary high spirits, and at other times severe anxiety, stubborn opposition to every therapeutic effort and frightening hallucinations of black snakes, which was how she saw her hair ribbons and similar things. . . . (Breuer, in Breuer & Freud, 1893–1895, p. 24)[1]

In addition to the emergence of an incipient dual personality, Bertha began to exhibit other forms of disturbance. She occasionally omitted necessary words from her spoken language. She gradually increased these omissions until her speech was rendered largely nonsensical, illogical, and ungrammatical. She even became totally mute for a period of two weeks. She struggled in vain to speak during this time.

Breuer finally guessed that something had recently annoyed and offended her. This resulted in her resolving not to speak about it. Somehow this resolution not to speak about a single topic had apparently caused her mutism. Breuer's insistence that they discuss the problem robbed Bertha's mutism of its efficacy. She began to speak again (Breuer, in Breuer & Freud, 1893–1895, p. 25).

Bertha, whose native tongue was German, now displayed a new symptom: She spoke *only English*. Nothing could convince Bertha, who seemed to be unaware of her change in language, that the German-speaking people to whom she spoke English were still unable to understand her—just as they had been during her weeks of silence.

"CLOUDS": SELF-INDUCED HYPNOSIS

Bertha's father died in April, nine months after her speech disturbances developed. "This [her father's death] was the most severe physical trauma that she could possibly have experienced. A violent outburst of excitement was succeeded by profound stupor which lasted about two days and from which she emerged in a greatly changed state" (Breuer, in Breuer & Freud, 1893–1895, p. 26).

Bertha's loss of feeling in her hands and feet as well as her paralysis returned, along with what would now be called **tunnel vision.** Her field of vision was greatly narrowed as when one looks through a keyhole. For example, ". . . in a bunch of flowers which gave her much pleasure she could only see one flower at a time."

> She complained of not being able to recognize people. Normally, she said, she had been able to recognize faces without having to make any deliberate effort; now she was obliged to do laborious "recognizing work" [she used this phrase in English] and had to say to herself "this person's nose is such-and-such, his hair is such-and-such, so he must be so-and-so." (Breuer, in Breuer & Freud, 1893–1895, p. 26)

Bertha's behavior varied with some regularity. She was usually upset during the early part of the day; she then presented a dismal picture. She hallucinated, talked incoherently, and experienced grave anxiety. Toward afternoon, Bertha usually became sleepy and quiet, sinking into a deep autohypnosis by sunset. She used the English word **"clouds"** to describe these sleepy, quasihypnotic states. Today we would term this waking-sleeping or sleeping-waking state a **hypnagogic state.** When Breuer visited Bertha in the evening,

---

[1]Reference citations throughout this chapter and the next that indicate the writings of Sigmund Freud (or, in this case of Josef Breuer) refer to the volumes of the *Standard Edition of the Complete Psychological Works of Sigmund Freud,* translated under the general editorship of James Strachey, with the collaboration of Anna Freud, and published by the Hogarth Press, London. Citations to the *Standard Edition* employ only the original publication date of the work, so that you may follow the chronology of Freud's thought.

she was able to recount to him her day's hallucinations, and it was in this state of "clouds" or hypnagogic state that Breuer and Bertha made a joint discovery.

Her family had noticed from Bertha's mumblings that the content of her daytime hallucinations seemed to resemble a fantasy story. Bertha's fantasies were sad, yet they were also pretty and poetic. They seemed to have been modeled on a book of Hans Christian Andersen's fairy tales with similar themes. After her father's death, her daytime hallucinations became even more tragic, and they usually involved, as at least one element of a complex structure, the character of an anxious young girl sitting near the bedside of a patient. Accidentally at first, a family member would repeat a few key words of Bertha's mutterings, and this response would draw her out to narrate an entire story or fantasy.

During her evening hypnagogic state, Breuer also began to prime a more complete rendition of Bertha's stories by repeating several words or phrases from Bertha's own fantasies. After Bertha recounted the full content of her daytime hallucinations and stories to Breuer, she became quieter, more lucid, and cheerful. She was almost symptom-free for the rest of the night. Little by little, through a combination of accident and intent, Bertha and Breuer together shaped a method to relieve Bertha of her anxiety and her symptoms, at least temporarily. By unburdening herself to Breuer in the evening, Bertha was able to achieve some respite from her torment. She and Breuer had thus made an important discovery, a "talking cure" that involved a kind of verbal **catharsis** (literally, a cleansing or purifying).

Aristotle had used the term *catharsis* to describe the emotional release and purification engendered in the audience during their viewing of a tragic drama. Bertha called the emotional release produced by her semihypnotic conversations with Breuer **"chimney sweeping."**

As the talking cure progressed, Breuer found that some of the symptoms of Bertha's illness permanently disappeared. He was particularly surprised when a long-standing symptom disappeared during an unplanned conversation with her. Breuer recounted this event:

> It was in the summer during a period of extreme heat, and the patient was suffering very badly from thirst; for, *without being able to account for it in any way,* she suddenly found it impossible to drink. She would take up the glass of water she longed for, but as soon as it touched her lips she would push it away like someone suffering from hydrophobia. As she did this, she was obviously in an *absence* [self-induced hypnotic state] for a couple of seconds. . . . This [condition] had lasted for some six weeks, when one day during hypnosis she grumbled about her English lady-companion whom she did not care for, and went on to describe, *with every sign of disgust,* how she had once gone into that lady's room and how her [the lady-companion's] little dog—horrid creature!—had drunk out of a glass there. The patient [i.e., Bertha] had said nothing, as she had wanted to be polite. After giving further *energetic expression to the anger she had held back,* she asked for something to drink, drank a large quantity of water without any difficulty and woke from her hypnosis with the glass at her lips; and thereupon the disturbance vanished, never to return. (Breuer, in Breuer & Freud, 1893–1895, pp. 34–35; italics added)

Here was the secret of the *origin* and the *form* of hysterical symptoms. An emotion had been experienced intensely, but it had been blocked from normal expression during the initiating event. The patient had been compelled to strangle, or bottle-up, the feeling. However, even though the emotion was not expressed, there was little cause, Breuer reasoned, to assume that the emotion had thereby ceased to exist. Indeed, the **strangulated affect,** as Breuer (and Freud) would later call these dammed-up emotions, remained to haunt Bertha. Bertha's suppressed disgust and anger were expressed in her symptom of disgust for water and a refusal to drink it. When the incident that had precipitated the original feelings had been recalled in hypnosis, Bertha's pent-up emotions were finally released and this symptom, at least temporarily, receded.

After this small success, Breuer systematically explored with Bertha the possibility that other precipitating but no longer remembered incidents lay at the root of her remaining symptoms. Breuer adopted the procedure of asking Bertha during hypnosis to tell him her thoughts about a particular symptom. This exploration was often difficult, and it required great concentration on the part of both Breuer and his patient. On some occasions, the whole process ground to a halt because the memory of the initiating cause of a symptom could not surface.

Eventually, concentrated effort relieved Bertha of many of her difficulties. Some visual disturbances, language problems, hallucinations, and the paralysis of her right arm were removed after she was able, under hypnosis, to recount the story of a particularly long and frightening night vigil she had spent at her sick father's bedside.

> She fell into a waking dream and saw a black snake coming towards the sick man from the wall to bite him. . . . Her right arm, over the back of the chair, had gone to sleep and had become anesthetic and paretic; and when she looked at it the fingers turned into little snakes with death's heads (the nails). (It seems probable that she had tried to use her paralysed right arm to drive off the snake and its anesthesia and paralysis had consequently become associated with the hallucination of the snake.) When the snake vanished, in her terror she tried to pray. But language failed her: *she could find no tongue in which to speak, till at last she thought of some children's verses in English, and then found herself able to think and pray in that language.* [Italics added]
>
> . . . on [another] occasion, when she was sitting by her father's bedside with tears in her eyes, he suddenly asked her what time it was. She could not see clearly; she made a great effort, and brought her watch near to her eyes. The face of the watch now seemed very big—thus accounting for her macropsia [tunnel vision] and convergent squint. Or again, she tried hard to suppress her tears so that the sick man should not see them. (Breuer, in Breuer & Freud, 1893–1895, pp. 38, 39, 40)

Breuer's account of the case history ends shortly after this incident is recounted, but that is not the end of the story. Bertha Pappenheim developed a new symptom that was to frighten and trouble Breuer.

Bertha's Treatment Ends

Symptom by symptom, feeling-event by feeling-event, the thread of Bertha's hysteria was unraveled with the assistance of Breuer and the cathartic method. During the course of the treatment, a period lasting almost two years, an intense relationship developed between Breuer and Bertha. Fraülein Pappenheim found herself in the hands of a caring, altruistic, humane, and fatherly physician, who was clearly interested in her suffering in ways that transcended the typical doctor–patient relationship.

Breuer's wife became jealous of her husband's involvement with this fascinating patient, and she provoked in Breuer a strong reaction of guilt. He decided precipitously to end his treatment of Bertha, a decision strengthened by her improvement, and he announced this intention to her. Ernest Jones, Freud's official biographer, provides an account, based on a conversation with Freud years later, of what followed Breuer's announcement to his patient:

> . . . that evening . . . [Breuer] was fetched back to find . . . [Bertha] in a greatly excited state, apparently as ill as ever. The patient, who according to him had appeared to be an asexual being and had never made any allusion to such a forbidden topic throughout the

treatment, was now in the throes of an hysterical childbirth (pseudocyesis), the logical termination of a phantom pregnancy that had been invisibly developing in response to Breuer's ministrations. Though profoundly shocked, he managed to calm her down by hypnotizing her, and then fled the house in a cold sweat. The next day he and his wife left for Venice to spend a second honeymoon. . . . (Jones, 1953, p. 224. Freud himself hinted at this story in *An Autobiographical Study*, 1925a, p. 26.)

There can be little doubt that Breuer had read the apparent meaning of Bertha's symptom, that at some level she believed he had had sexual intercourse with her and that he felt directly responsible and guilty for her (unconscious) belief. Breuer felt tremendously threatened by the pseudocyesis. He also, for the time being, lost almost all professional interest in hysterical neurosis.

Breuer could not have known, but his patient viewed him, as all future analytic patients were to view their therapists, as father, lover, confessor, friend, rival, villain, and hero. Her emotions toward the therapist were derived from previous relationships to important people in her life. This process of projecting inappropriate feelings and role images onto the therapist, known later in Freud's theory as **transference,** was a double-edged sword. For Bertha Pappenheim's transference of inappropriate love onto Breuer, there had to be Breuer's **countertransference** of similarly inappropriate emotions onto his patient. Knowledge of both transference and countertransference and how to deal with them in psychotherapy would eventually be one of Freud's major contributions. But that was years off.

The Posttreatment Bertha: Some Detective Work

The account of Bertha's illness and treatment by Breuer, and the historical additions provided by Jones (1953), seem to have been something less than complete. Ellenberger (1970, 1972) interviewed surviving relatives and acquaintances of Bertha Pappenheim and engaged in some clever detective work to find the sanitorium in which the patient sought refuge after the final episode with Breuer. In 1882 Bertha was far from cured, and the severity of her illness suggests that she was not a hysteric neurotic but, perhaps, a borderline patient with some psychotic features.

Breuer's hitherto unknown case history, although substantially different from the published version in *Studies on Hysteria* (with Freud, 1895), nevertheless matched the published case in lacking all reference to the hysterical childbirth. However, several new details about Bertha Pappenheim's life and illness are worth recounting here; the full document has not yet been published for reasons Ellenberger does not disclose.

In this version, Breuer more fully emphasized Bertha's "truly passionate love for her father," and revealed the strong antireligious sentiment Bertha harbored (Ellenberger, 1972, pp. 274–275). The death of her father, which had such a profound impact on Bertha, is now made more comprehensible.

> During the previous two months she had not been allowed to see [her father] and had continuously been told lies about his condition. . . . On April 5, at the moment when her father was dying, she called her mother and asked for the truth, but was appeased and the lie went on for some time. When Bertha learned that her father had died, she was indignant: she had been "robbed" of his last look and word. From that time on, a marked transformation appeared in her condition: anxiety replaced by a kind of dull insensitivity with distortions in her visual perceptions. Human beings appeared to her as wax figures. (Ellenberger, 1972, pp. 275–276)

At some time around the period of her father's death, Bertha made several suicide attempts (Ellenberger, 1972, p. 276). It might be possible, therefore, considering the severity of her reaction to the loss of her father, to equate her later loss of Breuer and its accompanying frightening symptom to the nearly psychotic mourning reactions she evidenced (Pollock, 1973).

Breuer's account mentions Bertha's quarrels with her brother and some difficulties with her "very serious" mother. Ellenberger quotes Breuer's assessment of the role of sexuality in Bertha's life as an "astonishingly undeveloped" element. Furthermore, "She had never been in love, 'insofar [as] her relationship to her father did not replace it, or rather was replaced by it' " (Ellenberger, 1972, p. 274).

The Bellevue Sanitorium doctors' follow-up report indicates that during her stay, Bertha became habituated to large doses of chloral and morphine, administered to relieve severe facial neuralgia. Among other comments, the report cites the patient's "unpleasant irritation against her family," and her "disparaging judgments against the ineffectiveness of science in regard to her sufferings." In the evenings, she again lost ability to speak in German, substituting English phrases for sentences begun in her failing native tongue. Last, the report mentions that the patient would sit for hours under a picture of her father, and she would speak of visiting his tomb.

Breuer's Contributions to Psychology

We should not overlook the major contributions provided by Breuer's scientific astuteness prior to the embarrassing episode leading to termination with Bertha. It was upon these contributions of Breuer that the young Sigmund Freud was to build the structure of psychoanalysis.

First, Breuer recognized that hysterical symptoms were *meaningful* and that they possessed a certain underlying logic.

Second, Breuer regarded the *origin* of the hysterical symptom as some intense, *emotionally abrasive experience* in the life history of the patient. Though no longer remem-

---

BOX 2.1   *The Contributions of Bertha Pappenheim*

Eventually, Bertha Pappenheim recovered from her illness to become an active feminist, supporter of Jewish causes, writer, and leading figure in social work in Germany. She campaigned against the oppression of women, coercive slavery of prostitutes, and for the betterment of conditions for poor and orphaned children. In her later years, she experienced a complete turnabout from her early antireligious attitudes to deeply religious and altruistic traits (Ellenberger, 1970, p. 481).

One can think of her cure as a two-step process. The first step was the therapy with Breuer, which *may* have freed her of some disabling symptoms. The second step consisted of her own actions, which she took to remedy the conditions around her. In trying to make the world a better place, she was remedying the very conditions that had led her— and other women—into a sense of uselessness and helplessness, if not actual paralysis.

By the end of World War II, Bertha Pappenheim was revered as a legendary figure and a founder of the field of social work, to the extent that, in 1954, the West German government issued a postage stamp bearing her picture (Ellenberger, 1970, p. 481). The full continuing story of Bertha Pappenheim's subsequent life is beyond the scope of our present purposes (see Freeman, 1972). She died in March 1936, in time to avoid being killed by the Nazis (Ellenberger, 1970), although she had stood up heroically under interrogation.

As we have seen, Bertha Pappenheim also played a major role in the early developments that led to psychoanalysis. Her ability to recover material hidden from conscious awareness and to access and express hidden emotions—the process of "chimney sweeping"—was crucial for Freud's subsequent development of psychoanalysis.

Figure 2.1 Fraülein Bertha Pappenheim (Anna O). Bertha was an attractive and intelligent, though deeply troubled, patient of Dr. Josef Breuer, Freud's mentor. She contributed to the development of the "talking cure" and went on to have a significant career in her own right.

bered, the past experience *actively operated unconsciously,* pressing for release and goading the patient to find symbolic means of expressing the discomfort. It is not easy to determine how much Sigmund Freud contributed to this interpretation of hysterical symptoms. Freud was always generous in giving most of the credit to Breuer for the early theory of hysteria that they proposed in their joint publications, the "Preliminary Communication" of 1893 and their full monograph, *Studies on Hysteria* of 1895.

Third, the discovery that symptoms could be removed by promoting the expression of the strangulated emotion dating from the past traumatic experience gave further force to the theory that symptoms were the result of dammed-up emotional (affective) energy. The cathartic method, a joint discovery of Breuer and Bertha, was a uniquely *psychological* method for dealing with hysterical disorder. In the terminology of the *Studies on Hysteria,* the goal of the cathartic method was to enable the patient to "abreact" the painful feelings, literally to "react away" the trapped energy. As Breuer and Freud expressed the idea in their "Preliminary Communication," *"The hysteric suffers mostly from reminiscences"* (1893, p. 7; italics added).

It was also Breuer's conviction that the essential precondition for the occurrence of hysterical symptoms was the presence of a tendency to self-induced hypnotic states of consciousness. Thus, for Breuer, any intensely experienced emotion that occurred during one of these states of "absence" and that was prevented from immediate expression could serve as the origin of a hysterical symptom. It was with this idea that Freud was later to disagree and that he would modify by the time *Studies on Hysteria* had been published.

THE CATHARTIC METHOD IN FREUD'S HANDS: HYPNOTISM

The young Sigmund Freud, a doctor in training at the University of Vienna, had been befriended by the older and more experienced Dr. Josef Breuer. In 1882, shortly after Breuer had terminated his treatment of Bertha Pappenheim, Freud heard the fascinating details of the important case. He was greatly interested and requested Breuer to tell him the story repeatedly (Jones, 1953, p. 226). It was not until some years later, however, that Freud and Breuer began to treat cases together, employing for the most part the cathartic method. Freud did not simply apply Breuer's (and Bertha's) technique mechanically. He was already experimenting with slight modifications on the application of hypnosis and the cathartic method to individual patients.

Jean-Martin Charcot

Freud's early reliance on the technique of **hypnotism**—a necessary adjunct to catharsis— had other roots besides Breuer's successful treatment of Bertha. In 1885, Freud was awarded a traveling grant to attend the lecture-demonstrations of the famous neuro-

Figure 2.2 Professor Jean-Martin Charcot in Paris. In this representation, he is demonstrating hypnosis and hypnotic anesthesia. Note the expressions of astonishment and wonder on the faces of the physicians in the audience.

pathologist Jean-Martin Charcot (1825–1893) in Paris, at the equally renowned Salpetriere Hospital (Freud, 1925a, pp. 12–16).

Charcot was investigating the symptoms and causes of hysteria. He had demonstrated that the behaviors associated with the disease could be removed and then restored under hypnosis at the suggestion of the physician. This famous French clinician had also demonstrated that hysterical symptoms parallel the hysteric's understanding of any given physical disorder. Thus, for example, the patient who has recently been involved in a frightening horse-drawn carriage accident, but who emerges unscathed, may nevertheless exhibit all the symptoms he or she *expects* to have. He or she might experience **glove anesthesia,** for example. In this disorder, it is as if all of the hand that could fit into an imaginary glove were anesthetized or without sensation. This disorder does not fit the distribution of nerves in the hand, even though it may fit the patient's notion of a disorder. As this type of numbness was not caused by any discernable organic or structural deficit, it was considered a functional disorder, a form of **functional anesthesia.** Hence, in Charcot's view, only *ideas,* rather than physical pathology, lie at the base of hysteria.

That a man of Charcot's professional standing could be scientifically interested in the clinical oddities of hysterical attacks was enough to impress Freud with the significance of the disease as worthy of investigation. He would, however, have a difficult time trying to convince the Viennese medical establishment to investigate what was then regarded as a malingerer's syndrome.

As if to underscore the incredulity with which the medical profession viewed the hysteric's suffering, the Viennese Society of Physicians greeted the young Freud's report of Charcot's work with open hostility. Freud recounted in his *Autobiographical Study* the cool and unpleasant reception his formal presentation of Charcot's findings engendered (1925a, pp. 15ff.).

Nevertheless, Freud had learned his lessons well with Charcot:

1. Hysterical conversion disorders were psychological in origin, not physical or physiological.
2. Male hysteria existed, eliminating the notion that hysteria was caused by a wandering womb or that it was based on female physiology.
3. Symptoms could be removed, modified, or reinstated by hypnotism.
4. Ideas underlay the patient's symptoms.

These ideas, which Freud learned from his contact with Charcot, formed a foundation upon which he could continue his further investigations.

Liebeault and Bernheim

Meanwhile, in another part of France, two physicians, Ambroise-Auguste Liebeault (1823–1904) and Hippolyte Bernheim (1837–1919), founded a clinic at Nancy that rivaled the Charcot school of Paris in its employment of hypnotism in the treatment of hysteria (cf. Watson, 1963, pp. 303–304; and Zilboorg, 1941, pp. 361–378). The physicians associated with the Nancy School, as it came to be known, differed from Charcot's group by their emphasis on the purely pragmatic efficacy of hypnotism as a cure for their hysteric patients. Liebeault and Bernheim were more interested in treating the disease than in developing theories to explain its origin, or the action of hypnotism. In contrast to Liebeault and Bernheim's practical viewpoint, Charcot was theoretically interested in both hypnotism and in hysteria as manifestations of altered mental processes. He conceived of hypnosis as an essentially pathological or diseased state in itself, a state to which hysterics were peculiarly susceptible. Hypnotic trance, Charcot believed, was the precursor and necessary biological foundation on which the disease of hysteria was built. (It was, incidentally, from Charcot that Breuer adopted the idea that hysteria required a "hypnoid state" or condition of "absence" in order for the damming up of feelings to take place.)

Liebeault and Bernheim held the rather different view that hysteria and hypnotism were not necessarily related. The members of the Nancy School believed, furthermore, that Charcot's findings about the malleability of hysterical symptoms were an artifact of hypnotism imposed by the physician, and, therefore, hypnotic states in themselves could not be the biological cause of hysterical disorder (Murphy & Kovach, 1972, p. 156). History seems to have supported the views of Liebeault and Bernheim.

In 1889, Freud traveled back to France, this time to visit the Liebeault-Bernheim clinic at Nancy in an attempt to refine his hypnotic technique (1925a, p. 17). He came away from Nancy with ". . . the profoundest impression of the possibility that there could be powerful mental processes which nevertheless remained hidden from the consciousness of men."

Hypnotism Fails

Throughout the late 1880s, Freud continued to employ the cathartic method, but the difficulties and the dissatisfactions he experienced in its use continued to mount. For one thing, not all his patients could be hypnotized. Some individuals could not achieve the trancelike state of somnambulism so necessary to reliving and releasing the strangulated emotion of the forgotten traumatic event. Furthermore, Freud had begun to understand that even in cases where hypnotism was successful, the success depended deeply on the personal relationship between the physician and the patient.

The efficacy of the hypnotic act was thus a function of the emotional quality of the person-to-person contact between himself and his patient. If for some reason or other this personal relationship was disturbed, "even the most brilliant results [of hypnotism] were likely to be suddenly wiped away . . ." (Freud, 1925a, p. 27). Breuer's unwitting intimate involvement with Bertha was proof enough of the partially erotic nature of the process.

Clearly, it was necessary for Freud to abandon hypnosis altogether if he was to pursue unimpeded his psychological investigations. Consequently, Freud was compelled gradually to reduce his reliance on hypnosis. His search for a new technique received its first important, if altogether unintentional, guidance from a new patient, Frau Emmy.

FRAU EMMY von N.

"Keep still—Don't say anything!—Don't touch me!" These words greeted Freud on an afternoon in May 1889 when he visited his new patient, Frau Emmy von N., for the first time.

Frau Emmy was lying on a couch when Freud entered, and she greeted her new physician. Interposed between perfectly coherent and logical, softly spoken amenities, came the striking utterance, "Keep still—Don't say anything!—Don't touch me!" She also evidenced several tic-like facial twitches, punctuated by grimaces of disgust and fear that contorted her pleasant face every time she repeated: "Keep still!—Don't say anything!—Don't touch me!" Frau Emmy had a tendency to stutter, and her speech was often accompanied by a smacking sound that Freud tried to convey to the reader by describing it as comparable to the call of a forest bird (Freud, in Breuer & Freud, 1893–1895, p. 49).

Figure 2.3 Fanny Moser (Frau Emmy von N) with her daughters. The formidable Madame Moser was Freud's first catharsis patient. "Keep still—Don't say anything!—Don't touch me!" she sporadically repeated as a magically protective phrase.

Freud's first suspicion was Frau Emmy's behaviors involved some form of protective ritual to ward off a repetitive hallucination.

The Real Frau Emmy von N.: Fanny Moser

Frau Emmy von N. was actually the 41-year-old Fanny Sulzer-Wart Moser, born in 1848 to a large aristocratic Swiss family (Appignanesi & Forrester, 1992, pp. 91ff.). Fanny was a middle child in the family with 13 brothers and sisters, the youngest born six years after her. Five of her siblings died when she was a child, including a brother addicted to morphine. Fanny eventually revealed to Freud that this brother was a central feature of her conflicts. At age 19, Fanny found her mother dead, probably of a stroke. At age 22, Fanny Sulzer-Wart married Heinrich Moser, a wealthy manufacturer who was 40 years her senior. Together they had two daughters, Fanny and Mentona, but Heinrich's two children by his first marriage treated Fanny as though she were an enemy.

When Heinrich died of a heart attack two days after the birth of their second daughter—Fanny was then 26 years old—her husband's children by the prior marriage accused Fanny of having poisoned him to take possession of his considerable estate and deprive them of their inheritance. The body was exhumed but no evidence of foul play was found. Fanny Moser became one of the wealthiest women in Europe.

Fanny Moser was seen as a scandalous woman in the more aristocratic social circles of European society. Rumors of her alleged complicity in the death of her husband persisted for many years. Nevertheless, Fanny Moser became a salon hostess. She entertained celebrity artists and intellectuals on a large estate in Switzerland and earned a reputation for colorful extravagance. By 1889, she was depressed; she was tortured by tics, hallucinations, insomnia, and pain (Appignanesi & Forrester, 1992, p. 91ff.). Indeed, she had been ill since the death of her husband. Accompanied by her daughters, ages 15 and 17, she traveled to Vienna for medical treatment. The prominent physician, Dr. Josef Breuer, recommended that she see Freud.

For the rest of the story, we return to Freud's case history of the woman he called Frau Emmy von N.

Tracing Symptoms to Their Origins

Freud suggested that Frau Emmy (i.e., Fanny Moser) place the girls with their governess and then enter a sanitarium, where he would visit her daily.

Fortunately, in this, one of the first cases that Freud treated by hypnosis and the cathartic method, Frau Emmy, unlike his later patients, proved to be an admirable subject. She was able to assume the sleeplike somnambulistic state readily, and she was cooperative in discussing her symptoms and their origins—to a point.

As the therapeutic relationship progressed, Freud attempted to trace each of Frau Emmy's symptoms to its root by asking her, under hypnosis, to explain its meaning. For example, Freud asked her to explain the meaning of her magical phrase, "Keep still!— Don't say anything—Don't touch me!"

> She explained that when she had frightening thoughts she was afraid of their being interrupted in their course, because then everything would get confused and things would be even worse. The "Keep still!" related to the fact that the animal shapes [hallucinations] which appeared to her when she was in a bad state started moving and began to attack her if anyone made a movement in her presence. The final injunction "Don't touch me!" was derived from the following experiences. She told me how, when her brother had been so ill from taking a lot of morphine—she was 19 at the time—he used often to seize hold of her; and how, another time, an acquaintance had suddenly gone mad in the house and had caught her by the arm; and lastly, how, when she was 28 and her daughter was very ill, the child had caught hold of her so forcibly in its delirium that she was almost choked. Though these four instances were so widely separated in time, she told them in a single sentence and in such rapid succession that they might have been a single episode in four acts. (Freud, in Breuer & Freud, 1893–1895, pp. 56–57)

Thus far, as Freud's account clearly indicates, he held to the conception of hysteria that Breuer had developed in working with Bertha Pappenheim. The patient's unconscious memory had to be searched through hypnotism for hidden emotional experiences that had not been fully expressed when they occurred. By allowing Frau Emmy to reexperience the strangulated affect of those events, catharsis was achieved. But Frau Emmy's list of traumatic experiences was endless.

Although Freud used hypnotic suggestion to remove her fears and the power of her memories to instill terror, Frau Emmy experienced relapses. She sometimes succumbed to new fears and hallucinations. Freud realized that his hypnotic suggestions and emotional catharsis were only partially successful. Tracing the symptom to its origin and freeing the choked emotional energy could not of themselves explain why a particular event had been traumatic or permanently cure the symptoms. It is worth noting again, in this regard, that Bertha Pappenheim herself had not been completely cured by Breuer's similar work.

FIRST CLUE IN THE DISCOVERY OF FREE ASSOCIATION: FREUD LEARNS TO LISTEN

Frau Emmy von N., the first patient with whom Freud employed the cathartic method, would also be the person who provided the first clue to the discovery of a new technique of conducting therapy, free association. That clue assumed great significance in later years, when Freud would have trouble with the hypnotic method.

Frau Emmy, despite Freud's hypnotic suggestions to the contrary, continued to recall frightening experiences with animals and terrifying hallucinations based on animal content. Freud, quite willing to accept the fact that each new instance of anxiety had to be removed separately, took to quizzing Frau Emmy closely on each occasion. She had reported intense stomachaches, and Freud noticed that reports of stomach pains coincided with each new animal terror. He questioned her under hypnosis on the possible origin of the stomachaches, but she seemed reluctant to continue examining each symptom with such exactness.

> Her answer, which she gave rather grudgingly, was that she did not know. I requested her to remember by tomorrow. She then said in a definitely grumbling tone that I was not to keep on asking her where this and that came from, but to let her tell me what she had to say. (Freud, in Breuer & Freud, 1893–1895, p. 63)

Frau Emmy's offhand and somewhat petulant remark was a momentous occasion in Freud's intellectual history. Jones, Freud's biographer, remarks with understatement worthy of Freud himself, that "he took the hint" and thus approached one step closer to a substitute for hypnosis (1953, p. 244).

In more concrete and immediate terms, Freud's acceptance of Frau Emmy's "suggestion" meant that he would allow more free rein in the handling of his patient. He would permit her feelings and strivings to direct the flow and content of their therapeutic conversation. He was moving away from hypnosis, in which the physician directs everything, to the concentration technique and eventually to free association. Each step increasingly relied on the autonomy of the patient.

False Connections: Deceptions of Memory

Freud had already begun to suspect that certain of the contents of mental processes revealed during hypnosis might be forms of self-deception designed to screen deeper and more threatening material. Thus he believed that one form of this self-protective deception involved an attempt by the unconscious mind to *falsely connect* one memory with another to obscure the real connections between thoughts. Such real connections, left undisturbed, might lead to the eventual recall of a threatening memory.

On one occasion, for example, Frau Emmy had a restless morning because she was worried that the hotel where her children and their governess were staying had a faulty elevator. She had recommended that the children use the elevator, and was now anxious over the thought that the elevator might fail. But a strange thing happened when Freud questioned Frau Emmy under hypnosis about the reason for her anxiety. Fully expecting to hear again the story of her concern for her children's safety, Freud was puzzled when

Frau Emmy related instead a worry that her massage treatments would have to stop because her menstrual period might begin. The explanation for this hypnotic non sequitur, Freud reasoned, might be found in the self-protective tendency of the mind to distort and to obscure connections between anxiety-arousing ideas. Ideas can be rearranged into sequences that block conscious recognition of the correct sequence of ideas, the sequence that is connected to some anxiety-provoking thought.

Freud was able to decipher the meaning of Frau Emmy's jumbled thought train. Her real concern was for her oldest daughter, who was having some difficulty walking because of a severe attack of ovarian neuralgia. Frau Emmy had just that morning solicitously inquired of the children's governess if the girl, in her pain, had used the elevator to descend from the upper floor of the hotel instead of walking down. Then, blotting out the true source of her anxiety, her daughter's illness, Frau Emmy recalled only its oblique connection with the elevator. By displacing the anxiety to the least threatening component of the sequence, the elevator, the thought sequence became transformed:

> Not afraid of consequences of daughter's illness, but afraid that elevator might fail.

The perceptive Freud noticed that the anxious impulse was not only displaced to another thought, but that the displacement had occurred along meaningful associative lines.

> Daughter's menstrual problem → her own menstrual problem → elevator fear

Consequently, during hypnosis only the topmost displacement, fear of the elevator, had given way to the next item in the sequence, Frau Emmy's own menstrual problem. Even though hypnotic exploration with her physician had enabled penetration one layer down through the sequence, the fundamental layer—anxiety over the daughter's menstrual problem—was left untouched.

Relapse: Intensification of Symptoms

Within seven weeks of the beginning of treatment, Frau Emmy's condition was sufficiently improved to warrant her dismissal from the sanitarium. It appeared that the cathartic method had once again worked its miracle. This happy outcome, however, did not last long.

Seven months later, Breuer received word from Frau Emmy that her oldest daughter had suffered a recurrence of her ovarian difficulties, and this time the daughter had succumbed to a "severe nervous illness" as well. The girl had visited a gynecologist for her difficulty. During the treatment, she had manifested all the signs of a severe emotional disturbance. Frau Emmy had concluded that Freud was responsible for the daughter's condition because he had treated the subject so lightly during his therapy with her. Thus, Frau Emmy relapsed into the state in which Freud had first encountered her. After much coaxing, Breuer persuaded Frau Emmy that Freud was not at fault, and one year elapsed before she again visited her old physician.

Overdetermination of Symptoms

Frau Emmy now began a period of self-inflicted semistarvation (anorexia). She refused to eat complete meals, and she drank very little. Freud ordered her to increase her intake of food and liquid, and there followed a somewhat uncharacteristic argument between patient and physician.

Two days passed and Frau Emmy mellowed a little. Freud put her into hypnosis and asked why she could not eat and drink normally.

> "I'm thinking how, when I was a child [Frau Emmy began], it often happened that out of naughtiness I refused to eat my meat at dinner. My mother was very severe about this and

under the threat of . . . punishment I was obliged two hours later to eat the meat, which had been left standing on the same plate. The meat was quite cold by then and the fat was set so hard" (she showed her disgust) ". . . I can still see the fork in front of me . . . one of its prongs was a little bent. Whenever I sit down to a meal I see the plates before me with the cold meat and fat on them. And how, many years later, I lived with my brother who was an officer and who had that horrible disease [venereal disease]. I knew that it was contagious and was terribly afraid of making a mistake and picking up his knife and fork" (she shuddered) ". . . and in spite of that I ate my meals with him so that no one should know that he was ill. And how, soon after that, I nursed my other brother when he had consumption so badly. We ate by the side of his bed and the spittoon always stood on the table, open" (she shuddered again) ". . . and he had a habit of spitting across the plates into the spittoon. This always made me feel so sick, but I couldn't show it, for fear of hurting his feelings." (Freud, in Breuer & Freud, 1893–1895, p. 82)

We can discern in Frau Emmy's reminiscences a phenomenon that Freud called *overdetermination*. Each symptom, Freud discovered, had not one cause, not one root, but multiple determinants that had become associatively bonded together in the patient's thoughts. Consequently, one overt symptom represented many emotional threads woven to a single pattern. Conversely, a branching network of emotionally related ideas, impulses, and meanings supported each symptom. In Frau Emmy's case, the unitary symptom of refusing to eat capped a latent amalgam of previous experiences that centered on the arousal of disgust for the act of eating; cold meat and fat; fear of contracting a "foul" disease through shared eating implements; and revulsion at the act of spitting into a spittoon over dinner.

Freud again helped his patient to *abreact* or express these repressed emotions. From that time on, Frau Emmy was able to eat relatively normally, and she began to recover her composure in most other respects as well.

THE THEORETICAL YIELD FROM FRAU EMMY'S THERAPY

The case of Frau Emmy von N. is important for a firm understanding of psychoanalytic theory because it provides a vivid illustration of the clinical data on which Freud exercised his powers of observation, imagination, and reason. There are at least five important features of the case that deserve consideration:

1. A doctor using a new method of treatment for the first time might rigidly adhere to the technique to gain facility with its use. In so doing, he or she would be concerned with maintaining the correct form and be temporarily blind to the method's shortcomings and limitations. This was not the case with Freud's use of Breuer and Bertha's cathartic method. Freud was sensitive to the limitations of hypnosis and to the shortcoming of catharsis in achieving an understanding of the network of strangled emotions.

2. We must not forget that it was Frau Emmy who provided for Freud a service similar to the one provided for Breuer by Bertha, namely, a timely hint about how to proceed. Frau Emmy's irritation with Freud's incessant probing, questioning, ordering, and badgering led to her modifying her physician's technique. She wished to be allowed to speak her mind without interruption. This hint was to stand Freud in good stead several years later as he searched about for a way to modify his procedure with patients not susceptible to hypnotic suggestion.

3. Freud had been led to hypothesize that the workings of the mind could be directed toward defending the person's conscious self or ego from the recognition of unpleasant, frightening, or unacceptable thoughts. Frau Emmy's concern over her daughter's illness had been obscured by a conscious, but associatively related, concern for the safety of her children in the hotel elevator. The link in the chain between the conscious fear that the elevator might not be safe and the unconscious anxiety over her daughter's ovarian difficulties was revealed during hypnosis as the non sequitur of Frau Emmy's worry that she might have to forgo massage treatment if her own menstrual cycle interfered. This worry was the last of a chain of displacements. The conscious shield-memories (elevator fear, menstrual-interference-with-massage) served to distract her thinking from the more threatening idea of her daughter's illness. Defense, not confusion, was responsible for the displacements.

4. We can see evidence from this early case that Freud's attention was directed to the importance of childhood incidents, childhood emotions, and childhood conflicts in establishing the basis of an intricate associative chain of ideas that influences adult behavior. Frau Emmy's childhood dinnertime experiences with cold meat and fat and her terrifying experiences with death and disease had certainly not passed from her memory with time.

5. Freud accepted only the permanent removal of that symptom as proof that a symptom had been fully explained and cured. He did not accept the patient's verbal expression of relief as sufficient evidence that a symptom had been traced to its fundamental cause. Only his patient's subsequent behavior could satisfy that requirement. In consequence, Freud puzzled over the recurrence of Frau Emmy's symptoms after he had employed hypnotic suggestion to remove the memory traces of the strangled emotions. Such symptoms, he discovered, were overdetermined. Multiple causes, complex chains of experiences, contributed to the formation of a single symptom. Hence, to account for the persistence of some symptoms in the face of massive hypnotic suggestion to abandon them, Freud found it necessary to hypothesize that the fundamental cause of the symptom had *not* been reached (cf. Freud, 1896c). Deeper probing often was necessary.

THE EVOLUTION OF METHOD: FRAÜLEIN von R.

In 1892, Freud faced an intensification of his difficulties with the cathartic method: Fraülein Elisabeth von R., a pseudonym for Fraülein Ilona Weiss, his latest patient, could not be hypnotized.

Hypnotism had been an invaluable adjunct in applying the cathartic method, widening the scope of the patient's consciousness and "putting within . . . [the patient's] reach knowledge which he did not possess in his waking life" (Freud, 1925a, p. 27). Freud had experienced the same difficulty with some of his other patients. In fact, some patients were not even willing to try to submit to hypnosis. Freud suspected that unwillingness to be hypnotized, whether verbally expressed or mutely evident in uncooperative behavior, formed the basis for all such failures (Freud, in Breuer & Freud, 1893–1895, p. 268).

Fraülein Weiss, therefore, posed a formidable problem because she was either unable or unwilling to achieve the customary somnambulistic state. Freud suspected that her hysterical symptoms of intense pain in her legs and her inability to stand or to walk for long periods were connected with some experience that she could recall if only she felt free enough. The greatest difficulty confronting Freud in the treatment of Fraülein Weiss was to devise a way to enable her to discuss her symptoms freely and without reservation in the absence of hypnosis.

The Real Elisabeth von R.: Ilona Weiss

Elisabeth von R. was actually Fraülein Ilona Weiss, the youngest of three daughters of a well-to-do Hungarian family (Appignanesi & Forrester, 1992, pp. 108ff.). She was an intelligent, ambitious, and independent young woman who wanted to pursue her education rather than the traditional role of wife and mother. Ilona had a close relationship with her father, who, by all accounts, treated her as the son he had wanted. Ilona nursed him until his death after he developed a heart condition. Her leg pains began at that time, but a full paralysis did not occur until about two years after his death.

Freud learned from Fraülein Ilona Weiss that she had nursed her father after his heart attack for a period of one-and-a-half years. She slept in her father's room, attended to his needs morning and night, and forced herself to remain cheerful and encouraging. Taking care of a sick person is often more stressful than being ill oneself. Ilona experienced an attack of severe pain in her legs during this period, an attack so intense that she had to take to her bed and become a patient herself. Two years after her father's death, her leg pains returned. They were unbearable, and Ilona was unable to walk at all.

Furthermore, because of the death of her father, family members were very unhappy. Ilona's eldest sister married a talented and ambitious man, who unfortunately did not respect their mother; Ilona was resentful both toward her new brother-in-law and toward her sister for deserting the family. Her other sister also married in this period. The married couple remained close to the family. This sister then became pregnant and died in childbirth. The widowed brother-in-law was overcome with grief, and he withdrew from Ilona's family. In the space of a few years, Ilona had lost by death or by alienation those most important to her. She now began a period of almost total social isolation.

For Freud, the case history as thus far related was hard to understand. It contained no overt indication of the cause of Ilona's hysterical symptoms. Freud was stymied. In the past, such obstacles had been overcome by the judicious use of hypnotism. His frustration was not helped much by Ilona's often biting remarks about his treatment's lack of effectiveness.

With candor and lack of defensiveness, Freud conceded, "I was obliged to admit that she was in the right" (Freud, in Breuer & Freud, 1893–1895, p. 145).

SECOND CLUE TO THE FREE ASSOCIATION METHOD: THE CONCENTRATION TECHNIQUE

Freud drew on his experiences with Bernheim at the Nancy Clinic. He remembered an unusual demonstration during which Bernheim had suggested to one of his patients under hypnosis that he, Bernheim, was no longer present in the room. Bernheim further encouraged the patient in the belief that she would not see him no matter what he might do. Bernheim followed this hypnotic suggestion with a variety of threatening gestures directly in front of the subject's face, but she behaved in every way as if Bernheim no longer existed. Bernheim then added to his previous instructions the command to remember nothing of what had transpired, a typical **posthypnotic amnesia** command.

Bringing the patient back to wakefulness, he proceeded to demonstrate that the patient could recall what had transpired, despite the hypnotic amnesia. All that the hypnotist had to do was to insist strongly, urgently, and convincingly enough that the subject do so. To aid the process of recall, Bernheim placed his hand on the forehead of the subject, who was awake, and pressed firmly, while insisting that the memory of the previous events return. Much to Freud's surprise, the subject could recall the events of the hypnotic session. Thus, Bernheim had shown Freud that the patient actually does have a memory of the events but does not know that she or he remembers until a strong suggestion to that effect was made. This was Freud's clue to finding his way out of his lack of therapeutic progress with the hypnotism-resistant Fraülein Ilona.

Willful concentration thus became the basis of Freud's new approach to therapy and the investigation of unconscious processes. It is worth noting that the new **concentration**

technique was no less dependent than hypnotism had been on the quality of the relationship between doctor and patient. The new method, in fact, was really another form of using the patient's suggestibility to achieve therapeutic progress. Freud described his new strategy as follows:

> I decided to start from the assumption that my patients knew everything that was of any pathogenic [disease-causing] significance and that it was only a question of obliging them to communicate it. Thus when I reached a point at which, after asking a patient some question such as "How long have you had this symptom?" or: "What was its origin?" I was met with the answer: "I really don't know," I proceeded as follows: I placed my hand on the patient's forehead or took her head between my hands and said: "You will think of it under the pressure of my hand. At the moment at which I relax my pressure you will see something in front of you or something will come into your head. Catch hold of it. It will be what we are looking for.—Well, what have you seen or what has occurred to you?" (Freud, in Breuer & Freud, 1893–1895, p. 110)

Using the new concentration technique with Fraülein Weiss brought immediate results. After a long silence, she admitted that the pressure of Freud's hand had brought forth an important recollection. She remembered an evening in which a young man had romantically escorted her home from the social affair they had attended, the pleasure of their intimate conversation during the walk, and her feelings of distress on returning home to nurse her father.

Freud found that approach had been as successful in obtaining results as had Bernheim's technique, which he was imitating. Apparently, even the reluctant Fraülein Weiss could recall events that seemed meaningful in context without hypnotism. Freud thought that whatever ideas were evoked by the pressure of the concentration technique *had to* be related to the symptoms at hand. He still had not discovered the actual relationship between these newly recalled incidents and the ongoing process of Ilona's neurotic symptoms.

Conflict, Symbol, Conversion

Freud observed that Fraülein Weiss's memories were conflicted. She had known the young man for a short time, and because he could not yet support a wife, and because Ilona was dutifully bound to her ailing father, she had resolved to wait until she and her young man were independent before marrying. But, at the same time, she felt that her feelings for the young man were somehow incompatible with her equally worthy resolve to care for her father. She recalled that the night of the social gathering, after which she had walked home with the man, marked the height of her awareness of the conflict between her affection for the young man and her responsibility to her father.

When Ilona returned home late that night, she found her father's condition worsened, and she reproached herself for having sacrificed her father's care to her own pleasure. Ilona never again left her father for a whole evening. As a result, she saw her young man only rarely thereafter.

At the death of Ilona's father, the young man withdrew from her. Eventually, he moved far away and contact between the two was not maintained. Not only was the loss of her first love a painful experience for Ilona. She had not resolved the conflict between her feelings for the young man and her sense of duty to her father. The emotional quality of Ilona's incompatible feelings remained untouched.

On the basis of these revelations developed through the concentration technique, Freud reasoned that Ilona's symptoms were a technique of defense by which she had unconsciously converted her painful conflicting emotions into a bodily manifestation. Fraülein Weiss confirmed Freud's interpretation by informing him that she now knew why her leg pains always began at the same point on her thigh: This was the exact place upon which her father rested his leg every morning while she changed the bandages on his swollen leg. Clearly, the pain in her own legs had arisen through association and symbolization with her father's painful leg. Furthermore, as Freud and Ilona discussed this interpretation, the pain in her legs intensified, or as Freud put it: "her painful legs began to 'join in the conversation' . . ." (Freud, in Breuer & Freud, 1893–1895, p. 148).

Freud followed up her several symptoms using the new concentration technique. When asked, for instance, why other areas of her legs were painful, Fraülein Weiss produced a series of recollections of other emotionally painful events. Moreover, each of these events was connected by association or by symbolization with her legs or with the act of walking. For the pain she felt while standing, she produced a memory of standing at the door when her father was brought home after his heart attack. In her fright on that occasion, she had been frozen in place. When Freud asked her what else the notion of "standing" meant to her, she reproduced a memory of standing "as though spellbound" by her sister's deathbed.

Yet, despite the insights that had been attained, there seemed to be some hesitation, some difficulty in recalling certain feelings, desires, or events. It was as if Ilona, though cooperating with Freud in the removal of her symptoms, was nonetheless resisting the recollection of some important ideas. Freud wondered whether the new concentration technique was already proving to be a failure. Perhaps, he reasoned, there might be yet another psychological process at work here?

Resistance: Defensive Barrier to Psychological Pain

On those occasions when Freud applied the concentration technique and Ilona reported that nothing had occurred to her, Freud detected behind her tense and preoccupied facial expression a hint that ideas had come to her. For some reason, Freud suspected, Ilona did not want to communicate her thoughts to him:

> I could think of two motives for this concealment. Either she was applying criticism to the idea, which she had no right to do, on the ground of its not being important enough or of its being an irrelevant reply to the question she had been asked: or she hesitated to produce it because—she found it too disagreeable to tell. (Freud, in Breuer & Freud, 1893–1895, p. 153)

Freud therefore decided to proceed as if he had the greatest confidence in his technique. He informed his patient that he knew full well that she had thought of something under the pressure of his hand, and that if she continued to conceal it, she would never be rid of her pains.

Freud had correctly surmised that the cause of her recalcitrance was emotional resistance. Ilona reluctantly complied:

ELIZABETH [ILONA]:   "I could have said it to you the first time."

FREUD: "And why didn't you?"

ELIZABETH [ILONA]:   "I thought I could avoid it, but it came back each time," or "I thought it wasn't what you wanted." (Freud, in Breuer & Freud, 1893–1895, p. 154)

It was at this point, using the concept of resistance, that Freud was able to gather the several threads of evidence he had been collecting from his patients into a new series of insights:

1. **Resistance** to recalling significant emotional events is another form of defensive maneuver that the conscious mind employs to ward off threatening thoughts and feelings.

2. But such thoughts, though consciously resisted, may nevertheless continue to exert unconscious pressure in their striving for expression, if not in their original form, then in disguised form.

3. Thus, Ilona's *symptoms* were not only the result of strangulated emotion; they were, indeed, the *unconsciously symbolic expression* of an unresolved **conflict.**

4. Her symptoms were substitute expressions of the conflicted emotions.

5. Ilona's conflict was pushed from conscious awareness because it had never been adequately resolved.

6. It continued to be a source of painful and unacceptable self-perceptions for Ilona.

Fraülein Weiss's conflict over her duty to her father and her incompatible desire for the companionship of her young man certainly fit this mold. Yet, Freud discovered, there had to be more to it because the expression of her emotions had not completely removed Ilona's symptoms. A still unresolved conflict had to be continuing to operate behind some formidable resistance to its recall.

Symptoms as Self-Punishment

Covering old territory, again from his new perspective, Freud began to question Ilona again about the origins of her pains. Her thoughts turned back to the summer resort where she had stayed just before her sister's death in childbirth, her worries over her father's illness, and her feelings of despair and loneliness at having been unable to accomplish anything in life. Particularly strong at this period had been her desire for love, a desire that, contrary to her previous resolve to do without men after her unhappy love affair, had begun to soften her "frozen nature."

With these feelings uppermost in mind, the marriage of her sister to a man who cared lovingly and tenderly for her made a profound impression on Ilona. She knew that her sister regretted becoming pregnant again so soon after her first child's birth. However, Ilona also knew and marveled at the way her sister bore the discomfort of the illness resulting from her pregnancy with absolute calm.

Ilona went on a walk with this brother-in-law at a summer resort. He had wanted to remain with his sick wife, but even she urged him to accompany Ilona, and he relented. Ilona enjoyed the afternoon she spent with her sister's husband tremendously because they talked freely and intimately, and, for the first time, she had the feeling that someone really understood her. In consequence, she became overwhelmed with the desire to possess a man with the qualities of her brother-in-law. In fact, so strong was this desire that, a few days after their walk, Ilona returned to the place in the woods where they had been together and, in a reverie, dreamed of a man like him who might make her as happy as her sister. She arose from the reverie with her legs in pain.

The nature of her hidden conflict had become crystal clear to Freud: Ilona desired her brother-in-law, but she felt guilty over such feelings, particularly so because his wife—her own sister—was now ill and helpless. As clear as the conflict was to Freud, it was obscure to Ilona. Because she had, apparently, never admitted the existence of these feelings, her guilty wish had remained utterly alien to her conscious personality. Ironically, several months after that fateful walk in the woods, Ilona's wish almost came true. She was called to her sister's sickbed but when she arrived, her sister was dead.

> At that moment of dreadful certainty that her beloved sister was dead without bidding them farewell and without having eased her last days with her care—at that very moment another thought had shot through Elisabeth's mind, and now forced itself irresistibly upon her once

more, like a flash of lightning in the dark: "Now he is free again and I can be his wife." (Freud, in Breuer & Freud, 1893–1895, p. 156)

Here was the confirmation of Freud's burgeoning speculations about conflict and emotional resistance. Ilona had converted a series of painful ideas into bodily symptoms to exact a kind of self-punishment. She had an illicit wish for her brother-in-law and was guilty for the feeling of gladness at the thought that her sister's death had freed him to marry her. By the time she had come to treatment with Freud, the memory of her love and guilt had already been defensively isolated from her awareness.

Fraülein Weiss was devastated at the eventual realization of her own feelings. Freud was kind to point out, however, that, strictly speaking, she was not responsible for her feelings and, more important, her symptoms and suffering were proof enough of her sound moral sense.

THE THEORETICAL YIELD FROM FRAÜLEIN WEISS'S THERAPY

Freud had progressed sufficiently in his use of the cathartic method with Fraülein Weiss to consolidate his observations into important theoretical concepts.

Concentration Technique

Fraülein Weiss's lack of susceptibility to hypnotism had initially prodded Freud into the search for a new therapeutic technique. Ilona thus provided the occasion for Freud's incorporation of a second clue in the process of developing his ultimate psychoanalytic method of free association. Freud recalled that Bernheim had demonstrated at the clinic in Nancy that a posthypnotic patient could willfully remember her previous hypnotic experiences if she was authoritatively pressured to do so. This had been the prototype for Freud's development of the concentration technique using hand pressure with the recalcitrant Ilona. (Freud's first clue was Frau Emmy's acid remark that he should allow her to speak her mind without interruption.)

Defense and Resistance

Freud discovered, through use of the concentration technique, that active resistance to unacceptable ideas directed Ilona's thought processes. Ironically, only through the loss of hypnotism as a therapeutic tool could the significance, cause, and direction of the process of resistance be uncovered. Because the patient in the hypnotic state is largely freed from active avoidance of unacceptable impulses and ideas, the defensive nature of this "forgetting" in the conscious state could not be discerned.

Freud's discovery clearly had brought about a drastic change not only in the way therapy was conducted, but also in the theoretical conception by which its effects were to be understood. Breuer's cathartic method focused on the problem of breaching the patient's conscious amnesia through hypnosis to reach dammed-up emotions. Once reached, these feelings could finally be spent in a therapeutic reenactment of the traumatic moment. Then, hypnotic suggestion was employed to help the patient forget the unpleasantness of his or her experiences and to conduct his or her life without the troublesome symptom. Freud, in contrast, was reshaping therapy by zeroing in, not on the symptom and its backlog of unexpressed emotion, but on the patient's unwillingness to recall painful or unacceptable thoughts.

The goal of psychotherapy for Freud became the examination and interpretation of the patient's resistances in an attempt to enable the patient to deal with conflicts that had festered, defensively protected from real resolution. Thus, by working with, rather than by circumventing, emotional resistance, Freud discovered that hysterical symptoms were a form of psychological defense against threatening ideas and wishes. The symptoms of the neurosis were symbolic and associative replacements for the pain of unresolved, "forgotten" conflicts.

Repression and Conflict

Fraülein Weiss could not willingly recall her desire for her sister's husband or her guilt feelings, and she vigorously resisted the thought when pressured. Therefore a psychological factor that actively keeps the memory out of consciousness must have been operating. Furthermore, this same counterforce must have been responsible for originally removing the memory from awareness. Freud labeled this hypothetical force *repression*.

Repression is a kind of motivated amnesia for certain impulses, ideas, or events. Resistance to recall is evidence of motivated forgetting or repression. However, as soon as the word *motivated* is used, it becomes necessary to ask what that motive might be. The answer, it seemed clear to Freud, lies in the nature of any underlying unconscious conflict(s).

Not just any unpleasant thought or any painful memory is repressed. Only memories, thoughts, and ideas that are somehow connected to impulses or wishes that are unacceptable to the individual's conscious ethical standards are capable of causing the intense anxiety needed to trigger repression (Freud, 1910b, p. 24).

Removal from consciousness is one way of avoiding the emotional pain of the conflict when a solution to the discord is unavailable. Therefore, the thought that Ilona was glad that her sister was dead because her sister's death freed her husband to marry again was a totally unacceptable idea to Ilona's ethical self. If the problem had been only a momentary desire for her sister's husband, Ilona would probably have only *suppressed* (not repressed) the thought. **Suppression** involves the conscious or deliberate avoidance of certain ideas with the individual's full awareness that he or she refuses to entertain them. Repression, on the other hand, is characterized by the unconscious, automatic nature of the "forgetting" that it accomplishes. When repression operates, the individual is not aware of avoiding certain thoughts or impulses. It is like forgetting that you have forgotten and what you have forgotten. Another way of thinking of repression is that the forgetting is somehow in advance of any overt awareness of the thought or impulse itself. You might not consciously know what you are repressing.

A Dynamic Unconscious

Though removed from consciousness by repression, emotions continue to operate unconsciously, thus comprising what Freud termed, the **dynamic unconscious.** Freud concluded that an emotion might produce symptoms that symbolically, or through association with other ideas, replace the expression of the emotion. Repression of wishes or impulses is not always an adequate response to conflict or strong enough to keep symptoms from emerging. A symptom, Freud discovered, could express the emotion in distorted form. In Fraülein Weiss's case, the symptoms of pain in her legs and the inability to walk or stand were shaped by a series of symbolic ("standing alone") and associative links:

- standing in shock by her dead sister's bed;
- walking with her brother-in-law;
- walking with her first love while she should have been caring for her father; and
- allowing her father to place his leg on her thigh to be bandaged.

Breuer had been right: The energy of the strangulated emotion had to be expressed somehow. But the cause of the neurotic's symptoms was not simply the damming up of emotional energy. First, Freud realized, there had to be a wish or an impulse that was incompatible with an individual's conscious self-perception. Such a wish would be at odds with his or her everyday ethical principles. Only this incompatibility could carry the conflict to an ego-threatening intensity. Then the conflict's associated emotions could be dammed up by repression. **Conflict** of a wish with a conscious ethical principle is the essence of defense by repression. It is an active, dynamic process giving painful, if mute, evidence of the power of unconscious forces.

It is interesting to note that some early attempts at experimental testing of the Freudian hypothesis of repression sorely missed the point. Some of these experimenters naively assumed, in their enthusiasm to design experiments, that any anxiety-provoking idea could trigger repression. Often, this unsophisticated version of the theory led to the creation of mild forms of anxiety or unpleasantness as experimental analogs of Freud's ideas. In a great number of cases, these attempts did not come close to the kind and the quality of anguish that Freud conceptualized as the basis of repression. The mechanism of repression remains a difficult phenomenon to study in the laboratory (see Monte, 1975, Chapter 3).

FREUD'S FINAL CLUE TO THE FREE ASSOCIATION METHOD

For his final modification of his developing therapeutic procedures, Freud followed yet another clue, a recollection from his own youth. One of his favorite authors, Ludwig Borne, had offered the following advice to those who wish to write creatively:

> Take a few sheets of paper and for three days on end write down, without fabrication or hypocrisy, everything that comes into your head. Write down what you think of yourself, of your wife, of the Turkish War, of Goethe, of Fonk's trial, of the Last Judgement, of your superiors—and when three days have passed you will be quite out of your senses with astonishment at the new and unheard-of-thoughts you have had. (Quoted in Freud, 1920b, p. 265. See also Jones, 1953, p. 246)

Borne's startling proposal apparently left a lasting impression on Freud, for he now began to follow Borne's advice, not for writing, but for allowing his patients free play for their thoughts during therapy. Freud developed a technique of therapeutic communication designed to permit patients to roam freely through their fleeting thoughts, verbalizing each idea as it occurred. He permitted his patients to omit nothing. Freud instructed each of his patients in the new technique of **free association** in the following way:

> You will notice that as you relate things various thoughts will occur to you which you would like to put aside on the ground of certain criticisms and objections. You will be tempted to say to yourself that this or that is irrelevant here, or is quite unimportant, or nonsensical, so that there is no need to say it. *You must never give in to these criticisms, but must say it in spite of them—indeed, you must say it precisely because you have an aversion to doing so.* . . . Finally, never forget that you have promised to be absolutely honest, and never leave anything out because, for some reason or other, it is unpleasant to tell it. (1913a, pp. 134–135; italics added)

Freud's **fundamental rule of psychoanalysis** was to say everything that came to mind without editing or censoring the stream of thought. Sometimes patients had great difficulty following the fundamental rule. In fact, patients would employ the most devious techniques of escaping the new fundamental rule. They would engage Freud in conversation about the decorations in his office, or in a discussion about the state of the weather, or they would pursue some abstract and irrelevant topic on which they considered themselves expert—anything rather than abandon logical and emotional censorship over their thoughts.

With careful prodding, urging, with constant reminders and corrections, Freud helped his patients see the importance of allowing the mind to take its own path. The associations that emerged did not prove to be random or accidental. Freud discovered that the sequence, content, and speed of the flow of ideas revealed an underlying logic.

COMPROMISE FORMATION: THE MEANING OF SYMPTOMS

Consider the following description of disordered behavior:

> An 11-year-old boy would not sleep each night until he had performed the following compulsive ceremony. He recounted to his mother every minute detail of the day; all scraps of paper, lint, or rubbish on the carpet in his bedroom had to be picked up; the bed had to be pushed up against the wall; three chairs, no more, no fewer, must stand by the bed; the pillows must be placed in a particular pattern on the bed. Finally, just before sleeping, the boy had to kick out with his legs a certain specified number of times and then lie on his side. Only then would sleep come. (Based on Freud, 1896b, p. 172)

The young boy's sleep ritual is evidence of a disorder known as **obsessional neurosis.** Obsessional neurotics practice a variety of ritualistic behaviors to avoid the experience of anxiety. When the obsessive is prevented from carrying out the behavior in question, he or she succumbs to an intense anxiety attack. The obsessive patient suffers from ostensibly unwanted, but continually intrusive, ideas that threaten to flood consciousness. Performance of a ritual-like series of behaviors temporarily alleviates the discomfort produced by the constant succession of the obsessive ideas. How could Freud make sense of the connection between the obsessive ideas and the compulsive anxiety-reducing ritualistic behaviors? Utilizing his new conception of **defense,** Freud sought to unlock the mystery of the obsessive person's behavior by attempting to understand the personal meaning of symptoms.

> The nature of obsessional neurosis can be expressed in a simple formula. Obsessional ideas are invariably transformed self-reproaches which have reemerged from repression and which always relate to some sexual act that was performed with pleasure in childhood. (1896b, p. 169)

Unable to sleep until his ceremonial acts involving chairs, pillows, bed, and rug had been accomplished, along with a detailed explanation to his mother of the day's events, the 11-year-old boy was able to reveal in analysis the defensive nature of these compulsive behaviors. Some years earlier, a servant girl had abused him sexually at bedtime. She had lain on top of him in the bed, and this memory was forgotten until a recent similar experience revived it. The defensive meaning of the ceremony became clear:

> The chairs were placed in front of the bed and the bed pushed against the wall in order that nobody else should be able to get at the bed; the pillows were arranged in a particular way so that they should be differently arranged from how they were on that evening; the movements with his legs were to kick away the person who was lying on him; sleeping on his side was because in the scene [with the servant girl] he had been lying on his back; his circumstantial confession to his mother was because, in obedience to a prohibition by his seductress, he had been silent to his mother about this and other sexual experiences; and, finally, the reason for his keeping his bedroom floor clean was that neglect to do so had been the chief reproach that he had so far had to hear from his mother. (Freud, 1896b, pp. 172n.–173n.)

Each of these compulsive behaviors served a double purpose. First, they served as a means of self-initiated, self-inflicted punishment for having engaged in behavior that was pleasurable but "bad." Second, performance of the ritual allowed the boy no time to think about the guilt-provoking memory or about possible future seductions. Thus, distraction as a type of avoidance as well as self-imposed penance formed the basis of his symptoms.

Paradoxically, the obsessive ideas and the compulsive acts were also a means of gratifying the pleasurable (yet anxiety-triggering) impulse involved in the taboo sexual activity. Each night, through the symptomatic ritual, the original seduction was recalled or relived. Freud therefore termed these symptoms **"compromise formations"**: they balanced the anxiety and the guilt of the conscious personality against the pleasurable gratifications sought by the unconscious.

Only by assuming the defensively altered form of the ritual acts could the repressed memory of the seduction take a place in consciousness. In effect, the symptoms symbolically substituted for the sexual gratification that the boy would not allow himself in reality (Freud, 1916, p. 368). The patient reproached himself for "bad wishes" and guilt-provoking experiences, expiating the guilt by ritual, while his symptoms achieved partial gratification of the very same wish that he sought to repudiate. In performing his defensive ritual against seduction, the young boy reenacted, not any the less completely, the very experience he struggled to escape. It was a way of "having one's cake" and "not having it" at the same time.

SEXUAL MOTIVES AS THE BASIS OF CONFLICT: ORIGINS OF THE HYPOTHESIS

The common denominator that Freud had discovered among his patients was the presence of erotic impulses from childhood that were frustrated or guilt-laden. Thus, to take but two examples, Fraülein Weiss suffered the pain of unacceptable desire for her brother-in-law because this desire clashed with her sense of moral responsibility; the 11-year-old boy's sleep ritual involved the stress produced by a pleasurable, yet anxiety-laden, seduction. Many of Freud's other patients revealed sexual themes in their free associations. In each such case, Freud was able to trace the themes back to incidents and experiences of childhood.

Freud recalled some years later in writing the "History of the Psychoanalytic Movement" (1914b) that offhand comments of Breuer, Charcot, and a gynecologist named Chrobak about the sexual nature of neurotic disorders in women had shown that the idea of the seduction hypothesis had fleetingly passed through the minds of other workers in the field. Chrobak and Breuer later denied any knowledge of such comments, and Freud concluded that Charcot, too, would have joined them in denial had he had the opportunity (Jones, 1953, p. 248).

Seduction Hypothesis

Intrigued by the direction his clinical investigations were taking, Freud asked the logical question: Why should sexual experiences and sexual motives be the common denominator in the cases he had observed? The answer, he suspected, could be found only by examining the neurotic's fundamental defensive response: repression.

Only emotional content intense enough to overwhelm the ego was ever subject to repression in the patients Freud had treated. One would, therefore, logically expect—if sexual motives were the common denominator—that any emotion connected with the sexual experience of patients would have been correspondingly intense. But there is a problem with this supposition. Most of Freud's patients were able through analysis to trace the critical sexual experiences to their childhood years when, presumably, their physical capacity for sexual stimulation had been undeveloped or nonexistent. Hence, the seduction by an adult in childhood could not have led to full understanding or to full sexual arousal with its normal accompaniment of emotional excitation. How, then, could these relatively mild childhood feelings ever have been intense enough to trigger repression?

The time sequence was wrong. Logically, the sequence should have been, first, some sexual experience like a forceful seduction by an adult; then, repression of the experience because of the intensity of the conflict between feelings of pleasurable arousal and feelings of guilt or anxiety; and, finally, the outbreak of neurotic symptoms in behalf of the repressed impulses. However, if the traumatic seduction had taken place in childhood, as many of his patients reported, this sequence was impossible. There could not have been sufficient sexual arousal or pleasure in a child to establish an intense enough conflict to trigger repression at that time.

In order for repression to have occurred, a new, inverted sequence had to be postulated, placing repression at the end of the process. Freud developed the following formulation of the **seduction hypothesis** to explain all cases of hysterical neurosis: The sexual experience (seduction) occurs first; then amnesia for it until some stimulus or situation triggers by its similarity recall of the incident at maturity; then, finally, repression and symptom formation after maturity has been reached. In other words, neurosis was not a product of childhood, but a process begun in those early years and brought to fruition in maturity (Freud, 1896b, 1896c, and 1898, pp. 279–285).

Logic of the Seduction Hypothesis

Freud examined the new hypothesis carefully. Ordinarily, he knew, when sexual fantasies or thoughts with sexual content are entertained, an adult becomes sexually aroused. This actual physical arousal is always more intense than any later, secondary memory of the experience. But if his reasoning up to this point was correct, a sexual seduction experienced before physical maturity (that is, before eight to ten years) would be experienced only as a somewhat faded recollection years later in maturity. It becomes necessary, therefore, to assume that the memory is intensified from some other source of energy (cf. Freud, 1954, Letter No. 52, p. 174).

Freud supposed that the source of energy was the bodily arousal associated with sexual excitation. Furthermore, he supposed that physical sexual arousal could be rechanneled into psychological emotional arousal. The result would be a conversion of physical, biological energy into mental, psychological energy. If such a process were possible, then the memory of the earlier experience (that is, the seduction) would initiate the deferred bodily arousal some years after the experience, when the individual had developed the biological capacity for appropriate somatic response. In this delayed version, it is the memory of the experience that leads to the kind of intense physical arousal that would be stronger than the original passive-seduction experience itself.

Proportionate adult anxiety and guilt would accompany and augment the memory image—intensifying it—to bring about the conflicting psychological state of affairs that was not possible during the actual experience in childhood (cf. Freud, 1896b, pp. 172–175 and pp. 166n.–167n; see also 1916, Lecture XXIII, pp. 361–371). Thus, Freud reasoned, a memory could actually be more potent than the actual experience it represented if there were a biological process that lagged behind the psychological development of children.

At maturity, there would be sufficient incremental emotional arousal, freshly fueled by the slower developing biological events, for repression to operate.

Freud had managed to answer a key question as to why sexual content, above all else, was the basis of the neurotic disorders he had seen. Only the sexual experiences of individuals are subject to the delay in physical development that human biology imposes. So, of all the experiences and motives of childhood, only the sexual among them would succumb to repression because only the sexual experiences become intensified by the developments of puberty. Neurotics, indeed, suffer from reminiscences.

Abandonment of the Seduction Hypothesis

The seduction hypothesis was an elegant one, for it accounted in one stroke for two observations:

- reports of childhood seductions by Freud's patients;
- the fact that his patients had been mentally healthy throughout childhood, succumbing to neurotic disorder only in adulthood.

However, new questions arose:

- What accounts for the period of childhood amnesia during which the seduction experience remains dormant?
- What stimulates the recollection of these early seductions in adulthood?

In supplying answers to these questions, Freud realized that he had made a major error.

Reviewing the evidence on which the seduction hypothesis had been based, Freud discovered that he had been a victim of his own naïveté. In a letter written to his friend Wilhelm Fliess on September 21, 1897, Freud revealed how some critical rethinking had caused the collapse of his seduction theory (1954, pp. 215–217). He enumerated the reasons:

- the high improbability of universal sexual abuse of children by their fathers, even though for a time it had seemed credible;
- the failure of his patients' revelations of such seductions to accomplish any lasting therapeutic effect;
- the hard-won insight that the unconscious cannot distinguish between reality and fantasy, an insight that had forced the conclusion that the reports of childhood seduction were not of real events but of imagined happenings;
- the discovery that, even in the severe psychoses, when the unconscious contents flood consciousness, no infantile sexual seductions are revealed.

Freud could only comment, years later:

. . . If the reader feels inclined to shake his head at my credulity, I cannot altogether blame him. . . . When, however, I was at last obliged to recognize that these scenes were only phantasies which my patients had made up or which I myself forced on them, I was for a time completely at a loss. (1925a, p. 34)

Toward a Revised Theory: Childhood Sexuality

Freud did not long remain in this bewildered state. He began to revise his thinking in the light of the new evidence that seduction tales were fantasies, products of the imagination.

> If hysterical subjects trace back their symptoms to traumas that are fictitious, then the new fact that emerges is precisely that *they create such scenes in phantasy*, and this psychical reality requires to be taken into account alongside practical reality. This reflection was soon followed by the discovery that these phantasies were intended to cover up the autoerotic activity of the first years of childhood, to embellish it and raise it to a higher plane. And now, from behind the phantasies, the whole range of a child's sexual life came to light. (1914b, pp. 17–18; italics added)

Freud was gradually coming to the view that children are not passive participants in erotic activities imposed on them, as the seduction hypothesis had it, but they are, instead, active initiators of autoerotic behaviors. He would thus replace the seduction theory with the idea of **childhood sexuality.** Moreover, Freud had begun to understand the importance of fantasy in the mental economy of his patients. Imaginary events, he realized, occupied the same status as real events *in the unconscious.*

FREUD'S INTEGRITY QUESTIONED— AND THE QUESTIONER QUESTIONED

Freud's own account of his reasons for abandoning the seduction hypothesis has been challenged by Jeffrey Masson (1984a, 1984b). Masson charged that Freud needed to abandon the seduction hypothesis to protect his professional standing and the professional image of his friend Dr. Wilhelm Fliess, a Viennese eye, ear, nose, and throat doctor.

Masson (1984b) marshals detailed historical evidence gleaned from his access to an unedited version of the letters between Freud and Fliess. The bulk of this evidence cannot be reviewed here, but we can briefly summarize the main features of Masson's argument.

Freud's experiences in Paris with Charcot exposed him to an eminent pathologist, Paul Brouardel, who taught fellow physicians about the brutal effects of child rape. Freud also had read several clinical texts on sexual abuse of children. Masson concludes that Freud was keenly aware of the reality of sexual seduction and assault.

Also, Masson considered the case of Emma Eckstein significant. One of Freud's earliest patients was Emma Eckstein, a 27-year-old woman who suffered a variety of hysteric symptoms and menstrual complaints. Freud referred Emma Eckstein to his friend Fliess for nasal surgery in an effort to control her menstrual difficulties. Fliess, apparently a quack, had developed an odd theory relating nasal difficulties with sexual functioning. His theory was that the functioning of the nasal mucous membranes was somehow causally connected to the activity of the mucous membranes of the vulva. The surgery apparently made sense to both Freud and Fliess.

Fliess botched the surgery by leaving a piece of surgical gauze in Emma's nasal cavity, and during the weeks that followed, Emma hemorrhaged profusely to a point of near death. Freud eventually consulted another nasal surgeon and Emma's life was saved, but poor Emma remained badly disfigured for the remainder of her life. When the second surgeon began removing the gauze, Freud actually became sickened and dizzy and had to retreat to the next room. Freud reported that another member of the household gave him a small glass of brandy, which restored his composure. He wrote to Fliess that when he returned still somewhat shaky to the room where Emma and the surgeon were working, "She greeted me with the condescending remark, 'So this is the strong sex' " (Freud, 1985, p. 117).

It is unclear whether it was the hemorrhage he observed that sickened him or whether his feelings of guilt and responsibility overcame him. Freud's opinion was expressed to Fliess in a letter:

I do not believe it was the blood that overwhelmed me—at that moment strong emotions were welling up in me. So we had done her an injustice; she was not at all abnormal, rather, a piece of iodoform gauze had gotten torn off as you were removing it and stayed in for 14 days, preventing healing; at the end it tore off and provoked the bleeding. That this mishap should have happened to you, how you will react to it when you hear about it; what others could make of it; how wrong I was to urge you to operate in a foreign city where you could not follow through on the case; how my intention to do my best for this poor girl was insidiously thwarted and resulted in endangering her life—all this came over me simultaneously. (Freud, 1985, p. 117)

It is fairly clear from the letter that Freud was overwhelmed by his feelings of uncertainty and, perhaps, guilt. He probably had serious doubts about Fliess's surgical treatment of someone he now realized was "not at all abnormal." Yet he avoids direct accusations or criticisms of Fliess.

Masson concludes that Freud needed to avoid blaming Fliess both for the strangeness of his treatment of Emma Eckstein's problems and for his lack of surgical skill. One way to defend Fliess and himself was to blame the victim. That is to say, Freud assumed initially that her continued nasal bleeding was another of her hysterical symptoms, not the result of Fliess's interventions. In this way, Freud abandoned the reality of sexual seduction as the cause of hysterical symptoms in favor of the patient's own fantasies and wishes. The stage was set to drop the seduction hypothesis in favor of seduction fantasies created by the patients themselves.

Masson argues that Freud abandoned the seduction hypothesis for these reasons:

- his realistic concern that the professional community would not look kindly on a psychiatrist who employed such data as the basis for his theories;
- his involvement in the Emma Eckstein case, and his consequent guilt and shame; and
- possible indirect pressure from Fliess to abandon the theory because of Fliess's advocacy of the idea of child sexuality. Masson asserted that Fliess was a possible child abuser/seducer, a pedophile, himself.

According to Masson's critique, Freud had to abandon the seduction hypothesis in favor of a theory that emphasized fantasy rather than the harsh facts of reality. Masson stated what he thought was the main consequence for psychoanalysis:

. . . by shifting the emphasis from an actual world of sadness, misery, and cruelty to an internal stage on which actors performed invented dramas for an invisible audience of their own creation, Freud began a trend away from the real world that, it seems to me, is at the root of the present-day sterility of psychoanalysis. (1984b, p. 144)

Many points cast doubt on Masson's conclusions, which have not gained general acceptance. For one thing, the Emma Eckstein case history (Freud, 1896c) shows no evidence of real seduction or brutality in Emma's history, and the same lack of brutal seductions is to be found in most of Freud's published cases (1896c).

It would appear to us that Freud was being honest when he reported that one of the reasons he abandoned the seduction theory was that he could not find a traumatic history in every patient who was hysterical (Freud, 1896b, 1896c).

Even some of the evidence that Masson cites in favor of his own argument maintains precisely the opposite viewpoint. For example, Masson (1984b, pp. 93–94) reproduces a previously unpublished letter from Freud to Fliess in which Freud recounts a case history of a young woman who learns that her brother kissed and licked a sister's feet at bedtime.

Clearly this memory is sexual, but it is hardly a memory of a traumatically abusive or assaultive event (cf. Storr, 1984, p. 35).

In the end, for better or worse, Freud's psychoanalysis was constructed along certain lines, and it is unlikely that contemporary analysts will alter the main forms of the theory if that alteration requires abandonment of the importance of personal meaning, wishes, and fantasies. Reality counts, but if Freud had not focused on fantasy in 1895, latter-day analysts would certainly have had to invent the idea. To what extent Freud may have assumed this focus to protect himself and Fliess is an issue that is not yet resolved.

It is noteworthy that, even today, the issue of the veracity of adult "memories" of having been sexually abused as children is still controversial. Even the testimony of children who state that they have recently been sexually abused is often false or questionable. Obviously, some such memories and accounts are valid. But some are not. The still unsolved problem, a century after Freud's efforts, is how to distinguish between those that are valid and those that are false memories or reports. Knowing the difficulty of this issue and our own lack of progress in this area, it is hard to blame Freud for the approach that he took.

PERSONAL SOURCES OF THE HYPOTHESIS: FREUD'S SELF-ANALYSIS

In the months before he announced to Fliess his not-quite-fatal error of the seduction hypothesis, Freud had begun to subject his own dreams and thoughts to careful scrutiny through the method of free association (Jones, 1953, pp. 319–323; Kris, 1954, p. 30). Beginning in the summer of 1897, Freud embarked on a process of self-exploration that was to occupy him for the rest of his life. Although we cannot trace the entire progress of his self-analysis here, several crucial discoveries deserve our consideration both for what they reveal about Freud and for the light they throw on the origins of some of his ideas. For, much to his own amazement, Freud uncovered a more-or-less erotic love for his mother and an equally disturbing hostility toward his father. These discoveries were later to be incorporated into psychoanalytic theory as central tenets (Freud, 1900, pp. 318, 583).

The triggering incident for Freud's application of psychoanalytic method to himself seems to have been the emotional aftermath of his father's death in October 1896. Though Freud did not at this time begin his "official" self-analysis, the emotional upheaval of the loss and some resulting family discord over proper funeral rites occasioned a dream about his father that provoked in him some residue of unexpected guilt. The dream led Freud to suspect that he was not as sorry for the loss of his father as he should have been. Yet, as he wrote to Fliess, he experienced a feeling of "being torn up by the roots," and he continued to be troubled in this way for some months (1954, Letter No. 50, p. 170). Some years later, in *The Interpretation of Dreams* (1900, p. xxvi), Freud acknowledged that his father's death was "the most poignant loss of a man's life" and had played a significant part in both his self-analysis and in the writing of that book. We take up the matters of Freud's ambivalent relationship to his father and the effect of that relationship on his theory in Chapter 3.

Another motive for Freud's undertaking the task of self-analysis was his discovery in himself of several neurotic symptoms (Schur, 1972, esp. Chapter 4). He had a disproportionate concern with the prospect of an early death, which was prompted by some cardiac symptoms. Freud also evidenced a phobia regarding travel. His concern for his health and the fear that he was developing severe heart disease may have included an element of neurotic anxiety even though his physical symptoms were certainly real enough (Jones, 1953; Schur, 1972). Freud also developed what, today, we would consider an addiction to

nicotine. He continued smoking his cigars even when faced with painful surgery operations for cancerous lesions in his mouth.

A somewhat different neurotic symptom involved Freud's behavior when setting out
on the journeys he professed to love so much. Throughout his life, he would frequently
turn up at a railway station hours before his train was scheduled to depart, apparently in
a compulsive attempt not to miss his train. But he would just as often enter the wrong rail
station or board the wrong train. Freud recognized that these were symptomatic acts suggestive of anxiety and an unconscious fear of embarking on a journey.

Freud was motivated by his awareness of some of his neurotic patterns to try to face
and accept whatever truths he could discover within himself. Freud wanted to have insight into the depths of his personality and to become master of his fate. He thus applied
to himself methods of self-exploration that were similar to the approaches he was so carefully shaping with his patients.

Self-Recognition of Oedipal Feelings: Freud's Two Mothers

During his self-analysis Freud discovered within himself several components of what he
would later call the "Oedipus complex." As his self-analysis progressed, he was able to
reconstruct and, with his mother's help, corroborate several memories from childhood.
These reconstructions allowed him to piece together a fairly accurate account of his own
emotional life in childhood. One such memory fragment concerned the recollection of the
elderly woman who had been the infant Freud's nanny along with the memory of a seemingly unconnected, but especially important, train ride with his mother:

> . . . the "prime originator" [of my troubles] was a woman, ugly, elderly, but clever, who told
> me a great deal about God Almighty and Hell and who gave me a high opinion of my own
> capacities; and that later (between the ages of two and two-and-a-half) my libido [sexual in-
> terest] was stirred up towards *matrem,* namely on the occasion of a journey with her from
> Leipzig to Vienna, during which we must have spent the night together and I must have had
> an opportunity of seeing her *nudam.* . . . (1897, Letter No. 70, p. 262)

This passage from Freud's correspondence with Fliess is notable for a number of
reasons:

1. It is a clear indication of the importance of an idea that Freud had been toying
with for some time: namely, that the child experiences sexual impulses toward his mother.
By "sexual", Freud meant to include all pleasurable and affectionate interactions, commonly called love, between mother and child (see, for example, Freud, 1925a, p. 38). In
this same letter, Freud hinted that his anxiety over traveling could be dated to the train
ride with his mother and the residue of guilt that remained from his feelings toward her.

2. The second important aspect of this memory fragment is Freud's admission of
such feelings himself. Notice, however, that both the word for "mother" (*matrem*) and the
word for "nude" (*nudam*) are in Latin, as though writing them in his native German would
have made them more threatening. Freud must have experienced firsthand the kind of
emotional resistance that his patients often exhibited.

3. Freud evidenced another characteristic typical of a patient undergoing psychoanalysis, an erring sense of time. Freud could not have been only two or two-and-a-half
years old, as he states. Ernest Jones, after careful research, places the date of the train ride
somewhat later, at around the age of four (1953, p. 13). Max Schur, Freud's more recent
biographer, concurs with Jones's estimate (1972, p. 120). Indeed, Schur suggests that it
is probable that the infant Freud had many times observed some intimate scenes between
his mother and father in the crowded conditions of their home.

4. The "prime originator" mentioned in the letter was the nursemaid who had cared for Freud as an infant and for several years of his childhood. This enigmatic old woman had popped in and out of Freud's memories for years. During his self-analysis, the memory finally yielded its secret. To substantiate his analysis, Freud asked his mother, now in her old age, to confirm the facts of his recollection. She confirmed that he had indeed had a nurse who was elderly but clever, and that she had been arrested for stealing his silver coins and toys. At the time of the incident, Freud's mother had relinquished his care to the nursemaid because she was in the last stages of pregnancy with Freud's younger sister, Bertha. Freud's self-analysis revealed that this nanny had a profound impact on his conception of himself, and that she had taught him a good deal about her religion. Paul Vitz has theorized that she even secretly baptized the baby Freud, who developed a "Christian unconscious" (Vitz, 1988). Moreover, this nanny was "my instructress in sexual matters, and chided me for being clumsy and not being able to do anything. . . ." (Freud, 1954, p. 220)

Thus, this "elderly but clever woman" was in charge of the young Freud, associated with sexuality in his memory, and most important, equated with his mother (Grigg, 1973; see also Gedo, 1976, pp. 298ff.). The identification in memory of the nanny and his mother had other determinants as well. Freud's older half brother, Philipp, had become a father substitute during the time of Freud's mother's pregnancy; and it was Philipp who had gone to fetch a policeman to arrest the nanny for her thefts. Freud's mother, helping her son to recollect these events, told Freud that Philipp's action had resulted in the nanny's imprisonment for 10 months. Thus, in the young Freud's mind, Philipp was responsible for the disappearance of one of his "mothers." Or, to put it another way, one of Freud's "fathers" enforced a separation between young Sigmund and one of his "mothers." With these facts in hand, Freud could focus his self-analysis on even more probing questions.

The Theme of Disappearing Persons

How had the equation between his nanny and his mother come about? Why was the nanny's disappearance so acutely felt? Freud's self-analysis provided the answers:

> I said to myself if the old woman disappeared so suddenly [on account of her imprisonment], it must be possible to point to the impression this made on me. Where is that impression, then? A scene then occurred to me, which for the last 29 years has occasionally emerged in my conscious memory without my understanding it. My mother was nowhere to be found: I was screaming my head off. My brother, Philipp, 20 years older than me, was holding open a cupboard for me, and when I found that my mother was not inside it either, I began crying still more, till, *looking slim and beautiful,* she came in by the door. What can this mean? Why was my brother opening the cupboard, though he knew that my mother was not in it, so that this could not pacify me? And then suddenly I understood. *I had asked him to do it. When I missed my mother, I had been afraid she had vanished from me just as the old woman had a short time before* [i.e., the maid's imprisonment]. Now I must have heard that the old woman had been locked up and consequently *I must have thought that my mother had been too*—or rather had been "boxed up"; for my brother Philipp, who is 63 now, is fond to this very day of talking in this punning fashion. *The fact that it was to him in particular that I turned proves that I knew quite well of his share in the nurse's disappearance.* (1897, Letter No. 7, pp. 264–265; italics added)

Freud's memory had condensed the account of the maid's disappearance with the memory of his mother's pregnancy. Analysis of the reconstructed memory was revealing. There was the implied accusation against Philipp to the effect that he had made Freud's mother vanish. Philipp was represented as a rival who controlled the whereabouts of Freud's mother—a rival, that is, who possessed adult authority. From other details of

Freud's life it was clear that Philipp also represented a specific father substitute. Note, too, that Freud's mother appeared in the memory as "slim and beautiful," emphasizing that her pregnancy was terminated.

Three elements, then, required interpretation:

- concern over Freud's mother's pregnancy;
- the demand that Freud's half brother open the cupboard; and
- an implied connection between Philipp causing the maid's disappearance and the disappearance of Freud's own mother.

Freud's self-analysis allowed him to clarify the relations among these three elements, as he reported some years later in *The Psychopathology of Everyday Life:*

> Anyone who is interested in the mental life of these years of childhood will find it easy to guess the deeper determinant of the demand made on the big brother [i.e., the request to open the cupboard]. The child of not yet three [i.e., Freud himself] had understood that the little sister [Bertha] who had recently arrived had grown inside his mother. He was very far from approving of this addition to the family, and was full of mistrust and anxiety that his mother's inside might conceal still more children. *The wardrobe or cupboard was a symbol for him of his mother's inside.* So he insisted on looking into this cupboard and turned for this to his big brother, who [as is clear from other material] *had taken his father's place as the child's rival.* Besides the well-founded suspicion that this brother had had the lost nurse "boxed up," there was a further suspicion against him—namely that *he had in some way introduced the recently born baby into his mother's inside.* (1901, p. 51n.; italics added)

The young Freud's disappointment when the cupboard was opened and his mother was not to be found inside was assuaged only by his relief when she reappeared "slim and beautiful," that is, without any other unwanted children. Key emotions contained in these disturbing memories involved the desperate fear of losing his mother to an adult rival, the vague understanding that men somehow put babies inside women, and the defensive telescoping of the maid's having been "boxed up" at the hands of the same adult rival with the memory of his mother's disappearance. Freud had thus discovered within himself the essential elements of the emotional constellation to be known later as the Oedipus complex.

Freud was singularly and passionately attached to his mother. He idealized her, and she, in turn, idolized him (Bernstein, 1976; Fromm, 1959; Gedo,1976; Grigg, 1973; Jones, 1953; Stolorow & Atwood, 1978). A good portion of his self-analysis had shown Freud, that, as a child, he wished to share his mother with no one, and that he had viewed, with enormous hostility, every potential rival for her attentions. His enforced separation from his real mother by virtue of her pregnancy, and his experience of a similarly imposed separation from his surrogate mother by a surrogate father figure helped Freud to comprehend the strength of a child's attachment to his mother and the child's desire for her exclusive attentions (Stolorow & Atwood, 1978). Freud was even able to face the enormity of his own aggression against rivals for his mother's love in his reconstruction of his death wishes against one such competitor, his younger brother Julius.

Julius did in fact die when Sigmund was only 19 months old, and to the young, wishful Freud this death must have seemed like the magical fulfillment of desire. As he was to theorize years later in works such as *Totem and Taboo* (1913b), the neurotic personality behaves as though thoughts were omnipotent. He had wished for the death of Julius, and it must have seemed the thought itself was sufficient to bring reality into line with desire. During his self-analysis, Freud reported this discovery to Fliess:

> . . . I welcomed my one-year-younger brother (who died within a few months) with ill wishes and real infantile jealousy, and that his death left the germ of guilt in me. (Freud, 1954, p. 219)

Figure 2.4 Sigmund Freud and his mother, Amalie Nathanson Freud, in 1872. Freud was 16 years old at the time this photograph was taken. The conventional pose with the distance between mother and son belies the deep attachment that Freud felt for his mother.

Source: Jones, E. (1953), by permission of Sigmund Freud Copyrights Ltd.

It is no wonder that the theme of disappearing persons held such significance for Freud. In his lifetime he had been exposed to the possibility of a "disappearing" previous wife of his father, to a disappearing mother substitute, to a disappearing mother, and to a disappearing younger rival for his mother's attentions. Thus, in short succession, through what must have been a painful self-exploration, Freud discovered in his own mental economy hostile wishes toward his father and toward his siblings; erotic wishes toward his mother; and a tangled series of anxieties and guilt that had forced these experiences out of consciousness.

Freud never ceased his self-analysis, reserving the last half hour of his day throughout his life for such self-exploration (Jones, 1953, p. 327). It was from the earliest self-analytic attempts that Freud derived his most fertile ideas, those which he sought to corroborate further with his patients. The implication of these early disturbing self-insights was clear: Children are capable of diffuse sexual feelings, and the first objects of their erotic endeavors and resulting jealous aggression are their parents, the people with whom they have had the most intimate contact.

It becomes necessary at this point to break off this essentially chronological treatment of psychoanalytic theory to gather together the several threads of Freud's continually evolving views of sexual development.

PSYCHOSEXUAL DEVELOPMENT: OEDIPUS AND ELECTRA

Human infants are born essentially helpless and vulnerable to all manner of painful and potentially lethal stimulation. It is only through the efforts of their caretakers that infants survive the first several years of life.

Erotogenic Bodily Zones

Consider the situation of the well-cared-for infant. When it experiences hunger, its cries bring its mother or caretaker with nourishment in the form of breast or bottle. The sucking response, with which it meets the nipple or bottle, though reflex at first, not only provides the needed nourishment to terminate the hunger pains, but also becomes a pleasurable source of stimulation. Gentle stimulation of the lips and mouth is quite satisfying and sensually pleasing. Even a thumb may become an object of sensual pleasure. The infant is finding satisfaction through the stimulation of its own body; it is, in Freud's terms, behaving *autoerotically* (1905, pp. 181–182).

The pleasurable activity of the mouth may be thought of as the prototype for various other potentially pleasurable zones of the body that yield satisfaction to rhythmic stimulation. Primary of such **erotogenic zones,** as they are called, are those areas of the body characterized by the presence of a mucous membrane, for example, the anus. But the infant's body pleasures are not restricted to mucous membrane areas. With time, these mucous membrane prototypes yield their dominance so that almost any part of the body may become an erotogenic zone. Thus the skin, when tickled or stroked, leads to great delight; the anus during elimination provides a sense of satisfaction at the pleasure of discharging tension, and so on.

Freud emphasized that children explore their own bodies, seeking sensations of pleasure. Consequently, Freud concluded, the infant's chief aim is the attainment of bodily or "organ pleasure" based on its experiences with the world, its body, and its caretakers. Food and the breast or bottle provided the first such experience and the mother or caretaker was the medium through which that learning took place. In Freud's day, the mother was directly connected with almost every other important—pleasurable and unpleasurable—activity of the infant's life. Freud therefore concluded that the mother would become the object of the child's constantly developing modes of seeking new pleasures.

The Widened Meaning of "Sexual"

The biological force underlying the child's pleasure-seeking activity is the sexual drive or **libido** (cf. Freud, 1905, p. 135; and 1916, p. 313). (Libido is a concept we give much more detailed consideration in the context of Freud's theory of instincts in Chapter 3.) The term "sexual" cannot be confined to the adult sense in which it is customarily used to indicate genital, procreative activity. Genital primacy, one component of the generalized sexual instinct, or libido, is a relatively late, postpubertal development. Genital sexuality has origins far more diffuse and deeply rooted in infantile pleasure-seeking activity than is ordinarily realized. Adult genital sexuality is only the final step in a long apprenticeship to pleasure.

The Oedipus Complex

The **Oedipus complex** occurs as a kind of emotionally climactic midpoint in the developmental sequence of the male child's ever-increasing interest in pleasurable sexual activity. In the first **psychosexual stages,** the child's dominant erotogenic zones are the oral and the anal areas. Eventually, however, through exploration of his own body, he discovers the pleasure to be derived from manipulation of a new zone, the genital area. It is at this point, when the mother first discovers the child's errant hand seeking out that taboo part of his body, that she is likely to take measures to prevent such "perversity." Her admonitions may take the form of direct or veiled threats to remove the tempting organ, or, more typically, she may delegate the responsibility to father (Freud, 1940, p. 189). Parental practices like these may have been widespread in Freud's post-Victorian age, but it is doubtful that a contemporary mother or father would resort to such extreme threats.

Even if such a threat is at first unbelievable, it easily becomes more real when it is reinforced by the sight, however accidental, of the female genitals. The young boy becomes convinced that castration is not only possible, but, in fact, has already been accomplished in some individuals. The distinction between the sexes is still obscure to the frightened and chastened boy.

In some diffuse and vaguely understood way, the pleasurable sensation produced by self-manipulation of the sexual organs is perceived by the child as connected with his relationship to his mother, displacing his earlier oral and anal interests.

> At this point in the developmental sequence, the child senses that his mother's attention and her warmly soothing ministrations are not exclusively his. Besides troublesome siblings, mother must be shared with father, and the child soon comes to resent and to be jealous of this interloper. Freud assumed that with increasing sophistication the child develops a belief that his father knows, or at least suspects, how much he would like to be rid of him. Anxiety-stricken and guilty, the young boy feels certain that his intense anger and avid pleasure-seeking are impossible to conceal. His submissive and overtly loving behavior, he feels, is but a transparent facade to an all-knowing, all-powerful father. What more appropriate retribution could father plan to exact than the removal of that organ that provides the most pleasure at this stage? Castration by the father becomes the overwhelming fear of the child's burgeoning ego, and this imagined outrage must be dealt with by the mechanisms of defense. Most notable of these is the mechanism of repression. (Monte, 1975, p. 100)

The period during which this emotional constellation of love, jealousy, and castration fear occurs is called the *phallic stage* of psychosexual development. Emotional ambivalence is the hallmark of the phallic stage, for the young boy not only must learn to give up his chosen love object, he must also reconcile his contradictory feelings of love for and anger at his father.

The Electra Complex

In the boy, it seemed clear that the Oedipus complex was dissolved by the real or fantasized threat of castration. However, since the girl, by virtue of her anatomical development, does not fear the loss of a penis, she must assume that its absence indicates that she has already been deprived. Consequently, for her the realization that she has been castrated initiates the Oedipus complex in the female or, as commonly labeled, the **Electra complex.** Freud alternately rejected and then accepted the term *Electra complex* for the distinctly different feminine version of this emotional constellation (cf. Freud, 1931, p. 229 for his arguments against the use of the term; and 1940, p. 194, for his apparent acceptance). Regardless of the term employed, the Electra complex in the female involves several highly distinctive processes that differentiate her from the male.

Attachment to the Mother: "Penis Envy"

Just as the little boy takes his mother as the first love object, the little girl likewise attaches herself intimately to her mother. Thus, like the little boy, she will also eventually

BOX 2.2 *Only Connect . . .*

Of course, Ruth Munroe's example of penis envy does not *prove* either the universality of penis envy in our own culture nor the Freudian assertion that penis envy is a consequence only of anatomy rather than of cultural factors. The social psycho-analytical theorist, Karen Horney, as indicated in Chapter 10, takes the point of view that penis envy occurs only if women are treated as inferiors. The anatomical differences between the sexes, in her view, are imbued with culturally defined meanings.

have to relinquish her first love object. More significantly, however, she will also have to relinquish her first erotogenic zone of pleasurable genital stimulation, the clitoris. When she first discovers that her clitoris is not a penis: ". . . she envies boys its possession; her whole development may be said to take place under the colors of envy for the penis" (Freud, 1940, p. 193).

An example of **penis envy** in a young child was provided by Ruth Munroe. Dr. Munroe, a psychologist was skeptical about Freud's theory until:

> . . . she observed her four year-old daughter in a bathtub with her brother. The daughter suddenly exclaimed, "My weewee (penis) is all gone,"—apparently comparing herself with her brother for the first time. Munroe tried to reassure her, but nothing worked, and for some weeks she objected violently even to being called a girl. (1955, pp. 217–218, as quoted in Crain, 1992, p. 233)

This example, however, by no means *proves* the universality of the experience of penis envy in little girls.

With the discovery that she lacks what, in her view, is an essential anatomical item, the girl at first tries to convince herself that her perception is wrong. She has seized on the clitoris as the nearest proximity to the external male genitalia, but the choice has not been successful. Maturation forces her to abandon even more fully any notion of a comparable external genital to that of boys. Ultimately, the girl is forced to the realization that she is lacking not only the penis, but also all the virtues of maleness that possession of such an organ implies.

> A variety of negative outcomes is possible: The girl, as she grows up, may develop a masculinity complex, in which she devoutly protests the injustice she perceives and comes to assume all the essential male personality characteristics in defiance of her alleged inferiority. On the other hand, she may eventually abandon sexual activity altogether in her attempt to avoid any reminder of her inferiority. (Freud, 1931, p. 230)

Devaluation of the Mother

In the light of her discovery that lack of a penis is a universal attribute of girls, devaluation of the mother and abandonment of her as a love object occurs (Freud, 1931, p. 233). Hostility accompanies this breaking off of the attachment for a variety of reasons. Some of these may include the real or fantasized idea that her mother deprived her of pleasures rightfully hers, or that her mother shortchanged her in affection, or, most important, that it was mother who deprived her of the envied organ. The hostility can reach a peak when a sibling is born:

> . . . what the child grudges the unwanted intruder and rival is not only the suckling but also all the other signs of maternal care. It feels that it has been dethroned, despoiled, prejudiced in its rights; it casts a jealous hatred upon the new baby and develops a grievance against the faithless mother. . . . (Freud, 1933, p. 123)

Consequently, it is to the father that the young girl now turns in her effort to obtain that which she "knows" her mother cannot provide.

Search for a Penis Substitute

Freud's earlier work with neurotic female patients had revealed the almost universal presence of a seduction-by-an-adult fantasy. In most of his published writings of the period he alluded to seduction, but Freud barely hinted that the seduction was accomplished by the patient's own father. He had, however, made the role of the father in the seduction tales of his patients known to his friend, Wilhelm Fliess, during the course of their correspondence (1897, p. 259; also in 1954, Letter No. 69, p. 215). In later published writings, Freud indicated that indeed it was the father who had been reported to have seduced his own child early in the child's life (1925a, p. 34). It was not until 1931, however, almost 35 years after his ideas on the role of childhood sexuality had replaced the original seduction hypothesis, that Freud revealed, in a paper on female sexuality, that mothers, too, had been indicted in the seduction fantasies (1931, p. 238; see also 1933, pp. 120–121).

Table 2.1   Successive Stages of the Oedipus and Electra Complexes Contrasted

Oedipus complex (boy)		
Motive	*Consequence*	*Outcome*
1. Attachment to mother (feeding, bodily care)	Jealousy of rivals, particularly of father	Feelings of hostility toward father
2. Castration fear (sight of female genitals; possible threats)	Fear of punishment by father for his desires to possess mother	Intensification of rivalry with father; development of need to camouflage hostility
3. Need to appease father and prevent imagined attack	Creation of facade of meekness and love for father	Repression of hostility and fear; relinquishment of mother; identification with father
"A mother is only brought unlimited satisfaction by her relation to a son; this is altogether the most perfect, the most free from ambivalence of all human relationships" (Freud, 1933, p. 133).		
Electra complex (girl)		
Motive	*Consequence*	*Outcome*
1. Attachment to mother (feeding, bodily care)	Jealousy of rivals	General feelings of inferiority; discovery of genital differences from males
2. Penis envy (sight of male genitals)	Jealousy of male organ and of male privileges	Devaluation of mother and of female role; adoption of male behaviors
3. Attachment to father as more powerful than mother	Seeking from father a penis substitute—a baby	Identification with female behaviors to appeal to father; slow fading of penis envy and mother devaluation
". . . girls hold their mother responsible for their lack of a penis and do not forgive her for their being thus put at a disadvantage" (Freud, 1933, p. 124).		

Of course, both types of seduction fantasy now made sense: In Freud's mind, they were products not of a perverse whimsy of hysterical patients, but of the female Oedipal stage of development. In the pre-Oedipal phase, the object of the seduction fantasy is the mother for both boys and girls. During the Oedipal period proper, the father becomes the focus of the girl's fantasy. She wishes for a penis from her father or a symbolic penis substitute, a baby. She cannot obtain a penis from her mother, who likewise lacks this vital equipment. With the wish for a "penis-baby," the girl fully enters the Oedipal phase (Freud, 1925b, p. 256).

Resolution of the Oedipus Complex and the Electra Complex

Freud summarized the dissolution of the boy's Oedipus complex:

> In boys . . . the complex is not simply repressed, it is *literally smashed to pieces by the shock of threatened castration*. Its libidinal cathexes are abandoned [i.e., the attachment to mother], desexualized and in part sublimated. . . . (1925b, p. 257; italics added)

In his final model of the mind, Freud extended this line of reasoning to show that the dissolution of the Oedipus complex results in the identification of the boy with his father and in the establishment of a "superego" or special agency of morality incorporated from the parents.

For the girl, however, the Electra complex has no such clear-cut, final outcome. Because the threat of castration, the motive for its dissolution in the boy, has affected the beginning of the Electra complex, the same fear cannot be the basis for its resolution. Instead, the female complex may undergo slow fading with time, or, in some cases, may meet its end through massive repression (Freud, 1925b, p. 257). Freud's view of the male Oedipus complex and the corresponding female Electra complex is summarized in Table 2.1.

Freud drew several conclusions that today would be considered antifeminist. Among these was the notion that women do not develop as strong a conscience (superego) as men. In Freud's view, only the fear of castration makes possible the development of a strong conscience, a topic we treat in Chapter 3.

PSYCHOSEXUAL STAGES: LIBIDINAL ORGANIZATION

Along with the discovery that sexuality is wider in scope than adult genital activities imply, Freud was able to discern a sequence in the development of the expression of libido or sexual energy. Characteristic patterns of sexual instinct organization prevail at each stage; each pattern centers on an erotogenic zone that dominates the given age.

Pregenital Organizations: Oral and Anal Periods

Libido is organized, in the first year of life, around the pleasurable activities of the mouth. Thus the attachment to the breast is a prototype of pleasurable behavior for the infant, a behavior that is, incidentally, clearly pregenital in character (Freud, 1916, p. 328).

The *oral* phase is marked, first, by the pleasure obtained from feeding, then by the development of purely sensual sucking in which the infant obtains oral pleasure by sucking nonnutritive objects like the thumb. In this way, the infant's own body provides sensual pleasure, justly characterizing this part of the oral period as autoerotic (Freud, 1905, pp. 179–181). Further development tends toward the decreasing importance of autoerotic activity and a search for an external love object. The dominant erotogenic zone during the oral phase is not genital. Freud noted that its flow of pleasure seemed analogous to sexual satisfaction:

> No one who has seen a baby sinking back satiated from the breast and falling asleep with flushed cheeks and a blissful smile can escape the reflection that this picture persists as a prototype of the expression of sexual satisfaction in later life. (Freud, 1905, p. 182)

With the development of the first teeth and with the possibility of chewing rather than simply swallowing food, children enter a phase of development characterized by a shift from a passive to an active orientation to their environment. From now on, the central concern for the infant is the attainment of self-mastery. From around the age of 18 months through the second year of life, children are subject to increased manipulation and discipline by the mother as she attempts to toilet train them. They discover that retention and expulsion of feces set a rhythmic pattern of tension and relief that is associated not only with pleasure but with social approval and motherly love. When they stubbornly retain their feces, or expel them in inappropriate places, they incur their mothers' wrath. When, on the other hand, they accomplish fecal elimination in a suitable place, at the appropriate time, each receives approval and other loving communications. The pleasures derived from retention and expulsion of feces are clearly pregenital (1905, pp. 186–187).

Transient Genital Organization: The Phallic Period

Sometime at the end of the third year or in the beginning of the fourth year of the child's life and extending into the sixth year, a phase of libidinal organization is entered in which the genital organs play a brief, but not yet, adult role. Through their bodily self-explorations and through the attentions of their mothers to their physical care and cleanliness, children discover that manipulation of the genital region produces pleasurable sensations. There ensues a period of infantile masturbation. Because children do not yet know shame, they express an unabashed curiosity about the genitals of others, along with a guiltless exhibitionism of their own (Freud, 1905, p. 194). As an example, the five-year-old nephew of one of the authors was playing in his bath. He stuck his penis into a small plastic container and proudly said, "Look, Uncle Bob, my 'pee-er' fits right in!" Such a vivid example, however, does not necessarily indicate or prove the universality of the type of behavior Freud had proposed for the phallic period.

It is during this period of "sexual researches" that the Oedipus complex arises (Freud, 1908a). Freud called this period the phallic stage of psychosexual development because for both the boy and the girl, in their own ways, it is the male organ that dominates their thinking and inquiry.

The Latency Period

In Freud's theory, the sexual forces dating from infancy become subject to mounting repression that require the sexual impulses to be rechanneled into nonsexual outlets. In the sixth year of life, the child's sexual activities, along with the Oedipus complex, are temporarily dethroned from their status as major elements of the child's developmental history, but the sexual drive does not cease to exist. Instead, libidinal impulses become latent, obscured by the overlay of learned shame, disgust, and morality. Freud, however, was of the opinion that the sexual impulses would become dormant at this stage even without cultural pressures because the phenomenon of latency is biologically determined (1905, pp. 177–178). In any event, the period of latency extends from the sixth to about the eleventh year of life, or roughly from the resolution of the Oedipus complex to the onset of puberty. At puberty, truly adult, primarily genital, sexuality emerges.

The Genital Period

Biologically capable of procreating because their hormonal and anatomical development permit the production of viable sperm and eggs, the pubescent child's sexuality is no longer dominated by its earlier infantile aim of the attainment of pleasure to the exclusion of all else. The adult sexual aim is the discharge of sexual products. This adult sexual aim also provides individual pleasure in addition to its essentially reproductive goal (Freud, 1905, p. 207).

The lengthy periods of development leading up to the adult's sexual status had as their ultimate goal the establishment of *genital primacy*. Genital arousal and the production of sexual tension is an early step toward the species-preserving goal of procreation. Three sources of sexual arousal are now possible for the adult. They include but are not limited to:

1. memories and impulses from the pregenital periods;
2. direct manipulation and stimulation of the genitalia and other erotogenic zones;
3. stimulation from the chemical hormonal discharges from within the interior of the body (Freud, 1905, p. 208).

Thus the genital period is the culmination of all those trends in the development of the libido, begun in infancy, and played out through the biological development of the mature organism.

We summarize the psychosexual stages with their chief developmental issues and love objects in Table 2.2.

Table 2.2   The Psychosexual Stages

Psychosexual stage	Libidinal zone	Chief developmental issue	Libidinal object
1. Oral [birth to 1 year]	Mouth, skin, thumb	Passive incorporation of all good through mouth; autoerotic sensuality.	Mother's breast; own body
2. Anal [2 to 3 years]	Anus, bowels	Active seeking for tension reduction; self-mastery; passive submission.	Own body
3. Phallic [4 to 6 years]	Genitals, skin	Oedipus and Electra conflicts; possession of mother; identification with same-sexed parent; ambivalence of love relationships.	Mother for boy; father for girl
4. Latency [6 to 11 years]	None	Repression of pregenital forms of libido; learning culturally appropriate shame and disgust for inappropriate love objects.	Repressed previous objects
5. Genital [adolescence onward]	Genital primacy	Reproduction; sexual intimacy.	Heterosexual partner

(Based on Freud, 1905 and 1916.)

Fixation

Fixation (of libido) may occur at any of the stages, thereby stunting and distorting the sequence of development that follows.

Fixation involves lagging behind or being stuck in the development of one of the components of the maturing sexual drive. One of the child's pregenital modes of attaining pleasure may cease its progression toward adult expression. It then becomes a dominant means of attaining satisfaction. For example, the pleasure of the anal phase, smearing and playing with feces, may be so great that the renunciation required by the child's toilet training program is very difficult for the child to accept. Though children eventually submit to the toilet training routine, their final socialization may be fixated on behaviors going back to the anal stage. As an adult, compulsively defensive traits like stinginess ("not letting go") and compulsive concern about filth make their appearance as a result of fixation regarding the struggles and issues of the toilet training period.

An Illustrative Type: "Anal-Erotic Personality"

One kind of fixated personality is the anal-erotic character. In adulthood, this person is characterized by the presence of a triad of related traits: orderliness, thriftiness, and obstinacy. Freud pointed out that he thought a common pattern of experiences occurred during the anal stage of their psychosexual development in all adults who exhibit a high degree of these traits. It is important to note that Freud did not actually *systematically* observe such toilet training but based his theory from the accounts of adult patients as well as personal observations and perusal of literature.

The anal-erotic types recalled more than the usual difficulty with toilet training as children, and they exasperated their parents by refusing to empty their bowels when, as Freud put it, "they were placed on the pot." Thus, these children expressed their defiance and self-mastery in an anal way, forcing their parents' use of increasingly extreme measures to accomplish this necessary act of socialization.

In Freud's view, anal-erotic children knew no shame or disgust at this early age, and therefore they found pleasure in examining or playing with feces and pleasure in retaining them until release of tension produces the greatest satisfaction. Eventually they succumb to parental pressures for rigid orderliness and cleanliness and to a learned disgust for unclean products of the body. By adulthood, therefore, anal-erotic children have had to develop defensive measures to guard against reemergence of the taboo pleasures. The result is a personality overladen with defensive reactions against its own impulses to obtain pleasure in anal, that is, "dirty," ways. The anal-erotic adult, consequently, becomes a model of cleanliness and orderliness, but a model who bears the hallmark of exaggeration in the pursuit of these desirable goals. Excessive, even compulsive, desire for order, neatness, and antiseptic spotlessness develops to ensure that the earlier and opposite traits remain submerged.

The trait of obstinacy is clearly related to children's attempts at self-mastery as indicated by their refusal to "go on demand." Instead, they prefer to "let go" only when they decide to experience the pleasure of tension reduction, and anal-erotic children prolong this release until an optimal amount of satisfaction can be obtained.

Thriftiness is also related to early developments in the anal period, as can be seen from the similar tendency of the stingy adult who "never lets go" of anything. Tightness with money may unconsciously represent earlier attempts to control fecal elimination against the demands by others to "let go." Stingy persons may even express unwilling-

BOX 2.3

Decades after Freud formulated the concept of regression, the ego psychologist, Anna Freud (Chapter 6) further elaborated his insights when she worked with children who had suffered loss and dislocation from World War II. Many had regressed to earlier levels of functioning but recovered quickly when she helped provide a secure and loving environment. Her observations and studies led to an elaborate model of child development.

ness to part with their money by saying, "Who would want the filthy stuff," or, "Money only brings ruin."

Tongue in cheek, Freud remarked in a letter to Fliess that, because he was immersed in working out the details of the anal period of libidinal development and because he had begun to see its wide significance for adult behavior, he considered himself to be the "new Midas," for everything he now touched turned to shit (1954, Letter No. 79, p. 240; Freud, 1985, p. 288; see also Freud, 1908b for a more detailed account of anal character types).

Regression

Another difficulty in psychosexual development may occur when there is cause for a return to an earlier stage's mode of response. Such a return is called **regression (of libido),** and it usually implies a primitivization of behavior in the service of the personality's defense against stress. For example, the six-year-old who, for one reason or another, finds their school experiences anxiety-provoking and intolerable may return to an infantile mode of attaining peace and tranquility by narrowing attention to pleasurable oral stimulation. He or she consequently regresses to thumb sucking, much to the dismay of parents and teacher.

Fixation and *regression* bear an important relationship to each other. The more intense the fixation of libido at early stages of development, the more susceptible that individual will be to regression (Freud, 1916, pp. 339–341).

Figure 2.5 Freud in Berlin in 1922 with his inner circle, "The Committee." This photograph was taken long after the departure of Jung and Adler from the Freudian psychoanalytic world. Note the evident pride of the members of this group.

EVALUATING CLINICAL PSYCHOANALYSIS

Much like the intimate relationships of the conflicted people he described so lucidly, Freud's theory has sustained a love-hate conflict with the rest of psychology. In 1934, the psychologist Saul Rosenzweig sent Freud reprints of some experimental studies that purported to support psychoanalysis. Freud responded in a brief postcard to Rosenzweig that psychoanalysis rested on so many reliable observations that it was independent of experimental verification. "Still," Freud added, "it can do no harm." This widely quoted anecdote has been taken as emblematic of Freud's ambivalent attitudes toward both the theory he created and the science he seemed to revere (e.g., Eysenck and Wilson, 1973, p. xi; Gay, 1988, p. 523n.; Postman, 1962, p. 702).

In fact, given the scope, breadth, and grand goals of psychoanalysis, it seems that Freud's attitude about the relevance of scientific verification to his theory was less a product of arrogance than it was a result of intellectual overload. By his own account, from the very beginning of his work, Freud wanted psychoanalysis to be a general psychology. Psychoanalysis was designed to encompass all of human action and thought. Normal and "abnormal" would yield to psychoanalytic principles. The net effect of this bigger-than-life ambition was a theory that "explained" virtually every human behavior or motive of which we can conceive.

We can admire Freud's ambition, but we have to temper our admiration with a dose of antigrandiosity. One of Christopher Monte's college professors, John M. Egan, had a memorable way of describing this tension between the intellectual attractiveness of Freud's majestic ideas and the rude requirement that such ideas be accurate. Egan used to say that it would take a hundred psychologists a hundred years just to devise experimental tests of one page of Freud's writing. At the time, I thought that was a very quaint apology for Freudian vagueness and a telling epitaph for a moribund psychoanalysis. With the passage of years, Egan's words have taken on deeper meaning. It was customary in psychology at the time to ask questions such as, "How good is Freud's theory?" or "How valid is psychoanalysis?" or, worse still, "Was Freud right about. . . . ?" Like Mark Twain, who ironically pointed out that the older he became, the wiser his father grew, personality psychology is older now and Freud is smarter. The questions have changed: "What is Freud's theory good for?" and "How useful is psychoanalysis for generating new ideas?"

For the purposes of this book, we introduced three main qualitative dimensions by which to compare theories of personality in Chapter 1: refutability, human agency, and idiographic-nomothetic focus. We also indicated many other dimensions on which to evaluate theories and by which to compare them. Because Freud's theory is presented in two large parts, the early clinical observations discussed in this chapter and the structural theoretical formulations in Chapter 3, we need to consider both the "early Freud" and Freud's later formulations in our analysis.

Refutability of Psychoanalysis

Freud's basic propositions are stated in terms that are most often not testable or refutable. It is hard to identify any Freudian variables that are directly observable. For example, consider the proposition of repression and the Oedipus complex. By definition, a repressed wish or thought is absent from awareness. And by definition, all boys have experienced an erotic attachment to mother and ambivalent feelings of love and hate toward father. But, again by psychoanalytic definition, all conscious memory of the Oedipal events is repressed. What evidence could count against the proposition that boys have Oedipus complexes if the very behaviors and memory that constitute this 'universal' emotional conflict are unavailable for examination by the person or by an outside observer? If an emotion or thought is unconscious, this means it is not conscious, not in a person's awareness.

Imagine telling the mythical "man on the street" that sometime between ages three and six years, he lusted after his mother, hated his father, and was terrified that his father would remove his penis. If our man on the street protests that this is nonsense or berates us for being offensive, we must point out to him that he is incredulous or offended precisely because he is repressing these experiences! And, indeed, the more he protests, the more we are prone to assume that he is threatened by these ideas precisely because he, like all males, has repressed his Oedipal strivings. What possible evidence could the man produce that would disconfirm our theoretical assertion that he was Oedipal as a child? By our psychoanalytic definition, both the hypothetical phenomenon and its evidence are not directly observable.

The problem is not that the psychoanalytic constructs of repression or of the Oedipus complex are fantastic, bizarre, or untrue. The real problem is that they are not readily testable in the form in which Freud proposed them. Someone, perhaps soon, may find a creative and scientifically acceptable way to do so. But for each failure of a concept to provide the possibility of disconfirmation, the theory is weakened as an acceptable scientific account of human action and thought.

On the whole, with exceptions, the history of classical psychoanalytic theory is a story of profoundly interesting and engaging ideas that are colossal monuments to untestability. But that is not the whole story. For there are also ideas in Freudian theory that are testable and that have received both experimental and observational tests. Even allowing for those few Freudian concepts that lend themselves to test and for those potentially testable ideas that some creative psychologist will fashion from Freud's work, psychoanalysis has to be rated low in scientific testability.

Freud's Conception of Human Agency

Freud painted a portrait of his early patients as shaped by reality. His neurological model conceptualized the human nervous system as a tension-reduction machine whose evolutionary history designed it for quick discharge of tension in response to mounting needs. Left to its own devices, the human nervous system is a passive discharger of tension. It strives to quell irritations such as hunger, thirst, and sexual desire. Seen in this way, drives are irritants, and the nervous system responds only when an itch must be scratched. "Reality makes much of us," Freud wrote, but he failed to see how much we make of reality.

The person who emerges from Freud's early clinical work is one who "defends" against threatening wishes, one who tolerates conflict until tolerance fails and then is "forced" to repress it. People "involuntarily" disavow their own frightening wishes only to find disguised or "compromise" ways to satisfy them in neurotic "symptoms." Human psychosexual development proceeds, in Freud's earliest conception, as a halting process of advance and retreat, development and fixation.

Balancing this picture to a certain extent, paradoxically, is Freud's development of psychoanalysis. This treatment was intended to help people become more aware of their psychodynamics and come to grips with the more frightening contents of their psyche. A psychoanalytic patient had to be highly motivated, persistent, and willing to be open to very uncomfortable and often unsettling insights. The analyst, in order to be effective, could not be at the mercy of unconscious dynamics but had to be aware of them. Goethe's insight that by recognizing limitations a person can become free applies here.

So, even though Freud saw humans as fundamentally reactive, he believed that some small portion of humanity could replace unknowing instinctually determined reactivity with clear insight and more rational behavior.

Freud's Balance of Nomothetic and Idiographic

Freud's intention was to create a theory that was universally applicable, a theory with a strong nomothetic emphasis. But he also intended a theory that could deal with the specifics of a given patient. As an example, he wanted to understand hysterical neurosis as a phenomenon and also the behavior of a given patient with hysterical conversion symptoms.

Many of his concepts, such as the *ego,* the *id,* and the *superego,* as well as *defense mechanisms, transference,* and *countertransference* are generally applicable. His writings refer to the application of such general or nomothetic concepts to specific individuals. Transference, for example, is considered a general phenomenon, but the specifics of any individual's transference are unique and tied in to his or her own experience. People may use many general defenses such as repression or denial, but the content of what is repressed or denied is often idiosyncratic.

Freud often demonstrated the value of theory by alluding to specific case histories. He also modified his theories based on his experience with cases. Thus, there was a dialogue between individual cases and Freud's more general theory. From Freud's point of view, such a case-by-case strategy facilitated his belief that what the analyst infers from his or her patient's behavior is generally of value.

We conclude, therefore, that Freud's theory balances the nomothetic with the idiographic. Early Freud was more idiographic and later Freud, as we shall see in Chapter 3, somewhat more nomothetic in emphasis.

SUMMARY

Fraülein Bertha Pappenheim's long array of hysterical symptoms was eventually viewed by her physician, Dr. Josef Breuer, as coherent, meaningful, and reflective of an underlying emotional logic. This was far from the conventional approach, which did not attribute any particular meaning to such symptoms. Breuer soon discovered in an unusual collaboration with his patient that the coherence and logic of her symptoms had its origins in strangulated emotions.

Dr. Sigmund Freud, Breuer's young colleague, was greatly interested in the case of Bertha, especially after his visit with Professor Charcot in Paris, during which he observed this renowned physician produce and remove hysterical symptoms through hypnosis. Applying Breuer and Bertha's method of catharsis, the "talking cure," Freud soon found that hypnosis could be achieved only with few of his patients. His search for a new method led, eventually, to the technique of *free association.*

With the method of free association in hand, Freud soon discovered the emotional resistances that had been hidden by hypnosis. Examining and removing these resistances revealed to Freud one of the fundamental notions of his psychology, the mechanism of repression. Freud concluded that repressed ideas and impulses require a continual outlay of energy to prevent their return to consciousness. He viewed the symptoms of neurotic disorder as the return of the repudiated material in compromise form, a form acceptable to the ego. Symptoms allow the simultaneous satisfaction and rejection of the unacceptable impulse or idea in symbolic form.

Much to his own amazement, Freud found that sexual impulses were the common denominator for classifying unacceptable thoughts. Freud found that, in practically every case, adults with hysterical symptoms had repressed often incestuous memories of sexual trauma that they had presumably experienced as infants and children. The theory based on this observation is termed the *sexual* hypothesis. Soon, however, Freud saw how untenable the idea of universal childhood seduction was, and simultaneously he faced a momentous conclusion: children are not merely passive recipients of sexual attentions by adults, but, rather, they are active sexual creatures who seek pleasure in a variety of diffuse ways before the onset of purely genital sexuality at puberty.

For the infant, pleasure seeking is connected with developing erotogenic zones in a sequence of psychosexual maturation that shows the sexual instinct to be very much broader than adult notions of genital sexuality ordinarily admit. An emotional climax in sexual development is the Oedipal phase, in which the male child focuses his pleasure-seeking activities on the mother, and he views siblings and father as hostile rivals. The girl, on the other hand, who also initially takes her mother as the first love object, relinquishes mother for father when she realizes that girls, including mother, do not possess a penis. The Electra and Oedipus complexes are only one part of Freud's scheme of psychosexual development, a scheme that involves five phases:

1. the *oral stage,* in which pleasurable activities center on the activities of the mouth;

2. the *anal stage,* in which the critical developments involve retention and expulsion of feces, as well as learning generalized self-mastery;

3. the *phallic stage,* the time period of the Oedipus and Electra complexes;

4. the *latency stage,* during which time the child's sexual interests and impulses lie dormant until puberty; and

5. the *genital stage* of adult sexuality and interest in the opposite sex.

Sometimes development does not proceed smoothly through the five stages because anxiety, threat, or frustration block further maturation. Such blocking is termed *fixation* in the Freudian scheme. It is intimately related to another phenomenon of development called *regression.* Regression is a partial return to an earlier form of impulse gratification when current stresses frustrate the normal progression of the sex drive's development.

When we examine Freud's early formulations on the dimensions of refutability, human agency, and idiographic versus nomothetic focus, we find:

- The theory is structured from many assumptions that are, for the most part, not testable because they do not have readily observable referents.

- The person in psychoanalytic theory is pictured as a passive receptacle rather than as an active agent. The process of psychoanalysis, however, enables the person to become aware of the workings of the psyche and reach a certain degree of self-understanding, if not mastery.

- Much of early psychoanalysis is focused on the unique characteristics and life events of individuals. However, it also refers to structures and processes that are general and universal, such as the *id,* the e*go,* the *superego,* and *repression.* Thus, one finds in psychoanalysis a balance between the idiographic and the nomothetic.

In the next chapter, we take up the matters of Freud's dream theory, his changing views of the instincts, and his final model of the mind.

FOR FURTHER READING

Freud's writings in psychology span over 43 years of theorizing and fill 23 volumes in the definitive translation of *The Standard Edition of the Complete Psychological Works of Sigmund Freud* edited by James Strachey (New York: Norton, 2000). Perhaps the single best overview of Freud's early ideas is contained in his *Introductory Lectures on Psychoanalysis* (New York: Norton, 1965). Another excellent introduction to Freud's ideas, written by Freud himself, can be found in *The Ego and the Id* (New York: Norton, 1990). *The Interpretation of Dreams* (New York: Avon, 1983) remains the most popular book Freud wrote; this early work of Freud's is still a fascinating book to read and shows Freud as a sleuth on the track of the unconscious workings of the mind. Freud's *Civilization and Its Discontents* (New York: Norton, 1989) was written in Freud's later years and focuses on the discrepancy between the requirements of civilization and happy lives for individuals.

Biographies and other books about Freud are plentiful. Two of the more interesting and well received in recent years are Paul Ferris's *Dr Freud: A Life* (Washington, DC: Counterpoint, 1997) and Louis Breger's *Freud: Darkness in the Midst of Vision—An Analytical Biography* (New York: Wiley, 2000). Both of these books try to penetrate and deconstruct the image that Freud presented to others as well as examine possible areas of his own self-deception. Breger's novel thesis is that Freud overemphasized the Oedipus complex in order to avoid the emotional pain he suffered from the many losses he experienced early in life.

The relation of Freud and Fliess is explored in *The Origins of Psychoanalysis: Letters to Wilhelm Fliess,* edited by Marie Bonaparte, Bertha Freud, and Ernst Kris (New York: Basic Books, 1954). A more recent and more complete translation of the Freud half of the correspondence to Fliess is provided by J.M. Masson (Ed.) in his *The Complete Letters of Sigmund Freud to Wilhelm Fliess: 1887–1904* (Cambridge, MA: Harvard University Press, 1986).

Laurence Miller makes the argument in *Freud's Brain* (New York: Guilford Press, 1991) that psychoanalysis can survive into the 21st century only by a return to its roots in neurophysiology, and attempts to show how contemporary neurophysiology can be integrated with fundamental psychoanalytic concepts.

The clinical evidence on which Freud based his early concepts is to be found in Josef Breuer and Sigmund Freud's *Studies on Hysteria* (1893–1895, Vol. II of *The Standard Edition;* also available in paperback from Beacon Press, Boston). Other case histories that have a bearing on Freud's developing theory of sexuality may be found in Vol. X of *The Standard Edition* under the titles "Analysis of a Phobia in a Five-Year-Old Boy" and "Notes Upon a Case of Obsessional Neurosis"; also available in paperback editions edited by Philip Rieff: *Dora: An Analysis of a Case of Hysteria* (New York: Simon & Schuster, 1997).

Two books explore some of the stream of information from the history of psychoanalysis that has become available for scholarly investigation. Lisa Appignanesi and John Forrester provide detailed accounts of Freud's early patients, colleagues, and family members in *Freud's Women* (New York: Basic Books, 1992). John Kerr's *A Most Dangerous Method* (New York: Knopf, 1993) details the complex relationship between Carl Jung, Sigmund Freud, and the nearly forgotten Sabina Spielrein, who was Jung's patient, lover, and nemesis.

An unusual opportunity is afforded the reader who would like to hear both sides of the story of a psychoanalytic patient's treatment by the publication of *The Wolf-Man* by the Wolf-Man (New York: Basic Books, 1972). This volume contains Freud's original case history of this young Russian nobleman whom he had treated for obsessional-compulsive neurosis and an account by the young man himself of his treatment with Freud.

Basic background reading into the details of Freud's personal life is best begun with Ernest Jones's three-volume masterwork, *The Life and Work of Sigmund Freud* (New York: Basic Books, 1953, 1955, 1957). Peter Gay's *Freud: A Life for Our Time* (New York: Norton, 1988) is a comprehensive biography that focuses on the personal sources of Freud's theoretical achievements. Max Schur, Freud's personal physician during the last years of his life, provides a glimpse into the personal incidents of Freud's life that shaped his attitude toward death in *Freud: Living and Dying* (New York: International Universities Press, 1972). Freud's correspondence with Carl Jung has been published as *The Freud/Jung Letters* (Princeton, NJ: Princeton University Press, 1974). These letters provide a rare glimpse into the personal lives of Freud and Jung, their attitudes toward their contemporaries (not always flattering), and the history of their early mutual admiration, ambivalent attachment, rivalry, and falling out.

Some previously unavailable personal documents and letters from Freud's early history have been made available. Especially noteworthy is the *The Letters of Sigmund Freud to Eduard Silberstein* (Cambridge, MA: Harvard University Press, 1992). This volume presents the picture of Freud as a young person, experiencing his first love, becoming disappointed with his mother, and assuming a typically adolescent intellectual pretentiousness in the safety of his correspondence with his friend.

For a sophisticated accounting of Josef Breuer's involvement with and abandonment of psychoanalysis, George Pollock's "The Possible Significance of Childhood Object Loss in the Josef Breuer-Bertha Pappenheim (Anna O)-Sigmund Freud Relationship" (*Journal of the American Psychoanalytic Association,* 1968, 16, 711–739; also reprinted in Gedo and Pollock [Eds.], *Freud: The Fusion of Science and Humanism, Psychological Issues,* Monographs 34/35, 1976 [New York: International Universities Press, 1976]) provides an abundance of fact and theory. Fourteen different accounts and analyses of Bertha Pappenheim's neurosis are provided in *Bertha,* edited by Max Rosenbaum and Melvin Muroff (New York: Free Press, 1984).

For those with a taste for psychoanalytic trivia, albeit historical, Freud's last 10 years of daily desk diary and notebook entries have been published with a wealth of photographs in *The Diary of Sigmund Freud 1929–1939* (New York: Scribner's, 1992).

Adolf Grunbaum's dense, but important, *Validation in the Clinical Theory of Psychoanalysis* (New York: International Universities Press, 1993) deserves the attention of the serious student of psychoanalysis. Grunbaum critically examines Freudian clinical concepts with reference to refutability and other logical tests of their validity.

Freud scholarship continues to be a vibrant area of scholarship and controversy. A recent exhibit of Freudian memorabilia at the Library of Congress aroused so much controversy that it was cancelled, only to be re-instated after protests by leading scholars. *The Freud Encyclopedia: Theory, Therapy and Culture,* edited by Edward Erwin, was published in 2001 by Routledge. It contains entries by over 200 scholars on numerous aspects of Freud's life and work and on his impact on society. In it, an entry by Barry Silverstein on "Psychoanalysis: Origin and History of Psychoanalysis" (pages 435–444) presents a perspicacious overview of the evolution of Freud's therapeutic approach.

Additional recommended readings for Freud's theory are provided at the end of Chapter 3 and concern his later theoretical contributions.

GLOSSARY

Catharsis: A release of emotions by expressing them.

Childhood sexuality: Freud's idea that children are active initiators of autoerotic behaviors designed to bring sensual pleasure; Freud replaced the seduction theory with the idea of childhood sexuality.

"Chimney sweeping": Bertha Pappenheim's term for recollection of emotionally charged memories and subsequent verbal catharsis in a semihypnotic state.

Clouds: The term that Bertha Pappenheim used to describe her hypnagogic states. She often felt as if she were floating on a cloud.

Compromise formations: Symptoms that balance the anxiety and guilt of the conscious personality against the pleasurable gratifications sought by the unconscious.

Concentration technique: Method first used by Bernheim to aid the patient in remembering hidden thoughts; the therapist placed his hand on the forehead of the subject and pressed firmly, while insisting that the memory of the previous events return.

Conflict: In Freud's theory, it occurs when an unconscious wish or an impulse is incompatible with the individual's conscious views and principles.

Countertransference: Similarly, the process of a therapist inappropriately projecting feelings or emotions from previous relationships onto a patient.

Defense: Any one of a number of psychological means used to keep anxiety-provoking material out of awareness in order to reduce or avoid anxiety.

Dynamic unconscious: A part of the mind in which thoughts and emotions removed from consciousness by repression continue to operate unconsciously; Freud concluded that they might produce symptoms that replace direct expression of the thoughts or emotions.

Electra complex: The psychological process during the phallic stage in which a female child detaches from her mother upon discovering that she too has no penis; she then devalues the mother and turns to her father; she starts identifying with female behaviors to appeal to her father and get a penis substitute from him—a baby.

Erotogenic zones: Pleasurable zones of the body that are a source of sensual pleasure.

Fixation (of libido): In the course of psychosexual development, an individual lags behind or becomes fixated in development at a specific stage. It may lead to oral, anal, or phallic personality types.

Free association: A therapeutic technique devised by Freud to encourage patients to report spontaneously any thoughts or fantasies that occur to them.

Functional anesthesia: Numbness of a part of the body, usually in one's hands or feet, without discernable physical cause.

Fundamental rule of psychoanalysis: Patients were to say everything that came to mind without editing or censoring the stream of thought.

Glove anesthesia: A disorder in which it is as if all of the hand that could fit into an imaginary glove were anesthetized or without sensation. This disorder does not fit the distribution of nerves in the hand, and was thus thought by Charcot to be caused by a person's ideas.

Hypnagogic state: A state between waking and sleeping. A person often has greater access to unconscious thoughts and is more open to suggestion in this state.

Hypnotism: A technique that Freud used to produce a state of consciousness that allows the patient to bring to the surface feelings or emotions that would otherwise be repressed.

Hysterical neurosis: A disorder involving various physical ailments such as paralysis and blindness without an apparent physical cause. Originally thought to be caused by a "wandering womb" in women and subsequently considered psychological in origin.

Libido: The biological force underlying the individual's pleasure-seeking activity.

Obsessional neurosis: A disorder in which individuals engage in ritualistic acts to keep from feeling anxiety.

Oedipus complex: The psychological process during the phallic stage in which a male child becomes sexually attracted to his mother and competes with his father for her attention; this stage is resolved when the boy identifies with his father due to fear of castration.

Penis envy: The envy that a girl presumably experiences toward boys when she discovers that she has no penis. Freud considered penis envy to be biologically based.

Posthypnotic amnesia: The induced forgetting of the material brought to the surface during hypnosis.

Pseudocyesis: A hysterical false pregnancy that evidences most of the usual signs of advanced pregnancy, but with no fetus in the womb.

Psychosexual stages: Stages of development in which a specific area of the body is sexualized and determines how a person interacts with others socially.

Regression (of libido): The return to an earlier stage of psychosexual development.

Repression: Motivated forgetting or amnesia characterized by its unconscious, automatic nature; repression serves to keep painful, undesirable, or anxiety-provoking thoughts out of consciousness.

Resistance: Defensive process to ward off threatening thoughts or feelings. Such threatening contents may continue to exert unconscious "pressure" in their striving for expression.

Seduction hypothesis: Freud's theory that all women who experienced hysterical symptoms had been sexually molested or seduced as children; Freud had found that all of his hysterical patients recalled an early sexual encounter under hypnosis.

Strangulated affect: Unexpressed or "dammed up" feelings or emotions, which are often the cause of hysterical symptoms.

Suppression: The conscious or deliberate avoidance of threatening ideas.

Transference: The process of a patient inappropriately projecting feelings or emotions from previous relationships onto a therapist.

Tunnel vision: A narrowing of the field of vision as though one were looking through a narrow cardboard cylinder.

Chapter 3

Sigmund Freud

Psychoanalysis:
The Dynamic Model of the Mind

Since I have started studying the unconscious, I have become so interesting to myself.

Sigmund Freud, *The Origins of Psychoanalysis*

But these two discoveries—that the life of our sexual instincts cannot be wholly tamed, and that mental processes are in themselves unconscious . . . amount to a statement that the ego is not master in its own house.

Sigmund Freud, (1917a, p. 143)

About Freud's Dynamic Model

Central to Freud's early clinical work was the concept that observable behavior is a disguised derivative of unconscious wishes. The derivatives included neurotic symptoms, slips of the tongue, and many self-defeating behaviors. Freud's story of exploration continues in this chapter with his study of dreams as disguised ways to satisfy taboo wishes.

Freud's struggle to understand the war between instinct and reason led to his model of a divided mind. He moved away from directly reporting clinical experiences with patients toward an increasingly complex intellectual representation of human self-division. The key achievements of psychoanalysis by the time of Freud's death include:

- *a picture of the means by which the conscious part of the mind allows the unconscious part to satisfy its urges in relatively nonthreatening ways;*

- *a disturbing portrait of childhood sexual and aggressive wishes drawn in part from Freud's own analysis of his personal history;*

- *a structural model of the mind that pictures the war between reason and instinct as a conflict of mental agencies each obeying its own rules of operation.*

DREAMS AS WISH FULFILLMENTS

Consider the following dream of Freud's daughter Anna:

> My youngest daughter, then 19 months old, had had an attack of vomiting one morning and had consequently been kept without food all day. During the night after this day of starvation she was heard calling out excitedly in her sleep: "Anna Fweud, stwawbewwies, wild stwawbewwies, omblet, pudden!" At that time she was in the habit of using her own name to express the idea of taking possession of something. The menu included pretty well everything that must have seemed to her to make up a desirable meal. (Freud, 1900, p. 130)

Clearly, as can be discerned in Anna's menu, children's dreams are relatively transparent embodiments of wishes come true. There is no disguise here to obscure Anna's craving for goodies. Anna's dream was of an undisguised wish receiving undisguised fulfillment.

Freud had already come to the conclusion that dreams are mental states designed for **wish fulfillment.** The dream, he reasoned in the "Project for a Scientific Psychology" (1895), is a hallucinatory state that serves to structure dream events, not as they are in the external world, but as we would like them to be. Sometimes, however, unconscious desires come up against conscious restraint, so the dream processes have to pursue devious or indirect paths to wish fulfillment. Freud stated the fundamental implication of this insight in the dictum "The interpretation of dreams is the royal road to a knowledge of the unconscious mind" (1900, p. 608). In other words, through examining and interpreting dreams, we can find out what desires and wishes are hidden in the unconscious.

By examining a dreamer's nighttime productions, the skilled observer can detect those motives and wishes that are hidden from view during waking life, motives and wishes that the dreamer can entertain only in the disguised, compromise form that dream imagery represents. Compared with the dreams of children, adult productions usually do not evidence the simplicity and directness of Anna's "stwawbewwies-and-pudden" fancy.

Disguised Wish Fulfillment

Compare the following adult dream with Anna's innocently lucid construction:

> The patient, who was a young girl, began thus: "As you will remember, my sister has only one boy left now—Karl; she lost his elder brother, Otto, while I was still living with her. Otto was my favorite; I more or less brought him up. I'm fond of the little one too, but of course, not nearly so fond as I was of the one who died. Last night, then, I dreamt that *I saw Karl lying before me dead. He was lying in his little coffin with his hands folded and with candles all round—in fact just like little Otto, whose death was such a blow to me.* (Freud, 1900, p. 152)

If it is true that dreams are the fulfillment of wishes, then surely this dream by one of Freud's patients must embody the wish that little Karl had died instead of little Otto.

Assured from his knowledge of his patient that she was not cruel, Freud considered the dream carefully. He asked her to tell him everything that came to mind when she thought of the separate elements of the dream. It is important to note that the interpretation of this particular dream is possible only when the analyst knows the past history of the dreamer, as well as the context provided by the dreamer's personality. In Freud's view, dreams usually fit into the unique experiences and circumstances of a dreamer's life.

Freud knew that, after his patient had been orphaned, she had been raised in the house of an elder sister. A particular male visitor to the sister's home, nicknamed "the professor" by virtue of his occupation as a professional lecturer, had made quite a romantic impression on Freud's patient. They made marriage plans, which were disrupted. He ceased to visit the sister's home. Freud's patient nonetheless secretly longed to see and to be with him. On the other hand, through hurt pride, she tried to convince herself to relinquish any romantic attachment to him. Her resolve was not an easy one to keep. Whenever she learned that he was to appear in a public lecture, she quietly became a part of the audience. Yet she would observe him only at a discreet distance, and she never allowed herself to confront him directly. In fact, she seized upon every opportunity, however trivial, to see this professor. She had even experienced a moment of happiness at the funeral of little Otto when her professor had made an appearance to express his condolences. It was this continual vacillation between approach and withdrawal that chiefly characterized the patient's behavior.

Here, of course, was the key to her dream. If little Karl were to die, his funeral would provide another opportunity to see her professor without any direct attempt on her part to bring about the meeting. Her wish, therefore, was not directly for Karl's death, but only for a meeting with her professor. The dream had created from her past history of associations a perfectly logical pretext for furthering the satisfaction of her ambivalent desire. Thus the lucidity and directness of Anna's "stwawbewwy dream" is not to be found here.

We can view adult processes and hysterical symptoms as similar if we make the assumption, as Freud did, that both dreams and symptoms conceal ideas that are not acceptable to the conscious personality. Freud found evidence in several of his own dreams that particularly threatening desires were frequently the kernels from which nighttime fantasies grew.

PERSONAL SOURCES: FREUD'S FATHER AND MOTHER DREAMS

We saw in Chapter 2 that Freud had begun a self-analysis in the summer of 1897, and that the precipitating incident for the task was his emotional distress over the death of his father. Throughout *The Interpretation of Dreams,* and in one or two of his other works, Freud employed his own dreams, elucidated by self-analysis, as examples of his concepts. Like his patient's Karl and Otto dream, Freud's own dreams also revealed how important it was for the analyst to understand the dreamer's personal symbols and meanings.

Immediately following his father's funeral, Freud had a dream about a sign hanging in a barbershop that he visited every day. The analysis given in *The Interpretation of Dreams* provides a detailed account:

> During the night before my father's funeral I had a dream of a printed notice, placard or poster [in a barbershop]—rather like the notices forbidding one to smoke in a railway waiting room—on which appeared either
>
>
>
> "You are requested to close the eyes"
>
> OR
>
> "You are requested to close an eye". . . .
>
>
>
>   Each of these two versions had a meaning of its own, and led in a different direction when the dream was interpreted. I had chosen the simplest possible ritual for the funeral, for I knew my father's own views on such ceremonies. But some other members of the family were not sympathetic to such puritanical simplicity and thought we should be disgraced in the eyes of those who attended the funeral. Hence one of the versions: "You are requested to close an eye," i.e., to "wink" or "overlook" [the simplicity of the services]. Here it is particularly easy to see the meaning of the vagueness expressed by the "either-or." (Freud, 1900, p. 318)

The dream was, upon analysis, clearly a form of self-reproach for not providing the "proper" full-fledged funeral that members of the family expected and desired.

Simultaneously, the dream represented the ultimate act of a son's duty toward his father; namely, the closing of his father's eyes at death. It was as though the dream condensed the idea of "failing to do your duty" with the idea of "filial duty" in a clever word picture.

Freud suspected that the dream was in some way connected with ever deeper feelings of guilt. Perhaps he did not love his father as much as he thought? There was evidence for this because on the day of the funeral Freud was actually late in arriving. He said he had been detained in a *barbershop*. The seemingly inexcusable lateness, coupled with his desire for relatively austere last rites for his father, must have seemed to members of Freud's family indications of supreme lack of respect. The important point is that to Freud, too, such behavior indicated some negativity toward his father.

Personal Sources of Freud's Ambivalent Love for His Father

During his extensive self-analysis, Freud uncovered some roots of his hostility toward his father and accompanying guilt pangs. The barbershop dream just discussed had emphasized the theme of filial duty—the duty of a son for a father. Instead of respect for his father, Freud had been neglectful. Freud's father died in October 1896; by 1899 Freud had included in *The Interpretation of Dreams* several pieces of his self-therapeutic efforts to cope with the complex emotions triggered by the loss and by Freud's concerns over his own neglectful behavior. By 1904, on a vacation to Greece with his brother Alexander, Freud's guilt over his father's death reached a crisis. Eight years after the event, Freud was still experiencing the painful reverberations of this experience.

The Acropolis Episode

In 1936, only three years before his own death, suffering terminal cancer of the jaw and mouth, Freud published an account of a crisis experience in Greece. Standing upon the Acropolis, surveying the majesty of the landscape and ruminating on the impressive history of the site, Freud was abruptly thrust outside of himself, as though he were suddenly two people. His own later description of the experience was that he endured a "splitting of consciousness." One part of himself was astonished to find that the fabled city of Athens existed! Freud thought, "So all this really *does* exist, just as we learnt at school!" (1936, p. 241). The other, more reality-oriented aspect of Freud's personality was astonished, too, as though unaware that Athens and its landscape had ever been the subject of doubt.

Freud interpreted his splitting of awareness as a form of derealization, a kind of defensive disbelief in the reality of things in an effort to ward off a segment of threatening experiences. He was able to analyze the experience to uncover the chain of associations that underlay his defensive maneuver; the chain led straight back to his guilt and hostility associated with his father. Schur (1972) has provided additional details that Freud was apparently unwilling to publish as part of his analysis.

From Freud's own account, we learn that as a child he harbored doubts, not of the existence of Athens, but of the possibility that he would ever see it with his own eyes. To see Athens had the personal meaning of "going such a long way," that is, becoming successful enough to make the dream of distant travel possible. Because his youth was one of poverty, the wish to travel to distant places was a desire to escape the privations of his real existence. Freud vividly expressed his sentiments, "When first one catches sight of the sea, crosses the ocean and experiences as realities cities and land which for so long had been distant, unattainable things of desire—one feels like a hero who has performed deeds of improbable greatness" (1936, p. 247). The symbolic meaning of travel to fabled cities, especially to the city of Rome, was, for Freud, intricately connected with a host of guilt-laden and aggressive feelings toward his father (for details of Freud's "Rome neurosis" see Grigg, 1973 and Schorske, 1975).

In the present instance, the visit to the Acropolis brought to Freud's mind the further association of Napoleon, during his coronation as emperor, turning to his *brother* to remark how pleasant it would be if their father could be present this day. But herein lay the crux of the defensive disbelief in Athens' reality. To "have come so far" was equivalent to success, the special success of having gone further than one's own father:

> The very theme of Athens and the Acropolis in itself contained evidence of the son's superiority. Our father had been in business, he had had no secondary education, and Athens could not have meant much to him. Thus what interfered with our enjoyment of the journey to Athens was a feeling of *filial piety*. (Freud, 1936, pp. 247–248)

Just as the barbershop dream after the funeral had contained an allusion to filial duty, the experience of derealization on the Acropolis embodied the sense of filial piety or reverence for his father. It was as though the trip to Athens had been not merely a surpassing of father but a betrayal of him as well. Such intolerable guilt and its implied hostility had to be defended against. As Freud put it, he was overcome with the unsettling sense that *"What I see here is not real."*

Suffering from terminal cancer, with thoughts of death nearly always in his mind, Freud concluded the Acropolis account with this sentence: "And now you will no longer wonder that the recollection of this incident on the Acropolis should have troubled me so often since I myself have grown old and stand in need of forbearance and can travel no more" (1936, p. 248). It is possible that at one level of his understanding, Freud was accepting his imminent end as fitting punishment for having surpassed his father; certainly, this last statement suggests his identification with the fate of his father, who similarly had grown old and stood in need of forbearance.

Freud's Death Fear

Schur (1972, pp. 225ff.) has shown that there were other important determinants of the Acropolis episode that involved Freud's relationship with Wilhelm Fliess. An eccentric Berlin physician, Fliess played the role of father figure and confidant during Freud's self-analysis in an extensive interchange of letters and a series of personal meetings, or "congresses," as Freud termed them. Through a complex system of biological numerology and critical-period theory, Fliess had predicted the year of Freud's death—completely wrongly, as it turned out—and in so doing fed directly Freud's already superstitious concern with the prospects of his own demise. Fliess's critical period calculations had set Freud's death near the age of 51; but Freud's superstitious turn of mind, after the death of his father, had its own chosen date. Freud was convinced that the year of his death would be between the ages of 61 and 62. He wrote jokingly, but revealingly, to Carl Jung of his trip to Athens with his brother Alexander:

> . . . It was really uncanny how often the number 61 or 60 in connection with a 1 or 2 kept cropping up in all sorts of numbered objects, especially those connected with transportation. This I conscientiously noted. It depressed me, but I had hopes of breathing easy when we got to the hotel in Athens and were assigned rooms on the first floor. Here, I was sure, there could be no No. 61. I was right, but I was given 31 (which with fatalistic license could be regarded as half of 61 or 62), and this younger, more agile number proved to be an even more persistent persecutor than the first. From the time of our trip home until very recently, 31, often with a 2 in its vicinity, clung to me faithfully. (Freud, in Freud/Jung, 1974, p. 219)

Freud's own analysis of his superstition centered on the fact that his conviction that death would come at 61 or 62 appeared in 1899, the year *The Interpretation of Dreams* (postdated to 1900 by the publisher) was issued. In 1899, Freud was 43 years old and had just received a new phone number (14362) that contained a "43." In his compulsive frame of mind, with his nets spread very wide, almost any incident would have been scrutinized for some indication of the year of his death. Similarly, the fact of the publication of *The Interpretation of Dreams* that year was brought into the service of his *Todangst,* or death fear. Because he believed that this book was his masterpiece, he harbored the despairing conviction that there was nothing more to accomplish in his life. In essence, he might as well die.

When the new phone number contained not only the 43 of his present birthday but another pair of numbers—62—his superstitious inclination allowed him to convince himself that 62 would be the year of his death. He would thus outlive the present, forestalling his *Todangst.* As Schur points out, Freud's preoccupation with his own demise received several reinforcements in 1904, the year of the trip to Athens. For in that year, Freud's long and intimate relationship with Fliess ended bitterly, ostensibly over Fliess's belief that Freud had provided crucial information about his periodicity theory to a plagiarist.

Freud made greater use of the personal sources of his ideas as later theoretical constructs than is generally acknowledged. It should perhaps be mentioned that this personalizing of theory sometimes took the form of generalizing his personal pain to *all humans.* In *Totem and Taboo* (1913b) Freud raised the father conflict of the Oedipus complex to a universal, evolutionary trend by which our early human forebears, having murdered the primal father of the tribe to possess his power and his women, proceeded guiltily to spoil the fruits of their ambition by erecting incest taboos. As Wallace (1977, pp. 79–80) expressed it so lucidly, "By raising a personal dynamic to the level of a phylogenetic universal based on a deed done long ago, Freud is on the one hand distancing himself from his patricidal rage . . . but on the other he is metaphorically expressing its importance (by calling it a primal fact of world history) in his own psychic life" (cf. Wallace, 1976 and Schur, 1972, p. 474).

Freud's Relationship to His Mother: The Birds'-Beaked-People Dream

Another of Freud's dreams indicates the complexity of the verbal linkages that may be employed defensively to obscure threatening wishes. In his seventh or eighth year, Freud's self-analysis revealed, he had dreamt of his mother with a "peculiarly peaceful, sleeping expression on her features." In the dream, he saw her being carried into a room by two or three people with birds' beaks. Then they laid her on a bed (Freud, 1900, p. 583). The bizarre creatures with birds' beaks brought to Freud's mind the association of the illustrations of bird-masked people in a particular edition of the Bible called the *Phillippson's* Bible.

BOX 3.1   *Only Connect . . .*

In the sense that Freud saw the Oedipus conflict as a universal part of the unconscious, he thereby put it in the same category as a Jungian archetype (see Chapter 4)—a pattern of meaning that does not reflect the experiences of a single individual, but is a common inheritance of humanity. Jung, in fact, considered the Oedipus conflict, with its mythic origins, to be the only archetype that Freud discovered (Jung, in Evans, 1976, p. 56).

Further analysis revealed an association to the name "Phillippson" in the form of a memory of an "ill-mannered boy" named Phillipp, who was the first person to reveal to the young Freud the vulgar word for sexual intercourse. In German, the word *vogeln* is slang for copulation, and it is derived from the proper form of the world *Vogel,* which means "bird." Hence, the associative chain from people with *birds'* beaks to the *Phillippson* Bible to the boy named *Phillipp* had revealed a sexual connotation to the dream images.

The expression of his mother's face in the dream reminds Freud of his dying grandfather, whom he had observed in a coma a few days before the grandfather's death. However, when the young Freud awoke from the dream, he had rushed into his parents' room to wake his mother and was quite relieved to discover that she was indeed alive.

Why, then, had the dream depicted her in a state similar to death—a state, that is, similar to his grandfather's coma? Surely the dream could not have been the representation of a wish that his mother die? On the contrary, Freud's anxiety at the thought of her death had forced him, upon awakening, to rush into her room to confirm that she was still alive. Perhaps, he thought, his anxiety over her death was a form of disguise to prevent recognition of the sexual longing the dream had really depicted, a sexual longing for his mother.

Another interpretation of this dream is that the anxiety Freud experienced was due to a death wish directed toward his mother. This interpretation proceeds from the well-established fact that Freud's relationship to his mother was an especially close one. Freud consciously held a very idealized conception of the relationship between a mother and a son, suggesting at one point in his writings that it was altogether the most perfect and free from ambivalence of all human relationships (Freud, 1933, p. 133). Robert Stolorow and George Atwood (1978) suggest that Freud had an intense need to preserve an entirely positive image of his mother, an idealistic vision of her that had to be defended at all costs. When, as a child, he experienced resentment and rage toward her for having more children and for deserting him to do so, his only means of dealing with his hatred toward a figure he so dearly loved was repression, followed by "splitting" his image of her into a good mother and a hateful mother. In his interpretation of the birds'-beaked-people dream, Freud avoided the obvious meaning of hostility toward his mother, and displaced the death wish interpretation onto his father.

Stolorow and Atwood (1978) pointed out that Freud's theory of psychosexual development views the origin of personal conflicts as lying in the child's own internalized, but universal, biological urges. Actual parental influences on the child were minimized:

> In Freud's theoretical view of infantile development, the sources of evil were located not in the parents (mother), but rather in the child himself, in his own sexual and aggressive drives. . . . Specifically, through the relocation of the sources of badness into the child, Freud absolved his mother from blame for her betrayals of him and safeguarded her idealized image from invasions by his unconscious ambivalence. Freud's wish to banish (destroy) the treacherous mother ["treacherous" because she disappeared and gave birth to rivals] was thus replaced in his theory with the child's need to repress his own evil wishes. (Stolorow & Atwood, 1978, p. 232; see also Stolorow & Atwood, 1979, p. 67)

Stolorow and Atwood are probably correct in their assumption that Freud needed to locate the "sources of badness" in his own internalized biological states. They are probably also correct in assuming that, in so doing, Freud exonerated his mother from the taint of his rageful impulses and defensive distortions. However, it seems clear that Freud also exonerated himself from guilt for these unacceptable impulses. By proposing that erotic attachment to mother and murderous rivalry with both father and siblings are biological and fixed universals (with a phylogenetic history, no less), Freud, in effect, absolved himself of personal responsibility.

It is also necessary to consider the fact that, even if Freud had angry feelings toward his mother, the depth of his displaced rage toward his father matched or surpassed them. In principle, consequently, we would have to assume that, whether defensively displaced or genuinely, Freud harbored hostile wishes toward nearly every significant member of his family. In either case, the evidence supports the view that Freud distanced himself from his conflicting feelings by conceptualizing them as human inevitables.

Freud's ambitious goal in the analysis of his dreams was not only self-therapy, but also the attempt to unmask the secrets of unconscious mental life. Freud's own dreams point up the difficult nature of the task. For Freud sought no less an accomplishment than the explanation of how dreams are structured to conceal significant but unacceptable motives from consciousness—how dreams can both satisfy real desires and, at the same time, keep them hidden from conscious awareness.

MANIFEST AND LATENT DREAM CONTENT: THE MASK

In light of the disguised nature of wish fulfillment in adult dreams, even the most elementary description of dream processes must include a distinction between the readily accessible disguise and the less accessible ideas that lie behind the distortion. Freud referred to the dream's facade or mask as consisting of all those recalled sights, images, ideas, sounds, and smells that compose the story of the dream. Behind the facade, *beneath the mask* of recallable elements, lie the "perverse," unacceptable impulses that, like "masked criminals," are far commoner in mental life than straightforward, undisguised urges (Freud, 1925c, p. 132).

Freud's use of the mask metaphor is an apt analogy for his more technical distinction between the manifest and latent content of the dream. The manifest or surface content corresponds to the mask, whereas the impulses, thus disguised like "masked criminals," are properly termed **latent content** or hidden content. The dreamer generally easily recalls **manifest content.** By contrast, the latent content can be arrived at only by careful interpretation of the manifest content.

The mental processes that convert strivings, wishes, and needs into the disguised images of the manifest content are collectively called dream work. In a sense, the analyst's interpretation of a dream is an attempt to undo the dream work, to unmask the manifest content, and reveal the more fundamental latent content from which the dream was constructed.

The Dream Work

Once distortion or disguise is recognized as a general phenomenon of dream imagery, it becomes necessary to search for a cause of the distortion. Freud postulated that the wishes or needs that initiate the dream are unacceptable to a special part of the conscious mind called the "censorship system." The censorship system is actually on the frontier of consciousness, a border guard, so to speak, between the unconscious and conscious systems of the mind.

The censorship system is very selective about the wishes and needs it allows the dreamer to entertain or remember consciously. Wishes that are morally unacceptable to the dreamer who is awake are also unacceptable to the sleeping dreamer's censor. In consequence, this ethical arm of the mental apparatus heavily censors wishes or urges that arise from the unconscious during sleep. Thus the distortion in those wishes as they appear in the manifest dream is a direct result of the efforts of the ever-watchful preconscious dream censor.

The two systems of the mind, the *unconscious system* from which the wishes emerge and the **preconscious censorship system** that prevents those wishes from freely entering consciousness, constitute the mechanism of **dream work** or dream formation (Freud, 1900, pp. 144–145). Unacceptable wishes can be prevented from gaining access to consciousness in only one way. The censorship system must selectively distort the wish, transforming it into an alternate form that does not clash with the conscious ethical standards of the personality. Conversely, the only way the unconscious can achieve satisfaction for its pressing urges is to evade the censor by masquerading the unacceptability of its wishes behind a facade of related but more neutral ideas. Hence the distortion in dreams is a joint product of two architects: the unconscious system and the censor.

FOUR PROCESSES OF DREAM WORK

Freud was able to isolate four separate processes in the dream work of these two architects that account for the form of the manifest dream:

1. condensation,

2. displacement,

3. visual representation, and

4. secondary revision.

The Work of Condensation

One of the mundane facts about the *interpretation* of a dream, but a fact that contains a significant clue about dream distortion, is that a remembered dream (i.e., the manifest content) can be recounted in relatively few words. In contrast, the *interpretation* of the manifest dream, penetrating to the latent content, may produce as much as 12 times the amount of information (Freud, 1900, p. 279). Freud concluded, therefore, that the manifest content is an unsurpassed model of compression, or **condensation** as it was called in Freud's technical vocabulary.

It might be possible to conclude hastily that the work of condensation is merely a one-way editing process whereby only a select few elements of the mass of unconscious material are chosen for representation in the manifest content. In this simplistic view, condensation is accomplished by a process of omission. But free association to the few manifest elements of a dream usually reveals that each manifest element has multiple, two-way relationships with every other element, and each component is, therefore, at least partially redundant.

Borrowing a concept from the study of hysterical symptoms, it can be said that the manifest dream content is **overdetermined.** Several unconscious ideas band together to contribute to one common manifest element. Simultaneously, each manifest element has connections to several other manifest elements, which, of course, have their own connections to other groups of unconscious, latent ideas that have similarly banded together. The picture that Freud paints of condensation is more like an associative web than it is like a chain.

Condensation, consequently, is not a process of simple omission. It is a technique of *creative compression.* Each segment of the manifest content is a nodal point upon which a great number of latent ideas converge (Freud, 1900, p. 283). The latent dream thoughts are thus condensed into the manifest dream content much as a composite photograph of a single person is constructed from the characteristics of several individuals: It may "look like A perhaps, but may be dressed like B, may do something that we remember C doing, and at the same time we may know that he is D" (Freud, 1916, p. 171). Freud's description sounds very much like the constructing of a "Mr. Potato Head" toy, building a composite from several elements.

The Work of Displacement

Displacement is a technique the censorship agency of the mind employs to replace a latent dream element in consciousness by a more remote idea, or to accomplish a shifting of the dream's recalled emphasis away from an important idea and toward an unimportant one. Thus displacement may proceed by two paths: replacement of one idea with a remote associate, or the shifting emotional accent from one thought to another. The dreamer is left with the impression of having dreamed a very strangely connected sequence of thoughts, or of having very absurdly made "much ado about nothing."

Freud employed an amusing anecdote in his *Introductory Lectures* to illustrate the concept of displacement:

> There was a blacksmith in the village, who had committed a capital offence. The Court decided that the crime must be punished; but as the blacksmith was the only one in the village and was indispensable, and as on the other hand there were three tailors living there, one of *them* was hanged instead. (1916, pp. 174–175)

Whereas condensation was responsible for compressing the latent thoughts into the abbreviated form of the manifest content, displacement is responsible for the "choice" of elements from which the manifest dream is constructed.

Beginning with the latent, unacceptable wish at the center, the dream work of displacement spins outward from this nucleus a web of increasingly remote associations. Each strand of this associative web is connected both to the central latent wish and to every other associated idea in the network. Hence, manifest elements are redundant in the sense that the unacceptable wish is dispersed simultaneously into many interconnected and mutually excitatory strands of the web. Because each of these strands shares a common origin, the nuclear wish, recollection of the ideas along any other strand excites recollection of nearby, connected strands of ideas.

One way to view the manifest dream, therefore, is to conceive of it as an associative "beating around the bush," whereby the unacceptable nucleus wish of the latent content is dispersed into any available channel of the web except one that leads directly back to the origin. The pattern of associatively connected, overlapping, and redundant ideas evoked by the dreamer during free association to a manifest element is evidence of this delicately tangled skein. Displacement robs the latent content of its normal sequence of ideas, substituting the sequence of the associative web, and it likewise rechannels the latent content's original focus of emotional intensity into the diffuse lattice of the web.

The Work of Visual Representation

Abstract ideas, wishes, and urges that form the latent thoughts of the dream are by themselves colorless and ephemeral. Within the scope of the dream, these abstract thoughts must be converted into concrete visual images with the kind of primitive pictorial quality that readily lends itself to the manipulations of condensation and displacement (Freud, 1900, p. 339). Although not all the elements of the latent content are converted into visual images, on the whole the translation of abstract thoughts into concrete pictures constitutes the essence of a dream (Freud, 1916, p. 175).

The translation of abstract thoughts into visual imagery typically follows the path of converting the symbolic labels representing the idea into a physical and concrete act. For example, the abstract idea of "possession" can be converted into the visually concrete act of "sitting on the object." Children often employ this strategy to protect a treasured possession from the grasp of an overwhelming playmate (Freud, 1916, p. 176n.).

To take another illustration, Freud reported the recollections of Herbert Silberer, who, in a sleepy, twilight state, often converted some abstract intellectual task into visual imagery. On one occasion, Silberer thought of having to revise an uneven or rough passage in an essay he was writing. He then pictured himself planing a piece of wood (Freud, 1900, p. 344). In another episode, Silberer had the experience of losing his train of thought so that he had to return to the beginning to pick up the thread of logic. Silberer subsequently had the visual image of a printer's typesetting form for a page with the last lines of type fallen away (Freud, 1900, p. 345).

Thus, one can see that the translation of abstract thoughts into visual imagery represents a process of personal, individualized symbolization. The dreamer creates concrete pictures to represent abstract thoughts. This process is opposite to the process often found in literature, that of transforming concrete acts into abstract symbols.

The Work of Secondary Revision

All the mechanisms of the dream work discussed thus far have as their common goal getting around or appeasing of dream censorship. The dream work can condense, displace, and represent in visual form the latent dream thoughts in its attempt to disguise them. For the most part, these three mechanisms distort and break apart the latent elements' form and organization. Thus, these dream mechanisms often produce an absurd or difficult to understand dream. When the dreamer tries to recall and make sense of the dream, however, the gaps, distortions, and substitutions seem lacking in harmony and logic.

The dreamer's waking need is for logical coherence and consistency in mental activities. Consequently, to bring order to what otherwise would be experienced as chaos, that part of the mind between unconsciousness and consciousness exerts an organizing, sense-making influence on the confused and bizarre stories that might emerge. In those twilight moments just before waking from a dream, it is the *preconscious mind* that struggles to mold the dreamer's creations into a form comprehensible to waking intelligence.

The preconscious mind thus attempts to patch together, into an understandable, coherent whole, the scattered and apparently nonsensical elements of the latent dream. In so doing, the preconscious is, in effect, subjecting the dream to an interpretation before the dreamer is fully awake. Whatever that interpretation is, the elements of the dream will be fitted to its outlines until what was scattered and diffuse becomes organized and reasonable.

It is this preinterpretation that introduces further distortion into the recalled manifest content. Freud called this process of constructing a coherent whole from the scattered dream elements **secondary revision.** In a sense, the preconscious treats the dream elements to a kind of further elaboration designed to mold what is patently unconnected and absurd into a logically consistent structure.

Sometimes the secondary revision occurs during the dream itself. For instance, a particular dream may be so laden with unpleasant emotional intensity that the various patterns of distortion introduced by the mechanisms of condensation and displacement are not sufficient to satisfy all the demands of the dream censorship. If the ever-watchful dream censor were to be aroused to action, the dreamer's sleep would surely be disturbed or disrupted in an effort to halt the dream. To lessen the impact of such a dream without recourse to interrupting the dreamer's sleep, there occurs instead a kind of judgmental interpretation on the part of the dreamer that, after all, *"It's only a dream"* (Freud, 1900, p. 489).

STUDY OF THE DREAM: THEORETICAL YIELD

Psychoanalytic dream interpretation is a careful labor of elucidating the apparent absurdities of the recalled dream by viewing such productions as evidence of the dreamer's nonconscious mental processes and contents. Accurate interpretation of the dream, therefore, lifts the disguise, makes intelligible the distortions, and replaces absurdity with understanding. The long hidden logic of the unconscious is made accessible. Freud considered the study of the dream one of his most fundamental and lasting achievements. A brief survey of the theoretical yield is in order.

Regressive and Archaic Nature of Dreams

The medium of dreams is visual imagery. It was Freud's opinion that visual imagery represents an earlier and more primitive mode of mental operation than verbal thought. Thus the dream is an archaic production—a return to a mode of thought characteristic of the early years of childhood before language achieves its prominence in our relations to the world. Each individual initially begins mental life, Freud asserted, with sensory impressions and memory images of such impressions. Words are attached to these images only later in development, so that, at the outset, the child does not code mental activities into language labels (Freud, 1916, pp. 180–181; see also Freud, 1900, pp. 189ff.).

Dreams are a return to this archaic mode of mental functioning, and often, "to our surprise, we find the child and child's impulses still living on in the dream" (Freud, 1900, p. 191). Dream processes, then, are a *regression* to the earlier years of the dreamer's mental life. Correctly translated, a dream's latent content may contain a wish that dates from childhood.

Sexual and Aggressive Motives of Childhood

On the whole, adults retain very few memories of the first five or six years of life. With rare exception, most of us can recall but one or two incidents that we now presume, precisely because they are remembered, to have been overwhelmingly important at the time. But key memories and feelings are conspicuously absent from adult consciousness. Recollection of our Oedipal sexual and aggressive strivings remains inaccessible to consciousness because **infantile amnesia** obscures them in addition to a great wealth of experiences of the childhood epoch.

However, it was Freud's discovery that these memories are not lost. Instead, they are only inaccessible or latent. Having become part of the unconscious, these childhood memories, strivings, and wishes may emerge during dreams when triggered by some current, thematically similar, incident.

The "Hellish" Unconscious

Consider the necessity of censorship in dreams. Dreamers entertain wishes and desires that would seem so perverse and unethical to them if awake that the dream work must disguise these thoughts beyond conscious recognition. What is the source of these monumentally "evil" inclinations? Obviously, since dreams are a product of the unconscious, the unconscious must be the source of the impulses that the conscious personality, the ego, finds objectionable. But during sleep, the censorship agency is less stringent, more easily pacified by partial disguise, and it allows the ego to be flooded with material that is customarily held in check.

The ego, freed from all ethical bonds, also finds itself at one with all the demands of sexual desire, even those that have long been condemned by our aesthetic upbringing and those, which contradict all the requirements of moral restraint. The desire of pleasure—the "libido," as we call it—chooses its objects without inhibition, and by preference, indeed, the forbidden ones: not only other men's wives, but above all incestuous objects, objects sanctified by the common agreement of mankind, a man's mother and sister, a woman's father and brother. . . . Lusts which we think of as remote from human nature show themselves strong enough to provoke dreams. Hatred, too, rages without restraint. Wishes for revenge and death directed against those who are nearest and dearest in waking life, against the dreamer's parents, brothers, and sisters, husband or wife, and his own children are nothing unusual. These censored wishes appear to rise up out of a positive Hell; after they have been interpreted when we are awake, no censorship of them seems to us too severe. (Freud, 1916, pp. 142–143)

Are we to conclude, on the basis of the seemingly reprehensible content of adult dreams, that dreams simply expose the inherently evil character of humanity? On the contrary, Freud protested. It is not that dreams expose evil, hellish strivings of adults, but that adults interpret such feelings in themselves as evil when they become aware of them. Actually, the egoistic, unrestrained sexual and aggressive urges found in dreams date from childhood, when ethical and realistic standards of conduct, which we attribute to adult understanding, were yet undeveloped.

Against the standards of adult ethics, such wishes as sexual desire for a parent and murderous intent directed toward rivals are absolutely wrong, shocking, and condemnable. But *for infants* such reactions are understandable, given that they are at once helpless, yet dominated by urgent needs for immediate gratification of their wishes. That gratification can come only from those persons who are in charge of their care, and who, therefore, are in intimate contact with them. For infants it is not morally outrageous to desire the exclusive possession of their mothers; it is not shocking that they expect this accustomed fulfiller of every pleasure also to be the object of their sexual explorations and curiosity; it is not a condemnable quality of infants that they harbor wishes for the annihilation of brothers, sisters, and father, along with anyone else who rivals their insistent and pressing commitment to mother, the satisfier. To the infant, unschooled in shame, disgust, or morality, such presumed desires would be the merely ordinary parts of daily existence. To the adult, recollecting these feelings in dreams, guilt and horror seem the only appropriate responses.

It is with these memories, wishes, and strivings that the ethical and realistic demands of later socialization will clash. The forces of repression will thrust them into the unconscious: " . . . what is unconscious in mental life is also what is infantile" (Freud, 1916, p. 210). Adult dreams regress to the archaic and amoral level of infancy, and they deceptively appear to shed light on the vileness of the adult unconscious.

The obvious question arises: "What triggers the reemergence of these latent, infantile strivings in adult dreams?" Freud suggested that something in the dreamer's current waking life—it could be an incident, a frustrated desire, the emotionally abrasive happenings of the day—connects by association with memories stored in the unconscious and, together with them, initiates a dream. Archaic wishes in the unconscious link up with these "day's residues," as Freud called them, to produce the dream thoughts. Dream thoughts are thus dominated by events that have given us pause for reflection during the day and which bear some associative similarity to the archaic wishes in the unconscious. The explanation, of course, may apply the other way round: Events that give us pause during the day do so because they are connected with repressed wishes in the unconscious (Freud, 1900, pp. 169, 174).

Indeed, in either case, dreams are the royal road to an understanding of the unconscious mind.

Counterwishes: Anxiety Dreams

If dreams are indeed wish fulfillments, then why do we sometimes dream dreams that apparently run counter to our most cherished desires? Indeed, why do our dreams sometimes contain elements of our most dreaded fears? To answer these questions, and to account for the apparent contradiction, we must ask a further question: "Whose wish is fulfilled by a dream?"

> No doubt a wish-fulfillment must bring pleasure; but the question then arises "To whom?" To the person who has the wish of course. But as we know, a dreamer's relation to his wishes is a quite peculiar one. He repudiates them and censors them—he has no liking for them, in short. So that their fulfillment will give him no pleasure, but just the opposite; and experience shows that this opposite appears in the form of anxiety. . . . Thus a dreamer in his relation to his dream-wishes can only be compared to an amalgamation of two separate people who are linked by some important common element. (Freud, 1900, pp. 580–581; this passage was added as a footnote in 1919; the same paragraph is included in Freud, 1916, pp. 215–216)

The amalgamated personage referred to in this passage describes, of course, the conflicting relationship between the dreamer's unconscious, the source of the wish, and the preconscious censorship agency, the source of the repudiation. Thus although the wish fulfillment embodied in the dream brings pleasure to the unconscious, the anxiety element introduced by the distortion of the dream work is meant to satisfy the ever-watchful censor.

If we conceive of the mind as divided between the two agencies—the unconscious pleasure-seeking system, and the preconscious censorship system—the compromise nature of anxiety dreams becomes apparent. On the one hand, the unconscious is allowed some expression and some satisfaction of its repressed urges in the dream. On the other hand, the ethical arm of personality is allowed some control over the unacceptability of the wishes (Freud, 1900, p. 581). Dreams, just like neurotic symptoms, are compromise formations that allow both an outlet for the discharge of the wish's tension and a censorship mechanism to repudiate the now gratified, but still unacceptable, wish.

Repression and the Unpleasure Principle

Consider once again the state of human infants. Striving to obtain satisfaction for their needs and to avoid mounting somatic tension, infants soon learn the distinction between a fantasized and a real satisfier. Frustration and unpleasure are the tutors in a curriculum that includes the lessons that imagined food cannot be eaten, hallucinatory milk cannot be drunk, and an ephemeral mother cannot be cuddled. In order to survive, the infant must learn that the wish fulfillments embodied in dream states and fantasies have to be pursued in reality.

When *real* satisfactions for its desires are not forthcoming, the infant experiences psychological and sometimes bodily pain that Freud termed *unpleasure*. Conversely, when the unconscious obtains gratification of its desires, the result is the physical and mental state of *pleasure*.

A further set of lessons, however, must be mastered to ensure a comfortable and safe existence. This "unpleasure principle" is a two-edged sword. It motivates infants to avoid the discomfort of hallucinatory need satisfaction. It also emphasizes the importance of actively avoiding painful or noxious stimulation as well. Hence, the newly developed preconscious reality-scanning system may operate to promote escape or flight from certain forms of excitation when, on the basis of past experience, it recognizes some stimuli as potentially threatening. This class of unpleasure-producing stimuli might include, for example, as the child matures, lighted matches, hot radiators, and an angry mother.

Furthermore, even the internal, mental representations of such stimuli would trigger avoidance responses in the mental apparatus. But in the case of internal stimulation, the mental apparatus cannot engage in the physical act of flight. Instead, mental withdrawal occurs that takes the form of an *anticathexis,* the removal of **cathexes,**[1] charges of mental energy, or the diversion of attention from the memory image of the noxious stimulus.

THE REALITY PRINCIPLE

The infant's newest mental attainment under the influence of the unpleasure principle is its ability to delay the motor activity that is normally employed in obtaining gratification. The infant will now wait until there is a clear indication of the existence of reality from its preconscious perceptual system. It is the reality-testing orientation to the world that provides the infant with a reliable income of pleasure. We might, therefore, redefine a wish in these terms: A wish is a quantity of unpleasurable excitation resulting from a need that can be completely satisfied only by a real object or by specific and instrumental activity in the external world.

Thus infants' intercourse with the world is governed not only by the pleasure-unpleasure principle, but by the **reality principle** as well. With the adoption of this more sophisticated mental strategy, external reality increases in importance in infants' mental lives. Infants will increasingly use their senses to scan the environment for appropriate objects of satisfaction demanded by the reality principle (Freud, 1911, p. 220).

Primary and Secondary Process Thought

Our description of the unpleasure and reality principles is incomplete because their joint functioning is more complicated than a simple picture might suggest. The unconscious system, for example, apparently knows no bounds to its wishfulness, and it is well satisfied with only hallucinatory wish satisfaction. Behaving as if reality did not exist, the unconscious does not by itself discriminate between real and imaginary objects. Its only interest is in the distinction between pleasure and unpleasure.

Moreover, as revealed in manifest dreams and in neurotic symptoms, the unconscious system's sum total of mental energy is highly mobile and capable of all sorts of shifts, condensations, and displacements. All of these mental acrobatics are, of course, directed to the attainment of satisfaction at all cost. Freud characterized this state of affairs in the unconscious as **primary process thinking.** The chief characteristics of primary process thinking are the urgency with which tension reduction is sought, the plasticity or mobility of its energy, and its disregard for reality.

---

[1]The term *cathexis* is a translation of a German term Freud had first used in his "Project for a Scientific Psychology" (1895). The project was a detailed neurological model of the mind in which Freud postulated coordinated systems of neurons with the brain as the basis of various psychological processes, including repression and dreams. Certain of the neurons in this model become permeable to the flow of energy (electrochemical discharges) within the nervous system and they "fill up" with quantities of it. Freud used the German word *Besetzung,* which roughly means "to fill up," or "to occupy," in describing the flow of energy in and out of the neurons. His translators converted the German word to the more technical sounding cathexis from a Greek root meaning "to hold on to." Freud abandoned the neurological model, but not the analogous idea of psychic energy systems that could fill up and discharge their quantities of energy, that is, their cathexis of excitation.

In contrast to the primary process functioning of the unconscious system, the preconscious system operates in accord with the reality principle by delaying gratification. This kind of mental functioning, characterized by an interest in the demands of reality and an ability to delay gratification, Freud termed **secondary process thinking.** Because secondary process mental functioning develops later than primary process thinking, and because such reality-oriented mental activity is characteristic of truly adult thought, Freud considered secondary process thought to be a clear developmental advance over primary process functioning.

THE MEANINGS OF *UNCONSCIOUS* IN PSYCHOANALYSIS

The way in which Freud had used the term, **unconscious,** in his early writings led to some confusion about the reasons for which an idea might be removed from consciousness. Freud, therefore, distinguished three ways in which the term unconscious was used in psychoanalysis.

The first meaning, indicating the existence of ideas that are not *now*—at this precise moment—in consciousness, is a purely *descriptive* one. Thus, for example, although few of us keep our own phone number in the forefront of our minds at every minute of the day, we can nevertheless recall that item when necessary. Our phone number is only temporarily out of immediate awareness. There is no a priori reason why it cannot be brought into consciousness at will. Such items that can easily be made conscious are conceptualized as residing in the preconscious system (Freud, 1912, p. 262). Hence, this first meaning of *unconscious* is descriptive of those occasions when the limitations of consciousness and the human attention span necessitate the simple omission of some content.

In contrast with this purely descriptive sense, there are memories of early childhood incidents, impulses, and desires that are unacceptable or threatening to the conscious ego and cannot be recalled. Such memories are repressed from consciousness. Hysterical symptoms owe their existence to such unconscious ideas that, despite their intensity and their activity, remain separate from conscious awareness. Repressed memories are never admitted to consciousness so long as repression operates successfully. There is a continual expenditure of energy required to keep threatening memories out of awareness. This type of unconscious, full of threatening desires and memories, is called the *dynamic* unconscious (Freud, 1912, pp. 263–264).

The unconscious is thus characterized by the high mobility of its cathexes of energy as evidenced in its ability to condense, displace, and distort ideas. Furthermore, the unconscious responds to the demands of the **pleasure principle** by its continual press for immediate gratification of wishes, in contrast with the delayed, inhibitory, reality-testing orientation of the preconscious. In consequence, the unconscious must be conceptualized as a unique system operating in accordance with its own local rules of conduct side by side with the other systems of the mind that, likewise, operate in conformity with their intrinsic standards of conduct. This usage of the word *unconscious* conveys the *systematic* meaning of the term, indicating the independent status of the unconscious as a system among systems.

In summary, Freud distinguished among three meanings of the term *unconscious:* the *descriptive,* the *dynamic,* and the *systematic*. Each of these usages might be thought of as corresponding to a question:

- What is unconscious? (descriptive)
- Why is it unconscious? (dynamic)
- Where is the unconscious idea? (systematic)

The Concept of "Metapsychology"

The complexity of the term unconscious led Freud to the useful strategy of distinguishing among its separate but interrelated meanings. Using a similar approach, Freud now began to distinguish among the various facets of any psychological event. He resurrected a term from his earlier work to describe the process of conceptualizing mental processes from multiple viewpoints simultaneously. **Metapsychology** (meaning "above" or "beyond" psychology) was the technical term to be used whenever a psychological process was understood from its descriptive, systematic, and dynamic aspects. Unfortunately, Freud introduced some confusion into the concept by changing his vocabulary each time he wrote about metapsychology (cf. Freud, 1915c, p. 181; 1933, pp. 70ff.).

The *systematic* meaning was sometimes identified as the **topographic** viewpoint, indicating not only Freud's conception of different systems but also that he viewed the systems as spatially arrayed. At this point in his career, Freud pictured the unconscious, preconscious, and conscious systems as three adjacent compartments (see 1900, Chapter 7). Hence, the topographic viewpoint referred not only to the unique properties of a particular system of the mind but also to its particular location with respect to the other systems and the paths of its access to consciousness at any moment in time.

In a similar way, Freud enlarged the meaning of the term dynamic by suggesting that not only are there competing and conflicting forces behind psychological processes but also that their relative magnitudes or quantities of energy may be measurable. Hence, the term *economic* was coined to indicate the differing degrees of intensity with which dynamic interactions take place (1915c, p. 180).

Other psychoanalysts have pointed to another component of metapsychology inherent in Freud's way of understanding behavior. Any symptom, dream, or act has a psychological history within the life history of a person's life. By reconstructing the many events (or memories of them) that coalesced into one mental process, the origins of symptoms, ideas, beliefs, resistances, feelings, and so on are reached. This life history viewpoint is what Freud called the genetic approach, and it constitutes another facet of metapsychology (A. Freud, 1969a, p. 153).

Finally, analysts who followed Freud have also stressed the nonconflictive aspects of some psychological events. Thus Hartmann (1939, 1964) emphasized the adaptive

Table 3.1   Components of Freud's Metapsychology

Metapsychological viewpoint	Clinical referent
1. **Descriptive**	Momentary absence from awareness of particular ideas or feelings that can easily be made conscious at will.
2. **Systematic** (or **topographic**)	Special quality of a mental event due to the unique characteristics of the psychological system in which it originates, presently occupies, or to which it has access by virtue of its location.
3. **Dynamic**	Energetic mobility of the competing, conflicting forces that prevent an idea or feeling from becoming conscious or allow it to enter awareness only in disguised form.
4. **Economic**	Relative intensities or quantities of the competing dynamic forces, and their changes in strength over time.
5. **Genetic**	Reconstruction of the multiple origins of any psychological event in the life history of the person.
6. **Adaptive**	Degree to which a psychological process or act functions in resolving unconscious conflicts and in the healthy management of life events.

quality of psychological processes that function not only to resolve individuals' personal conflicts but also serve them in a healthy way to fit comfortably into the life they and their environment create. Hence, the **adaptive viewpoint** is added alongside the others as a component of metapsychology.

It is clear that the Freudian way of viewing any human event requires attention to the complex interplay of a host of determinants. Metapsychology requires that each person be regarded as an intricate, but understandable, organism. The various facets of metapsychology are summarized in Table 3.1.

METAPSYCHOLOGY OF REPRESSION

Repression, you may recall, is the way in which the mental apparatus deals with wishful impulses from which physical flight is impossible. Instead, these inescapable and unacceptable impulses are not admitted to awareness. Consider the paradox involved in proposing a mechanism like repression. Wishful impulses demand satisfaction and, when it is forthcoming, pleasure is the usual result. But in the case of a repressed impulse, something has happened to a wishful idea that makes satisfaction so unpleasurable that denial of its existence is the only means of dealing with it. Yet the impulse continues to press for release.

It thus seems that one of the preconditions for an impulse to be subject to repression is that satisfaction of the impulse be simultaneously pleasurable and unpleasurable. The only way to account for this disparity of aims is to assume that the reason a repressed impulse has been denied release into consciousness is because its satisfaction would create pleasure for one mental system at the expense of the even more grave unpleasure evoked in a competing system. This is the conflict between unconscious wishful demands and conscious restraint.

A Balance of Pleasure and Unpleasure

Freud clearly conceived of repression as the expression of a balance between these two motives: the seeking after pleasure and the avoidance of unpleasure. In the case of a repressed impulse, however, the motive force of unpleasure is more intense than the pleasure to be obtained from satisfaction of the impulse. Repression occurs, consequently, when the balance between pleasure and unpleasure is tipped in the direction of unpleasure.

The process of **repression** requires that the preconscious system prevent the emergence of the unconscious impulse into awareness by withdrawing a sum of mental energy (cathexis) from the offending impulse. However, having lost the cathexis of the preconscious, the unacceptable impulse may still retain the cathexis of energy from the unconscious, where it originated. Consequently, the repressed impulse can continue to make assaults on the preconscious system indefinitely, drawing on its reserve of energy in the unconscious. The simple expedient of withdrawing preconscious energy from the impulse is not sufficient to prevent the impulse from unendingly repeating its attempts at entry into consciousness (Freud, 1915c, p. 180).

What is needed to accomplish the permanent subjugation of the impulse is another, opposing quantity of energy, strong enough to resist the unconsciously endowed impulse's cathexis of energy. Such an opposing supply of energy would, in effect, serve as a barrier against the reemergence of the rejected impulse. Freud called this barrier that is set up by the preconscious an **anticathexis.** Anticathexis is the primary mode of dealing with unacceptable unconscious content. Clearly, to enable repression to remain effective, an anticathexis requires a continual expenditure of energy by the preconscious.

Primal Repression and Repression Proper

With the development of the theoretical concept of anticathexis, Freud could account for the creation and presence of repressed derivatives in consciousness, like symptoms and seduction fantasies. He now conceived of repression as a two-stage process to effect this theoretical advance.

In the first stage, the ideational representative of the unacceptable impulse is denied access to consciousness by the preconscious setting up an anticathexis as a barrier. The first stage is called **primal repression.** The immediate result of primal repression is that the repressed idea or impulse is fixated or frozen in development. No further modification or maturation of the repressed content can occur (Freud, 1915b, p. 148). Significant acts of primal repression occur during the first six or eight years of life, and in their role of immobilized, unconscious memories they become important sensitizing or predisposing factors for later acts of adult repression.

The second stage of repression is called **repression proper,** and it is directed against any derivatives or associates of the originally repressed impulses that may enter consciousness. Repression proper is rather like an "after pressure," to use Freud's descriptive phrase, whereby ideas, trains of thought, or perceptions that are associatively linked to the primally repressed impulse are also denied access to consciousness. Repression proper consists of the preconscious system's withdrawing its cathexis (energy) from the derivative. Repression proper thus cooperates with primal repression to ensure that unacceptable impulses and associated ideas remain out of consciousness awareness.

Thus repression is not a unitary act. Or, more precisely, repressions of primal derivatives that occur after infancy depend on the mass of primally repressed impulses already present in the unconscious. An idea or an impulse cannot be removed from awareness by repression proper unless there has already been an act of predisposing primal repression to exert a "pulling effect" on subsequent derivatives. At the same time, the preconscious system actively strives from its vantage point on the threshold of awareness to eject these offending ideas by pushing them away from consciousness (cf. Freud, 1900, p. 547n.).

INSTINCTS OF THE UNCONSCIOUS

Terms like "excitation," "impulse," "wish," and "tension," dating almost from the very beginning of Freud's psychological writing, were replaced in his later work by the term *instinct.*

In his 1915 metapsychological paper, "Instincts and Their Vicissitudes," Freud carefully delineated two distinctions between stimuli and instincts:

- Freud pointed out that physical stimuli impinge on the organism from the external environment, whereas instinctual urges develop from within the organism. Although the organism, through the use of reflexes, may escape or even terminate external stimulation, internal instinctual demand cannot be escaped by flight. An organism cannot flee the demands of its own body.

- A second distinguishing feature is that stimulation originating in the environment is only temporary in its impact on the organism. Instinctual, internal excitation terminates only when the tissue need that gives rise to the instinct is satisfied. Thus instincts may be thought of as needs seeking appropriate satisfactions (Freud, 1915a, p. 119).

Freud returned in his discussion of instinct to his earlier idea of the nervous system as an apparatus that functions to reduce stimulation and excitation to the lowest possible level. In Freud's view, the nervous system is assigned the task of "mastering stimuli" by discharging excitation almost as soon as it builds up (1915a, p. 120). Called the principle of constancy by Breuer and Freud, this idea of the nervous system repeatedly returning to some optimal state of minimum arousal is similar to the modern biologist's concept of **homeostasis.** It follows, in consequence, that this essential task is complicated in the case of an instinct because the nervous system cannot master instinctual demands by the expedient of flight. Furthermore, because the nervous system is governed by the **pleasure principle**—the seeking after pleasure by the discharge of unpleasurable mounting tension—instincts must not be dealt with in a way that merely avoids their demand; the nervous system must find a way to reduce the biological deficit (or to satisfy the urge) that the demand represents.

For Freud, then, the concept of instinct was both a psychological and a biological one, on the border between bodily and mental phenomena. An instinct is a mental representation of a physical or bodily need (1915a, p. 122).

CHARACTERISTICS OF INSTINCTS

Freud distinguished four characteristics of an instinct:

1. **Pressure:** The amount of force or strength of the demand made by the instinct on the mind is described as pressure. Thus, for example, deprivation of food for 24 hours produces greater instinctual pressure (hunger) than deprivation for only four hours.

2. **Aim:** Instinctual impulses all strive toward one goal or aim: satisfaction or tension reduction. Whereas satisfaction is clearly the universal aim of an instinct, a given instinct may operate to achieve its aim in differing ways. Freud distinguishes, therefore, between *ultimate aim,* the immediate gratification of demand, and *intermediate aim,* the substitute forms of satisfaction for which an instinct may strive when blocked from a directly suitable goal. The sexual instinct is particularly prone to this widening of its aims. For example, the aim of the sexual instincts is "organ pleasure," a pleasing sensation attached to a particular part of the body when stimulated. With maturation, the sexual instincts become focused on the aim of reproduction (Freud, 1915a, p. 126).

3. **Object:** To obtain its ultimate aim of satisfaction, the instinct must seek some concrete, usually external, object that has the power to reduce its tension. For example, an infant's hunger drive is directed toward the object of food. The object of an instinct is its most variable characteristic. Thus displacement from one satisfying object to another, a process so characteristic of the wish fulfillments in dreams, is possible. Some prisoners, for example, confined with members of their own sex, might resort to homosexual gratification as a substitute for heterosexual satisfaction, only to return to exclusive heterosexual gratification upon release.

4. **Source:** The source of instincts reside in the physical-chemical processes of the body. The sexual instincts, for example, have their physiological sources in hormonal secretions, central nervous system activity, and genital arousal; the hunger instinct originates in the viscera (and also in some parts of the central nervous system).

DUALISTIC DIVISION OF THE INSTINCTS: HUNGER VERSUS LOVE

It is clear that Freud viewed the instincts, though biologically based, as essentially malleable and plastic in the course of an organism's life history. During their collision with life's circumstances, the instincts may undergo modifications or reversals of expression. These vicissitudes, to use Freud's translators' term, share the common motive of avoiding the psychological or biological discomfort that would result from free, undisguised expression of an instinctual urge. Repression, as we have seen, is one of the vicissitudes that an instinct may undergo.

Although instincts may be expressed and satisfied in diverse ways, Freud was hesitant to catalog a seemingly infinite list of biological demands and their mental representatives. Instead, he proposed a concise, bipolar division of all instincts into two great classes: instincts in the service of the preservation of the individual's life, and instincts directed toward the attainment of pleasure. *Life maintenance* and *pleasure* are the two poles around which the operations of the mental apparatus are organized.

According to this dualistic scheme, Freud asserted that the ego was the seat of the organism's instincts for self-preservation, whereas striving for pleasure was a function of the child's developing sexual equipment. Though Freud did not provide a name for the energy of the ego instincts, he employed the term **libido** to denote the energy of the sexual or pleasure instincts (e.g., 1916, p. 313). Libido was broadly conceived as general pleasurable stimulation rather than as restricted to genital, sexual pleasure. Thus Freud's original dualistic classification of the instincts pitted the ego instincts against the sexual (pleasure) instincts: survival versus libido.

The ego instincts have as their main goal the preservation and continuance of the safety and bodily integrity of the individual. Sexual (pleasure) instincts, on the other hand, are directed to the preservation of the species. Consequently, in Freud's original dualism, the ego instincts are individual-centered and the sexual instincts are, ultimately, species-centered. This dichotomy, Freud pointed out, is roughly similar to the division between *hunger* (individual self-preservation) and *love* (other-centered pleasure).

Freud introduced this division of the instincts in a paper in 1910 (1910b, p. 214; see editor's footnote), and he maintained the dualism of which he was so fond for a number of years. The bulk of his writing in subsequent years, however, was focused on the sexual instincts with the effect of obscuring by neglect the role of the ego instincts. But the ego instincts were to come into their own in psychoanalysis as Freud's clinical practice revealed some disconcerting anomalies and violations of the dualistic hunger-love scheme.

Exceptions to the Hunger-Love Model: Narcissism

In the dualistic conception of the instincts, libido, the energy of the sexual or pleasure instincts, should be a separate quantity from that of the ego instincts. Freud noted a disconcerting exception to this separation hypothesis in the case of some psychotic patients.

One of the main characteristics of some forms of schizophrenia is the withdrawal of the patient's interest from the external world. They behave as if reality no longer existed and in every way as though only their own ideas, feelings, or urges mattered. Freud's instinct theory would characterize such withdrawal as the retraction of libido from external objects and persons. Simultaneously with this retraction of libido, however, there occurs what seems to be an expansion of ego instinctual energy, an increase in the ego's self-interest. In short, psychotics overvalue their own ideas, their own bodies, and their own person. Why should this reciprocal increase in ego instinct occur at the same time as outwardly directed libido is diminished—unless the two forms of energy are not separate? Freud had to conclude that libido could be turned back on the ego and that libido could donate to the ego's disposal some of the energy normally expended outwardly:

> The libido that has been withdrawn from the external world has been directed to the ego and thus gives rise to an attitude that may be called **narcissism.** (1914a, p. 75)

Clearly the energies of the ego and sexual instincts are not separate. They commingle, one drawing on the reserves of the other at various times. Freud had thus introduced a new distinction into his theory of instincts. He postulated that in the earliest stages of life there is a supply of libidinal energy in the ego that produces a primary state of narcissism or self-love. It is from this pool of primary ego libido that the later, external object libido emerges. But the original pool of ego libido remains in the ego, and it is this supply that is expanded or contracted in the narcissism of psychosis. In consequence, ego instinctual energy and sexual instinctual energy are not completely independent, but initially emerge from a common pool. Thus in the beginning all instinctual energy was one libido. Later developments cause the differentiation into **ego libido** and **object libido.**

Freud had thus revised his dualistic notion of the instincts, altering the nature of the conflict from that of a clash between ego instincts and sexual instincts to that of a clash between two forms of libido: ego libido conflicts with object libido. Freud was fond of dualistic, bipolar explanations of events and certainly ego and object libido fit the favored pattern.

Return to a Dualism: Life Against Death

By considering the narcissistic pool of ego libido the primal source of all significant interactions with the world, Freud had virtually erected libido as the unitary scheme of explanation. He was not, as some of his critics accused, attempting to sexualize all human behavior. His distinction between the self-preservation nature of ego libido and the pleasure-seeking orientation of object libido had maintained and paralleled his original division between ego and sexual instincts. But the problem for Freud was that his clinical experience had uncovered the essentially conflict-ridden nature of human behavior and neurosis. A unitary scheme of instinctual dynamics based solely on libido deprived psychoanalytic theory of the ability to specify the elements of the conflict precisely. What

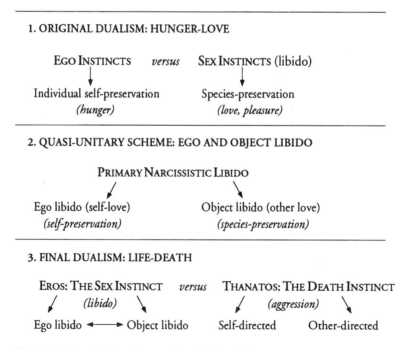

Figure 3.1 Freud's changing models of the instincts.

was needed was a new dualistic scheme in which libido (both object and ego libido) could be contrasted against some other, independent pool of instinctual energy.

In 1920, Freud solved the problem. He published a startlingly speculative account of a profoundly revised instinct theory whereby libido was contrasted with a newly discerned instinctual energy, the *death instinct*. Thus Freud returned to a dualistic conception of mental energy. At the same time, he traveled beyond his earlier model of the mind by transcending even the seemingly secure dominance of the pleasure principle. For in revising his instinct theory, Freud replaced the pleasure principle as the fundamental mental rule with an even more basic "law," the *repetition compulsion*. It is no wonder that Freud entitled the book in which he made these radical, and for some psychoanalysts disturbing, revelations *Beyond the Pleasure Principle*. Consequently, we turn now to a survey of the evidence on which Freud predicated his final, most radical revision. It may be of some help to refer to Figure 3.1 to obtain an overview of the sequence of changes in Freud's three revisions of his instinct theory.

BEHAVIORS BEYOND THE PLEASURE PRINCIPLE: THE CLINICAL EVIDENCE

Ernst's "Gone" Game

At one-and-a-half years, Freud's eldest grandson, Ernst, played a strangely symbolic game. He would momentarily take hold of any available small object, throw it into a corner of the room or under the bed, and croon loudly the German word for "gone" (*fort*) with a peculiarly long, drawn-out "o-o-o-o" pronunciation. Immediately upon throwing his toys away from himself, Ernst would retrieve them only long enough, it seemed to Freud, to begin the dispersal again. Freud soon realized that the sole use Ernst made of his toys was to play this strangely compelling game of "gone."

Ernst was singularly attached to his mother and especially sensitive to periods of her absence. Not that Ernst ever cried or showed any other obvious form of protest to separation from his mother. In all respects, Ernst was a "good" child. In September 1915, while Freud was spending several weeks with his daughter Sophie at her home in Hamburg, he had the opportunity to observe Ernst's extraordinary game (Jones, 1957, p. 267). Freud found himself peculiarly moved by Ernst's pastime.

As if to confirm his growing apprehension that the "game" was somehow strangely symbolic of Ernst's sense of loss at his mother's absence, Freud was able to make the following further observation: Ernst had as one of his toys a wooden reel (probably similar to a thread spool) with a piece of string firmly attached.

> It never occurred to [Ernst] to pull it along the floor behind him, for instance, and play at its being a carriage. What he did was to hold the reel by the string and very skillfully throw it over the edge of his curtained cot, so that it disappeared into it, at the same time uttering his expressive "o-o-o-o." He then pulled the reel out of the cot again by the string and hailed its reappearance with a joyful "da" ["there"]. This, then, was the complete game—disappearance and return. (1920a, p. 15)

On another occasion, when Ernst's mother had been away for several hours, her return was greeted by her son's exclamation, "Baby o-o-o-o!" In the light of Freud's earlier observations, such an utterance could only be meant to communicate: "Ernst (baby) was gone!"—an interpretation that was confirmed when it was discovered that Ernst had tried a variation of his "gone" game with a full-length mirror. Not quite reaching the floor, the mirror had provided the inventive Ernst with the opportunity to make himself "gone" each time he crouched below its bottom edge (Freud, 1920a, p. 15n.).

"Gone" was more than a game. It was a form of self-discipline by which Ernst had sought to master the unpleasurable prospect of his mother's periodic absences. He could not, however, symbolically act out the pleasurable return of a missing love object until he had first staged its unpleasurable disappearance. In his "game," Ernst was particularly successful because the disappearance and return of his toys were directly under his control, as contrasted with the absences of his mother, which he could experience only as a circumstance imposed from without.

Ernst had developed a technique of symbolically repeating an unpleasurable experience. In its original form, the experience had to be endured passively. By his re-creations, Ernst could *actively* control the event, and he could express a kind of defiance: "All right, go away—I don't need you!" Sadly, when Ernst was almost six years old, his mother died of pneumonia; in his terms, she was permanently "gone."

On the theoretical level, Freud offered Ernst's game as one example of a violation of the pleasure principle. It showed clearly that unpleasurable events could be reworked, repeated, and relived, despite their painful quality, until they were mastered. Yet, Ernst's game was not a definite example. Freud pointed out that such cases could be interpreted as consistent with, rather than beyond, the pleasure principle because the eventual outcome was pleasurable. He searched about for another example of a behavior beyond the pleasure principle.

Recurring Posttraumatic Dreams

In the dreams of patients suffering from hysterialike paralysis and apparent physical illness following upon some life-threatening accident like a railway collision or exposure to stress on the battlefield, Freud found another illustration of an urge to repeat unpleasant experiences. Traumatic neurosis resembles hysterical symptomatology in that the afflicted individual shows no organic basis or demonstrable physical cause for the symptoms. But, more important, in many such cases the individual experiences recurring dreams that each night re-create the traumatic situation of the accident or battlefield. By contrast, such patients in their waking state are usually more concerned with forgetting the trauma than with reliving it. The dream, however, instead of pleasurably fulfilling some wish, returns the patient to the situation and to the fright that was once helplessly endured.

Reliving Painful Memories

As a last example of an apparent violation of the dominance of the pleasure principle, Freud cited an observation from the realm of psychotherapy. Often, during psychoanalysis, patients treat analysts as if they were particular authority figures from the patients' own past. They thrust onto their therapist attitudes and desires that would be appropriate only to the real figures of their past lives. In effect, the patients relive significant experiences and attitudes of their life histories with the therapist as their present target. ". . . [The patient] is obliged to repeat the repressed material as a contemporary experience instead of, as the physician would prefer to see, remembering it as something belonging to the past" (Freud, 1920a, p. 18).

Transference is the name that Freud gave to this tendency of patients to react to their therapists with emotions reproduced from childhood. Because the material that is thus repeated originates in the unconscious, and because the conscious ego is occupied with the repression of that material, Freud concluded that the compulsion to repeat must also originate in the unconscious. Therefore, in the conflict between the ego and the unconscious, reexperience of the repressed material must figure as a potent source of unpleasure for the beleaguered ego.

For every instance cited—Ernst's game, traumatic dreams, transference in therapy—the common denominator is individuals are acting under the compulsion endlessly to repeat unpleasurable experiences.

REDUCTION OF THE PLEASURE PRINCIPLE TO A PLEASURE "TENDENCY"

Freud had in mind cases like Ernst's game, transference, and traumatic dreams when he modified his conception of the pleasure principle from a dominating influence to that of a trend in mental life:

> If such a dominance [of pleasure] existed, the immense majority of our mental processes would have to be accompanied by pleasure or to lead to pleasure, whereas universal experience completely contradicts any such conclusion. The most that can be said, therefore, is that there exists in the mind a strong *tendency* toward the pleasure principle, but the tendency is opposed by certain other forces or circumstances, so that the final outcome cannot always be in harmony with the tendency towards pleasure. (1920a, pp. 9–10)

The opposing forces were, of course, those underlying the compulsion to repeat unpleasurable experiences until, like Ernst's, they are mastered. Freud was now prepared to embark on a speculative reexamination of his previous accounts of the mental apparatus. His intention was to bring his discrepant findings about violations of the pleasure principle into harmony with the rest of psychoanalytic theory.

The Nirvana Principle

The overwhelming necessity governing the operation of the mental apparatus is the reduction of excitation, tension, or drive, and the need to maintain a relatively stable state of stimulation-free existence. Freud, following Breuer, had originally adopted the term "constancy principle" to describe the tension reduction efforts of the nervous system. Breuer had borrowed the term from the psychophysicist Gustav Fechner.

In *Beyond the Pleasure Principle,* Freud incorporated some new terminology from Barbara Low to replace the constancy principle. Freud now employed the **Nirvana principle** to indicate the homeostatic trend of nervous system functioning whereby it attempts to divest itself of disturbing tensions and excess stimulation. In fact, Freud had thought that the Nirvana principle and the pleasure principle were essentially intimately related so that the nervous system's adherence to the Nirvana principle was guaranteed by the operation of the pleasure principle. That is, reduction of tension and the maintenance of an almost stimulation-free state implied by the Nirvana principle are pleasurable. However, in a paper written in 1924, Freud changed his mind and distinguished between the two principles.

The distinction was necessary, Freud thought, because certain states of pleasure require increases in excitation rather than the reduction of excitation. One state, for example, that would violate the Nirvana principle, but accord with the pleasure principle, is sexual excitation, in which rising amounts of bodily tension in the genitals produce pleasurable sensation (Freud, 1924a, p. 160). Therefore, the Nirvana principle and the pleasure principle were distinguishable as separate, but complementary, trends in mental life.

Conservative Nature of Instincts

As Ernst played his evocative game of "gone," and as traumatic neurotic patients relive their frightful experiences in nightly dreams, so too the instincts, when viewed from the perspective of the nervous system's ultimate goal of tension reduction, seem to function to repeat the past. Instincts operate to return to an earlier state—to the excitation-free state prior to stimulation.

> *It seems, then, that an instinct is an urge inherent in organic life to restore an earlier state of things* which the living entity has been obliged to abandon under the pressure of external disturbing forces . . . or, to put it another way, instincts are the expression of the inertia inherent in organic life. (Freud, 1920a, p. 36; italics added)

Freud was postulating that mental life is essentially conservative in quality. The mental apparatus is periodically disturbed by outside stimulation and internal needs but, on the whole, strives to maintain itself in the state of quietude that characterizes its functioning prior to such disturbances. A "Nirvanalike" state of peaceful freedom from need is the principal goal of the mental apparatus, for it is this satiety that conforms faultlessly to the pleasure principle.

As primitive organisms evolved, however, their trend toward maintaining a constant state and inertial resistance to change would have been overcome by the continuous flux of external conditions, the constant change of environmental pressures, which make their demands on living things. Thus the instincts developed in unison with the increasing biological complexity of the evolving primitive organisms in order to maintain the capacity of the organism perpetually to restore an internal state of harmony in the face of a changing environment. The hunger instinct is a good example. When hunger tension mounts, we seek food and achieve satisfaction, but within a few hours, food again must be sought to return to the state of satisfaction, and so on.

Such striving is always returning to or repeating the earlier state of quietude before the world or internal needs made their demands. In its most fundamental form, the compulsion to repeat is the ultimate conservative trend: an urge to gain complete quietude, total freedom from stimulation and need, and absolute independence of the world. In short, the aim is death.

> It would be in contradiction to the conservative nature of the instincts if the goal of life were a state of things that had never been attained. On the contrary, it must be an *old* state of things, an initial state from which the living entity has at one time or other departed and to which it is striving to return by the circuitous paths along which its development leads. If we are to take it as a truth that knows no exception that everything living dies for internal reasons—becomes inorganic once again—then we shall be compelled to say *"the aim of all life is death"* and, looking backwards, that *"inanimate things existed before living ones."* (Freud, 1920a, p. 38)

In Freud's view, accidental death arising from external causes would cheat the organism of the completion of its cycle by merely terminating organic life. The organism would be deprived of achieving a return to the earlier state of inorganic existence that is an intrinsic part of its cellular structure. In consequence, accidental death, illness, and injury merely short-circuit the process and circumvent the aim of life. The organism must gain death in its own way—the gradual burning out of the life energies.

REVISION OF INSTINCT THEORY: EROS AND DEATH

Freud's bold proposal of a death instinct brings the new theory into direct conflict with his original dualistic model of the instincts whereby one-half of the dichotomy was asserted to be constituted of self-preservation ego instincts. Of what use to the organism are self-preservation instincts if the ultimate aim of life is death? Freud ingeniously answered this question by placing the ego instincts in the service of the death instincts as their agent of successful discharge:

> [Self-preservative instincts] . . . are component instincts whose function it is to assure that the organism shall follow its own path to death, and to ward off any possible ways of returning to inorganic existence other than those which are immanent in the organism itself. . . . What we are left with is the fact that the organism wishes to die only in its own fashion. Thus these guardians of life [i.e., self-preservative instincts] too, were originally the myrmidons of death. (Freud, 1920a, p. 39)

Although Freud himself never, except in conversation with colleagues, used the term **Thanatos** to refer to the death instinct, his followers have almost universally adopted the term as the official name (Jones, 1957, p. 273). (*Thanatos,* incidentally, is the name of the Greek god of death and was first used to refer to the death instinct by Freud's pupil Paul Federn.)

The other half of the original dualistic classification of the instincts, the sexual instincts, presented yet another problem to the hypothesis of a death instinct. How could instincts that serve the continuity of life, the longevity of a species, be brought into line with the penultimate conservatism of the death instinct in its striving toward the dissolution of life? The answer is that these two forces conflict.

Eros and Immortality

The instincts that guard the development of the germ cells, sperm, and egg, that provide them with safety during their time of generativity, and that motivate the union of male and female are the sexual instincts, collectively termed *libido.* Clearly the sexual instincts are the true-life instincts since they operate against the forces of death and dissolution by attempting to immortalize the organism through its progeny. Paradoxically, the other class of instincts, ego instincts, subserve death by striving to promote the self-preservation of the organism until it dies in its own way, of its own immanent causes. Thus, in *Beyond the Pleasure Principle,* the ego instincts presented Freud with a problem of classification. In which group, life or death, should the ego instincts be included? Freud eventually combined the ego instincts with the sexual instincts and considered them to be part of the libido's press for the continuity of life while they nevertheless serve the inexorable aims of death.

Freud had retained much of his desired dualistic classification by opposing the death instincts to be combined life instincts (ego and object libido) (1920a, p. 41). In honor of the changed scheme, Freud assigned to the unified sexual and ego instincts the term **Eros,** the name of the god of love and passion. Consequently, the dichotomy in Freud's theory was changed from the conflict between love and hunger to the opposition between life and death. All organisms die. If they bear the spark of immortality, it is evidenced only in their ability to confer equally transient life.

Eros and Bisexuality: Return to Unity

Freud had one further problem that had to be solved before his life-death dualism could be brought into the main body of psychoanalytic theory. How is Eros governed by the compulsion to repeat, a compulsion that is basic to all instincts? The death instinct operates to return the organism to the prior evolutionary state of inorganic existence. But what is Eros attempting to repeat; to what does it seek to return?

Figure 3.2 A 1937 photograph of Freud in his study with his prized dog, Lun Yug. Nineteen thirty-seven was a difficult time for Freud. Suffering from cancer of the jaw, he would shortly be forced by Nazi persecution to leave Vienna. He would die in London in 1939.

The answer, Freud speculated, lies in the origin of the two sexes. He suggested, hesitantly at first, that Plato's myth of the origin of the human race might be a poetic representation of a fundamental truth. In the *Symposium,* Plato, speaking through the character of Aristophanes, recounts a myth in which the original human sexes existed in three varieties: male, female, and the union of the two. Those bisexual humans had double sets of hands, feet, and sexual organs, but, because they offended the gods, Zeus decided to cut them into two. After the division, each half human, desiring its missing component, sought out its mate. They threw their arms about each other, eager to merge again into unity. Freud commented,

> Shall we follow the hint given us by the poet-philosopher, and venture on the hypothesis that living substance at that time of its coming to life was torn apart into small particles, which have ever since endeavored to reunify through the sexual instincts? that these instincts, in which the chemical affinity of inanimate matter persisted, gradually succeeded, as they developed through the kingdom of protista, in overcoming the difficulties put in the way of that endeavor by an environment charged with dangerous stimuli—stimuli which compelled them to form a protective cortical layer? that these splintered fragments of living substance in this way attained a multicellular condition and finally transferred the instinct for reuniting, in the most highly concentrated form, to the germ cells? (1920a, p. 58)

Freud had returned to the concept of the inherently bisexual nature of the human constitution as the basis of the compulsion to repeat in Eros. Humans are striving in their sexual activity to attain the wholeness of sexuality that once was the hallmark of the earliest organisms. The compulsion to repeat is evidenced by Eros in the active striving of males and females to consummate sexual union—that is, in their striving to repeat evolutionary history.[2]

---

[2]It is interesting that Freud later rejected this formula of the *compulsion to repeat* in Eros. In one of his last considerations of the subject, "An Outline of Psychoanalysis" (1940), Freud came to the conclusion that the hypothesis that living substance was once a unity that, having been separated, now struggles toward reunion could not be supported by biological fact (1940, p. 149n.). He did not, however, offer an alternative basis for Eros's repetition compulsion, and by his omission, he left himself open to the criticism that Eros no longer fits his own definition of an instinct (cf. Fromm, 1973, Appendix).

Death Derivatives: Aggression and Hate

Operating silently and invisibly, the death instinct is rarely observable in pure form. The existence of the death instinct can only be inferred from the operation of its more observable derivatives: namely, a tendency in humans to behave aggressively and their capacity to harbor destructive intent. These more observable derivatives of the death instinct emerge when the life instinct, Eros, succeeds in preventing the full self-destructive expression of Thanatos. Thus when Thanatos is deprived of expression within the individual, it emerges as other-directed, displaced aggression. Eros succeeds in preventing the death instinct from achieving the destruction of the individual by diverting the death instinct's energy to other individuals. The price of Eros's success is high.

Yet it was Freud's opinion that the death instinct and Eros are generally mingled throughout life. He believed that Eros generally succeeds in preventing Thanatos from attaining the organism's dissolution at the cost of creating outwardly directed human hate and aggression. Where Eros succeeds in constructive unification of humans, the death instinct wins a victory for human misery (Freud, 1930, p. 119).[3]

Freud's changing views of how the instincts were organized, from the original hunger-love dualism to the final Eros-Thanatos dichotomy, are summarized in Figure 3.1.

THE FINAL, STRUCTURAL MODEL OF THE MIND

In 1923, in a book entitled *The Ego and the Id,* Freud again embarked on a major theoretical adventure. During the course of his career, he had constructed two major models of the mind. The first was a neurological model (1895), which he soon abandoned. The second, proposed in Chapter 7 of the *Interpretation of Dreams* (1900), was a distinctly psychological theory based on a spatial or topographical analogy. It was from this topographical model that terms like *unconscious* and *preconscious* originated. Both of these previous models, however, had serious flaws and ambiguities, chief of which was their inability to depict unambiguously the interplay of combining and competing forces within the personality.

In *The Ego and the Id* (1923a), Freud created a final, **structural model** of the mind that no longer represented mental functioning as divided among sharply separated and rigidly compartmentalized subsystems. One can think of the personality that results as a *composite.* The different parts operate, to some degree as separate psychic entities, sometimes functioning autonomously, even while interacting. Three newly named agencies, the *id,* the *ego,* and the *superego,* subsumed all of the mental functions previously assigned to the unconscious and the preconscious.

---

[3]The concept of a death instinct aroused enormous controversy and criticism from sources within and outside psychoanalysis.

Ernest Jones, Freud's biographer and himself a psychoanalyst, found very little support in biology or in medicine for the death instinct. He suggested that Freud's proposal of the concept could be understood only in terms of Freud's personal reaction to the prospect of death. That eventually was periodically impressed on Freud's mind by the loss of members of his own family, some early recurring cardiac problems, and by his ultimately fatal protracted illness of cancer of the jaw and mouth (Jones, 1957, p. 278; see also Wallace, 1976). Max Schur, Freud's personal physician during the latter part of his life, also criticized the death instinct along much the same lines as Jones in his insistence that the concept of the death instinct served an important role in Freud's personal mental economy (1972, Chapter 12). Erich Fromm, a leading psychoanalytic thinker, argued that the concept of the death instinct was not consistent with Freud's definition of an instinct, which emphasized the achievement of bodily satisfaction through tension reduction. The death instinct strives not for tension reduction within the organism, but for *the actual dissolution* of the organism's life integrity (Fromm, 1973, p. 366).

In conversation between Anna Freud and Christopher Monte in July 1974, Anna Freud insisted that contemporary presentations of psychoanalysis, like this one, should exclude the neurological model from consideration because psychoanalysis is a *psychological theory,* not a modified form of neurological science. She conceded that her father's early training in neurology had been influential in shaping his thinking and that his habit of framing his thoughts in biological terms was not easily overcome. When Dr. Monte suggested that, were her father alive today, he might adopt for his use some of the recent advances in biology and neurology, she stated that her father had created a psychology, and not merely a neurology, that had been translated into psychological language. She reemphasized that her father would not have returned to his neurological ideas under any circumstances.

Id, Ego, Superego Terminology

Because the unconscious could no longer be restricted to a distinct region of the mind, and because it could not be employed solely as a description of momentarily latent thoughts, the term **id** would from now on indicate that part of selfhood that is alien to or isolated from the conscious self, or **ego.** Freud adopted the Latinized term id (originally, the simple German pronoun *das es,* meaning "it"—referring to the impersonal nature of this part of the psyche) from Georg Groddeck (1922), a physician who had become interested in psychoanalysis. Freud's translators converted the terminology to Latin equivalents to preserve in English translation the technical flavor of the terms.

In a similar way, Freud's translators converted his other plain German pronouns to Latin equivalents, so that the simple German for "I" (*Ich*) became the Latin *ego,* and the German for "over-I" became **superego.**

THE ID

Developmentally, the id is the oldest portion of personality. The existence of the id dates from birth. "Originally, to be sure, everything was id . . ." (Freud, 1940, p. 163). Because the id is the most archaic portion of personality, already operative before the infant has had much in the way of transactions with the world, it must contain all of the unlearned, innate strivings that we have come to know "psychoanalytically" as the instincts. Thus Freud characterized the id as a "cauldron full of seething excitations," fueled by the energies of the organic processes of the instincts and striving toward one goal: immediate satisfaction of its wishes.

The id is to be regarded as the pool of mental representatives of the biological processes underlying bodily needs, a pool populated, therefore, by Eros and the death instinct: ". . . but it has no organization, produces no collective will, but only a striving to bring about the satisfaction of the instinctual needs subject to the observance of the pleasure principle" (Freud, 1933, p. 73).

Like its precursor, the unconscious, the id is an untrammeled, primeval chaos free of the laws governing logical thought. Contrary impulses exist side by side without canceling each other; the passage of time exerts no influence on the id; and wishful impulses, after the passage of decades, behave as if they had just occurred (Freud, 1933, p. 74). Freud summarized the characteristics of the id in much the same way as he had previously spoken of the unconscious:

The id of course knows no judgments of value: no good and evil, no morality. The economic or, if you prefer, the quantitative factor, which is intimately linked to the pleasure principle, dominates all its processes. Instinctual cathexes seeking discharge—that, in our view, is all there is in the id. It even seems that the energy of these instinctual impulses is in a state different from that in the other regions of the mind, far more mobile and capable of discharge. . . . (1933, p. 74)

Because it is ruled by primary process thinking, condensations and displacements of its energy are not only possible for the id, they are an inevitable result of the id's striving for satisfaction without due regard for the goodness, evilness, realness, or appropriateness of its objects. In many ways, the id operates on the principle that whatever brings satisfaction to a want, desire, or wishful impulse is good; whatever hinders or frustrates such satisfaction is bad. "The id obeys the inexorable pleasure principle" (Freud, 1940, p. 198).

THE EGO

Left to itself, the id's unbridled striving would bring about the destruction of the organism. The id's lack of organization, its diffuseness and disregard for reality must be tamed in the service of survival. It is to the ego that the task of self-preservation falls.

The ego develops out of the id. In fact, the ego is a differentiated part of the id that has become specialized and organized in response to its constant exposure to external stimulation. Thus the ego is conceived as having an intimate relationship with the outermost layer of the organism, the perceptual and conscious systems that are localized in the cortical layer of the brain.

Clearly, Freud pictured the ego as developing from the id in response to the organism's need for a mediator between its internal needs and the demands of reality. The ego is thus the reality-oriented arm of the mental apparatus, though it is simultaneously responsive to internal conditions as well.

With reference to the external environment, the ego's functions are familiar ones: to become aware of stimuli and their location; to avoid excessively strong stimulation; and to learn to bring about changes in the external world that would be to its own advantage in pursuing survival. For this last activity, the ego must govern the muscular apparatus of the organism (Freud, 1933, p. 75).

Correspondingly, with reference to the internal environment, including the id, the ego functions to gain control over the expression of the instincts. The ego must decide whether the instincts are to be immediately satisfied as the id demands, or if their satisfaction is to be postponed to later times more favorable to wish fulfillment, or, finally, whether the instinctual demand should be totally denied expression, that is, whether the instinct should be repressed.

With the development of the ego as a specialized and efficiently organized portion of the id, the organism correspondingly increases in the degree of sophistication with which it approaches the tasks of life. For one thing, the pleasure principle is "dethroned" by the **reality principle** as the ego seeks to provide safe and realistically appropriate pleasures for the id. "To adopt a popular mode of speaking, we might say that the ego stands for reason and good sense while the id stands for the untamed passions" (Freud, 1933, p. 76).

Metaphorically, the ego is fighting a battle on two fronts: It must not only protect the organism from excessively strong demands from within, it must also seek to satisfy these demands in an external world fraught with danger. Such external dangers can be dealt with by flight, that is, by the removal of the organism from the dangerous situations. Internal threats to the integrity of the organism, that is, impulses whose satisfaction would bring the organism into contact with external dangers, are dealt with by the ego in an analogous way, namely, by mental flight or repression.

Thus there is a portion of the id-ego amalgam that becomes separated from the conscious functioning of the ego. That separated part, the repressed, then behaves in every way as if it were part of the unconscious. This zone of alien content is nevertheless part of the ego, though functionally, dynamically separated from it.

It is important in this context of defense by repression to note that it is the id that is the great reservoir of libido or sexual energy. In his previous writings, Freud had characterized the ego, in his then broad usage of the term, as the reservoir of libido. But actually there is no contradiction, for the ego is a specialized aspect of the id, and while it is only the very tip of a deep iceberg, the ego is nonetheless an integral part of that mass (Freud, 1923a, pp. 30, 38).

In the original state of being at birth, the total energy of Eros, libido, is available to the undifferentiated id-ego amalgam. Eros's presence serves to neutralize the death instinct (Freud, 1940, p. 149). The ego is, therefore, primarily narcissistic at this stage, and it cathects itself with libido. Only when the ego becomes differentiated from the id will it direct its cathexes of libido to external objects. Once a quality of its libido is externalized as object libido, the ego's remaining store of libido comes into opposition with the death instinct. Ego libido, as contrasted with the externalized object libido, thus works in the service of the organism's own preservation, and ego libido operates to keep the organism from premature harm that might cheat the death instinct of its opportunity to bring the organism to its immanent destiny. Thus it is the particular developmental stage that determines whether it is the undifferentiated id-ego unity or the id alone that occupies the focus of attention as the reservoir of libido.

While the ego is fighting a two-front battle with the internal and external worlds, there is yet a third front that the ego is compelled to consider during its intercourse with life and death. This third front is the superego.

THE SUPEREGO

When the id is forced by circumstances beyond its control to give up its love objects, as for example, in the boy's renunciation of the mother at the resolution of the Oedipus complex, it is compensated for the loss by the ego (Freud, 1916, p. 249; 1923a, p. 23ff.). The ego undergoes an alteration by which it takes on the characteristics of the lost love object. An analogous process can be seen more clearly in adulthood when one marriage partner is widowed. The surviving spouse may then unconsciously adopt the habits or the speech patterns of the deceased, or an item of the deceased's apparel, as if to compensate for the loss by reinstating at least a part of that person's identity in the survivor's own behavior.

> When the ego assumes the features of the [lost] object, it is forcing itself, so to speak, upon the id as a love-object and is trying to make good the id's loss by saying: "Look, you can love me too—I am so like the object." (Freud, 1923a, p. 30)

This process of modeling itself on the lost love object, as the ego attempts to pacify the id, is called **identification.** Identification is an important part of the processes by which the superego is formed. Freud emphasized the importance of the process of renunciation of a love object for the process of identification with a parent and subsequent development of the superego. Freud de-emphasized the importance of simple imitation learning and role-modeling in the identification process (see Chapter 16).

Freud was clearer in his elucidation of the development of the superego in boys than in girls. As indicated in Chapter 2, Freud thought that a less painful process of renunciation occurred in girls than in boys, one that led to a weaker supergo or conscience. This process was less painful and marked in girls than in boys for two reasons. First, girls, unlike boys, did not have to renounce their close relationship with the mother. The Electra complex involved desire for the father and competition with the mother, but repressing these desires did not mean giving up an already close relationship with the mother. In addition, the little girl did not have the fear of castration by the parent of the opposite sex.

In Freud's model, during the phallic stage of libidinal development, the young boy seeks his mother as a desirable love object and begins to perceive his father as a competitor. Without recapitulating the entire progress of the Oedipal situation (Chapter 2), you may recall that the boy relinquishes his mother as love object, identifies with his father in order to be like him because father possesses desirable objects, and the child represses his libidinal cathexes toward mother.

Freud's formulation of identification is self-contradictory, as Roger Brown (1965, p. 379) pointed out. According to Freud's account, since the boy must relinquish his mother as a love object, he should identify with her, not with his father. Likewise, the girl, having relinquished her father, should identify with him. Obviously this sequence will not do since boys usually assume a masculine sexual identity and girls similarly identify with their mothers. Freud noted the discrepancy between his proposed mechanism of identification and the actual outcome (1923a, p. 32). As a result, he returned to one of his longstanding ideas, the inherent bisexuality of human nature. In this view, because most boys are more male than female, they thus identify only partially with mother but largely with father. The converse is true for girls. Such bisexual identification is not necessarily hidden or unconscious. Many people are aware of traits they have that are like their father and other traits that are like those of their mother. Commenting on Freud's theory of inherent bisexuality, Brown stated, "if that assumption is acceptable to Freud he does not need all the rest of his theoretical apparatus . . ." (1965, p. 379).

Undaunted by his own discovery of the inconsistency and relying on the concept of bisexuality, Freud proposed that the Oedipus complex is comprised of both positive and negative aspects. It is positive in the sense that the boy actively strives to be like his father, to identify with him. But the Oedipus complex may also have negative properties because of a boy's inherent feminine components. The boy may behave passively or "girlishly" toward the father because he has partially identified with mother when he was forced to renounce her as love object. In this way, the boy may also attempt to appease his father by an overtly submissive attitude. For girls, of course, the opposite set of behaviors dominates, for the girl has partially identified with father and so behaves in subtle masculine ways (Freud, 1923a, p. 33). The final outcome, however, is as expected: Boys identify with their fathers, and girls model themselves on their mothers.

Sometime around the age of five, a child goes through a process of **internalization** in becoming like the father or mother. Children thus internalize the standards of adult

---

BOX 3.3 *Only Connect . . .*

Carl Jung (see Chapter 4) also concluded that personality contained bisexual elements. His concepts of *animus* and *anima* indicated the male and female aspects of the *psyche* in both genders. Jung said that in males the animus was conscious and the anima unconscious, whereas in females the reverse was true.

authority, but more important they also internalize (identify with) the parental standards of rightness, morality, and goodness. A new internal agency continues from within to exercise these judgmental functions autonomously, without parental input. In terms of psychoanalytic theory, a superego has been formed. Through the process of identification with the parent of the same sex, the development of the superego represents the resolution of the Oedipal complex in the boy and the Electra complex in the girl.

Freud elaborated the dynamics of resolving the Oedipal crisis in some detail. The boy's ego not only must strive to be like the all-powerful father who possesses the all-desirable mother, it must also establish the boundaries that limit the degree to which he acts the role of the father (Freud, 1923a, p. 34). Out of fear of his competitor, the boy must not carry the identification as far as actual possession of the mother. Hence, the boy internalizes the prohibitions that he imagines his father might enforce. As a direct result, the superego is formed. The development of the superego in a boy is a combination of the active striving to be like the father and the anxiety-motivated attempts to anticipate the father's proscriptions.

The next step in the sequence is the repression of his Oedipal strivings. Repression of desire for mother and hostility toward father is not an easy undertaking for the boy's ego and must occur outside of any conscious awareness. The force that such repression requires is a measure of the strength of the internalized superego. For it is the superego that embodies the anxiety and resultant identification with authority that remain after the Oedipal strivings are repressed. To say it another way, the superego replaces the strength of the Oedipal wishes in the mental economy with the equal or stronger energy of the father identification. Or, as Freud repeatedly stated it, "The superego is the heir of the Oedipal complex." (Freud, 1923a, p. 48).

Superego as Conscience

An important quantitative relationship may be inferred from the fact that the superego becomes the repository of the quantity of energy that was required to master and to repress the incestuous desires (Freud, 1923a, pp. 34–35; 1930, p. 123). The greater the instinctual gratification that is renounced in both the girl and the boy, the more severe the superego grows in its judgments of the ego (Freud, 1923a, p. 54; 1930, p. 129).

In effect, the intensity of the impulse or desire that is mastered is assimilated by the superego, increasing its supply of energy for future moral judgments. In less technical language, the greater the temptation to which persons fail to yield, the greater will be the pangs of their consciences in future temptations. In short, the superego is fed by the energy of the renounced id impulse, and it grows more scrupulous with each moral triumph.

The paradox is clear: The more aggression you virtuously renounce, the more your conscience reproaches you. Common sense, contrary to psychoanalytic theory, suggests that the stronger a person's conscience, the more virtuous he or she will be. Freud reversed the temporal sequence in this apparent truism, and he suggested that

> . . . the more virtuous a man is, the more severe and distrustful is . . . [the behavior of his conscience], so that ultimately it is precisely those people who have carried saintliness furthest who reproach themselves with the worst sinfulness. (1930, pp. 125–126)

Clearly, Freud meant to emphasize that once the superego was established within the personality to be fed by the energy of renounced id impulses, it could be as harsh and unyielding in its demands as the id in its relationship to the ego. "From the point of view of instinctual control, or morality, it may be said of the id that it is totally non-moral, of the ego that it strives to be moral, and of the superego that it can be super-moral and then become as cruel as only the id can be" (Freud, 1923a, p. 540).

ID, EGO, SUPEREGO INTERACTIONS

Because the superego was formed at a stage in developmental history when children usually idealized their parents and saw in them every kind of perfection, it follows that the standards of the superego will likewise have the character of the parents' idealized image (Freud, 1933, p. 64). Conscience is thus a standard of perfection, an ideal, rather than a realistic appraisal of behavior. Consequently, in their rearing of children, parents exemplify not so much a standard of experience tempered by a realistic appraisal of life, but rather the idealistic standard of their own superegos (Freud, 1933, p. 67).

Freud employed a diagrammatic summary of his new structural model that, reproduced here as Figure 3.3, is helpful in recapitulating the essential points.

Figure 3.3 shows the location of the three mental structures: id, ego, and superego. It also indicates the important relationships that bind them.

The ego is situated near, and oriented toward, the perceptual-conscious end of the organism, and it is thus in direct contact with the external world. But the diagram also clearly indicates a segment of the ego that functions *dynamically* like the unconscious system.

In Figure 3.3, this ego-alien segment is illustrated in its separation from conscious ego activity by two diagonal lines that define the boundary of repressed content. The ego is thus both conscious in its orientation toward the perceptual end of the apparatus and dynamically unconscious by virtue of its repressions.

Although Freud did not include the superego in the diagram that he used in *The Ego and the Id* (1923a, p. 24), by the time he had written his *New Introductory Lectures,* almost ten years later, he found a way to include the superego in such diagrammatic summaries. Lying along the left-hand margin of the drawing in Figure 3.3, the superego clearly merges into the unconscious id, for, as "the heir of the Oedipus complex it has intimate relations with the id; it is more remote than the ego from the perceptual system" (Freud, 1933, p. 79).

The superego, therefore, is structured of both conscious and unconscious components, and, as a moral or ethical agency, it functions both consciously and unconsciously. That is to say, the superego has relations with both the ego and the id.

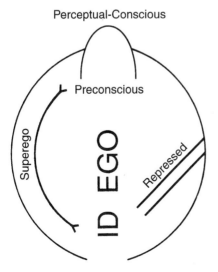

Figure 3.3 The dynamic model of the mind.

Note that the diagram depicts the three agencies of the mind with no sharp boundaries between them. In Freud's last model, the mind was represented as an amalgam of blending, combining, and competing forces. See text for explanation.

Based on Freud, 1933, p. 78.

In several respects, Freud pointed out, the diagrammatic summary of Figure 3.3 is misleading. On the one hand, the space occupied by the unconscious id should be greater than that of the ego or preconscious. On the other hand:

> In thinking of this division of the personality into an ego, superego, and an id, you will not, of course, have pictured sharp frontiers like the artificial ones drawn in political geography. We cannot do justice to the characteristics of the mind by linear outlines like those in a drawing or in a primitive painting, but rather by areas of color melting into one another as they are presented by modern artists. After making the separation we must allow what we have separated to merge together once more. (Freud, 1933, p. 79)

The ego's task is to balance the instincts of the id against the censure of the superego while it simultaneously appraises reality and its exigencies. In Freud's words, for the ego *"Life is not easy!"* When the ego is compelled to recognize its own weaknesses in carrying out successfully its often overwhelming tasks, anxiety results. There are three forms of such anxiety:

1. **Realistic anxiety**—the result of fear of the *external world*.
2. **Neurotic anxiety**—fear of being overwhelmed by the *id's instincts*.
3. **Moral anxiety**—fear of the *superego's censure*.

FREUD'S CHANGING CONCEPTIONS OF ANXIETY

In the earliest days of Freud's theorizing, he came to view anxiety as the result of unexpressed or dammed-up libido. The neurotic's badly distorted relations with the world and its people, he found, are often expressed in sexual difficulty. Normal, satisfying sexual relations are frequently foregone as a welter of neurotic symptoms and other defensive measures sap the individual's capacity for joyous living. Unexpressed libido, the dammed-up energy of the sexual impulses that have thus succumbed to repression, is then explosively released in a transformed state, the state of anxiety. In short, in Freud's early thinking, repression of sexual impulses is the cause of anxiety (cf. Freud, 1894; 1896a; 1896b; 1896c; and 1898).

According to this early view, anxiety was instinctual, arising from repressed unconscious sexual urges. But if it were true that such feelings were restricted to unconscious origin, the conscious ego as depicted in the new structural model with its separation from the repressed would never experience the unpleasant affect of anxiety. Furthermore, if the ego did not experience the anxiety, it would never trigger repressive counterforces to cast the unacceptable, anxiety-producing impulses from consciousness in the first place (Freud, 1926a, pp. 140, 161). Freud's new structural model demanded that the ego be the seat of anxiety, and so Freud was required to rethink the problem.

Birth Trauma as the Prototype of Adult Anxiety

Through a slow return to and development of his neurological ideas, Freud renounced the view of anxiety as transformed libido. In his early neurological model of the "Project for a Scientific Psychology," Freud had experimented with the idea that anxiety originates from a sense of overwhelming helplessness (1895). The ego experiences the perception of being overpowered or flooded with too much stimulation. In infancy, the first of such experiences is the act of birth. The newborn infant has been thrust from its warm, dark, safe existence in the mother's body into the confusing, demanding, changing, and irritating external environment (Freud, 1926a). In successive stages of life, other situations will evoke the same emotional response of helplessness, stimulus flooding, and the experience of being overpowered. Separation from the mother (recall Ernst's "gone" game) provokes distress in most infants, and such separation is a good example of a later life situation that harbors the threat of helplessness.

The common denominator in all such cases of anxiety is the sense of abandonment and the concern that life's demands will overwhelm the isolated, helpless ego. When anxiety mounts to a frightening level, neurotic symptoms may be formed as attempts to stifle the tide of mental confusion and emotional pain. Adult neurotics develop symptoms to control their anxiety over threats that they perceive as truly life threatening, just as life threatening as early abandonment by mother. Overt symptoms thus unconsciously replace what they can no longer consciously bear (Freud, 1933, p. 85). The question of significance thus changed for Freud from how libido could be transformed into anxiety, to how anxiety was produced from the ego's perceptions.

As early as 1909, in a footnote to the *Interpretation of Dreams,* Freud pointed out that ". . . the act of birth is the first experience of anxiety, and thus the source and prototype of the affect of anxiety" (1900, pp. 400–401). In effect, Freud was postulating that the birth situation and the ensuing **birth trauma** is every individual's first experience with the unpleasurable state of anxiety, and that it is the first experience that serves as the model against which the ego compares future situations in making its responses to reality and to the demands of the id and superego.

A colleague of Freud's, Otto Rank, broadened the concept of birth trauma beyond its status as the prototype for anxiety. Rank established the birth trauma as the central event in all psychological development (Rank, 1929; 1932). In emphasizing the significance of the birth trauma for neurotic symptomatology, Rank dethroned the main psychoanalytic concepts of the Oedipus complex and sexual strivings from their central role. For Rank, the birth trauma was the nucleus from which all human development, neurotic and normal, proceeds. Freud subsequently repudiated Rank's heretical ideas.

Freud's Chronology of Danger Situations

As the child's ego develops, Freud reasoned, anxiety becomes less and less an experience of flooding helplessness and more and more a signal to avoid such danger. The prototype for the danger situation of the ego disruption is birth. If an ego were present at birth, it would be helpless. Only through the care of the mother does the infant survive, feel comforted, and become eventually tension-free. But at base, the danger situation of birth is the fear of death.

Throughout infancy, the child learns that survival depends on this "love object," the mother, being present to minister to its needs. When she is absent—loss of the object—the burgeoning ego experiences potential danger, and senses that mounting needs will go unsatisfied to the point of annihilation.

Later, after the first year of life during the anal period of two to three years, the toddler recognizes that absence of mother does not mean abandonment. Instead, what now counts for survival is getting the mother's love. For it is only by her loving anticipations of its needs that the child receives gratifications that assure safety and survival. An angry or aloof mother does not care. The danger situation for the ego is now transformed into a fear of the loss of the mother's love.

At the phallic phase, the time of the Oedipus complex around ages three to five, the male child learns that father can retaliate for his secret wishes to possess mother exclusively. Furthermore, beginning sexual interest has become vaguely attached to the person of the mother, and this interest becomes a source of additional fear should father detect these taboo wishes.

The fear that assails the child's ego now is a fear of castration, for what more appropriate punishment could father exact than removal of the offending organ? In more general terms, the child experiences this new danger situation not only as an Oedipal fear but also as a broader fear of injury and physical insult to the body. What the analogous process for girls may be, Freud did not say. But the implication from his writing is that girls experience similar danger signals because they interpret their discovery that they do not have a penis as meaning that they have already been injured.

Finally, in the post-Oedipal period persisting until adulthood, the ego responds to ever more sophisticated danger signals. Having internalized the moral standards of the parents in the form of the superego, the ego responds with anxiety to judgments of the superego that a particular id impulse is dangerous. Thus the final danger situation is fear of one's own self-evaluations.

Two common features are shared by all the danger situations.

1. The experience of helplessness is the central core of anxiety: feeling helpless to manage internal needs, helpless to cope with external threats and signals of disintegration, and feeling helpless to maintain survival.

2. Second, each danger situation is a derivative or a representation of the experience of loss. In order, these losses are loss of complete dependence (birth), loss of the love object, loss of the object's love, loss of a body part, and loss of self-esteem or self-love.

We should mention that this final experience of loss contained in the fear of one's own self-judgments is strikingly similar to Freud's earliest theory of repression discussed in Chapter 2: Namely, wishes that clash with one's self-image are very threatening. Table 3.2 summarizes the chronology of the danger situations, and it should be apparent that Freud's scheme implies that anxiety takes its meaning from the development processes active at a given moment in time.

Table 3.2   Freud's Chronology of Danger Situations

Development period	*Danger situation*	*Ego experience of anxiety*
Birth	Global feelings of flooding, distress, helplessness	No awareness of outside world, but survival is threatened.
First year (Oral phase)	Fear of loss of the love object (mother)	Feelings of helplessness occur when mother is out of sight, understanding that she is needed for survival.
Two to three years (Anal phase)	Fear of loss of the object's love	Learns that survival and need satisfaction depend on mother's loving and caring.
Four to six years (Phallic phase)	Castration fear and anxiety over injury	Oedipal dynamics result in castration fear because of desire to possess love object exclusively, attack anticipated.
Post-Oedipal through adulthood	Fear of superego censure: fear of negative self-judgments	After internalization of parental standards, superego judges ego's efforts to satisfy id, and may condemn some wishes or ideas. Fear of self-evaluation.

Based on Freud, 1926a and 1933.

EVALUATING THEORETICAL PSYCHOANALYSIS

In Chapter 2, clinical psychoanalysis was evaluated in terms of its poor scientific testability, conception of human agency as passive, except for the very existence of psychoanalysis itself, and its acknowledgement of both nomothetic and idiographic aspects of the human personality. These conclusions are relevant for the psychoanalytic model of the mind.

In this section, we focus on the question of whether testable propositions can be drawn from the more *theoretical* psychoanalytic psychology.

While considering some of the limitations of psychoanalytic theory and practice, we should also indicate some of the lasting contributions of Freud's work:

1. He established that many disorders that had previously been considered organically caused actually had psychological causation, that is, they had to do with an individual's personal *experiences*.

2. He demonstrated that verbal psychotherapy or a *talking cure* might be a means of treatment, rather than physical measures.

3. His work indicated that, in addition to conscious thought, unconscious mental processes could also occur.

4. His work indicated the importance of drives, especially the sexual drive, in the human makeup.

5. He emphasized insight and patients' own activity in finding answers to their problems.

6. His many useful concepts including transference, countertransference, defense mechanisms, and many others have relevance far beyond the confines of psychoanalysis per se. Even down to the institution of the 50-minute psychotherapeutic hour, with its roots in Freud's work, the helping professions have been affected by Freud's foundational innovations.

Refutability of Psychoanalysis

As Freud built increasingly complex abstractions to represent his clinical observations, psychoanalysis grew more distant from clinical experience. Freud thought of his theoretical abstractions from about 1914 onward as a "metapsychology" ("beyond psychology") in the sense that the theoretical concepts evolved out of, but surpassed, the psychological observations on which they were based.

Freud sometimes regarded his metapsychological creations as metaphors for unmapped brain processes and structures, not as "internal agents" in a literal sense. Rather, he seems to have hoped that his structural metaphors would someday be anchored to brain function and location when the sciences of neuroanatomy and neurophysiology had progressed. He was open to the medical and physiological knowledge of his day. In fact, the hypothalamus and structures of the limbic system have—subsequent to Freud's theorizing—been found to be associated with the desires Freud attributed to the id, such as hunger, sexual desire, and aggression. The frontal lobe is associated with a sense of reality, an ego function. Higher cortical functions also relate to activities that Freud attributed to the ego (Miller L., 1991).

Yet there are lengthy theoretical discussions in some of Freud's major books where he intellectually manipulates metapsychological concepts as if they were real, as if they were to be understood as reality. In his popular lectures and essays, for example, he treats his model of the mind quite dramatically so that ego, id, and superego are described in terms of war metaphors, battle strategies, and advances and retreats, and as having motives and expectations of their own (Freud, 1910a, 1916, 1933, 1940). For his popular audience, he treated these "structures" as if they were individual people inside the person.

But in his more professional writings Freud clearly is aware that these "structures" are metaphors (e.g., 1923a, 1926a). The puzzle for scholars and scientists is to discover the nature of what underlies the metaphors (see the answers proposed by Parisi, 1987, 1988; Silverstein, 1985, 1988, 1989a, 1989b; Sulloway, 1979). The eminent psychoanalyst Roy Schafer (1976, 1983) has shown the many ways in which Freud's followers have taken his metaphors as literally true and as replacements for the actual experiences that they represent. In this view, the id, for example, is not more than a *reification* of human passions and desires. The term *reification,* in this context, refers to the transformation of human experience into an object or a thing. So, for example, the concept of an *id* is substituted for a whole array of sexual desires and experiences. (For the difficulties such literalizing causes, see also Leites, 1971, for a compelling analysis of the confusion between Freudian concepts and experiential reality in psychoanalytic theory.)

So we are left with a continuing intellectual conversation continuing long after Freud's death. Freudian concepts such as id, ego, superego, and the various defense mechanisms are drawn from human experience and, in a sense, can be seen as representing nothing more than different aspects of such experience. In this sense, there is *really* no id, ego, or superego; they are merely indications of major subsets of experience. At the same time, and seemingly in a contradictory fashion, findings in neuroanatomy and neurophysiology correspond to many Freudian concepts. So, perhaps they are not *merely metaphors.* They might also represent underlying physiological realities, at a different level from personal experience.

In summary, our view is that many of Freud's terms are metaphorical expressions that he originally derived from his knowledge of human experience. They also have turned out to point to underlying brain structures and processes and, in this sense, are more than merely overly concise metaphors for areas of experience.

The testability of Freud's theory is another area deserving mention. Large parts of his theory have to do with the presumed experiential life and perceptions of infants and children who are at a preverbal level and who have a very limited means of expressing their feelings and perceptions other than in a very global way. Numerous inferences about the specifics of their inner life are made from Freud's own adult recollections, and his work with clients. Whether Freud's ideas about the workings of the infant's mind (for example, the apprehensions and emotional life of the infant), are more than the result of the imagination of adults is difficult to determine. Infants cannot be interviewed to find out.

There is one more major limitation regarding the refutability of Freud's ideas. His observations were all made within the particular social and cultural framework of his times. His clients were largely from an upscale class of Europeans. His findings about personality may not reflect universal content or processes but simply aspects of human nature manifest in a particular culture, place, and historical epoch. Certainly, ideas regarding sexuality and the roles of men and women have changed since his day. Some of Freud's ideas could very well turn out not to be valid or at least not relevant in twenty-first century North America. Such results would not necessarily indicate that his concepts would not have been valid in the Europe of the early 1900s.

Some Illustrative Studies in Psychoanalysis

Freudian theory rates high for motivating people to do research. If we rate the quality, coherence, and reliability of the research results associated with this theory, the results are less promising. The nature of research connected with psychoanalysis has been summarized in two anthologies of such work.

Hans Eysenck and Glen Wilson (1973), two psychologists well known for their anti-Freudian views (see Chapter 17), collected 19 empirical studies of psychoanalytic theory that ranged from tests of oral sexuality to castration anxiety to dream wishes. In every instance, they identified methodological flaws that invalidated the results of the study. Moreover, even in studies that evidenced only minor methodological flaws, Eysenck and Wilson questioned whether the hypothesis tested really needed Freudian theory as its basis.

By contrast to Eysenck and Wilson, Paul Kline (1972), a psychologist with a favorable estimation of Freudian theory, examined several hundred observational and experimental studies that tested psychoanalytic ideas. In many cases, Kline found the same flaws as had Eysenck and Wilson. However, for a substantial number of studies, especially those concerned with repression and the Oedipus complex, Kline interpreted the outcomes as verifying some major psychoanalytic concepts.

Who is right here? Is the skepticism of Eysenck and Wilson too negative? Is the enthusiasm of Kline too positive? In some cases, both the Eysenck and Wilson book and the Kline book examine identical studies and draw opposite conclusions. How can opinion count so much? How can there be such disagreement if the evidence, experiments, and research designs being reviewed adhere to acceptable scientific criteria? The answer is that it depends on who is reviewing the evidence and the criteria that are being used for evaluation.

Refutability: Some Positive Findings

Seymour Fisher and Roger Greenberg (1996) arrived at what seems to be a balanced assessment of the scientific status of Freud's ideas. These reviews are very thorough and they deserve some consideration. Here are a few of Fisher and Greenberg's conclusions:

- Freud's notion that the experience of loss is the trigger for depression receives little support from the scientific literature. There is some evidence that accumulated early and late losses over a lifetime are linked to depression, but the evidence is weak. Freud's related idea that non-nurturing or disapproving parents make a child vulnerable to depression receives moderate support. The strongest support was for Freud's notion that depression is linked to a passive orientation marked by feelings of oral dependency and fixation to the oral stage of psychosexual development.

- Freud's concept of the existence of an orally dependent personality type prone to the use of repression and denial was supported by factor analytic research that demonstrated meaningful clustering of the personality traits described in Freud's theory.

- Freud's "anal-retentive" and "anal-erotic" personality types likewise received substantial support from factor-analytic studies that demonstrate a clustering of the relevant traits.

- The Oedipus theory advanced by Freud, including his hypotheses about the origins of homosexuality and the severity of individual moral self-judgment, had *no support* in the scientific literature. However, derivations of Oedipal theory based on the concept of "penis envy" in females, surprisingly, received some support in Fisher and Greenberg's view (possibly because they conducted some of the very studies they reviewed).

- Freudian dream theory, especially his notion that dreams were disguised fulfillment of taboo wishes, was largely contradicted by current dream research.

Greenberg and Fisher (1996, p. 267) point out that they did not review what seem to be supportive studies of Freud's concepts of repression and the unconscious. On the whole, they conclude that Freud's theory *has more* scientific support than widespread stereotypes about its failings suggest, but much of the theory still either defies scientific testing or has failed the tests made.

Even though much of Freudian theory is not easily tested, there is still the promise that further aspects of the theory can be tested and either validated or contradicted by empirical findings.

SUMMARY

Anna Freud's "stwawbewwies" dream reveals the essential nature of dream processes: the fantasized fulfillment of wishes. As Freud investigated dream processes of adults, however, he soon learned that their productions differed from the lucid creations of children. Distortion and disguise are introduced into the story of the dream by the mechanisms of dream work, including displacement, condensation, visual representation, and secondary revision. Thus, Freud found, dreams have both a latent and a manifest content.

Freud next embarked on a revision and a tightening of his psychological theory in a series of important "metapsychological" papers. Freud now saw repression as a two-stage process: primal repression against early unacceptable impulses and repression proper against later adult derivatives.

Because of the basic conflict underlying the neurotic behavior of the patients he observed, Freud contrasted the self-preservative instincts (e.g., hunger) with the instincts of pleasure (sex, libido). The dualistic classification of hunger versus love eventually had to be revised when Freud's speculations revealed the presence of an even more fundamental dichotomy in instinctual life: life versus death.

In *Beyond the Pleasure Principle* (1920a), Freud created a new picture of the workings of the mind. This altered view included Freud's argument that the nervous system had evolved in such a way as to minimize the excitatory level of the organism by directing the organism's efforts to satisfy needs immediately. The ultimate aim of an instinct is to return the organism to the unresponsive state of inorganic matter, namely, to the state of death. Since the death instinct cannot be directly observed, its derivatives of hate, anger, and aggression are the only overt evidence of its existence. When the life instincts, or *Eros* as Freud now called the combined ego and sexual instincts, oppose the death instinct, the energy of destruction is turned outward from the individual and displaced onto other individuals.

Freud proceeded to a total revision of his conception of the mind. He created a structural model that depicted the mind as a blending, merging amalgam of forces. The structural model had three divisions: id, ego, and superego.

1. The id, formerly the unconscious, is the seat of the instincts, and is a cauldron of fury, striving to gain immediate satisfaction of its urges.

2. To accommodate the id's desires and needs, a specialized portion, the ego, emerges from the id to steer a safe course through reality and to maintain satisfactory relations with the world.

3. By the age of five or six, another agency, the superego, is internalized within the child. The superego is the "heir of the Oedipal complex," for it is based on identification with the parents, and assimilates the energy of the renounced Oedipal desires. The superego is the moral or ethical arm of personality, and it has final say in matters of ego-id relations.

Freud's conception of anxiety changed over the years from the view that anxiety is the result of dammed-up sexual impulses to the concept that the ego responds to a variety of danger situations with signals of unpleasure. Freud experimented with the idea that the prototype of anxiety is the trauma of birth and, more generally, that anxiety is an ego reaction to perceptions of being overwhelmed or flooded by intense stimulation.

As we saw in Chapter 2, Freud's theory does not easily lend itself to scientific testing. Reviews of research based on Freudian ideas indicate that much of it is flawed, but that some propositions derived from Freudian theory are demonstrably correct.

Though the scope of our two chapters on Freud is extensive, it should not surprise you that the material presented merely scratches the surface of the mass of ideas and hypotheses that are to be found in Freud's collected works. For that reason, you are encouraged to pursue topics of interest in Freud's own writings.

ADDENDUM: LIMITATIONS OF CLASSICAL FREUDIAN THEORY

The crucial subject of interest for Freud was the id. He envisioned this mental province as ceaselessly pursuing gratification for its sexual and aggressive urges. Freud consistently maintained that his central contribution was the elucidation of unconscious instinctual dynamics. "The power of the id," Freud wrote, "expresses the true purpose of the individual organism's life" (1940, p. 148). Although the ego assumed increasing importance in Freud's theory from the 1920s onward, it nevertheless always remained secondary in importance to the id. The id and its biological processes thus persistently occupied center stage in Freud's thinking.

In comparison to the monolithic id, Freud considered the ego a "facade" of the unconscious. The ego owed its unique properties to the more extensive id from which it initially emerged (Freud, 1926b, pp. 195 and 200). Its development of the reality principle was designed to serve the needs expressed in the id:

> If we accept the distinction which I have recently proposed of dividing the mental apparatus into an ego, turned towards the external world and equipped with consciousness, and an unconscious id, dominated by its instinctual needs, then psychoanalysis is to be described as a psychology of the id (and of its effects upon the ego). (1924c, p. 209)

> . . . [The ego] is not only a helper to the id; it is also a submissive slave who courts his master's love. Whenever possible, it tries to remain on good terms with id. . . . (1923a, p. 56)

Freud stretched drive theory to explain human strivings that are beyond its realm. One example was the Freudian explanation of Picasso's artistic achievements as merely a sublimation of an anal-stage urge to smear excrement. Such reductionistic explanations ignore all but the most primitive causes of behavior. They also uncritically dismiss the importance of manifest levels of thought and meaning.

Freud himself finally proposed the concept of a desexualized libido, which implied a broadened independence of the ego from the id's drives (1923a, pp. 43–45). In its desexualized form, libido provided the ego with a neutral and displaceable form of energy. Freud went so far as to apply this concept of desexualized libido to the task of explaining thinking and the judgmental processes of the ego. However, even with its neutral status, Freud conceived of desexualized libido as arising from the ego's original pool of narcissistic libido and as obeying the pleasure principle (1923a, p. 45). Freud still did not allow the ego full independence from the id's drives, for even thought itself was still to be interpreted as a result of "the sublimation of erotic motive forces" (Freud, 1923a, p. 45).

Freud's Compartmentalized Model of the Mind

Freud constructed a theory of the mind that pictured the psyche as a house divided against itself. In Freud's view, such compartmentalization was the best way that paradoxical self-deceptions could be explained. Let's look at an example of a self-deception that is paradoxical. When a person says the exact opposite of what was meant, as in a slip of the tongue: "I would like to prevent, uh, present, our next Governor . . ." —the slip seems to indicate that the person knows what he or she does not intend (Fingarette, 1974). In the case of a repressed impulse, one can observe the enigma of persons who intend what they do not know.

Freud was acutely alert to such a paradox, for its existence seemed to reveal that a person could be literally of two minds. One part did not know some threatening material and the other knew exactly what it was. In the case of the manifest dream content, to take one more example, the dreamer has fooled her- or himself by disguising the latent content of strong desires so successfully that when awake he or she seems not to know what was avidly wished for while asleep:

> ". . . I can assure you that it is quite possible, and highly probable indeed, that the dreamer does know what his dream means: only he does not know that he knows it and for that reason thinks he does not know it" (Freud, 1916, p. 101).

In order to explain such apparent self-division, Freud conceptualized seemingly whole personalities as a congregation of compartmentalized agencies. Each agency, in Freud's view, is capable of only imperfect knowledge of the others and quite able to disavow their existence. The psychological portrait that emerges is an abstraction of a person, what Schafer (1976, p. 86) calls an "assembly of minds." This composite has been referred to as a "Mr. Potato Head" model of the psyche. As a result, Freud was forced into a curious anthropomorphism, treating each of the agencies as though it were a human entity with feelings, wishes, motives, blind spots, and goals of its own. In short, the abstractions—designed initially only to represent observable conflict—became personified. To illustrate, consider some of Freud's more memorable statements:

> When the ego assumes the features of the [lost] object, it is forcing itself, so to speak, upon the id as a love-object and is trying to make good the id's loss by saying: "Look, you can love me too—I am so like the object." (1923a, p. 30)

> The poor ego has things even worse. . . . Its three tyrannical masters are the external world, the superego and the id. When we follow the ego's efforts to satisfy them simultaneously—or rather, to obey them simultaneously—we cannot feel any regret at having personified this ego and having set it up as a separate organism. (1933, p. 77)

Ironically, one difficulty to which later psychologists had to address themselves is the impersonalization that resulted from Freud's theorizing. Intended only to communicate in a facile way a natural science, mechanistic conception of psychology, the divided agencies became homunculi ("little people") inside the person. Presumably, each homonculus has a little person within, and so on in a never-ending succession. The metaphors and personifications accomplished their end, conveying Freud's meaning clearly: *Persons are partitioned systems powered by biological energies.*

"The Project for a Scientific Psychology"

By 1895, Freud's apprenticeship to Josef Breuer and his own tentative, searching efforts to understand his neurotic patients confronted him with the first of a host of intellectual dilemmas. On the one hand, Freud now understood that the hysteric's suffering and symptoms made psychological sense. Indeed, symptoms had their origins in the patient's personal emotional history. On the other hand, Freud was schooled in the deterministic and mechanistic faith of nineteenth-century science that all phenomena are reducible to their physical, material components (Jones, 1955; McCarley & Hobson, 1977; Schur, 1972). Psychological events, like other biological functions, have their seat of origin in material bodily processes and in measurable flows of energy. Freud thus conceived a way out of his dilemma by proposing a "Psychology for Neurologists." That is to say, he attempted to construct a neurophysiological model of psychological processes that would bear the "serious stamp of science" to legitimize his "strange case histories."

Freud implicitly conceived of the mind as functionally and (initially, at least) anatomically related brain systems. Freud's goal, almost from the beginning of his work with hysterical patients, was to mine those bizarre disturbances for what they would yield in universal scientific knowledge about all mental functioning. He thought that the dramatic case histories of the *Studies on Hysteria* were not at the level of scientific work:

> . . . I have not always been a psychotherapist. . . . It still strikes me myself as strange that the case histories I write should read like short stories and that, as one might say, they lack the serious stamp of science. (Freud, in Breuer & Freud, 1893–1895, p. 160)

His first model of the mind was a complex and elegant scheme of neuron cell systems and their mutual interchange of metabolic energy. Within the 150 or so pages of his "Psychology for Neurologists" may be found the kernel of nearly every important idea that occupied Freud for the next 44 years of theorizing (Basch, 1975; Gill, 1977; Holt, 1963; Kris, 1954, p. 364; McCarley & Hobson, 1977; Solomon, 1974). Freud wrote to Wilhelm Fliess that the model he was constructing was his tyrant. Yet, upon completion, Freud's tyrant had become Freud's castoff. He now described it to Fliess as a momentary "aberration" to be abandoned as a failure (1954, p. 134).

The neurological model, undertaken near the beginning of Freud's psychoanalytic work, demonstrates clearly his intention to create a scientific theory of neurosis that would at the same time be a general psychology of human behavior.

Freud understood the sterility of restricting his conceptualizations to abnormal behavior. A successful neurophysiological model should also be capable of explaining the broad range of normal human psychology. But Freud must have felt unsuccessful in his goal of utilizing neuroanatomical concepts for the task of psychological explanation. He turned away from explicit neurologizing of his clinical findings, but he never abandoned the implicit model of brain systems as his abiding hypothesis for rendering clinical observations scientifically sensible. The terminology in Freud's writing became psychological, but the traces of neurological concepts remained evident.

Enduring Limitations of Freud's Implicit Neurological Model

It is nearly impossible to turn to any of Freud's later work without catching a glimpse of hypotheses formulated originally in neurological terms. The most general premise that mental activity is an economics of energy transfer among neuronal systems was, of course, the basis for the concept of instinctual energy transfers among agencies of the mind. Implicit in this general postulate is the more fundamental premise that the nervous system is a passive receptacle of energy from the environment or from bodily processes that convert environmental energy into mental energy. Once received, the prime goal of the nervous system, in Freud's view, is to discharge this stimulation as quickly as possible. Because in Freud's dated neurological thinking neurons have no energy sources of their own, they inherently treat inputs of external energy as irritations to be discharged at all costs, with all possible speed. In effect, the nervous system strives to be completely passive, for total inertia is its ultimate goal.

Modern neurophysiology conceptualizes nerve cells as active processors of energy that they themselves generate biochemically. Moreover, they stress that Freud's conception of the nervous system pictured no mechanisms of active inhibition of discharge whereby neurons could deliberately prevent responses. Freud had only the concept of the ego diverting energy from particular pathways and redirecting it to alternate pathways to prevent some neurons from discharging. In Freud's scheme, therefore, inhibition is a relatively passive process requiring specialized neurons to redirect, but not stop, energy flows. By contrast, it is now known that neurons can cancel excitation by altering their threshold sensitivity to stimulation, an active process of metabolic inhibition.

This conception of the nervous system as a passive processor of externally derived energies and as a protector of the organism's normally quiescent state was carried over into all of Freud's later theory, and it was based on what we now know was an erroneous neurological formulation. Freud's classical picture of the personality in distress was built psychologically from his clinical experiences but conceptualized neurologically along the lines of nineteenth-century deterministic, materialistic physiology. Picturing the mind as a collection of competing agencies, Freud was forced into a number of dubious assumptions about the nature of human mental functioning.

What Had Freud Left Undone?

Freud thought that his own greatest accomplishment had been the exploration of the drives of the unconscious id. The ego was, for the most part, conceptualized as the helpless rider of the spirited id horse, directing the horse where the horse wants to go. If we ask the inevitable question, "What had Freud left undone?" we can provide at least three answers:

1. He neglected the individual's direct relationships to interpersonal reality, especially to the reality of the mother in her role as the nurturing, shaping,

esteem-building, trust-building influence in development. Freud's focus had been on conflict, with the powerful id drives seen as the foundation of all human endeavors.

2. Freud failed to complete his picture of the ego as the executive of the personality, capable of more than safe and reliable id satisfactions. Although Freud implied that the ego could function relatively autonomously, his theory sorely lacked a coherent account of how persons adapt to the reality that they themselves helped to create. Without the id pulling the strings in the background, there is no way in classical Freudian theory to explain logically and convincingly the various ways that persons master obstacles beyond instinctual conflict or derive satisfactions from enterprises other than conflict resolution. Not every personal achievement, not every human satisfaction, not every human urge or pain can be derived from the war of sexual and aggressive impulses.

3. The "assembly of minds" that is Freudian structural, dynamic theory runs the risk of losing sight of the whole person, the overall synthesizing, integrating, coordinating function. In Freud's theory, the ego was to be the seat of an overall integrating and coordinating function, but he failed to develop this idea beyond simple and scattered statements of its existence.

Building on Freud's achievements with increasing sophistication and heightened concern for whole persons rather than partitioned minds, we shall see in subsequent chapters that Anna Freud and other ego psychologists who followed Freud stressed the autonomy and self-sufficiency of the ego. In contemporary ego psychology, humans are viewed as neither completely drive-bound nor fully emancipated from their biological heritage.

By contrast, in classical Freudian theory, as we have seen, drives predominate, and the ego is, to use Freud's own metaphor, like the rider of a spirited horse heading through a small town. After a person asks the rider where he is going in such a great hurry, the rider answers, "Don't ask me. Ask the horse!" (Freud, 1923a, p. 25; 1933, p. 77). For Freud, the id horse was far more powerful than the ego rider. The ego was merely a necessity of the id's survival, a means to the end of tension discharge. A mind that always struggles to meet all-consuming inner and outer pressures is a mind that never acts to create its own environment. It is a mind whose ". . . cogs meshed . . . [and] really seemed to be a machine which in a moment would run of itself . . ." (Freud, 1954, p. 129).

What had Freud left undone? He had left the picture of the ego's own functions incomplete—particularly how it was able to deal with external reality. And Freud omitted from consideration the fact most riders *can and do* control and direct their mounts.

FOR FURTHER READING

The best overviews in Freud's own writings of his later theory are to be found in two complementary sets of lectures. The first of these dates from his pre-structural model of the mind and is entitled *Introductory Lectures on Psychoanalysis,* Vol. XV and XVI of *The Standard Edition* (or in paperback under the title *A General Introduction to Psychoanalysis* [New York: Washington Square Press, 1960, or Norton, 1989]). The second set of lectures dates from his development of the id-ego-superego model and can be found in Vol. XXII of *The Standard Edition* under the title *New Introductory Lectures on Psychoanalysis* (also available in paperback [New York: Norton, 1964]).

Possibly the simplest and clearest introduction to psychoanalysis ever written and one that can claim some measure of authority is Anna Freud's, *The Harvard Lectures* (New York: International Universities Press, 1992).

Freud's own historical accounts of the development of his system bear scrutiny. *An Autobiographical Study (The Standard Edition,* Vol. XX; paperback edition, Norton, 1989) was Freud's attempt to survey personal and intellectual factors that shaped his theorizing. A further historical effort by Freud, dating from somewhat earlier in his career (1914), can be found in *On the History of the Psychoanalytic Movement (The Standard Edition,* Vol. XIV [London: Hogarth, 1957]; also *in The Basic Writings of Sigmund Freud,* translated and edited by A. A. Brill, New York: Modern Library, 1995).

Freud considered *The Interpretation of Dreams* to be his masterpiece (Vols. IV and V of *The Standard Edition,* London: Hogarth, 1953; also in *The Basic Writings of Sigmund Freud,* edited by A. A. Brill, New York: Modern Library, 1995). The serious student of psychoanalysis will also want to consult a series of papers collectively termed Freud's "Metapsychology," and published as "Instincts and Their Vicissitudes" (1915); "Repression" (1915); "The Unconscious" (1915); "Metapsychological Supplement of the Theory of Dreams" (1917); and "Mourning and Melancholia" (1917) (all contained in Vol. XIV of *The Standard Edition*). These papers form the heart of Freud's midcareer theorizing and his attempts to reconcile ambiguities and inconsistencies in his early formulations.

Freud's final model of the mind is to be found in his *The Ego and the Id* (New York: Norton, 1990). Anna Freud elaborated her father's conception of neurotic defense mechanisms in a book that has now become a psychoanalytic classic and essential reading for all students of psychoanalysis, *The Ego and the Mechanisms of Defense,* revised edition (New York: International Universities Press, 1971). Robert Stolorow and George Atwood's *Faces in a Cloud: Intersubjectivity in Personality Theory* (New York: Aronson, 1994) considers the subjective sources of Freud's psychosexual theory.

Critical commentaries and summaries of Freud's thinking abound. A survey and analysis of the experimental study of Freudian concepts is provided by Paul Kline in *Fact and Fantasy in Freudian Theory* (New York: Harper & Row, 1972, originally published in Great Britain by Methuen). Where Kline is relatively optimistic about the empirical testability and validity of Freud's ideas, Hans Eysenck and Glen Wilson in their *Experimental Study of Freudian Theories* (New York: Harper & Row, 1973) reproduce and sharply criticize several "classic" experiments purporting to demonstrate the validity of Freudian hypotheses.

GLOSSARY

Adaptive viewpoint: Point of view that some psychological processes have the purpose of healthy adaptation.

Aim: Instinctual impulses strive toward satisfaction or tension reduction. An *ultimate aim* is the immediate gratification of an instinctual demand, and an *intermediate aim* is the substitute form of satisfaction when an instinct is blocked from obtaining a suitable goal.

Anticathexis: The barrier that is set up by the preconscious to deal with unacceptable unconscious content through repression. Also, the removal of charges of mental energy (cathexes), or the diversion of attention from the *memory image* of a noxious stimulus; a form of mental withdrawal from threatening stimuli.

Anxiety: Feelings arising from the ego's sense of being overwhelmed and helpless. Freud defined three types: **Realistic anxiety** is triggered by real and objective sources of danger in the *external world*. **Neurotic anxiety** is caused when *id's instinctual impulses* threaten the ego. **Moral anxiety** is felt when the individual disregards moral and ethical concerns and fears the *superego's censure*.

Birth trauma: The anxiety the infant experiences when leaving the safety of the womb and being flooded with too much stimulation upon birth. The birth trauma is an individual's first experience, which serves as the model against which the ego compares future situations.

Cathexis: (from a Greek root, meaning "to hold on to") A term used to describe the attachment of mental energy to a variety of thoughts, feelings, or objects. One example is the attachment of libido to external objects.

Condensation: In dream interpretation, the idea that manifest content is a model of compression, or condensation. Many latent meanings are hidden in one manifest image.

Displacement: A technique the censorship agency of the mind uses to replace a latent dream element in consciousness by a more remote idea, or to accomplish a shifting of the dream's recalled emphasis away from an important idea and toward an unimportant one.

Dream work: Dream formation; the various mechanisms or mental processes used to transform latent strivings, wishes, or impulses into more acceptable forms by distorting or disguising their true meaning in manifest content.

Ego: Arising from the id, it is that part of the personality that is in contact with reality. It acts as a mediator between the urges of the id and the demands of the superego. It uses reason and problem-solving strategies to solve the often-incompatible demands of the id and superego.

Ego libido: That portion of the original pool of libido remaining in the ego.

Eros: (a term derived from *Eros,* the Greek god of love and passion) The combined sexual and ego instinct. Preservation of the self and of the species are involved in this instinct.

Homeostasis: A state of balance or equilibrium. Applied to the nervous system, it indicates an optimal state of minimal arousal and physiological equilibrium.

Id: The unconscious and the oldest component of the personality. It contains mental representations of the instincts and leads to urges to satisfy instinctual needs. It operates according to the pleasure principle.

Identification: The process of modeling itself on the lost love object, as the ego attempts to pacify the id. Identification is an important part of the processes by which the superego is formed as part of resolution of the Oedipal complex. More generally, identification refers to taking on the characteristics of another in order to soothe anxieties and alleviate internal conflicts.

Infantile amnesia: A type of amnesia or blanket forgetting that prevents recollection of any Oedipal sexual and aggressive strivings of childhood as well as other memories. These memories are not really lost but remain in the unconscious.

Internalization: The process by which children identify with the standards of rightness, morality, and goodness originally enforced by their parents. A new internal agency, the superego, functions autonomously and continues from within to exercise moral judgments.

Latent content: Repressed or disguised thoughts or wishes expressed in a dream, the hidden meaning behind the storyline of a dream.

Libido: In Freudian theory, the energy of the sexual or pleasure instincts. Later theorists such as Carl Jung and Alfred Adler would develop alternative definitions of *libido*.

Manifest content: The surface meaning of a dream, that is, images, storylines, and symbols as observed and remembered by the dreamer. The pictures or stories as they appear to be.

Metapsychology: Literally, "beyond psychology", metapsychology is the term used by Freud whenever a psychological process is understood from its descriptive, systematic, and dynamic aspects. One must look at the complex interplay of multiple determinants.

Narcissism: The process in which some libidinal energy is directed toward a person's own ego.

Nirvana principle: The homeostatic trend of the nervous system to divest itself of disturbing tensions and excess stimulation. The associated mental processes also strive to reduce excitation and tension, and maintain stability. It is an urge to gain or retain complete quietude.

Object: A concrete, usually external, object that has the power to reduce or to satisfy an instinctual need. Appropriate objects may be changed many times to satisfy a specific instinct.

Object libido: That portion of the original pool of libido used to bond to a variety of external objects.

Overdetermined: In dream interpretation, the idea that several unconscious ideas band together to contribute to one common manifest element.

Pleasure principle: The seeking after pleasure by the discharge of unpleasurable mounting tension. The nervous system must find a way to reduce the biological deficit (or to satisfy the urge) that an instinctual demand represents.

Preconscious censorship system: The mental system that prevents those wishes that are morally unacceptable to an individual from entering waking, postdream consciousness. It also attempts to patch together the scattered and apparently nonsensical elements of a latent dream into an understandable, coherent, and acceptable whole.

Pressure: The amount of force or strength of the demand made by the instinctual need on the mind.

Primal repression: The fixating or freezing of unacceptable ideas or impulses. Significant acts of primal repression occur during the first six or eight years of life.

Primary process thinking: The id satisfies bodily needs in two ways. Through reflexive action, it reduces tension. And through wish fulfillment, it imagines the object to satisfy the need. The imagery or fantasy temporarily reduces the tension linked to the need. The unconscious knows no bound to its wishfulness and fantasized objects. Primary process thinking does not take reality into account.

Reality principle: The principle that directs the ego's activities. It causes the ego to interact realistically with the environment to satisfy the id's sensual appetites and the superego's moral concerns.

Repression: The processes by which unconscious impulses and memories are kept out of awareness. Unlike *suppression, repression* occurs outside of conscious awareness. There are two types of repression: *primal repression* and *repression proper.*

Repression proper: The process whereby ideas, trains of thought, or perceptions that are associatively linked to the primally repressed impulse are also denied access to consciousness. Repression proper thus cooperates with primal repression to ensure that unacceptable impulses and associated ideas remain buried.

Secondary process thinking: Deals with the ego's efforts to bring about genuine biological satisfaction. The ego takes the demands of reality into consideration and delays gratification of the need until an appropriate object is found. It tries to match the object to the person's need.

Secondary revision: The process by which a dream is reconstructed or reshaped into a coherent whole from fragmented and chaotic elements.

Source: The origin of all instincts is located in the physical-chemical processes of the body.

Structural model: The model of the mind that divides it into three agencies—the id, ego, and superego. It subsumes all of the mental functions previously assigned to the unconscious and the preconscious.

Superego: An internal agency, formed in the resolution of the Oedipal complex, which internalizes the values of society and the standards originally enforced by parents. The superego criticizes the ego for acting against its injunctions.

Thanatos: (a term derived from *Thanatos,* the Greek god of death) The death instinct. It is a desire to return to a state of inorganic existence in which there are no biological demands to be met. Two derivatives of this instinct are aggression and destruction—desire to destroy others or destroy the self.

Topographic/systemic model: The model of the mind that divides it into the unconscious, the preconscious, and conscious systems.

Transference: A term Freud gave to patients' tendencies to react to their therapists with emotions reproduced from childhood. Patients *transferred* feelings that often originated with their parents to their therapists.

Unconscious: A term Freud used to describe that part of the mind containing instincts, thoughts, and emotions that were not part of or acceptable to the conscious mind. Freud attached three different meaning to the term *unconscious:* the *descriptive unconscious,* the *dynamic unconscious,* and the *systemic unconscious.*

Wish fulfillment: Freud's concept that dreams bring about the fulfillment of often, but not always, unacceptable wishes or desires.

Chapter 4

Carl Gustav Jung

Analytical Psychology

It seemed to me that I was high up in space. Far below, I saw the globe of the earth, bathed in a gloriously blue light.

C.G. Jung, *Memories, Dreams, Reflections*

[Whether He is] Called or not, God is present.

Translation of the Latin carving over the doorway of Jung's home at Kussnacht

There are more things in heaven and earth, Horatio,
Than are dreamt of in your philosophy.

William Shakespeare, *Hamlet*

Carl Gustav Jung	Born: 1875	Kessnil, Switzerland
	Died: 1961	Kussnacht, Switzerland

About Jung's Analytical Psychology

Carl Gustav Jung was for a short time Freud's hand-chosen successor. But personal and intellectual differences eventually led to a break between Freud and Jung, with Jung subsequently developing his own theories and therapeutic approach. Much of Jung's picture of the human personality was derived from his affiliation with Freud, so the familiar concepts of unconscious motivation, neurotic defenses, and human conflict will also be found

117

here. Jung's importance lies very much in the many ideas that differed markedly from Freud's. Some basic Jungian concepts are these:

- *Jung agreed with Freud that energy dynamics were important to the psyche, but he thought the fundamental energy, or libido, was not specifically sexual in nature but, rather, a more general type of energy.*

- *The personal unconscious described by Freud overlays what Jung termed the "collective unconscious," which consists of universal images and inherited behavioral proclivities (instincts).*

- *All aspects of a person's psychological makeup, including all conscious and unconscious aspects, are part of a whole, the psyche.*

- *Personality is an important but largely surface aspect of the psyche.*

- *The psyche is guided toward becoming a harmonious and integrative whole. Many crises and conflicts can be considered part of the teleological or purposive process of growth and development instead of merely as forms of pathology.*

- *Spiritual growth is central to personality development.*

- *Jung developed a typology of personality or temperaments to help understand and categorize differences in how people experience and approach life.*

Much of Jung's thinking emerged from his personal experiences. Even though many clinicians would consider these experiences, which included visual and auditory hallucinations, to be pathological, Jung used them creatively and productively in developing his theories. Jung maintained an often tenuous hold on reality while exploring worlds of meaning emerging from the collective unconscious.

EXPERIMENTAL STUDY OF ASSOCIATIONS

Jung and Freud exchanged a number of letters and published articles. After a visit by Jung to Freud's home early in 1907, Freud began to consider Jung his successor. That visit involved an intense exchange of ideas between Jung and Freud. On April 7, Freud wrote to Jung, "that you have inspired me with confidence for the future, that I now realize that I am as replaceable as everyone else and that I could hope for no one better than yourself, as I have come to know you, to continue and complete my work" (Freud & Jung, 1974, p. 27). Thus transpired what would turn out to be a relatively brief period of mutual admiration between the two theorists. However, along with his overt enthusiasm about Freudian theories, Jung held quiet doubts or "mental reservations" about some of Freud's main concepts, especially regarding Freud's views about the primary importance of sexuality. Jung also believed that he had a broader education than Freud and was more knowledgeable in the field of philosophy (Jung, 1959; McLynn, 1997).

Part of Freud's enthusiasm for his younger colleague rested in part on Jung's published acknowledgment that Freud's ideas had been useful in his own clinical work. Jung had also conducted extensive experiments with his cousin, Franz Riklin, which demonstrated unconscious mental processes. Various grammatical forms were included among the various stimulus words. The list was arranged in a specific sequence that Jung's experience had shown was suitable for eliciting maximum emotional reaction. In later experiments, Jung and his colleagues used additional procedures beside the simple stopwatch timing of the subject's reactions. Sometimes the subject's respiration rate was measured along with a recording of galvanic skin response (GSR). The GSR measures the skin's decrease in resistance to electrical current during sensory and emotional changes, a variable akin to one of the measures used in the modern "lie detector" or polygraph.

Table 4.1   Jung's List of Stimulus Words

1. head	26. blue	51. frog	76. to wash
2. green	27. lamp	52. to part	77. cow
3. water	28. to sin	53. hunger	78. friend
4. to sing	29. bread	54. white	79. happiness
5. death	30. rich	55. child	80. lie
6. long	31. tree	56. to pay attention	81. department
7. ship	32. to prick	57. pencil	82. narrow
8. to pay	33. pity	58. sad	83. brother
9. window	34. yellow	59. plum	84. to fear
10. friendly	35. mountain	60. to marry	85. stork
11. table	36. to die	61. house	86. false
12. to ask	37. salt	62. darling	87. anxiety
13. cold	38. new	63. glass	88. to kiss
14. stem	39. custom	64. to quarrel	89. bride
15. to dance	40. to pray	65. fur	90. pure
16. village	41. money	66. big	91. door
17. lake	42. stupid	67. carrot	92. to choose
18. sick	43. exercise book	68. to paint	93. hay
19. pride	44. to despise	69. part	94. contented
20. to cook	45. finger	70. old	95. ridicule
21. ink	46. dear	71. flower	96. to sleep
22. angry	47. bird	72. to beat	97. month
23. needle	48. to fall	73. box	98. nice
24. to swim	49. book	74. wild	99. woman
25. journey	50. unjust	75. family	100. to abuse

From Jung, 1909a, p. 440.

The word association experiment was not unique to Jung's laboratory (cf. Woodworth & Schlosberg, 1954, Chapter 3 for a brief history of the method; and Jung, 1909a). Individual differences in **reaction time,** respiration rate, **galvanic skin response (GSR),** and ideational content were the rule prior to Jung's work. Jung made the discovery that, in experiments with neurotic and psychotic patients, the word association method could also aid in uncovering latent psychological difficulties. This was done by recording and exploring content areas that produced hesitation, perseveration, or total inhibition of response. The **word association test** was a precursor of using standardized stimuli in psychological testing to discover the makeup of specific individuals.

EMOTIONAL COMPLEX INDICATORS

Usually, the stimulus word that triggered the subject's hesitation or inability to respond was connected symbolically with a deeply personal and threatening set of ideas or experiences. Jung's word association test was tapping the same phenomenon as Freud's method of free association—experiences that were threatening were found to resist conscious awareness. Because such latent difficulties were often collections of various thoughts held together by common themes, Jung and Riklin termed them *complexes.* A **complex** is thus a personally disturbing constellation of ideas connected together by common feeling-tone (Jung, 1913, p. 599). For example, the individual caught up in a conflict over relations with his or her father would be said to have a "father complex"; the individual

**Table 4.2   Educational Level
and Reaction Time (in seconds)**

	Educated subjects	*Uneducated subjects*
Men	1.3	1.6
Women	1.7	2.2
Average	1.5	1.9

From Jung, 1905, vol. 2, p. 227.

experiencing anxiety and frustration in sexual matters would be characterized as having a "sex complex."

Complexes are revealed in word association experiments through a number of diagnostic signs:

- Longer than average reaction time
- Repetition of the stimulus word by the subject
- Mishearing of the stimulus word as some other word
- Expressive bodily movements like laughing, twitching
- Reaction composed of more than one word
- Very superficial reaction to stimulus word, as in rhyming to the sound: e.g., to sin—subject responds with "to win"
- Meaningless reaction: made-up words
- Failure to respond at all
- Perseveration of response: continuing to respond to previous word even after new stimulus word is presented
- Major alteration of responses when list is administered for second time
- Slips of the tongue or stammering

In addition to these 11 unique patterns of response, Jung also discovered characteristic and stable differences between men and women and between more educated and less educated subject's responses. Consider Table 4.2. In Jung's laboratory, women characteristically took longer to respond to the stimulus words than their male counterparts at both educational levels. Generally, Jung found that more educated people responded faster than less educated ones.

DISCOVERING A CASE OF CRIMINALLY NEGLIGENT HOMICIDE THROUGH THE WORD ASSOCIATION TEST

One of Jung's clinic patients, a 30-year-old woman, had been diagnosed as a depressed schizophrenic. Most of the hospital staff agreed that the prognosis for her recovery was poor. Jung thought otherwise. To obtain more insight into her personality, he administered a form of the association test.

Some of her responses are graphically indicated in Figure 4.1. Each of the words graphed in Figure 4.1 has a reaction time that exceeds the average reaction time for an educated woman. The height of the bars indicates the relative differences in length of reaction time above the mean for educated women. Most outstanding of the woman's responses was her inability to offer any reply to the word "obstinate."

Jung proceeded by confronting the patient with the results of her word association test. He asked her to comment on the various stimulus words that had produced the longest

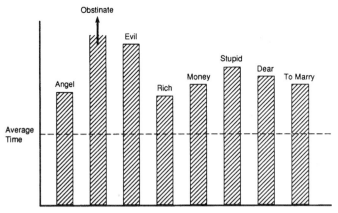

Figure 4.1 Relative reaction time for critical stimulus words.

reaction times. To "angel," the woman replied, "Of course, that is my child whom I have lost." She then displayed great emotional upheaval. To "obstinate," she responded, "It means nothing to me." To "evil," she again refused to comment. But to the word "blue" (not illustrated in the graph) she replied, "Those are the eyes of the child I have lost." Jung asked her why the child's eyes had so impressed her: "They were so wonderfully blue when the child was born." Jung noticed that this last reply was accompanied by much emotion. He again asked her why she was upset: "Well, she did not have the eyes of my husband."

A tragic story unfolded: The child's eyes had so upset her mother because they resembled the eyes of a former lover. In her hometown, the woman had fallen in love with a wealthy young aristocrat. Coming from a "common" background, the girl and her parents had concluded that an engagement and then marriage with the aristocrat was not feasible. At the insistence of her family, she married another young man. She was happy until the fifth year of the marriage. At that time, a friend from her hometown visited her and brought upsetting information: her present marriage had hurt and displeased the wealthy aristocrat she had once loved. For the first time she realized that he had also loved her. She realized that she could have fulfilled her dreams by getting married to him. Her mind quickly repressed these hard-to-accept thoughts and associated feelings.

Two weeks later, she was bathing her two children, a small boy and the blue-eyed girl. She noticed the girl sucking on a bath sponge. The woman knew she should stop the child because the town's water supply was thought to be infested with typhus, and she had not boiled the bath water. She hesitated to take the sponge away from the girl's mouth. She consciously allowed the little girl to continue sucking on the sponge. Shortly thereafter, the girl got typhoid fever and died.

The act was symbolic—a denial of her marriage through murder of the first child. Jung knew that he was obligated to confront her with the fact of her crime, the significance of which she did not at first seem to understand. She began to experience guilt as she finally realized what she had done. Within three weeks she was sufficiently recovered from her depression to be released from the hospital.

> I traced her for fifteen years, and there was no relapse. That depression fitted her case psychologically; she was a murderess and under other circumstances would have deserved capital punishment. Instead of going to jail she was sent to the lunatic asylum. I practically saved her from the punishment of insanity by putting an enormous burden on her conscience. For if one can accept one's sin one can live with it. (Jung, 1968, p. 61)

USES OF THE WORD ASSOCIATION TEST

Jung became quite adept in the use of the word association test for *diagnosis of unconscious complexes*. He used a variation of the test even for criminal cases. The guilt or innocence of an accused person often could be established by careful interrogation with the help of word lists that included critical words relating to key aspects of the crime (Jung, 1905, pp. 318 ff.). Jung and his associates also employed the word association tests for comparisons of unconscious complexes among members of a family. Thus, for example, Jung (1909b, pp. 466 ff.) investigated the associations of the members of 24 families, collecting in the process some 22,000 responses. The resulting data were analyzed in a variety of ways, but the outstanding overall result was the similarity of content among members of a single family. For example, the associations of a mother and daughter in different sessions to the same stimulus words were quite revealing:

Stimulus Word	Mother	Daughter
law	God's commandment	Moses
potato	tuber	tuber
strange	traveler	travelers
brother	dear to me	dear
to kiss	mother	mother
merry	happy child	little children

From Jung, 1909b, p. 469.[1]

Not only do the content of this mother's and daughter's word associations match, but also the choice of response word was found to be virtually identical in several other cases. Jung had thus inadvertently touched upon a phenomenon found in family dynamics, which would not be more thoroughly studied for many decades.

JUNG'S CONCEPT OF LIBIDO

Jung quickly saw that his word association studies could offer empirical support for some of Freud's psychoanalytic concepts. Subject's inhibitions and long reaction times to the stimulus words, along with their heightened physiological responsivity, could serve as quantitative evidence of latent ideas that could not be directly expressed but nonetheless produced demonstrable effects. Jung realized that he had developed a method of exploring the unconscious comparable to Freud's investigations of it with free association. In the early days of their association, Jung and Freud agreed on what was to be found there: namely, repressed, unacceptable sexual and aggressive strivings and threatening experiences.

As Jung continued his explorations of the unconscious, he found it increasingly difficult to accept Freud's insistence that sexual motives were the only basis of neurosis (Jung, 1961, Chapter 5). Jung questioned the central Freudian concept of libido as a general pleasure drive rooted exclusively in sexuality. Early in their relationship Jung wrote to Freud and inquired,

> Is it not conceivable, in view of the limited conception of sexuality that prevails nowadays, that the sexual terminology should be reserved only for the most extreme forms of your "libido," and that a less offensive collective term should be established for all the libidinal manifestations? (Freud & Jung, 1974, p. 25)

---

[1](1909b). The psychological diagnosis of evidence. In Vol. 2 of *The Collected Works of C.G. Jung*. Princeton, NJ: Princeton University Press, 1973.

Figure 4.2 Jung in 1910. This photo was taken when Jung was in his mid-30s, around the time he conducted his word association experiments and about three years before his unsettling break-up with Freud.

For Jung, then, the fundamental psychic energy was still to be termed **libido,** but his conception of this primal force differed from the classical psychoanalytic view. For Jung, libido was a neutral and nonsexualized or general psychic energy (1912, p. 137). Libido is a form of energy, and, as in Freud's theory, may be channeled, suppressed, repressed, blocked, or expressed. In all cases, however, it is to be understood as a dynamic life force not purely as a sexualized energy.

THE PRINCIPLES OF EQUIVALENCE AND ENTROPY

If libido is dammed up, or repressed, an equivalent or substitute expression must occur in consciousness. Hence, for Jung, as for Freud, repressed libido obeys what Jung called the **principle of equivalence:** Following the laws of thermodynamics, Jung agreed with Freud that psychic energy never ceases to exist, despite transformations in form. Repressed ideas embodying psychic energy simply find substitute expression in equivalent symbolic forms (Jung, 1948, p. 19; 1912, pp. 143–144). Unlike Freud, Jung did not regard these transformations as necessarily neurotic. Rather, Jung defined such modifications as potentially healthy "canalizations of libido," that is, as transfers of psychic energy to mythic symbols.

A symbol is therefore considered a "libido analog." Throughout history, people have practiced religious and magical rituals that center on unconsciously created symbols. Jung found evidence that the process of converting libido into symbolic expressions occurs in contemporary patients as he thought it did in our prehistorical and ancient ancestors.

Jung's principle of equivalence had been based on the first law of thermodynamics— that energy is neither created nor destroyed but only transformed. According to this law, repressed libido is not destroyed but turns up elsewhere in the psyche. A good example is a student who represses sexual fantasies may redouble efforts at community service. This represents not the destruction of energy but a shift of an equivalent amount of energy elsewhere in the psyche.

Jung also formulated a psychological principle based on the second law of thermodynamics, the law of entropy, which states that, in a physical system, energy will flow from the more energized matter to the less, eventually achieving a state of balance. The **principle of entropy** implies that psychic energy flows from the most intensely energized ideas, archetypes, and complexes to those that are less energized. Ultimately, the mental system strives to an equalization of differences (1948, p. 26). Thus, for example, an individual who overemphasizes one way of approaching life will find, over the years, that other areas receive more energy. For example, a "macho" male may gradually get in touch with his more sensitive and artistic side; a compliant young woman may get in touch with her more combative sense of self.

LEARNING FROM UNLIKELY SOURCES

The Sun's Phallus

Staring out the window of the hospital corridor, a young schizophrenic patient beckoned Jung to his side. If you half shut your eyes, he told Jung, and stared at the sun, you could see the sun's phallus, or penis. If you then moved your head side to side, the sun's phallus would also move. The young man concluded his strange remarks to Jung with the matter-of-fact assertion that *the movement of the sun's phallus was the origin of the wind* (Jung, 1931, pp. 151–152; 1912, pp. 100, 157; and 1936, pp. 50–51).

Jung had this enigmatic encounter with a psychotic 30-year-old clerk in 1906. Jung originally dismissed the episode as one more strange hallucination or fantasy characteristic of schizophrenia. Four years later, however, in 1910, while researching in the field of mythology, Jung came across a book that reproduced the rituals of the ancient Mithraic Greek religious cult. Professor Albrecht Dieterich, the author of the book, quoted one of the cult's visions:

> *And likewise the so-called tube, the origin of the ministering wind.* For you will see hanging down from the disc of the sun something that looks like a tube. And towards the regions westward it is as though there were an infinite east wind. But if the other wind should prevail towards the regions of the east, you will in like manner see the vision veering in that direction. (Quoted in Jung, 1931, pp. 150–151; italics added)

Jung was startled by the almost exact similarity between this ancient pre-Christian myth and the young schizophrenic clerk's hallucinatory vision. The clerk could not have read Dieterich's book since he had been institutionalized before its publication. Nor could Jung explain the similarity as a product of the young man's educational and cultural experience. He had, after all, only the equivalent of a secondary school education and he had not engaged in foreign travel. Further mythological study convinced Jung that the notion of a sun phallus, or its equivalent, a divine phallus, was a common theme in many cultures of the past. Jung wondered how to account for the presence of this myth in the unconscious and conscious mind of a contemporary schizophrenic.

The Snake Dream

Another of Jung's patients, a young military officer, succumbed to a hysterical neurosis characterized by three symptoms. First, he suffered severe attacks of pain in the chest. Second, he experienced several episodes of choking "as if there were a lump in his throat."

Finally, he was unable to walk normally because of stabbing pains in his left heel (Jung, 1931, p. 146).

In psychotherapy with Jung, the source of the first two symptoms was uncovered and followed the usual patterns of hysterical neurosis. The young man had been hurt and humiliated by a love affair that terminated when the girl became engaged to another man. He had denied his hurt and shattered self-esteem, but unconsciously he felt that "his heart was broken," and the idea that she had terminated the affair was "hard to swallow." Thus, as Freud had suggested, a painful experience had been converted into a painful and symbolic cluster of bodily symptoms. Though the pain in the throat and the choking attacks, along with the chest pains, were eliminated when these feelings were made conscious, the young soldier's third symptom, a stabbing pain in his left heel, remained intractable.

Jung turned to analyzing the man's dreams. The officer reported a dream in which he was bitten in the heel by a snake and instantly paralyzed. Analysis of the dream revealed the expected associations of the girl as a "snake" who had betrayed him; of a mother who had overprotected and thus "crippled" him; of a certain tendency to "girlishness" in himself for which he overcompensated by joining the military. But Jung thought that he detected something more fundamental, more primitive and universal in the man's dream. It was as though the Genesis saying: "And I will put enmity between thee and the woman, and between thy seed and her seed; it shall bruise thy head, and thou shalt bruise his heel . . ." had been transformed by the man's unconscious mind into a personal mythic symbol of his recent romantic upset.

For some reason, this nonreligious soldier had needed mythic expression of inner pain. Jung concluded that the man's knowledge of the Bible, scanty though it was, was dormant until his unconscious seized upon it (1931, p. 147). For the Bible story had provided just the right medium for conversion of a personal conflict into an opportunity to express a deeper sentiment in allegorical fashion (Jung, 1968, p. 116). The soldier's unconscious chose a universal myth to express his pain.

Consequently, Jung was convinced that a part of the unconscious mind, as exemplified by the sun's phallus fantasy, transcends the personal experiences of the individual. This unconscious subsystem embodies some of the past experiences of the humanity. Moreover, that same transpersonal unconscious domain may *also* employ personal experience as a vehicle for mythological, allegorical expression of age-old themes, as exemplified by the soldier's snake dream. Jung wrote that, ". . . for the dream of the snake reveals a fragment of psychic activity that has nothing whatever to do with the dreamer as a modern individual . . ." (Jung, 1931, p. 148). Such a dream could not be a product solely of the soldier's personal experiences. Fantasies like the sun's phallus and the snake dream could have originated only in the individual's resonance with the cumulative experiences of the humanity. Jung gave the name *collective unconscious* to the part of the mind involved in unconscious myth transmission.

VISIONARY AND CREATIVE OR JUST CRAZY?

Jung's writings are studded with a seemingly endless array of mythological examples and their similarities to dreams, paintings, and fantasies of normal as well as abnormal personalities. But there was an even more fundamental source of Jung's conviction that a suprapersonal unconscious exists. In his autobiography, *Memories, Dreams, Reflections,* written just before his death in 1961, Jung provided his readers with a series of rare and penetrating glimpses into his inner life. The entire book is laden with gods, spirits, and fantasy figures that populated Jung's inner mental life. One event in particular is relevant in the context of our discussion of the collective unconscious, because out of it grew Jung's conviction that ". . . there are things in the psyche which I do not produce, but which produce themselves and have their own life" (1961, p. 183).

Jung reported that between 1913 and 1917 he was seized by a series of vivid dreams, visions, fantasies, and mystical experiences. Many of these would have met the formal characteristic of hallucinations, that is, "the apparent perception of sights, sounds, etc., that are not actually present." Jung envisioned several personages during these experiences. Several of these figures subsequently had long conversations together with Jung about topics of which Jung could have consciously known very little. One particular figure, whom Jung named Philemon, arose from the metamorphosis of an earlier fantasy figure, Elijah:

> Philemon was a pagan and brought with him an Egypto-Hellenistic atmosphere with a Gnostic coloration. His figure appeared to me in the following dream. There was a blue sky, like the sea, covered not by clouds but by flat brown clods of earth. It looked as if the clods were breaking apart and the blue water of the sea [was] becoming visible between them. But the water was the blue sky. Suddenly there appeared from the right a winged being sailing across the sky. I saw that it was an old man with the horns of a bull. He held a bunch of four keys, one of which he clutched as if he were about to open a lock. He had the wings of a kingfisher with its characteristic colors. (1961, pp. 182–183)

At first, Jung did not understand the dream. He tried to impress it upon his memory by painting it. During the time he was painting that memory, he discovered in his garden a dead kingfisher bird. "I was thunderstruck, for kingfishers are quite rare in the vicinity of Zurich and I have never since found a dead one" (1961, p. 183).

For Jung, the significance of the Philemon figure lay in the insight that such apparitions represented a force beyond himself—beyond his personal experiences and personal unconscious mind. He "heard" Philemon say things during the fantasies that Jung realized he himself had not consciously thought. "He confronted me in an objective manner, and I understood that there is something in me which can say things that I do not know and do not intend, things which may even be directed against me" (1961, p. 183).

The Philemon fantasy occurred between the middle of December and early January 1913, approximately one year after Jung's acrimonious break with Freud. Jung had been extending his theoretical talents in directions that Freud found unacceptable. Jung's ideas clashed with his own, and Freud was sure Jung was heading in a mystical direction. Freud had concerns that an association of psychoanalysis with mysticism would undermine its already fragile credibility and scientific status in the medical world.

Jung saw himself poised on the edge of a precipice. Visions and fantasies or, more clinically, visual and auditory hallucinations, had been bombarding his consciousness and threatening to overwhelm him. Jung knew that he might be on the verge of being overwhelmed by the unconscious contents of his mind. He was in danger of being engulfed by a full-blown psychosis. Jung was faced with a momentous decision: Should he attempt to fight off these assaults of the unconscious or should he voluntarily descend into the depths of the unconscious and attempt to make rational sense of his experiences? He was aware that, in others, such a descent into unknown experiences, could lead to insanity.

> My enduring these storms was a question of brute strength. Others have been shattered by them. . . . But there was a demonic strength in me, and from the beginning there was no doubt in my mind that I must find the meaning of what I was experiencing in these fantasies. When I endured these assaults of the unconscious I had an unswerving conviction that I was obeying a higher will, and that feeling continued to uphold me until I had mastered the task. (Jung, 1961, p. 177)

and

> It was most essential for me to have a normal life in the real world as a counterpoise to my strange inner world. . . . My family and my profession remained the base to which I could always return, assuring me that I was actually an existing, ordinary person. The unconscious contents could have driven me out of my wits. (Jung, 1961, p. 189)

Opinion is divided over whether Jung's descent into his dreams and fantasies was voluntary, or whether it was an involuntary form of psychopathology. One school of opinion is represented by writers like Aniela Jaffé (1971) and Laurens Van der Post (1975), who have accepted Jung's own view that his 1913 to 1917 "stormy period" was a careful and deliberate voyage of exploration that would be "unpopular, ambiguous and dangerous" (Jung, 1961). According to them, Jung was a visionary, who skillfully charted unknown inner realms with courage and determination. Jung phrased it this way:

> It is of course ironical that I, a psychiatrist, should at almost every step of my experiment have run into the same psychic material that is the stuff of psychosis and is found in the insane. This is the fund of unconscious images that fatally confuse the mental patient. But it is also the matrix of a mythological imagination, which has vanished from our rational age. (Jung, 1961, p. 188)

On the other hand, writers such as Paul J. Stern (1976) and Henri Ellenberger (1970) were convinced that Jung's voyage was not visionary but rather psychotic, not voluntary but uncontrollable. It must immediately be pointed out, however, that the question cannot be definitively answered on the basis of the published evidence. Each of us will form our own opinion, but it is important that such opinion be informed. For even if we decide that Jung had indeed undergone a psychotic episode, we cannot deny that he emerged from his descent with ideas and concepts that stand as creative, though still controversial, contributions to psychology. The 1913 to 1917 period of engulfment was not an isolated episode of visionary experience for Jung. From childhood, Jung engaged in confrontations with his own, seemingly independent, inner life. Many of the concepts of his later theoretical writings can be traced to Jung's gift for universalizing and externalizing his inner experiences. (cf. Atwood & Stolorow, 1977b; Jaffé, 1979).

Interestingly, there is a long history of people who dealt creatively with the very ingredients that would make most people mad. Emily Dickinson, Vincent Van Gogh, Friedrich Nietzsche, and William Blake are but four examples. Such individuals are antedated by the role of shamans in traditional tribal society. Shamans would enter into the worlds of dreams, fantasies, and visions and emerge not only intact but also with information important to society. In the West, the long tradition of saints, prophets, and healers goes back to Biblical times. The history of religion would not be the same without the influence of visionaries and their visions or other sources of inner knowledge.

The prophetic, shamanic role is one that Jung assumed for the modern world. Based on the dreams of his patients, he prophesized World War I and the demise of Communism and commented extensively on what he considered basic aberrations in the modern way of life (Jung, 1959). Shortly before his death, he expressed concerns about the possibility of a nuclear holocaust: "We need more understanding of human nature because the only real danger that exists is man himself" (Jung, 1959).

Themes of Jung's Boyhood

From the evidence of his memoirs and from information provided by his biographers, two related themes arose in Jung's experience before the age of 12. The first theme was his experience and conviction that he was actually two persons: the child he objectively seemed to be and also an authoritative wise old man who had lived in the eighteenth century. The precise imagery of Jung's other personality seems to have been adopted from a piece of terra cotta sculpture that depicted a well-known medical doctor of the day and his patient. So powerful was his sense of a past life that, in doing schoolwork, he would occasionally write "1786" instead of the correct date, 1886. The second theme was contained in Jung's secretly held belief that certain thoughts, dreams, visions, and fantasies he periodically experienced were truly important, externally derived revelations, secret wisdom that only a few, rare people were privileged to acquire.

The Stone

Between the ages of seven and nine, Jung had several experiences that helped form his belief that he actually had two distinct personalities. The first experience involved a game that Jung played with a large chunk of stone jutting from a garden wall. Frequently, when alone, Jung would mount the stone and pass the time in reverie:

> "I am sitting on top of this stone and it is underneath." But the stone also could say "I" and think: "I am lying here on this slope and he is sitting on top of me." The question then arose: "Am I the one who is sitting on the stone, or am I the stone on which he is sitting?" This question always perplexed me, and I would stand up, wondering who was what now. The answer remained totally unclear, and my uncertainty was accompanied by a feeling of curious and fascinating darkness. (Jung, 1961, p. 20)

Jung thought his apparent ability to shift his sense of his center of awareness to this chunk of stone was his first discovery of the "mysterious" in life. This sense of a deep connection with what was mysterious and hidden to others made him less open to the formal religious doctrines he heard. When the very religious adults around him (his father was a minister and his mother a minister's daughter) tried to "pump" religious teachings into him, Jung would inwardly resist: "Yes, but there is something else, something very secret that people don't know about" (1961, p. 22).

Jung realized that a self-calming motive lay behind his sometimes thinking that he was a stone rather than a person:

> . . . it was strangely reassuring and calming to sit on my stone. Somehow it would free me of all my doubts. Whenever I thought that I was the stone, the conflict ceased. "The stone has no uncertainties, no urge to communicate, and is eternally the same for thousands of years," I would think, "while I am only a passing phenomenon which bursts into all kinds of emotions, like a flame that flares up quickly and then goes out." I was but the sum of my emotions, and the Other in me was the timeless, imperishable stone. (Jung, 1961, p. 42)

The Mannequin

When Jung was ten years old, he carved from a wooden ruler a small male figure, a mannequin approximately two inches long. With ink and small bits of wool, Jung fashioned a miniature frock coat, shiny black boots, and a top hat for this mannequin. He also devised a little bed for the figure from a pencil case. Jung deposited in the pencil case, along with the mannequin and makeshift bed, a blackish oblong stone that he had painted with watercolors: "This was *his* [the mannequin's] stone. All this was a great secret. Secretly I took the case to . . . the attic at the top of the house . . . and hid it with great satisfaction on one of the beams under the roof—for no one must ever see it! . . . I felt safe, and the tormenting sense of being at odds with myself was gone" (Jung, 1961, p. 21).

Thereafter, whenever Jung was under stress, he would visualize his hidden mannequin and feel more at peace. Sometimes he would devise small scrolls of paper on which, in a secret language of his own invention, he would write a particularly pleasing saying. Each addition of a scroll to the mannequin's case was treated as a solemn ceremonial act to be guarded as an inviolable secret, "for the safety of my life depended on it" (1961, p. 22).

The dialogue with the stone and the creation of the wooden mannequin can be seen as attempts by Jung to concretize and thereby control his perhaps unsettling sense that he had two personalities. We can think of the stone and the mannequin as externalizations of the second personality that Jung was convinced that he harbored.

Let us look now at the family environment in which Jung grew up. Perhaps some insights might emerge regarding the origins of his unusual childhood (and lifelong) experiences.

Jung's father, the Reverend Dr. Paul Jung, had many disappointments. Failing to become a university professor in his field of Oriental languages, he settled for becoming a country parson. His wife was stronger willed than he and was constantly worried about his health. Jung reports that his father's depressed spirits and morose personality were due to a deep crisis of faith (1961, p. 73). Toward the end of his life, Jung's father became extremely hypochondriacal and believed that he suffered from a variety of diseases. Jung's father also had a more positive side. Jung described him as tolerant and approachable. His religious views as a pastor of the Swiss Reformed Church were traditional but not at all fanatical. Jung described him as reasonable and kind (Jung, 1959).

Jung's mother, Emilie, was, on the surface, an opposite personality to his father. Some of Jung's childhood sorrow stemmed from his experience of frequent parental disputes. Jung was convinced that his mother also possessed or was possessed by two personalities: one, the observable character of the pleasant, plump housewife. The other personality was that of a witch, prophetess, and seeress who communicated with spirits. Jung described his mother in this way:

> By day she was a loving mother, but at night she seemed uncanny. Then she was like one of those seers who is at the same time a strange animal, like a priestess in a bear's cave. Archaic and ruthless; ruthless as truth and nature. (1961, p. 50)

The "uncanny" personality in his mother seems to have emerged only at special moments. "She would then speak as if talking to herself, but what she said was aimed at me and usually struck to the core of my being, so that I was stunned into silence" (1961, p. 49). Early on, Jung decided to keep his own inner life hidden from his mother because he was unsure just how much control the uncanny personality exerted over the housewife personality (cf. Atwood & Stolorow, 1977b, p. 199).

Jung's propensity for endowing people with two personalities may have had its origins in his need to cope with feelings of vulnerability. His mother's uncanny personality emerged frequently when she was scolding young Carl or trying to instill in him good manners so that he would not embarrass the family with friends. It may have been easier for him to believe that a second personality within his mother administered these lessons. Likewise, his conviction that he himself consisted of two different individuals seems to have emerged originally during a scolding he received from a friend's father for some misbehavior related to the man's boat.

> . . . I was seized with rage that this fat, ignorant boor [i.e., the friend's father] should dare to insult ME. This ME was not only grown up, but important, an authority, a person with office and dignity, an old man, an object of respect and awe. Yet the contrast with reality was so grotesque that in the midst of my fury I suddenly stopped myself, for the question rose to my lips: "Who in the world are you, anyway?" . . . Then, to my intense confusion, it occurred to me that I was actually two different persons. One of them was the schoolboy who could not grasp algebra and was far from sure of himself; the other was important, a high authority, a man not to be trifled with. . . . This "other" was an old man who lived in the 18th century, wore buckled shoes and a white wig, and went driving in a fly with high, concave rear wheels. . . . (Jung, 1961, p. 34)

At one point, Jung was thoroughly challenged and almost overwhelmed by two dreams that revealed to him secrets that were so frightening and even blasphemous that he was terrified at first even to think of them.

The Phallus-God

The first of these secret dreams about the phallus-God occurred when Jung was three years old. Descending a stone stairway, he came upon a rounded archway closed off by a green curtain. In the dream, he pushed aside the curtain to expose a large rectangular chamber constructed of stone. In the center of the chamber stood a magnificent golden king's throne:

> Something was standing on [the throne] which I thought at first was a tree trunk 12 to
> 15 feet high and about one and a half to two feet thick. It was a huge thing, reaching almost
> to the ceiling. But it was of curious composition: it was made of skin and naked flesh, and
> on top there was something like a rounded head with no face and no hair. On the very top
> of the head was a single eye, gazing motionlessly upward. (Jung, 1961, p. 12)

Jung was paralyzed with terror at the sight of this huge column of flesh and was consumed with the fear that at any moment it would crawl off the throne. "At that moment I heard from outside and above me my mother's voice. She called out, "Yes, just look at him. That is the man-eater!'" (1961, p. 12). The dream haunted Jung for years, causing him nightmares when he could sleep, and enormous fear on those nights when sleep would not come.

Jung later interpreted the dream as a condensation of his childhood fears of Jesuits, members of a Catholic order about whom he had heard some frightening things. The column of flesh on the throne was an erect penis or phallus, a phallus-god, in fact. For Jung, Jesus was the aboveground counterpart of this subterranean monster. "Lord Jesus never became quite real for me, never quite acceptable, never quite lovable, for again and again I would think of his underground counterpart, a frightful revelation that had been accorded me without my seeking it" (1961, p. 13).

The Throne

Jung experienced an additional dreamlike vision relevant to this discussion. One afternoon, his mind was focused on the beauty of the day, the beauty of the nearby cathedral roof glinting in the sunlight, and the magnificence that God displayed in such creations. The image of God sitting on his golden throne in the beautiful clear blue sky came into Jung's mind. Suddenly he froze. No other images would come, but Jung intuitively knew that something monstrous and blasphemous was about to emerge. For days, he went about in a fog as he attempted to ward off the dreaded image. He feared that, were he even to entertain it a little, he would be plunged immediately into hell.

Three nights later, awaking from a restless sleep, Jung was struck with the thought: "Now, it is coming, now it's serious! *I must think*. It must be thought out beforehand. . . . Who wants to force me to think something I don't know and don't want to know?" (1961, p. 37). Jung finally convinced himself that it was God who intended that he think the unthinkable as a critical test of faith. Gathering his courage, Jung allowed the image he had been choking back for three days and nights to flood into awareness:

> I saw before me the cathedral, the blue sky. God sits on His golden throne, high above the
> world—and from under the throne an enormous turd falls upon the sparkling new roof,
> shatters it, and breaks the walls of the cathedral asunder. (1961, p. 39)

Jung immediately experienced relief from his turmoil. He explained to himself that his image of God befouling his own cathedral was God's way of revealing to him that

"God could be something terrible." Jung kept this dream secret during his boyhood. It motivated him to explore his father's theological books in search of further understanding of it. These studies would lead to his belief that even wise scholars and theologians could not fully explain or be a substitute for his first-hand religious and visionary experiences. One possible interpretation of Jung's dream is that God was no longer satisfied with the traditional forms of religion with which Jung was familiar. Such an interpretation is consistent with one of the themes of Jung's work—to preserve a sense of spirituality outside of the forms of organized religion.

SUMMARY OF SOME MAJOR THEMES OF JUNG'S LIFE

We can now review some major themes of Jung's life:

1. The first theme was that Jung's dreams, visions, and secrets resulted in a sense of isolation and independence of viewpoint beginning during his boyhood.

> My one great achievement during those years was that I resisted the temptation to talk about it with anyone. Thus the pattern of my relationship to the world was already prefigured: today as then I am a solitary, because I know things and must hint at things which other people do not know, and usually do not even want to know. (1961, pp. 41–42)

2. A second theme was Jung's conviction that he consisted of two separate persons. Some of the motives that shaped this odd belief: Jung's family dissatisfaction, his sense of inferiority, his religious skepticism in a home where religion was paramount, and his desire for the alleviation of stressful situations. This second theme includes the idea that some inner experiences may be truthful revelations. This idea later became one basis for many of Jung's ideas—including the *collective unconscious, archetypes* or inherited images that reside there, and the *synchronicity* between internal psychic events and external equivalents. He viewed his sense of being two persons, his visions and his dreams as gifts full of knowledge and wisdom bestowed by a truthful and holy source. He was convinced that his personalities were not evidence of a psychopathological "split personality" or schizophrenic dissociation (1961, p. 45).

3. Jung was also sure that his descent into the unconscious was a foray after truth, not a psychotic folly.

Whatever one's opinion on these matters, the fact remains that Jung's theorizing was shaped by his experiences of two personalities and his dreams, fantasies, and intuitions, which eventually included a vivid dream experience of being many miles above the earth:

> Far below my feet lay Ceylon, and in the distance ahead of me the subcontinent of India. My field of vision did not include the whole earth, but its global shape was plainly distinguishable and its outline shone with a silvery gleam through that

---

BOX 4.1   *Only Connect . . .*

Jung's view of some (not all) dreams and visions as gifts to be experienced, reexperienced, and cherished is far from Freud's idea of dreams as disguised transformations of taboo thoughts and feelings. Jung's view is very similar to that of traditional cultures, which viewed dreams as gifts from the spirits or gods. In such cultures, a dream or vision might be a sought-after and treasured experience with possible significance for the entire society. Alfred Adler (Chapter 5) had a more practical view of dreams as assisting the ego to act.

> wonderful blue light. . . . Later I discovered how high in space one would have to be to have so extensive a view—approximately a thousand miles! The sight of the earth from this height was *the most glorious thing I had ever seen.* (Jung, 1961, pp. 289–290, italics added)

In his memoirs, Jung reports that, when he was 69 years of age, he had a dream of seeing a yogi meditating:

> When I looked at him more closely I realized that he had my face. I stared in profound fright, and awakened with the thought: 'Aha, so he is the one who is meditating me. He has a dream, and I am it.' I knew that when he awakened, *I would no longer be.* . . . In the opinion of the "other side" our unconscious existence is the real one and our conscious world a kind of illusion, an apparent reality. (Jung, 1972, p. 323, italics added)

Toward the end of his life, Jung was fully able to accept both the rational and the irrational as co-partners in the events of the psyche. He was, furthermore, capable of welcoming the mysterious with a relish no less than his acceptance of the merely logical.

JUNG AND FREUD

It is necessary, at least very briefly, to discuss the development of the relationship between Jung and Freud. Their ideas are intertwined and share much in common. Jung drew much from Freud's concepts. In fact, after Freud's death, he wrote, "Without Freud's psychoanalysis, I wouldn't have had had a clue" (as quoted in McLynn, 1997). After a period of cooperation with Freud, however, Jung began to question Freud's ideas and further develop his own.

After an initial period of mutual admiration, there was growing and intense ambivalence between the two men. Meeting in 1909, Freud, for example, thought Jung harbored a death wish against him and fainted in Jung's presence (McLynn, 1997, p. 135). By 1913, the break with Freud and the Freudians had become permanent. As we have seen, this period also signaled Jung's development of the most distinctive aspects of his own theorizing and his own personal voyage into the depths of the collective unconscious.

Finally, in the 1930s, after many years of bitterness between the two camps, Jung wrote anti-Freudian and apparently anti-Semitic statements. Though not an outright Nazi, many people saw Jung as, at the very least, morally neutral when it came to fascism. His theory of archetypes allowed him to see many aspects of a vicious totalitarian system as simply the expression of long hidden archetypal themes, such as that of the mythical Teutonic personage Wotan (McLynn, 1997). Jung said Hitler was "just a hero myth" (Jung, in Evans, 1976, p. 86).

Jung and Freud thus ultimately came to see their theories as opposed and themselves as rivals. There was, to the end, no reconciliation between the two, even though Jung tried to donate funds to help Freud leave Vienna to flee from Nazi persecution. In spite of his decades-long competition with Freud, Jung thus attempted to aid him. In a poignant scene, Freud refused to accept the money that Jung's cousin brought to his door (McLynn, 1997).

STRUCTURE OF THE PSYCHE:
EGO, PERSONAL, AND COLLECTIVE UNCONSCIOUS

In light of his clinical observations with schizophrenic patients such as the young visionary clerk, along with his own self-analysis, Jung's approach to personality theory was necessarily different from Freud's. In Jung's view, the chief problem that Freud had not solved was how to explain the individual's construction of fantasies and dreams that embody symbols and themes unlikely to be part of an individual's strictly personal experiences. He began by formulating the existence of a *collective unconscious* in addition to Freud's ego and *personal unconscious* as part of the psyche. He also significantly modified Freud's ideas of the *personal unconscious* and its functions.

Let us first consider what Jung meant by **psyche.** The *psyche* ["soul" in Greek] is the total of all the conscious and unconscious contents of the mind including the conscious ego, thoughts and feelings, memories, surface and deeper emotions, the personal unconscious, the collective unconscious, and a multitude of archetypes including the most spiritual. It is important to indicate that the psyche is far more extensive than the individual's own conscious sense of his or her personality, or than the images an individual would project to the world. These comprise the archetype of the persona, which is only one, mostly surface, aspect of the psyche. Within the psyche, there is space for all the psychodynamics, transformations, and growth about which Jung theorizes.

The Conscious Ego

The **conscious ego,** for Jung, corresponds roughly to what Freud meant by the same term. Functioning as the conscious part of personality, the ego includes all external sense impressions, thoughts, and awareness of feelings and bodily sensations. Consciousness consists of all those internal and external events that are within our awareness at a given moment.

The Personal Unconscious

Jung's second division of the mind, the **personal unconscious,** is partly similar and partly different from what Freud termed the *unconscious.* Jung conceived of the personal unconscious as the necessary surface aspect of the unconscious.

Jung agreed with Freud that the personal unconscious contains ideas and impulses that have been actively withdrawn from consciousness by repression. Such content is kept unconscious because it involves repressing motives, the awareness of which would be threatening to the ego (1931, p. 151). This part of Jung's personal unconscious corresponds in a general way to Freud's *dynamic unconscious.*

Jung also included mental content which, through disuse or inattention, does not at the moment occupy awareness, but which can become conscious at will. (Freud would have called such momentarily latent content *preconscious.*) Even out of awareness, however, all the activities that normally take place consciously also are recorded unconsciously (Jung, 1931, p. 144). Therefore, the personal unconscious also consists of all those contents that became unconscious simply because they lost their intensity and were not attended to or forgotten. This aspect of Jung's personal unconscious is equivalent to *long-term memory* in contemporary cognitive psychology.

Despite areas of agreement with Freud, Jung viewed the personal unconscious as having different functions from Freud's dynamic unconscious mind. For Jung, the personal unconscious has both retrospective and prospective aspects. It is oriented not only by the individual's past but also by anticipations of the future. Jung noted that his patients often had dreams that could aptly be described as "forward looking" in the sense that, though the individual was not yet aware of his or her decision or feelings, a dream revealed that the unconscious had already solved some problem or made some decision (1916, p. 255).

Jung's personal unconscious also has a **compensatory function.** When an individual's conscious attitude leans too one-sidedly in a single direction, the unconscious may

---

Jung's concept of archetype anticipated the concept in evolutionary psychology (Chapter 18) that organisms, including humans, have inherited proclivities to behave in certain ways. This concept is very similar to Jung's concepts of archetypes and the collective unconscious. Jung's ideas include, more explicitly than does evolutionary psychology, the idea of the inheritance of proclivities for developing specific forms of imagery and subjective experiences.

---

compensate for the imbalance by producing dreams or fantasies that emphasize the opposite tendency (Jung, 1916, pp. 252–253). For example, a person with a sedate existence may have dreams involving exciting adventures. Compensation may also be seen in dreams that make available to consciousness all that was subliminal or not attended to during the day.

The function of prospection may aid the individual's adaptation to life, as for example when the individual is confronted with a difficult problem. In the morning, the solution may pop suddenly into mind as if the problem had been continuously worked on while the individual was sleeping. Jung also thought that people could have accurate precognitive hunches about future events, sometimes based only on intuitive, inner knowing (Jung, 1961).

The Collective Unconscious

At a deeper level than the personal unconscious lies the *impersonal* or *transpersonal* unconscious. This transpersonal domain is "detached from anything personal and is common to all men, since its contents can be found everywhere" (Jung, 1917, p. 66). Jung termed this layer of the unconscious the **collective unconscious.**

Stored within the recesses of the collective unconscious are the primordial images and ideas that have been common to human beings. These images represent *possibilities* of action; *predispositions* to respond to external events in specific ways, and *potentialities* of shaping experience in certain directions. They are, in short, flexible templates, or models, for current experience to follow (Jung, 1936, pp. 66 ff.).

Jung termed these images of the collective unconscious **archetypes,** in the sense of *prototypes,* or molds, of reaction. As a kind of template or model, the archetypes organize and shape the course of an individual's interactions with the external world and with the inner world of the personal unconscious.

ORIGIN OF THE ARCHETYPES

The collective unconscious did not develop in any one person's lifetime. Jung asserts that its contents are inherited from the sum total of all human experience. Jung noted that, within the course of the history of humanity, certain fundamental day-to-day events had to be experienced by all members of the human family. For example, the rising and setting of the sun surely did not escape the notice of even the most primitive humans.

> One of the commonest and at the same time most impressive experiences is the apparent movement of the sun every day. We certainly cannot discover anything of the kind in the unconscious, so far as the known physical process is concerned. What we do find, on the other hand, is the myth of the sun-hero in all its countless variations. It is this myth, and not the actual physical process, that forms the sun archetype. The same can be said of the phases of the moon. The archetype is a kind of readiness to produce over and over again the same or

similar mythical ideas. Hence it seems as though what is impressed upon the unconscious were exclusively the subjective fantasy-ideas aroused by the physical process. We may therefore assume that the archetypes are recurrent impressions made by subjective reactions. (Jung, 1917, p. 69)

Archetypes, in this view, are the cumulative effect of perpetually repeated experiences on the human nervous system's development. It is not the memory of the actual physical experience itself that is inherited. The repetitive subjective reaction to the event is impressed on unconscious mental processes. It is this internal state, this predisposition to react in a similar way to repetitions of the physical event, that is transmitted to future generations. Thus the archetypes in the collective unconscious are residues of ancestral emotional life (Jung, 1917, p. 77).

Jung's concept of the development of the collective unconscious and its contents are closely related to the discredited Lamarckian theory of evolution, which asserted that acquired characteristics can be inherited. In Lamarck's view, parental experiences or at least the learning that accrued from them could be transmitted to offspring. Modern biologists do not accept the view that characteristics or experiences acquired in an organism's life can be biologically or genetically passed on to offspring.

Jung's critics interpreted his concept of the formation of the collective unconscious as an instance of inheriting acquired characteristics. Jung's repeated explanations did not help much in dispelling this conclusion, for Jung often treated the subject abstractly and with vague, imprecise language that definitely seemed to support a Lamarckian view. In the last decade, the pendulum has begun to swing a direction more sympathetic to Jung's ideal of the collective unconscious even though Lamarckian notions are still discredited. Contemporary evolutionary psychological theories agree that people have complex instincts but do not agree with a Lamarckian explanation (see Chapter 18). The mechanism for this evolutionary process is not considered to be the inheritance of acquired characteristics as Lamarck—and probably Jung also—theorized, but rather selected variations in the genetic makeup and neural wiring of people, an explanation in keeping with modern biological understanding.

Symbol-Making Processes

Jung himself asked the most significant question of his theory: ". . . why does the psyche not register the actual process, instead of mere fantasies about the physical process?" Jung's answer centered on some well-known hypotheses about the mind of primitive people, namely, James George Frazer's concept of sympathetic magic and Lucien Lévy-Bruhl's treatment of the "participation mystique."

Frazer postulated that early humans interpreted their world magically by assuming that events, though separated in time or space, could nevertheless affect one another. Frazer called this assumption of a type of parapsychological phenomenon, "sympathetic magic." Such mental functioning is based on the idea that, through some mysterious or unknowable means, events and objects may exert a mutual reaction without any physical cause and effect. For example, some early people believed that the fingernail clippings and hanks of hair they stole from an enemy could be used to gain control over that individual. What was done to the nail fragments and hair, would, mysteriously, affect their owner (Frazer, 1963). Lévy-Bruhl went a step further and suggested that what he considered the "primitive mind" could not clearly distinguish between self and object, between what is "me, mine" and what is external. For the primitive person, what happens outside *is* happening inside (Jung, 1931, p. 154).

For early humans, then, what was of supreme importance was not the external physical event, or an objective conception of cause and effect. They may not even have made such distinctions. Their ultimate reality was the self, its emotions, and its desires. Crucial for the early human was the emotional significance of events, for "his emotions are more important to him than physics; therefore what he registers is his emotional fantasies. . . . It is not thunder and lightning, not rain and cloud that remain as images in the psyche, but the fantasies caused by the affects they arouse" (1931, pp. 154–155).

In this view, people do not store within their brains the exact photographic copies of their ancestors' experiences. Each successive culture, each individual, creates afresh the myth and the associated symbolism of the sun god, or the hero, or the god of thunder when external events demand reaction. The *mythological tendency,* the predisposition to respond to these external events in specific ways, and the disposition to be deeply affected by such events are the real legacy of past generations. "The primitive mentality does not *invent* myths, it *experiences* them" (Jung, 1940, p. 154).

Jung subsequently devoted a significant part of his life to discovering and elucidating specific archetypal images as they appeared in mythological stories, dreams, fantasies, and in paintings. Presumably, there is no preexisting limit to the number of archetypes that are possible. Among the most frequently appearing, however, are the following.

Child-God Archetype

The Christ child and personifications of children as elves or dwarfs are depicted throughout legend and religious lore as having divine or mystical powers. Jung discovered this archetype in female patients who had an imaginary child. Such a child may symbolize anticipation of future events and is likely to make its appearance as an archetype when an individual is in the process of beginning an initiative or new direction (Jung, 1940, p. 164). The infant symbolizing the New Year is a popular example of this archetype.

Mother Archetype

The Mother archetype may be elicited from an individual's collective unconscious in response to a real mother, mother-in-law, grandmother, or stepmother. Even figurative mothers may provoke the emergence of the Mother archetype as symbolized by a wife, Divine Mother (Virgin Mary), an institution, or any event, place, or person associated with fertility and fruitfulness. Most students react to their college or university (Alma Mater) in terms of this mother archetype. The Mother archetype can be positive or negative, light or dark, good or evil. For example, the goddess of fate (Moira) can be kind and generous, or remorseless and heartless. Evil-Mother archetype symbols abound: the witch, the dragon (or any devouring and entwining animal) (Jung, 1938, p. 82). Thus the Mother archetype includes both the loving and the terrible mother.

Trickster or Magician Archetype

Jung explored the figure of the Trickster or Magician through a variety of myths, most notably in Native American mythology. A characteristic of this mythical figure is his fondness for sly jokes, malicious pranks, and his dual nature: half animal, half human. The demonic figures of the Old Testament, even the characterization of Yahweh himself as Trickster undergoing transformation into a divine savior, embody this age-old myth (Jung, 1954, p. 256).

Hero Archetype

According to Jung, the finest expression of the symbol-making capacity of the collective unconscious is the figure of the Hero, or its opposite, the demon (e.g., Anti-Christ, Satan). Hero myths are common to many cultures and tend to share the same characteristics. The Hero defeats evil, slays the dragon or monster, usually near water, suffers punishment for another, or rescues the vanquished and downtrodden (Jung, 1917, p. 99). To provide only one of scores of examples in popular culture, Luke Skywalker played the hero role in *Star Wars*.

Shadow as Archetype

Within our personal unconscious there are repressed, unacceptable motives, tendencies, and desires. There is thus within us an inferior, undesirable aspect to our personality. Jung calls this side of our inner life the **Shadow,** the "dark half" of personality. It is the side of ourselves that we would prefer not to recognize. The Shadow is common to all people. It is both a personal and a collective unconscious phenomenon (Jung, 1968, pp. 21–22).

Mythologically, Shadow symbols include demons, devils, and evil ones. This archetype may be evoked in our relations with another when we feel terribly uncomfortable with a person but are unable to specify exactly what provokes the distress. We might sense, for example, an immediate dislike for some people we hardly even know. In such cases we may be projecting our shadow side onto them because we recognize in these persons something that we do not like in ourselves (Jung, 1917, p. 95). In the case of war, one side may project their shadows upon the enemy, who might be seen as cunning, treacherous, and sinister. People usually see their own side as clever, courageous, and righteous. In popular culture, the *Star Wars* character Darth Vader is a good example of the Shadow archetype; he contains unacceptable qualities of evil and cunning.

It is difficult to deal with the Shadow archetype. If we fail to recognize the "inferior" dark side of ourselves, there is the possibility of separation of the Shadow from the conscious experience of the ego. In this case, our personality would be incomplete, truncated. Harmonious and balanced psychological development involves becoming aware of and accepting the existence of our shadow qualities. We may come to recognize that we are not entirely free of what we consider the bad or evil traits we see in others.

Animus and Anima Archetypes

During the period when Jung was experimenting with the descent into his unconscious, he asked himself the question "What am I really doing?" Abruptly, a "voice" within said: "It is art." Jung was astonished and somewhat annoyed—astonished because the voice was a woman's, and annoyed because he did not agree with her assessment.

> Then I thought, "Perhaps my unconscious is forming a personality that is not me, but which is insisting on coming through to expression." I knew for a certainty that the voice had come from a woman. I recognized it as the voice of a patient, a talented psychopath who had a strong transference to me [i.e., an inappropriate but strong attachment to her therapist]. She had become a living figure within my mind. (Jung, 1961, p. 185)

Jung struck up a conversation with this new feminine personality, which rapidly turned into an argument over whether Jung's exploration of his unconscious was science, art, or something else. The conflict was resolved when Jung insisted to his inner feminine personality that what he was doing was neither science nor art; it was nature. He now encouraged her to speak through himself and felt both awed and perturbed:

> I was greatly intrigued by the fact that a woman should interfere with me from within. My conclusion was that she must be the "soul," in the primitive sense, and I began to speculate on the reasons why the name "anima" was given to the soul. Later I came to see that this inner feminine figure plays a typical, or archetypal, role in the unconscious of a man, and I called her the "anima." The corresponding figure in the unconscious of woman I called the "animus." (Jung, 1961, p. 186)

Once again, Jung found his own interior world divided and populated by autonomous personalities. It was only a short step from this experience of personal division to proposing universal, gender-based opposites: Accordingly, no man could be entirely masculine or exclusively male. Feminine elements, attitudes, and intuitions are part of every man's character. This is not often apparent because, traditionally, men strive to repress their weak, soft, feminine traits.

Jung presumed that repression of feminine qualities would lead to a buildup of libidinal tension within the male's unconscious. In striving to win a woman as a mate, a man unconsciously projects these feminine traits and the feminine image of himself that he has so actively repressed (Jung, 1917, p. 189). This internalized feminine image is based on his real experiences with women (his mother, sister, etc.) and on the collective experiences of men throughout history (Jung, 1917, p. 190). The projected image of femininity from a man's collective unconscious is his **anima** as is a woman's conscious experience of what are considered feminine qualities. The anima determines a man's relationship to women throughout his life and shapes his understanding of those relationships. In a sense, a man's first repressed and then projected anima compensates for the otherwise one-sided masculine nature of his personality.

Likewise, the woman has her inherited masculine image, her **animus,** which is also the conscious sense of masculine qualities in a male.

> If I were to attempt to put in a nutshell the difference between man and woman in this respect, i.e., what it is that characterizes the animus as opposed to the anima, I could say only this: as the anima produces moods [in the male], so the animus produces [in the female] *opinions* . . . (Jung, 1917, p. 207)

Jung suggested that the opinions of a woman's animus have the character of solid convictions with unassailable validity. The moods of the man's anima are often expressed in sudden changes in temperament, or character, so that a man may say, "I was not myself today."

The woman's animus, unlike the man's anima, usually does not consist of a single personification, but rather of a plurality of masculine figures. "The animus is rather like an assembly of fathers or dignitaries of some kind who lay down incontestable 'rational' *ex cathedra* judgments" (Jung, 1917, p. 207). The animus is thus the embodiment of all of a woman's ancestral experiences of man.

A danger of the anima and the animus lies in the possibility that the entire psyche may come under the exclusive sway of these images so that a man loses his masculinity and a woman her femininity (Jung, 1917, p. 209). Yet, without recognition of their inherent opposites, man and woman run the risk of being permanently incomplete.

One can question the degree to which Jung's formulation of the animus and anima archetypes reflected the role of men and women in Western society in the nineteenth and early part of the twentieth century. In a society with a greater opportunity for women to be more autonomous and independent, Jung's model seems to express mostly traditional gender roles. It is possible to disengage the meanings of anima and animus from the specifics of gender and refer to them as more general psychological characteristics, which may be conscious to one extent or another in both men and women.

The Persona Archetype

Persona is Latin for the mask that actors in Roman and Greek drama wore to depict their roles (see Chapter 1). Thus the **persona** in Jung's theory is the front we present to others because social living makes demands for certain kinds of behavior. Society establishes certain expectations and certain roles around which we must shape our public selves, and behind which we hide our "private" selves (Jung, 1917, p. 192).

There is danger in the persona, for "people really do exist who believe they are what they pretend to be" (Jung, 1917, p. 193). When the mask and the ego become identical, the personal unconscious must find an alternate means of expression and representation for its demands in consciousness. Thus, "Whoever builds up too good a persona for himself naturally has to pay for it with irritability" (Jung, 1917, p. 193).

As described thus far, the persona is an individual creation, rather than an archetypal form. But there is also an impersonal or transpersonal aspect to the persona. It comes into existence to smooth the individual's collective existence as an individual among individuals. "It is, as its name implies, only a mask of the collective psyche, a mask that feigns individuality, making others and oneself believe that one is individual, whereas one is simply acting a role through which the collective psyche speaks" (Jung, 1917, p. 157).

Fundamentally, therefore, the content and form of the individual's persona is a projection of the collective unconscious. There are individual differences only in the choice of collective unconscious themes that the individual will role-play, but the themes themselves are born of universal and impersonal archetypal images. The persona is an ideal image, a desirable actor's part, a compromise between the individual and humanity as a whole, past and present, as to what a person should appear to be (Jung, 1917, p. 158).

To understand the importance of the persona in the psyche, all one has to do is think of all the energy and thought each of us puts into honing the image that we present to the world and how much we depend on others presenting us with their personas. When we meet someone for the first time, we are uncomfortable unless we have clues as to their identity, who and what they are. A person who has not formed a clear persona image can be seen as drifting or aloof. A person too attached to some aspects of his persona may view everything he or she experiences too narrowly in terms of a specific social role.

Other Archetypes

Jung discovered a whole array of archetypes in his work with clients, his personal introspective work, and his study of mythic and religious symbols and themes. Just for starters, there are the Eternal Child (a youthful and creative Peter Pan-like archetype), the Wise Old Man, the Trickster, Wotan, and the Hero archetypes. A sensual Bacchus-like figure is another archetype, as are a Venus- or Aphrodite-like archetype. One clue to archetypal identities is the panoply of ancient or tribal gods and goddesses, each representing a different aspect of the psyche. Another way of uncovering archetypes is to examine the themes behind the most popular and energized figures of contemporary popular culture. People like Elvis Presley, Marilyn Monroe, John F. Kennedy, and Michael Jackson have elicited projections of archetypal themes by the public.

ARCHETYPES AND SYNCHRONICITY

Archetypes can channel great emotion. Jung pointed out that sometimes an archetype might even take control of the personality so that individual behavior from that point onward is actually modified and directed by the collective unconscious. In fact, Jung thought that groups of people, even whole civilizations, might project the meanings of a given archetype at a given point in history. The course of that civilization may then move in the direction of the archetypal theme that emerges. For example, a satanic or demonic archetype may have made its appearance during the years of the rise to power of the Nazis. The reverse may, of course, also occur. A return to religious commitment or faith may be preceded by an emergence of the God archetype. This might have been the case, for example, during the "Great Awakening" in American history, a religious revival in the early 1800s that transformed American society and led to the abolitionist movement.

Jung proposed the principle of **synchronicity** to account for events that are related through meaning but with no apparent physical cause-and-effect sequence. For example, one might dream of the death of a relative with whom little contact has been had in recent years. A day after the dream, word arrives announcing that relative's death. The two events, dream and relative's death, are not related causally. The dream did not cause the relative's death any more than the future demise could have caused an anticipatory dream. The two events are related through *meaningful simultaneity* without apparent physical cause and effect. Jung termed such a phenomenon *synchronicity* (1952).

Jung's explanation of synchronistic events involved the emergence of an archetype from the collective unconscious. An individual's collective unconscious, containing the wisdom of humanity, knows more than the individual does. In the case cited, the dream and death, the archetypal figure of death had begun to penetrate into the dreamer's consciousness and real-life experience as well. For the collective unconscious, time is relative. Future, present, and past are one. For the dreamer, the dream and subsequent death are uncannily coincidental, but, from the standpoint of collective unconscious, the dream and the death are both part of an integral whole.

What are the implications of Jung's ideas about synchronicity for our lives? If you accept his theory, synchronicities point to deeper meanings to which we should pay attention. An incidence of synchronicity is like a universal exclamation point that makes us attend to the meanings that are entering our experience. On the other hand, one might consider such events to be mere randomly determined coincidences, without any particular meaning. Jung's assumptions concerning his concept of synchronicity seem impossible to prove or disprove empirically. Whether one is attracted to the idea of synchronicity or not seems more a question of personal belief than of scientific evidence.

IMAGINING THE CLINICAL PERSPECTIVES OF FREUD AND ADLER

Jung was concerned with the differences between the views of Sigmund Freud and Alfred Adler (Chapter 5) and presented a case of a distressed neurotic person to be analyzed from the viewpoint of each theory.

> A young woman begins to have attacks of anxiety. At night she wakes up from a nightmare with a blood-curdling cry, is scarcely able to calm herself, clings to her husband and implores him not to leave her, demanding assurance that he really loves her, etc. Gradually a nervous asthma develops, the attacks also coming during the day. (Jung, 1917, p. 35)

A strictly Freudian approach to this woman's difficulty, according to Jung, would begin by eliciting from the patient her associations to the nightmare, exploring her past anxiety dreams, and by investigating the circumstances of her childhood and familial relations. With such a thorough evaluation of the patient the following facts would be discovered:

- Her prior dreams involved ferocious bulls, lions, tigers, and evil men attacking her.
- She had lost her father when she was 14; before his death, when she was on an outing in Paris with him at the *Follies Bergeres,* a dancer had looked at her father in a brazen way, and he had returned her gaze with an "animal look."

- From then on, the girl's relationship with her father changed. The patient reported that the dancer's gaze and her father's return stare had reminded her of the look in the wild animals' eyes in her dreams, and of the look of a former lover of her own who had treated her badly.

- The first appearance of her neurosis came when she had her second child and discovered that her husband evidenced a "tender interest" in another woman.

- After her father's sudden death, she succumbed to fits of uncontrolled weeping followed by equally uncontrollable episodes of hysterical laughter.

Jung pointed out that the Freudian interpretation of this information would center on the woman's inability to break with her father as a young girl, her Electra complex, and on the sexual imagery of the animals in her dreams in relation to her father's animal-like stare at the dancer. Her husband's feelings for another woman—after she herself had become a *mother* for the second time—bore a powerful unconscious similarity to the relationship between her own mother and father. Her hysterical laughing and weeping fits betrayed the ambivalence she experienced toward her husband, and more fundamentally, toward her father.

What would happen, Jung wanted to know, if the same case history were subjected to a different theoretical analysis? Alfred Adler, one of Freud's early colleagues, developed a different way of approaching such cases. For Adler, the key human motivation was a struggle to compensate for any perceived sense of inferiority. Compensation for inferiority feelings takes the form of a struggle for its opposite, superiority, and emerges as a fight for power in human relationships (Adler, 1959; we discuss Adler's theory in Chapter 5). According to Jung, Adler would see in this case various techniques of interpersonal domination and striving for power such as the woman's plea for her husband not to leave her, her demand for assurances of love, and her asthma. Her sense of loneliness and helplessness was provoked by the dancer episode and repeated by her reaction to her husband's interest in another woman (Jung, 1917, p. 39).

Whether Adler and Freud would have agreed with Jung's application of their viewpoints is not known. What is important, however, is that Jung was interested in the fact that major differences in interpretation would result from different personality theorists viewing the same case. Each would approach the personality of his patients from the perspective of his or her own theory. Jung began to see the differences between the views of Freud, Adler, and himself as an interesting and important problem to be solved. He eventually began to see that not only were Freud and Adler different in intellectual skills and theoretical viewpoint, but also, more important, each was a distinctly different type of personality. What emerged from this effort to understand the differences between theories was first an understanding of the personality theorists themselves and finally, Jung indicated, to his theory of psychological types (Jung, 1921).

JUNGIAN ATTITUDE TYPES: FREUD THE EXTROVERT AND ADLER THE INTROVERT

According to Jung, the Freudian interpretation of the case just discussed centers on the woman's problem with unresolved sexual and emotional dependence on the father. That pattern of dependence on a significant external love object is repeated, in the Freudian view, throughout the woman's life (e.g., with her husband). For Freud, according to Jung, the key element is the individual's conscious and unconscious relationship to people and things in the external world (1917, p. 41). For Adler, on the other hand, the focus is more subjective with the accent on the individual's striving for inner security and compensation for perceived personal inferiority, as interpreted by Jung.

Jung formulated a problem out of his ruminations on the differences in approach of Freud and Adler:

> The spectacle of this dilemma made me ponder the question: are there at least two different human types, one of them more interested in the [external] object, the other more interested in himself? (1917, p. 43)

Adler, it seemed to Jung, was an *introvert* whereas Freud appeared to be more of an *extrovert.* Jung described **introversion,** which he considered the first attitude and **extroversion,** which he termed "the second attitude."

> The first attitude [introversion] is normally characterized by a hesitant, reflective, retiring nature that keeps itself to itself, shrinks from objects, is always slightly on the defensive and prefers to hide behind mistrustful scrutiny. The second [extroversion] is normally characterized by an outgoing, candid, and accommodating nature that adapts easily to a given situation, quickly forms attachments, and, setting aside any possible misgivings, will often venture forth with careless confidence into unknown situations. (Jung, 1917, p. 44)

Thus Freud and Adler were bound by their own personality type to see only one viable interpretation of the psychology of others.

It is possible that Jung's explanation of how Adler and Freud's personal differences gave rise to his own notion of two fundamental personality types is incomplete. Perhaps Jung's own history of experiencing competing personalities within himself and in those close to him also contributed to his development of the idea of psychological types. His conclusions may result more from inner reflection than from abstract theorizing.[2]

Jung also proposed that the differences between introverts and extroverts in relation to subjective and objective experience were not absolute. In some cases, introverts will be more interested in the objective, external world, when that world affects their inner lives. Conversely, extroverts are more interested in the subjective world when the objective world has caused them disappointment. Then, the extrovert will withdraw into moodiness and subjective, egocentric behavior.

At all events, it is clear that Jung was not satisfied with the simple division of personality into two rigid types (1921, p. 6). He postulated, in addition to the attitude types of introversion/extroversion, four functional types: (1) sensation; (2) intuition; (3) thinking; (4) feeling. Thus, the introvert and extrovert personalities have gradations and variety. In all, disregarding the infinite variety that degree of expression may provide, there are eight combined attitude-function types of introvert and extrovert. A brief consideration of the four functions is in order before we undertake a survey of these eight types.

THE FUNCTIONS OF THE PSYCHE

Jung postulated that the mind has a number of specific functions, directed on the one hand to mediating intercourse with the external world and, on the other, focused on relations with one's own inner world, the world of the personal and collective unconscious. To those functions of consciousness directed outwardly to the world, Jung gave the name ectopsychic. To the functions of the unconscious in its relations with the ego, Jung gave the name endopsychic (1968, p. 11). The endopsychic functions were not emphasized in Jung's theory and we omit them in the present discussion.

---

[2]Christopher Monte's student, Cynthia Dowd, shared this insight.

Ectopsychic Functions

The **ectopsychic functions** were those that Jung emphasized in constructing his introversion/extroversion typology. The first ectopsychic function is *sensation,* "which is the sum total of external facts given to me through the functions of my senses" (Jung, 1968, p. 11). Thus sensation is concerned with orientation to reality: "Sensation tells me that something is; it does not tell me *what* it is" (Jung, 1968, p. 11; 1921, p. 461, definition 47).

The second ectopsychic function is *thinking* and is complementary to sensation, for thinking "in its simplest form tells you what a thing is. It gives a name to the thing" (Jung, 1968, p. 11; 1921, p. 481, definition 53). For Jung, the term thinking was to be restricted to "the linking up of ideas by means of a concept, in other words, to an act of judgment, no matter whether this act is intentional or not" (1921, p. 481).

The third ectopsychic function is *feeling.* For Jung, the concept of feeling had a somewhat restricted meaning. "Feeling informs you through its feeling-tones of the values of things. Feeling tells you, for instance, whether a thing is acceptable or agreeable or not. It tells you what a thing is worth to you" (1968, p. 12). Feeling may give rise in isolated circumstances to mood, an emotional state of acceptance or rejection. Thus feeling is a subjective process that is independent of external stimuli (Jung, 1921, p. 434, definition 21).

The fourth and last ectopsychic function is *intuition.* Sensation tells us that a thing is; thinking tells us what that thing is; and feeling tells us what that thing is worth to us, whether we like or dislike it. The only conscious function left is an awareness of time, the past and the future of a thing, where it has come from, and where it is going. Intuition is composed of hunches about the origins and the prospects of a thing (Jung, 1968, p. 13). Jung found it very difficult to define intuition, but he pointed to the conditions, familiar to almost everyone, under which we use intuition: "Whenever you have to deal with strange conditions where you have no established values or established concepts, you will depend upon that faculty of intuition" (1968, p. 14). Intuition is therefore the psychological function that mediates perceptions in an unconscious way so that our experience of intuitive problem solutions is that they spring on us suddenly, without conscious intent (Jung, 1921, p. 453, definition 35).

Rational Versus Irrational Functions

The four ectopsychic functions can be further classified as either **rational or irrational functions** depending on how much reasoning or judging is involved. Hence, **sensation and intuition** are classified as *irrational* because conscious reasoning is, by Jung's definitions, virtually absent in these functions. By contrast, **thinking and feeling** are classified as *rational* functions because both involve the judgmental process and the "supremacy of reason" (Jung, 1921, pp. 359ff.; 1968, p. 12). Feeling is therefore considered a rational function in this typology, at variance with the commonly held conception that feelings are often irrational.

During the course of his famous Tavistock Lectures, Jung employed the diagram shown in Figure 4.3 to summarize the four ectopsychic functions and their relationships in the psyche. In the central circle of Figure 4.2 is the ego, the center of conscious self-awareness and possessor of the psychic energy. At the top of the compasslike diagram is thinking (T) and its direct opposite on the lowest spoke, feeling (F). Thus the diagram represents the type of person whose *superior function* (topmost in the diagram) is reason or thought, and whose *inferior function* (lowermost spoke) is feeling, "for when you think you must exclude feeling, just as when you feel you must exclude thinking" (Jung, 1968, p. 16).

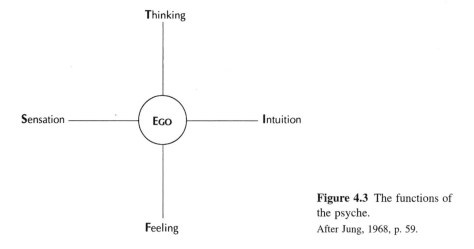

Figure 4.3 The functions of the psyche.
After Jung, 1968, p. 59.

To represent the opposite type of personality, the individual for whom feeling is the superior function and thinking the inferior, the T and F spokes would be reversed. The two other possible types of personality may be represented, depending on the dominance of either sensation (S) or intuition (I), by rotating the spokes of the compass accordingly.

Each of these four functional types may dominate the basic introvert or extrovert attitude orientation. The eight resulting personality types are summarized in Figure 4.4. Psychological types are not fixed. Jung suggested that an individual's type might change over time (1921, p. 405). Which function that is superior or most fully differentiated at a given time depends on the psyche's need for auxiliary or compensatory functions to adapt to external circumstances and to develop in a harmonious and balanced fashion.

THE EXTROVERT TYPES

From our discussion thus far, it is clear that Jung's typology is not a gross classification of individuals into mutually exclusive categories. Rather, Jung pictured his typology as having the breadth and flexibility to allow for any number of possible permutations of function, attitude, and degree. In order to most clearly exemplify the characteristics of pure types, Jung employed extreme cases as the dominant illustrations of his scheme.

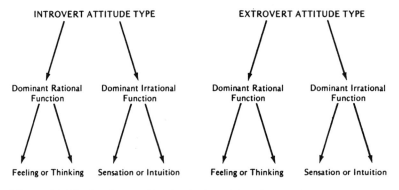

Figure 4.4 The Jungian combined attitude and function typology.

As we have seen, the extrovert is focused on external objects instead of subjective experience. Extroverts are strongly influenced by their social surroundings, and their beliefs are therefore shaped by the opinions and values of those close to them. The extreme extrovert can be overly focused on objects and might completely lose the sense of an autonomous self in them (Jung, 1921, p. 336). Thus, in Jung's view, the most typical neurosis of the extrovert is hysteria, as hysterical reactions are essentially attention getting, dependent attitudes toward people and things in the environment. Eysenck (e.g., 1953a, 1953b, 1967) has marshaled a good bit of empirical evidence that supports this view.

Extrovert Thinking Type (Rational)

Thinking extroverts are also "captured" by external ideas and objects; they are unable to escape their influence in solving problems. They may give the impression of a certain shortsightedness or lack of freedom in the drawing of logical conclusions because they refuse to go beyond the objective facts at hand.

Thinking extroverts subjugate everything to the intellect, refusing to see any other principle for themselves or others to follow than the power of their own decision making. Their moral code is correspondingly rigid and intolerant of exception. Their struggle is for objective and valid universal truths (Jung, 1921, p. 347). "Oughts" and "musts" dominate the thinking extroverts' approach to values, and their thinking tends to be dogmatic.

Since thinking is their superior function, the feeling side of their lives is suppressed. They may, therefore, give the impression of being cold or indifferent. Key concise trait descriptions are that they are *objective, rigid,* and *cold.*

Extrovert Feeling Type (Rational)

According to Jung, dominance by the feeling function is most characteristic of women, (Jung, 1921, p. 356). Like thinking extroverts, *feeling extroverts* seek harmony with the external world. Their thinking function is hidden behind a facade of loud gushing talk and intense displays of extravagant emotionality. They have a tendency to make friends easily and to be influenced by the feeling-tone of social situations. They are often described as *intense, effervescent,* and *sociable.*

Extrovert Sensation Type (Irrational)

The *sensation extrovert's* lifestyle is a search for new sensory experiences (1921, p. 363). They may refine their sensory powers to a high pitch so that they are not merely gross sensual types, but rather connoisseurs of fine wines, discriminating judges of art. Sensation extroverts are usually good company, for they suppress any tendency to introspection and self-concern, favoring instead minute attention to objective, external detail. They tend to be well adjusted to reality and concerned for the welfare of others. Key trait descriptions are *realistic, sensual, jolly.*

Extrovert Intuitive Type (Irrational)

The *intuitive extrovert* has difficulty maintaining an interest in any one thing for very long. Usually, this type of person flits from one new idea to another and stays with each only until the novelty wears off. This individual tends to make decisions without much conscious, reflective thought. Yet such persons' decisions are likely to be good ones because intuitive extroverts can use their intuition to access the wisdom of their own unconscious.

Their consideration for the welfare of others is weakly developed. However, intuitive extroverts are valuable to society because they have the capacity to inspire confidence and enthusiasm for new causes and undertakings. Key trait words describing the intuitive extrovert are *visionary, changeable,* and *creative.*

THE INTROVERT TYPES

The introvert attitude, you may recall, implies that, even though such individuals are aware of external conditions, they are focused on their subjective reactions. The introverts' orientation to life in modern society may be characterized as an exhausting struggle to keep themselves free of external influences and tugs. Typically, if the extreme introvert succumbs to neurosis, it will be to what was called psychasthenia in Jung's day. This neurosis is, as might be expected, characterized by intense anxiety reactions, chronic fatigue, and exhaustion. The diagnosis of "psychasthenia" is no longer used. Some combination of the diagnoses of *anxiety disorder* and *dysthymic disorder* (neurotic depression) would probably be assigned to Jung's "neurotic" introvert. Eysenck has marshaled evidence that this neurotic disposition was more than a haphazard guess on Jung's part.

Introvert Thinking Type (Rational)

The introvert's whose consciousness is dominated by the thinking function presents a picture of the stereotypical intellectual. Concerned with abstractions and with the creation of theories, the *thinking introvert* has a tendency to ignore the practicalities of everyday living. "His judgment appears cold, inflexible, arbitrary, and ruthless, because it relates far less to the [external] object than to the subject [himself]" (Jung, 1921, p. 384).

The thinking introvert develops an intense desire for privacy. Some key terms to describe the introverted thinking type are therefore *intellectual, impractical,* and *private.*

Introvert Feeling Type (Rational)

Dominance of consciousness by feeling in the introvert produces a picture of cold indifference to others. The extreme *feeling introvert* seems to have no concern for the feelings or opinions of others. There is an air of superiority and critical neutrality in the feeling introvert's relations with others. Emotional expression is kept to a minimum, for the feeling introvert's emotions are intense and troublesome. Key trait descriptions are *silent* and *indifferent.*

Introvert Sensation Type (Irrational)

The *introvert sensation* type is focused on changing flux of external events. Their subjective reactions are of paramount importance, for the only thing that matters to the sensation type of introvert is their personal reaction to objective sensory events. Such individuals' thinking and feeling functions are not developed. They evaluate their sense impressions in terms of clear-cut categories of good and evil—only in terms of what seems good and evil *for them.* They sometimes are distant from the outer world and misinterpret reality. They remain calmly undisturbed under most circumstances. They are often described as *passive, calm,* and *artistic.*

Introvert Intuitive Type (Irrational)

The introvert intuitive type of person tends to be aloof and unconcerned about concrete reality or external events. They present the stereotypical picture of the "peculiar artist" or the slightly "mad genius" whose productive efforts result in beautiful but strange creations. Inaccurate perception is the main problem for *intuitive introverts*. They often interpret their perceptions in ways that will satisfy the inner self. Thus they may become estranged from those around them and be viewed as a "wise person gone wrong" or as a "crank and oddball." Key descriptive traits are *mystic, dreamer,* and *unique*. Incidentally, Jung saw himself as an introvert intuitive type (Jung, 1959).

THE PROCESS OF INDIVIDUATION: ENANTIODROMIA

Given Jung's emphasis on the collective unconscious, inherited archetypal images, and on the classification of personality types, it might seem that he was uninterested in individual personality development. In fact, Jung also spent a good deal of the latter part of his life exploring the processes by which a person becomes a complete individual. He investigated the process of individual psychological **differentiation,** by which each person develops their own pattern of traits as well as an idiosyncratic relationship with their personal unconscious and the collective unconscious. He called the process of harmonizing the unconscious with the conscious ego and accessing the meaning of the variety of the components of the psyche, **individuation** (1939, p. 287).

Jung also thought that each person has an innate tendency, the **transcendent function,** to pursue inner harmony. The transcendent function is the motive force for the individual to come to terms with all aspects of the self. It guides the need to accept the content of the unconscious as "mine" (Jung, 1916, p. 73). Individuation and the transcendent function are two sides of the same coin. Individuation refers to the attainment of full development of all sides of oneself into a unique whole. The transcendent function is the guiding force behind this process.

Jung's method of helping his patients to attain individuation involved the process of **active imagination.** Jung instructed his patients in the art of consciously focusing on dream images or on fantasy figures. Active imagination might best be considered a form of visualization or meditation for the purpose of attaining self-knowledge. Through the process of active imagination, Jung's patients could examine many formerly hidden aspects of their psyches.

Within every personality, Jung discerned many usually conflicting, discordant, and antagonistic opposites. Thus, for the anima, there is the animus; for the good mother archetype, there is the evil opposite; for introversion, there is extroversion; for thinking, sensation; for sensation, feeling; and the Shadow is opposite to the persona archetype. Sometimes, Jung approached opposites as complementary aspects of reality. For example, causal explanation should be balanced by acausal, synchronistic explanation; dreams can be analyzed not only in terms of the dreamer's past, but also in terms of their future.

Jung employed a term from Heraclitus, the fifth-century B.C. Greek philosopher, to label the usually opposed themes of the human condition. Jung referred to these opposites as examples of **enantiodromia,** literally as "running counter to" (1921, p. 425, definition 18). Initially, Jung restricted the term to mean only the emergence of an unconscious function or idea that was opposite to a conscious dominant function. Eventually, however, Jung began to see the development of personality as a goal-directed enterprise, marked by a striving toward the equal development of all parts of the psyche. Thus, opposites must surface and coalesce in the psyche. Each of us should not only develop the function of rationality, but also should accept our irrationality. We should not only be aware of qualities we have that we think are ideal but also recognize the shadow characteristic in ourselves. Failure to recognize the opposite tendency within ourselves can lead only to the feeling of being torn apart (Jung, 1917, p. 73; 1957, pp. 302 ff.). Success at individuation means the acceptance of inherent enantiodromia or play of opposites.

Individuation is such an involved process that it necessarily can come to fruition only in one's mature years. Throughout life, the psyche's development is focused on the attainment of the reconciliation of opposites. Within the fully differentiated, individuated psyche, a final psychological organization develops that embodies all the discordant elements, slighting none, emphasizing all equally. Jung gave the name **self** to that psyche in which all the aspects have been reconciled and balanced and has become a harmonious whole. He also applied the term *self* to the part of the psyche that provided guidance toward such wholeness (1950b, p. 267).

DEVELOPMENT OF THE SELF: A TELEOLOGICAL VIEW OF LIFE

Jung treated a variety of middle-aged patients who, although not mentally ill by any definition, were nonetheless discontented. They were ill at ease with themselves and alienated from any possible satisfaction in life. Jung thought that these patients had developed one-sidedly. In short, the process of individuation, the creation of the self as reconciler of opposites, had not occurred for them. For Jung, individual psychological development does not proceed haphazardly. It is purposive or **teleological,** and thus shaped by goals. The purpose of an individual's life is attained when that person is fully integrated, completely in harmony with the self. Some individuals find their purpose in religion, some discover their life's goal in helping their fellow humans, and yet others find purpose in simply living each day with care. However, in every case, the self-actualized individual has accepted the basic enantiodromia, or play of opposites, of life.

The Self as an Archetype

Jung asserted that the perfect mythological symbol of the self is Christ

"He [Christ] is our culture hero, who regardless of his historical existence, embodies the myth of the divine Primordial Man, the mystic Adam. . . . *Christ exemplifies the archetype of the self.* He represents a totality of a divine or heavenly kind, a glorified man, a son of God *sine macula peccati,* unspotted by sin" (Jung, 1950b, pp. 36–37).

Even the divine archetypal figure of the self is a composite of opposites: Christ and Anti-Christ, God and Satan, the Prince of Light and the Prince of Darkness (1950b, p. 44). Thus the self, that totality of opposites, that unique combination of perfection and baseness, was prefigured in humanity's mythology and religion by symbols of the God-man. The early Christian concept of Christ implied an "all embracing totality that even includes the animal side of man" (1950b, p. 41). It is clear, therefore, that Jung regards humans' need for religion, for God, as an inherent motive directed toward self-fulfillment. Without God or a symbolic equivalent (such as an ideal or even a political figure who is seen as godlike) of God to which to aspire, people are forever condemned to the incompleteness of their own existence. For Jung's theory, the question of God's existence is nearly irrelevant because it can never be answered with certainty. What is important in Jung's view is humanity's belief in God's existence, for without the inner belief in an omnipresent, omniscient, and omnipotent reality, the inherent need for wholeness is denied.

This aspect of Jung's theory reveals one of the most important functions of Jungian psychology in the modern world, to preserve a sense of the spiritual outside of the traditional formulations and institutions of religion. Jung was steeped in traditional Christianity as a child (Jung, 1959), but the spirituality of his psychological theories includes, but is not restricted to, a single religious approach.

Expressions of the Self's Harmonies: Mandala Paintings

Jung found in his explorations of mythology and alchemy that the self, or harmonious personality, was often archetypically symbolized by a **mandala.** *Mandala* is a Sanskrit word meaning "circle." In various mythologies, religious rituals, and in the dreams and fantasies of his patients, a variety of mandalalike figures could be observed. Sometimes the mandala is divided into four segments, around which is drawn the characteristic circular enclosure. Figure 4.5 illustrates a mandala drawing by one of Jung's patients. The coiled snake within the circle is seemingly trying to wend its way out of the enclosure. Jung himself was seized on occasion with the compulsion to create mandala figures in paint:

> My mandalas were cryptograms concerning the state of the self, which were presented to me anew each day. In them I saw the self—that is, my whole being—actively at work. . . . I had the distinct feeling that they were something central, and in time I acquired through them a living conception of the self. The self, I thought, was like the monad which I am, and which is my world. The mandala represents this monad [i.e., unity], and corresponds to the microcosmic nature of the psyche. (Jung, 1961, p. 196)

Three of Jung's own mandala paintings are reproduced in Figure 4.6. *Picture a* in Figure 4.6, a group of interlocking circles, with human figures in the four most peripheral circles, was intended by Jung to illustrate four complementary aspects of the self. To the right and left of center are two female figures, with the left woman representing the "dark" side of the anima and the right one symbolizing the nurturing aspect. The top and bottom peripheral circles contain the Wise Old Man archetype and the Trickster archetype, respectively. The sixteen "globes" surrounding the center star are symbolic "eyes," and stand for "observing and discriminating consciousness" (Jung, 1950a, p. 374).

Picture b in Figure 4.6, a star-shaped motif within which lie concentric circles and mazelike compartments, was designed by Jung to represent a medieval city with walls,

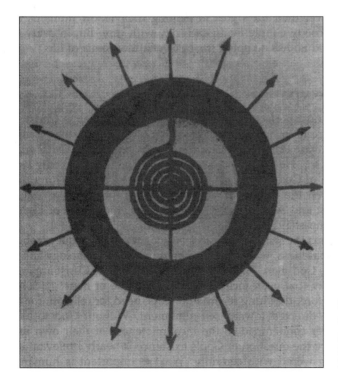

Figure 4.5 A mandala drawing by one of Jung's patients.

Source: Jung, 1950b, "Concerning Mandala Symbolism."

Figure 4.6a Four archetypes of the self, painted by Jung. Source: Jung, 1950a.

moats, streets, and churches, arranged in units of four. The buildings all open inward, facing center, which in turn is a castle with a golden roof. Black-and-white tiles, representing united opposites (i.e., the self), surround the castle center.

Picture c in Figure 4.6 is the most interesting of Jung's mandala paintings because it was the last mandala he painted, and because he reported fully the circumstances surrounding its creation.[3] Entitled "Window on Eternity," *picture c* was produced following a dream Jung had in which he found himself in the city of Liverpool, traveling with three younger companions. He had the impression in the dream of a dirty, sooty city; it was dark and raining. His companions were Swiss, and together they climbed a plateau to a broad square illuminated dimly by streetlights, into which many city streets converged. All of the parts of the city were arranged radially around the square in which Jung and his companions stood. In the center of the square was a round pool with an island in its middle, strangely blazing with sunlight. On the island stood a single tree, with a shower of reddish magnolia blossoms; but the tree itself seemed to be the source of the sunlight. Jung's traveling companions commented on the bad weather they were experiencing and apparently did not see the sunlit tree. They spoke of another Swiss person who lived in the city of Liverpool, and they were surprised that he had settled there. Jung's dream ended with the feeling, "I know very well why he has settled here" (Jung, 1961, p. 198; see also 1950a, p. 364).

> This dream represented my situation at the time. I can still see the grayish yellow raincoats, glistening with the wetness of the rain. Everything was extremely unpleasant, black and

---

[3] Jaffé (1979, pp. 91–93) has published Jung's own paintings with his marginal notations, and it is clear that "Window on Eternity" was not his last. Jung's (1961, pp. 197–198) contradictory statements about this picture's finality in the sequence may have been a reflection only of his sense of emotional finality as expressed in the dream that provoked the painting of "Window on Eternity." The picture was painted in 1927, and "The Medieval City" was finished in 1928.

Figure 4.6b Medieval
city, painted by Jung.
Source: Jung, 1950a.

"opaque"—just as I felt then. But I had a vision of unearthly beauty, and that was why I was able to live at all. Liverpool is the "pool of life." The "liver," according to an old view, is the seat of life—that which "makes man live." This dream brought with it a sense of finality. I saw that here the goal had been revealed. One could not go beyond the center. The center is the goal, and everything is directed toward that center. Through this dream I understood that the self is the principle and archetype of orientation and meaning. Therein lies its healing function. (Jung, 1961, pp. 198–199)

Jung's own mandala paintings show his efforts at healing the painful self-division he harbored. His paintings demonstrate his strivings to mold unity and order from the chaos within himself, and Figure 4.6c represents the culmination of the self-therapy. The "Window on Eternity" painting is at once the final and the most harmonious of Jung's mandalas.

In the delicately balanced harmonies of the mandala, Jung discerned a mythic expression of the self as the reconciler of opposites. The precise juxtaposition of colors and shadings and the fourfold spatial division of the circle symbolize the harmony of the self. This fourfold division of many mandalas is the instinctive expression of human desire to create organization from chaos, to plot on a schema of four coordinates the confusing flux of the inner and outer life. Each individual's approach to the attainment of self-harmony is unique and occurs only once in time, as the Christ figure symbolizes. But even the Christ figure has to be expressed in antagonistic terms, a complementary of opposites.

Figure 4.6c Window on eternity, painted by Jung. Source: Jung, 1950a.

Figure 4.7 expresses an analogy of the self through the historical and mythical figure of Christ. "As an historical personage Christ is unitemporal [once in time] and unique; as God, universal and eternal. Likewise the self: as the essence of individuality it is unitemporal and unique; as an archetypal symbol it is a God-image and therefore universal and eternal" (Jung, 1950b, p. 63). Christ alzso embodied another fourfold division of opposites: *good* (Christ) versus *evil* (Anti-Christ) and *spiritual* (divine) versus *material* (human). Thus, Jung illustrated this composite of opposites with another set of coordinates, shown here in Figure 4.8.

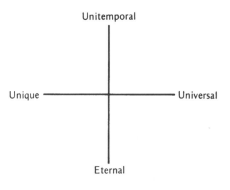

Figure 4.7 Christ as an archetype of the self—the first set of opposites.
After Jung, 1950b, p. 63.

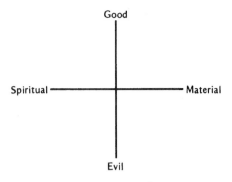

Figure 4.8 Christ as an archetype of the self—
the second set of opposites.
After Jung, 1950b, p. 63.

Because the self is a totality, it must embody both light and dark, good and evil. Fully individuated persons can freely accept both aspects of their psyches and can willingly strive to unite the two into wholeness. For Jung, the goal of psychotherapy, indeed, the goal of the well-lived life, is the attainment of wholeness, balance, and harmony.

EVALUATING CARL JUNG

Jung's work has had a continuing influence, not so much on scientific psychology, but in psychotherapeutic practice and in the humanities and creative arts. There are numerous Jungian institutes throughout the world. Many scholarly investigations are animated by Jungian theory. Expressive artists and writers find inspiration in Jungian archetypal explorations. Jung's work did anticipate, in particular with its emphasis on instincts, the work of evolutionary psychologists. He was also far ahead of his time in emphasizing cross-cultural approaches to personality.

Jung's reputation has been tainted among those who are convinced that he either unwittingly or deliberately contributed to Nazi anti-Semitism. How relevant this factor is for evaluating his work and his theories is a very difficult question. One conclusion is that his theories, in their acceptance of all facets of human behavior—both good and evil—provide neither a complete nor a satisfactory moral, ethical compass.

Refutability

Of all the theories we present, Jung's is the one that best fits Henri Ellenberger's (1970) idea that some theories emerge from a thinker's "creative illness." The historical and biographical evidence, as well as the content of the theory itself, link most of Jung's more controversial ideas to his attempts to resolve his own substantial conflicts. However, unlike other theorists, for whom the same relationship exists between their ideas and their lives, Jung's personal difficulties included periods of hallucination, suicidal depression, and regression, as documented in his autobiography, *Memories, Dreams, Reflections* (Jung, 1961). Consequently, Jung's critics often dismiss his ideas without serious consideration.

In our view, a theory should not be dismissed simply because it has demonstrable links to the personal distress or interests of its creator. The theory should be tested against reality, not against opinion. In fact, we could easily argue that a psychological theory originating in the personal distress of its creator is likely to be a more accurate description of *some* aspects of human personality than if it had originated only in the laboratory.

Not surprisingly, like Freud's theory, Jung's is also a composite of empirical and non-empirically based ideas. Jung's early work with the word association test was certainly empirical, and though the standards of evidence have grown more stringent than they were in Jung's day, his basic research technique would qualify as a refutable way to test his hypothesis of psychological complexes.

Jung's conception of personality types, especially the fundamental dimension of introversion-extroversion, is eminently testable. Eysenck's work (e.g., 1967; Eysenck & Eysenck, 1985), which we review in Chapter 17, has certainly established the basic dimension and its correlates in the laboratory. However, beyond only the most elementary trait descriptions, Eysenck's concepts of introversion and extroversion differ from those of Jung. Nevertheless, taking Jung's ideas about this dimension, there is at least one paper-and-pencil personality test devoted to measuring the Jungian personality types and their attitudinal correlates (Myers, 1972). Moreover, we should point out, the descriptions that Jung gave of the types, subtypes, and attitudinal variations lend themselves to a variety of empirical tests using already available psychological instruments.

What of Jung's most original and central ideas? The *collective unconscious, archetypes, synchronicity,* to name a few of Jung's major concepts, are not stated in empirically testable form. By definition, synchronicity is a non-empirical, acausal concept, and we really cannot get much further from refutability than that. The scientific problem with each of these ideas is that none of them has a measurable referent. For the phenomena that Jung indicates as belonging to any one of these main concepts, it is possible to generate alternative and simpler explanations. The burden of proof, then, lies with Jung and his followers to show that their explanation covers the facts.

Jung's Conception of Human Agency

Jung's work anticipated much of the later ideas of existentialist and humanist theorists, such as Rollo May, Abraham Maslow, and Carl Rogers (Chapters 12 and 13), in their emphasis on the person's active creation of meaning. The ideas of Jung's later years focus on the self, on actualizing the self, and on a holistic conception of personality that is quite consistent with humanistic psychology in flavor and conception. Jung believed, apparently, in determinism, the determinism of our primordial ancestry and our personal history. However, he emphasized that the person's responsibility lies in an active synthesis of the discrete parts of his or her life into a harmonious whole. This synthesis is an activity, not merely of the *persona,* but of the whole *psyche,* guided in the process of individuation by the archetype of the *self.*

Jung's emphasis on the spiritual side of life, his concern with teleology or goal-oriented behavior, and his willingness to see the determinants of behavior in a person's remote past, personal past, and future strivings certainly argue for a complex, largely active conception of human agency.

Jung's Combined Idiographic-Nomothetic Emphases

Jung envisioned his theory as providing a nomothetic basis for understanding behavior by transcending the individual, by going beyond the immediate past, and by allowing for the influence of the future. In a way, his concepts of the collective unconscious and synchronicity are the clearest examples of a nomothetic or universal focus in personality theory. Concepts such as enantiodromia, the various archetypes, the collective unconscious, the principles of entropy, equivalence, and opposites are also nomothetic or generally applicable. As we have indicated here, they are very difficult if not impossible to test.

On the other side of the coin, Jung clearly proposed idiographic concepts that have fared better in empirical research. His word association procedure is an idiographic one by definition. His psychoanalytic-like analysis of dreams and symptoms is, like its psychoanalytic cousin, highly individualized. And Jung's conception of the self as the psychological structure that harmonizes the conflicting pulls of an individual life proceeding toward self-actualization is largely idiographic.

SUMMARY

Beginning his career in the tradition of classical clinical psychiatry, Carl Gustav Jung soon developed a tool of investigation that brought his thinking close to that of Sigmund Freud. The word association test, in Jung's innovative hands, revealed that normal and neurotic subjects harbored latent and inexpressible ideas and feelings. These *complexes,* as Jung called them, could be objectively demonstrated in the pauses, hesitations, and inhibitions of the subjects as each reacted to a list of stimulus words.

Eventually, however, Jung pursued a path different from Freud's when he found himself unable to accept the exclusively sexual nature of Freud's *libido.* With his own patients, Jung discovered residues of human history and prehistory in their fantasies. His own childhood experiences with visions and alternative personalities had prepared him to accept the possibility that some psychic content might arise from sources external to the individual. His self-analysis (from 1913 to 1917) of the dreams, visions, and nightmares that flooded his consciousness convinced him more strongly that a higher power was responsible for at least some of the content of mental life. He therefore postulated a personal unconscious similar to Freud's concept, and a collective unconscious that transcends the personal experiences of the individual.

Within the collective unconscious, there are stored inherited predispositions to respond with great emotion to specific events. These predispositions, which Jung called *archetypes,* include the animus and anima, the hero, God, the shadow, and the persona. Jung considered the archetypes solid evidence of the innate symbol-making tendency humans had inherited from their ancestors.

In trying to resolve the differences between himself and Freud, and between Freud and Adler, Jung postulated two personality types: the introvert and the extrovert. Introverts are characterized by their withdrawal from social stimulation, their intensely subjective interest in things intellectual, and their reliance on the power of their own feelings. The extrovert, much the opposite, is dominated by objective, external reality and is socially oriented. In addition to these attitude types, Jung proposed four functions: thinking and feeling (rational), and intuition and sensation (irrational). Introverts and extroverts each can be dominated by one or more of these functions, leading to an eightfold combined typology.

In his later years, Jung came to emphasize the spiritual side of humanity's existence. Jung postulated that to achieve full individuality, or *individuation* as he called it, the person must form a psychological organization that can reconcile all of the opposing and contradictory trends within the psyche. To this reconciler of opposites, Jung gave the name *self.*

An evaluation of Jung's theory indicates that some parts are, in principle, testable, especially his early work on word association and his conception of his theory of personality types. Jungian theory is essentially an active agent theory that anticipated much of the concerns of the American existentialists who focused on the person's capacity to create meaning actively from reality. We should note, however, that the active agent in Jung's theory is not the egoistic personality or persona, but the entire psyche, itself, including both unconscious and conscious elements. Jung's theory is a complex blend of nomothetic universals (e.g., collective unconscious, archetypes) and idiographic particulars (e.g., introversion, the self).

FOR FURTHER READING

Jung's popular *Memories, Dreams, Reflections* (New York: Vintage, 1989) is a wonderfully readable, unpretentious, and intriguing autobiography. It is open, well-written, and reveals much about Jung's personal experiences. Calvin Hall and Vernon Nordby's *A Primer of Jungian Psychology* (New York: New American Library, 1999) is a most sympathetic, straightforward, and uncritical account of Jungian psychology.

Jung wrote three relatively concise introductions to his work. In order of value to the serious student, these introductions are *Analytical Psychology: Its Theory and Practice* (New York: Pantheon, 1968), which is the published version of Jung's Tavistock Lectures, and the most readable of his writings; *Two Essays on Analytical Psychology* (Vol. 7 of *The Col-*

lected Works of C.G. Jung [Princeton, NJ: Princeton University Press, 1967]), a work that is somewhat more difficult but also more characteristic of Jung's style; *and Man and His Symbols* (New York: Laurelleaf, 1997), which is a lavishly, though at times superficially, illustrated compendium of Jungian thought by both Jung and several of his collaborators.

To gain some of the flavor of Jung's religious and spiritual researches, *The Archetypes of the Collective Unconscious* (Vol. 9 of *The Collected Works of C.G. Jung* [Princeton, NJ: Princeton University Press, 1969]) will introduce you to his characteristic form of presenting hypotheses drawn from clinical, mythological, and historical sources.

The complexity of Jung's personality and theoretical contributions (as is also the case with Freud) has led to diverse appraisals of his life and works. Five biographical accounts of Jung present drastically different pictures of the same man. F.J. McLynn's *Jung: A Biography* (New York: St. Martin's Press, 1996) portrays Jung, warts and all. It covers some of the more controversial and darker sides of this theorist. Jung does not emerge as a "nice person" in this portrait. Aniela Jaffé, Jung's longtime student and colleague during the later part of his life, attempts to explicate some controversial aspects of Jung's thinking and career in *From the Life and Work of C.G. Jung* (New York: Harper & Row, 1971). Jaffé's essays are particularly worthwhile in the areas of attempting to explain Jung's alleged anti-Semitism and his apparent sympathy for the Nazi philosophy. Laurens Van der Post's *Jung and the Story of Our Time* (New York: Pantheon, 1975) is a spiritual rather than intellectual account of Jung's life and influence based on Van der Post's personal relationship with Jung. Very sympathetic and mystical, approaching almost hero worship, Van der Post emphasizes Jung's image as a "wise old man." A somewhat more realistic view that sometimes borders on hostility is provided by Paul J. Stern in *C.G. Jung: The Haunted Prophet* (New York: Braziller, 1976). Stern attempts to make the case for Jung's personal psychotic episodes as the basis of his

later theoretical ideas. Vincent Brome's *Jung: Man and Myth* (New York: Atheneum Books, 1981) offers a balanced account of Jung's life and work.

Further personal insights may be gleaned from *The Freud/Jung Letters,* edited by William McGuire (Princeton, NJ: Princeton University Press, 1994), in which the development, course, and final breakup of Freud and Jung's relationship may be witnessed. For fans of scandal and psychoanalytic soap opera, John Kerr's well-written and researched *A Most Dangerous Method: The Story of Jung, Freud, and Sabina Spielrein* (New York: Knopf, 1993) recounts in detail the nature of the relationship between Freud and Jung, and the story of one of Jung's lovers who had also been his patient. One of Richard I. Evans's interviews with Jung is contained in *Conversations With Carl Jung and Reactions From Ernest Jones* (New York: Van Nostrand, 1964), or in condensed form in Evans's *The Making of Psychology* (New York: Knopf, 1976). Gerhard Adler's *Studies in Analytical Psychology* (New York: Routledge, 1999) shows Jungian therapy at its best through studies of dreams and detailed case histories. A view of how the contemporary Jungian analyst operates may be obtained from E.C. Whitmont and Y. Kaufmann's "Analytical Psychotherapy," in Raymond Corsini (Ed.), *Current Psychotherapies* (Itasca, IL: Peacock, 1995).

GLOSSARY

Active imagination: The conscious process of focusing on dream images or on fantasy figures to facilitate psychological insight and personal transformation.

Anima: Female component of the psyche. Includes the positive characteristics of warmth and intuitive understanding and the negative components of moodiness and irrationality.

Animus: Male component of the psyche. On the positive side it includes the ability to reason and use logic to solve problems, and on the negative side it leads to argumentativeness and social insensitivity.

Archetypes: Universal themes or symbols that are a residue of ancestral emotional life. They lead to predispositions to behave and to experience reality in certain ways.

Collective unconscious: For Jung, that part of the psyche that is presumed to contain representations of the collective experiences of humanity. It is the depository of instincts and archetypes that go beyond one's own personal experience.

Compensatory function: The activities of the unconscious to compensate for the imbalance that

occurs when an individual's conscious attitude leans too one-sidedly in a single direction. The unconscious may compensate for this imbalance by producing dreams or fantasies that emphasize the opposite tendency.

Complex: In Jungian theory, a set or collection of interrelated ideas or fantasies that are highly valued by the individual and which reside in the personal unconscious. Such thoughts are usually united by a common underlying theme.

Conscious ego: The conscious part of the psyche. It consists of all those internal and external events that are within our awareness at any given moment, including all sense impressions and self-awareness.

Differentiation: The psychological process by which individuals develop their unique patterns of traits and idiosyncrasies.

Ectopsychic functions: The four functions of consciousness that are directed outwardly to the world. Those functions are sensation, thinking, feeling, and intuition.

Enantiodromia: The play of opposites within every personality. Jung discerned a multiplicity of conflicting themes, discordant opposites, and antagonistic forces that individuals faced in their pursuit of individuation or wholeness.

Extroversion: The tendency to be externally oriented, confident, outgoing, and fun-loving.

Galvanic skin response (GSR): The skin's decrease in resistance to electrical current during sensory and emotional changes.

Individuation: The process by which the unconscious is harmonized with the ego. In this process, the individual comes to recognize the various components of his or her psyche, and express them in the context of his or her life. This is the full development of all aspects of the psyche into a unique and harmonious whole.

Introversion: The tendency to be internally oriented, reserved, reflective, and socially inhibited or circumspect.

Libido: In Jungian theory, the libido is a general life energy, of which sexual urges are only one aspect. This life force or energy manifests itself in our diverse feelings, thoughts, and behaviors. Libidinal energy can be shaped, channeled, suppressed, repressed, blocked, or expressed.

Mandala: In Jung's theory, a circular figure that represents the synthesis or union of opposites within the psyche that takes place when individuals reach self-realization. It is the symbol of wholeness, completeness, and perfection. It can be imagined as a symbolic representation of the self.

Persona: The archetype that consists of the mask we wear in order to function adequately in interpersonal relationships. This mask or public face takes as many forms as the roles we engage in on a regular basis.

Personal unconscious: The region of the mind or psyche that contains the individual's experiences that have been blocked or repressed from conscious awareness. It is comparable but not identical to Freud's *dynamic unconscious*.

Principle of entropy: Second law of thermodynamics, which states that there is a tendency to equalize energy within a system. Thus elements of unequal strength seek psychological equilibrium within the psyche.

Principle of equivalence: First law of thermodynamics, which states that the amount of energy in a system is fixed. Thus an increase in psychic functioning in one area of interest or preoccupation will lead to a compensatory decrease in functioning in another part of the psyche.

Psyche: In Jung's theory, the sum total of all aspects of the personality, including all conscious and unconscious components. To Jung, the psyche transcends time and space.

Rational versus irrational functions: The four ectopsychic functions can be further classified as rational or irrational, depending on the degree of judgment or reasoning involved.

Reaction time: The time an individual takes to respond to a stimulus word in the word association test.

Self: In Jung's theory, a psyche that has achieved balance and has developed into a harmonious whole. In addition, it is a term used for the part of the psyche that provides guidance toward wholeness.

Sensation/intuition: Modes of apprehending the world without evaluation or interpretation. Those two manners of responding are classified as irrational because conscious reasoning is virtually absent. They do not involve logic thought processes.

Shadow: The archetype that represents the dark, evil, and repulsive side of human nature. The shadow archetype is universal, but its specific contents vary individually. It is often projected onto other people.

Synchronicity: The meaningful coincidence of two or more outer or inner events (e.g., dreams or visions). They may occur around the same time but have no apparent cause-and-effect connection.

Teleological: Goal-directed. In Jung's theory, the development of the psyche is directed toward the goals of balance and harmony.

Thinking/feeling: Modes of making judgments or evaluations of events. These types of responding are classified as rational because they involve the supremacy of reason, and the assessment of the worth of an experience.

Transcendent function: The driving force behind individuation, the innate tendency to pursue inner harmony.

Word association test: A test developed by Jung in which individuals are presented with stimulus words and asked to give responses to them. This method helps to uncover latent emotional difficulties by exposing content areas that produce hesitation, perseveration, or total inhibition of response.

Chapter **5**

Alfred Adler
Individual Psychology

The most important question of the healthy and the diseased mental life is not whence? but, whither?

Alfred Adler, *The Individual
Psychology of Alfred Adler*

If life gives you lemons, make lemonade.

Anonymous

Alfred Adler   **Born: 1870**   **Penzing, Austria;**
              Died: 1937   **Aberdeen, Scotland**
                         (while on a speaking tour)

Adler's Individual Psychology

Alfred Adler began as an adherent of Freud's theory. After almost a decade, as a result of major disagreements, the two men ended their collaboration. Subsequently, Adler devoted himself to the development of his own theoretical and therapeutic approach, which he called individual psychology to distinguish it from other approaches. Some ideas central to Adler's theory are:

1. *Each person strives for superiority or personal competence.*

2. *Each person develops a style of life and a life plan that are partly deliberate and partly unconscious.*

> ***a.*** *A person's style of life indicates a consistent approach to many situations. For example, one person might be typified as avoidant, another enthusiastically collaborative, a third combative, and so on.*
>
> ***b.*** *The life plan that is developed directs the person's choices and leads to goals that the person strives to accomplish.*

3. *The most important qualities of a healthy personality are an acquired capacity for "fellow feeling" (what Adler called* Gemeinschaftsgefuhl*), and accompanying concern to foster the well-being of others or what Adler termed, social interest.*

4. *The ego is that part of the psyche that is creative. It creates new realities through the process of setting goals and bringing them into fruition. This is called* fictional finalism.

THE NONEXISTENT CEMETERY: ADLER'S FEAR OF DEATH

One purpose of this textbook is to show, when possible, how some aspects of a theorist's view of human nature reflect their own life experience. This is evidently the case with the prolific personality theorist, Alfred Adler.

As child of five through the age of 35, Adler had what we would today term a "false memory" (Adler, 1959, pp. 179–180). This false memory was of Adler as a child mastering the fear of death.

> I remember that the path to the school led over a cemetery. I was frightened every time and was exceedingly put out at *beholding the other children pass the cemetery without paying the least attention to it, while every step I took was accompanied by a feeling of fear and horror.* Apart from the extreme discomfort occasioned by this fear I was also annoyed at the idea of *being less courageous than the others.* One day I made up my mind to put an end to this fear of death. Again, I decided upon a treatment of hardening. I stayed at some distance behind the others, placed my schoolbag on the ground near the wall of the cemetery and ran across it a dozen times, until I felt that I had mastered the fear. (Adler, 1959, italics added)

Only at the age of 35, in conversation with a childhood school chum, did Adler learn that there had never been a cemetery on the way to their school (Adler, 1959, p. 180; Orgler, 1963, p. 37). Adler's unconscious mind, dealing with feelings of fear and horror, had woven what Freud called a *screen memory.* It dealt with events related to an imagined cemetery.

This "memory" was apparently the result of a series of actual childhood brushes with death. As a young boy, Adler had twice been run over by a car and recalled regaining consciousness on the living room sofa (Orgler, 1963, p. 2). Also, Adler's younger brother died in a bed beside his when he was only three. At the age of five, the period to which the cemetery pseudo-recollection dates, Adler became so profoundly ill with pneumonia that the family physician gave him up for lost. However, he beat the odds and eventually recovered.

Adler recounted the impact of this brush with death on his career choice:

> From that time on I recall always thinking of myself in the future as a physician. *This means that I had set a goal from which I could expect an end to my childlike distress, my fear of death.* . . . I came to choose the occupation of physician in order to overcome death and the fear of death. (Adler, in Ansbacher & Ansbacher, 1956, p. 199; italics added)

As an adult physician, Adler was still beleaguered by proximity of death. Hertha Orgler (1963), Adler's biographer and friend, reports that Adler gave up his general medical practice after the death of several of his diabetic patients. Practicing before insulin was discovered, Adler found himself powerless to prevent these patients' deaths.

In 1929, Adler indicated his preoccupation with the topic of death and his awareness of the importance of death for personality development. The connection to his own experiences is evident:

> In all probability none but human beings are conscious of the fact that death is in the destiny of life, and this consciousness alone is enough to give mankind a sense of being terribly overpowered by Nature. If a child experiences a brusque contact with death at an early age, the whole style of life may be largely molded by that single impression. In such a case the importance of death to life is invariably over-valued, and we can often perceive how the child's actions and reactions are so directed as to find relief from this oppressive idea, or compensate for it. (Adler, 1929b, p. 145)

Adler further suggested that confrontation with death could have far-reaching consequences for the direction a person's life might take. Some people may seek a type of immortality through their descendants. Others may seek to defy death through the attainment of personal greatness in art or science. Believing in the actual immortality of one's soul may also allay the fear of death. Adler himself chose to become a physician to be able to struggle directly against death.

Alfred Adler was a chronically sick and weak child. He suffered from rickets, a nutritional deficiency disease that results in softening of the bones. He was thus unable to compete well in many areas with his older brother or with peers (Bottome, 1957; Orgler, 1963). Another of Adler's childhood recollections drawn from the age of two again indicates his special sensitivity to feelings of inferiority:

> I remember sitting on a bench bandaged up on account of rickets, with my healthy elder brother sitting opposite me. He could run, jump, and move about quite effortlessly, while for me, movement of any sort was a strain and an effort. Everyone went to great pains to help me, and my mother and father did all that was in their power to do. (Quoted in Bottome, 1957, pp. 30–31)

Also, Adler was resentful toward his mother over the birth of his younger brother, for this child "dethroned" him and became his mother's favorite (Mosak & Kopp, 1973, p. 158).

In summary, three features marked Adler's early personality development:

- His boyhood involved exposure to and attempts to master the fear of death.
- His frailty contributed to his sense of being inferior to his older brother and peers.
- His resentment toward his mother for transferring her affections to his infant brother.

ADLER'S, FREUD'S, AND JUNG'S CHILDHOOD PERCEPTIONS OF DEATH

Adler was not the only personality theorist whose experience of death was an important influence. Adlerian psychologists, Harold Mosak and Richard Kopp (1973) compared Adler's early recollections with several of Freud's and Jung's early memories. Freud reports an incident that involved his first awareness of the inevitability of death.

> When I was six years old and was given my first lessons by my mother, I was expected to believe that we were all made of earth and must therefore return to earth. This did not suit me and I expressed doubts of the doctrine. My mother thereupon rubbed the palms of her hands together—just as she did in making dumplings, except that there was no dough between them—and showed me the blackish scales of epidermis produced by the friction as a proof that we were made of earth. My astonishment at this ocular demonstration knew no

bounds and I acquiesced in the belief which I was later to hear expressed in the words: *"Du bist der Natur einen Tod schuldig"* [*"Thou owest Nature a death"*]. (Freud, 1900, Vol. IV, p. 205)

This reported incident is relevant to Freud's later theory of the death instinct as an inexorable force. (See Chapter 3 for a discussion of Freud's death instinct.)

Jung was not afraid of death and was even fascinated by it. He recounted two memories from approximately his fourth year of life which were indicative of his attitude:

> And once there was a great flood. The river Wiese, which flowed through the village, had broken its dam, and in its upper reaches a bridge had collapsed. Fourteen people were drowned and were carried down by the yellow floodwater to the Rhine. When the water retreated, some of the corpses got stuck in the sand. When I was told about it, there was no holding me. I actually found the body of a middle-aged man, in a black frock coat; apparently he had just come from church. He lay half covered by sand, his arm over his eyes. Similarly, I was fascinated to watch a pig being slaughtered. To the horror of my mother, I watched the whole procedure. She thought it terrible, but the slaughtering and the dead man were simply matters of interest to me. (Jung, 1961, p. 15)

Musak and Kopp contrasted the significance of each theorist's early recollections regarding death for understanding the approach to life of Adler, Jung, and Freud as adults:

> Although all three show an interest in death, they differ in their approach to it. Jung is intrigued by death, Freud is awed by death's inevitability, while Adler resolves to work to overcome death. . . . Finally, the dominant life goals of each man emerge from their recollections. *Adler's goal is to overcome inadequacy through effort and resolve.* Freud strives to comprehend through analysis and interpretation, while Jung moves toward communion with nature through sensual awareness. (1973, pp. 164–165, italics added)

For Adler, death was the ultimate enemy, the paramount symbol of helplessness against which one must struggle at all costs. For Freud, death was an inevitable biological process he struggled to understand. For Jung, death was a fascinating part of reality, the meaning of which he wanted fully to explore.

FREUD AND ADLER: DISSENT OVER THE FUNDAMENTAL HUMAN MOTIVE

Adler disagreed drastically with Freud over the issue of the central motive in human personality. He was convinced that human motivation could not be subsumed under the category of pleasure or sexuality. He thought that a new model of personality was needed, a model that accorded more weight to other fundamental human strivings. Like other neo-Freudians, Adler replaced the instinct model of personality with an interpersonal model. Neo-Freudians considered many goals, such as achievement, success, freedom from a sense of helplessness and personal completeness, as more important than fulfillment of the sexual drive. Adler considered the striving to compensate for a sense of helplessness and perceived inferiorities as a primary motivating factor.

In 1902, Adler wrote a defense of Freud's *Interpretation of Dreams* that was published in one of Vienna's foremost newspapers. Freud subsequently invited Adler and several others to meet with him for a series of informal seminars (cf. Ansbacher & Ansbacher, 1973, p. 336n.; Furtmüller, 1973; Jones, 1955). Adler did join the select group of intellectuals surrounding Freud, but he never became as completely committed to the Freudian viewpoint as most of the others.

Nine years later, at the culmination of continually widening personal and theoretical differences, Adler resigned from Freud's group to pursue his own psychological formulations. Some of Freud's correspondence with Jung reveals the depth of personal and intellectual animosity that arose between Freud and Adler. For example, shortly before Adler's resignation, Freud wrote to Jung, vividly expressing his disappointment at the direction he believed Adler's theorizing was taking:

> I see now that Adler's seeming decisiveness concealed a good deal of confusion. I would never have expected a psychoanalyst to be so taken in by the ego. In reality the ego is like the clown in the circus, who is always putting in his oar to make the audience think that whatever happens is his doing (Freud, in Freud & Jung, 1974, p. 400).

Freud was convinced that Adler's psychology was too superficial, too concerned with conscious functioning, and too neglectful of the most fundamental tenet of psychoanalytic motivation theory, the importance of unconscious determinants of behavior. He was also concerned that Adler's views would affect the unity of the thinking of the psychoanalytic movement and thus obstruct the impact Freud wanted to make on society. Freud expressed himself quite frankly to Jung:

> The crux of the matter—and that is what really alarms me—is that [Adler] minimizes the sexual drive and our opponents will soon be able to speak of an experienced psychoanalyst whose conclusions are radically different from ours. Naturally in my attitude toward him I am torn between my conviction that all this is lopsided and harmful and my fear of being regarded as an intolerant old man who holds the young men down, and this makes me feel most uncomfortable. (Freud, in Freud & Jung, 1974, p. 376)

The members of the informal seminar group, who now called themselves the Vienna Psychoanalytic Society, decided to clear the air by having a formal debate on the differences between Freud and Adler. Adler was therefore invited to give a systematic presentation of his ideas, beginning on January 4, 1911, and extending over the course of the next several sessions. On February 22, after the members of the group had discussed Adler's ideas and Freud had commented on the differences between their two viewpoints, Adler resigned from the presidency of the Vienna Psychoanalytic Society. By May 24, he terminated all contact with the group and, at Freud's suggestion, withdrew as co-editor of the *Zentralblatt,* an important psychoanalytic journal. Freud wrote to Jung in early June. He did not mince words:

> *I have finally got rid of Adler.* After I had pressed Bergmann [the journal's publisher] to dismiss him from the *Zentralblatt,* he twisted and turned and finally came up with a strangely worded statement, which can only be taken, as his resignation. At least, this interpretation is supported by his announcement that he is leaving the Psychoanalytic Society. And then he came out with what he had been holding back: "Despite its unprecedented resolution at one time to that effect, the Society has not had sufficient moral influence on you to make you desist from your old personal fight (!!) against me. Since I have no desire to carry on such a personal fight with my former teacher, I hereby announce my resignation." The damage is not very great. Paranoid intelligences [referring to Adler] are not rare and are more dangerous than useful. As a paranoiac of course he [Adler] is right about many things, though *wrong about everything.* (Freud, in Freud & Jung, 1974, p. 428; italics added)

For Adler's part, the society's meetings devoted to the differences between his views and those of Freud had allowed him to formulate and crystallize the essential tenets of his own developing viewpoint. His break from Freud also enabled him to develop his own views and to train other therapists in his new approach. Before undertaking a study of Adler's theory, we briefly explore Adler's own presentation of his divergence from orthodox psychoanalysis.

ADLER'S VIEW OF HIS DIFFERENCES WITH FREUD

Years after Adler's original dispute with Freud, he published an essay summarizing his differences with orthodox psychoanalysis (Adler, 1931). In it, He expressed his views on the limitations of Freudian theory and the direction his own ideas were taking. Some major topics he covered were the ego, the Oedipus complex, narcissism, drives/goals, and the meaning of dreams.

The Ego

Adler viewed the **ego** not as the servant of the id's desires but as an independent aspect of the psyche. Adler believed that creative activity, bringing ideas into fruition, was the primary function of mankind. He viewed the ego as that part of the personality responsible for such creativity. Adler viewed the ego as the seat of the individual's sense of wholeness, of the person's identity (1931, in 1973, p. 206). On the other hand, Freud emphasized the ego's relationship to the unconscious. Freud also believed that the ego had to adapt to external demands. Thus, to Freud, the ego's main functions were psychological survival and adjustment—not creativity.

The Oedipus Complex

In Adler's view, the **Oedipus complex** was not a purely sexual phenomenon in which the male child vainly attempts to possess the mother. Rather, Adler thought that equal, if not greater, weight should be attached to the child's striving to overcome his sense of weakness and inferiority. This leads to competition with the father in order to secure equal or greater strength and power. Adler affirmed "that the boy wants to grow beyond himself, wants to attain a superiority over his father" (Adler, 1931, in 1973, p. 207).

Narcissism

When Freud developed the concept of narcissistic ego libido, he had in mind a protective channeling of energy into the self—a healthy self-interest or self-love. Adler, however, thought that the Freudian notion of narcissism indicated a personality turned in on itself. Thus it led to a style of life that necessarily excluded healthy social interest. Adler believed that the narcissistic attitude, contrary to Freudian theory, is neither innate nor instinctual, but learned or acquired. In Adler's view, narcissistic people fear that they are essentially too weak and too powerless to survive, and they try to control this fear by avoiding any sense of obligation to others (1931, in 1973, p. 208). Adler viewed such an approach as a pathological style of life.

Drives or Goals?

Adler thought that Freudian theory had fragmented the person into competing parts rather than being a complete functioning unity. Adler emphasized that personality has a fundamental, innate, evolutionary tendency to grow and to become whole. A person, he affirmed, seeks happiness not by satisfying discrete drives but by fulfilling his or her potential. For Adler, human motivation cannot be understood in terms of attempts to reduce the discomfort of mounting biological tensions like sex, hunger, and fatigue. Rather, persons strive toward goals they have chosen. Adler put the matter this way:

> The main problem of psychology is not to comprehend the causal factors as in physiology, but the direction-giving, pulling forces, and goals which guide all other psychological movements. (1931, in 1973, p. 216)

The Meaning of Dreams

According to Freud, a dream is a disguised fulfillment of a wish that would be quite unacceptable or unattainable in the waking state (cf. Chapter 3). Thus dream stories are often bizarre, confused, and incomprehensible to the dreamers. The distortion and disguise of the manifest content is a protective mask defensively obscuring threatening meanings.

For Adler, dreams were not to be interpreted as disguised unacceptable wishes. Instead, they represent attempts to resolve problems that dreamers have not mastered with their conscious powers of reason (Adler, 1973, p. 214). Like Freud, Adler believed that the dream was disguised. In contrast to Freud, however, he was convinced that the *purpose* of a dream had to do with the mood that it evoked.

> It is the intention of the dreamer not to understand his dreams. He wants to withdraw the dream from understanding. This must mean that something happens in the dream, which he cannot justify with reason. *The intention of the dream is to deceive the dreamer.* The person attempts in a certain situation to deceive himself. I have also understood why one does not understand the dream. Its purpose is only *to create a mood.* This emotion must not be clarified; it must exist and act as an emotion, created from the individuality of the dreamer. This apparently corresponds to the desire to solve a problem by an emotional episode and in accordance with his lifestyle, since he is not confident of solving his problem in accordance with the common sense. (Adler, 1973, p. 214; italics added)

Thus, for Adler, a dream is an attempt by the dreamer's unconscious mind to create a mood or emotional state that, upon waking, will enable the dreamer to take an action that they had been reluctant to attempt. For example, a person may wake up with the energy and enthusiasm to tackle a new project or to take a new direction in life. In Freud's theory the dream itself is a focus of attention and a source of insights into the depths of one's personality. For Adler, however, the dream is a means of assisting the ego and its activities.

This difference of view regarding the function of dreams is consistent with the different emphases of the two theorists. Insight into unconscious dynamics was most important for Freudian theory, but Adler emphasized the creative achievements of the ego. Freud correspondingly saw dreams as the "royal road" to the unconscious, but Adler viewed them as helping the ego to take action.

Adler's approach to personality has many differences with Freud's; some of these will become apparent in subsequent sections. Those concepts of Adler most different from Freud's are:

- the ego as mediator of social reality,
- the Oedipus complex as a striving for superiority,
- narcissism as unhealthy self-centeredness,
- goal striving of the unified person versus an emphasis on separate drives, and
- dreams as aids to action.

Freud and Adler did not reconcile their differences. As Freud's theory and therapeutic approach continued to evolve, Adler's disenchantment with his former teacher grew. Freud's increasing pessimism and fatalism about human nature was in direct contrast to Adler's view that people are basically good and capable of genuine altruistic social

---

BOX 5.1 *Only Connect . . .*

In Chapter 18 we shall find that one tenet of evolutionary psychology is that much altruistic behavior has been selected as part of the evolutionary process. Freud based his ideas on classical Darwinian evolutionary theory, which focused on reproduction and aggression and did not include the possibility of biologically determined altruism. The more recent "selfish gene" hypothesis indicates selective advantage to those genes that lead to altruistic behaviors.

---

concern. Depending on where one stands oneself, one might view Adler as expressing a healthy optimism and Freud as darkly pessimistic; or Freud as realistic and Adler as naïve. Adler seems to be expressing how people are at their best and Freud as how people unfortunately often behave. Given two bloody world wars and the associated killing of civilians, ethnic cleansing, and genocide, Freud's attitude should not be dismissed out of hand. In fact, he did have to flee as a refugee from Nazi Germany. Adler died in 1937 in Scotland, before the horrors of World War II took place.

In 1930 Freud gave vent to his pessimism and negative view of human nature in a remarkable passage in *Civilization and Its Discontents,* in which he commented on the age-old precept: "Thou shalt love thy neighbor as thyself":

> Not merely is this stranger in general unworthy of my love; I must honestly confess that he has more claim to my hostility and even my hatred. He seems not to have the least trace of love for me and shows me not the slightest consideration. . . . Indeed, if this grandiose commandment had run "Love thy neighbor as thy neighbor loves thee," I should not take exception to it. . . . The element of truth behind all this, which people are so ready to disavow, is that men are not gentle creatures who want to be loved, and who at the most can defend themselves if they are attacked; they are, on the contrary, creatures among whose instinctual endowments is to be reckoned a powerful share of aggressiveness. As a result, their neighbor is for them not only a potential helper or sexual object, but also someone who tempts them to satisfy their aggressiveness on him, to exploit his capacity for work without compensation, to use him sexually without his consent, to seize his possessions, to humiliate him, to cause him pain, to torture and to kill him. *Homo homini lupus* [*Man is a wolf to man*]. (Freud, 1930, pp. 110–111)

Adler was genuinely shocked by this statement (Orgler, 1963). To him, it was contrary to all reasonable views of human nature to assume that humans were inherently evil. He attributed Freud's outlook to his personality makeup. In Adler's view, Freud's psychology was indicative of his having been pampered as a child:

> And, indeed, if we look closely we shall find that the Freudian theory is the consistent psychology of the pampered child, who feels that his instincts must never be denied, who looks on it as unfair that other people should exist, who asks always, "Why should I love my neighbor? Does my neighbor love me?" (Adler, 1931, p. 97)

TRANSITIONAL SUMMARY

Paul Stepansky (1983) has reviewed the available evidence on the dissolution of the relationship between Freud and Adler, and he has summarized the features of Adler's developing theory that most concerned Freud:

1. Freud initially regarded Adler's focus on concepts such as organ inferiority (early Adlerian theory) as "too biological" to qualify as a psychological contribution (Stepansky, 1983, pp. 99 and 131).

2. Adler focused on what Freud considered surface issues rather than on the unconscious (Stepansky, 1983, p. 132). For Freud, the ego's struggle with the unconscious was central; for Adler, the creative activities of the ego in regard to external reality were most important.

3. Freud was concerned about Adler's move away from the idea that sexual libido was the key motivating force in human behavior (Stepansky, 1983, p. 132 ff.). Adler, it seemed to Freud, was more concerned with personal "safeguarding" strategies than he was with the threat of libidinal impulses to overwhelm the ego.

Of the three objections he had to Adler's ideas, Freud apparently considered the second one, what he considered to be the superficial focus of Adler's psychology, most important (Stepansky, 1983, p. 127). It is not difficult to understand why. At the time, and probably for many years to come, Freud thought his most unique contribution in creating psychoanalysis was his investigation of the unconscious and its power. Here was Adler, to all intents and purposes, saying that complex psychopathology and behavior could be understood without emphasizing that contribution.

INFERIORITY-SUPERIORITY:
FROM MINUS TO PLUS SELF-ESTIMATES

In light of Adler's childhood infirmities and his experiences of helplessness in the face of death, it is not surprising that he developed the concept of the **inferiority complex** (1927, 1929a, 1931, 1964). Adler was acutely aware that a sense of powerlessness in the face of death is not the only way that an inferiority complex may arise. Physical inferiorities in the form of damaged or diseased organs may also be contributing factors. These defects may impede or prevent successful competition. Children, merely by virtue of their small size, limited knowledge and ability, and lesser strength, often feel weak, helpless, and inferior in regard to adults.

Adler himself embarked on a lifelong struggle to compensate for his sense of inferiority. Adler, like some other personality theorists we will examine, generalized his understanding of his own strivings to humanity in general. In his theory, the struggle for superiority, whatever its origin, is an inherent characteristic of all living things, a product of organic evolution: "Set in motion at one time or other the material of life has been constantly bent on reaching a plus from a minus situation. . . . This movement is in no way to be regarded as leading to death; on the contrary, it is directed towards achieving the mastery of the external world and does not by any means seek a compromise with it or a state of rest" (Adler, 1964, p. 97). Thus, for Adler, the basic striving is not to achieve satisfaction of drives. For Adler, life is goal-directed and aims toward mastery and a sense of superiority.

It is interesting to note that Adler's theory itself constantly developed. The concepts of superiority and inferiority underwent several transformations as Adler refined his theory. Adler began with the view that a sense of inferiority is rooted in physical organ defects. Slowly, this medical conception was modified toward a psychological emphasis on the person's perception of his or her own physical inferiorities. Finally Adler emphasized the strivings of individuals to compensate for their inadequacies. By focusing on individual's subjective perceptions of their inferiorities, cultural and social factors came to be included in the theory. New Adlerian concepts such as the masculine protest, superiority strivings, and perfection strivings rapidly took their respective places as successive transitions of Adler's developing personality theory. An overview of these transitions is provided in Table 5.1. Please review it as a prelude to the more detailed discussions that follow.

Table 5.1   An Overview of Adler's Changing Views of the Fundamental Human Motive

Organ Inferiority

Least or most poorly developed organ succumbs fastest to environmental demands. Disease strikes only such predisposed organs.

$\downarrow$

Aggression Drive

Hostile attitude toward perceived helplessness in obtaining satisfactions. May be reversed into an opposite drive of humility or submission.

$\downarrow$

Masculine Protest

Every child desires to be competent, to be superior, and in control of their own life. Overcompensation to be "manly" and admired results.

$\downarrow$

Superiority Striving

Inherent biological urge toward self-expansion, growth, and competence.

$\downarrow$

Perfection Striving

Seeking after a chosen goal, or dream, fulfillment. Based on subjective or fictional estimates of life's values.

Organ Inferiority: Compensatory Strivings

Adler had fought his own childhood battles with **organ inferiority** in struggling to compete with his older brother and other children in physical activities. He later chose the vocation of physician in his continuing efforts to combat his own sense of helplessness by aiding others who needed help. He correspondingly decided to locate his first medical office in a neighborhood where many of his patients would be working men and women. Situated near the famous Prater amusement park of Vienna, Adler's practice also happened to include entertainers, acrobats, and artists of the Prater. Furtmüller (1973) has suggested in his biographical essay on Adler that these patients directed Adler's attention to the relevance of physical strength and weakness for patterns of adaptation.

> All these people [i.e., Prater entertainers], who earned their living by exhibiting their extraordinary bodily strength and skills, showed to Adler their physical weaknesses and ailments. It was partly the observation of such patients as these that led to his conception of overcompensation [for perceived inferiority]. (p. 334)

In 1907 Adler published a novel theory of disease that would now be considered a contribution to the then nonexisting field of psychosomatic medicine. Entitled "Study of Organ Inferiority and Its Psychical Compensation," the essay asserted that all persons succumb to disease in whichever organ is least well developed, less successfully functioning, and generally "inferior" from birth. Whatever the inherent bodily weakness, environmental demands and stresses have their greatest impact on the inferior organ. At the psychological as well as the physical level, the way individuals adapt to life is likely to be shaped by their reactions to their organ inferiorities.

At first, Adler had postulated that, because the entire organism is governed by a principle of equilibrium or balance, the inferior organ, guided by the central nervous system, would compensate for the defect of underdevelopment or damage. Undergoing increased growth and functioning power, the initially inferior organ or related organs might overcompensate for the previous deficit. For example, individuals with a speech defect may become so involved learning how to master it that they transform the inferiority into the basis for a career. Becoming a speech therapist, or an orator, or an actor, the individual can overcompensate for what had been a perceived inferiority (1907, p. 29).

Adler did not yet include his characteristic later emphasis on the individual's subjective perception of inferiority. He still thought of **compensation** and **overcompensation** as merely biological-environmental processes in the service of equilibrium or homeostasis. Adler's notion of organ inferiority did not mean that the individual suffers disease only through inherited organ defects. Sometimes the demands made upon them by the environment can cause an organ to become diseased.

Adler later saw that an individual's reaction to his or her physical infirmities, rather than the infirmities themselves, determined his or her type of compensatory behavior. Finally, Adler realized that organ inferiority, attempts to compensate for it, a person's sense of self-worth, and his or her unique reactions to the social environment are all inextricably "woven together."

The Aggression Drive

Adler's next step, taken in 1908, was to assert the existence of an inherent **aggression drive.** Freud himself was not yet ready to admit the possibility that aggressive strivings were equal in strength to the drive of sexuality. Adler, still working from a generally psychoanalytic framework, wanted to maintain the importance of Freud's basic pleasure principle. Thus Adler proposed that *both* the drives of sexuality and of aggression were fundamental. Along with these two primary biological urges, a number of diverse secondary drives associated with sensory processes like seeing, smelling, and hearing also had to be included in any account of motivated behavior. Adler's unique contribution was the idea that no drive stands alone, that there is a **confluence of drives** that enter into an **integrative amalgam** whereby each separate component drive is subordinated to the whole (Adler, 1908, p. 30).

Furthermore, Adler thought that drives could be displaced from their original form and goals and transformed into new types of expression. Some changes that were possible in his model of personality included:

- *Transformation of a drive into its opposite:* the unconscious drive to eat, for example, becomes the conscious refusal to eat.

- *Displacement of a drive to another goal:* the unconscious love for father becomes a conscious love for a teacher or other authority figure.

- *Redirection of a drive to one's own person:* the unconscious repressed drive to see becomes the conscious drive to be looked at; in other words, exhibitionism.

- *Displacement onto a second strong drive:* the repression of one drive may enhance the expression of another. Thus, blocking of the sex drive's direct expression may increase the drive to "look" at sexual objects. (Adler, 1908, pp. 32–33).

In his paper "Instincts and Their Vicissitudes" (1915a), Freud elaborated the first two of these transformations, for which he gave Adler some credit. Adler, however, developed the concept of "confluence of drives" in a different direction from Freud. He saw the aggression drive as the dominant and governing force shaping the confluence of drives:

> From early childhood, we can say from the first day (first cry) we find a stand of the child toward the environment which cannot be called anything but hostile. If one looks for the cause of this position, one finds it determined by the difficulty of affording satisfaction for the organ [i.e., the sites of drive; e.g., hunger]. This circumstance as well as the further relationships of the hostile, belligerent position of the individual toward the environment indicate a drive toward fighting for satisfaction which I shall call "aggression drive." (Adler, 1908, p. 34)

Adler continued,

> Pure expressions of this superordinate striving toward aggression take form as fighting, beating, biting, and outright cruelty. But aggression, following the principle of transformation or plasticity of drives, may also be expressed in less direct form. Athletic competition; religious conflict; social, national, and race struggles; politics; and even art embody this fundamental human motive. When the aggression drive is turned inward, the individual displays the resultant opposite traits of humility, submission, or in the extreme case, masochism. (Adler, 1908, p. 35)

In contrast to his emphasis on aggression, Adler also pointed out the importance of love and affection in the development of the child's personality. Parts of the drives to look, to touch, and to listen join in a unique confluence called the **need for affection:**

> Children want to be fondled [i.e., to be touched], loved, and praised [i.e., to be looked at]. They have a tendency to cuddle up, always to remain close to loved persons, and to want to be taken into the bed with them. (Adler, 1908, p. 40)

Adler found the striving for affection in some areas in which Freud perceived only sexual drives. Given these drives for affection, prudent parenting can have positive results. By partially satisfying children's love needs, their behavior can be shaped in the direction of social interest or concern for others. By partially denying them, they can be taught healthy independence.

MASCULINE PROTEST: NOT FOR MEN ONLY

Adler's theorizing to this point emphasized the biological nature of the organism and its defects: organ inferiority and the confluence of drives. In 1910, Adler shifted his focus to the psychological level. His psychological formulations were derived from his early physiological concepts of inferiority and aggression, but now he was interested in the *experience* and *perceived significance* of organ inferiorities. Adler first connected the biological fact of organ inferiority with its psychological counterpart, the feeling of inferiority. Thus children with marked defects like stuttering, clumsiness, deafness, visual deficits, or disfigurement develop a feeling of inferiority in relation to others. "Such children are thus often placed in a role which appears to them as unmanly. All neurotics have a childhood behind them in which they were moved by doubt regarding the achievement of full masculinity" (Adler, 1910, p. 47).

Adler identified superiority feelings with masculinity and inferiority feelings with femininity. Masculinity and femininity were to be understood as culturally accepted meanings rather than simply in terms of gender: Today, we may see identification of inferiority with femininity and masculinity with superiority as a poorly chosen set of terms, but early in the twentieth century, they were common metaphors in Western culture.

> . . . any form of uninhibited aggression, activity, potency, power, and the traits of being brave, free, rich, aggressive or sadistic can be considered masculine. All inhibitions and deficiencies, as well as cowardliness, obedience, poverty, and similar traits, can be considered as feminine. (Adler, 1910, p. 47)

Neither boys nor girls, according to Adler, wish to be locked into the "minus" role then assigned to the traditional concept of the female. The "feminine tendency" toward passivity itself provokes in the child a need to overcome a sense of inferiority. All persons, girls as well as boys, therefore, may engage in the protest to be superior. **Masculine protest,** or compensatory striving to demolish dependency, to assert autonomy, and to achieve superiority, emerges in both genders.

RELATION BETWEEN INFERIORITY AND SUPERIORITY

The core of the **inferiority complex** is organized around a network of traits that have in common the feelings of "smallness" and "powerlessness." The masculine protest overlays a defensive network of compensatory traits, as illustrated in Table 5.2. Striving for superiority is a two-phase process. In the first phase, children's sense of inferiority in relation to the adults around them fosters a timid, passive, and insecure feeling of smallness. In the second phase, a superordinate **striving for superiority,** for autonomy, and for assertive expression of "masculinity" compensates for these inferiority feelings. At a later point in his theorizing, Adler understood that compensatory "superior" traits could also be indicators of persons' interpretations of their inferiority.

The Mask Must Fit the Drama

An individual's life takes shape and direction in accordance with an unconscious plan to overcome sensed inferior traits. People create, to use Adler's later terminology, *fictional goals,* that is, subjective guiding ideals that represent mastery of their sense of inferiority. The ideal of mastery, furthermore, becomes the achievement toward which, throughout life, every fantasy, thought, and action are directed. The mask of compensatory

Table 5.2   Traits of Superiority Striving

Inferiority character traits	Masculine protest compensatory traits
timidity	impudence
indecision	stubbornness
insecurity	rebelliousness
shyness	impertinence
cowardliness	courage
increased need for support	defiance
submissive obedience	fantasy of hero, warrior, grandeur
fantasies of smallness	
masochism	

Based on Adler, 1910, p. 53.

"superior" traits must be consonant with this abiding life goal and must, in an unconscious fashion, foreshadow this desirable life outcome.

> The fictional, abstract ideal is the point of origin for the formation and differentiation of the given psychological resources [of the individual] into preparatory attitudes, readiness, and character traits. The individual then wears the character traits demanded by his fictional goal, just as the character mask (*persona*) of the ancient actor had to fit the finale of the tragedy. . . . The self-ideal [i.e., fictional goal] . . . carries within itself all abilities and gifts of which the so-disposed child considers himself deprived. (Adler, in 1956, pp. 94–95)

AN ILLUSTRATIVE CASE: LYING FOR SUPERIORITY

Philip, age nine, tells lies that portray him as a fearless hero, able to master all obstacles, willing to enter on new and bold adventures. "For example, he says, 'I was in England. From where I was standing I looked around the corner of a wall, and I saw a tiger'" (Adler, 1930a, p. 97; italics added). Adler commented:

> In itself, this is a big lie. But what interests me particularly is that he does not just look, he looks "around the corner of a wall." . . . This is virtuosity. Not everyone can do it. And it tells us even more: The boy's interest is particularly marked, and he is eager to conquer difficulties—difficulties which would be insurmountable for anyone else. (1930a, p. 97)

Philip has a visual problem; he is cross-eyed. For this acutely felt organ inferiority, Philip has learned to compensate with fantastic lies that involve impossible visual feats: "I looked around the corner of a wall." He turned a handicap into a marvelous feat. His mother describes Philip as a "problem child" because he is terribly restless and a poor student. In school, Philip feels unsure and "unequal to the demands of the situation." But he misses little in his life out of school. He is paradoxically incompetent at tasks favored by his parents and teachers, and quite competent at those of his own choosing. His mother further describes him as cowardly: "He is afraid of everything and runs away from any kind of danger."

Philip's mother understands that he would like to be brave and smart in school, and to be a person that everyone admires. She tries to help him, but Adler reveals that her "help" is more like pampering. She makes his decisions for him; she decides what dangers force her to protect him; she cares for his every need. Her husband confirms Adler's conclusion, for he too feels that she "spoils" Philip. Adler was very specific in his definition of the pampered child:

> A pampered child is one who has been relieved of his independent functioning. Someone else speaks for him, recognizes the dangerous situations, and protects him from them. In short, the child is taken in tow by someone else. He has another person at his disposal, and he builds his life in symbiosis with her. Such a child has a parasitic trait: he tries to get everything he wants through the aid of his mother. (Adler, 1930a, p. 97)

Despite his mother's attention, Philip is unlikely to give up his lies, for lying is the only source of independent superiority. In fact, the sole route open to Philip is to construct ever more subtle lies in an effort to avoid losing what remains of his own sense of selfhood: ". . . he cannot give up his lying and run the risk of appearing to be a 'zero' . . ." (Adler, 1931, p. 99).

Philip's lies continued to grow. For a school theme he wrote about a trip he and his father had made to a cemetery. The entire account was fictional, but Philip went so far as to indicate that he had even surpassed his father in courage: His father had cried, but "I didn't cry. A man doesn't cry."

Unable to win any sense of personal worth without lying for superiority, Philip's response was flight into a fantasy of superiority.

FICTIONALISM: THE PHILOSOPHY OF "AS IF"

To a considerable extent, the young Philip lived by a fiction. Philip's fiction was not identical with the lies he told but rather with the motive underlying his specific tales: namely, his desire to be brave, assertive, aggressive, and independent. Despite their contradiction of reality, idealistic fictions often serve us well as working hypotheses in daily living (Ansbacher & Ansbacher, 1956, p. 77).

The philosopher Hans Vaihinger (1911) published a book devoted to explaining the ways in which people create and live by the process of hypothetical or "as if" thinking. Entitled, *The Philosophy of "As If,"* Vaihinger's book so impressed Adler that he modified and adopted several of its concepts for his theory.

For Vaihinger, fictions are working hypotheses—useful theories and interpretations of reality that are valuable in making sense of life and guiding one's actions. Thus, although Vaihinger was skeptical regarding religion, he acknowledged that behaving "as if" there were a God lent meaning to people's lives. Similarly, the legal profession must operate "as if" corporations were persons. Physicists sometimes proceed "as if" electricity were a fluid or "as if" light consisted of discrete packets of energy. In his book, Vaihinger indicated that both science and ordinary life proceeded by inventing and testing "as ifs" or hypotheses to see if they are of value (1911).

The fiction or hypothesis may or may not coincide with the "truth" or objective fact it seeks to represent, but it may prove to be useful to the thinker. For Vaihinger, "truth is merely the most expedient degree of error, and error the last expedient degree of ideation"; but all such ideation is nevertheless fictional—hypothetical, invented, or made-up. What counted to the pragmatic Vaihinger is the degree of usefulness of any idea, the degree to which an idea helps one to deal with the demands of life.

What seemingly attracted Adler's interest in Vaihinger's philosophical position was Vaihinger's emphasis on the subjective perceptions and views of the thinker. Moreover, Adler was impressed by Vaihinger's stress upon the active individual nature of the process of creating fictions. All individuals create fictions that are unique to them, that result from their personal inventiveness. Vaihinger even made it clear that the creation of fictions was sometimes "carried on in the darkness of the unconscious," a proposition for which Adler's psychoanalytic experience readied him to accept (cf. Ansbacher & Ansbacher, 1956, p. 88). As in the case of Philip, each person can be most fully understood when we explore the fictions that underlie his or her goals and dreams, passions and promises.

PERSONALITY AS UNIFIED GOAL STRIVING: FICTIONAL FINALISM

Vaihinger's concept of fictions became for Adler the means to understanding the goal-directedness of personality and the creative process of the ego. He adopted the notion of a fictional final goal in the sense of an ultimate ambition at the center of a person's existence. Although Adler eventually dropped the term *fictional* from his designation of this

---

BOX 5.2 *Only Connect . . .*

Vaihinger's ideas are also similar to those of the psychologist George Kelly (Chapter 15). Kelly was a constructivist personality theorist, who also saw people as inventing, developing, and testing models of reality. Vaihinger's ideas were an early forerunner of the constructivist approach.

ultimate goal, three meanings of the concept derived from Vaihinger remained in his usage (Ansbacher & Ansbacher, 1956, p. 90):

- The goal is subjective and personally meaningful.
- The individual creates the goal to deal with the challenges of life.
- The goal is unconscious.

The immediate motive underlying the creating of the fictional goal is the need to gain superiority, to attain a state of "plus existence" from a position of minus:

> . . . the movement of the psyche is analogous to the movement of organic life. In each mind there is the conception of a goal or ideal to get beyond the present state, and to overcome the present deficiencies and difficulties by postulating a concrete aim for the future. *By means of this concrete aim or goal the individual can think and feel himself superior to the difficulties of the present because he has in mind his success of the future.* (Adler, 1929a, p. 2; italics added)

Adler pictured the creation of this *superordinate* goal, or process of **fictional finalism** (invented goal-directed activity), as beginning in early childhood. The child, from the base of his early **feelings of inferiority,** formulates a "prototype" of his later mature personality:

> A child, being weak, feels inferior and finds itself in a situation that it cannot bear. Hence it strives to develop, and *it* strives to develop along a line of direction fixed by the goal that it chooses for itself. . . . Children look for the strongest person in their environment and make him their model or their goal. It may be the father, or perhaps the mother, for we find that even a boy may be influenced to imitate his mother if she seems the strongest person. . . . Later on, the ideal may become the doctor or the teacher. For the teacher can punish the child and thus he arouses his respect as a strong person. (Adler, 1929a, pp. 3–4)

Thus Adler strongly emphasized the **teleological** or goal-directed character of the human personality. In Adler's own words, the creativity of the personality is "that power which expresses itself in the desire to develop, to strive, and to achieve—and even to compensate for defeats in one direction by striving for success in another" (1929a, p. 1). In 1912 Adler introduced new terminology for this final fictional goal. He referred to a "guiding self-ideal" as the unifying principle of personality, as in the idea of the role models referred to in the previously quoted passage. Consequently, Adler's view of personality began to emphasize more strongly the wholeness or unity of personality centered around a guiding goal.

How do these concepts apply to daily life? Let us say that a college student, let's call her Sally, would like to become a practicing attorney. She imagines a future in which she is a lawyer, and decides to take pre-law courses. She develops skills and bones up for the LSAT in her junior year. In short, she acts *as if* her goal were to become a reality. Finally, after many years of purposive effort, she enters the bar and begins the practice of law. Her dream has become a reality. How did this happen? It was through the planning and goal-directed activities of the ego, through the process of *fictional finalism*. For Adler, this is the creative process of humanity. The concepts of fictional finalism and the ego as creative apply to practically everything—the course you are taking, this textbook, the university you attend. All of these realities are the results of the dreams, goals, and ego activities of many people.

STRIVING FOR PERFECTION: FOCUS ON THE NEUROTIC PERSONALITY

Adler had described the core of the neurotic personality as a balance between inferiority and the striving for compensatory superiority as expressed in gaining power over others.

Neurotic personalities struggle with an exaggerated sense of their importance, their "god-likeness," in their efforts to win security:

> All neurotic symptoms have as their object the task of safeguarding the patient's self-esteem and thereby also the life-line [later, lifestyle] into which he has grown. To prove his ability to cope with life the patient needs arrangements and neurotic symptoms as an expedient. He needs them as an oversized safeguarding component against the dangers that, in his feeling of inferiority, he expects and incessantly seeks to avoid in working out his plans for the future. (Adler, 1913b, p. 263)

In Adler's view, the essential characteristics of neurotics are their self-centeredness, their inflated perception of self, and their overcompensation for their feelings of inferiority. For the neurotic, the dominant goal is self-security through personal superiority. A healthy interest in the being of others, in their welfare, in their commonality with the self, is excluded from the neurotic's personality development and life plan.

STRIVING FOR PERFECTION: "SAFEGUARDING" THE NEUROTIC PERSONALITY

All persons have feelings of inferiority, in Adler's view, but only the neurotic has blown them up to become the central fact of existence. Whereas normal individuals are capable of giving up their fictional goals as they mature, neurotics are defensively rigid and often unable to budge:

> More firmly than the normal individual does the neurotic fixate his God, his idol, his personality ideal, and cling to his guiding line, and with deeper purpose he loses sight of reality. *The normal person, on the other hand, is always ready to dispense with this aid, this crutch.* In this instance, the neurotic resembles a person who looks up to God, commends himself to the Lord, and then waits credulously for His guidance; the neurotic is nailed to the cross of his fiction. The normal individual, too, can and will create his deity, will feel drawn upward. But he will never lose sight of reality, and always takes it into account as soon as action and work are demanded. *The neurotic is under the spell of a fictional life plan.* (Adler, 1912, pp. 246–247; italics added)

Adler clearly had evolved a new scheme for interpreting the striving for superiority. He now saw this motive as a ceaseless yearning for perfection, a yearning that is inherent to organic life:

> The origin of humanity and the ever-repeated beginning of infant life impresses with every psychological act: "Achieve! Arise! Conquer!" This feeling, this longing for the abrogations of every imperfection, is never absent. . . . The unreluctant search for truth, the ever-unsatisfied seeking for solution of the problems of life, belongs to this longing for perfection of some sort. (Adler, 1956, pp. 103–104)

The striving for perfection in one's life is inherent to the processes of life itself, "something without which one could not even conceive of life" (Adler, 1973, p. 31).

Neurotic Self-Absorption

Adler portrayed the neurotic person as self-involved and self-absorbed.[1] Feelings of inferiority are intensified in the neurotic person because real or imagined threats to

---

[1]It must be remembered that the term *neurosis* was used by Adler, and by most clinicians of the period, as a generalized term for a broad range of psychological dysfunction. Today, *neurosis* is not a currently acceptable official diagnostic label for treatment or for insurance purposes.

self-esteem abound in every interaction with another, in every task attempted, and in every memory recalled. The neurotic becomes focused on self-protection:

> When scrutinized, the neurotic will be found to be an individual placed in a test situation who is attempting to solve his problems in the interest of his own personal ambition rather than in the interest of the common welfare. This holds true of all neuroses. All neuroses grow out of the psychic tensions of an individual who is not socially well prepared when he is confronted with a task which demands for its solution more social interest than he is capable of. (Adler, 1932, p. 91)

Safeguarding self-esteem and personal security become paramount to the neurotic person. Neurotic symptoms may be thought of primarily as tools for safeguarding:

> All neurotic symptoms are safeguards of persons who do not feel adequately equipped or prepared for the problems of life, who carry within themselves only a passive appreciation of social feelings and interest. (Adler, 1932, p. 95)

Neurotic Safeguarding Strategies

Because the neurotic person's self-esteem is so vulnerable, a "far-flung net of safeguards" becomes part of the person's coping style (Adler, 1913c, p. 264). **Safeguarding strategies** are defense mechanisms. Unlike the Freudian version of defense mechanisms, which are focused most on protecting the ego from instinctual (internal) dangers, Adler's safeguards are aimed more at protecting self-esteem from external, usually interpersonal, threats. Adler enumerated three classes of safeguarding strategies, each with its own subtypes:

1. **Excuses or rationalizing strategies**
2. **Aggressive strategies**
3. **Distancing strategies**

Excuses or Rationalizing Strategies

The neurotic develops symptoms that inhibit or impede some kinds of interpersonal functioning. He or she feels secure because a certain freedom to do less, achieve less, and demand less of self develops. It is as if the neurotic were excusing self from the usual demands of life by saying, "See, I have this illness or this symptom, so I cannot be expected to perform at my best." In Freudian theory, neurotic symptoms not only solve the neurotic conflict, but also provide *secondary gains* in the form of sympathy from people and a lessening of demands. Adler's concept of "excuses" is akin to the Freudian concept of secondary gain. Table 5.3 summarizes Adler's safeguards and provides a listing of comparable Freudian mechanisms. The similarities between safeguards and defense mechanisms range from substantial to superficial, and it might be helpful to consult Chapter 6 for a more complete account of Anna Freud's classic defense mechanisms.

Aggressive Strategies

In order to safeguard self-esteem, a neurotic person can express either open or disguised hostility to others and to self. Adler distinguishes between three main categories of aggressive safeguarding.

1. Depreciation is a strategy that the neurotic employs to devalue other people so that in comparison to self they are not seen as superior or as threats. A similar maneuver involves overvaluing self in relationship to others. Instead of expressing hostility directly toward competitors, the neurotic can accomplish the same end by inflating their own importance relative to others. Other people are perceived as inferior, just as when they are

Table 5.3   Adler's Safeguards and Freud's Defense Mechanisms

Adlerian "safeguard"	Description	Comparable Freudian defense mechanism
Excuses	Neurotic symptoms used as reasons to escape life's demands, cannot perform at one's best.	• Rationalization • Secondary gain
Aggression	1. *Depreciation:* strategies for feeling superior by making others feel inferior, or overvaluing self relative to others or being overly solicitous of others' welfare as a way to control them.	• Reaction formation • Altruistic surrender • Reversal
	2. *Accusation:* unconscious feelings of deprivation lead to blaming others for one's own feelings of inferiority and frustration. Sometimes person blames fate.	• Displacement • Rationalization • Projection
	3. *Self*-accusation (guilt): blaming self, "cursing" self, and suicidal thoughts and acts sometimes to gain attention, sometimes as a displaced intention to really hurt someone else. Or sometimes self-blame is a way of punishing others by making them feel guilty.	• Turning against self • Reversal • Asceticism
Distancing	Reflects the basic neurotic conflict between feelings of inferiority and strivings for superiority.	
	1. *Moving backward* by using symptoms to avoid social obligations, being helpless, "can't do anything."	• Fixation • Regression
	2. *Standing still* by refusing to do anything or participate in life, especially when demands are made.	• Inhibition • Regression
	3. *Hesitation and procrastination* around a self-created difficulty and attempts to master it. Obsessions and compulsions.	• Rationalization • Undoing
	4. *Constructing obstacles* by focusing on a symptom and blaming failure on it. Usually the least severe form of safeguarding because there is some success.	• Rationalization • Inhibition

depreciated directly, but the neurotic can console the self by implying they are not disparaging other people, only comparing them to their own magnificent self (1913c, p. 268).

In a similar way, the neurotic can depreciate others subtly by comparing real people to impossible ideal standards. The neurotic says to self, "I must be careful not to yield to submission; what I want is a wife (or husband) who is strong (or smart, or powerful, etc.)." But, of course, no real person ever lives up to the ideal, somewhat magical standard, and the result is depreciation of most candidates for an intimate relationship.

Finally, Adler describes another, more subtle, even backhanded form of depreciation. He observes that neurotic people can be overly solicitous for the welfare of others. They behave as if they are altruistically concerned that the people in their lives are exposed to dangers, confusions, and demands that only they can help them master. The neurotic seems to believe that without his or her help, other people are incapable of caring for themselves:

> They always give advice, want to do everything themselves, find new dangers and never rest until the other person, confused and discouraged, confides himself to their care. Neurotic parents thus create much damage. . . . The neurotic aspires to make the laws for the others (1913c, p. 269).

This kind of loving concern hurts. With friends like the neurotic people Adler is describing, we do not need enemies.

2. Accusation involves a more direct expression of anger. The neurotic feels unconsciously deprived and frustrated by others, and embarks on subtle blaming of others. The person blames parents, siblings, or fate for their own difficulties. Adler referred to this strategy as the "Cinderella" fantasy because, like Cinderella, the person looks for someone, a "Prince Charming," to take responsibility and to be the source of well-being and happiness. In Freud's terms, *accusation* may be considered a form of displacement and is often found combined with the defense of rationalization in some people to avoid a sense of responsibility.

3. Self-accusation is putting the blame for one's misfortunes on self, but doing it in such a way that it attracts attention, sympathy, concern, or help from others. Unconsciously, the neurotic person who accuses self also provokes guilt as a kind of atonement for being inferior. Self-accusation, making oneself a pitiable target of criticism can also be a way of inducing guilt in others—trying to make them feel guilty for one's misery. The comparable Freudian mechanisms are turning-against-the-self, reversal, and asceticism.

Distancing Strategies

The person can also safeguard self-esteem by restricting his or her participation in life. The person protects his or her self-image by avoiding challenging situations where there is some risk of failure. Adler described four overlapping **distancing strategies.** There is not much difference among them, even though Adler gave them four different names:

1. *Moving backward* is a strong indicator of the basic conflict of the neurotic person because he or she is caught between wanting success and wanting to avoid failure. As a result, the person becomes motivationally frozen. The person "moving backward" can either do nothing or develop symptoms that are equivalent to doing nothing, such as mutism (can't talk), hysterical paralyses (can't move), abulia (can't decide), agoraphobia (can't go out into the world), anorexia (can't eat), or amnesia (can't remember). According to Adler the person can also display severe anxiety attacks or even criminal behavior. The major point, however, is that the neurotic symptoms put a great deal of distance between the person and the demands of life. Comparable, but not identical Freudian defenses are fixation and regression.

2. *Standing still* is not much different from "moving backward"; the person shows the same motivationally frozen attitude, but the symptoms are less dramatic. The person again uses the neurotic symptom as a way of not putting self in jeopardy of evaluation. Examples are complaints of weak memory, insomnia that produces fatigue and prevents work, or premature ejaculation that prevents a sustained intimate relationship. The trigger for such behaviors is some life demand, such as an examination, a job task, or a relationship demand that all serve to prompt the person to find a way of "standing still" and not participating. When the external demand or test is removed, the safeguarding strategy disappears. Analogous Freudian defenses are inhibition and regression.

3. *Hesitation* is a "back and forth" strategy of safeguarding by procrastinating so that whatever effort the person makes, it is "too late." The person may unconsciously create his or her own difficulties, and then, just as unconsciously, create a way of mastering it that becomes a neurotic symptom. Washing compulsions, touching compulsions, leaving things unfinished, destroying nearly completed work because it has to be done over to be right are all ways of wasting time and never committing oneself to be evaluated. Analogous Freudian mechanisms are undoing and rationalization.

4. *Construction of obstacles* is similar to hesitation and to the strategy of excuses because the person looks for problems that will prevent him or her from expending effort.

Table 5.4   Transitions in Adler's Conception of Human Motivation

Motive or personality goal	*Antecedent or cause*
1. Organ inferiority	Physiological-environmental interaction
2. Aggression drive	Frustrated biological needs and perceived helplessness
3. Masculine protest	Cultural attitudes toward "maleness," and feelings of passivity or inferiority
4. Superiority striving	Evolutionary trend toward successful adaptation; personal feelings of inferiority
5. Perfection striving	Subjective interpretation of life's meaning, life's values, the fictional final goal

However, this version is usually the least restrictive form of the safeguarding strategies, because the person has some successes, some achievements. But the person rationalizes by saying, "If only I wasn't handicapped by such and such, I could have achieved so much more." The person does not use the obstacle to break off his or her efforts. Rather the obstacle is a challenge that can be overcome even with partial success (and therefore partial effort) so that the person can say, "Oh, what I could have done had I not been ill."

Adler pointed out that there is a complex relationship between anxiety and the safeguarding tendencies. The safeguards are attempts to avoid the anxiety of perceived low self-esteem. But anxiety can also be a person's first response to any new challenge, such as looking for a job, leaving home, looking for a companion. All the person can think about is the anxiety, not the task, and in this way is already distanced from life. The safeguards that the person will develop will be maintained by this anxiety at the same time that the anxiety serves as a distancing mechanism.

The Completed Transition

Adler viewed the striving for perfection as consistent with the Darwinian principle of adaptation to the environment. He viewed the striving for perfection as more than minimal adaptation but rather a "victorious adaptation to the external world." With the concept of perfection-striving as a basic evolutionary process of adaptation to life's circumstances, Adler had maintained continuity with his earliest notions of organ inferiority and the striving to compensate and win a sense of superiority. By the assumption of an inherent biological trend toward better adaptation (i.e., toward perfection), Adler also maintained the goal-seeking or teleological aspect of his personality theory. The steps involved in this final conception of perfection-striving as the superordinate or overriding goal of life are summarized in Table 5.4. It may be of some help to compare the contents of Table 5.4 with the items outlined previously in Table 5.1.

SOCIAL INTEREST: THE TASKS OF LIFE

Even though the striving for perfection is common to normal and neurotic personality alike, the neurotic's motives are isolated from any interest in the rest of humanity. Indeed, they are isolated from any interest, even in those closest to them. Adler indicated the essentially normal sympathy of feeling for one's fellow humans by a German term he coined **Gemeinschaftsgefuhl.** He favored the term **social interest** as the best English translation (Ansbacher & Ansbacher, 1956, p. 134).

Adler thought that the normal person's trait of social interest is missing in the neurotic person:

Figure 5.1 Aldred Adler speaking to a receptive audience in Sweden. Consistent with his concepts of *Gemeinschaftsgefuhl* (literally "fellow feeling") or social interest, Adler believed it was important to reach out to the public in many countries with his ideas. He no doubt would use television or the Internet to reach people if he were alive in today's world.

> It is always the want of social feeling, whatever be the name one gives it—living in fellowship, co-operation, humanity, or even the ideal-ego—which causes an insufficient preparation for all the problems of life. (Adler, 1964, p. 110)

Adler asserted that only a person with strong social interest could successfully solve these problems of life. Adler conceived each of these life tasks as a universal life problem that all humans are called upon to master. He grouped them under three categories. Adler's ideas here are very similar to Erik Erikson's concept of *generativity* (Chapter 8). Both of them are very concerned with the overall impact of the person's life on the world.

- *Occupational Tasks.* In the selection and pursuit of a vocation as a productive mode of existence, a person "arrives at a feeling of his worth to society, the only possible means of mitigating the universally human feeling of inferiority. The person who performs useful work lives in the midst of the developing human society and helps to advance it."

- *Societal Tasks.* In this instance the goal is to make a positive difference in the society in which one finds oneself. One works with others to build a better community, society, or world.

- *Love Tasks.* The relationship between the sexes is the last significant "task" to be mastered. "On his approach to the other sex and on the fulfillment of his sexual role depends his part in the continuance of mankind" (Adler, 1933, p. 132).

Adler emphasized the relatedness of the three tasks:

> The three problems are never found apart, for they all throw cross lights on one another. A solution of one helps toward the solution of the others, and indeed we can say that they are all aspects of the same situation and the same problem—*the necessity for a human being to preserve life and to further life in the environment in which he finds himself.* (Adler, 1933, pp. 132–133; italics added)

The individual who embodies a healthy social interest is expressing an empathic attitude toward life: *"To see with the eyes of another, to hear with the ears of another, to feel with the heart of another"* (Adler, 1956, p. 135; italics added).

STYLE OF LIFE: INDIVIDUAL PSYCHOLOGY

Adler chose the phrase **individual psychology** to identify his system. He emphasized the subjective nature of the individual's goal striving, the creativity of human psychological adaptation, and the wholeness of personality. And then, individuals subordinate all drives, needs, and strivings to the context of their entire **style of life,** the very pattern of their existence as social beings as they create it:

> The goal of superiority, with each individual, is personal and unique. It depends upon the meaning he gives to life; and this meaning is not a matter of words. It is built up in his style of life and runs through it like a strange melody of his own creation. . . . Understanding a style of life is similar to understanding the work of a poet. A poet must use words; but his meaning is more than the mere words he uses. The greatest part of his meaning must be guessed at; we must read between the lines. . . . The psychologist must learn to read between the lines; he must learn the art of appreciating life-meanings. (Adler, 1931, pp. 57–58)

To the degree that individuals have developed healthy social interests, their strivings for superiority will be shaped into a style of life that is warmly receptive of others and focused on friendship and interpersonal ties. They will be characteristically expectant that other people are similarly warmly receptive of them and are therefore sources of satisfaction and pleasure.

Style of life, then, is based on each individual's unique interpretations of his or her inferiority. Adler illustrated his meaning of *style of life* with the following analogy:

> Perhaps I can illustrate this by an anecdote of three children who were taken to the zoo for the first time. As they stood before the lion's cage, one of them shrank behind his mother's skirts and said, "I want to go home." The second child stood where he was, very pale and trembling, and said, "I'm not a bit frightened." The third glared at the lion fiercely and asked his mother, "Shall I spit at it?" The three children really felt inferior, but each expressed his feelings in his own way, consonant with his style of life. (1931, p. 50)

One's style of life is the product of a *creative* personality trend to overcome one's unique sense of inferiority. The goal that beckons one becomes the guiding force in life. A person decides to shape one' s life in the direction of that goal because one's own feelings of inferiority form a unique constellation with one's' own striving for superiority.

> Every individual represents both a unity of personality and the individual fashioning of that unity. The individual is thus both the picture and the artist. He is the artist of his own personality, but as an artist he is neither an infallible worker nor a person with a complete understanding of mind and body; he is rather a weak, extremely fallible, and imperfect human being. (Adler, 1956, p. 177; see also 1930c, p. 24)

In Adler's view, therefore, the individual is a creative artist of personality, an active constructor of their life events.

ADLER'S TYPOLOGY OF PERSONALITY

Adler developed a theory of personality types based on the degree of social interest and activity level. For Adler, the important fact was not whether a person had to overcome a deep sense of inferiority. According to him, such a sense of inferiority was universal. It applied to everyone. What was most important was to what extent a person developed a constructive rather than a destructive style of life.

In addition to the all-important, constructive-destructive dimension, Adler further defined and categorized an individual as either a **ruling-dominant type, getting-leaning type, avoidant type,** or **socially useful type.** Clearly the socially-useful type would be the most constructive. Descriptions of the four specific types of this typology are:

1. *The Ruling-Dominant Type.* These personalities are assertive, aggressive, and active. They manipulate and master the life situation and the people in it. Their activity levels are high but are combined with minimal social interests. The danger is that the activities will be directed into antisocial behaviors.

2. *The Getting-Leaning Type.* These types of individuals expect others to satisfy their needs and to provide for their interests; they may be said to "lean on" others. The getting-leaning types are combinations of low social interests and low activity levels.

3. *The Avoidant Type.* These individuals are inclined to achieve success by circumventing a problem, by withdrawing from it. In effect, they achieve mastery by avoiding defeat. Their social interests are as low as those of the getting-leaning types, but their activity levels are even lower.

4. *The Socially Useful Type.* This personality type is the healthiest of them all in Adler's view. The socially useful person attacks problems head on with a realistic appraisal of their difficulty. This type is socially oriented and prepared to cooperate with others to master the tasks of life. Thus the socially useful person has a combination of high activity level and high social interest (based on Adler, 1935, pp. 167–168).

An important consideration was the degree of empathy and social interest embodied in a particular type. Adler considered the capacity for empathy as necessary for a life that avoids self-centered neurotic striving.

EARLY RECOLLECTIONS AS INDICATORS OF STYLE OF LIFE

Adler thought that one of the most significant ways of understanding patients was to explore their earliest recollections. We have already seen an application of this technique to aspects of Adler's own life. The incidents, feelings, and people that an individual recalls from early in life are significant as a result of the selectivity of such memories. Current meanings and understandings are expressed in the memories that are available for recall. Thus, if one lives one's life "as if" others are always trying to humiliate one, the memories one is likely to recall are those of humiliation or those that can be interpreted as humiliating experiences (Adler, 1956, p. 351). A person's memories "represent his 'Story of My Life'; a story he repeats to himself to warn him or comfort him, to keep him concentrated on his goal, and to prepare him by means of past experiences, so that he will meet the future with an already tested style of action" (Adler, 1931, p. 73).

Adler considered the most significant early recollection as the one that a person chooses to verbalize first. This incident will reveal the basic life attitude, "his first satisfactory crystallization of his attitude." Adler in no way accepted the individual's recollections as statements of fact. He seems, rather, to have treated them more as a form of a projective test whereby the individual's *perceived meanings,* not the objective truth of the memory, are the key indicator. Therefore Adler considered even false or distorted "memories" to be significant as reflections of personality. "What is altered or imagined is also expressive of a patient's goal . . ." (Adler, 1956, p. 352).

Adler treated a 32-year-old man, suffering for two years with hysterical aphasia. He accidentally fell against the window of a taxi. For two days, he vomited and suffered intense headaches—probably from a concussion. At this time he lost his voice, although his throat showed no organic changes and no signs of injury from the accident. Eventually, the man decided to sue the taxi company for his injuries. As Adler diplomatically stated, "We can understand that he is in a much better situation with his lawsuit if he can show some disability. We need not say that he is dishonest; but he has no great stimulus to speak loudly" (1931, p. 86).

To help him understand this patient, Adler asked for his earliest memory: He responded,

> "I was hanging in the cradle, lying on my back. I remember seeing the hook pull out. The cradle fell and I was badly hurt." (1931, p. 87)

Adler viewed the man's recollection as revealing an important aspect of his style of life: His mother had been horrified when she discovered the mishap in the cradle, and she showered him with atypical attentiveness. It was the man's opinion that he had deserved the increased concern and attention because, before the accident, "She did not take good enough care of me." In the man's opinion, the childhood accident occurred largely because his mother had failed to prevent it. The taxi incident many years later followed the same pattern, for he thought the company and the cab driver "did not take good enough care of him" (Adler, 1931, p. 87).

The character of these recollections suggested to Adler that the man had been a "pampered child," a favorite descriptive phrase for Adler. For Adler, such a child was one whose daily life involved the delegation of responsibility for living to others. Allowed to make none of his own choices, protected from every danger, the child soon fails to develop genuine autonomy, and he resents people who do not shower him with favor. The case history we presented earlier of Philip, "the liar," is a similar example of a pampered child.

The man's next recollection was along the same lines: "At the age of five I fell twenty feet with a heavy board on top of me. For five or more minutes I was unable to speak" (1931, p. 87). Again, his mother was horrified and then very attentive. Adler's interpretation needs no elaboration:

> He was a child who wanted to be pampered, to be the center of attention. We can understand how he wants to be paid for his misfortunes [i.e., the taxi accident]. Other pampered children might do the same if the same accidents happened. Probably, however, they would not hit on the device of having a speech defect. This is the trademark of our patient; it is part of the style of life he has built up out of his experiences. (1931, pp. 87–88)

ORDINAL POSITION WITHIN THE FAMILY AS INDICATOR OF STYLE OF LIFE

Adler used the **birth order** of children within a family as a diagnostic indicator. Adler pointed to the myriad differences that exist between the first born and the last born, to the differences between an only child and a child with many siblings, and so on. *First born, second born, youngest child,* and *only child* are considered significant roles by Adler.

Adler's observations seem to describe some aspects of the behavior of many people, but they are by no means universally relevant. Merely examining birth order does not elucidate the pattern of relationships within a family nor does it take account of the personalities of the parents, the nature of their parenting, or many other factors. Adlerian birth-order analysis is transparently a very generalized and often inaccurate approach to understanding a given individual. We present Adler's typology with the understanding that it has many limitations. One of the problems is that Adler assumes a standard married, two-parent household with traditional roles. Many changes have occurred in typical family structure since Adler's time. Increased numbers of divorces, blended families, stay-at-home-fathers, working mothers, and single-parent families have limited the applicability of Adler's theory. We might consider preserving Adler's general idea that a child's role in the family affects his or her development of life style, but such a role is based on much more than simply birth order. Family history and the complexity of relationships within the family must be taken into account.

First Born (Oldest)

Because it is first born, the oldest child lives a favored existence for a time as an only child. It is given central place until another child is born to remove its favored status. Adler comments,

> Now he must share the attention of his mother and father with a rival. The change always makes a great impression and we can often find in problem children, neurotics, criminals, drunkards, and perverts that their difficulties began in such circumstances. They were oldest children who felt deeply the arrival of another child; and their sense of deprivation had molded their whole style of life. (1931, p. 144)

Though skillful at gaining attention, the oldest child eventually learns that mother is too busy, too harassed, or too unconcerned to tolerate its demands. It turns to father. By directing attention-getting behaviors to father, the deprived oldest child seeks to "reproach his mother" (1931, p. 146). The outcome of this family struggle is that the oldest child "trains himself for isolation." It masters the technique of surviving alone and independently of the need for anyone's affection or attention. Because the happiest time of life was before the birth of the new child, oldest children often show an unusual interest in the past. "They are admirers of the past and pessimistic over the future" (1931, p. 147).

A healthy outcome is also possible. An oldest child may imitate father and mother in their attentions to the other children. As such imitation progresses, the oldest becomes a helper to the younger children or a mother or father figure to playmates.

Second Born

From birth, a second-born child is raised in a world in which mother divides her attention and ministrations between her two children. This second child's existence is the more favored of the two since it has, so to speak, a pacemaker in the form of an older brother or sister. It is thus stimulated, or perhaps provoked, to match the older child's exploits:

> He behaves as if he were in a race, as if someone were a step or two in front and he had to hurry to get ahead of him. He is under full steam all the time. (Adler, 1931, p. 148)

When, however, the oldest child, the pacemaker, beats the younger sibling, the younger child is likely to feel incompetent. The most difficult combination occurs when the oldest is a boy and the second child is a girl. If the girl beats the older boy at his own game, he fares worse than if the younger child had been another boy. On the other hand, if the older child sets a pace to which the girl cannot match her stride, her personal and culturally reinforced feelings of inferiority will be intensified. Generally, however, the second child is the conqueror, using direct and devious means to surpass the pacemaker (Adler, 1929b, p. 106).

The Youngest Child

Although in a large family each succeeding child dethrones the previously born one, the last or youngest can never be removed from its pampered position. This child has many pacemakers, but because it retains the position of the thoroughly *pampered child,* the baby of the family group, it often outstrips its brothers and sisters in achievements.

Adler thought, however, that the second largest proportion of problem children come from the group of youngest:

> The reason for this generally lies in the way in which all the family spoils them. A spoiled child can never be independent. He loses courage to succeed by his own effort. Youngest children are always ambitious; but the most ambitious children of all are the lazy children. Laziness is a sign of ambition joined with discouragement; ambition so high that the individual sees no hope of realizing it. (1931, p. 151)

Because of the multiplicity of its pacemaker models, the youngest child is driven to desire success in everything. Because universal accomplishment is unlikely, he or she may be discouraged and give up.

The Only Child

The only child's rival is the father. Pampered by the mother because she is afraid of losing her child, the only child becomes "tied to the mother's apron strings." In later life, when no longer the center of attention, this enforced timidity and passivity will operate to the child's detriment.

> Only children are often very sweet and affectionate, and later in life they may develop charming manners in order to appeal to others, as they train themselves in this way, both in early life and later. . . . We do not regard the only child's situation as dangerous, but we find that, in the absence of the best educational methods, very bad results occur which would have been avoided if there had been brothers and sisters. (Adler, 1929b, pp. 111–112)

EVALUATING ALFRED ADLER

Adler's Legacy

A large portion of what Adler wrote and thought that was criticized by the orthodox Freudians has become mainstream ego psychology or accepted into humanistic psychology. It was Adler, striving to promote his own unique theory, who focused on some of the blind spots in the psychoanalytic conception of human beings well before the "orthodox revisionists" within psychoanalysis also expanded the theory into the arena of ego psychology. Adler's chief contribution was to provide the framework for a unified, holistic account of personality. His view of people as creative was along the lines that Carl Rogers, Abraham Maslow, and other humanistic theorists (Chapter 13) would later pursue. Adler's work thus anticipated many later developments in psychoanalytic theory, humanistic theory, cognitive psychology, and even social learning theory (Mosak & Maniacci, 1999).

Adlerians train therapists in institutes and in professional graduate programs around the world. Recent trends in psychotherapy including the method of coaching and focusing on formulating and reaching goals follow in Adler's footsteps. Adler's optimistic approach to the possibility of change in people who have had difficult early circumstances facilitates the development of therapeutic programs for the disadvantaged.

Refutability of Adler's Concepts

It is of some historical interest that Karl Popper's criterion of refutability was created in part as his response to the ideas of Adler and Freud. Popper conceived of the idea of refutability when he realized that Freud's, Adler's, and Karl Marx's theories could explain any kind of human behavior. Popper's account of how he first came to the concept of refutability is instructive both for its historical value and for its relevance to Adler's work. Popper (1965, p. 35) said that he was, in fact, "much impressed" by his experience of working with Alfred Adler in 1919 when he discussed a case with Adler and found that Adler could account for a child's behavior easily with his theory of inferiority feelings. Popper asked Adler how he could be so sure of his interpretation, and Adler replied, "Because of my thousand fold experience." Popper responded wryly, "And with this new case, I suppose, your experience has become thousand-and-one-fold" (1965, p. 35). Popper was not simply being sarcastic. The interchange with Adler set Popper thinking:

> . . . every conceivable case could be interpreted in the light of Adler's theory, or equally of Freud's. I may illustrate this by two very different examples of human behaviour: that of a man who pushes a child into the water with the intention of drowning it; and that of a man who sacrifices his life in an attempt to save the child. Each of these two cases can be explained with equal ease in Freudian and in Adlerian terms. According to Freud the first man suffered from repression (say, of some component of his Oedipus complex), while the second man had achieved sublimation. According to Adler the first man suffered from feelings of inferiority (producing perhaps the need to prove to himself that he dared to commit some crime), and so did the second man (whose need was to prove to himself that he dared to rescue the child). *I could not think of any human behaviour which could not be interpreted in terms of either theory.* It was precisely this fact—that they *always fitted,* that they were always confirmed—which in the eyes of their admirers constituted the strongest argument in favor of these theories. (Popper, 1965, p. 35, italics added)

What Popper realized is that precisely the apparent comprehensiveness of the theories—that they apply to and are confirmed by so much—is their greatest weakness. To be compatible with any outcome is to predict no one outcome (see also Stepansky, 1983, pp. 37ff. for a similar view of Adler's difficulties with refutability).

Adler's theory, like Freud's and like the theories of the other psychoanalytically oriented thinkers, is largely unrefutable. The basic concepts, such as superiority striving, or the inferiority complex, or even the safeguarding strategies, are empirically empty. None of these concepts specifies measurable, observable consequences that ought to exist if they are inaccurate. In Popper's language, such concepts are not falsifiable.

There are sections of Adler's thinking that, in principle, are empirically testable. For example, his ideas on the effects of birth order should lead to some measurable consequences in the real world. And, in fact, a great deal of research has been done on the personality effects of birth position. The results of such research do indicate in a general way that there is some impact on personality of a person's birth-order in a family, but the effect clearly depends on many factors including the subjective perceptions of the family members, cultural and economic factors, and the specific dynamics and history of an individual family.

Adler's Conception of Human Agency

Almost from the beginning, Adler argued that a person was not trapped by personal history, biology, or social circumstances. Each person has the ability to alter or adapt creatively to these conditions. When we read Adler's essays, our impression is that he was angered by people who passively accept their limitations or who create their own obstacles in order to safeguard their self-esteem.

It might be argued, however, that Adler allowed for a balance between environmental determinism and choice as, for example, in his concept of organ inferiority. But by the final phases of his theory construction, it is quite clear that Adler placed the greatest emphasis on a person's power to choose, capacity to interpret, and willingness to try to change the conditions of his or her life in the direction of social interest. Genetic, physical, or environmental limitations were there as challenges for the individual to overcome. "If life gives you lemons, make lemonade," was his approach to life.

The Idiographic Versus Nomothetic Nature of Individual Psychology

As the very term *individual psychology* suggests, the major focus of Adler's theory is idiographic. For the same reasons discussed under his conception of human agency, Adler stressed the individual's unique and creative interpretation of reality as the most important element of his understanding of psychology. And, like the other thinkers who share psychoanalytic propositions, Adler's own efforts were largely clinical and educational, working with individual cases and using such work as support for his ideas. There are also some nomothetic aspects to his theory. For example, his thoughts about birth order represent a nomothetic typology. Also, concepts such as the inferiority complex and superiority strivings are viewed as generally applicable, although the specific content of an inferiority complex or superiority strivings can be individualized.

SUMMARY

As a child, Alfred Adler had been singularly sensitized to cues indicating his own frailty and powerlessness. Poor health prevented him from competing successfully with his older brother and peers in the athletic pursuits of boyhood. Repeated brushes with death impressed Adler with the fragility of human nature and with the necessity for struggling against imposed helplessness. His resentment toward his mother and brother led to his conviction that hostility had to be controlled and replaced by a healthy concern for others. In his later theory of personality, Adler referred to this essential quality of the healthy personality as *Gemeinschaftsgefuhl* (social interest).

Having joined Freud's intellectual circle in Vienna in 1902, Adler, never completely committed to psychoanalysis, slowly drew further apart from orthodox Freudian theory. By 1911 the split between Freud and Adler reached a climax, and Adler set off to develop his own school of individual psychology. His differences from Freud were many, but key theoretical discrepancies can be discerned in the following six areas:

1. The ego was not merely the handmaiden of the id, but an independent, creative entity mediating intercourse with social reality.

2. The Oedipus complex was not exclusively a sexual phenomenon but an indication of the boy's attempts to gain superiority and power as possessed by the father.

3. Narcissism was not a retraction of energy into the ego as a protective self-interest, but an unhealthy, antisocial, and egocentric withdrawal of interest in others.

4. Personality could not be studied piecemeal or in fragments of discrete id, ego, or superego functioning; *the human person is a whole entity,* striving toward self-determined goals.

5. Dreams are attempts to create a mood that will induce awake dreamers to take action they were previously reluctant to pursue; dreams are not satisfactions, as Freud held, but attempts to solve problems from waking life.

6. Freud's view of the inherent evil of human nature offended Adler's optimistic philosophical convictions of innate human goodness.

For Adler the central core of personality is a state of perceived inferiority for which the individual feels compelled to compensate by striving for superiority. The notion of inferiority compensation underwent several changes in Adler's thinking. In order of their development, they are:

1. **Organ inferiority**

2. **Aggression drive**

3. **Masculine protest**

4. **Superiority striving**

5. **Perfection striving**

Adopting Vaihinger's concept of *fictional finalism,* Adler postulated that all persons have a fictional final goal. The meaning of individuals' lives can be understood only by comprehending the goals toward which they strive.

Adler developed a typology of personality organized on the principles of activity level and degree of social interest. Four personality types were described: ruling-dominant, getting-leaning, avoiding, and socially useful. Adler believed that only the socially useful personality type, embodying a high degree of social interest and a high degree of activity, was healthy enough to master successfully the three types of life tasks: occupational tasks, societal tasks, and love tasks.

Adler's diagnostic indicators employed in psychotherapy included the analysis of early recollections and the interpretation of the child's ordinal position within the family. Early recollections are important indicators because they reveal the central concerns and unconscious goals (fictions) of the personality through its conscious choice of key memories. Positional or ordinal psychology is concerned with the child's relationship to parents and siblings. The first born is independent and initially favored; the second born is also favored because it has the "pacemaker" older sibling to model itself after, though there is the danger that it may feel incompetent by comparison, as had Adler with his older brother; the youngest child has many pacemakers to follow and is customarily the "most pampered"; and, finally, the only child, who, like the first born, learns to be independent, is initially pampered, but may ultimately become timid and passive because it lacks pacemakers and siblings with whom to compete.

Evaluation of Adler's theory indicates that many, but not all, of its concepts are nonrefutable. In fact, Karl Popper created the criterion of refutability largely out of consideration for the capacity of Freud and Adler's theories to be compatible with nearly any human behavior. Adler is a strong proponent of an active agency conception of human motivation and behavior, as evidenced in his adoption of Vaihinger's "as if" process of creativity. Many aspects of individual psychology are highly individualized or idiographic. Other aspects, such as Adler's typification of the differential psychologies of people with different birth orders, are nomothetic.

FOR FURTHER READING

Two readily accessible paperbacks by Adler that express his ideas in a very clear way are *What Life Could Mean to You* and *Understanding Human Nature.* Both were published by Hazelden Information and Education Services (Center City, MN, 1998). *Adler For Beginners* by Anne Hooper and Jeremy Holford (New York: Writers and Readers, 1998) is an excellent, deceptively simple comic-book style summary of Adler's life and work.

Adler's definitive work is *The Practice and Theory of Individual Psychology* (London: Routledge, 1999). It was originally published in 1924. Two biographical accounts are worth pursuing for what they reveal of the sources of Adler's ideas on inferiority and superiority. The most comprehensive biography is Phyllis Bottome's *Alfred Adler: A Portrait From Life* (New York: Vanguard, 1957). More concerned with explicating Adler's concepts than his life is Hertha Rogers' *Alfred Adler: The Man and His Work* (New York: Putnam, 1963).

Harold Mosak, an eminent Adlerian therapist, and Michael Maniacci have recently written a book that highlights the connections between Adler's thought to current trends in psychological theory and practice— *A Primer of Adlerian Psychology: The Analytic-Behavioral-Cognitive Psychology of Alfred Adler* (New York: Brunner/Mazel, 1999). An older book, edited by Mosak, places Adler's work in historical perspective and evaluates his influence: *Alfred Adler: His Influence on Psychology Today* (Park Ridge, NJ: Noyes Press, 1973). Some of the papers in this collection seek to extend Adlerian theory to family and child therapy.

Heinz and Rowena Ansbacher collected some of Adler's writings and edited them into a coherent account of his theory in *The Individual Psychology of*

Alfred Adler (New York: Harper & Row, 1956); this volume serves as an excellent sourcebook for students of Adlerian psychology. The Ansbachers have performed the same service with a collection of Adler's later writings in *Superiority and Social Interest: A Collection of Later Writings* (New York: Viking, 1973), and this volume contains Furtmüller's previously unpublished biography of Adler. An interesting collection of case histories with Adler's comments is provided in *The Problem Child* (New York: Putnam, 1963) and in *Problems of Neurosis,* which is edited by Philip Mairet (New York: Harper, 1929).

For contrasting points of view on why Adler and Freud ended their relationship, consult Vol. 2 of Ernest Jones's, *The Life and Work of Sigmund Freud* (New York: Basic Books, 1955) for the Freudian camp's opinion. The Adlerian consensus on the breakup may be gleaned from Harold Mosak and Rudolf Dreikurs's "Adlerian Psychotherapy," in Raymond Corsini (ed.), *Current Psychotherapies* (Itasca, IL: Peacock, 1973).

GLOSSARY

Accusation: Blaming others for one's own short-comings and failures.

Aggression drive: (Adler) One of the two major drives, along with the sex drive.

Aggressive strategies: Strategies involving feeling or expressing hostility toward others or self in order to safeguard self-esteem. This hostility can consist of depreciation, accusation, and self-accusation.

Avoidant type: Individuals who consistently avoid or ignore problems or challenges.

Birth order: Different birth orders create different situations to which children must adjust, and that adjustment may influence personality development and adherence to specific lifestyles.

Compensation/Overcompensation: A process by which a perceived weakness or frailty is both denied and converted into a strength.

Confluence of drives: Drives enter into a "confluence", an amalgam of interaction whereby each separate component drive is subordinated to the whole.

Depreciation: A devaluing of the accomplishments of others in order to safeguard one's own self-esteem.

Distancing strategies: The neurotic strategy of safeguarding self-esteem by restricting one's participation in life. The person protects his self-image by not exposing himself to challenge, or by not entering a situation where there is some risk of failure.

Ego: (Adler) The center of a person's sense of wholeness; the source of autonomy and creative processes.

Excuses/Rationalizing strategies: Excuses to escape life's demands or to avoid performing at one's best.

Feelings of inferiority: A sense or feeling one has of being inferior, which Adler asserted was universal.

Fictional finalism: The process of inventing or formulating a goal and working toward its fulfillment.

Gemeinschaftsgefuhl (literally "fellow-feeling"): The feeling of connectedness with and sympathy for one's fellow humans, translated by Adler as *social interest.*

Getting-leaning type: Individuals who expect others to satisfy their needs. They attain personal goals by relying on others for help.

Individual psychology: A term used to identify Adler's theory to distinguish it from other approaches. It stresses that each person, as an integrated whole, engages in goal-directed behavior.

Inferiority complex: An individual's sense of helplessness, of powerlessness, beginning in infancy and childhood.

Integrative amalgam: A term used to indicate the confluence of drives.

Masculine protest: Attempt by both males and females to compensate for feelings of inferiority. Overcompensatory striving to demolish dependency, to assert autonomy, and to achieve superiority.

Need for affection: An amalgam composed of a confluence of parts of the drives to look, to touch, and to listen.

Oedipus complex: (Adler) An only partly sexual rivalry felt by a son toward his father. Much of this rivalry has to do with overcoming a sense of inferiority and attaining a sense of power and superiority.

Organ inferiority: A damaged, diseased, or defective organ, usually accompanied by inferiority feelings.

Perfection striving: The desire to develop, to strive, and to achieve perfection.

Philosophy of "as if": According to the philosopher Hans Vaihinger, the idea that terms, concepts, hypotheses, goals, theories, laws, generalizations, etc., are fictional inventions.

Ruling-dominant type: Individuals who are assertive, aggressive, and active. They strive for personal superiority by trying to exploit or control others.

Safeguarding strategies: Adlerian defensive strategies to protect self-esteem from interpersonal threats. They come in three classes: *excuses* or *rationalization strategies*, *aggressive strategies,* and *distancing strategies.*

Self-accusation: Putting the blame for one's misfortunes on self, but doing it in such a way that it attracts attention, sympathy, concern, or help from others.

Social interest: Adler's preferred translation of *Gemeinschaftsgefuhl,* desire to contribute to the welfare of others and to society. It has a different meaning than *sociability*.

Socially useful type: Individuals who actively confront and solve problems in a pragmatic and thoughtful manner. Such people are socially oriented and prepared to cooperate with others.

Striving for superiority: Striving for autonomy and masculinity to compensate for a sense of inferiority. The fundamental urge to achieve a sense of competence and self-fulfillment.

Style of life: The consistent approach people take to pursue their life plans. This term, in Adler's theory, does not refer to consumer behavior.

Teleological: Goal-directed, purposeful; examining behavior in terms of its goals.

Chapter 6

Freud   Mahler

Two Mothers of Psychoanalytic Ego Psychology: Anna Freud & Margaret S. Mahler

The Psychoanalytic Heritage: Ego Psychology

Instinctual danger makes human beings intelligent.

Anna Freud

. . . the prerequisite for personality development . . . is contact with a human love object.

Margaret S. Mahler

[I] continued to crave a conventional female role even as I moved ahead with "male" pursuits.

Margaret S. Mahler

About Ego Psychology

By the time of Freud's death, psychoanalysis began to focus on the unique properties of the ego in guiding a person's capacity to master life's demands and not just react to them.

Psychoanalytic ego psychology emerged as an attempt to extend and complete Freudian theory. It addressed itself to the inconsistencies between the classical Freudian drive theory of competing energy systems and the clinical observations that people often are able to transcend their drives and impulses.

In this view, satisfaction comes not only from passive tension reduction but also from the sense of active mastery in surmounting life's obstacles.

Maladjustment is not exclusively the result of a clash among id, ego, and superego; neurosis may also be present in persons who have no life goals, who have been unable to establish a sense of harmony and order between themselves and their social world.

Anna Freud began the development of this approach in her efforts to work psychoanalytically with children. She gradually altered the theory of the ego from that of the helpless rider of the id horse described by Sigmund Freud into a more intelligent rider concerned with the best routes to travel.

Margaret Mahler explored the early roots of ego development in the interaction between infant and mother. Her work established a theoretical sequence of the formation of important ego skills, such as the capacity for empathy, restraint of action, and tolerance for being a separate person. With Mahler, early cognitive and emotional developments as well as object relations were emphasized. Mother-child love grew in stature in psychoanalytic ego psychology, taking a place alongside the classical emphasis on mother-child-father conflicts.

Anna Freud **Born: 1895 Vienna, Austria**
Died: 1982 London, England

LEGITIMIZING EGO PSYCHOLOGY

Whereas Sigmund Freud reconstructed his patients' childhoods from their adult recollections, Anna Freud observed her child patients in the act of constructing their adult reminiscences. Sigmund Freud liberated his patients from ignorance of their own pasts. Anna Freud labored to nurture her patients' mastery of the past they had yet to live. In many ways, Anna followed directly in her father's footsteps yet she also developed new directions of theory and practice.

Beginning officially in 1922, with the publication of her first psychoanalytic paper, Anna Freud devoted nearly 60 years to the application of analytic technique to children and adolescents, whereas her father did not do a great deal of psychoanalytic work with children or younger adolescents. Along the way, almost inadvertently it seems, she lent her prestige and her talents to legitimizing the direct study of the ego. Close inspection of her writings, however, reveals that Anna Freud's conception of ego psychology is consistent with orthodox Freudian theory. The ego, in her view, is a legitimate object of psychoanalytic study if the analyst remembers that fundamentally the ego is inescapably bound to the id and unavoidably regulated by the superego. For Anna Freud, the chief theoretical justification for study of the ego is that: "It is, so to speak, the medium through which we try to get a picture of the other two institutions" (A. Freud, 1936, p. 6).

For Anna Freud, widening the scope of psychoanalysis means applying the fundamental discoveries of her father to new realms of behavior, to children, to adolescents, to pediatrics, to family law, and to modified techniques in education and child care (A. Freud, 1972, 1978). A widened psychoanalytic theory of the ego does not include leaving behind her father's conception of the power of id instincts, his portrait of the ego as a survival-contingent outgrowth of the id, and his conviction that, after all, the ego rider leads the id horse where the id horse wants to go. But the story of Anna Freud's work is not the history of a student rigidly devoted only to her teacher's maxims. It is a narrative of innovation, revision, and creation accomplished almost reluctantly but with brilliance (Young-Bruehl, 1988, p. 208ff. and Chapter 11). Viewing her psychoanalytic career in 1964 as part of her acceptance speech for an honorary doctorate from Jefferson Medical School, Anna Freud pictured an essential difference between herself and many other contemporary psychoanalytic theorists:

> In contrast to many colleagues, I was never concerned one-sidedly with id, ego, or superego, but always with the interactions between them. The dynamics of mental life which fascinated me, to my mind, found their clearest expression in the defense organization of the ego, with the attempts of the rational personality to deal with the irrational. (1967, pp. 514–515)

Within the body of Anna Freud's work we can detect the tension that inevitably must arise when an innovative student struggles to preserve the theoretical fundamentals of her teacher while hesitantly demanding fair consideration for new and independent ideas. For in the end, Anna Freud's position in contemporary psychoanalysis, indeed, in the overall history of the discipline, must be forever unique and exquisitely contradictory. In her primary role as Sigmund Freud's self-chosen, self-trained intellectual heir, she was the keeper of the keys, custodian of the faith, and conservator of tradition. Balanced against these protective but understandable daughterly motives is her competing role as an independent theorist whose explorations into new territories must inexorably reduce the usefulness of old maps. Her family heritage not only ensured a protective attitude toward classical psychoanalysis, it also supported an adventuresome curiosity to make new discoveries. She was, after all, not a neo-Freudian; she was a Freud.

PERSONAL SOURCES: FROM BEING UNWANTED TO BECOMING INDISPENSABLE

By the time Sigmund and Martha Freud realized that Martha was again pregnant, they had already agreed that their fifth child, Sophie, was to be their last. Indeed, the initial phase of Martha's pregnancy was misinterpreted and welcomed as an early onset of menopause (Roazen, 1969, p. 40; 1971, pp. 52 ff. and pp. 436 ff.; Young-Breuhl, 1988, p. 35 ff.). When it became clear that the pause in Martha's menstruation was not the end of fertility but the beginning of new life, Freud found himself hoping for another son. He wrote to his friend, Wilhelm Fliess, in October 1895, "You will not have any objection to my calling my next son Wilhelm! If he turns out to be a daughter, she will be called Anna" (S. Freud, 1954, p. 130). He was she, as Freud and Martha learned on the afternoon of December 3, 1895. Freud resignedly announced Anna's birth to Fliess in this most curious way:

> If it had been a son I should have sent you the news by telegram. But as it is a little girl of the name of Anna, you get the news later. (S. Freud, 1954, p. 136; see alternate form of this quotation in Freud, 1985, p. 153)

Despite this birth announcement to Fliess, Freud seems to have become fond of all of his children. Anna, his youngest and last child, would mature to become the intellectual heir Freud was unable to find in Jung, Adler, Rank, or in any of his other male psychoanalytic colleagues.

On the basis of his extensive researches in the unpublished material of Jones's archives, his interviews with surviving relatives, colleagues, and former patients of Freud, Paul Roazen (1968, 1969, 1971) has pieced together the probable personal history of Anna Freud's eventual entrance into her father's discipline. Roazen's research and conclusions have not gone unchallenged. (Anna Freud herself found Roazen's work objectionable, as reported by Young-Bruehl, 1988, p. 432ff.). We follow Roazen's account supplemented with some of Sigmund Freud's letters here.

Young Adulthood: Training Analysis with Freud

Sometime before 1918, when Anna was in her early twenties, she entered into analysis with her father. This unique relationship apparently continued for several years (Dyer, 1983, p. 26, feels that the duration was somewhat shorter; Roazen, 1971, p. 439; Young-Bruehl, 1988, gives the most complete and compelling account. See especially Young-Bruehl, 1988, p. 171). Thus, with no formal academic training or credentials in medicine or psychology, Anna Freud was nevertheless committed to psychoanalysis by the strongest of bonds: She was engaged in intellectual and emotional self-exploration with the founder of psychoanalysis, her own father, who had to function in the acutely contradictory roles of professional and paternal intimate. Roazen described the consequences for Anna Freud's development in this way:

> Freud's motives may have been the very best, but medically and humanly the situation was *bizarre.* As her analyst, he would inevitably mobilize her feelings of overvaluation, while at the same time invading the privacy of her soul; he added new transference emotions to their relationship, without the possibility of ever really dissolving them. A genius who was also naturally an immense figure in his daughter's fantasy life, as her analyst he tied her permanently to him. (1971, p. 440; italics added)

Freud broke the rules he himself created for the proper conduct of a psychoanalyst by taking his own daughter into such a relationship. Why did he break such rules? One possibility is that he must have placed special importance on having a trustworthy and competent intellectual heir. By teaching his daughter the techniques of his profession, Freud bequeathed to her his place as leader of the psychoanalytic movement.

One source for understanding the meaning of her analysis with her father is Anna Freud herself. In a letter advising a friend, Eva Rosenfeld, to enter treatment with her father, whom Eva already had known in a social context, Anna made these poignant remarks:

> You know, there is no contradiction in your undergoing analysis in a place that you would prefer to come to for love's sake alone. I did the same thing, and perhaps because of it, the two things became inextricably bound together for me. In the end you will realize: it is the only way to go into analysis. Right now you are troubled by the feeling that where you love you would like to be especially good. You will see that being good and being in analysis finally amount to the same thing. (A. Freud, 1929/1992, letter 8, p.112)

Anna Freud began attending her father's lectures, and she was permitted to join the famous Wednesday seminars of the Vienna Psychoanalytic Society (Roazen, 1971, p. 438). She was even given her first exposure to classical psychiatry by being allowed to attend rounds in the psychiatric teaching hospital of Vienna, under Professor Wagner-Jauregg, a friend of Sigmund Freud's from his own medical school years (A. Freud, 1967, p. 512). Heinz Hartmann, known later as the father of ego psychology, served as a second assistant on these psychiatric rounds. In May 1920, two years after her training analysis by one account, Sigmund bestowed one of his famous rings on his daughter. Freud gave such rings to members of his inner circle, and it was certainly his way of confirming Anna's special place as a full-fledged and accepted member of the Vienna Psychoanalytic Society (Dyer, 1983, p. 32).

Anna as an Early Analyst

By 1923, having already presented her first psychoanalytic paper to the society the previous year, Anna Freud was ready to enter psychoanalytic practice (A. Freud, 1922). Unfortunately, 1923 was also the beginning of the end for Sigmund Freud. His cancer of the upper palate was first detected and operated on that year, and the complications resulting from its removal were to mark the start of a 16-year struggle with pain.

Her first paper was an extension of one of her father's own essays on "beating fantasies" devised by children. The elder Freud (1919) had written a paper entitled "A Child Is Being Beaten" in which he described the fantasies of several of his female patients for what they reveal of the plasticity of sexual motives. Freud's analysis shows that the fantasylike daydream of his patients, which pictured an older person beating or punishing a child, is a disguised substitute for a repressed sexual wish.

Anna Freud's (1922) own first published contribution to psychoanalysis is an extension of the beating fantasy analysis with a major difference from her father's work. The female patient she describes in the paper is most certainly herself (Young-Bruehl, 1988,

Figure 6.1 Anna Freud and her famous father in the Dolomite region of Italy, 1927. They appear happy together. Anna was devoted to her father.

pp. 103ff.). Anna Freud describes the progressive fantasy stories of a girl from preschool age through adolescence in which the central theme is "a child is being beaten." We will not trace the details of her analysis here. The essential point, however, for our discussion of the personal sources of Anna Freud's ideas is that this 1922 paper reveals some of the personal experiences on which Anna Freud based her therapeutic method for working with children. The girl described in her paper eventually developed a set of "nice fantasies" that she thought had little or no connection with the "beating fantasies" she found so distressing. In fact, the nice fantasies were more deliberate on the surface, more under voluntary control. But, as Anna Freud reveals in the paper, through analysis, the "patient" learns that the "nice stories" are thinly disguised continuations of the beating fantasies. Like her father, she interprets the beating fantasy as an intermediate level of disguise for taboo, incestuous sexual wishes toward an adult figure, most likely the girl's father. What makes this paper so poignant is that Anna Freud is apparently describing herself.

Anna Freud analyzes the progression from the beating fantasies to the "nice stories" as a study in repression and sublimation, two defense mechanisms she would later describe in much detail. She implies that the girl is developmentally more mature at the point when she can recognize the connection between the earlier unwanted beating fantasies and her even more defensive "nice stories." Anna Freud points out that the girl eventually turned her combination beating fantasies and "nice stories" into a creative and more rationally controlled enterprise by writing a compelling short story that she could share with others. In this early paper, the theme of creative mastery of conflict as a basic motive is already clearly in evidence, a theme that she later extended in the theoretical concept called "developmental lines." She concludes the paper with these words:

> By renouncing her private pleasure in favor of making an impression on others, the author has accomplished an important developmental step: the transformation of an autistic into a social activity. We could say: she has found the road that leads from her fantasy life back to reality. (A. Freud, 1922, p. 157)

Anna's Adulthood: Anna's Antigone Played to Freud's Aging Oedipus

Through those 16 years of the battle with cancer, Anna Freud became indispensable to the ailing but uncomplaining Sigmund. She was his emissary to psychoanalytic societies throughout the world, and she delivered his papers when his prosthesis, designed to replace excised oral tissue, impaired her father's ability to speak. She typed his correspondence daily and administered to his personal and medical needs. That task required daily inspection of Freud's surgically brutalized mouth for any signs of new growth. Anna Freud accompanied her father on his journeys to Paris for radium treatments, on visits to his surgeon in Berlin, and on much-needed holidays in the woods to pick mushrooms and wild strawberries (Jones, 1957; Schur, 1972; Young-Bruehl, 1988, p. 118). Anna Freud was devoted to her father's comfort and care.

Sigmund Freud himself understood how dependent he had become on Anna. He chose an appropriate metaphor to describe the relationship between them. In his correspondence of the mid-1930s, Freud would refer to Anna as his "faithful Antigone," alluding to the dutiful and courageous daughter of the blind and ill Oedipus in Sophocles' plays. For example, to Arnold Zweig in 1934, Freud wrote,

> But it cannot have remained concealed from you that fate has granted me as compensation for much that has been denied me the possession of a daughter who, in tragic circumstances, would not have fallen short of Antigone. (Freud/Zweig, 1970, p. 66)

Thus, in Freud's mind, with Anna as his Antigone, he was the ailing and aged Oedipus. Freud also wrote despairingly to Zweig that,

> My mood is bad, little pleases me, my self-criticism has grown much more acute. I would diagnose it as senile depression in anyone else. I see a cloud of disaster passing over the world, even over my own little world. I must remind myself of the one bright spot, and that is that my daughter Anna is making such excellent analytic discoveries just now and—they all tell me—is delivering masterly lectures on them. An admonition therefore not to believe that the world will end with my death. (Freud/Zweig, 1970, pp. 110–102)

"My own little world," referred to by Freud in this letter, is the world of psycho-analysis that he had constructed. Freud here implicitly acknowledged Anna as his successor. Like the blind Oedipus led by his faithful Antigone, Sigmund Freud's contacts with the outside world were made through Anna's skilled touch. In a letter to Lou Andreas-Salome, he also managed to express fatherly pride in a peculiarly objective—almost depersonalized—way that echoes the equally curious tone of his announcement of her birth to Fliess 40 years before:

> I of course rely more and more on Anna's care, just as Mephistopheles once remarked:
>
> > In the end we depend
> > On the creatures we made.
>
> In any case, it was very wise to have made her. (Freud [1935], 1960, p. 425)

From an unexpected and unwanted daughter, Anna Freud had finally matured into an indispensable Antigone, among whose virtues was the ability to clarify what other potential psychoanalytic "heirs" had managed only to cloud:

> She has grown into a capable, independent person who has been blessed with insight into matters that merely confuse others. To be sure, for her sake I would like—but she must learn to do without me, and the fear of losing vital parts of my still intact personality through old age is an accelerating factor in my wish. (Freud/Zweig, 1970, p. 140)

Freud partly expressed his wish not to die and, in so doing, indicated his concern that Anna required his continued presence. But the wish for immortality gave way to a more realistic appraisal. Freud finally realized that the ravages of his illness and age would ultimately render him unable to act as protecting father to Anna and as founding father of psychoanalysis. Anna's growing independence and mastery of psychoanalytic theory and practice assured him that she would continue to prosper and so, in consequence, would aid his other "creation"—the psychoanalytic endeavor itself.

Throughout the period of Freud's illness, Anna increasingly assumed authority around the household in her role as her father's private nurse, companion, and colleague. Her role became a source of conflict between Anna and Martha Freud. Roazen (1971, p. 452) quotes Martha as commenting that: " 'she was such a tender child,' but that the hardness in her had come out." Anna resented that her mother did not assume more responsibility for the care of her father, but seemed instead to become less and less capable of coping with the increasingly difficult situation. "The more incapable Martha became, the more Anna's feelings of being an unwanted child were reinforced, and thus the more her father meant to her" (Roazen, 1971, p. 452). An escalating cycle of family interactions had developed.

The Central Themes: Devotion, Protection, and Reluctant Innovation

Three fundamental themes governing the course of Anna Freud's work emerge from our brief look at her life history. First, Anna found her whole life centered in one person and became intellectually and emotionally focused on her relationship with her father. Freud's own need for emotional and intellectual intimacy intensified the momentum of their growing mutual dependence.

The second relevant theme of Anna Freud's life history is her understandably protective and conservative approach to psychoanalytic theory. Anna Freud regarded her father's basic discoveries as foundation stones that cannot be discarded or greatly modified without demolishing the entire edifice they support. She cogently argued that psychoanalysis historically achieved its uniqueness and value as the study of the whole personality in both its unconscious and conscious components (A. Freud, 1936, pp. 3–5; 1969a). Restricting investigation to one aspect of personality functioning or ignoring instinctual factors in favor of environmental-cultural ones severely distorts and violates psychoanalytic procedure and theory.

The third and last theme that is discernible in Anna Freud's life history follows from her first two themes and her own creativity and innovativeness. Anna Freud was caught between genuine loyalty to and belief in her father and his work and the compelling evidence of her own discoveries in child analysis and ego function. Thus, she never presented her contributions as revisions or modifications of psychoanalytic theory. She envisioned her own work as more in the nature of subtle refinements, sophisticated clarifications, or shifts in emphasis. Yet, despite her tendency to minimize the newness of her ideas as a solution to the conflict between her loyalty and creativity, genuinely new discoveries and fresh ideas are found in Anna Freud's writings. Some of these ideas have profoundly influenced other psychoanalytic workers to alter the course of contemporary psychoanalysis, moving the evolution of theory in directions never contemplated by Sigmund Freud in his lifetime.

There is no better way to illustrate and to summarize this enduring conflict between Anna Freud's loyal protectionist attitude and her own hard-won discoveries than to quote an instance of her own vacillating prose:

> . . . It is important to remember that some forty years ago, long before the time when co-operation with academic workers could have played a part, psychoanalytic child study itself had already *transgressed the strict confines* of the psychoanalytic technique and situation, and had created its own field of direct observation, in its own way. It is true that all the important data on which psychoanalysis has built its view of childhood . . . were derived from the analytic setting itself, reconstruction from the analyses of adults, and later from the analyses of children. But immediately after the discoveries were made, a host of observers set to work, outside of the analytic setting, unsystematically indeed, and following the opportunities offered by life situations as they arose, but providing in time a mass of useful data, which served to check and countercheck, add to or refute the analytic findings proper. (A. Freud, 1951a, pp. 139–140; italics added)

Anna Freud's muted claims for originality and independence of child analysis, her special branch of the discipline, are inseparably interwoven in this passage with her dutiful recognition of the primacy of classical psychoanalysis. Yet she ends the passage with the admonition to remember that the data of child analysis have the special status of serving as the "countercheck" by which classical theory is confirmed or refuted.

WIDENING THE SCOPE OF ANALYSIS: LITTLE PATIENTS' PROBLEMS

By extending psychoanalytic technique from the reconstruction of childhood events in adults to direct exploration of children's life histories as they live them, Anna Freud quickly made two discoveries. Little patients are often exuberant free spirits but lackadaisical free-associates. As might be expected, the use of disciplined verbal-analytic technique with small children, with small vocabularies and limited verbal skills, is not a promising undertaking. Furthermore, unlike adults, child patients typically do not perceive themselves as needing aid, do not comprehend the role of a psychoanalyst, and present themselves for treatment only at the urging or command of parents. Because traditional psychoanalysis required that patients be intellectually and emotionally engaged in their own treatment, child patients constituted a formidable challenge (A. Freud, 1927, p. 6; 1945, p. 8).

How do we decide when a child requires psychoanalysis? One viewpoint, represented by other child analytic workers in the 1920s and 1930s, was that any emotional or intellectual disturbance in the child would benefit from psychoanalytic treatment. Anna Freud's own early view during this same period was that psychoanalysis was indicated only for children in whom a full-blown childhood neurosis was strangling further development (A. Freud, 1927).

After considerable experience, Anna Freud conceptualized the criteria for treatment of children. For adult patients, the severity of neurotic disturbance is indicated by the degree of damage to their capacities to lead a conflict-free love life and to work productively with satisfaction (A. Freud, 1945, p. 15). These criteria are inapplicable to children. Childhood involves cognitive, emotional, and behavioral development:

> In childhood there is only one factor of such central importance that its impairment through a neurosis calls for immediate action; namely, the child's ability to develop, not to remain fixated at some stage of development before the maturation process has been concluded. (A. Freud, 1945, p. 17)

The broadening in theory to encompass the facts of childhood change was required by the demands of child patients whose unconscious processes were not accessible by strictly verbal procedures. The refocusing of theory was necessitated by the shift from treatments for outright pathology to therapy for developmental, transitional impairments (A. Freud, 1968). Thus the criterion by which a child's need for analytic treatment was to be assessed was no longer the presence of explicit neurotic symptoms. Threatened fixation to some single phase of development became a sufficient indicator to warrant analytic intervention.

MAKING THE CHILD ANALYZABLE: THE PREPARATORY PHASE

Prior to Anna Freud's work with children, Melanie Klein (Chapter 7) of the Berlin School of Psychoanalysis had used a method for treating children almost exactly the same as adult psychoanalysis (Sayers, 1991, p. 153). Anna set about to develop a therapeutic method more suited to children. Many of the approaches and methods she developed were fundamentally different from the more orthodox or conventional Freudian approach developed by Klein. It could be argued that, even though Anna Freud's techniques with children differed from her father's techniques with adults, that her work was still nonetheless in keeping with Freudian theory. This was possible because children were not simply little adults. There were major differences between the psyches of children and the adults with which Sigmund Freud was more familiar. Melanie Klein, following the letter of Freudian technique, may have not "gotten it" as well as Anna Freud.

Coming from her experiences as a teacher of children (A. Freud, 1952), Anna Freud understood the importance of engaging children's interest at the outset and the necessity of winning their respect for the superior skills of the adult participant. In the early years of formulating usable principles of child analysis, Anna Freud felt the necessity of a lengthy preparatory phase of give-and-take relationship building before analytic work was begun. This preparatory phase was made more elaborate later with her addition of a "metapsychological assessment" procedure based on direct observation of a child and reports by others who were able to observe the child's family interactions.

Engaging the Child's Self-Interest; Establishing the Analyst's Usefulness

Initially, Anna Freud undertook a preparatory period of "breaking the child in" for analysis by helping the child see the need for the treatment, view the analyst as helpmate and ally, and develop a genuine resolve to endure the difficulties of self-exploration. In practice, these goals are transformed into creative strategies. The analyst helps the child gradually develop insight into the child's difficulties and elicits greater and greater cooperation. In these efforts, the analyst expresses sincere interest and good wishes for the child's eventual self-management. To illustrate, consider Anna Freud's skillful approach to a 10-year-old boy presented for treatment by his parents for a variety of anxieties, nervous states, tendency toward lying and fabrication of stories, and for a series of thefts. With some children, the analyst may assume the role of helpful ally against a hostile adult world or of potential helpmate in dealing with inner misery. For this child, no such partnership could be proposed. His attitude from the outset was one of hostile rejection of his proposed analyst, and, on the surface at least, he was not interested in looking at or changing any aspect of himself.

At first, therefore, Anna Freud spent their time together merely mirroring his moods. When he appeared cheerful, she was cheerful; when he was serious or depressed, she acted seriously. At one point, he preferred to spend the entire session under a table in the room, an activity that Anna Freud treated with no special attention. She merely lifted the tablecloth to speak with him as though it were the most ordinary conversation. Simultaneously, however, she also subtly demonstrated the superiority of her adult skills and wisdom:

> If he came with a string in his pocket, and began to show me remarkable knots and tricks, I would let him see that I could make more complicated knots and do more remarkable tricks. If he made faces, I pulled better ones; and if he challenged me to trials of strength, I showed myself incomparably stronger. (A. Freud, 1927, p. 12)

Throughout their conversations, Anna Freud followed his every whim and choice of topic, with no subject too delicate or too adult for discussion. "My attitude was like that of a film or novel meant to attract the audience or reader by catering to their baser interests" (1927, p. 12). Thus, Anna Freud succeeded not only in making herself interesting to the boy but also in learning about his interests, attitudes, and typical behaviors and activities.

A second stage in this preparatory work began when Anna Freud demonstrated that she could be useful to the boy in many small ways, such as by typing letters for him, by eliciting and writing down his daydreams, and by making small toys during their therapy sessions. In the process of recording daydreams, the analyst could also learn something about the child's fantasy life. Anna Freud remarked concerning another of her patients, ". . . I zealously crocheted and knitted during her appointments, and gradually clothed all her dolls and teddy bears" (1927, p. 13). If we take this last statement as typical, it suggests that such a preparatory phase is relatively long-lived and requires much patience until the child patient finally becomes committed to the therapeutic process.

Establishing the Analyst's Power and the Child's Vulnerability

The third stage of the preparatory period had its origins in yet another skillful maneuver designed to augment the boy's growing value for his analyst. "I made him realize that being analyzed had great practical advantages; that, for example, punishable deeds have an altogether different and much more fortunate result when they are first told to the analyst, and only through him to those in charge of the child" (A. Freud, 1927, p. 13).

Eventually the boy relied on Anna Freud to protect him from punishment for his rash acts, to confess to his parents for him, and to restore stolen money before he was caught. The chief result of this stage of preparation was that Anna Freud had now become not only interesting, helpful, and wise, but powerful as well, a person "without whose help he could no longer get along" (1927, p. 13). At this point came the crucial moment when Anna Freud could finally request his complete cooperation in unveiling his treasured and guarded secrets. She could demand of him the equivalent of the adult analytic rule: Tell all. Keep no secrets.

The preparatory phase concludes when children have developed sufficient insight to recognize the necessity of external aid for their difficulties. Indeed, child patients must learn to understand that they have difficulties. The only clear signal of sincere willingness to attempt extended and painful self-exploration comes when the child has experienced his or her own vulnerability and needs to invest the analyst with complete and trusting dependence. In short, the analyst works very hard during the preparatory stage to establish a strong, positive transference relationship.

The analyst must become the child's ego ideal in order for treatment to proceed and eventually to succeed. The analyst then displaces the parents from this role and usurps much of their authority: "Before the child can give the highest place in his emotional life, that of ego ideal, to this new love object which ranks with the parents, he needs to feel that the analyst's authority is even greater than theirs" (A. Freud, 1927, p. 60). In some cases, where the parents themselves are either the source of the child's difficulties or are negatively disposed to the treatment, it becomes necessary for the child analyst to work actively against their influence.

THE CHILD ANALYSIS PROPER: TECHNIQUES

Once an affectionate and dependent attachment to the analyst is established, analytic treatment of the child, with its special focus on the unconscious, may begin. The success of the analysis depends heavily upon the firmness of this attachment, for "Children, in fact, believe only the people they love, and make efforts only for the love of such people" (A. Freud, 1927, p. 40). The question naturally arises of how to provide analytic interpretations in the absence of free-associative verbal products. What does the analyst interpret?

Interpretation of Fantasy and Dreams

One avenue of approach that immediately suggests itself is the play activities of the child. The Berlin school of child analysis headed by Melanie Klein employed the technique of play interpretations. Anna Freud rejected this road to the child's unconscious because it implies that a child's manipulations of toys and construction of play fantasies are equivalent to adult verbal productions in the analytic situation, a proposition for which there seemed little justification (1927, p. 38). Compared to verbal expressions, the analyst dealing with play may have difficulty understanding when a behavior is symbolic and when it is merely play.

At the beginning of her work with children, Anna Freud employed two tools adopted from adult psychoanalysis but in greatly modified form. The first of these approaches was the reliance on the child patients' verbal reports of their fantasies and dreams. As in adult analysis, these productions were treated as symbolic derivatives of unconscious processes, and they were therefore subject to interpretation. In this activity, Anna Freud clearly drew on her own experience analyzing her own "beating fantasies" and "nice stories." With some children, direct encouragement of fantasy stories was employed, as in the case of a little girl patient who was asked to close her eyes and "see pictures" that she would then describe to Anna Freud. In a similar way, the analyst and child patient discuss the child's dreams, and with practice, the child becomes accustomed to seeking hidden meanings in his or her own productions.

Maintaining and Interpreting the Child–Analyst Relationship

The second tool of child analysis in the initial period of Anna Freud's development of the technique was the interpretation of the relationship between herself and her patient. In adult analysis, the transference relationship and the development of a full-blown transference neurosis was necessary for therapy to succeed. With a child patient, as we have seen, the transference relationship embodies an essentially positive, affectionate quality that is not inherent to adult psychoanalysis. In fact, though negative feelings toward the analyst will eventually emerge, Anna Freud regarded these as temporary interferences that should be dealt with promptly to prevent rupture of the delicate bonds that hold the child to the therapist (1927, p. 41). The only really productive work with children, she concluded, takes place in an atmosphere of positive emotional attachment.

The child's transference relationship to the analyst is different from the adult's in other important ways. Unlike adult counterparts, child patients are still in the formative stages of their real relationships with their parents or guardians and other important people. They do not recall, reexamine, and relive these relationships in analysis as part of the

Figure 6.2 Anna Freud at her desk. The books and objects in this photograph indicate Anna's wide-ranging interests and scholarly activities. Like her father, she was a theorist and a prolific writer in addition to her psychotherapeutic role.

past; they live them in the present. Outside the analytic room, their pleasures and pains still largely depend on those who affect them in daily life. Analysts who attempt to interpose themselves in this scheme of things have to share the children's affection for their parents as well as the hostilities, disappointments, and idealizations they have for their parents. By contrast, the analyst of adult patients becomes the full target of feelings reconstructed from the patient's past. The adult analyst becomes momentarily a blank screen onto which the patient can project unresolved and unrealistic feelings carried over from the patient's early parent–child interactions.

The situation is further complicated in cases where children have little or no real affection from their parents. Emotionally deprived children may obtain a caring and affectionate relationship from their analysts that they have not experienced at home. Such children do not project a fantasized reenactment of their emotional relationships onto the analyst (A. Freud, 1927, p. 45).

> For these reasons the child forms no transference neurosis. In spite of all his positive and negative impulses toward the analyst, he continues to display his abnormal reactions where they were displayed before—in the home. Because of this the child analyst must not only take into account what happens under his own eye, but also direct his attention to the area where the neurotic reactions are to be found—the child's family. (A. Freud, 1927, p. 46)

Child analysis involves understanding and interpreting interpersonal bonds both in and outside of the analytic situation. In addition to understanding these relationships from the child patient's view, the analyst might also be able to explore the viewpoint of the adults with whom the child has their most intimate contacts. Child analysts often violate a rule of adult analysis in their reliance on and active seeking of information about the patient from outside sources.

Delicate Balance Between Permissiveness and Authority

If, as Anna Freud was discovering, children's neurotic disturbances were so dependent on their present relationship to the people and things in their own worlds, then it must follow with inevitable logic that:

- Childhood neurosis is not limited to conflicts among the id, ego, and superego but includes the distorting and paralyzing influences of the environment;
- Children's egos and superegos are not only weak by virtue of unconscious conflict but also as a result of lack of maturation.

As a result of these factors, the results of child analysis would appear to be fragile. One might ask, "If the analyst succeeds in liberating the conflicted instinctual forces of the child's id, will the environment provide a healthy context for continued growth? If the superego and ego are not fully mature and are not sufficiently experienced in modulating these liberated unconscious forces, will the environment, especially the parents, provide understanding acceptance and support for this unruly transition to emotional health?" In the case of an adult, the analyst need not be overly concerned with the fate of impulses freed from repression, because the normal adult's ego is able to take charge of them, manage them, and accept them for what they are. In the child's case, however, liberated impulses may easily find themselves translated into action.

To illustrate: A young girl that Anna Freud was treating had gotten to a stage of her analysis in which she was producing a wealth of anal fantasies, marked by use of particularly vulgar imagery and language. The child saw her analytic sessions as a period of freedom, a "rest hour" during which all of this repressed and suppressed anxiety-producing fantasy material could be openly expressed in the seclusion of the analytic room. However, she eventually began to carry her fantasies, her "dirty" jokes, and her anal language into situations beyond the analytic "rest hour." Alarmed, the parents consulted Anna Freud, who took the matter lightly, suggesting that they neither reject nor condone such misbehavior but merely let it pass unnoticed. The advice backfired! Without external condemnation, the little girl reveled in her anal verbalizations, especially at the dinner table, where they produced the most dramatic effect:

> I had to acknowledge that I had made a mistake, in crediting the child's superego with an independent inhibitory strength that it did not possess. As soon as the important people in the external world had relaxed their demands, the child's superego, previously strict and strong enough to bring forth a whole series of obsessional symptoms, suddenly had turned compliant. . . . I had changed an inhibited, obsessional child into one whose "perverse" tendencies were liberated. (A. Freud, 1927, p. 63)

It is clear that the child analyst cannot depend on the strength of the patient's ego to stay out of trouble. Experienced child analysts learn to steer skillfully between two

Figure 6.3 Anna Freud at age 85 with her dog, Jo-Fi. This photograph indicates the affectionate and caring side of Anna Freud's personality.

dangerous extremes. On one side, they have to tease unconscious material into consciousness. On the other side, the child analyst must somehow prevent the freed impulses from creating total anarchy in the child's life, a real threat in the light of the child's underdeveloped superego. They must educate children to employ healthy strategies for dealing with their heretofore frightening impulses. "The analyst accordingly combines in his own person two difficult and diametrically opposed functions: he has to analyze and educate, that is to say, in the same breath he must allow and forbid, loosen and bind" (A. Freud, 1927, p. 65).

THE THEORETICAL YIELD: NEW MEANINGS FOR FAMILIAR ANALYTIC CONCEPTS

It became increasingly clear to Anna Freud that child analysis involved more than merely applying orthodox psychoanalytic theory to children. Her earliest work with the technique laid the groundwork for important new areas that promised not only to establish child analysis as an independent, special branch of psychoanalysis but also to open the door to fundamental modifications of classical theory.

The Therapeutic Alliance: Awe and Trust

The first theoretical yield derived from the fact that child analysis could not be undertaken with the usual methods of free association, dream interpretation, and transference analysis. Children's strivings to grow, to mature, to change, to master inner and outer reality could lead to the modification of classical techniques or to the development of new ones. Anna Freud learned the importance of a long preparatory phase designed to establish the analyst as an important, dependable, even indispensable person. With a mixture of awe and trust, the child would come to accept the analyst as a very special kind of teacher, namely, as a specialist in self-knowledge and as an ally. Although the adult analytic patient may fantasize this kind of relationship with the therapist, it is only the child patient who lives it.

Beyond Structural Conflict: Developmental Vulnerability

Second, the fact of a child's plasticity, the continual growth toward maturity, forces the child analyst to focus not on overt neurotic symptoms but on the distant goal of future healthy functioning. Anna Freud and her colleagues soon recognized that crystallized neurotic syndromes were only a small fraction of the problems of childhood. Developmental disturbances, threats to continued maturing, both physical and psychological, were most often areas of concern. Moreover, even when overt indicators of serious pathology were present, these often had a very different significance in the context of a child's life than they did in an adult, whose psychological makeup was largely formed.

What Anna Freud and her co-workers eventually developed was a formalized system of diagnosis for children. It emphasized the developmental sequence of personality formation and malformation. The diagnostic system highlighted serious threats to the completion of personality growth while minimizing those that were less serious (A. Freud, 1970b, pp. 163ff.). In effect, doing analytic therapy with children had enabled Anna Freud to go beyond the classic conception of neurosis and maladjustment as primarily a result of intrapsychic conflict. Children often have disturbances that stem from difficulties in the process of psychological maturation.

Metapsychological Assessment

Third, Anna Freud had learned an important lesson from the length of the preparatory period required to make a child analyzable. Not only do child patients need a relatively long time to convince them of the value of analysis, but therapists also need a substantial period of assessment to understand each child's conflicts, deficits, and strengths. What was needed was a way to make such assessments at the outset. In general, psychoanalysts did not favor observational and formal interviewing techniques modeled on the academic tradition of psychological testing. However, the new field of child analysis seemed to require some compromise with formal academic psychology. Eventually, just such an assessment procedure was developed and formalized into what is termed, "a metapsychological profile" (A. Freud, 1965a, 1965b; W.E. Freud, 1972; Laufer, 1965).

The **metapsychological profile** is a psychoanalyst's way of organizing all of the information obtained about a patient during a diagnostic assessment. *Metapsychological* is applied as a descriptive term to this procedure because the diagnostician attempts to integrate the findings into a coherent picture of the person's dynamic, genetic, economic, structural, and adaptive functioning (see Chapter 3 for a discussion of metapsychological viewpoints).

Recall that the:

- *dynamic* meaning of a psychological event refers to the conflictful nature of the competing drive energies as the ego attempts to provide satisfaction for the id;

- *genetic* viewpoint refers to the multiple developmental experiences in the course of a person's life history that converge to produce a particular symptom, meaning, or defense;

- *economic* is meant to indicate the degree of drive intensity and changes in quantity of instinctual energy over time;

- *structural* (or, earlier, topographical) viewpoint seeks to understand the interactions among the various structures or agencies of the mind as the ego, id, and superego perform their tasks; and

- *adaptive metapsychological perspective* focuses attention on the ego's capacity to enable the person to resolve inner conflict and "fit in" with external reality's demands in a healthy way.

Metapsychological profiles have been developed for infants (W.E. Freud, 1972), for adolescents (Laufer, 1965), and for adults (A. Freud, 1965a; A. Freud, H. Nagera, & W.E. Freud, 1965). The baby, adolescent, and adult profiles require somewhat different kinds of data from those required by the child profile. For example, the baby profile requires assessments of bodily functions such as sleeping, eating, and elimination. Adult profiles focus on the possible interferences of the patients' conflicts and regressions with their sexual functioning and with their ability to work productively.

The version we present here was designed for children (A. Freud, 1965b). Table 6.1 outlines the major categories of the child's metapsychological profile. The categories in Table 6.1 range from biographical information, such as family background and current environmental situation, to descriptions of drive functioning to diagnosis based on an integration of all preceding metapsychological viewpoints.

The significance of the metapsychological profile is threefold:

- It is standardized. It provides a uniform set of explicit instructions to gather specific behavioral and psychological data.

Table 6.1 Outline of Metapsychological Profile of the Child

I. REASON FOR REFERRAL—arrests in development, behavior problems, symptoms.

II. DESCRIPTION OF CHILD—personal appearance, moods, manner.

III. FAMILY BACKGROUND AND PERSONAL HISTORY—life history, family constellation.

IV. POSSIBLY SIGNIFICANT ENVIRONMENTAL INFLUENCES

V. ASSESSMENTS OF DEVELOPMENT

   A. Drive Development

   Libido and aggression distribution toward self and others.

   B. Ego and Superego Development

   Ego functions, age appropriate behavior, defensive balance, emotional balance.

VI. GENETIC ASSESSMENTS (Regression and Fixation)

Behavior, fantasy, and symptoms from which can be inferred the level of psychosexual development that has been reached or whatever regression or fixation to earlier stages is indicated.

VII. DYNAMIC AND STRUCTURAL ASSESSMENTS

Classify internal and external conflicts as to source in ego-id, ego-superego, or ego-reality clashes.

VIII. ASSESSMENT OF GENERAL CHARACTERISTICS

   A. Frustration Tolerance

   Ability to ensure tension, drive blocking, and capacity to employ adaptive defenses.

   B. Sublimation Potential

   Ability to neutralize sexual and aggressive urges and channel them into healthy activities.

   C. Attitude to Anxiety

   Use of defenses against fears of external and internal stimuli; degree of capacity to master inner and outer fears and stress situations.

   D. Progressive versus Regressive Forces

   Estimate ability to continue to develop, to profit from learning and treatment, to move forward to next developmental level.

IX. DIAGNOSIS

Integrate findings on degree of ego health, conflicts, frustrations, developmental level, superego severity, presence of organic disease, role of environment.

Based on A. Freud, 1965b, pp. 138–147.

- It requires the diagnostician to integrate those observations and supplementary life history data into a picture of the overall functioning and developmental status of the child's personality. Patterns of consistency and inconsistency emerge, as do areas of adequate and deficient development.

- It requires sophisticated use of psychoanalytic developmental theory, drive theory, and ego theory to derive metapsychological meaning from it. Psychoanalytic theory is used as a conceptual guide to diagnosis and as a predictive guide to specific therapy.

The metapsychological profile thus integrates theoretical propositions and observable clinical phenomena into a coherent psychological "map."

The Inescapable Limits of Child Analysis: Unchangeable Lives

The fourth theoretical yield from Anna Freud's work with children was her discovery that one could pursue therapeutic exploration too far. Other analysts who entered the field of child therapy often pursued personality disturbances in children to their very roots in the first year of life. In trying to go beyond manifest disturbances to the earliest antecedents of personality, the child analyst runs the risk of prolonging the analysis indefinitely. Furthermore, such analyses, extending to the very beginning of the child's short life, may very well run headlong into *unchangeable* constitutional or environmental givens of personality:

> In my opinion, these earliest environmental influences on the child create states that are comparable to deficiency illnesses on the physical side. While the effects of such early deprivation can be mitigated by later favorable influences, they cannot be undone or reversed or solved in a new more age-adequate way, as conflicts can: this means that they are not in the true sense of the word a legitimate object of analytic effort. (A. Freud, 1970a, pp. 18–19)

Anna Freud thus acknowledged that child analysis does not prevent all psychological misery. Certain environmental and constitutional givens cannot be undone. Specific elements of the human condition may mar a child's life, yet remain beyond the reach of even the most well-intentioned efforts. Failure to recognize these real limits leads to the unrealistic aspiration of extending a child's analysis through the full period of development and well into adulthood.

Significance of Contemporary Social Reality: Bulldogs Bank Children

A fifth theoretical yield from Anna Freud's work was her discovery that the analytic practitioner must recognize that, unlike adults, children are more dependent on and more easily influenced by their current external realities. The child analyst must be prepared to accept the proposition that child patients' current dependencies on parents, their conflicts with siblings and peers, and their relationships to teachers and other authority figures are all reflected in their disturbances. Unlike adult analytic patients whose neurotic disturbances are almost entirely internalized and have their causes largely in past relationships or prior unresolved conflicts, children can be disturbed to a great degree by their present relationships in present reality:

> In treatment, especially the very young reveal the extent to which they are dominated by the object world, i.e., how much of their behavior and pathology is determined by environmental influences such as the parents' protective or rejecting, loving or indifferent, critical or admiring attitudes, as well as by the sexual harmony or disharmony in their married life. . . . *The child analyst who interprets exclusively in terms of the inner world is in danger of missing out on his patients' reporting activity concerning his—at the time equally important— environmental circumstances.* (A. Freud, 1965b, pp. 50–51; italics added)

The child analyst must recognize that the little patient's disturbances do not necessarily exclusively reflect what has gone wrong, been distorted, or been blocked in the realm of the child's internal world. A child's disturbances may very well reflect his or her links to reality (A. Freud, 1958, p. 127).

The importance of children's external environments and their abilities to cope with grave threats was impressed on Anna Freud in her work with children separated from their parents during World War II in the London bombing raids. Children, with the consent of their parents, were evacuated from areas of extreme danger and relocated in safer foster homes outside the bombing zone. Suddenly, thousands of children who had never before been separated from home and family were under the guardianship of strangers (A. Freud, 1953, p. 511). Other less fortunate children experienced the death of a family member or members through the devastation wreaked on London by German air attacks. Such children had witnessed death and destruction firsthand and, therefore, had been even more traumatically separated from their parents or other loved ones.

In 1940 Anna Freud collected financial contributions from several sources to open and staff a children's center in Hampstead, London. Eventually a babies' rest center and a country house in Essex were also opened and were filled with evacuated children. Collectively known as the Hampstead Nurseries, Anna Freud's residential homes were designed not as institutional settings but as substitute homes that would provide security, mothering, and love for the children (A. Freud & D. Burlingham, 1944).

The effects of separation took their greatest toll on the youngest children and infants. Children between 5 and 12 months responded with all manner of bodily disorders, ranging from eating difficulties, sleep disturbances, and feeding problems to respiratory troubles and loss of recently acquired abilities such as talking and walking. Other children evidenced uncontrollable grief reactions and resisted all contact. When reunited with their mothers or provided with a substitute mother, most of these grief-stricken infants returned to normal emotional responsivity and behavior. In Anna Freud's view, the disaster of war and evacuation had demonstrated the validity of psychoanalytic hypotheses concerning the central importance of the mother–child relationship (1958, p. 515).

Some years later, in August 1945, six young children finally reached England. They were German-Jewish orphans whose parents had been killed in gas chambers shortly after their births and then were evacuated from one place and one family to another. For three years they had actually been held in a German concentration camp. One can only imagine their sufferings under such conditions. A former contributor to Anna Freud's Hampstead Nurseries donated a year's tenancy of a country house in Sussex named Bulldogs Bank. Together with Sophie Dann, one of the nurses in charge of Bulldogs Bank, Anna Freud published an account of their group life (A. Freud, 1951c).

> The Bulldogs Bank children functioned as a unit; no child wished to be separated from the others, nor would the group allow any of its members to be parted. Their insistence on being constantly together caused some difficulty in the staff's plans to treat them as individuals. For example, John, the oldest (3 years, 10 months), needed only to push away his plate at dinner for the other five children to cease eating. Unlike normal children, this group of orphans showed no envy, jealousy, or rivalry among themselves. They would spontaneously take turns at games, equally share every treasure, and were acutely sensitive to each other's needs and feelings. (A. Freud, 1951c, p. 174)

The **Bulldogs Bank children** rarely attacked or hurt one another during their first few months at the country house. Disputes were typically word battles, which ended in a massed attack against any outsider, such as an interfering adult. Their way of expressing aggression was less sophisticated than would be expected for children of their age. Biting and spitting were the usual modes of expressing anger, although sometimes they urinated on the floor or into their clothes to express their feelings. All of these behaviors are regressive, that is characteristic of much younger children. But after a few weeks, they were able to add hitting and smacking adults to their growing repertoire.

Positive relations with adults were first made on a group basis. They began to expect that adults should act the way they did. For example, the children eventually began to insist that the adults take their turns or share. Then they expressed concern about the adults' feelings. Finally, individual personal attachments to the adults began to appear and had the quality of child–parent relationships.

The children had been exposed to terror and deprivation during their stay in concentration camps. Though they usually expressed no clear memories of their past, they evidenced signs of their experiences. For example, all six children were terrified of dogs, probably because of the concentration camp guard dogs. "Once, when he met a strange large dog on a walk, John bit his lip in his terror and thought that the dog had bitten him when it bled" (A. Freud, 1951c, p. 216). In a similar way, the children were afraid of large trucks, presumably because they resembled concentration camp vans. That the children did not show an even greater range of fears and anxieties is probably attributable to their close cohesion and mutual support, through which each member drew strength from the others. Anna Freud and Sophie Dann summarized their observations in this way:

> They were deprived of mother love, oral satisfactions, stability in their relationships and their surroundings. They were passed from one hand to another during their first year, lived in an age group instead of a family during their second and third year, and were uprooted again three times during their fourth year. . . . The children were hypersensitive, restless, aggressive, difficult to handle. They showed a heightened autoeroticism and some of them the beginning of neurotic symptoms. But they were neither deficient, delinquent, nor psychotic. They had found an alternative placement for their libido [i.e., each other] and, on the strength of this, had mastered some of their anxieties and developed social attitudes. (1951c, pp. 228–229).

Thus, even in children who were severely deprived and traumatized, Anna Freud recognized the efforts they made for psychological survival in a devastating environment.

Mastery of Life Tasks: Developmental Lines

The sixth and last theoretical yield from Anna Freud's child analytic work was her observation of how the ego masters problems posed by life. **Developmental line** is Anna Freud's term for a developmental sequence of id-ego interactions. As they proceed along these developmental lines, children outgrow, in gradual steps, their dependence on external controls and gain in **ego mastery** of internal and external reality (A. Freud, 1965b, p. 63). The focus is not only on the ego's growing mastery, for the id drives are the primary impetus for the ego's alertness to inner and outer demands.

Developmental lines may be thought of as reliable sequences in the child's maturation from dependency to relatively complete independence, from irrationality to rationality, and from passivity to activity. These lines of development reveal the ego's attempts to confront life situations successfully, without painful retreat and without overly defensive inhibition. Such life situations include separation from mother, birth of a brother or sister, illness, school, peer relations, play, emergence of sexual interest at puberty, and, of course, love (A. Freud, 1962, p. 34).

The six developmental lines (Table 6.2) are:

1. From Dependency to Emotional Self-Reliance
2. From Suckling to Rational Eating
3. From Wetting and Soiling to Bladder and Bowel Control

BOX 6.1 *Only Connect . . .*

When you examine Table 6.2, you will notice that some of the items reflect actual behaviors that can be observed, such as "Being nursed by schedule or on demand." Other items reflect imagining what a child must be thinking and feeling, such as "Preoedipal, clinging stage, marked by fantasies of dominating the love object." This hybrid combination of operationally defined observable items and other items that can only be inferred indicates both Anna Freud's immersion in psychoanalytic theory as well as her attention to the actual behaviors of infants and children as they respond to their surroundings.

Table 6.2   Six Developmental Lines

I. Dependency to emotional self-reliance	*II. Suckling to rational eating*
1. Biological dependence on mother; no recognition of separation between self and other. 2. Need-fulfilling relationship, with mother seen as partially externalized satisfier. 3. Object-constancy phase, in which image of mother is retained even when she is not present. 4. Pre-oedipal, clinging stage, marked by fantasies of dominating the love object. 5. Phallic-oedipal phase, marked by possessiveness of parent of opposite sex and rivalry with same-sexed parent. 6. Latency phase with lessening of drive urgency, denigration of parental models, transfer of libido to peers, groups, authority figures. 7. Preadolescent phase of return to early attitudes of need-fulfilling relationship with love object. 8. Adolescent phase, marked by struggle to win independence and break ties with childhood love objects (parents), and need for establishing genital primacy.	1. Being nursed by schedule or on demand. 2. Weaning from breast or bottle initiated either by infant or by wishes of mother; new food difficulties. 3. Transition from being fed to self-feeding; "food" and "mother" still identified with each other. 4. Self-feeding, disagreements with mother about quantity; meals as battlegrounds for other difficulties of mother–child relations. 5. Infantile sexual theories shape attitude toward food: fantasies of impregnation through mouth, pregnancy fear (fear of getting fat). 6. Fading of sexualization of feeding, with pleasure in eating regained or increased; more self-determination of eating habits.
III. Wetting and soiling to bowel-bladder control	*IV. Irresponsibility to responsibility in body management*
1. Complete freedom to wet and soil is controlled by mother, not self. 2. Anal phase of child's direct opposition to control of elimination by others; feces treated as precious "gifts" to mother; battle of wills for toilet training. 3. Identification with parental rules, self-control of bladder and bowel; cleanliness concerns based on learned disgust and shame. Orderliness and tidiness interests based on anal regularity. 4. Cleanliness concerns pursued for their own sake, regardless of parental pressures; autonomous ego and superego control of anal drives.	1. Aggression turned from self to external world. Self-injury from biting, scratching, picking limited by focus on external objects; child recognizes causes of self-induced pain. 2. Ego advances of understanding cause-effect principles, delay of dangerous wishes, recognition of external dangers such as fire, heights, water. 3. Voluntary endorsement of rules of hygiene and medical necessity; avoidance of unwholesome foods, bodily cleanliness, compliance with doctor's orders only when fear or guilt enforces it. Belief that mother can restore endangered health.

(continued)

Table 6.2   *(continued)*

V. Egocentricity to companionship	VI. Body to toy and play to work
1. Selfish, narcissistic outlook, in which other children do not matter or are seen as disturbers and rivals for parental love.	1. Infant play is body sensuality in fingers, skin, and mouth of own or mother's body with no clear distinction between the two.
2. Other children related to as lifeless objects or toys, to be manhandled and roughly treated with no response expected from them.	2. Sensual properties of own and mother's body transferred to some soft object; e.g., teddy bear, blanket.
3. Other children seen as helpmates in tasks; duration of partnership determined by task requirements.	3. Clinging to one specific "soft" object grows into general liking for such cuddly things; but all are inanimate objects and do not retaliate for toddler's ambivalent handling.
4. Other children seen as equals and partners in their own right; they can be admired, feared, or competed with, loved, hated, or identified with. True companionship desired.	4. Cuddly objects used now only at bedtime; other toys for day play.
	5. Pleasure in finishing play activities, and pleasure in achievement.
	6. Play grades into work via hobbies, daydreams, games, proficiency sports. Child can inhibit own impulses.

Based on A. Freud, 1965b, pp. 64–85.

4. From Irresponsibility to Responsibility in Body Management

5. From the Body to the Toy, and From Play to Work

6. From Egocentricity to Companionship

Anna Freud's introduction of the concept of developmental lines is an original contribution to psychoanalysis. The concept of lines of development as formulated by Anna Freud focuses attention on the ego's capacity to adapt to life's demands; those demands can be situational, interpersonal, or personal. Thus, Anna Freud has brought classic psychoanalytic theory closer to looking at the world of relationships and away from an exclusive focus on intrapsychic dynamics.

THE EGO DEFENDS ITSELF: PROFILES OF MASTERY AND VULNERABILITY

In the early phase of her development of a modification of the analytic method for application to children, Anna Freud searched for a way to shorten the diagnostic stage of the preparatory period. The first step in that direction came with her investigation of ego defenses as indicators of instinctual change. Although the instinctual dynamics themselves are not directly observable, the ego's reaction to them is apparent from an examination of the individual's defenses.

In 1936 Anna Freud published her classic monograph, *The Ego and the Mechanisms of Defense*. This book was largely responsible for legitimizing the interest of psychoanalysts in ego functioning. She stated the justification for interest in ego defenses:

> If we know how a particular patient seeks to defend himself against the emergence of his instinctual impulses, i.e., what is the nature of his habitual ego resistances, we can form an idea of his probable attitude toward his own unwelcome affects. (A. Freud, 1936, p. 32)

Anna Freud began to systematize and expand the whole range of Sigmund Freud's many writings and pronouncements on the topic of ego defenses. These ranged from his earliest conception of repression as the fundamental ego maneuver in the face of instinctual threat to his later elaboration of secondary defense strategies. For the first time, the patients' maneuvers for adjusting to their social and biological needs, and their typical techniques of expressing emotional reactions came under direct scrutiny. All of these ego functions, many of them involving observable behaviors, had been largely ignored or neglected by analysts in favor of what they presumed to be more valuable knowledge to be gained by study of unconscious drives. Defenses had been viewed merely as obstacles to a clear view of the unconscious.

Defenses as Diagnostic Indicators

Consider the paradox that confronts the psychoanalyst treating patients who navigate the obstacles of their lives with the aid of massive psychological defenses. Such patients have come to therapy because they feel that their lives are constricted, joyless, and devoid of spontaneity. Yet, so long as a patient's defenses hold, the analyst confronts an apparently intact personality, which does not need psychoanalysis. It is ironic that only when the defenses fail and unconscious material reemerges into awareness that the analyst may discern trouble in the depths:

> So long as the defenses set up by a person's ego are intact, the analytic observer is faced by a blank; as soon as they break down, for example, when repression fails and unconscious material returns . . . a mass of information about inner processes becomes available. (A. Freud, 1969a, p. 125)

Defenses are successful protectors of the personality precisely because the ego remains unaware that it is defending itself.

In Anna Freud's terms, the ego's defenses are silent and invisible (1936, p. 8). Repression, for example, is only apparent by the absence of drive components that we expect to be present in a normal person. The child who is all sweetness and goodness, with no evidence of hostility, jealousy, or anger is most likely one whose ego has been enfeebled by massive repression against anger and aggression. Thus, the ego defenses are observable only by inference when the individual's behavior evidences signs of missing customary id derivatives. Looked at from the developmental point of view, people's defenses reveal their personal history of ego development, that is, life stories of mastering or succumbing to their passions, needs, wishes, and urges (1936, p. 21; Sandler & A. Freud, 1985).

Motives for Defense

Following her father's lead (S. Freud, 1926a), Anna Freud distinguished three sources of danger to which the ego responds defensively.

First, in the case of the adult neurotic, there is the danger of superego dissatisfaction with the way the ego seeks to provide gratifications to id sexual and aggressive strivings. The irony of this form of anxiety is that the ego itself does not regard the sexual or aggressive impulses against which it so actively defends itself as dangerous or condemnable. "The instinct is regarded as dangerous because the superego prohibits its gratification, and if [the instinct] achieves its aim, it will certainly stir up trouble between the ego and superego" (A. Freud, 1936, p. 55). Because the superego is capable of setting up a rigid and unattainable ideal standard, the neurotic's ego works to renounce all sexual and aggressive impulses to a degree that is incompatible with good mental health. The neurotic ego thus serves the superego to an exaggerated extent, even at the cost of internal conflict.

Second, in the case of the child neurotic, who has not yet formed a severe superego, the ego may come to fear the danger of the outside world. Fearing the instincts because the parents have prohibited their expression, the child's ego is reacting to fear of their displeasure. This more "objective" anxiety is nevertheless sufficient to trigger the ego's defensive maneuvers against sexual and aggressive impulses (A. Freud, 1936, p 57).

Third, there is the ego's fear of the danger of the strength of unconscious impulses. Sigmund Freud thought that this fear resulted from the ego's differentiation from the id in infancy and its gradual separation from the id's primary process by the development of its own reality-oriented secondary process of logical thought. Thus, when an instinct becomes too strong, the ego experiences the impulses as a threat to its independence, as a signal of the danger of being flooded by id primary process chaos (S. Freud, 1923a, p. 57). Rather than submit helplessly to invasion, the ego brings defenses into play. In a few sentences, Freud concisely summarized the three kinds of anxiety that trigger ego defenses and the difficult situation in which the id finds itself:

> Thus the ego, driven by the id, confined by the superego, repulsed by reality, struggles to master its economic task of bringing about harmony among the forces and influences working in and upon it; and we can understand how it is that so often we cannot suppress a cry: "Life is not easy!" If the ego is obliged to admit its weakness, it breaks out in anxiety— realistic anxiety regarding the external world, moral anxiety regarding the superego, and neurotic anxiety regarding the strength of the passions in the id. (S. Freud, 1933, p. 78)

In Anna Freud's hands, analysis of ego defensive functioning became a very sensitive diagnostic tool. For the child analyst, severely limited in the use of free association, defense analysis became the indispensable means to an understanding of the child's personal history of instinctual development (A. Freud, 1936, pp. 37–39; Sandler & A. Freud, 1985). By permitting the deduction of the specific id passion, the period of life when it emerged, and the specific kind of blockage erected by the ego against it, defense analysis opened the way to the hidden depths of the child's life history.

Anna Freud listed ten ego defenses hinted at or described by her father, and five elaborations of her own. Table 6.3 provides a definition and an illustration of each of these **classic defenses.** It should be pointed out that other psychoanalysts have many others, so that the total number of possible ego defenses is considerably larger than those represented in the table.

A FINAL WORD ON ANNA FREUD

Anna Freud's work represents one possible solution, or more precisely, a group of solutions, to the unfinished problems bequeathed by Sigmund Freud. The character of Anna Freud's solutions was threefold.

First and foremost, she attempted to enlarge the boundaries of classical psychoanalysis with direct considerations of ego functioning in social reality without abandoning the bedrock of psychoanalytic instinct theory. For Anna Freud, the ego is still in partnership with the id, still bound primarily to fulfill its tasks at the id's behest. But the ego is also capable of some independent functioning in the areas of life mastery.

Second, Anna Freud systematized what had been insights scattered throughout her father's work. Thus her attention to ego defenses, her adaptation of the psychoanalytic method for therapy with children, and her metapsychological classification scheme is all based on classic theoretical formulations. At the same time each of these achievements

Table 6.3   Anna Freud's Ten Ego Defenses

Defense mechanism	Definition and characteristics	Illustration
1. REPRESSION [Motivated Forgetting]	Abrupt and involuntary removal from awareness of any threatening impulse, idea, or memory. Most dangerous and one of the most archaic defenses, repression or denial is the prerequisite for any of the other defense mechanisms listed below.	Adolescent girl feeling guilty over her sexual impulses, frequently "blocks" on her boyfriend's name when introducing him to family and friends.
1A. DENIAL [Motivated Negation]	Blocking of *external* events from entry into awareness, when perception of such stimuli is symbolically or associatively related to threatening impulses. Denial abolishes dangers "out there" by negating them.	A recent widow continues to set a place at the table for her deceased husband. She also fantasizes frequently about conversations she is having with him.
2. ASCETICISM [Renunciation of Needs]	Characteristic of puberty, asceticism is more of a character style than a defense. Preadolescents feel over-whelmed by their emerging sexual impulses and protect themselves by repudiating *all* desires, *all* pleasures. In extremes, adolescents may "mortify" themselves by limiting sleep and food intake, and retaining urine and feces as long as possible.	The adolescent who embarks on what seems to be a "fad" diet, or "fad" interest in rigorous physical exertion *may* be attempting to control his or her impulses.
3. PROJECTION [Displacement Outward]	Attribution to another person or object one's own unacceptable impulses, wishes, or thoughts. Then, these impulses become "ego-alien" as though not a part of self.	A husband who has barely resisted the temptation to be unfaithful to his wife, begins to be chronically suspicious about her fidelity to him.
3A. ALTRUISTIC SURRENDER [Sacrifice Self]	A form of projection in which the person fulfills his or her own needs vicariously by identifying with the satisfactions of another; in extreme form, person may even give up own ambitions to allow another to be fulfilled.	An employee who was too timid to ask for a raise for herself became a militant advocate on the rights of another worker, expressing extreme assertiveness.
3B. DISPLACEMENT [Redirection of Impulse]	Redirection of impulses, usually aggressive ones, onto a substitute target when the appropriate target is too threatening.	A young woman, who in childhood was very envious of her brother's relationship with their mother, could only express her feelings of rage toward other females, typi-cally other female relatives.
4. TURNING-AGAINST-SELF [Self-as-Object or Target]	Redirection of impulses inwardly against oneself instead of outwardly toward the appropriate target. Usually results in masochistic feelings of inadequacy, guilt, depression.	Same woman as above (3B) also turned her hatred toward mother inward, becoming self-accusatory, passive, surrendering, and inferior feeling.
5. REACTION-FORMATION [Believing the Opposite]	Transformation of unacceptable impulses into their opposites and more acceptable forms; usually has the quality of "The Lady doth protest too much." Hate into love; love into hate.	A child who had been aggressive toward her mother became overly concerned for her safety, for her mother's welfare, and became excessively worried that some harm would befall her mother.

(continued)

Table 6.3 *(continued)*

Defense mechanism	Definition and characteristics	Illustration
5A. REVERSAL [Active into Passive]	Similar to reaction-formation, reversal transforms an impulse from an active to a passive mode. Also similar to Turning-Against-Self.	Sadistic impulses may become masochistic, with the self as passive target of aggression and sexual impulses.
6. SUBLIMATION [Acceptable Substitutes]	Transformation of an impulse into a socially productive and acceptable form.	A Vietnam veteran who, as a Green Beret, had enjoyed his soldiering, became a policeman who preferred assignments in the most dangerous neighborhoods.
7. INTROJECTION [Taking Within]	Incorporating into one's own behavior and beliefs the characteristics of some external object or admired person.	The adolescent who adopts the traits, mannerisms, and speech of an admired teacher. The widow who adopts items of apparel from her deceased husband, along with his tastes in food and entertainments.
7A. IDENTIFICATION-WITH-THE-AGGRESSOR [Adopting Feared Traits]	Adopting the traits or mannerisms of a feared person or object.	Hostages in skyjackings often feel protective of their captors. A little girl who was afraid to walk down the dark hallway of her house for fear meeting a ghost solved the problem by "booing" her way down the hall: "You just have to pretend that you're the ghost who might meet you."
8. ISOLATION [Stripping of Emotion, Meaning]	Characteristic of obsessive-compulsive neurosis, unacceptable impulses are retained in consciousness but divested of emotion and separated from connecting ideas to achieve an emotional-intellectual quarantine.	Seventeen-year-old boy with acute masturbation guilt, divided all his thoughts into acceptable and unacceptable ones. Both categories of ideas could not be thought simultaneously without unacceptable ideas contaminating acceptable ones. (Fenichel, 1945)
9. UNDOING [Magical Cancellations]	Characteristic of obsessive-compulsive personality, who performs magical gestures, or rituals, to cancel unacceptable thoughts, or acts, once the thought or act has been completed.	Same boy as above (8), had to perform rituals whenever unacceptable and acceptable thoughts occurred together. For example, he had to recite the alphabet backward whenever he had a sexual thought, or turn around and spit whenever he met another boy he knew also masturbated.
10. REGRESSION [Developmental Retreat]	Probably not really a defense, so much as a primitivization of behavior in face of stress: return to earlier modes of response when confronted with anxiety.	At his first separation from mother upon hospitalization for a tonsillectomy, Timmy began thumb-sucking and soiling his pants, deeds he "outgrew" two years earlier.

Based on A. Freud, 1936; Undoing and Isolation examples from Fenichel, 1945; Sandler & A. Freud, 1985.

transcends classical theory in significant but sometimes subtle ways. The key modification was her emphasis on viewing personality development as more affected by the environment, as more easily shaped by interpersonal relations, and as more fluid than classical theory would have it.

Third, Anna Freud's work is far removed from the implicit neurological assumptions of Sigmund Freud's creation. For Anna Freud, children, and presumably also adults, are active, assertive, and masterful. They need not be perpetual victims of their internal conflicts or of their overwhelming environments.

THE LEGACY OF ANNA FREUD

Anna Freud has bequeathed an enormous multifaceted legacy. While she preserved the important findings of her father, she also developed his ideas to studying the ego's pattern of activity with external reality. Her psychotherapeutic work with children was pioneering. She can be credited for beginning the work of psychoanalytically informed child psychotherapy. This approach involved considerable creative and thoughtful modification of adult psychoanalysis. Her idea of measuring stages of child development in many areas, which she termed "developmental lines" was an innovative study of child development and a forerunner of an abundance of developmental theories and measures that are still applied today. Her "metapsychological analysis" which looked at many areas of an individual and their functioning was very similar to the work of contemporary psychologists and psychiatrists. Most important, her thoughtful compassion and attention to the needs of children modeled such behavior on the part of generations of mental health professionals working with children.

Later in her life, Freud extended her work to informing the legal system, particularly the area of family law, to take into account what had been the largely ignored emotional and developmental needs of children (A. Freud & Burlingham, 1973; Sayers, 1991, pp. 190–195). She emphasized, not the parents' wishes, but the maintenance of the child's attachments. Her foray into jurisprudence endeavored to have a positive impact on quality of the environments with which children would have to cope. Her ideas in this regard do not seem so striking today, but they represented a real advance over the practices of the time.

Margaret S. Mahler   Born: 1897   Sopron, Hungary
                              Died: 1985   New York, New York

PSYCHOTIC AND HEALTHY EGOS:
SYMBIOSIS AND SEPARATION THEMES

Margaret S. Mahler's work began with her observation of severely damaged ego functioning in psychotic children whose cardinal difficulty seemed to be a total lack of comprehension of what human beings are (Mahler, 1968, p. 3). Such children, sometimes described as "autistic," seem to be encased inside a shell that is untouched by the outside world. Mahler was eventually able to differentiate the autistic child, as described by Kanner (1949), from the symbiotically psychotic child.

Truly autistic children seem from birth unable to utilize their mothers as auxiliary egos; that is, they show no interest in relating to mother, or to any person, as a needed partner in becoming oriented to inner and outer reality (Mahler, 1968, p. 67).

> [The autistic child's] . . . most conspicuous and characteristic behavior patterns are the classical features described by Kanner (1942, 1944): an obsessive desire for the preservation of sameness; a stereotyped preoccupation with a few inanimate objects or action patterns toward which he shows the only signs of emotional attachment. As a consequence, he shows utter intolerance of any change in his inanimate surroundings. . . . The primarily autistic child differs from the organic, as well as from the predominantly symbiotic psychotic child, by his seemingly self-sufficient contentedness—if only he is left alone. These autistic children behave like omnipotent magicians if they are permitted to live within, and thus to command, their static and greatly constricted segment of inanimate environment. (Mahler, 1968, p. 68)

Thus, in Mahler's view, the autistic child has regressed to the most primitive stage of life possible outside the womb. Such autistic children shut out the interpersonal world, which is the part of reality that demands emotional and social responses.

Symbiotic children, by contrast, are psychotic in a much different way. They are attached to their mothers; but the attachment is global fusing with her, so that they cannot tell where they begin and she ends.

> [Symbiotic psychotic] . . . children may be described by their mothers as "cry-babies" or as oversensitive infants. Their disturbance becomes apparent either gradually or fulminately at those crossroads of personality development at which maturation of the ego would usually effect separation from the mother, and would enable the child to master an ever-increasing segment of reality, independently of her. As soon as ego differentiation and psychosexual development confront the child and thus challenge him with a measure of separation from and independence of the mother, the illusion of symbiotic omnipotence is threatened and severe panic reactions occur. (Mahler, 1968, p. 72)

Symbiotic psychotic children evidence their profound psychosis only around the third and fourth years. At this time, their increased motor coordination leads to physical distance from their mothers; the demands of the beginning Oedipal period force them to face a sense of psychological distance. They are threatened with what to them is a dangerous possibility of becoming more independent.

While autistic children cannot cope with unexpected stimulation from the external world, symbiotic psychotic children fuse themselves with one agent, usually the mother, of that world. Autistic children fail to break out of their protective shells or primitive isolation, whereas symbiotic psychotic youngsters fail to create any distance between themselves and their mothers. For autistic children, the potential intrusion of outer human reality is unthinkable and intolerable; but symbiotic psychotic children regard one portion of outer human reality and themselves as narcissistically joined.

What has happened during the brief lives of each of these disturbed children to so fragment their egos? Why have each of these children, in their own way, failed to become individuals? To put these questions into more answerable form—can some reliable sequence of development be observed in the formation of a healthy child's ego that is somehow missing or injured in these disturbed children? Margaret Mahler set out to answer this question by gathering observational data on normal children and their relationships to their mothers from birth through the period when children establish themselves as separated and individuated persons. The sequence of her investigations proceeded from trying to understand disordered children by then studying normal development.

PSYCHOLOGICAL BIRTH: SEPARATION AND INDIVIDUATION

Mahler had hypothesized (1968, pp. 32ff.) that the central issue in the fragmentation of these disturbed children's egos was their failure to develop a normal symbiotic relationship with their mothers from which could emerge a strong, integrated, independent ego able and ready to treat self and others as persons: "The salient feature in childhood psychosis is that individuation, i.e., a sense of individual identity, is not achieved" (1968, p. 35).

From her study of severely disturbed children, Mahler turned to an investigation of normal children and their mothers at the Masters Children's Center in New York. In 1939, Mahler and her colleagues set up an observation room containing an observation booth, a play area, and a separate sitting area for mothers. Groups of children and their mothers could be watched as they interacted with one another, played with toys, or experimented with their opportunities for separation from mother. Children from four months old through four years old were, at one time or another, participants with their mothers in the study.

With increasing experience in natural observation, Mahler and her colleagues devised a number of data-gathering techniques that revolved around several important questions. How does a mother carry her child when she arrives? Like a part of herself? Like another human being? At what stage of growth does the child become aware of his mother? Is there an invisible bond between mother and baby? How does she separate herself from her child? Gradually? Abruptly? When separated from mother, how does the child bridge the gap between them? Visually? Vocally? By physically approaching? How does the mother respond to the child's needs? Quickly? Consistently? Reluctantly? Neglectfully? And so on.

From the mass of data gathered over the years, Mahler began to construct a picture of the normal sequence of stages in normal growing up, a process that had gone so sadly awry in her disturbed child patients. In essence, Mahler was studying the phenomenon of "psychological birth" (Mahler, Pine, & Bergman, 1975, p. 3). She discovered that a **separation-individuation** process is required for normal ego functioning. This process begins optimally around the fourth month and climaxes at or near the end of the third year of life. Before separation-individuation begins, however, there are two "forerunner" phases, **normal autism** and **normal symbiosis,** in which the mother and child mutually lay the groundwork for the child's subsequent "hatching" in psychological birth as a potential person. Therefore, six interdependent phases are required altogether for normal ego development. The two forerunner phases and the four subsequent stages of the individuation-separation process are summarized with their approximate age ranges in Table 6.4 as a prelude to the discussion that follows.

First Forerunner of Separation-Individuation: Normal Autism

During the first month of life, infants' physiological rhythms and needs outweigh all psychological processes. They spend most of the day in a half-sleeping, half-waking state, broken by full wakefulness only in moments of hunger or pain (Mahler et al., 1975, p. 41). In Freud's (1895; 1920a) language, the infant's stimulus barrier is strongly erected, enforcing a relative absence of cathexis of external objects.

Using another of Freud's concepts, Mahler and her colleagues characterize this normal autistic phase as a stage of absolute primary narcissism: Infants have no recognition of their mothers as external agents of satisfaction. As the first few weeks after birth proceed, this infantile absolute primary narcissism normally gives way to a dim recognition that needs are satisfied from somewhere outside the self (Mahler et al., 1975, p. 42). This secondary narcissism of the autistic phase might be termed "conditional hallucinatory omnipotence," for though infants recognize external need satisfiers, they nevertheless are convinced that their own desires alone are sufficient to assure their presence.

Although there is a relative disinterest in external reality, some stimuli may fleetingly penetrate the autistic shell of the stimulus barrier and evoke crude, global responses from

Table 6.4   **Forerunners and Subphases of Separation-Individuation**

The two forerunners

1. Normal Autism (First month)	2. Normal Symbiosis (2 to 4 months)
a. strong stimulus barrier	a. dim recognition of mother as object.
b. absolute primary narcissism	b. good (pleasure) and bad (pain) distinguished
c. conditional hallucinatory omnipotence	c. no real separation of self from mother
d. *achievement:* homeostatic balance of physiological mechanisms	d. *achievement:* formation of inner core of self established through mother's handling of infant's needs

The four subphases

1. Differentiation and Development of Body Image (5 to 9 months)	3. Rapprochement (14 to 24 months)
a. hatching process of tentative differentiation of self from mother	a. increased awareness of separateness from mother
b. checking back to mother pattern	b. shadowing of mother
c. stranger anxiety	c. darting-away games
d. *achievement:* movement toward active and separate functioning	d. rapproachement crisis, "losing" mother, and conflict between urge to separate and fear of loss
2. Practicing (10 to 14 months)	e. splitting mechanism of defense
a. interest in early phase in inanimate objects supplied by mother	f. *achievement:* ego eventually integrates good and bad images; beginning of gender identity
b. expanded locomotor capacity	4. Consolidation of Individuality (2 to 3 years)
c. low-keyed behavior when mother is absent; imaging mother	a. verbal form of communication dominant
d. *achievement:* building fear resistance to separation from mother and increased exploration of world	b. time concepts
	c. emotional-object constancy
	d. *achievement:* formation of a stable self-concept, a notion of "me" separate from love object

Based on Mahler, 1968; and Mahler et al., 1975.

the infant, but such responses show no precision of specificity, suggesting that the infant's various bodily reactions are all of a piece. Infants respond to every stimulus that can penetrate the barrier with the whole body, with their entire physical being (1975, p. 45). In effect, the stimulus barrier and its enforced autism protect the infant against extremes of stimulation fairly reliably, a situation similar to the fetal state, with the same goal of promoting unbroken biological growth.

The main achievement of the autistic phase is the infant's gradual attainment of physiological stability in the new, demanding world outside the mother's body. Restricted only for the moment to bodily homeostatic mechanisms, the infant will nevertheless shortly cross the frontier into the realm of psychological functioning. The purely biological balancing mechanisms of the body will now be supplemented by a series of psychological harmonizing processes designed to adapt infants to their world, to themselves, and to the meanings they create themselves.

By the second month of life, the dim awareness of the external mother marks the transition to the next, symbiotic phase. For all practical purposes, the infant now behaves as though it and its mother were a dual unity within a common boundary (Mahler, 1968, p. 8).

Second Forerunner of Separation-Individuation: Normal Symbiosis

From the second month onward through the third month, the autistic shell begins to crack, and the child's ego begins gearing up for its sensory and perceptual tasks that require alertness to the outside world. But infants cannot differentiate between their own tension-reducing efforts and those of the mother in their behalf. Thus their own tension-relieving activities such as urinating, defecating, coughing, sneezing, spitting, regurgitating, and vomiting are indistinguishable at this point from their mothers' attentions to the wet diapers, to providing food and cuddling, and to supplying warmth and cleanliness (Mahler et al., 1975, p. 43). The combined result of the infant's and the mother's actions is the gradually developing ability to distinguish between good (pleasure) and bad (pain) aspects of experience.

Thus the normal relationship during the second and third months of life between mother and infant is symbiotic, a term drawn metaphorically from biology to indicate the life-sustaining quality of two organisms living together.

> It is obvious that, whereas during the symbiotic phase the infant is absolutely dependent on the symbiotic partner, symbiosis has a quite different meaning for the adult partner of the dual unity. The infant's need for the mother is absolute, while the mother's need for the infant is relative. . . . The term "symbiosis" in this context is a metaphor. It does not describe, as the biological concept of symbiosis does, what actually happens between two separate individuals. . . . It was chosen to describe that state of undifferentiation, of fusion with mother, in which the "I" is not yet differentiated from the "not-I," and in which inside and outside are only gradually coming to be sensed as different. (Mahler, 1968, pp. 8–9)

The crude differentiation between good and bad, between pleasure and pain, allows the symbiotic child to deal with painful perceptions in only one way: projection of the bad outside the realm of the symbiotic partnership, in the same way that sneezing, coughing, urinating, vomiting, and defecating expel pain-producing material into the external world to provide tension-reducing pleasure. But the external world, for the symbiotic child, is everything outside of mother-self; it does not yet include mother alone.

> The essential feature of symbiosis is hallucinatory or delusional somatopsychic omnipotent fusion with the representation of the mother and, in particular, the delusion of a common boundary of the two actually and physically separate individuals. This is the mechanism to which the ego regresses in cases of the most severe disturbance of individuation and psychotic disorganization, which I have described as "symbiotic child psychosis. . . ." (Mahler, 1968, p. 9)

Through their continued experience of pleasure and pain, infants begin to differentiate a sense of their own bodies and a sense of the distinction between "inner" and "outer." These perceptions are still somewhat fused with perception of the mother's body. The beginning experience of inner sensations now forms the core of the infant's sense of self. The primary narcissism of the autistic phase yields to the secondary narcissism of the pleasures to be derived from the infant's own and its mother's body (Mahler, 1968, p. 10; Mahler et al., 1975, p. 47). While, in the autistic phase, the mother's breast was experienced as part of self, it is now seen symbiotically as a "satisfying object" located outside the self but not independent of the self.

The mother's "holding behavior" during feeding shapes the infant's own style of reacting to the human environment. Thus a mother who feels proud and self-sufficient because she is able to breast-feed her child is likely to handle the infant differently and communicate different meanings from the handling and communications of a mother whose puritanical upbringing makes her feel uncomfortable nursing her infant with her own body (Mahler et al., 1975, p. 49).

A mother who genuinely enjoys her children, who smiles and talks to them during their intimacies, will encourage a smiling and talkative baby, who pleasurably anticipates human contacts of all kinds. For this reason, Mahler describes the holding behavior of mothers as "symbiotic organizers" of psychological birth.

We turn now to the first subphase of the separation-individuation process proper, beginning where symbiosis leaves off, at four months of age.

First Subphase: Differentiation and Development of the Body Image

At four to five months of age, when symbiosis is at its peak, infants have already begun to show signs of differentiating themselves out of the symbiotic orbit. Called the "hatching process," it marks the beginning of the child's emergence as a permanently alert, perceptually aware creature.

Hatching is psychological birth, for this first subphase marks the start of the child's tentative and healthy efforts to break away, in a strictly bodily sense, from the previously passive "lap-babyhood" during symbiotic unity with mother (Mahler et al., 1975, p. 55). The entire subphase of differentiation and development of the body image lasts from approximately four or five to nine months of age.

At the six-month mark, infants show beginning **differentiation and development of the body image.** A variety of new behaviors are apparent: pulling mother's hair, ears, and nose; putting food into her mouth; straining back from her arms to better see her or other interesting things outside their orbit. The infant spends a good deal of time exploring the external environment when awake, and these investigations include examinations of the contours of mother's face, her eyeglasses or earrings, and any other object that can be grasped, mouthed, or yanked. Infants may even enjoy games of peekaboo, signaling in their delighted, throaty laughter vague comprehension that mother may disappear and reappear unexpectedly, that is, her presence and absence are independent of the infant's bodily control.

At seven or eight months, a "checking back to mother" behavior pattern emerges, in which a baby seems to compare his or her mother with other people, feature by feature: "He seems to familiarize himself more thoroughly, as it were, with what is mother, what feels, tastes, smells, looks like, and has the 'clang' of mother" (1975, p. 56). "Stranger anxiety" is also a development of this period, and the child is both apprehensive under a stranger's gaze and wondrously fascinated with the details of this "other-than-mommy" person.

From the period of this first subphase of separation-individuation onward, the child has embarked on a course that has two developmental tracks. The first track is the development of separation from mother, distancing with confidence, forming boundaries to the self, and a slow disengagement that results in subjective awareness of separateness as a positive, satisfying state. The second track is the development of individuation through the internal maturation of independent ego functions in the areas of perception, memory, cognition, and reality testing. Individuation is literally the psychological process of assimilating one's recognition of physical separateness from the mother into an intrapsychically harmonious acceptance of oneself as an individual. Separation is becoming a discrete entity; individuation is becoming a functioning person.

Second Subphase: Practicing

From approximately 10 to 14 months, children build on their accomplishments of the first subphase. They are now able to differentiate their bodies from those of their mothers, they recognize their own mothers as special, unique persons, easily detectable as different from all "non-mommies," and their egos have begun to develop autonomous perceptual, cognitive, and reality-testing capacities.

In the early practicing subphase, interest becomes partially focused on inanimate objects supplied by mother: a diaper, bottle, toy, or blanket, left with the child as they part for the night. But though children explore these objects visually, tactually, perhaps even tasting them, their primary interest remains centered on mother. Simultaneously, however, they are developing increased facility in locomotor coordination.

> Expanding locomotor capacity during the early practicing subphase widens the child's world; not only does he have a more active role in determining closeness and distance to mother, but the modalities that up to now were used to explore the relatively familiar environment suddenly expose him to a wider segment of reality; there is more to see, more to hear, more to touch. (Mahler et al., 1975, p. 66)

The way children interpret their experiences in this new world will be subtly shaped by their still close relationship to mother. Her reactions to brief separations will amplify or minimize any apprehensions they might have. In all such separations, the mother remains the "home base," an emotional refueling stop on the road to increasingly lengthy, increasingly distant separations.

The **practicing subphase** proper begins with the shift to upright walking near the age of 10 or 12 months. Now a child is truly physically independent and free to roam widely and proudly. Children become interested in the accomplishments of their own bodies and are more easily able to resist the knocks and bruises that new adventures will inevitably bring. Familiar adults other than "Mommy" are easily accepted as substitutes. Some children seem diminished when they become aware of mother's absence. Motility and other performances slow, interest in surroundings decreases. When a person other than mother offers comfort, toddlers may lose their emotional balance and burst into tears. Mahler hypothesized that such a child had been concentrating on an image of the mother in order to resist the fear of love-object loss.

Third Subphase: Rapprochement

In the third subphase, **rapprochement,** lasting from about 14 months to 2 years, children become more aware of their separateness and are able to make greater use of cognitive faculties to resist frustration. Paradoxically, however, there is also an increase in sensitivity to mother's absences, expressed in the child's nearly constant concern over mother's whereabouts (Mahler et al., 1975, p. 76). "As the toddler's awareness of separateness grows . . . he seems to have an increased need, a wish for mother to share with him every one of his new skills and experiences, as well as a great need for the [mother] object's love" (1975, pp. 76–77).

During this subphase, toddlers begin to "shadow" their mothers, exhibiting continuous vigilance by following every move. They also begin games of "darting away" so that they can be caught after a chase and swept into her arms. It is possible that darting-away games express both the child's wish for reunion with the love object and fear of reengulfment by her (1975, p. 77).

This rapprochement phase is a period of contradictions. As toddlers become aware of their separateness, they devise strategies for denying it, for preventing it, and for maintaining close contact. But they also "dart away." Verbal communication becomes easier and supplements gestural and bodily contact as the only ways to express meaning; yet toddlers find it difficult to give up their sense of preverbal omnipotence and self-grandeur long enough to recognize that adults do not respond automatically to their magical wishes. Even though they can barely bring themselves to be parted from their mothers, they discover new love objects in their lives. They begin to become aware of their fathers as unique persons, with special and interesting characteristics of their own.

Sometime near the 18-month mark, extending through the second year, a rapprochement crisis develops in which the toddler is nearly overwhelmed by a resurgence of separation fear. Rapid mood changes may be evident, temper tantrums may occur, or prolonged bouts of whining and clinging behavior suddenly make their appearance. This usually occurs when a child seems just at the point of readiness to assert independence. It is as though toddlers struggle acutely with a conflict between wanting to push away a mother and also desperately wanting to cling to her. At the same time, there appears a resurgence of stranger fear, sometimes interpreted by adults as "shyness."

An odd reaction may also surface in the child at the crisis phase of the rapprochement stage. Toddlers may suddenly become intensely anxious because they believe their mothers have left the room, even though they are sitting next to each other. Mahler and her colleagues (1975, p. 96) suggest that this peculiar anxiety over "losing" mother is a form of projection on the child's part, stemming from a conflict between independence and separation fear: "The desire to function by one's own self may be particularly threatening to the child at the very point in development when one's own feelings and wishes and those of mother are still poorly differentiated. The wish to be autonomous and separate from mother, to leave her, might also mean emotionally that the mother would wish to leave him . . ." (Mahler et al., 1975, p. 96).

Most often in the 20- to 21-month range, the child discovers the bodily differences between boys and girls. The boy's discovery of his penis takes place earlier. New knowledge and awareness has to do with the differences between boys and girls, and between parents and children. Generally, Mahler found, this discovery seemed to be more difficult for girls than boys to assimilate into their growing sense of identity (1975, p. 106). Consistent with Freudian theory, girls in the rapprochement crisis tended to blame their mothers for the anatomical difference between girls and boys, "to blame her, to demand from her, to be disappointed in her, and still be ambivalently tied to her" (1975, p. 106).

Boys, by contrast, seemed to be confronted with the classical conception of anxiety about the possibility of being castrated by the father, but only later, after the rapprochement crisis had ended. As a result, boys were better able than girls to cope with their separation conflict and to find some restorative security in their growing gender identification with father.

From the viewpoint of ego development, the rapprochement phase may be crucial to the child's ability to internalize conflict and to reconcile clashes between an "all good" mother and an "all bad" one. The good mother is the person who has provided all pleasures, all securities, all warmth, and all companionship. In the symbiotic phase, this "good love object" was viewed as a part of self. But now the child's growing psychological sophistication confronts a serious conflict. Mothers unavoidably have their dark sides. Sometimes mother is a need-frustrator, or a pain-inflictor, or an indifferent and distracted caretaker, or, most painful of all her shortcomings, mother is sometimes absent altogether. For the child's newly developing ego, the "good mother" and the "bad mother" cannot be one and the same love object. She, who was once so long ago a part of me, cannot be bad; yet, undeniably, mother is not always good. If the good mother and the bad mother are one person, then, I too, must harbor some bad within me. That is not possible, for, "I am all good."

The rapprochement child may employ the defense mechanism termed **"splitting"** of the ego to deal with such contradictory love objects by treating them in all-or-none fashion. Thus mother cannot be both good and bad simultaneously. There is a good mother, and there is a bad mother. The good mother is the love object that was internalized as part of the child's own narcissistic ego during symbiosis. The bad mother is externalized, projected to the outside world, outside me, where all pain-producing, threatening objects belong.

After all, one's mother cannot be both loving and unloving, cannot be loved and hated, approached and avoided at one time. "Hence the toddler may displace aggression onto the world-outside-of-mother while exaggerating his or her love for, overidealizing, the absent, longed-for mother. When mother returns she disrupts the ideal image, and reunions with her are often painful, since the young ego's synthetic function cannot heal the split" (Mahler et al., 1975, pp. 292–293). In the case of the normally developing child, however, the ego gradually gains the ability to synthesize good and bad, to integrate divided feelings and perceptions into a unified, "synthetic" whole.

Fourth Subphase: Consolidation of Individuality— "On the Way to Object Constancy"

Toward the end of the second year, and extending through the third year of life, the image of the mother as a separate entity in the outside world is consolidated with the "good" and the "bad" images of her. As a result of this **consolidation of individuality,** the beginnings of the child's own individuality also emerge with a gradual recognition of separate personhood.

In psychoanalytic language, the child is said to have achieved a fair degree of emotional **object constancy.** Internally, mentally, such children are able to maintain an image of the mother even when she is not present. They cognitively grasp, however vaguely, that mother does not cease to exist just because she is out of sight, nor does her absence imply that she has stopped loving her child.

> But the constancy of the object implies more than the maintenance of the representation of the absent love object. . . . It also implies the unifying of the "good" and "bad" object into one whole representation. This fosters the fusion of the aggressive and libidinal drives and tempers the hatred for the object when aggression is intense. . . . In the state of object constancy, the love object will not be rejected or exchanged for another if it can no longer provide satisfactions; and in that state, the object is still longed for, and not rejected (hated) as unsatisfactory simply because it is absent. (Mahler et al., 1975, p. 110)

For the healthy child to achieve emotional object constancy, two prior essential steps are necessary. The first step is the establishment of basic trust in mother and self that comes from reliable, immediate, loving gratification of need. The second step is the cognitive development of mental imagery to allow the child to form internal representations that abstractly and symbolically embody external reality in relatively permanent memories.

Verbal ability, developed in rudimentary form during the third subphase, now assumes complete dominance as the means of communication. Play becomes more imaginative and purposeful, taking on aspects of role-playing and dramatic fantasy. The concept of time (later, tomorrow, before) is meaningful to children in terms of their mothers' comings and goings, an attainment achieved in a similar way by Freud's grandson Ernst in his masterful "gone game" (see Chapter 3).

The main accomplishment of this last phase of separation-individuation is the attainment of a self-concept organized around a stable sense of "me." The process of forming a unique identity, the core of individuality, is not completed at the end of the third year, but continues throughout the later Oedipal phase. In Mahler's view, the normal child has an intrinsic drive toward growth and personality integration:

> It bears special emphasis . . . that our study convinced us that the maturational pressure, *the drive for and toward individuation* in the normal human infant, is an innate, powerful given, which, although it may be muted by protracted interference, does manifest itself all along the separation-individuation process. (Mahler et al., 1975, p. 206, italics in original)

PERSONAL SOURCES OF MAHLER'S SEPARATION-INDIVIDUATION HYPOTHESIS

The central feature of Mahler's theory is the development of a helpless, symbiotically dependent, and unthinking biological creature into a quasi-independent, self-reflective psychological entity capable of other-recognition. Abstracted in this way, Mahler's description of the maturation of the pre-Oedipal ego is a narrative on becoming a person. We can ask, therefore, from what personal origins does Mahler's focus on autonomy stem?

Rejecting Mother, Confounding Father: Self-Sufficiency Is Everything

Mahler's childhood memory of her mother was that she was a "deeply unhappy woman":

> I came far too early—nine months and six days after the wedding—and was very much unwanted by my mother, who was a mere girl of nineteen at the time. Very beautiful, very narcissistic, and greatly pampered, she blamed my father for my untimely arrival. . . . In her anger, she had as little to do with me as she could. During my first year of life, when I was quite sickly and had sleep disturbances, it was my father who, with my nurse, arose at night to attend me. My symbiotic stage of life was difficult: I must have been full of frustrated rage at the rejecting mother whom I greatly loved nonetheless. (Mahler, 1988, p. 4)

Born in the Hungarian village of Sopron in 1897, Margaret Mahler née Schoenberger grew up speaking two languages. Her Hungarian-speaking father, Gustav Schoenberger, was a physician in general practice and chief public health officer of his district. Eugenia Wiener Schoenberger, Margaret's mother, spoke primarily German at home. Much to the adult Margaret's amazement, during psychoanalysis she realized that she and her younger sister had spoken Hungarian with their father and switched automatically to German when their mother would enter the room (Mahler, 1988, p. 2). Mahler recalls that her father was socially prominent and active, especially in the political life of their town, whereas her mother devoted herself primarily to being an "excellent cook and homemaker."

Fueled by her own feelings of rejection, the four-year-old Margaret became a keen observer of her mother's elation at the birth of a second daughter. From Margaret's point of view, her new baby sister Suzanne was greeted with affection and delight—maternal responses Margaret now understood had been denied her. Indeed, the young Mahler began to assume that her mother wanted her dead (1988, p. 5).

In what appears to be utter candor, Mahler states in her memoirs that it was this harsh contrast with the loving acceptance and attention her sister received that inspired her own interest in pediatrics, psychoanalysis with children, and especially the study of mother–child relationships (Mahler, 1988, pp. 4–5). Out of frustration, Mahler turned to her father. She recalls that at age four-and-a-half, she observed her mother treating her sister lovingly, saying to her child, "I have brought you into this world, I love, I adore you . . ." and other endearments, to which the young Margaret is reported to have said, "And I, I was born by my father" (Mahler, 1988, p. 6).

Her mother did not like visitors or Margaret's friends or even her husband's patients to "intrude" into the house. On one occasion, Mahler recalled that her mother would permit her to have a birthday party only if she consented to give away her precious collection of chocolate animal figures as a prize for one of the party games. Reluctantly, Margaret consented, but in the end her mother gave the entire collection to a child who was distantly related to her. Mahler recalls crying "inconsolably" at the end of the party (1988, p. 7).

Her Father's "Son": Gender Confusion as Self-Confidence

Out of such frustrations, rejections, and hurts, Margaret turned to the world of her father. Medicine, science, politics, and mathematics captured her interests and intelligence, and supported by her father's enthusiasm, Mahler became the "son" her father wanted: ". . . it was my father's eager adoption of me as his 'son,' and my willing acceptance of this role, that confounded my childhood gender identity." Mahler reports that it never occurred to her that she might be a "pretty young girl," and her father's attention to her intellectual development did nothing for the development of her feminine self-esteem. To erode her tenuous grip on feminine identity further, her father would greet her schoolgirl avowals of admiration or love of a male teacher with the remark, "You are man enough for yourself" (1988, p. 8). Mahler's intellectual prowess provided for an intimidating reputation during the dating years of adolescence. When her sister attracted young suitors, Margaret was off reading Einstein's ideas on relativity. In what should have been a simple conversation, which she later regretted, she startled one young man who had taken her to a dance with the proposition that God existed in the fourth dimension! There was no second date.

> . . . I tended to deny my own femininity entirely. I refused to believe that any man worth having could love me; if one perchance expressed any feeling for me, he was instantly devalued. Never having learned how to compete with other women as a woman, I learned instead how to avoid defeat as a woman in a world of men. In short, I developed a strong drive for independence at an early age. . . . (Mahler, 1988, p. 9)

Years later, when the adult Margaret would return to Sopron and talk with her family about the young men who now courted her, her father voiced his unchanging refrain: "Why did I need to marry, he would ask, when I was so self-sufficient. I was really much 'better' than the average man" (1988, p. 77). When, at age 39, she introduced Paul Mahler to her father as the man she was going to marry, her father said to the startled young man: "You must know what you are doing; she is not average . . ." (1988, p. 10). From Mahler's psychoanalytic point of view in later years, she interpreted her father's comment to the erstwhile Paul Mahler as reflecting his deep resentment of her marriage:

> Psychoanalytically speaking, my father meant [to warn Paul]: "Watch out, for whatever her strengths and weaknesses, she is not castrated, and you had better watch out not to get castrated by her." (Mahler, 1988, p. 10)

Medical School: The Compromise Solution

It is not surprising that Mahler chose a career in medicine, in part to emulate the father who had so strongly, if inappropriately, nurtured her and in part to pursue her own intellectual strengths. During her early preparation, she came into contact with psychoanalysis through friends and acquaintances, and her interest was sparked.

It is noteworthy that so many of the early psycho-analysts as well as other personality theorists were not only Jewish but affected by anti-Semitism. They shared in the culture and the education of the general society, but did not accept many of the assumptions and values of the general culture. Margaret Mahler was also one of the few women in a primarily male profession. Perhaps Mahler's occupational, ethnic, and religious status as an outsider was a factor that predisposed her to want to look at behavior from a more objective or analytic stance. This is probably not the whole explanation, but it is interesting to consider the role of gender, religion, and ethnicity in the development of personality theories.

In 1917, she gained admission to the medical school of the University of Budapest. Throughout her schooling, her father was supportive, but he tried to persuade his daughter to avoid certain medical specialties that he felt were not suited to a pioneering woman pursuing a medical career. He especially tried to dissuade his daughter from a career in psychiatry, which he regarded as a more or less academic and custodial branch of medicine. But when he learned that his daughter was interested in Freud, he read Freud (Mahler, 1988, p. 22).

Anti-Semitism in the Communist regime that ruled Budapest was intensifying, and if the chances that a Jewish medical student would be permitted to finish medical school were small, then the chances for a Jewish female medical student were practically nil. At about the same time, Mahler's younger sister, who was somewhat immature, wanted to move to Munich to study music. Mahler's parents would grant the younger sister permission only if the older Margaret would accompany her and serve as substitute parent.

So in 1919, Mahler entered the university in Munich. She became a star student and several young men became interested in her romantically. But she recalls that she was still under the influence of her father's disapproval of any interactions with the opposite sex and did not believe that she could really be attractive to men. As she recalls, "I had effectively embraced the meaning of my father's devaluation of my feminine strivings: that I was neuter" (1988, p. 25).

Consistent with her self-analyzed personal history, Mahler chose the medical specialty of pediatrics. "Pediatrics, I should perhaps explain, represented a compromise of sorts: it would enable me to be what my father was [i.e., a practicing physician], while simultaneously accommodating my desire—perhaps my outstanding 'feminine' trait—to work with children" (1988, p. 23).

Conditions in Munich deteriorated for Margaret and her sister. Anti-Semitism grew more blatant, and at one point, to encourage Jews to leave Munich, apparently random arrests were made of Jewish students. Mahler and her sister found themselves briefly in jail (1988, p. 28). By 1920, mounting indignities and aggressive prejudice, as well as a growing resentment that she was trapped in this situation by her sister's needs, led Mahler to the decision that it was time to transfer to the University of Jena in southern Germany near Weimar. Mahler's sister was forced to return to Vienna.

As assistant to an eminent pediatric researcher in Jena, Mahler got her first exposure to the serious illnesses and psychosomatic disorders of childhood. One case in particular left an enduring impression. A woodcutter brought his child for treatment with symptoms of failing to thrive and loss of weight, but with no other medical disorders apparent. The father and child had what Mahler would later recognize as a symbiotic relationship. Persuaded to leave his child overnight, the woodcutter returned home and dreamt that night in a symbolic dream that he had felled a tree and that the tree was his son. When the father returned to the clinic the next morning to reclaim his son, he was told that the child had died during the night. Mahler understood intuitively, and later psychoanalytically, that the father had been everything to the child, and when that symbiotic bond had been disrupted, the child could no longer survive (Mahler, 1988, p. 31). The significance of emotional and psychological variables was becoming salient to Mahler, a pediatrician training in a medical specialty that could be blind to the critical importance of psychology.

Despite the intellectual excitement and enjoyment Mahler was experiencing in Jena, the anti-Semitism continued unabated. At one point, despite academic excellence, Mahler was in danger of being expelled because she was an "East European Jewess" whom the general student body organization thus deemed unfit. Fortunately, influential friends intervened in Mahler's behalf and she was able to graduate magna cum laude from the University of Jena two years later, completing her final semester at the University of Heidelberg, a "fun" city where anti-Semitism was not yet rife.

Because she was not a citizen of Germany, Mahler's medical diploma did not entitle her to a German medical license. But she had acquired Austrian citizenship in preparation for this event, and she now returned to Vienna (close to her home village of Sopron) to obtain her license, to continue her training in psychoanalysis, and to begin the practice of pediatrics.

As part of her continued training, she became an assistant in a famous pediatric institute under the eminent Viennese pediatrician von Pirquet. Professor von Pirquet had created a well-known feeding system for very ill infants called the "nem system." An infant was placed in a sterile cubicle with one or more glass walls and fed precisely measured portions of milk called "nems." A nem is a unit of measurement that corresponds to the caloric value of one gram of breast milk. The entire feeding procedure involved no human contact with the infant!

In total contrast, Mahler spent her summer months in a rival pediatric institute that stressed the importance of the mother's nurturance of the sick child and the critical "communication" between the two in the care of its small patients. Well ahead of its day, the Leopold Moll Institute admitted sick children for treatment with their mothers, and operated strictly on the philosophy that "a baby not only 'belonged' to its mother but that the presence of the mother . . . was essential if a sick baby was to get well" (Mahler, 1988, p. 47). Babies were routinely assigned to special student nurses to provide "maternal" care so that both the nurse-in-training and the baby received nourishment from the experience. So dedicated and loving were these nurses that they would frequently don surgical masks and spend an entire night holding, cuddling, and talking to a dying child. To Mahler's amazement, many of these children recovered under this regimen. The contrast with the von Pirquet Institute and its nem feeding was stark. Mahler's own childhood experiences had exquisitely sensitized and prepared her to absorb these crucial lessons about the power of the intimacy in the mother–child dualism.

Cinderella in Psychoanalysis Land

Mahler's interest in psychoanalysis continued. She met August Aichhorn, the child guidance movement leader and psychoanalyst. Aichhorn was an elusive and "mysterious man" who spoke frequently of his contacts with the criminal elements of Viennese society, especially among the adolescent gangs. He spoke the language of "delinquents" and seemed to earn their trust easily both in therapy and in institutional settings by communicating that he would always give them the benefit of a doubt. He was able, apparently, to attend meetings of gang members as they plotted their activities, and frequently "predicted" a particular crime well in advance of the actual event. Aichhorn's therapeutic approach to these children was a mixture of psychoanalysis and commonsense humanism. He understood them not as criminals but as abused and misunderstood children. In his counseling technique, Mahler recalled him as a master of drawing out the unconscious motivations in the child's recounting of circumstances and then showing the child how he had "chosen" a certain course of action. Making rounds and attending consultations with Aichhorn gave Mahler her first real exposure to child psychiatry and a firsthand experience with psychoanalytic method.

By 1926, Mahler entered a training analysis with the well-known analyst Helene Deutsch, but the match of patient and therapist was not made in heaven. Deutsch, acting somewhat authoritatively and regally, made it clear to the enthusiastic Mahler that she had agreed to accept her for analysis mostly because of a professional favor. At the time, Mahler was financially impoverished and had arranged a modified fee with this eminent analyst. What Mahler did not know at the time was that Helene Deutsch resented treating her for less than her usual fee. At the time, Mahler interpreted Deutsch's arrogant attitude as a personal rejection and was crushed. She spent the next 50 or 60 sessions trying to prove her worth to her analyst. Accustomed to being treated as special and intellectually gifted, Mahler chafed under the Deutsch regime of being treated like a "second-class citizen." After a series of missed appointments (canceled by the ambivalent Helene Deutsch), Deutsch terminated Mahler's training analysis, informing the patient that she was "unanalyzable."

What followed was a series of negative appraisals of Mahler by members of the analytic community in Vienna. Anna Freud wrote to Mahler informing her that her candidate status at the Vienna Psychoanalytic Institute was terminated until she undertook a therapeutic analysis to resolve her difficulties, at which point she might reapply to the Institute. By a circuitous route, Mahler sidestepped the officially recommended analysts and appealed to her friend August Aichhorn. He agreed to take her as a patient and evolved a characteristically secret plan whereby he would rescue and restore her to acceptable status in the professional psychoanalytic community. Seriously depressed and demoralized, Mahler was ready to be rescued by Prince Charming. In the end, she was in analysis with Aichhorn for almost three years, and during that time analyst and patient fell in love. With her usual candor, Mahler describes the familiar essence of the situation in which she found herself:

> Under Aichhorn's analytic care, I became a sort of Cinderella, the love object of a beautiful Prince (Aichhorn) who would win me the favor of a beautiful stepmother (Mrs. Deutsch). At the same time, my analytic treatment with him simply recapitulated my Oedipal situation all over again—I was the daughter of both a rejecting mother (Mrs. Deutsch) and a father (Aichhorn) very partial to me. (Mahler, 1988, p. 68)

Realizing that the analytic work they accomplished together was far from classical, Aichhorn and Mahler decided that she should continue her training analysis with another analyst. In the meantime, Aichhorn, as promised, secured Mahler's readmission to the Vienna psychoanalytic establishment.

Other difficulties ensued. As a member of Anna Freud's training seminar in child analysis, Mahler recalled that her relationship with Freud's daughter was "unpleasant" and distant. In general, Mahler's experience with the psychoanalytic establishment in Vienna was abrasive and disappointing for her. By the time the Nazis had risen to power, Margaret and her husband, as well as a host of other Jewish intellectuals, began to emigrate from Europe. Mahler and her husband Paul arrived in the United States in 1938, where she began the work that secured her place in psychoanalytic history. She died in 1985, at the age of 88.

A FINAL WORD ON MARGARET S. MAHLER

Unlike nearly any other theorist for whom we have personal source information, Mahler has done our work for us. She candidly identified the three main themes of her early life that led to her interest in child psychiatry and eventually to the theory of separation-individuation:

- Maternal indifference and rejection coupled with strong, frequently inappropriate, emotional support from her father.
- Gender and personal identity confusion shaped by her father's attempts to treat her as the son he did not have.
- Prematurely enforced self-sufficiency based on her father's need to have a son and her mother's need to distance her daughter.

Coupled with these self-identified themes, we might add the obvious underlying themes of insecurity and feelings of inferiority that Mahler strove so successfully to master. She had struggled firsthand with the experience of early rejection, with the pain of finding her own specialness unwelcome in the wider world, and with the belief that, as a woman, she could not ever be "good enough." Out of these experiences came her focus on pediatrics, on the emotional consequences of adequate "mothering," and her interest in what it takes to be a competent, self-sufficient person.

Margaret Mahler reached a few major conclusions based on her clinical observations and theoretical considerations:

- Grave maladjustment of psychotic proportions has its ego origins in developmental failures to separate from mother as an autonomous agent, or in failures to use mother as a living aid in making sense of the living world. The symbiotic psychotic child exemplifies the former and the autistic child the latter form of ego pathology.
- Psychological birth as a human person can be accomplished only by children whose inherent strivings toward individuality are undamaged and whose mothers encourage, however reluctantly, their burgeoning struggles toward separation, without overwhelming their capacities to endure aloneness.
- The height of ego individuation embodies the ability to synthesize not only aggressive and libidinal strivings toward mother, but also the capacity to draw sustenance from an internalized representation of her.

Thus, Mahler's work has shown, contrary to Freud's classical scheme, that the roots of identity, conflict resolution, and ego strength lie much earlier in development than the Oedipus complex; and these ego functions are more influenced by the mother than Freud's paternalistic viewpoint would allow.

EVALUATING THE EGO PSYCHOLOGISTS

Much of our evaluation discussion of Freud's classical psychoanalysis is pertinent to the work of his daughter, Anna, and Margaret S. Mahler. Like Freud's classical approach, ego psychology represents a collective attempt to understand both normal and abnormal human functioning. And like Freud's work, ego psychologists, like Anna Freud and Mahler, aimed to clarify the connection and the conflict between reason and passion. But unlike Freud, these ego psychologists gradually shifted psychoanalysis away from its focus on drives and instinctual satisfaction and more toward a concern with reason and masterful coping with life.

Refutability of Ego Psychology

It is necessary to understand that ego psychologists are different in aim and method from those theorists identified as "neo-Freudians," some of whom we study in later chapters. Anna Freud and Margaret Mahler explicitly attempted to preserve classical psychoanalysis insofar as that was possible. They certainly developed radical ideas that would qualify as "neo-Freudian" in the sense of being "new," but they invariably did not claim originality. By contrast, the neo-Freudian thinkers we examine later had no great concern for the preservation of classical analysis. Thinkers such as Horney, Fromm, and Sullivan aimed to change classical analysis. Instead, Anna Freud and Margaret Mahler tried hard to show that their ideas were derived from Freud's theories.

Anna Freud and Margaret Mahler did little to provide a basis for the empirical researcher. There is much in what we have seen that cries out for testing, but there are so few ways to translate ego psychology into testable hypotheses. To take one example, D. N. Stern (1985) has reviewed basic empirical findings from developmental psychology and has tried to correlate these data with Mahler's concepts of normal autism and normal symbiosis. What was the result? Stern finds literally no evidence to support any of Mahler's concepts. An exception appears to be Anna Freud's concept of developmental lines, which is based largely on observations of children and is inherently refutable or testable.

What can we conclude? For the issue of refutability, concepts such as *symbiosis, ego synthesis,* and *Self object* are not much improved over Freud's *libido, id,* or *repression.*

Ego Psychology's Conception of Human Agency

The greatest difference between classical psychoanalysis and the two ego psychologists considered in this chapter concerns the issue of active versus passive human agency. Whereas in the classical theory the person is essentially a passive receptacle for reality, there can be discerned a steady progression away from this concept beginning with Anna Freud. Her conception of developmental lines emphasizes themes of mastery that partially free the ego from its passive stance in relation to the id and to reality. With the ego psychologists, humans are seen, in part, as active agents who, in part, influence the nature of the reality with which they interact.

Anna Freud and Margaret S. Mahler's Largely Idiographic Focus

Again, as in classical psychoanalysis, the focus in ego psychology is largely clinical, almost exclusively idiographic, and more or less completely aimed at understanding the dynamics of the individual. Despite Mahler's aspirations to understand broad human developments, close examination of the two approaches in this chapter reveals no real difference from the classical analytic obsession. Anna Freud and Margaret Mahler both focus on the unique dynamics of one person at a time.

SUMMARY

Anna Freud, Freud's self-chosen psychoanalytic conservator, legitimized ego psychology by her publication of a book devoted to examining the ego defenses for what they could reveal of the history of instinctual conflict.

Through her work with child patients, with war orphans, and with children separated from their parents temporarily, Anna Freud was able to transcend classical drive theory without demolishing it. She developed a diagnostic classification system predicated on the plasticity of the child's healthy strivings toward increased maturity. Her most original contribution to psychoanalytic theory has been her elucidation of developmental lines, sequences of psychological and physical growth organized along the paths of dependency to independence, from irrational to rational, and from passive to active relations with reality. Developmental lines suggest an important interactionist vantage point from which to account for psychological functioning, a viewpoint neglected in classical Freudian theory.

Margaret S. Mahler, in line with mastery themes, has chronicled the six stages through which a child's ego develops on the road to separation and individuation, that is, on the complex and winding pathway to becoming a self-reliant and unique person. Beginning in "forerunner" phases of normal autism and normal symbiosis, the infantile ego matures from its initial absolute narcissistic shell of isolation to dim recognition of an external, satisfying object world. Then, progressing in graduated steps, the child passes through symbiotic fusion with mother to a stage of primitive differentiation of self, then toward the practicing and rapprochement stages, marked by increasing awareness and acceptance of separateness from the love object. In the final subphase, children consolidate matured verbal, locomotive, and cognitive skills into a coherent unity, self-reliantly able to function apart from mother, and, free of fear, capable of the recognition that each is a center of awareness, an "I."

Our evaluation of the ego psychologists suggests:

- In general, the ego psychologists' concepts are not generally refutable or empirically verifiable. This was also the case for classical psychoanalysis—and largely for the same reasons. Anna Freud's model of developmental lines is, however, largely based on observable behaviors.

- Human agency is conceptualized as more active and interactive than in classical Freudian theory.

- There is a strong idiographic emphasis.

FOR FURTHER READING

General background exploration of ego psychology is best begun with two classic papers by David Rapaport: "The Autonomy of the Ego" (*Bulletin of the Menninger Clinic,* 1951, *15,* 113–123); and "The Theory of Ego Autonomy: A Generalization" (*Bulletin of the Menninger Clinic,* 1958, *22,* 13–35). Helpful for its historical breadth and comparative approach, Daniel Yankelovich and William Barrett's *Ego and Instinct: The Psychoanalytic View of Human Nature—Revised* (New York: Vintage Books, 1970) provides a clear theoretical account of classical theory's shortcomings, alternatives that have been proposed, and a lucid treatment of the philosophical underpinnings of classical and contemporary theory. With more emphasis on the therapeutic applications of contemporary ego psychology, Gertrude and Rubin Blanck's *Ego Psychology: Theory and Practice* (New York: Columbia University Press, 1974) provides relatively clear insights into the work of the major ego theorists and a close view of how ego pathologies are therapeutically treated. Thomas Parisi's "Why Freud Failed" (*American Psychologist,* 1987, *42*[3] 235–245) is a well-reasoned account of why Freud abandoned biological, evolutionary, and neurological concepts in constructing his psychology.

Anna Freud's most important books and papers have been collected into the seven-volume *The Writings of Anna Freud* (New York: International Universities Press, 1965–1974). Essential readings in these volumes are *Introduction to Psychoanalysis* and *Lectures for Child Analysts and Teachers* (Vol. 1, 1974); *The Ego and the Mechanisms of Defense* (Vol. 2, 1966); *Normality and Pathology in Childhood: Assessment of Development* (Vol. 6, 1965); and the collection of papers in Part I of *Problems of Psychoanalytic Training, Diagnosis, and the Technique of Therapy* (Vol. 7, 1971). A biographical account of Anna Freud emphasizing her constructive and caring approach can be found in Chapter IV of Janet Sayers' *Mothers of Psychoanalysis: Helene Deutsch, Karen Horney, Anna Freud, Melanie Klein.* (New York: Norton, 1991).

Margaret S. Mahler's classic monograph, *On Human Symbiosis and the Vicissitudes of Individuation* (New York: International Universities Press, 1968) is somewhat difficult reading, but still the best introduction to her concept of symbiotic psychosis. Her collaborative effort with Fred Pine and Anni Bergmann, *The Psychological Birth of the Human Infant* (New York: Basic Books, 2000), contains a more readable introduction to both symbiotic psychosis and to the stages of the separation-individuation process.

GLOSSARY

Anna Freud

Bulldogs Bank children: The collective name given to six children who were survivors of a concentration camp. Anna Freud cared for them in a house called Bulldogs Bank. She learned much about the resiliency of the personality from them.

Classic defenses: Repression, denial, asceticism, projection, altruistic surrender, displacement, turning-against-self, reaction formation, reversal, sublimation, introjection, identification-with-aggressor, isolation, undoing, and regression.

Developmental lines: Reliable sequences of development during which children outgrow dependence on external controls and gain in ego mastery of internal and external reality. Anna Freud listed six separate developmental lines:

1. From Dependency to Emotional Self-Reliance
2. From Suckling to Rational Eating
3. From Wetting and Soiling to Bladder and Bowel Control
4. From Irresponsibility to Responsibility in Body Management
5. From the Body to the Toy, and From Play to Work
6. From Egocentricity to Companionship

Ego mastery: The ego's ability effectively to deal with both internal drives and external reality. Ego mastery involves the individual's growing awareness of inner and outer demands.

Metapsychological profile: Developed first by Anna Freud, it is the psychoanalyst's way of organizing all of the information obtained about a patient during a diagnostic assessment. It integrates the findings into a coherent picture of the person's dynamic, genetic, economic, structural, and adaptive functioning.

Psychoanalytic ego psychology: An approach that focuses on the unique properties of the ego in guiding a person's capacity to master the demands of life, not just react to them. An extension of Freudian theory, it addressed inconsistencies between the classical Freudian drive theory and observations that people often are able to transcend their drives and impulses.

Margaret S. Mahler

Consolidation of individuality subphase: Toward the end of the second year and extending through the third year of life, this subphase involves integrating or consolidating the image of the mother with both good and bad images of her as a separate entity in the outside world. The child's own individuality also begins to emerge with a gradual recognition of separate personhood.

Differentiation and development of body image subphase: Beginning from four or five months of age to approximately nine months, this subphase of separation-individuation is characterized by the early exploration of the external world, including the mother and her face.

Normal autism: A stage of absolute primary narcissism. Infants have no recognition of their mothers as external agents of satisfaction. The infant is unable to recognize the outside world as the source of need fulfillment.

Normal symbiosis: Describes "the state of undifferentiation, of fusion with mother," in which the "I" is not yet differentiated from the "not-I", and in which *inside* and *outside* are only gradually sensed. The dim recognition of mother as object comes slowly.

Object constancy: The sense or concept that another person, in particular the mother, continues to exist even when out of view. Children who have acquired object constancy are able to maintain an image of the mother even when she is not present.

Practicing subphase: The phase, from approximately 10 to 14 months, during which children become able to differentiate their bodies from those of their mothers. They recognize their own mothers as special, unique persons, easily detectable as different from all "non-mommies," and their egos have begun to develop autonomous perceptual, cognitive, and reality-testing capacities.

Rapprochement subphase: Lasting from about 14 months to two years, this stage involves children becoming more aware of their separateness and able to make greater use of cognitive faculties to resist frustration.

Separation-individuation: Beginning around the fourth month, this stage involves the process of developing an individual identity, a stable sense of "me", and separating the self from the parental figure—the mother. *Separation* is the realization that one is a discrete entity, and *individuation* requires that the child's ego has begun to develop autonomous perceptual, cognitive, and reality-testing capacities. It occurs in four subphases.

Splitting: A psychological defense used during the rapprochement subphase, splitting involves the inability to see the good and bad properties of another at the same time. Mother, then, may be seen at different times as all good or all bad.

Chapter 7

Klein

Winnicott

Kohut

Melanie Klein, D. W. Winnicott, & Heinz Kohut

The Psychoanalytic Heritage: Object-Relations Theory

. . . the infant's longing for an inexhaustible and ever-present breast stems by no means only from a craving for food . . .

Melanie Klein, *Envy and Gratitude*

It is certain that envy is the worst sin that is; for all other sins are sins only against one virtue, whereas envy is against all virtue and against all goodness.

Chaucer, *The Parson's Tale*

. . . you teach your child to say "thank you" out of politeness and not because this is what the child means. In other words, you start up teaching good manners and you hope that your child will be able to tell lies. . . .

D. W. Winnicott, "The Concept of the False Self"

. . . the normal child's Oedipal experiences . . . contain, from the beginning and persisting throughout, an admixture of deep joy. . . .

Heinz Kohut, *The Restoration of the Self*

About Object Relations Theory

Object relations theorists sought to revise Freud's classical psychoanalysis and psychoanalytic theory.

Melanie Klein pictured the subjective world of the infant as a chaotic mixture of internalized images of people and parts of people. The child's imagination, spurred by anxiety and anger, transforms these images into sometimes terrifying phantasies of good and bad objects.

D. W. Winnicott, a pediatrician and child psychoanalyst, learned from Melanie Klein about the infant's internal world of object relations. Winnicott advanced beyond Kleinian ideas and thought of children as persons capable of healthy spontaneity.

Heinz Kohut focused on the constructive and destructive properties of human relationships, especially those in childhood. He pictured optimal personality development as based on loving and empathic parenting.

SO, WHO ARE THE OBJECT RELATIONS THEORISTS?

By the time of Freud's death, Freudian psychoanalysis was experiencing growing pains both from friendly attempts to update it and unsympathetic efforts to dismantle it. Ego psychologists such as Anna Freud and Margaret Mahler worked to modernize psychoanalysis. Object relations theorists started with modest revisions but eventually transformed Freudian theory and practice.

The label *object relations theorist* is difficult to assign with precision. In contemporary psychoanalysis, the term **object relations** is used sometimes as a synonym for interpersonal relations. However, to qualify as a psychoanalytic object relations theory, the theory must reach beyond social transactions to include associated private and unconscious meanings.

One meaning of the term *object relations* is derived from Freud's (e.g., 1917b; 1921; 1923a) use of the term *object* in his drive theory, as we discussed in Chapter 3. Freud referred to the specific actual satisfiers of drives as the "objects" of the drive. For example, different foods are objects of the hunger drive.

Later, in *The Ego and the Id,* Freud theorized that the ego could incorporate lost or renounced love objects as internal images. By creating such images, the ego diminishes the id's frustration at the loss. Freud concluded that the very character of the ego—one might say its "personality"—is formed by incorporating lost love objects. The ego can assume the features of the lost love object "Look, you can love me too—I am so like the object" (Freud, 1923a, pp. 29 and 30; see also Freud, 1917b).

Freud specified that the ego's makeup is thus largely shaped by its history of object choices. The ego incorporates the qualities of the people it loves, hates, and sometimes loses.

The interpersonal emphasis of the term *object relations* gradually evolved. Whereas Freud's main efforts had been spent explaining how the ego achieved the aims of the id drives, theorists such as Melanie Klein and David W. Winnicott focused on the infant's interpersonal strivings for safety, love, empathy, admiration, and trust. Freud's drive model was thus supplanted by a theory of intimate relationships. The term *object relations* was thus understood as: the person's actual relationships with "objects" (mostly people) beyond the subjective world of the self, and the enduring changes that accrue to the developing person's inner world.

Some theories are also about object relations in the interpersonal sense, but in addition are simultaneously structural drive theories (Kernberg, 1976, 1992; Klein, 1932, 1946,

1975c; Mahler, Pine, & Bergman, 1975). Margaret Mahler's approach provides a relevant example. With some justification, Mahler could be considered an object relations theorist. Her description of the development of the ego from birth to 36 months of life certainly focuses on interpersonal events, with the infant–mother relationship as its centerpiece.

However, we classified Mahler as an ego psychologist in Chapter 6. It was Mahler's intention to describe the ego as a central structure in personality and its development as crucial. That is why we have classified her as an ego psychologist rather than as an object relations theorist.

In selecting theorists for this chapter, we have applied the term *object relations* to psychodynamic theories that focus more on intimate interpersonal relationships and people's conceptions of them and less on personality structure and drives. By our criteria, the three main theorists we consider in this chapter, Melanie Klein, D. W. Winnicott, and Heinz Kohut, are thus psychoanalytic object relations theorists.

By other standards, they have been considered ego psychologists or even neo-Freudians. According to some, Anna Freud, the mother of ego psychology, is also an object relations theorist, and so, we might add, was Sigmund Freud (the father of the mother of ego psychology). Clearly there are often overlapping and divergent classifications of approaches as object relations theories, ego psychological theories, and/or neo-Freudian theories.

Melanie Klein   Born: 1882   Vienna, Austria
Died: 1960   London, England

PSYCHOANALYSIS AS PEDAGOGY: EDUCATING ERICH

Melanie Klein would eventually become a leading object relations theorist and therapist, but her starting point was in classical psychoanalysis. She began without an M.D. or a Ph.D. and had only a personal analysis as preparation for a career. Klein's analyst, Sandor Ferenczi (1873–1933), encouraged her to engage in one of the few professional roles open to her: observing children's educational development and relating the observations to psychoanalytic theory. Using her own son Erich as her first subject, Klein's earliest contributions were largely enthusiastic confirmations of prevailing psychoanalytic theory and uncritical ideas about the liberating effects of psychoanalysis on children.

In her early efforts, Klein took Freud at his word when he proposed that every adult neurosis has origins in a childhood neurosis. Freud had even argued for the special theoretical importance to psychoanalysis of such childhood neuroses (Freud, 1918, p. 9). In what would become a Kleinian hallmark, she often greatly amplified Freud's intent:

> . . . if however we wish to get hold of and remove those [neurotic] traits, then the earliest possible interventions of analytic observation and occasionally of actual analysis becomes *an absolute necessity.* (Klein, 1921/1975a, p. 52)

From her limited experience linked to seemingly boundless enthusiasm, Klein saw an "upbringing with psychoanalytic features" as a means of ensuring and enhancing normal development. Perhaps more important, Klein believed that neurosis—or more generally, psychopathology—gets its first foothold in the personality as an anxious inhibition or a constriction of development (Klein, 1931/1975a). Psychoanalysis as education is not only liberalizing, it can be preventive, a kind of prophylaxis for the mind.

Among the achievements from her early observations of her own and friends' children, three stand out for their subsequent elaboration by Klein into fundamental concepts of her object relations theory. From the beginning, Klein emphasized the child's imaginative reconstruction of reality in phantasy, the necessity for plain talk, adultlike interpretations and explanations, and the power of interpretation to liberate and protect a child's development from the inhibiting influences of anxiety. She also sought to rectify Freud's emphasis on the psychodynamics of the male with her own maternalcentric view of infancy as a period dominated by the child's relationship to the breast.

KLEIN'S DISCOVERY OF "PHANTASY"

Melanie Klein discovered that from the very earliest moments of life, children construct what she termed *phantasies*—Klein used the word **phantasy** to mean the infant's unconscious world of the "unreal real" (Klein, 1937/1975a, p. 221). Phantasy with the "ph" spelling, as distinguished from fantasy, describes for Klein unconscious thoughts and wishes that are not necessarily reality (cf. Mitchell 1986, p. 22). Presumably, she reserved the alternate spelling of the word *fantasy* for conscious, imaginative constructions.

In Klein's concept, phantasy emanates from within and imagines what is without, it creates the world of imagination. Through phantasizing, the baby tests out and primitively construes its experiences of inside and outside. External reality can gradually affect and modify the unrealistic sense of reality that phantasy creates (Mitchell, 1986, p. 23).

Klein's Adultlike Interpretation of Phantasy

From the beginning, Klein's interpretations of children were direct and adultlike. Her overly blunt style probably began as a product of inexperience (Klein, 1961). With increasing sophistication and accumulated clinical experience over a long period, however, Klein's bluntness eventually became transformed into skillfully phrased and timed interpretations.

Klein believed that direct interpretation and sympathetic acknowledgment of the child's phantasies strengthened the child's ability to deal with conflicting feelings. Klein had in mind such normal developmental issues as learning to balance love and hate for the same person (cf. Segal, 1992, p. 59).

One prominent feature of Klein's interpretative style is that she treated the child's verbal expressions during play as equivalent to adult free associations. She encouraged verbalization by providing an assortment of toys, including human and animal figures, building blocks, and toy vehicles of all kinds. She even used ordinary objects in the therapy room. Klein did not limit her interpretations only to what the child said. She thought that the child's actual behavior with the toys represented, sometimes even symbolized, unconscious ideas, wishes, and phantasies. Klein believed that the themes expressed in play are similar to those in dreams and thus are especially suitable for interpretation (Klein, 1926/1975a, p. 134).

Correcting Freud's Male Emphasis

Klein made every effort to correct Freudian theory when she thought it was in error. She believed that Freud had taken a giant misstep in his theoretical neglect of the mother's role. She correctly thought that Freud's version of psychosexual development focused on the male. For example, he emphasized the significance of the penis for both genders in castration anxiety and penis envy, Oedipal strivings, superego formation, and the boy's guilt in competing with and surpassing his father. By contrast, Klein assigned over-whelming significance to the loving, or rejecting, breast, which became the enduring core of Klein's maternalcentric psychoanalytic point of view (cf. Hughes, 1989; pp. 174–175). It has become conventional wisdom to point out that Melanie Klein intended in this way to level the balance with a focus on the female (cf. Sayers, 1991, pp. 3–20 and pp. 261–268).

Freud, however, had not ignored the importance of the breast in his writings. Consider his well-known passage:

> A child's first erotic object is the mother's breast that nourishes it; love has its origin in attachment to the satisfied need for nourishment. There is no doubt that, to begin with, the child does not distinguish between the breast and its own body; when the breast has to be separated from the body and shifted to the *"outside"* because the child so often finds it absent, it carries with it as an *"object"* a part of the original narcissistic libidinal cathexis. This first object is later completed into the person of the child's mother, who not only nourishes it but also looks after it and thus arouses in it a number of other physical sensations, pleasurable and unpleasurable. By her care of the child's body she becomes its first seducer. In these two relations lies the root of a mother's importance, unique, without parallel, established unalterably for a whole lifetime as the first and strongest love-object and as the prototype of all later love-relations-for both sexes. (Freud, 1940, p. 188)

Klein is generally portrayed as having corrected Freud's gender-induced tunnel vision. Although, she began with Freud's concepts from her analyses of her own and her friends' children, Klein drew conclusions that expanded Freud's ideas and created entirely new, often controversial, meanings for fundamental psychoanalytic concepts.

LOVE AND HATE AT THE BREAST

The most important object in the world for the infant, initially the only object, is the breast. Concerned exclusively with the gratification of needs, the infant is limited to two major categories of experience: pleasure (gratification) and pain (frustration). Riveted in this way to a rudimentary hedonism, infants gradually perceive a world populated by **good objects** (satisfying and pleasurable) and **bad objects** (frustrating and painful). However, the "goodness" or "badness" of an object is never a simple product of the amount of pleasure or pain it provides. Good (gratifying) objects are idealized in phantasy, elevating them to absolute and superlative goodness. Bad objects are phantasized into representations of distilled hate. Because mother is sometimes a satisfier, sometimes a frustrator of the infant's self-preservative needs, she is the first and most enduring influence in the way the child learns to manage love and hate beyond this first object relationship.

Mother as Part-Object

An infant's undeveloped cognitive abilities permit it to attach to a part of a person or even to parts of his or her own body. The infant treats the part as the whole. Most of the infant's early relationships have this phantastic, sometimes fragmented, and unrealistic character. The experience of the mother in early infancy thus need not be the whole, real person. Initially, the experience of mother is little more than a nipple protruding from a breast (Klein, 1936/1975a, p. 290). That **part-object** is experienced as the source of all goodness or, sometimes, the agent of all that is frustrating:

> The baby's mother is both desired and hated with all the intensity that is characteristic of the early urges of the baby. In the very beginning he loves his mother at the time when she is satisfying his needs for nourishment. She alleviates his feelings of hunger, and gives him

sensual pleasure, which he experiences when he is sucking at her breast. This gratification is the initial part of the child's sexuality. The meaning of the situation suddenly is altered when the baby's desires are not gratified. Hatred and aggressive feelings are aroused and he becomes dominated by the impulses to strike out at the object of all his desires and who, in his mind, is linked with everything he experiences—good and bad alike (Klein, 1937/1975a, p. 306).

When babies feel frustrated at the breast, in their phantasies, they attack this breast; but if the baby is being gratified by the breast, the baby loves it and has phantasies of a pleasant kind in relation to it. In these aggressive phantasies, the baby wishes to bite up and to tear up his mother and her breasts, and to destroy her in other ways (Klein, 1937/1975a, p. 308).

The essence of phantasy building is that wish and reality are blurred. Unable to distinguish reliably between what phantasy squeezes from desire and what experience constructs from reality, the infant, for a time, is magically omnipotent, able to generate hallucinatory satisfaction from the mere presence of the urge.

Devouring the Breast: Persecution and Guilt

Love and hate at the breast join the blur between phantasy and reality. The infant's relationship to the breast, and therefore to the world, is nearly completely oral, almost exclusively a passive-incorporative orientation with very little reality-based active initiative or differentiation between self and not-self. Consequently, the child's phantasy building takes aim at its "object of constant desire." The breast is possessed by incorporation:

> In phantasy, the child sucks the breast into himself, chews it up and swallows it; thus he feels that he has actually got it there, that he possesses the mother's breast within himself, in both its good and bad aspects. (Klein, 1936/1975a, p. 291)

The baby phantasizes that the breast-in-the-mouth is part of self. Breast is baby and baby is breast. Concealed by the influence of inborn aggressiveness in the form of the death instinct, the infant's angry or destructive wishes toward mother are equivalent to death wishes: the urge to annihilate a frustrator by making it "gone." The wish itself is all-powerful, and the baby can believe that it has actually killed or destroyed the object; but the object, recall, is the relatively undifferentiated fusion of breast and baby. Thus, the "object" that is killed or destroyed is breast-baby, mother-baby, or both. Kleinian infancy is scary.

The object world of the very young infant thus consists of part-objects, some of which are gratifying, some frustrating, some welcoming and some hostile, some inside and some outside. Hostile objects are interpreted by the infant as persecuting and attacking (Klein, 1936/1975a, p. 293). To defend itself, the infant incorporates as much of the safe and gratifying good breast as possible, eventually extending its "greedy" impulses to the mother's entire body. Erotic and aggressive impulses are fused into **infantile sadism,** an actively aggressive stance toward love objects.

Parallel with maturation in the infant's emotional life is the child's growing sophistication in perceiving its love-objects. Some time after four or five months of life, mother is transformed from a collection of part-objects to a **whole object.** Good and bad breasts become experienced as good and bad mothers. Now the clash of love and hate—the fear of being attacked by a gratifying but frightening object—is transferred to the mother as a whole person.

The infant now experiences an intensification of its conflict about good and bad objects. How can I cope consistently with a good-mother-who-is-also-sometimes-a-bad-mother? One strategy might be to protect the good object with a preemptive first strike against the bad. Annihilate bad mommy before she attacks you. However, such infantile logic clashes with infantile good sense. *Good* and *bad* are no longer separate part-objects. Mommy is a whole person. Therefore, it is possible, the infant must calculate, to destroy the loving good object even when one intends to destroy only the persecutory bad object. The dim awareness that the love-object is in danger sharpens the infant's realization that it is he or she who actually has created that danger (Klein, 1936/1975a, p. 295).

The experience of guilt feelings is thus added to the pain of the conflict between love and hate. The infant's array of fears has grown to include the fears of:

- persecution by the internalized bad object, its own persecution of the hated bad object;
- losing control of its own aggression toward the bad object;
- damaging or annihilating the good object; and
- death or loss of the mother, who is now perceived as a whole but endangered person.

SADISM AND THE OEDIPUS COMPLEX

Klein's observations led her to believe that the Oedipus complex is triggered at the time of weaning from the breast, when sadistic oral and anal impulses are dominant. In her earliest papers, Klein (1921/1975a; 1928/1975a) had first reported observations that indicated the presence of a sadistic superego as early as age two. In contrast to Freud's view of genital dominance in the Oedipal phase, Klein believed that the dynamics of the classic Oedipus complex emerge only when they build on these earlier, more amorphous and more unruly sadistic impulses (Klein, 1929/1975a, p. 212; 1933/1975a, p. 251). Under the influence of the death instinct, an extremely sadistic, self-punishing version of the Oedipus complex was already being enacted, according to Klein, as much as three years earlier than Freud had envisioned. Eventually, Klein (1933/1975a) located the origins of the superego and a rudimentary Oedipus complex even earlier in development—in the first half of the first year of life. Put more simply, Freud saw the Oedipus complex as developing during the phallic stage with a male child's sense of rivalry with his father. Klein thought it was a response to frustration during the oral stage.

The Epistemophilic (Love of Knowledge) Instinct

The infant's ego is undeveloped and poorly equipped to understand the nature of the oral and anal impulses that are mounting in intensity. Feeling overwhelmed in the face of these unruly urges, the infant's ego is nevertheless intensely curious about them. Because of the importance she attributed to the child's sexual curiosity, Klein called it the *epistemophilic* (love of knowledge) *instinct*.

But about precisely what is the child so curious? Klein's interpretations of older children's phantasies led her to believe that infants, as well as younger children, caught up in a confusing swirl of oral, anal, and emerging genital impulses, are curious about those same processes in the love-object. Therefore, the child's urge to know is directed at first to the mother's body, which the child believes is the site of all sexual processes. In Klein's theory, the young child phantasizes that inside the mother's body are feces, sexual organs, and even father's penis. Still incorporative in its relation to the world and dominated by aggression, the child is not only curious about mother's body and its contents, but desires strongly to take possession of it. Klein called this phase of development the **femininity phase** because infants of both genders actively identify with the mother they seek to possess (Klein 1928/1975a, p. 189). Both infant boys and infant girls desire to possess the mother's "special sexual organs." Put another way, children of both genders experience "breast envy" and "womb envy."

The infant's intense sexual curiosity meets initially only with frustration because the primitive ego lacks language with which to ask questions about sexual urges and body parts and how they work. Even somewhat later, when the child can formulate rudimentary questions, frustration is rekindled because the child realizes that most of the interesting questions are still unanswered (Klein, 1928/1975a, p. 188). Early and late frustrations turn to anger and indignation. Inhibition of the child's sexual curiosity can generalize over time to include all forms of curiosity. Haunting general feelings of being inept and incapable may result. Anger over "not knowing" may impede the child's development of generalized intellectual competency and skills needed to meet the demands that life makes.

The Oedipus Complex in Boys

Klein thought that *womb envy* was more important than penis envy as a universal Oedipal motive. The breasts and vagina were also sexual organs of interest to the boy. Full of aggressive and sadistic urges as well, the male infant not only wants to learn about these organs and to possess them, but also to injure or destroy them. Yet, the infant also is fearful of retaliation for its hatred. In addition, Klein suggests that the mother, too, can be part of the male child's castration fears:

> The boy fears punishment for his destruction of his mother's body, but, besides this, his fear is of a more general nature. . . . He fears that his body will be mutilated and dismembered, and that he will be castrated. Here we have a direct contribution to the castration complex. In this early period of development the mother who takes away the child's feces signifies also a mother who dismembers and castrates him. Not only by means of the anal frustrations which she inflicts does she pave the way for the castration complex: in terms of psychic reality she is also already the castrator. (Klein 1928/1975a, p. 190)

One can imagine, to illustrate these fears for oneself, an infant lying frightened and helpless as his mother, perhaps forcefully, cleans his behind of fecal material. Such a scene is very different from the picture of an infant sucking contentedly at the breast.

Klein further hypothesized that infants of both genders phantasize that the mother incorporates orally one or more of father's many penises. As a result, infants envy the mother, but also fear what might be inside her. For the boy, the mother-who-incorporates-father's-penis is a "woman with a penis," that is, an amalgam of father and mother. It does not go unnoticed by the boy that mother has "taken" a penis from a man. In short, mother can be a dangerous, castrating person (Klein, 1928/1975a, pp. 131, 245).

Overlapping toilet training, during which the mother must at least partially frustrate the child's anal impulses as she sometimes has frustrated its earlier oral urges, the femininity phase rekindles feelings of intense anger toward the frustrator. Klein (1928/1975a, p. 189 ff.) believed that this new **anal frustration** is in fact a "second trauma" that prompts the child eventually to devalue the frustrating love-object. Children of both genders may thus be prompted to withdraw from the mother and move toward the father.

Under the influence of his emerging genital impulses, the boy desires his mother as a love-object. He already experiences her as a frustrator of his oral and anal needs, and his accumulated feelings of hatred are now amplified to encompass genital urges. To make matters more difficult, an early and incomplete version of castration anxiety in the form of jealousy and fear of the father makes itself known, although full castration fear at the hands of the father will not materialize until later, around the ages of four and five years.

Now, however, as early as age one or two years, the male child is caught on the horns of a three-pronged dilemma: desire to possess the mother, hatred of her as a frustrator-castrator, and an amorphous fear that father will take revenge.

The boy's sexual curiosity grows. His insecurity over not being able to have a baby because he has no womb is concealed behind a facade of ever-escalating curiosity about wombs. He can become an expert on where babies come from even if he cannot have one. Hence, the boy directs his sexual urges and fears into curiosity and information gathering. In this way, intellectual challenges, at which eventually he can feel superior, displace the anatomical deficiencies that made him feel inferior (Klein, 1928/1975a, p. 191). The use of his mind helps him deal with his "womb envy."

The Oedipus Complex in Girls

After weaning, the girl turns away from her frustrating mother and is further encouraged to devalue her mother by the anal deprivations she feels mother imposes. Klein proposed that the girl infant unconsciously senses her vagina and other sexual equipment as soon as the stirrings of the Oedipal impulses begin (Klein, 1928/1975a, p. 192). Unlike her male counterpart, Klein believed that the female infant gains little gratification from masturbation for these newly emerging genital impulses. Envy and hatred of the mother arise because the girl believes that mother not only possesses the father but also the father's penis. As time progresses, the more classical form of Oedipal dynamics (actually *Electra* dynamics) appear as the girl grows more attached to father, experiences his attentions erotically, and becomes increasingly resentful of mother.

The little girl's epistemophilic impulse is first roused by the Oedipus complex; the result is that she discovers her lack of a penis. She feels this lack to be a fresh cause of hatred for the mother, but at the same time her sense of guilt makes her regard it as a punishment. This embitters her frustration in this direction, and, in its turn, exercises a profound influence on the whole castration complex (Klein, 1928/1975a, p. 193).

> Analogous to the boy's castration anxiety in the full Oedipus complex described by Freud, the girl, too, has a primal fear. She desires to empty her mother's body of all its goodness, including the father's penis she imagines within it, feces, and other children. Nevertheless, the girl phantasizes that the mother may turn the tables on her to retaliate by emptying the child's body of these good things. In short, the mother can attack the self and destroy, devour, or annihilate it. Klein regarded this terrible fear of being destroyed by mother to be the fundamental and universal danger situation among woman. At later stages of development, this fear of an attacking mother is transformed into a fear of losing the real mother (Klein, 1929/1975, p. 217).

Mother-as-love-object is thus closely associated with guilt and anxiety. Consequently, Klein thought that the infant girl finds that she can identify with the father more easily than with the mother. The plot thickens as the female infant's guilt leads her to try to form a new love relationship with mother. This effort bears the hallmarks of overcompensation and reaction formation. She overdoes it to the point of being saccharine and ungenuine. This new attempt at a loving relationship is doomed as the girl experiences a fresh round of hatred and rivalry with her mother for father's attentions. The girl finally gives up her attempts to identify with father. Instead, she comes to view father as a love-object from whom she can obtain love and to whom she may give love without necessarily being like him. More or less by default, mother becomes the girl's object of identification (Klein, 1928/1975a, pp. 193–194).

In the end—and there is an end—the girl, unlike the boy, has to come to grips with unrelenting frustration. Despite the boy's fears to the contrary, he does actually possess a penis; but the girl must endure permanently unfulfilled desire for a penis and deferred desire for a baby.

HOW IT ALL TURNS OUT: KLEIN'S FIRST THEORY OF THE SUPEREGO

Ultimately, the girl models herself on her *phantasy* of the mother in both its cruel and nurturing aspects. "From the early identification with the mother in which the anal-sadistic level so largely preponderates, the little girl derives jealousy and hatred and forms a cruel super-ego after the maternal imago" (Klein, 1928/1975a, p. 195). Fortunately, as the little girl matures and as her genital impulses assume dominance over the oral and anal sadism of early infancy, she identifies more and more with mother's nurturing, kind, and generous qualities. She even phantasizes an idealized image of the "bountiful mother" who may be more a product of wish than reality.

The boy's development is along similar lines with a slightly different outcome for his superego. Initially, the boy also acquires a severe superego modeled on the cruel-sadistic image he has constructed of mother-breast in phantasy. Moreover, like his female counterpart, maturity finds the boy incorporating in a more modest way the kinder, nurturing aspects of the maternal image. But boys ultimately have to identify more strongly with *father*. The idealized father image now becomes dominant in the boy's superego.

Klein (1927/1975a; see especially 1928/1975a, pp. 197 ff.) argued early in her career that her account of the Oedipus complex, including the infant's hatred and its origins in an early, cruel superego, did not contradict Freud's model. She believed that her ideas extended Freud's without substantially challenging his basic views. As Klein's ideas continued to evolve, she began gradually to consider hatred as a less important factor in development than did Freud. Other psychoanalysts could see that she was taking Freud's ideas and transforming them into her own (e.g., A. Freud 1927, pp. 37–40; and A. Freud, 1952/1992, p. 63; Freud & Jones, 1993, pp. 621 ff., see especially Freud's letters to Jones, #508, p. 624; and letter #509, pp. 627 ff).

"RICHARD": EXTRACTS FROM AN ILLUSTRATIVE CASE

At the height of World War II in 1941, Klein moved to Scotland to treat two children and simultaneously evade the London bombings. Her published account of parts of the case of one of these children, referred to as "Richard," is an effective illustration of Klein's thinking. In *Narrative of a Child Analysis,* Klein (1961) presented her detailed session notes along with some of the child's drawings from almost one hundred daily sessions. The case is strikingly detailed and an especially clear expression of Klein's diagnostic and therapy techniques. The case also serves as an excellent account of how Klein translated her early theoretical concepts into interpretations that she made to a 10-year-old boy (Figure 7.1).

Richard's Presenting Problem and Family Background

Richard's mother referred the child to Melanie Klein because he had been unable to relate normally to other children in school, was aggressive and hard to control. He eventually refused to go to school altogether. The anxious mother evidenced both love and resentment toward her difficult son. Richard's father appears to have been largely uninvolved with the child's daily care. An older brother by 11 years, then serving in the army, had been the preferred child.

Figure 7.1 Melanie Klein's ten-year-old patient "Richard."
(From: Grosskurth, 1986, following page 372.)

Richard's older cousin, "Dick," had been in analysis with Melanie Klein, and the report of his treatment is widely regarded as the first published psychoanalysis of a psychotic or possibly autistic child (Klein, 1929/1975a; see Grosskurth, 1986, p. 266n). It was "Richard," however, who became the subject of Klein's most extensive published case. Younger than Dick by six years, Richard exhibited severe interpersonal difficulties, confused thinking, and catastrophic levels of anxiety regarding the ongoing war around him. Richard's anxieties also included a paranoid quality that centered on fears of being poisoned and worries about being spied upon. Klein soon found such anxieties to be linked to the images of his internal phantasy world. Klein eventually concluded that neither cousin had been given the close, warm, and empathic mothering she regarded as essential to normal development.

Dick's mother had convinced Klein to join her and her son in order for Dick to resume his analysis with Klein. Around the same time, cousin Richard and his mother were evacuated to Scotland, and Richard became Klein's patient. Shortly after leaving London, Richard's home was bombed, a sad and frightening event that intensified his feelings of vulnerability. From the outset, Klein knew that the period of treatment could be no more than four months, a relatively brief course of analysis for such serious presenting problems. Nevertheless, she undertook the task and saw Richard several times a week in a rented "hut" or cottage that was used by the Girl Guides (an organization similar to the American Girl Scouts) as their headquarters. The setting was a bit unusual because a variety of Girl Guide artifacts, such as wall maps, pots and pans, and such, could not be removed from the room, but Klein's own living quarters were even more unsuitable for treating a child. To begin a session, Klein had to unlock the "hut," as it was called, gain entry, light a fire, and keep track of Richard.

Richard's First Session: Anxieties and Worries

Richard immediately established a workable rapport with Klein. He told her how frightened he was of going to school, how he often could not sleep because he was worried about his mother's health, and how interested but worried he was about the ongoing war. He described his experiences of the London bombings, and reported the results of a detonated bomb near his home. He did not see much physical damage but noted that the family's cook had been alone in the house at the time and was badly frightened. Richard spoke about Hitler's cruel treatment of conquered people. He mentioned that Hitler was himself an Austrian but treated the Austrians very badly.

Richard also described how he worried that a "tramp" might break in during the night and kidnap his Mummy. He envisioned himself going to her rescue and making the tramp unconscious by scalding him with boiling water. He said he would not mind being killed except for the fact that it would prevent him from saving his mother. Klein interpreted to Richard that there was a parallel between his fears about Hitler's treatment of the Austrians and what he imagined was happening at night in his parents' bedroom:

> At night he might have been afraid that when his parents went to bed something could happen between them with their genitals that would injure Mummy. . . . *Mrs. K.* Interpreted that he might have contradictory thoughts about Daddy. Although Richard knew that Daddy was a kind man, at night, when he was frightened, he might fear that Daddy was doing some harm to Mummy. (Klein, 1961, p. 21)

One might suppose that the immediacy, adult level content, and directness of Klein's interpretations drove Richard screaming from the Girl Guides' hut. On the contrary, Klein reports that after she had clarified the meaning of *genitals* to him, Richard became thoughtful and appeared impressed with her interpretation.

And so it went for the next several months. Klein and Richard developed a close, almost tender relationship through which Richard learned the Kleinian vocabulary for inner distress. As he became more adept in the new idiom, Richard's verbal tolerance for anxiety seemingly strengthened, but his conversational stories and crayon drawings grew primordial. Klein thought that her interpretations assisted Richard to detoxify and assimilate increasingly deeper unconscious phantasies.

Overview of Richard's First and Last Sessions

As always, Klein had available some toys and drawing materials in the Girl Guides' hut, but after a time Richard chose to focus on constructing a series of drawings. Figure 7.2 reproduces Richard's first and last sessions.

The first drawing actually required two sessions, 12 and 14, to complete. The last drawing, of a total of 74 pictures reproduced in Klein's *Narrative of a Child Analysis,* was done in session 90. Beneath each picture is an extract of Klein's commentary on and interpretation of the drawing to Richard as she recorded in her daily notes. The subject matter of Richard's first drawing makes clear the degree to which the reality of the war fueled the boy's anxieties. Klein's approach is to tell Richard that his war stories are also a medium through which he expresses his phantasies. For example, Klein interpreted the British ships as representing Richard's own family, whereas the German U-boats stand for Richard and another child patient, John Wilson. According to Klein, Richard unconsciously senses that he and John Wilson are dangerous to the family, especially to mother. Klein explained to Richard that his drawing of U-boats and ships thus expresses his unconscious conflict: He desires both to protect and to attack his parents.

After four months, near the end of his analysis, Richard produced the simply graceful and metaphorical Drawing 74, shown as the second picture of Figure 7.2. He identified the picture as a railway, and he ran his pencil through the curves repeatedly while drawing it. On its face, the drawing expresses far less anxiety than his earlier drawings. Even Richard's demeanor during the final sessions is far more reserved, almost melancholy, as he prepares to end his analysis. On the basis of Richard's associations, Klein interprets to him that the railway drawing is a representation of his mother's body, especially the breast, nipple, and stomach. The caption for Figure 7.2 elaborates the details of her interpretation.

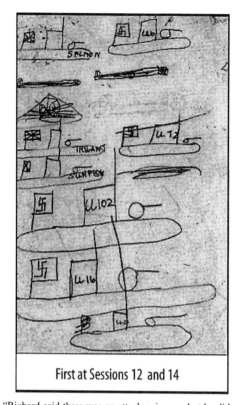

First at Sessions 12 and 14

"Richard said there was an attack going on, but he did not know who would attack first. . . . He pointed at U 102 and said that 10 was his own age; and to U16 he associated the age of John Wilson [another of Mrs. Klein's patients whom Richard knew]. He was . . . extremely interested to find that drawing could be a means of expressing unconscious thoughts. Mrs. K. pointed out that the number also indicated that he and John were represented by German U-boats, and were therefore hostile and dangerous to the British . . . , [and] that the British represented his own family and that he had already recognized that he not only loved and wished to protect, but also wished to attack them. . . ."

(Klein, 1961, p. 56)

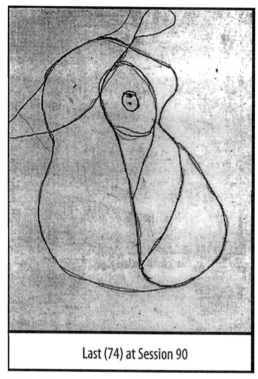

Last (74) at Session 90

"[Richard] . . . said it was a railway line and made his pencil go over it repeatedly; this stood for a train traveling. Mrs. K. interpreted the exploration of Mummy's (now Mrs. K.'s) inside and pointed out that the drawing of the railway line was in the shape of a female body. After Mrs. K.'s interpretation he pointed to the circle near the top and said that this was the breast. The smaller circle was the nipple. He suddenly pounced on it with his pencil, making the dot in the centre, but at once restrained himself from making further dots—obviously preventing himself from destroying Mrs. K.'s breast and body."

(Klein, 1961, p. 451)

Figure 7.2 First and last drawings by Melanie Klein's ten-year-old patient "Richard."

A crucial difference reflected in the first and last drawings of Figure 7.2 is the great change in the way Richard copes with anxiety. It is clear that some positive emotional change has occurred in this child. Klein thought that Richard's first and last artistic efforts reveal a developmental progression from a worried, vulnerable-feeling, and chaotic child to a calmer, certainly more introspective ten-year-old child who is more skillful in containing his fears.

Beginning Phase of Richard's Analysis: The Starfish Drawings

Richard's feelings toward his mother, father, and brother, and his conflicts about them are central beginning issues of his analysis. His first "starfish" drawing, reproduced in

Figure 7.3, shows Richard's anxious interest in the ongoing war. The war has also become a metaphor for his own inner conflicts. Richard freely associates to the elements of his picture that the topmost fish is Mummy, who has swallowed a ragged-edge starfish who hurts her by breaking through her body with its sharp edges. The U-boat attacking the submarine in the drawing, Klein suggests to Richard, is Richard attacking Daddy to punish Hitler-Daddy for putting such a dangerous thing inside Mummy.

A similar drawing made in the next session began with Richard's exclamation that he was making a "wild picture." The starfishes surrounding the British ship, *Emden,* had grown "greedy." Klein pointed out to Richard that each starfish in the cluster was more jagged than previous ones. Perhaps, she proposed, these "greedy" destructive starfish represent teeth that want to attack Mummy's breasts (the ship's two funnels). Equally significant,

Drawing 7 at Session 15

Drawing 8 at Session 16

"[Richard said] . . . the starfishes were babies, the fish was Mummy who had put her head above the periscope so that the U-boat should not see the British ship. It would be deceived because it saw nothing but yellow. . . . The fat fish on top was also Mummy. She had eaten a starfish, which was now breaking through with its edges and hurting her. . . . Mrs. K. interpreted that the upper U-boat which was attacking the submarine represented Richard attacking Daddy. . . . Richard wanted to punish the Hitler-Daddy for having put such a dangerous starfish genital into Mummy—the fat fish on top—which injured her inside."

(Klein, 1961, p. 70)

"[Richard said] he was making a 'wild picture' . . . Richard explained that the starfishes were 'very greedy'; they were all round the sunk Emden and wanted to attack her. They hated her and wanted to help the British. . . . Mrs. K. interpreted that Richard's need to make a 'wild' picture was expressed by the starfishes having so many more jagged edges that in former drawings and, since Richard said that they were 'very greedy,' Mrs. K. suggested that these edges represented the teeth of the greedy babies. They came so close to the Emden because they attacked her breasts (the two funnels). The sunk Emden stood for Mummy who died because she was eaten and destroyed by the children. . . ."

(Klein, 1961, p. 70)

Figure 7.3 Starfish/War drawings by Melanie Klein's ten-year-old patient "Richard."

Richard had drawn the *Emden* sunk below the surface of the water, a feature that Klein thought was worth interpreting. The caption to the second picture (Drawing 8) in Figure 7.3 indicates the meaning that Klein attached to "sunk Mummy."

Early Middle Phase of Richard's Analysis: The Empire Drawings

By the 17th session, Richard's starfish had become larger and more colorful. Starfish became the central elements of his drawings. Drawing 9, shown as the first picture in Figure 7.4, has a rather pointy, multicolored creature inside a circle. Klein reminded Richard of their work together in previous sessions, in which she had suggested that the starfish creature represented Daddy's genital inside mommy. Now Klein said that the encircled paternal genital was making mommy bleed, as shown in the red circular border around the creature. Klein pointed out to Richard that the starfish actually has a double meaning, as related in the caption to the first picture in Figure 7.4.

Drawing 9 at Session 17

Drawings 12 and 13 at Session 23

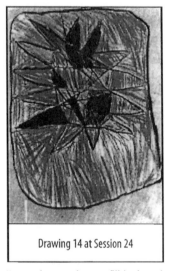

Drawing 14 at Session 24

"Mrs. K. reminded [Richard] that two days ago . . . a starfish had represented Daddy's devouring genital which the fish-Mummy had eaten, and he drew that at the time when Mummy had a sore throat. . . . In today's drawing the big starfish also seemed to represent Daddy's devoured genital which made her bleed because it ate her inside; this was shown by the red border round the starfish. The starfish also stood for the greedy and frustrated baby—himself—injuring and eating Mummy's inside when he wanted her and she did not come."

(Klein, 1961, p. 79)

"[Richard] . . . said this was an empire and the various colours represented different countries. . . . Mrs. K. suggested, referring back to the first drawing in this session, that this empire again represented the family. Richard at once agreed. He said that the nasty black was Paul, the light blue was Mummy, the puple was the maid (Bessie) and the cook. The very small area of heliotrope blue in the centre was himself, and the red was Daddy. Suddenly he said, 'And the whole is a greedy starfish full of big teeth.'"

(Klein, 1961, pp 107–108)

". . . as he was about to fill in the red sections [Richard] . . . announced, 'This is me, and you will see what a large part of the empire I get.' Then he coloured some sections light blue, and while doing so he looked up at Mrs. K. and said, 'I feel happy'. . . . A moment later . . . he said, 'Can you see how Mummy has spread herself. She has got much more of the empire'. . . . He left a few sections near the centre blank and now filled them in with black, saying that Daddy was squeezed in. . . . When he finished, he paused . . . and asked, 'Do I really think this of all of you? I don't know if I do. How can you really know what I think?'"

(Klein, 1961, p. 111)

Figure 7.4 "Empire" drawings by Melanie Klein's ten-year-old patient "Richard."

By session 23, the compartmented starfish drawings are transformed to "empire draw-ings," which depict countries with all their various parts. "There was no fighting. 'They come in but the smaller countries don't mind being taken' " (Klein, 1961, p. 107). Most likely Richard's interest in the daily reports of the ongoing war and the maps on the walls of the therapy room stirred his imagination in the direction of a geography metaphor. Draw-ings 12 and 13, shown as the second picture in Figure 7.4, employ various colors to rep-resent different countries but now the countries are like the various members of Richard's family. The topmost "empire-starfish" (Drawings 12, 13) was done in session 12, but the empire-starfish located at the bottom of the picture was added in the following session. Richard's color code for the various members of his family is given in the caption to the picture. Klein's interpretations to Richard throughout this period emphasize Oedipal themes and persecution by internalized bad objects.

By the 24th session, Richard shows some indications of resistance, including arriv-ing late for his appointment, remaining silent much of the time, and generally looking un-happy (Klein, 1961, p. 110). Richard finally speaks about his current worry over a possible German invasion he has heard about from news broadcasts. He asks Klein whether she could continue to see him if there were an invasion. As the conversation progressed, Richard completed Drawing 14, shown as the third picture in Figure 7.4. The empire-starfish became expansive, and the sections assigned to Mummy and to Richard himself had grown in size. Richard told Mrs. Klein that he was happy.

With a child's wisdom, Richard then asks, "Do I really think this of all of you? I don't know if I do. How can you really know what I think?" (Klein, 1961, p. 111). Richard's remark points up the dilemma for the skeptical reader of a case involving such interpre-tive leaps as this. According to Klein, her interpretations elicit agreement from the child, promote further associations, and appear to have a positive effect on Richard's anxieties. Richard's remark raises another possibility, that of a child eager to please his therapist by colluding in a peculiar game involving drawing pictures and mutually coming up with in-terpretations regarding his parents. If he improved, a skeptic would see the improvement as being the result of a relationship with an attentive therapist rather than by the content of her interpretations.

Terminating Richard's Analysis: Portraits of Mrs. K.

Toward the end of the analysis, Richard's anger toward Klein was surfacing. At session 65, Richard drew a portrait of his therapist (Drawing 55), shown as the first picture in Figure 7.5. The picture is hand-labeled and portrays Mrs. Klein with breasts but no arms. She has a small "v" above the right leg and a large "V" closed at the top placed between the breasts and extending the length of the trunk. Klein understood the victory letters to be not only expressions of Richard's Oedipal rivalry with his father but also a feeling of triumph of Richard over his therapist (Klein, 1961, 424). The caption to Drawing 55 in Figure 7.5 gives the details of Klein's interpretation of her portrait to Richard in her own words.

By session 83, Richard expressed his anger by scribbling and tearing pages during the session. He completed the portrait shown as the second picture (Drawing 68) in Figure 7.5, a rather primitive figure drawing showing Mrs. K. with breasts *and* a penis. The picture is labeled "sweet Mrs. Klein," and Richard has written "lovely eyes" on Mrs. K.'s forehead. Klein's interpretation is given in the caption to Drawing 68 in Figure 7.5, and indicates that she was alert to Richard's attempts to hide his anger toward her. As the session progressed, Richard's face became red, he scribbled furiously with far less control than usual, and he referred several times to the scribblings as showing Mrs. K. "in bits." Richard was angry with Klein both for symbolic and for real reasons. Symbolically, she had come

Drawing 55 at Session 65

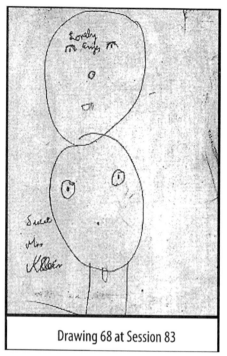

Drawing 68 at Session 83

"Mrs. K. asked what the uncompleted triangle had meant. Richard replied that it was V for victory. Mrs. K. interpreted that there was also a small V above the right leg, and asked who the bigger victory belonged to. Richard replied that it was his, and Daddy had the smaller victory."

(Klein, 1961, p. 323)

"[Richard] . . . leaned forward, looking into Mrs. K.'s eyes, and said that she had such lovely eyes. (This sounded entirely false and artificial.) After saying this, Richard added the penis on the drawing and asked Mrs. K. what the "tops of the breasts" (meaning the nipples) were called. Mrs. K. interpreted that her tummy was also a face—actually Hitler's—inside her, and that the penis he had added seemed to be Hitler's."

(Klein, 1961, p. 421)

Figure 7.5 Views of Melanie Klein by her ten-year-old patient "Richard."

to represent his parents, toward whom he had conflicted feelings. Simultaneously, Richard had become attached to Mrs. Klein and was aware that their work together was ending. He discussed the train that she would take to leave Scotland, and he expressed his worries about what would happen to her in the bombings when she had gone back to London. Overall, Richard was an unhappy, angry, and anxious boy about to lose his therapist.

In the few remaining sessions, Richard was alternately sad and exuberant. Klein relentlessly continued to interpret the material Richard presented. Both therapist and patient were aware of the approaching termination. By session 93, on August 23, 1941, which Klein lists as the last session, therapist and patient were determined to get the most out of their last meeting. Klein entered the following private notes after the last session:

> 23rd Aug. 1941. Last day. Let's get the most out of it.—K. sad?—K. very sorry etc. R. Pleased—Is she going to cry? [His eyes watering]—R. pleased.—Should not kiss him, parting.—Some days ago when so clinging, asked to be kissed.—To-day's mood—serious, some depression, but determined & resolved. . . . (quoted in Grosskurth, 1986, pp. 268–269)

Her final note also indicates that Richard spent part of the last session arranging two chairs under a table to represent himself and Mrs. K. staying together. Richard expressed his desire to return to London with his therapist. Klein actually considered the possibility, but Richard's mother opposed the idea. Eventually, Klein and Richard decided to keep in touch with postcards.

For the next year or so, Richard's mother wrote to Klein. She reported that he had continuing difficulties in relating to other children. He displayed aggressive, even violent behavior toward other children and animals and had a tendency to be "deceitful" and disobedient (Grosskurth, 1986, p. 276). Despite these problems, Richard's mother wrote to Klein that she thought the analysis had some positive effect because Richard did show some indications of gaining insight into himself. Klein occasionally responded to Richard's mother's insistent questions by offering pragmatic parenting advice or an optimistic reframing of Richard's aggression as something positive. By January 1942, the flow of letters subsided. Richard's mother grew more accepting of him (Grosskurth, 1986, p. 277).

IMPLICATIONS OF THE "RICHARD" CASE

The main features of Klein's early theory are clearly discernible in her work with Richard. Direct interpretation of Richard's angry feelings toward family members are interwoven with Klein's educational explanations about sexuality, childbirth, and death.

Kleinian Oedipal Themes

Much of Klein's therapeutic work with Richard centers on his rivalry with his father and sometimes with his older brother. Klein's concept that the child internalizes phantasized object-images was directly interpreted to Richard using the medium of his "starfish-empire" drawings. Klein tells Richard that he believes Mummy will be injured by the objects Richard imagines that are inside her, that he believes Daddy's penis has been incorporated into Mummy, and that he has even portrayed himself inside Mummy in the form of a hurtful "starfish." Furthermore, Richard is introduced to the idea that he both wants to injure and protect Mummy and Daddy just as the war raging outside injures some and protects others.

Disagreements between Melanie Klein and Anna Freud

Klein was permissive and supportive of her child patients. For example, she made a variety of toys available to Richard from the outset, but he preferred the medium of drawing, which Klein permitted and even encouraged at several points by joining in. She used virtually every activity as a source of interpretation, and every interpretation embodied ideas drawn from Klein's vision of the unconscious. For Klein, the child's play is an equivalent to free association in the adult and is thus suited for direct interpretation.

As we saw in Chapter 6, Anna Freud did not regard child analysis as a simple equivalent of adult psychoanalysis. She insisted on a specialized technique, a phase of preparation for analysis, and only then did she interpret the child's verbal associations elicited by play. Anna Freud avoided interpreting the play activity itself. In all respects, Anna Freud emphasized the unique developmental requirements that make working analytically with children different from working with adults. Given this fundamental divergence in orientation to the task, Melanie Klein's play technique seemed utterly wrong to Anna Freud on three counts.

First, Klein's interpretations were often based on symbolic meanings derived from her theory. She treated the child's games and play with toys as direct representatives of the phantasy objects her theory postulates in the child's unconscious. In working with children, Klein used the child's play with toys and objects in the room for interpretation of symbolic meanings. Anna Freud thought that symbolic interpretations imposed meanings on the child's actions rather than elucidating their inherent meaning. Such a technique, she thought, amounted to "wild analysis," in which the child's thoughts and actions would be steered into compliance with Kleinian theory. Anna Freud's own technique for child analysis (see Chapter 6) emphasized the child's actual verbal productions during play or story telling. Interpretations were limited to the immediately available evidence emerging from the child's associations after a period of preparation in which the child is made comfortable with and instructed in the procedure. Very young children were not considered suitable candidates for psychoanalysis precisely because they were not yet sufficiently verbal.

Second, for Anna Freud, the transference relationship with a child is different from adult transference because the child's past relationships are necessarily also its current relationships (A. Freud, 1927, pp. 39 ff. and p. 45). From Melanie Klein's point of view, transference is transference. Object relationships begin almost from birth in Klein's view of infancy. Thus early object relations, real and phantastic, are sufficiently plentiful to form the basis of a child's transferential relationship to the therapist. Just as in adult analysis, the analyst must interpret the transference (A. Freud, 1952/1992, p. 63).

Third, Klein suggested that Anna Freud saw children as very different from adults, whereas she herself saw very little reason to treat a child patient differently from an adult patient. Using her own play technique with toys and drawings, Melanie Klein thought that she had been able to access the most primitive layers of the child's unconscious, an achievement that lay outside the range of Anna Freud's more verbal technique. It seemed to Klein that Anna Freud's method minimized the analyst's role as the interpreter of the child's unconscious conflicts. Instead, the analyst operating with Anna Freud's technique becomes an educational role model who encourages a positive, even submissive, transference relationship with the child. Because of the analyst's failure to establish a "true analytic situation," the child becomes unable and unwilling to make its deepest feelings known (Klein, 1927/1975a, pp. 153–154, 167).

The dispute between Anna Freud and Melanie Klein resulted in permanent divisions in the profession of child analysis in London, with students and analysts becoming Kleinians, Anna-Freudians, or Middle-groupers.

Strengths and Weaknesses of Klein's Technique

On the positive side of the ledger, Klein demonstrates the skillful management of a child patient whose cooperation and motivation she enlists and maintains throughout the treatment. She is warm, empathic, permissive, tolerant, supportive, and caring, and knows well how to communicate these attitudes to her patient. Richard obviously makes a strong emotional connection to "Mrs. K.," one that he is reluctant to end when the agreed upon time arrives.

The behavioral evidence provided by Klein's reports of Richard's responses, supported by his drawings, suggests a certain progress in anxiety tolerance through the course of the treatment. Richard begins treatment with intensely disorganizing feelings of anxiety and anger, and he expresses these in highly detailed, highly compartmentalized, intensely colored, almost frantic war and "empire" drawings. By the end of treatment, his artistic productions are calmer, more organized, less frenetic, less intense, and more graceful. Compare the drawings in Figures 7.2 and 7.3 with the portraits of Mrs. K. in Figure 7.5. Alternatively, compare Richard's first and last drawings, as shown in Figure 7.2.

On the negative side of the ledger, the sophistication of the drawings, from beginning to end, remains at a more cognitively primitive level than expected for a boy of ten years.

There are indications of serious psychopathology in the portraits of Mrs. K. and the "empire" drawings. Aspects of these drawings reflect substantial disturbances of thinking, compulsive needs to compartmentalize anxieties and other feelings, and wishes felt so intensely as to be almost beyond Richard's ability to endure. Klein, however, apparently does not clinically conceptualize this child at such a severe level of dysfunction. She appears to believe that Richard is psychologically more intact than either his behavior or his drawings indicate. Summers (1994, pp. 118 ff.) has succinctly summarized criticisms of Klein, three of which we can apply to Richard's analysis:

Over-Pathologizing

Criticism   For Klein, the world of the infant's phantasies is akin to psychotic thinking. Recall the interpretations she made to Richard of his Oedipal beliefs, expressed in a nightmarish vision of parts of people, mutilation, fear of attacking and being attacked, and fantastic delusions of poisoning, penetrating, and puncturing. Klein argued that the infant's phantasies were only *psychotic-like,* composed of the very stuff that the normal infant will eventually learn to moderate, assimilate, and control. Richard is told, for example, that he believes Mummy's insides can be devoured by the starfish, that the starfish is himself, that the starfish is also other "greedy babies" trying to devour Mummy, and that Daddy's penis is also inside Mummy's body because Mummy devoured it. To many observers, interpretations such as these seem extraordinary, eccentric, and excessively pathological. To Richard, apparently, they were reasonable, thought provoking, and calming.

Response   Although Klein's account of the case can be challenged on this point, at the very minimum, her interpretations were tolerated by Richard. He adopted her vocabulary, usually followed her lead, and appeared to have found something of value in the relationship.

Seeing Aggression Almost Everywhere

Criticism   Klein's concept of the death instinct as the fountainhead of all aggression is theoretically fuzzy. In Klein's theory, the death instinct is used virtually always as a simple synonym for aggression or hate. Used in this loose way, the death instinct is divested of its evolutionary and instinctual links and is therefore theoretically irrelevant. A related problem of fuzzy definition is that *any* behavior of the child can be interpreted as aggression or one of its derivatives. The distinctions between hate for another, envy of another, sadism for its own sake, and destructiveness for its own sake are not clear or precise in Klein's application of her theory to children. Thus, Richard's presumed conflict over wanting to hurt his mother and father at the same time that he fears their retaliation is the common interpretative theme applied to nearly all of his "empire-starfish" drawings. Even Klein's transference interpretations to Richard more frequently target his anger and envy than his obvious affection for Mrs. K. One fact is certain. In Klein's psychological universe, there is no shortage of aggression.

Response   The main response to this criticism is that aggression and angry feelings are fundamental and underlie many psychological phenomena. This concept is consistent with Freudian theory, even if Klein's techniques do not seem to be.

"Wild" Analysis

Criticism   Some of Klein's interpretations to Richard are criticized as wild speculations driven by a theory that is not always linked to the clinical observations at hand. Some of Richard's drawings, for example, lend themselves to other interpretations along the lines of distressed feelings rather than destructive phantasy. Critics could argue that Richard's therapy consists of learning Klein's vocabulary, which he then uses to generate compatible ideas and drawings in order to preserve his attachment to her.

Response   One counterargument mounted by Kleinians points out that people find her conclusions alienating and fantastic precisely because they are unconsciously accurate. Labeling such unconscious content absurd or fantastic is merely a defense against recognizing that truth.

ANXIETY: FIRST MODIFICATIONS TO THE THEORY OF DEVELOPMENT

With growing experience and an increased number of observations from child analyses, Melanie Klein modified her basic formulations about the development of the superego and Oedipus complex. The changes took three forms. She added detail about the content of the child's phantasies, changed the developmental timing of them, and slightly reduced the role of aggression in all of them. The first change resulted in a significant population explosion of the infant's internalized objects whereas the second change pushed back the origins of personality structure to the earliest days of life. Klein postulated the existence at birth of a rudimentary ego, superego as well as innate Oedipal-like motives. Klein supplemented her emphasis on the importance of aggression as the primary motive of infancy with some small degree of consideration of envy, guilt, anxiety, and love.

Fear of One's Own Destructive Impulses: Projection

In amplifying her reasons for the severity of the infant's superego, Klein elaborated her theory of internalized objects. Her observations led her to believe that a regular part of a child's life centers on fears of phantastic frightening figures who threaten to dismember, devour, or "tear the child to pieces." Klein believed that the terrifying characters of fairy tales are transformed by phantasy into personalized constructions of real objects in the child's life:

> I have no doubt from my own analytic observations that the real objects behind those imaginary, terrifying figures are the child's own parents, and that those dreadful shapes in some way or other reflect the features of its father and mother, however distorted and phantastic the resemblance may be. (Klein, 1933/1975, p. 249)

If a child unconsciously equates the parents with wild beasts and fairy tale monsters, then the child clearly is not identifying with actual parents as they exist in reality. Instead, the child is identifying with transformed images of the parents unconsciously created by the child. The cruelty and sadism of the child's superego thus derives secondarily from identifying with the cruelty of these transformed and imaginary objects. The primary transformation of the objects into malevolent persecutors, recall, was a product of the child's innate sadism. But how does a child's fear mount to a level that can transform loved ones into menacing object images?

Klein's answer is that the child's immature ego is frightened of its own innate sadism. The danger of being destroyed by one's own death instinct is so terrifying that the immature ego mobilizes against the death instinct what libido or life instinct it has available (Klein, 1932/1975b, pp. 126 ff.) Then, using the relatively primitive defense of projection, the ego directs the uncontainable aggression outward onto external objects. In this way, the infant's fear of its own internal impulses becomes, in part, a fear of external objects (Klein, 1932/1975b, p. 128). Now the infant believes that the objects want to destroy self rather than vice versa. Projections grow into persecutors. The infant's internalized and externalized objects have become ravaging terrorists within. In reality, the fear that the infant experiences is the dread of its own destructive urges toward love-objects. Consequently, ". . . his fear of his objects will always be proportionate to the degree of his own sadistic impulses" (Klein, 1933/1975a, pp. 251).

The weapons of the child's sadism are ordinary infantile equipment and activities mutated by phantasy into agents of destruction. Thus wetting by urination becomes equivalent to drowning, cutting, stabbing, and burning; feces are equated with missiles and direct-contact combative weapons. With development, the more knowledgeable child can perceive feces as poisons and toxins of all sorts. The penis itself can be a target of injury or a weapon with which to inflict it. And there are the always available standbys of biting, chewing, and spitting, which can become interchangeable equivalents of devouring, dismembering, and annihilation (Klein, 1930/1975a, pp. 219–220, 226).

With the focus thus firmly on sadism and fear as the motivating force, Klein moved the timing of the origins of the superego to the child's first oral introjections of objects, that is, to the first few months of life.

Oral, Urethral, and Anal Sadism: Cannibalizing Mother

In her reformulation, Klein continued to rely heavily on innate aggression as a primal motive. However, she tempered this reliance with a consideration of the child's fears of its own aggression and its displacement of that aggression onto phantastic internalized and external objects. She eventually tempered sadism further with considerations of love and guilt. For now, however, the content of the child's sadistic phantasies was given greater elaboration and increased developmental precision.

Taking Freud at his word once again, Klein distinguished between an early oral-sucking aggressive phase and a later oral-sadistic phase. In the first part of the first year of life during the oral-sucking phase, the child phantasizes taking the breast within itself; in the somewhat later oral-sadistic phase, the child imagines chewing it up, devouring the breast cannibalistically. In this later phase, presumably late in the first year, oral and aggressive needs are simultaneously gratified by the same phantasy. In the second and third years of life, the child enters the anal-sadistic phase in which the necessary focus on elimination becomes tied to aggressive urges once more. Klein believed that elimination of feces took on the meaning for the child of eliminating the love-object—a "forcible ejection" of it—linked to destructive desires (1933/1975a, p. 253). Between the oral-sadistic phase and the anal-sadistic phase, Klein discerned a transitional urethral-sadistic phase and its associated phantasies.

In its oral-sadistic phantasies the child attacks its mother's breast, and the means it employs are its teeth and jaws. In its urethral and anal phantasies it seeks to destroy the inside of the mother's body, and uses its urine and feces for the purpose. In this second group of phantasies the excrements are regarded as burning and corroding substances, wild animals, weapons of all kinds, etc.; and the child enters a phase in which it directs every instrument of its sadism to the one purpose of destroying its mother's body and what is contained in it. As regards choice of object, the child's oral-sadistic impulses are still the underlying factor, so that it thinks of sucking out and eating up the inside of its mother's body as though it were a breast (Klein, 1933/1975a, pp. 253–254).

When the child phantasizes attacking the insides of the mother, he or she thereby attacks a great many internalized objects. By extension of its infantile phantasy logic, Klein argued, the infant is attacking an entire world peopled by objects hostile to the self, including the father, mother, brothers, and sisters. "The world, transformed into the mother's body, is in hostile array against the child and persecutes him" (Klein, 1929/1975a, p. 214). Destroy or be destroyed becomes the infant's strategy, but it is a strategy fraught with guilt and anxiety.

HATE VERSUS GUILT: REPAIRING THE RAVAGES OF SADISM

As the child matures toward the genital phase of development in the fourth and fifth years of life, innate sadism diminishes because life-affirming and creative motives take precedence. With these normal developments comes the emergence of the child's capacity for pity, sympathy, and empathy (Klein, 1929/1975a, p. 214). In short, authentic object love becomes possible.

From Part-Object Introjections to Whole Object Identification

Initially, as we have seen, the infantile ego is capable only of identifying with **part-objects,** and often these partial persons are equated in phantasy with body processes and products such as feces, breasts, and penises. With development, the infantile ego becomes capable of perceiving and identifying *with* **whole objects** that more closely approximate reality. More important, given the choice, the ego more readily identifies with and incorporates good rather than bad objects because good objects can provide pleasure for the id and because bad objects installed into the self are likely to create pain. From the ego's point of view, preservation of the good internalized object is synonymous with survival of the ego (Klein, 1935/1975a, p. 264). Said differently, the ego is now capable of understanding that loss of or damage to the good object threatens its own existence.

> With this change in the relation to the object, new anxiety-contents make their appearance and a change takes place in the mechanisms of defense. The development of the libido also is decisively influenced. Paranoid anxiety lest the objects sadistically destroyed should themselves be a source of poison and danger inside the subject's body causes him, in spite of the vehemence of his oral-sadistic onslaughts, at the same time to be profoundly mistrustful of the objects while yet incorporating them. (Klein, 1935/1975a, p. 264)

The infant repeats again and again the act of incorporating the good object. Each repetition is also a compulsive test of an object's goodness as the infant tries to disprove its fears about the object. In this way, the infant fortifies itself against persecutory objects and can phantasize about protecting the good objects by safeguarding them within the self.

Protecting the Good Object: Paranoid Versus Depressive Anxiety

To the child's dismay, repetition does not lead to success or finality. The child soon discovers that he or she cannot protect internalized good objects from the sadism of internalized bad ones. Anxiety develops about the dangers that lie in wait for internalized good objects, including a phantasy that the inside of the body can be a poisonous place in which good objects perish (Klein, 1935/1975a, p. 265). Every real and imagined act of destruction that objects have enacted against one another, including parental sexual relations, which the child views as an act of violence, are seen as sources of continuing danger to the good object.

One irony, lost on the child, is that its new capacity to identify with whole objects occurs simultaneously with the development of its awareness that it cannot protect them from persecuting bad objects or from the id.

It requires a fuller identification with the loved object, and a fuller recognition of its value, for the ego to become aware of the state of disintegration to which it has reduced and is continuing to reduce its loved object. The ego then finds itself confronted with the psychic reality that its loved objects are in a state of dissolution—in bits—and the despair, remorse and anxiety deriving from this recognition are at the bottom of numerous anxiety-situations. To quote only a few of them: there is anxiety how to put the bits together in the right way and at the right time; how to pick out the good bits and do away with the bad ones; how to bring the object to life when it has been put together; and there is the anxiety of being interfered with in this task by bad objects and by one's own hatred, etc. (Klein, 1935/1975a, p. 269)

Another irony is the close link between love and destruction:

For at this stage of his development, loving an object and devouring it are very closely connected. A little child who believes, when its mother disappears, that he has eaten her up and destroyed her (whether from motives of love or of hate) is tormented by anxiety both for her and for the good mother which he has absorbed.

It now becomes plain why, at this phase of development, the ego feels itself constantly menaced in its possession of internalized good objects. It is full of anxiety lest such objects should die. Both in children and in adults suffering from depression, I have discovered the dread of harbouring dying or dead objects (especially the parents) inside one and an identification of the ego with objects in this condition. (Klein, 1935/1975a, p. 266)

Thus, for Klein, even the apparent love and empathic concern that develops with the maturation of the infant's ego has a selfish basis. The child fears that its good objects may die and is terrified that such dead objects will reside within the self. Every event that signals loss of the real, good mother in the world of reality also indicates the potential loss of the internalized good mother in the world of phantasy. The feelings of sadness or remorse that result from imagining loss of the loved object is what Klein initially called depressive anxiety. At its core, depressive anxiety is a kind of sadness about the fate of the good object.

However, paranoid anxiety over what the objects might do to the self also develops. Never secure in their possession of the good object, children cannot be certain about the goodness and stability of the good object. Instead, paranoid fears and doubts can prevail. Even if good objects of the real world are not actually lost, it is nevertheless possible, the anxious and suspicious child believes, that bad objects of the phantasy world can still mount an assault on them. In Klein's account, the alternatives the child faces in viewing the world are a lose-lose proposition.

PARANOIAC AND DEPRESSIVE POSITIONS: KLEIN'S FIRST THEORY

A child's self-involved fears take one of two forms. When the central anxiety assumes the form of persecution of the ego itself—a fear that one's own ego is at risk of attack—then the anxiety is described by Klein as the **paranoic position.** If, however, the central fear is that the good object is at risk because internalized bad objects might destroy it, the prevailing feeling is melancholy and therefore is considered the **depressive position** (Klein, 1935/1975a, p. 269).

Persecution and Pining

The feelings of sorrow in the depressive position reflect a desire to regain or repair the lost or damaged love-objects. Klein called this whole constellation of melancholy emotions "pining." The depressive position constitutes anxiety that internalized bad objects will per-secute and destroy internalized good objects, defends against these fears, and subjectively experiences longing or pining (Klein, 1945/1975a, p. 349). It is characteristic of the depressive position to be anxious and remorseful about the plight of the damaged loved object, whereas the person in the paranoiac position is vigilant and fearfully alert to the possibility that a disintegrated object may reunify to emerge again as a persecutor (Klein, 1935/1975a, p. 272).

Positions of Development from Paranoid to Depressive

Fear of one's own annihilation, the paranoiac form of anxiety, is the developmentally ear-lier and more primitive form because its danger situation—annihilation—is innate. Fear of losing the good object by destruction or mutilation, the depressive form of early anx-iety, is developmentally later and more complex because its danger situation requires a comprehension of whole objects, empathy for them, and a sense of guilt for one's own role in the process of loss. The depressive and paranoiac forms of early anxiety to per-ceived danger situations are actually a normal developmental personality progression, but one that is never completely surpassed with age or totally resolved in the sense that or-dinary developmental stages are customarily outgrown. For that reason, Klein referred to these personality processes as the depressive position and the paranoid position, rather than "stages" of melancholy and persecutory anxiety (Klein, 1935/1975a, p. 275n; see es-pecially the last paragraph of the end notes in 1952/1975c, p. 93).

MANIC AND DEPRESSIVE POSITIONS IN ADULT PSYCHOPATHOLOGY

Klein theorized that the adult psychopathologies of manic excitation and depression could be understood as derivatives of the paranoiac and depressive positions of childhood. In clas-sical theory, Freud had argued that manic behavior was the ego's way of defending itself against feelings of depression at the loss of a love-object. Klein held the view that the ego is seeking refuge from depressive feelings and trying to escape its tortured relationships with internalized love-objects. To do so, the ego attempts to take control of its love-objects by dominating them. The ego supplements the familiar paranoid and depressive positions by adopting a manic position that serves the additional defensive aim of denial.

Omnipotence and Denial

The sense of omnipotence observable during some adult manic episodes is the central fea-ture, Klein suggested, of this psychotic level of psychopathology. For Klein, the normal developmental version of the "manic position" also hinges on the child's belief in its own omnipotence. The person destined to be manic in adulthood attempted early in infancy to deny the presence of the internalized persecuting objects it had incorporated into the self. Even more painfully, the infantile ego of the person heading toward mania denied its dependence on good objects as well. This defense of denial also has to accomplish an ad-ditional aim. The manic person uses denial to obliterate all recognition of danger to good objects from the persecution of internalized bad objects. Freud had pictured personality dynamics as conflict between the id, ego, and superego. Klein widened the war to include conflicts between real and internalized phantasy objects:

> What in my view is quite specific for mania is *the utilization of the sense of omnipotence* for the purpose of *controlling and mastering objects*. This is necessary for two reasons: (a) in

order to deny the dread of them which is being experienced, and (b) so that the mechanism (acquired in the previous—the depressive-position) of making reparation to the object may be carried through. By mastering his objects the manic person imagines he will prevent them not only from injuring himself but also from being a danger to one another. His mastery is to enable him particularly to prevent dangerous coitus between the parents he had internalized and their death within him. (Klein, 1935/1975a, pp. 277–278; italics in original)

Infantile denial no longer works for the manic adult, even though the infantile sense of magical omnipotence lingers. Adult psychopathology results when the manic patient believes that he or she has destroyed the internalized love-objects and also magically believes he or she can reconstitute them at will.

Omnipotence and Devaluation: The Power of Life and Death

Omnipotence is coupled with the defense of *devaluation* whereby the adult belittles the worth and importance of its internalized objects. Contempt replaces love. "This *disparagement of the object's importance and the contempt for it* is, I think, a specific characteristic of mania and enables the ego to effect that partial detachment which we observe side by side with its hunger for objects" (Klein, 1935/1975a, p. 279; italics in original). By detaching itself from its loved objects, the ego advances its development beyond the more dependent depressive position, but it does so at the price of increased anxiety and the need for perpetual vigilance. The new burden that has been presented to the ego is that it must gain mastery over its objects. Merely hungering for them and worrying about their safety are no longer sufficient. Sometimes, however, mastery over the persecuting and malevolent internalized objects includes killing them—with the intention, perhaps, of resurrecting them later.

At a deeper level, the dynamics of the manic position reveal the fundamental ambivalence of children toward their internalized objects. Klein argued, as we have seen, that the infant eventually has to form a more realistic perception of the parents as real objects in the real world. To do so, it must maintain the separation between incorporated good and bad phantasy objects. However, learning and development are making clear to the infantile ego that good and bad are often aspects of the same object, not separate objects as it once thought.

Splitting in Normal Development

As the child relates with increasing appropriateness to the real mother, there is the danger that the phantasy good and bad mother-breast will also unite into one contradictory and unmanageable object. To prevent this intolerable and confusing internal state, the ego splits the *imagos,* as Klein describes the process, into permanently separate and opposite object images. Notice that the splitting mechanism is aimed at the internal world of phantasy objects rather than the external world of actual people. Now the child can treat the internalized objects as simple instances of good or bad, loved or hated, while it puts increased trust in the more complicated real people who exhibit both qualities simultaneously (Klein, 1935/1975a, p. 287).

The child now vacillates between depressive worry and manic omnipotence. Troubling thoughts that the good objects will be destroyed are warded off by manic efforts to exert mastery over them. Splitting the phantasy objects into separate good and bad images helps confine this vacillation to the internal world of phantasy objects, and paves the way for the child to relate appropriately to its real objects. In Klein's view, when splitting is used as a strategy to protect the internalized good objects from the internalized bad ones, it is a normal component of personality development. Healthy adaptation to reality requires that the child perceive its real objects accurately and trust them more than its primitive phantasy objects as it matures to adolescence (Klein, 1945/1975a, pp. 348 ff.). This concept is consistent with Freudian theory, even if Klein's techniques do not seem to be.

Splitting as a "Flight to the Good"

Klein described a secondary defense as a "flight to the good" by which the child can vacillate between its external love-objects and its internalized love-objects. If the flight is directed inwardly to the good but internalized phantasy objects, then the result is separation from reality and potential psychosis. On the other hand, if the person's flight is directed outwardly to the good but external real objects, there is the potential either for normal development or for slavish and neurotic dependence on others. In either case, the flight mechanism is the child's way of resolving its depressive and paranoiac anxieties. Thus development of the defense of splitting, for Klein, is a normal developmental process.

At this stage of her thinking, Klein used the term **splitting** in a narrow way to refer to the separation of good and bad *objects* in the child's phantasy. Subsequently, as we shall see, Klein (1946/1975c) elaborated her account of splitting to include *structural splits* in the child's id, ego, and self. In fact, she later makes clear that the infant cannot split its image of the love-object without splitting its own ego into good and bad components as well. A particular split-off part of the id, Klein will later propose, becomes the prison of psychoticlike and terrifying object images that seek to devour the child.

Triumph and Guilt in the Manic Position

If psychological development is normal, a balance is achieved between love and hate as the child's objects are unified into whole and more realistic images. With time, the child develops the desire to outgrow its dependencies, to rival the achievements of its admired love-objects, and to master fears of its own destructiveness. Eventually, mastery strivings become dominant. The child wants to reverse the parent–child relationship so that it can attain power over the parents, exceed their achievements, and even subjugate them in phantasies of power and humiliation. Envisioning a time when the parents will have changed into helpless beings, like little children, as they become weak, old, and frail adults, the child relishes its future triumph. But the ego also experiences these phantasies of triumph with feelings of guilt (Klein, 1945/1975a, 351–352).

Triumph and guilt can impede the child's progression out of the depressive position because they compete with and block the ego's reparative work of restoring the damaged loved objects. Without the reparative work of normal mourning for lost or abandoned love-objects, normal emotional development and healthy independence are put at risk. This destructive aspect of the manic position mobilizes the child's sadism and focuses it not only on healthy urges to be masterful, but also on desires to humiliate and destroy the parental figures. Nevertheless, there is good news as well as bad. Triumph over one's objects can also promote emotional, intellectual, and physical growth. "The child's growing skills, gifts and arts increase his belief in his constructive tendencies, in his capacity to master and control his hostile impulses as well as his 'bad' internal objects" (Klein, 1940/1975a, p. 353). Triumph thus can lead to genuine mastery and ultimately to the capacity for authentic love.

Of the three positions—paranoiac, depressive, and manic (psychotic)—Klein regarded the depressive position as the central feature of infantile development. The ways in which the child learns to resolve its depressive anxieties and establish real relationships with real objects is crucial to normal personality functioning (Klein, 1935/1975a, p. 289).

LOVE, GUILT, AND REPARATION

By the late 1930s, Klein was expanding her analysis of love and guilt. Klein began to emphasize that infants have spontaneous feelings of love and empathy for others, a different stance from her previous pronouncements. In addition to all of the negative emotions that infants experience, she pointed out, they can routinely feel love and gratitude toward the mother for the care she provides. Klein now introduced the importance of the concept of love. Following Freud's lead, Klein viewed the emotion of love as a derivative of the life instincts, ever present and opposing the destructive urges of the death instinct:

> Side by side with the destructive impulses in the unconscious mind both of the child and of the adult, there exists a profound urge to make sacrifices, in order to help and put right loved people who in phantasy have been harmed or destroyed. In the depths of the mind, the urge to make people happy is linked up with a strong feeling of responsibility and concern for them, which manifests itself in genuine sympathy with other people and the ability to understand them, as they are and as they feel. (Klein, 1937/1975a, p. 211)

Restoring the Good Object: Restitution as Self-Serving Love

Guilt drives love in the Kleinian world. Because the child's ego is identified with the good object and can empathize with its plight, the ego is motivated to make restitution to the good object for all of its previous acts of sadism against it. As the superego develops, furthermore, the child's phantasies of attacking its objects are met with guilt. Feelings of regret surface in the child's awareness for the imagined damage it has inflicted. Desires to "make good"—engaging in the processes of **reparation/restitution**—emerge in the infant mental economy, fueled equally by love and guilt (Klein, 1933/1975a, p. 254).

The infant's empathy for and identification with the love-object also permits it to profit from its concern for the love-object's welfare. Whatever sacrifices the child makes for the sake of the loved one, it is simultaneously making for itself because it identifies with the love-object. As adults, we complete the circle by assuming the role of caring parents where once we were cared-for children. In so doing, we reenact the love we received from our own mothers and now give to our children. In Klein's view, we also expiate our infantile guilt for the damage we imagine we, so long ago, inflicted on our mothers (Klein, 1937/1975a, p. 314). When successful, the infant's reparative efforts open the child to the possibility of loving new objects without fear or guilt. "Thus making reparation—which is such an essential part of the ability to love—widens in scope, and the child's capacity to accept love and, by various means, to take into himself goodness from the outer world steadily increases" (Klein, 1937/1975a, p. 342).

The mother who turns the tables and excessively identifies with her child presents an alternative scenario. Caught up in a resurgence of her own infantile unconscious guilt for the harm she once wished on her love-objects, the mother is attempting to revive a loving relationship to her own mother through her child. She becomes overly self-sacrificing because she sees far too much of herself in the child and far too much of her mother in the role she plays toward her child. Instead of repairing the damage to her own phantasy objects, however, the overly indulgent mother deprives her child of those experiences that will permit it to mature and become psychologically differentiated. "It is well known that a child who has been brought up by a mother who showers love on him and expects nothing in return often becomes a selfish person" (Klein, 1937/1975a, p. 318).

PROJECTION + IDENTIFICATION = SPLITTING REVISITED

Klein revised her earlier views by concluding that splitting was a universal process of defense against normally occurring, psychoticlike anxiety states. Klein wanted to make the implicit link between splitting and the paranoiac and depressive forms of anxiety more explicit.

Revision of the Paranoiac Position to the Paranoid-Schizoid Position

In an earlier version of Klein's theory, the infant splits the love-object into a good and bad object to isolate its own sadism to one aspect of a part-object rather than risk destroying the whole. The infant also splits its relationships with the object into love and hate-love for the good and hate for the bad object. Klein now elaborated this twofold concept of splitting and extended its reach from the early splitting of object relationships to the splitting of personality structures, the self, and feelings.

To reflect the changes, she renamed the "paranoiac position," now to be called the **paranoid-schizoid position.** Schizoid personality phenomena—dysfunctions of empathy, love, and hate in relating to objects and to the self—became for Klein a convenient synonym for all manner of personality pathologies; thus she included the term *schizoid* in the newly named *paranoid-schizoid position.*

How Shall I Split? Let Me Count the Ways

From the very beginning of life, Klein now asserted, the ego's experience of its own fear of annihilation is the foundation of anxiety. Anxiety is always experienced in connection with objects. In the paranoid-schizoid position, the infant projects all of its fears onto part-objects, transforming them into hated persecutors. Other significant sources of anxiety included in Klein's new view are the trauma of birth and the frustration of bodily needs. Even these anxieties are experienced from the earliest moments as linked to objects or projected onto them (Klein, 1946/1975c, pp. 4–5; Klein, 1958/1975c, pp. 23 ff.).

Splitting the Object: *Defending Against Annihilation*

In the early days and weeks of life, the normal state of the early ego is a lack of cohesiveness. Its natural tendency toward integration alternates with a tendency toward disintegration when confronted with the enormity of its own destructiveness (Klein, 1946/1975c, p. 4). This vacillating pair of opposite tendencies underlies the mechanism of splitting.

Some of the infant's annihilation fear is not projected outwardly onto objects. A residual component of the death instinct lurks within and magnifies the primitive ego's feelings of helplessness. As such helplessness mounts, the ego's natural tendency toward disintegration is accelerated. Thus threatened, the ego attempts to defend itself in one of three ways: by externalizing (projecting) the threat, by denying it altogether, or by **splitting the object** perceived to be the source of the threat into good and bad images. Klein regarded this most elementary form of splitting as a defense directed to the control of annihilation anxiety under the impact of the death instinct. Splitting dichotomizes the internalized phantasized and the perceived external object into good and bad. Splitting also bifurcates the child's relationships to these images into love-and-hate/desire-and-fear. The destructive impulse and its associated anxiety is thus defensively dispersed, deflected, and isolated from the good objects and from self-identified-with-good-objects.

Splitting the Ego: *The Idealized Breast and the Superego*

In her revised formulation, Klein suggested that the ego could not split the object without also **splitting the ego** itself (1946/1975c, pp. 5–6; see also 1958/1975c). When the infant takes into himself the "good" and satisfying breast, this phantasy object is experienced as whole or integrated. In contrast, the split-off "bad" and frustrating breast is experienced as fragmented, "broken into bits." Good feelings that derive from having a satisfying object inside one can be disrupted by the anxiety of having a fragmented and poisonous bad object also inside. To enhance the effectiveness of splitting as a defense against the bad objects, the infantile ego idealizes the goodness of the good object images. "Idealization is bound up with the splitting of the object, for the good aspects of the breast are exaggerated as a safeguard against the fear of the persecuting breast" (Klein, 1946/1975c, p. 7).

A secondary motive also governs idealization of the good object. Because the infant is also driven by its instinctual needs for food and love, it strives for unlimited gratification from an inexhaustible and always bountiful object, the idealized breast. Klein proposed that the process of idealization of split-off parts of the ego underlies the formation of the earliest superego. By the end of the first six months of life, splitting the breast into good and bad images, idealizing the good aspect, and identifying with it constitute the formation of the earliest and most primitive superego (Klein, 1958/1975c, p. 239). Said another way, one aspect of splitting the ego is the creation of the superego.

> In my view, the splitting of the ego, by which the super-ego is formed, comes about as a consequence of conflict in the ego, engendered by the polarity of the two instincts [i.e., life and death]. This conflict is increased by their projection as well as by the resulting introjections of good and bad objects. The ego, supported by the internalized good object and strengthened by the identification with it, projects a portion of the death instinct into that part of itself which it has split-off—a part which thus comes to be in opposition to the rest of the ego and forms the basis of the superego. (Klein, 1958/1975c, p. 240)

For Klein, the superego is a product of very early splitting of the ego and phantasized incorporation of the good (satisfying) and bad (frustrating) mother, rather than, as Freud's version would have it, the repository of the image of the father who punishes by castration.

The bad object is kept as distant as possible from the bountiful object. Toward this end, the infant's ego may use denial to obliterate awareness of the very existence of the bad object, along with any frustrating situations linked in phantasy to the bad object. But this very selective obliteration of reality works only because the infant temporarily experiences itself as all-powerful—capable of materializing gratification by the mere experience of desire.

In the process of annihilating recognition of the bad object, an entire set of object relations is obliterated and along with them a part of the ego that supported those relations (Klein, 1946/1975c, pp. 7). In short, phantasy objects, reality objects, the relationship to both, and the part of the ego active in the process are all split off and denied.

Splitting the Id: *Dividing Conscious From Unconscious*

Another structural split is needed to cope with the incorporated and terrifying bad object images that the infant has split off from the sadistic strivings of its ego—**splitting the id.** In this way, the unmanageable terrifying persecutory objects—derived, you will recall, from the phantasy transformations of the mother and father—are "relegated to the deeper layers of the unconscious", to the split-off section of the id (Klein, 1958/1975c, p. 241). Two benefits result. First, the split-off aspect of the ego destined to become a superego is better tolerated once these horrific images are dissociated into the deeper unconscious. Second, "extremely bad" images are not assimilated or accepted into either the superego or the ego. They remain dissociated as split-off id contents, or what Freud considered primal repressions.

Klein pointed out that ego splitting is different from id splitting. The ego has to fuse together contradictory images and drives to create its split-off part of the superego. When the id splits, in contrast, images have to be "defused" so that the bad images are divorced from the good and then split off or dissociated. In short, the first kind of splitting associated with the ego ultimately results in a synthesis whereas the second kind associated with the id results in dissociation or in primal repression (Klein, 1958/1975c, pp. 243 ff.).

For Klein, even the adult defense mechanism of repression is a kind of splitting whereby the fully integrated adult ego "divides itself off" from unconscious threat. Consequently, one might suppose that yet another sense in which Klein used the concept of splitting is the division of conscious from unconscious mental *content* as contrasted with defensive structural splitting.

Splitting the Self: *Projective Identification*

As development proceeds, Klein theorized that the early oral incorporative and aggressive impulses are joined by anal and urethral aggressive impulses. The good object—idealized breast—and the mother's body as an extension of the breast become the targets of the infant's attacks. This is termed **splitting the self.**

> The phantasized onslaughts on the mother follow two main lines: one is the predominantly oral impulse to suck dry, bite up, scoop out and rob the mother's body of its good contents. . . . The other line of attack derives from the anal and urethral impulses and implies expelling dangerous substances (excrements) out of self and *into* the mother. Together with these harmful excrements, expelled in hatred, split-off parts of the ego are also projected on to the mother or, as I would rather call it, into the mother. These excrements and bad parts of the self are meant not only to injure but also to control and to take possession of the object. In so far as the mother comes to contain the bad parts of the self, she is not felt to be a separate individual but is felt to be *the* bad self. (Klein, 1946/1975c, p. 8; italics in original)

There is even a bonus to be had in all this projection and splitting: To the degree that the infant can idealize the good parts of self it has projected, it can reincorporate not only the original good aspects but the intensified and idealized ones it has created. It is truly a give and take world for the infant. Normal development, Klein suggested, is an exquisitely delicate balance of optimal degrees of introjection and projection (Klein, 1946/1975c, p. 11).

Because the infant can project self-content into the object and then take it back by identification, Klein termed the process **projective identification.** In a way, the infant gets what it gives: predominantly hostile projections result in primarily hostile identifications. But another aspect of projective identification is that the intention of the infant is forcibly to enter the object to take control of it. This strategy can backfire during the identification part of the cycle. When identification is at its height, the infant ego may feel that others are controlling it, or can take retribution for the violent intrusion, or that its own body and mind can be controlled by others (Klein, 1946/1975c, p. 11).

Schizoid Object Relations: Guilt, Narcissism, and Projective Identification

Because the infant projects the split-off hated part of the self into the object, it eventually realizes that it has placed the object in jeopardy. The infant feels guilty, at least to the

Table 7.1   The Meanings of Splitting in Klein's Theory

Splitting type	Definition and functions
Object	Good-satisfying breast split from the bad-persecuting breast. *Infant's earliest defense against "bad" objects.*
Object relations	The infant can "hate" the bad and "love" the good object (breast). *Defense against guilt for sadistic urges to destroy the good object.*
Ego	Because the infant "incorporates" objects into itself, there is necessarily a split in the ego that parallels splits in the object and relations to the object. *Structure building: Split-off parts are destined to become the superego but only if they can be reintegrated.*
Id	Terrifying and persecuting phantasy objects that the infant has projected onto the parents are "split off" from the rest of the unconscious and pushed to the "deepest" area of the id. *Defensive dissociation: These split-off images are never reintegrated and are like "primal repressions."*
Self	Split-off and hated "bad" parts of the ego and self are split off and projected into the mother to injure her and take possession/control of her. Some good parts of self are also split off and projected into mother: excrements intended as "gifts of self." *Structure building through projective identification and defensive protection against bad objects.*

small degree that it can experience responsibility, for others who are representatives of the sadistic parts of the self. On the other hand, the projection and splitting enable the infant to permit the "bad" object to carry some of the guilt.

There is also a narcissistic element in projective identification. The infant, after all, is also projecting good aspects of the self, often idealized, into the object. Objects are loved and admired because they are so like the self. Correspondingly, the despised parts of the self can be "split off" and projected into others. Perceived as resembling the unacceptable self, objects embodying the unacceptable projections are transformed into targets of hatred. In either case, the schizoid position from which some infants never emerge assures that their later object relations will be marked by themes of control. For narcissistic self-protection, the infant must dominate the people who carry its projected, split-off self-fragments.

If the infant fails to resolve the paranoid-schizoid position on its way to the depressive position, there is also the possibility that later character development will be marked by a degree of artificiality and lack of spontaneity in relating to others. This characteristic "coldness" of the schizoid style reflects a severe disturbance of a self that has failed to reintegrate the split-off and projected aspects by identification with the available good objects. The various ways in which Klein applied the term *splitting* to the developmental process are summarized in Table 7.1

REPARATION: THE LINK BETWEEN POSITIONS

The depressive position is the central feature of normal development, for the way in which the infant resolves its depressive longings sets the pattern for its later intimate interpersonal relationships. When the infant can introject a "complete" object near the end of the first six months of life, the split between good and bad (and those corresponding splits in the self and ego) are narrowed. The infant begins to construct a more realistic picture of people. Because loved and hated aspects of the breast and mother are now not so widely separated, the infant experiences a sense of loss or mourning when the whole object is not available. An increased sense of guilt for sadistic urges toward the object is the price to be paid for this achievement, a developmental advance that marks the infant's entry into the depressive position (Klein, 1946/1975c, p. 14).

The Drive to Reparation Promotes Ego Integration

The depressive position, Klein now proposed in more detail, has a beneficial early effect of integrating the fragmented ego that has been weakened by its earlier paranoid-schizoid phase of excessive projection and splitting. Depression, an infantile reaction to the phantasized damage inflicted on the love object, engenders strivings to repair or restore the object. This "drive to reparation" exhibited by the infantile ego during the second six months of life will remain in effect for the next several years of childhood. As the child's growing ability to process reality more realistically enhances its adaptation to the world, the depressive position is "worked through" as part of normal emotional development. However, if the earlier paranoid-schizoid position has not been successfully navigated, a successful resolution of the depressive position is also jeopardized. Under these circumstances, the impact of the depression and anxiety of the depressive position may thus mark not a developmental progression but the onset of a vicious circle:

> For if the persecutory fear, and correspondingly schizoid mechanisms, are too strong, the ego is not capable of working through the depressive position. This forces the ego to regress to the paranoid-schizoid position and reinforces the earlier persecutory fears and schizoid phenomena. Thus the basis is established for various forms of schizophrenia in later life; for when such a regression occurs, not only are the fixation-points in the schizoid position reinforced, but there is a danger of greater states of disintegration setting in. Another outcome may be the strengthening of depressive features. (Klein, 1946/1975c, p. 15)

Klein was adamant that during normal development no precise line could be drawn between the feelings of persecution experienced in the paranoid-schizoid position and guilty anxiety in the depressive position. One slowly grades into the other, and elements of both positions persist in later life.

ENVY AND GRATITUDE: THE FOREVER GENEROUS, TOLERANT, AND BOUNTIFUL BREAST

From the infant's point of view, the good breast is an inexhaustible and ever-present source of all that is satisfying. The good breast is the most powerful ally the infant can recruit to protect itself from its own destructive urges. So powerful, so generous, so satisfying is the good breast that the infant envies it and suspects that the good breast selfishly keeps for itself some of its unlimited milk, love, and power (Klein, 1957/1975c, p. 183).

Envy, Jealousy, and Greed Distinguished

Klein distinguished among the meanings of three related terms: envy, jealousy, and greed. **Envy** is an angry feeling that another person possesses and enjoys something desirable. The envious person wants to take away the object of desire, and failing that, to spoil the object of envy so that no one can enjoy it. **Jealousy,** by contrast, is found in the love relationship between two people. When one of the people feels that love is in danger of being taken away by a rival, he or she becomes *jealous* of the rival. The loved object itself is not the target of the emotion and is in no danger of being harmed. **Greed,** a related term, indicates an impetuous and insatiable craving that exceeds what the loved object can give and what the greedy person actually needs (Klein, 1957/1975c, p. 181). In short, the envious person cannot tolerate someone else's possession of the good, the jealous person is fearful of losing the good, and the greedy person is never satisfied by any amount of goodness.

Primary Envy of the Breast

Klein now extended her earlier descriptions of the effects of frustration to include the infant's feelings of envy for a mean and grudging breast that is seen as depriving the infant by keeping for itself what the infant wants: milk, care, love. But the good breast can also be envied. "The very ease with which the milk comes—though the infant feels gratified by it—also gives rise to envy because this gift seems something so unattainable" (Klein, 1957/1975c, p. 183).

Envy Expressed as Grievances in Analysis

Klein pointed out that a parallel to this infantile envy exists within the transference relationship to the analyst in therapy. For example, when the analyst provides an interpretation that brings relief and changes the patient's mood from despair to hope, some patients respond with angry and destructive criticism of the analyst. The interpretation, initially experienced as enriching and nourishing, is quickly experienced as "not good enough." Focusing on often trivial details, the envious patient is full of criticisms of the analyst:

> The envious patient grudges the analyst the success of his work; and if he feels that the analyst and the help he is giving have become spoilt and devalued by his envious criticism, he cannot introject him sufficiently as a good object nor accept his interpretations with real conviction and assimilate them. (Klein, 1957/1975c, p. 184)

Feeling guilty for devaluing the help given him in analysis, the envious patient also feels unworthy to benefit from the analysis.

A different but related devaluing maneuver is typical of the paranoid person. Particularly prone to concealing the split-off hostile and envious parts of self from the analyst, the paranoid patient exacts a kind of sneaky revenge against the helpful therapist who expects the patient to be grateful. The paranoid patient cannot permit the self to experience any gratitude to the therapist or incur any psychological debts to the therapist. Instead such patients have abundant needs to devalue the therapist by defeating the analyst's efforts and spoiling whatever good might come of the process. A kind of perverse sadistic, but self-defeating, pleasure is experienced by disparaging the analyst's efforts. This strategy of spoiling the therapeutic relationship is fed by split-off feelings of envy the patient experiences relative to the therapist. Pathological envy thus prevents any possibility that the analyst's interpretations can be meaningfully assimilated.

A defense against recognizing unbearable envy is employed by patients who become confused and express their open doubts about the meaning of interpretations. Their confusion is a way of substituting expressions of doubt for open criticism of the analyst. Klein hypothesized that such confusion stems from the earliest possible object-relationship disturbances. Such patients, as infants, were unable to keep apart the images of the good and bad breast because the strength of their paranoid-schizoid and depressive fears were overwhelming. Such infants do not separate feelings of love and hate and are thus confused about what might be a good (safe) breast and what might be a bad (persecuting) breast.

Infants who cannot adequately maintain the split between good and bad never know whether they will suck or be sucked dry, bite or be bitten.

For both kinds of patients, the infantile origins of their contemporary envy include feelings that the breast was not available when wanted or that it provided milk too quickly or too slowly. Such infants may have turned away from the breast to suck their own fingers for a time. When they finally accepted the breast, they may not have drunk enough to satisfy hunger. Some infants overcome their grievances and eventually enjoy feeding, but others seem unable ever to be satisfied even by a satisfactory breast, just as some patients seem unable to accept what good the analyst can provide (Klein, 1957/1975c, p. 185). At the core, however, what the infant most wants from the bountiful breast, and entertains grievances for not having gotten, is a sense of safety and, in addition, security from its own destructive and frightening urges.

Excessive Envy: Spoiling the Breast

Envy aims to spoil the primary envied object. Sadistic attacks on the breast are intensified by envy, sometimes to the point that the object utterly loses its value. The breast has become "bad" by being bitten. Greed, envy, and persecutory anxiety, all linked together, intensify one another and increase the level of the infant's destructive impulses toward the mother. The good object is never completely or reliably introjected. Doubts about the reliability, goodness, and generosity of the good object have repercussions for later object relationships. Adults who have been unable to completely introject the good object exhibit poor judgment about others, sliding into and out of inappropriately intimate relationships repetitively.

Gratitude and Love: Breast Bliss and Self-Trust

The infant who can overcome its own destructive impulses, incorporate a stable and nurturing object image of the good breast and good mother, can love. There is, Klein acknowledged, some pleasure to be had at the breast for most infants. Full gratification at the breast means that the infant feels it has received from its loved object a unique gift (Klein, 1957/1975c, p. 188). Gratitude is also the basis of trust. When the infant feels grateful for the sustenance and security provided by the breast, it begins an object relationship based on positive feelings for and trust in the object. Such feelings become the foundation for later feelings of connectedness with other people, pleasure in their happiness, and trust in their capacities to reciprocate. Reliable mothering increases the likelihood that such trust will develop.

Freud (1905) described the infant's "bliss" in sucking at the breast as the prototype of all later sexual satisfactions. Klein expanded this Freudian concept to suggest that bliss at the breast is even more widely influential in permitting later intimate relationships, feelings of love for others, and feelings of being fully understood by others. Perhaps even more important, she theorized that investing the good object with one's feelings of trust permits the infant to begin developing a sense of trust in self (Klein, 1957/1975c, p. 188).

DEFENDING AGAINST ENVY: THE MOST DEADLY OF SINS

Klein proposed her new central ideas on envy and gratitude toward the end of her career. They replaced her earlier emphasis on sadism and hatred. One indicator of the importance she placed on these new concepts was her insight into the reasons why envy has been classed as one of the "seven deadly sins."

There are very pertinent psychology reasons why envy ranks among the seven "deadly sins." I would even suggest that it is unconsciously felt to be the greatest sin of all, because it spoils and harms the good object which is the source of life. . . . The feeling of having injured and destroyed the primal object impairs the individual's trust in the sincerity of his later relations and makes him doubt his capacity for love and goodness. (Klein, 1957/1975c, p. 189)

When the infant's ego feels overwhelmed by envy, it may resort to an array of primitive defenses against envy. Some of these defenses may develop into adult personality features that have the potential to disrupt interpersonal relationships. Klein enumerated eight defenses against envy:

- *Idealization.* Klein originally described the infant's efforts to idealize the good breast as a protection against the persecution of the bad breast. Now she expanded her concept to include **idealization** as a means of protecting self from envy of the good object. She indicated that for children in whom the normal splitting process of the object into good and bad has failed, "Strongly exalting the object and its gifts is an attempt to diminish envy" (Klein, 1957/1975c, p. 216).

- *Confusion.* Recall the confusion and doubting of the resistant patient in therapy. For the infant who cannot achieve the normal splitting of the object, confusion between good-and-bad/love-and-hate is the result. "By becoming confused as to whether a substitute for the original figure is good or bad, persecution as well as the guilt about spoiling and attacking the primary object by envy is to some extent counteracted" (Klein, 1957/1975c, p. 216). In extreme form, such confusion may lay the groundwork for psychotic-level states of delusion and obsessive indecision later in adulthood.

- *Flight from mother to other.* Both infants and adults may learn to avoid admired people because they are reminders of the primary envied object, mother. In this way, they protect the breast (and mother) from the destructiveness of their envy. Somewhat later in life, such behavior may lead to promiscuous relationships as the person flees from one love-object to the next (Klein, 1957/1975c, p. 217).

- *Devaluing of the object.* Spoiling and **devaluation** are inherent in envy. A devastated or spoiled love-object need not be envied. Even idealized objects are subject to such devaluation. Indeed they may be especially vulnerable to such devaluation. A sense of ingratitude and the expression of complaints about the object's failings accompany devaluation.

- *Devaluing of the self.* Some adults are unable to use or exploit their own talents and abilities. By denying their own competencies, they avoid envy of and rivalry with admired figures who may provide occasions for unflattering competitive comparisons. As we have seen, even in analysis, the patient may admire and therefore envy the analyst. Only by further devaluing the self can some patients maintain any relationship with the analyst.

- *Greed for the good.* By greedily and rapaciously incorporating the good and admired object, the infant can believe that it possesses the object and controls it totally. Therefore, all the object's good attributes have become its own.

- *Arousing envy in others.* A frequent adult maneuver to conquer envy is to arouse it in others. In one stroke, the situations of envious subject and envied object are reversed. Klein suggested that this method is particularly ineffective because it backfires, creating worries of being persecuted. Another reason why this defense is so fragile, Klein suggested, is its link to the depressive position. "The desire to make other people, particularly loved ones, envious and to triumph over them gives rise to guilt and to the fear of harming them. The anxiety stirred up impairs the enjoyment of one's own possessions and again increases envy" (Klein, 1957/1975c, pp. 218–219).

- *Stifling love and intensifying hatred.* One way to prevent envy is to deny love for the admired object and express hatred for it instead. Freud had referred to such transformations of impulses into their opposites as the defense of reaction formation. In this way, the most painful combination of love, hatred, guilt, and envy is avoided. On the surface, the hatred may not be evident, but a degree of studied indifference or coldness toward others is observable. An allied maneuver is simply to withdraw from all intimacy.

For the infant who cannot work through the paranoid-schizoid persecutory position adequately, these defenses may signal later severe disturbances of personality. However, for the infant who achieves the depressive position and is able to work through its feelings of depression and guilt, the outcome is more favorable. Such an infant can learn not only to contain its own destructive impulses, but also to care for, rather than envy, the admired object.

SOME PERSONAL SOURCES OF KLEIN'S VISION OF THE INFANT'S WORLD

Klein's conclusions about the infant's subjective world are speculative and inferential. But what was her sense of the experience of infancy that guided her inferences? Klein envisioned the infant's subjective world as a frightening place of psychoticlike phantasy, need, and wish. Driven by fear, sadism, hate and more hate, triumph, and envy, the Kleinian infant seemingly experiences little happiness. Even triumphs lead, not to ultimate satisfaction, but to guilt. For the Kleinian infant, life is hard: frighteningly difficult to endure or master, nearly impossible to comprehend, and stingy in its rewards. Small wonder that Klein thought infants were angry.

Childhood: No Breast for Melanie

The youngest of four children, Melanie Reizes had reason to believe that she had been an unexpected and unwanted child (Grosskurth, 1986, pp. 10, 15, 57; Segal, 1992, p. 3). Her older siblings apparently resulted from planned pregnancies. Emilie, Emanuel, and Sidonie were born in the three consecutive years from 1876 to 1878. Melanie, born in 1882, was the exception to the pattern. She followed her nearest sibling, Sidonie, by four years. Her mother actually told her that she had been unexpected. In addition, Melanie's father openly revealed that he preferred his oldest daughter Emilie to Melanie. This was another hurtful revelation, made more painful by Melanie's realization that her father could voice his preference without realizing its impact on her (Grosskurth, 1986, p. 11).

Melanie Klein claimed little significance for these experiences in her autobiography, written in her seventies. Klein even asserted in her autobiography that she had been untouched by her parents' disclosures: "I have no particular feeling that I resented this because there was a great deal of love towards me" (quoted in Grosskurth, 1986, p. 10).

Klein was also aware that she had been the only child of the four Reizes siblings who had not been breast-fed. She had been handed over to a "wet nurse," who was, in her memory of it, a more than satisfactory substitute. The theoretical importance she later placed on the role of the breast as the first object, and the significance she attached to breast-feeding as the first object relation, lend weight to Grosskurth's surmise that she harbored substantial resentment about her childhood despite her denials (1986, pp. 10 ff.).

Melanie Klein's belief that she had been less than intimately and joyously cared for and was initially unwanted is apparent. Her denial of any resentment suggests the operation of a defense mechanism. Perhaps, like the anxious and angry infants she spent a lifetime describing, Melanie Klein also experienced the same need to protect her primary love-objects from the destructiveness of her own anger. Her autobiographical account portrays her mother and father in the idealized fashion that Klein had observed in her patients in order for them to have safe recall.

When Melanie was four years old, her nearest sibling in age, Sidonie (age 8), died from a particularly virulent form of glandular tuberculosis. The two had enjoyed an especially close relationship. Sidonie treated her younger sister with memorable kindness, in sharp contrast with their older siblings, who had less tolerance for their youngest sister and often made Melanie the target of their teasing.

Sidonie's death was the first of many that Melanie Klein would experience through her long life, and each of the losses she endured fed her earliest fears of illness and death (Grosskurth, 1986, p. 15). Substantial periods of unresolved mourning, feelings of anxious vulnerability over her own health, and episodes of overt depression recurred throughout her adult life. These symptoms probably had their origins in these early experiences of illness and death (cf. Sayers, 1991, p. 206). As we shall see, young Melanie's feelings of physical vulnerability and susceptibility to illness were often preyed upon, if not actually manipulatively concocted, by her mother.

An Intrusive Mother and Detached Father

Libussa Deutsch Reizes (1852–1914), Melanie's mother, was a smart, strong-willed, energetic but very intrusive person. Twenty-four years younger than her husband, Libussa was in her mid-twenties when the couple settled in an Austrian town to raise their first three children. By 1882, the year Melanie was born, the family had relocated to the capital city of Vienna. Moriz Reizes (1828–1900), Melanie's father, was a general medical practitioner. Melanie and her mother noted that his family was of lower status than the maternal side of the family. Melanie regarded her mother's clan as "full of knowledge and education," whereas the paternal relatives were largely the objects of scorn (Grosskurth, 1986, p. 7).

Melanie wanted to feel close to her father and to note things about him she could admire, such as his knowledge of at least ten languages. But she had few memories of happy moments with him and no recollections of her father ever playing with her. She attributed this neglect largely to his age (an "old fifty") during her childhood. A favorite childhood anecdote about her father told of his brave conduct during a cholera epidemic in a Polish village. Her father volunteered to go to the village, and unlike the other doctors who stood at the windows of the villager's cottages and shouted directions to them, Moriz Reizes bravely entered their homes to treat the victims (Grosskurth, 1986, p. 6). The historical authenticity of the cholera story is unknown, but it gave Melanie something of the heroic father most children would want.

Nevertheless, as a Polish-Jewish doctor in an anti-Semitic Vienna, Moriz's medical practice failed. He eventually set himself up as a dentist. The women in the family, most notably Libussa, communicated their disappointment to the children. Although no one said it aloud, Moriz was regarded as ineffectual, invisible, and irrelevant.

Libussa Reizes was clearly the dominant member of the family. Melanie grew up observing firsthand a matriarchy that no doubt shaped much of Melanie's attitude toward her mother, motherhood in general, and herself in particular (Grosskurth, 1986, pp. 7, 18). To bolster the family's finances, Libussa opened a shop where she sold both plants and reptiles with substantial success. In Melanie's view, her mother's efforts were crucial to the family's survival (Sayers, 1991, p. 206).

As he aged, Melanie perceived her father growing increasingly ineffectual and detached. In her recollection, her father had grown not only old but also became senile. Moriz Reizes died of pneumonia on April 6, 1900, and his passing created even greater financial stresses for the family. Libussa seems to have spent the rest of her life worrying about money and about Melanie's alleged poor health.

Melanie was 17 years old when her 21-year-old second cousin, Arthur Klein, proposed marriage (Grosskurth, 1986, p. 19). Melanie was quite a beauty, and some of her older brother's friends had indicated their interest in her. But Melanie and her cousin, Arthur, had eyes only for each other. Even brother Emanuel was initially impressed with Arthur's intellect. Melanie had plans to go to medical school like her father, but she abandoned these when she met Arthur.

Arthur and Melanie decided to postpone their marriage for a few years, until economic circumstances stabilized and Arthur could earn a comfortable living. He was then a student preparing for his degree in chemical engineering, and his prospects seemed very good. Over a period of years, however, Melanie found herself trapped in a long engagement to a man she found she actually did not love. Her mother was more committed to the idea of Arthur as Melanie's husband than was Melanie.

Emanuel's Death, Melanie's Guilt

After the death of their father, Melanie's brother, Emanuel, thought that Emilie and Melanie were being given preferential treatment by Libussa. Both sisters had the full attention of their mother and were the beneficiaries of what money she had. For her part, Libussa spent what she had to make the young women attractive to suitors. Emanuel, on the other hand, received little money and was given his dead father's old clothes. He had an "artistic temperament" and had been known to brood and become depressed, but after his father's death his behavior became even more eccentric. Emanuel also suffered from rheumatic heart disease. Emanuel became involved with drugs and alcohol and traveled to Italy where his romantic entanglements became very complicated and stressful.

Melanie and Emanuel corresponded frequently, but his letters created worries about his health and sanity. Emanuel grew discontented with a young woman with whom he was romantically involved, and they broke off the relationship. Emanuel descended further into depression, broken periodically by maniclike episodes. Melanie's plans for further education were stymied. Libussa did what she could to discourage Emanuel from returning home. She explained to him that his health would suffer more (!) if he returned to the hot summer weather of Vienna. Libussa also implied that Melanie might not love him as much in his present state (Grosskurth, 1986, pp. 24–25). Libussa's machinations were making Emanuel more depressed and angry, and he communicated those feelings through Melanie to his mother. Sensing defeat, Libussa designed a new strategy to keep Emanuel away. She attempted to persuade Emanuel to stay through the summer of 1901 with Melanie at the home of her prospective in-laws in a Viennese suburb.

In the end, Emanuel did return to Vienna, where, for lack of space, he had to sleep in the same room as his mother. Denying the seriousness of Emanuel's erratic behavior, Libussa nevertheless observed firsthand how Emanuel did not sleep at night, ate little, and fluctuated wildly in his moods. By 1902, Emanuel resumed a restless life that seemed to suit him. He moved to Switzerland, but kept in touch with the family, requesting increases in his allowance and advising Melanie on her upcoming wedding. Emanuel gambled with the money he received, and quickly squandered all of his resources. Libussa pressured Melanie to send him what money Melanie had.

Melanie wrote to Emanuel that her fiancé, Arthur, had obtained a job and that they were ready to marry. In an extraordinary letter to his sister, Emanuel revealed true feelings about the wedding, about Arthur and, surprisingly, about Melanie. He clearly was jealous of his sister's romance and also of her place in the family. He informed Melanie that ". . . I rejoice in the awareness that Mother will be relieved now of the heaviest burden among her loving concerns, which she has always hidden with her pride and secrecy. I am almost as grateful to you for her sake as for mine!" (quoted in Grosskurth, 1986, p. 30). Melanie was again being informed that she was an unwanted burden. This time the impact of the message was heightened because it originated, despite its obvious anger, from a most trusted and admired source.

The Reizes' family crises continued through 1902. Emanuel became even more involved with drugs, more reckless with money, and increasingly depressed and angry. He wandered from place to place throughout Europe, unable to go home to die (Grosskurth, 1986, p. 35). On December 2, 1902, one day after his arrival in Genoa, Emanuel Reizes, age 25, died of heart failure, alone in his hotel room. His failing rheumatic heart may have received a substantial push from the combined effects of the deteriorated state of his health, malnutrition, and the catastrophic combination of drugs and alcohol he was consuming. Some years later, Melanie wrote in her autobiography that Emanuel had been "the best friend I ever had" (quoted by Grosskurth, 1986, p. 39).

Melanie's Marriage: The Matriarchy Continues

Still in mourning for Emanuel, Melanie Reizes married Arthur Klein on March 31, 1903. Melanie was 21 years old. In an autobiographical story written some 10 years later, Melanie described a fictional young woman who is shocked by her wedding night experience: "And does it therefore have to be like this, that motherhood begins with disgust?" (quoted in Grosskurth, 1986, pp. 40–41). The young heroine of the story, Anna, is consoled by her husband that decent women have a natural dislike for "these things," but Anna is haunted by unexpressed longings for unnamed fulfillment. Melanie was pregnant with her first child within two months of the wedding, and spent several weeks nauseated and miserable. Nausea, misery, and anxious apprehension were to be the dreaded hallmarks of Melanie's subsequent pregnancies. Emanuel's threatening innuendoes were proving to be eerily true.

Libussa was delighted to learn that she would be a grandmother again (Emilie had already bestowed grandmother status on Libussa), but she suggested to Melanie that a boy would be preferable. Instead, to Melanie's delight, a baby *girl,* Melitta, was born January 19, 1904. She took eagerly to being breast-fed. During this period of Melitta's childhood, the Klein family's prospects were looking up. Arthur's career was advancing steadily. Never one to miss an opportunity, Libussa pressured Melanie and Arthur repeatedly with letters about the poor state of her own finances. Libussa's intrusion into Melanie's marriage was not restricted to money matters, nor was money the only topic about which she reshaped truth to fit her aims.

When Melanie confided to her mother that even though she was fundamentally unhappy with Arthur, she wanted to be pregnant again, Libussa encouraged her to do so. But Libussa also expressed the wish that the next child be more like Emilie and "less nervous" than Melanie herself. Three years after Melitta's birth, on March 2, 1907, Melanie gave birth to her second child, Hans. During her pregnancy with Hans, Melanie was sick, depressed, nauseated, and felt increasingly confined in her marriage. Arthur moved the family to Krappitz, a small town in Upper Silesia, now Poland, to take a new job as director of a paper mill, but Melanie experienced the move as one more burden enforced upon an already dismal existence. Nevertheless, Arthur's new financial security permitted him to quiet Libussa's continual complaints by settling most of her debts. They invited Libussa to live with them, a move Melanie initially relished, but one that gave Libussa more of an opportunity to control Melanie's marriage.

Arthur began traveling frequently, and Melanie suspected that he was often unfaithful to her. Libussa became the not-so-diplomatic link for letters between Melanie and her forever-traveling husband. She even took command of the Klein household, as Melanie became angrier, withdrawn, and depressed. Libussa did everything she could to keep Arthur away from Melanie, even suggesting to both of them that it would be bad for Melanie's health for them to spend time together. She encouraged her daughter to travel to distant places "for her health," and told Arthur any story that was momentarily expedient to keep him away from home as he traveled on business.

> According to Libussa, Arthur blossomed when [Melanie] was away, the children were much better off without her, and her own mother needed the absence in order to achieve serenity. Melanie was a pampered object, not a loved daughter, but treated like a trained and obedient lap dog. (Grosskurth, 1986, p. 58)

Libussa tried to control each person's perception of the others. Melanie's eldest daughter Melitta, for example, was made to understand by grandmother Libussa that Melanie was so emotionally crippled and physically vulnerable that she had to abandon her daughter repeatedly just to survive (Grosskurth, 1986, p. 53). Libussa also made it clear to Melitta that Hans was her preferred grandchild.

Arthur eventually negotiated a new job that required the family to move to Budapest, a compromise move that Melanie could tolerate better than Arthur's original proposal for a move to another small Silesian town bleaker than Krappitz. The move to Budapest had clear benefits for everyone. Arthur's career was advanced by the move. Also, the cosmopolitan atmosphere of Budapest momentarily diminished Melanie's depression, and Libussa could enjoy unbroken security in her living arrangements.

But Budapest also had its inevitable downside. World War I was raging and would quickly separate Melanie both from her husband and her psychoanalyst, as both were called into the military. On July 1, 1914, Melanie gave birth to her third child, Erich, with whom we are already familiar. He became the subject of Melanie's first published case history.

After a relatively brief illness that did not initially appear to be serious, Melanie's mother, Libussa Reizes, died. Libussa had been losing weight and vigor for some time with undiagnosed cancer. Her death was hastened by a bronchial infection that ended her life only two weeks after the diagnosis of cancer.

Melanie was bombarded with devastating losses. She was deprived by the war of her husband and her analyst and had lost forever the mother on whom she had become dependent. Almost simultaneously, she had become a new mother for the third time.

At some point in this period, around 1914, Melanie read Freud's (1900 and 1901) brief essay "On Dreams" and became convinced that she had found the answer to her own personal distress. In addition to the emotional relief that Freudian therapy seemed to promise, psychoanalysis as an intellectual pursuit might provide a substitute way to achieve her long blocked professional interests in a medical career (Grosskurth, 1986, p. 68).

Melanie sought psychoanalytic treatment for her ongoing depression, recently intensified by the death of Libussa, with the eminent Hungarian analyst Sandor Ferenczi (1873–1933). Ferenczi was not just another Budapest analyst. For a long period, Ferenczi

Figure 7.6 A sad-looking Melanie Klein. This photograph was taken around the time Melanie Klein suffered a series of losses and sought psychotherapy for depression with the analyst, Sandor Ferenczi.
(Grosskurth, 1986, opp. p. 148)

was a confidant and close associate of Sigmund Freud. Ferenczi underwent personal analysis with Freud in 1914 and 1916. Sometime around 1914, it was Sandor Ferenczi who first suggested to his patient Melanie Klein that child analysis would profit from her unique skills. Figure 7.6 shows Melanie around the period of her analysis with Ferenezi.

Divorce

By 1916, toward the end of the war, an anti-Semitic revolution had turned the social climate in Budapest against Jews. Arthur Klein had been wounded and permanently injured, and he lost his job. In 1919, Arthur moved to Sweden where he was able to find work, leaving Melanie to care for their three children. Melanie understood that they would never again be together as a couple. For the remainder of his life, Arthur was not able to rise to the heights of success he had experienced prior to the war.

Melanie left Budapest with the children and returned briefly to Austria. By 1921, she moved again, this time to Berlin. The precise date of Melanie and Arthur's divorce is unclear. Melanie claimed 1922 or 1923 as the year in different autobiographical accounts, but Grosskurth (1986, p. 90) makes the case that the divorce could not have been final until 1926.

The divorce marked an energetic beginning for Melanie Klein. She focused her newfound energy on making an impact in the psychoanalytic community and to build a professional life that would sustain her and the children. In subsequent decades, her reputation as a pioneering child analyst and her body of work grew enormously.

The Implications of Klein's Personal Sources

Melanie's experiences with the dominating and intrusive Libussa Reizes surely fueled her anger. The utter detachment of the nearly invisible Moriz Reizes could only facilitate

Libussa's fabrication of the Reizes matriarchy. Melanie's yearning for a competent father was thwarted. Her mother and brother convinced Melanie that she had been an "unexpected" child and the "heaviest burden" to her mother. Like so many theorists we examine in this book, Klein also felt unwanted. Rejection, too, breeds anger.

As an adult, Melanie's experiences with her own children led to the discovery that mothers can be seen as evil, devouring witches, or as trustworthy, comforting companions.

The concept of mother-as-evil-devouring-witch was not entirely unprecedented in her experience and not all that difficult to accept. She understood that the maternal phantasy image created by children was determined in large part by the character of the relationship between mother and child at that time. And so it must be, she reasoned, for all children. There can be little doubt that Melanie applied this reasoning to her own conflicted feelings toward Libussa, and thereby insulated her mother from a great deal of anger. Used in this way, the concepts of phantasy and split objects are both theoretical constructs and personally protective rationalizations.

As a mother herself, Klein was often depressed and distracted, with the apparent result that her children created angry phantasies about her. As she had experienced her own mother, Melanie Klein must have been experienced as intrusive and manipulative by those of her children she employed as psychoanalytic patients. It is small wonder that Klein proposed the fear of being attacked, devoured, or annihilated by mother as the fundamental and universal danger situation among women.

Klein's belief that she had been the unplanned and begrudgingly loved child among her more favored siblings instilled deep curiosity, a motive beyond anger. We will see the same motivation again among other personality theorists who felt unwanted as children and in the search for self-knowledge and healing chose psychology or psychiatry as their life work. For Klein specifically, the path to psychoanalysis was paved with chronic depression and intolerable feelings of unworthiness. She was especially alert to those feelings in others. If anger is the first reaction to feeling unwanted or inferior, the second is curiosity.

Creative thinkers transcend the immediate grievance to question the meaning of what they experience. Such people want to know if others share similar personal pain, and if so, *how* is it similar? Klein found herself focusing on this version of the puzzle: How can relationships be so contradictory? It was clear to her that even the earliest relationships generate pleasure along with pain. They generate chaos and thereby instigate a need for order. Relationships trigger rage, but rage provokes guilt and anxiety. Love and admiration put the infant on the fast track to envy. These contradictory experiences were the ones Melanie Klein knew best and most intimately and chose to universalize.

Klein understood from her own experience the great complexity of object relations. For example, the mother she loved and admired nevertheless dominated and manipulated her. More painful still, Libussa contributed substantially but covertly to the failure of Melanie's marriage. Emanuel Reizes, the much admired but fatally vulnerable brother, evoked taboo feelings in her. Their adult brother–sister relationship is described by Klein's chief biographer as all but overtly incestuous (Grosskurth, 1986, pp. 31 ff.).

A FINAL WORD ON MELANIE KLEIN

Melanie Klein learned from her own relationships that the people to whom one is most attached are also the people who can provoke the most profound anger and the deepest envy. Hatred of one's nearest intimates inevitably leads to guilt. More painful still, when these people are gone, through death or alienation, only the residue of unresolved guilt grounded in the finality of loss remains constant. The raw power of feeling, not reason, is at the heart of the Kleinian worldview. Melanie Klein's emphasis on the irrational is evident in her insistence on chaotic infantile phantasy, aggression, love, and guilt-driven reparation.

D. W. Winnicott Born: 1896 Plymouth, England
Died: 1971 London, England

A COMMONSENSICAL AND CREATIVE CHILD ANALYST

Pediatrician turned child analyst, Donald Woods Winnicott brought common sense and a wry spontaneity to the treatment of children. Compared to such luminaries as Melanie Klein and Anna Freud, D. W. Winnicott was restrained in his rhetoric, pragmatically playful in his clinical style, and fiercely protective of his intellectual independence. Above all other qualities, Winnicott was gifted in the art of communicating with children. He could be playful with youngsters, even ironic, without patronizing them. And he had the knack of helping them feel safe and secure in his presence.

Winnicott, unlike Klein, viewed the child as a collaborator not an antagonist (Phillips, 1988, p. 52). Winnicott positioned himself as a sympathetic witness to a child's distress, acknowledging a child's need for "holding" in both realistic and metaphorical ways. In short, Winnicott was like a good mother to his patients. A measure of the man can be had in three anecdotes. The first provides a glimpse into Winnicott's down-to-earth, use-what-you-got technique with children. The second displays Winnicott's charm, a graceful mix of whimsy and wit. The third provides a close-up view of the flinty side of Winnicott's personal style.

The Squiggle, the Spatula, and the Niffle

When beginning to work with a child, Winnicott often drew a random-appearing line or an elaborate but ambiguous doodle on paper. He then invited a child to "make something" from this squiggle and then encouraged the child to talk about the drawing and what it might mean. Then it was Winnicott's turn. He encouraged the child to create a squiggle, which Winnicott, with his talent for drawing, could turn into a meaningful picture. Winnicott's creations were often better than anything the child could accomplish with squiggles, and he was not reticent about pointing out this fact. Figure 7.7 illustrates Winnicott's use of squiggles with a 12-year-old patient named Patrick.

Winnicott sometimes enjoyed completing the child's squiggle with a wry or comic picture accompanied with humorous comments or even patently absurd, Dr. Seuss-like word play. Squiggle by squiggle, Winnicott permitted the child to tell the story of his or her world without hurry, often disjointedly, always interactively. After several "consultations" with Dr. Winnicott, inhibited children learned to express themselves and to do psychotherapeutic work through play.

The Spatula

Winnicott invented a different but equally creative technique to enable infants to communicate. The waiting room outside his office in the Paddington Green Hospital was often full to bursting with mothers and their infants. One by one, they entered Winnicott's

Figure 7.7 Squiggle drawings of a 12-year-old boy.

Patrick made the elephant in the left frame (1) from a squiggle drawn by Winnicott. The middle frame (3) shows Winnicott's transformation of Patrick's squiggle into what Patrick called "mother holding a baby." Sometime later, Patrick made the unusual picture on the right (11) from Winnicott's squiggle. He described it as person "who slipped into some dog food," and was probably mocking someone, perhaps Winnicott. The bottom corner inset of each frame shows the probable outlines of the starting squiggles, which are more apparent in the originals as variations of line density.

(Winnicott, 1965b, pp. 344, 346).

consulting room to make a rather lengthy walk from the door to the desk and chair where the mother was invited to sit with her infant on her lap. The long walk provided Winnicott with an opportunity to observe the mother's handling of her child and the demeanor of both as they entered for the consultation.

He then invited the mother and her infant to sit together next to a table on which he had placed a shiny, steel tongue depressor called a "spatula." Winnicott instructed the mother and any observers present in precisely how to behave, especially about the necessity to restrict their natural eagerness to prompt the infant.

> . . . I ask the mother to sit opposite me with the angle of the table coming between me and her. She sits down with the baby on her knee. As a routine, I place a right-angled shining tongue-depressor at the edge of the table and invite the mother to place the child in such a way that, if the child should wish to handle the spatula, it is possible. Ordinarily, a mother will understand what I am about, and it is easy for me gradually to describe to her that there is to be a period of time in which she and I will contribute as little as possible to the situation, so that what happens can fairly be put down to the child's account. You can imagine that mothers show by their ability or relative inability to follow this suggestion something of what they are like at home; if they are anxious about infection, or have strong moral feelings against putting things to the mouth, if they are hasty or move impulsively, these characteristics show up. (1941/1992, pp. 52–53)

Eventually, Winnicott's "set situation," as he called it, grew into a process suitable for personality assessment of mother and child. Despite Winnicott's instructions to remain silent and motionless, some mothers did not go along with the stated guidelines. Winnicott observed, for example, mothers who "have a rooted objection to the child's mouthing and handling of objects," and communicated their disgust to their infants in subtle and not so subtle ways. Impulsive-anxious mothers could not restrain their eagerness to reassure and comfort their babies. Such over-eager reassurance often had the paradoxical effect of interfering with the child's spontaneous efforts to cope with the situation. Competitive mothers saw the set situation as a test of intelligence. These mothers intrusively coached and prodded their infants toward what they thought was "success" in grasping the spatula (1941/1992, p. 59).

Based on his observations of infants ranging from 4 to 13 months, Winnicott described three stages. The beginning one, called the period of hesitation, consists of initial stillness and expectancy with little overt action. In the second stage, the infant grasps the spatula and exhibits confidence and satisfaction in taking possession of and exerting control over it. Finally, the infant becomes playful, deliberately dropping the makeshift toy to hear it clang on the floor. Some infants in this third stage even engage the collaboration of an adult to "lose" and "find" the dropped spatula repeatedly. Table 7.2 provides a more detailed summary of a typical child's progress through the three stages.

Winnicott thought that the first stage in Table 7.2, or period of hesitation, was especially significant in revealing infants' typical emotional reactions to unfamiliar situations. For most normal infants, the period of hesitation can be more precisely described as only a moment of expectation. Normally infants, Winnicott observed in thousands of instances, rapidly overcome their initial hesitancy because desire and curiosity grow more intense than anxiety. As self-confidence grows, action replaces indecision. Delight displaces delay. Anxiety evaporates. The prize is seized. Drooling and cooing accompany the spatula

Table 7.2   Behavior of Normal 4- to 13-Month-Old Infants in Winnicott's "Set (Spatula) Situation"

Stage	Infant behavior	Evidence of anxiety
1. Period of hesitation (*Expectation and stillness*)	• Holds body still. Expectant but not rigid. • Touches spatula, hesitantly, warily. • Wide-eyed with expectation, watches adults. • Sometimes withdraws interest and hides face. • Momentary hesitation to summon courage and accept reality of own desire to touch the spatula.	Inhibited. Buries face in mother's lap. Ignores spatula completely or immediately seizes and throws spatula.
2. Confident and collaborative play (*Possession and control*)	• Reaches for spatula decisively. • Excitement and interest mirrored in changes in baby's mouth: inside becomes flabby, saliva flows copiously, tongue looks thick and soft. • Explores spatula with mouth. • Free/flexible body movements linked to the spatula. • Exhibits confidence that he/she possesses the spatula and is in (magical?) control of it. • Plays with spatula, bangs it on table or on nearby metal bowl to make as much noise as possible. • Wants to play at being fed with adult as collaborator, but is upset if adult "spoils" game by really taking spatula into mouth. • Not obviously disappointed that spatula is inedible.	Persistent, prolonged hesitation. Brute force needed to bring spatula close to infant or put it in baby's mouth with resulting distress, crying, colic, or screaming.
3. Riddance and restoration (*Loss and return*)	• Drops spatula as if by mistake. • Pleased when it is retrieved. • Deliberately drops it after restoration. • Enjoys aggressively getting rid of spatula, especially if it makes sound when dropped.	Persistent (compulsive) repetition of riddance and restoration, with no evidence of boredom or waning interest.

(Based on the description in Winnicott, 1941/1992).

as it enters the baby's mouth. Winnicott also observed that anxious infants had difficulty mastering their hesitation and often prolonged their delay indefinitely. In contrast, some anxiously impulsive infants circumvented the period of hesitation altogether and immediately seized the spatula to throw it to the floor.

When Winnicott wrote his first paper describing his deceptively simple observational technique, he was still in the early phases of learning about child psychoanalysis. Melanie Klein's ideas loomed large in Winnicott's training, and he attempted to interpret the symbolic meaning of the spatula for the child. He hypothesized that the spatula signified to the infant a breast, a penis, and even a person or "bits" of a person (1941/1992, p. 61). Fortunately, Winnicott's empirical predilections and good sense eventually prevailed over his early enthusiasm for Kleinian speculations. He could see that the "set situation" was a window on the infant's interpersonal transactions and emotional maturity (1941/1992, pp. 64–65).

The Niffle

Five-year-old Tom was injured while on vacation with his family and evacuated to a distant city to be hospitalized. His mother accompanied him, but eventually left Tom alone in the hospital. Tom found it hard to sleep without what he called his "niffle." His niffle was a square of woven material derived from a wool shawl. In fact, there had been three niffles, but only one of them was Tom's special niffle. He could distinguish his special niffle from the other two even in the dark (Winnicott, 1996a/1996, p. 105). Returned home, Tom's mother tried to ship the special niffle to her son's hospital, but the niffle failed to arrive and was never seen again.

Eventually Tom recovered and rejoined his family, but he seemed not to be the same child. He became oppositional toward his mother, and resisted being dressed and cleaned by her. Tom acted in an annoying way and spoke with a peculiar high-pitched voice. Tom's mother was especially irritated by this voice. When questioned by Winnicott, Tom summed it all up: "But I wish I had this little niffle. It makes me feel . . ."—at which point Tom was at a loss for words. Winnicott understood the strength of Tom's emotional reaction to his loss.

We have all seen children attached to their teddy bears, comforted by soft blankets they drag around with them, and their delight in other cuddly things. Winnicott understood that the teddy bears, blankets, and niffles of this world had the function of bridging the gap between children's dependence on their mother's and their capacity for independence. Winnicott termed such objects **transitional objects.** Tom experienced the disappearance of his niffle as a profound loss of love, security, and trust.

UNCONVENTIONAL PSYCHOANALYSIS: THE PEDIATRIC CONSULTATION MODEL

Winnicott's primary professional training was in pediatrics. Throughout his career, even after years of preparation as a child analyst, Winnicott thought of himself as both a pediatrician and a psychoanalyst. Each professional identity, he believed, informed and enhanced the other (e.g., Winnicott, 1965a, pp. 140–141; Kahr, 1996; Phillips, 1988). He faced obstacles on both sides. As a pediatrician, Winnicott encountered the refusal of his medical colleagues to consider the psychology of physical illness or the relevance of unconscious processes (Winnicott, 1931a/1992, p. 20). As a child analyst, Winnicott was expected to leave pediatric medicine behind. The analyst does not take detailed histories of the patient and patient's family, does not physically examine the patient, nor does the analyst directly observe the child-rearing environment provided by the parents. The child analyst's role does not include brief consultation to provide child-rearing advice to the parents or make focused, often educational, interventions (Winnicott, 1963a/1965a; 1958/1965c). Except for Winnicott, such forays outside the analyst's traditional role were simply not done.

"I am a paediatrician who has swung to psychiatry," Winnicott wrote, "and a psychiatrist who has clung to paediatrics" (1948c/1992, p. 157). He sought nothing less than his own synthesis of two antagonistic traditions. Successful management of this novel, not to say subversive, blending of clinical roles elevated Winnicott to a unique position in medical and psychiatric circles. He became *the* pediatric child analyst (see Jacobs, 1995 for a similar view; and Phillips, 1988, pp. 48 ff.; Winnicott, 1971, "Introduction").

Elements of a Winnicottian Consultation

Much of Winnicott's experience was gained in relatively brief consultations with parents and children, especially during the time of World War II, and frequently in a hospital clinic setting. In these consultations, Winnicott provided a number of services, including diagnosis, advice on child care, and recommendations for placement or specialized treatment. Khan (1975/1992, p. xvii) places the number of children and family members seen by Winnicott in consultation over a period of four decades at an amazing sixty thousand. Winnicott (1948c/1992, p. 158) himself reported that he had personally taken histories from over twenty thousand mothers.

Although Winnicott (1972/1986; Little, 1990) conducted a fair share of the more traditional one-on-one analyses, his pediatric training and personal preferences steered him in the direction of a consultative style characterized by precision focus, rapid tempo, and brief duration. Such encounters, sometimes episodically repeated, might consist of a single "diagnostic-history-taking-recommendation-session" or a series of comparatively leisurely meetings with a child, typically over the span of several weeks or months, but sometimes extending for years (Winnicott, 1957/1965c). Winnicott viewed few of the children for whom he consulted as appropriate candidates for standard psychoanalysis. One size, Winnicott believed, does not fit all: ". . . by and large, analysis is for those who want it, need it, and can take it" (1962a/1965a, p. 169).

Straddling the two worlds of pediatric psychiatric consultation and child psychoanalysis demanded that Winnicott develop a singularly flexible perspective. The real world constraints of distressed children, and the living conditions provided for them by their parents, achieved special significance in Winnicott's thinking. A composite picture of the Winnicott consultative method highlights these techniques and assumptions.

Take a History, Make a Diagnosis

Winnicott believed it was necessary to obtain a complete and chronologically ordered narrative of the child's life. Such history taking included the usual elements of presenting problem, chronology of developmental landmarks, parental descriptions of the child's problem, the child's description of the problem, and sometimes even direct observation of mother and child (or father and child) playing together. But the purpose of taking the history was not the mere gathering of data:

> It was as a practicing paediatrician that I found the therapeutic value of history taking, and discovered the fact that this provides the best opportunity for therapeutics, provided that the history-taking is not done for the purpose of gathering facts. Psycho-analysis for me is a vast extension of history-taking, with therapeutics as a by-product. (Winnicott, 1963a/1965a, pp. 198–199)

Diagnosing the patient's difficulty correctly was a central feature of Winnicott's work. His diagnosis began by taking the patient's history, but continued throughout their work together. Changes in the patient's behavior, alterations to the patient's circumstances, and changes in the quality of the therapeutic relationship signaled Winnicott to alter his diagnosis and sometimes his therapeutic strategy.

Take Charge, Take Notes, Take Your Time

From the vantage point of medical practice, Winnicott was a firm believer in taking charge of the consultation. As both a pediatrician and as a psychodynamic psychotherapist, Winnicott assumed that it was his responsibility to provide a structured setting in which both the child and parents felt safe enough to communicate the meaning they placed on the child's distressing symptoms. The responsibility of the clinician is to be reliable, truthful, calm, and authoritatively knowledgeable (Winnicott, 1961b/1990, p. 235).

Use What Is Available: As Little as Needed, as Simply as Possible

Winnicott was creative in enlisting the aid of the child's parents, teachers, or caseworker to carry out treatment plans in the child's daily environment. Winnicott was sensitive to the need for economy and efficiency in the treatment of childhood disorders, a sensitivity that he carried over into his psychoanalytic practice as well (Winnicott, 1955/1989). Even when working analytically, Winnicott strove to make his interpretations as brief as possible. He usually limited himself to one interpretation per session (1962a/1965a). He did not hesitate to mix standard analytic method with other procedures that met the needs of specific patients. He sometimes intervened directly into the patient's daily life. He aimed to provide more stability and security for those who were fragile and in need of such support (e.g., Little, 1990).

Don't Be Eager to Be Clever. Don't Talk Too Much. Listen.

Winnicott learned a lesson then very unusual in medical education from a teacher of pediatrics—Dr. Thomas Horder—at St. Bartholomew's Hospital. The lesson was to listen to his patients. Horder told Winnicott: "Don't you go in with your wonderful knowledge and apply it all. Just listen. They'll tell you quite a lot of things. You'll learn if you listen" (C. Winnicott, 1983/1991, pp. 188–189). Winnicott took the advice both for his pediatric consultations and, later, for his approach to psychoanalysis. When he was tired, he sometimes found himself talking too much in analytic sessions. At such times, he described himself as having drifted into a "teaching session" rather than "doing psychoanalysis." He even quipped that whenever he found himself using the word *moreover*, he knew he had drifted again (Winnicott, 1962a/1965a, p. 167). As Winnicott put it toward the end of his life,

> If only we can wait, the patient arrives at understanding creatively and with immense joy, and I now enjoy this joy more than I used to enjoy the sense of having been clever. I think I interpret mainly to let the patient know the limits of my understanding. (1968b/1989, p. 219)

Normal Life Is Normally Difficult. Symptoms Are Easier.

Winnicott recognized that even a child's aberrant behavior often had multiple functions. Symptoms can communicate various meanings that are not always abnormal. Bed-wetting, for example, is

> . . . a common enough symptom which almost everyone has to deal with who has to deal with children. If by bed-wetting a child is making effective protest against strict management, sticking up for the rights of the individual, so to speak, then the symptom is not an illness; rather it is a sign that the child still hopes to keep the individuality which has been in some way threatened.
>
> Or take refusal of food—another common symptom. It is absolutely normal for a child to refuse food. I assume that the food you offer is good. The point really is that a child cannot always *feel* the food to be good. A child cannot *always* feel that good food is deserved. (Winnicott, 1964a, p. 127; italics in original; see also 1964c)

Sometimes, Winnicott stated, the best course of action for the child therapist is to do nothing. Waiting for the child's growth and maturity to attenuate the problem is often effective. Active intervention in what appears to be seriously pathological behavior is sometimes not necessary if the parents can provide an adequate and loving environment for the child to master his or her distress.

> A normal child can employ any and all of the devices nature has provided in defence against anxiety and intolerable conflict. The devices employed (in health) are related to the kind of help that is available. Abnormality shows in a *limitation* and *rigidity* of the child's capacity to employ symptoms, and a relative lack of relationship between the symptoms and what can be expected in the way of help. (1964a, p. 126–127; italics in original)

Winnicott repeatedly emphasized that symptoms are often indicators of the healthy child's ability to battle against disease and other adversities. Only when such symptoms are linked to failure of the child's natural defenses can we assume the presence of abnormality.

Why Normal Life Is Difficult: From Illusion to Disillusion

Under the best of circumstances, the developing infant is challenged by a succession of disappointments. Winnicott first pointed to the child's experience of the clash between its inner world of fantasy and the outer world of reality. With varying degrees of disappointment, babies learn that what they want is not always provided. Wishes are frustrated by the facts of reality (1964a, p. 128).

Second, babies learn that destructive urges and thoughts that are frightening sometimes accompany the feeling of excitement (1964a, p. 128). As the infant slowly recognizes and increasingly loves the person who supplies food, care, and affection, its spontaneous urges to devour and use up the good it receives from that person become increasingly troubling. "And, along with this, there comes a feeling that there will be nothing left if everything has been destroyed; and what happens then, should hunger return?" (Winnicott, 1964a, pp. 128–129). Consequently, the baby's eagerness for food disappears. Inhibition can replace the infant's healthy greediness for food. Wise mothers intuitively know that simply "playing for time" is all that is needed to allow the baby to overcome its inhibitions.

Third, the infant quickly discovers a new source of life's difficulties. "Only too soon, added to other troubles are those that belong to the child's recognition that there is also father to be reckoned with" (Winnicott, 1964a, p. 129). Perhaps, the discovery of siblings adds additional fuel to the fire. Jealousy rears its ugly head. The illusion of exclusive possession of mother dissolves into the disillusionment of a shared, sometimes unavailable, love-object.

Fourth, the child's inner world of imaginary friends and foes, fantastic fairies and animals, and magical battles won and lost is an illusion that the child can omnipotently control. With time however, the stresses and strains of controlling this inner world are revealed in all manner of bodily aches, pains, and upsets (Winnicott, 1964a, p. 130). Such aches, pains, and upsets are normal reflections of internal ups, downs, triumphs, and failures. The wise mother and father support the child's struggle to reconcile inner and outer worlds. They might, for example, acknowledge that they, too, could see an imaginary friend. Imaginative play need not be shameful. Setting a place at the table for the friend, or at bedtime even tucking child and companion in for the night strikes some as pandering to the child's eccentricity, but the alternative is to invalidate the child's healthy childishness. Hence, parents who scoff at their child's imaginary world and its creatures are expecting maturity to occur prematurely.

In Winnicott's description of it, life is hard. Early experiences are fraught with difficult things to learn, and often evoke disappointment because disillusionment is unavoidable. Such experiences, however, are normal, and momentary signs of psychological distress are not indications of abnormality. The degree to which a child remains sufficiently able to be playful through all of the adversities and disappointments of early life is a measure of that child's normality.

Commitment to Pediatrics

Winnicott's early papers consisted of pediatric medical advice, admonitions to parents to trust their own abilities and those of their children, and psychological insights about development drawn from Freud (e.g., Winnicott, 1931a/1992, 1931b/1992, 1936/1992, 1944/1992). Winnicott had a wry, homey, avuncular style honed to perfection in a series of radio broadcasts during World War II. That same style, an entertaining and disarming mix of authority, wit, and soothing nurturance, continued to serve him well in print when his broadcasts were turned into papers and books (Winnicott, 1993, especially Chapter 1). He was widely in demand as a speaker throughout his career, and he never failed to provide a humorous and psychologically informed slant on practical pediatric problems and issues.

Winnicott's knowledge and experience as a pediatrician broadened his vision as a child psychiatrist and supported his understanding of child psychology. Pediatric practice taught him the importance of patience in treating children. Most important, Winnicott was realistic and had reasonable expectations for the children he treated:

> The best that can happen is that the person who is being analyzed gradually comes to feel less and less at the mercy of unknown forces both within and without, and more and more able to deal in his or her own peculiar way with the difficulties inherent in human nature, in personal growth, and in the gradual achievement of a mature and constructive relationship to society. (Winnicott, 1945b/1996, p. 12)

Winnicott gradually theorized more and more based on his own clinical experience and insights. He got away from being influenced very much by the theories of others and finally developed an object relations theory that, more often than not, stands traditional ideas on their heads.

EARLY THEORY: THE KLEINIAN INFLUENCE

At the outset of his psychoanalytic career, Winnicott had also assimilated the classic formulations of Freud both from his reading and from his personal analysis with James Strachey (1887–1967), an eminent British analyst and Freud's chief translator. During the analysis, Strachey recommended to Winnicott that he seek out Melanie Klein to learn more about the application of psychoanalysis to children (Winnicott, 1962b/1965a). Winnicott took Strachey's advice and made contact sometime in 1932, about two years before the end of his analysis (Kahr, 1996, p. 58).

Winnicott's View of Melanie Klein

Winnicott found that Klein's work provided important insights about emotional functioning at the very earliest periods of infancy. As we have seen, Klein was extending psychoanalysis to earlier and earlier periods of infancy on an almost daily basis. For a time, Winnicott found this Kleinian direction a congenial and enlightening path to follow. His own observations as a pediatrician had already paved the way for his ready acceptance of the idea that children could be emotionally ill with roots extending well before the Oedipal period of ages five and six.

Winnicott saw Klein as an admirable teacher who could be flexible and attentive to the details of the cases he brought for supervision. He retained Melanie Klein as a clinical supervisor for the better part of six years, from 1935 to 1941 (Kahr, 1996, p. 59). More than 20 years later, Winnicott summarized the significance of his experiences with Melanie Klein:

> Klein was able to make it clear to me from the material my patients presented, how the capacity for concern and to feel guilty is an achievement, and it is this rather than depression that characterizes arrival at the depressive position in the case of the growing baby and child.
>
> Arrival at this stage is associated with ideas of restitution and reparation, and indeed the human individual cannot accept the destructive and aggressive ideas in his or her own nature without the experience of reparation, and for this reason the continued presence of the love object is necessary at this stage since only in this way is there opportunity for reparation.
>
> This is Klein's most important contribution, in my opinion, and I think it ranks with Freud's concept of the Oedipus complex. (1962b/1965a, p. 176)

In a narrative 20 years later, Winnicott alluded to his growing independence from Klein's thinking and from her approach:

> Since those days a great deal has happened, and I do not claim to be able to hand out the Klein view in a way that she herself would approve of. I believe my views began to separate out from hers, and in any case I found she had not included me in as a Kleinian. This did not matter to me because I have never been able to follow anyone else, not even Freud. (1962b/1965a, p. 176)

On December 4, 1935, Winnicott presented his membership paper entitled "The Manic Defence" to the British Psychoanalytic Society. This, his first psychoanalytic paper, was largely an elaboration of one of Melanie Klein's central concepts. Giving such a presentation carried the weight of a commencement ceremony in psychoanalytic circles. It marked the culmination of Winnicott's long preparation to become a qualified psychoanalyst and indicated his acceptance as a full member of the society.

Candidates for membership were required to present original theoretical or clinical ideas, but the wise aspirant understood that the content of the presentation had to fall within specified parameters. Applicants first had to demonstrate that their ideas were derived from or consistent with Sigmund Freud's concepts. A candidate also had to acknowledge intellectual debts to the influential senior analysts in the candidate's area of specialization. There was a demand for originality within the context of a developing tradition of psychoanalytic thought. One's ideas should be original but not too original or too threatening.

The Manic Defense: Inner and Outer Reality

In his original paper on this topic, Winnicott (1935/1992) artfully redefines Klein's manic position to moderate her emphasis on the absolute power of the internal world. He argues that the developmentally normal manic defense against depressive feelings compels the defender to minimize, not maximize, as Klein would have it, the influence of internal object representations.

> Omnipotent fantasies are not so much the inner reality itself as a defence against acceptance of it. One finds in this defence a flight to omnipotent fantasy, and flight from some fantasies to other fantasies, and in this sequence a flight to external reality. This is why I think one cannot compare and contrast fantasy and reality. (Winnicott, 1935/1992, p. 130)

Winnicott was subtly paving the way for a fundamental alteration to Klein's ideas. Recall his argument that life is normally difficult. Winnicott asserted the importance of the difficult realities of life in development. As a direct consequence, he normalized the pathological-sounding—manic and depressive—developmental positions. Winnicott reasoned that manic defenses, for example, are part of ordinary living. They are inherent in the struggles all people make against the daily abrasions and sorrows of life.

> For instance, one is at a music-hall and on the stage come the dancers, trained to liveliness. One can say that here is the primal scene, here is exhibitionism, here is anal control, here is masochistic submission to discipline, here is a defiance of the super-ego. Soon or later one adds: here is LIFE. Might it not be that the main point of the performance is a denial of deadness, a defence against depressive "death inside" ideas, the sexualization being secondary.
>
> What about such things as the wireless [i.e., radio] that is left on interminably? What about living in a town like London with its noise that never ceases, and lights that are never extinguished? Each illustrates the reassurance through reality against death inside, and a use of manic defence that can be normal. (Winnicott, 1935/1992, p. 131)

For Winnicott, inner reality is an equal partner with outer reality, the world of ordinary life. "Life is hard," but that does not mean for Winnicott that strenuous coping with life's difficulties, including the struggle to feel alive in the face of death, is inevitably pathological. Winnicott depathologizes Klein's concept of manic defense by reframing it to encompass coping with life's unavoidable miseries. He elevates the external world to equal status with the inner world as a determinant of emotional development.

Depathologizing the Depressive Position: The Ruth and the Ruthless

In a later paper, Winnicott applied the same strategy to a fuller discussion of the Kleinian depressive position (Winnicott, 1954–1955/1992). He proposed that the Kleinian term *depressive position* was a poorly conceived name and suggested that the term, **stage of concern,** would be more accurate. Winnicott thus took a Kleinian concept that implied abnormality and changed it to indicate a more normal process. Winnicott agreed with Klein that the infant begins its relationship to the external object more or less "pre-ruth," that is, ruthless (pitiless) in attempting to satisfy its needs. With the whimsy of Lewis Carroll, Winnicott points out that the infant gradually passes from the pre-ruth stage to the stage of ruth (capable of pity).

PRIMITIVE PERSONALITY DEVELOPMENT, WINNICOTT STYLE

Despite his disagreement with some of Klein's concepts, Winnicott incorporated many of her ideas about the psychology of the earliest days of life. Winnicott's own observations as a pediatrician suggested that a series of important cognitive and emotional achievements occurred during the first five or six months of life. His observations of babies exploring the spatula had convinced him that infants of five months understood that the object for which they reach is localized in space and separate from themselves. Furthermore, the baby who thrusts the spatula into its mouth is necessarily aware that there is an "inside me." Deliberately dropping the spatula demonstrates that "he knows he can get rid of something when he has got from it what he wants from it" (1945a, p. 148). Parallel to these achievements, the infant of five or six months

> . . . assumes that his mother also has an inside, one that may be rich or poor, good or bad, ordered or muddled. He is therefore starting to be concerned with the mother and her sanity and her moods. In the case of many infants there is a relationship as between whole persons at six months. Now, when a human being feels he is a person related to people, he has already traveled a long way in primitive development. (Winnicott, 1945a, p. 148)

Winnicott concluded that Klein's depressive position involves cognitive and emotional developments that have nothing to do with defensive maneuvers against depression. Winnicott began describing what happens before the stage of concern at five or six months. He eventually determined that the five- or six-month-old child has developed in three areas: personality integration, personalization, and realization.

Personality: From Muddled to Cuddled

Winnicott hypothesized that at the very beginning of life, personality is in a primal state of "unintegration." With absolute literalness, Winnicott meant that in the earliest days of life there is no *person* to embody an integrated personality. There are only biological needs and potentials. "What is there is an armful of anatomy and physiology, and added to this a potential for development into a human personality" (Winnicott, 1968a/1987, p. 89). Unintegrated infants do not comprehend themselves or others as whole people. **Unintegration** has a different significance than the term, **disintegration.** Disintegration lies on an altogether different conceptual dimension—the dimension of psychopathology—rather than occupying the opposite end of the same dimension as unintegration. *Unintegration* is a nonpathological term.

Personality integration begins quickly and spontaneously after birth, and requires two sets of experiences to go forward smoothly. The first is the baby's own internal world of need and drive, which by their infinite repetition become the stabilizing routines of life around which a personality can form. Needs and drives provide reassuring experiences that signal one is alive. As long as mother and other caretakers satisfy the infant's needs reliably, survival is not threatened, and the natural process of integration proceeds unhindered. The inexorable repetition of appetite arousal and satisfaction gradually grows familiar and welcomed.

The second organizing area of experience is the care the infant receives. The baby is handled, bathed, fed, rocked, named, called by name, and cuddled. Each of these repetitive events helps bring order to internal confusion. From these scattered fragments of need, maternal response, cuddling, and predictable care, a gradual synthesis of identity emerges. "Me" and "not-me" begin to have meaning for the infant. Mother can provide physical and a kind of emotional cuddling, or what Winnicott termed **holding.** As Winnicott used the term, holding elevates cuddling to a primary means of communication between infant and mother. Holding the infant securely in both the physical and psychological senses of the term enables the securely held infant to organize its urges, wishes, and fears into predictable experiences.

Personality integration continues to evolve with time, but the feeling of being not quite whole does not frighten the securely held infant:

> "There are long stretches of time in a normal infant's life in which a baby does not mind whether he is many bits or one whole being, or whether he lives in his mother's face or in his own body, provided that from time to time he comes together and feels something" (Winnicott, 1945a, p. 150).

Personalization: From Cleaning to Weaning

Satisfactory **personalization** leads to the feeling that the infant is in his or her own body. *Personalization,* as Winnicott employed the term, is the achievement of a personality completing the process of integration by taking possession of the body in which it finds itself and becoming increasingly comfortable with ownership. As with integration, biological needs and maternal care guide the process of personalization so that the evolving personality has a "place" to reside. Mother's attention to physical care and cleanliness quietly helps the infant reach the understanding that he or she has a body, resides in it, and is sometimes in control of it. In short, the infant achieves a sense of personalization.

Put another way, the infant particularizes its inventory of recognizable physical equipment by personalizing each component. The particular "person" is either self or not-self. This waving digit is *my* finger because I can make it go in my mouth for a good suck, but this digit tickling my tummy is not mine because I can't stop it. This wiggling pink thing that lies just out of reach is *my* toe, but this bigger one that I can reach—and bite— is not mine because I don't feel bitten and because Daddy is doing the yelling.

Schizophrenic and near-psychotic people, who may abruptly feel uncomfortable with their own bodies or develop the delusion that they are not in their bodies, sometimes experience **depersonalization.** A less pathological variation of depersonalization is the belief that something is alarmingly and abruptly different, "not right," or "not real" about my body. An even less serious variation of depersonalization, in fact a common occurrence of childhood, is the creation of imaginary companions. Some children even use an imaginary companion as a magical defense to bypass the anxieties of childhood associated with eating, digestion, retention, and expulsion (Winnicott, 1945a, p. 151). One of the authors of this text, in fact, had a friendly and playful imaginary companion named Mortimer, who accompanied him at mealtime quite often.

Realization: From Dreaming to Scheming

The third major early personality development is learning to take account of external reality. Rather than employ the standard psychoanalytic term, "reality testing," Winnicott chose to call this achievement **realization.** Winnicott explained how he thought such realization could be achieved in the nursing situation. Mother and baby each bring to the nursing situation their own capabilities and needs. The mother brings knowledge, tolerance, and adult judgment. The baby brings absolute dependence, need, and a readiness for hallucinatory gratification. Sights, sounds, smells, and touches experienced with each real feeding teach the baby what it can and cannot conjure up when the real object is not present but real need is exerting itself (1945a, p. 153). Eventually, over substantial periods of time, the mother helps her infant accept and tolerate the limitations of reality, and to enjoy the real satisfactions that such acceptance makes possible.

In the earliest phase of life, objects seem to act according to magical laws. The object exists when desired, approaches when approached, and vanishes when not wanted. Vanishing is a terrifying experience for the infant because it represents annihilation. From this dreamlike world of magic the infant progresses to the real world of planned actions.

The change from dreaming to scheming is paralleled by the nature of the changes in the infant's relationship to the object. Initially, following Klein, Winnicott proposed a "ruthless" stage prior to the stage of concern in which the infant expects mother to tolerate its aggressiveness in play. Without this experience of a tolerant caretaker, the infant can show its ruthlessness only in dissociated states. In later life, ruthlessness can be shown only in states of disintegration marked by abrupt regression to the primitive and magical world of infancy. In short, ruthless relations to objects may reappear in psychotic-level psychopathologies.

"THERE'S NO SUCH THING AS A BABY"

"I once risked the remark, 'There is no such thing as a baby'. . . . A baby cannot exist alone, but is essentially part of a relationship" (Winnicott, 1964a, p. 88; 1969d/1989, p. 253). This instance of vivid expressiveness is a landmark in both object relations theory and in the public presentation of Winnicott's original views. Contrary to orthodox Freudian theory, Winnicott put the focus of child emotional development on what he termed the *nursing couple:* a child in an adaptation-enhancing relationship with a mother.

> "*There is no such thing as a baby.*" I was alarmed to hear myself utter these words and tried to justify myself by pointing out that if you show me a baby you certainly show me also someone caring for the baby, or at least a pram with someone's eyes and ears glued to it. One sees a "nursing couple."
>
> In a quieter way today I would say that before object relationships the state of affairs is this: that the unit is not the individual, the unit is an environment-individual-set-up. By good-enough child care, technique, holding, and general management, the shell becomes gradually taken over and the kernel (which has looked all the time like a human baby to us) can begin to be an individual. (Winnicott, 1952, p. 99)

Winnicott's insistence that babies can be understood psychologically only in relation to their environments, specifically the "ordinary devoted mother," was an important corrective to Melanie Klein's often one-sided emphasis on the infant's instincts.

Holding: Primary Maternal Preoccupation of the Ordinary Devoted Mother

Winnicott hypothesized the existence of a special psychological state called "primary maternal preoccupation." Among its characteristics are:

> It gradually develops and becomes a state of heightened sensitivity during and especially towards the end of pregnancy.
>
> It lasts for a few weeks after the birth of the child.
>
> It is not easily remembered by mothers once they have recovered from it. I would go further and say that the memory mothers have of this state tends to become repressed. (Winnicott, 1956/1992, p. 302)

Winnicott thought that the **primary maternal preoccupation** provides a specific adaptive context for her newborn to flourish and mature. The mother is sensitized to the newborn's state and she can empathically put herself in the infant's place. She comes to know her infant's needs and capabilities as she knows her own. In short, the primary maternal preoccupation results in a close identification of mother with her infant (Winnicott, 1960c/1965a, p. 147).

For their part, infants bring their biological constitution, innate developmental tendencies (conflict-free ego functioning), motility, and drives. Mother's heightened empathy permits the kind of silent communications that enable the infant's "innate equipment" to unfold, helps the infant experience free movement for the first time, and encourages the child to take ownership of its body and sensations (personalization). In short, the mother provides a "good-enough" adaptation to the infant's absolute dependency.

> . . . from these silent communications we can go over to the ways in which the mother makes real just what the baby is ready to look for, so that she gives the baby the idea of what it is that the baby is just ready for. The baby says (wordlessly of course): "I just feel

like . . ." and just then the mother comes along and turns the baby over, or she comes with the feeding apparatus and the baby becomes able to finish the sentence: ". . . a turn-over, a breast, nipple, milk, etc., etc." (Winnicott, 1968a/1987, pp. 100)

Winnicott grouped maternal caretaking practices under the general, and metaphorical, label of **holding.** In its literal sense, the mother holds her infant securely in her arms while feeding, cleaning, and playing with it. This tight and intimate physical closeness provides the initial and most basic level of holding. At a metaphorical level, holding involves a number of interconnected, more emotional communications from mother to child. Holding communicates to the infant that it is alive—"I am seen and I exist"—as the child feels mirrored in the mother's facial expressions and reactions (Winnicott, 1962c/1965a, p. 61). Inherent in these mirroring experiences are the infant's gradual realization that there is another, someone who is *not me,* who reacts to me. Personality integration, as we have seen, gets its impetus from these "holding" communications.

Holding and the Unthinkable Anxieties

Holding provides a safety net for the infant to survive the earliest and most terrifying first fears. Influenced again by Klein, Winnicott described a series of infantile **unthinkable anxieties,** or primordial fears, that date to the earliest days of life. Unlike Klein, Winnicott saw these "anxieties" as normal developmental phases, not as derivatives of the death instinct. More important, unthinkable anxieties are precursors of psychopathology only with the failure of mother's holding functions. Typically, however, the combination of maternal holding and an unthinkable anxiety leads to normal personality integration, personalization, and realization. The unthinkable anxieties are:

- Going to pieces
- Falling forever
- Having no relationship to the body
- Having no orientation
- Complete isolation because there is no means for communication

Winnicott added the last item in the list some years after his initial formulation (1962c/1965a, p. 58; and 1968a/1987, p. 99). Maternal holding is the totality of the mother's loving physical and emotional care that, to extend Winnicott's metaphor, prevents the infant from toppling over the abyss of unthinkable anxiety.

Winnicott pointed out the parallel to the analyst's "holding" interpretations in therapy. The analyst's words sometimes are less significant than the nonverbal and spontaneous message that the analyst and the patient are both alive and continue to be real. For example, Winnicott related the incident of the patient who dug her nails into the back of his hand during an intense moment in therapy.

My interpretation was: "Ow!" This scarcely involved my intellectual equipment at all, and it was quite useful because it came *immediately* (not after a pause for reflection) and because it meant to the patient that my hand was alive, that it was part of me, and that I was there to be used. Or, shall I say, I can be used if I survive. (Winnicott, 1968a/1987, p. 95)

A good-enough mother, in Winnicott's vocabulary, provides encouragement and support for the infant's "going on being" (Winnicott, 1956/1992, p. 303). The mother protects the infant from "impingements." Impingements are any experiences that jeopardize "going on being." They can stem either from the external environment or originate in occasional maternal failures to provide "good-enough" care. Unreliable need satisfaction, prolonged separation, intolerance of infantile neediness and aggression, or an inability to make the infant feel safe are all forms of impingement because they threaten spontaneous and normal developmental progress (Winnicott, 1968a/1987, p. 95). Winnicott's focus in this part of his theory is on maternal actions that enhance healthy personality formation. The infant must feel safe enough to be spontaneous, secure enough to be able to take risks vis-à-vis the difficulties of reality, even to be able to "afford to die" (Winnicott, 1956/1992, p. 304). The good-enough mother makes "normally difficult life" tolerable, manageable, and capable of being mastered:

> . . . without the initial good-enough environmental provision, this self that can afford to die never develops. The feeling of real is absent and if there is not too much chaos the ultimate feeling of futility. The inherent difficulties of life cannot be reached, let alone the satisfactions. If there is not chaos, there appears a false self that hides the true self, that complies with demands, that reacts to stimuli, that rids itself of instinctual experiences by having them, but that is only playing for time. (Winnicott, 1956/1992, pp. 304–305)

Winnicott's concept of the **False Self** seems to have originated from two sources. First, Winnicott had a keen interest in working therapeutically with severely regressed adult patients who were psychotic or near psychotic. Winnicott saw the dependency needs of the infant reemerge in an exaggerated form in a type of personality splitting in his adult schizophrenic and borderline patients. In particular, one patient described to Winnicott how she had felt all her life that she had not been real, and felt as though she had been looking for her true self (1960c/1965a, p. 142). From the patient's point of view, the first two years of her analysis had been conducted between what she called her "caretaker self" and Winnicott. This caretaker self had sought out treatment, protected the patient during the early phases, gradually handed over its role to Winnicott, and hovered nearby to resume caretaking whenever Winnicott failed to "hold" the patient safely.

The second basis of Winnicott's concept of the False Self was his experience with apparently cheerful children who visited his hospital clinic. Nevertheless, these children were, at the same time, presented for psychological treatment by their parents, often with maternally described problems of depression, listlessness, anger, and apathy. The marked discrepancy between direct observation and maternal report caught Winnicott's attention:

> It took me years to realise that these children were entertaining me as they felt they must also entertain their mothers, to deal with the mother's depressed mood. They dealt with or prevented my depression or what might be boredom in the clinic; while waiting for me they drew lovely coloured pictures or even wrote poems to add to my collection. I have no doubt that I was taken in by many such cases before I eventually realised that the children were ill and were showing me a false self organisation and that at home the mother had to deal with the other side of this, namely the child's inability to keep up counteracting the mother's mood all of the twenty-four hours. Indeed the mother had to endure the hatred belonging to the child's sense of having been exploited and of having lost identity. (Winnicott, 1969c/ 1989, pp. 247–248)

Winnicott discovered that some of these entertaining children had developed their False Selves not only to cheer up their depressed mothers, but also to fend off her hatred of them (1969c/1989, p. 249; 1948d/1992, pp. 91–92). We return to the concept of the mother's unconscious hatred of her child shortly. It is of some benefit at present, however, simply to note that Winnicott links the three concepts of maternal depression, hatred, and the False Self.

Origins of the False Self: The "Not-Good-Enough" Mother

Winnicott eventually hypothesized that the primary purpose of the False Self is defense of the True Self. It is like a mask or a shell that others perceive as real, and can totally conceal the True Self.

The origins of the False Self are in failures of the mother–infant relationship during the phase prior to the integration of the infant's personality (1960c/1965a, p. 145). The "not-good-enough" mother fails to hold her infant securely and reliably. She may permit external reality to "impinge" on the infant's world before the infant is ready. Or she herself may intrusively impinge on that world in a way that the infant cannot tolerate. Such "errors" of maternal care fail the infant in two ways. First, the "not-good-enough mother" does not validate or help make real her infant's spontaneous gestures. She does not mirror in her responses her empathic understanding of the infant's needs or wonderment at her infant's successes. In Winnicott's terms,

> The mother who is not-good-enough is not able to implement the infant's omnipotence, and so she repeatedly fails to meet the infant gesture; instead she substitutes her own gesture which is to be given sense by the compliance of the infant. This compliance on the part of the infant is the earliest stage of the False Self, and belongs to the mother's inability to sense her infant's needs. (1960c/1965a, p. 145)

The second failure of the not-good-enough mother is that she does not help her infant link its spontaneous gestures with observable effects in reality, including her own reactions. Thus the infant is unable to reach the stage of giving up a sense of omnipotence in an imagined or hallucinatory world in favor of dealing with the real world. In extreme cases, where the maternal failures occur from the very beginning of existence, the infant's survival may be in question. More often, however, the not-good-enough mother is not "bad enough" to disrupt infant survival totally. Instead, the infant complies with the maternal environment by creating the mask of the False Self:

> Through this False Self the infant builds up a false set of relationships, and by means of introjections even attains a show of being real, so that the child may grow to be just like mother, nurse, aunt, brother, or whoever at the time dominates the scene. The False Self has one positive and very important function: to hide the True Self, which it does by compliance with environmental demands. (Winnicott, (1960c/1965a, pp. 146–147)

Ultimately, the chief defensive efforts of the False Self are directed to protecting the True Self from exploitation, manipulation, and unjust demands. The most "unthinkable" anxiety of all is thus fended off: annihilation of the True Self.

Levels of Organization of the False Self

Winnicott distinguished five different "levels" of False Self personality organization. They are organized along a spectrum of severity extending from gross maladaptation to ordinary healthy adaptation. Table 7.3 summarizes the levels of False Self organization.

Extremely Maladaptive: Mask

In this instance the False Self is organized as real and observers see and relate only to this real False Self as it takes over relationships in work, love, play, and friendships. The True Self is completely masked. With time, however, the False Self shows signs of failure because life continues to present situations in which a whole person is required.

Table 7.3 Winnicott's Levels of False Self Organization

False self	True self	Consequence
Extremely Maladaptive: *Mask*	Completely hidden beneath an utterly compliant False Self.	False Self fails when life demands a whole spontaneous person.
Moderately Maladaptive: *Caretaker*	Permitted secret life, regarded as potential self.	Preservation of individual in abnormal environments. Minimal spontaneity, aliveness.
Minimally Adaptive: *Defender*	Waits for safe/desirable conditions to reveal True Self.	Possible suicide if hope for safe conditions is lost; little aliveness.
Moderately Adaptive: *Imitator*	Identifies with caring or productive objects as models.	Successful life, but without realness, aliveness.
Adaptive: *Facilitator*	Normal socialization for politeness and self-restraint.	Humility, modesty, social success.

Moderately Maladaptive: Caretaker

The False Self defends the True Self and even serves as its protector or caretaker. The True Self is dimly acknowledged as a potential self and is permitted, in Winnicott's terms, to have a "secret life." Winnicott's constant search of the healthy silver lining exhibited itself most clearly when he wrote of the moderately pathological False Self that it is: ". . . the clearest example of clinical illness as an organization with a positive aim, the preservation of the individual in spite of abnormal environmental conditions" (1960c/1965a, p. 143).

Minimally Adaptive: Defender

The False Self can serve as a defender against exploitation of the True Self, biding its time until proper conditions for the emergence of the True Self can be found. If safe conditions are not encountered, the False Self may defend the True Self literally to death: suicide. When there is no hope left that the True Self can emerge safely, then the False Self can mobilize the psychological equivalent of a scorched earth policy. The False Self attempts or carries out suicide with the paradoxical intention of preventing the annihilation of the True Self by accomplishing the absolute destruction of the entire self.

Moderately Adaptive: Imitator

A False Self is organized within the personality, but is modeled on caring, productive, and protective people. Although the person feels as though he or she is sometimes not really real, or continually searching for him- or herself, the False Self comprised of benign identifications can negotiate a very successful life.

Adaptive: Facilitator

The False Self is organized normally as ordinary elements of socialization, including polite behavior, personal restraint, false-but-charming modesty, and deliberate control over personal wishes and urges. Without this benign False Self, a kind of socially sophisticated alter ego, the unvarnished True Self would not achieve a place in society as successful or as satisfying.

The True Self: Aliveness

The **True Self,** in Winnicott's view, is real, spontaneous, and creative. It originates in the "aliveness" of the body tissues and functions, especially the beating of the heart and the regularity of breathing (Winnicott, 1960c/1965a, p. 148). At the beginning, the True Self is linked to the primary process thinking of the unconscious and is therefore not responsive to external reality (see the discussion of primary process thinking in Chapter 3). At core, True Self is a synonym for the "experience of aliveness."

Initially little more than sensory motor aliveness, the True Self grows more complex and develops its own links to reality. At first, reality is understood as a projection of the inner world. Somewhat later, reality is actually "real" in the sense of having an objective, outside-the-self, existence. Finally, the strengthened True Self becomes able to tolerate two kinds of momentary breaks in personal continuity. First, physical trauma such as brief separations from mother or physical illness do not have the devastating effect after the emergence of the True Self that they would have had prior to it. Second, normal False Self experiences, such as being taught to say "thank you" when the child hardly feels thankful, are taken in stride as part of ordinary socialization without the integrity of the True Self. In this sense, everyone develops a normal social mask or False Self which functions to provide superficial compliance in social contexts where conformity is routinely required (Winnicott, 1964d/1986, p. 67). Functioning in this way, the False Self is a social compromise.

An intermediate level of functioning of the False Self that lies between healthy compromise and pathological defense is to be found between dreaming and reality. People who develop a compliant self, a self capable of manipulating symbols and language can use their skills to play roles deliberately, entertainingly, and convincingly in the world of drama. The False Self becomes a sublimation of the True Self rather than a defender. However, when the split between the True and False Selves is large, the person is impoverished in the use of symbols, language, and cultural skills.

The greatest danger of the successful False Self is that it will be too successful. By hiding the True Self, the False Self may bury its potentialities so deep that they are no longer accessible, no longer constitute the core of the person's "going on being." A "too successful" False Self ironically may result in the very obliteration of the True Self that it was originally created to prevent.

Transitional Objects and Transitional Phenomena

A transitional object, in Winnicott's sense, is anything—even a part of the child's own body, such as a fist or thumb—to which the child relates (Winnicott, 1959/1989, p. 53). It is, in Winnicott's phrase, the child's "first not-me possession." Early on, the infant's own tightly balled fist in the mouth is explored with tongue and lips in pretty much the same way as the breast or bottle are explored and comprehended. Later in development, external objects—rattles, stuffed toys, and the like—will become transitional objects with which the infant, guided by the sensitive assistance of the attuned mother, establishes a relationship.

At first, when the infant's needs are aroused, it provides its own objects on demand (the fist or thumb in the mouth). Sometimes the infant's crying and other signs of distress or excitement prompt the mother to provide the nipple or bottle. From the child's point of view, the very desire to have something actually causes the satisfaction of that desire. To the infant it appears that the subjective wish is sufficient to create the gratification. The infant thus has a sense of magical omnipotence. On some occasions, the infant will "conjure" up an image of what it wants, and because the sensitive mother is attuned and can read her child's signals of curiosity or distress, she provides in a seemingly magical way the exact object desired: a teddy bear, rattle, blanket, or the like. Winnicott calls this seemingly magical satisfaction of a wish the "moment of illusion."

> The mother, at the beginning, by an almost 100-per-cent adaptation affords the infant the opportunity for the *illusion* that her breast is part of the infant. It is, as it were, under the baby's magical control. The same can be said in terms of infant care in general, in the quiet times between excitements. Omnipotence is nearly a fact of experience. The mother's eventual task is gradually to disillusion the infant, but she has no hope of success unless at first she has been able to give sufficient opportunity for the illusion.
>
> In another language, the breast is created by the infant over and over again out of the infant's capacity to love or (one can say) out of need. A subjective phenomenon develops in the baby, which we call the mother's breast. The mother places the actual breast just where the infant is ready to create, and at the right moment. (Winnicott, 1971, pp. 12–13)

Besides the breast, other "objects," such as a teddy bear or a favorite blanket, are dimly recognized by the infant as not belonging to the infant's body ("not me"). However, they are not necessarily fully comprehended as belonging to the outside world or to another person either (Winnicott, 1971, p. 2). Such objects are *transitional* in the senses of:

- *Place:* bridging inner and outer
- *Agency:* bridging hallucinatory omnipotence and dependency on a real external agent
- *Separateness:* bridging not-me and me

What is important for Winnicott is not the object itself, but the process of transition between subjective hallucination and objective reality testing. These objects are not completely magical nor are they completely real. They are transitional.

> I have introduced the terms "transitional object" and "transitional phenomena" for designation of the intermediate area of experience, between the thumb and the teddy bear, between the oral erotism [*sic*] and true object relationship, between primary creative activity and projection of what has already been introjected, between primary unawareness of indebtedness and the acknowledgement of indebtedness (Say: ta! [i.e., "thanks"]). (Winnicott, 1951/1992, p. 230)

Thus, for Winnicott, transitional objects and phenomena are fundamentally intermediate between reality and illusion, landmarks on the road to full acceptance of the real. However, there are "rules of ownership" over the transitional object that the infant carefully exercises:

- The infant assumes rights over the object, and we agree to this assumption. Nevertheless, some abrogation of omnipotence is a feature from the start.
- The object is affectionately cuddled as well as excitedly loved and mutilated.
- It must never change, unless changed by the infant.
- It must survive instinctual loving, and also hating, and, if it be a feature, pure aggression.
- Yet it must seem to the infant to give warmth, or to move, or to have texture, or to do something that seems to show it has vitality or reality of its own.
- It comes from without from our point of view, but not so from the point of view of the baby. Neither does it come from within; it is not an hallucination.
- Its fate is to be gradually allowed to be decathected, so that in the course of years it becomes not so much forgotten as relegated to limbo. By this I mean that in health the

transitional object does not "go inside" nor does the feeling about it necessarily undergo repression. It is not forgotten and it is not mourned. It loses meaning. . . . (Winnicott, 1951/1992, p. 233)

Winnicott assumed, that at least for some infants in some circumstances, the transitional object served as a symbol for a part-object. That is, a piece of cherished blanket might symbolize the nurturing breast for some infants; for others it may symbolize feces (1951/1992, p. 236). Yet the fundamental purpose remains the same: Transitional objects are the infant's first tools in negotiating the gap between the illusion of magical creation of desired objects and the disillusion that such objects have their own existence.

The infant eventually learns to distinguish between "me" and "not-me," between "inner" and "outer," and between illusion and reality. Reality in the form of external frustration and obstacles makes itself known. And the mother herself will become a real object with whom the infant establishes a mutual relationship. Out of this relationship will come important psychological understandings about trust in self, trust in others, and how to relate to people.

Transitional phenomena are not restricted to infancy. Even as adults the task of relating inner to outer reality continues to make its demands felt. Is there anyone, for example, who does not have photographs of loved ones in his or her wallet? How many of us treasure some "keepsake" possession given to us by a distant loved one? Special letter or poem? A baseball card signed by Cal Ripken or a Tiger Woods golf ball?

SEVERE PSYCHOPATHOLOGY AND FAILURES OF ADAPTATION

Winnicott (1966b/1996; 1967/1996), late in his career, extended his model of maternal holding and infantile adaptation to childhood autism and schizophrenia. He hypothesized that these catastrophic disorders of childhood were failures in the adaptive context provided by "not-good-enough" mothering. Following the general outlines of a theory advanced by Bruno Bettelheim (1967) in his well-known book, *The Empty Fortress,* Winnicott insisted that the psychotic emotional and intellectual manifestations of autism and schizophrenia were not evidence of a disease in the medical sense (Winnicott, 1969b/1989, p. 246n). Bettelheim's psychological formulation and claims of treatment efficacy were themselves controversial in their time and have grown increasingly suspect (Sutton, 1996, pp. 10, 304, and especially 424–427). In his own description of these disorders, Winnicott did nothing to make a purely psychological model less controversial:

> The illness is a disturbance of emotional development and a disturbance that reaches back so far that in some respects at least the child is defective intellectually. In some respects the child may show evidence of brilliance.
>
> I am hoping that what follows may strengthen the argument that the problem in autism is fundamentally one of emotional development and that autism is not a disease. It might be asked, what did I call these cases before the word autism turned up? The answer is that I thought of these cases, and I still think of them, under the heading "infant or childhood schizophrenia." (Winnicott, 1966b/1996, p. 200)

Winnicott here condenses the two syndromes of schizophrenia and autism into one family of adaptive failures. By itself, this one theoretical maneuver puts Winnicott at odds with more contemporary thinking about these disorders (e.g., APA, 1994, pp. 75, 77, 273–285). Beyond the classification issues, however, Winnicott's hypothesized etiology for these disorders emphasizes failures in emotional attachment at the cost of dismissing biological causes. Most contemporary thinkers regard childhood-onset schizophrenia and childhood autism as neurological, probably neurochemical, disorders of the brain linked to a modest degree of genetic predisposition (e.g., Andreasen, 1984; Andreasen and Munich, 1995; Heinrichs, 1993; Torrey, Bowler, Taylor, and Gottesman, 1994).

EXPLORING DEEPER QUESTIONS

Near the end of his life, Winnicott turned his attention toward paradoxical aspects of living and dying. The concepts of survival, creation, and annihilation had renewed fascination for the aging pediatrician. Always the master of puns and paradoxes, Winnicott now grew increasingly philosophical. His thinking became more abstract and drawn toward the philosophical implications of psychoanalytic concepts. In this frame of mind, Winnicott introduced a distinction between *using* and *relating to* an object. The distinction embodied his last concerns in a formulation that elevated psychological paradox into metaphysical existentialism. The theme of survival was placed squarely at the center of the circle of creation, destruction, and recreation—the universal cycle of birth, death, and renewal.

The Cycle of Aliveness: Using an Object

Winnicott's formulation of transitional objects and phenomena already had laid the foundations for the recognition of the significance of paradox in object relations:

> I should like to put in a reminder here that the essential feature in the concept of transitional objects and phenomena . . . is the *paradox, and the acceptance of the paradox:* the baby creates the object, but the object was there waiting to be created and to become a cathected object. I tried to draw attention to this aspect of transitional phenomena by claiming that in the rules of the game we all know that we will never challenge the baby to elicit an answer to the question: did you create that or did you find it? (Winnicott, 1968b/1989, p. 221)

What Winnicott had accomplished in formulating the concept of transitional phenomena was to diffuse the usual psychoanalytic focus. Instead of the traditional understanding of the external world as interesting only to the degree that it is a projection of the internal world, Winnicott studied the external world on its own terms. Transitional phenomena are the bridge between inner and outer worlds. To exist at all, they require an interaction between subjective and objective reality. Transitional objects are paradoxically both projections and discoveries. Part illusion, part perception, transitional phenomena belong to the middle ground between unreal and real. They are projections sent into the objective world by an infant who creates them in the subjective world; but projections are, by definition, projected onto something. That suitable something is always also an accessible something. It is a something that happens to be available at exactly the moment the baby is ready to create. In this metaphysical sense, then, the baby repeatedly creates and recreates its image and experience of the breast as love-object (Winnicott, 1951/1992, p. 238).

Winnicott now argued that a baby progresses from relating to using the love-object. The transition between relating and using presupposes destroying the object in fantasy. The specific sequence follows this logic: In the first phase, **relating to the object** requires that the infant advance from magical understanding of the object's existence as a projection under omnipotent control to realistic comprehension of the object as a real, independent, objectively existing entity. Mother becomes a person. At that point, following

Melanie Klein's hypotheses, the baby's innate destructiveness meets an obstacle it had never before encountered. Real objects *survive* fantasies of destruction.

Indeed, the most significant developmental advance in distinguishing between fantasy and reality comes from this very stubborn refusal of real objects to be obliterated by wishing. "Aha!" says the infant, "total destruction is not total destruction" for objects that really exist and continue to exist. The attempt at destruction—and most important, the failure of the attempt—is the trigger for the infant to place the object outside subjective reality and squarely into the world (Winnicott, 1968b/1989, p. 223). Winnicott summarized the paradoxical logic of his hypothesis in this way:

> This is a position that can be arrived at by the individual in early stages of emotional growth only through the actual survival of cathected objects that are at the same time in process of becoming destroyed because real, becoming real because destroyed. . . . (1968b/1989, p. 223)

and

> *There is no anger* in the destruction of the object to which I am referring, though there could be said to be joy at the object's survival. From this moment, or arising out of this phase, the object *is in fantasy always* being destroyed. This quality of "always being destroyed" makes the reality of the surviving object felt as such, strengthens the feeling tone, and contributes to object-constancy. The object can now be used. (1968b/1989, p. 226; italics in original)

A main effect of Winnicott's hypothesis was to shift the emphasis in psychoanalysis away from the theory that the infant's understanding of external reality is based primarily on its own projections. In accord with his long-standing emphasis on the facilitating environment, Winnicott's **using the object** concept split the focus equally between internal and external reality.

But what, precisely, does it mean to say that the infant progresses from relating to using the object? Winnicott argued that the infant's realization that the object survives its attacks—without retaliating—enables the baby not only to believe in its external existence, but also to trust the object. An object that survives the most intense destruction the infant can muster and that does not strike back is a "good-enough" mother whose reliability and trustworthiness are usable—helpful—in learning how to cope with life.

Reactions to Winnicott's Later Ideas

Late in his career, when Winnicott first presented these ideas to a meeting of the New York Psychoanalytic Society, they were not welcomed with enthusiasm. For one thing, Winnicott was understood to be equating object *relating to* subjective reality and object *using* to external reality. In Winnicott's scheme, the ability to use the object in the external world was the more sophisticated phase of emotional development. Thus some psychoanalysts perceived Winnicott's concepts as diminishing the importance of the internal world.

Even more disagreements with Winnicott's ideas related to therapeutic technique. Winnicott implied that psychoanalytic treatment was not exclusively a matter of interpretation. "Holding" and "good-enough" therapeutic parenting that enable the patient to "use" the analyst as a collaborator in the search for maturity were at least equally important. Implications such as these were given a hostile reception by the New York analytic community in 1968, and Winnicott, who was already in declining health, suffered a heart attack the day after his presentation that prevented his return to London for more than a month.

PERSONAL SOURCES FROM WINNICOTT'S CHILDHOOD

The majority of Winnicott's biographers agree that he had a strong identification with his mother and an empathic bond with all mothers (especially C. Winnicott, 1978, 1989; see also Goldman, 1993; pp. 47ff.; Jacobs, 1995; Kahr, 1996; Phillips, 1988). Winnicott's own childhood has been described by his second wife Clare as "too good to be true" in the particular sense that Donald was loved, knew he was loved, and thought of himself as lovable (1989, p. 9). He grew up fundamentally happy and secure. To judge from the substance of the theory he left behind, his vision of humanity was certainly individualized by his experiences—even, necessarily, idiosyncratic ones—but it does not appear to have been driven by psychopathology.

Mothered by Many

Donald Winnicott was born in 1896 in Plymouth, England. He was the youngest of three children and the only son born to John Frederick Winnicott and Elizabeth Martha Woods. The Winnicott family belonged to the Wesleyan Methodist Church (Phillips, 1988, p. 23). Clare Winnicott (1983/1991, p. 184) pointed out that the Methodist tradition is one of strong independence, self-reliance, and nonconformity, characteristics that certainly describe Winnicott himself.

Winnicott recalled as an adult that: ". . . in a sense I was an only child with multiple mothers and with a father extremely preoccupied in my younger years with town as well as business matters" (quoted in C. Winnicott, 1989, p. 8). Clare Winnicott recalled that Donald had thought he did not have enough contact with his own father: "So he says, 'I was left too much to all my mothers. Thank goodness I was sent away at thirteen!'" (1983/1991, p. 185). In fact, the members of the Winnicottian household in which Donald grew up were almost exclusively female. Two older sisters, his mother, a nanny, sometimes a governess for his sisters Violet and Kathleen, his Aunt Delia and another aunt, a cook, and several parlor maids populated the Winnicott household, and all "doted" on Donald (Kahr, 1996, p. 5). All the Winnicott females loved children and all of them, well into their elderly years, maintained the knack of playing and talking with youngsters (C. Winnicott, 1983/1991).

This unusual childhood situation of being a little boy enveloped by mothers and virtually deprived of a father seems to have left an indelible impression on Winnicott's psychological development, resulting in a powerful female identification. First of all, because young Donald received so much affection from so many women with whom he interacted in a reliable manner, he felt protected, safe, and secure, and this emotional stability provided him with a solid foundation for a sturdy, productive, and creative adult life. Secondly, the preponderance of women in Winnicott's childhood stimulated his fascination with the inner world of the female (Kahr, 1996, p. 6).

Donald's Mother: Elizabeth Woods

Donald's actual mother is a biographically indistinct figure about whom few details are known. There is some evidence that Elizabeth Woods struggled with episodes of depression throughout her life and that Donald's distant father expected his son to care for and cheer up his mother (Kahr, 1996, p. 10). Clare Winnicott quoted her husband's observation that ". . . it is probably true that in the early years [my father] left me too much to all my mothers. Things never quite righted themselves" (C. Winnicott, 1989, p. 8; see also

C. Winnicott, 1978, p. 24). At the age of 67, Winnicott wrote a poem about his mother entitled "The Tree," which he sent to his brother-in-law with a note acknowledging the hurt he felt in composing it:

> Mother below is weeping
> weeping
> weeping
> Thus I knew her
> Once, stretched out in her lap
> As now on dead tree
> I learned to make her smile
> to stem her tears
> to undo her guilt
> to cure her inward death
> To enliven her was my living.
>
> (quoted in Phillips, 1988, p. 29)

The tree referred to in the title was the special place to which the young Donald retreated to do his homework. Phillips (1988) points out that there is religious symbolism in Winnicott's choice of metaphor:

> In the poem Winnicott clearly identifies himself with Christ, and the Tree of the title is the Cross. . . . The chilling image of himself 'stretched out on her lap/As now on dead tree,' by omitting the definite article suggests that once it is dead it is no tree in particular, as anonymous as dead wood. (Phillips, 1988, pp. 29–30)

His poetry alludes to the role that the young Winnicott played in combating his mother's "deadness." The poem also poignantly expresses themes that occupied Winnicott professionally for his entire career:

- feeling fully alive versus feeling dead numbness,
- maternal depression experienced by the child as aggression,
- the needs of the child for maternal holding,
- the protective role of a superficially compliantly cheerful False Self, and
- the False Self as caretaker.

Winnicott understood that at the beginning and at the end of his life that he had made ". . . a living out of keeping his mother alive" (Phillips, 1988, p. 30).

Donald's Father: Sir John Frederick Winnicott

John Frederick Winnicott was a successful merchant, specializing in women's corsets. He was a religious man with a strong faith who attended church regularly. John Winnicott was twice elected mayor of the town of Plymouth and was knighted in 1924 (Phillips, 1988, p. 23). "Sir Frederick," as he became known, was active in town politics and the business community, and even became Manager of the Plymouth Hospital and Chairman of the Plymouth Chamber of Commerce. Despite these accomplishments, John Frederick felt insecure throughout his adult life about his lack of formal education (Phillips, 1988, p. 23). His aspirations to become a member of Parliament foundered on lifelong learning difficulties, which John Frederick believed had robbed him of the confidence to enter the world of politics outside his local community (Kahr, 1996, p. 4).

For all of his success in local business and politics, John Frederick was a distant parental figure and not a good or close father to Donald. His relationship with Donald was formal rather than intimate, and sometimes surprisingly authoritarian. Indeed, John Frederick could be so insensitive to his son's needs that Donald risked the humiliation of his father's rejection for even minor infractions of proper decorum. On one occasion, 12-year-old Donald used the word *drat* as an expletive during the noonday meal:

> . . . my father looked pained as only he could look, blamed my mother for not seeing to it that I had decent friends, and from that moment he prepared himself to send me away to boarding school, which he did when I was thirteen. (quoted in C. Winnicott, 1989, p. 8)

There is some indication that the nature of John Frederick's rejection and teasing was linked to issues of Donald's masculinity or sexuality. When Donald was only three, he ascended the grassy slope in the garden armed with his child-sized croquet mallet prepared to exact revenge and make a piece of personal family history. In the tall grass, he bashed flat the nose of a wax doll called "Rosie" that belonged to his sisters. Rosie was a particular source of irritation to young Donald because his father often teased him with the doll by parodying a popular song of the day in a voice intended to taunt:

> Rosie said to Donald
> I love you
> Donald said to Rosie
> I don't believe you do.
>
> (quoted in C. Winnicott, 1989, p. 7)

Winnicott (1989, p. 7) says that he "knew the doll had to be altered for the worse, and much of my life has been founded on the undoubted fact that I actually did this deed, not merely wish it and planned it." Ironically, his father relieved some of his son's guilt by heating the wax of the doll's head with a series of matches and remolding it into a more or less recognizable face.

> This early demonstration of the restitutive and reparative act certainly made an impression on me, and perhaps made me able to accept the fact that I myself, dear innocent child, had actually become violent directly with a doll, but indirectly with my good-tempered father who was just then entering my conscious life. (Winnicott, quoted in C. Winnicott, 1989, p. 8)

Winnicott clearly and defensively presents the memory of his father as an admirable, even-tempered, helpful man for whom he felt only admiration and love. Yet it was the father who provoked humiliation by repeated teasing of his son.

Implications of Winnicott's Childhood

At least three inferences can be drawn from the sample of episodes we have reviewed from the early life of D. W. Winnicott. First, compared to most of the theorists we examine in this book, Winnicott had a happy, secure, healthy childhood in a warm and loving family. For this reason, Winnicott's vision of personality development emphasizes spontaneous collaboration between children and their parents rather than the conflicts that are enacted between them.

Second, Winnicott's freedom from childhood insecurity was not immunity from other forms of maternal rejection. Although the definitive biography has yet to be written, the existing body of life history data make it clear that Winnicott's sensitivity to failures in maternal "holding" stemmed from his own experiences trying to vitalize an emotionally numbed and depressed mother.

Third, Winnicott's theory mentions the contributions of fathers to the development of their children—but just barely. Fathers are not in the Winnicottian spotlight just as

Sir Frederick was not in his son's daily life. Winnicott's affinity for and empathy with mothers, his tight focus on mothering, rather than parenting, and his own impressive talents "mothering" and "holding" his patients clearly had their origins in his family traditions of interest in children and in his personal experiences with "multiple mothers."

A FINAL WORD ON D. W. WINNICOTT

D. W. Winnicott followed a line of independent thinking as he blended approaches from pediatric medical practice and psychoanalysis. More than the other object relations theorists, he was a careful observer of the actual behavior of infants and children. Like Anna Freud (Chapter 6), he adjusted his behavior so as to strengthen the relationships between his young clients and himself. He also emphasized the healthy aspects of behaviors that Melanie Klein and other theorists might have dismissed as simply pathological.

Heinz Kohut   Born: 1913   Vienna, Austria
Died: 1981   Chicago, Illinois

BEYOND THE EGO: PSYCHOANALYTIC SELF-THEORY

Heinz Kohut found the need to extend psychoanalytic theory beyond the ego concept to be capable of conceptualizing the reasons for a patient's narcissistic vulnerability. Such narcissistically disturbed individuals seemed not to be suffering from castration anxiety or from conflicted id strivings in the classical sense; they seemed to be fixated at a stage in development where fear of the loss of the love-object prevails (Kohut, 1971, p. 20).

In the psychoanalytic relationship, such patients form a unique kind of transference to the analyst. An **idealizing transference** develops in some patients, who behave toward their therapists as though they were the all-good, all-powerful parent who is still part of the self. Such patients are projecting onto their therapist their idealized images of the good love-object as though they were still searching and yearning for fusion with it. A possible explanatory hypothesis is that such patients suffered severe trauma in a stage of early development when the love-object had not yet been entirely distinguished from self:

> Adolescents and adults who have suffered such traumas are forever attempting to achieve a union with the idealized object. In view of the insufficient idealization of their superego, their narcissistic equilibrium is safeguarded only through the interest, the responses, and the approval of present-day (i.e., currently active) replicas of the traumatically lost self-object (Kohut, 1971, p. 55).

Idealizing transferences may occur in a variety of forms, ranging from most archaic and primitive to most mature, depending on the point in development at which narcissistic injury took place. The key point is that such a narcissistically injured person was unable to form internalized capacities for self-control, for self-judgment, and for the maintenance of self-esteem as an independent entity.

A second kind of narcissistically disturbed patient forms a different kind of **mirroring transference** relationship with the analyst. In this form, the patient is regressing to an even earlier stage of development during which **absolute narcissism** prevails.

> The mirror transference . . . constitute[s] the therapeutic revival of that aspect of a developmental phase (roughly corresponding to the condition which Freud referred to as the "purified pleasure ego") in which the child attempts to save the originally all-embracing

narcissism by concentrating perfection and power upon the self—here called the grandiose self—and by turning away disdainfully from an outside to which all imperfections have been assigned. (Kohut, 1971, p. 106)

In the mirror transference, the roots of pathology go further back in development to the period before any recognition of the external love-object (mother) was formed. The grandiose self is formed by internalizing "all good" and externalizing "all bad" experiences. Good (pleasure) is part of me; bad (pain) belongs out there. This process of assimilating "good" and expelling "bad" is thus a form of splitting in its most fundamental and autistic form.

In the *idealizing transference,* the experience of the mother's help in satisfying tension needs revolves around the mechanism: "You are perfect, but I am part of you" (Kohut, 1971, p. 27). By contrast, the more archaic *mirror transference* involves the mechanism: "I am perfect" in order to avoid any experience of "the bad" as part of self. In the idealizing transference, the therapist becomes the perfected mother-self image; in the mirroring transference, the therapist functions as a reflector of the archaic self-perfection of the patient. From the patient's viewpoint in a mirroring transference, the therapist is a looking glass in which can be seen displayed the patient's own grandiose, exhibitionistic self.

Origins of the Self

The idealizing and mirroring transference relationships that emerged in psychoanalysis with narcissistically wounded patients served as an important clue to the processes of development. Kohut began to understand that such patients used the therapist as a **Selfobject** rather than seeing the therapist as an independent human being.

> Selfobjects are objects [people] which we experience as part of our self; the expected control over them is therefore closer to the concept of the control which a grown-up expects to have over his own body and mind than to the concept of control which he expects to have over others. (Kohut & Wolff, 1978, p. 414)

Like the mirroring and idealizing transferences observed in the treatment of patients with wounded selves, Kohut envisioned normal development as a process of interaction between the growing infant and his or her mirroring and idealizing Selfobjects. The mother serves as a **mirroring Selfobject** when she is able to confirm and admire the child's sense of strength, health, greatness, and specialness. The key ingredient, of course, is the mother's capacity to be attuned emphatically to her child's needs for such personal confirmation and admiration.

Mother also serves as an **idealizing Selfobject** somewhat later in development when she encourages and permits the child to merge with her own strength and calmness as a powerful and caring adult. From the child's point of view, the idealizing Selfobject is a model of perfection, power, and soothingness—experienced in part as a component of self.

Unlike the classical psychoanalytic model, Kohut's theory of development pictures the mother's relationship with her child not in terms of drive satisfactions but in terms of emphatic, warm, loving responsiveness to the whole child. As a consequence, the child will experience self as a joyful, competent, and valuable person, or as a rejected, depleted, empty self. When the Selfobject–child relationship is seriously deficient, as with a latently psychotic mother, the child is as unable to survive psychologically in a loveless relationship as he or she would be unable physically to survive in an oxygenless environment. Human warmth, responsiveness, and empathy are the oxygen, the crucial survival elements in the development of a self that is neither grandiosely isolated from reality nor delusionally idealizing of magical love-objects (Kohut, 1977, pp. 75–76).

The essence of the healthy . . . [parental relationship] for the growing self of the child is a mature, cohesive parental self that is in tune with the changing needs of the child. It can, with a glow of shared joy, mirror the child's grandiose display one minute, yet, perhaps a minute later, should the child become anxious and overstimulated by its exhibitionism, it will curb the display by adopting a realistic attitude *vis-à-vis* the child's limitations. Such optimal frustrations of the child's need to be mirrored and to merge into an idealized selfobject, hand in hand with optimal gratifications, generate the appropriate growth-facilitating matrix for the self. (Kohut & Wolff, 1978, p. 417)

Structure of the Bipolar Nuclear Self

Kohut hypothesized that an adequate relationship with a healthy Selfobject results in the formation of a **bipolar nuclear self** that has three components:

1. **Nuclear ambitions,** which are the child's learned strivings for power and success mirrored admiringly by the Selfobject;

2. **Nuclear ideals,** which are the idealized goals and images derived from the child's recognition of the satisfying and soothing power modeled by the Selfobject; and

3. **Basic talents and skills,** which lie metaphorically between the two poles of ambitions and ideals and which form a kind of metaphorical "tension arc" of psychological activity as the person is "driven" by ambitions and "led" by ideals in the pursuit of life goals using what talent and skills he or she possesses (Kohut, 1977, p. 188).

The nuclear ambitions are formed early in life, at or around the second or third year, whereas the nuclear ideals are incorporated into the self as a second pole around the ages of four or five years (Kohut, 1977, p. 179). Kohut envisioned the nuclear self as a bipolar entity, with the ambitions and ideals anchoring opposite poles. The central process in the formation of these two poles, as we have seen, is the relationship with empathic Selfobjects. The nuclear self, however, is not simply a direct copy of the Selfobjects. It is an assimilation of some aspects of their personality characteristics, but the main features of the Selfobject are depersonalized and generalized in a process Kohut calls "transmuting internalization."

Transmuting internalization is a kind of psychological digestion by which the usable and good features of the Selfobject are incorporated into the child's self in a pattern that is unique to that child. Mild frustrations and failures in empathy by the Selfobjects encourage the child to see them as "only human." Such occasional failures in empathy on the part of the Selfobjects permit the child to build his or her own self-structures without the need to incorporate the total personality of others.

Unlike Freud's emphasis on drive conflict, Kohut's emphasis is clearly on person-to-person interactions. Kohut suggests that one way to conceptualize the difference between classical psychoanalysis and his own self-psychology is to contrast the traditions of "Guilty Man" and "Tragic Man."

Guilty Man is the concept of persons as always struggling toward the satisfaction of their drives. They are pictured in classical psychoanalysis as living under the domination of the pleasure principle, striving endlessly to reconcile inner conflict. They are frequently blocked from their goal of tension reduction by their own inadequacies or those of the people who raised them.

Tragic Man, by contrast, is Kohut's picture of people struggling to fulfill the aims of their nuclear selves. That is to say, Tragic Man is attempting to express the pattern of his or her very being, the pattern of the ambitions and ideals that comprise the self-expressive goals of a human life (1977, p. 133). Where Guilty Man is driven, Tragic Man yearns.

An Illustration: Reinterpretation of the Oedipus Complex

As an example of the differences between Kohut's self-psychology and classical psycho-analysis, consider Kohut's interpretation of the child's experiences during the phallic phase of development.

In classical theory, this central development-instinctual conflict is the source of a variety of weaknesses and unresolved guilt in the area of identity. Kohut, on the other hand, prefers to view the Oedipus conflict as the source of potential strengths. Without a firm sense of self, a cohesive and continuous realization of "who I am," an Oedipus conflict cannot take place (1977, p. 227). "Unless the child sees himself as a delimited, abiding, independent center of initiative, he is unable to experience the object-instinctual desires that lead to the conflicts and secondary adaptations of the Oedipal period" (1977, p. 227).

With the focus on the positive aspects of the Oedipal period, Kohut suggested that the typical Oedipal desires are experienced by the child as assertive-possessive, affec-tionate-sexual urges to possess the opposite-sexed parent, combined with assertive, self-confident, competitive feelings toward the same-sexed parent. Parents will typically react to both sets of feelings with different, contradictory feelings of their own. On the one hand, they will become counteraggressive toward the child's aggression, and on the other they will "react with pride and joy to the child's developmental achievement, to his vigor and assertiveness" (1977, p. 230).

When parents are able to respond in both ways to the child's Oedipal feelings—neither overdoing the aggression nor exaggerating the joy and pride in assertiveness—they promote the child's mental health and capacity for self-confidence. "If the little boy, for example, feels that his father looks upon him proudly as a chip off the old block and allows him to merge with him and with his adult greatness, then his Oedipal phase will be a decisive step in self-consolidation and self-pattern-firming . . ." (Kohut, 1977, p. 234).

> What, in other words, is the Oedipus complex of the child who has entered the Oedipal phase with a firmly cohesive self and who is surrounded by parents who themselves have healthy cohesive and continuous selves? It is my impression . . . that the normal child's Oedipal experiences . . . contain, from the beginning and persisting throughout, an admixture of deep joy that, while unrelated to the content of the Oedipus complex in the traditional sense, is of the utmost developmental significance within the framework of the psychology of the self. (Kohut, 1977, pp. 235–236)

Parents who themselves are cohesive personalities will pass along their joy in living to their child. Kohut, in essence, asks whether the Oedipus complex is not more joyful, less conflicted, less violent, and less wounding to self-esteem than classical theory would have it (Kohut, 1977, p. 246). Could it be, he asks, that the classical version of the Oedipus complex exists only in the case of the child whose parents are themselves narcissistically wounded?

When Selfobjects Fail: The Injured Self

Psychological disorder from the perspective of Kohut's theory is no longer viewed in terms of the ego's failures to balance reality, id wishes, and superego judgments. Abnormal psychological functioning is pictured in Kohut's theory as the result of defects in the formation of a cohesive self. Such defects represent developmental insults to normal narcissism. When the insult or injury is sufficiently intense, characteristic pathological distortions are introduced into the infant's developing self. Kohut has described five such distortions that correspond to five different kinds of Selfobject failure (Kohut & Wolff, 1978):

1. The **understimulated self** that develops in the child whose Selfobjects are seriously unattuned to his or her self-needs for mirroring and idealizing. The self loses vitality, and in later life, the mirrorless and ideal-less self experiences itself as deadened, empty, and numbed. Such people may turn to momentary and risky ways of experiencing "aliveness" in the abuse of drugs and alcohol, sexual adventurism, or compulsive gambling. But all such artificial "self-stimulants" can provide only fleeting experiences of an alive self, and even those flashes of aliveness may be experienced as alien intrusions from the outside world. The person's self even has a quality of alien, depersonalized existence.

2. The **fragmenting self** is formed in the child whose Selfobjects have inflicted some definite narcissistic injury on the child at a particularly vulnerable moment. The child's self-esteem is overtaxed in the face of humiliation that proves permanently damaging. As a result, the person experiences self as fragmented, uncoordinated, and lacking balance and cohesion. Hypochondriacal complaints of vague pains and chronic but undefinable illness may characterize the person's daily life. At base, the person experiences self as sickened, weakened, and at the mercy of life.

3. The **overstimulated self** develops in the child who is exposed to Selfobjects who inappropriately stimulate either the child's ambitions or ideals. If the grandiose ambitions pole of the self is stimulated intensely, the result is a self that attempts to avoid situations where the person may become the center of attention. Archaic "greatness fantasies" stimulated by the Selfobjects arouse much anxiety in adulthood and push the person to hide the self from scrutiny. If, on the other hand, the ideals pole of the self was inappropriately responded to by the Selfobjects, the result is a persistent need to merge with idealized people and share in their greatness. But such a need to merge with them can also be experienced as threatening because one loses one's self in a fusion with another.

4. The **overburdened self** is embodied in the child whose Selfobjects did not provide opportunities for the child to merge with their strength and calmness. The overburdened self that develops lacks an ability to soothe itself, and the person experiences the world as a threatening, dangerous, inimical place. Any stimulation is overwhelming and fearful, and there is no place to turn for comfort.

Kohut moved away from a drive model of psychological functioning toward a more interpersonal and phenomenological viewpoint. In fact, Kohut argued in his last and posthumously published book that the curative ingredient in psychoanalytic treatment is the analyst's ability to teach the patient how to look for and use healthy Selfobjects. The essence of the psychoanalytic cure resides in a patient's newly acquired ability to identify and seek out appropriate Selfobjects—both mirroring and idealizable—and to be sustained by them (Kohut, 1984, p. 77).

A FINAL WORD ON HEINZ KOHUT

Heinz Kohut's self-theory is the attempt to view personality development and the various ways in which it can go wrong in the light of the person's own evaluation of his or her success or failure in mastering the obstacles of life. The narcissistically injured patient, with whom Kohut primarily deals, evidences the kind of deficits and misinterpretations of reality that only make sense if a narcissistically damaged nuclear-self is postulated beyond the three agencies of the ego, id, and superego. Kohut perhaps summarized his own contribution best when he explained the goal of psychoanalytic therapy with the narcissistically wounded personality:

> The successful end of the analysis of narcissistic personality disorders has been reached,
> when, after a proper termination phase has established itself and has been worked through,

the analysand's formerly enfeebled or fragmented nuclear-self—his nuclear ambitions and ideals in cooperation with certain groups of talents and skills—has become sufficiently strengthened and consolidated to be able to function as a more or less self-propelling, self-directed, self-sustaining unit which provides a central purpose to his personality and gives a sense of meaning to his life. (Kohut, 1977, pp. 138–139)

Kohut wished to preserve the essence of psychoanalysis; but there is little doubt that he also moved psychoanalysis toward the humanistic position of such theorists as Abraham Maslow and Carl Rogers (Chapter 13) to whom integration and personal purposiveness are the criteria of personality health.

EVALUATING OBJECT RELATIONS THEORY

Indebted as they were to classical psychoanalysis, Klein, Winnicott, and Kohut, each in their own way, advanced psychoanalysis from a drive theory to an interpersonal, transactional, and highly developmental model of personality. But intellectual debts are still debts. Like the parent theory from which these object-relations models emerged, each of them shares the strengths and weaknesses of psychodynamic formulations.

Refutability of Object Relations Theory

It is ironic that the great strength of object relations theory—a concern with the developmental consequences of intimate relationships—is also its greatest scientific weakness. Because the major focus of each theorist in this chapter was the unconscious dynamics rather than the observable interpersonal transactions of relationships, most of Klein's, Winnicott's, and Kohut's hypotheses are untestable. What presumably transpires in the mind of the baby as it interacts with its mother is largely inferential.

Some inferences are more reasonable than others, but reasonableness is not equivalent to refutability. Klein's formulations appear on close examination to be wanting both in the consistency of their logic and in the vast distance between her inferences and the observations on which they are presumably based. Winnicott's proposals, influenced by Klein, lie closer to pragmatic common sense. Unfortunately, however, with the exception of the concept of the transitional object, Winnicott's hypotheses are also inferences about unconscious dynamics that are far from the possibility of empirical test. Kohut's formulations, more philosophical than his colleagues, are nevertheless similarly speculative.

What can we conclude? In some respects, object relations theory represents no improvement in refutability relative to classical psychoanalysis. Indeed in some ways—including reliance on the death instinct, emphasis on innate aggression, reliance on paradoxical formulations—object relations theory represents a regression.

Human Agency in Object Relations Theory

If we ranked the three theorists from the least-active to the most-active conception of agency, the order would be: Klein, Kohut, and Winnicott. Klein's formulation preserves substantial elements of the classical drive theory and its reliance on a reactive model of the nervous system. Kleinian babies are tense infants who reactively discharge their drives onto available objects. Kohut's model clearly pictures humans as active constructors of their social reality, but his aim, necessarily, was a clinical one that emphasized the aberrant functioning of wounded people reacting to significant others who inflict their wounds. Winnicott, by far, is the theorist who most completely comprehends people from the earliest days of their lives as collaborative constructors of social reality. Winnicott's concepts of the infant's progress from omnipotent magical thinking to object relating and on toward using the object by constructing it, destroying it, and happily rediscovering it surviving in reality are active agent concepts. They are even interactive concepts of human agency.

The Idiographic Emphasis of Object Relations Theory

Shared with orthodox psychoanalysis is the goal of understanding the individual. Personality development, and the ways in which it can go wrong, are strictly "one person at a time" phenomena for object relations theorists. It could hardly be otherwise for any theory with psychodynamic aspirations. A goal, however, is also to generate clinical data that will eventually lead to nomothetic laws or rules of predictable behavior.

SUMMARY

Object relations theory advanced Freud's orthodox model in two ways. First, a more ambitiously developmental perspective based on direct clinical work with children was introduced into psychoanalysis. Second, Freud's passing references to the ego's propensity to retain the character of its lost objects were expanded substantially. Intimate relations, rather than drive gratification, became both the medium and the message of psychoanalysis. Unlike the neo-Freudians, whom we consider in later chapters, the object relations theorists wanted to preserve as much of orthodox psychoanalysis as they could.

Melanie Klein

Beginning with the observations of her own children, Melanie Klein's earliest formulations were more or less overly enthusiastic educational applications of classical theory. She initially presented her formulations as "psychoanalytic educational upbringing" designed to be a kind of prophylaxis of the child's mind. In a number of other ways, Klein took Freud at his word, and then extended the words beyond anything Freud intended. She soon pushed psychoanalytic understanding backwards in time to the earliest days of life, where eventually she found a fully functioning ego, superego, and a remarkably active aggressive drive. She credited even the youngest children with an active unconsciously imaginative capacity, called "phantasy." Phantasy images are real to the infant, as real as the people from whom they are derived and on whom they will eventually be projected. Klein's work is sometimes seen as a feminist corrective to Freud's male-dominated theory. In contrast to Freud's emphasis on the importance of the penis for both genders, Klein placed the female breast, the child's first love and most enduring love-object, at the center of her psychological world.

Klein's conception of the infant pictures an inherently aggressive, sadistic, and opportunistic creature who becomes frightened by its own aggression. To protect itself from the retaliation it imagines its love-objects might enact, the infant splits objects into good and bad. The worried infant anticipates persecution from its bad objects and idealizes its good ones for protection.

With time, Klein moderated the role of aggression in her theory, supplementing it with formulations of anxiety, guilt, envy, and reparation. The infant was now understood as envying the good object (breast) because of its bountiful goodness. Phantasies of destroying the good object not only evoke anxiety but also provoke guilt feelings. The need to repair the love-object emerges and the infant omnipotently believes that it can accomplish this magical feat.

These various landmarks in the infant's progress toward conceptualizing the mother as a real person were called "positions" by Klein to emphasize that they are ongoing, lifelong processes. The first developmental position was called the *paranoid position* because the central anxiety is the infant's fear of its own annihilation. By a convoluted twist of logic, Klein argued that the infant fears that the destroyed object may reconstitute itself inside the infant and reinitiate its persecution. At a later moment in development, anxiety or concern for the welfare of the object becomes dominant. When the infant comprehends that the mother-as-a-person is in jeopardy from its own rage, the *depressive position* is entered. Now the baby's central concern is to protect the good object from its own attacks and those mounted against the mother by internalized bad objects. To supplement the reparative defensive strategy, the ego may temporarily adopt what Klein called the *manic position*. This developmental phase is marked by the need to take omnipotent control over the object, dominating it by exerting the power of life and death over it, and protecting it from its own sadistic impulses.

Although Klein originally proposed *splitting* as an elementary and primitive infantile defense against the recognition that good and bad object are one, she elaborated the concept into a series of complex developmental maneuvers. *Splitting* eventually referred to object division (good and bad), ego defensive splitting or repressive dissociation, object relations splitting (love and hate), and even splitting of enduring personality structures such as the id and superego. A supplementary and related defense is *projective identification,* whereby the infant identifies with the split-off good object and distances itself from the split-off bad object. But the target of the projection, mother, may find that the infant behaves in ways that subtly coerce her behavior into conformity with the infant's projection. Projective identification can thus be a kind of self-fulfilling prophecy by which the projector manipulates the projectee to comply with the wish embodied in the projection.

Klein's model of infant development relies on major inferences about the infant's mind. It strikes many observers that Klein's specific deductions tell us less about the infant's mind than they do about what was on Klein's mind. To the extent that this is true, they are Klein's own projections.

D. W. Winnicott

Trained as a pediatrician, Donald Woods Winnicott brought to psychoanalysis a pragmatic sensibility rooted in common sense. He had a gift for communicating with children and often could employ the simplest of games as diagnostic assessments. The squiggle game and his observations of babies mouthing a shiny tongue depressor (the "spatula") were part of Winnicott's consultative approach to child psychiatry.

He transferred that same flexible, spontaneous attitude to his psychoanalytic clinical work and to his theoretical formulations. Influenced by Melanie Klein, Winnicott was nevertheless adamant in trying to maintain his intellectual and creative independence. He understood infants as collaborators rather than as sadistic aggressors. While he found value in Klein's developmental "positions," he made every effort to depathologize them by focusing on the achievements of the infant in coping with its interpersonal world. Life is normally difficult, Winnicott argued, and most babies momentarily display some forms of behavior that appears pathological. But on closer examination, coupled with a willingness to tolerate momentarily eccentric or disruptive behavior, adults soon discover that most children can cope with life's real difficulties if their mothers can provide sufficiently secure and comforting *holding.*

The basic developmental tasks for the infant whose mother provides the physical and metaphorical holding that facilitates development are threefold: integration, personalization, and realization. *Integration* refers to the organization of personality facilitated by the mother's attention to satisfying her infant's needs reliably. Unintegration, the Winnicottian opposite of integration, is a primordially natural phase of development that the infant does not find distressing. *Personalization* is Winnicott's term for the infant's achievement of linking inner and outer reality by recognizing the boundaries of its own physical body. By this he meant that the baby "personalizes"—takes possession of—its body with help from mother's ministrations so that "this is my finger" begins to have real meaning. Finally, *realization* was Winnicott's term for the baby's acceptance of external reality as real, as objective and as enduring contrasted with the inner world of fantasy. Here the mother helps her child achieve "disillusionment": the understanding that illusion, however satisfying, is simply not shared reality.

Winnicott suggested that the *"good-enough mother"* provides enough security to permit her child to master its own aggression, come to grips with life's real difficulties, and develop a spontaneous, authentic self that he termed the *True Self.* By contrast, "not good-enough" mothering, exhibited, for example, by the depressed, psychiatrically ill, or neglectful mother, promotes the development of a protective masklike self, called the *False Self.* Children can develop differing levels of False Self protection that vary in degree of maladaptiveness. At the extremely maladaptive end of the continuum is the False Self, which functions to conceal completely the spontaneous True Self in an effort to protect it from manipulation in social contact. At the opposite end of the spectrum, most children develop a kind of socially cooperative False Self that serves to facilitate social success rather than to wall off the True Self. Between these extremes, children find healthy and not-so-healthy ways of protecting their inner lives from "impingement" and potential betrayal. But it was Winnicott's belief that the more protectively powerful the False Self grew, the less "alive," spontaneous, and playful could the True Self feel.

As part of her skilled and empathic "holding," the good-enough mother provides just those things that the baby needs at just those moments when the baby is ready for them. In Winnicott's famous phrase, "There's no such thing as a baby," babies are best understood as an integral part of the "nursing couple."

Winnicott envisioned the mother–child relationship as a collaboration of two very unequal partners. The mother's task is to "shrink down" to baby size to understand her infant's needs because the baby cannot expand to adult size to tell her what they might be. The good-enough mother provides sufficient holding for the baby to master its most primitive fears, the unthinkable anxieties:

- Going to pieces,
- Falling forever,
- Having no relationship to the body,
- Having no orientation, and
- Complete isolation because there is no means for communication.

Along the way, the infant learns the difference between those parts of self and mother that belong to "me" and those that are "not-me." Once this division between inner and outer reality is achieved, the infant can tolerate increased separation from its love-objects. To bridge the separation, *a transitional object,* the infant's first "not-me" possession will be "created" in collaboration with the mother. A bit of soft blanket, a stuffed toy, even a handkerchief or piece of clothing ("the niffle"), can serve the role of transitional object. It is baby's choice in cooperation with a mother who facilitates and supports the choice.

Toward the end of his life, when personal survival was at issue, Winnicott created one final developmental distinction between relating to and using an object. On the basis of a dream evoked by reading Jung's autobiography, Winnicott came to the insight that the infant has to fantasize destroying its love object to discover that the object in reality nevertheless survives. This infantile discovery permits the infant not only to relate to the object in a dependent way, but also to trust sufficiently in the reliability and durability of the object to *use* the object to facilitate its own growth toward independence. As Winnicott pointed out, the progression from relating to using involves creation by destruction.

Heinz Kohut

Heinz Kohut proposed a psychoanalytic self-theory in which the classical tripartite division of the mind is not considered adequate to the task of accounting for the development of a person's ambitions and ideals. Beginning his work with narcissistically wounded patients, Kohut argued that classical drive theory excludes from its account of normal development some important interpersonal interactions responsible for the emergence of empathic understanding, self-esteem, and healthy adaptation to life.

The nuclear-self, in Kohut's formulation, is structured around the bipolar anchor points of ambition and ideals. Between these poles lies a tensions arc of psychological activities representing the forces that drive the individual to attain his or her goals. Classical psychoanalytic theory regards humans as struggling under the domination of the pleasure principle to reduce the tension of their instincts. A picture of a person as *Guilty Man* emerges from such a viewpoint, whereas Kohut's self-formulation portrays *a Tragic Man* conception of personality, whereby persons are interpreted as struggling to fulfill the aims of the ambitions and ideals contained in the bipolar nuclear-self.

In all, ego psychology has greatly expanded the confines of classical theory. No longer is a human being an "assembly of minds" or a battlefield on whose terrain the battalions of the mind erect obstacles, conduct assaults, and sustain defeats. No longer is psychoanalytic psychology restricted to study of unhealthy personalities. The whole span of life, from birth through adulthood, and the whole range of possible adaptations, from inhibited and fearful withdrawals to psychotic and fragmented separations from reality to masterful and efficacious coping, are accepted as suitable areas for a general psychoanalytic psychology to explore.

Taken as a loosely related group of ideas, object relations theories share the strengths and weaknesses of their parent model, classical psychoanalysis. They rely on untestable, irrefutable inferences about the infantile mind. The three theorists in this chapter represent advances over orthodox psychoanalysis in conceptualizing humans as active agents, but ranked on their conceptualizations from least active to most active, the list puts Klein at the bottom, Kohut in the middle, and Winnicott at the top rank. Idiographically focused on the individual case, objects relations theorists intend to generate universal or nomothetic, law-like principles, but they have not done so thus far.

FOR FURTHER READING

Scope and History of Object Relations Theories

A thorough and readable overview of the history and variety of object relations theories is given by Frank Summers in his *Object Relations Theories and Psychopathology* (New York: Academic Press, 1994). Judith M. Hughes provides a comparison of the lives and works of Klein, Winnicott, and Fairbairn in her *Reshaping the Psychoanalytic Domain* (Berkeley, CA: University of California Press, 1989). Jay R. Greenberg and Stephen A. Mitchell survey the details, philosophy, and metapsychology of a wide range of object relations theories in their *Object Relations in Psychoanalytic Theory* (Cambridge, MA: Harvard University Press, 1983). Roy Schafer's edited volume, *The Contemporary Kleinians of London* (New York: International Universities Press, 1997) fulfills the aims of its title.

Melanie Klein

The most detailed and compelling biography of Klein is Phyllis Grosskurth's psychologically insightful and monumental *Melanie Klein: Her World and Her Work* (Cambridge, MA: Harvard University Press, 1989). Klein never wrote a simple overview of her fully developed theory, but two of her books taken together provide a good introduction. The first is Klein's *Envy and Gratitude: The Writings of Melanie Klein* (Vol. III, pp. 176–235; New York: The Free Press, 1975). The second is Klein's *The Psycho-Analysis of*

Children: The Writings of Melanie Klein (Vol. II; New York: The Free Press, 1975). Julia Segal's *Melanie Klein* (London: Sage Publications, 1992) gives a sympathetic overview of Klein's life and work.

D. W. Winnicott

The best introduction to Winnicott's own writings consists of the papers collected into D. W. Winnicott's *The Maturational Processes and the Facilitating Environment* (Madison, CT: International Universities Press, 1965). Winnicott's *Playing and Reality* (Harmondsworth, Great Britain: Penguin, 1971; a variety of paperback editions available) is easy reading and a worthwhile supplement to Winnicott's professional papers.

Heinz Kohut

Heinz Kohut's chief publications include *The Analysis of the Self* (New York: International Universities Press, 1971), which presents the concept of the narcissistic personality; and *The Restoration of the Self* (New York: International Universities Press, 1977), which more comprehensively elaborates his theory of the self, treatment for the narcissistic disorders, and his speculations on the flaws in classical psychoanalytic theory. Kohut's final statement in which he answers his critics has been posthumously published as *How Does Analysis Cure?* (Chicago: University of Chicago Press, 1984) and contains some important clarifications of his position.

GLOSSARY

Melanie Klein

Anal frustration: During toilet training, the mother partially frustrates the child's anal impulses. This experience prompts the child to devalue the frustrating love-object.

Bad objects: Objects that are frustrating, unfulfilling, or painful and often experienced as persecuting and attacking.

Depressive position: The prevailing melancholy or depressive feeling that is derived from the fear of losing the good object by destruction or mutilation.

Devaluation: Belittling the worth and importance of internalized objects. Contempt replaces love. Such devaluation enables the ego to effect partial detachment from the love-object.

Envy: An angry feeling that another person possesses and enjoys something desirable. The infant develops feelings of envy when the mother's breast is begrudging, depriving him or her of ample milk, care, and love.

Femininity phase: A phase in which infants of both genders actively identify with and envy the mother they seek to possess.

Good objects: Objects that are gratifying, satisfying, or pleasurable. Such objects are idealized in phantasy.

Greed: An impetuous and insatiable craving that exceeds what the loved object can give and what the greedy person actually needs. The greedy person is never satisfied by any amount of goodness.

Idealization: The infantile ego's attitude of "strongly exalting the object" and what it provides. The good breast is idealized as a protection against the persecution of the bad breast. Klein also added that idealization serves to diminish envy of the good object.

Infantile sadism: An actively aggressive stance toward love-objects. In their imagination, children attack the object, rob it of everything it contains, and devour it.

Jealousy: An attitude that occurs when a person feels that love is in danger of being taken away by a rival.

Object relations: In Freud's theories objects were considered aims of id drives; later theorists defined object relations as the person's actual relationships with and subjective views of "objects" (mostly people) beyond the subjective world of the self.

Paranoic position: The fear of one's own annihilation, fear that one's own ego is at risk of attack.

Paranoid-schizoid position: Dysfunctions of empathy, love, and hate in relating to objects and to the self may be found in schizoid personality phenomena. The infant "splits" its relationships with the object into love and hate—love for the good and hate for the bad object.

Part-object: A part of a person, often the mother's breast, that itself becomes an object with which the infant or child relates

Phantasy: For Klein, the infant's unconscious world of the "unreal real." The child's phantasy world, which may not correspond to external reality, is nonetheless the child's reality.

Reparation/restitution: A desire to protect the object or person that was once mutilated or annihilated in sadistic phantasies. It is guilt-driven reparation. Destructive impulses in the unconscious mind mingle side by side with spontaneous feelings of love and empathy for others in the conscious mind.

Splitting: Originally used by Klein to indicate the separation of good and bad objects in the child's phantasy. Subsequently, Klein elaborated to include *structural splits* in the child's id, ego, and self.

Splitting the ego: The split that occurs when good feelings arise from internalized satisfying objects, but anxiety arises from internalized fragmented and poisonous bad objects.

Splitting the id: Unmanageable, terrifying, persecutory objects, derived from the phantasy transformations of the mother and father, are "relegated to the deeper layers of the unconscious." The horrific images are dissociated into the deeper unconscious.

Splitting the object: The splitting of the object perceived to be the source of the threat into good and bad images.

Splitting the self/projective identification: Identification with external objects. The infant projects self-content into the object and takes it back by identification.

Whole object: An object seen as having both good and bad qualities and having its own continuing existence.

D. W. Winnicott

Depersonalization: The feeling of being mildly or extremely uncomfortable with one's body. A person might develop the delusion that he or she is not "in" his or her body. In a milder variation, there can be the belief that something is alarmingly different, "not right," or "not real" about one's own body.

Disintegration: A frightening unintegrated state caused by developmental failure. This state is often associated with psychotic-level psychopathology.

False Self: A sense of self in which the feeling of being real is absent. The False Self masks and hides the True Self. The True Self does not feel secure enough to surface and display its facets spontaneously. The False Self may serve as *caretaker, defender, imitator,* or *facilitator* of the True Self.

Good-enough mother: A mother who "holds" her infant securely in her arms while feeding, cleaning, and playing with it. She provides warmth, reliability, and sameness.

Holding: A physical and psychological process that enables the infant securely to organize his or her muddled urges, wishes, and fears into predictable experiences. The mother's holding promotes comfort and stability. It fosters the beginnings of personality integration.

Personalization: The process of becoming increasingly comfortable with ownership of the body and its sensations. Satisfactory personalization leads to the feeling that the infant is "in" his or her own body.

Primary maternal preoccupation: The mother's sensitization to the infant's needs toward the end of pregnancy and shortly after birth. It results in a close identification of the mother with her infant.

Realization: Learning to take account of external reality. Sights, sounds, smells, and touches experienced with each real feeding teaches the baby what it can and cannot conjure up when the real object is not present. The baby learns to accept and tolerate the limitations of reality.

Relating to the object: Realistic comprehension of the object as a real, independent, objectively existing entity. Mother becomes a person. In Kleinian terms, real objects survive fantasies of destruction.

Stage of concern: Winnicott proposed that the Kleinian term "depressive position" be renamed the "stage of concern" to indicate the greater awareness of the good object. The infant begins to feel concern and empathy for its love-objects.

Transitional objects: Objects that bridge the gap between the child's dependence on its mother and its need to progress to independence. Teddy bears, blankets, and other cuddly things are often transitional objects.

True Self: The core self, or, the True Self is a synonym for the "experience of aliveness." The True Self is real, spontaneous, and creative.

Unintegration: At the beginning of life, the stage before a "person" begins to exist. All that exists is a bundle of biological needs and potentials. Winnicott said, "There is no such thing as a baby."

Unthinkable anxiety: Those anxieties having to do with going to pieces, falling forever, having no relationship to the body, having no orientation, or complete isolation due to inadequate communication. The mother's loving physical and emotional care prevents the infant from unbearable anxiety.

Using the object: The infant's realization that the object survives its attacks—without retaliating—enables the baby not only to believe in its external existence, but also to trust the object.

Heinz Kohut

Absolute narcissism: Mahler's term, which emphasized that infants have no recognition of their mothers as external agents of satisfaction. The infant exists in a state of perfect and cozy self-love, and believes that bodily fulfillment stems from its own perfection and power.

Basic talents and skills: These lie between the two poles of ambitions and ideals. They form a "tension arc" of psychological activity as the person is "driven" by ambitions and "led" by ideals in the pursuit of life goals.

Bipolar nuclear self: The model of the nuclear self as a bipolar entity, with ambitions and ideals anchoring opposing poles. The central process in the formation of these two poles is the relationship with empathic Selfobjects. It is the foundation of an individual's personality.

Fragmenting self: A pathological condition in which the person feels fragmented, uncoordinated, and lacking balance and cohesion because the parents inflicted some definite narcissistic injury on the child at a particularly vulnerable moment.

Guilty Man: The concept of people as struggling toward the satisfaction of their drives. In Freudian terms, they are dominated by the pleasure principle or id strivings.

Idealizing Selfobject: From the child's point of view, the idealizing Selfobject is a model of perfection, power, and comfort who can be experienced in part as a component of the self.

Idealizing transference: A patient's behavior toward the therapist as though he or she were the all-good, all-powerful parent who is still part of the self. Such behavior is an idealized image of the "good love-object."

Mirroring Selfobject: Selfobjects are objects or people who we experience as part of our self. The mother serves as a mirroring Selfobject when she is able to confirm and admire the child's sense of strength, health, greatness, and specialness.

Mirroring transference: A patient's seeking of approval or reflective mirroring from the therapist. Such a patient may be compensating for early experiences in which the father or mother failed to mirror them or withheld approval.

Nuclear ambitions: The child's learned strivings for power and success mirrored admiringly by the Selfobject.

Nuclear ideals: Idealized goals and images that are derived from the child's recognition of the satisfying and soothing power modeled by the Selfobject.

Overburdened self: A pathological condition in which the individual lacks the ability to soothe itself in times of stress because the parents did not provide opportunities for the child to merge with their strength and calmness. Such a person is easily overwhelmed and experiences the world as a threatening and dangerous place.

Overstimulated self: A pathological condition in which the individual was inappropriately stimulated in his or her ambitions or ideals. Disproportionate admiration, attention, and approval were given by the parents to the child's grandiose and idealizing needs. The individual now lives in fear of these grandiose ambitions.

Tragic Man: The concept that people are attempting to express the pattern of their very being, the pattern of the ambitions and ideals that comprise the self-expressive goals of a human life. Where Guilty Man is driven, Tragic Man yearns.

Transmuting internalization: A kind of psychological digestion by which the usable and good features of the Selfobject are incorporated into the child's self.

Selfobject: A mental representation of people or things that exist within the self. The individual experiences this as an integral part of the self.

Understimulated self: Pathological condition in which individuals feel empty, bored, and numbed because their parents were unattuned to their self-needs for mirroring and idealizing.

Chapter 8

Erik Homburger Erikson

Psychoanalytic Ego Psychology:
The Centrality of Identity

. . . healthy children will not fear life if their elders have integrity enough not to fear death.

Erik H. Erikson, *Childhood and Society*

The youth of today are not the youth of twenty years ago.

Erik H. Erikson, *Identity, Youth and Crisis*

Erik Homburger Erikson   Born: 1902   Frankfurt-am-Main, Germany

Died: 1994   Harwich, Massachusetts

About Erikson's Ego Psychology

Erik Homburger Erikson's work consists of two major and closely related contributions: a psychoanalytic ego psychology and a psychosocial life span theory of development. The focus for Erikson, as for the other ego psychologists, is on the person's interactions and relationships with others. Instincts and needs are seen as important, but the chief concern for Erikson is how the person interprets and acts upon them. He also accords to the environment an important role in facilitating or obstructing healthy psychological development.

Central to Erikson's formulation are his concepts of:

1. Ego identity formation by which Erikson means the development of a clear sense of who and what one is within the cultural and environmental framework in which one finds oneself.

2. Epigenetic stages of psychosocial development. These were originally derived from Freud's psychosexual stages but go beyond them by considering ego development within the context of a person's psychosocial environment.

3. The developmental progression of the human life cycle from infancy to old age.

4. Ego strengths, which mark each of eight stages of human development; they are virtues such as hope, will, purpose, and wisdom.

Erikson's work led to a psychotherapeutic focus on an important aspect of personality not strongly emphasized by prior theorists: What is the person's conception of him- or herself? It also led to reconsidering much psychopathology in terms of the process of identity formation.

Each stage of Eriksonian personality development includes different insights and emphases. Erikson's contributions thus constitute one of the most comprehensive personality theories.

EGO IDENTITY: CENTRAL TO PSYCHOLOGICAL DEVELOPMENT

Erik Erikson proposed that the individual's ego progresses through a reliable sequence of stages in the development of personality from infancy to adulthood. The ego adds new abilities as it learns to face the challenges of each new phase of life. By adolescence, the central developmental task for the ego is to develop a sense of **ego identity.** Knowing "who I am, what my role in society is, and who I am to become" is a crucial aspect of the ego's task. The concept of ego identity includes the sense of continuity of self, including one's values, purposes, and role in society. A clear sense of identity—either positive or negative—enables a person to sort out the relevant from the irrelevant and to have a clear guide to behavior.

The concept of ego identity is complex and continually under refinement in Erikson's thinking. Thus Erikson has wisely avoided providing any single restrictive definition of ego identity:

> I can attempt to make the subject matter of identity more explicit only by approaching it from a variety of angles. . . . At one time, then, it will appear to refer to a conscious sense of individual identity; at another, to an unconscious striving for a continuity of personal character; at a third, as a criterion for the silent doings of ego synthesis; and, finally, as a maintenance of an inner solidarity with a group's ideals and identity. (1959, p. 102)

Let us review some personal and clinical experiences relevant to Erikson's development of the concept of ego identity.

LIFE HISTORY SOURCES OF THE IDENTITY HYPOTHESIS

In 1970, Erikson published an autobiographical essay in which he traced some aspects of his own identity formation. Erikson employed the facts of his own life history to illustrate the concept of **identity crisis** and the ultimate resolution of his crisis in forming an acceptable personal identity. Erikson provided glimpses into the motives that underlaid his own intense interest in the concepts of identity and identity crisis.

Erikson's biological father abandoned his mother, Karla (maiden name *Abrahamsen*), before Erik's birth. She then got divorced before Erik was born. She subsequently married Theodor Homburger, a physician, also before Erik's birth. Throughout childhood, Erikson's mother and stepfather Theodor "kept secret from me the fact that my mother had been married previously . . ." (Berman, 1975, p. 27). Both Karla and Theodor were Jewish, whereas Erik's biological father apparently was a tall, light-skinned gentile.

Sometime after the age of three, Erikson developed the beginnings of his later identity crisis. Further intensification of his identity crisis was produced when, as a schoolboy, he was referred to as a "goy" (gentile) in his stepfather's temple, whereas his schoolmates identified him as a Jew (Berman, 1975, p. 27). Erikson thus developed a sense of "being different" from other children, and he entertained fantasies of being the son of "much better parents" who had abandoned him. Because his mother and stepfather, Dr. Homburger, were Jewish, Erikson's Scandinavian heritage of blue eyes, blond hair, and "flagrant tallness" enforced and intensified his feeling of somehow not belonging to his family. Thus, a conflicting family heritage, discordant social expectations and prejudices, and his own sense of not belonging to the family in which he grew up combined to create for Erikson an acute sense of identity confusion.

Erikson's kindly stepfather, Dr. Homburger, allowed young Erik to take the last name "Homburger." His eventual choice of a last name, "Erikson," reflected his wish to create his own identity. In effect, the name "Erik Erikson" signified, "Erik, son of Erik." It was a way of saying, "I have created my own identity." Erik kept "Homburger" as a middle name.

At puberty, Erikson rebelled against his stepfather's expectation that he would follow in his footsteps and also become a doctor. After graduation from a Gymnasium, the equivalent of high school in the United States, Erikson entered art school. Later, as a young man with the tentative identity of an artist, Erikson moved frequently throughout Europe. He was, like many a hippie later in the 1960s, independent of social pressures for success and conformity: "I was a 'Bohemian' then" (1975, p. 28). At around this time, young Erikson was in the throes of what he would later term an "identity crisis."

> . . . the choice of the occupational identity of "artist" meant, for many, a way of life rather than a specific occupation . . . and, as today, it could mean primarily an anti-establishment way of life. Yet, the European establishment had created a well-institutionalized social niche for such idiosyncratic needs. A certain adolescent and neurotic shiftlessness could be contained in the custom of *Wanderschaft* [journey or excursion]. . . . To be an artist, then, meant to have at least a passing identity, and I had enough talent to consider it for a while an occupational one. The trouble was, I often had a kind of work disturbance and needed time. *Wanderschaft* under those conditions meant neurotic drivenness as well as a deliberate search, even as today dropping out can be a time either of tuning in or of aimless negativism. . . . No doubt, my best friends will insist that I needed to name this crisis and to see it in everybody else in order to really come to terms with it in myself. (1975, pp. 25–26)

With the help of a youthful friend, Peter Blos, who later became a psychoanalytic expert on adolescence (e.g., Blos, 1962, 1970), Erikson finally overcame his crisis. He learned to work regular hours. Joining the faculty of a school in Vienna, Erikson met the circle around Anna Freud and her father, Sigmund Freud. Erikson must have been a brilliant and impressive young man because, to his own surprise, he was quickly accepted by Freud's psychoanalytic circle. At first, he tenaciously held on to his identity as "artist" rather than changing it completely to "psychoanalyst." The fact that psychoanalysis then "collected at least a few men and women who did not quite belong elsewhere" admirably suited Erikson's unconsciously formed identity of "outsider."

> It must be obvious now what Freud came to mean to me, although, of course, I would not have had words for it at the time. Here was a mythical figure and, above all, a great doctor

who had rebelled against the medical profession. Here also was a circle which admitted me to the kind of training that came as close to the role of a children's doctor as one could possibly come without going to medical school. What, in me, responded to this situation was, I think, some strong identification with my stepfather, the pediatrician, mixed with a search for my own mythical father. (Erikson, 1975, p. 29)

Erikson's professional association with the early Freudians was the outcome of a set of unique personal and historical circumstances. Psychoanalysis was at that period in its history when it was outside of the medical establishment. Erikson found in this group of brilliant outcasts a congenial solution to the conflict between his "Bohemian" identity and his growing need for commitment to a productive cause. If medicine treated psychoanalysis as an unwanted stepson, leading psychoanalysts, including Freud, accepted Erikson wholeheartedly.

Erikson sought neither a Ph.D. nor an M.D. He was accepted into Freud's circle not by virtue of his educational background but because of the recognition of his brilliance and insightfulness. Erikson did receive formal training under Anna Freud in psychoanalysis with children (she was also his training analyst).

Erikson's eventual identification with the field of psychoanalysis fit his psychological makeup. As a psychoanalyst, Erikson would be able to remain aloof from medicine in accord with his own need to be a creative outsider, yet he still was able to engage in clinical work like his stepfather. Erikson's successful resolution of his identity crisis was the psychological basis for nearly 50 years of productive clinical and theoretical work.

CLINICAL SOURCES OF THE IDENTITY HYPOTHESIS: WAR VETERANS

Erikson left Europe in 1933 to come to the United States. He taught at Harvard for three years. Later, during World War II, he worked for a time at Mt. Zion Veterans' Rehabilitation Clinic in San Francisco. In treating soldiers sent there largely from the Pacific front, Erikson first coined his now famous phrase "identity crisis." This term described the chaotic, profoundly confused mental state of soldiers hospitalized for "battle neurosis," or what we would today term "posttraumatic stress disorder." Erikson described these soldiers as having lost their sense of identity and also suffering from anxiety and vulnerability to different types of stimuli (1968, p. 66).

> Anxiety and anger were provoked by anything too sudden or too intense, a sudden sensory impression from outside, an impulse, or a memory. A constantly "startled" sensory system was attacked by external stimuli as well as by somatic sensations: heat flashes, palpitation, cutting headaches. Insomnia hindered the nightly restoration of sensory screening by sleep and that of emotional rebinding by dreaming. . . . Above all, the men felt that they "did not know any more who they were": there was a distinct loss of ego identity. The sense of sameness and continuity and the belief in one's social role were gone. (1968, p. 67)

Erikson reported a case of a marine who had suffered loss of ego identity sometime after discharge from the service. The soldier told Erikson of a particular incident during an assault on a beachhead under enemy fire. Lying in the darkness, the soldier had experienced intense anger, rage, disgust, and fear at the military's failure to provide supportive air cover and naval reinforcements. He was stunned to realize that he and his group of marines had to take the enemy's fire "lying down." As a medical officer, Erikson's patient had been unarmed on that beachhead. His memories of the rest of the night on the beach were vague and incomplete. The soldier stated that medical corpsmen were ordered to unload ammunition instead of attending to medical duties. One night, he recalled, he was forced to take a submachine gun—an unusual weapon for a medic. The remainder of what transpired was a blank. He woke up the next morning in an improvised field hospital. He was suffering from severe fever. That night, the enemy attacked from the air. He found that he was unable to move or to help others. He did not go blank at this time and was aware of his fear. After evacuation from the beach, he succumbed to raging headaches, chronic anxiety, and "jumpiness" in response to any sudden sound or sensory impression.

Later, in therapy with Erikson, the young ex-marine was able to trace his difficulties back to the time he had been forced to brandish a submachine gun. At this time, he had also observed his superior officer violently angry, swearing, and perhaps a little afraid. He told Erikson that the officer's behavior had disillusioned him. He thought such an outpouring of rage and anger by an officer was shocking conduct. Erikson wondered why this soldier was so outraged by anger in others. Was it necessary for him to see himself and others as such paragons of strength that they were immune to anger or fear?

The soldier's free associations led back to a critical childhood incident in which his mother, in a drunken rage, had pointed a shotgun at him. He took the gun from her, broke it in half, and threw it out the window. He subsequently sought the protection of a fatherly person, his school principal. Remorseful and frightened by the violent episode, he promised never again to drink, swear, indulge sexually, or touch a gun (Erikson, 1950, p. 41). Later, as a soldier faced with the stress of battle, his sense of personal identity as a good, moral, and benevolent person crumbled. Standing with a submachine gun in his hands and watching his superior officer explode with violent oaths were behaviors inconsistent with the identity he had formed as a civilian.

In Erikson's view, three factors conspired to provoke the young man's battle neurosis. First, his sense of having a shared identity with other soldiers was threatened by their panic and anger on the beachhead. Second, the constant assault on the soldier's bodily integrity by the real dangers of the battle, combined with his fever, led to a breakdown of his ego's capacity to ward off and control external stimuli. Third, there was loss of his inner sense of personal continuity or ego identity. His officer's anger and fear along with his own possession of a gun served further to undercut his sense of identity, his sense of who he was and what his values were.

His lifelong adherence to idealized moral values had served as a defensive bulwark against disturbing life circumstances. Now, in battle, these defenses were crumbling as he began to feel fear, rage, and panic (Erikson, 1950, p. 43). Erikson summarized his findings in this way:

> What impressed me most was the loss in these men of a sense of identity. They knew who they were; they had a personal identity. But it was as if, subjectively, their lives no longer hung together—and never would again. There was a central disturbance of what I then started to call ego identity. At this point it is enough to say that this sense of identity provides the ability to experience one's self as something that has continuity and sameness, and to act accordingly. In many cases there was at the decisive time in the history of the breakdown a seemingly innocent item such as the gun in our medical soldier's unwilling hands: a symbol of evil, which endangered the principles by which the individual had attempted to safeguard personal integrity and social status in his life at home. (1950, p. 42)

Thus Erikson's developing concept of ego identity helped him understand the psychological impact of soldiers' involvement in combat.

ANTHROPOLOGICAL SOURCES OF THE IDENTITY HYPOTHESIS: OGLALA SIOUX

After the war, Erikson accepted an appointment with the Yale Institute of Human Relations within the medical school. Under the leadership of John Dollard, Erikson was able to secure financial support for a field trip to South Dakota to study child-rearing practices among the Oglala Sioux Tribe at the Pine Ridge Indian Reservation.

Teachers in the government-sponsored education program complained of a variety of character defects in the Native American children they taught:

> Truancy was the most outstanding complaint: when in doubt Indian children simply ran home. The second complaint was stealing, or at any rate gross disregard of property rights, as we understand them. This was followed by apathy, which included everything from lack of ambition and interest to a kind of bland passive resistance in the face of a question or of a request. Finally, there was too much sexual activity, a term used for a variety of suggestive situations ranging from excursions into the dark after dances to the mere huddling together of homesick girls in boarding-school beds. . . . The discussion was pervaded by the mystified complaint that no matter what you do to these children, they do not talk back. They are stoical and non-committal. (Erikson, 1950, p. 125)

Erikson detected in his discussion with these teachers a deep and unconscious "fury" that clouded their professional judgments. So disappointed, so discouraged, and so disillusioned were many of the teachers at their lack of success with these children that they had come to regard their failures as the fault of some inherent "Indian" personality flaw. Erikson surmised that the difficulty lay elsewhere.

Erikson undertook a historical investigation of Sioux tribal identity. The members of the Oglala Tribe lived on land allotted to them by the federal government. They had been militarily defeated and subdued. When the Sioux had ranged over their land, the buffalo was central to their nomadic hunting existence. The early white settlers disturbed the hunting grounds with their homesteads and domesticated cattle, and they "playfully, stupidly, slaughtered buffalo by the hundred thousands" (Erikson, 1950, p. 116). When gold fever struck Americans, they invaded the Sioux's holy mountains, game preserves, and winter refuge. An appeal by Sioux leaders to U.S. Army generals was of little help in setting matters right. The government would usually break any treaties shortly after they were signed.

The outcome of the resulting chronic warfare between settlers and Sioux was epitomized in the tragedy of two massacres. General Custer's decisive defeat by Sioux warriors was avenged years later at Wounded Knee by the Seventh Army cavalry's massacre of a small band of Sioux they outnumbered four to one. Erikson summarized this climax to the gradual erosion of tribal identity.

> The young and seething American democracy lost the peace with the Indian when it failed to arrive at a clear design of either conquering or colonizing, converting or liberating, and instead left the making of history to an arbitrary succession of representatives who had one or another of these objectives in mind—thus demonstrating an inconsistency which the Indians interpreted as insecurity and bad conscience. (1950, p. 117)

Sioux culture came under massive assault. Government policies of establishing reservations, controlling the education of Sioux children, and imposing the values of larger society undermined Sioux identity. In fact, even Native American religious practices were illegal during the time Erikson was working with them. Dependency, fearfulness, chronic suspicion, and despair were some results of U.S. government policies.

In Erikson's estimation, the crux of the problem was primarily the shock of contact between the two cultures. White, middle-class, competitive values modeled by the educators and government advisers were singularly inappropriate to the needs and traditions of Native Americans. Teachers undermined traditional child-rearing practices, and families were forced to reconsider the meaning and the value of their existence. Erikson recounted many examples of the psychologically confusing and harmful effects of the government educational system. One poignant illustration serves here:

> During school time the child is taught cleanliness, personal hygiene, and the standardized vanity of cosmetics. While having by no means fully assimilated other aspects of white female freedom of motion and of ambition which are presented to her with historically disastrous abruptness, the adolescent [Indian] girl returns home prettily dressed and clean. But the day soon comes when she is called a "dirty girl" by mothers and grandmothers. For a clean girl in the Indian sense is one who has learned to practice certain avoidances during menstruation; for example, she is not supposed to handle certain foods, which are said to spoil under her touch. Most girls are unable to accept again the status of a leper while menstruating. (1950, p. 131)

Thus, as in his clinical work with American soldiers, Erikson found that the concept of identity was essential for understanding the plight of the Oglala Sioux children.

THE EGO IDENTITY HYPOTHESIS AND PSYCHOANALYTIC THEORY

As we shall note in the coming sections, the development of a sense of identity is an important ego activity. Erikson observed in the cases of the traumatized World War II soldiers that their disorders could not be traced to their earliest psychosexual stages. A Freudian model of the psychiatric disorders of war veterans would have traced them to such vulnerabilities. Erikson believed that their war experiences were sufficient to explain their pathology. He developed what would be termed, the **ego identity hypothesis.** The experiences were such as to undermine the ego's efforts to maintain a consistent, meaningful sense of ego identity. In other words, the soldiers' pathology occurred because of disruptive events during adult life—not as a result of events during infancy or early childhood. Likewise, with the Oglala Sioux, Erikson did not trace the psychopathology he found to poor parenting of Sioux infants, but rather to events that took place mostly during latency or early adolescence. It was difficult for Sioux youngsters to form coherent ego identities out of discordant experiences.

The psychotherapeutic implications of Erikson's insights are profound. A therapist who applies Erikson's theory is encouraged to consider the environmental challenges at each stage of life and how the person has dealt with and is dealing with them. Also worth considering is the nature and adequacy of the specific identity that an individual has formed.

Much of this therapeutic work can refer to contemporary behavior and current environmental challenges as well as characteristic coping patterns. Similarities to the approaches of Anna Freud, Karen Horney, and Alfred Adler are apparent in Erikson's work.

PSYCHOSOCIAL DEVELOPMENT: AN EPIGENETIC SEQUENCE

Although Erikson was trained as a psychoanalyst, indeed his training analyst was Anna Freud, he emphasized different personality dimensions from those of classical psychoanalytic doctrine. Erikson worked to broaden Freud's emphasis on *psychosexual* development and instinctual dynamics with a consideration of *psychosocial* development.

Erikson received wide recognition for his specification of the stages through which the ego develops. In response to the crises initiated by the biological and social givens of life, the child's ego matures in an **epigenetic** sequence of combined psychosexual and **psychosocial stages.** The term *epigenetic* is drawn from biology. It is used wherever there is a stepwise sequence of development that is genetically determined but requires specific environmental conditions for successful completion. For example, gardeners know that a plant requires certain conditions to sprout from seeds and to develop roots, stems, and finally produce seeds of its own. The structures that develop are predetermined by the plant's genetic makeup, but their successful unfolding is made possible by the presence of environmental factors, such as sunlight and rain.

For Erikson, it is the social environment that influences how the biologically determined psychosexual characteristics of the infant develop. To Freud's oral, anal, phallic, and genital stages, Erikson couples interpersonal crises that guide the flowering of these biologically determined developments. For Erikson, the person's interpersonal milieu is the psychosocial half of the developmental equation, an aspect that pre-ego psychologists neglected. Freud interpreted human behavior largely as the result of a clash between the ego and the biological drives of the id on one side and the requirements of the superego on the other. Ego psychologists, such as Erikson, focus on the interaction between the ego-id-superego, taken as a whole, and the external, social world.

Let's examine here Erikson's recasting and broadening of the meaning of Freud's oral stage in his epigenetic model of psychosocial development.

For Freud, the nursing relationship between mother and infant was of lasting importance in the development of personality. In supplying the infant with breast or bottle, the mother not only relieves its accumulated hunger tension, she also establishes a reliable sequence of pleasurable stimulation. The pleasurable activities of feeding, cuddling, touching, and sucking are all motivated, in Freud's scheme, by the same generalized sexual or pleasure drive: libido. As a result, hunger reduction becomes the model for all later libidinal (pleasurable-sexual) satisfactions. The theoretical importance of the oral stage for Freud was the light it shed on the interaction between the biological drives of the id (e.g., hunger) and the ego's efforts to secure satisfaction and pleasure from the external world (in the form of the mother).

Like Freud, Erikson regards the nursing relationship as crucial for personality development. Unlike Freud, Erikson does not restrict his theoretical considerations to id-ego interactions or to the result of id satisfactions by the ego. Instead, the feeding situation in Freud's oral stage is, for Erikson, a model of developmentally significant social interaction between the infant and others. Hunger is certainly a biological (id) manifestation, but the consequences of its satisfaction by the mother transcend immediate pleasure. Reliable and timely satisfactions of the infant's hunger make it more likely for the infant to develop a sense of basic trust, a sense that external reality is trustworthy. Irregular and unpredictable responses of the caretaker make it harder, if not impossible, for the infant to develop a sense of basic trust. Whereas Freud emphasizes the consequences of biological drive reduction for the development of id-ego relations, Erikson stresses the impact of such interaction for the infant's psychosocial development. Once established, basic trust endures as an independent ego characteristic, free of the id drives from which it originated. Figure 8.1 illustrates basic differences between the classical psychoanalytic view and psychoanalytic ego psychology.

It is possible at this point to discern within Erikson's work several trends that are characteristic of psychoanalytic ego psychology:

- Erikson has conceptualized the ego as the source of the person's awareness of self. The ego also develops a sense of continuity. The ego has a realization of itself as an "I."

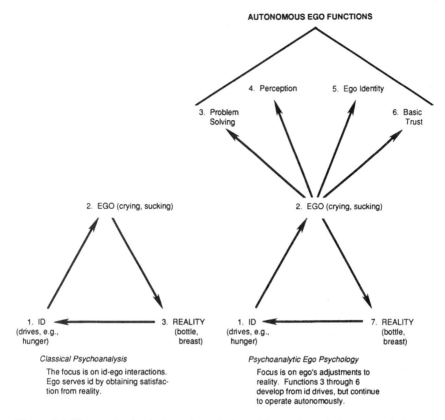

Figure 8.1 The ego in classical psychoanalysis and in psychoanalytic ego psychology.

- One of the ego's major tasks is to develop and maintain a sense of personal identity.

- Erikson emphasizes the individual's conscious adjustments to interpersonal influences.

- Erikson builds upon the instinctual theoretical framework developed by Freud, by adding his own epigenetic psychosocial conception of personality development.

- Motives may originate in unconscious or repressed id impulses, yet these motives may become free of the id drives from which they originated. This idea, as we shall see in Chapter 11, is very similar to Gordon Allport's concept of "functional autonomy." It recognizes that, even though adult behaviors might have originated from early drives and immature motives, they could have subsequently become motivated by mature goals.

THE LIFE CYCLE: EIGHT STAGES OF HUMAN DEVELOPMENT

The center of Erikson's developmental model of personality is a sequence of **eight stages of ego development.** The first five stages in Erikson's scheme build on and broaden Freud's psychosexual stages (Erikson, 1950, 1959, 1968). In Erikson's model, relatively successful resolution of a specific crisis is the necessary preliminary to advancement to the next. These eight crisis periods can be grouped into four broad life periods: The four divisions of Table 8.1 represent a condensation of Erikson's scheme in which he distinguishes between early and later childhood, and between young adulthood and adulthood proper (cf. Erikson, 1959, p. 120).

Table 8.1   Life Cycle Ego Crises

Infancy	Childhood	Adolescence	Adulthood
1. Trust versus mistrust (oral)	3. Initiative versus guilt (phallic)	5. Identity versus role confusion (early genital)	6. Intimacy versus isolation (genital)
2. Autonomy versus shame, doubt (anal)	4. Industry versus inferiority (latency)		7. Generativity versus stagnation
			8. Ego integrity versus despair

Note: Corresponding Freudian psychosexual stages appear in parentheses.

Each of the eight psychosocial crises includes both positive and negative elements. It is sometimes mistakenly assumed that negative and positive outcomes are mutually exclusive. Erikson has pointed out, however, that it is important to experience and incorporate *both* negative and positive aspects of each crisis. A degree of mistrust, of shame, of guilt, and other negative aspects of development are normal consequences of dealing with the challenges of life. Without any degree of suspicious caution or mistrust, for example, a child would be very vulnerable to harm. Each crisis is favorably resolved when there are more positive than negative elements incorporated into the person's identity (Erikson, 1968, p. 105).

Ritualization Versus Ritualism: The Way We Do Things

Erikson hypothesized a pair of **ritualizations** and **ritualisms** for each of the eight psychosexual stages. A ritualization, the positive member of each pair, is a custom that is part and parcel of the pattern of life within a culture. Stemming initially from the ego's capacity for playfulness, ritualizations confirm one's sense of identity, one's sense of belonging to a particular culture. A good way to understand what Erikson meant by ritualization is to consider its origins in evolutionary biology. Erikson borrowed the term ritualization from Julian Huxley's description of the "ceremonial" acts of certain animals, such as the greeting ceremonies of some bird species (Erikson, 1982, p. 43). Erikson emphasizes in his uses of the term ritualization the "informal and yet prescribed interplay between persons. While such interplay may not mean much more . . . than 'this is the way we do things,' it has, we claim, adaptive value for all participants and for their group living" (1982, p. 43). An example might be the friendly interaction that occurs as part of a family meeting. This idea anticipated some concepts of the field of evolutionary psychology, which will be covered in Chapter 18.

On the negative side, each ritualization is balanced by ritualism, which is a form of behavior involving estrangement from self and from one's community. Ritualisms indicate the ambivalent character of all human relationships. The loving mother, for example, also has a potentially dark side that threatens abandonment and separation. A ritualism is a ritualization that has become stereotyped and mechanical, an empty ceremony devoid of meaning and lacking the power to bond individuals. It is a pattern of coldly going through the motions without the appropriate emotions.

The balance between love and the fear of separation can have either a positive or negative balance. The ideal balance for each ritualization, in each developmental stage occurs when the negative or ritualistic aspect is present but outweighed by positive aspects. This is parallel to the ideal balance between trust and mistrust.

The Psychosocial Ego Functions of Ritualization

Ritualizations serve at least seven important psychosocial functions:

1. *Social function:* Ritualization elevates need satisfaction to a communal context by joining personal desire and right to the group's shared sense of the importance and justice of its desires and rights.

2. *Destiny function:* In teaching a sanctioned way of doing simple and daily things, ritualization transforms the infantile sense of omnipotence into a joint sense of destiny.

3. *Worthiness function:* Ritualization deflects feelings of unworthiness onto outsiders, both in and out of one's culture.

4. *Interpreting function:* Ritualization puts emerging cognitive patterns in the service of a general vision shared by the community; it also cultivates the cognitive capacity to discern the "right" class of things and people from the "wrong" one.

5. *Sanctification function:* Each successive stage of ritualization helps develop essential aspects of all ritual sense.

6. *Moral function:* Ritualization develops the experience of social differentiation between good behavior and wrongful acts.

7. *Identity function:* Ritualization provides the psychosocial foundation for the gradual development of an independent identity.

ACQUIRING A SENSE OF *TRUST VERSUS MISTRUST: HOPE*

The earliest sense of identity arises from an infant's contact with its mother or caregivers in the feeding situation (Erikson, 1968, p. 105). Throughout the first year of life, an infant's most crucial contacts with reality are those mediated by the person attending to the infant's needs. When these attentions have been given willingly, lovingly, and reliably, and in quick response to the infant's cries, it is more likely that the infant will develop a sense of the environment as trustworthy and predictable (Erikson, 1950, pp. 247 ff.; 1959, p. 56). The opposite is also true: Erratic and unreliable parenting is more likely to result in an attitude of mistrust.

The trusting infant's experiences have been marked by consistency, continuity, and sameness in the mother's or caregiver's responses:

> Such consistency, continuity, and sameness of experience provide a rudimentary sense of ego identity which depends, I think, on the recognition that there is an inner population of remembered and anticipated sensations and images which are firmly correlated with the outer population of familiar and predictable things and people. (Erikson, 1950, p. 247)

When the baby's first teeth begin to emerge, a parent's patience is often tested. Seeking to bite and to grasp desirable objects and persons, infants explore the boundaries of their capacities to trust and be trusted. Consequently, Erikson stressed that the sense of basic trust is not restricted to a perception of the outer world as trustworthy, "but also that one may trust oneself and the capacity of one's own organs to cope with urges; and that one is able to consider oneself trustworthy enough so that the providers will not need to be on guard lest they be nipped" (Erikson, 1950, p. 248).

The infant's sense of trust is often robust enough to withstand parental restrictions or prohibitions, especially if they are consistent and reasonable. As long as parental commands and prohibitions communicate to the infant that the parents know what they are doing, minor frustrations and repeated "no, no"s are not harmful. Only discipline that

---

BOX 8.1 *Only Connect . . .*

Such an attitude of basic trust as well as Erikson's ideas of a sense of competence lead to a sense of what could also be termed *optimism,* or more technically, as elaborated by the psychologist Albert Bandura (Chapter 16) *positive outcome expectations* or *positive efficacy expectations*—predispositions to expect that one's behavior will lead to positive results in a given environment. As Bandura indicated, people with such expectations are most likely to take risks and show initiative.

---

is administered without confidence and without consistency can result in damaged trust (Erikson, 1950, p. 249). On the opposite side of the coin, an infant who has failed to experience predictable parenting behavior may develop a basically mistrusting attitude. Successful development during the first year of life involves acquiring a preponderance of basic trust. The trusting infant looks forward eagerly to new challenges.

Erikson proposed a developmental schedule of psychological virtues (1964, pp. 111 ff.). Successful resolution of the crisis at each stage leads to the attainment of a specific virtue. For example, the infant who acquires a sense of basic trust has also acquired the virtue of hope. The acquisition of various virtues indicates the ego's growing capacity for strength, restraint, and courage (Erikson, 1964, p. 113). In Erikson's own words, "I will call 'virtue,' then, certain human qualities of strength, and I will relate them to that process by which **ego strength** may be developed from stage to stage and imparted from generation to generation" (1964, p. 113).

For the infant who finds itself and its environment trustworthy,

Hope is the enduring belief in the attainability of fervent wishes, in spite of the dark urges and rages which mark the beginning of existence. (Erikson, 1964, p. 118; italics in original)

Because, at the first stage of development the trusting infant's desires and wishes have met with reliable and generally positive responses from a trustworthy interpersonal environment, the future development of the person is marked by hope—for all types of positive experiences, achievements, and successes.

The ritualization characteristic of the trust-mistrust stage centers on the significance of the interaction of mother or caregiver and child. Every day the infant is exposed to the repeated ritual of its mother's approach, her smiles, her voice, her nursing behavior, her cuddling. The infant experiences the **ritualization of the numinous** (or awesome) quality of the mother's presence as evidenced by her facial expression, voice quality, and the feel of her touch. The whole series of infant care events is highly stylized and superimposed on the periodicity of the infant's physical needs. By her care and reliable concern, the mother confirms the infant's "I-ness" while she also helps the infant to overcome fears of aloneness (Erikson, 1977, pp. 86ff).

According to Erikson's theory, the ritualism possible at this stage is **idolism,** a distortion of the numinous reverence into adulation or worshipful adoration. An illusory image of perfection binds the idolizing infant to the mother. Instead of the mutuality of affirmation and recognition, idolism results in dependence and in an inflexible attribution to the mother of impossibly unreal human perfection.

ACQUIRING A SENSE OF *AUTONOMY VERSUS SHAME AND DOUBT: WILL*

Near the age of 18 months, the infant gains more precise control over its muscles. An increased capacity for self-control accompanies this development. The child begins to experiment with two modes of muscular action: holding on and letting go (Erikson, 1950, pp. 251 ff.). Such an infant may repeatedly drop an object to the floor and then repeatedly grab and drop it again when it is retrieved.

This period of muscular exertion and experimentation occurs during the Freudian anal stage. Besides holding on to and letting go of objects, the child also begins to learn how to retain feces and urine until an appropriate, parentally approved, time and place is reached to let them go. Depending on the way the parents handle this pivotal experience, the child learns either that holding on and letting go are powerful weapons to be employed against overly demanding parents, or that elimination is "a relaxed 'to let pass' and 'to let be' " (Erikson, 1950, p. 251). Parental guidance at this stage should ideally be firm and at the same time protective of that sense of trust achieved during the previous oral stage:

> Firmness must protect [the child] against the potential anarchy of his as yet untrained sense of discrimination, his inability to hold on and to let go with discretion. As his environment encourages him to "stand on his own feet," it must protect him against meaningless and arbitrary experiences of shame and of early doubt. (Erikson, 1950, p. 252)

The crisis of this stage of ego development revolves around the child's need to achieve a sense of independence or willful autonomy in controlling its bodily functions and physical activity. Early experiences of self-control will set the pattern for the capacity to make free choices. A child that has been repeatedly and excessively *shamed* is most likely to become an over-controlled adult.

"Shame supposes that one is completely exposed and conscious of being looked at: in one word, self-conscious. One is visible and not yet ready to be visible . . ." (Erikson, 1950, p. 252). Thus the child who has learned control over self by having been made to feel small or shameful for unavoidable lapses wins only a "hollow victory." Shamed beyond the limits of its trust, such a child learns to distrust those who are doing the shaming. Instead of learning to regard the products of its body as dirty or evil, the child may come to regard its tutors as evil. Harsh parental demands for self-control have a further negative consequence: *Doubt.*

Erikson vividly explicates this sense of doubt concretely as a form of "watching one's butt":

> Where shame is dependent on the consciousness of being upright and exposed, doubt . . . has much to do with a consciousness of having a front and a back—especially a "behind." For this reverse area of the body, with its aggressive and libidinal focus in the sphincters and in the buttocks, cannot be seen by the child, and yet it can be dominated by the will of others. The "behind" is the small being's dark continent, an area of the body which can be magically dominated and effectively invaded by those who would attack one's power of autonomy. (Erikson, 1950, p. 253)

The child who attains a favorable ratio of autonomy to shame and doubt is likely to develop a capacity for willful self-control. Reasonable tolerance and realistic firmness shown to the child by the parents result in reasonable self-tolerance and realistic self-firmness (Erikson, 1959, p. 70). The quality of ego strength that emerges during the establishment of a sense of autonomy corresponds to the virtue of *will:*

> *Will . . . is the unbroken determination to exercise free choice as well as self-restraint, in spite of the unavoidable experience of shame and doubt in infancy.* (Erikson, 1964, p. 119; italics in original)

In this stage of autonomy versus shame, the ritualization that develops centers on the ego's capacity to discriminate good from bad. Erikson terms this capacity **judicious ritualization;** here the child learns what is culturally sanctioned and what is out of bounds (Erikson, 1977, p. 92). During this stage, autonomous behavior may test the limits of peer and adult tolerance. Before this stage, the child's deeds and misdeeds were the responsibility of the parents; now he is trained to "watch itself."

Sometimes, parents predict the child will turn out badly unless the limits of good behavior are followed. Such negative prophecies may be the self-fulfilling roots of an adolescent's negative identity. The child may very well develop in accordance with parental fears, not their hopes.

> Behind the dreaded traits, of course, are often images of what the parents themselves had been tempted to become and therefore doubly fear the child might turn out to be—*potential traits,* then, which the child yet must learn to imagine in order to be able to avoid them. (Erikson, 1977, p. 95)

The ritualism that parallels judicious ritualization is **legalism:** "the victory of the letter over the spirit of the word and the law" (Erikson, 1977, p. 97). Legalism is marked by self-centered displays of righteousness and a moralistic insistence on right over justice. A legalistic individual may learn to use the letter of the law to justify bad behavior. Such an individual might be motivated not by a sense of rightness but by shrewdly manipulative selfishness.

ACQUIRING A SENSE OF *INITIATIVE VERSUS GUILT: PURPOSE*

Resolving the crisis of autonomy, the child of age four or five enters the next phase of ego development with a firm sense that he or she is a person, an "I" (Erikson, 1959, p. 74). The child now also discovers what kind of person he or she is. The crucial question for the child is to decide which of the parents will be the object of identification. Freud characterized this stage of development as phallic, and the chief crisis as the solution of the Oedipus or Electra complex.

Three important developments during this stage bring the child closer to the point of crisis:

1. The range of movement is widened by the capacity to walk rather than crawl;
2. The use of language is more precise "to the point where he understands and can ask about many things just enough to misunderstand them thoroughly;"
3. Language and locomotion combine to permit the child to expand the imagination, even to the point of being frightened by his or her own thoughts (Erikson, 1959, p. 75).

The key characteristic of this stage is the child's growing capacity to initiate actions, thoughts, and fantasies. The child develops the capacity to plan and to reflect on the consequences of self-initiated activities. He or she can experience jealous rage against siblings or others who are perceived as threats. For the male child in a traditional two-parent family, the sense of exclusive domination of mother's attention is imperiled when he realizes that father is a stronger, more powerful competitor. To resolve these Oedipal strivings, the boy internalizes the imagined prohibitions of his father. The prohibitions become the basis of the superego or conscience (see the discussion of the superego in Chapter 3). With the formation of the superego, the child usually consolidates its identification with the same-sexed parent and acquires the gender-specific behaviors of that model.

During this stage, too, the child learns to cooperate with other children. The child may plan projects and participate actively in games and social interaction. The child also imitates desirable adult role models. Hopefully, a favorable balance between initiative and guilt is established. As the child discovers what it can do, it also continues to realize what is permitted, what it may do (Erikson, 1959, p. 75). Nowhere is this balance between ability and expectancy more apparent than in imaginative play:

> Play is to the child what thinking, planning, and blueprinting are to the adult, a trial universe in which conditions are simplified and methods exploratory, so that past failures can be thought through, expectations tested. (Erikson, 1964, p. 120)

The main addition to the ego's strength that results from a successful resolution of the crisis during this stage is the virtue of *purpose:*

> *Purpose . . . is the courage to envisage and pursue valued goals uninhibited by the defeat of infantile fantasies, by guilt and by the foiling fear of punishment.* (Erikson, 1964, p. 122; italics in original)

Purpose requires the internalization of the sense of right and wrong, that is, with the inner adoption of external moral and ethical guidelines. The child's ego may now make judgments and plans that in the past had to be made for it.

The initiative versus guilt stage of development incorporates a **ritualization of a sense of authenticity.** Entering the play stage of childhood, girls and boys learn to create dramatic elaborations of their inner and outer conflicts. This dramatic element allows a child to relive, correct, re-create, and rework past experiences, and to anticipate future ones. The child can experiment dramatically with a variety of roles. A genuine sense of inner guilt—the capacity for self-condemnation—develops as the child toys with fantastic events and roles it could not possibly enact in "real life."

An awareness of congenial roles, comfortable situations, and satisfactory coping strategies emerge during play. Finally, a sense of authenticity emerges. Such authenticity involves a feeling of what "I *want* to be" and what "I realistically *can* be."

Impersonation is the ritualism of the dramatic element. It is a form of disconnected role-playing that is untempered by realistic shame and guilt. "To be denied a true chance of authenticity . . . can force children (and youths) to compulsively assume the role of shameless evildoers—as preferable to being either nameless or overly typed" (Erikson, 1977, p. 103). Such an impersonating child lacks and does not develop a genuine commitment to any one role.

ACQUIRING A SENSE OF *INDUSTRY VERSUS INFERIORITY: COMPETENCE*

In the first stage of basic trust, personality focuses around the conviction, "I am what I am given." During the crisis of the second stage involving autonomy, personality is centered on the belief that, "I am what I will." At the third stage, when the sense of initiative reaches critical proportions, the nucleus of personality is, "I am what I can imagine I will be."

With the emergence of the fourth psychosocial crisis of industry versus inferiority, the central theme for personality development becomes "I am what I learn" (Erikson, 1959, p. 82). This fourth stage takes place along with the child's first school experiences.

In school, the child is expected to focus on often impersonal and abstract subjects and, at least in class, taming imagination in the service of productive learning (Erikson, 1950, p. 258). Corresponding to the Freudian latency period, the child in this stage discovers that how one is valued in school is becoming increasingly important.

Children ideally realize that completing a task requiring steady attention and diligence is intrinsically rewarding (Erikson, 1950, p. 259). They learn to use tools of the culture and to become familiar with current technology. The key danger here is that some children may despair of success. They may develop a sense of inadequacy and inferiority and may even lose some of the accomplishments of their previous ego crises. Such children may not be able to identify with productive adult models.

A successful resolution of the crisis between industry and inferiority leads to the development of a new strength, the virtue of *competence:*

> Competence . . . is the free exercise of dexterity and intelligence in the completion of tasks, unimpaired by infantile inferiority. (Erikson, 1964, p. 124; italics in original)

Children learn "by virtue of" their trust, autonomy, initiative, and industry that confident, independent, and active productivity is satisfying.

The industry versus inferiority stage is marked by the **ritualization of formality.** Becoming accustomed to school tasks and the necessity for successful "making" and "producing," the youngster learns the value of methodical performance (Erikson, 1977, p. 103).

> [In school] . . . with varying abruptness, play is transformed into work, game into competition and cooperation, and the freedom of imagination into the duty to perform with full attention to the techniques which make imagination communicable, accountable, and applicable to defined tasks. (Erikson, 1977, p. 104)

School introduces children to the socially appropriate forms of producing, competing, and cooperating. When children master the formal aspects of work, they learn to feel worthwhile, deserving of praise, success, gain, and acceptance. They learn that hard work, initiative, and perseverance are necessary for meaningful accomplishments.

The ritualism side of formality is **formalism,** the forgetting of the purpose of methodical performance in favor of mere proficiency. As Karl Marx suggested, a "craft-idiot" is one who denies the human significance of his or her skills and becomes enslaved to the trappings of efficient method (Erikson, 1977, p. 106). Formalism is adherence to technique and blindness to purpose and meaning.

ACQUIRING A SENSE OF *IDENTITY VERSUS ROLE CONFUSION: FIDELITY*

By the time childhood is over, the child's ego has ideally assimilated a grown-up sense of industry. In reaching this point in development, the adolescent has constructed a sense of his or her own sameness. This sense of continuity is the foundation of ego identity.

At this time, the earlier developmental crises are echoed and the person's sense of sameness is questioned all over again.

> In their search for a new sense of continuity and sameness, adolescents have to refight many of the battles of earlier years, even though to do so they must artificially appoint perfectly well meaning people to play the roles of adversaries; and they are ever ready to install lasting idols and ideals as guardians of a final identity. . . . The sense of ego identity, then, is the accrued confidence that the inner sameness and continuity prepared in the past are matched by the sameness and continuity of one's meaning for others, as evidenced in the tangible promise of a "career." (Erikson, 1950, pp. 261–262)

In Erikson's view, the adolescent period is a socially sanctioned interval of role experimentation. A full and healthy ego identity can emerge only when previous identifications are integrated. The varying senses of identity formed in infancy, childhood, and in the school years can merge to become a comfortable and workable whole. Identity is not formed in a vacuum, however. The identity ideally should be formed in such a way as to fit within the framework of society. A youngster may want to be a rock star, but in order to become one, his musical style must attract an audience. Erikson has contributed thoughtful idiographic studies of Mahatma Gandhi (Erikson, 1969) and Martin Luther (Erikson, 1962). In these studies, he explored their creative formation of historically important identities.

In proper perspective, the **psychosocial moratorium** of adolescence (and occasionally, young adulthood) permits a young person to explore a range of opportunities without the necessity of immediate commitment. For the adolescent who has failed to integrate all previous crisis solutions, the moratorium on final role choice permitted by society to its young is extended to a paralyzing and interminable era of confusion. Like Erikson with his own youthful identity crisis as an outsider, confused adolescents cannot become what their lives have prepared them to be:

> The prime danger of this age, therefore, is identity confusion, which can express itself in excessively prolonged moratoria; in repeated impulsive attempts to end the moratorium with sudden choices, that is, to play with historical possibilities, and then to deny that some irreversible commitment has already taken place. . . . The dominant issue of this, as of any other stage, therefore, is that of the active, the selective, ego being in charge and being enabled to be in charge by a social structure which grants a given age group the place it needs—and in which it is needed. (Erikson, 1963, p. 13)

Thus the sense of identity means "being at one with oneself," and harboring an affinity for one's community, both for its history and for its future (Erikson, 1974, p. 27). But with this positive sense of identity there is necessarily a negative aspect to one's sense of self. Each adolescent consequently harbors a negative identity. Healthy resolution of the identity crisis enables adolescents to discard their negative identity. However, for the adolescent who does not develop a positive ego identity,

> The loss of a sense of identity often is expressed in a scornful and snobbish hostility toward the roles offered as proper and desirable in one's family or immediate community. Any part or aspect of the required role, or all parts, be it masculinity or femininity, nationality or class membership, can become the main focus of the young person's acid disdain (Erikson, 1959, p. 129).

Negative identity choices are most easily discerned among troubled or "disturbed" adolescents. Such young people willfully choose to become everything that parents and teachers had expressly indicated as undesirable. A **negative identity** is thus "an identity perversely based on all those identifications and roles which, at critical stages of development, had been presented to the individual as most undesirable or dangerous, and yet also as most real" (Erikson, 1959, p. 131). For example:

> A mother who is filled with unconscious ambivalence toward a brother who disintegrated into alcoholism may again and again respond selectively only to those traits in her son which seem to point to a repetition of her brother's fate, in which case this "negative" identity may take on more reality for the son than all his natural attempts at being good: he may work hard on becoming a drunkard and, lacking the necessary ingredients, may end up in a state of stubborn paralysis of choice. (Erikson, 1959, p. 131)

According to Erikson, vindictive choices of negative roles around which to integrate one's sense of self represent a desperate attempt to regain some control over one's fate. Many adolescents faced with chronic **identity diffusion,** an unclear and often fluctuating sense of who one is and what one's purpose is, I would "rather be nobody or somebody bad, or indeed, dead—and this totally, and by free choice—than be not-quite somebody" (Erikson, 1959, p. 132).

Despite the dangers of adolescent identity diffusion, the majority of ego-integrated youth evidence attainment of another form of ego strength, the virtue of *fidelity:*

> *Fidelity is the ability to sustain loyalties freely pledged in spite of the inevitable contradictions of value systems.* (Erikson, 1964, p. 125; italics in original)

Healthy youths, from their springboards of firm self-identities and strong egos, develop a high sense of duty to the tasks of rendering reality faithfully to themselves and to their culture. For youths who have attained the strength of fidelity, life becomes the living out of their established core identities. They actually are the roles they play.

Like other theorists, Erikson employed the theatrical imagery of the actor and his mask of roles. For healthy "faithful" adolescents, the actor's mask is adjusted precisely to the actor's face. The danger in the roles to which adolescents turn in their experimentation with the multiple identities their life offers is that the role may become more real than the actor's core:

> But what if role-playing becomes an aim in itself, is rewarded with success and status, and seduces the person to repress what core-identity is potential in him? Even an actor is convincing in many roles only if and when there is in him an actor's core identity—and craftsmanship. (Erikson, 1974, p. 107)

The ritualization of the adolescent identity-formation period is **commitment to an ideology.** Adolescence is the time to integrate the conflicting self-images that have developed since infancy in some formal "confirmation" procedure. A formal rite of passage is needed to mark clearly the adolescent's transition from childhood to adulthood. Adolescents must be made to experience what Erikson calls "solidarity of conviction," that is, a sense that they belong to the generation of youth as distinguished from their elders (Erikson, 1977, p. 107). Adolescents often develop their own rituals of belonging, marked outwardly by the distinction of their clothes, preferences for music and literature, and sometimes hostility to adults. By their adoption of the work ethic of their culture, adolescents implicitly adopt its ideological style. They are ready to exclude and repudiate all alien ideologies (Erikson, 1977, p. 107).

The ritualism of this phase is **totalism,** "a fanatic and exclusive preoccupation with what seems unquestionably ideal within a tight system of ideas" (1977, p. 110). Ritualism is a partial regression to the idolism of infancy. Adolescents now find themselves a cause, an idea, a group to which they can totally commit themselves unthinkingly and in which they run the risk of losing themselves.

ACQUIRING A SENSE OF *INTIMACY VERSUS ISOLATION: LOVE*

With entrance into young adulthood, the person becomes willing to risk his or her newly established identity by fusing it with the identities of others. "He is ready for intimacy, that is, the capacity to commit himself to concrete affiliations and partnerships and to develop ethical strength to abide by such commitments, even though they may call for significant sacrifices and compromises (Erikson, 1950, p. 263).

A firm sense of personal integrity based on the fusion of past bodily and social identifications allows the young adult to face the fear of ego loss in situations and relationships that call for self-sacrifice. Thus the young adult can experience intimate social interactions ranging from intense friendships or physical combat to hesitant sexual experimentation.

The danger of this period is that young adults may not be ready for the demands of

BOX 8.2   *Only Connect . . .*

Freud was once asked what he thought the healthy person should be able to do well. His curt answer was "Lieben und arbeiten" (to love and to work) (Erikson, 1950, p. 265). Compare this answer with Erikson's fourth and sixth developmental stages. Freud's formula, "to love and to work," is more complicated than is at first apparent. Freud and Erikson meant to indicate that the healthy adult personality is able to absorb himself or herself in intimate sexual fulfillment while simultaneously maintaining the independence of spirit necessary for productive and fulfilling work.

intimacy. They may be unwilling to lend themselves to intimate sharing with another, and thus retreat into personal isolation.

In the shift among combative, cooperative, and intimate interpersonal relationships, new adults must learn not only to adopt personal formulas for intimate cooperation, but also their own unique modes of productivity.

In Erikson's view, healthy genital sexuality that marks this stage is characterized by:

1. mutuality of orgasm
2. with a loved partner
3. of the other sex
4. with whom one is able and willing to share a mutual trust
5. and with whom one is able and willing to regulate the cycles of
   a. work
   b. procreation
   c. recreation
6. so as to secure to the offspring, too, all the stages of a satisfactory development. (Erikson, 1950, p. 266)

Some aspects of this part of Erikson's theory now seem very dated and even biased. His specifications regarding healthy genital sexuality can be seen as unfairly excluding same-sex couples and couples who do not engage in child-rearing. Erikson's assertion that mutuality of orgasm is a necessary indication of genuine intimacy is an assertion without empirical evidence.

The key virtue attending the successful resolution of the conflict between intimacy and isolation in this stage is *love:*

> Love . . . is mutuality of devotion forever subduing the antagonisms inherent in divided function. (Erikson, 1964, p. 129; italics in original)

Love is thus the ego strength to share one's identity with another for "mutual verification."

Growing from the core of intimacy achieved in this stage is the **affiliative ritualization** (Erikson, 1977, p. 110). Affiliation indicates that the identity achieved thus far is compatible with the identities of people in one's life. The young adult finds a partner with whom to share enthusiastic opinions and scathing judgments, and with whom to establish an enduring affiliation promising a productive and procreative life (1977, p. 110).

The ritualism counterbalancing the affiliative element is **elitism,** a sense of narcissism shared with others that leads to membership in formal or informal groups that exclude others. According to Erikson, such elitism is an isolating trend rooted in infantile idolism.

ACQUIRING A SENSE OF *GENERATIVITY VERSUS STAGNATION: CARE*

"Mature man needs to be needed, and maturity needs guidance as well as encouragement from what has been produced and must be taken care of" (Erikson, 1950, p. 267). Mature adults thus need to feel some concern for the next generation, especially as exemplified by their own offspring. Because children are the products of the intimate fusion of bodily and personal identities of the parents, each has a "libidinal investment" in their offspring.

Being a parent does not, in itself, ensure the attainment of a sense of generativity. What is needed is the ability to extend oneself, literally to give oneself to the future. Erikson chose the term *generativity* to indicate the capacity to transcend immediate self-related interests in favor of generations to come (Erikson, 1968, p. 138).

The main danger of this stage lies in the inability of some otherwise mature adults to find value in guiding and aiding the next generation. A pervasive sense of stagnation or boredom then characterizes their approach to a variety of life tasks. Life is viewed as unsatisfying and without much meaningful activity. A feeling exists that accomplishments and even interpersonal intimacies lack relevance to one's sense of identity.

The ego's strength in meeting the necessities of life is increased in the generative adult by the development of the virtue of *care:*

> Care is the widening concern for what has been generated by love, necessity, or accident; it overcomes the ambivalence adhering to irreversible obligation. (Erikson, 1964, p. 131; italics in original)

By postulating the stage of generativity and the attainment of the virtue of care, Erikson has extended the Freudian psychosexual stages beyond genital sexuality. Care assures for the mature ego the right to be needed and the privilege to need the young. Thus care includes not only work for those persons whom one has created, but for all of humanity's created works as well.

The hallmark of the adult generative period is what Erikson calls the **generational ritualization** (1977, p. 111). This ritualization is a composite of a variety of adult ritualizations, including the parental, the teaching, and the curative. *Generational* means that the adult must be prepared to exercise authority with a conviction that "I know what I am doing" and receive reassurance from the various cultural images of authority, such as God, kings, and one's own parents, that "I am doing it right."

The corresponding ritualism of the adult period is **authoritism,** a self-convinced but spurious seizing of authority. Instead of functioning as a just transmitter of ideal values and as a sanctioned judge of evil, the adult who yields to authoritism becomes an oppressive model of insensitivity.

BOX 8.3   *Only Connect . . .*

The possible evolutionary basis for a generative stage of development has been highlighted by evolutionary psychology (Chapter 18). In addition to working for the survival of one's own progeny, the *inclusive fitness* theory indicates the selective advantage accruing to genes of people who enhance the overall fitness of those around them. The *kin selection* concept indicates the evolutionary value of aiding those who are related, especially young offspring. Thus, altruism directed toward the next generation (generativity) would be selected in the evolutionary process.

ACQUIRING *EGO INTEGRITY VERSUS DESPAIR: WISDOM*

The climax of the life cycle is reached when the foundations of infantile trust have made possible their adult counterpart: ego integrity. Adults who have been cared for, who have cared for others, can now care for themselves. The fruit of the previous seven stages ripens in adults whose egos can accept their life cycles "as something that had to be and that, by necessity, permitted of no substitutions: it thus means a new, a different love of one's parents" (Erikson, 1950, p. 268).

Adults in whom ego integrity has fully blossomed realize that their individual lives are but one life cycle in the flow of history. They are convinced that what had to be, was—and was satisfying. The danger is that the ego may have failed to integrate the crisis resolutions of the previous seven stages. The fear of death that emerges means that the individual is unable to accept his or her life cycle as the ultimate and one and only meaning that living embodies. Despair of what has been implies that what has been, has been in vain. Despair is the protest of a person who is not yet satisfied with a life that has never been satisfying. Despair indicates unwillingness, paradoxical as it may be, to end a life that has failed to achieve fulfillment and that now culminates as the sum of a thousand little miseries.

The most important gift parents can provide their children is the strength, shown in their own example, to face ultimate concerns like death without the disintegrating effects of fear: "Healthy children will not fear life if their elders have integrity enough not to fear death" (Erikson, 1950, p. 269). Thus the virtue that serves as the hallmark of the climactic stage of the life cycle is wisdom:

> Wisdom . . . is detached concern with life itself, in the face of death itself. (Erikson, 1964, p. 133; italics in original).

Adults who embody the kind of integrity that Erikson describes are wise in the sense that they view their limited lives as a totality that transcends petty disgust at the feeling of

Table 8.2   Crises, Ego Strengths, and Ritualizations of the Life Cycle

	Ego crisis	*Ego strength*	*Ritualization range*
Infancy	1. Trust versus mistrust	Hope	Mother–child mutual recognition: Numinous to idolism
Early childhood	2. Autonomy versus shame and doubt	Will	Good-bad discrimination: Judicious to legalism
Childhood (play age)	3. Initiative versus guilt	Purpose	Dramatic elaboration: Authenticity to impersonation
Childhood (school-age)	4. Industry versus inferiority	Competence	Methodical performance: Formality to formalism
Adolescence	5. Identity versus role confusion	Fidelity	Solidarity of conviction: Ideology to totalism
Young adulthood	6. Intimacy versus isolation	Love	Complementarity of identities: affiliative to elitism
Mature adulthood	7. Generativity versus stagnation	Care	Transmission of values: Generational to authoritism
Old age	8. Ego integrity versus despair	Wisdom	Affirmation of life: Integral to sapientism

(Based on Erikson, 1950, 1977, 1978.)

"being finished." They are able to transcend the despair "of facing the period of relative helplessness which marks the end as it marked the beginning" (Erikson, 1964, p. 134).

This last stage of the life cycle brings us to the **integral ritualization,** literally an ability to integrate the previous phases into a confirmation of the life thus led. To have achieved the ego strength of wisdom means that the important achievements of the previous seven stages are synthesized and consolidated into the awareness that new ideas, new meanings, new persons have been personally created. In a real way, these creations are immortality—for the individual and for the human group. The ego that has achieved the ritualization of the integral affirms life, and the person of old age realizes a new affinity for what was childish. This paradox is expressed beautifully in the lines of William Blake that Erikson used as his book epigraph and title: "The Child's Toys and the Old Man's Reasons Are the Fruits of the Two Seasons" (Erikson, 1977).

The ritualism of this stage is a distortion of wisdom that Erikson names **sapientism,** "the unwise pretense of being wise" (Erikson, 1977, p. 112).

Table 8.2 summarizes the eight stages of the life cycle and their various crises, strengths, and ritualizations.

IS THERE A NINTH STAGE?

After Erikson had died, his widow, Joan M. Erikson, wrote an extended version of *The Life Cycle Completed* (1997) in which she proposed a ninth stage of development: **gerotranscendence.** This stage occurs toward the end of life and involves a number of factors that have to do with a fundamental shift, a "shift . . . from a materialistic and rational vision" (Erikson & Erikson, 1997, p. 125) in one's experiencing and thinking: One comes to experience oneself as part of a greater whole, one not limited to the sense of being a particular individual in time and space. There is a sense of a cosmic connection and a sense of consciousness outside of time and space. Such gerotranscendence or even gerotransecen*dance*

> . . . Speaks to soul and body and challenges it to *rise above* the . . . clinging aspects of our worldly existence that burden and distract us from true growth and aspiration. (Erikson & Erikson, 1997, p. 127; italics added)

This potential of a spiritual stage toward the end of life is reminiscent of the spiritual focus that we reviewed as part of Jungian personality theory (Chapter 4) and is also similar to Abraham Maslow's concepts, which will be presented in Chapter 13.

APPLYING ERIKSON'S STAGE THEORY

When we apply Erikson's stages to our lives or to the lives of other people, some interesting conclusions emerge. First, it is not necessary to resolve each stage completely one hundred percent positively. For example a good amount of healthy mistrust is a beneficial trait as is the capacity to identify those situations in which either trust or mistrust is warranted. A certain degree of basic trust does need to be established in order to provide a foundation for further development. Otherwise, trust-mistrust issues might continue to dominate a person's experience.

The stages seem more flexible than Erikson actually proposed. The timing of stages is not necessarily strictly sequential or invariant. Individual and cultural differences play a role in determining the course of development. Some people may put off the stage of developing an occupational identity until later in life or even go through a whole new identity crisis while switching to a new field in midlife. In many instances, adult women who have finished child-rearing go through the same soul-searching that Erikson indicated is typical for younger people. Adolescents and young adults may demonstrate generativity in the form of community service projects or other ways of improving the world. Even the virtue of wisdom may be found in those younger people who are, "wise beyond their years."

When applied in a flexible manner, Erikson's developmental model provides general categories and guidelines by which we can more fully understand the patterns of psychological growth. Knowledge of them is a rich resource for anyone trying to understand psychological development over a lifetime.

SOME CONCLUDING REMARKS ON ERIKSON

Erikson's psychosocial scheme of the life cycle has provided the conceptual tools for the analysis of the lives of significant historical figures. Erikson has thus examined the process of identity development in the lives of Martin Luther (1962) and of Mahatma Gandhi (1969). In both cases, Erikson sought to identify the historical, social, and psychological forces that uniquely combined with accidental circumstance to produce a human personality that changed the course of history.

Psychohistory, as this form of psychological and historical investigation has come to be called, has gained a wide foothold in a broad array of academic disciplines. It is not within the scope of this chapter to review this literature. But it is important to recognize the far-reaching acceptance Erikson's ideas have had. The concepts of identity, identity crisis, life cycle, ego strength, and psychosocial development, all pioneered by Erikson, have found their way into quarters where orthodox psychoanalytic doctrine would be most unwelcome. Perhaps one reason for the great respectability of Erikson's concepts in the eyes of critics lies in the stimulating impact of Erikson's ideas in many fields.

EVALUATING ERIK ERIKSON

Erikson's theory is a most widely read, taught, and written-about theory. We would be hard put to find a general psychology text or an adolescent or child psychology text in the United States that does not give substantial space to his ideas. Erikson's ego psychology has been welcomed in places where Freud's theory would be most unwelcome. People from different disciplines, with vastly different expectations about psychological theories of human nature, find in Erikson what they are looking for, even if each of them seeks something different. Developmental psychologists find a stage-phase theory of psychological growth; psychoanalysts find a Freudian account of identity formation; humanists find a holistic conception of the life span; theologians find cogent observations on aging and death; and social learning theorists find a cognitive translation of Freudian developmental tasks. The list could be expanded. But the point is that Erikson was a man of great erudition, with the humanist's eye for the uniqueness of personality, the psychoanalyst's ear for the unconscious personal meaning, and the artist's flair for bold but elegant statement.

Refutability of Erikson's Concepts

Erikson's concepts are easily translated into cognitive and emotional constructs, independent of the psychoanalytic assumptions from which he started. The most research productive of Erikson's concepts has been his notion of identity and identity formation. Some years ago, James Marcia (1966) devised a set of criteria and a way to measure various degrees of crystallized identity formation in young people. Since then, there have been a variety of empirical, sometimes predictive, studies based on the Marcia-Erikson measures of identity status (e.g., Marcia, 1993; Marcia & Friedman, 1970; Rowe & Marcia, 1980).

In principle, there are other fundamental Eriksonian concepts that should be refutable because they are measurable. For example, Donald Hamachek has developed a social cognitive translation (see Chapter 16) of some of Erikson's ego strengths and other features of the developmental stages. Such a translation should pave the way for empirical testing.

In summary, Erikson's theories thus score relatively high in refutability. However, much of the theory is so philosophical and general that large portions appear not to be testable.

Erikson's Concept of Human Agency

Erikson has a balanced conception of human agency. On the one hand, as a Freudian theorist, Erikson regards unconscious processes and social reality as determining variables that shape the person. But, as we have seen, Erikson also portrays development as a matter of some personal choices, which implies an active agent view. How shall we characterize Eriksonian theory, then? It is a matter of judgment, based largely on whether one emphasizes the Freudian component to the theory or the cognitive component. Because Erikson has stressed repeatedly his allegiance to the basic psychoanalytic formulations, especially for the first four developmental stages, we can speculate that Erikson's view of people is more of a passive agent view—people are shaped by reality—than an active agent view. But it is a close call.

The Idiographic-Nomothetic Balance in Erikson's Theory

Erikson's theory deals with universals. His conception of the stages/phases asserts a universal human developmental scheme. As we have seen, Erikson even reiterated Freud's "anatomy is destiny" dictum and thereby earned a great deal of criticism. His conception of identity formation clearly has nomothetic components, some of which have received testing, as we discussed.

By the same token, Erikson has argued convincingly that each of us solves the crisis of a given developmental stage uniquely, in terms of our given social, historical, and familial context. His early clinical work with soldiers, Native American children, and his own psychoanalytic patients, along with his interest in psychohistory (Martin Luther and Gandhi, for example) are testimony to the idiographic, single-case concerns of his work.

In Erikson, as in few other theories, we find the idiographic perspective well balanced with the potential for nomothetic or generally applicable "laws" that can be tested.

SUMMARY

Erik Homburger Erikson's work falls within the realm of psychoanalytic ego psychology by virtue of the theory's stress on the ego's integrating and stabilizing influences in the person's life history, but he might just as well be considered an object relations theorist. Identifying himself closely with orthodox psychoanalysis, Erikson nevertheless has transcended classical Freudian instinct theory. He portrays the ego from a psychosocial perspective as the hub of individual identity. As the ego matures through life crises, it gains strength to master in increasingly sophisticated ways the puzzles posed by inner and outer reality. Perhaps Erikson's continued self-identification with psychoanalytic theory and his desire to preserve its essential elements were fostered by his own gratefulness for his early acceptance into the Freudian mainstream. His adolescent role confusion, the culmination of his development as an outsider, was greatly reduced by his commitment to the role of psychoanalyst. Feeling neither completely Jewish nor completely Scandinavian, the young Erikson had long wondered who his real father was, why he did not fit in either with his Jewish family or his non-Jewish schoolmates, and what he would ever become.

Erikson conceptualizes the healthy personality as one who, in Freud's words, is able to work and to love. That is, the healthy functioning personality has the capacity to share intimacy with another and to work fruitfully, with personal satisfaction. A healthy social milieu, initially provided by the parents, aids the individual to accept the inexorability of his or her own development. Erikson calls such acceptance of one's life a "sense of ego integrity."

Erikson has proposed that such integrity or ego strength is achieved in an unalterable sequence of psychosocial stages. Beginning in infancy, the child's ego must first learn to trust itself and others to become autonomous and self-sufficient. With trust and autonomy come the virtues of hope and will, forms of ego strength that foster sufficient security for the child to risk the potential disappointment that hope entails, and sufficient independence of spirit for children to dare to initiate willingly their personal adaptation to their inescapable realities. Once these fundamental ego strengths are acquired, the child is able to acquire, in sequence, a sense of initiative (purpose), a sense of industry (competence), a sense of identity (fidelity), a sense of intimacy (love), a sense of generativity (care), and, finally, a sense of integrity (wisdom).

During the various phases in the acquisition of these ego strengths or virtues, the maturing person will also be exposed to age-appropriate ritualizations and ritualisms through which comes a special kind of learning, the mastery of "the only proper way to experience and to do things" in that person's culture. In the trust-mistrust stage, there is the ritualization of mother–child recognition; in the autonomy-doubt stage, the child learns good-bad discriminations, followed by acquisition of the ability to elaborate dramatically conflicts and concerns in the initiative-guilt phase of middle childhood. By the school-age years, the ritualization of methodical performance is acquired, allowing the child to progress into adolescence with a more or less perfectly formed "worker" image that will be further shaped by the ritualization of shared convictions with other adolescent children. Young adulthood brings exposure to the complementary identity of one's intimate partner, with whom, by mature adulthood, the person seeks to perform the ritualization of transmitting values to the next generation. Old age, finally, sees a return, in Erikson's view, to the playfulness of childhood in the wise old person's affirmation of the life he or she has led.

An evaluation of Erikson reveals a theory that has the potential for refutable constructs and an established capacity for generating productive research. Erikson also achieves a balanced view of human agency in which social, biological, and cultural variables are seen as determinants, but the individual is capable of choice within these limits. Erikson's theory embodies a well-balanced concern for nomothetic or universal psychological "laws" with some traditional psychoanalytic concern for the uniqueness of the individual, especially in the areas of clinical application and psychohistory.

FOR FURTHER READING

Erikson's most comprehensive treatment of both his early and later theorizing is contained in *Childhood and Society* (New York: Norton, 1993). In *Insight and Responsibility* (New York: Norton, 1994) Erikson considers the various "virtues" that may arise through healthy resolution of the eight psychosocial developmental crises.

Robert Coles has provided a detailed account of the personal and historical influences that shaped Erikson's ideas in *Erik Erikson: The Growth of His Work* (Boston: Little, Brown, 1970). More recently, he has put together *The Erik Erikson Reader* (New York: Norton, 2000), which contains a wide spectrum of Eriksonian writings. Richard I. Evans, in Vol. 8 of his famous "Dialogs" series, interviews Erikson and provides commentary on his work. Evans' interview comprises *Dialog with Erik Erikson* (New York: Harper & Row, 1996).

A good summary of his stages (including an introduction to a ninth stage) can be found in *The Life*

Cycle Completed (New York: Norton, 1997). This book is worth consulting for the new emphases that have emerged as Erikson himself writes from the perspective of old age; the extended edition was co-authored posthumously by his widow, Joan Erikson, and contains a brief introduction to a possible ninth stage. A more artful and literary approach to Erikson's conception of the eight stages may be witnessed in the collection of papers, including his own analysis of an Ingmar Bergman movie, edited by Erikson under the title *Adulthood* (New York: Norton, 1978).

Young Man Luther (New York: Norton, 1993) and *Gandhi's Truth: On the Origins of Militant Nonviolence* (New York: Norton, 1993) are two of Erikson's books that transcended the world of psychology and dealt with historical events and cultural change from the perspective of individual development and life history.

Two volumes give some indication of the scope of Erikson's research and thinking on the concept of identity and some of its philosophical underpinnings. The collection of papers edited by Jane Kroger in *Discussions on Ego Identity* (Hillsdale, NJ: Lawrence Erlbaum, 1993) presents a wide range of interpretations of identity. The compendium edited by J. E.

Marcia and his colleagues, *Ego Identity: A Handbook for Psychosocial Research* (New York: Springer-Verlag, 1993) provides a thorough survey of recent research, Marcia's most recent thinking, and several samples of ongoing projects.

GLOSSARY[1]

Autonomy versus shame and doubt: Second psychosocial stage. With increased voluntary muscular control comes the capacity for increased self-control. The child begins to experiment with holding on or letting go. If the parents mishandle toilet training, a sense of shame and doubt will result instead of a sense of willful autonomy. If the developmental task is resolved positively, the virtue of **will** emerges.

Ego identity: A person's clear sense of "who I am, what my role in society is and who I am to become." The sense of ego identity includes the sense of continuity of self, including one's values, purposes, and role in society. A clear sense of identity—either positive or negative—enables a person to sort out the relevant from the irrelevant and to have a clear guide to behavior.

Ego identity hypothesis: Erikson's theory that much adult pathology, originally that of wartime veterans, occurred because life experiences undermined the ego's efforts to maintain a consistent, meaningful sense of identity. In other words, their pathology occurred because of disruptive events during adult life—not as a result of events during infancy or early childhood.

Ego integrity versus despair: Eighth psychosocial stage. Those who have adapted successfully to the triumphs and disappointments of life can look back on a constructive journey with a sense of completion and fulfillment. The person who has led an overly disappointing life is not contented, and thus will experience despair. If the outcome of this stage is positive, the resulting ego strength is **wisdom.**

Ego strength: A virtue that could develop from each of Erikson's eight developmental stages. Those virtues—states of goodness or growth orientedness—are: *hope, will, purpose, competence, fidelity, love, care,* and *wisdom.*

Eight stages of ego development: These refer to a series of sequential psychosocial stages that begin in infancy and extend through life to old age. Each psychosocial stage involves a developmental crisis that can be resolved positively (strengthening the ego) or resolved negatively (weakening the ego).

Epigenetic: A term drawn from the field of biology. It is used wherever there is a stepwise sequence of development that is genetically determined but requires specific environmental conditions for successful completion. Erikson applied the concept of epigenetic stages to human psychological development.

Generativity versus stagnation: Seventh psychosocial stage. This stage of adulthood involves finding meaningful activities by extending one's sense of self into future generations. It involves passing on one's skills, knowledge, experience, and even possessions to the next generation. The main danger of this stage lies in the inability of some adults to find value in guiding and aiding the next generation. A sense of stagnation or boredom then sets in. If the outcome is positive, the virtue is **care.**

Gerotranscendence: The proposed ninth psychosocial stage of life. In this stage, a person comes to experience himself or herself as part of a greater whole, one not limited to the sense of being a particular individual in time and space. There is a sense of a cosmic connection and a sense of consciousness outside of time and space.

Identity crisis: An inner conflict, usually during adolescence, during which a person's identity in one or more areas of life is unclear.

Identity diffusion: An unclear and often fluctuating sense of who one is and what one's values and goals are.

Identity versus role confusion: Fifth psychosocial stage. Individuals strive to find out who they are

---

[1] In the glossary for this chapter, the definitions for the various *ritualizations* are paried with terms defining the corresponding *ritualisms.* So, for example, the definition for the *ritualization of the numinous* is paried with the definition of *idolism,* its corresponding ritualism.

and who they are not. They must sort out their sexual, ideological, and occupational orientation. Identity confusion may include problems of a conflicting self-image, an inability to establish intimacy with others, an inability to adhere to tasks, and a rejection of family or community values. If the outcome is positive, the virtue that ensues is **fidelity.**

Industry versus inferiority: Fourth psychosocial stage. The child learns to complete tasks with diligence and perseverance, and to acquire new intellectual and technological skills as well as social skills for cooperative endeavors in the future. If the outcome is positive, the ego strength is **competence.** If the child is ridiculed in his or her efforts, or does not receive praise and appreciation, the child will acquire a sense of inadequacy and inferiority.

Initiative versus guilt: Third psychosocial stage. If the parents encourage the child's self-initiated fantasies, ideas, and behaviors, it develops a lively curiosity and a strong sense of initiative. If they stifle or ridicule the child's behavioral or ideational initiative, it will develop guilt feelings whenever it strives for independence and goal-orientedness. If the outcome is positive, the ego strength is **purpose.**

Intimacy versus isolation: Sixth psychosocial stage. In this stage, a person becomes willing to risk his or her newly established identity by fusing it with the identities of others. It is the capacity to commit oneself to concrete affiliations and partnerships. If one avoids close contacts and withdraws into oneself, a feeling of isolation ensues. If the outcome is positive, the virtue that emerges is **love.**

Negative identity: Refers to a commitment to aspirations, values, and roles that are deemed unacceptable by society. The individual makes undesirable or dangerous choices. A person may be inclined to choose a negative identity to relieve a state of chronic identity diffusion.

Psychological moratorium: A period during which a person, usually an adolescent or young adult, explores a range of opportunities without the need for immediate commitment.

Psychosocial stages: Four childhood and four adulthood stages of development that Erikson added to Freud's oral, anal, phallic, latent, and genital psychosexual stages. The combined psychosexual and psychosocial stages are epigenetic stages of development.

Ritualisms: Mechanical and stereotyped activities—just "going through the motions" without including feelings or a sense of deeper meanings. Ritualisms lead to an individual's estrangement from the self and from the community.

Ritualizations: The "informal and yet prescribed interplay between persons, with adaptive value for all participants and for their group living." These patterns of behavior confirm the meanings held by individuals and by the larger society.

The affiliative ritualization versus elitism: The ritualization in which a young adult finds others with whom to share enthusiastic opinions and scathing judgments, and with whom to establish an enduring affiliation—promising a productive and procreative life. The comparable ritualism is elitism, which is a sense of shared narcissism with a few select people. It leads to exclusion and isolation.

The generational ritualization versus authoritism: This ritualization is a composite of a variety of adult ritualizations, including the parental, the teaching, and the healing. **Generational** indicates that the adult must be prepared to exercise meaningful authority with conviction. The corresponding ritualism, **authoritism,** indicates that the adult becomes insensitively authoritarian.

The integral ritualization versus sapientism: The integral ritualization involves the ability to unify all the previous phases into a confirmation of the life thus led. It synthesizes all the important achievements of the previous stages. The corresponding ritualism is a distortion of wisdom called sapientism, "the unwise pretense of being wise."

The judicious ritualization versus legalism: The judicious ritualization is one in which the child learns the significance of rules, laws, and societal norms. The comparable ritualism is legalism, which is marked by self-centered displays of righteousness and moralistic insistence on right over justice.

The ritualization of a sense of authenticity versus impersonation: The child tries on a variety of roles, and both positive and negative roles are used to reconfirm appropriate behaviors and frown upon inappropriate behaviors. Eventually the child discovers the role that is just right for him or her. This is called the ritualization of a sense of authenticity. The comparable ritualism is impersonation, which occurs when the child uses ungenuine role-playing, that is, becomes the role he or she is playing without shame or guilt.

The ritualization of commitment to an ideology versus totalism: The ritualization of commitment to an ideology involves the search for a religious, political, or other set of beliefs that give meaning to his or her life. The adolescent is faced with integrating all the conflicting self-images that have developed since infancy. The corresponding ritualism is **totalism,** "a fanatic and exclusive preoccupation with what seems unquestionably ideal within a tight system of ideas" Adolescents now find themselves a cause, an idea, a group to which they can totally commit themselves unthinkingly and in which they run the risk of losing their sense of self.

The ritualization of formality versus formalism: The ritualization of formality occurs when the youngster learns the appropriate ways of doing tasks, and learns the value of methodical performance, which includes real skills and knowledge. The comparable ritualism is formalism, which occurs when the person ignores or forgets the human significance of his or her skills, and becomes overly concerned purely with technological proficiency.

The ritualization of the numinous versus idolism: In the mutual recognition and affirmation of the mother and child interaction, the infant experiences the ritualization of the numinous (awesome) quality of her presence. If the infant's normal respect for the mother becomes distorted, the ritualism of idolism unfolds. Such idolism involves a kind of hero worship or putting the mother "on a pedestal."

Trust versus mistrust: First psychosocial stage. When the mother's attentions have been given willingly, lovingly, and reliably, the infant is more likely to develop an attitude of basic trust. The infant who failed to experience reliability, continuity, and sameness is much more likely to develop a sense of basic mistrust. The ego strength that emerges is the capacity to **hope.**

Chapter 9

Harry Stack Sullivan

Interpersonal Theory

A multiple personality is in a certain sense normal. . . . What we have here is a situation in which there can be different selves, and it is dependent upon the set of social relations that is involved as to which self we are going to be.

George Herbert Mead, *Mind, Self and Society*

Properly speaking, a man has as many social selves as there are individuals who recognize him *and carry an image of him in their mind. To wound any of these images is to wound him.*

William James, *Principles of Psychology*

Harry Stack Sullivan	Born: 1892	Norwich, New York
	Died: 1949	Paris, France (at a mental health conference)

About Sullivan's Interpersonal Theory

For Sullivan, personality arises in interpersonal exchanges. A person does not "possess" personality so much as reflect one in responding to the perceptions of significant others. Sullivan was among the most eclectic of the neo-Freudians, and one of the first psychodynamic theorists to see the importance of non-Freudian thinkers. Among the most important organizing elements in Sullivan's thought are these concepts:

- *Sullivan's "one-genus" hypothesis emphasized the fundamental humanity of all people: "We are all much more simply human than otherwise."*

- *Psychological development proceeds through three modes of experiencing the world: prototaxic, parataxic, and syntaxic. Such development centers on the increasing use of cause-and-effect logic to structure reality.*

- *The "self system" arises out of interpersonal experiences. The most significant of these is the mothering–infant relationship.*

- *The ways in which the mothering one responds to the infant's behaviors shapes the three personifications of the self, called the "Good-Me," "Bad-Me," and the "Not-Me."*

- *Avoiding anxiety is an important motive of behavior. Sullivan does not conceptualize anxiety in a Freudian manner but, rather, as socially and interpersonally based.*

MODES OF EXPERIENCE: PROTOTAXIC, PARATAXIC, SYNTAXIC

Sullivan proposed a developmental theory that focused on what he thought was the way infants and young children and adults experienced the world. In reviewing this theory, it is necessary to realize that Sullivan's earlier modes of experience may continue to co-exist with those that are more mature. In their psychological development, people do not necessarily abandon one mode when they move on to another.

Prototaxic: Serial Sensation

The simplest, crudest, and most exclusive mode of experiencing reality at the beginning of life is what Sullivan called the **prototaxic mode** (1953b, p. 29). For the first few months of life, the infant's world is composed of a stream of sensory experience upon which it is unable to impose order or consistency. Generally, each sensory experience in the prototaxic mode is isolated from and uncoordinated with all other sensory experiences. As a result, the world is perceived, or "prehended" as Sullivan would say, as a flux of unconnected and discrete moments of sensation (1953b, p. 108). Even though some sensory events may be repetitive, the infant is unable to generalize from one event to another. Experiences occur in succession, but the infant does not comprehend that one event "goes with," "goes before," or "comes after" another. The world is a "buzzing, blooming confusion."

When it is hungry, "mother-with-bottle" appears. Sullivan called this personification of mother the "mouth mother." The infant does not understand that its crying is a causal signal to mother that feeding time is at hand. If the infant were left unfed, its crying would increase. It would not necessarily comprehend that it was the mother's failure to bring the bottle that was responsible for its frustration. In this stage, its own existence is everything that exists. It does not have a working conception of cause and effect in the external world.

Parataxic: Sequential Sensation

At the point when the infant begins to perceive events as having a temporal connection, Sullivan speaks of an emerging **parataxic mode** of experience. The cycle of mounting hunger tension and its reduction when food is available leads eventually to the child's fore-sight or anticipation of satisfaction when it experiences hunger (Sullivan, 1953b, p. 38). Before this achievement, the infant's experience of tension and its eventual satisfaction after eating seem unrelated. With the establishment of the ability to predict or anticipate one event from another's presence, the dimension of time is imposed on the infant's universe. Temporal contiguity, the occurrence of one event immediately after or immediately before another event, comes to the center of the infant's attention. This dominance of the awareness of temporal sequencing as the conception of causality is what Sullivan calls the *parataxic mode of experience*. When an infant enters the parataxic mode of experience, it has progressed to the point at which it can generalize experiences and identify similarities and differences among events. The infant is thus now able to respond differentially to different stimuli based on experience (Sullivan, 1953b, pp. 82–83).

For example, the infant is able to see that the same person might minister to different needs: The mother who produces a nipple when the baby cries with hunger is the same mother who produces a blanket when it cries with cold. In the previous prototaxic mode, the baby could identify a person only by the bodily zone through which satisfaction was obtained: Thus, there was a "mouth mother," a "skin mother," an "anus mother," and so on.

Though the child's egocentrism is diminished during the stage of elementary externalization, it still tends to judge events only by their effects on itself. For example, though it realizes there are other people in the world, and that it, like them, is a member of an even larger universe, the only importance others have is in terms of what they do for and to the child. Sullivan proposed that parataxic thinking is accompanied by the ability to differentiate the body from the rest of the world (1953b, p. 163). Out of this differentiation gradually emerges a personification of self called the "Not-Me."

Parataxic thinking may occur in older people as well as in infants. For example, many superstitions are based on parataxic reasoning. If a gambler on a losing streak at the roulette table suddenly strikes it lucky, he or she is likely to assume that the person who just sat down nearby was the cause of the good fortune.

Syntaxic: Causal Sensation

The **syntaxic mode** of experience corresponds to adult, logical, analytical thought. Syntaxic experience of reality thus requires the ability to understand physical and spatial causality and the ability to predict causes from knowledge of their effects. It involves a logical synthesis of past, present, and future experience. Syntaxic experiencing is characteristic of much adult functioning.

Sullivan pointed out the importance of the use of language at this stage:

> . . . the first instances of experience in the syntaxic mode appear between, let us say, the 12th and the 18th month of extrauterine life, when verbal signs—words, symbols—are organized which are actually communicative. (Sullivan, 1953b, p. 184)

and

> . . . I should stress that syntaxic symbols are best illustrated by words that have been consensually validated. A consensus has been reached when the infant or child has learned the precisely right word for a situation, a word which means not only what it is thought to mean by the mothering one, but also means that to the infant. (Sullivan, 1953b, pp. 183–184)

Sullivan also emphasized the predictive function of syntaxic thought (1953b, p. 233). Language allows children to store information from experiences for use in understanding future novel events. Not only can they generalize from their experience, syntaxic thinkers can choose to focus on only certain events that make sense in terms of their past accomplishments.

JUNGIAN ASPECTS OF SULLIVAN'S THEORY

Some of Carl Gustav Jung's concepts (Chapter 4) were major building blocks from which Sullivan constructed many of his important conceptions of personality dynamics.

First, Jung's approach emphasized the possibility that certain feelings and thoughts could be split off from the bulk of conscious functioning, yet remain in consciousness in an isolated, encapsulated form. In a sense, the disassociation of these ideas and feelings was a case of repression in reverse. Instead of submergence to the unconscious, these unacceptable feelings were separated from the ego but kept within awareness as isolated fragments deprived of apparently meaningful connection with each other and with the self, or ego. Sullivan construed schizophrenic functioning in much the same way. But Sullivan extended the idea of **dissociation** to include normal personality development. Each of us, Sullivan postulated, develops an aspect of self that is dissociated from the bulk of our self-concepts. Called the "Not-Me," this personification of self embodies all the unacceptable behaviors that are accompanied by "uncanny" feelings of anxiety. These emotions prevent our recognizing some behaviors as "ours."

Second, Jung saw no reason to assume that the processes of schizophrenic thought were different in kind from normal thought. As Freud saw neurotic and normal mental processes lying on the same continuum, Jung thought that

> when we penetrate into the human secrets of our patients, the madness discloses the system upon which it is based, and we recognize insanity to be simply an unusual reaction to emotional problems that are in no way foreign to ourselves. (1908, p. 165)

Compare to Jung's formulation Sullivan's later statement of his position:

> In approaching the subject of mental disorder, I must emphasize that, in my view, persons showing mental disorder do not manifest anything specifically different in kind from what is manifested by practically all human beings. . . . From my viewpoint, we shall have to accept as a necessary premise that what one encounters in various stages of schizophrenia—the odd, awe-inspiring, terror-provoking feelings of vastness and littleness and the strange strewing-about of relevance—are part of the ordinary experience of these very early stages of personality development in all of us [namely, parataxic thinking and the Not-Me]. Most of us, however, experience these processes in later life only as strange fragments carried over from sleep or in our fleeting glimpses of what I call anxiety. (Sullivan, 1956, p. 3)

Sullivan was quite explicit that **schizophrenia** was to be regarded as lying within the range of processes found in normality:

> Schizophrenic thinking shows in its symbols and processes nothing exterior to the gamut of ordinary thinking, including therein that of reverie and of dreams. . . . It is, as a whole, a peculiarly inadequate adaptation of the cognitive processes to the necessities of adult life. . . . (Sullivan, 1962, p. 92)

Sullivan's idea that the normal personality experiences something similar to the mental state of schizophrenics only in dreams is reminiscent of Jung's conceptualization. Sullivan took matters a step further than Jung by establishing a developmental chronology of events leading to **schizophrenia.**

Furthermore, Sullivan's emphasis on the continuity of mental processes from normality through psychosis led him to a rather important philosophical statement of human similarities. "Everyone and anyone is much more simply human than otherwise, more *like everyone else* than different" (1962, Frontispiece). This concise statement was originally called the species identity theorem by Sullivan in his early unpublished notebooks, and later expanded to the **one-genus postulate.**

BOX 9.1   *Only Connect . . .*

Sullivan's one-genus theory seems to be confirmed by the findings of modern genomics, the study of the genome. Of the 3 billion-or-so-long molecular chemical code for the human genome, only an average of 0.01% distinguishes one person from another. We are almost completely alike in terms of our genetic makeup. We are, in fact, 99.99% similar. This 0.01% that is different may account, however, for major physical and behavioral differences—such as sickle cell anemia and schizophrenia.

. . . the differences between any two instances of human personality—from the lowest-grade imbecile to the highest-grade genius—are much less striking than the differences between the least-gifted human being and a member of the nearest other biological genus. *Man— however undistinguished biologically—as long as he is entitled to the term, human personality, will be very much more like every other instance of human personality than he is like anything else in the world.* (1953b, pp. 32–33; italics added)

Because "everyone and anyone is much more simply human than otherwise," Sullivan thought it necessary to rescue psychiatry from the "ivory tower myth" of objective, uninvolved commitment to "scientific" truth finding (1964, p. 15). For Sullivan, the psychiatrist is certainly a scientific observer of behavior, but he is also a **participant observer** who is no less human, no less involved, no less of a participant, and no less changed than the patients he treats. As Sullivan pithily summarized his concept, "The crying need is for observers who are growing observant of their observing" (1964, p. 27). The one-genus postulate also led to more interactive and humane treatment of schizophrenics and other mental patients, who were often treated in isolated long-term wards.

The third implication of Jung's work for Sullivan's theory was Jung's emphasis that the wish-fulfilling tendencies observed in the schizophrenic's bizarre speech and thoughts are derived from important concerns of his or her life before his illness began. Jung had summarized his view in this way:

. . . we can assert that the pathological ideas dominate the interests of the patient so completely because they are derived from the most important questions that occupied him when he was normal. In other words, what in insanity is now an incomprehensible jumble of symptoms was once a vital field of interest to the normal personality. (Jung, 1908, p. 173)

Sullivan's later conceptualization of schizophrenic personality development is nearly identical to Jung's:

The disorder [i.e., schizophrenia] is one in which the total experience of the individual is reorganized. . . . It is a disorder that is determined by the previous experience of the individual—regardless of whether it is excited by emotional experience (psychic traumata), by the toxemia of acute disease, by cranial trauma, or by alcoholic intoxication. (Sullivan, 1962, p. 12)

and

Schizophrenia is considered tentatively as an evolution of the life process in which some certain few motivations assume extraordinary importance to the grave detriment of adjustive effort on the part of the individual concerned. This disturbance of adjustive effort is shown as an interference in the realm of social experience. (Sullivan, 1962, p. 160)

Jung was not the only theorist whose ideas led up to Sullivan's theories. Sullivan read widely in the psychiatric literature and adopted for his own purposes the conceptions that most suited his interpersonal theory. To name just a few of Sullivan's intellectual antecedents and influences, we can list Jean Piaget, Sigmund Freud, Carl Jung, Alfred Adler, William Alanson White, George Herbert Mead, and Kurt Lewin. Sullivan drew on such influences in the creative development of his own unique theory of personality.

ANXIETY: THE STATES OF EUPHORIA AND TENSION

Sullivan had observed the effects of dissociated systems of experience in extreme form in his work with schizophrenics. The cause, it seemed clear, was the patient's struggle to master unacceptable and anxiety-provoking interpersonal situations. With the goal of forming a model of personality development, Sullivan's chief questions became "How does the experience of **anxiety** originate?" and "How does the experience of anxiety cause dissociation of certain feelings and ideas?"

> It is demonstrable that the human young in the first months of life . . . exhibits disturbed performance when the mothering one has an "emotional disturbance." . . . Whatever the infant was doing at the time will be interrupted or handicapped—that is, it will either stop, or it will not progress as efficiently as before anxiety appeared. . . . I have reason to suppose, then, that a fearlike state can be induced in an infant under two circumstances: one is by the rather violent disturbance of his zones of contact with circumambient reality; and the other is by certain types of emotional disturbance within the mothering one. (Sullivan, 1953b, pp. 8–9)

Sullivan had embarked on a theoretical assumption that anxiety was communicable from mother to child, and from child to mother. Sullivan conceptualized anxiety, however, in a very specific way. He distinguished between two hypothetical states: **absolute euphoria** and **absolute tension.** Absolute euphoria is roughly similar to total peace, complete freedom from desire and need, a state of utter well-being experienced, for example, by the infant in the state of deep sleep (Sullivan, 1953b, p. 35). Absolute tension is defined as the "maximum possible deviation from absolute euphoria" as, for example, being in a state of terror or panic. These bipolar opposites are hypothetical extremes that are only rarely experienced by an individual. Much of a person's life is spent in states of experience lying near the middle of the extremes.

Sullivan's next major assumption about personality development concerned the reciprocal relationship between mother's and child's tensions: "The observed activity of the infant arising from the tension of needs [e.g., hunger, thirst] induces tension in the mothering one, which tension is experienced as tenderness and as an impulsion to activities toward the relief of the infant's needs" (1953b, p. 39). In simpler language, Sullivan conjectured that bodily tensions of hunger cause the infant to cry, and this pattern of behavior induces a state of tension in the mother that can be satisfied only by attending to the infant's needs. Thus, from the earliest moments of life, anxiety and tension involve interpersonal relationships.

THE COMMUNICATION OF ANXIETY

Because tension arising in the infant can induce tension in the mother, then it follows that tensions arising in the mother are likewise communicable to the infant: *"The tension of anxiety, when present in the mothering one, induces anxiety in the infant"* (Sullivan, 1953b, p. 41). Since the infant experiences reality in the prototaxic mode, its experience of anxiety is diffuse and fragmented, isolated from other experiences. From the infant's perspective, the tension of anxiety seems similar to tensions produced by needs like hunger and thirst. The infant does not yet differentiate itself from its environment, but experiences itself and its world as one global, fused mass. So the anxiety of the mother or mothering person seems the same to the infant as its own anxiety. They are linked by **empathy,** or a kind of empathic resonance, the capacity of the child to feel the mother's feelings, and vice versa.

Since it cannot differentiate the experience of anxiety from other unpleasurable tensions, the infant possesses as yet no specific means of reducing the anxiety. To reexperience the comforting state of euphoria, the infant must rely on the mothering one to reduce his or her anxiety as the infant relies on her to satisfy bodily needs. But because she is the origin of the anxiety, she cannot of herself reduce the infant's tension until she eliminates her own:

> . . . the infant's capacity for manipulating another person is confined, at the very start, to the sole capacity to call out tenderness by manifesting needs; and the person who would respond to manifest need in the situation in which the infant is anxious is relatively incapable of that response because it is the parental anxiety which induces the infant's anxiety. . . . Therefore, there is, from the very earliest evidence of the empathic linkage, this peculiar distinction that anxiety is not manageable. (Sullivan, 1953b, p. 43)

Once experienced, the feeling of anxiety cannot be removed, nor destroyed, nor escaped for the remainder of the person's life (Sullivan, 1953b, p. 53). Having been inoculated with the first dose of this unmanageable emotion, the human organism is transformed into a sensitive, vulnerable, and insecure human person. Anxiety is the most potent, the earliest, and the most pervasive interpersonal force that can affect the human infant.

NURSING AS THE PROTOTYPE OF INTERPERSONAL SITUATIONS

Because the infant experiences reality in the prototaxic mode, the sum of its perceptions is no more than momentary and fleeting states of sensory awareness. One of the most important sensory experiences for the infant is nursing, or more specifically, the experience of "nipple-in-the-lips." The infant comprehends or, in Sullivan's term, "prehends" the nipple-in-the-lips event as a series of discrete bodily sensations including tactile, thermal, and olfactory stimuli.

From the repetitive nature of the experience, the infant slowly begins to develop a rudimentary conception of the person attached to the nipple—the mothering person. The infant's conception of the mothering person is far from a full picture. Instead, the infant's prototaxic, and later parataxic, experience of discrete sensations leads to a personification of the mother or mothering person. This person becomes identified with the primary transactions with the infant in the feeding situation and the infant's experience of it.

Depending on the degree of satisfaction supplied by the mothering person's feeding behavior, the infant develops one of several different **personifications** of the nipple-in-the-lips mothering one:

1. *Good-and-satisfactory nipple* personification is the nipple in the lips that supplies milk when the infant is hungry [Good Mother].

2. *The good-but-unsatisfactory-nipple* personification is the nipple that supplies milk when the infant is not hungry [Good Mother].

3. *Wrong-nipple-in-the-lips* is an unsatisfactory nipple because it does not supply milk when the infant is hungry; infant rejects this nipple and searches for a better nipple [Bad Mother].

4. *Evil-nipple* is the nipple of an anxious mother who communicates a profound degree of anxiety and tension; this tension is a signal for avoidance; "not that nipple in my lips" [Bad-Anxious Mother]. (Based on Sullivan, 1953b, p. 80.)

Thus, the nursing situation is an important prototype for the development of the infant's relationships with future "significant others":

> . . . the infant is bound to have two personifications of any mothering person (Good and Bad Mother), barring the most incredible good fortune, and . . . the infant in the earliest stages of life need have only two personifications for any number of people who have something to do with looking after him. (Sullivan, 1953b, p. 122)

For example, feelings associated when others are giving unnecessary or unwanted support or advice, according to Sullivan's theory, could be traced back to "the good-but-unsatisfactory-nipple" experience. Likewise, feelings that occur if one's professor is not supportive or caring when one needs guidance can be traced to the "wrong-nipple-in-the-lips" situation. Whether Sullivan's portrayal of infant-nipple relationships is anything more than a striking metaphor for nurturance or lack of nurturance in human relationships has not been empirically verified. Some critics have even called his theory a "fairy tale." Tracing back feelings in adult situations to infantile experience might be seen as an example of a reductionistic approach to personality.

One can also see in Sullivan's theory something akin to a behavioral analysis, in which early conditioning has a great influence on later behavior.

DIFFERENTIATION OF SELF FROM THE UNIVERSE

Toilet training is a clearly interpersonal situation that involves the learning of new personifications about oneself and about one's own body. The way in which the mothering one responds to the infant's body—with disgust, with delight, or with simple acceptance—will be the key determinant in the infant's personification of itself. Coupled with these interpersonal effects are the infant's first clues that it is an independent object in the universe.

For example, the infant lies in the crib and studies the movement of its own hands. The infant may grasp an object, bring it unsteadily to its mouth, and then insert it into its lips. The infant soon discovers that it is not a nipple; but it also discovers that its own hand has brought about the event. When, moreover, it brings an empty hand to its mouth, and sucks the thumb, the infant learns an even more important lesson:

> . . . That the thumb is uniquely different from any nipple by reason of being *in itself* a source of zonal sentience. *The thumb feels sucked.* (Sullivan, 1953b, p. 136; italics added)

Sucking the thumb is also different from the nursing situation in an important way: Unlike an attempt to bring mother-with-satisfactory-nipple on demand, the infant's attempts to bring the thumb to his or her mouth are always successful and unvaryingly satisfying.

> The thumb-in-the-lips is dependable, and is independent of evoking the good mother; the infant can bring it into being, as it were, without cooperation—in isolation from any of his personifications, whether of the good mother or the bad mother. (Sullivan, 1953b, p. 139)

By its experiences with self-evoked satisfactions, the infant learns to foresee and to control some of its own behaviors. More important, the infant learns that it exists—that it has a certain independence. However, when the infant seeks further exploration of its body in the genital or anal zones, it unwittingly brings the personification of the bad mother, the anxious mother, into play:

> The hand manipulating the anus, as any mother knows, will shortly be the hand that is in the mouth; thanks to the great development of the doctrine of germs and to the doubts about physical and sexual purity and cleanliness . . . many mothers feel that a finger conveying anything from the perineal region to the mouth would be disastrous. . . . And even if these

things are not so regarded by the mothering one, she will know that they are so regarded by a large number of other people. (Sullivan, 1953b, pp. 143–144)

Thus, the infant quickly discovers that he or she is not independent of the mothering one's "forbidding gestures" directing the infant not to experience certain parts of itself.

PERSONAL SOURCES OF SULLIVAN'S EMPHASIS ON HUMAN RELATIONSHIPS

Harry Stack Sullivan's early life may very well have sensitized him to the theme of boyhood loneliness and to the pain of the sensitive child who is ridiculed or ignored by his peers because he is somehow ineffably different. For Harry Stack Sullivan *was* different from other boys in his rural village. He was an Irish Catholic in an all-Protestant community; he was an only child, emotionally isolated from unaffectionate parents; and most important, he was homosexual in a place and at a time when there was no shred of acceptance for gays and lesbians. When he later wrote, "everyone and anyone is much more simply human than otherwise, more like everyone else than different," Sullivan was stating in theory ideals that came from his experience as an outsider.

A. H. Chapman was the first to pull together the known facts and speculations about Sullivan's early life, and Helen Swick-Perry (1982) published the first complete biography of Sullivan. We draw from both of their accounts here.

The other children at school and in his rural village never accepted young Harry. Sullivan's social isolation seems to have been a mixture of shyness that triggered withdrawal and compensatory disdain for his schoolmates (Swick-Perry, 1982; cf. Thompson, 1962). He was thus shy, socially awkward, and eccentric. Perry reports a poignant image of the lonely boy standing in a pressed serge suit in the church courtyard after attending Sunday Mass:

> He seemed miserable. . . . This standing alone on the edge of a group is a picture of Sullivan that persists. While close friends remember him as merry and witty in a social setting, people who saw him in situations of less intimacy think of him as testy and caustic—and often obviously miserable. Junior colleagues, who saw him usually in seminars, are apt to discount the idea that he could be kind and merry. (Swick-Perry, 1982, p. 89)

Boyhood on an isolated New York farm was lonely, and the one enduring value Harry seems to have taken from it was a fascination with horses. He used the symbol of two horses' heads, one facing up and the other facing down, intertwined within a circle as his personal emblem throughout his life. The covers of his books always bear this design (Chapman, 1976, p. 21). Swick-Perry (1982, pp. 342–343) has suggested that the horse symbol may have embodied a number of personal meanings for Sullivan by serving as a visual metaphor for evil versus good, male versus female, and homosexual intimacy.

Sullivan's Relationship with His Parents

Harry's mother was the dominant figure in his early life. He had been her third child, but the two previous children died in infancy. Mrs. Sullivan was a semi-invalid who appears to have been profoundly depressed and sufficiently disturbed to require periods of hospitalization (Swick-Perry, 1982). Among her chief concerns was her belief that she had married below her social station, and she communicated this belief to Harry in a variety of ways.

Harry's mother mysteriously disappeared when he was about two-and-a-half years old. Swick-Perry (1982) has been unable to determine the exact cause of the disappearance, but it is clear that Harry's mother was in some way too ill to care for her son. Her

Figure 9.1 Harry Stack Sullivan with his parents, Ella and Timothy, about 1925. All three seem reserved and self-contained. The image of Timothy's dour expression and folded arms is consistent with Harry's description of his father as "remarkably taciturn."
Source: Perry, H. S. (1982). *Psychiatrist of America: The life of Harry Stack Sullivan.* (Cambridge, MA: Belknap Press of Harvard University.)

own mother took over Harry's care, but the demands of farm life resulted in a somewhat distant and detached form of childcare. Harry's own mother may have suffered a "mental breakdown," or possibly attempted suicide (Swick-Perry, 1982, p. 39). Eventually, however, mother and son were reunited. Harry's relationship with his father was distant, and Sullivan described him as "remarkably taciturn." Harry was nearly 30 years old before he was able to establish a somewhat closer relationship with his father. At this late date, Sullivan had come to understand that his mother had gotten in the way of his getting to know his father.

Figure 9.1 shows Sullivan with his mother and father. One can note the empty, cold, and distant expression on his father's face and his folded arms and legs. Sullivan and his mother seem more relaxed than the father, but neither Harry nor his father has a trace of a smile.

Sullivan's First Intimate Relationship

At the age of eight-and-a-half, Harry found friendship with an older boy of 13. Chapman (1976) suggests that the relationship was probably homosexual. However, Swick-Perry (1982, p. 89) has argued on the basis of more thorough research that the relationship was not homosexual. At the time, however, the relationship between Sullivan and Clarence Bellinger was widely regarded as homosexual by the people of Sullivan's hometown. This notoriety added to the boys' sense of ostracism and increased their sense of unity in the face of outsiders.

For Harry, the relationship with Clarence was one of trust and tenderness. Clarence, on the other hand, seems to have been a manipulative bully. Years later, Harry recalled that early relationship with more pleasure than pain, whereas Clarence appears to have come to hate his one-time chum.

Both Clarence and Harry became psychiatrists. Perhaps their own experiences of psychological pain and stress steered them into professional careers in search of answers to personal puzzles.

In his first book, withheld from publication for a variety of reasons until 23 years after his death, Sullivan wrote of the sexual adjustment of the isolated preadolescent:

> Three special cases of isolation call for comment. The first and most unfortunate is that of boys who, because of serious deviation of personality growth, are excluded from gangs and chumships. Those whose progress was fair into the juvenile era are one class. One of these boys is usually clearly conscious of his "difference" from the other boys, of being an "outsider," of his being distrusted, if not despised, by the "regular fellows." Often he has earned a nickname cruelly indicative of the most conspicuous social manifestation of his limitation. . . . His self-respect is gravely impaired. His authority-attitudes are upset. His schoolwork suffers. If he can he becomes loosely associated with some other "failures," often under quasi-leadership of an older, badly beaten boy. It may be that the boy is so unhappy that he submits to manipulation for criminal purposes. It may be that, while he is incapable of submitting himself thus far, he is glad to participate in activities clearly damaging to those who "belong." (Sullivan, 1972, pp. 177–178)

The autobiographical nature of this theoretical discussion is further strengthened by a later passage in which he describes the case of boys isolated merely by virtue of their geographical location. The typical rural community enforces this kind of loneliness, Sullivan states, and the boy usually suffers a prolongation of adolescence:

> Fantasy processes and the *personification of subhuman objects* are called on. Loyalty is developed to abstract ideals, more or less concretely embodied in fanciful figures, rather than to concrete groups. The capacity for sympathy becomes peculiarly differentiated because of the elaboration of its underlying tendencies in loneliness, among fanciful objects. (Sullivan, 1972, p. 180; italics added)

In this passage may lie the explanation for Sullivan's adoption of the horse emblem as his personal symbol. His own loneliness as a child may have resulted in loyalty to "personified subhuman objects" who could neither reject nor ridicule their chum.

In an earlier passage in the same book, Sullivan was even more overtly autobiographical in speaking of a rural community where he had observed firsthand the matter of gang sexuality:

> . . . a large number of the early adolescents participated in overt homosexual activities during the gang age. Most of them progressed thereafter without let or hindrance to the customary heteroerotic interest in later adolescence. Some of the few boys in this community who were excluded from the gangs as a result of their powerful inhibitions, who missed participation in community homosexual play, did not progress to satisfactory heterosexual development. (Sullivan, 1972, p. 171)

It is not unreasonable to assume that Sullivan was writing here about his own exclusion from gang friendships. One can also see that he not only felt stigmatized by a homosexual identity but that he internalized such stigmatization as a lack of "satisfactory heterosexual development."

Sullivan's College Years

Having won a state scholarship to Cornell University in the fall of 1908, Sullivan entered college at the age of 16. After only two terms at Cornell, he was suspended for failure in all his subjects. He also seems to have been involved in some illegal activities that included tampering with mail sent to other students (Swick-Perry, 1982). Another version depicts young Harry as selling something illegal through the mail. The exact facts are not known, but Swick-Perry (1982, p. 146) suggests that he may have been involved in the schemes of older students who attempted to obtain chemicals illegally by ordering them on stolen drugstore stationery.

In any event, Harry left Cornell and dropped out of sight for two years. Swick-Perry (1982) reports that Sullivan suffered a schizophrenic psychotic episode during this time and was probably hospitalized at Bellevue in New York for an indeterminate period. Throughout his writings, Sullivan (see especially 1972) makes oblique reference to the fact that he had personal experience with "schizophrenic states." Also, his first professional contributions involved the treatment of schizophrenic patients.

In 1911, having never returned to college, Sullivan gained entrance to a medical school in Chicago. Only 19 years old, he was barely able to afford tuition. Education at this medical school included little psychiatric study. Incidentally, this was a subject in which Harry received some of his lowest grades. Although graduating within four years, he was not given his diploma because he could not pay his final tuition bill. Sullivan worked as a physician for insurance and steel companies in Illinois and Indiana. After two years, he was able to save enough to redeem his diploma.

Eventually, he became affiliated with a branch of the federal government that worked with war veterans. In 1921, he accepted a position as liaison officer at St. Elizabeth's Hospital in Washington, D.C. At St. Elizabeth's, Sullivan received wide exposure to psychiatric cases and seems to have acquired his knowledge of psychiatric procedure by on-the-job training. By 1923, Sullivan had moved to Baltimore to work at Sheppard and Enoch Pratt Hospital, under the direction of Ross McClure Chapman. He developed a reputation for remarkably empathic contact with male schizophrenics and established a special ward from which females were barred. Sullivan thought that the presence of women made his patients uncomfortable. One might speculate that Sullivan himself was uncomfortable among women or, perhaps, that he was more sensitive to the inner world and feelings of schizophrenics than others. He devised a number of novel procedures for working with schizophrenic patients that soon established his reputation in American psychiatry.

He carefully selected six male aides and intensively instructed them in the art of relating to patients. Sullivan's goal was to establish healthy human relations between the staff and patients as a therapeutic procedure. He reasoned that schizophrenia had its origins in initially unhealthy interpersonal relations (Chapman, 1976, p. 45). He also assumed that many male schizophrenic patients had prior homosexual conflicts, and even indicated that he himself had firsthand experience with that kind of stress (Swick-Perry, 1962, p. xii).

Sullivan encouraged the staff members to share their own experiences of any preadolescent homosexual activity and to indicate that such activities are not depraved but simply part of the human condition. On the basis of his personal experience, Sullivan firmly believed that a period of homosexual interaction in puberty was part of healthy male development. Thus, his special ward at Sheppard-Pratt was, in a sense, a corrective preadolescent society. This concept provided an underlying logic for the exclusion of women. (Swick-Perry, 1962, p. xxi; see also Sullivan, 1962, pp. 104 and 251).

Sullivan's procedures brought remarkable success. Approximately 80 percent of his patients were substantially improved as a result of his treatment and were able to resume more normal interpersonal functioning. We cannot ascertain whether the effectiveness of his treatment actually specifically validated his theories of schizophrenia. For one reason, his patients were selectively chosen, a factor that might have increased his success rate. Patients may have improved because there was a high level of interaction with staff. They received a lot attention and were treated sensitively and with an expectation that they would improve. This was far from the indifferent treatment and low expectations that usually greeted schizophrenic patients in ward settings.

As a therapist, Sullivan held daily interviews with his patients and demonstrated a "fine disregard" for the rules and procedures of classical psychiatry (White, 1977, p. 317). Excerpts of verbatim transcripts of Sullivan's sessions with three patients at Sheppard-Pratt during the period 1923 to 1930 have been published (Schulz, 1978). Sullivan frequently had a stenographer present to record the interviews, and at one point had a microphone concealed on his desk so that his secretary could record the sessions from another part of the building (Swick-Perry, 1962, p. xxi).

As Clarence Schulz (1978) points out, Sullivan's style was not focused on "helping" the patient or on trying to make him feel more comfortable. Rather, the patient was treated as a collaborator who knew his problems better than the psychiatrist. Sullivan would often confront a patient directly with the illogicalities of his statements or with his deliberate untruths. He would attempt to show the patient the nature of his evasions, and Sullivan could sometimes be deliberately sarcastic to make a point.

In considering Sullivan's approach, one might keep in mind other therapists who have relied, to one extent or another, on the patient's own efforts to seek health. Freud, as we have seen in Chapters 2 and 3, first started with hypnotic techniques but then increasingly relied on his patients' own activities, first using the concentration techniques and then in free association.

Theorists as varied as Anna Freud, George Kelly, Carl Jung, Carl Rogers, Gordon Allport, and Erik Erikson, in different ways, emphasized a person's own inclinations toward mastery and growth.

Sullivan's Last Years

In 1927, Sullivan adopted unofficially a 15-year-old boy who lived with him until Sullivan's death on a trip to Paris in 1949. There is some confusion surrounding the circumstances of the "adoption," but Swick-Perry (1982, p. 209) reports that the boy had been brought to Sullivan for treatment after he had been found in a kind of catatonic pose on the street. For more than 20 years, this young man, James Inscoe Sullivan, served as confidant, household staff, cook, and office staff combined. Sullivan regarded Jimmie as his "beloved foster son," and there is no doubt that the relationship was genuinely intimate for both men (Swick-Perry, 1982, p. 211).

Sullivan moved to New York in 1930 to open a Park Avenue private practice. During this period, he received what was probably his first psychoanalysis with Clara Thompson. Chapman (1976) has shown that Sullivan's statements that he had about 75 hours of psychoanalysis much earlier were probably not true but merely an attempt to win needed prestige among colleagues.

On January 14, 1949, while attending a meeting of the World Federation of Mental Health in Paris, Sullivan suffered a brain hemorrhage and died. In the course of his life, he had transformed the loneliness and isolation of his childhood into a career that helped many other vulnerable people and contributed to a more sympathetic understanding and compassionate treatment of mental illness.

PERSONIFICATIONS OF SELF: GOOD-ME, BAD-ME, NOT-ME

For Sullivan, it was clear that the most important kinds of learning occur in the discovery that some behaviors eliminate or reduce the intensity of interpersonal anxiety (1953b, p. 152). The great steersman of development is the **gradient of anxiety** attached to different behavioral situations. An infant can gauge the desirability of particular behaviors in its repertoire. The gradient of anxiety ranges from relatively mild tension-evoking behaviors to behaviors that elicit such intense feelings of emotion that they are best described as "uncanny," "*awe*-full," or "*dread*-full."

Good-Me Personification

All those infant behaviors to which the mothering one has responded with tenderness, praise, emotional warmth, or physical reward become amalgamated into a self-perception of **Good-Me.** The Good-Me personification is thus a product of satisfying or pleasing interpersonal relations with this significant other, the mothering one (1953b, p. 162). The Good-Me personification is largely conscious and usually indicated in verbal behavior by everything to which a person can freely apply the pronoun "I," as in "I am . . ." or "I would like to be . . ." or "I have. . . ."

Bad-Me Personification

Increasing degrees of anxiety and tension on the part of the mothering one are often responses to certain behaviors of her infant: touching objectionable parts of its body, unruly crying, refusing to eat certain foods, struggling over bodily care such as bathing. All those behaviors that cause increasing tension in the mother also evoke anxiety in the infant. Over time, these undesirable, anxiety-provoking behaviors become amalgamated into the personification of the **Bad-Me.** The Bad-Me personification is also conscious to a large degree, but it may merge into behaviors that are unconscious because they evoke stronger degrees of anxiety.

Not-Me Personification

The **Not-Me** personification is an elusive concept The Not-Me is the dissociated cluster of feelings and images that exists side by side with the more neutral content of consciousness but which seemingly does not belong to one's everyday self. It is the part of personality that is rarely experienced consciously by the normal person, except perhaps during dreaming. For the schizophrenic, on the other hand, experience of the Not-Me personification is continual. Thus the Not-Me lies outside the realm of description by language. It is a product of intense, "uncanny" emotion in the parataxic mode:

> This [Not-Me] is a very gradually evolving personification of an always relatively primitive character—that is, organized in unusually simple signs in the parataxic mode of experience, and made up of poorly grasped aspects of living which will presently be regarded as "dreadful," and which still later will be differentiated into incidents which are attended by awe, horror, loathing, and dread. (Sullivan, 1953b, p. 163)

The feelings of dread and terror, disgust and loathing that attend the Not-Me personification are difficult to place in words. These feelings were originally attached to certain behaviors and perceptions that resulted from forbidding gestures and expressions of anxiety from the mothering one. To a greater or lesser extent, all personalities have a Not-Me personification, a part of one's own self that seems alien and hideous.

BOX 9.2	*Only Connect . . .*

Sullivan's concept of the "Not-Me" personification corresponds in many ways to Carl Jung's (Chapter 4) idea of the Shadow archetype. In both cases, it is the part of the psyche that normally does not get incorporated into the person's sense of self and consists of qualities that the individual considers very negative. It is interesting to note that the purported origins of the Not-Me personification differ from Jung's idea of the origins of the Shadow archetype. The Not-Me personification is presumably a result of experiences in early infancy. Jung thought, however, that the Shadow, like other archetypes, arose out of the experiences of humanity during its long history, although the content of a person's Shadow reflected individual differences.

In the development of the normal personality, according to Freud's theory, incestuous and erotic impulses of childhood are repressed along with autoerotic wishes at the time of the resolution of the Oedipus complex. In addition, the child's normally uninhibited desire to play with and to smear his own feces is abandoned after "education" in the shame and disgust lessons of parental example and horror. In one of Sullivan's patients, most of these impulses lingered on in consciousness, but only in a dissociated form that intruded into his conscious fantasies and delusional thinking This psychotic patient evidenced, among other dissociated systems, strong homosexual and incestuous impulses so loathsome and frightening that they had been split off from the rest of consciousness. Particularly problematic was his habitual masturbation accompanied by fantasies that could be described in the normal personality only as Not-Me:

> He masturbated frequently, to the accompaniment of homosexual anal phantasies. *On an occasion when about 17,* he, having inserted a candle into the rectum "to increase satisfaction," as the orgasm approached, withdrew the candle and thrust it into his mouth. The orgasm, he remembers vividly, was very powerful. This recollection was strongly resisted. He had never repeated the procedure. (Sullivan, 1962, p. 36; italics in original)

The revulsion we experience upon reading of this schizophrenic person's behavior is some evidence of the uncanny Not-Me nature of the oral-anal impulses. Because of the negative reaction of the mothering one, most normally socialized adults have acquired a sense of loathing and disgust for anything connected with anal or fecal content.

Ordinarily, the close association between the mouth and the anus for the infant is not connected with disgust or revulsion until shame, learned through anxiety, is established. From that point, the early willingness to manipulate feces, to smear them, or to raise them to the mouth evokes intense horror. Any connection between oral and anal impulses and genital sexual activity is likewise deeply submerged. In effect, these impulses have become Not-Me:

> The not-me is literally the organization of experience with significant people that has been subjected to such intense anxiety, and anxiety so suddenly precipitated, that it was impossible for the then relatively rudimentary person to make any sense of, to develop any true grasp on, the particular circumstances which dictated the experience of this intense anxiety. (Sullivan, 1953b, p. 314)

As in some other parts of Sullivan's theory, much of what he says here seems to be related to specific cultural and societal norms. In today's culture, some parents take a more relaxed, less anxious, and certainly less punitive response to an infant's touching his or her genitals or anus or playing with feces than did parents during Sullivan's childhood. No doubt, this change has been caused by a greater acceptance of bodily functions and sexuality. Such increased acceptance in turn has come about, at least in part, by the efforts of theorists such as Freud and Sullivan. Sullivan's theory would predict an impact of such changes in parenting on the personality of today's adults.

THE SELF-SYSTEM: SECURITY OPERATIONS

From its experiences with reward and anxiety, with forbidding and tender gestures, the infant learns important lessons: Its own anxiety can be reduced by certain specific behaviors that are approved by the mothering one; and its own anxiety is sometimes increased to an unbearable degree by behaving in ways that she disapproves. In effect, it learns that it is desirable to be the Good-Me; undesirable to be the Bad-Me; and unthinkable to be the Not-Me.

To maintain the division between "good" and "bad" forms of living, the infant learns to interact only in certain ways with the significant others of its world. The habitual pattern of behaviors that the infant develops to gain the greatest satisfaction and to keep anxiety at a minimum in dealing with significant others is the **self-system,** or **self-dynamism.** The self-system is thus a cluster of **security operations.**

In Sullivan's attempt to establish a scientific conception of interpersonal relations, he chose the term **dynamism** to indicate habitual patterns of behavior like the self-system because he thought it was a term indicating objective, neutral observation. For Sullivan, the study of the personality is based on understanding the organism's energy transactions with the world of things and people. Sullivan defined dynamism in psychological and biological terms:

> . . . the ultimate entity, the smallest useful abstraction, which can be employed in the study of the functional activity of the living organism is the dynamism itself, the relatively enduring pattern of energy transformations which recurrently characterize the organism in its duration as a living organism. (1953b, p. 103)

The concept of dynamism may be thought of in psychological terms as a habitual reaction pattern. Sullivan again emphasized his fundamental belief that we are all "much more simply human than otherwise" by suggesting that minor variations in habitual reaction patterns were relatively unimportant. It was his opinion that such variations were merely "the envelope of insignificant particular differences." Thus his earliest definition of personality was constructed along these same lines:

> Personality is the relatively enduring configuration of life-processes characterizing all of the person's total activity pertaining to such other persons, real or fantastic, as become from time to time relevant factors in his total situations. (1972, p. 47)

In Sullivan's final, definitive lectures on his conceptualizations, he changed the definition of personality somewhat to emphasize the concept of person-to-person contact as the fundamental unit of study:

> Personality is the relatively enduring pattern of recurrent interpersonal situations that characterize a human life. (1953b, pp. 110–111)

Personality is thus composed of a series of interpersonal dynamisms, habitual patterns of relating to others. Originally founded on the need to reduce anxiety and obtain satisfaction for needs, the self-system is the dynamism of "educative experience called into being by the necessity to avoid or to minimize incidents of anxiety" (1953b, p. 165). The self-system's sole function is to aid the infant in reducing anxiety, first with the mothering one and later, as an adult, with all significant others.

Unfortunately, the self-system also embodies some troublesome characteristics. Since it is the product of parental censure and praise, it embodies the prevailing cultural standards by which the parents themselves have been molded. The self-system, therefore, functions to screen the child's repertoire of possible behaviors and to focus them into a smaller number of socially acceptable ones. Thus, the self-system narrows attention to those aspects of living that generate praise and blame, and it attempts to perpetuate only those experiences that are least likely to generate anxiety. In this sense, the self-system is a stumbling block to growth:

> [The self-system] permits a minute focus on those performances of the child which are the cause of approbation and disapprobation, but, very much like a microscope, it interferes with noticing the rest of the world. When you are staring through your microscope, you don't see much except what comes through that channel. So with the self-dynamism. It has a tendency to focus attention on performances with the significant other person which get approbation or disfavor. (Sullivan, 1953a, p. 21)

The self-system prevents awareness of all experiences, all impulses, that are not relevant to parental approval and disapproval. Experiences that generated parental approval become part of the Good-Me; experiences that generated disapproval become part of the Bad-Me. Experiences that generated large doses of disapproval or intense disfavor are dissociated from the personality and relegated to the Not-Me. The self-system is a selective filter, restricting attention, and consequently personality growth, to the reflected appraisals of others (Sullivan, 1953a, p. 29). Sullivan called this process of filtering **selective inattention.**

SELECTIVE INATTENTION

Selective inattention may occur in emergency situations, for example, when it is necessary to focus awareness only on the problem at hand. In this case, selective inattention is a very adaptive and useful response. But when selective inattention to important aspects of living is habitual in the service of allaying anxiety, it is a mechanism of defensive perception, a security operation. Sullivan added this concept to the long list of defenses developed by Freud, Anna Freud, and others.

To illustrate, Sullivan reported an experience with a patient who provided an elegant and extreme example of selective inattention. Sullivan had been seeing this patient every week for a number of years and soon became accustomed to the man's ritualistic way of beginning the therapeutic hour. Each week the patient would recount an experience he had while on the train en route to Sullivan's office. Each week it was the same experience. And each week the man reported the experience with the same fresh amazement, as if none of the other reported experiences had happened. Sullivan commented,

> I had heard it perhaps two hundred times when one day, for some reason or other, all the factors added up in my mind and I interrupted before he finished. After he had recounted his fantasy of kissing some man and then biting a piece out of his ear I said, "And you were amazed!" He said, "Yes, what do you mean? . . . I was amazed. But why did you say so? What do you know about it?" [Sullivan responded:] "Why, only that you have told me the same story two or three hundred times. . . ." (1956, pp. 44–45)

To a large extent, selective inattention resembles Freud's mechanisms of denial and repression. But Sullivan saw selective inattention as an integral part of the self-system's functioning. On this basis, Sullivan proposed a **Theorem of Escape:**

> The self-system unlike any of the other dynamisms . . . is extraordinarily resistant to change by experience. This can be expressed in the theorem that the self-system from its nature . . .

tends to escape influence by experience which is incongruous with its current organization and functional activity. (1953b, p. 190)

As maturity is attained, whole segments of activity related to anxiety are kept away from the self-system. As with the train-riding man, parts of the self are isolated from the rest of the personality. Though we behave in particular ways, we may be reluctant to recognize all our actions as our own or to incorporate new experiences into the self.

ME-YOU PERSONIFICATIONS

Even in maturity, the individual's self-system and its processes of selective inattention shape conceptions of the self and of significant others. For example, consider the possibilities inherent in the multiple relationships of Mr. A to Mrs. A in the course of their married life. Both partners' self-systems are differently attuned to reality. To maintain self-images founded on others' reflected appraisals, they may respond to **personifications** of the other, not to the reality of the other's presence. As the conditions of the interpersonal situation change, Mr. A's image of his wife will shift. He may personify her one moment as the illusory image "loving and tender wife-mother" and in the next situation she will become for him the illusory image "feminine viper and tauntress." Likewise, Mrs. A responds not to the objective Mr. A but to a series of multiple "you's" she has created in relationship to her personification of herself, her "me" image.

In a sense, at least eight personages are involved (based on Sullivan, 1964, pp. 46 ff.):

Mr. A and Mrs. A as they really are

Mr. A[1] as his wife personifies him [loving husband]

Mr. A[2] as his wife personifies him in another situation [selfish and despicable husband]

Mrs. A[1] as her husband personifies her [loving wife]

Mrs. A[2] as her husband personifies her in another context [viper and tauntress]

Mr. A[3] as he sees himself [peacemaker; long suffering]

Mrs. A[3] as she sees herself [victim; belittled wife]

Additionally, the list of personifications might be supplemented with the subsequent changes in self-perception as the other's "you" image changes the situation and is reflected in changed self-images: Mr. A[4,5,6,7 ···] and Mrs. A[4,5,6,7 ···] and so on.

If we could observe a quarrel between Mr. and Mrs. A, we could record the shift in me-you patterns that takes place. In the quarrel, Mrs. A has assumed the role of victimized wife; she resents frequently being left alone on her husband's nights out. Mr. A, on the other hand, remarks to his wife that her choice of friends is so utterly boring and ridiculous that he can barely tolerate being present. That is why he seeks out his own friends.

Mrs. A now unleashes some pent-up fury to inform the man she now views as an utterly selfish belittler of women not to "judge my friends by the fools you spend your evenings with" (Sullivan, 1964, p. 45). In response, Mr. A assumes the role of wounded husband, a long-suffering peacemaker who has finally suffered enough at the hands of this malicious person. In his view, Mrs. A has become "the epitome of malicious persecutions, a human viper whom the law protects while she taunts him with her ability to destroy his every chance of happiness" (Sullivan, 1964, p. 45).

The interaction between Mr. A and Mrs. A has shifted among mutual illusory "me-you" patterns. The fact that the partners can respond to each other, to each other's image of self, and to their own illusory personifications of the other led Sullivan to propose that

. . . the incongruity in the coincident me-you patterns may grow to such a point that [Mr.] A comes to think "something is wrong" with Mrs. A, and consults a psychiatrist about her. He reports that "she seems to have undergone a complete change. She misunderstands everything I do, thinks I deceive her about everything. . . ." (1964, p. 47)

Thus the label "mental illness" may be applied to one partner on the basis of discrepant mutual and illusory me-you personifications. For Sullivan, the goal of psychiatry is "the study of the phenomena that occur in interpersonal situations, in configurations made up of two or more people, all but one of whom [the psychiatrist-observer] may be more or less completely illusory" (1964, p. 33).

DEVELOPMENTAL EPOCHS: FROM INFANCY TO LATE ADOLESCENCE

Sullivan divided the course of personality development into six epochs. Each of these is marked by a distinctly different quality of interpersonal relations and by functioning in one of the three modes of experience.

The six epochs and the predominant mode in each epoch are:

1. infancy   (prototaxic mode)
2. childhood   (parataxic mode)
3. juvenile   (mostly syntaxic mode, partly parataxic)
4. preadolescence   (syntaxic mode)
5. early adolescence (syntaxic mode)
6. late adolescence (syntaxic mode)

Infancy

Extending roughly from birth to the development of language, the period of infancy is primarily prototaxic in nature. The infant experiences reality as a discrete flux of momentary states. The infant does not differentiate self from the world; his or her experience of reality is global, diffuse. Most significant of the developments of infancy are the personifications of self and significant other. Good-Me, Bad-Me, and Not-Me have already been surveyed as well as the personifications of the Good and Bad Mother (nipple). Out of its experiences with the significant others of its world, the infant develops a particular orientation to the world. These dynamisms can include apathy and somnolent detachment when the infant's experiences with the mothering one have been anxiety-provoking and frustrating.

The term **apathy** refers to the capacity of the infant to deal with emergency situations of unsatisfied needs by developing a withdrawing "I don't care" orientation to its own experiences of hunger, thirst, and pain (Sullivan, 1953b, p. 55).

Somnolent detachment literally means the separation from reality that occurs by being sleepy. In effect, the infant's withdrawal response of apathy may be extended to cope with anxiety situations that are persistent and prolonged. From the infant's point of view, somnolent detachment involves not only a "don't care" attitude about objects of need satisfaction but also a forthright indifference to the significant persons who are responsible for neglect of desires. Apathy is called out by aggravated and unsatisfied needs; somnolent detachment is evoked by prolonged anxiety in interpersonal contacts (Sullivan, 1953b, p. 57).

Childhood

The childhood epoch extends roughly from the acquisition of language to the appearance of a need for playmates or what Sullivan termed "compeers" (1953b, p. 33; 1953a, p. 37). Though language is present, it is sometimes used in some very magical, parataxic ways:

> . . . in so far as a verbal statement by a child is taken by the acculturating adults to have a superior quality of reality to other of his behavioral acts, the child is being trained to be incapable of dealing with life. . . . In a good many homes, the following kind of statement is a conspicuous ingredient in the alleged education of the young: "Willie, I told you not to do that. Now say you are sorry." . . . If Willie dutifully says he is sorry, that is supposed to markedly mitigate the situation, although it is something that Willie is almost absolutely incapable of understanding. (Sullivan, 1953b, pp. 200–201)

Another important development of the childhood epoch is the possibility for the child to undergo what Sullivan called a **malevolent transformation** (1953b, p. 213):

> A child may discover that manifesting the need for tenderness toward the potent figures around him leads frequently to his being disadvantaged, being made anxious, being made fun of. . . . Under those circumstances, the developmental course changes to the point that the perceived need for tenderness brings a foresight of anxiety and pain. The child learns, you see, that it is highly disadvantageous to show any need for tender cooperation from the authoritative figures around him, in which case he shows something else; and that something else is the basic malevolent attitude, the attitude that one really lives among enemies. . . . (Sullivan, 1953b, p. 114)

Later, in adolescence, some children have learned that their world is hostile and unfriendly. They may, therefore, deliberately behave in ways that make it difficult for anyone to show them affection and kindness. They have learned not to express any need for tenderness, and they often treat others in a hostile manner.

On the positive side, the epoch of childhood is marked by a number of "as if" performances or role-playing the significant behaviors modeled by parents. "As if" performances may eventually be practiced as defensive maneuvers by a child who has been exposed to manipulative and anxiety-provoking parenting.

Instead of a healthy identification with parents, children may play roles to conceal their real feelings in the dramatization of behaviors demonstrated by mother and father (1953b, p. 209). In a dramatization, the "as if" performance shifts to children acting as if they actually were the parents. For the most part, however, dramatizations are an essential and normal part of the childhood epoch, and they facilitate adoption by the child of each one's appropriate male or female role.

The second kind of "as if" performance is the technique of seeming preoccupied with something in order to be left alone. Children learn to behave "as if" some activity were highly important to them, riveting their attention and demanding all their energy. In actuality, the seeming preoccupation is really a technique of avoiding disturbing and painful interactions with anxiety-provoking significant others, or it is a means of escaping their demands (1953b, p. 210).

The changing role of playmates clearly marks the transition from childhood to the juvenile epoch. In childhood, the need for a playmate was essentially **egocentric,** even selfish. Children play side by side, but they do not necessarily interact. A child's awareness of a playmate or playmates is usually less important than the child's own ideas and pursuits. The child may even invent an imaginary playmate to satisfy his or her own wishes. A need for genuinely cooperative play and for mutuality of experience emerges during the juvenile period (Sullivan, 1953b, p. 226).

The juvenile epoch extends from the grammar school years through that phase when the child experiences a need for an intimate relationship with a same-sexed "chum." Most of the juvenile's experiences are in the syntaxic mode; language has become the chief tool for coping with the demands of authority.

Education and the authority figures of the school play a significant role in the juvenile's life. The chief contributions to personality development occur through two avenues of social activity.

1. *Social subordination* occurs when the child learns to respect and to obey a succession of parental authority substitutes: a teacher, a crossing guard, the gym coach, and so on.

2. *Social accommodation* involves learning to accept and tolerate familial and social diversity through exposure to a variety of new and significant others.

Preadolescence

The key characteristic of preadolescence is the strong emergence of a trend already present in the juvenile epoch: the need for a close friend or what Sullivan termed a "chum" of the same sex. The preadolescent epoch begins with the establishment of a friendship with a same-sexed peer to the emergence of an interest and a need for a partner of the opposite sex.

The significance of the need for a chum is in the character of the relationship. For the first time, the chum is a person who has equal importance to self. His or her interests, needs, and fantasies are on the same level of importance as those of the preadolescent. The preadolescent has developed a real sensitivity to the needs of the other person.

> And this is not in the sense of "what should I do to get what I want," but instead "what should I do to contribute to the happiness or to support the prestige and feeling of worth-whileness of my chum." (Sullivan, 1953b, p. 245)

The relationship that develops between chums is termed *collaboration* because each of the chums validates the personal worth of the other. They collaborate mutually to validate desires, conceptions of the world, and interpretations of the self:

> Because one draws so close to another, because one is newly capable of seeing oneself through the other's eyes, the preadolescent phase of personality development is especially significant in correcting autistic, fantastic ideas about oneself or others. (Sullivan, 1953b, p. 248)

Early Adolescence

Early adolescence is characterized by feelings of "lust" (1953b, p. 263). Most adolescents have experienced orgasm, and the feelings of sexual arousal are a new and continual component of the self-image. A variety of collisions between the feelings of lust and the needs for security and intimacy often occur. It is typical of adolescence in modern secular society that burgeoning sexual needs cause a reevaluation of the self-image in the light of growing doubts about sexual competence and proficiency.

> Ridicule from parents and other elders is among the worst tools that are used on early adolescents. Sometimes a modification of ridicule is used by parents . . . and this modification takes the form of interfering with, objecting to, criticizing and otherwise getting in the way of any detectable movement of their child toward a member of the other sex. (Sullivan, 1953b, p. 268)

There are also collisions between the need for intimacy and lustful feelings. Adolescents often feel awkward and clumsy in their first advances to a member of the other sex, particularly so when that person has already been idealized and idolized. Groups of male adolescents may distinguish between "good" girls and the more permissive ones. When there is a double standard, sexual intercourse or genital stimulation is thought to apply only to the latter group, with the "good" girls reserved as more or less potential marriage partners.

Biographical material on Sullivan's childhood indicates that his description of the whole adolescent epoch was consistent with his own painful struggle in the area of male sexuality. One might question to what extent his developmental theory of early adolescence largely reflects *culturally determined behaviors* rather than being universal.

Late Adolescence: The Mask

Late adolescence extends from the focused expression of genital sexual activity through the establishment of a full repertoire of adult interpersonal relations (1953b, p. 297). The predominant mode of experience is syntaxic. The most important behavioral characteristics of late adolescence are the establishment of vocational identity or the decision to pursue an educational course leading to some professional role.

For the first time, adolescents may experience real "restrictions in living." Inhibitions or hindrances based on past developmental failures or other handicaps stemming from their past emotional interactions may curtail their range of adult choices for a job, for education, or for a mate. Respect for self must be based on learned respect for others. Without this mutuality of concern and performance, the adolescent is likely to develop a variety of techniques for isolating and preventing further development to full maturity.

To cope with the puzzling inner and outer changes that they experience, adolescents on the threshold of adulthood may experiment with aspects of all the "selves" they have been up to now. Sullivan described this compartmentalization of character with the metaphor of the mask in the first book he wrote:

> The adolescent may begin the "life behind a mask" that tends to characterize numbers of our urban denizens. The mask, however, requires so much energy for its successful maintenance that personality growth is apt to end with its successful construction. As the necessities for masking certain motivations vary from one to another interpersonal situation, it may be easier to avoid further integration of the self, and to develop, from this point onward, specialized accommodations and interests for various groups. (Sullivan, 1972, p. 201)

In effect, such an adolescent has failed to integrate the many self-conceptions and reflected appraisals that constitute the personality into a functioning unity. Instead, an artificial facade that may fit into some peer groups is developed.

EVALUATING HARRY STACK SULLIVAN

Harry Stack Sullivan is frequently considered a neo-Freudian, but he does not fit that label easily. Unlike the other neo-Freudians, Sullivan did not actually rebel against Freud's ideas, rather, he merely ignored those he found uncongenial. Sullivan was an eclectic borrower from many other theorists. He had a broad range of interests in the social sciences, linguistics, and anthropology. Findings or concepts from each of these fields are, in some way, integrated into his theory. But Sullivan was first and foremost a psychiatrist whose primary duty was the treatment of patients, and much of his focus was clinical rather than theoretical. Out of this clinical, social, and scientific mixture arose his interpersonal theory.

Refutability of Sullivan's Concepts

Because the main thread that runs through Sullivan's ideas is a psychodynamic one, he shares with other psychoanalytically oriented theorists a general lack of refutability that such theories embody. Many of his main concepts, however, are in principle testable, but not in the form he stated them. For example, his conception of the self-system as a group of self-protective processes with selective inattention as the "motor" of self-protection could be reconceptualized in testable cognitive and perceptual terms. But his more abstracted and psychodynamic constructs, such as the "Not-Me" and the "Bad-Me," are couched in nonobservable referents and are beyond empirical testing. Sullivan's theory, however useful clinically, has not generated empirical research.

Sullivan's emphasis on the psychological causation of schizophrenia has been largely refuted. Recent research and clinical advances have pointed to a superabundance of dopamine as being a major causal factor in schizophrenia. Medications that reduce dopamine levels reduce schizophrenic symptoms. To what extent environmental or psychological factors, such as ones to which Sullivan alludes, may result in too much dopamine has not been determined. As far as improving the life of schizophrenic patients, demonstration of the value of Sullivan's work in therapeutic wards is handicapped by the lack of comparison or control groups. Given that many of Sullivan's patients improved, we therefore do not know whether such improvement is a result of the specifics of his treatment approach or simply of a kind, caring, and respectful environment. He should, in any case, be given a good deal of credit for not "giving up" on or warehousing his schizophrenic patients.

Sullivan's Conception of Human Agency

Sullivan has an essentially interactive viewpoint with respect to personality functioning. He emphasized that personality develops in social interaction, so that without the multiple perspectives of others' views of self, the self would be empty. But Sullivan also acknowledged that each person constructs his or her own interpretations of others, the "personifications" supported by selective inattention, and he believed that each person acts on that set of beliefs. The balance, therefore, appears to be toward an active and even interactive agency viewpoint. Interpersonal relationships shape us, and we have the power to shape our relationships.

The Nomothetic Aims of Sullivan's Theory

More than other psychodynamic theorists, Sullivan emphasized the importance of human relationships and the influence of cultural variables. His theoretical focus was nomothetic. But, as a clinician, his focus on individual psychopathology and its treatment raised idiographic issues.

On balance, Sullivan's theory would be classed as nomothetic, but, unfortunately, a nomothetic theory that has yet to generate empirical validation for its generalizations. His scheme of development through the various epochs from infancy to adolescence would certainly lend itself to nomothetic research, but no one has taken up the challenge of conducting such research.

SUMMARY

Sullivan viewed personality as the set of characteristic and habitual interpersonal relations that mark a human life. The most significant of these is the mothering–infant relationship. Because the mother or mother figure can communicate anxiety to the infant, and because the infant's needs arouse in her a corresponding need to show her infant tenderness, Sullivan characterized the relationship as an "empathic linkage." The ways in which the mothering one responds to the infant's behaviors shapes the three personifications of the self: Good-Me, Bad-Me, and the uncanny Not-Me.

Sullivan also emphasized the unity of human endeavor in his one-genus postulate: "We are all much more simply human than otherwise." Thus, even the activities of psychotherapists are to be conceptualized as *participant* observation, for they, too, bring to the therapeutic relationship strictly human experiences and qualities.

As infants progress through the various stages of growth and psychological development, they experience reality in vastly more abstract ways than were possible in their first months of existence. Sullivan conceptualized three levels or modes of experiencing in the earliest years:

1. The infant's first perceptions of self and the universe are fused, vague, and in continuous flux. Called the *prototaxic mode,* this early form of experience is primarily sensory and predominantly egocentric.

2. In the *parataxic mode,* temporal contiguity is interpreted as causality.

3. Finally, the child begins to enter the *syntaxic mode* in which reality is interpreted on its own terms,

and the most important tool that the child brings to bear is language.

Sullivan's conception of me-you patterns of personification was yet another indication of his growing sense of the importance of social interaction for psychiatry. Sullivan's emphasis on the importance of interpersonal experiences along with his understanding of early stages of thought and experience led to his insightful, humane, and empathic approach to schizophrenic patients.

Sullivan divided personality development into six epochs: infancy, childhood, juvenile, preadolescence, early adolescence, and late adolescence. The significant advances represented by the successive stages center on the increasing emphasis on more sophisticated modes of experiencing reality and on its growing need for intimate relationships with significant others.

Our evaluation of Sullivan's theory suggests that it is a largely untestable one, with a few exceptions, such as his concept of selective inattention, his developmental scheme, and his notion of "personifications." These concepts would require creative research to derive an empirically testable version from Sullivan's imprecise theoretical prose. Sullivan aimed to be nomothetic in his theory-building, but large segments of the theory are fundamentally idiographic.

The most important aspect of Sullivan's view of personality was that he pointed out that, from early infancy, this is a world of interpersonal relations. Our feelings and emotions—both painful and joyful—are tied up with our interactive relations to significant others. In his view, our basic ways of dealing with life emerge from our earliest and deepest experiences with others.

FOR FURTHER READING

During his lifetime, Sullivan published rarely. His major work, *The Interpersonal Theory of Psychiatry* (New York: Norton, 1968), is actually a series of lectures skillfully edited into a coherent work. To gain some historical perspective on the development of Sullivan's ideas, you will find *Personal Psychopathology: Early Formulations* (New York: Norton: 1984) quite illuminating. Sullivan had postponed the publication of this volume several times during his career, until it was finally published posthumously.

Some of Sullivan's early papers on schizophrenia and psychotic disorganization have been organized into a single volume under the title *Schizophrenia as*

a Human Process (New York: Norton, 1974); a careful reading of these papers will reveal Sullivan's debts to Jung and to Freud. Another collection of Sullivan's papers, *The Fusion of Psychiatry and Social Science* (New York: Norton, 1964), more clearly exposes his methodological assumptions, including his one-genus (species identity) theorem. Sullivan's other published works are cited throughout the chapter, and a careful reading of any of them will repay the effort involved.

A reading of George Herbert Mead's *Mind, Self and Society from the Standpoint of a Social Behaviorist* (Chicago: University of Chicago Press, 1934;

available in paperback) will reveal another source of Sullivan's ideas on the nature of selfhood.

Indirectly influenced by Sullivan, Jurgen Ruesch has written two books that emphasize the power of language in shaping a person's worldview. The two volumes are *Disturbed Communication and Therapeutic Communication* (New York: Norton, 1957 and 1961, respectively).

The papers published in Patrick Mullahy's *The Contributions of Harry Stack Sullivan: A Symposium on Interpersonal Theory in Psychiatry and Social Science* (New York: Jason Aronson, 1995) attempt to place Sullivan's work in historical perspective.

The style of Sullivan's psychotherapy is treated by Mary Julian White in her "Sullivan and Treatment" (*Contemporary Psychoanalysis*, 1977, *13,* 317–347), and by C. G. Schulz in his publication of some verbatim transcripts of Sullivan's patient interviews at Sheppard-Pratt in "Sullivan's Clinical Contribution During the Sheppard-Pratt Era—1923–1930" (*Psychiatry,* 1978, *41,* 117–128).

GLOSSARY

Absolute euphoria: A state of complete well-being, roughly similar to total peace, complete freedom from desire and need. Like *absolute tension,* a hypothetical extreme that rarely occurs.

Absolute tension: The "maximum possible deviation from absolute euphoria" as, for example, experiencing terror or panic.

Anxiety: Sullivan asserted that the experience of anxiety has its origins in an infant's interpersonal experiences. A mother who is tense and fearful passes on those feelings to her vulnerable infant.

Apathy: A withdrawn "I don't care" orientation to an infant's experiences of unsatisfied needs such as hunger, thirst, and pain.

Bad-Me: A personification that is made up of those experiences that have been punished or disapproved of by the mother. It stems from unpleasant or embarrassing interpersonal relationships, and it contains those behaviors of which we are ashamed. This self-image is associated with feelings of anxiety.

Dissociation: The process of keeping impulses, desires, fantasies, and needs out of awareness. Those disorganized thoughts and urges are split off from waking consciousness and are thus not under ego control.

Dynamism: Energy transformations that become habitual behavioral patterns of relating to others that characterize the individual throughout life.

Egocentric: Being absorbed in one's own ideas or needs; lacking awareness or attentiveness to the reactions or experiences of others. In Sullivan's theory, such developmentally based egocentricity is characteristic of childhood.

Empathy: The capacity to resonate with and understand the feelings of other people.

Good-Me: A personification that consists of those aspects of ourselves we feel good about, and for which we have been praised in the past. This self-image is associated with feelings of security resulting from a nurturing, satisfying, and pleasing relationship with a mothering figure.

Gradient of anxiety: A means of an infant's gauging the desirability of its various behaviors. The gradient of anxiety ranges from relatively mild tension-evoking behaviors to behaviors that elicit intense negative emotions.

Malevolent transformation: The development of a malevolent attitude toward others. This change in attitude can occur when children have been denied tenderness and affectionate care. They come to repress any need for tenderness and treat others with hostility and unfriendliness.

Not-Me: A personification that is made up of those inchoate and threatening aspects of ourselves, from which we dissociate and keep in the unconscious. This personification of self embodies all the unacceptable behaviors that are accompanied by "uncanny" feelings of anxiety.

One-genus postulate: The concept that, "Everyone and anyone is much more simply human than otherwise, more like everyone else than different." Sullivan focused on the continuity of mental processes from normality through psychosis.

Parataxic mode: The perception of events in a temporal sequence, one after the other. The infant comes to expect an event by what immediately precedes or follows it.

Participant observer: Sullivan's concept that the clinical investigator is not only a scientific observer but also an involved participant who is insightful regarding his or her own reactions.

Personality: A series of interpersonal dynamisms, habitual patterns of relating to others, originally designed to reduce anxiety and obtain satisfaction.

Personifications: Mental images we have of ourselves and other people. Also, conceptions of the self that are formed in the relationship with the mothering figure.

Prototaxic mode: The simplest and crudest mode of experiencing reality at the beginning of life in which the infant's experience is limited to a constant stream of sensory events over which it cannot impose order or consistency.

Schizophrenia: A disorder that is characterized by bizarre, seemingly unconnected cognitive and verbal processes and often can be of psychotic proportions. Sullivan focused on psychological causation, whereas contemporary psychiatry emphasizes the biochemistry involved in this syndrome.

Security operations: The process of denying or distorting interpersonal experiences that contradict or upset an individual's self-image.

Selective inattention: A method of ignoring or rejecting stimuli, which serves to alleviate the influence of anxiety-provoking stimuli. This defense mechanism may lead to distortion of reality.

Self-system/self dynamism: A cluster of security operations. It begins when the infant begins to develop an habitual pattern of behaviors, in dealing with others, to keep anxiety minimal and to gain the greatest satisfaction.

Somnolent detachment: Literally, the separation from reality that occurs by being sleepy. From the infant's point of view, somnolent detachment involves not only a "don't care" attitude but also a forthright indifference to those who are seen as responsible for neglecting the infant's desires.

Syntaxic mode: Adult, logical, and analytical thought processes. The experience of reality in the syntaxic mode includes the ability to predict cause and effect.

Theorem of Escape: Sullivan's theorem that the self-system tends to escape the influence of experiences that are incongruous with its current organization and functional activity.

Chapter 10

Karen Horney

Psychoanalytic Social Psychology

For the very reason that love in our civilization is so rarely a genuine affection, maltreatment and betrayal abound.

Karen Horney, *Our Inner Conflicts*

Karen Horney	Born: 1885	Blankenese, Germany
	Died: 1952	New York, New York

About Horney's Social Psychoanalytic Approach

Karen Horney began as a psychoanalytic theorist. However, she soon found classical Freudian ideas too restrictive in their emphasis on sexual and aggressive motives.
    Karen Horney widened classical psychoanalysis with her concepts of:

1. *Childhood as a period of anxious helplessness and hidden anger toward all-powerful but indifferent adults.*

2. *Strategies to cope with the anxiety and anger that alienate the person from the true self; the neurotic person is not comfortable in his or her own skin but must avoid, attack, or completely comply with others.*

3. *A desexualized Oedipus complex in which the key issues are power and love instead of sexuality and guilt.*

Horney transcended Freudian classical theory in her search to understand people based on factors other than the gratification of sexual and aggressive drives.

COPING APPROACHES AND NEUROTIC[1] TRENDS

Neurotic individuals differ in the way they view the world and in their patterns of relating to others. Although nearly everyone occasionally adopts each of these interpersonal stances to some extent, neurotics are usually both more inflexible and extreme.

Some are human doormats who allow others to tread on them. These compliant personalities try to please and pacify others. At the opposite extreme, some persons are typically hostile toward others. These aggressive persons view the world as dangerous. They believe that only constant vigilance can thwart the continually hostile efforts of others. Yet a third form of interpersonal strategy is exemplified by individuals who remain coldly aloof and withdrawn from genuine interaction with significant others. These detached personalities seem to construe the world and other people as essentially troublesome and unjustly demanding. The only reasonable solution, they feel, is avoidance.

On the basis of theoretical assumptions derived partly from psychoanalytic theory and partly from her own clinical observations, Karen Horney further elaborated that the neurotic personality is governed by one or more of ten **neurotic trends.** Each neurotic trend is directed toward interpersonal control and coping. Horney distinguished her theory from those of the other theorists with whose ideas she was most familiar:

> Freud believed that the [neurotic] disturbances generate from a conflict between environmental factors and repressed instinctual impulses. Adler, more rationalistic and superficial than Freud, believes that they are created by the ways and means that people use to assert their superiority over others. Jung, more mystical than Freud, believes in collective unconscious fantasies, which, though replete with creative possibilities, may work havoc because the unconscious strivings fed by them are the exact opposite of those in the conscious mind. *My own answer is that in the center of psychic disturbances are unconscious strivings developed in order to cope with life despite fears, helplessness, and isolation. I have called them "neurotic trends."* (1942, p. 40; italics added)

Neurotic needs differ from those experienced by psychologically more normal people. Such needs:

- evidence disproportionate intensity,
- are indiscriminately applied to others,
- evidence an extreme disregard for reality, and
- show a tendency to provoke intense anxiety when they remain unsatisfied.

---

[1] The term *neurotic* is not a current diagnostic label. Many people formerly labeled as neurotic would be considered to be suffering from some form of anxiety disorder, a more behaviorally defined term. Horney often used the term *neurotic* to indicate patterns of extreme and inflexible approaches to life. The current diagnostic term most similar to Horney's meaning is *personality disorder*. Such a label indicates a deeply ingrained, inflexible, and maladaptive pattern of behavior. The person usually has little or no insight into such a behavior pattern (APA, 2000, 685–729). Three personality types very similar to Horney's descriptions are *dependent personality disorder, obsessive-compulsive personality disorder,* and *avoidant personality disorder.*

These ten neurotic "needs" (Horney, 1942, pp. 54–60) are as follows:

1. *The neurotic need for affection and approval:* an indiscriminate desire to please others and to be liked and approved of by others. The person's "center of gravity" is in others, not in self.

2. *The neurotic need for a "partner" who will take over one's life:* a partner who will fulfill all expectations the neurotic has in life; who will take responsibility for good and evil, success and failure. The neurotic so inclined has a tendency to overvalue "love" because love can solve everything.

3. *The neurotic need to restrict one's life within narrow borders:* a necessity to be undemanding and contented with little; a need to remain inconspicuous, belittling one's potential.

4. *The neurotic need for power, for control over others, and for a facade of omnipotence:* domination over others craved for its own sake; essential disrespect for others; indiscriminate adoration of strength and contempt for weakness; belief in the power of reason and intelligence; extreme value placed on foresight and prediction; tendency to relinquish wishes and to withdraw because of dread of failure.

5. *The neurotic need to exploit others and get the better of them:* others evaluated primarily according to whether they can be exploited or made use of; dread of being exploited or made to look "stupid."

6. *The neurotic need for social recognition or prestige:* self-evaluation dependent entirely on public acceptance; all things and people evaluated only in terms of prestige value.

7. *The neurotic need for personal admiration:* inflated image of self; need to be admired not for what one possesses or presents in the public eye but for the imagined self.

8. *The neurotic ambition for personal achievement:* self-evaluation dependent on being the very best lover, athlete, writer, worker—particularly in one's own mind—recognition by others being vital too, however, and its absence resented.

9. *The neurotic need for self-sufficiency and independence:* necessity never to need anybody, or to yield to any influence, or to be tied down to anything; necessity to avoid any closeness that involves the danger of enslavement.

10. *The neurotic need for perfection and unassailability:* ruminations or recriminations regarding possible flaws; relentless driving for perfection; feelings of superiority over others because of being perfect.

Some overlaps and similarities can be found among the ten needs or trends. Horney devoted a great deal of her later theoretical efforts to grouping these ten discrete trends into clusters and categories descriptive of particular personalities.

BASIC ANXIETY AND BASIC HOSTILITY

Horney, like Alfred Adler (Chapter 5), asserted that one of children's most important experiences is an awareness of their vulnerability and dependence. In the face of powerful "giants" such as parents and other adults, children correctly perceive themselves to be weak and small. Children quickly learn that satisfaction of their needs, their safety, and their comfort are dependent on these powerful people.

Parental Indifference: The "Basic Evil"

To Horney, a coldly indifferent, perhaps hostile, rejecting attitude of a child's parents is the source of later neurosis:

> The basic evil is invariably a lack of genuine warmth and affection. A child can stand a great deal of what is often regarded as traumatic—such as sudden weaning, occasional beating, sex experiences—as long as inwardly he feels wanted and loved. . . . *The main reason why a child does not receive enough warmth and affection lies in the parents' incapacity to give it on account of their own neuroses.* . . . We find various actions or attitudes on the part of the parents which cannot but arouse hostility, such as preference for other children, unjust reproaches, unpredictable changes between overindulgence and scornful rejection, unfulfilled promises, and not least important, *an attitude toward the child's needs which goes through all gradations from temporary inconsideration to a consistent interfering with the most legitimate wishes of the child,* such as disturbing friendships, ridiculing independent thinking, spoiling its interest in its own pursuits . . . *altogether an attitude of the parents which if not in intention nevertheless in effect means breaking the child's will.* (1937, pp. 80–81; italics added)

A child who is subjected to such parental indifference, interference, and inconsistency usually develops an attitude of **basic hostility** as a result.

Basic Hostility: Repression for Survival and Security

Like mature persons, children sense and rightfully resent the injustice of their treatment at the hands of emotionally manipulative elders. Many such children repress such feelings—drive them right out of awareness—in the service of continued survival. Repression of hostility is triggered by a combination of feelings on the child's part: feelings of helplessness, fear, love, or guilt (Horney, 1937, p. 85). But whatever the motive for repression, the result consists of feelings of increased unworthiness and anxiety. Children may be caught between dependence on their parents and a growing feeling of hostility toward them. It is as if the child's behavior says to the adult, *"I have to repress my hostility because I need you"* (Horney, 1937, p. 86). Repressing any expressions of hostility to adults, a child may then turn those hostile feelings against a safe target, his or her own self.

Some parents actively strive to dominate their children by teaching them to be fearful. They impress their children with the "great dangers of life": germs, cars, strangers, other children, and on and on. In consequence, such children become apprehensive lest they be unable to survive in such a dangerous world without their parents' help. Furthermore, they learn to fear the parents themselves because they have the awesome power to evoke images of dangers. For such children, repression of hostility is a product of their fear. Their behavior signifies that, *"I have to repress my hostility because I am afraid of you"* (Horney, 1937, p. 86).

Other families without real affection and warmth may be full of substitute expressions of love. These may consist of protestations by the parents of how much they are sacrificing for the child. In such a case, a child may cling desperately to his parent's superficial emotions and feel *"I have to repress my hostility for fear of losing love"* (Horney, 1937, p. 86).

In all these situations, a child's fundamental motive is to sustain satisfying contact with parental figures. A thread of helplessness runs through the child's patterns of behavior and coping. This comprises what Horney termed the child's **basic anxiety.**

<table>
<tr><td>

BOX 10.1   *Only Connect . . .*

Some of Alfred Adler's (Chapter 5) ideas served as the jumping-off point for Horney's conception of basic hostility and inferiority. Horney's concept of *basic anxiety* is similar to Adler's notion of the inferiority feelings of childhood. Consider her definition of basic anxiety: "It [basic anxiety] may be roughly described as a feeling of being small, insignificant, helpless, deserted, endangered, in a

world that is out to abuse, cheat, attack, humiliate, betray, envy" (Horney, 1937, p. 92). Adler, however, did not think that "basic hostility" was *the only outcome* of inferiority feelings. He thought that more constructive choices were possible. Adler's *The Practice and Theory of Individual Psychology* (Totowa, NJ: Littlefield, Adams, 1999) provides some basis of comparison with Horney's ideas.

</td></tr>
</table>

Basic Anxiety: Lonely and Helpless in a Hostile World

Children may generalize their anxious helplessness and repressed hostility:

> The condition that is fostered or brought about by the factors I have mentioned . . . is an insidiously increasing, *all-pervading feeling of being lonely and helpless in a hostile world.* . . . This attitude as such does not constitute a neurosis but it is the nutritive soil out of which a definite neurosis may develop at any time. Because of the fundamental role this attitude plays in neuroses I have given it a special designation: the *basic anxiety*; it is inseparably interwoven with a *basic hostility.* (Horney, 1937, p. 89; italics added)

The most immediate consequence of the combination of basic hostility and the resultant basic anxiety is the creation of a characteristic mode of reacting to the world and to significant others.

If children come to feel that they can survive only by *complying with others* and by placating them—*"If you love me, you will not hurt me"*—they may solve their survival problems by offering the world a passive, nonassertive, appeasing personality (Horney, 1937, p. 97).

Other children may develop the attitude that life is a struggle, which must be fought by maintaining an aggressive stance toward others: *"If I have power, I shall not be hurt"* (Horney, 1937, p. 97). These children's characteristic interaction with others involves keeping others at arm's length or by exerting dominance over them.

Last, children may solve the conflict between unexpressed basic hostility and anxiety by withdrawal from others: "If I withdraw, nothing can hurt me" (Horney, 1937, p. 99). Such children avoid *any* significant emotional interactions.

Transitional Summary

We can trace Horney's ideas about the importance of basic hostility and basic anxiety to neurotic personality development.

A child's feelings of helpless and repressed hostility lead to various approaches to coping with others. Horney initially proposed ten such values or neurotic trends. She later grouped them in terms of the three categories of *compliance, aggression,* and *withdrawal.*

The child has been made aware that his or her feelings of hostility and anger cannot be openly displayed; he or she represses them, thus avoiding further parental indifference, inconsistency, or withdrawal of love. The child comes to anticipate the world and its people as a source of pain and anxiety. Out of these anticipations the child develops rigid, compulsive, and indiscriminate strivings to predict, control, and survive a hostile world.

Karen Horney's lucid portrait of a child's resentment to parental indifference and of helplessness in the face of a hostile world may have been based on her own experiences. We turn next to a biographical study of Karen Horney to trace the roots of her special sensitivity to children's feelings of rejection and their strategies for coping with them.

PERSONAL SOURCES OF THE BASIC ANXIETY AND BASIC HOSTILITY HYPOTHESES

Like many other personality theorists, Karen Horney felt she had been an unwanted child. This theme is prevalent in the life histories of people who later made important contributions to psychology. Sigmund Freud, Anna Freud, Harry Stack Sullivan, Alfred Adler, Carl Jung, Gordon Allport, and Erik Erikson all evidenced this theme of feeling unwanted. Rubins (1978) and Quinn (1987) have written the first full-length biographies of Horney, and they provide much insight into the personal sources of her theoretical concepts. In what follows, we rely on Rubins and Quinn and on Horney's (1980) own diaries and letters.

Karen Horney was born on September 16, 1885, to a ship's captain, Berndt Wackels Danielson, and his second wife, Clotilde. Captain Danielson already had four children by his previous marriage, and his search for a second wife may have been motivated by the desire to have a mother for them (Quinn, 1987, p. 20; Rubins, 1978, p. 8). However, Captain Danielson's children never accepted his new wife, and they resented the two new children born into the marriage, Berndt and his younger sister, Karen. Moreover, the marriage between the gruff and masterful sea captain and his 18-year-younger bride, despite all appearances, was not made in heaven. In August 1904, Clotilde Danielson could stand her husband's tyrannical personality no longer and, with her two children, separated from Captain Danielson completely.

Young Karen's Unhappy Family Life

When Karen's brother Berndt was born, he fulfilled the family tradition by carrying on the family name. He was a boy, he was wanted, and he became his parents' darling (Rubins, 1978, p. 10). Karen's birth, four years later, came at a time when the relationship between her parents had grown abrasive. "Karen questioned whether she had really been wanted" (Rubins, 1978, p. 11).

Captain Danielson was an authoritarian personality, drawing his rigidity and tyrannical style from his avid fundamentalist religious beliefs. He sought to impose a strict interpretation of Biblical teachings on his wife and children. On occasion, after a long period of silent Bible reading, he would erupt into one of his frequent explosions of anger and throw his Bible at his wife. The children later referred to their father as *der Bibelschmeisser* (Bible-thrower), when he was not present (Rubins, 1978, p. 11). Captain Danielson believed that men were created intellectually and morally superior to women and should have more privileges and status. In the Bible, "What was permitted the male could not be tolerated in the female. His son Berndt would be allowed freedom, privilege, education; these were not necessary for his wife or youngest daughter" (Rubins, 1978, p. 11).

Danielson's wife, nicknamed "Sonni," was beautiful and a more sophisticated person than her husband. Karen's relationship with her mother was close, loving, and devoted. Sonni often came to the girl's rescue in disputes with the father. Rubins (1978, p. 13) speculates she identified with her daughter's talents and wishes, thus vicariously fulfilling her own blocked ambitions. As the children grew older, they—along with their mother—formed a "protective alliance" against their father (Rubins, 1978, p. 13).

On the whole Karen felt rejected by her father and less loved than her brother Berndt. Nonetheless she did have some positive feelings toward her father and had some good times with him. She admired and respected him and was caught up in the romantic vision of his far-ranging sea travels. For his part, Captain Danielson took his daughter on at least three lengthy voyages aboard his ship, and he occasionally brought her gifts from exotic places. As an adult in her thirties, she took to wearing a captain's style cap. Perhaps this indicated that she had some positive memories of her father (Rubins, 1978, p. 12).

In her childhood, Karen generally felt deprived of affection. Her coping style up to the age of eight was to behave "like a little lamb" (Rubins, 1978, p. 13). Once, she even placed some of her toys on the street for some poorer child to find. She told no one about her altruistic deed because self-sacrifice was her way of being the good child she hoped her parents would love. (See Horney's semi-autobiographical case history and comments in Horney, 1950, p. 20, and 1942, pp. 190 ff.)

During her school years, Karen was an unhappy child. She found her home life intolerable. She was also self-conscious and displeased with her appearance even though she was considered strikingly good-looking. She seized upon schoolwork and achievement as a way of compensating for her unhappiness at home and with her appearance. "As she said years later to her daughter, 'If I couldn't be beautiful, I decided I would be smart'" (Rubins, 1978, p. 14A).

At puberty, Karen displayed open and excessive affection toward her brother Berndt. Such displays were her attempts to cope with her more genuine feelings of resentment toward him. Berndt found his sister's loving protestations embarrassing and rebuffed her. His rejection proved overwhelming for Karen: "It was a blow to her pride; . . . she felt ashamed and humiliated" (Rubins, 1978, p. 14). She became depressed. The family doctor told her parents that the strain of schoolwork caused her depression so they transferred her to a lower grade. As a result, Karen vowed to be first in her class always!

By the age of 12, she had decided on a career in medicine. This career was almost unheard of for women at the time. Karen's stern father predictably opposed her pursuit of a medical career, but Karen's mother was encouraging. Karen, with the help of her brother and mother, finally convinced her father to provide the tuition to enter a preparatory program. Karen promised in writing to ask nothing more of her father if he would help her attain the goal of a medical education (Rubins, 1978, p. 21).

An Antireligious Rebellion

Given her family background, it is not surprising that Karen became hostile to religion in adolescence. She was a skeptic who doubted fundamental religious beliefs. Immersing herself in religious studies, she even began to question the divinity of Jesus. At one point, Berndt lovingly guided her to one way of understanding the contradiction contained in the belief that Jesus was both man and God. Karen confided to her diary: "'Something like a stone fell from my heart. . . . He [Jesus] became dearer to me'" (Rubins, 1978, p. 18).

Her religious skepticism, nonetheless, continued to grow. At the time of her confirmation, religious authority merged in her thinking with her father's domineering and abusive authoritarianism. They were both targets of her despair and anger. Karen wrote in her diary:

> It must be grand to have a father one can love and esteem. The Fourth Commandment stands before me like a specter, with its "Thou shalt." I cannot respect a person who makes us all unhappy with his hypocrisy, egocentricity, crudeness and illbreeding. . . . [These are] indescribable days for Mother and us under the fearful domination of the master of the house and our pastor. Pen and paper would rebel against writing down anything so coarse

and mean. Confirmation was no blessing for me. On the contrary, it was a great piece of hypocrisy, for I professed belief in the teachings of Christ, the doctrine of love, while carrying hatred in my heart (and for my nearest at that). I feel too weak to follow Christ. Yet I long for the faith, firm as a rock, that makes oneself and others happy. (Quoted by Rubins, 1978, p. 19; see also Horney, 1980, p. 37)

As Rubins notes, such hostile feelings could not be expressed openly, for Karen was rebelling against her father, his edicts, and her own deepest childhood beliefs (1978, p. 19). As she confided years later to her friend Franz Alexander, such grave doubts meant " 'standing up to the frightening gaze of my father's blue eyes' " (Rubins, 1978, p. 19).

Horney's Relationship with Her Husband and Children

In 1906, Karen entered one of the few medical schools that admitted women, one in Freiburg, Germany. Even in an all-male environment, Karen nevertheless relished her newfound sense of freedom and independence. During this exciting time, she became friends with Oskar Horney, an economics student on vacation from his own studies at the University of Brunswick. Karen was attracted to the strong but stern Oskar, who radiated emotional and physical strength, intelligence, and independence. She wrote letters to him for the next year in which she expressed her most private feelings, including her changing attitudes toward her mother. Sonni had become, in her daughter's less idealized view, basically a good person but one who was also coldhearted and lacking in self-control (Rubins, 1978, p. 31).

In 1909 Karen and Oskar were married. He had graduated law school and was employed by an investment firm. She was finishing college—in preparation for medical school. By 1910, Karen was pregnant with her first child, Brigitte. Shortly before Brigitte's birth, Sonni suffered a stroke; she died one week later in February 1911. Karen graduated from medical school in 1913. Thus, in a relatively short space of time, Karen had experienced profound changes—her marriage, a death, and the giving of new life. She also successfully pursued her career goals. Not surprisingly, she became depressed.

At this time, she was also undergoing her own personal psychoanalysis with Karl Abraham in preparation for a career in psychiatry. The net effect of all these experiences, along with the reexamination of childhood conflicts necessitated by the analysis, has been well summarized by Rubins (1978, p. 38):

> Karen's ambivalent feelings toward her father, her dependency upon her mother and her struggle to free herself from this dependency, her longstanding resentment at playing a secondary role to her brother, the conflict within herself between the roles of assertive professional woman and the compliant childbearing homemaker—all these had to be confronted.

The outcome of her psychoanalysis was not satisfying. Karen remained depressed. She even asked in a letter to her analyst, " 'Does not the real work begin after the analysis? The analysis shows one her enemies but one must battle them afterwards, day by day' " (Quinn, 1987, pp. 157 ff. and pp. 193 ff; Rubins, 1978, p. 39).

The Horneys eventually had three daughters. Oskar was as severe and demanding as Karen's own father had been with her. Karen did not intervene, even when he became physically abusive. One Christmas dinner, Marianne, the middle daughter, leaned back too far in her chair at the table. Grabbing hold of the tablecloth, she pulled with her to the floor an entire new dinner service and the elaborate meal as well. Oskar spanked Marianne viciously with a dog whip. Brigitte, the eldest, cried in sympathy, but Karen showed no outward reaction to her daughter's plight (Rubins, 1978, p. 51). All three of the girls recalled that Karen generally exhibited a detached indifference toward them.

> She would not interfere with their growing up, with their comings and goings. But the children felt that this noninterference might have bordered at times on neglect: Their clothes were often too long or too short; their stockings did not fit. A governess was no longer needed now that they were all in school, and the maids did not look after them personally. (Rubins, 1978, p. 83)

And this cold and indifferent behavior was that of a mother who herself had been so desperate for parental warmth and affection as a child.

Karen's marriage gradually began to disintegrate over personality differences and the burden of professional obligations. In 1923, Oskar's investments collapsed and his salary (in inflated currency) from his bankrupt firm was worth little. He borrowed heavily, contracted encephalomeningitis during a business trip to Paris, and eventually returned home as a broken, defeated, spiritless man. He became morose, withdrawn, and argumentative. As their finances deteriorated, so did their marriage. In 1926, Karen and her daughters separated from Oskar by moving into a small apartment with their few possessions. Some ten years later, Karen filed for divorce, which finally became official in 1939.

Berndt's Death

Throughout her life, beginning with her brother's rejection of her effusive protestations of love for him in adolescence, Karen Horney suffered periodic bouts of dejection bordering on depression. In 1923, at the height of her husband's financial difficulties, her brother Berndt died of pulmonary infection. He was 40 years old, and she was devastated at the senselessness of his death. Profound depression was the consequence. Writing to Georg Groddeck some months after Berndt's death, Karen expressed a curiously ambivalent kind of acceptance.

> . . . in the beginning I considered [the death of my brother] as something totally senseless—he belonged to those people who seem to burst with the joy of living. In the face of this, after many weeks I arrived at the conclusion: something in him had wanted to die. That insight I tend to accept in general and I have only one suspicion about it, and that is that it is too much of what we want to believe. (Quoted in Rubins, 1978, p. 72)

The loss of her idealized yet resented brother was overwhelming for Karen. Shortly after Berndt's death, while on vacation at the beach with her family and friends, Karen went alone for a swim. When she failed to return after more than an hour, Oskar found her clutching a piling in deep water, ruminating on whether to end her life or swim back to the beach (Rubins, 1978, p. 87). Oskar and his friends had to plead to convince Karen that her life was worth living.

The death of her brother evoked profound depression in Karen. A possible explanation was that Berndt's death fulfilled her darkest childhood wishes for his death and simultaneously triggered the most intense adult guilt: self-punishment in suicidal longings.

Summarizing Karen Horney's Personal Problems

Overall, the central issues in Karen Horney's life centered around her profound sense of inadequacy and guilt-provoking resentment toward her parents and her brother for making her feel that way. In summary, three related themes emerge in her life history.

First, her sense of her own unwantedness and unattractiveness initially had produced a compliant, meek, over-eager-to-please child. From this stance of selflessness emerged a rebellious, skeptical, and defiant young woman, who sought by her intellectual achievements to compensate for her presumed weaknesses and to exact revenge with the evidence of her hard-won competence.

Second, Karen found herself almost unwittingly married to a man who bore more than superficial resemblance to the authoritarian father she so resented. Avoiding confrontation, she proved unable to stand up to her husband's abusive behavior toward one of her daughters.

Third, achieving in a frowned-upon profession for women in the early 1900s, Karen adopted psychoanalytic theory, drew what intellectual and emotional sustenance she could from it, and then abandoned some of its central tenets in favor of her own insights. She rebelled against paternalistic psychoanalysis in much the same way as she had rebelled against religion and her father's conception of it, and through that revolt, against the father himself. As Rubins (1978, p. 113) tactfully phrased it: "It was the same old conflict within her that she had experienced so often before, how to be aggressive yet friendly and loving at the same time."

We turn now to the case history of "Clare", which, there is some reason to believe, contains some thinly disguised autobiographical elements of Karen Horney's own life. According to Rubins (1978, p. 17), we can catch a glimpse of Karen Horney's view of her own struggle in this case.

AN ILLUSTRATIVE CASE: CLARE, AN UNWANTED CHILD

Despite several of her mother's abortion attempts, "Clare" was born into an unhappy marriage. Her parents' first child, a boy, had been born at a time when the marriage was a happy one, and in some ways he remained the main object of parental approval and affection. Not that Clare was in any material way mistreated or abused. She always received the same quantity and quality of gifts, trips, lessons, and educational opportunities as her brother.

> But in less tangible matters she received less than the brother, less tenderness, less interest in school marks and in the thousand little daily experiences of a child, less concern when she was ill, less solicitude to have her around, less willingness to treat her as a confidante, less admiration for looks and accomplishments. (Horney, 1942, p. 49)

Always away from home, Clare's father, a doctor, became the object of the mother's ridicule and loathing. Clare's mother was so bitter that she often expressed open death wishes against her husband. Clare felt that the safest course was meekly to acquiesce to her mother's expressions of rage (Horney, 1942, p. 49). The most immediate result of the family atmosphere on Clare's development was her lost opportunity to develop a sense of confidence and self-trust. As Clare matured, her feelings of unworthiness and her sense of total unlikableness grew:

> This shift from essentially true and warranted accusations of others to essentially untrue and unwarranted self-accusations had far-reaching consequences. . . . *And the shift meant more than an acceptance of the majority estimate of herself. It meant also that she repressed all grievances against the mother. If everything was her own fault, the grounds for bearing a grudge against mother were pulled away from under her.* (Horney, 1942, p. 50; italics added)

Clare thus relinquished any possibility of genuine rebellion against the injustice of her own treatment at the hands of her family. Instead, she became a "joiner," a compliant member in the circle of admirers surrounding her powerful mother. "By admiring what in reality she resented, she became alienated from her own feelings. She no longer knew what she herself liked or wished or feared or resented" (Horney, 1942, p. 51). In short, she began to act on the premise "that it is safer to admire others than to be critical."

BOX 10.2	*Only Connect . . .*

The distinction between the mother's treatment of Clare and of her brother is illustrative of Erik Erikson's (Chapter 8) concepts of *ritual* and *ritualization*. *Ritualization* involves meaningful participation and real bonding, but Erikson used the term, *ritual,* to describe stereotyped, mechanical, empty and fundamentally meaningless interactions. Rituals involve no more than "going through the motions."

Clare was overly modest and had a tendency to "put herself in second place," and to judge herself more critically than others did. On the surface, she lived life largely to appease and placate others. But beneath the surface, she developed a need to surpass others, to beat them at their own game. That need remained out of consciousness. It would have been dangerous to express and thus had to remain submerged.

At the age of 30, Clare felt the need for psychoanalytic treatment. As an editor for a magazine, she had not fulfilled her ambition to write fiction. Her life and interests had become so constricted in the service of her compliant approach to others that she was able to perform only the routine editing work that her employer requested but was unable to engage in her own creative writing.

Fortunately, an incident occurred that helped Clare in her psychoanalysis to develop insight into the degree of her compliant and self-effacing behavior. She had developed a plan for improving the magazine, a plan she knew to be sound but that would occasion much protest and argument from other members of the staff. During the staff meeting at which she was to present her plan, Clare experienced several moments of panic. She even had to leave the room at one point because of a sudden, apparently psychogenic, attack of diarrhea. However, when the discussion began to favor her proposal, she was able to control herself and the panic diminished. After her plan proved successful in operation, she received much recognition and acclaim. Instead of viewing her success as an important milestone, however, she viewed it only as a lucky escape from great danger.

Eventually, with continued analytic treatment, Clare was able to recognize that a striving for security motivated her self-effacing behavior. She came to enjoy her successes and to take pride in her considerable abilities. A final indication of her slowly burgeoning self-confidence and realistic pride was embodied in a dream she had during the final phase of her psychoanalysis:

> . . . she drove with her friend in a strange country and it occurred to her that she, too, might apply for a driver's license. Actually she had a license and could drive as well as the friend. The dream symbolized a dawning insight that she had rights of her own and need not feel like a helpless stranger. (Horney, 1942, p. 84)

DESPISED REAL SELF, IDEAL SELF, AND THE ACTUAL SELF

When children are confronted by the intense conflict between their feelings of helplessness and repressed hostility toward their parents, they develop a defensive way of perceiving themselves. When parents are inconsistent and indifferent in their reactions toward their children, children are made to feel that their self is despicable, unlovable, and unworthy. This results in what Horney considered the **despised real self.** Children's repressed hostility turns against the self to further buttress the notion that they are unlovable and unworthy. This despised real self is not real at all. Since the picture they hold of their self is based on *false* evaluations by others, it is "real" only to the extent that they believe it

(Horney, 1945, p. 98). When their image of this *real self* is this negative, it would more appropriately be designated as the *despised real self.*

Children necessarily begin to defensively restructure the image of the despised real self into an image of the **idealized self** or **ideal self** they should be. They do this in order to survive in a hostile world and gain needed love and approval.

> In contrast to authentic ideals, the idealized image has a static quality. It is not a goal toward whose attainment he strives but a fixed idea, which he worships. . . . The idealized image is a decided hindrance to growth because it either denies shortcomings or merely condemns them. *Genuine ideals make for humility, the idealized image for arrogance.* (Horney, 1945, p. 99; italics added)

The idealized self substitutes for genuine self-confidence and pride. It is based on a wishful-thinking style. This unrealistic ideal fills the mind of the adult neurotic with a population of "shoulds":

> Forget about the disgraceful creature you actually *are* [i.e., the despised real self]; this is how you *should* be. . . . He should be the utmost of honesty, generosity, considerateness, justice, dignity, courage, and unselfishness. He should be the perfect lover, husband, and teacher. He should be able to endure anything, should like everybody, should love his parents, his wife, his country; or, he should not be attached to anything or anybody, nothing should matter to him, he should never feel hurt, and he should always be serene and unruffled. He should always enjoy life; or, he should be above pleasure and enjoyment. He should be spontaneous; he should always control his feelings. He should know, understand, and foresee everything. He should be able to solve every problem of his own, or of others, in no time. He should be able to overcome every difficulty of his as soon as he sees it. He should never be tired or fall ill. He should always be able to find a job. He should be able to do things in one hour which can only be done in two to three hours. (Horney, 1950, p. 65; italics in original)

This seemingly endless list of things neurotics feel they ought to be or do was termed by Horney the **"tyranny of the should"** (1950, pp. 65 ff.). The idealized self-image eventually becomes converted into an ideal self, no longer to be recognized as a fiction. It is now seen as a state of being that is nearly impossible to attain (Horney, 1950, p. 158). Nevertheless, the neurotic is compelled to strive toward this unreachable ideal in what Horney called the "search for glory" (1950, p. 23). Indeed, the ideal self slowly becomes more real to the neurotic than the "real" despised self ever was. The idealized self becomes the **comprehensive neurotic solution,** for it actualizes the fantasized image by which all problems can be solved and all difficulties surmounted. With the creation of the ideal self, the neurotic "solves" the conflict between feelings of basic anxiety and hostility; he or she learns to deal with the world and its people through the shoulds of the ideal self.

In writing about the *tyranny of the should,* it seems as though Horney was alluding to her father's rigid standards of conduct and impossible demands for moral perfection. Horney, no doubt, was expressing to some degree her own experience of these demands, as well as her striving to surpass her more favored brother.

In her later work, Horney created a further distinction among the images neurotics have of themselves. Originally Horney used the term *real self* to indicate the damaged self-image produced in children by indifferent parents. Horney later changed the usage somewhat by employing **real self** to designate the true core of a person's being, his or her very center of existence. The real self harbors all the potential for growth and health: "clarity and depth of his own feelings, thoughts, wishes, interests; the ability to tap his own resources, the strength of his will power, the special capacities or gifts he may have; the faculty to express himself, and to relate to others with his spontaneous feelings" (Horney, 1950, p. 17). It is this core that is damaged by parental indifference. The goal of the

Table 10.1   Horney's Conception of the Self

1. **Despised real self:** False conceptions of one's competence, worth, and lovability based on belief in others' evaluations, especially those of the parents. Negative evaluations may reinforce one's sense of helplessness.
2. **Real self:** The true core of one's being, containing potential for growth, happiness, will power, special capacities and gifts, and the urge for "self-realization," that is, the need to be spontaneously what one truly is.
3. **Actual self:** Distinguished from the subjectively perceived real self as the objectively existing person, physically and mentally, independent of anyone's perceptions.
4. **Ideal self:** The damaged real self, hurt by negative evaluations and indifference from parents, struggles with the "tyranny of the shoulds," that is, strives to be perfect in a wishful way as a compensation for feelings of inadequacy and unlovability.

real self is the striving for self-realization, that is, the accomplishment of the person's own values and aims in life. In this sense, Horney began to use the term *real self* to indicate a "possible self," that is, a self that the individual can realistically learn to express. To a large extent, this real self is a product of the person's own perceptions, his or her own interpretations of what he or she is. Horney distinguished this subjectively real self from the person's objective reality as observed by others. Horney used the term **actual self** to describe the totality of everything that the person "really" is.

In summary, the real self is the core of the person's existence as he or she perceives it and perhaps despises it; the ideal self is a glorified image of what he or she should be, an image that is impossible to attain; the actual self is the sum of objectively observable characteristics of the person at one moment in time.

It should be pointed out that for Horney the goal of psychotherapy was to provide the individual with the means to free the real self, to accept its character, and to allow it full and spontaneous expression without the curtailment of learned defensiveness (Horney, 1946, pp. 202 ff.). Table 10.1 summarizes the differences among the real, actual, and ideal selves.

THE CORE NEUROTIC CONFLICT: ALIENATION FROM REAL SELF

The pervasive anxiety and helplessness experienced in childhood, coupled with basic hostility that cannot be expressed, causes an alienation of the individual from his or her real self. This **core neurotic conflict** is furthered by the adoption of an idealized self at the expense of one's spontaneity, self-trust, and independence. Since other people are dangerous actors in what is seen as a dangerous world, neurotics adopt defensive strategies for dealing with them: "He feels what he *should* feel, wishes what he *should* wish, likes what he *should* like" (Horney, 1950, p. 159; italics added).

BOX 10.3   *Only Connect . . .*

Carl Rogers' later development of his personality theory (Chapter 13) included many ideas very similar to those engendered by Horney. For example, his concepts of conditions of worth, perceived self, and ideal self are very consistent with Horney's formulations, even though his outlook on life was much more optimistic. In a very real sense, Horney's work is a precursor of humanistic psychology.

In other words, the tyranny of the should drives him frantically to be something different from what he is or could be. And in his imagination he *is* different—so different, indeed, that the real self fades and pales still more. Neurotic claims, in terms of self, mean the abandoning of the reservoir of spontaneous energies. Instead of making his own efforts, for instance, with regard to human relations, the neurotic insists that others should adjust to him. (Horney, 1950, p. 159; italics in original)

Three consequences of the individual's alienation from his or her real self can be discerned in the neurotic's feelings of being removed from himself or herself (Horney, 1950, pp. 159–161). These are the ways in which a neurotic person's relation to his or her own real self can be distorted:

1. *Abandonment of responsibility for one's own behavior:* The neurotic comes to feel that "I am driven instead of being the driver" (1950, p. 159).

2. *Active moves away from the real self:* The person's creative forces lie fallow as he or she succumbs to the idealized self and the search for glory embodied in "shoulds"; the ideal image must be the ever unreachable goal since only by investing all energy in such strivings can the despised real self be left behind.

3. *Active moves against the real self:* The individual experiences bouts of self-hate, with the idea of "being oneself" becoming terrifying and appalling. The neurotic has an unconscious interest in not being him- or herself, in not having a clear self-perception.

INTERPERSONAL COPING STRATEGIES: MOVES TOWARD, AWAY FROM, AND AGAINST OTHERS

Unlike Freud, who saw conflict between repressed instincts and the forces of the ethical side of personality as the core of neurosis, Horney viewed her concepts of interpersonal and intrapersonal conflict as central:

They [i.e., the conflicts] operated between contradictory sets of neurotic trends, and though they originally concerned contradictory attitudes toward others, in time they encompassed contradictory attitudes toward the self, contradictory qualities and contradictory sets of values. . . . (1945, p. 15)

Horney thought that neurotic symptoms and interpersonal strategies are attempts to resolve basic conflicts. Compulsive and indiscriminate strivings, contradictory and conflicted needs for perfection, power, affection, and independence are all anxiety-allaying techniques with the purpose of maintaining the alienation between the despised real self and the ideal self, and between the real self and significant others. The ten neurotic trends or needs began to be more comprehensible to Horney as *clusters of strivings* directed toward dealing with people and their demands. Horney organized the ten needs into three patterns of traits, illustrated by the three hypothetical personalities with which we began this chapter. Let us now examine those three character types from the perspective of Horney's concept of self-alienation.

Moving Toward People: The Self-Effacing Solution

You may recall that the first solution to neurotic conflict that Horney described was originally termed **moving toward people** (Horney, 1945, pp. 48 ff.). This type of individual manifests the neurotic traits that are conducive to compliance, as in the case of "Clare".

These traits include intense needs for affection and approval, a need for a partner in the form of friend, husband, wife, or lover, and a necessity to be undemanding, restricting one's life within narrow borders:

> In sum, this type needs to be liked, wanted, desired, loved; to feel accepted, welcomed, approved of, appreciated; to be needed, to be of importance to others, especially to one particular person; to be helped, protected, taken care of, guided. (Horney, 1945, p. 51)

The goal of the **compliant type** is a surface need to be in harmony with others, to avoid friction. But contradictory trends may also be served by this strategy. Compliance on the surface may mask a strong inner need to compete, to excel, to dominate (Horney, 1945, p. 56). Below the surface, within the real self, unrecognized rage, anger, and residual hostile sentiment boils. Occasionally, repressed anger will explode into fits of irritability or into temper tantrums. Or this individual may make demands on others to help "poor me." Of course, the compliant person never recognizes that such demands are manipulative of others, or that they are attempts to satisfy his or her aggressive strivings: "He cannot help feeling at times that he is so unfairly treated that he simply can't stand it any longer" (Horney, 1945, p. 58).

In her later statement of neurotic conflict (1950, pp. 214 ff.), Horney referred to the "moving toward others" strategy as the **self-effacing solution** to neurotic conflict. In effect, the self-effacing person has identified the ideal self with the restricted and subdued despised self:

> He is *his subdued self;* he is the stowaway without any rights. In accordance with this attitude he also tends to suppress in himself anything that connotes ambition, vindictiveness, triumph, seeking his own advantage. In short he has solved his inner conflict by suppressing all expansive attitudes and drives and making self-abnegating trends predominant. (Horney, 1950, p. 216)

The self-effacing type has idealized the qualities of suffering, helplessness, and martyrdom. Only by viewing oneself as "saintly" can one supply oneself with a good reason to endure the basic hostility one has never allowed oneself to express. If one is a saint, then it is reasonable that one must suffer. And suffering becomes even more enjoyable if one can spread the misery to others. Horney felt that the self-effacing "solution" was the most damaging because this strategy involves the most intense unhappiness.

Moving Against People: The Expansive Solution

The aggressive, expansive solution to neurotic conflict is based on a different view of life: on a belief that the world is a hostile place and that life "is a struggle of all against all . . ." (Horney, 1945, p. 63). Individuals with this view characteristically behave toward others in aggressive ways; they are best described as **moving against people.** They may have a facade of suave politeness and good fellowship that is designed to facilitate satisfaction of their needs for control and power. Aggressive individuals need to excel by exploiting others, to attain recognition by exerting dominance and power over those they perceive to be underlings. Success and prestige are the yardsticks to their sense of self-worth.

> Any situation or relationship is looked at from the standpoint of "What can I get out of it?"—whether it has to do with money, prestige, contacts, or ideas. *The person himself is consciously or semiconsciously convinced that everyone acts this way,* and so what counts is to do it more efficiently than the rest. (Horney, 1945, p. 65; italics added)

Where the compliant types who move toward others have a need for a mate or partner stemming from their feelings of helplessness, aggressive types desire a partner who can enhance their prestige, power, or wealth.

Horney later described this type who "moves against" people as the **expansive solution** to neurotic conflict: the appeal of mastery (1950, pp. 187 ff.). In almost every respect, the expansive solution is the direct opposite to the self-effacing solution. The expansive type glorifies and cultivates in himself or herself everything that leads to mastery of others (1950, p. 214).

> The appeal of life lies in its mastery. . . . He should be able to master the adversities of fate, the difficulties of a situation, the intricacies of intellectual problems, the resistances of other people, conflicts in himself. The reverse side of the necessity for mastery is his dread of anything connoting helplessness; this is the most poignant dread he has. (Horney, 1950, p. 192)

Unlike the compliant, self-effacing type who identifies with the despised real self, the aggressive person has come to believe that he or she is the ideal self, that he or she is the glorified image toward which he or she strives. All the behaviors of the **aggressive type** can be understood as attempts to actualize the ideal self (Horney, 1950, p. 192).

Moving Away from People: The Solution of Resignation

Those individuals who develop a protective "I don't care about anything" attitude practice the third "solution" to neurotic conflict, the **solution of resignation.** They become detached from human affairs and resigned to an emotionally flat life. For if they do not allow themselves to care about anything or anyone, they think that they will never be hurt. Horney characterized this individual's dominant strategy as **moving away from people** (1945, pp. 73 ff.). Resigned individuals evidence intense needs of self-sufficiency, perfection, and unassailability. They tend to restrict their lives within narrow confines much as the compliant types do, but for resigned individuals the motive is the need never to be dependent on anyone.

Neurotic detachment is considerably different from the normal feelings each of us experiences on those occasions when we would like to be alone with our own thoughts. The neurotic has *persistent* feelings of indifference and withdrawal based on an "intolerable strain in associating with people" (Horney, 1950, p. 73).

> What is crucial is their inner need to put emotional distance between themselves and others. More accurately, it is their conscious and unconscious determination not to get emotionally involved with others in any way, whether in love, fight, co-operation, or competition. They draw around themselves a kind of magic circle, which no one may penetrate. (Horney, 1945, p. 75)

By their resigned attitudes and detachment, neurotic individuals who move away from others have removed themselves from the "inner battlefield" of their own conflicts. Their "don't care" demeanor provides them with a sense of superior distance, haughty removal from their own and others' "petty" problems. They become onlookers at themselves and their lives to the degree that even in therapy they remain detached and view the process of their own inner explorations as "fascinating entertainment" (Horney, 1950, p. 261).

A consequence of this "moving away from others" is the total lack of any striving for achievement or success. They are considered the **detached type.** Unconsciously, they deny any desire to achieve success or to exert effort on their own behalf. They are hypersensitive to coercion or advice and they reject both in their attempts to remain independent.

Horney identified three modes of stilted and joyless living that characterize various subtypes of the resigned neurotic:

1. *Persistent resignation:* These individuals are characterized by a continual emotional inertia. They fulfill as few of the tasks of life as are necessary to guarantee their freedom. They may pass for essentially normal, though without any observable joy in living. Their persistent resignation may be only a mask covering a feeling of rebelliousness.

2. *Rebelliousness:* The appeal of freedom and independence from others is so strong for these individuals that they actively resist the "trivia" of life. They may turn their rebellion against the self and struggle against their own inner tyrannies and shoulds. In this sense, their rebellion may actually become liberating and therapeutic.

3. *Shallow living:* This type of individual "moves to the periphery of life;" he or she is without hope or any positive commitment. In worse condition than the persistently resigned type, the one engaged in "shallow living" finds life worthless. Eventually he or she will settle for superficial enjoyments, "high living," without meaning or direction, or will pursue opportunistic success in business. But beneath the mask of sociability, this individual is merely a "well-adapted automaton" (Horney, 1950, pp. 286–287). He or she goes through the motions of life, but is without genuine concern or involvement.

The common denominator that binds the three types of resigned neurotic is vacillation between identification with the despised real self and identification with the glorified ideal self. Detached neurotics strive halfheartedly toward actualization of the ideal self, but fundamentally they have surrendered any hope of making the glorified image come true. In effect, they are unsatisfied with the despised self, but simultaneously afraid to strive toward the goals of the ideal self. They desire to be free *from* all demands, rather than to be free *for* the pursuit of desirable activities.

Horney's description of the three patterns of neurotic conflict-solution points to an important premise of her theory. Each of the patterns is designed to minimize anxiety in dealing with people. Thus, Horney's conceptualizations emphasize her position that the

Table 10.2 "Solutions" to Neurotic Conflict

Self-effacing solution: Love "moving toward" (compliance)	*Expansive solution:* Mastery "moving against" (aggression)	*Resignation solution:* Freedom "moving away" (detachment)
Need for	*Need for*	*Need for*
1. Affection and approval	4. Power, omnipotence, and perfection	3. Restrictions of life to narrow borders[a]
2. Partner to take control	5. Exploitation of others	9. Self-sufficiency
3. Restriction of life to narrow borders	6. Social recognition and prestige	10. Perfection and unassailability
	7. Personal admiration	
	8. Personal achievement	
"If you love me, you will not hurt me."	*"If I have power, no one can hurt me."*	*"If I withdraw, nothing can hurt me."*
Identification with the despised real self	Identification with the ideal self	Vacillation between despised real self and ideal self

[a]Need 3 is repeated from the Self-effacing solution.

Based on Horney, 1945, Chapters 3, 4, 5; 1942, Chapter 2; and 1950, Chapter 3.

neuroses are evidence of damaged interpersonal processes. Horney summarized the three attitude types in these terms:

> As we have seen, each of the basic attitudes toward others has its positive value. In moving toward people the person tries to create for himself a friendly relation to his world. In moving against people he equips himself for survival in a competitive society. In moving away from people he hopes to attain a certain integrity and serenity. As a matter of fact, all three attitudes are not only desirable but also necessary to our development as human beings. *It is only when they appear and operate in a neurotic framework that they become compulsive, rigid, indiscriminate, and mutually exclusive.* (1945, p. 89; italics added)

The three attitude types are presented together with their dominant neurotic needs in Table 10.2.

AUXILIARY CONFLICT SOLUTIONS

In addition to the basic attitudes for dealing with others, Horney suggested that several secondary or **auxiliary conflict solutions** might be employed by neurotic personalities in their striving for security. These techniques can be conceptualized as **secondary defenses.** The secondary defenses are techniques to buttress neurotic solutions to the core neurotic conflict. Unlike Freudian defenses, they are not designed to deal with id impulses but rather to protect the person from seeing what we would consider his or her character flaws.

Externalization

Though the neurotic personality seeks to bridge the distance between the idealized self and the real self, efforts to do so paradoxically broaden the gap. In the most extreme instance, the gap between the idealized self and the real self becomes so great that the person can no longer tolerate the discrepancy. He or she must turn to external factors for the solution: "The only thing left then is to run away from himself entirely and see everything as if it lay outside" (Horney, 1945, p. 116).

Externalization is the auxiliary neurotic defense technique by which individuals shift their "center of gravity" from the self to others. Although somewhat similar to the defensive technique described by Freud as projection, externalization is much more comprehensive, for it involves the shift outward to others not only of unacceptable feelings, but of all feelings, all emotion. Other people become the center of all the neurotic's emotional life; these external individuals become the nucleus of all important strivings that would normally be directed to and experienced by the self, from the self to others. Other people become the center of all the neurotic's emotional life. One focuses not on how what one thinks or feels but on the thoughts and feelings of others.

Thus, one may be angry with oneself but instead attribute the anger to another: *He is angry with me.* A profound consequence for dealings with others emerges from this tendency to externalize:

> When a person feels that his life for good or ill is determined by others, it is only logical that he should be preoccupied with changing *them,* reforming *them,* punishing *them,* protecting himself from *their* interference, or impressing *them.* . . . Another inevitable product of externalization is a gnawing sense of emptiness and shallowness. . . . Instead of feeling the emotional emptiness as such, the person experiences it as emptiness in his stomach and tries to do away with it by compulsive eating. Or he may fear that his lack of bodily weight could cause him to be tossed about like a feather—any storm, he feels, might carry him away. He may even say that he would be nothing but an empty shell if everything were analyzed. (Horney, 1945, p. 117; italics added)

Such an individual can forgo any feelings of humiliation, self-hate, or self-contempt, merely assigning these damaging functions to others. He or she still feels unworthy but now has provided a rational reason for the self-hatred: Others have no use for him or her since he or she is *nothing*.

Creation of Blind Spots

The magnitude of the difference between neurotics' ongoing behaviors and the idealized picture of themselves can sometimes be so great that outsiders marvel that they never detect the discrepancy. The fact that neurotics never consciously admit the difference is evidence for the existence of a **blind spot,** that is, the creation of a defensive "refusal to see" their own defenses.

> A patient, for example, who had all the characteristics of the compliant type and *thought of himself as Christlike,* told me quite casually that at staff meetings he would often shoot one colleague after another with a little flick of his thumb. True enough, the destructive craving that prompted these figurative killings was at that time unconscious; but the point here is that the shooting, *which he dubbed "play,"* did not in the least disturb his Christlike image. (Horney, 1945, p. 132; italics added)

Compartmentalization

Similar to blind spots, **compartmentalization** involves pigeonholing one's life into rigid and exclusive categories: Thus, there is a compartment for friends, for enemies, for family, for outsiders, a compartment for professional activities separate from personal life, and so on (Horney, 1945, p. 133). The important point is that anything that occurs in one compartment cannot contradict, influence, or support what transpires in another. "Compartmentalizing is, thus, as much a result of being divided by one's conflicts as a defense against recognizing them" (Horney, 1945, p. 134). A widely cited example is that of the man who ruthlessly runs his business affairs during the week, taking no real interest in the hurt or humiliation he causes his competitors, and on Sunday serves as the deacon of his church. Religion and business are in separate compartments, and so too, unfortunately, is his humanity. Horney herself may be viewed as someone who compartmentalized. Her professional life involved helping people overcome the very conflicts that she continued to express in her personal life.

Rationalization

Horney treated the defense of **rationalization** pretty much as had other theorists, including Freud. "Rationalization may be defined as self-deception by reasoning" (Horney, 1945, p. 135). Thus, when the person rationalizes, he or she invents a good reason for some action where the actual reason would be unacceptable to his or her self-esteem. For example, the compliant type offers as the reason for "giving in" to others the desire to make *them* happy when, in fact, he or she seeks to bring them under his or her control. Where an altruistic reason is consciously offered, a desire for dominance lurks.

Excessive Self-Control

In her clinical practice, Horney found that the tendency for **excessive self-control** was so pervasive that she originally classed it among the ten neurotic trends or needs: *the need* *to restrict one's life within narrow borders*. Individuals who are exerting excessive self-control are attempting to avoid emotions: They "will not allow themselves to be carried away, whether by enthusiasm, sexual excitement, self-pity, or rage. . . . In short, they seek to check all spontaneity" (Horney, 1945, p. 136).

Arbitrary Rightness

Because the inner conflicts that have shaped the individual's life always produce doubt and hesitation, the individual is sometimes unable to take any course of action. All energy is spent in keeping the conflicts under control. Therefore, almost any outside influence will tip the scales, even temporarily, in one direction or another. To an outsider, it appears that the neurotic decides important events arbitrarily and then defends the decision with rationalizations.

Horney felt that the most fertile soil for such rigid **arbitrary rightness** was the development of aggressive tendencies coupled with feelings of detachment from others (1945, p. 138). For example, a neurotic may end a family dispute by preemptively declaring that he will do what he has already decided to do since he is right. He then storms off, effectively ending the argument by absenting himself to pursue a course of action chosen more in spite than by reason.

Elusiveness

Sometimes the only way neurotics can avoid the inherent contradictions of their lives is through **elusiveness**—to avoid making any decisions whatsoever. Completely opposite to the arbitrarily right neurotic, the *elusive* neurotic seeks never to be pinned down to anything, never to state any issue or opinion clearly. "They have a bewildering capacity to becloud issues. It is often impossible for them to give a concrete report of any incident; should they try to do so the listener is uncertain in the end just what really did happen" (Horney, 1945, p. 138).

Cynicism

To defend against the recognition of inner conflict, the neurotic may adopt **cynicism,** a *cynical* stance toward life and its traditional moral and ethical values. By treating such issues derisively, the neurotic can forestall any conflict over deciding what his or her own position is. In effect, he or she adopts the attitude "Do what you please, so long as you don't get caught" (Horney, 1945, p. 140).

In summary, the character attitudes of compliance, aggression, and withdrawal, coupled with secondary defenses or auxiliary conflict solutions, constitute what Horney termed a **protective structure.** This protective structure is designed to provide a sense of security, however falsely based, and the means to fend off threats to a person's idealized self-image. Neurotics pay a heavy price for having a strong and rigid protective structure: They do not realize their true potentialities and do not express their authentically felt needs. They fall short of what they could become.

MODIFICATION OF FREUDIAN PSYCHOANALYSIS

Horney's jumping-off point was traditional psychoanalytic technique and theory. She accepted, for example, Freud's orientation toward psychological determinism. For Horney, as for Freud, every mental event had a cause (1939, p. 18). Furthermore, the idea that the cause of each mental event lay in the unconscious mind, another basic Freudian tenet, was a postulate Horney also accepted. The basic concept of unconsciously motivated defenses against self-disturbing perceptions also was borrowed from psychoanalysis by Horney, as can be seen in her list of defensive strategies for coping with others.

Horney radically differed from Freud, however, in the area of motivation. For example, she reinterpreted the Oedipus complex as culturally rather than biologically determined. She saw it as resulting from jealousy and aggression within some families (1939, p. 84). For Horney, the roots of the Oedipal situation consisted largely of *interpersonal attitudes:*

> If a child, in addition to being dependent on his parents, is grossly or subtly intimidated by them and hence feels that any expression of hostile impulses against them endangers his security, then the existence of such hostile impulses is bound to create anxiety. . . . The resulting picture may look exactly like what Freud describes as the Oedipus complex; passionate clinging to one parent and jealousy toward the other or toward anyone interfering with the claim of exclusive possession. . . . *But the dynamic structure of these attachments is entirely different from what Freud conceives as the Oedipus complex. They are an early manifestation of neurotic conflicts rather than a primarily sexual phenomenon.* (1939, pp. 83–84; italics added)

Thus Horney desexualized the Oedipal conflict and transferred the dynamics of its emotional constellation into the realm of disturbed interpersonal relations.

Some years before Horney rejected the orthodox Freudian interpretation of the Oedipus complex, she applied it rather tellingly in the classic manner to the topic of marriage. Her comments contain echoes of her own marriage to Oskar Horney:

> In his paper on a case of female homosexuality, Freud says that there is nothing about which our consciousness can be so incomplete or false as about the degrees of affection or dislike we feel for another human being. This is quite especially true of marriage, it being often the case that the degree of love felt is overestimated. . . . Once again, the relation to the Oedipus complex provides a very much deeper explanation. For we see that the commandment and the vow to love and cleave to husband or wife with which one enters into matrimony are regarded by the unconscious as a renewal of the fourth commandment ["Honor thy father and thy mother"] in relation to the parents, and in this respect also—the suppression of hate and the exaggeration of love—the earlier experiences are compulsorily repeated with exactness in every detail. (Horney, 1967, p. 88)

The reference to the fourth commandment is reminiscent of Horney's diary entry on the same theme with reference to her difficulties with her father and with religious doubt. In the just-quoted passage, Horney, in a paper entitled "The Problem of the Monogamous Ideal," is apparently trying to justify to herself ill-fated marriages on the basis of resurrected Oedipal themes. Not surprisingly, she reworked this basic tenet of Freudian theory during her period of rebellion from psychoanalysis into a more interpersonal concept with which she had personal experience.

Along these same lines, Horney found Freud's libido theory to be a grossly inaccurate representation of feminine psychology. Freud used his concept of penis envy to explain women's feelings of inferiority and subsequent development into the role of motherhood. Horney found this notion to be based on inadequate and biased interpretations of "evidence" from neurotic women (1939, pp. 104 ff.). Horney also pointed out that, while psychoanalyzing men, she uncovered "womb envy" and formed

> . . . a most surprising impression of the intensity of this envy of pregnancy, childbirth, and motherhood, as well as of the breasts and of the act of suckling. (1967, pp. 60–61).

Horney differed with Freud on other issues in personality theory, but the central distinction that divided the two theorists was Horney's resculpting of human motivation theory in cultural terms. Consequently, for Horney, personality development cannot be understood exclusively in terms of *instinctual* or biological dynamics. Personality is meaningful only when individuals' cultural settings, familial interactions, and wider interpersonal relationships are taken into account. Basic anxiety and basic hostility can be conceptualized only as interpersonal outcomes; masculinity and femininity can be understood psychologically only as cultural products.

A FINAL WORD ON KAREN HORNEY

Karen Horney, in recent years, has become the unwarranted object of neglect among students of personality theory. Her contributions have been less valued, less frequently studied, and more rarely applied by researchers than those of other neo-Freudian theorists. The reason for this narrowing of interest in Horney's writings is difficult to understand. Certainly other theorists whose contributions were of lesser magnitude have retained their popularity. It would be difficult to find another personality theorist with whom to compare her lucid and brilliant descriptions of neurotic misery and excessive and compulsive striving for imaginary and defensive self-excellence. That her lucidity and attention-compelling style derive their potency from her self-explorations should, in coming years, rearouse at least scholarly historical interest in Karen Horney's body of writings. But, as may be said of any personality theory, until the creative researcher devises an empirical way of testing or applying Horney's ideas, it is unlikely that her work will become influential outside the clinical realm of intuitive and artistic understanding of troubled people.

Refutability of Horney's Concepts

Horney's elegant, lucid, and nearly behavioral descriptions of neurotic misery and the conflicts underlying neurotic striving beg for translation into empirically testable concepts. At the least, the psychometrically minded psychologist could develop personality assessment tests, based on her descriptions. Beyond those descriptions, her lucid synthesis of neurotic "styles" (moving toward, away from, and against) have an empirical power that is waiting to be tapped.

Horney's Conception of Human Agency

Horney emphasized personal freedom and autonomy as ways in which we give up our freedom. Had Horney pursued her interest in Eastern philosophy, she would, no doubt, have come to grips with the issues of human agency and determinism more clearly than she had thus far. On the whole, she portrays human agency as active, subjective, and only partly determined by drives, needs, or environmental pressures. Many adults have the potential to make free decisions, freely interpret their world, and freely make the kind of mistakes for which they suffer the burden of anxiety and alienation. For some, however, the early environmental influences are so strong that they have little ability to be aware of or to change their patterns of relating.

The Idiographic Emphasis of Horney's Approach

Horney clearly focused on clinical issues of psychopathology. Normal development is an afterthought in her work, and while she describes personality functioning with empathy and brilliance, her most dazzling concepts are those related to neurosis. With such a clinical perspective, it is not surprising that her theory is almost wholly focused on individual functioning and idiographic, almost phenomenological, concepts. Despite her concern with cultural differences and effects, the body of her work is idiographically focused.

She also was interested in patterns of coping and behavior. In looking at the similarities underlying behavior and the general types of choices that people make, there was also a nomothetic aspect to her work.

SUMMARY

Karen Horney developed a psychoanalytically oriented interpersonal theory of personality and psychopathology. Fundamental to her conception of personality development and its distortion by neurotic strivings are two basic emotions: anxiety and hostility. When the parental attitude toward the child is cold, inconsistent, or abusive, the foundation is laid for the child to develop a sense of basic hostility toward the parents, and perhaps toward people at large. Because children cannot openly express their anger for fear of abandonment by these powerful "giants," they repress these dangerous feelings. Unable to recognize the hostility that boils below the surface, the child develops a facade of pleasing lovableness, a strategy Karen Horney herself had used as a child to cope with her anger and resentment toward her parents for favoring her brother. But such a strategy is usually doomed to failure, for the child's fear of abandonment and the resulting chaos of utter helplessness provoke a basic and enduring anxiety that shapes all dealings with significant people in the child's world. Compulsive, indiscriminate, and unrealistic "neurotic needs" make their appearance in the child's character as desperate means to control self and others. Horney eventually grouped these ten needs (affection and approval; partner; restriction of life; power and omnipotence; exploitation of others; social recognition;

personal admiration; personal achievement; self-sufficiency; and perfection-unassailability) into three compulsive patterns: moving compliantly *toward,* detachedly *away* from, or aggressively *against* others.

For Horney, too, the central neurotic conflict is alienation from self, a personal estrangement that has its roots in the stranglehold of the neurotic needs and coping strategies. The real self, in Horney's conception, is the source of all spontaneous personal growth toward happiness, health, and genuine love for others.

Horney conceptualizes neurotic individuals as developing idealized self-images, typically composed of a long list of things they *should* be. She wrote brilliantly of the "tyranny of the shoulds" by which the neurotic's life becomes distorted and constricted in an unending struggle to attain what is humanly impossible. Horney speaks of the person's alienation from real self in futile attempts to identify with an idealized and tyrannical self-image.

Horney's theories are largely nonrefutable, although some of Horney's concepts regarding personality style are more than ripe for translation into empirical referents. Horney's theory strongly emphasizes active human agency, and demonstrates a largely idiographic focus in her emphasis on specific case histories.

FOR FURTHER READING

Karen Horney did not publish as extensively as did some of the other personality theorists. Her first book, *The Neurotic Personality of Our Time* (New York: Norton, 1994), contains lucid descriptions of neurotic coping mechanisms. She elaborated her differences from Freud and criticized fundamental psychoanalytic tenets in *New Ways in Psychoanalysis* (New York: Norton, 2000). By far the most comprehensive presentation of her thinking is to be found in her *Neurosis and Human Growth* (New York: Norton, 1991).

A collection of Horney's papers that show both her agreement and disagreement with the Freudian

view of women is in *Feminine Psychology* (New York: Norton, 1993). Janet Sayers' *Mothers of Psychoanalysis* (New York: Norton, 1991) devotes a chapter to Karen Horney in which she indicates the importance of Horney's introduction of such concepts as "womb envy" (to counter Freud's idea of penis envy). Jack L. Rubins' *Karen Horney: Gentle Rebel of Psychoanalysis* (New York: Dial Press, 1978) is the first full-length biography of Karen Horney and merits attention for the light it sheds on the personal sources of Horney's emphasis on parental indifference as the root of self-alienation. Susan Quinn's *A Mind of Her*

Own: The Life of Karen Horney (New York: Summit Books/Simon & Schuster, 1987) is a relatively complete and penetrating look at Horney's personal history. Horney's very personal glimpses of her own life and motives can be found in *The Adolescent Diaries of Karen Horney* (New York: Basic Books, 1980).

Two volumes edited by H. Kelman, *New Perspectives in Psychoanalysis: Contributions to Karen Horney's Holistic Approach* (New York: Norton, 1965) and *Advances in Psychoanalysis: Contributions to Karen Horney's Holistic Approach* (New York: Norton, 1964), will provide some indication of Horney's influence in psychiatry. A critical examination of her modification of psychoanalysis is provided by Benjamin Wolman in "Psychoanalysis Without Libido: An Analysis of Karen Horney's Contribution to Psychoanalytic Theory," *American Journal of Psychotherapy* (1954), *8*, 21–31. Georg Simmel shaped some of Horney's ideas on social influences; his *Conflict and the Web of Group Affiliations* (New York: Free Press, 1964) will give some indication of his thought.

GLOSSARY

Actual self: The person physically and mentally as he or she actually exists, independent of anyone's perceptions.

Arbitrary rightness: The secondary neurotic defense technique through which the individual chooses one solution or one position rigidly to ward off indecision or doubt.

Basic anxiety: A child's all-pervasive sense of being lonely and helpless in a hostile world.

Basic hostility: Children's often hidden anger toward all-powerful but indifferent and manipulative adults. Many children must repress their anger and feelings of hostility to survive, resulting in internalized hostility.

Blind spot: The secondary neurotic defense technique through which the person refuses to see his or her own defenses. It deals with a marked discrepancy between one's actual behaviors and one's idealized self-picture.

Compartmentalization: The secondary neurotic defense technique by which the individual pigeonholes his or her life into rigid and exclusive categories. Anything that occurs in one compartment cannot contradict, influence, or support whatever transpires in another.

Comprehensive neurotic solution: The resolution of the conflict between feelings of basic anxiety and hostility by dealing with the world and its people through the shoulds of the ideal self.

Core neurotic conflict: The alienation of the individual from his or her real self. It leads the person to adopt an idealized self at the expense of one's spontaneity, self-trust, and independence.

Cynicism: The secondary neurotic defense technique through which the individual adopts a cynical stance toward life and society's traditional moral and ethical values. By believing in nothing in particular, the person avoids hurt or disappointment by others.

Despised real self: The child's view of him- or herself as despicable, unlovable, and unworthy. This is a false conception of self that is derived from false negative evaluations by others of one's ability, worth, and lovability.

Elusiveness: The secondary neurotic defense technique that involves avoiding making any decisions whatsoever. Completely opposite to the arbitrarily right neurotic, the *elusive* neurotic seeks never to be pinned down to anything, never to state any issue or opinion clearly.

Excessive self-control: The secondary neurotic defense technique by which the individual seeks to check all spontaneity. Emotional impulses are kept under control.

Externalization: The secondary neurotic defense technique by which the individual shifts his "center of gravity" from the self to others. Other people become the center of all the neurotic's emotional life; one focuses not on what one thinks or feels but on the thoughts and feelings of others.

Idealized or ideal self: The false sense of self constructed by the individual hurt by negative evaluations and parental indifference. This person strives for perfection in a wishful way to compensate for feelings of inadequacy and unlovability.

Moving against people: An **expansive solution** to the core neurotic conflict. The person handles the neurotic conflict by adopting an aggressive approach, which includes the tendency toward mastery and control, to dominate and exploit others. Such a person is viewed as an **aggressive type.**

Moving away from people: The adoption of a protective **solution of resignation** to the core neurotic conflict. Such an approach includes the tendency to become detached from human affairs and resigned to an emotionally flat life. Such a person is perceived as a **detached type.**

Moving toward people: A self-effacing solution to the core neurotic conflict. The person identifies with the despised real self. Horney described such an individual as a **compliant type.**

Neurotic trends: Strategies in the neurotic individual directed toward interpersonal control and coping, designed to overcome fears, helplessness, and sense of isolation experienced by the neurotic person.

Protective structure: The protective structure in a person consists of character attitudes of compliance, aggression, or withdrawal as well as secondary defenses or auxiliary conflict solutions. In neurotics, the protective structure, developed to protect against threats to their idealized self-images, hinders personal growth.

Rationalization: The secondary neurotic defense technique through which the individual uses self-deception by reasoning. It offers plausible but inaccurate explanations to excuse one's failures or unacceptable tendencies, thus warding off anxiety.

Real self: In Horney's later theorizing, the essential core of a person's being and very center of existence. The real self contains all the potential for growth and health, including "the ability to tap his own resources, the strength of his will power, the special capacities or gifts he may have; the faculty to express himself, and to relate to others with his spontaneous feelings."

Secondary defenses/auxiliary conflict solutions: Techniques to buttress neurotic solutions to the core neurotic conflict. Unlike Freudian defenses, these are not designed to deal with id impulses, but rather to protect the person from seeing major aspects of his or her character and personality.

Tyranny of the should: Domination by an often unrealistic view of what one should do and what one should be.

Chapter 11

Gordon W. Allport

Humanistic Trait and Self Theory

Whoso would be a man must be a nonconformist.

Ralph Waldo Emerson, *Essays*

Personality is like nothing else in the world, there is nothing with which it can be compared, nothing which can be placed on a level with it.

Nicholas A. Berdyaev, *Slavery and Freedom*

Gordon W. Allport   **Born: 1897   Montezuma, Indiana**
Died: 1967   Cambridge, Massachusetts

About Allport's Trait and Self Theory

Gordon Allport was a founder of the field of personality psychology in the United States. His emphases on the uniqueness of each person and the importance of individuality have enduring value. Among his core ideas are:

   1. Personality can be understood as a system made up of traits. As a dynamic system, the whole (personality) is more than the additive sum of is parts (traits), and each part is affected by its participation in the system.

   2. A personality trait is an actual neuropsychic structure that disposes a person toward specific kinds of action in certain circumstances.

3. *A person's experience of self and sense of purpose are unifying aspects of personality. Allport replaced Freud's use of the term ego with the broader concept of "proprium."*

4. *The concept of functional autonomy indicates that motives may develop as a person matures. Although originally set in motion by infantile or childish motives, behaviors may function autonomously in new ways for new reasons in new situations.*

5. *A psychologist understands another person most adequately by examining that person's life history—gathering information about the person from various sources and encouraging the person to contribute a thoughtful self-evaluation. This is far from the psychoanalytic approach of distrusting an individual's consciously held explanations of his or her own behavior. It also differs from the behavioral approach of emphasizing the history of environmental conditioning.*

Allport worked within the tradition of the Harvard psychological clinic and in the spirit of personologists such as Henry Murray and Robert White. His contributions influenced the thinking of several generations of personality theorists and clinicians toward considering whole human lives in addition to specific motives, wishes, and actions. He stood for consideration of the organized complexity of the individual against the prevailing intellectual climate, which favored reductionistic psychoanalytic or behavioral approaches.

WAS YOUNG ALLPORT MISUNDERSTOOD BY FREUD HIMSELF?

After graduating college, where he took as many psychology courses as were available, Gordon Allport taught for a year at a college in Turkey. On his way back from Turkey, he had an opportunity to be in Vienna. Allport recounts that, at the age of 21, he sent Sigmund Freud a note announcing that while he, Allport, was visiting Vienna, Freud would no doubt be glad to make his acquaintance. In response to what Allport afterward labeled his "callow forwardness," Freud invited the assertive young American to his office with a reply in his own handwriting. Over four decades later, Allport recalled his recollection of his visit with Freud to a class on Personality and Religious Development at the Boston University School of Theology:

> I went there, to the famous red burlap room with pictures of dreams on the wall. He opened the door and invited me into the inner sanctum, and sat there silent. You may not believe this possible, but I was not prepared for silence. It occurred to me it was up to me to say something, so I fished around in my mind and I told him about an episode on the tram car coming out. I had seen a little boy about four years old and the little boy, obviously, was developing a real dirt phobia. His mother was with him. She was a starched Hausfrau, terribly clean and purposive looking. And the little boy was saying: "I don't want to sit *there!* Don't let *him* sit near me, he's *dirty*." He kept this up all the time, and I thought it might interest Freud how early a phobia of dirt can get set. (Allport, 1962, p. 2; emphasis in original)

Freud responded by interpreting Allport's remarks.

> When I finished my story Freud fixed his kindly therapeutic eyes upon me and said, "And was that little boy you?" Flabbergasted and feeling a bit guilty, I contrived to change the subject. While Freud's misunderstanding of my motivation was amusing, it also started a deep train of thought. I realized that he was accustomed to neurotic defenses and that my manifest motivation (a sort of rude curiosity and youthful ambition) escaped him. For therapeutic progress he would have to cut through my defenses, but it so happened that therapeutic progress was not here an issue. (Allport, 1968, pp. 383–384)

Allport later told the Boston University class,

> . . . *this time* he made a mistake, a bad mistake, thinking that I was a pathological case. (I may have been, but not in that particular respect.) I don't think he had ever seen a *well* person, if you know what I mean. He was so busy, he had all these neurotics coming around. So, he was not prepared for a normal personality—for a brassy young American tourist. He was prepared for the pathological, unconscious, resistant, defensive type of person. I don't think I perceived the importance of this experience until a few years later. (Allport, 1962; emphasis in original)

Allport further commented that the experience with Freud, ". . . taught me that depth psychology, for all its merits, may plunge too deep, and that psychologists would do well to give full recognition to manifest motives before probing the unconscious" (1968, p. 384). One might see in Allport's report of his early encounter with Freud evidence that he must have had an aversion to psychoanalytic interpretations even before he became a psychologist.

In his accounts of this episode with Freud, Allport did not indicate awareness that he might have been projecting his feelings about his meeting with Freud on the "little boy" (Allport) and the "dirty" man (who would have been Freud) that he had seen earlier that day. If so, then Freud's upsetting interpretation, "And was that little boy you?" would have been correct. Years later, Allport would tell his students, "As far as the unconscious was concerned, Freud went down deeper, stayed longer, and came up dirtier than anybody else." He *did* see Freud, at least to a certain extent, as a "dirty man."

"HOW SHALL A PSYCHOLOGICAL LIFE HISTORY BE WRITTEN?"

Allport stated the guiding questions that shaped his work in personality: "How shall a psychological life history be written? What processes and what structures must a full-bodied account of personality include? How can one detect unifying threads in a life, if they exist?" (1968, p. 377). Although these were questions that governed his lifelong theorizing and research, Allport modestly admitted toward the end of his life: "I still do not know how a psychological life history should be written" (1968, p. 377). The individual person was a subject of enduring mystery and fascination for Allport.

As a mature scholar, Allport championed research and assessment strategies that emphasized exploration of readily accessible information, thoughts and feeling:

> When we set out to study a person's motives . . . I see no reason why we should not start our investigation by asking him to tell us the answers as he sees them. (1960, p. 101)

Allport believed that direct questioning frequently results in more information than either projective testing or psychoanalytic interviewing. Commenting on the prevailing motivational theories in the 1950s, Allport pointed out that psychologists thought that conscious verbal reports were untrustworthy. Indeed, psychologists were often interested in the roots of patients' motives rather than trying to understand present strivings. Allport did not deny the existence or significance of unconscious motives or the importance of infantile experiences. Rather, he wanted to supplement such a focus with an emphasis on a person's current conscious self-evaluation.

Allport taught that reliance on theories of personality should be tempered with a willingness to apply them flexibly and nondogmatically. He emphasized that whole persons are more complex than our often over-simplifying explanations. Allport urged psychologists to abide by two principles (1968, p. 23):

1. *"Do not forget what you have decided to neglect."* If a theory accounts for some findings, do not lose sight of what remains unexplained.

2. *"Theorize in such a way that what is true in any region of mental life can be verified to be so."* This is Allport's statement of the important principle of *refutability.*

TOWARD A PERSONALISTIC PSYCHOLOGY

Allport was challenged by the difficulty of combining science's traditional interest in universal laws with psychology's presumed focus on the unique individual. In *Personality: A Psychological Interpretation* (1937), his first book on the field of personality, Allport wrote:

> The outstanding characteristic of man is his individuality. He is a unique creation of the forces of nature. Separated spatially from all other men he behaves throughout his own particular span of life in his own distinctive fashion. It is not upon the cell nor upon the single organ, nor upon the group, nor upon the species that nature has centered her most lavish concern, but rather upon the integral organization of life processes into the amazingly stable and self-contained system of the individual creature. (1937, p. 3)

Allport indicated that, in its attempts to seek regularities in nature, science has focused on whole classes of phenomena. From this perspective, the individual is regarded only as an instance or an example of a universal principle. For scientific psychologists, processes like intelligence, perception, and learning are regulated by general laws. It is their job to discover how these laws apply despite individual differences among subjects.

In contrast to the classic scientific strategy, Allport preferred the rationale and methods of **personalistic psychology:**

> The chief tenet of [personalistic psychology] is that every mental function is embedded in personal life. In no concrete sense is there such a thing as intelligence, space perception, color discrimination or choice reaction; there are only *people* who are capable of performing such activities and of having such experiences. . . . Nor can motives ever be studied apart from their personal setting; they represent always the striving of a total organism toward its objective. (Allport, 1937, p. 18; italics in original)

Idiographic and Nomothetic Approaches

The distinction between the investigation of general or universal laws, and the application of such laws to the individual case occupied Allport's attention throughout his career. He adopted from the philosopher Wilhelm Windelband (in Allport, 1937, p. 22) the term **idiographic** for the study of individuals and **nomothetic** to describe a concern for general principles. Probably to correct a perceived imbalance in research methodology, Allport asserted that his chief interest was the development of methods and concepts that take account of the complexity of individual cases. But, as a personalistic psychologist, or personologist (Murray, 1938), Allport also took the point of view that idiographic (particular) and nomothetic (general) methods and concepts should ultimately be combined:

> [The psychological study of individuality] will not be content with the discovery of laws pertaining to mind-in-general, but will seek also to understand the lawful tendencies of minds-in-particular. The personologist seeks to understand individual consistency; that is, uniformities and regularities in individual behavior. The concern is always for the whole of personality as it exists in real people (Allport, 1960, pp. 146–147).

Suggestions for an Adequate Theory of Personality

Allport's emphasis on the importance of the individual case and the necessity to understand the whole person led him to formulate criteria by which to judge the adequacy of any personality theory (1960, pp. 20 ff.):

1. Does the theory construe the human personality as actually existing within the functioning organism? To Allport, personality is more than a hypothetical construct. It actually *is*. Personality, for Allport, is not explainable exclusively in situational terms or in terms of others' opinions of the person. An adequate personality theory recognizes that personality is *biophysical,* having both psychological and physiological components (Allport, 1960, p. 21). It ". . . has internal structures and substructures which 'cause,' or partially cause, behavior" (1960, p. 25). This view is contrary to the behavioral approach, which focuses on observable stimuli and responses to the exclusion of inferred internal processes or structures.

2. An adequate personality theory will regard motivation "as normally a fact of present structure and function, not merely as an outgrowth of earlier forces" (Allport, 1960, p. 20). Allport disagreed with psychoanalytic theories that regarded motivation largely as a product of the person's past. Such formulations reduce the multiplicity of human motives to a few basic drives, needs, wishes, or vectors. Allport's view was that such reductionism does not aid in understanding any actual personality (1960, p. 27).

3. The satisfactory personality theory will employ units of analysis "capable of living synthesis" (Allport, 1960, p. 20). Allport criticized the method of reducing personality to a set of measurable variables without the eventual goal of resynthesizing the measurements into a whole picture: "To say that John Brown scores in the eightieth percentile of the 'masculinity-femininity' variable, in the thirtieth percentile on 'need for achievement' and at average on 'introversion-extroversion' is only moderately enlightening. Even with a more numerous set of dimensions, with an avalanche of psychometric scores, patterned personality seems to elude the psychodiagnostician" (1960, p. 30).

4. The acceptable personality theory will "allow adequately for, but not rely exclusively upon, the phenomenon of self-consciousness" (Allport, 1960, p. 20). "[S]elfhood is the central presupposition we must hold in examining the psychological states of human beings" (Allport, 1960, pp. 34–35).

Allport advocated an *open system* model of personality (1960, Chapter 3). Such a theory stresses past, present, and future-oriented motives and goals. The individual is viewed as proactive as well as reactive. The open-system approach acknowledges that people sometimes strive for more than the status quo. Allport's view was that people strive toward self-enhancement and growth rather than act largely from a sense of deficiency.

PERSONAL SOURCES OF ALLPORT'S EMPHASIS ON UNIQUENESS AND INDEPENDENCE

Allport did not go along with Freudian or behavioral reductionism regarding adult motives. Someone's motives could no doubt have had childish origins, yet that person could function adaptively or creatively in the present. In his mature theorizing, Allport called this conception of motivation "functional autonomy." Allport may have drawn the concept of functional autonomy at least in part from his own life, where it is clearly relevant.

On Swallowing a Dictionary: Competing for Recognition

Gordon Allport was born November 11, 1897, in Montezuma, Indiana, to a Scottish American medical doctor, John Edwards Allport, and his wife, Nellie Edith Wise. Gordon was the youngest of four brothers. Family life was marked by "plain Protestant piety and hard work" (Allport, 1967, p. 4). Allport's father stressed a humanitarian outlook on life, expressed in his fundamental rule: "If every person worked as hard as he could and took only the minimum financial return required by his family's needs, then there would be just enough wealth to go around" (1967, p. 5).

Allport's brothers were much older than he was. Gordon was introverted and had few boyhood friends, "for I never fitted the general boy assembly. I was quick with words, poor at games." At the age of 10, a schoolmate expressed the prevailing opinion of young Gordon: "Aw, that guy swallowed a dictionary" (1967, p. 4). Allport then knew he was an "isolate," though "I contrived to be the 'star' for a small cluster of friends."

For Allport, the road to acceptance as a valued individual was intellectual achievement. But even this avenue was fraught with competition. His high-achieving, older brother, Floyd, graduated from Harvard about the time Gordon finished high school. Floyd suggested that Gordon attend Harvard, and though he made the decision to apply belatedly, Gordon was accepted "after squeezing through the entrance tests." After his first final examinations produced an array of D's and C's, young Gordon redoubled his efforts to earn all A's at the year-end exams.

After college graduation, when Allport returned from his travels, including his visit with Freud, his work for the doctorate in psychology at Harvard seemed less challenging: "Back at Harvard I found that the requirements for the Ph.D. degree were not stiff (not nearly stiff enough), and so with only two years' additional course work, a few examinations, and the thesis, I qualified for this degree in 1922 at the age of 24" (1967, p. 8). He had, at last, mastered Harvard's academically challenging environment and was now on a par with his brother Floyd.

When Floyd published a classic textbook on social psychology, Gordon's view was critical: "His *Social Psychology* (1924) was too behavioristic and too psychoanalytic for my taste" (1967, p. 12). Gordon and Floyd Allport rarely collaborated professionally, and they published only two papers together. Gordon Allport commented "Apart from these two papers we never collaborated, even though we have occasionally helped each other with criticism" (1967, p. 12).

Atwood and Tomkins (1976) have pointed to the pattern in Allport's life of first following in his brother's footsteps and then striving for autonomy:

> If we assume that this pattern of similar behavior [by Gordon imitating Floyd] was the outcome of an identification based on envy, it would mean that Allport's education and career choice were, in large measure, "functionally dependent," i.e., motivated by the infantile aim of participating in his brother's greatness and thereby overcoming his own feelings of inferiority. Some insight into why it should have become necessary for him to abandon this aim and make his work functionally autonomous is suggested by another emphasis in his theoretical writings—the uniqueness of the individual. To the extent that his life was directed and determined by the emulation of his brother, his own identity as a separate person (his uniqueness) was likely to have been compromised. In the service of asserting his identity, then, he opposed the identification with his brother by declaring that his interests had become independent of their origins. (Atwood & Tomkins, 1976, p. 175)

Atwood and Tomkins therefore suggested that Allport's emphasis on his own personal uniqueness was an ego defense. They thus presented a Freudian analysis of Allport, who was himself critical of Freud's ideas.

Allport's View of His Own Personal Uniqueness

Throughout his autobiography, Allport mentions his poor ability in the hard sciences. He considered Floyd talented in these subjects and others: "Floyd was a stricter logician and more systematic in his use of method than I. It should also be said that he had artistic, musical, and manual giftedness that I lacked" (1967, p. 12). What special talent, then, did Gordon himself possess? He hints that he and his brother differed drastically but then ambivalently withdraws the distinction: "Over the years we pursued our own ways, but because of our common and unusual surname and divergence of points of view we managed to confuse students and the public. Were there one or two Allports?" (1967, pp. 12–13).

Most emphatically, there were two. But one of them was a social psychologist and the other was a personality psychologist who struggled to wrest his chosen, self-created field from that of social psychology:

> In my thinking there is a sharp distinction between personality and social psychology. One must think of personality as a biophysical or biopsychical structure. It may be modified by the field, but it *is* something. Social psychology is everything else. (Allport, paraphrased by Brewster-Smith, 1971, p. 353; italics in original)

Allport dismissed the genetic fallacy of disproving a proposition by demonstrating its personal origins in the believer's life experiences. It is difficult to read his statement without seeing some degree of personal justification in it:

> The plain truth is that origins can tell nothing about the validity of a belief. Neither can origins characterize the mature belief as it now exists, nor explain its part in the present economy of life. One of the best musicians I know took up his profession originally, in part at least, because he was taunted in childhood for what seemed to be his tone-deafness. In psychological parlance, he "overcompensated" for the defect. But that incident has absolutely nothing to do with the present structure or dynamics of his life-absorbing interest. . . . Were we to gauge our evaluations by origins we would disparage the eloquence of Demosthenes because his oratory served as a compensation for his tendency to stammer. . . . And the fact that many psychologists take up their science because of personal maladjustments would make psychology worthless. (Allport, 1950, pp. 109–110)

Allport himself created a valuable and unique theory of personality out of his unique constellation of personal experiences and motives. His theory's validity is not lessened by an examination of its personal origins. Allport followed his brother to Harvard as an undergraduate and then followed him again through Harvard graduate study, even imitating his brother's field of specialization. But Gordon Allport's study of psychology was deliberately a world apart from Floyd's brand of psychology. In organizing the field of personality study, Gordon sought to rescue his special domain from the hands of his brother, the social psychologist. In one stroke, he built a theory to reflect the uniqueness and independence of the person and, at the same time, established his own uniqueness and independence among the Allports.

PERSONALITY: ALLPORT'S DEFINITION

Allport's emphasis on an open-system personality theory was an outgrowth of his earliest conceptualization of **personality**:

> Personality is the dynamic organization within the individual of those psychophysical systems that determine his unique adjustments to his environment. (1937, p. 48)

In devising his definition, Allport devoted a good deal of effort to synthesizing the varied usages of the term *personality* into a coherent and workable concept. Allport's definition of personality has four major criteria:

1. The first emphasis involves the usage of the term **dynamic organization**. Allport meant to stress that personality is always an organized whole, a whole that is constantly changing (dynamic). Personality is thus self-regulating and continually evolving (1937, p. 48).

2. The phrase *within the individual* was intended to indicate that personality is something "real"—something that resides within the skin. Personality is not an abstraction, nor is it a scientifically convenient fiction or hypothetical construct. It really exists.

3. The term **psychophysical systems** was meant to convey a recognition of the fact that personality has roots in the physical, chemical processes of the body's glands and nervous system. The term *psychophysical* reminds us that personality is neither exclusively mental nor exclusively neural.

4. The phrase *unique adjustments to his environment* emphasizes both Allport's conviction that psychology must attend to the individual personality as the individual adapts to changing psychological or physical environments.

In his 1961 revision of his major work, Allport modified his personality definition by substituting a new phrase for the previous "unique adjustments to his environment." The modified definition now ended with the phrase, "characteristic behavior and thought" (1961, p. 28). The alteration broadened the concept of personality as involving more than adjustment to personal and physical environments. Thus Allport recast his definition in 1961: "We not only adjust to our environment but we reflect on it. Also, we strive to master it, and sometimes succeed. Behavior and thought, therefore, make both for survival and for growth."

The Concept of Traits: Personal Consistency

The basic component in Allport's concept of personality was the **personality trait.**

> A trait is . . . *a neuropsychic structure having the capacity to render many stimuli functionally equivalent, and to initiate and guide equivalent (meaningfully consistent) forms of adaptive and expressive behavior.* (1961, p. 347; italics in original)

In this definition Allport asserted that traits are indeed real, that they are rooted in nervous system functioning, and that they guide behavior. A trait lends consistency to personality by allowing the person to respond similarly to a wide array of situations, that is, renders diverse stimuli "functionally equivalent." For Allport, traits are rather complex enduring dispositions to respond to one's environment in particular ways. A trait is always

---

BOX 11.1   *Only Connect . . .*

Contemporary cognitive psychology's concept of *schema* is very similar, if not identical, to Allport's concept of trait. A cognitive schema is capable of evaluating stimuli in a way that leads to certain actions. It identifies patterns in stimuli and it may lead to meaningfully consistent patterns of behavior. We might well consider Allport an incipient cognitive psychologist, ahead of his time.

established within the personality through a combination of innate physical attributes and acquired environmental habits (1937, p. 292).

Allport illustrated his conception of trait development and function with the following example:

> A young child, finding that his mother is nearly always present to satisfy his wants, develops for her an early affective attachment (conditioning). But later other social contacts likewise prove to be conducive to this child's happy and successful adjustment: playmates, for example, or family gatherings, or crowds at the circus. . . . The child gradually comes to seek people, rather than to avoid them. A trait (not an instinct) of gregariousness develops. The child grows eager for social intercourse; he enjoys being with people. When isolated from them for some time, he misses them and becomes restless. The older he grows the more ways he finds of expressing this gregarious interest. He seeks to ally himself with groups of people at the lodge, at the theater, at church; he makes friends and keeps in touch with them, often entertains them, and corresponds with them. . . . Sociability has become a deep and characteristic quality of this individual's personality. Its expression is variable; a wide range of equivalent stimuli arouse it. (1937, pp. 292–293)

Thus the child's trait of gregariousness or sociability renders many stimuli equivalent and guides many behaviors into equivalent forms of expression. The way in which Allport conceptualized a trait's mediation between diverse stimuli and the individual's characteristic and uniform responses to them is illustrated in Figure 11.1.

As Figure 11.1 indicates, the child's trait of gregariousness allows diverse situations like theater-going, church-going, letter-writing, and family gatherings to be occasions in which an individual may express his or her pervasive outgoing social involvement. The behaviors that constitute personal style are varied because they are particular responses to the specific characteristics of each social situation. But all behaviors share the common denominator of gregariousness or sociability. Thus, the trait of gregariousness indicates a person's "characteristic behavior and thought" in the face of diverse circumstances. In

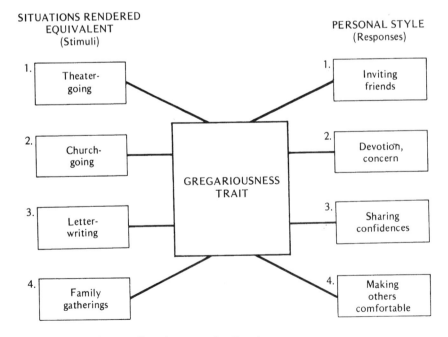

Figure 11.1 Trait as mediator between stimuli and responses.

commonsense terms, we often say that John or Jane did something "typical" of them. To be able to make such a judgment, it was first necessary to have observed John or Jane behaving in a consistent fashion in different situations. Traits are inferred as the basis of this personal consistency over situations.

Cardinal, Central, and Secondary Traits

Allport indicated that, within the context of an entire network of traits that compose a personality, some traits play major roles and some play minor roles. In rare cases, a particular trait is so outstanding, so pervasive that nearly all of an individual's activities can be traced to it. A trait of this significance is readily apparent. Such pervasive, dominantly influential traits are termed **cardinal traits** (Allport, 1937, pp. 337 ff.).

A cardinal trait, such as *Christlike* or *Machiavellian,* is so unifying that all other traits are subordinate to it. A cardinal trait is not found in a large percentage of people. Cardinal traits are not necessarily good, nor is it necessarily good to have a cardinal trait. Some saintly people like Mother Teresa and some tyrants such as Hitler are examples of people with cardinal traits. What they have in common is only a highly focused personality.

Central traits have an important role in the personality. They represent patterns of behavior that typify major areas of a person's functioning. "Central traits are those usually mentioned in careful letters of recommendation, in rating scales where the rater stars the outstanding characteristics of the individual, or in brief verbal descriptions of a person" (Allport, 1937, p. 338). Some typical characteristics that would likely be central traits are conscientiousness, level-headedness, laziness, industriousness, sense of responsibility, or irresponsibility.

Secondary traits are less generalized, less consistent, and less influential in the overall guidance of behavior than central traits. Such secondary traits are evoked by a narrower range of equivalent stimuli and direct a more restricted range of equivalent responses than central traits (1937, p. 338). Some typical secondary traits might refer to tastes in food, music, or clothing. Being well-groomed is usually considered a secondary trait. But determining whether a trait is central or secondary depends not so much on the trait itself, but of its importance within the personality.

Depending on the specific person or life situation, a given trait may be cardinal, central, or secondary. For example, a comedian's sense of humor might be central to their identity or even to their career whereas, for another person, a sense of humor may be less important. A given trait, such as love of music, might be a central trait in a musician and a secondary trait for someone else. An accountant's precision with numbers might be a central trait, whereas, for an artist, the same trait of precision might be of secondary importance. The fact that you shine your shoes regularly might represent a secondary trait; yet for a person who is obsessively concerned about neatness and cleanliness, such behavior might represent a central trait.

Individual and Common Traits; Personal Dispositions

Allport distinguished between individual and common traits. **Individual traits** are those unique to an individual whereas **common traits** are those shared by many people. Allport accurately noted that two people could not have precisely the same trait (1937, p. 297). Thus, even though two individuals may be said to possess the trait of politeness, the personal style with which this common trait will be expressed is at least a little different in each person. In this sense, every trait is an individual trait. Yet, for all practical purposes, individuals do share some patterns of behavior. It is possible, for example, to speak of generally polite people. In this more practical sense Allport concluded that the term *common trait* may be applied. In 1961 Allport introduced some terminological changes into his theory of traits. To emphasize his fundamental distinction between individual and common (aspects of) traits, Allport chose to relabel the individual trait as a *personal disposition* (1961, p. 358). Allport employed the following definition of **personal disposition:**

> *A personal disposition is a generalized neuropsychic structure (peculiar to the individual), with the capacity to render many stimuli functionally equivalent, and to initiate and guide consistent (equivalent) forms of adaptive and stylistic behavior.* (1961, p. 373)

Allport emphasized that,

> Every man is in certain respects: a. like all other men (universal norms), b. like some other men (group norms), c. like no other men (idiosyncratic norms). (1961, p. 13)

He continued by indicating that this individuality is not only a matter of individual traits, but represents the unique organization and dynamics of each and every person:

> Although we accept the formula of three sets of norms, we should guard against one pitfall. This approach might mistakenly imply that the individual as such is only a handful of residual, and perhaps negligible, idiosyncrasies. . . . The facts are otherwise. [A given person] Sam, to be sure has many attributes characteristic of the human species, and many that resemble his cultural fellows: *but he weaves them all into a unique idiomatic system. . . .* The organization of the individual life is first, last, and all the time a primary fact of human nature. (1961, pp. 14–15; italics in original)

This is a clear statement of Allport's idiographic focus. Each person is viewed as unique, one of a kind. The study of an individual, in his view, is the proper and most appropriate area of investigation for psychology. We will see how this view is applied in his single case strategy for studying individuals.

PERSONAL DOCUMENTS: AN IDIOGRAPHIC APPROACH TO LIFE HISTORY

Personal documents may take many forms: autobiographies, diaries, letters, interviews, even literary productions (Allport, 1942, 1961). "The personal document may be defined as *any self-revealing record that intentionally or unintentionally yields information regarding the structure, dynamics, and functioning of the author's mental life*" (Allport, 1942, p. xii; italics in original).

Individuals create self-revealing personal documents out of a variety of motives. For example, adolescents often keep detailed diaries or personal journals recounting their innermost thoughts, feelings, and aspirations. Such a document is often so revealing that the most grievous sin a parent can commit is to violate its secrecy.

The motives that impel individuals to create self-revealing productions are varied. Allport described 13 motives that might underlie such productions (1942, pp. 69–75):

1. *Special pleading:* To argue in a convincing way some self-serving or self-justifying premise.

2. *Exhibitionism:* A single-minded desire to display one's virtues and vices.

3. *Desire for order:* Compulsive need to record the circumstances of one's day.

4. *Literary appeal:* Desire for aesthetic and artistic satisfaction.

5. *Securing personal perspective:* A personal "taking stock" of one's life, achievements, failures, and so on.

6. *Catharsis:* A need to secure relief from tension and anxiety by writing when relief through direct action is unattainable.

7. *Monetary gain:* Personal revelations for prize competition, for payment in an experimental investigation, and so forth. Payment does not rule out, however, the validity of the self-revelations.

8. *Assignment:* School task imposed for some educational or therapeutic reason.

9. *Assisting in therapy:* Production of personal document for therapist to assist in one's own cure.

10. *Redemption and social reincorporation:* "Confessions" of an ex-criminal, spy, alcoholic, and so on. Generally such confessions are motivated by a genuine desire for forgiveness and acceptance.

11. *Public service:* Desire to achieve public or social reform.

12. *Desire for immortality:* "Battle against oblivion," or a desire not to be forgotten after death.

13. *Scientific interest:* Though not necessarily created for this reason, personal documents sometimes are donated to psychologists with the intention of furthering science.

This diverse array of motives suggests the methodological problems that historians, sociologists, anthropologists, or psychologists face when they decide to study evidence of this sort. All of these personal documents suffer from varying degrees of lack of candor, defective recollection on the part of the writer, and from conscious or unconscious self-concealment. Nonetheless, it was Allport's conviction that personal documents were a valuable source of answers to the question: "How shall a psychological life history be written?"

To assess the value of a personal document, the psychologist must ask how useful it is in meeting three goals of science: understanding, prediction, and control beyond the level of unaided common sense (1942, p. 148). It was Allport's judgment, after a thorough survey of the literature relating to research on personal documents, that their use was well justified.

> Personal documents are good if they serve the comparison of lives, one with another, leading to statistical generalizations and to an understanding of uniformities of behavior. But they are good also if standing one by one they provide concrete evidence of the nature of single lives from which all psychological science is derived; if they yield evidence of pluralistic causation; if they give clinicians and practitioners a sounder basis for work; and if they enhance the understanding, prediction, and control of individual lives (which is all that science ultimately demands). (Allport, 1942, p. 59)

Allport's evaluation suggests that personal documents may be treated in research with a variety of conceptualizations and methods. Analyses ranging from impressionistic characterizations, psychoanalytic hypothesizing, and direct content analysis to sophisticated statistical and factorial assessments are, in principle, possible. But two significant points about Allport's advocacy of personal document research bear mention: First, by definition, the study of personal documents is the idiographic strategy of assessing the unity, uniqueness, and consistency of the individual. Second, this single-case approach treats personality investigation as an attempt to comprehend the person from a subjective perspective—that is, trying to understand the viewpoint and experience of each individual.

AN ILLUSTRATIVE CASE:
ANALYSIS OF JENNY GOVE MASTERSON'S LETTERS

Within four years of the publication of his monograph on the use of personal documents in psychology, Allport published a series of letters that revealed the story of a mother–son relationship from the mother's point of view (Allport, 1946). The letters were presented to Allport by a young couple, identified as Glenn and Isabel, because they felt the letters might be valuable for the field of psychology. A psuedonymous "Jenny Gove Masterson" wrote the letters. The correspondence between Glenn and Isabel and Jenny began in March 1926, when Jenny was 58 years old, and ran its course of 301 letters. The correspondence ended with Jenny's death at the age of 69.

In 1965, Allport made the "Jenny Masterson" letters more widely available by publishing some of them in book form along with several types of psychological analysis of Jenny's personality. Allport posed the following challenges to psychologists:

> To me the principal fascination of the Letters lies in their challenge to the reader (whether psychologist or layman) to "explain" Jenny—if he can. Why does an intelligent lady behave so persistently in a self-defeating manner? When and how might she have averted the tragedy of her life? Could proper guidance or therapy at an appropriate time have helped alter the rigid course of her conduct? Was the root of her trouble some wholly unconscious mechanism? (Allport, 1965, p. viii)

Some brief details about "Jenny's" life are in order here. "Jenny Gove Masterson" was born in Ireland of Protestant parentage in 1868. Migrating to Canada when Jenny was five years old, the Gove family took up residence in Montreal. Her mother worked hard to preserve the family's sense of Irish culture and tradition. Jenny grew up in a family with five younger sisters and one younger brother. Her father died when Jenny was 18. Jenny became a telegrapher to support her family. Unfortunately, Jenny and her siblings did not get along well. By the time Jenny was 27 years old, bitter quarrels and disputes resulted in disintegration of the family. Jenny married an American railway inspector, Henry Masterson, a marriage that angered her family because he was divorced.

Jenny and Henry Masterson moved to Chicago, where Jenny found herself in an enforced idle existence. "She complained that she was being 'kept' by a man. She quarreled more than once with her husband over this issue, but he, like most men of his day, was firmly set against a wife seeking employment" (Allport, 1965, p. 3). The issue was not resolved at the time of Henry Masterson's death in 1897, when Jenny was 29 years old. A month after her husband's death, Jenny gave birth to her only child, a son named Ross.

After many years of a close relationship with his mother, Ross left home for college "back East" at Princeton. Jenny continued to work to support Ross's tuition and miscellaneous expenses. In Ross's sophomore year, the United States entered World War I, and Ross enlisted in the ambulance corps. At his departure for France, Jenny visited Ross and met his college friends, including Glenn and Isabel, her later correspondents. When Ross returned from France in 1919, he found himself disoriented. Ross returned to college, obtained his college degree, and subsequently failed in some business endeavors.

Ross and Jenny had many quarrels. One encounter occurred after Jenny learned of his marriage, which he had kept secret from her, ". . . she drove him out of her room with violent denunciations and a threat to have him arrested if he ever tried to see her again" (Allport, 1965, p. 6).

Jenny later renewed her contacts with Ross's college friends, Glenn and his wife Isabel, and requested permission to "keep in touch" with them. Her motives for this renewed acquaintance with Glenn and Isabel seem to have been a mixture of nostalgia for the days when "Ross was all hers" and a need to maintain a source of information about Ross's whereabouts.

Jenny's Personality: Samples of Her Letters

Writing to Glenn and Isabel on the occasion of Ross's visit to her room with his second wife, Jenny described the scene as follows:

> Ross brought this same woman and her brat to my house one Sunday evening and I was angry and told him that if he ever brought any more prostitutes to my house I would have them both arrested. Anyone, short of a fool, would know what she was at one glance. (Allport, 1965, p. 9)

In her letter of January 5, 1927, Jenny recalled her childhood:

> My father dropped dead one day, and had no provision made for his family—7 of them, all under 18. Not one in the house capable of earning a penny. It was my salary that kept the house going. . . . No one ever denied it, or pretended to think otherwise, and when I dared to marry the man I had been in love with for years, but dreaded to take my money out of their house . . . why, they said I was like the cow that gave the milk and then kicked the pail. (Allport, 1965, p. 27)

In June 1928, Jenny gave vent to one of her characteristic outbursts of pessimism and martyrdom:

> Anyway I am firmly convinced that I am "through" and ought to step out. I have done all, of any use, that it is possible for me to do in this world. Whether it was for good or bad it is over and done and nothing can change it now, "The moving finger writes, and having writ moves on" and my days for possible usefulness are past. I should step out, but am a coward. To suppose that Ross needs me would be indeed a joke. (Allport, 1965, p. 50)

In 1929 Ross underwent surgery for a tumor on his inner ear and for an "abscess on the outer covering of the brain." During his convalescence, he stayed with "one of his women." About two months after the operation, Jenny received word that Ross had died in a sudden relapse. She was to outlive her son by eight years. Glenn was summoned to attend the funeral and cremation of Ross's body. After the ceremony, Glenn accompanied Jenny back to her room. Ending an hour of respectful silence, Jenny spoke, "The body is consumed, now we'll have a good steak dinner" (recollection of Isabel, in Allport, 1965, p. 153). Jenny wrote to Glenn and Isabel, following Ross's death:

> After a while I shall count up all my riches—after the horror of this loss becomes blunted a bit—you know "the years roll by and on their wings bear healing"—wounds do not remain open for always—and then I shall count up my riches—such wonderful friends—*such* friends—the glory of the sun and the stars—the sigh of the sea—the laughter of little children. (Allport, 1965, p. 73; italics in original)

An Analysis of Jenny's Personal Dispositions

Allport's perennial question: "How shall a psychological life history be written?" can, as always, be answered on two levels. A psychologist may decide to analyze the letters with regard to nomothetic (general-universal) results. Jenny's letters could be analyzed today to see to what extent she fits within some *DSM-IV* diagnostic category, such as Paranoid Personality Disorder. This diagnosis would indicate overall patterns of behavior but would not be adequate for understanding Jenny as an individual. The psychologist who wished to form an impressionistic portrait of Jenny as a unique person might take a different approach. Such a psychologist might ask a series of judges to read the Masterson letters and to put Jenny's outstanding traits in their own words. Then a "trait portrait" could be formed. It would be based on areas of agreement among the judges.

Allport reported the results of the latter type of investigation undertaken by himself with 36 judges. These 36 people used a total of 198 trait names to characterize Jenny. Loosely clustered, the 198 items fell into nine categories (Based on Allport, 1965, pp. 193–194):

1. *Quarrelsome-Suspicious* (e.g., distrustful, paranoid, opinionated)
2. *Self-centered* (e.g., selfish, jealous, possessive, martyr complex)
3. *Independent-Autonomous* (e.g., hardworking, stubborn, calculating)
4. *Dramatic-Intense* (e.g., emotional, rigid, serious, violent)
5. *Aesthetic-Artistic* (e.g., intuitive, fastidious, expressive)
6. *Aggressive* (e.g., ascendant, domineering, self-assertive)
7. *Cynical-Morbid* (e.g., pessimistic, sarcastic, despondent)
8. *Sentimental* (e.g., loyal, affectionate, maternal)
9. *Unclassified* (e.g., intelligent, witty, whimsical)

Clearly, some of the categories are contradictory, and some overlap. Yet nearly all the judges agreed that the prominent traits in Jenny's personality were: *suspiciousness, self-centeredness, autonomy, a dramatic nature, aggressiveness, morbidity, and sentimentality.*

Allport reported a more elaborate study of Jenny's letters by one of his students. Jeffrey Paige (in Allport, 1965, pp. 199 ff.) used a computer lexicon of social science terms to analyze Jenny's letters. Containing nearly 3,000 items, the coding system used by Paige reduced Jenny's letters to a small number of labels that summarized large classes of phrase usage in Jenny's writing. For example, Jenny employed many phrases to express her aggression, hostility, open rage, and opposition to Ross and his women. All of these phrases were coded into a single category signifying aggression. Once programmed in this way, the computer was asked to sort out several kinds of data from Jenny's letters.

Paige found, using the first 56 letters up to the death of Ross, eight factors that embodied Jenny's most prominent traits (1965, pp. 200–201). Listed in order of decreasing frequency of expression, these traits were

1. aggression
2. possessiveness
3. need for affiliation
4. need for autonomy
5. need for familial acceptance
6. sexuality
7. sentience (love of art, literature, natural beauty)
8. martyrdom

Clearly, there is much overlap between the judges' impressionistic analyses of Jenny's letters and the computer-derived traits.

Computer-derived data reveal further information. Jenny expresses more affection for Glenn than for Isabel; she makes more requests of Glenn for advice than of Isabel. But the computer had some trouble with items tagged "Good" and "Bad." For example, the statement: "I have a truly noble son, an honor to his college, his friends, his family"—

a sarcastic comment—is labeled "Good" by the computer. Apparently sarcasm was not labeled by the computer's programming.

One can see why Allport concluded that little is gained by sophisticated statistical and factorial analyses of individual persons. The impressionistic judgments of Jenny's personality provide as much information on most issues as the computer-derived traits. Yet analysis with the aid of a computer program does lead to more detailed results. The two approaches could readily become complementary.

CRITICISMS AND ALLPORT'S RESPONSES

Allport's insistence that an adequate personality psychology must be based on attempts to understand the individual case evoked a great deal of criticism. The main issues in the controversy centered on Allport's distinctions between the idiographic and nomothetic scientific strategies. Part of the controversy, too, concerned Allport's conceptualization of traits as the fundamental units of study.

Falk (1956), whose ideas were repeated by later critics, suggested that there is no real dispute between nomothetic and idiographic goals in science. Study of unique events is not essential to the formulation of scientific theory. Furthermore, Falk argued, the idiographic approach is a necessary preliminary method to the development of generalizations, for the observation of single events always precedes the construction of laws. But, Falk suggested, general laws are adequate, when properly applied, to the task of understanding the unique personality.

Robert Holt (1962) extended the objections to Allport's emphasis on the idiographic in his idiographic-nomothetic distinction. He labeled Allport's point of view a "romantic personology." Holt concluded that there was no logical basis for establishing a special branch of natural science for the study of the unique personality because such a study is, by definition, not scientific. Holt suggested that Allport had confused art and science in his attempts to achieve comprehensive understanding of single persons. The feeling of fully understanding a person is more suitable to an artist. Scientists, by contrast, are satisfied when they can reliably predict and control the events they study.

Holt also pointed out that it is theoretically impossible to conceptualize something that is unique. If a given personality were unique, heretofore never experienced, a totally unique trait name would have to be coined or some unique combination of existing trait names would have to be employed. A combination of trait names, though, would hardly satisfy Allport because it would fail to capture the personal element in personality.

The concept of traits as the fundamental units of personality has also been subject to its share of criticism. B. F. Skinner, in the tradition of radical behaviorism (see Chapter 14), objected to postulating inner mechanisms to explain observable behaviors. From a behavioral viewpoint, traits, needs, or instincts are not necessary to explain observed responses.

> When we say that a man eats *because* he is hungry, smokes a great deal *because* he has the tobacco habit, fights *because* of the instinct of pugnacity, behaves brilliantly *because* of his intelligence, or plays the piano well *because* of his musical ability, we seem to be referring to causes. But on analysis these phrases proved to be merely redundant descriptions. A single set of facts is described by the two statements: "He eats" and "He is hungry." A single set of facts is described by the two statements: "He smokes a great deal" and "he has the smoking habit." (Skinner, 1953, p. 31; italics in original)

Thus, from the behaviorist point of view, postulating traits of personality is merely a redundant statement of the behavior that has already been observed.

Allport was aware of these criticisms of his trait theory and responded to what he considered to be the valid points of his critics. He wrote in his autobiography, "I know in my bones that my opponents are partly right" (1968, p. 405). He eventually came to the conclusion that ". . . my earlier views seemed to neglect the variability induced by ecological, social, and situational factors. This oversight needs to be repaired through an adequate theory that will relate the inside and outside systems more accurately" (1966, in 1968, p. 63). He subsequently revised his trait theory to make it more adequate.

"TRAITS REVISITED": HEURISTIC REALISM

In a 1966 restatement of trait theory, Allport conceded that trait theory would have to be made more sophisticated, more predictive, and more empirically testable if it was to survive as a useful construct in contemporary psychology. To further this aim, he proposed a new approach to theory building, which he termed **heuristic realism.** Heuristic realism has two guiding assumptions. First, the personologist *chooses* to believe that "the person who confronts us possesses inside his skin generalized action tendencies (or traits) and that it is our job scientifically to discover what they are" (1968, p. 49). Second, heuristic realism asserts that owing to the complexity of the objects or events observed, and because present methods are not completely adequate, the goal of scientifically conceptualizing personality's realness cannot be fully successful. Yet the heuristic realist proceeds "as if" success were possible, for only by making the attempt will progress toward knowledge of the person be attained. By introducing the concept of heuristic realism, Allport held to the position that it was worthwhile to try to understand the individual personality, even though complete, perfectly accurate understanding might be out of reach.

Recently, many of Allport's most criticized views have been vindicated. Thomas Pettigrew, a leading social psychologist and former student and colleague of Allport, has recently written,

> . . . many of Gordon's initial proposals for addressing basic problems now exist in our literature with new labels and enlarged meanings. . . . Consider the much derided concept of functional autonomy. The notion that motives can become independent of their origins was widely considered heretical in 1937. Slowly, psychology came to accept the phenomenon if not the formulation. (1999, p. 415)

Pettigrew also mentions the fact that Allport's trait theory was in fact more interactionist and dynamic than portrayed by his contemporary critics.

THE MATURE, HEALTHY PERSONALITY

In his 1937 statement of his position, Allport criticized psychology's lack of interest in the **mature or healthy personality** and elaborated on the concept of maturity. One characteristic of maturity is the capacity to defer momentary needs, pains, or desires in favor of reaching long-term goals. Setbacks or defeats do not easily deter mature persons. The pursuit of personally meaningful goals represents **self-extension** (1937, p. 213). A mature person is capable of going beyond self to invest energies in pursuits beyond immediate self-interest. Allport related his concept of maturity to limitations in the thinking of behaviorists. He wrote, ". . . true maturity leads us to do things for reasons that are not mechanically enslaved to the principle of reward and punishment" (1961, p. 96).

The psychologically mature person also has the capacity for **self-objectification** (1937, p. 214). Allport defined self-objectification as "that peculiar detachment of the mature person when he surveys his own pretensions in relation to his abilities, his present objectives in relation to possible objectives for himself, his own equipment in comparison with the equipment of others, and his opinion of himself in relation to the opinion others hold of him" (1937, p. 214). The capacity for self-objectification is tied to insight and to a sense of humor. A third attribute of being mature is the development of *unifying philosophies of life*. Mature people live their lives according to guiding principles.

Allport proposed a developmental model to account for maturity. It appears to be generally relevant, although it is not the only model on the scene (see Erikson, Chapter 8).

Emergence of the Self in Infancy

The first sense of self to evolve, according to Allport, is the **bodily self.** To illustrate, consider the infant of five or six months who manages to get its foot into its mouth for a two- or three-toothed bite: "If he hurts his foot he cries but has no idea at all that *he* has hurt *him*" (1961, p. 112). But with the passing of time, many such bodily sensations are experienced as recurrent and reliable aspects of *me*. Combined with these sensations are the frustrations of desires and wants that originate in external agents, like mother. "A child who cannot eat when he wants to, who bumps his head, soon learns the limitations of his too, too solid flesh" (1961, p. 112).

The emerging certainty that "I am the *same person*" as time passes is what Allport termed **self-identity.** He thought that self-identity depends on the child's developing capacity for language. For with the possibility of employing words to think and to communicate, the regularity, the solidity, and the sameness of existence become apparent. "He hears constantly 'Where is Johnny's nose?' 'Where are Johnny's eyes?' 'Good Johnny,' 'John naughty' " (1961, p. 115). With the repetition of his name in various contexts, the child develops the capacity to refer to himself with a name. He also becomes aware of the continuity of his self-identity.

Parents often have difficulty with the two- to two-and-a-half-year-old because the child resents anyone taking over his or her prerogatives:

> A two-year-old went to the bathroom with his father to have his face washed. Saying, "Let me," he struggled to turn on the faucet. He persisted without success. For a time the father waited patiently, but finally "helped" the child. Bursting into screams of protest the child ran from the bathroom and refused to be washed. His father had spoiled everything. (Allport, 1961, p. 118).

A sense of **self-esteem** begins to acquire importance near the end of the second year of life and becomes critical for healthy development in the third year. At the same time the child undergoes what parents call negativism, saying "No!" to nearly every important demand that the parents make. In effect, the child regards every adult proposal or demand as a threat to its integrity. "To him it seems safer to resist any adult proposal in advance, as a protection to dawning self-esteem" (Allport, 1961, p. 119). So, by the end of the third year of life, three aspects of self have emerged: the bodily self, self-identity, and self-esteem (with accompanying pride and stubbornness).

Emergence of Self in Later Childhood

From four to six years of age, the child consolidates and refines the three aspects of self that have already emerged. At this time, the child's cognitive and emotional egocentricity is readily apparent. As Piaget described, the child believes that the sun follows it, "that God, or Santa Claus is a Being whose primary duty is to serve his interests" (Allport, 1961, p. 122). Slowly, however, the child experiences the fourth aspect of selfhood, **self**

extension. For example, the child begins to understand the meaning of possession: "This ball is mine, he is my Daddy" and so on. The "ball" and the "Daddy" are each seen as an extension of self. Important during this period, too, is the developing awareness of the child that its parents want it to be a certain kind of self. The child's **self-image** begins to become important and definite. The child of five or six years begins to realize the difference between being "good" and being "naughty."

From ages six to twelve, the child's sense of an extended self and its self-image are enhanced by experiences with peers in the school setting. The child learns what is expected of it in regions beyond the security of the family situation. The child learns to shift gears as it moves from family to outside situations so that, for example, rough-and-ready talk with peers is restrained to a more polite form of conversation at home. By the 12th year the child is capable of reflective thought and hypothetical or "as if" reasoning, and this achievement also marks the child's realization that self is a thinker and a judger—in short, a "rational coper" (1961, p. 124).

The **self-as-rational-coper** corresponds in Allport's view to Freud's "ego." This aspect of the self, like the Freudian ego, attempts to deal with external reality, mediate between the demands of one's impulses, and act according to the restraints of society (parents, teachers). In this sense, not all of the self-as-rational-coper's activities are conscious. Some of its attempts to mediate between need and reality may be unconscious and defensively oriented in its striving to maintain self-esteem. In this area, Allport has incorporated much of Freudian thinking.

Identity and Beyond

The period of adolescence is marked by what Erikson (Chapter 8) calls an "identity crisis." The central question for the adolescent is: "Just who am I?" or "Am I a child or an adult?" In attempts to form an identity, adolescents play various roles, trying on each for size and discarding those with which the emerging sense of self-identity clashes.

> The search for identity is revealed in the way an adolescent tries on different masks. He first develops one line of chatter, then another, one style of hairdress and then another (always within the range permitted by the peer group). He imitates one hero and then another. He is still searching for a garb that will fit. What he really wants is not yet fully present—his adult personality. (Allport, 1961, p. 125)

After adolescence, choosing to direct one's life into realistic and appropriate channels eventually becomes a central concern. "Paring down the self-image and aspirations to life-size is a task for his adult years" (1961, p. 126). This last aspect to emerge within the slowly evolving self is what Allport calls **propriate striving,** meaning literally, "self-governing motivations." In addition to its other aspects, the self (proprium) is the proprietor or governor that has ownership and responsibility for the outcome of one's life. The central theme of a life, the dominant goals of a life history, are the essence of propriate striving. Thus the content of a person's propriate strivings consists of who a person wants to be and what he or she wants to become.

Propriate striving is a process that leads to the unification of personality and is characteristic of healthy functioning.

> Propriate striving distinguishes itself from other forms of motivation in that, however beset by conflicts, it makes for unification of personality. . . . The possession of long-range goals, regarded as central to one's personal existence, distinguishes the human being from the animal, the adult from the child, and in many cases the healthy personality from the sick. (Allport, 1955, pp. 50–51)

"Me, Myself, and I" and More: The Proprium

Because each of the emerging aspects of self is experienced as relevant, as personal, as "owned," Allport suggested substituting the term **proprium** for the term self or ego (1955, p. 40). The first seven aspects of the proprium consist of the bodily self, the self-identity, self-esteem, extended-self, self-image, self-as-rational-coper, and self-as-proprietor. Table 11.1 summarizes the ages at which different aspects of the proprium develop.

A key characteristic of the proprium is its warm or intimate quality, the feeling of being really a part of *me:*

> Personality includes these habits and skills, frames of reference, matters of fact and cultural values that seldom or never seem warm and important. But personality includes what is warm and important also—all the regions of our life that we regard as peculiarly ours, and which for the time being I suggest we call the *proprium.* The proprium includes all aspects of personality that make for inward unity. (Allport, 1955, p. 40)

A last aspect, **self-as-knower,** goes beyond the first seven aspects of the proprium and unifies them as objects of awareness:

> "Who is the I who knows the bodily me, who has an image of myself and sense of identity over time, who knows that I have propriate strivings?" I know all these things and, what is more, I know that I know them. But who is it who has this perspectival grasp? (Allport, 1961, p. 128)

Allport indicated that the self-as-knower is inherent to the structure of the person. It was not to be conceptualized as a "little man" or *homunculus* inside the person, but *rather as the totality of the person as process, as an entity that is becoming* (1961, p. 130; 1955, p. 53). Yet Allport readily admitted that the concept of self-as-knower still left a residue of mystery.

> It seems on the whole sounder to regard the propriate functions of wanting, striving, willing as interlocked with the total personality structure. They are felt as self-relevant, but are not caused by a separate agent within the personality. As for the knower, whether it is simply an inference we make at a high level of complexity . . . or whether it is necessary to postulate a pure knower, a continuing transcendental self . . . is a riddle we have not solved. (1961, p. 138)

Table 11.1   Aspects of the Proprium

Development period	Proprium characteristic	Personality function
First year	Bodily self	Sensation-perception of physical pains, pleasures, and limitations.
Second year	Self-identity	Continuity of experience made possible through language.
Third year	Self-esteem	Pride in accomplishment; independence and negativism.
Four to six years	Self-extension	Abstract concept of possession: "mine."
Four to six years	Self-image	"Good" and "naughty" selves; sensitivity to praise and blame.
Six to twelve years	Self-as-rational-coper	Realistic solving of life's tasks; mediator between needs and reality.
Twelve years through adolescence	Propriate strivings	Ownership and acceptance of feelings, needs, thoughts; self-defined life goals.
Adulthood	Self-as-knower	The totality of all previous aspects of the proprium: awareness of self.

FUNCTIONAL AUTONOMY: ALLPORT'S THEORY OF MOTIVATION

Allport objected to prevailing trends in motivational theory, particularly Freudian explanations, that rely almost exclusively on the person's past unconscious needs to account for his or her present status (1960, Chapters 6, 9). Allport preferred, in keeping with his emphasis on individuality, to view adult motives in terms of the person's contemporary situation and feelings. The most important concept he developed in this regard was that of **functional autonomy.** Allport proposed that new sets of motivations for behaviors may develop that are functionally autonomous or freed from their original motivations.

Allport pointed to a variety of everyday motives, freed of their initial sources, which continued to function as ends in themselves. "An ex-sailor has a craving for the sea, a musician longs to return to his instrument after an enforced absence, a city-dweller yearns for his native hills, and a miser continues to amass his useless hoard" (1937, p. 196). Although the sailor may have first gone to sea to earn a living, he is now financially secure. Yet, he continues to desire to go to sea.

Allport indicated that his development of the concept of functional autonomy was a direct response to his early encounter with Freud:

> . . . you can see the impact of my encounter with Freud as the origin of my idea that adult motivation is not necessarily a channeling or conditioning, or overlay of cathected instincts or infantile motivations or fixations. The result was the concept of functional autonomy. . . . This was a direct answer to Freud, for Freud had thought that I was suffering from an infantile trauma. I wasn't. . . . He didn't perceive my contemporary motivation. His error impressed me very much, so that I kept working on the problem of motivation from a point of view of the developing adult. (Allport, 1962, p. 5)

In his presentation to a class at Boston University in 1962, he continued:

> I'm not denying or disparaging at all the Freudian contribution. But, Freud's theory to my mind just is not adequate, because some people *do* grow up *sometimes,* in *some* respects and be adult and normal in personality function. That is the focus of my concept of functional autonomy . . . as well as much subsequent writing. (Allport, 1962, p. 5).

Allport presented the **Zeigarnik effect** as an example of functional autonomy. Bluma Zeigarnik (1927) noted that subjects will often spontaneously resume tasks that they failed to complete during an experiment. Working with the task has become functionally autonomous of the original experimental requirements.

Peter Bertocci (1950) criticized Allport's conception of functionally autonomous motives for its all-inclusiveness. Bertocci questioned the logic of Allport's concept because it seemed to imply that any motive could become autonomous if repeated often enough. Furthermore, Bertocci suggested that even if motives could become functionally autonomous with repetition, there was no limiting principle to prevent the creation of completely independent, competing motives.

In the light of these and other criticisms, Allport restated his concept to bring it into line with other developments of his theory. In 1961, he defined functional autonomy more broadly:

> *Functional autonomy . . . refers to any acquired system of motivation in which the tensions involved are not of the same kind as the antecedent tensions from which the acquired system developed.* (1961, p. 229; italics in original)

To modify his original conception further Allport proposed two types of functional autonomy: **perseverative functional autonomy** and **propriate functional autonomy.** In each of these forms of functional autonomy, the original motivational system is replaced by a new one. But there is a major difference between the two.

BOX 11.2   *Only Connect . . .*

Allport was proposing a distinction similar to Maslow's later notion of the difference between deficiency and growth motivation (cf. Chapter 13). Propriate functionally autonomous motives may be viewed as goal-directed growth motives; perseverative functionally autonomous motives would be viewed as deficit motives in Maslow's hierarchy of needs.

A motive becomes perseverative or self-repeating by developing roots in some biochemical or neurological process. Forms of perseverative functional autonomy include addictions to drugs, alcohol, or tobacco, the tension induced by the Zeigarnik effect, and a child's circular activities like dropping a spoon repeatedly as long as mother returns it. For example, a person may begin smoking to gain the acceptance of peers. A short time later, the underlying motivational system may involve nicotine dependence and physiologically based withdrawal symptoms.

Propriate functional autonomy, by contrast, does not depend directly on any feedback mechanism or biochemical processes. Here, the self (proprium) determines which motives will become functionally autonomous. Consider, for example, a student who originally undertakes a field of study because it is required. He may continue to study it beyond the externally enforced requirements. He may discover the field is connected toward his ideals and plans for the future. A miser who begins to hoard and amasses a huge fortune—perhaps on the basis of a Freudian fixation at the anal level—may ultimately increase his wealth with philanthropy in mind.

Propriate functionally autonomous motives come about, according to Allport, for three main reasons:

1. *Principle of organizing the energy level:* People need new motives to consume their available energies. If existing motives have been satisfied, new ones will develop. For example, one might be a successful businessperson who enters the world of politics or a middle-aged employee who begins a new enterprise.

2. *Principle of mastery and competence:* People have the need to do more than passively react to their environment. They have the need to master it and thus experience a sense of competence in tackling the tasks of life.

3. *Principle of propriate patterning:* The self, or proprium, is the pattern or template on which functionally autonomous motives are shaped, directed, and unified.

EVALUATING GORDON ALLPORT

Gordon Allport was a founder of the academic field of personality psychology. It was his 1924 college course in personality, followed by his 1937 book, *Personality: A Psychological Interpretation* that put the subject of personality on the academic psychology map. He wrested the study of personality from the field of psychopathology and from the clinic and hospital. The present course you are taking and others like it are descendants of Allport's original Theories of Personality course taught at Harvard.

In his teaching, Allport emphasized the dynamic organization of the components of personality. He was convinced that personality was complex and could not be studied piecemeal. He first proposed the concept of refutability (testability) of theories, the active-passive dimension in evaluating human agency and the idiographic-nomothetic distinction. As evidenced by this text, these concepts continue to be of value in the field of personality theory.

The third force, humanistic psychology (see Chapter 13), which would emphasize individuality and growth rather than pathology, has some roots in Allport's ideas. He wrote, ". . . how wrong we have been in viewing the process of growth as a reaction to past and present stimuli, neglecting the dynamics of futurity: of orientation, intention, and valuation" (Allport, 1955, p. 76).

The newly developing positive psychology movement also owes much to Gordon Allport's pioneering work. He had the insight that, ". . . we have paid more attention to the pathology of becoming than to its normal course, focusing upon disease rather than health, upon bad citizenship rather than good, and upon prejudice rather than tolerance and charity" (Allport, 1955, p. 33).

Allport pioneered the study of normal and psychologically healthy individuals and people's strengths as well as pathologies. He opposed the reductionistic psychoanalytic and behavioral approaches at a time when they predominated.

Allport's concept of trait was an incipient cognitive formulation and, as such, decades ahead of its time. Intensive studies of individuals, begun by Allport and other personologists, continue to have a very modest place in published research. The idiographic approach is more important in confidential applications such as executive selection, clinical assessment, and classified studies of powerful world leaders for governmental purposes.

In addition to his work in the area of personality, Allport also pioneered the study of the psychology of religion. His theory of intrinsic and extrinsic religiosity has generated continuing research and theoretical discussion. His own interest in religiosity as an area of study countered the fashions of his day and provided a foundation for the later work of many others. Allport also contributed to the understanding of prejudice and discrimination.

From the beginning, Gordon Allport was a ruggedly independent thinker who did not conform to the prevailing Freudian and behavioral emphases in psychology. He spent his professional life as a scholar with a serious commitment: to study the normal person in a way respectful of individuality. His work affirmed the human capacity for development and personal growth.

Refutability of Allport's Theory

Allport's ideas were largely refutable and intentionally so. After all, he was the person who first stressed the importance of the refutability of psychological theories. Accordingly, his work did lend itself to research, to experimental design, and to observational and correlational tests. Nonetheless, Allport's theories did not always withstand empirical tests. As we have noted, refutable theories may, at times, be refuted. For example, Allport's original concept of traits had to be modified on empirical grounds. Early research showed that situational factors (rather than traits) seemed largely responsible for people's often inconsistent behavior. Allport eventually developed a more sophisticated theory emphasizing interaction between traits and environment.

Emphasis on Active Human Agency

Allport's conception of personality included an elegant affirmation of active human agency. He rebelled against the determinism of Freudian psychology and was also opposed to behavioral reductionism. Allport's conception of personality as an open system stressed the human capacity for rational decision making and for creative problem solving. Like leading humanists such as Abraham Maslow and Carl Rogers, Allport emphasized the human capacity for seeking and overcoming challenges and for continued and active growth.

Allport's Focus on the Idiographic

Allport first brought the terms *idiographic* and *nomothetic* into psychology from philosophy. He also argued for combining idiographic with nomothetic factors in the field of personality psychology. Later, Allport's humanism and his interest in and respect for the individual pushed his efforts in the direction of the development of idiographic research methods—an area that had not been emphasized by other psychologists. His book, *Letters from Jenny* (1965), is a case in point. In it, Allport exemplified the use of personal documents as research data, a method that by definition is idiographic.

SUMMARY

Allport's early experience in an interview with Freud that he himself had engineered seemingly had lasting effects on his conceptualization of people and their motives. Refusing to accept the Freudian thesis that all motives can be reduced to a few basic unconscious drives, Allport proposed that motivational research should at least begin with an assessment of the individual's own estimates of his or her motives. *"How shall a psychological life history be written?"* became, for Allport, the abiding focus of his personality theory. Perhaps the single most important advice Allport had for psychologists was "Do not forget what you have decided to neglect." Allport's emphasis on individuality led him to adopt from the philosopher Windelband the distinction between idiographic and nomothetic strategies of acquiring knowledge. Allport argued that the two strategies should be blended to achieve what he called "full-bodied understanding of personality." Yet Allport's emphasis was largely on the idiographic. Allport conceptualized traits as the fundamental units of individual consistency.

Distinguishing between common traits and individual traits, Allport stressed that any individual possesses a unique organization of these personal dispositions to characteristic behavior and thought. A trait functions to mediate between larger classes of stimuli and equally large classes of response. The trait of sociability, for example, serves to render many diverse situations functionally equivalent by initiating a range of meaningfully consistent behaviors. Allport was careful to stress that traits are conceptualized as neuropsychic structures, that is, as real biophysical processes existing within persons.

The concept of traits was further organized into a hierarchy of cardinal, central, and strategies of acquiring knowledge. Cardinal traits are the master dispositions of personality, so pervasive and influential that they seem to color every activity of the person.

Central traits are somewhat less pervasive and influential, but nevertheless exert strong directive influences on the person's characteristic ways of behaving. Secondary traits are the least influential forms of personal disposition.

Allport's abiding concern with the individual (idiographic) approach and with the concept of trait was criticized. Allport's restatement of his trait concepts stressed the need for heuristic realism in conducting research of an individual personality. The heuristic realist first recognizes that though he or she may be wrong, it is better to proceed as if traits were real entities residing in real, unique personalities. Second, though it is always a matter of approximation, and success is never certain, the heuristic realist realizes that it is better to make the attempt to understand individuals than to dismiss the idea as absurd.

Allport's personality theory also stresses the importance of individual personality unity and the fact that the person is always becoming, not just being. The sense of self that characterizes the mature, healthy individual is a gradual acquisition that proceeds through eight stages: (1) sense of bodily self, (2) sense of self-identity, (3) sense of self-esteem, (4) extension of self, (5) self-image, (6) self-as-rational-coper, (7) propriate striving, and (8) self-as-knower. The proprium, for Allport, is the final sense of self that develops in which the individual is capable of knowing and capable of knowing that he or she knows. In short, the self-as-knower poses the ultimate riddle of personality: How does the individual recognize that *he* or *she* is the person who is?

Closely connected with his concept of proprium was Allport's motivational theory of functional autonomy. Functional autonomy asserts that motives may continue to operate even when the original tensions on which they were based no longer operate. To modify the construct in the light of its subsequent criticism, Allport distinguished between two kinds of functional autonomy: perseverative and propriate. Perseverative functional autonomy involves biochemical or neurophysical processes that continue to operate through their own momentum or rhythm in the absence of the original deficit need that provoked them. Propriate functionally autonomous motives are those activities that serve some function of the self in its active striving for fulfillment.

Allport definitely took the position of human beings as active constructors of their lives. He supported the blending of idiographic and nomothetic strategies. In his own research, however, he encouraged idiographic methods more wholeheartedly, perhaps to correct for an existing imbalance in the field of personality studies.

FOR FURTHER READING

Allport's small volume, *Becoming: Basic Considerations for a Psychology of Personality* (New Haven, CT: Yale University Press, 1955), expresses in clear form Allport's views on individuality and personal growth. It is a very popular and readable book and is in its umpteenth edition. It contains a historical survey of the use of the concept of self and Allport's recommendations for adopting the analogous concept of the proprium.

Allport's most comprehensive work in personality theory is to be found in two successive editions of the same work: *Personality: A Psychological Interpretation* (New York: Henry Holt, 1937) was his first major contribution and continues to be valuable as an introduction to his early ideas; *Pattern and Growth in Personality* (New York: Holt, 1961) is a revision of the former work and reflects Allport's changing views of such important concepts as functional autonomy and individual traits. A collection of Allport's midcareer papers may be found in *The Person in Psychology* (Boston: Beacon Press, 1968).

Allport's publication of Jenny Masterson's letters, *Letters From Jenny* (New York: Harcourt, Brace & World, 1965), provided psychologists with raw data on a unique personality that deserves the reader's careful attention. In a similar vein, Allport presents the benefits and limitations of personal documents in psychological research in *The Use of Personal Documents in Psychological Science* (New York: Social Science Research Council Bulletin, No. 49, 1942).

Allport's views on the crucial function of religion in the mature, healthy personality may be gleaned from his *The Individual and His Religion* (New York: Macmillan, 1971). Allport's book *The Nature of Prejudice* (Reading, MA: Addison Wesley, 1958) contributed much to the cause of social justice and civil rights and is still considered a classic in the field. A recent whole volume of the *Journal of Social Issues* (Fall 1999, Vol. 55, 3, Malden, MA: Blackwell Publishers) is devoted to reviewing and honoring Allport's contributions to psychology.

An interview of Allport is to be found in R. I. Evans's (Ed.) Dialogue with Gordon Allport (New York: Praeger, 1981) or in condensed form in Evans's *The Making of Psychology* (New York: Knopf, 1976).

GLOSSARY

Bodily self: That sense of self based on one's physical senses and bodily reactions.

Cardinal traits: Traits that are pervasive, outstanding, and dominating. Only a few individuals have cardinal traits.

Central traits: Those five or ten traits that best describe an individual's personality. Such attributes are used to describe another person or to write a letter of recommendation.

Common traits: Generalized dispositions or shared traits, such as the capacity for gregariousness or aggressiveness.

Dynamic organization: The type of organization that characterizes personality, which Allport viewed as an organized whole that is constantly changing.

Functional autonomy: A process by which a behavior that was once set in motion by a basic motive comes to operate even when the original motive on which it was based is no longer present.

Heuristic realism: The useful working assumption that traits really exist even though the theorist realizes that this may not literally be true.

Idiographic: An approach in psychology that is concerned with identifying the unique combination of traits and other characteristics that best accounts for the personality of specific individuals.

It consists of in-depth analyses of individuals, usually for clinical or evaluative purposes.

Individual traits: A term that can be applied to all traits. Each person has a personal style in expressing a common trait, such as gentleness. Moreover, a trait is always individual in that it must be viewed within the context of a person's unique organization of traits.

Mature or healthy personality: In Allport's view, a person who focuses on long-term goals over momentary needs or goals. Such a person has sense of self-extension, self-objectification, and a unifying philosophy of life.

Nomothetic: An approach to psychology that seeks to establish general laws of human functioning, that is, to understand the general variables and the behavior of people in general or groups of people. Most psychological research is nomothetic.

Perseverative functional autonomy: A behavior that becomes perseverative or self-repeating because it develops new motivational roots in some biological or neurological process. For example, a person who originally smokes to get the approval of peers may continue because of the development of an addiction to nicotine.

Personal disposition: Unique trait of an individual, a trait not shared with others.

Personalistic psychology: An approach to psychology that looks at every psychological process in terms of its occurrence within specific individuals. For example, instead of examining cognition or perception in general, the personalistic psychologist would focus on Jill's cognitions and cognitive process of Jack's perceptual field.

Personality: The dynamic organization within the individual of those psychophysical systems that determine his or her characteristic behavior and thought.

Personality traits: Continuing dispositions to respond to one's environment in meaningfully consistent ways. Personality traits consist of neuropsychic structures that render stimuli functionally equivalent and lead to equivalent forms of adaptive and expressive behaviors.

Propriate functional autonomy: A behavior that continues because it develops new motivational roots that express the individual's propriate strivings or most cherished self-wishes or desired goals. A person who originally plays the violin

because of parental pressure may continue as an adult because of a deep love of music.

Propriate striving: Striving for the attainment of personally meaningful goals.

Proprium: Allport's term for the self; it consists of the bodily self, self-identity, self-esteem, extended-self, self-image, self-as-rational-coper, and self-as-proprietor.

Psychophysical systems: The physical and chemical structures and processes of the body's glands and nervous system, as well as associated psychological processes.

Secondary traits: Characteristics that are peripheral to the individual's personality, such as specific tastes in clothing, preferences for certain foods, or different musical affinities.

Self-as-knower: The last aspect of the proprium that surpasses, transcends, and unifies the other seven parts of the self through its awareness of the parts of the proprium. It is that sense of self that is aware of being, and existing.

Self-as-rational-coper: That aspect of self that solves problems rationally and efficiently; knowledge that one is able to initiate strategies to attain present and future goals.

Self-esteem: Feelings about one's worthiness in the eyes of others and in one's own eyes. Based on a sense of competence or lack thereof.

Self-extension: Extension of one's sense of self. A person may extend his or her sense of self to his or her possessions, family, home, fellow humans, and country.

Self-identity: The aspect of the proprium that represents self-continuity. The regularity, the solidity, and the sameness of existence are apparent in self-identity.

Self-image: The reflected appraisals of others that have become internalized; it also indicates one's own appraisal of one's virtues and weaknesses.

Self-objectification: Ability to perceive and measure realistically one's own abilities and shortcomings.

Zeigarnik effect: Named after Bluma Zeigarnik, the tendency of people to be motivated to complete an unfinished task. For Allport, the Zeigarnik effect was an example of a type of behavior that was functionally autonomous of its original motive.

Chapter 12

Rollo May

Existential Phenomenology

How are you able to live in a world where we are all alone,
where we all die?

Rollo May (1989)

Freedom must be loving, and loving must be free.

Nicholas Berdyaev, *Slavery and Freedom*

Rollo May   **Born: 1909   Ada, Ohio**
                 Died: 1994   Tiburon, California

About Rollo May's Existential Phenomenology

Some theories in personality psychology focus on narrow but manageable issues that can eventually be synthesized into a bigger picture. Rollo May has focused on broad, historically enduring, and deeply philosophical issues central to human experience. Some topics of ultimate meaning that May has addressed are indicated by some words in the titles of his books: Being, Death, Love, Evil, and Destiny.

Rollo May can be credited with bringing the ideas of largely European existential and phenomenological theorists to the attention of psychologists. Through the anthologies of writings that he edited and through his own contributions to existential phenom-

enological psychoanalysis, May shaped the thinking of psychologists, psychotherapeutic social workers, and other mental health professionals.

Central to May's conception of humanity are these ideas:

- *Human beings are not like inanimate objects in that they experience themselves as conscious beings who experience a meaningful world.*

- *An individual's experience of the world—the physical world, the world of thoughts and ideas, and the interpersonal world—can be described directly, without the use of abstract concepts that refer to impersonal processes or entities (such as repression, the id, the superego, or drive).*

- *Human beings can become aware of their own mortality. Such awareness that a person's life is finite emphasizes the importance of choice and commitment in the present.*

- *Anxiety is more than a form of psychopathology. One form of anxiety, existential anxiety, involves an individual's confrontation with the possibility of nonbeing, the possibility of being engulfed by a meaningless life.*

- *Human beings are always capable of change and development.*

- *People are, to a large extent, responsible for the meanings they experience and create. They have a great potential for good and evil, for creativity and destruction.*

A LONELY YOUNG MAN, LOOKING FOR ANSWERS TO DEEP QUESTIONS

Rollo May described himself as having been an angry adolescent and rebellious in school. During his college years at Michigan State College, May irked the school authorities with a student literature magazine he started and transferred to Oberlin College in Ohio, a small liberal arts college, at the suggestion of a friend. His experience at Oberlin was positive and fed his interests in the humanities, especially Greek art and literature. He was hired by a Gymnasium (a kind of high school and junior college) in Greece to teach English to boys between the ages of 12 and 18. He stayed in Greece for about three years teaching and studying art and painting.

> The boys were effusive, lovable, emotionally changeable. It was a case of an immediate love affair between the students and myself, but I was later to learn how unstable such adoration could be. . . . All this seemed to make my first year happy enough. But as the year went on I found that my habits and principles, coming from a typical small-town, midwestern childhood, such as hard work, fidelity, honesty and so on, stood by me less and less as the year progressed. (May, 1985, p. 6)

May grew lonely. There were only a few other Americans at the Greek college, and they soon ran out of things to talk about. Two new American teachers came on staff and ". . . the boys in the school found these new teachers to lavish their inconstant affection and charm upon" (May, 1985, p. 8). We can assume that feelings of rejection were now added to the loneliness May felt. May tried to work harder but found that the more effort he expended, the less effectively he taught. The loneliness was overwhelming:

> Finally in the spring of that second year I had what is called euphemistically a nervous breakdown. *Which meant simply that the rules, principles, values by which I used to work and live simply did not suffice anymore.* I got so completely fatigued that I had to go to bed for two weeks to get enough energy to continue my teaching. I had learned enough psychology at college to know that these symptoms meant that something was wrong with my whole way of life. I had to find some new goals and purposes for my living and to relinquish my moralistic, somewhat rigid way of existence. (May, 1985, p. 8; italics in original)

Had he been in America, May wrote that he would have sought psychotherapy at this time. Instead, a sympathetic couple teaching at the same college invited May to spend time at their home.

One late night in March, after a long talk with these new friends, May left the house and walked toward Mt. Hortiati—about ten miles away. May continued up the mountain alone in spite of a freezing rain. About six hours later he reached a plateau in the darkness and heard the barking of wolves. A pack of wolves circled around May a few times, but he reports that he was absorbed in his own inner turmoil and paid little attention to them. Fortunately for him, the wolves eventually left. May spent the rest of the night alone on the mountainside. At dawn, he made his way to the small village of Hortiati, woke up the café owner, and arranged to rent an upstairs room. After some sleep, May went down to the café, where some of the village men gathered around a stove to eat roasted fish, drink, and talk. May sat as near to them as he could "to keep warm" (1985, p. 10). He spent hours writing on the back of laundry slips he had carried from the school in his coat. Soon the village men became curious and asked about what May was writing. After his night in lonely contemplation, their reaction must have been quite jolting for the sensitive and impressionable May:

> I knew they would not understand if I talked about philosophy, and furthermore it wasn't quite true that I was writing that anyway. So I answered in my halting Greek, "I write, *what is life?*" They all leaned back with guffaws of laughter. One of them spoke out, "That's easy! If you have bread you eat, if you do not have bread you die." (May, 1985, p. 10)

May was far from familiar surroundings. He was distressed, lonely, feeling rejected and confused. In addition, the villagers' earthy philosophy, which was focused on meeting basic physical needs, must have been even more alienating. Young Rollo May was struggling for the survival of his own identity and searching for familiar landmarks by which to navigate this alien existence that threatened his understanding of the world and self. He climbed up the mountain again to contemplate the meaning of his existence. After two days, May started down Mt. Hortiati, this time to return to the home of his friends.

May spent some time around his friends' home walking in surrounding hillsides and meadows. On one day, he climbed a hill and found himself suddenly knee-deep in a field of poppies that were so beautiful, their "perfect movements seemed like children in a ballet" (1985, p. 11). He sketched those poppies that morning in 1932, and he made an important discovery that was to stay with him for many years:

> I realized that I had not listened to my inner voice, which had tried to talk to me about beauty. I had been too hard-working, too "principled" to spend time merely looking at flowers! It seems it had taken a collapse of my whole former way of life for this voice to make itself heard. (May, 1985, p. 13)

The drawing of the poppies, reproduced here in Figure 12.1 from May's book *My Quest for Beauty* (1985, p. 13), is a black-and-white pencil sketch of about a dozen flowers and

---

BOX 12.1 *Only Connect . . .*

Maslow's theory of the hierarchy of needs (Chapter 13) can be applied to Rollo May's experiences with the local people in Greece. They seemed to be interested only in meeting physical or physiological needs, whereas May was focused on trying to find beauty in his environment, thus trying to satisfy a higher level need or what Maslow would call a *B(eing)-need.*

Poppies, drawn at "White House,"
May 22, '32

Figure 12.1 Rollo May's drawing of a field of poppies in Greece, 1932, during his time of emotional crisis.
Source: May, 1985, used by permission.

foliage. Despite his description of his emotional state on that morning, the drawing is suggestive of a melancholy mood in the drooping stems of the flowers and the somewhat isolated quality of each of the individual flowers. Contrasted with other May drawings and paintings in the same book from other times in his life, the poppy drawing shows clear signs of the profundity of his distress and the depth of his depression at that time.

Ironically, the chapter of the book following the one that describes this emotional crisis is "Beauty Has Kept Me Alive," which May hastily informs the reader is only a metaphorical statement, not a literal one. Yet the close association of the description of that depressed episode in his life and his later concern with nonbeing leads us to speculate about how closely May examined the issue of continued living during his crisis.

Beauty is harmony, as May explains later in the book, and harmony within himself, oneness with his own identity, with his fellows, and with nature (*Eigenwelt, Mitwelt,* and *Umwelt*) were to be theoretical concepts that would occupy most of May's later professional life. May's discovery of the beauty and peace that lay around him was his salvation.

Some years later, May recalled that, when he returned to America after his summer of crisis and searching in Greece, his interest in psychology centered on substantive issues and profound questions that he could not find addressed in most graduate psychology programs.

> American psychology, to which I came back, seemed naive and simplistic, omitting exactly what made life most rich and exciting. I longed for some community in which one could ask questions about the meaning of despair, suicide, and normal anxiety. . . . (May, 1973, p. 2)

May was looking for an approach outside of the traditions of American psychology. He was to find it in the writings of two related schools of thought, the existentialists and the phenomenologists.

The personal uncertainty he experienced had brought the young Rollo May to the edge of personal dissolution. There is every reason to believe that these experiences permanently sensitized May to the issues of existence, identity, and death, themes that were to occupy him for many years in his career as a psychologist and writer.

EXISTENTIAL PHENOMENOLOGICAL PSYCHOLOGY AND PSYCHOTHERAPY

The two philosophical traditions that inspired May, **phenomenology** and **existentialism,** were combined into a single approach to human nature, **existential phenomenological psychology.** The phenomenological tradition, pioneered by Edmund Husserl and Martin Heidegger, focused on the description of human experience as it appeared or unfolded without the application of explanatory or theoretical concepts. The idea of this approach was to "get back to the experience" itself. Concepts important in this approach, which we will define shortly, include terms such as *Dasein, Welt* (German for "world") *Mitwelt, Umwelt,* and *Eigenwelt.* The meanings of these terms, we will discover, are simpler and more basic than that of many psychological terms with which most people are more familiar. The existential philosophical tradition can be traced to thinkers such as the Russian novelist Fyodor Dostoyevsky, the Danish philosopher Søren Kierkegaard, and the French thinker Jean-Paul Sartre. The major emphasis in this tradition was that people had a responsibility for creating the meanings that they lived and for their commitments in various areas of life. In this view, people are in the ongoing process of **becoming.** In this process, people explore and develop their potentials and should bear responsibility for the choices they make. In a given situation, a person may choose to act creatively, courageously, generously, considerately, cowardly, or selfishly. Existential philosophers asserted that people should not deny their responsibility as conscious agents by referring to deterministic forces, whether they be internal drives or external intimidation.

The two threads came together in the work of psychiatrists such as the German émigré Ludwig Binswanger and the Swiss psychiatrist Medard Boss. Rollo May has been the most prominent exponent and popularizer of existential phenomenology in American psychology. For the existential phenomenologist, the central problem of human psychology is *being* and the person's awareness that someday he or she will *not be.* In metaphysics, a branch of philosophy, the study of being and reality is termed **ontology.** Many of Rollo May's (1958a, 1983) concepts and those of other existential phenomenological thinkers are ontological in character. That is to say, although the vocabulary sounds like familiar psychology—for example, *anxiety, guilt,* and *repression*—the terms are interpreted by the existential phenomenologist as reflecting the core processes of being and nonbeing.

May received his psychoanalytic training at the William Alanson White Institute and became a senior training analyst there. The White Institute was co-founded by Harry Stack Sullivan. How, then, did May reconcile the interpersonal psychoanalytic approaches of Sullivan and existential-phenomenological approaches? Rollo May achieved an integration by synthesizing those parts of psychoanalysis that are experientially based with an interest in the person's own view of reality. By avoiding the abstract psychoanalytic metapsychology of Freud's later years, May created a form of analytic existential phenomenology.

CONTRIBUTIONS OF EUROPEAN PHILOSOPHY

Rollo May began doing psychotherapeutic work and theorizing with the basic assumption that Freud's contributions to understanding human behavior, especially clinical phenomena, were largely correct (May, 1950/1970, 1960/1965). He gradually reached the conclusion, however, that Freud's concepts were philosophically unsophisticated and inadequate.

May wanted to broaden the psychoanalytic horizon and emphasize a view of human nature that incorproated the ideas of a number of nineteenth and twentieth century existential and phenomenological European philosophers.

Modes of Being in European Existentialism

Ludwig Binswanger and other European existentialists and phenomenologists employed the German word *Dasein* to express an essential quality of human life. *Dasein* can be translated literally as "being" (*sein*) and "there" (*da*) (Binswanger, in May, 1958a, p. 315). The meaning of the term *world* (originally the German word *welt*) in this philosophical context is the structure of meaning and meaningful relationships in which a person exists (May, 1958b, pp. 56–59).

Dasein indicates that humans are beings who exist in relation to a specific time and place and in relation to specific meanings. Humans are actively involved in forming the meanings lived out in their existence. (May, 1958a, p. 41). The existential phenomenologists refined their concept of *Dasein* or *being-in-the-world* by distinguishing three modes of world:

Umwelt, translated literally as "around-world," includes the biological drives, needs, and instincts of the individual. *Umwelt,* considered alone, corresponds to what we mean by the physical aspects of the world, including our body. May also be defined **Mitwelt:**

> *Mitwelt* is literally the "with-world," the world of being-with-others, one's fellow humans. My *Mitwelt* includes the meaning I make out of my relationships with others, and they are also finding their own meanings in their relationships with me. (May, 1958b, p. 63).

Eigenwelt, or "one's own world," is the mode of relationship to one's self. "It is a grasping of what something in the world—this bouquet of flowers . . . means to me" (May, 1958b, p. 63). Thus, the concept of *Eigenwelt* is not restricted to the inner, subjective world but includes one's subjective reactions to the world at large.

According to this viewpoint, the way to understand a person and their experience is to grasp these three worlds of experience *as they are experienced by the individual,* in a non-reductionistic fashion. One needs to understand how a person actually perceives and experiences the physical world, including his body, how the person experiences interpersonal relationships and the interpersonal world, and what constitutes the person's often private thoughts, feelings, and inner reactions. Existential phenomenologists are not interested in reducing or explaining such experiences by resorting to explanatory concepts such as *drives, cathexes* or *libido.*

ONTOLOGICAL PRINCIPLES: "MRS. HUTCHENS"

May wanted to replace Freudian concepts with terms that more simply and directly referred to human experiences and that indicated the possibility of personal choice. For example, he reshaped Freud's concept of **the unconscious.**

> The "unconscious," then, is not to be thought of as a reservoir of impulses, thoughts, wishes which are culturally unacceptable; I define it rather *as those potentialities for knowing and experiencing which the individual cannot or will not actualize;* that it cannot be adequately comprehended in *"ego"* and *"not-ego"* terms, or even "self" and "not-self"; and that it inescapably raises the question of the human being's margin of freedom with respect to his potentialities, a margin in which resides his responsibility for himself which even the therapist cannot take away. (May, 1960/1965, p. 178; see also May, 1983, pp. 17–18; italics in original)

It is clear that for May there is much value in psychoanalytic ideas, but that the concepts have to be transformed into first-person actions from their status as theoretical, third-person "things." The unconscious, in this example, is not a place, not a reservoir, not an internal structure. It is, rather, the process of the whole person in the acts of *wishing, fearing, knowing,* and *choosing not to know.* By these standards, a person does not "have defenses"; he or she defends against threats. Similarly, a "neurotic" person is not a person "with" a psychological disorder, nor can he or she be said to "have" symptoms. Rather, the person, along with all of his or her other human qualities, behaves anxiously or with a great deal of conflict because of the way he or she decides to interpret his or her life. A neurosis is not a condition that a person *has.* Rather, the term "neurosis" is a term that represents an ongoing pattern of choices that a person makes in order to preserve his or her own way of being or adjusting to perceived threat.

We can obtain an initial orientation to the six **ontological principles** that governed May's early views by following his account of the difficulties of "Mrs. Hutchens," one of the first patients May wrote about.

Principle One: Phenomenal Centeredness

May argues, as the European existential phenomenologists do, that genuine understanding of a person comes not from seeing people as composites of drives and deterministic forces nor by conceptualizing people as individual statistical units in the group we call humanity. If people are defined in this way for psychological understanding, "you have defined for study everything except the one to whom these experiences happen, everything except the existing person himself" (May, 1960/1965, p. 179).

May offers the extended example of one of his patients. "Mrs. Hutchens" is a woman in her thirties who presents herself as sophisticated, in control, and poised. But in her eyes, May detected "something of the terror of a frightened animal or lost child." She was referred for psychotherapy by her neurologist because of an hysterical tenseness of the larynx so severe that she could speak only in a hoarse whisper. May administered a Rorschach projective inkblot examination:

> I have been given the hypothesis from her Rorschach that she has felt all her life, "If I say what I really feel, I'll be rejected; under these conditions it is better not to talk at all." (May, 1960/1965, p. 178)

As Freud discovered by the beginning of the twentieth century, hysterical symptoms rest on personal meanings, some of which are unconscious. A symptom is not random but is meaningfully related to the person's life experiences. Mrs. Hutchens's life history reveals an intimidating relationship with her authoritarian mother and grandmother, along with experiences that resulted in becoming guarded: choosing not to reveal any "secrets" at all. This background information is helpful in understanding some of the reasons why Mrs. Hutchens behaves as she does. But May argues that mere historical understanding is incomplete. Tracing the events in the development of Mrs. Hutchens's hysterical hoarseness does not provide an understanding of Mrs. Hutchens as she experiences her world. Her experience cannot be reduced to her history. Mrs. Hutchens must be grasped as an *existing person* with the "terror of a lost child" in her eyes along with her unique *continuing* reasons for *choosing to be* hoarse, controlled, guarded, and distressed. Ontological principle number one, **phenomenal centeredness,** describes the profoundly significant human core of subjectivity:

Phenomenal Centeredness:

Every person is centered in self and therefore lives, loves, hates, is creative or destructive, flexible or rigid, blind or perceptive by reason of that center.

Mrs. Hutchens can be understood only by grasping the world as *she sees it and lives it*. For Mrs. Hutchens, like every other existing person, organizes her understanding of reality and self through her experience of it. If we do not understand her experience, we do not understand her. Only by empathy and by avoiding theoretical abstractions can the observer get a glimpse of Mrs. Hutchens's world.

Principle Two: Courage for Self-Affirmation

May defines self-affirmation as the "courage to be," relying on the concepts of Paul Tillich, a theologian who influenced him greatly (May, 1973; Tillich, 1952). Without courage, according to Tillich, a person "loses being." It is courage that permits choice. Courage to be does not remove anxiety, according to Tillich. Nor can courage, by itself, lead to personality health. Rather, courage permits the healthy person to confront anxiety and avoid despair, as given in ontological principle number two, **self-affirmation and courage:**

Self-Affirmation and Courage:
Every existing person has the character of self-affirmation, which is the need to preserve his or her centeredness, and can mobilize courage to do so.

In Mrs. Hutchens's case, the possibility exists that she was confronted with three choices as she grew up. She could succumb to the authoritarian and frightening relationships and become what her elders wanted her to be. Or, second, she could rebel against their wishes and pressure, acting out her anger in some destructive way. Or, third, she could yield to despair, giving up hope and retreating from reality and life into nonbeing. What actually happened appears to be an outcome combining all three possibilities. Mrs. Hutchens has somehow found a way to avoid destructive rebellion, complete despair, and complete capitulation. What might conventionally be labeled as hysterical neurosis is, from this point of view, to be understood as an act of courage, an act of dignity, as well as a process of psychological dysfunction. Paul Tillich made these points well:

> Anxiety turns us toward courage, because the other alternative is despair. Courage resists despair by taking anxiety into itself. . . . He who does not succeed in taking his anxiety courageously upon himself can succeed in avoiding the extreme situation of despair by escaping into neurosis. He still affirms himself but on a limited scale. *Neurosis is the way of avoiding nonbeing by avoiding being.* In the neurotic state self-affirmation is not lacking; it can indeed be very strong and emphasized. But the self which is affirmed is a reduced one. (Tillich, 1952, p. 66; italics in original)

Mrs. Hutchens's previous therapist had, in fact, informed his patient that she was "too controlled" and "too proper." She became very upset and broke off treatment. The therapist, in a way, was correct, but he missed the essence of this controlled and proper person. Although these qualities can be seen as part of the "neurotic" process, the existential point is that they are Mrs. Hutchens. "Controlled" and "proper" and even the hysterical hoarseness are the adjustments to her life as she interprets it out of the center of her being. To interpret her personality qualities and behaviors as her "problem" is to attack precisely those ways of being in which she is centered and those ways of being that she has chosen to protect herself as a person.

There is to be found in Mrs. Hutchens's actions a further act of self-affirmation, **participation in other beings.** Mrs. Hutchens gathers the courage to seek out another therapist who could also demand that she change this center of being.

Principle Three: Participation in Other Beings

In seeking out her new therapist, Mrs. Hutchens confronts a new risk of losing her identity. "If the neurotic [person] is so afraid of his own conflicted center that he refuses to go out but holds back in rigidity and lives in narrowed reactions and shrunken world space, his growth and development are blocked" (May, 1960/1965, p. 181). Mrs. Hutchens sits with her new therapist:

> Now as Mrs. Hutchens talks hoarsely, she looks at me with an expression of mingled fear and hope. Obviously a relation exists between us not only here but already in anticipation in the waiting room and ever since she thought of coming. She is struggling with the possibility of participating with me. (May, 1960/1965, pp. 180–181 and 1983, p. 27)

Ontological principle number three, participation in others, formalizes this conclusion:

Participation in Other Beings:

All existing persons have the need and possibility of going out from their centeredness to participate in other beings.

May points out that it is also possible for the "neurotic" person to cope with the experience of threat to self by "overparticipating" in others. The neurotic might "lose self" by diffusing it in overidentification with others. In Mrs. Hutchens's case, she has enacted neither of these losses of self. She has acted from courage and pain to confront her conflicts. Understanding her in terms of a diagnostic classification would get in the way of a real understanding of her personal qualities and strengths (May, 1967/1979, p. 8).

Principle Four: Awareness

As May uses the term, **awareness** means alertness or vigilance. The person is wary of external threats and dangers. In the first few therapy sessions with May, for example, Mrs. Hutchens regards him as a threat. Lifelong vigilance underlies Mrs. Hutchens's guardedness. Ontological principle number four is:

Awareness:

The subjective side of centeredness is awareness.

In May's definition "awareness" is a form of self-protective, but not uniquely human vigilance (May, 1953, p. 75 ff.), which May believes has numerous counterparts in the vigilance systems of animals. It is probably best understood as an "early warning system" common to both animals and humans who feel themselves in danger. In humans, a more sophisticated level of awareness, the development of self-consciousness, has also been formed.

Principle Five: Self-Consciousness

Only a human can be self-conscious. Self-consciousness permits the person to transcend the immediate, concrete situation, to live in terms of the possible, and to use abstractions (May, 1960/1965, p. 182). But there are two sides to self-consciousness, for not only can a person be conscious of self as an active subject, a person can also be conscious of self as a passive object (May, 1967/1979, pp. 8 ff.).

As an example, May cites his own experience of writing a book under the pressure of a deadline. His first state of self-consciousness is bound by attention to externals. He looks at the clock, decides how much longer he will spend writing that morning, wonders how best to get the most done before his afternoon consultation hours begin, and he continues working. He realizes that something he has written might be criticized by a colleague and wonders whether to change the wording. He criticizes himself for worrying about what his colleague will think. He is aware that this thought is intruding on his writing. He refocuses on the writing, asking himself what is the best way to write this, what is the most efficient way to get it done, meet the schedule, make the ideas palatable to others?

As he continues to write, May becomes excited by a new idea. He enters a second state of self-consciousness. "Ah, here is something that has been playing around the fringes of my consciousness for years—what an alluring prospect to work it out now, form it, see where it leads!" (May, 1967/1979, p. 7). For a while, he is engaged in reorganizing the writing around the new idea. He wonders briefly whether his colleague will approve, then suddenly does not care because the idea is a good one. He looks at the clock and discovers that it is half an hour later than he had planned to stop.

In this brief episode, May has shown both kinds of self-consciousness. During the first part of the writing, musing about how to meet the deadline, setting time limits for himself, and wondering how best to phrase something so as not to offend a colleague, May has thought of himself as an object. But in the second phase of his writing, when the exciting idea has emerged, he becomes engaged in the idea and the process of working the idea through its many implications. His thinking reflects the change because he no longer experiences self as a "slave of time." In the second state, he is an active subject who is absorbed and engaged in what he does. Hence, we arrive at ontological principle number five, **self consciousness:**

Self-Consciousness:
The uniquely human form of awareness is self-consciousness.

In a parallel way, May points out, a psychotherapist can be aware of his or her patient as an object or as a subject. If May were to be aware of Mrs. Hutchens as an object, he would focus on her life history, on the diagnostic category that best describes her difficulties, and on the information reported by her neurologist. Consequently, Mrs. Hutchens would be an object of his thought, but little empathic understanding of Mrs. Hutchens as an existing person would result. (May, 1967/1979, p. 8)

Principle Six: Anxiety and Nonbeing

From the existential point of view, human beings are unique in their capacity not only to be aware of self but also in their realization that the self will ultimately come to an end. Consciousness of death, of the possibility of the state of nonbeing is a powerful influence on the person's experience of self. Nothing so heightens the meaning of life as awareness of the possibility of dying.

> Death is . . . the one fact of my life which is not relative but absolute, and my awareness of this gives my existence and what I do each hour an absolute quality. (May, 1958b, pp. 48–49; see also May, 1961)

We come now to May's next ontological principle, **anxiety and nonbeing:**

Anxiety and Nonbeing:
Anxiety is the state of the person in the struggle against what would destroy his or her sense of meaningful being.

This understanding indicates that much of human anxiety arises from threats to one's sense of self and to the meanings to which one is committed. In the case of Mrs. Hutchens, May interprets her anxiety as arising from her confrontation with the imminent possibility of the death of a meaningful life. Her relationships to her mother and to her grandmother caused her to forfeit her independence and identity. May saw Mrs. Hutchens's anxiety as a sign that she realizes the threat of nonbeing in these relationships. Forfeiting one's identity is a descent into nonbeing—the death of the meanings important to the self (May, 1960/1965, pp. 183–184).

Transitional Summary

The six ontological principles we have discussed in the context of Mrs. Hutchens's therapy are a road map of the concerns that occupied Rollo May from the late 1950s until the end of his life almost 40 years later. The main themes of May's work are largely represented in these six major themes:

1. Every person is centered in self and lives life through the meaning he or she places on that center.

2. Every person is responsible for mobilizing the courage to protect the self, to affirm it and enhance its continued existence.

3. People need other people with whom they can empathize and from whom they can learn.

4. People are vigilant about potential dangers to their sense of selfhood.

5. People have self-consciousness; they experience themselves as both subject and object.

6. Anxiety originates, in part, out of a person's awareness that one's existence or sense of meaningful being can end.

THE PROBLEM OF NOTHINGNESS

"To grasp what it means to exist, one needs to grasp the fact that he might not exist . . ." wrote May, voicing one of the central concerns of the existential movement (1983, p. 105). As we have seen, such awareness is a dialectical process, for the awareness of death enhances one's sense of living. Life becomes real, vivid, and flavorful only when one confronts the possibility of nothingness. From this understanding of the significance of death comes May's definition of anxiety:

> Anxiety is *the experience of the threat of imminent nonbeing.*

and

> Anxiety is the subjective state of the individual's becoming aware that his existence can become destroyed, that he can lose himself and his world, that he can become nothing. (May, 1983, pp. 109–110; italics in original)

This ontological meaning of the term *anxiety* derives in part from the philosopher Kierkegaard, who, along with Freud and other European thinkers, used the German word **Angst** to describe this feeling of "losing being" (May, 1950/1970, p. 36), and in part the definition derives from theologian Paul Tillich's ideas (1952). *Angst* is not adequately translated into English by the word *anxiety,* for *angst* carries the connotations of "anguish" and "dread." As Tillich conceptualized the problem, "The basic anxiety, the anxiety of a finite being about the threat of nonbeing, cannot be eliminated. It belongs to existence itself" (1952, p. 39).

Ontological Anxiety in Contrast to Fear

May distinguishes between **ontological anxiety** and **fear:**

> The difference is that the anxiety strikes at the central core of his self-esteem and his sense of value as a self, which is the most important aspect of his experience of himself as a being. Fear, in contrast, is a threat to the periphery of his existence; it can be objectivated and the person can stand outside and look at it. (May, 1983, p. 110)

Anxiety has more profound effects than fear, according to May, for the experience of this emotion can overwhelm the person's "discovery of being," demolish the person's sense of time, dull the memory of the past, and even "erase the future" (May, 1983, p. 110). Anxiety can occur when a possibility for a new way of being opens for a person. That very possibility, even the possibility of positive change, is often anxiety-laden because it carries with it the seeds of destruction for the person's old way of being (May, 1950/1970, p. 36; 1983, p. 111). To give up the old is to give up security and induce angst. By the same token, to close oneself off from the possibility of change is to risk losing freedom.

Ontological Guilt

To pursue new possibilities of living is anxiety-provoking as we give up the familiar and with it our security. But to deny those possibilities, to deliberately fail to fulfill them to preserve security provokes what May termed **ontological guilt** (May, 1983, pp. 112 ff.). May points out that his conceptions of guilt and anxiety are both *ontological* conceptions. It other words, they are derived from basic qualities of "human being-ness." We can experience ontological anxiety precisely because we have choices, and our choices involve change and uncertainty. We can have ontological guilt because we might not have made the choices that were open to us, or that we might not have made the best choices. Ontological guilt is a non-neurotic form of guilt that accompanies awareness of our responsibility for our choices. Experiences of ontological anxiety and guilt stem from fundamental qualities of the human being and not from psychopathology, particular relationships, failures, or rule violations (May, 1983, p. 115).

May distinguishes among three ontological levels of guilt that correspond to the three modes of being discussed earlier in this chapter. Recall the *Umwelt* or the "world around" of natural drives and needs, the *Mitwelt* or the "with world" of being with others, and the *Eigenwelt* or one's "own world" of subjective meaning.

1. The first form of ontological guilt, then, corresponds to the *Umwelt* and is referred to as "separation guilt" in the sense of alienation or separation from the natural world. Our own technology continually distances us from nature, but the process is subtle and insidious so that we remain unaware of this kind of ontological guilt (May, 1958b, p. 54; 1983, p. 115).

2. The second form of ontological guilt corresponds to the *Mitwelt* (with world) and arises from ". . . the fact that since each of us is an individual, he necessarily perceives his fellow man through his own limited and biased eyes. This means that he always to some extent does violence to the true picture of his fellow man and always to some extent fails to understand fully and meet the other's needs" (May, 1958b, p. 54). May asserts that this kind of guilt is inescapable because we each have no choice but to see the world through our own eyes.

3. The third form of ontological guilt is equivalent to the *Eigenwelt* and returns us to our starting point of the person who forfeits potentialities in order to preserve security. That forfeiture produces ontological guilt at the most personal level.

Ontological guilt has four characteristics (May, 1958b, p. 55; 1983, pp. 115 ff.):

1. Everyone participates in ontological guilt because each of us distorts the reality of others and each of us fails to fulfill some of our possibilities.

2. Ontological guilt does not rely on cultural prohibitions. "Ontological guilt does not consist of I-am-guilty-because-I-violate-parental-prohibitions, but arises from the fact that I can see myself as the one who can choose or fail to choose" (May, 1958b, p. 55).

3. Ontological guilt is not neurotic or morbid. If a person can become aware of his or her ontological guilt, the person has an opportunity to accept it rather than repress it.

4. Ontological guilt does not necessarily lead to symptom formation. It might be the basis for constructive personality development. One possibility is that awareness of ontological guilt, an alertness to the vulnerability and universality of the human condition, leads to humility (May, 1958b, p. 55).

PERSONAL SOURCES OF MAY'S EXISTENTIALISM

If we take a step back from the ideas of Rollo May presented thus far, three broad themes emerge:

- First, May emphasizes the fragility of human life as well as its beauty. Like so many other personality theorists, much of May's professional concerns grew from his clinical work. There is, then, a thread of concern for the vulnerability of people to anxiety and despair and the struggle against helplessness. As we have seen, May's dissertation was the study of anxiety.

- The second theme that emerges from the theory thus far presented is May's profound concern with ultimate existence and death. His close association with theologian Paul Tillich is ample testimony to the importance of this theme in his work (May, 1973).

- The third theme we can trace is May's concern with loneliness and alienation in human existence. His ideas on the nature of ontological guilt that we have explored thus far can be understood as a concern with alienation from others and self, but a kind of alienation that is universal, inescapable, and experienced as profound loneliness.

These three themes are related. They evidence a great deal of coherence. Put succinctly, May's view of self, of others, and of the world emphasizes the needs for intimacy and acceptance, the human struggle against uncertainty and helplessness, and the confrontation with death and meaninglessness (nonbeing).

At the beginning of this chapter, we described the crisis that Rollo May experienced as a young man in Greece and indicated the important impact of these events and experiences. Now we are going to focus on some other aspects of May's biography. Additional personal roots of the themes in his work as a psychologist emerge as we review his life history.

May's Needs for Intimacy and Acceptance

Rollo May's childhood and family life were discordant and lonely. He was born April 21, 1909, in a small town in Ohio; the family moved to Michigan early in May's life. His father was a secretary for the YMCA and moved his family frequently. Rollo's immediate family consisted of five brothers and a sister who later became psychotic. The marital relationship was "discordant" with a rather unhappy family life as the result (Rabinowitz et al., 1989, p. 436). His experience of this family discord sparked May's interest in psychology and counseling and provoked escapes to the shores of the St. Clair River to watch the ships go by. May suggested that he learned more from the river than from his school years because the river was a "clean, deep, demonic, and beautiful friend" (quoted by Rabinowitz et al., 1989, p. 436). As a boy, Rollo found peace at the river, away from the sooty, noisy, industrial Detroit area in which he lived.

May's Confrontation with Helplessness and Death

After the emotional crisis we reviewed at the beginning of this chapter, May was on summer vacation from his job in Greece. He traveled to Vienna to study with Alfred Adler. His experience there was very positive. He even commented that Adler was "absolutely psychic in his therapy with children" (May in Rabinowitz et al., 1989, p. 67). May was also inspired by the work of Freud, Jung, and others, who were pioneers in developing psychoanalysis and related approaches.

He returned to America in 1933, with the intention of becoming a psychologist by taking a graduate degree at Columbia University. But the psychology program at Columbia was behavioral, not psychodynamic. Issues such as war, death, love, and hate were the questions that Rollo May wanted to investigate. So, after looking into the Columbia program, he decided not to apply (Rabinowitz et al., 1989, p. 436; May, 1973, p. 2).

May enrolled instead at Union Theological Seminary, where the questions in which he had become interested were being discussed by some of the many professors who had fled Nazi persecution in Europe. At this time, May began what was to be a long-lasting friendship with the theologian Paul Tillich, one of the European émigrés. At Union, May earned a bachelor's degree in divinity, but initially had no intention of a career in the ministry.

He was called home after graduation to "hold the family together" after his father left his mother (Rabinowitz et al., 1989, p. 437). Once home, he accepted a combined teaching and church position at Michigan State College in 1936. His interest in psychology and counseling combined, along with his brief studies with Alfred Adler (see Chapter 5), led to his lecturing on counseling procedures and to writing a book on counseling (May, 1939/1967a). May decided to return to graduate school again to study the process of counseling in more detail and enrolled in the clinically oriented psychology program at Teachers College of Columbia University.

Working hard in graduate school, researching his dissertation, and trying to earn a meager living by teaching part-time, May came down with tuberculosis. At that time, tuberculosis was a killer disease for which the only, usually ineffective treatment was complete rest. May spent most of the next two years in upstate New York in a tuberculosis sanatorium. During this extended period in the sanatorium, May had to confront the possibility of death from a disease about which medical science could do little. He gradually came to believe that his helpless and passive attitude was actually enhancing the disease process and decided to combat it. He reports that only when he took this more active stance did he recover:

> For a year and a half I did not know whether I would live or die. As best I could, I tried to do what my doctors instructed me to do. This meant, as I then interpreted it, accepting the program of rest and giving my healing over to others. I could only lie in bed, tracing with my eye patterns of light on the ceiling of my room, waiting for the monthly X-ray, which would tell whether the cavity in my lung had enlarged or decreased.
>
> But I found, to my moral and intellectual dismay, that the bacilli were taking advantage of my very innocence. This innocence had transformed my helplessness into passivity, which constituted an open invitation to the bacilli to do violence to my body. I saw, too, that the reason I had contracted tuberculosis in the first place was my hopelessness and sense of defeatism. . . . I could see in the apparently innocent patients around me in the sanatorium that passively accepting their powerlessness in the face of the disease meant dying. Not until I developed some "fight," some sense of personal responsibility for the fact that it was I who had the tuberculosis, an assertion of my own will to live, did I make lasting progress. (May, 1972, pp. 13–14; see also May, 1969, p. 239)

May described three types of patients he observed in the sanatorium. Some patients became passive and helpless. According to May, such patients "invite their own deaths" by essentially giving up the struggle for life (May, 1953, pp. 140 ff.). Other patients in the same sanatorium adhere to the prescribed regimen, but spend most of their time resenting their misfortune. Such people don't die, May observed, but they do not recover either. "Like rebels in any area of life, they remain on a plateau perpetually marking time" (1953, p. 141). Finally, there are those patients (one presumes this was the way May thought of himself) who confront the fact of their illness. They reflect on the meaning of their lives and try to understand what was wrong with their way of living before their illness. These patients use the illness as a means to new self-knowledge and self-discipline. "They are the ones who not only achieve physical health, but who also are ultimately enlarged, enriched, and strengthened by the experience of having had the disease" (May, 1953, p. 141).

He quotes the letter of a patient with tuberculosis. Given the allusion to overwork and three jobs, the letter could very well have been written by May himself:

> The disease occurred not simply because I overworked, or ran athwart some T.B. bugs, but because I was trying to be something I wasn't. I was living as the "great extrovert," running here and there, doing three jobs at once, and leaving undeveloped and unused the side of me which would contemplate, would read and think and "invite my soul" rather than rushing and working at full speed. The disease comes as a demand and an opportunity to rediscover the lost functions of myself. It is as though the disease were nature's way of saying, "You must become your whole self. To the extent that you do not, you will be ill; and you will become well only to the extent that you do become yourself." (May, 1953, p. 95)

May's confrontation with illness and the possibility of death led not to his demise but to a personal reorientation and to a productive and successful struggle to survive.

LOVE AND WILL

People have long sought either love or will power as the solution to many of the problems of existence. But, as May (1969) pointed out, these solutions no longer are effective in our society.

According to May, contemporary people usually believe that love and will are illusions. Contemporary life, according to May, has produced a schizoid withdrawal. He is not using the term *schizoid* in its diagnostic psychopathological meaning. Rather he is referring to a kind of empty numbness or apathy that people experience and can use as a way of avoiding or defending against the dilemmas of existence (May, 1969, pp. 27 ff.). If a person feels powerless or helpless to change his or her life, the concepts of will and love have little meaning. What is immediately lost is a concern for other people and a sense of concern for self.

Apathy and Violence

Violence can erupt out of such apathy. The person does not merely stagnate; he or she becomes increasingly apathetic and emotionally calloused.

> When I use the term "apathy," . . . it is because its literal meaning is the closest to what I am describing: "want of feeling; lack of passion, emotion or excitement, indifference." Apathy and the schizoid world go hand in hand as cause and effect of each other. (May, 1969, p. 29)

May defines apathy as: "a condition in which men and women find themselves experiencing a distance between themselves and the objects which used to excite their affection and their will" (May, 1969, p. 29). A kind of numb indifference sets in as a protection against the depersonalizing, schizoid world. Such numbness breeds violence because

> When inward life dries up, when feeling decreases and apathy increases, when one cannot affect or even genuinely touch another person, violence flares up as a daimonic necessity for contact, a mad drive forcing touch in the most direct way possible. (May, 1969, pp. 30–31)

FOUR FORMS OF LOVING

From May's point of view (1969, p. 29), the opposite of apathy is love in its different forms. May distinguishes among four different **types of love:**

1. *Agapé* or *Caritas* or *Care,* the love devoted to the welfare of others; the prototype for which is the love of God for man. It is the foundation for all of the other forms of love.
2. *Sex* or lust, or what Freud called libido.
3. *Eros,* the biological drive to procreate.
4. *Philia,* or brotherly love and friendship.

Care or Agapé

For the person who evidences **Agapé** or who *cares,* things matter, people matter. There is a sense of relatedness between the person who cares and the object of care. The ancient Romans' Latin word is the root of our own: *Caritas.* Sometimes in theology the word *Agapé* is applied, as in the biblical account of God's *caring or love for humankind.* At the more human level, one cannot be indifferent if one cares. Care is essential from birth because the infant whose mother does not care will not survive. And caring can be directed toward self as well. If we do not care for ourselves, we neglect our health and well-being, producing injury and disease.

Care is associated with compassion and with empathy. It is likely that as infants we learn to care for others by the care we are shown. Care is also the foundation for wishing and willing, for we would not wish or will anything unless we care for it. But we must not assume that care is simply a feeling. It is, according to May (1969, p. 292), an onto-logical state, a state of being. It might lead to feeling and passion and even to motivated action, but the phenomenon of *caring* is part of being and the source of love and will. Caring is a form of intentionality in which the carer "throws his or her weight on the side" of another person. Caring is the prerequisite for love as it manifests itself in the remaining three forms: Sex, Eros, and Philia.

Sex: The Flight from Eros

May asserts that it is only in relatively recent times that **sex** has become as important as it is in our sexually obsessed culture. Up to Victorian times, the topic of sex was difficult to talk or write about. In Freud's day, sexuality was targeted for both personal and social repression. But, May argues, in the 1920s a revolution occurred. A belief developed in liberal circles that the opposite of sexual repression would have healthy effects. "In an amazingly short period following World War I, we shifted from acting as though sex did not exist at all to being obsessed with it" (May, 1969, p. 39). But, according to May, There are ironies in our newfound freedom with sex. Guilt and performance anxiety have been increased by the new emphasis on good technique and the implication that health requires a vigorous sex life. If you don't perform well, so this distortion goes, you are not healthy. There is also what May calls the new "puritanism" (spelled with a lowercase "p" to distinguish it from the historical Puritans):

> I define this puritanism as consisting of three elements. First, *a state of alienation from the body.* Second, the separation of emotion from reason. And third, *the use of the body as a machine.* (May, 1969, p. 45; italics in original)

This new Puritanism, according to May, involves depersonalized sexual activity that is devoid of caring, love, and passion. People use impersonal terms ("having sex" or "getting laid" rather than "making love" or, more simply, "love") to describe sexual intercourse. May's picture of sexual attitudes and behavior is one of depersonalized, mechanized, obsessive human interaction devoid of caring, relatedness, and joy.

What motives underlie such depersonalized, confused, and uncaring sexual preoccupations? May offers three major answers:

1. There is the motive of *trying to prove one's identity* based on a misguided egalitarianism of the sexes. "Egalitarianism is clung to at the price of denying not only biological differences—which are basic, to say the least—between men and women, but emotional differences from which come much of the delight of the sexual act" (May, 1969, p. 54).

2. Also involved is the need behind some sexual behavior to overcome isolation, loneliness, and feelings of emptiness: ". . . partners pant and quiver hoping to find an answering quiver in someone else's body just to prove that their own is not dead; they seek a responding, a longing in the other to prove their own feelings are alive" (May, 1969, p. 54).

3. Also, the need to prove oneself competent is often an underlying motive. A man, for example, may feel inferior or very insecure if his "technique" is unpracticed or not in line with the "latest" advice of media experts. Sex therapists have developed many remedies for sexual performance difficulties, some of which, in May's opinion, are more demeaning than the original sexual problem itself. Obsessive concern with performance ironically lessens sexual enjoyment.

What is missing in all of this, May asserts, is true passion—a desire to make love to one's partner because there is healthy lust, mature caring, and satisfying communication between the two people. In May's terms, sex has become superficial and disconnected from both the deep yearnings of *Eros* and the connectedness of *Caritas*.

Eros and Death

According to May, people have learned to anesthetize their deeper emotions in order to achieve better sexual performance. May sees sex as being used as a test of competence, and asserts that people often give up their identity in the search for intimacy. "We fly to *the sensation of sex in order to avoid the passion of* **eros**" (1969, p. 65; italics in original).

May explains that, in Greek mythology, Eros is the god of more than simply eroticism. Eros was one of the four original gods: Chaos, Mother Earth (Gaea), and Tartarus (the pit of Hell). According to the myths, Eros created life on earth. Eros is thus a progenitor, a creator, and the source of life. Eros involves yearning and a desire to transcend ourselves. Sex, for some people, is equivalent to orgasm, but Eros involves a sense of union with one's partner. Sex is surface satisfaction, whereas Eros involves delight in the beloved.

But there is a dark side to Eros as well. To love another, one must open the self to the possibilities of grief, sorrow, disappointment, and loss. To "fall" in love, one's reason is suspended in the service of Eros's passion. May pits the positive delight of love against the possibility of nonbeing or death:

> For death is always in the shadow of the delight of love. . . . When we love, we give up the center of ourselves. We are thrown from our previous state of existence into a void; and though we hope to attain a new world, a new existence, we can never be sure. . . . This experience of annihilation is an inward one and, as the myth [of Eros] rightly puts it, is essentially what *eros* does to us. To love completely carries with it the threat of annihilation of everything. This intensity of consciousness has something in common with the ecstasy of the mystic in his union with God: just as he can never be *sure* God is there, so love carries us to that intensity of consciousness in which we no longer have any guarantee of security. (May, 1969, p. 101; italics in original)

According to May, the relationship between love and death can be viewed in a number of different ways:

- Recognition of our own mortality heightens our appreciation of those things that give us pleasure.
- Both mythology and popular figures of speech ("I love you so much, I could die!") and psychotherapy patients' dreams and associations provide a metaphorical connection between love and death. The experience of orgasm, May suggests, is possible only when one can "let go" completely or surrenders one's being completely, as in death.
- There is a defensively disguised connection between love and death. It is possible, for example, to pursue obsessive concern with sex as a way of avoiding the fear of death. Or, along a different defensive pathway, the person may invest self so completely in sexual love that he or she can simply repress the fear of death. In contemporary society, whereas we rarely speak about death openly, it is usually easier and more acceptable to talk about sex.
- Sexual love is a way of "making ourselves infinite" in the face of our own mortality, the eventuality we fear most and speak of least (May, 1969, p. 106).

In short, May believes that many factors underlie a profound connection between love and death.

Philia: Brotherly Love and Friendship

Philia is friendship or *brotherly love.* It involves a kind of acceptance, in which the lover accepts, and enjoys, simply being with the beloved. In a way, Philia provides Eros with time to grow stronger and sink deeper roots (May, 1969, p. 317).

In turn, as Philia supports Eros, Agapé supports Philia. Agapé, recall, is a kind of esteem for the other in which there is no intention of getting something from the other. It is a genuinely disinterested love for another, modeled on the Biblical accounts of God's love for humans (May, 1969, p. 319). The New Testament renders the concept of Agapé as *charity,* which may be a poor translation but nevertheless conveys its selfless and altruistic quality. Philia needs Agapé in order to flourish, for the mutuality and acceptance embodied in Philia can flourish only when it is truly selfless. And, as we might expect, all three kinds of loving—Sex, Eros, and Philia—ideally rest on a foundation of Agapé— unselfish caring love.

GOOD AND EVIL

Through his many writings, May grapples with enduring and profound aspects of experience. Fear, anxiety, love, sex, death, being, and nothingness constitute just a partial list. May pictures humans neither as saints nor as sinners. He has consistently taken the position that humans are both good and evil, People are involved in a continuing struggle between good and evil, being and nonbeing, creation and destruction because of what May has emphasized is a *daimonic* element in human nature.

The Daimonic

The word *daimon* is to be distinguished from the more typical word *demon.* May is not using the term with any implication of some substantive thing or entity, such as a demon or devil, and he has clearly distinguished between the two (May, 1986b).

> The word can be spelled "demonic" (the popularized form), or "daemonic" (the medieval form often now used by the poets—Yeats, for example), or "daimonic" (the derivative from the ancient Greek word "daimon"). Since this last is the origin of the concept, and since the term is unambiguous in its including the positive as well as the negative, the divine as well as the diabolical, I use the Greek term. (May, 1969, p. 123n.)

The **daimonic** in May's usage is *"any natural function which has the power to take over the whole person"* (1969, p. 123). It can be a creative "taking over," as in lovemaking, or it can be destructive, as in sexual compulsion. What is daimonic in people can be the

---

BOX 12.3 *Only Connect . . .*

Recall a similar concept to Philia in Harry Stack Sullivan's "chum" relationships of adolescence (see Chapter 9). The chum is the developing person's first opportunity to care for someone as much as he or she cares for self. Sullivan believed that prior to the "chum period" (approximately ages 8 to 12), the child is not capable of genuine love. Without the chum experience, Sullivan felt that heterosexual love relationships would be difficult to form (Sullivan, 1953b, pp. 223 ff.). In a way, Sullivan, and May are both pointing to the necessity for learning mutuality and cooperative interaction with peers as a sound basis for loving, adult relationships. Out of the experience of "brotherly love" grows the possibilities of truly loving another.

best that they are capable of, such as poetry, art, dance, literature, and ethical and religious convictions. The daimonic can be contagious, as when a charismatic figure exhorts others to his or her cause. The daimonic in us can even lead to ecstasy, as in the feeling of lovers for each other or the religious mystic's feeling of being swept away in the presence of the divine. But the daimonic can also be an expression of the worst in humans, the void of nothingness or nonbeing. The daimonic can assert itself in psychosis, or in a destructive cause.

According to May, when the daimonic is repressed in us, it tends to erupt in some other way. Violence is the daimonic unleashed without the balancing forces of reason and love. Freud's idea of the instinctual drives of the id is very similar to May's notion of the daimonic. May rightly credits Freud with detailing the power of the daimonic in his description of the dark urges and fantasies of which we are capable. When the daimonic takes over, the person's sense of self is no longer in control. Such a condition is revealed in psychotherapy when the patient says, "I felt like I had no control. I couldn't help myself" (May, 1969, p. 146 ff.).

WILL

Is it accurate to conclude that the daimonic is responsible for our actions, for our decisions? Are we the creatures of fate? Or do we intend our actions and therefore assume responsibility for our thoughts and actions? This is a question that May raises, the question of the existence of **will.**

Are We Responsible Agents?

May believes that Freud's greatest contribution was to peel away the illusion of what Victorians had termed "will power" to show that unconscious urges, drives, and wishes prompt much of our behavior. "Under his penetrating analysis, Victorian 'will' did, indeed, turn out to be a web of rationalizations and self-deceit" (May, 1969, p. 183).

Freud and other intellectuals fostered a tendency for people to view themselves as passive, pushed by forces for which they have little responsibility. This picture itself can undermine a sense of will and responsibility. It can become a self-fulfilling prophecy. People sometimes believe that even if they make decisions, exert effort, their actions will inevitably be futile in the face of deterministic forces that they cannot control.

Intentionality: The Subject-Object Bridge

May's proposed alternative to the deterministic conception of human action rests on European phenomenological philosophers' analysis of a way of knowing termed **intentionality.** Intentionality is a bridge between subject and object, between knower and known. It refers to the inextricable connection between our awareness and objects of awareness, the idea that there is no act of consciousness without an object of consciousness. One meaning of this concept is that our consciousness does not exist independent of the meanings and meaningful world we experience. Intentionality, therefore, is the person's ongoing and inevitable application of meaning to objects and people in his or her world, and to the experience of the world itself.

> [Intentionality] . . . is the structure of meaning which makes it possible for us, subjects that we are, to see and understand the outside world, objective as it is. In intentionality, the dichotomy between subject and object is practically overcome. (May, 1969, p. 225)

The concept of intentionality is a way of saying that we really cannot know a thing, unless we have, in some way, already participated in it. "I take this to mean that in the process of knowing, we are in-formed by the thing understood, and in the same act, our intellect simultaneously gives form to the thing we understand" (May, 1969, p. 225).

How does the concept of intentionality undermine the idea of determinism? The answer is that, from this point of view, the events in the world cannot be external causes of human behavior. Rather, even in the very experience of such events, acts of awareness and assignment of meaning are involved. The external events do not have inherent meaning. They are meaningful only as objects of intentional acts of consciousness.

May asserts that we inevitably impose our meanings on the people and things we observe. He (May, 1969, p. 224) gives the example of examining a house to rent. If the house hunter approaches the search for a suitable house in which to spend the summer months, issues such as how much sun the house gets, how soundly it is built, and whether there are guest rooms for friends will be paramount in shaping the meaning of *house* as "shelter." But if the house hunter examines houses from the viewpoint of a real estate speculator, then issues such as can a rundown house be fixed cheaply and resold for more than its purchase price, and can the house be made attractive to a particular group of buyers transform the meaning of *house* into "profit." Or, finally, if our house hunter is an artist looking for an aesthetically pleasing arrangement of house, hillside, and trees, the meaning of *house* becomes "beauty."

While considering the example given above, it is good to keep in mind that intentionality is an ontological concept, one rooted in our very being, regardless of whatever are the particular meanings that we might experience.

Will and Intentionality

Will and intentionality are linked. The connection between them is the fact that an intention and the resulting action are part of the same process. A willed action is implied by an intention, and an intention leads to the willed action. The only difference is when they occur. In the present, we are capable of intending a specific future action, as when we say, "I *will* go to England next week." The fact that the traveler projects an action for the future means that the meaning of this action already exists in his or her mind. When a person wills the action to be carried out—that action will embody the intention that preceded it.

May asserts that, in acts of intentionality and will, a person experiences his or her identity as an existing person. According to May, "I conceive—I can—I will—I am" (May, 1969, p. 243). The depression of some patients in therapy can be usefully understood as an incapacity to imagine their own futures: In effect, the patient says "I can't," and the therapist's job is to help the patient see the possibility for "I can." For it is in the "I will" and the "I can" that we are most authentically ourselves, most fully aware of our own existence, and most completely conscious of our identities.

Love and Will United

Loving and willing are not complete opposites, according to May. They are similar in that they both involve reaching out to someone or something and attempting to produce an effect. Love and will aim at influencing others. Both love and will are ways of molding, forming, relating to the world (May, 1969, p. 276). Love and will do not become united without our intention to unite them. An important task for adults is to unite love and will in their actions and in their speech to a variety of parental demands.

As any parent knows, children often exert their will in opposition to love. They say "no" loudly and clearly think of these developments as the emergence of individuality and independence. We usually think of these developments in a positive light. But, without the eventual development of the capacity to love and to care for others, children would grow into self-centered, narcissistic, and selfish individuals. Instead, most children learn also to deny self in a variety of tempting situations and to express caring, love, and consideration. Development involves learning to reach out to others, giving as well as getting.

As adults, we need to relearn, time and again, to combine love and will. May sees unifying love and will as an important developmental task. When it is accomplished, the result is mature integration and harmony.

FREEDOM

Freedom is defined as the capacity to make choices. If we do something without having made a choice, it is not a free action and does not have the same significance as a free choice would have. To take one example, May asks what value we would place on a person's love if we knew that the person was forced to love us (1981, p. 6). Unless love is given freely, it loses much of its value as love. In fact, one might question whether it would be love at all. People sometimes deny their freedom. One aspect of contemporary life is that people often say that they had no choice when anyone can see that they did choose a particular course of action.

Freedom of Doing

Freedom of doing is defined by May as ". . . the capacity to pause in the face of stimuli, from many directions at once, and, in this pause, to throw one's weight toward this response rather than that one" (May, 1981, p. 54). It is the kind of freedom we experience in everyday activities when we make the myriad choices and decisions that constitute a day's activities. When we select one product rather than another from the supermarket's shelves, or when we watch one TV program rather than another, we are experiencing freedom of doing. One of the most interesting examples of freedom of doing is our ability to ask questions. The fact that questions occur to us implies that the question has more than one answer, or there would be no point in asking the question.

Freedom of Being

May distinguishes **freedom of being** as a second category of freedom that may also be called "essential freedom." Freedom of being is the origin of freedom of doing and goes to a deeper level of human existence. Instead of focusing on the act, or on the process of

---

BOX 12.4   *Only Connect . . .*

There is a fundamental difference between May's idea of freedom of action and behavioral (see Chapter 14) or psychodynamic views (see Chapters 2 and 3). The behaviorist would be inclined to look at a person's conditioning history in order to explain his or her choice of a product at a supermarket, whereas the analyst might refer to the satisfaction of a drive. Thus, a person with a proclivity to drink sodas might be seen as conditioned or as having oral cravings. The existentialists are open to the idea of individual freedom and choice, although they do not ignore the possibility that compulsions to behave in certain ways might occur in some cases.

decision, freedom of being is concerned with the context of acts and the ability to choose one's attitude toward events whether one acts or not (May, 1981, p. 55).

May offers as an example the accounts of psychoanalyst Bruno Bettelheim, who was imprisoned in a Nazi concentration camp during World War II. Bettelheim had no freedom of action whatsoever, but he could choose his attitude toward his captors. Bettelheim could reflect, ponder, and ask spoken or unspoken questions about the situation and the people who controlled his daily life. Thus freedom of being is an inner, spiritual freedom that may or may not be reflected by external behavior.

DESTINY

Cooperating with Destiny

May resolves the conflict between determinism and freedom by conceptualizing these apparent opposites as dialectical, that is, as involved in reciprocal interaction. May is saying that the meaning of the terms *freedom* and *determinism* is each dependent on the other: One cannot be free from determinism unless determinism is possible, and one cannot be determined unless it is possible to remove a person's freedom (1981, p. 95).

> *Freedom and determinism give birth to each other. Every advance in freedom gives birth to a new determinism, and every advance in determinism gives birth to a new freedom.* Freedom is a circle within a larger circle of determinism, which is, in turn, surrounded by a larger circle of freedom. And so on *ad infinitum.* (May, 1981, p. 84; italics in original)

May thus acknowledges the possibility of determinism, but he prefers to use the term *destiny* to describe the limits of freedom for human beings. Billiard balls struck by other billiard balls are "determined" in the flight across the table. But humans are limited by their "destinies."

May defines **destiny** as the "pattern of limits and talents that constitutes the 'givens' in life" (1981, p. 89). May believes that it is through our very confrontation with these limits, with these "givens," from which our creativity and freedom emerge.

Destiny's Different Forms

Destiny (May's term for the limits of human freedom) has many levels, and each of the levels differs in the degree to which it yields to human intervention. May distinguishes four levels:

1. Cosmic destiny, sometimes termed "acts of God." Included here are birth, death, earthquakes, volcanoes, and other relatively unpredictable natural events that affect our lives but about which we can do nothing.

2. Genetic destiny, our inherited genome, which governs many of the physical traits with which we are born, including the color of our eyes or skin and our gender. Genetics may also play a role in the talents we have for art, music, mathematics, and so on. We can enhance or cooperate with our genetic givens to a degree, but there is little we can do to change what we inherit.

3. Cultural destiny, which includes the family, society, and culture into which we are born. We do not get to choose these "givens," although, through our attitudes and actions, we may greatly influence their effects.

4. Circumstantial destiny, which includes human events over which we individually have no control, such as the rise and fall of the stock market, or a terrorist act.

The Dimension of Destiny

Figure 12.2 Degrees of human intervention in destiny.
Drawn from a description in May, 1981, p. 91.

Figure 12.2 summarizes the spectrum of limitations that May envisioned as forms of destiny. As you move across the spectrum in Figure 12.2 from left to right, the degree of human control or choice increases.

May states that there are at least five ways that a person can relate to his or her destiny:

1. *Cooperate with destiny* and accept that one's life is shaped by it.

2. *Acknowledge destiny* in our limitations, such as height, weight, and death.

3. *Engage destiny* by actively seeking out the challenge of our limitations and trying to transcend them.

4. *Confront and challenge destiny* by attempting to see the most productive path that destiny provides and trying to overcome the destructive directions destiny tries to enforce.

5. *Rebel against destiny* by refusing to accept it or cooperate with it. We can, for example, rage against death. It is not clear, however, what such "rebelling" can do to affect destiny.

Even if we cannot change certain limitations, we are free in how we relate to them.

EVALUATING ROLLO MAY

May's approach borrows heavily from psychoanalysis, ego psychology, philosophy, and theology. What he has created is an approach to human experience that includes an understanding derived from philosophical as well as psychological insights. The result is a set of ideas that encourages us to see ourselves as conscious beings capable of free choices. Many problems formerly considered psychopathological are viewed by May as inevitable consequences of having awareness and choice.

During the years since May's death, there has been a continuing interest in existential phenomenological psychology. At least one doctoral psychology program, at Duquesne University, is committed to this approach. It is also emphasized at the Saybrook Institute and by some scholars scattered throughout the United States and Europe. In addition, the past decade has shown an increase in the acceptance of the value of qualitative psychological research. Much of this research is in the phenomenological tradition of direct inquiry of subjects concerning their experiences. Such research might involve eliciting subjects' own accounts or narratives.

Refutability of May's Approach

Almost by definition, the existential phenomenologist would find the concept of scientific refutability inappropriate, if not irrelevant. However, because May has attempted to synthesize psychoanalytic ideas into his theory, there are some questions about refutability that pose themselves.

In May's earliest work on anxiety, the definitions he provides of normal and neurotic anxiety, and the hypotheses drawn loosely from psychoanalytic theory, surely lend themselves to empirical test. In fact, May's own doctoral dissertation, a part of which found its way into May's 1950 book on anxiety, was just such an attempt. But then there is the rest of May's work. What scientific psychological sense can we make of concepts such as *ontological principles, nonbeing,* and *will?* Because these terms and their associated ideas deal with unobservables, and with processes that do not have measurable empirical referents in action or thought, they remain outside the scope of refutability altogether. We are not even certain that the concept of refutability is the right question to ask about concepts such as these.

But even in this thicket of metaphysics there lurk some ideas that have a possibility of translation into refutable statements. *Destiny* may not of itself be a refutable concept, but what about the person's conception of destiny? Using May's hypothetical dimension of destiny, as illustrated in Figure 12.2, could we not devise a measure of people's reactions to the limitations that life hands them? Could we not develop a way of measuring the subjective reaction to destinies, such as the chance events of earthquakes, and the social constraints of other people's reactions to our handicaps and infirmities? In a way, the social learning theorists have begun to consider the power of destiny in shaping our perceptions of our lives. The social cognative theorist, Albert Bandura (1986, 1989) avoids the term *destiny* in favor of either the term *chance* or *fortuitous events* (see Chapter 16).

On the whole, May's theory is comprised of a composite of largely nontestable ideas, with small pockets of potentially empirical constructs.

May's Conception of Human Agency

May's ideas on will, intentionality, destiny, and helplessness make it clear that he regards the person as capable of both active and passive agency. May's philosophical argument puts the body of his work on the side of an active agency conception of the person. May asserts that intentionality is an inherent aspect of the human being from which active willing emerges. May views much psychopathology (alienation, depression, despair, and violence) as the result of blocking the person's freedom. Mature personality integration is possible, therefore, in May's estimation, only when the person is free to exercise will in decision and in action.

May's Idiographic Focus

May's focus is a composite of particular and general, of specific and universal. At the most abstract, he deals with universals: existence, being, nonbeing, destiny, freedom, and so on. But he places the highest value on understanding the *individual's* unique embodiment of these universals. In fact, May's particular version of the existential phenomenological position emphasizes individual meanings, individual perceptions, and centeredness in the individual self.

May also borrows much from psychoanalysis, itself a highly idiographic account of people. Also, because such a large portion of May's work has centered on the clinical issues of treatment for psychological disorder, we would expect his focus to be idiographic rather than nomothetic. And because so much of the theory is couched in untestable terms, the usual relationship between degree of idiography and testability prevails: The more idiographic a theory is, the less likely will it generate empirical referents to permit its concepts to be tested.

SUMMARY

Rollo May attempts to blend the more clinical and experience-near ideas of psychoanalysis with the philosophical issues raised by the European phenomenologists and existentialists. His earliest efforts involved introducing existential phenomenological theory into American psychology. This approach focuses on ontological issues, that is, issues involving the conceptions of being. The person is conceptualized in such a way as to emphasize the ongoing, continuously becoming aspects of human personality. The existential phenomenological philosophers and psychologists distinguish among three modes of being:

- *Umwelt,* or the "around-world," meaning the natural world of biological urge and drive;

- *Mitwelt,* or the "with-world," meaning the social, interactive, interpersonal aspects of existence; and

- *Eigenwelt,* or the "one's own world," meaning the subjective, phenomenal world of the self.

May proposed six ontological principles, discussed in the context of the case of his patient, Mrs. Hutchens:

1. Every person is centered in self and lives life through the meanings he or she places on that center.

2. Every person is responsible for mobilizing the courage to protect the self, to affirm it, and enhance its continued existence.

3. People need other people with whom they can empathize and from whom they can learn.

4. People are vigilant about potential dangers to their sense of selfhood.

5. People have self-consciousness; they experience themselves as both subject and object.

6. Anxiety originates, in part, out of a person's awareness that one's existence or sense of meaningful being can end.

May defined anxiety as the active confrontation with nonbeing. Only the human person, he points out, is capable of envisioning a time when he or she will not be. The realization of one's own mortality is a powerful determinant of our behavior. When a person yields to anxiety and refuses to make choices or retreats from living, the result is feelings of helplessness, despair, and ontological guilt. Ontological guilt parallels the three kinds of being in the world, so that we can feel ontological guilt in a separation from the natural world (*Umwelt*), or experience guilt as alienation from self (*Eigenwelt*), or be aware of ontological guilt as alienation from others (*Mitwelt*).

We can trace the personal sources of May's interest in European existential and phenomenological philosophy in terms of his early discordant family life and subsequent sensitivity to loneliness, his personal confrontation with death when suffering from tuberculosis, and his personal desire to struggle against feelings of helplessness and despair at all costs.

May dealt with the theme of apathy in his discussion of love and will. He distinguishes among four kinds of loving:

1. *Agapé* or *Caritas* or *Care,* the love devoted to the welfare of others, the prototype for which is the love of God for man. It is the foundation for all of the other forms.

2. *Sex* or lust, or what Freud called libido.

3. *Eros,* the drive to procreate.

4. *Philia,* or brotherly love and friendship.

May argued that modern society has trivialized sexuality, separated it from passion, undermined the human motivation for procreation contained in Eros, and forced people into uncaring and indifferent attitudes toward each other.

The issues of good and evil occupied May at some length. He argued that human nature is a composite of both good and evil, and he wrote metaphorically about this composite in his conception of the *daimonic,* which is defined as any natural human function which can reach such intensity that the person is overcome by it. On the positive side, the daimonic is the force underlying creativity and self-affirmation. On the negative side, the daimonic can be destructive addiction to power or fascination with death.

May addressed the issues of freedom, responsibility, and determinism with his conception of destiny. In his view, destiny is a kind of dimension ranging from cosmic acts that affect us but over which we have no control to the inheritance of talents and handicaps, about which we may exert some choice. He argued that ultimately people are free in being, if not in action, because they can choose the meaning they will place on what reality provides. Intentionality, to be distinguished from intention, is a kind of subjective bridge between the passive and the active, between the subject and object in existence. Reality may provide its own input into our lives, but we make much of the reality that we interpret.

Our evaluation of May indicates that his blend of existential phenomeonolgy and psychoanalysis focuses on broad, philosophical questions. As such, May's theory is largely, but not completely, untestable. It is strongly pushed toward the idiographic end of the idiographic-nomothetic spectrum, and it conceptualizes people as largely active agents with the freedom to act or to choose how they will permit fate or destiny to affect them.

FOR FURTHER READING

The clearest overview of existential phenomenology in psychology that May provides is to be found in an anthology he co-edited entitled *Existence: A New Dimension in Psychiatry and Psychology* (R. May, E. Angel, & H. F. Ellenberger [Eds.], New York: Basic Books, 1958). A more recent presentation of much of the same theoretical material may be found in May's *The Discovery of Being: Writings in Existential Psychology* (New York: Norton, 1994). To round out the historical and philosophical picture, William Barrett's classic *Irrational Man: A Study in Existential Philosophy* (New York: Doubleday Anchor, 1962) remains a scholarly and readable approach. Existential phenomenological psychiatrist Medard Boss's *Existential Foundations of Medicine and Psychology* (New York: Jason Aronson, 1995) is similar to May's approach in that it is another comprehensive existential phenomenological theory informed by psychoanalysis. Boss's discussion of the psychological issues surrounding perception of one's own mortality is especially clear and engaging.

May's earliest theoretical writing on anxiety (*The Meaning of Anxiety* [New York: Norton, 1996]) gives some indication of the development of his thinking. For comparison purposes, the reader might want to consult May's later writings, which expand upon many of the fundamental issues with which he began. A good starting place is May's *Love and Will* (New York: Norton, 1989).

Glimpses into May's personal history can be most efficiently accomplished by examining May's *My Quest for Beauty* (Dallas: Saybrook, 1985). This book also includes a sample of May's paintings and drawings, which are well worth more than a casual glance.

Viktor E. Frankl's *The Unheard Cry for Meaning: Psychotherapy and Humanism* (New York: Simon & Schuster, 1997) gives a concise overview of yet another way to interpret existential phenomenological philosophy in personality psychology.

GLOSSARY

Agapé: Caring. In May's theory, *caring* is more than a feeling; it is a state of being that is the source of love and will.

Angst: The feeling of "losing being," anguish, dread. It is, in May's theory, the basic anxiety of a finite being about the threat of nonbeing.

Anxiety and nonbeing: Anxiety is the state of the person in the struggle against what would destroy his or her being. At a deep level, anxiety always involves a confrontation with the possibility of nonbeing.

Awareness: The subjective side of centeredness is awareness. For May, this term means vigilance. The person is wary of external threats and dangers.

Becoming: The process in which an individual is continually struggling to develop and discover what his or her potentialities are, and assume responsibility for their expression.

Circumstantial destiny: Human events over which we individually have no control, and which we cannot ignore, undo, or avoid.

Cosmic destiny: Unpredictable, natural events that affect our lives, but about which we can do nothing.

Cultural destiny: The family, society, and culture into which we are born. We do not choose those givens, but we may influence their effects to some extent.

Daimonic: Any natural function that has the power to take over the whole person. This force can be either creative or destructive.

Dasein: (German for "being there") Human being, being-in-the-world. The term *Dasein* indicates that a human being does not exist apart from his or her experience of the world at a particular time in a specific place.

Destiny: May uses the term *destiny* to describe the limits of freedom. These limits or "givens" have four levels: *Cosmic, genetic, cultural,* and *circumstantial.*

Eigenwelt: (Means *one's own world*) One's experience of thoughts and feelings, involving self-awareness and self-relatedness.

Eros: The passionate desire to unite with another person. It leads people to search for a tender relationship within a sexual context and to seek wholeness with that partner.

Existentialism: A philosophical approach emphasizing that people have a responsibility for their actions, beliefs, and commitments. Søren Kierkegaard and Jean-Paul Sartre are two philosophers associated with this approach.

Existential phenomenological psychology: An approach to psychology that combines the emphases of existentialism and those of phenomenology.

Fear: The emotions accompanying the sense of a threat to the periphery of one's existence; the person can stand outside and look at it objectively.

Freedom: The capacity to make choices. May distinguished between *freedom of doing* and *freedom of being*.

Freedom of being: An essential freedom, the deeper origin of the freedom of doing. It is concerned with the context of acts and the ability to choose one's attitude toward events—whether one acts or not. It is an inner spiritual freedom.

Freedom of doing: May stated that it is "the capacity to pause in the face of stimuli, from many directions at once, and in this pause, to throw one's weight toward this response rather than that one. It represents the myriad of choices and decisions we make on a daily basis."

Genetic destiny: That which is embodied in our genetic makeup.

Intentionality: A person's ongoing application of meaning to objects and people in his or her world, and to the experience of the world itself.

Mitwelt: (Means *with-world*) One's experiential world of interpersonal relationships and interrelatedness. It includes the meaning the individual attaches to those relationships.

Ontological anxiety: The emotion accompanying the sense of a threat to the core of a person's self-esteem and sense of value as a self.

Ontological guilt: The sense of guilt that arises because we might not have made the choices that were open to us, or that we might not have made the best choices. This is a non-neurotic form of guilt.

Ontological principles: Six principles or guidelines that May thought are necessary to understand human behavior: *phenomenal centeredness, self-affirmation and courage, participation in other beings, awareness, self-consciousness,* and *anxiety and non-being.*

Ontology: A branch of philosophy that seeks to understand the nature of being. It studies the processes of *being* and *nonbeing,* and the person's own view of reality.

Participation in other beings: All existing persons have the need and possibility of going out from their centeredness to participate in other beings.

Phenomenal centeredness: Every person is centered in self and therefore lives, loves, hates, is creative or destructive, flexible or rigid, blind or perceptive because of that center.

Phenomenology: The philosophical approach pioneered by Edmund Husserl and Martin Heidegger, which focuses on the description of human experience as it appears or unfolds, without the application of explanatory or theoretical concepts.

Philia: Friendship or "brotherly love." It is a love that accepts and enjoys the other person.

Self-affirmation and courage: Every existing person has the character of self-affirmation, which is the need to preserve his or her centeredness, and can mobilize courage to do so.

Self-consciousness: The uniquely human form of awareness is self-consciousness. Self-consciousness permits the person to transcend the immediate, concrete situation, to live in terms of the possible, and to use abstractions. The person is conscious of self both as an active subject and as a passive object.

Sex: One of the biological drives, the biological aspect of love. It is often described as libido or lustful love.

The unconscious: According to May, those potentialities for knowing and experiencing that the individual cannot or will not actualize.

Types of love: May distinguished between four types of love: *Agapé, Sex, Eros,* and *Philia.*

Umwelt: (Means *around-world*) The experience of the physical aspects of the internal and external environments. The *umwelt* is that aspect of the experienced world that includes biological needs, drives, and instinct. It is one mode of being-in-the-world.

Welt: (*World* in German) Indicates the experiential world of a person in phenomenological philosophy and psychology. It has three modes or components: the *Umwelt,* the *Mitwelt,* and the *Eigenwelt.*

Will: The application of meaning to objects and people, which allow individuals to make decisions willfully. The capacity to organize one's thoughts and movements toward a goal or person.

Chapter **13**

Maslow

Rogers

Abraham Maslow
& Carl Rogers

Humanistic Self-Actualization Theory

Be all you can be.

United States Army Recruiting Poster

Evaluation by others is not a guide for me.

Carl Rogers, *On Becoming a Person*

About Maslow and Rogers' Humanistic Psychologies

Abraham Maslow and Carl Rogers were both pioneers of the humanistic psychological approach to understanding personality, a major alternative to both psychoanalysis and behaviorism.

From his research with primate and human subjects and drawing upon his in-depth and broad knowledge of personality and motivational theories, Maslow developed these main themes:

1. *Personality health is not merely the absence of pathology. It consists of many positive qualities and can be a subject of study in its own right.*

2. *His theory of the hierarchy of needs indicated that behavior is not motivated entirely by physiologically based drives for food or sex. Once these basics are satisfied, other needs such as those for security, belongingness, and self-esteem become prepotent. Eventually, what Maslow termed "metaneeds" may develop. These steer the person toward a search for beauty, knowledge, justice, and truth.*

3. *Self-actualization is the full development of a person's positive potentials. Very few people become fully self-actualized.*

4. Peak experiences are altered states of consciousness in which a person has a deeper grasp of the meaning of his or her life or of existence. They are often significant confirmatory experiences or turning points in a person's life history.

Carl Rogers' theory developed out of his life experiences, his knowledge of contemporary philosophical traditions, and developments in the field of psychotherapy and his psychotherapeutic work with troubled children and their parents. Rogers emphasized understanding individual experience and the importance of personal freedom and choice. Some of the main tenets of his approach are:

1. The core of personality is the phenomenal self, the private world of experience and personal meaning.

2. In the absence of empathic understanding and unconditional love, a person's sense of self is shaped by qualified or conditional love and acceptance. Trying to meet the conditions of value may alienate the developing individual from being aware of and acting on his or her deepest and most authentic promptings.

3. Psychotherapy from the Rogerian point of view requires the establishment of a relationship in which the therapist has unconditional positive regard for the client, attempts to see the world as the client sees it, and is able to provide genuine empathic warmth for the client. When these conditions are met, the person is able to access his or her deeper feelings and desires and can begin to act more autonomously.

Both Maslow and Rogers emphasize the importance of the experience of the individual and the process of personal growth.

Abraham Maslow   **Born: April, 1908   New York, New York**
                      Died: June, 1970   Menlo Park, California

---

WHAT ABOUT THE NORMAL OR HEALTHY PERSONALITY?

Most people generally are psychologically healthy, even though at times they may have difficult adjustments to make. Yet, many personality theories have been about maladjustment, personality flaws, and psychopathological behavior. Knowledge derived from this nonrepresentative sample of behavior has often served to obtain a pool of principles, which are then applied universally. What can we learn from studying the healthy personality?

Abraham Maslow, the first theorist we consider in this chapter, focused his attention on those rare persons who are on the verge of, or who have already achieved, psychological health. Maslow preferred to think of this state of exemplary personality development as **self-actualization.** Maslow's concern with such atypical individuals also established a nonrepresentative sample of personalities as the basis of psychological generalizations, but this sample may serve as a much-needed corrective to a long history of focusing on psychopathology. Only by including the psychologically healthy as a subject of study can a comprehensive personality theory be developed.

> Health is not simply the absence of disease or even the opposite of it. Any theory of motivation that is worthy of attention must deal with the highest capacities of the healthy and strong man as well as with the defensive maneuvers of crippled spirits. (1970, p. 33)

Maslow regarded the truly healthy personality as one that possesses sufficient personal fortitude and creativity to be spontaneous and innocent. **Innocence,** according to

Maslow, refers to the healthy personality's capacity to live without pretense, to be self-lessly focused on a creative goal. Creative, innocent, and healthy people are able to devote themselves completely to whatever task is at hand. They are able to free themselves from the distractions, fears, and petty influences imposed by other people, for they are in the process of becoming completely themselves, becoming more real, authentic, and less influenced by a need to placate others. Maslow used the metaphor of the actor, the mask, and the audience to portray these qualities:

> This [freedom from the influence of others] means dropping masks, dropping our efforts to influence, to impress, to please, to be lovable, to win applause. It could be said so: if we have no audience to play to, we cease to be actors. With no need to act we can devote ourselves, self-forgetfully, to the problem. (1971, p. 65)

In becoming more our real selves and less the persons we expect others want us to be, we approach closer to our potential.

THE ORIGIN OF MASLOW'S INTEREST IN EXCEPTIONAL PSYCHOLOGICAL HEALTH AND STRENGTH

Maslow's original training was in experimental psychology, and he completed his doctoral thesis under Harry Harlow at the University of Wisconsin. Harlow was then (circa 1933) just beginning to set up his primate laboratory for the study of monkey behavior. Maslow's research involved a great many observational investigations of animal interaction and group affiliations. In fact, his doctoral study was concerned with the establishment of dominance hierarchies in a colony of monkeys.

Maslow noted throughout his early researches (e.g., 1936a, 1936b, 1937, in Maslow, 1973) that dominance of one animal over others was only rarely established through overt physical aggression. To Maslow it seemed rather that the dominant animal exhibited a kind of internal confidence or **dominance-feeling** that communicated to less assertive cagemates that he would prevail (1936b, p. 45). The more dominant monkeys displayed very different behaviors from those lower in the dominance hierarchy, and subsequent research has shown that they differ hormonally and physiologically from those lower down on the ladder of influence.

Dominance-Feeling in Humans

When Maslow later applied his animal research findings and methods to the investigation of human behavior, he again employed the notion of dominance-feeling: "If we were forced to choose a single synonym or definition for dominance-feeling, we should say that it was chiefly the evaluation of, or confidence in, the personality (self-confidence)" (1937, p. 53). Maslow also indicated that people often wish for psychological health and effectiveness:

> . . . it is possible that the most parsimonious way of treating this concept is to think of it in specific, rather than general terms. It may be possible and even desirable to speak *not* of a craving for dominance, but of craving for health *per se*. . . . Or one may crave to be free of timidity, not because of an attempt to increase self-evaluation, but simply for vocational efficiency; e.g., in order to be a better teacher or a more efficient physician. (1937, p. 64; italics in original)

To study dominance-feeling, Maslow developed a method he termed **conversational probing.** Conversational probing is intensive interviewing of a subject after satisfactory rapport is established: "This meant mostly a frank, trusting, friendly relationship, resembling somewhat the transference of the psychoanalysts" (Maslow, 1939, p. 75). Maslow studied approximately 130 women and a few men in this fashion. Of these, the majority of subjects were college students between the ages of 20 and 28; 75 percent were Protestant, 20 percent were Jewish, and 5 percent were Catholic.

The interview data were organized around a basic premise: *What personality variables correlate with dominance-feeling?* Dominance-feeling was now redefined in human terms as a form of self-evaluation:

> High dominance-feeling empirically involves good self-confidence, self-assurance, high evaluation of the self, feelings of general capability or superiority, and lack of shyness, timidity, self-consciousness or embarrassment. (Maslow, 1939, p. 74)

In addition to the traits Maslow listed as characteristics of high-dominance individuals, he also found evidence they were unconventional, less religious, extroverted, and, surprisingly, more hypnotizable than low-dominance subjects (1942, pp. 108 ff.). Furthermore, Maslow discovered a number of variables that were rarely found in high-dominance persons. If a subject was high in dominance-feeling it was unlikely that she was anxious, jealous, or neurotic. The high-dominance subjects appeared to be very psychologically healthy.

Sexual Behavior and Attitudes of High-Dominance Women

In a later study, Maslow focused attention on the sexual behavior of his subjects. He reported a wide range of impressionistic and statistical data about his high-dominance subjects' sexual preferences, but one particular phenomenon is striking. When one considers the findings of Maslow today, they very much seem to be a reflection of American culture in the early 1940s rather than the discovery of enduring psychological characteristics. Certainly, our attitudes about sexuality and the respective roles of males and females have markedly changed in the past 60 years.

The women of high dominance-feeling that Maslow studied, according to him, had very specific ideas about the "ideal man" and about the "ideal lovemaking situation." For the high-dominance woman, only a high-dominance man is attractive. Preferably, he should be even more dominant than she is. This paragon of masculinity was described as "highly masculine, self-confident, fairly aggressive, sure of what he wants and able to get it, generally superior in most things" (Maslow, 1942, p. 126).

In contrast, women of medium to low dominance-feeling stressed qualities like kindness, amiability, and love for children, along with gentleness and faithfulness as desirable masculine traits.

In Maslow's view, ideal lovemaking for the high-dominance woman involved a preference for:

> . . . straightforward, unsentimental, rather violent, animal, pagan, passionate, even sometimes brutal lovemaking. It must come quickly, rather than after a long period of wooing. She wishes to be suddenly swept off her feet, not courted. She wishes her favors to be taken, rather than asked for. In other words she must be dominated, must be forced into subordinate status. (Maslow, 1942, p. 127)

Maslow was also interested in the preferences of the middle- and low-dominance woman. He found that women lower in dominance-feeling were repelled by the kind of "ideal man" that attracted high-dominance subjects. Middle-dominance women preferred an "adequate" rather than a superior man, "a comfortable and 'homey' man rather than a man who might inspire slight fear and feelings of inferiority" (Maslow, 1942, p. 126). In short, high-dominance women seek a good lover; middle- and low-dominance women are more interested in a good husband and father.

The Good Specimen Strategy: "Exceptional" Primates

Maslow conceptualized the distinction between high-dominance and low-dominance individuals as a difference between relatively secure and relatively insecure personalities (1942, p. 133). He later developed an interest in the extremely secure personality, an individual completely accepting of self. People in whom dominance-feeling has come to complete fruition he later conceptualized as "most fully human."

Maslow eventually came to develop a strategy of research with what he considered exceptionally psychologically healthy personalities:

> I proposed for discussion and eventually for research the use of selected good specimens (superior specimens) as biological assays for studying the best capability that the human species has. . . . What I am frankly espousing here is what I have been calling "growing-tip statistics," . . . taking my title from the fact that it is at the growing tip of a plant that the greatest genetic action takes place. (1971, pp. 5–7)

Thus Maslow initiated the study of what he considered the "best" that human nature has to offer, the most "saintly," the wisest, most actualized human personality. In order to do so, he turned to a group of selected historical and contemporary figures who seemed to embody the traits he associated with this "good specimen." We shall see that the observational data Maslow collected tended to be similar, in some cases identical to, his early findings on dominance-feeling.

PERSONAL SOURCES OF THE HYPOTHESIS: "IN PURSUIT OF ANGELS"

Maslow (1971) reported the personal sources of his interest in the self-actualizing (SA) personality. Devotion to and admiration of two of his teachers, Max Wertheimer, a founder of Gestalt psychology, and Ruth Benedict, the eminent cultural anthropologist, sparked the young Maslow's interest in the exceptional person. Maslow's teachers had impressed him with their calm acceptance of life and with their special capacity to take delight in intellectual and cultural pursuits. Yet, at the same time, Benedict and Wertheimer were something of an enigma to Maslow. In trying to ferret out the sources of Benedict and Wertheimer's approach to life and its people, Maslow embarked on a private and informal investigation of self-actualization:

> [My investigation on self-actualization] . . . started out as the effort of a young intellectual to try to understand two of his teachers whom he loved, adored, and admired and who were very, very wonderful people. It was a kind of high-IQ devotion. I could not be content simply to adore, but sought to understand why these two people were so different from the run-of-the-mill people in the world. These two people were Ruth Benedict and Max Wertheimer. They were my teachers . . . and they were most remarkable human beings. My training in psychology equipped me not at all for understanding them. It was as if they were not quite people but something more than people. My own investigation began as a prescientific or nonscientific activity. I made descriptions and notes on Max Wertheimer, and I made notes on Ruth Benedict. When I tried to understand them, think about them, and write about them in my journal and my notes, I realized in one wonderful moment that their two patterns could be generalized. I was talking about a kind of person, not about two noncomparable individuals. . . . I tried to see whether this pattern could be found elsewhere, and I did find it elsewhere, in one person after another. (1971, pp. 41–42)

Begun as a private and informal undertaking, Maslow's interest in psychologically healthy, self-actualized people soon became a serious professional interest. It is clear that this concern with the exceptional organism, "the good specimen," was an extension of Maslow's early work with dominant animals and then dominant people he had interviewed.

Subsequently, Maslow began to develop criteria of normality and psychological health. From his observations of personal acquaintances who might embody such qualities, Maslow was able to develop an impressionistic sketch of the exceptionally psychologically healthy person. With time, Maslow developed a definition of the self-actualizing person:

> . . . [self-actualization] may be loosely described as the full use and exploitation of talents, capacities, potentialities, etc. Such people seem to be fulfilling themselves and to be doing the best that they are capable of doing, reminding us of Nietzsche's exhortation, "Become what thou art!" (Maslow, 1970, p. 150)

Using biographical information on historical figures, and on some contemporary public ones, Maslow discovered only nine living individuals in whom he was "fairly sure" that self-actualization was well under way. The historical figures he chose as self-actualized subjects were Abraham Lincoln in his last years and Thomas Jefferson. Additionally, Maslow discovered seven "highly probable" figures: Albert Einstein, Eleanor Roosevelt, Jane Adams, William James, Albert Schweitzer, Aldous Huxley, and the philosopher, Benedict de Spinoza. Ultimately, 37 public and historical figures were selected as possible cases of self-actualization. Among these figures were Adlai Stevenson, Ralph Waldo Emerson, George Washington, Walt Whitman, Martin Buber, and Johann Wolfgang von Goethe (Maslow, 1970, p. 152).

In the course of his work, Maslow interviewed and studied more than 3,000 individuals, of whom he considered only a "handful" to have the potential for self-actualization. In fact, only one individual who was self-actualized in the fullest sense was found. Maslow's analysis of those individuals with whom he was directly familiar was different from the usual clinical-experimental investigation. Because subjects tend to freeze up when informed they are being studied as examples of exceptional psychological health, most of Maslow's observations had to be surreptitious (1970, p. 152). Therefore, the data took the form of impressionistic analyses of informal conversations and easily observable behaviors.

From Dominant Monkeys to Near-Perfect People

Maslow's childhood, like that of so many personality theorists, had been lonely:

> With my childhood, it's a wonder I'm not psychotic. I was the little Jewish boy in the non-Jewish neighborhood [see Erik Erikson, Chapter 8]. It was a little like being the first Negro enrolled in the all-white school. I was isolated and unhappy. I grew up in libraries and among books, without friends. (Maslow, in Hall, 1968, p. 33)

As a student, Maslow not only sought out the most esteemed people in his chosen field, but he attached himself to them in the most personal ways:

> I was young Harry Harlow's first Ph.D. And they were angels, my professors. I've always had angels around. They helped me when I needed it; fed me; Bill Sheldon taught me how to buy a suit. I didn't know anything of amenities. Edward L. Thorndike was an angel to me. Clark Hull was another. (Maslow, in Hall, 1968, p. 33)

As with his relationship with Wertheimer and Benedict, Maslow chose idealizing words to describe his attachments to his professors. Maslow idealized his professors as superhuman in more than one way. Once, for example, having stood beside his philosophy professor at an adjoining urinal, Maslow was shocked at the realization that even professors needed to urinate from time to time: ". . . it stunned me so that it took hours, even weeks, for me to assimilate the fact that a professor was a human being and constructed with the plumbing that everybody else had" (Wilson, 1972, p. 138).

Maslow described his fantasy of participating in the greatest academic procession in the most astounding commencement exercise of all time:

> I was in a faculty procession here at Brandeis. I saw the line stretching off into a dim future. At its head was Socrates. And in the line were the ones I love most. Thomas Jefferson was there. And Spinoza. And Alfred North Whitehead. I was in that same line. Behind me that infinite line melted into the dimness. (Maslow, in Hall, 1968, p. 35)

In this fantasy, Maslow saw himself among the company of the best minds in civilization.

The transition of interest from studying monkeys to focusing on self-actualized individuals thus now seems more understandable. Central in Maslow's life history was the clash between feelings of childhood isolation, inferiority, and powerlessness and yearnings for intellectual superiority and eminence (Maslow, 1979, pp. 101 ff.). His first goal, intellectual superiority, could be obtained by an academic career, whose prime research interest was focused on dominant "best specimens." While Maslow was among the academic behaviorists, monkeys were the best-specimen subjects. The second goal, personal eminence, could be had only vicariously, only through association with eminent teachers, who would presumably reveal the secret of their renown. While he was among the "angels," near-perfect-people were the best-specimen subjects (Maslow, 1979, p. 115).

Commenting on his techniques for handling critics of his life work, Maslow revealed this not-unexpected strategy:

> . . . I have worked out a lot of tricks for fending off professional attacks. . . . I have a secret. I talk over the heads of the people in front of me to my own private audience. I talk to people I love and respect. To Socrates and Aristotle and Spinoza and Thomas Jefferson and Abraham Lincoln. And when I write, I write for them. This cuts out a lot of crap. (Maslow, in Hall, 1968, p. 36)

Upon the birth of his son, Maslow also had an intuitive insight that was related to his shift from behavioristic studies of monkeys to the exploration of human experience. He reports that he had a growing disaffection with behaviorism, which stemmed initially from his reading of philosophers and psychoanalytic psychology, and reached a crisis at the birth of his son:

> . . . [W]hen my baby was born that was the thunderclap that settled things. I looked at this tiny, mysterious thing and felt so stupid. I was stunned by the mystery and by the sense of not really being in control. I felt small and weak and feeble before all this. I'd say that anyone who had a baby couldn't be a behaviorist. (Maslow, in Hall, 1968, p. 36)

Oedipus Against the Windmills

The theme of dominance was an enduring passion for Maslow. In a self-revealing class in a seminar at Brandeis University in January 1963, Maslow expressed his own identification with and projections about the Saul Steinberg drawing shown in Figure 13.1.

Steinberg's drawing evokes a wealth of meanings and serves admirably as a kind of projective test. Maslow began the class discussion with the admission that he thought the Don Quixote-like figure represented himself: ". . . because I think it expresses me very much. Somehow I identify with it" (Maslow & Chiang, 1977, p. 241). To encourage his students to participate in this venture into self-knowledge, Maslow provided some of his own, apparently spontaneous, free associations to the drawing. These associations included

Figure 13.1 "I think it expresses me very much"—Abraham Maslow. Copyright © 1960 by Saul Steinberg.

From the book *The Labyrinth,* Harper & Row. Originally published in *The New Yorker* magazine.

the fact that when he saw the picture for the first time, he had laughed and laughed, and wanted to share it with his wife and friends. The geometrical objects toward which the figure on horseback seems to be proceeding reminded Maslow of something cold and bloodless, mechanistic, "just the sort of thing that I'm fighting against in the American Psychological Association" (Maslow & Chiang, 1977, p. 247). Maslow referred to his fight for recognition of humanistic psychology as an independent discipline of equal value to the mechanistic Freudian and behavioristic branches of APA. Thus, Maslow saw himself as a quixotic figure tilting at the windmills of establishment.

> That is, Don Quixote, or whoever this figure with his spear is, it's all very nice. The association with me is of bravery, a kind of hopeless bravery, you might say—the ship going down with the flag flying and so on. Because this looks stronger and he can't break them—the spear isn't big enough for that—it isn't strong enough or powerful enough. So there's that kind of fundamental absurdity about the effort itself—of Don Quixote, or a Don Quixote-ish figure. I like Don Quixote, and I like that it seems like a nice thing to do. His spear will get bent, or he can't crack it or break it or anything, but the fact is that he is in a certain sense stronger, you might say, because he sees how absurd all these self-important blocks are, all puffed up with pride and solidity. (Maslow & Chiang, 1977, pp. 247–248)

Maslow then followed his associations on tilting absurdly against the mechanists with the thought of a friend with whom he played a game involving Freud's book *Totem and Taboo.* This book contains Freud's hypothesis on the evolutionary origin of the Oedipus complex in the primal patricide of the primitive horde's father and leader by his sons in

BOX 13.1 *Only Connect . . .*

Maslow is similar to some of the other personality theorists we are considering in seeing himself as an outsider. This sense of oneself seems to be a characteristic of many creative people. Certainly, the same was true of Sigmund Freud and Erik Erikson who, in spite of their fame, never felt completely accepted.

In 1965, the co-author of the present text, Robert Sollod, wanted to study with Maslow at Brandeis University. Maslow informed him that he felt isolated at Brandeis and that the other professors in the psychology department did not like his ideas, thus making Brandeis University not a good place to pursue Maslowian studies. Maslow died five years later.

order to obtain his power and his women. In the game, apparently, his friend saw himself as one son against a horde of primal fathers, a reversal of Freud's hypothesis. Maslow went on to suggest that Freud never took his own version seriously:

> It's a myth. It's a kind of a way of saying something, just the way this cartoon is. He was trying to say that you have to overthrow the dominant one or else you'll never be a man, and if you're not a man you don't deserve a woman and so on. (Maslow & Chiang, 1977, p. 248)

Maslow's further associations involved his current guilt feelings at not doing rigorous experimentation in support of his work:

> I felt uneasy about all these big things without data, without support and all sorts of theories and hypotheses. A big, big balloon, and there's always the thought, Which needle is going to prick that balloon? (1977, p. 248)

Maslow was quite fearful of criticism when delivering one of his papers to an audience. In fact, his pre-presentation jitters were often so intense that immediately following his public recital he would privately take to his bed for several days to recover (Maslow, 1979, p. 99; Wilson, 1972, p. 139).

Maslow's associations to the Don Quixote-like figure with whom he identified included three elements. First, the feeling of fighting absurdly against overwhelming and cold-blooded adversaries was interpreted as nevertheless quixotically meritorious. Second, the theme of overtaking the father's power and the threat of being defeated in turn by him was interpreted as a Freudian allegory on manhood. Third, the ever-present theme of dominance emerged overtly, centering on the proposition that one has to overthrow those who are already dominant in order to be dominant.

Maslow's Disappointing Parents

Maslow's extraordinary lifelong interest in dominant and exceptional personalities may have been related to his early disappointment with his own parents, whom he viewed as inadequate in many ways. Maslow described his mother as "a pretty woman—but not a nice one"; and he portrayed his father as a "vigorous man, who loved whiskey and women and fighting" (Wilson, 1972, p. 131). Maslow retained as little affection for his mother in adulthood as she had shown him in childhood, and his fondly ironic description of his father's "loves" was tempered by a strong measure of fear of the man. A maternal uncle cared for young Maslow when his mother and father were no longer interested in their children (Wilson, 1972, p. 131).

In his journal, Maslow recorded thoughts he had at the age of 61 about his mother. He had been speaking that evening with his wife about how she reacted against some aspects of her childhood with opposite behaviors now. That discussion brought these thoughts to mind:

> And suddenly it dawned on me that it had been the same thing for me & my mother (father too). What I had reacted against & totally hated & rejected was not only her physical appearance, but also her values & world view, her stinginess, her total selfishness, her lack of love for anyone else in the world, even her own husband & children, her narcissism, her Negro prejudice, her exploitation of anyone, her assumption that anyone was wrong who disagreed with her, her lack of concern for her grandchildren, her lack of friends, her sloppiness & dirtiness, her lack of family feeling for her own parents & siblings, her primitive animal-like care for herself & her body alone, etc., etc. I've always wondered where my Utopianism, ethical stress, humanism, stress on kindness, love, friendship, & all the rest

came from. I knew certainly of the direct consequences of having no mother-love. But the whole thrust of my life-philosophy & all my research & theorizing also has its roots in a hatred for & revulsion against everything she stood for which I hated so early that I was never tempted to seek *her* love or to want it or expect it! (Maslow, 1979, p. 245; italics in original)

It may very well have been that Maslow believed he disappointed his father as much as his uneducated father had disappointed him. Maslow wanted to be superior, and the only road he knew to that goal was the intellectual road, a journey his father could neither comprehend nor condone. Maslow rejected the option of law school. To be a lawyer meant, in the elder Maslow's eyes, that education could be applied to something practical and success-making. To be an intellectual meant—what? But that was Maslow's identity; "a young intellectual," he called himself (Maslow, 1971, p. 41).

The achievements he eventually won for himself did not dispel his insecurities. He was a pioneer in an area of psychology that defied rigorous experimentation. Would his critics understand his professional intentions without hard data to back them up? Would the established profession of psychology understand his efforts to be different, to be humanistic in a mechanistic discipline, to be somebody? Would they understand and esteem his passion better than his father had? (Maslow, 1979, p. 101)

Maslow's enduring concern with the theme of personal dominance and superiority, including his conception of the "best human specimens" as self-actualized individuals, was probably a reflection of his own need to justify his search for heroes from whose power and eminence he could draw sustenance.

CHARACTERISTICS OF SELF-ACTUALIZERS

From his observations, interviews, and partial test results, Maslow developed a picture of the self-actualizing personality. The self-actualizing pattern consists of fifteen characteristics that are positive or favorable and five negative (from the viewpoint of other people) traits. All 20 items have been summarized in Table 13.1 with a brief description of the meaning of each item. In addition, the 20 separate items have been grouped into seven classes where overlap and similarity permit such redistribution. To preserve the essence of continuity in Maslow's original list, the number of the item in that list is indicated in parentheses (see Maslow, 1970, Chapter 11).

From Table 13.1 it can be seen that self-actualizing people are generally characterized by independence and self-trust. They are accepting of others and self, and most important, accepting of what life holds in store for them. They are people in whom basic needs for food, shelter, and sexual intimacy have been satisfactorily met. Self-actualizers, consequently, are functioning in response to higher needs, needs for the classic "Goods" of the well-lived life. Beauty, Truth, Justice, and many other capitalized virtues are the very essence of the self-actualizer's existence. People therefore strived *for* meaningful existence. The question that now occupied Maslow was, *How do such higher motivations develop to engage the self-actualizer's being?*

Some Problems with the Self-Actualizing Construct

The concept of self-actualization has a good deal of appeal as a corrective to reductionistic thinking. After all, the reduction of human motivation to sexual and aggressive instincts appears illogical and oversimplifying. However, simply because Maslow is able to repudiate and go beyond such theories does not make his theory correct. A major flaw in Maslow's concept of self-actualization is its circularity: Maslow first chose individuals, either those he knew, public figures, or historical figures who had qualities or characteristics he admired and then found the qualities that they had in common. In short, the qualities he discovered in such individuals were precisely the qualities that he admired and that reflected his own values. One wonders why certain people were chosen and others were omitted. Your listing of what you consider to be self-actualized people might differ greatly from that of someone else. Perhaps you would include characteristics of tenacity and personal courage in picking your heroes. Your list of self-actualized people would then be different from Maslow's, and the traits you would discover would also be different.

Another problem with the concept of self-actualization is its elitism. As indicated earlier in this chapter, Maslow was able to find *only one* fully self-actualized person out of 3,000 he personally interviewed and studied. So the idea of self-actualization is an unattainable, or at least unattained, goal for practically everyone. Such elitism, the idea of the superiority of a very few, is one which most people would find goes against their value system. What is more to the point, though, is that there is little or no evidence for the validity of such elitism. Rather it appears to be a value-laden assumption.

LEARNING FROM ALMOST EVERYBODY WHO WAS ANYBODY IN PSYCHOLOGY

In the 1930s, Maslow was living in the New York City area as a professor of psychology at Brooklyn College. This location gave him a chance to meet many psychologists and engage in exchanges of ideas with them.

> I never met Freud or Jung, but I did meet with Adler in his home where he used to run Friday night seminars, and I had many conversations with him. . . . As for many of the others, I sought them out—people like Erich Fromm and Karen Horney and Ruth Benedict and Max Wertheimer and the like. . . . I think it's fair to say that I have had the best teachers, both formal and informal, of any person who ever lived, just because of the historical accident of being in New York City when the very cream of European intellect was migrating away. . . . There has been nothing like it since Athens. And I think I knew every one of them more or less well. . . . I cannot say that any one of them was any more important than any other. I was just learning from everybody and from anybody who had anything to teach . . . I learned from all of them. So I could not be said to be a Goldsteinian nor a Frommean nor an Adlerian or whatever. . . . I learned from all of them and refused to close any doors. (Maslow, 1968 in Goble, 1970)

Maslow's remarkable openness to such diverse creative thinkers enabled him to put different theories of motivation into a single conceptual framework in his development of the concept of the hierarchy of needs.

THE HIERARCHY OF NEEDS: FROM DEFICIENCY TO BEING MOTIVATION

Maslow conceptualized a **hierarchy of needs.** Needs lowest in the scale are prepotent to needs lying above them. Such prepotency indicates that higher needs cannot emerge until lower ones have first been satisfied. Thus, basic needs or what Maslow terms **deficiency needs** shape an individual's behavior *before* the higher needs, and continue to have a major impact until satisfied. The physiological needs, safety needs, love and belongingness needs, and esteem needs are included in the category of deficiency needs.

In this view, for example, people whose every biological need is satisfied are capable of turning to poetry, photography, art, or music to have some meaningful way of spending their energies and occupying their time.

Table 13.1   Maslow's Self-Actualization (SA) Pattern

Self-actualization characteristic	Description
Reality (1) and Problem-centered (4)	More efficient and accurate perception of reality; unusual ability to detect the fake, phony, and dishonest; focus on problems external to self; invests energies in "causes."
Acceptance of self and others (2); Spontaneity and simplicity (3)	Accepts own nature in stoic style; accepts what cannot be changed; is spontaneous and always natural; prefers simplicity to pretense and artificiality in self and others; conventional on surface to avoid hurting others.
Need privacy (5); Independence of culture and environment (6); Resists enculturation (15)	Relies on own judgment; trusts in self; resists pressure from others and social norms; able to "weather hard knocks" with calm; resists identification with cultural stereotypes; has autonomous values carefully considered.
Freshness of appreciation (7); Creativeness (14)	Maintains constancy for awe and wonder; ability to marvel at and enjoy the good things of life: food, sex, sports, travel; thousandth baby seen is as wonderful as first; creative in daily tasks of living; inventive and original in childlike way.
Unhostile sense of humor (13); Democratic (11); *Gemeinschaftsgefühl* (9); Intimate personal relations (10)	Does not enjoy jokes at expense of others; prefers a philosophic humor that pokes fun at the human condition; enjoys company of all people regardless of social or racial origins; Adler's *Gemeinschaftsgefühl* means "fellow-feeling" or social interest; strong interest in others' welfare; small number of intense and intimate friendships.
Peak (mystical) experiences (8); Discrimination between means and ends (12)	Has experienced mystic states characterized by feelings of limitless horizons opening, being more powerful and more helpless simultaneously, with loss of time sense; strong ethical-moral sense but not in conventional ways; discriminates between moral means and ends differently from average person; means can be ends.
Imperfections: Unexpected ruthlessness; occasional absentmindedness; overkindliness; non-neurotic guilt and anxiety	"There are no perfect people"; SA individuals can display surgical coldness when called for in situations of betrayal; overkindliness gets them into trouble by letting others impose on them; uninterested in social "chatting" or party-going; anxiety and guilt present, but from realistic not neurotic sources; sometimes philosophical concerns cause a loss of sense of humor.

Based on Maslow, 1970, pp. 153–176.

> It is quite true that man lives by bread alone when there is no bread. *But what happens to man's desires when there is bread and when his belly is chronically filled?* (Maslow, 1943, in 1973, p. 157; cf. 1970, p. 38; italics added)

The answer, of course, is that higher needs emerge to shape people's strivings. The cycle continues indefinitely, for once needs for Beauty, Truth, Justice, and so on are fulfilled, even "higher" needs emerge. The highest of the needs in the hierarchy are the **B-values (Being-values),** or **metaneeds** as Maslow termed them. The metaneeds will be considered shortly, but it is important to note that the 15 metaneeds are *not* hierarchically arranged. Having reached the self-actualization step in the hierarchy, the individual experiences needs for the B-values like Beauty, Truth, and Justice more or less simultaneously, though not necessarily with equal intensity. The basic hierarchy may be schematized as in Figure 13.2 (based on Maslow, 1970, pp. 35–46).

When a lower-order need predominates—for example, hunger in the physiological step—then all behavior is directed to the fulfillment of that need. If its satisfaction is a chronic problem, then the next highest need in the hierarchy will fail to develop full potency.

When all four levels in the hierarchy, the basic needs, are satisfied, the highest needs for self-actualization emerge. Collateral with self-actualization needs are the uniquely human desires to know, to understand the world, and to enjoy its beauty. Although Maslow was not particularly clear on the matter, he seems in the final revision of his definitive work (1970) to have intended the aesthetic and knowledge needs to be grouped with self-actualization as equal potency motives.

For Maslow, **satisfaction striving,** rather than deficiency motivation, is the motor of personality. Maslow construes the organism not as pushed by drives, but as pulled by the need to be fulfilled.

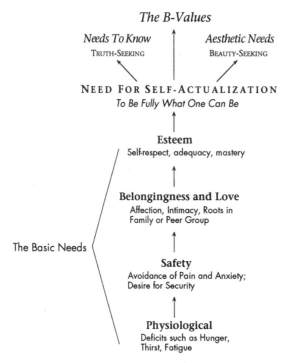

Figure 13.2 Maslow's hierarchy of needs.

Hierarchy of Needs: Uses

Maslow's concept of the hierarchy of needs has had great value for a variety of purposes. Let us take the case of a college student who might be having some trouble with studying and getting good grades. A self-analysis of need satisfaction might quickly reveal that the student was not getting his or her needs for belongingness met, so the self-esteem related goal of achievement seemed irrelevant. In other words, getting good grades was not motivating for this lonely student. The answer would be not simply to study more but to take some steps to meet his or her social needs. Likewise, a manufacturing company might be having a problem with employee morale in spite of high wages. Institutional research might reveal that workers do not feel either a sense of pride or self-esteem in their work. Nor is there much of a sense of belongingness. Merely increasing the workers' pay will not solve these problems or meet these needs. Instead, efforts to enhance the sense of belongingness and to bolster a meaningful sense of achievement seem like a good idea.

Hierarchy of Needs: Flaws with the Idea

The idea of the hierarchy of needs has some fundamental flaws. First, it is not true that people must have "lower-level" needs met before going on to the higher ones. For example, the famous Russian novelist, Alexander Solzhenitsyn, was writing excellent novels while being imprisoned in a Siberian camp. He was given little food, spare clothing and flimsy shelter, exposed to the harsh elements, and subjected to physical intimidation. He was often isolated from other prisoners. In spite of this, he worked on producing excellent works of politically important literature. Such a vivid example is far from unique, and most of us have known people and can think of other examples of those who have accomplished a great deal while some of their basic needs remained unmet.

Another illogical aspect of Maslow's hierarchy-of-needs theory is the very real question of what constitutes a need. A person may work to maintain a six-bathroom mansion, whereas another person lives in a studio apartment. How much of our so-called "need" for food, shelter, companionship and the like is not a need but a preference or wish. A final aspect worth questioning is whether the hierarchy of needs is as Maslow proposes them. For example, whether belongingness or love is lower in any sense than self-esteem is questionable. A person might consider meeting his belongingness needs as a means to the ends of self-esteem and self-actualization, but one would question how his loved ones might respond to such a notion. Many people see intimacy as a part of life more valuable than achievement leading to self-esteem. As Erik Erikson (Chapter 8) indicated, intimacy often *follows* establishment of a satisfactory identity. Again, we find what appears to be an expression of Maslow's value system rather than an empirical finding.

BEYOND SELF-ACTUALIZATION: THE B-VALUES

Self-actualized people develop B-values and metaneeds. They have already successfully progressed through the hierarchy of basic needs. They now embark on the growth processes of living to *enhance their being, to expand their knowledge of self and others, and to operationalize their self-actualized personalities* in any activity that they undertake.

In this sense, Maslow proposed the further set of Being-needs that emerge at the point of self-actualization in the basic hierarchy. To these B-values, Maslow assigned the name *metamotives.* "Self-actualizing people are not primarily motivated by basic needs; they are primarily metamotivated, by metaneeds or B-values" (1971, p. 311).

With the B-values, Maslow proposed that individuals may satisfy all their basic needs through to the esteem levels in the hierarchy and yet not be self-actualized. To be fully self-actualized, one must be committed to long-reaching goals: the B-values. Thus, Maslow revised his definition of the self-actualizing personality:

> . . . it may turn out to be useful to add to the definition of the self-actualizing person, not only [a] that he be sufficiently free of illness, [b] that he be sufficiently gratified in his basic needs, and [c] that he be positively using his capacities, but also [d] that he be motivated by some values which he strives for or gropes for and to which he is loyal. (1971, p. 301)

Originally, Maslow proposed a list of 14 B-values (1962, p. 78), only later to add one more (1971, pp. 318–319). The 15 B-values are listed in Table 13.2 along with the "deficiency diseases" or metapathologies that result when one of the B-values is unsatisfied.

The B-values in Table 13.2 overlap to some degree. In Maslow's opinion, the overlap is an essential characteristic of Being-values:

> It is my (uncertain) impression that any B-value is fully and adequately defined by the total of the other B-values. That is, truth, to be fully and completely defined, must be beautiful, good, perfect, just, simple, orderly, lawful, alive, comprehensive, unitary, dichotomy-transcending, effortless, and amusing. . . . It is as if all the B-values have some kind of unity, with each single value being something like a facet of this whole. (Maslow, 1971, p. 324)

Table 13.2 B-Values and Metapathologies

B-Value or metaneed	Pathogenic deprivation	Specific metapathologies (motivation disease)
1. Truth	Dishonesty	Disbelief; mistrust; cynicism
2. Goodness	Evil	Utter selfishness; hatred, reliance only on self; disgust, nihilism
3. Beauty	Ugliness	Vulgarity; loss of taste; tension; fatigue
4. Unity-Wholeness	Chaos, atomism	Disintegration; arbitrariness
4A. Dichotomy-Transcendence	Black/White dichotomies; forced choices	Either/or thinking; seeing everything as dualistic; a simplistic view of life
5. Aliveness; process	Deadness; mechanizing of life	Robotizing; feeling totally determined; loss of zest in life
6. Uniqueness	Sameness; uniformity	Loss of feeling of individuality or being needed
7. Perfection	Imperfection; sloppiness	Discouragement (?); hopelessness
7A. Necessity	Accident; occasionalism; inconsistency	Loss of safety; unpredictability
8. Completion; finality	Incompleteness	Cessation of striving; no use trying
9. Justice	Injustice	Insecurity; anger; cynicism; mistrust
9A. Order	Lawlessness, chaos	Insecurity; wariness; loss of safety
10. Simplicity	Confusing complexity	Overcomplexity; confusion; loss of orientation
11. Richness; totality	Poverty	Depression; uneasiness; loss of interest
12. Effortlessness	Effortfulness	Fatigue; strain; clumsiness
13. Playfulness	Humorlessness	Grimness; depression; paranoid humorlessness
14. Self-sufficiency	Accident; occasionalism	Dependence upon the perceiver and others
15. Meaningfulness	Meaninglessness	Despair; senselessness of life

Condensed from Maslow, 1971, pp. 318–319.

PEAK EXPERIENCES
AS MOMENTARILY INTENSE B-VALUE STATES

In 1902, William James published his Gifford Lectures under the title *The Varieties of Religious Experience.* In a series of 20 lectures, James surveyed from a variety of poetic, theological, and biographical writings the diversity of ways in which individuals reported experiencing God. One particular subclass of such experiences called the "mystical state" occupied James at some length. From his researches, James was able to distinguish four characteristics of the mystical experience that separated it from states of normal consciousness. Maslow accepted James's descriptive criteria as adequate characterization of **peak experiences** undergone by self-actualizing people (see Maslow, 1964; 1970, p. 164). James listed the following characteristics of the mystical experience (1902, pp. 371–373):

1. **Ineffability:** "The subject of [a mystical experience] immediately says that it *defies expression,* that no adequate report of its content can be given in words. It follows from this that its quality must be directly experienced; it cannot be imparted or transferred to others."

2. **Noetic quality:** The word "noetic" is based on a Greek root meaning "mind" or "intellect." James employed the term to indicate the essentially intellectual, "truth-finding" quality of a mystic experience.

3. **Transiency:** "Mystical states cannot be sustained for long. Except in rare instances, half an hour, or at most an hour or two, seems to be the limit beyond which they fade into the light of common day."

4. **Passivity:** ". . . the mystic feels as if his own will were in abeyance, and indeed sometimes as if he were grasped and held by a superior power."

Maslow initially thought that only self-actualizing people underwent these peak experiences with any appreciable regularity (1964, p. 22). But as he became more skilled in interviewing subjects and in phrasing questions to elicit the information, Maslow discovered that most people have had some peak experiences.

When peak experiences are sought, actively induced, or otherwise treated as a commodity to be acquired, the value of the experience is lost. Maslow cautioned that drugs, meditation rituals, and shortcuts of all kinds cheapen the peak experience (1971, p. 345). Maslow suggested that people may approach even the deepest peak experiences with apathy or superficiality, a tendency to desanctify or *desacralize* life.

The Psychological Defense of Desacralizing

Desacralizing, a term adopted from the philosopher, Mircea Eliade (1961; see also 1958), was used by Maslow to indicate the process of denying the awesome, marvelous, beautiful, and sublime aspects of people and the universe. In effect, the desacralizer has learned to "reduce the person to the concrete object and to refuse to see what he might be or to refuse to see him in his symbolic values or to refuse to see him or her eternally" (Maslow, 1971, p. 49). A 1970 popular song written by Joni Mitchell, "Big Yellow Taxi," included the sentence, "They paved paradise and put up a parking lot." This song mocked our society's desacralizing attitudes and materialistic values.

Along with the concept of desacralizing, Maslow introduced the notion of the **Jonah complex.** In this syndrome, a person, like the prophet Jonah in the Bible, avoids the deeper pursuits of which he or she is capable. It is a pattern of running away from one's calling. Such a person prefers to stay on the surface of life, and he or she pays a huge price in the sense of subsequent meaninglessness, unfulfillment, and guilt.

Maslow has suggested that one characteristic of the self-actualizing personality is the ability to *resacralize* people and things, to bring the sense of the sacred back into experience. The self-actualizing person has learned to be awe-inspired, to marvel at the beauty, mystery and infinite complexity of life, to include an appreciation of the cosmic and the spiritual as well as the material.

Extending his criticism of desacralization to the domain of the sciences, Maslow found the social sciences in particular to be wanting in their treatment of persons:

> Briefly put, it appears to me that science and everything scientific can be and often is used as a tool in the service of a distorted, narrowed, humorless, de-eroticized, de-emotionalized, desacralized, and de-sanctified *Weltanschauung* [philosophy of life]. This desacralization can be used as a defense against being flooded by emotion, especially the emotions of humility, reverence, mystery, wonder, and awe. (1966, p. 139)

Particularly for those who work in the fields of psychology, sociology, and anthropology, classical scientific method may serve the function of a defense mechanism. Maslow thought that, by abstracting, objectifying, and generally dehumanizing their human subjects, social scientists unknowingly seek to separate themselves from the all-too-human failings, emotions, anxieties, and confusion they investigate in others (Maslow, 1966, p. 33).

> More than any other kind of knowledge we fear knowledge of ourselves, knowledge that might transform our self-esteem and our self-image. . . . While human beings love knowledge and seek it, they are curious they also fear it. The closer to the personal it is, the more they fear it. So human knowledge is apt to be a kind of dialectic between this love and this fear. Thus knowledge includes the defenses against itself, the repressions, the sugar-coatings, the inattentions, and the forgettings. (Maslow, 1966, p. 16)

Maslow suggested that the acquisition of knowledge about the experience of others is fraught with anxiety and can amount to a "cognitive pathology." For example, when the need to know is based on a compulsive seeking after certainty rather than on enjoyment of discovery, it is pathological. Or, when individuals compulsively deny their doubts, ignorance, and mistakes from a fear of confessing human fallibility, their scientific skills and knowledge are serving pathological ends. Or, when individuals feel that knowledge makes them "tough-minded," "hard-nosed," and "scientifically rigorous," they may defensively close themselves off to the tender, romantic, poetic, and spiritual aspects of the people they study.

Maslow summarized his view of the desacralizing tendency by indicating the directions that a new and more humanistic scientific enterprise should pursue:

> If humanistic science may be said to have any goals beyond sheer fascination with the human mystery and enjoyment of it, these would be to release the person from external controls and to make him less predictable to the observer (to make him freer, more creative, more inner-determined) even though perhaps more predictable to himself. (1966, p. 40)

Hence, for Maslow, the sciences, and psychology in particular, are value-laden enterprises in which the psychological makeup and needs of the investigator become mingled with the virtue of the investigated.

The Effects of Peak Experiences

The B-values—Truth, Beauty, Goodness, Unity, and so on—that assume such significance for the self-actualized person are intensified in states of peak experience. The individual who has undergone such moments comes away from them feeling that the world "looks different." A peak experience may change the course of a person's life. Maslow isolated 16 aftereffects of the peak experience (Based on Maslow, 1962, pp. 97–107). The person who has undergone a peak experience feels

1. more integrated, whole, and unified;
2. more at one with the world;
3. as if he or she were at the peak of his or her powers, more fully her or himself;
4. graceful, without strain, effortless;
5. creative, active, responsible, self-controlled;
6. free of inhibitions, blocks, doubts, self-criticisms;
7. spontaneous, expressive, innocent;
8. creative, self-confident, flexible;
9. unique, individualistic;
10. free of past and future limits;
11. free of the world, free to be;
12. undriven, unmotivated, nonwishing, beyond needs;
13. rhapsodic, poetic;
14. consumed, finished, closed, complete, subjectively final;
15. playful, good-humored, childlike;
16. lucky, fortunate, grateful.

In short, the peak experience is evidence that

> Man has a higher and transcendent nature, and this is part of his essence, i.e., his biological nature as a member of a species which has evolved. (Maslow, 1971, p. 349)

HUMANISTIC PSYCHOLOGY: THE THIRD FORCE

Both Maslow and the second theorist we consider in this chapter, Carl Rogers, considered themselves to be *humanistic psychologists*. Humanistic psychology emphasizes human capacity for goodness, creativity, and freedom. Unlike the strictly deterministic and somewhat mechanistic views of humans to be found in Freud's psychoanalysis and in contemporary behaviorism, **humanistic psychology** construes the human being as rational, purposeful and autonomous, capable of creativity and able to experience deep insight into reality. Maslow, like Rogers (and Allport) emphasized wholeness; in particular, Maslow—much more than Rogers—emphasized the spiritual or transcendent aspects of the person:

> If I had to condense the thesis of this book into a single sentence, I would have said that *in addition* to what the psychologists of the time had to say about human nature, man also had a higher nature and that this was instinctoid, i.e., part of his essence. And if I could have had a second sentence, I would have stressed the profoundly holistic nature of human nature in contradiction to the analytic atomistic Newtonian approach of the behaviorisms and of Freudian psychoanalysis. (1970, p. ix; italics in original)

The work of Maslow and Rogers, and many others, has been called the **third force** of psychology to emphasize its stature as a viable viewpoint that is distinctive from both psychoanalysis and behaviorism. Toward the end of his life, Maslow emphasized that he had not intended to be either pro-Freudian or anti-Freudian, pro-behaviorist or anti-behaviorist:

> In my opinion all such loyalty-positions are silly. Our job is to integrate these various truths into the whole truth, which should be our only loyalty. (1971, p. 4)

One piece of evidence of his futuristic thinking was his vision of a psychological utopia in which healthy, self-actualized people would live and work in harmony. Called *Eupsychia,* this utopia would represent an attempt to blend what is godlike in our nature to what is most fully human, to actualize what Maslow saw as our inherently "good being." For Maslow, Eupsychia would attempt to provide the environment in which humans could become all that they could be (1970, p. 277).

TOWARD A TRANSPERSONAL VIEWPOINT

Maslow is considered one of the founders of the field of **transpersonal psychology,** an area that emphasizes the spiritual dimension of human experience (Vaugan & Walsh, 2000). He labeled transpersonal psychology as the "fourth force" of psychology. Psychodynamic approaches are generally considered the "first force," behaviorism the "second force," and humanistic psychology the "third force." This emphasis grew out of Maslow's interest in altered states of consciousness and self-actualization (Hoffman, 1988). One branch of transpersonal psychology focuses on research with altered states and another branch focuses on working out models of consciousness and personality associated with the highest levels of human functioning. In addition, some aspects of transpersonal psychology are involved with the normative processes of psychospiritual development. The connection of these efforts with Maslow's earlier work is evident.

Carl Rogers   **Born: January, 1902**   **Oak Park, Illinois**
Died: February, 1987   **La Jolla, California**

A HARBINGER OF THINGS TO COME

In 1961, Carl Rogers recounted an event that occurred while he was a student at Union Theological Seminary. At the time, Rogers was 22 years old, and he was in the first year of Divinity School. He and a number of other students formed a group to explore their own ideas. Rogers explained,

> A group of us felt that ideas were being fed to us, whereas we wished primarily to explore our own questions and doubts and find out where they led. We petitioned the administration that we be allowed to set up a seminar for credit, a seminar with no instructor, where the curriculum would be composed of our own questions. . . . The only restriction was that in the interests of the institution a young instructor was to sit in on the seminar, but would take no part in it unless we wished him to be active. (1961, p. 8)

Because of the discussions and soul-searching that occurred during this group, most of the members, including Rogers, decided to abandon the vocation of the ministry:

> The majority of the members of that group, in thinking their way through the questions they had raised, thought themselves right out of religious work. I was one. (1961, p. 8)

Rogers himself went on to study psychology at Teachers College, Columbia University, which was in the immediate neighborhood of the theological seminary.

His account indicates the importance of personal freedom in his choice of career:

I felt that questions as to the meaning of life, and the possibility of the constructive improvement of life for individuals, would probably always interest me, but I could not work in a field where I would be required to believe in some specified religious doctrine. My beliefs had already changed tremendously, and might continue to change. It seemed to me it would be a horrible thing to have to profess a set of beliefs, in order to remain in one's profession. (1961, p. 8)

This incident reveals certain themes and emphases in Rogers' life that were established even before his graduate training in psychology had begun. As in client-centered therapy, which Rogers would develop over a decade later, the authority figure was seen as someone whose role is to help and who does not act in a directive manner. Significant change in their life paths arose as a result of the free exploration and discussion (Sollod, 1978). In this incident Rogers already demonstrated that he valued personal freedom and in the possibility of exploring options and making choices. He distrusted authority, though the for-credit seminar he participated in was not a total repudiation of authority. Rather, authority was used to legitimize free discussion and choice.

In the ensuing years, Rogers would gradually realize that his approach to issues in his own life might also be helpful to others within a professional framework.

PSYCHOTHERAPIST AS SELF-ACTUALIZATION FACILITATOR

Unlike Maslow, Rogers began his study of human nature with troubled personalities. As a clinical psychologist, Rogers explored the potential for change in the therapeutic relationship. Rogers found that what is considered as psychopathology results when persons are prevented or do not have the chance to become who they truly are.

Rogers' personality theory emerged in part from his careful and exacting psychotherapeutic studies. He was among the first therapist-researchers to record psychotherapeutic sessions. Along with his willingness to commit the process of therapy to scientific scrutiny, Rogers pioneered a pervasive change in the way the clinical relationship could be used to induce personality change and in the ways personality data could be derived from the relationship.

Consider, on page 468, fragments of two recorded counseling interviews with college students. They are printed side by side to facilitate direct comparisons. The left-hand transcript is of a client and a therapist who view the therapeutic situation as structured, problem-centered, and under the direct control of the therapist. The right-hand column contains the transcript of a similar client-therapist interview in a situation with a counselor who recognizes that therapeutic processes are very much person-centered.

Focus on the Client's Feelings

There are significant and easily discernible differences between the two counseling interviews. The essence of the directive counselor's effort is information gathering and dispensing. The flow of communication between counselor and client tends to be one way: from counselor to client. Responsibility for the direction and outcome of the relationship implicitly lies with the authoritarian counselor. Restricted to the role of question answerer, the client is led through a series of diagnostic queries and away from any confrontation with his or her feelings, confusions, and anxieties. To the degree that client feelings are mentioned at all, they are *talked about* rather than genuinely experienced or forthrightly made the focus of concern. The counselor goes so far as to summarize by assuming the "wise knower" role: "It seems to me that your problem is you want to learn more about yourself." It is a rational, perhaps even correct statement. But it is the counselor's statement, one not arrived at or formulated by the client.

The second counseling transcript has a different emotional flavor. Here, the client is encouraged to express a wealth of feelings. In all replies, the counselor responds to the emotional content of the client's statements, not to the cognitive aspects or the information provided. The nondirective counselor tried to respond to the troubled *person* by helping him or her to clarify his or her feelings: "It's a situation you've really got to face" or, "It'll be fairly hard for you to tell them." When the counselor is successful in detecting the emotional meaning of a client remark, rephrasing the client's statements allow the client to examine his or her feelings openly. When the counselor is unsuccessful at mirroring the emotional tone of the client's statements, the client sometimes feels that the counselor "does not understand" or is "putting words into my mouth." But even when mistaken, the counselor's attitude communicates to the client a genuine concern about the experience of the client.

Directive Counseling Transcript	**Nondirective Counseling Transcript**
COUNSELOR: I noticed that you stated you enrolled in Psychology 411 [study habits course] because you didn't know how to study well enough uh and then I checked over the problem list, and I saw that you went rather heavy on you worried about low grades and poor memory and so on. How well did you do in high school?	STUDENT: I haven't written to my parents about this at all. In the past they haven't been of any help to me in this respect, and if I can keep it away from them as much as possible, I'll do so. But there's a slight matter of grades to explain, and they're not good, and I don't know how I'm going to explain without telling them about this. Would you advise me to tell them about it?
STUDENT: Well, I was just an average student.	COUNSELOR: Suppose you tell me a little more about what you had thought about it.
COUNSELOR: And what major did you have there?	STUDENT: Well, I think I'm compelled to, because
STUDENT: Ah, you mean	COUNSELOR: It's a situation you've really got to face.
COUNSELOR: In high school, you took college preparatory or commercial?	STUDENT: Yes, there's no use getting around it, even if they can't take it the way they should, because I've already flunked my gym course, I just haven't come. . . .
STUDENT: It was an academic course. I took languages and English and history.	COUNSELOR: It will be fairly hard for you to tell them.
COUNSELOR: What course did you like the best? [Student presumably answers; later in session counselor summarizes:]	STUDENT: Yes. Oh, I don't know if they're going to sort of condemn me. I think so, because that's what they've done in the past. . . .
COUNSELOR: It seems to me that your problem is that you want to learn more about yourself. We'll be getting all these tests back, and there are those [study] projects, and the way we do, I see you each week at this time and you'll begin to get a little better picture and then I'll help you check it and I'll tell you if it's right (Laugh)	COUNSELOR: You feel that they'll be unsympathetic and they'll condemn you for your failures.
STUDENT: Mm-hm.	STUDENT: Well, I'm pretty sure my father will. My mother might not. He hasn't been he doesn't experience these things; he just doesn't know what it's like. . . .
COUNSELOR: So we can work it out. I would suggest I would more or less work this project out because you say you are having difficulties concentrating. . . .	COUNSELOR: You feel that he could never understand you?
(From Rogers, 1942, pp. 116–117)	(From Rogers, 1942, pp. 135–136)

These differences between these two counseling interviews are only a small sample of the insights about the counseling relationship systematized by Rogers. His development of a personality theory is so inextricably interwoven with his clinical therapeutic work that some consideration must be given to the slow development of what Rogers came eventually to call *client-centered counseling and theory* as a replacement for the original "nondirective" label.

DEVELOPMENT OF THE NONDIRECTIVE VIEWPOINT

In 1974, as part of his address to the American Psychological Association on the occasion of receiving its Distinguished Professional Contribution Award, Rogers traced his impact on psychology. In particular, he formulated from his perspective of nearly half a century of therapeutic work the kernel of the central hypothesis that had initiated and guided his theoretical development:

> . . . the gradually formed and tested hypothesis [was] that the individual has within himself vast resources for self-understanding, for altering his self-concept, his attitudes, and his self-directed behavior and that these resources can be tapped if only a definable climate of facilitative psychological attitudes can be provided. (1974a, p. 116)

The similarity to Maslow's conception of human nature is obvious. Both theorists regard humans as inherently good, as self-directed, and as striving toward increased autonomy. Rogers' theory, then, can be understood as the attempt to discover the conditions that foster the individual's utilization of *his or her own* powers for health and understanding.

Early Pragmatism: "If It Works, Do It"

Rogers began his career as a clinical psychologist trained in empiricism. He was granted an internship at the newly founded Institute for Child Guidance while in doctoral training, and in the atmosphere of this clinic Rogers was exposed to a multiplicity of theoretical viewpoints. Members of the staff at the guidance clinic were largely psychodynamic in their orientation, and a contrast to the statistical, objective atmosphere of graduate school. Rogers later recalled ". . . I was functioning in two completely different worlds, 'and never the twain shall meet'" (1961, p. 9; cf. 1974c, p. 7).

The conflict of intellectual traditions was an important learning experience for Rogers, opening him to the possibility that experts differ drastically in their interpretations. Before completion of his doctorate, Rogers obtained a position in the Child Study Department of the Society for the Prevention of Cruelty to Children in Rochester, New York (1961, p. 9). For the next 12 years, Rogers was engaged in the application of psychological services to delinquent and underprivileged children. Many of the staff at the Rochester facility were trained in the Philadelphia School of Social Work and operated from the neopsychoanalytic viewpoint developed by Otto Rank. Rank focused on the individual exploring and expressing his or her own inner experiences:

> I conceive of human help for the individual not as a planned method of psycho-therapeutic techniques with respect to a control of his stimuli and responses but as *his experiencing of the irrational forces within himself* which he has not heretofore dared to express spontaneously. (1941, p. 47; italics added)

Rogers later commented that his own early emphasis on responding to the feelings of the client sprang from the influence of Rank and his followers at the Rochester facility (Rogers,

1966, in Hart & Tomlinson, 1970, p. 515). Most important of all, however, was the lesson to be learned from his colleagues' attitude toward therapeutic technique: "There was only one criterion in regard to any method of dealing with these children and their parents, and that was, 'Does it work?'" (1961, p. 10).

This emphasis on effectiveness was reinforced for Rogers when his careful psychodynamic prodding and questioning to uncover the sexual conflicts of a young arsonist did not prevent the boy from repeating his illegal behaviors. On probation after therapy with Rogers, the boy continued to set fires (1961, p. 10).

Insight into the Dignity of the Individual Person: A "Failure"

Another influence that shaped Rogers' slowly developing theoretical formulations occurred during an interview with a client's mother. The boy was something of a "hellion," and Rogers could clearly see that the mother's early rejection of the boy was responsible. Despite repeated attempts at directing her flow of conversation toward the attainment of this insight, he could not accomplish a successful breakthrough. His report of the experience is particularly instructive:

> Finally I gave up. I told her that it seemed we had both tried, but we had failed. . . . She agreed. So we concluded the interview, shook hands, and she walked to the door of the office. Then she turned and asked, "Do you ever take adults for counseling here?" When I replied in the affirmative, she said, "Well then, I would like some help." She came to the chair she had left, and began to pour out her despair about her marriage, her troubled relationship with her husband, her sense of failure and confusion, all very different from the sterile "case history" she had given before. Real therapy began then. . . . (Rogers, 1961, p. 11)

From this experience Rogers learned an important lesson about the nature of the ideal psychotherapeutic experience and about the dignity of the person:

> ". . . it is the *client* who knows what hurts, what directions to go, what problems are crucial, what experiences have been deeply buried" (1961, pp. 11–12)

Thus Rogers slowly came to the viewpoint that authoritative, directive, and diagnostically oriented psychological service was far less important than allowing the client to speak freely, feel freely, and think freely.

PERSONAL SOURCES OF ROGERS' EMPHASIS ON FREEDOM AND SELF-WORTH

Rogers' theory of personality, like other humanistic approaches, such as those of Maslow or Allport (Chapter 11), stresses the dignity and worth of the individual. The accent is on the inherent capacity of the person to direct his or her own life when the interpersonal environment provides sufficient freedom from both subtle and overt coercion. In Rogers' view, the primary, indeed essential, ingredient of the well-lived life is, simply, *freedom* to be, to choose, and to act.

The core of Rogers' approach to personality is the belief that every individual requires freedom from coercion—from, as Karen Horney (Chapter 10) had written, internalized "shoulds" and "oughts." His own experience growing up in a strict family appears to be one source of his emphasis on personal freedom.

Rogers' Growing-Up Years: Faith and Rebellion

Carl Rogers was born in 1902 in a Chicago suburb as the fourth of six children of parents he described as "highly practical, 'down to earth' individuals" (Rogers, 1967b, p. 344). His father was an engineer and his mother had finished two years of college. Despite their level of educational achievement, Rogers describes his parents as being "rather anti-intellectual, with some of the contempt of the practical person toward the long-haired egghead" (1967b, p. 344). Both parents were hard workers, convinced that there was no virtue higher than hard work and no problem that could not be solved by even harder work.

Rogers' mother, who wore her religion on her sleeve, shaped the family atmosphere. Among her frequently uttered biblical expressions according to Rogers, were "Come out from among them and be ye separate"; and, "All our righteousness is as filthy rags in thy sight, oh Lord."

> The first [saying] expressed her conviction of superiority, that we were of the "elect" and should not mingle with those who were not so favored; the second her conviction of inferiority, that at our best we were unspeakably sinful. (Rogers, 1967b, p. 344)

The main consequence of such convictions was a pervading sense in the Rogers family children that they were specially set apart from the children of other families, and that most typical enjoyments were faintly "sinful." For example, Rogers wrote, "I remember my slight feeling of wickedness when I had my first bottle of 'pop' " (1961, p. 5).

Rogers remembers both parents as extremely loving but subtly controlling:

> I do not remember ever being given a direct command on an important subject, yet such was the unity of our family that it was understood by all that we did not dance, play cards, attend movies, smoke, drink, or show any sexual interest. (1967b, p. 344)

One major result of this stringent upbringing was that Rogers had little social life. Rogers reports that he never had a "real" date until his junior year in high school, when he nervously asked a girl he had admired "from afar" to a school dinner-dance.

Rogers was a very good student. He took an active interest in doing research at a very young age. He became a "student of scientific agriculture" at the age of 14. His early research provided an early grounding in empirical scientific methodology. He learned,

> . . . how experiments were conducted, how control groups were matched with experimental groups, how conditions were held constant by randomizing procedures . . . how difficult it is to test a hypothesis. (1961, p. 6)

During Christmas vacation of his college sophomore year, Rogers pursued his religious interests by attending a conference of student volunteers for evangelical work.

> I decided at this conference that I should change my life goal and go into Christian work. . . . Having made this decision, agriculture no longer seemed to be a very suitable field. I felt that I should shift to some subject which would prepare me for the ministry. . . . (1967b, p. 350)

In his junior year of college, Rogers was selected as one of ten students to travel to what was then called Peking, China, as a representative of the World Student Christian Federation. The other members of the group were mostly young intellectuals with far more liberal backgrounds than Rogers. The long voyage provided Rogers with much needed social interaction and intellectual exchange. Decades later, Rogers speculated that there might be an Eastern aspect to his thinking that traced back to this early trip:

> In more recent years, I have wondered about the possibility of the effect of my trip to China. Prior to that trip and on the ship going over, we held many discussions about China and its

history and undoubtedly about its philosophy. I don't remember any of those. It is quite possible, however, that some of the ideas were taken in but did not seem real to me until I had experienced them myself. . . . So the Oriental influence on my thinking may go back to 1922. (Rogers, 1978)

The key element in the rift with his family centered on a fundamental theological tenet that separated more liberal from more conservative Christians. One evening, aboard ship, a traveling companion, Dr. Henry Sharman, a student of the sayings of Jesus, made some provocative remarks. Rogers later indicated that this event led him to doubt the divinity of Jesus. Rogers left behind his family's conservative religious views by coming to the conclusion that Jesus was a man. Rogers had freed himself from parental authority, and he attempted to minimize his experience of conflict at the time by asserting that the rift was accomplished with minimal pain.

Rogers kept a journal of his personal reactions to his new acquaintances and their ideas. He sent a copy to a girl he had been seeing and who was to become his fiancée upon his return. But he also, without realizing the upsetting impact his new ideas would have on his religiously conforming family, sent a copy home to his family:

> Since we did not have the benefit of airmail it took two months for a reply to arrive. Thus I kept pouring out on paper all my new feelings and ideas and thoughts with no notion of the consternation that this was causing in my family. By the time their reactions caught up with me, the rift in outlook was fully established. Thus, with a minimum of pain I broke the intellectual and religious ties with my home. (Rogers, 1967b, p. 351)

In 1924, Rogers set out to study for the ministry at Union Theological Seminary in New York. Union Theological Seminary had then, as it does now, a reputation for liberality, the kind of radical liberalism of which Rogers' father disapproved.

> Knowing my plan to go to Union, my father had made one offer that was very close to a bribe. I suspect he was not proud of himself afterward for this. Certainly I rejected it indignantly. He told me that he would pay all the expenses for both of us [Rogers and his wife] if I would go to Princeton Seminary, which was at that point a center of fundamentalist thinking. (Rogers, 1967b, p. 353)

During this period a child was born to Rogers and his wife, and they attempted to raise him by "the book of Watsonian behaviorism [see Chapter 14], strict scheduling and the like" (1967b, p. 356). Rogers' recent experience with freedom had not yet worked its way down to the second generation.

As we have seen, Rogers stayed only briefly at Union. He thought his way out and became a psychologist instead.

The Importance of the Intellectual Climate

In addition to personal and professional experiences, ideas were very important to Carl Rogers. He was affected by philosophical and ideological currents that emphasized personal responsibility and choice and evidenced a deep trust in the ability of individuals and free societies to solve their own problems. Such ideas were congruent with Rogers' own personal proclivities.

Rogers appears to have been influenced by the ideas of the American philosopher John Dewey, and the leader of the progressive education movement, William Kilpatrick. Dewey's functionalism and Kilpatrick's progressive education movement emphasized the importance of an individual's own experience in coming to grips with and solving problems in his or her own life. The ideal in progressive education was to work in accordance with a child's readiness rather than to impose tasks that did not interest him or her. This theme of working in accordance with a person's readiness was to be central in Rogers' subsequent development of therapeutic approaches (Sollod, 1978).

But Rogers did not apply these ideas in his early professional work. After graduate school at Columbia, Rogers worked at the Child Study Department of the Society for the Prevention of Cruelty to Children in Rochester, New York. He followed the conventional directive techniques he had been taught in his work with delinquent and underprivileged youngsters. He was unhappy with the results and with his approach and experienced, "disillusionment with authority, with materials, with myself (1951, p. 10). He continued, "There were mistakes in authoritative teachings and that there was still new knowledge to discover." At this point he began to rediscover the ideas of John Dewey and William H. Kilpatrick and to search for kindred spirits in the psychotherapeutic world.

It was also at this point he discovered the work of Jesse Taft, a social worker in Philadelphia who had developed what she termed a "controlled relationship" method. Rogers (1942) drew on her ideas liberally in his first book. Taft (1951) emphasized that there should be a lack of control or coercion in psychotherapy and that the patient should be allowed to express whatever thoughts or feelings he or she wished. Taft emphasized the importance of the patient focusing on the feelings he or she was experiencing at any given time. The therapist should do nothing more than facilitate such exploration.

A leading educator and psychologist, Goodwin Watson (1940), presented ideas at a 1940 conference, "Areas of Agreement in Psychotherapy," that Rogers took part in. Watson emphasized the expression of feelings in psychotherapy as well as the importance of rapport between the therapist and patient. He stressed the value of "a relationship in which the therapist tries not to let his own values influence the patient" (1940, p. 708). He said, "We do not believe that mere catharsis of feelings is therapeutic. We distrust advice and exhortation" (1940, p. 709). The influence of these ideas is apparent in Rogers' subsequent development of nondirective psychotherapy (Sollod, 1978).

In summary, some central themes of Rogers' formulation of a theory of personality stressing freedom to be self-actualized, and his theory of psychotherapy stressing the creation of an atmosphere of permissiveness and warmth, have deep and broad roots. Rogers' personal and professional experiences and his intellectual background were the foundations for the development of his emphasis on personal freedom and his creative contributions in personality theory and in the field of psychotherapy. His personal outlook and professional contributions are connected.

EARLY NONDIRECTIVE VIEW: TOO MUCH FREEDOM

In 1940 Rogers accepted a position with The Ohio State University to teach graduate students about counseling. As he taught, he was forced to focus his views more sharply, in the process forming a perspective of psychotherapy that was unique. Up to this point, Rogers thought that he was simply writing and teaching about clinical techniques that all clinicians were using (1959, p. 187). But when invited to deliver a lecture at the University of Minnesota chapter of the *Psi Chi* Society entitled "Newer Concepts in Psychotherapy," Rogers soon discovered from the furor and controversy the lecture aroused that he was indeed saying something new (1974c, p. 8).

It was from this Minnesota lecture that Rogers derived the second chapter of his book on **nondirective therapy.** In *Counseling and Psychotherapy* (1942), Rogers emphasized four important principles of the "new" psychotherapy:

1. The newer therapy "relies much more heavily on the individual drive toward growth, health, and adjustment. Therapy is not a matter of doing something *to* the individual, or of inducing him to do something about himself. It is instead a matter of freeing him for normal growth and development . . ." (1942, p. 29).

2. ". . . this newer therapy places greater stress upon the emotional elements, the feeling aspects of the situation, than upon the intellectual aspects" (1942, p. 29).

3. ". . . this newer therapy places greater stress upon the immediate situation than upon the individual's past" (1942, p. 29).

4. The newer approach ". . . lays great stress upon the therapeutic relationship itself as a growth experience. . . . Here the individual learns to understand himself; to make significant independent choices, to relate himself successfully to another person in a more adult fashion" (1942, p. 30).

Thus, the central concept in Rogers' first formulation of his views was that people have within themselves the capacity to solve their own problems, as previously pointed out. The task of the therapist is to establish the conditions that allow people to attain this insight themselves: *Attainment of insight* was, therefore, one of the key goals of nondirective therapy in the 1940s. To enable the client to achieve self-insight, the counselor's chief tool was the *clarification of feelings* through rephrasing the emotional content of the client's statements (cf. Hart, 1970, pp. 6 ff.). Rogers summarized his early view of the counselor's role in this way:

> *Effective counseling consists of a definitively structured, permissive relationship which allows the client to gain an understanding of himself to a degree which enables him to take positive steps in the light of his new orientation.* (Rogers, 1942, p. 18, italics in original)

Though controversial, Rogers' techniques and philosophy were widely adopted by practitioners. The problems that followed in the application of nondirective counseling and therapy were due in part to two crucial aspects of this early formulation:

1. Little or no *explicit* theory had been developed to guide the counselor's efforts;

2. In the hands of an unskilled or inadequately trained therapist, the permissive and accepting attitude was construed by his clients as a threatening "don't care" attitude or as a directionless, disorganized relationship.

Rogers believed that the difficulty lay in the tendency of some counselors to interpret his formulations too literally (1951, p. 26). In effect, some counselors supposed that their role was to be merely passive and to adopt a laissez-faire policy: "the passivity and seeming lack of interest . . . is experienced by the client as a rejection, since indifference is in no real way the same as acceptance" (Rogers, 1951, p. 27).

The criticisms of Rogers' nondirective psychotherapy as well as his own awareness of its shortcomings led to Rogers' modification and further development of his psychotherapeutic approach.

CLIENT-CENTERED THERAPY: EMPATHIC UNDERSTANDING

In 1951, Rogers published a second major work on counseling, carefully delineating his views on what he now termed **client-centered therapy.** The book's title, *Client-Centered Therapy,* was meant to emphasize the new rationale of his approach: "The client, as the term has acquired its meaning, is one who comes actively and voluntarily to gain help on a problem, but *without any notion of surrendering his own responsibility for the situation*" (Rogers, 1951, p. 7n.; italics added).

Thus the publication of *Client-Centered Therapy* marked the beginning of a second phase in Rogers' thinking (cf. Hart, 1970). The focus had shifted to the counselor's efforts to be *empathic* in understanding the client's world, and to the *communication* of that understanding to the client. The technique of reflection of feelings, though present from the first nondirective period, now assumed more importance. Reflection of feelings was not merely to be used to help the client attain insight and clarification of his or her emotions, but also to communicate the counselor's understanding of the client's inner world. In mirroring back the client's feelings, the counselor simultaneously transmits the desire to perceive the world as the client perceives it. In effect, the goal of the counselor is to achieve the *internal frame-of-reference* of the client:

> . . . it is the counselor's aim to perceive as sensitively and accurately as possible all of the perceptual field as it is being experienced by the client . . . and having thus perceived this internal frame of reference of the other as completely as possible, to indicate to the client the extent to which he is seeing through the client's eyes. (Rogers, 1951, p. 34)

This approach on accurate empathy goes along with Rogers' view of the individual's subjective experience, his or her **phenomenal world,** as the fundamental psychological reality. As Rogers stated this proposition, *"Every individual exists in a continually changing world of experience of which he is the center"* (1951, p. 483). The individual's experience is his or her reality (1959, p. 222). For this reason, the effort to empathically understand the experiential world of the client takes on central importance in Rogers' approach to psychotherapy.

Thus, by 1951, two of the three major elements that characterize Rogers' view of personality were present to his thinking. First was the necessity for the counselor to provide a warm and permissive relationship; second was the necessity for the counselor to assume the internal frame of reference of the client and to communicate empathic understanding of the client's world.

EXPERIENTIAL THERAPY: THE CONDITIONS OF PERSONALITY CHANGE

The third element characteristic of Rogers' view of personality emerged during the third aspect of the development of client-centered theory. Joseph Hart (1970) and Eugene Gendlin (1964, 1968, 1970) have characterized this phase of Rogers' and their own work as the "experiencing" phase or as *experiential therapy.*

By 1957 the focus had again shifted to a *mutual expression of feelings* by both client and counselor. *Experiencing* became the technical term to describe the internal, directly experienced emotional processes that the client and counselor struggle to put into words. Because tangled and latent feelings are the core of psychological maladjustment in Rogers' view, the tasks of learning to experience one's own distorted and trapped emotions and of learning to communicate them to oneself and to the counselor became the central goals of experiential therapy.

One of the key causes of this shift in emphasis from pure verbal transactions to direct emotional experience can be found in a research effort undertaken by Rogers and his colleagues at the University of Wisconsin. Working with nonverbal, often uncooperative, schizophrenic patients in a state hospital required the radical shift in therapeutic strategy (see Rogers, 1967a; Gendlin, 1966). If psychotherapy from the client-centered framework had been a verbal interchange between a willing client and a warmly accepting therapist, it now had to be something more direct, less verbal, and increasingly experiential.

Along these lines Rogers had already provided a theoretical rationale for personality change in therapy, which implied that constructive alterations in personality could occur regardless of the specific verbal techniques employed by the counselor. If six operationally defined conditions of relationship were met, then any person-to-person contact embodying them could promote personality growth. The six conditions postulated by Rogers (1957) were:

1. *Two persons are in psychological contact* so that each of them is aware, even if in only the dimmest fashion, that the other's presence makes a difference.

2. *The first person, the client, is in a state of self-incongruence,* being vulnerable or anxious. **Self-incongruence** means that a discrepancy exists between the client's self-image and his or her ongoing experiences, between the actor and the mask. Any experience that threatens the self-picture will be defensively distorted.

3. *The second person, or therapist, is self-congruent* or integrated in the relationship. **Self-congruence** means that the therapist is genuinely him- or herself, totally free to express what he or she actually feels, positive or negative, in the situation with the client. Such spontaneity includes the ability to express feelings that are not particularly pleasing: "I am afraid of this client;" or "I am bored with this client."

4. *The therapist experiences unconditional positive regard for the client.* **Unconditional positive regard** means that the counselor warmly accepts the client. It is unconditional. The counselor prizes the person in a nonjudgmental way.

5. *The therapist experiences an empathic understanding of the client's internal frame of reference and endeavors to communicate this experience to the client.* The counselor tries to see the world as the client sees it and to communicate that he or she does so.

6. *The communication to the client of the therapist's empathic understanding and unconditional positive regard must be minimally achieved.* If the client does not perceive acceptance and understanding, they are not real for him or her.

When these six conditions are fulfilled in a relationship, intentionally therapeutic or otherwise, personality change in a positive, healthy direction will occur. Clients who experience these conditions will be more able to accept their feelings and perceptions freely as their own; they will grow in the direction of their idealized self-images; they will become more autonomous in their decision making. The emphasis is clearly not on the counselor's technique, nor on the specifics of verbal interchange. Crucial to personality change is the quality of the directly experienced relationship. Unlike directive approaches in which there is an effort to shape the client's behavior, the client-centered approaches is one that facilitates change.

PERSONALITY CHANGES EVOKED BY THE THERAPEUTIC RELATIONSHIP

Rogers and his colleagues formulated a conceptualization of the specific process of personality change that occurs when these six conditions exist between two persons. From hundreds of recorded therapeutic sessions and from his own experiences, Rogers was able to discern the basic similarities of the client's progressive changes in experience within the therapeutic relationship. Rogers proposed that such personality changes might be thought of as a continuum of experience. One end of the continuum is personality or experiential rigidity; the opposite end is fluidity or psychological flow (Rogers 1958, 1961). Clients with differing degrees of personality difficulty may be conceptualized as initially occupying different positions between the two extremes. As therapy progresses, the client progresses toward the fluidity end of the spectrum.

In all, Rogers identified seven steps in the process. The first three phases through which clients pass involve their initial inability to see their difficulties, a gradual dim recognition that some problem exists, and a tendency once a problem is recognized to speak of themselves as objects without a real feeling. Thus, the first three stages of personality change in Rogerian psychotherapy are identified as:

1. *Rigidity of self-perception:* no recognition of need to change self

2. *Dim recognition of problem:* problem exists in others, not self

3. *Self treated as object:* does not own his or her feelings

In the fourth stage, there is some movement in the direction of greater flexibility. But clients continue to discuss emotions of their past rather than feelings they now experience. Some questioning of their own interpretations also occurs and consequently anxiety and distrust of their own perceptions begin to develop. This fourth or middle phase may be identified as:

4. *Partial recognition of feelings:* tendency to treat feelings as colorless objects

In the last three phases of the process of personality change, the client progressively approaches accurate recognition and ownership of feelings, acceptance of self, with reevaluation of personal interpretations, and finally, in the seventh phase, experiencing of feelings with richness and clarity. These last three phases of the process of personality change may be identified as:

5. *Improved recognition of feelings:* feelings of wanting to be the "real me"

6. *Acceptance of feelings with richness:* self is free to "own" feelings

7. *New feelings experienced freely:* self is totally flexible, trustworthy, and capable of change and growth

The seven phases outlined here provide an instructive scheme by which to understand Rogers' developing conception of personality. It is easy to see that Rogers views the psychologically maladjusted personality as one who is defensively rigidified, constricted in his or her experiencing of self, and conflicted in his or her willingness to "own" his or her feelings. To describe this phenomenon, Rogers, too, employed the metaphor of the actor and the mask, for the rigid, defensive person is adopting a series of false fronts or masks to deceive others and him- or herself. In the warm and accepting empathic relationship of psychotherapy, the person

> . . . begins to drop the false fronts, or the masks, or the roles, with which he has faced life. He appears to be trying to discover something more basic, something more truly himself. (Rogers, 1961, p. 109)

The task that remains is to explore how Rogers systematized these discoveries into an explicit theory of personality.

THE FULLY FUNCTIONING PERSON: IDEAL MENTAL HEALTH

From his experience in psychotherapy, and from the consistency of the changes he observed as his clients grew toward more personal freedom, Rogers formulated a concept of the ideally free and self-accepting person. He first committed his ideas to paper during the winter of 1952–1953, but the journal editor to whom he submitted them rejected them. The

BOX 13.2   *Only Connect . . .*

Rogers' concept of the fully functioning person is similar to Maslow's notion of the self-actualized (SA) personality. Maslow used a greater range of descriptive terms than Rogers does, and Maslow's SA person seems slightly more autonomous with a possibility of ruthlessness. Nevertheless, the two concepts can be compared as seen in the accompanying table.

Rogers' Fully Functioning Person and Maslow's Self-Actualized Person Compared

Rogers' Fully Functioning Person	Maslow's Self-Actualized Person

1. More fully open to experience
    Unafraid of own feelings
	1. Reality and problem-centered
	    Accepting of self
	    Unexpected ruthlessness

2. More existential living
    Nondetermined, independent
	2. Spontaneity and simplicity
	    Freshness of appreciation
	    Discrimination between means and ends
	    Need for privacy

3. Increased trust in own organism
    More creative, nonconformist
	3. Acceptance of others
	    Resistance to enculturation
	    Creative
	    Unhostile sense of humor
	    More intimate personal relations
	    Gemeinschaftsgefühl (social interest)

[cf. Alfred Adler, Chapter 5]

paper was finally published in original form in 1964 (see also Rogers, 1961, Chapter 9), and it presented Rogers' view of what he called "the fully functioning person."

Rogers approached the problem of defining a **fully functioning person.** In order to do so, Rogers characterized the traits of a person who successfully completes psychotherapy and exhibits in his or her behavior the highest goals of the best and most effective psychotherapy available. Rogers distinguished three primary characteristics of the fully functioning person, who Rogers viewed as a person after successful therapy:

1. The fully functioning person is *more fully open to experience* (1964, p. 18). He or she has become freed of the need to distort defensively both inner and outer reality and is able to listen perceptively and unanxiously to the demands of his or her body and mind.

2. The fully functioning person has the capacity to experience life *in an existential fashion* (1964, p. 20). He or she lives each moment of life more spontaneously, enjoying the exuberance and the joy of seeing life as one new moment following another. The person realizes that "What I will be in the next moment, and what I will do, grows out of that moment, and cannot be predicted in advance either by me or by others" (1964, p. 20).

3. Fully functioning people experience an *increased trust in their own organisms* (1964, p. 20). They feel free to do what "feels right" at any given moment, fully expecting that they will prove competent to meet any challenge, judge accurately any obstacle, and regulate their behavior realistically as the situation demands.

Three secondary personality characteristics are connected with Rogers' concept of the fully functioning person:

1. Fully functioning people grow unafraid of their own feelings; emotions become important but not overwhelming personal experiences.

2. They are neither determined nor controlled by external influences.

3. With increased trust in their own cognitive and emotional processes, these people find themselves more creative in their relationships. They are able to harmonize themselves with the needs of others because they find themselves trusting human nature in general.

ROGERS' MODEL OF DEVELOPMENT

The most basic, innate tendency of the human infant is a drive toward "actualizing his organism." Instead of postulating a long list of needs or drives, Rogers chose to hypothesize that most biological functions and psychological urges could be subsumed under one major heading: a need to maintain and to enhance one's life (1951, p. 488):

> We are talking here about the tendency of the organism to maintain itself, to assimilate food, to behave defensively in the face of threat, to achieve the goal of self-maintenance even when the usual pathway to that goal is blocked. We are speaking of the tendency of the organism to move in the direction of maturation, as maturation is defined for each species. . . . [The organism] moves in the direction of limited expansion through growth, expansion through extending itself by means of its tools, and expansion through reproduction. It moves in the direction of greater independence or self-responsibility. (1951, p. 488)

As the infant develops biologically, its psychological maturation tends to keep pace through increasing self-awareness. Gradually, a part of the infant's phenomenal world becomes differentiated and recognized as "me," "I," or "myself." From the total global mass of perceptual stimuli, the infant learns slowly and cautiously to identify itself as an independent agent (Rogers, 1951, p. 497; 1959, p. 233).

THE IMPORTANCE OF APPROVAL

The infant develops its picture of "me" through its interactions with significant others. Much as Harry Stack Sullivan (Chapter 9) had described, Rogers indicated the importance of the child's sensitivity to the praise and blame of the adults in its world. These evaluations of its behavior are assimilated to the infant's self-structure, and as socialization continues, the infant's perceptual field continues to grow in complexity. Many behaviors consistent with its parents' conception of what it should be will be praised; a variety of behaviors that are disapproved of by its parents will be punished or responded to by them with emotionally abrasive communications.

> [The child] . . . experiences words and actions of his parents in regard to these satisfying behaviors, and the words and actions add up to the feeling "You are bad, the behavior is bad, and you are not loved or lovable when you behave in this way." This constitutes a deep threat to the nascent structure of the self. The child's dilemma might be schematized in these terms: "If I admit to awareness the satisfactions of these behaviors and values I apprehend in these experiences, then this is inconsistent with my self as being loved or lovable." (1951, p. 500)

Thus, to preserve the continuity of parental love in its world, the child must fend off threats of withdrawal of that affection. Rogers hypothesized that the infant must deal with those of its behaviors that arouse parental disapproval by removing both the threat and the motive for the behavior from its awareness. For example, the infant may distort its experience of the situation: "The accurate symbolization would be 'I perceive my parents as experiencing this behavior as unsatisfying to them.' The distorted symbolization, distorted to preserve the threatened concept of self, is '*I* perceive this behavior as unsatisfying' " (Rogers, 1951, p. 500).

In short, the child learns to experience reality secondhand. It adopts not its spontaneous feelings and perceptions as guides to its behavior, but the defensively safe feelings that maintain parental love and approval. Experience is thus distorted in the service of "self" survival. The **self-structure** becomes "an organized configuration of perceptions of self which are admissible to awareness" (Rogers, 1951, p. 501). Threatening self-perceptions are excluded.

As the self-structure develops, a need for approval, or what Rogers termed **positive self-regard,** grows in intensity. Positive regard is the experience of feeling accepted, loved, and "prized." The source of the infant's sense of positive regard is located in the approval of others.

People feel good when they realize that others are approving and prizing them: "when an individual discriminates himself as satisfying another's need for positive regard, he necessarily experiences satisfaction of his own need for positive regard" (1959, p. 223). Satisfying another's need for love and acceptance is in itself satisfying. Rogers' description of the infant's developing need for positive regard bears quoting:

> The infant learns to need love. Love is very satisfying, but to know whether he is receiving it or not he must observe his mother's face, gestures, and other ambiguous signs. He develops a total gestalt as to the way he is regarded by his mother and each new experience of love or rejection tends to alter the whole gestalt. Consequently, each behavior on his mother's part such as a specific disapproval of a specific behavior tends to be experienced as disapproval in general. So important is this to the infant that he comes to be guided in his behavior not by the degree to which an experience maintains or enhances the organism, but by the likelihood of receiving maternal love. (1959, p. 225)

The infant gradually acquires a knowledge of relevant **conditions of worth.** That is, the infant "understands," however dimly at first, that only under certain conditions is he or she positively esteemed by others, by self in response to others, and most important, by his or her parents. The infant realizes that certain behaviors are the conditions of worth that provide acceptance or provoke rejection.

How is it possible for any infant ever to develop a healthy, spontaneously natural, self-concept? Rogers suggested that three parental characteristics foster healthy self-structure formation: (1) ability to accept the child's feelings and strivings; (2) ability to accept one's own feelings that certain of the child's behaviors are undesirable; (3) and communication of acceptance of the child as a person (based on Rogers, 1951, p. 502). The child who experiences a relationship with its parents based on the three previously listed qualities experiences no threat to itself as a loved or lovable person.

INCONGRUENCE BETWEEN SELF AND EXPERIENCE

Rogers emphasized the importance of an individual protecting his or her sense of **self-regard** and developed the concept of self-incongruence.

> Because of the need for self-regard, the individual perceives his experience selectively, in terms of the conditions of worth that have come to exist in him.
>   a. Experiences that are in accord with his conditions of worth are perceived and symbolized accurately in awareness.
>   b. Experiences which run contrary to the conditions of worth are perceived selectively and distortedly as if in accord with the conditions of worth, or are in part or whole, denied to awareness. (1959, p. 226)

Rogers suggested that the conditions of worth by which the individual has learned to navigate his or her world serve as selective filters in screening new experiences. Those experiences that are denied access to awareness because they violate the self-structure form

BOX 13.3   *Only Connect . . .*

Rogers' idea of filtering experiences so that one is aware only of those that protect one's self-regard is his version of a defense. This is not an ego defense as in Freudian psychology but a defense against one's often unrealistic sense of self. Thus the experiences not consistent with one's idea of self are warded off or, as Rogers terms it, *subcepted.*

the foundation of potential psychological maladjustment. The resulting self-incongruence means that one's actual core of experience, which constitutes the **real self,** is discrepant with the self-picture or **perceived self** and denied to awareness. The individual is thus vulnerable to anxiety every time a fresh experience threatens to trigger perception of the discrepancy.

Experiences that are threatening to one's self-structure are said to be "subcepted." **Subception** means that the individual perceives the threat but does not admit it to full awareness in the higher cognitive brain centers (Rogers, 1959, p. 200; see also McLeary & Lazarus, 1949). Subception of threatening discrepancies between self-structure and new experiences begins the process of defensive personality disorganization.

PERSONALITY DISORGANIZATION

When the discrepancy between self-structure and experience becomes so great that subception no longer functions with complete success, the result for some people can be personality disorganization (Rogers, 1959, pp. 228–229). This may arise if the perception of a threatening experience occurs suddenly and so forcefully that further denial is impossible. Because the perception is accurately symbolized in awareness, the gestalt of the self-structure is broken by the intrusion of discrepant data (Rogers, 1959, p. 229). This Rogerian concept is reminiscent to Erik Erikson's discussion of the loss of a sense of ego identity among "shell-shocked" combatants of World War II (Chapter 8).

Rogers offered an example of this kind of maladjustment:

> . . . take the familiar picture of a mother whom the diagnostician would term rejecting. She has as part of her concept of self a whole constellation that may be summed up by saying, "I am a good and loving mother. . . ." With this concept of self she can accept and assimilate those organic sensations of affection which she feels toward her child. But the organic experience of dislike, distaste, or hatred toward her child is something that is denied to her conscious self. The experience exists, but it is not permitted accurate symbolization. . . . Since the good mother could be aggressive toward her child only if he merited punishment, she perceives much of his behavior as being bad, deserving punishment, and therefore the aggressive acts can be carried through, without being contrary to the values organized in her picture of self. (1951, pp. 511–512)

At times of great provocation, such a mother might scream at her child, "I hate you." But almost in the same breath she would rush to explain that "she was not herself."

Sometimes the individual experiences psychological maladjustment when the total self-structure is founded on the evaluations of others. Since these alien values have no genuine connection with the person's own experiences, he or she may perceive him- or herself as a "nothing," as a "zero" (Rogers, 1951, p. 512).

SOME CRITICISMS OF ROGERS' APPROACH

Rogers' ideas have been criticized in terms of the values expressed by his theories. There is no doubt that Rogers asserts the quintessential importance for mental health of individual freedom and choice, but one can question whether this emphasis is empirically based or rather a reflection of his own values. Certainly, many mentally healthy and happy people have made commitments and stuck to them in spite of their own personal wishes (Sollod, 1978). Rogers and other humanistic psychologists have been criticized for promoting selfishness and egoism (Wallach & Wallach, 1983). What one feels like or wants to do, for most people, is only one aspect of their decision-making process. For religiously committed people, a question they might consider is what they believe is the correct course of action or, after prayerful consideration, what they feel God wants them to do. Rogers has been criticized for abandoning a God-centered approach to values and decision making in favor of an unqualified "selfist" or self-centered approach (Vitz, 1977).

OPERATIONALIZING THE CONCEPT OF SELF: Q-SORT METHODOLOGY

Rogers' reliance on the concepts of self, self-incongruence, and ideal self emerged from his experiences with patients in therapy. Often, when he had allowed clients to express their problems in their own fashion, without guidance or interpretation, they would refer to the *self* as the core of their experience: "I feel I'm not being my real self"; "I never had a chance to be myself"; or, "It feels good to let myself go and just be myself here" (1959, p. 201).

As a consequence of their therapeutic efforts, Rogers and several of his students and colleagues mounted an early research project to investigate the individual's changing conception of self in therapy (Rogers & Dymond, 1954). The process of psychotherapeutic change seemed to be directly expressible in terms of changes in the individual's perceived self and movement toward the **ideal self.**

At about the time that Rogers had begun to conceptualize the self as the key element in any description of the person's experience, a colleague at the University of Chicago, William Stephenson, developed a rationale and a statistical method uniquely applicable to a study of the **phenomenal world,** or the individual's experienced world of perceptions and meanings. Called a *Q-sort* technique, Stephenson's procedures were applied to a variety of social and personal processes (1953). Rogers and his research team adopted Q-sort methods to operationalize the conception of self.

Essentially, the **Q-sort** technique involves providing a person with a large number of written statements and asking him or her to sort them into a deliberately determined number of piles. The array of categories into which the subject places his or her statements is purposefully constructed to approximate a statistically normal distribution. Printed on cards, the statements describe various aspects of a person's self. In the most widely used version, the subject is asked to sort 100 statements into nine piles ranging from "least like me" to "most like me." Other variations involve the inclusion of additional categories: "what I most would like to become," or "what I most dislike about me." A typical arrangement of a Q-sort distribution looks like this:

	Least Like Me			Undecided			Most Like Me		
Pile No.	0	1	2	3	4	5	6	7	8
No. of Cards (Total: 100)	1	4	11	21	26	21	11	4	1

(Based on Dymond, in Rogers & Dymond, 1954, p. 77.)

The criteria by which the self-statement cards may be sorted are nearly limitless. One very instructive example of a subject's card-sorting responses before and after therapy is provided in Table 13.3.

Table 13.3   Mrs. Oak's Changes in Perceived Self in Terms of Q-Sort Statements

Before therapy	After therapy
"Most characteristic"	
I usually feel driven.	I express my emotions freely.
I am responsible for my troubles.	I feel emotionally mature.
I am really self-centered.	I am self-reliant.
I am liked by most people who know me.	I understand myself.
I am intelligent.	I feel adequate.
"Least characteristic"	
I feel comfortable while talking with someone.	I have few standards and values of my own.
I make strong demands on myself.	I feel helpless.
I am optimistic.	I often feel guilty.

From Rogers, in Rogers & Dymond, 1954, p. 275.

In the left-hand column of Table 13.3 is a small sample of "Mrs. Oak's" statements chosen as *most characteristic* of herself before therapy. In the right-hand column are her statements describing herself after therapy. The bottom half of the table contains an additional sample of Q-sort statements that were chosen before and after therapy by Mrs. Oak as least characteristic of herself.

The items of Table 13.3 show that before therapy, Mrs. Oak regarded herself as driven, insecure, and disorganized. After therapy, by the time of the five-month follow-up interview, she viewed herself as more in control and more secure. The items that Mrs. Oak considered to be least characteristic of herself before therapy included an ability to be independent and comfortable with others. After therapy, Mrs. Oak perceived herself to be less helpless and less guilty.

The correlation between the perceived self before and after therapy was low: .30. In another Q-sort, Mrs. Oak was asked to sort the items in order of importance to her for the *person she would like to be,* thus providing an estimate of her ideal self. After therapy, Mrs. Oak again sorted the items in relation to her ideal self. The before self-ideal included "I feel emotionally mature"; "I can live comfortably with people around me"; "I am a rational person." The after self-ideal included the following items: "I understand myself"; "I express my emotions freely"; and, "I am poised" (Rogers, 1954, p. 274). The degree of similarity for Mrs. Oak's self-ideal before and after therapy was great: The correlation for before and after ideal selves was .72. The key question is whether Mrs. Oak perceived her actual self to have become more like her ideal self after therapy. The correlation between her perceived self and ideal self before therapy was .21, a very low degree of relationship. Thus before therapy Mrs. Oak perceived a large discrepancy between what she was and what she would like to be. After therapy, the correlation between her ideal self and her actual self, that is, the self she thought she had become was .69 at termination and .79 within several months after therapy (1954, p. 282). Thus the Q-sort method had shown that Mrs. Oak believed herself to be more like her ideal self after therapy than before.

Rogers and his colleagues used a variety of other assessment techniques; but in all cases the client's consistent movement in the direction of greater freedom, more independence, and more congruence between perceived self and ideal self was measurably real.

EVALUATING ABRAHAM MASLOW AND CARL ROGERS

Both Maslow and Rogers were independent thinkers, who in their different ways tilted at windmills. Both thinkers had their share of successes and failures as they struggled against established ideas drawn from behaviorism and psychoanalysis. Rogers, for example, was instrumental in the political fight for psychologists and social workers to practice psychotherapy alongside their medical colleagues. And Maslow struggled against depersonalizing educational institutions. We could say that both were committed to and lived the ideas they espoused.

Both Maslow and Rogers have left a major legacy in the way our society thinks about human nature and in the way psychotherapy is practiced. Maslow's idea of the hierarchy of needs and self-actualization has had a transformative impact on the workplace, and many of the therapeutic approaches that Rogers developed are now widely used in the mental health professions.

Refutability of Maslow and Rogers' Concepts

Maslow grew up in a largely empirical branch of psychology, and for a time, even practiced a kind of naturalistic behaviorism. Rogers was one of the first, if not the very first, clinicians to open the doors of the consulting room and expose psychotherapy to scientific scrutiny.

Maslow created a great wealth of ideas, most of which lack the rigor and empirical referents that would permit them to be tested. This chapter has noted some major flaws with two of his most important theoretical contributions: the concept of the self-actualized person and the hierarchy of needs. Some of Maslow's ideas, in principle, are highly testable, such as the hierarchy of motivational needs, at least up to, but not necessarily including, needs such as the need for beauty, truth, and self-actualization. But on the whole, Maslow's humanistic psychology has not attracted empirically minded psychologists to create empirical translations of his ideas.

Rogers opened the process of psychotherapy to research, and under his leadership, a whole program of empirically based research on the therapeutic process, the characteristics of the helping relationship, and the characteristics of the helping person was done. Studies of empathy, warmth, directiveness versus nondirectiveness, pre- and postmeasures of personality, and even attempts to use client-centered therapy to aid schizophrenic people have been researched. So, on the clinical side of the enterprise, Rogers gets high grades for stimulating hypothesis testing and for refutable therapeutic concepts.

On the downside, the theory that underlies Rogers' clinical practices is frequently vague, subjective, and not tied to empirical referents. Concepts such as the phenomenal self, conditions of worth, and "fully functioning" person are not easily testable in the precise form in which they exist in Rogers' theory. Some of these concepts could be translated into operations that lend themselves to measurement. The difficulty seems to be that few psychologists are willing to test Rogers' theories of personality although many have tested his clinical strategies.

Maslow and Rogers' Conception of Human Agency

Both Maslow and Rogers regard people as capable of active decision making. Rogers, early on, was even reluctant to take a clinical history with his clients or perform diagnostic testing because he believed that whatever information would be needed in treatment would emerge as the client decided to communicate it. Maslow argued that human motivation is more of a "pulling" *toward* goals than it is a "pushing" by human drives. People set their own standards and discover their own paths to achieving them. When life events intervene to block pursuit of self-chosen goals, the person is frustrated but no less free to make new decisions. In short, both Maslow and Rogers picture people as active determiners of their lives rather than as passive receptacles of reality.

The Idiographic/Nomothetic Nature of Humanistic Psychology

Rogers' theory is largely a phenomenological model of human personality, which is to say that its focus is on the subjective meanings a person lives by, although he indicates universal factors that are important for everyone. Rogers' emphasis can be characterized as largely idiographic. Maslow is less focused than Rogers on clinical work with individuals and more on abstract ideas such as the hierarchy of needs or the concept of self-actualization, so his approach is more nomothetic in its emphasis.

SUMMARY

Maslow's interests in psychological health followed his early work on dominance-feeling in infrahuman primates and from his interview research of dominant women. Rogers developed his conceptualization of the self-actualizing nature of human motivation from his experiences in psychotherapy. The ideas of both converged in the direction of a humanist approach that emphasized the full development of the individual.

Maslow's central concept is the growth of the health-striving character of human personality. Proceeding through a hierarchy of basic needs, the individual progresses toward ultimate health and fully spontaneous expression of the self. At the lowest level of the hierarchy are the physiological needs such as hunger and thirst. These having been satisfied, the individual's behavior becomes directed by his or her needs for safety, then by needs for love and esteem. Finally, when these basic motives have been fulfilled, the need for self-actualization emerges.

Rogers discovered essentially the same rule of human growth from his observations of clients in therapy. In the earliest stages of his work, Rogers' central concern was to allow clients to feel warmly accepted and fully free to express themselves. Slowly, Rogers developed this nondirective orientation to include the necessity for the counselor to enter the client's phenomenal world or internal frame of reference. In order for constructive personality change to occur, the counselor must communicate an understanding of the client's internal frame of reference to the client.

Maslow's conceptualization of the self-actualizing person as independent, creative, and growth-motivated corresponds to Rogers' notion of the fully functioning person who emerges from a successful psycho-

therapeutic relationship. Maslow has gone further than Rogers in one respect. Specifically, Maslow has postulated that the self-actualizing person embarks on a further course of metamotives. These Being-values, or B-values as Maslow termed them, include the classic virtues like Beauty, Truth, Justice, Honesty, and Freedom. When denied or frustrated, these B-values show evidence of being innate, for the frustrated individual succumbs to metapathologies.

Maslow's development of the construct of peak experiences was closely connected with William James' exploration of spiritual experiences. James was one of the founders of the field of transpersonal psychology, which explores the psychology of spirituality, including transcendent and anomalous experiences.

In Maslow's theory, the motor of personality is the drive toward self-actualization, toward psychological health, toward fully accepted humanness. In Rogers' theory, the same innate striving toward enhancement and expression of one's spontaneous urges and feelings constitutes the fundamental layer of personality. In both theories, psychological maladjustments are the product of learned tendencies to subvert or block the spontaneous and natural expression of self.

Our evaluation of Maslow and Rogers indicates that both theorists constructed largely nonrefutable theories, although Rogers' clinical work did produce empirically testable therapeutic strategies. Human agency, from the viewpoint of both theorists, is active rather than passive. Rogers' theory, with its clinical emphasis, is more idiographic and Maslow's approach, with its emphasis on general constructs, is more nomothetic.

FOR FURTHER READING

Maslow's definitive statement of his position is located in *Motivation and Personality* (New York: Addison-Wesley, 1987). His early papers on dominance-feeling with primates have been collected into a single volume by J. Lowry and entitled *Dominance, Self-Esteem, Self-Actualization: Germinal Papers of A. H. Maslow* (Monterey, CA: Brooks-Cole, 1973). A collection of Maslow's later papers, including a semi-autobiographical account of the sources of his interest in self-actualization, is *The Farther Reaches of Human Nature* (New York: Arkana, 1993). Sometimes bitter, sometimes ironic, Maslow's criticism of classical scientific method in application to persons may be found in his *The Psychology of Science: A Reconnaissance* (New York: Harper & Row, 1966). The collection of papers in Chiang and Maslow's (Eds.) *The Healthy Personality* (New York: Van Nostrand, 1977) demonstrates the application of humanistic psychology to a wide variety of fields and provides accounts of some of the personal sources of Maslow's, Rogers', and Allport's humanistic leanings.

A fascinating book is *Abraham H. Maslow: A Memorial Volume,* compiled with the assistance of Bertha G. Maslow, his widow (Monterey, CA: Brooks/Cole 1972). It consists of some of his writings, reminiscences of those who knew him well, and many intimate photographs. Frank Goble's *The Third Force: The Psychology of Abraham Maslow* (New York: Grossman, 1970) was published shortly after Maslow's death and is an excellent review of the ideas that he was working on at that time, including his thoughts about mental health and more enlightened management practices. Edward Hoffman has written a largely adulatory biography of Maslow, now in paperback: *The Right to Be Human: A Biography of Abraham Maslow* (New York: McGraw-Hill, 1999). *Maslow on Management,* written by Deborah Stephens with Abraham Maslow (New York: John Wiley & Sons, 2000) contains a number of writings of Maslow that have to do with the transformation of management practices and the business world.

William James' lectures on mystical experience bear a strong similarity to Maslow's views on peak experiences. James' very readable lectures are located in *The Varieties of Religious Experience* (New York: MacMillan Publishing Company, 1997). For Maslow's own account of peak experiences, see *Religions, Values and Peak-Experiences* (New York: Viking, 1994).

Two of Rogers' early works set forth his initial strategy and philosophy: *Counseling and Psychotherapy* (Boston: Houghton Mifflin, 1942) and *Client-Centered Therapy* (Boston: Houghton Mifflin, 1951).

To bring Rogers' perspective on theory and therapy up to date, two volumes should be consulted. The first of these is a collection of research and theory papers edited by J. T. Hart and T. M. Tomlinson under the title *New Directions in Client-Centered Therapy* (Boston: Houghton Mifflin, 1970) and is, perhaps, the better of the two. The second collection of papers is in David Wexler and Laura North Rice's (Eds.) *Innovations in Client-Centered Therapy* (New York: Wiley, 1974).

Rogers gives a definitive statement of his position in "A Theory of Therapy, Personality and Inter-Personal Relationships as Developed in the Client-Centered Framework," in S. Koch (Ed.), *Psychology: A Study of a Science,* Vol. III, *Formulations of the Person in the Social Context* (New York: McGraw-Hill, 1959). A current survey of Rogerian method and philosophy is provided by Betty Meador in "Client-Centered Therapy," in Raymond Corsini (Ed.), *Current Psychotherapies* (Itasca, IL: Peacock, 2000). A personally revealing account of Rogers' early career is in *On Becoming a Person: A Therapist's View of Psychotherapy* (Boston: Houghton Mifflin, 1995). *Carl Rogers on Personal Power* (New York: Delacorte Press, 1977) contains Rogers' updated views on the self-actualization motive and its political implications for personal knowledge. *A Way of Being* (Boston: Houghton Mifflin, 1995) by Rogers and Irvin Yalom is a personal and direct statement of Rogers' approach to human experience.

Rogers' own expansion of his ideas to the field of marriage and to other two-person intimate relationships is contained in his *Becoming Partners: Marriage and Its Alternatives* (New York: Dell, 1972). The efficacy and process of encounter groups are treated to a sympathetic examination by Rogers in *Carl Rogers on Encounter Groups* (New York: Harper & Row, 1970). An interview with Rogers, along with a reprint of his ongoing debate with B. F. Skinner and one of his previously unpublished papers, are located in R. I. Evans' *Carl Rogers: The Man and His Ideas* (New York: Dutton, 1975). The interview in condensed version may also be found in Evans' *The Making of Psychology* (New York: Knopf, 1976). Howard Kirschenbaum has written a biography of Carl Rogers with Rogers' and his wife's cooperation, but *On Becoming Carl Rogers* (New York: Delacorte Press, 1979) is marred by its uncritical, almost worshipful, appraisal. Rogers' autobiography (in E. G. Boring and Gardner Lindzey's *A History of Psychology in Autobiography,* Vol. 5, New York: Appleton Century, 1967) is far more revealing. Robert Sollod's "Carl Rogers and the Origins of Client-Centered

Therapy" (*Professional Psychology,* 1978, *9,* pp. 93–104) explores in depth the sources of Rogers' psychotherapeutic approach.

Psychology's Sanction for Selfishness: The Error of Egoism in Theory and Therapy by Wallach & Wallach (San Francisco, CA: W. H. Freeman, 1983) presents a critical view of the values expressed by humanistic psychologists. Paul Vitz's *Psychology as Religion: The Cult of Self Worship* (Grand Rapids, MI: William B. Eerdmans, 1994) critically evaluates what he terms Rogers' "selfism" from a religious perspective.

GLOSSARY

Abraham Maslow

B-values/metaneeds: Growth needs that deal with the quality and nature of beingness. They include striving for goodness toward others, seeking truth and justice, yearning for knowledge, and trying to create beauty and order.

Conversational probing: A qualitative research method Maslow developed that involves establishing rapport with a subject and engaging in an intensive interviewing process.

Deficiency needs: The physiological drives, safety needs, love and belongingness needs, and the esteem needs are comprised in this part of Maslow's hierarchy of needs.

Desacralizing: The denial of the awesome, marvelous, beautiful, sublime aspects of people and the universe. Leads to a tendency to be cynical and disrespectful, and steers the individual to focus on others' weaknesses and disregard of their strengths and virtues.

Dominance-feeling: A sense of oneself that involves good self-confidence, self-assurance, high evaluation of the self, feelings of general capability or superiority, and lack of shyness, timidity, self-consciousness, or embarrassment.

Hierarchy of needs: A scale in which the deficiency needs are prepotent to needs lying above them. It begins with basics such as physiological needs, survival, safety, and self-esteem and steers toward a search for beauty, knowledge, justice, and truth.

Humanistic psychology: An approach that emphasizes the dignity and worth of the person. It presumes that the individual advances creatively toward growth and psychological health.

Ineffability: A term indicating that something cannot be described, imparted, or transferred to others. It defies words—it defies expression.

Innocence: The healthy personality's capacity to live without pretense, to be genuinely spontaneous and free of guilt.

Jonah complex: Maslow's term for the pattern of avoiding challenges and of not fulfilling one's potential or one's calling. This term is an allusion to Jonah, the Bible's reluctant prophet.

Noetic quality: The word "noetic" is based on a Greek root meaning "mind" or intellect." The term indicates an essentially meaningful, "truth-finding" quality. Maslow used this term to describe a peak experience.

Passivity: A term indicating that mystics feel as if their own wills were not active and that they were under the control of a superior power.

Peak experiences: Intense, mystical experiences in which a person exists momentarily in a state of joy, awe, and wonderment. The qualities of such experiences are their noetic quality, transiency, passivity, and ineffability.

Satisfaction striving: The motor of personality. The individual is pulled by the need to be fulfilled.

Self-actualization: A state of exemplary personality integration; the full development of one's abilities and potentialities; the process of seeking one's essential nature.

Third force: A term that refers to the humanistic approach, as opposed to psychoanalysis, often referred to as the *first force.* Behaviorism is referred to as the *second force.*

Transiency: A term used, in this instance, to indicate that peak experiences are not usually sustained for long periods of time.

Transpersonal psychology: An approach to psychology that studies spirituality, higher states of consciousness, and ego transcendence. It is often referred to as the *fourth force.*

Carl Rogers

Client-centered therapy: An approach to counseling and psychotherapy that potentiates the client's own ability to discover and resolve problems. The therapist provides unconditional positive regard, accurate empathy, and a genuine relationship.

Conditions of worth: Conditions applied to a person to determine whether he or she receives approval or not. Parents and other people important in one's life may either give or withhold approval depending on one's behavior.

Fully functioning person: A person who is engaged in self-realization or self-actualization. Such a person is growth motivated, open to new experiences, and uses his or her potential maximally.

Ideal self: The individual's description or visualization of how he or she would like to be or become.

Nondirective therapy: An approach to counseling and therapy that relies on the individual's resources. The therapist uses techniques empathically to facilitate self-insight and clarification of feelings and refrains from unnecessary directness and advice.

Perceived self: The self, as perceived by an individual; how one perceives oneself.

Phenomenal world: The private world of experience and personal meaning, the individual's subjective reality.

Positive self-regard: The process of viewing oneself positively. A person with high self regard is open to the warmth and respect of others.

Q-sort: A technique used by Rogers to measure a person's self-concept. Rogers used it, for example, to assess the discrepancy between an individual's perceived self and ideal self.

Real self: A person's actual core of experience.

Self-congruence: The absence of any discrepancy between an individual's experiences and his or her self-concept.

Self-incongruence: The discrepancy between a person's experiences and his or her self-concept.

Self-structure: Parental conditions of worth (praise or blame) become internalized. They eventually form the basis of a person's self-structure.

Subception: The process of keeping an experience inconsistent with one's self-structure outside of awareness.

Unconditional positive regard: A relationship involving prizing or valuing another person without reservations or conditions of worth.

Chapter **14**

Watson

Skinner

John B. Watson & B. F. Skinner

Radical Behaviorism

Does the name Pavlov *ring a bell?*

Anonymous

Someday we shall have hospitals devoted to helping us change our personality because we will be able to change the personality as easily as we can change the shape of the nose, only it takes more time.

John B. Watson, Behaviorism

I am sometimes asked, "Do you think of yourself as you think of the organisms you study?" The answer is yes. So far as I know, my behavior at any given moment has been nothing more than the product of my genetic endowment, my personal history, and the current setting. That does not mean that I can explain everything I do or have done.

B. F. Skinner, A Matter of Consequences

About Radical Behaviorism

Radical behaviorism *began with John B. Watson's rejection of the method of introspectionistic psychology, the method of using inner states as explanations of behavior. Watson wanted to make psychology an experimental science, so he radically eliminated any attempt to study mind, conscious state, or other items that cannot be observed publicly.*

Following in this tradition, B. F. Skinner elevated behaviorism to a major orientation in psychology. Studying the behavior of single organisms in situations where their actions were instrumental in obtaining a desired effect, Skinner developed a reinforcement or operant theory of behavior.

The term radical behaviorism *began in regard to Watson's theories as an indication of what were considered Watson's extreme views. The term also became a formal designation for Skinner's approach to the science of behavior. Today, the term* radical behaviorism *still has a negative connotation for some psychologists but, for most psychologists, merely indicates a high degree of consistency and thoroughness (Schneider & Morris, 1987).*

In this chapter, the conceptual history of behaviorism's development is selectively traced by focusing on areas of interest to students of personality. Watson and Skinner did not see themselves as personality theorists per se, but rather as behavioral scientists who studied observable behaviors.

John B. Watson   **Born: 1878   Greenville, South Carolina**
Died: 1958   New York, New York

THE TRADITION OF RADICAL BEHAVIORISM

The theorists we have studied thus far picture the human mind as the inner cause of a person's actions. From Sigmund Freud through Carl Rogers, personality puzzles were solved with the presumption that *thought,* either conscious or unconscious, causes action. John B. Watson (1878–1958), the founder of behaviorism, found such solutions puzzling.

"The time seems to have come," wrote Watson in his characteristically direct way, "when psychology must discard all reference to consciousness; when it need no longer delude itself into thinking that it is making mental states the object of observation" (1914/1967, p. 7). In contrast to Freud's concern with hidden wishes and thoughts, Watson chose to study what people actually do:

> The behaviorist asks: Why don't we make what we can *observe* the real field of psychology? Let us limit ourselves to things that can be observed, and formulate laws concerning only those things. Now what can we observe? We can observe behavior—what the organism says or does. . . . (Watson, 1924/1930, p. 6)

Watson was reacting to the tradition of introspection in psychology, an approach that emphasized the importance of an individual's introspecting ("looking within") and then describing his or her thoughts and mental states (Buss, 1978). Watson considered any such approach to be unscientific and unreliable. In addition, Watson was particularly critical of the additional Freudian emphasis on unconscious mental processes.

To Watson, Pavlov's just published work on the conditioned reflex (1927, 1928) held the scientific key to all complex human action. Watson understood Pavlovian **classical conditioning** as automatic and involuntary. Animals and people could acquire conditioned behaviors without their awareness, provided the appropriate conditions were arranged. Whether mental processes somehow mediated such learning was a question Watson, like Pavlov, considered irrelevant to explaining or understanding the causes of behavior (Bandura, 1974; Shevrin & Dickman, 1980). Table 14.1 summarizes the main Pavlovian concepts.

For Watson, human beings are malleable and trainable by the proper arrangement of environmental conditions. Watson endeavored to explain even strong emotional responses as chains of conditioned associations with demonstrable causal links between stimuli and the responses. He made the challenging claim:

> Give me a dozen healthy infants, well formed, and my own specified world to bring them up in and I'll guarantee to take any one at random and train him to become any type of specialist I might select—doctor, lawyer, artist, merchant-chief and yes, even beggar man and thief, regardless of his talents, penchants, tendencies, abilities, vocations and race of his ancestors. I am going beyond my facts and I admit it, but so have the advocates of the contrary and they have been doing it for many thousands of years. (Watson, 1924/1930, p. 104)

In support of his emphasis on the importance of **conditioning,** Watson began a comprehensive study of newborns "to catalog the birth equipment of the human young," that

Table 14.1   Summary of Key Pavlovian Concepts

1. UNCONDITIONED STIMULUS (UCS): *Unlearned Input*

Before conditioning, this event reliably and automatically triggers a response that does not require prior experience with the stimulus.

EXAMPLE: AIRPUFF to eyelid elicits a FULL EYEBLINK.

UCS (airpuff) → UCR (full eyeblink)

2. UNCONDITIONED RESPONSE (UCR): *Unlearned Output*

Before conditioning, this behavior, usually a reflex, is reliably and automatically elicited by the UCS.

EXAMPLE: Airpuff to eyelid elicits a FULL EYEBLINK.

UCS (airpuff) → UCR (full eyeblink)

3. CONDITIONED STIMULUS (CS): *Learned Input*

Before conditioning, CS is a neutral event and elicits no reliable response; but arranged so that CS precedes UCS by a fraction of a second for a number of trials, the CS will evoke a response that resembles the UCR in anticipation of the UCS, but which is reduced in magnitude and slower in response time.

EXAMPLE: Tone comes before airpuff 20 times and then elicits a REDUCED, SLOWER EYEBLINK without the airpuff on 21st trial.

For 20 times: CS (tone) + UCS (airpuff) → UCR (eyeblink)

Then on 21st trial: CS (tone) → CR (reduced eyeblink)

4. CONDITIONED RESPONSE (CR): *Learned Output*

Learned response elicited by the CS in anticipation of the UCS; but the CR only resembles the reflex UCR because its magnitude and latency (response time) are reduced.

EXAMPLE: Tone that comes before airpuff elicits a REDUCED EYEBLINK.

CS (tone) → CR (reduced eyeblink)

5. EXTINCTION:

Withholding the UCS (airpuff) while presenting the CS repeatedly (tone) until the CS no longer elicits the CR (reduced eyeblink). Organism stops blinking at the sound of the tone.

is, to ascertain what innate or unlearned behaviors were present. He hoped to demonstrate that the increasingly complex behaviors of growing infants came about through the development of more complex conditioned responses out of an initial base of a few simple instinctual behaviors.

POSSIBLE PERSONAL ASPECTS OF WATSON'S RADICAL BEHAVIORISM

Admitting to a strong negative emotional reaction toward maternal expressions of affection, Watson confessed: "When I hear a mother say 'Bless its little heart' when it falls down, or stubs its toe, or suffers some other ill, I usually have to walk a block or two to let off steam" (Watson & Rayner, 1928, p. 82). According to Watson, kissing, cuddling, and patting a child on the head constitute a "dangerous experiment" conducted by mothers, who themselves are "starved for love." Such maternal "interference," Watson believed, robs the child "of its opportunity for conquering the world."

In Watson's view, a widespread detrimental parental practice is "coddling," an emotional indulgence that he believed deprives the child of precious time during development to learn how to conquer its world. The infant "must have time to pull his universe apart and put it together again" (Watson & Rayner, 1928, pp. 79 and 80). Instead, Watson encouraged mothers to treat their children in what he termed a more "sensible" way:

> Treat them as though they were young adults. Dress them, bathe them with care and circumspection. Let your behavior always be objective and kindly firm. Never hug and kiss them, never let them sit in your lap. If you must, kiss them once on the forehead when they say good night. Shake hands with them in the morning. Give them a pat on the head if they have made an extraordinarily good job of a difficult task. (Watson & Rayner, 1928, pp. 81–82)

The expression of positive emotions and even ordinary caring feelings and affection troubled Watson throughout his life (cf. Buckley, 1989, pp. 120–121). Early on, he started to think of such feelings as habits that could be controlled or avoided. As already indicated, though, he had little trouble feeling negative emotions when observing open expressions of affection. There is nothing inherent in radical behaviorism itself to indicate that children should not be shown affection by their mothers; it was Watson's personal views that led to such assertions. Knowing something about his family background, we can have more of an understanding of the context in which his way of approaching positive feelings and emotions developed.

Watson's Childhood: Long-Suffering Mother, Explosive Father

Born fourth among six children in 1878, John Broadus Watson was named for John Albert Broadus, a prominent South Carolina Baptist minister-theologian. Emma Roe Watson, Watson's mother, hoped and prayed that her son John would follow in his namesake's footsteps to a career in the ministry (Buckley, 1989, p. 4). Her influence shaped John's ambitions until nearly the end of his college years, when he applied to Princeton Theological Seminary.

Pickens Butler Watson, Watson's father, was a notorious character in South Carolina. He left home at age 16 to enlist in the Confederate Army, where he earned a reputation for reckless impulsiveness. A brawling alcoholic, Pickens's explosive anger found targets among family, friends, and neighbors. He was an erratic, possibly abusive, spouse and an unpredictable, explosive, and frequently absent father. From a contemporary perspective, these symptoms lead one to wonder if he had developed posttraumatic stress disorder from his Civil War experiences. By the time of John Broadus Watson's birth, Emma and Pickens Watson were social outcasts. The neighbors shunned Pickens Watson for his aggressive, impulsive behavior. He failed at farming and at a number of other jobs, and eventually took to being a "wanderer," who would return only occasionally and briefly at that (Buckley, 1989, p. 3).

Emma Watson's strong religious faith helped her cope well in her difficult circumstances. She wanted more for her children than a life of poverty, loneliness, and adversity. In 1890, she sold the farm and moved the family to Greenville, South Carolina, where better educational and economic opportunities existed.

The young John's rural ways and different manner made him the butt of his classmates' jokes in Greenville. He reacted aggressively and earned a nickname of "Swats" for his propensity to get in fights with his tormentors and others (Buckley, 1989, p. 7). John was arrested once for fighting, and a second time for discharging firearms within the city limits. As his biographer Kerry Buckley concludes, Watson's adolescence was a troubled time (1989, p. 7). Like his father, he was overtly aggressive and impulsive.

Watson's Ambitious College Years

In 1894, at the age of 16, Watson entered the college prep program of Furman University. At that time, there were no public high schools in South Carolina and colleges offered "sub-freshman" programs for those students wanting to continue their education (Buckley, 1989, p. 9). Watson was an intelligent and ambitious adolescent, and college was the path to his goals. In spite of this, he had low grades, and graduated 16th in a class of 22 from Furman five years later. He earned both an undergraduate and master's degree from this university.

Watson's biographer explained that, even though he was intelligent, he was ambivalent toward success. "Watson's constant striving for achievement and approval was often sabotaged by acts of sheer obstinacy and impulsiveness more characteristic of a flight from respectability" (Buckley, 1989, p. 12). An example is Watson's (1936) reported relationship with one of his psychology professors, Gordon B. Moore. Moore had studied at the University of Chicago under the prominent philosopher, John Dewey. According to Watson, Moore told his class that any student who turned in his final examination with its pages in reverse order would fail the course. Out of contrariness, Watson did just that and was promptly flunked. His graduation was delayed for over a year.

Despite his bad grades, Watson composed a letter to the president of the University of Chicago asking to be accepted to the school as a doctoral student. He described himself accurately in the letter as a poor student but eager for "advanced work in a real university" (Buckley, 1989, p. 15). He was able to get the president of Furman University to write a strong letter of recommendation for him, and largely as a result of this personal endorsement, Watson was awarded a partial scholarship at the University of Chicago. The future pioneer of radical behaviorism was on his way to graduate school.

Watson in Academia: Toward the Breaking Point

The University of Chicago provided an intellectual milieu where a newly emerging experimental approach to psychology was blossoming. Watson took courses with Jacques

Loeb, an eminent zoologist who taught that scientific knowledge was the road to understanding and controlling the behavior of organisms. Watson was attracted to and quickly grasped the ideas of Loeb and the experimental psychologists at Chicago. As a graduate student, he began to develop and conduct a pioneering series of experiments that led to the development of radical behaviorism.

In the year before he earned his doctorate, however, Watson experienced what he later called a "breakdown" (Watson, 1936). He had several jobs at once to support himself and was simultaneously struggling to be a top student in the department. At around the same time, a young woman with whom he wanted a relationship rejected him. The symptoms he reported appear to have been a combination of anxiety, insomnia, and depression. Today, one might say that he was "stressed out." He endured weeks of not being able to sleep, followed by a need to have the lights on during those few times when he could sleep. Watson bounced back with long walks and academic and laboratory pursuits.

Watson saw a silver lining in his dark experience. He wrote that it taught him to accept a "large part" of Freud's ideas, just as it had taught him to be more cautious in life or, as he put it, "watch his step" (Watson, 1936, p. 272ff.; Buckley, 1989, pp. 43–44). Watson reinvested himself more fully in his work, and the pattern of exercise and intellectual activity continued through much of his life.

Watson's biographer suggests that at least part of the cause of his breakdown was his discovery that his new professional world was fraught with competition (Buckley, 1989, pp. 43–44). In Buckley's view, Watson suffered from both fear of failure and fear of success. Watson's self-discipline was sometimes overwhelmed by conflict, anxiety, and uncertainty. Small wonder that Freudian ideas began to make some sense to this father of behaviorism.

Watson the Cad

Watson's personal life at the university was stormy. He presented himself as a daring, charmingly romantic young man but privately deeply distrusted intimacy in any form (Buckley, 1989, p. 49). According to all accounts, he acted like a cad. On the rebound from one of his relationships, Watson became interested in Mary Ickes, a 19-year-old student from a very prominent family. Mary's brother, Harold Ickes, a successful attorney who eventually became a member of Franklin Roosevelt's presidential cabinet, despised Watson and made no secret of his feelings. Harold profoundly distrusted Watson and thought that he was an unprincipled social climber (Buckley, 1989, p. 51).

Watson and Mary Ickes were secretly wed in 1903 against the wishes of her brother. They did not live together for the first year of their marriage because Harold intervened to separate them and sent Mary to live with an aunt. Apparently, Harold Ickes thought that Watson and Mary were not yet married but only engaged. A young woman who had previously rejected Watson reentered his life during this period of separation. John and Mary at last had a public marriage ceremony in 1904. At this time, he confessed to her the entire episode with the other woman (Buckley, 1989, p. 50).

Watson received his doctorate from the University of Chicago in 1903 at the age of 25 and became the University's youngest PhD. For the next four years Watson worked as an instructor in psychology. Other professional offers soon were coming in for this pioneer in behavioral psychology. Eventually, he received an offer from Johns Hopkins University for a full professorship at a salary of $3,500, a large sum for the day. Watson set out for Johns Hopkins, where he was to make psychological history with his laboratory work and writings. By 1913, Watson was ready to publish a famous paper declaring the birth of the new orientation of radical behaviorism in psychology. This paper, "Psychology as the Behaviorist Views It," was of great interest to both academic psychologists and the more general intellectual community.

The End of Watson's Career in Academe

In Baltimore, Watson would not only make his mark in the field of psychology but he would become involved in one adulterous affair too many, which would lead to a highly publicized divorce trial that subsequently ended his career at Johns Hopkins.

Sometime during 1906–1907, Watson's former girlfriend reappeared in his life. His brother-in-law, Harold Ickes, hired a private detective who reported that Watson was seeing this woman regularly (Buckley, 1989, p. 55). Ickes tried to persuade his sister to divorce Watson, and he even tried to have Watson fired from the University, but Ickes failed at both enterprises thanks to the intervention of one of Watson's colleagues at the University.

The events of the winter of 1919–1920, however, proved too scandalous for the University. Watson and his graduate assistant Rosalie Rayner began work on conditioned emotional reactions with the infant "Little Albert B." in a series of studies destined to add to Watson's fame. This work is described in more detail later in the chapter. Watson regarded these experiments as demonstrating that emotions were simply acquired conditioned reflexes. But as Watson's scientific reputation was nearing its zenith, he and his assistant became adulterously involved.

In this latest instance of unfaithfulness to Mary, Watson went beyond what his personal and professional community could tolerate. The affair between the young graduate student, Rosalie Rayner, and Professor John B. Watson became public knowledge and led to a plethora of newspaper stories. The fact that Rosalie's family was prominent in Baltimore political and economic circles and that Watson was a leading professor at Johns Hopkins and in the field of psychology simply added fodder to the public's craving for a juicy scandal. Mary Watson, still embittered from her husband's earlier liaisons, stole some of Watson's love letters to Rosalie Rayner. The resulting divorce trial with its revelations resulted in the destruction of Watson's career at Johns Hopkins. His former colleagues shunned him.

After Watson's divorce in 1920, he married Rosalie Rayner. In the meantime, he worked at establishing a career outside of academic life. Eventually, he secured a position with a prominent advertising agency, where he brought to bear the same intelligence and tenacity that had proven so successful in changing the face of psychology. He was, at the same time, also able to write popular and professional psychology books and articles that kept his name before the public and the academic community.

Transitional Summary: Watson's Life and His Radical Behaviorism

Watson did not want to be ordinary. He struggled and succeeded to make himself into something exceptional. He was brilliant and worked tirelessly and successfully to become a star in the field of psychology. At the same time, his ardent and, at times, adulterous pursuits of women led to an unstable and scandalous personal life. Finally, he was able to enter and to achieve success in the field of advertising, to which he had to retreat as a result of rejection by the academic world.

Is there a connection between Watson's life history and his behavioral approach to psychology? Perhaps Watson's approach to psychology was connected to his way of understanding the origins of his own behavior and emotions. He might well have concluded

---

It is interesting to try to understand the life of a personality theorist by using the theories of other theorists. In the case of Watson, for example, Alfred Adler's (Chapter 5) concept of inferiority feelings and superiority strivings, which in Watson appear very marked, is relevant. Also, the Jungian theory of psychological types (Chapter 4) can usefully be applied. Watson shows every indication that he was a "thinking" not a "feeling" type, "sensing" not "intuitive," and an "extroverted" not an "introverted" individual. His behavior appears to correspond closely to the ISTP (introverted, sensing, thinking, perception) type. You can see descriptions of this profile on the Internet by entering ISTP type on a search engine such as at the Internet address: www.google.com

---

that his rejecting father and difficult and unpredictable environment during an impoverished childhood led to his instability, rage, and alienation. Certainly, his life history indicates that, though he was a brilliant thinker and a great achiever, he did not seem be able to change some of his most self-destructive behaviors. One might also speculate that Watson's avoidance of the softer side of human behavior, feelings, and emotions in his scientific work reflected just such a blind spot toward feelings and empathy with others in his overall experience.

CONDITIONING LITTLE "ALBERT B."

Watson and his second wife, Rosalie Rayner Watson, applied Pavlov's conditioning methods to a nine-month-old child (Watson & Rayner, 1920). "Albert B.," as he was named for the report, was raised from birth in a children's hospital where his mother worked as a "wet nurse." Described as "stolid and unemotional," little Albert served as an experimental subject for the Watsons from his ninth month well past his first birthday. One aim of the experiments was to demonstrate that complex emotional responses, in this case *fear,* are developed through the principles of Pavlovian or classical conditioning.

Thus, at approximately nine months of age, Albert was supported on a tabletop equipped with a mattress, while John Watson successively presented the child with a white rat, rabbit, dog, monkey, costume masks with and without hair, ball of white cotton wool, and burning newspapers. As Albert had no experience with such stimuli, his reaction was one of curiosity or eagerness to touch the objects. According to the Watsons, Albert showed no fear and never cried.

When Albert was 11 months and 3 days old, the Watsons began their conditioning regimen. Previous research had shown that abrupt loud sounds such as that made by a hammer struck against a metal bar called forth a sharp fear reaction in most infants. Here was the opportunity to follow Pavlov's method: combine an **unconditioned stimulus** (loud sound) that reliably elicits an **unconditioned response** (startle, crying) with a neutral **conditioned stimulus** (white rat, for example), and wait to see whether the conditioned stimulus will eventually elicit a **conditioned response** similar to the original unconditioned response (startle, crying). The sequence is summarized in Figure 14.1. Watson and Rayner described their first attempt at conditioning in this way:

> White rat suddenly taken from the basket and presented to Albert. He began to reach for rat with left hand. Just as his hand touched the animal the [metal] bar was struck [with a

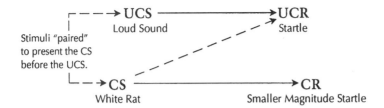

UCS = Unconditioned Stimulus
UCR = Unconditioned Response

CS = Conditioned Stimulus
CR = Conditioned Response

Figure 14.1 The Pavlovian paradigm for Watson's Little Albert studies.

hammer] immediately behind his head. The infant jumped violently and fell forward, burying his face in the mattress. He did not cry, however. (Watson & Rayner, 1920, p. 8)

A second trial was conducted, and then Albert was given a week's rest. About a week later, the white rat was presented suddenly to Albert without the loud sound, and gradually brought nearer to the infant. He did not cry, but he withdrew his hand. Then Albert was exposed to a series of conditioning trials "to freshen" the conditioned responses. Rat and loud sound were paired for several trials, with the expectable result that Albert cringed, withdrew his body sharply away from the rat, and "puckered his face" while whimpering. Eventually, presentation of the white rat alone was sufficient to cause Albert to display the full range of fear responses reliably without the loud sound accompanying the rat.

In ensuing weeks, Albert was presented with a variety of new stimuli, all of which were white: a white rabbit, a fur seal coat, a dog, a ball of white cotton, and even John Watson's own head of white hair. On the whole, Albert's fear responses and withdrawal efforts became generalized to all of these stimuli, presumably because of their similarity to the original conditioned stimulus of the white rat. There were differences in degree of reaction, with the dog eliciting the least fear and withdrawal. Watson and Rayner's definite conclusion was that Albert had learned these emotional responses as a generalized reaction to a known history of Pavlovian conditioning.

By the age of 1 year, 21 days, after a 31-day rest interval, Watson and Rayner exposed Albert to a Santa Claus mask, fur coat, and white rat with somewhat reduced but still detectable fear and withdrawal reactions. The Watsons also noted Albert's propensity for the "compensatory blocking" behavior of thumb sucking during stressful moments of testing. So successful was Albert's self-soothing thumb sucking that the Watsons had to remove Albert's thumb from his mouth to obtain the conditioned fear responses. Among the conclusions that Watson drew from his work with Albert and from other observational studies of infants were these two:

1. Freud was wrong about the primacy of sexual urges as motives. Clearly, Watson thought that Albert's conditioning history demonstrated at least an equally important place for learned fears in shaping personality development.

2. Phobic disorders (irrational and inappropriately intense fears of objects, places, persons) can be explained by straightforward conditioning principles without resort to hypothetical unconscious associations, wishes, or conflicts. Thus Little

Albert's apparently bizarre fear of white, furry objects can be explained in light of his learning history.

The Watsons concluded their report with this imaginary account of what might happen if, decades later, little Albert, now a young man, were to be treated with Freudian psychoanalysis:

> The Freudians 20 years from now, unless their hypotheses change, when they come to analyze Albert's fear of a seal skin coat—assuming that he comes to analysis at that age—will probably tease from him the recital of a dream which upon their analysis will show that Albert at three years of age attempted to play with the pubic hair of the mother and was scolded violently for it. (We are by no means denying that this might in some other case condition it.) If the analyst has sufficiently prepared Albert to accept such a dream when found as an explanation of his avoiding tendencies, and if the analyst has the authority and personality to put it over, Albert may be fully convinced that the dream was a true revealer of the factors which brought about the fear. (Watson & Rayner, 1920, p. 16)

In other words, a Freudian would falsely conclude that a fear of incest was the source of Albert's experimentally conditioned fear of a sealskin coat.

It is interesting to note that, even though Watson and Rayner were critical of Freudian explanations, they concurred with Freud that infancy and childhood were important periods in the development of behavior and that the early childhood environment played a crucial role.

BASIC ASSUMPTIONS OF WATSON'S RADICAL BEHAVIORISM

There were four main assumptions underlying Watson's approach:

1. Evolutionary continuity: Human and animal behavior are not different in kind. The Watsonian behaviorist "recognizes no dividing line between man and brute" (Watson, 1916/1967, p. 1). Human behavior differs from animal behavior only in the degree of its complexity. Natural selection shaped the human species to adapt to increasingly complex environments, but such behavior is behavior, no matter the organism. Study of the simpler behavior of animals holds the promise of shedding light on the more complex behavior of humans.

2. Reductionism: This approach looks at behavior in terms of the simplest physical components. Watson believed that all human behavior is understandable as the workings of glandular and nervous systems. And the workings of the nervous and glandular systems may be traced to the biochemical processes that operate within these structures. Watson believed that behavioral processes are always to be understood in terms of their constituent parts, whether the parts are at the structural level of the brain or at the molecular level of events in brain cells. A psychologist may observe gross behavior, but what he or she is studying is really the effect of the activity of electrons in atoms in molecules in cells! Viewed in this way, behavior is "nothing but" biochemistry.

3. Determinism: At the behavioral level, every response is determined by the external events (current stimuli, previous conditioned responses) that precede it. No organism behaves spontaneously or whimsically or completely freely. Behavior, strictly speaking, is never accidental. There is always some causal chain of physical events ultimately responsible for the observed behavior.

Table 14.2   The Assumptions of Watson's Radical Behaviorism

Principle	Rationale	Influence on psychology	Interpretation of psychopathology
1. Evolutionary continuity	Behavior is behavior. Humans and animals differ only in degree of complexity.	Fostered study of animal behavior as simple model of complex human responses.	Abnormal behavior is maladaptive responding in a particular situation compared to other members of species.
2. Reductionism	Behavior is analyzable into component physiologic and biochemical events in the central nervous system and peripheral musculature.	Biology and chemistry are crucial sources of knowledge about behavior; nonmaterial explanations of behavior are nonscientific.	Behavior and its supportive biology and biochemistry lie on a single dimension so that changes in one variable are reflected in changes in the other. Normal and abnormal behavior lie on a single dimension, with abnormal differing only in degree of adaptiveness.
3. Determinism	Behavior is caused by prior stimulation and is never accidental, random, or "free." Mental states are epiphenomenal, and never causal.	Goal of scientific psychology is the prediction and control of human behavior by knowledge of stimulus-response relationships.	Normal and abnormal behavior are learned, and necessary and sufficient conditions of learning are found in principles of conditioning.
4. Empiricism	Only observable, measurable events have impact on organisms; only observables can be scientifically verified.	Experimental method became the key tool of psychology. Introspective and subjective data and methods are suspect.	Symptoms are not signs of hidden unconscious conflict or disease states. Symptoms are the disorder and are changed by new conditioning.

Note: A common denominator underlying these four principles in their radical Watsonian form is the exclusion, on scientific grounds, of subjective data and methods from psychology and psychopathology.

    4. Empiricism: Watson insisted on experimental method. He considered only measurable and controllable phenomena suitable as the objects of study for a psychology aspiring to natural science status. For Watson, research had two fundamental aims: ". . . to be able to predict and to control human activity" (Watson, 1924/1930, p. 11).

    Table 14.2 summarizes basic assumptions of Watson's approach.

WATSON'S COMMONSENSE VIEW OF PERSONALITY

    In a clear exposition of his ideas, Watson summarized his definition of behaviorism and his views on instinct, emotions, habits, thinking, verbal behavior, and personality (Watson, 1914/1967). Here we will briefly present his way of thinking about personality. Watson defined what we call personality as consisting of our observation of a person's activities:

> *Personality is the sum of activities that can be discovered by actual observation of behavior over a long enough time to give reliable information. In other words, personality is but the end product of our habit systems. Our procedure in studying personality is the making and plotting of a cross section of the activity stream.* (Watson, 1914/1967, p. 274, italics in original)

Watson continues by indicating that our habit systems are elicited by environmental factors:

> . . . *the situation we are in dominates us always and releases one or another of these all-powerful habit systems.* . . . In general, we are what the situation calls for—a respectable person before our preacher and our parents, a hero in front of the ladies, a teetotaler in one group, a bibulous good fellow in another. (Watson, 1914/1967, p. 276, italics in original)

Watson follows with a brief exposition of very commonsensical ways of studying personality, in which he puts an emphasis on the actual behavior patterns, or "track record," of an individual. He mentions examining the educational background of an individual, the accomplishments of the person, ascertaining not only the person's ability through testing, but also the person's work habits. He writes about examining how the person gets along with others in daily life and finding out about his or her recreational activities. He indicates that interviews have some value but that people often overestimate their ability to make sound personality judgments based on interviewing alone:

> The voice of the person under observation, his gestures, his gait, his personal appearance—all of these I think are significant. You can tell in a moment whether the individual is or is not a cultivated individual, whether or not he has good manners. One individual will come in for an interview and will keep his hat on his head and his cigar in his mouth; another will be so scared that he cannot even talk; still another will be so boastful that you want to escape his presence immediately. . . . But personal interviews tell us nothing about work habits and nothing about the honesty of the individual, nothing about the steadfastness of his principles and little about his ability. Here again we have to fall back upon a study of the life history of the individual . . . (Watson, 1914/1967, pp. 286–287)

and

> Why is it, then, that office managers and the public general believe that they can read personalities? Probably the main reason is that it flatters them to think that they can . . . at best the selection of personnel today is little better than a hit or miss affair. This is the reason the psychological faker gets along so easily. (Watson, 1914/1967, p. 287)

In his exposition, Watson discusses human foibles, a reluctance to admit to weakness, our "susceptibility to flattery and human self-centeredness and self aggrandizement," which Watson calls, "our constant strife to become kings and queens" (Watson, 1914/1967, p. 192).

> . . . every man can watch his own way of acting and he will often be surprised when he comes to face the real stimuli that touch off his actions. Susceptibility to flattery, selfishness, avoiding difficult situations, unwillingness to show or to confess weakness, inadequacy or lack of knowledge, jealousy, fear of rivals, fear of being made the scapegoat, hurling criticism upon other to escape it oneself—make up an almost unbelievable part of our natures. The individual when he really faces himself is often almost (if not quite) overcome by what is revealed—infantile behavior, unethical standards, smothered over by the thinnest veneer of rationalization. Nakedness of "soul" can be faced only by the truly brave. (Watson, 1914/1967, p. 291)

And what about personality change? Here again, Watson is clear, if not oversimplifying:

> There must be both unlearning the things we have already learned (and the unlearning may be an active *unconditioning* process or just *disuse*) and *learning* the new things, which is always an active process. Thus the only way thoroughly to change personality is to remake the individual by changing his environment in such a way that new habits have to form. The

Only Connect . . .

Watson's view of personality, as might be expected, is one that emphasizes observable behaviors and puts the greatest stock in persistent, habitual patterns. In this way, it can be related from Gordon Allport's concept of traits (Chapter 11). Even though Allport considered traits to be more than hypothetical constructs and actually to reside *within* the individual, he relied on the observation of regularities of behavior and life history.

more completely they change the more personality changes. (Watson, 1914/1967, p. 302, italics in original)

Reading these passages, we infer that Watson's emphasis on the laboratory for developing his research findings did not get in the way of a very commonsense approach to personality. His understanding is not removed from the experiences of daily life and provides a perspective that can be very useful and practical. Watson's own personality and values also emerge in these passages. He seems to be a no-nonsense individual who is achievement-oriented and values that characteristic in others.

RADICAL BEHAVIORISM AND PSYCHOPATHOLOGY

Watson extended his principles to the phenomena of abnormal behavior. He provided an illuminating example of his thinking on abnormal psychology in the case of his "psychopathological dog." The case shows how strongly he believed that abnormal behavior could be understood and cured through behavioral means alone, without any idea of cognitive or emotional factors:

To show the needlessness of introducing the "conception of mind" in so-called mental diseases, I offer you a fanciful picture of a psychopathological dog. . . . Without taking anyone into my counsel suppose I once trained a dog so that he would walk away from nicely ground, fresh hamburg steak and would eat only decayed fish (true examples of this are now at hand). I trained him (by use of electric shock) to avoid smelling the female dog in the usual canine way—he would circle around her but would come no closer than 10 feet. . . . Again, by letting him play only with male puppies and dogs and punishing him when he tried to mount a female, I made a homosexual of him. . . . Instead of licking my hands and becoming lively and playful when I go to him in the morning, he hides or cowers, whines and shows his teeth. . . . He sleeps only two hours per day and sleeps these two hours leaning up against a wall rather than lying down with head and rump touching. He is thin and emaciated because he will eat no fats. He salivates constantly (because I have conditioned him to salivate to hundreds of objects). This interferes with his digestion. Then I take him to the dog psychopathologist. His physiological reflexes are normal. No organic lesions are to be found anywhere. The dog, so the psychopathologist claims, is mentally sick, actually insane; his mental condition has led to the various organic difficulties such as lack of digestion; it has "caused" his poor physical condition. Everything that a dog should do . . . he does not do. And everything that seems foreign for a dog to do he does. The psychopathologist says I must commit the dog to an institution for the care of insane dogs; that if he is not restrained he will jump from a 10-story building, or walk into a fire without hesitation. I tell the dog psychopathologist that he doesn't know anything about my dog; that, from the standpoint of the environment in which the dog has been brought up (the way I have trained him), he is the most normal dog in the world; that the reasons he calls the dog "insane" or mentally sick is because of his own absurd system of classification.

> I then take the psychopathologist into my confidence. He becomes extremely angry. "Since you've brought this on, go cure him." I attempt then to correct my dog's behavior difficulties, at least up to the point where he can begin to associate with the nice dogs in the neighborhood. . . . I use behavioristic methods. I uncondition him and then condition him. Soon I get him to eating fresh meat by getting him hungry, closing up his nose and feeding him in the dark. This gives me a good start. I have something basal to use in my further work. I keep him hungry and feed him only when I open his cage in the morning; the whip is thrown away; soon he jumps for joy when he hears my step. In a few months' time I not only have cleared out the old but also have built in the new. (Watson, 1924/1930, pp. 298–300).

Watson's view of psychopathology focused on learned patterns of habit, pain-avoidance, and appetite. The dog psychopathologist, in his imagined scenario, was lured into the Watsonian trap of postulating a series of unobservable mental states causing the dog's "diseased" behavior. Watson's point is that the dog's conditioning history makes the psychopathologist's explanations irrelevant.

Watson's story of a dog with abnormal behavior patterns illustrates a number of basic aspects of his approach:

1. It is clear from Watson's willingness to use an animal example of psychopathology that his belief in *evolutionary continuity* of behavior applies to abnormal behavior as well as to normal behavior.

2. One aspect of Watson's *reductionism* is exemplified in his assertion that there is a direct connection between the dog's learned pathological behavior and the biologic ("organic") symptoms that it develops. Certainly, those responses that interfere with normal eating and digestion have a direct negative effect on the dog's health.

3. Watson's thoroughgoing *determinism* is shown by his insistence that the dog's behavior is completely explicable in terms of its conditioning history. Behavior is determined and lawful. Manipulation of the proper sequence of stimuli and responses could produce the desired outcome, even when such an outcome consisted of behavior that was considered abnormal or pathological. Moreover, the application of conditioning principles should also be able to undo the original learning and/or replace it with new learning.

4. Watson's *empiricism* is found in his assumption that the dog's psychopathology is not a sign of some underlying, hypothesized "mental disease." Symptoms are behaviors. They are not signs of unconscious conflicts. They do not reflect unobservable mental events. Symptoms do not reflect anything but the conditions under which complex behavior is learned. The dog's observable symptoms *are* its psychopathology.

From Watson's point of view, the solutions created by Freud to the puzzles of psychopathology are no solutions at all. In his view, Freud merely constructed more cumbersome puzzles. Watson's approach to Freud's puzzles aimed at ruling them out of existence. For, if pathology is to be found in the organism's behavior, problems such as self-deception, symbolic meaning, and unconscious conflict cease to be real problems in themselves.

B. F. Skinner   Born: 1904   Susquehanna, Pennsylvania
Died: 1990   Cambridge, Massachusetts

SKINNER'S (LESS) RADICAL BEHAVIORISM

By the late 1930s, behaviorism was about to undergo a major change. A young experimental psychologist at the University of Minnesota had, years before, found the answer to a personal crisis in the hard-nosed empiricism of John Watson. The theory and methods he would develop provided the scientific rationale for a theory of behavior that dominated psychology until the 1960s. Burrhus Frederic Skinner (1938) extended Watson's behaviorism beyond the level of Pavlovian conditioning into the more complex arena of voluntary behavior.

In our study of Skinner's behaviorism, we will focus on those features that are most relevant to the subject matter of personality. In the example that follows, the main theme of Skinner's account of human behavior and some differences from John Watson's behaviorism are highlighted. The child's behavior is not reflex behavior. There is no identifiable triggering stimulus. And there are a host of possible responses that the child can make, each of them having different consequences.

Behaviors and Their Consequences

It is difficult to specify precisely what prompts a child to treat a tall set of bookshelves as if it were a ladder. But the fact that its climb to the top shelf is successful leads us to predict increased furniture climbing on this and on other heart-stopping pieces of temptation in the future. It is the *consequence* of the child's behavior—successfully reaching the top—that increases the frequency of such behavior.

Unlike Watson's little Albert, for whom a specific stimulus triggered a specific and *automatic* response, the immediate trigger for our little bookcase climber's behavior is not clear. Certainly the bookcase itself is a stimulus to action, but what action? For this child, the action is climbing. For another child, the bookcase might be a stimulus to touching, or scattering books on the floor, or running small toy cars on the shelves. It is the same stimulus in each case, but knowledge of the stimulus does not predict different children's behaviors.

For our climber, the act of climbing was strictly voluntary, and it was "emitted" behavior not "elicited" by the stimulus of the bookcase. Another way to state that distinction is to say that the bookcase provided the occasion for the response, but it did not cause the response to occur. From a whole repertoire of potential responses, this child climbed on the bookcase. The bookcase itself, unlike little Albert's frightening loud sound, did not, by itself, produce this child's climbing response.

What, then, determines the probability that such climbing will continue? For the first and successful climb, it is the consequence of reaching the top that *increases* the probability that the child will behave the same way again. A fall or an anguished parental scream is other potential consequences that will *reduce* the frequency of climbing. But for both positive and negative consequences, this voluntary, exploratory behavior can best be predicted (and controlled) by describing (or arranging) the consequences of the behavior.

E. L. Thorndike and the Law of Effect

Edward L. Thorndike (1874–1949) had shown that a cat generates a great wealth of responses trying to release itself from a cagelike puzzle box to reach a dish of food just outside the door. At first, the cat roams around the box, sniffs at the corners, scratches at various points on the wall, and may even bite at the slats of the door. Eventually, all of this trial-and-error behavior accidentally results in triggering the simple latch mechanism of the door, which springs open, thus permitting the cat to escape and to reach the food dish. On subsequent trials, the cat spends less and less time on behaviors that were ineffective attempts to escape, and more and more time scratching and pawing at the door. Those of its responses that were closest in time to actual escape (i.e., behavior directed to the door latch) had the rewarding consequence of reaching food. By the 13th or 16th trial, the cat's escape time drops from nearly three minutes on the first trial to a scant five seconds (Thorndike, 1911). At this point, the cat has learned to escape. In Thorndike's vocabulary, the cat has "dropped out" of its repertoire those "random" responses unrelated to escape, and has repeated only those responses instrumental in securing release. Such successful responses are "stamped in" or "strengthened" by the pleasurable consequences of the food reward.

From studies such as these, Thorndike formulated a set of "Laws of Learning." For present purposes, Thorndike's most famous law, The **Law of Effect,** will be sufficient to show the most immediate intellectual precursor of Skinner's work. Thorndike's Law of Effect states that a response that leads to a "satisfying state of affairs" is strengthened, whereas responses that are less satisfying or "annoying" are weakened and will occur less frequently. Thorndike was stating an observable relationship between behavior and its consequences. It is the effect produced by a behavior that determines the behavior's future probability of occurrence.

Skinner's Empirical Law of Effect

In the late 1930s, B. F. Skinner, in the tradition of John Watson and Edward Thorndike, was able to show that a broad range of behavior can be acquired, changed, and regulated by manipulating its consequences in the laboratory. But Skinner, in the tradition of Watson, preferred to avoid mentalistic terms such as pleasure and satisfaction in favor of the direct description of the observable events. Whereas Thorndike attributed pleasurable properties to the food reward, Skinner would prefer to say simply that food "strengthens" (increases the probability of) the cat's pawing at the latch to open the puzzle box door (1938/1966). All that can be observed is that the cat behaves in a particular way, that food follows latch-pawing behavior that opens the door, and that on future trials, latch-pawing behavior increases in both speed and frequency. We can observe neither the cat's presumed satisfaction with escape and with food nor its equally hypothetical annoyance should it fail to escape.

Skinner, therefore, suggested that Thorndike's Law of Effect be relabeled as the *"Empirical Law of Effect"* and be thus limited in meaning to a simple statement of the relationship between an observable behavior and its consequences (Skinner, 1950, 1953, 1974). For the next four decades, Skinner devoted himself to a specification of these relationships, and the body of his work is often referred to as reinforcement theory. Whereas Thorndike spoke of rewards and punishments as key consequences shaping behavior, Skinner preferred the more descriptive and neutral terms *positive* and *negative* to describe reinforcers. Skinner's scientific style became a model of radical empiricism and determinism.

Unlike Watson, however, Skinner was not limited to explaining complex behavior in

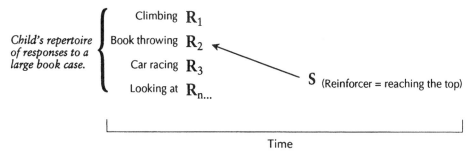

Figure 14.2 Increasing the probability of one voluntary response from a whole repertoire of potential responses.

terms of the stimulus-substitution model of Pavlovian conditioning. Voluntary behavior and the **reinforcers** that shape it became Skinner's focus. Skinner (1938, 1953) pointed out that Pavlovian conditioning was very much overworked as an explanation of behavior. After all, the Pavlovian model is a reflex process in which there is a necessary and unvarying connection between the stimulus and the response:

$$S \rightarrow R$$

Both the sequence (stimulus before response) and the connection between them (autonomic nervous system pathways) are "wired" into the organism. Skinner refers to Pavlovian conditioning as **respondent behavior** to emphasize the rigidity of the stimulus-response relation. But voluntary behavior is not reflexive, is not invariably triggered by antecedent stimuli, and is instrumental in operating upon the environment to produce some effect. Furthermore, the sequence is different from Pavlovian conditioning and the variability of behavior far greater (see Figure 14.2).

Out of all the possible responses in a child's voluntary repertoire, our little athlete's climbing the bookcase was positively reinforced ("rewarded," Thorndike would say) by safely reaching the top shelf. Note that in this sequence of what Skinner calls **operant behavior** (from "operate"), the response must occur before the reinforcing stimulus can be reinforcing. Figure 14.3 illustrates this principle.

The key feature that permits a reinforcer to be effective in shaping behavior is that the reinforcing stimulus be *contingent* on the response. That is to say, every time Thorndike's cat *correctly* pawed the latch mechanism, the puzzle box door opened to permit

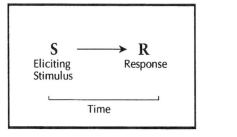

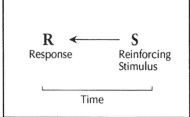

PAVLOVIAN PARADIGM
The eliciting stimulus literally triggers the involuntary response.

OPERANT PARADIGM
The reinforcing stimulus is a consequence of the voluntary response and occurs after it.

Figure 14.3 Pavlovian and operant paradigms of conditioning.

access to food. In operant vocabulary, we say that the food was contingent on (dependent upon) the latch-pawing response. **Positive reinforcers** (such as food, praise, money) are said to strengthen a response because they increase its frequency.

Negative reinforcers also strengthen responses by increasing their frequency, but the negatively reinforced response is one that prevents or terminates the negative reinforcer.

Table 14.3 Summary of Key Reinforcement Concepts

Concept	Definition	Examples
1. POSITIVE REINFORCER "Reward"	Any stimulus event that "strengthens" (increases the probability of) the response it follows.	Parent's praise when child shares toy with younger sibling increases sharing in future.
2. NEGATIVE REINFORCER "Relief"	Any stimulus event that "strengthens" (increases the probability of) the response that removes the negative reinforcer.	Criticism about being "chubby" is stopped or prevented by dieting.
3. POSITIVE PUNISHMENT "Pain"	Aversive or painful stimulus applied to response to reduce its frequency. Not the same as a negative reinforcer because behavior is weakened not strengthened, and punishment may continue during the behavior.	Slapping child's hand for reaching into cookie jar suppresses reaching-in-jar response.
4. NEGATIVE PUNISHMENT "Removing Reward"	Punishment may also involve the removal of a positive reinforcer.	Suspending a child's allowance as a punishment for lying.
5. EXTINCTION	Withholding a reinforcer while subject makes the previously reinforced response until probability of response drops to baseline levels.	Withholding praise for sharing behavior even when child calls attention to it.
6. OPERANT	Any voluntary behavior that can "operate" on the environment to make changes instrumental in securing reinforcements.	Walking, talking, any manipulative behavior.
7. SHAPING	"Molding" a final, complex response from "bits and pieces" of responses by reinforcing successively more precise approximations of the final desired response.	Driving instructor praises increasing precision of student as he or she guides car straight ahead, withholding praise for any performance that is less precise than last best approximation.
8. PARTIAL REINFORCEMENT "Schedules"	Delivering reinforcements on a schedule so that not every response is reinforced. Schedules may follow time patterns so that reinforcement is available only after a specific interval, or a schedule may be based on number of responses required before reinforcement is available. Time schedules are Interval Schedules, and response-based schedules are Ratio Schedules. Behavior maintained by partial reinforcement is more resistant to extinction.	*Interval Schedule:* Receiving a paycheck once a week. *Ratio Schedule:* Auto salesman who is paid by the number of cars sold.

Based on Bandura, 1997, Chapter 5.

For example, if the cat's pressing a lever in the puzzle box stopped electric shock, the removal of the electric shock is a negative reinforcer that increases the frequency of lever pressing.

Punishing stimuli are not negative reinforcers. Punishers suppress behavior. Punishers may be painful, such as a spanking. The presentation of an aversive stimulus constitutues a **positive punishment.** A punisher may also be the *removal* of a positive reinforcer, as when we deprive a child of a favorite television program because he told a lie. Such removal of a positive reinforcer is termed **negative punishment.** Table 14.3 contains complete definitions and examples of the main reinforcement-theory concepts.

To make these concepts easier to keep clear, remember that both positive and negative reinforcers always increase the frequency of antecedent behaviors, whereas punishment always suppresses the frequency of antecedent behavior, whether it involves addition of an aversive stimulus or removal of a positive reinforcer.

AN ILLUSTRATION OF OPERANT CONDITIONING

To see how behavior can be shaped and maintained by reinforcement contingencies, we can borrow and modify an example from two theorists whose work we discuss more thoroughly in Chapter 16 (Dollard & Miller, 1950, pp. 26–30). The point of our lengthy example is simply to foster familiarity with the vocabulary of reinforcement theory.

Suppose we tell a six-year-old girl that we want to play a special hide-and-seek game. We tell her that she can earn candy kisses, which we know are her favorite treat, by finding plastic poker chips, "tokens," that we will hide. For each token the girl finds, she will receive one candy kiss.

The child is not present when we hide the first token under the bottom edge of the center book on the lowest shelf of a small bookcase in the room. We take her to the room and tell her that the token is someplace in the bookcase to reduce the sheer wealth of possible behaviors she is likely to emit. She is excited and eager to begin.

On her first trial, she enters the room and walks immediately to the bookcase. First, she looks under several randomly chosen books on the middle shelf. Then, on tiptoes, she shuffles several books on the top shelf. No tokens. She then drops to her knees and examines books on the lowest shelf. Finding nothing, she stops for a moment and eyes the entire bookcase. The pause is not long. She is eager and hungry. With a shrug, she starts looking under books on the bottom shelf again. By our count, she has picked up 37 books at the point when she finds the token with a shriek of discovery. Total elapsed time on this first trial is 210 seconds.

With a shout of joy, the girl hands the experimenter the token and receives one candy kiss, which she devours as soon as she can remove the wrapper. To the question: "Do you want to play again?" we receive a delighted "Yes!" On the next trial, we hide the token with incredible scientific cunning under the same middle book on the bottom shelf. The little explorer examines 12 books before she tries the familiar book. Total elapsed time on the second trial is 86 seconds.

On the third trial, the girl goes directly to the same book, and is not disappointed. Total elapsed time is 11 seconds.

On the fourth trial, believing that we must be more sophisticated than we are, the little girl overturns 15 books before her suspicion is aroused sufficiently to look under the middle book on the bottom shelf again. Total elapsed time on the fourth trial is the same as it was on the second trial, 86 seconds. Total candy kiss consumption: four. Girl's opinion of behavioristic psychological experimenters: simple-minded.

Secure in our scientific empiricism, we continue to hide the token under the middle book on the bottom shelf for all of the remaining trials through the 10th. Equally empirical in her strategy, the middle book on the bottom shelf is now the first place the girl looks. Average time per trial is now reduced to a mere 3 seconds, just long enough to enter the room, kneel down, and lift the book. At this point, we might say that book-lifting behavior has been shaped from approximate responses to the one specific bottom-shelf-middle-book response by the positive reinforcer of candy kisses. What of the tokens? Tokens are positive *secondary* reinforcers. They cannot themselves be eaten, but they can be redeemed for the primary positive reinforcer of candy. The little girl "works" for the token because this "currency" has the value of "buying" a more direct reward. We now turn to a discussion of the reinforcement theory concepts that are illustrated by this procedure.

Shaping

From the girl's entire repertoire of behavior, we selected the response of "examining-bottom-shelf-middle-book." All other book-examining responses went unreinforced, and although it may have seemed unchallenging to her, only one response had positively reinforcing consequences. By the fifth or sixth trial, all other responses were reduced in probability, and the desired response increased in probability. This process of rewarding successive approximations to a desired behavior is termed **shaping.**

Positive Reinforcement

In our present example the reason why candy kisses are positive reinforcers is that the little girl can eat them and satisfy her hunger. But positive reinforcers need not be biological drive reducers to be reinforcing. All that is necessary is to observe what stimulus increases a behavior's probability to be able to describe that stimulus as a positive reinforcer. David Premack (1965) has shown, for example, that one can establish very powerful positive reinforcers solely on the basis of observing a person's differential preferences for one rather than another activity.

Premack demonstrated that a child who initially prefers watching television cartoons to playing with a pinball machine may be shaped into playing pinball if the more preferred cartoons are used as the reinforcer. To watch a cartoon, the child *must* spend a specific amount of time playing pinball.

Another child who prefers the pinball game to the cartoons can be shaped to watch the less preferred television cartoon by permitting the child to play pinball *only* when he or she has spent a specific amount of time watching the cartoon. Reinforcers are clearly relative, not absolute, commodities.

The **Premack Principle** states that a reinforcer can be defined in terms of the relationship between behaviors of different initial probabilities: A behavior of initially higher probability (preferred action) can be contingent on performing a behavior of initially lower probability (less preferred action). The behavior of higher probability is the reinforcer (Premack, 1965).

Skinner's point in defining reinforcers in terms of their observable effects on the frequency of behavior is that we need not make assumptions about what is "pleasurable" or "annoying" for a given creature. The Premack demonstration is therefore consistent with Skinner's empirical strategy.

Negative Reinforcement

We could change the rules of the game so that instead of earning tokens redeemable for candy, the girl's behavior of finding the hidden token turns off a loud, blaring siren. In this case, although the girl would be much less motivated to play the game at all, her correct responses would be increased in frequency by the *removal* of the negative reinforcer of painfully loud sound.

Punishment

Another change in the rules of the game would make it very much less appealing. We could tell the child that for every *incorrect* response (selecting the wrong book), she will receive a mild electric shock from the electrode wired to her leg, or a **punishment.** We doubt whether this child would persist at the game at all, but for present purposes assume that she has no choice. Or, we could play the "game" with this rule: Every wrong response costs one previously earned token. Here, loss of prior positive reinforcements is punishing. In both cases, the emotional side effects are damaging to motivation, and in both cases, the behavior we aim to suppress (wrong responses) might better be eliminated by simply allowing wrong responses to be extinguished. In the original version of the game with tokens for correct responses and no consequences for wrong ones, that is precisely what happens to the wrong responses. They "drop out" of the girl's repertoire because they are not reinforced—and the game was fun.

Extinction

A simple change in procedure can lead to the **extinction** of the bottom-shelf-middle-book response. We change the location of the token. After several trials of no reinforcement for selecting the middle book on the bottom shelf, the girl stops providing or "emitting" that response. Or, we could extinguish the broader behavior of "playing-the-token-finding-game" by not hiding any tokens. After several totally unsuccessful, candy-kissless trials, the appeal of the game will drop to zero, that is, the probability of game-playing behavior is progressively diminished.

Partial Reinforcement Schedules

In addition to providing a reward for each behavior, Skinner explored **partial reinforcement schedules.** When the game-playing routine is firmly established by having every successful response reinforced by a candy kiss, we could make the game more challenging. We tell the girl that to receive her usual candy kiss, she must now find the token three times in a row. In other words, we have scheduled reinforcements on a 3:1 ratio so that the child has to make three times as many responses to get the one reinforcement she previously received.

The 3:1 ratio is unchanging, although we may choose to hide the tokens under different books each time. However, as long as the schedule demands three responses for one reinforcement it remains a **fixed ratio schedule.** The child will probably proceed at a steady pace trial after trial to earn her candy kisses.

But we could tell her that the game is going to get harder. Under a new rule, she must find as many tokens as possible before earning a candy, and that sometimes it will take three tokens, sometimes five, and sometimes only two; however, she will not be able to predict which **contingency** (three, five, or two) applies at a given moment. This schedule is still a ratio schedule (the ratios are 3:1, 5:1, and 2:1), but it is a **variable ratio schedule.** The child's best strategy, especially if she is hungry, is to work as fast as she can to build up as big a supply of tokens as she can.

We would also schedule reinforcements by establishing time limits punctuated by a buzzer and a clock we install in the room. We tell the girl that she must find the hidden token within 10 seconds or she will not receive the candy for her token. But if she finds the token before 10 seconds elapse, she must wait until the 10th second before getting the token. This schedule is called a **fixed interval schedule** because the availability of reinforcement is governed by intervals of time that remain constant from reinforcement to reinforcement. Such constant time limits encourage a steady pace of responding.

But we could speed things up by continually changing the time limits in a fashion that, from the girl's point of view, is unpredictable. We might arrange for the buzzer to sound after five seconds, then after three seconds, then after ten seconds, and then back to five seconds, and so on. This schedule is called a **variable interval schedule** because the time limits for the availability of reinforcement are continually changing. Such a schedule generates very high and very rapid rates of responding. Our little girl's best strategy under such rules would be to overturn books very rapidly and continually to beat the clock.

All of these schedules produce response rates that are more resistant to extinction than behavior maintained by continuous reinforcement (one reinforcement for every correct response). The reason is easy to understand. When the girl was reinforced for every correct response, an extinction contingency (no token available) is quickly detected. Within one or two trials it will be obvious to the girl that no reward is forthcoming and she will cease responding. But when the availability of tokens is less predictable, as on the variable schedules, it will take a considerably larger number of trials for the child to detect that reinforcement is not available at all. Her behavior persists, therefore, in the face of no reward for a longer time. Or, more correctly put, an intermittently reinforced response resists extinction.

Generalization

The capacity for organisms to emit a learned behavior in environments that resemble the original learning environment is called **generalization.** As a rule of thumb, the more similar a stimulus is to the reinforced stimulus the more likely it will be to elicit similar behavior. To demonstrate generalization, we could modify our simple game by having a number of trials in which we hide tokens under red and near-red colored books, and never under black, yellow, or green ones. As we observe the child responding, her likelihood of choosing red or near-red colored books will increase. If we let a number of trials continue in which no tokens are present, the child will continue to respond at a decreasing frequency. The number of times a book is picked up will depend on how similar its color is to the original bright red. Such a diminishing pattern regarding how close each book chosen is resembles the color red is called the gradient of generalization.

Discrimination

The girl withholds responding to stimuli that are perceptibly different from the reinforced stimulus. In terms of our game, she does not lift green, black, or yellow books to find the token because they are not sufficiently similar to the red book that always has the token. This capacity to detect the difference between stimuli associated with reinforcement and those that are not is called **discrimination.** The little girl discriminates one book from another through color cues, and she responds differently to red books than she does to yellow ones. For the behaviorist, it is the girl's differential *responding,* not her presumably perceptual distinction between red and other colors, that is the essence of discrimination. As with generalization, discrimination is more or less governed by a rule of increasing dissimilarity. The more stimuli differ on some relevant dimension, the more probable is the subject's discrimination.

This rather lengthy example illustrates the major terms of reinforcement theory and their application in a specific setting. We have not yet called attention to other aspects of this illustration that will serve us well toward the end of this chapter when we review the strengths and weaknesses of the behavioral paradigm.

We now turn to some basic applications of Skinner's work, for the puzzles of personality first described by Freud have alternative solutions.

SKINNER'S SOLUTIONS TO FREUD'S PUZZLES

Skinner, like Watson, conceptualizes psychopathology as maladaptive responding, but the principles by which he conceptualizes such behavior are drawn from operant theory. The widely accepted distinction between operant (instrumental) and Pavlovian (classical) conditioning is the major difference between Watson's theories and those of Skinner.

Skinner's approach to Freudian puzzles is to accept as legitimate data the observations of psychodynamic theorists while discarding their explanations of the meaning of those data. He has accepted the observations of psychodynamic theorists as legitimate while rejecting their explanations. Skinner restates the basic clinical facts of disordered human behavior in testable, empirically rigorous, and measurable terms. And, like Watson, Skinner views the environment as the key determinant of behavior.

In this section, we review the central puzzles described and explained by Freud (see Chapters 2 and 3) and see how they are approached from a Freudian psychodynamic and a Skinnerian behavioral perspective. The contrast is very instructive.

Freud's account of psychopathology revolves around explaining three central puzzles of psychopathology: repressed wishes, unconscious conflict among internal agencies, and the experience of anxiety as the ego's experience of its own helplessness. Skinner also developed approaches to thinking about all three of these central puzzles.

Repressed Wishes and Urges

Freud's Puzzle Solution

Wishes and urges seethe unrestrained in the unconscious mind, finding, from time to time, disguised expression in behavior metaphorically related to the disavowed and threatening wishes. Symptoms are, for example, compromise formations because they both symbolize *and* deny the wish-repudiate *and* gratify sexual and aggressive urges that are too painful to act on or to recognize consciously.

Skinner's Puzzle Solution

The assumption that behavior is related to inner mental forces that have causal properties in shaping behavior is untestable, unobservable, and unnecessary. The same behavior (i.e., a symptom), can be explained more simply and more verifiably by looking for the *contingencies* of reinforcement under which that behavior was punished or rewarded:

> A [Freudian] wish that has been repressed as the result of aversive consequences struggles to escape. In doing so it resorts to certain devices which Freud called "dynamisms"—tricks which the repressed wish uses to evade the effects of punishment. . . . The Freudian wish is a device for representing a response with a given probability of occurrence. Any effect of "repression" must be the effect of the variables which have led either to the response itself or to the repressing behavior. . . . Where in the Freudian scheme, behavior is merely the symptom of a neurosis, in the present formulation it is the direct object of inquiry. . . . Let us say that two brothers compete for the affection of their parents and for other reinforcers

which must be divided between them. As a result, one brother behaves aggressively toward the other and is punished, by his brother or by his parents. Let us suppose that this happens repeatedly. Eventually any situation in which aggressive action toward the brother is likely to take place or any early stage of such action will generate the conditioned aversive stimulation associated with anxiety or guilt. This is effective from the point of view of the other brother or the punishing parent because it leads to the self-control of aggressive behavior; the punished brother is now more likely to engage in activities which compete with and displace his aggression. In this sense he "represses" his aggression. The repression is successful if the behavior is so effectively displaced that it seldom reaches the incipient state at which it generates anxiety. It is unsuccessful if anxiety is frequently generated. (Skinner, 1953, pp. 375–376)

In Skinner's formulation, repression is not the construction of inner mental agencies at war with one another. He sees a punished behavior (even a verbal response) as being avoided in favor of less anxiety-provoking responses. Behaviors already in the punished brother's repertoire are used as substitutes for direct aggression. By generalization, the punished brother "selects" similar but less painful responses. He can, for instance, *fantasize* killing his brother, or if that activity is still too anxiety-provoking, he can fantasize killing brother substitutes, such as cousins or friends (Skinner, 1953, p. 376). Perhaps the punished brother can spend his anger in unpunished (maybe even rewarded) activities such as police work, or military service.

Repression for Skinner is not "forgetting" threatening ideas and wishes. Skinner's explanation avoids all assumptions about hidden wishes evoking anxiety. Behavior increases in frequency, ceases altogether, or remains constant because of the reinforcement contingencies to which it is exposed. When the contingencies are aversive, anxiety results. But what a person thinks about those contingencies is unimportant. What he or she *does* about them is everything. Note that Skinner is not reluctant to consider human fantasy and wishing. He is reluctant to conceptualize such unobservables as causal. Behavior, not thoughts, can be predicted and controlled.

From Freud's point of view, the difficulty with this explanation of repression is the failure to take account of the path of the displacements (substitutions). Subjective meanings govern the "choice" of substitute behaviors. Humans, in Freud's clinical experience, create substitutes not merely to avoid painful consequences, but also to symbolize their unspoken thoughts in ways far more complicated than those predicted by simple similarity generalization.

Unconscious Conflict

Freud's Puzzle Solution

Contradictory and self-deceptive behavior reflects the universal personality structure of internalized unconscious passion (id), social intelligence and reason (ego), and ethical-moral restraint through guilt (superego). It is possible for a person to be self-divided, wishing for the opposite of what he or she really wants, and to remain unaware of the self-deception because each agency has different aims and each may at various times overpower the others.

Skinner's Puzzle Solution

Again, Skinner does not dismiss Freud's clinical observations of conflicted behavior. Instead, he prefers to couch the explanation of such behavior in terms of observable variables and the principles of operant conditioning:

In Freud's great triumvirate, the ego, superego, and id represent three sets of contingencies which are almost inevitable when a person lives in a group. The id is the Judeo-Christian "Old Adam"—man's "unregenerate nature," derived from his innate susceptibilities to reinforcement, most of them almost necessarily in conflict with the interests of others. The superego—the Judeo-Christian conscience—speaks in the "still small voice" of a (usually) punitive agent representing the interests of other people. . . . [But the superego] . . . is mainly the product of the punitive practices of a society which attempts to suppress the selfish behavior generated by biological reinforcers, and it may take the form of imitating society ("serving as the vicar of society") as the injunctions of parents, teachers, and others become part of its repertoire. The ego is the product of the practical contingencies in daily life, necessarily involving susceptibilities to reinforcement and the punitive contingencies arranged by other people, but displaying behavior shaped and maintained by a current environment. It is said to satisfy the id if it achieves a certain amount of biological reinforcement, and the superego if it does so without risking too much punishment. We do not need to say that these archetypal personalities are the actors in an internal drama. The actor is the organism, which has become a person with different, possibly conflicting, repertoires as the result of different, possibly conflicting, contingencies. (Skinner, 1974, pp. 150–151)

Conflict, as reinterpreted by Skinner, is the result of incompatible contingencies of reinforcement. In place of Freud's internal warfare of competing mental agencies, Skinner prefers to look at the **reinforcers** that establish and maintain incompatible behaviors. Conflict is not *inside* the person; it is outside in either the social or natural environment's arrangement of reinforcements and punishments. There are no metaphorical inner personalities causing the observable conflicted behaviors. There are only learned behaviors, some of which are based in age-old traditions of social ethics that may conflict with an individual's biological needs. Nothing is gained, according to Skinner, by replacing the external view of the person with a hypothetical internal view of persons within a person.

For Freud, the difficulty with a behavioristic account of conflict is not the emphasis on learning. Freud himself spelled out a rather detailed formulation by which social and ethical learning takes place. Rather, the difficulty lies in localizing the causes and the controls exclusively in the environment. Freud assumed that learning has permanent or at least enduring effects on the person, and that these effects *are* enduring precisely because they are located *within* the person as persistent structures of personality that transcend time and generalize across situations. In a real way, Freud regarded some kinds of learning history as virtually permanent, so that wishes and ideas dating from crucial experiences in childhood are "frozen" in time within the unconscious id. And such motives remain isolated from reality. Direct environmental manipulation of a person's behavior would do little, if anything, to modify these internalized, unchanging motives.

Skinner, on the other hand, makes no such assumptions of permanence. For the behaviorist, changes in the environmental contingencies, the patterns of reinforcement and punishment, have the capacity to change the behavior they maintain. As we noted in our discussion of partial reinforcement schedules, some patterns of reinforcement may generate more persistent behavior than others. For Freud, a person is the sum total of his or her internalized images, experiences, and wishes; for Skinner, a person is his or her behavior.

Anxiety as a Signal of Impending Helplessness

Freud's Puzzle Solution

Anxiety is an aversive signal generated by the ego when it perceives that either external or internal threats will overpower it. The nature of anxiety experienced by the ego changes over time with development, as we discussed in Chapter 3. But by the time the child has resolved the Oedipus complex, around the age of six or seven, learned standards of self-evaluation for "good" and "bad" behavior regulate the ego's vulnerability to anxiety. Freud called the sum total of those learned standards the superego. For Freud, wishes and ideas that violate the superego's standards trigger anxiety in the ego, and it is the ego's attempts to control the anxiety that result in psychopathology.

Skinner's Puzzle Solution

Anxiety is emotion, and emotions are merely special cases of involuntary behavior. Generally, Skinner argues, when a person reports that he or she is feeling anxiety, a certain class of bodily events is being described. Thus the frightened man reports feeling frightened because he detects his own sweating, rapid heart rate, and "goose pimples." But what, Skinner asks, is the causal status of such bodily states?

Skinner's answer is that anxiety (or any emotion) is not a *cause* but a reflex consequence of reinforcement contingencies. A behavior exposed to a negative reinforcer or to punishment becomes a conditioned signal that unpleasant consequences will occur again in similar situations. During our evolutionary development such automatic reactions to aversive or painful stimuli may have had adaptive effects. Certainly the organism that could learn to anticipate the negative consequences of coming close to a predator would survive longer. But the organism learns to flee to avoid being eaten, not to avoid the unpleasant bodily state of fear (Skinner, 1953, pp. 178 ff.; 1974, p. 62). In fact, the particular label a person is likely to place on the bodily arousal felt as emotion depends on the situation in which negative reinforcement or punishment has occurred:

> What a person feels when he is in a situation in which he has been punished or when he has engaged in previously punished behavior depends upon the type of punishment, and this often depends in turn upon the punishing agent or institution. If he has been punished by his peers, he is said to feel shame; if he has been punished by a religious agency, he is said to feel a sense of sin; and if he has been punished by a governmental agency, he is said to feel guilt. If he acts to avoid further punishment, he may moderate the condition felt as shame, sin, or guilt, but he does not act because of his feelings or because his feelings are then changed; he acts because of the punishing contingencies to which he has been exposed. (Skinner, 1974, pp. 62–63)

Like a rat in an operant chamber that learns to avoid electric shock by pressing a lever to turn off the current, people learn to avoid punishing and other aversive consequences associated with some of their behavior. Neurotic symptoms may thus be interpreted, not as compromise formations designed to appease combative internal agencies, but as learned avoidance behavior maintained by the negative reinforcement of preventing painful consequences. To control anxiety it is necessary to manipulate the environmental stimuli that are painful. It is of no help whatsoever to focus on the personal meanings and subjective bodily states associated with aversive stimuli.

From Freud's point of view, anxiety is developmentally progressive, changing its meanings as the infant proceeds toward maturity. And it is precisely those personal meanings that are the heart of psychopathology. Freud would not find Skinner's focus on environmental rewards and punishments at all relevant to the crux of the problem. For, in Freud's worldview, emotion is not merely correlated with behavior. Feelings are the springs of action. We act to block, change, distort, and reduce states of inner emotional tension. And of these states, anxiety is the most pathologically motivating.

A NEW ELEMENT IN SKINNER'S BEHAVIORISM

Skinner introduced an element in his behavioral approach that was not present in Watson's radical behaviorism. That is a concern with what he termed *private events*—

behaviors such as thinking, remembering, or even having an emotional reaction that are not observable or necessarily apparent to an external observer.

> When we say that behavior is a function of the environment the term "environment" presumably means any event in the universe capable of affecting the organism. But part of the universe is enclosed within the organism's own skin. . . . The individual's response to an inflamed tooth, for example, is unlike the response which anyone else can make to that particular tooth, since no one else can establish the same kind of contact with it. . . . With respect to each individual, in other words, a small part of the universe is *private*. (Skinner, 1953, p. 257, italics in original)

Skinner also referred to the role of thinking and the possibility of what he termed, *self-control*. In Skinner's view, thinking was not the ultimate cause of behavior but could enable a person to select stimuli that influence or control behavior:

> . . . to a considerable extent an individual does appear to shape his own destiny. He is often able to do something about the variables affecting him. Some degree of self-determination of conduct is usually recognized in the creative behavior of the artist and scientist, in the self-exploratory behavior of the writer, and in the self-discipline of the ascetic. (Skinner, 1953, p. 228)

For Skinner, however, such private events were not the ultimate causes of behavior, which, to him as to Watson, resided in the nature of environmental reinforcement.

WERE THERE PERSONAL SOURCES OF SKINNER'S BEHAVIORISM?

The behaviorist looks outside people to explain the primary causes of their behavior. The ultimate causes of action are in the environment, not in the person's beliefs or feelings. The environment selects behaviors by reinforcing them, and we do what we do in accord with these external selection principles (e.g., Skinner, 1987a, 1989). From the viewpoint of the behaviorist, the concept of motivation, like that of personality, is not needed to explain the causes of behavior.

Skinner redefines popular concepts such as choice, freedom, responsibility, mind, and dignity in terms of the effect of an environment, including its cultural aspects, on its population (Skinner, 1953, 1971, pp. 96ff., 1974). He did consider the possibility of a role for thought and even self-control, but these were always secondary to the fundamental importance of the environment.

From a commonsense point of view, one problem with this explanation is trying to determine where responsibility for behavior lies (Skinner, 1971, pp. 70ff.). Does it lie with the person? With the environment? With the institutions that construct the environment? With the parents who initially constructed the child's first environment and first set of reinforcement contingencies? As we consider these possibilities, we wonder if, perhaps, the concept of responsibility is itself irrelevant.

Skinner emphasizes external factors influencing human behavior. We can therefore ask, what about this view is a result of or connected with Skinner's own life history?

Skinner's Autobiography: Applying Behaviorism to Self

From 1976 to 1983, Skinner published three volumes of autobiography, totaling more than 1,100 pages. On the face of it, Skinner has provided historians and psychologists, more than any other theorist, with a greater quantity of personal information than anyone had a right to ask for. But the 1,100 pages consist largely of detailed, functional descriptions of his life, the same kind of descriptions of behavior that are useful in the laboratory study of reinforcement. The three volumes of autobiography contain only a few statements of personal feeling, and an infrequent mention of intention, wish, or expectation. At the end of the last volume of his autobiography, Skinner appended an epilogue in which he explained his strategy for writing about himself. On the subject of his feelings, Skinner wrote:

> There are several reasons why I have not often reported my feelings. Occasionally I have said how I felt (or, more accurately, how my body felt to me) either literally ("I was angry, happy") or metaphorically ("I was stunned, shaken"), but I have not tried to "convey my feelings" in other ways—as by describing other situations which evoke the same feelings. . . . Paleontology is a science of bones, teeth, and shells because the softer parts of organisms have disappeared, and feelings are softer parts too. Only when I recorded how I felt at the time have I accepted it as part of the story.
>
> I also do not think feelings are important. Freud is probably responsible for the current extent to which they are taken seriously. . . .
>
> Rather than tell my readers how I felt, I have left them to respond as I myself may have responded. It is the reader who must be judged warm or cold. (Skinner, 1983, p. 399)

Consistent with the behavioral theory that occupied his professional life for nearly a half century, Skinner dismisses the importance of feelings in his account of himself. Readers of his autobiography, not the subject of it, "must be judged warm or cold," for Skinner believes that his feelings are irrelevant. Or to say it another way, we will feel the relevant feelings, not he.

Skinner makes no claims to individuality: "If I am right about human behavior, I have written the autobiography of a no person" (Skinner, 1983, p. 412). "If I am right about human behavior, an individual is only the way in which a species and a culture produces more of a species and a culture" (1983, p. 413). Above all, Skinner applies his method to himself, as indicated in the quotation that opens this chapter:

> I am sometimes asked, "Do you think of yourself as you think of the organisms you study?" The answer is yes. So far as I know, my behavior at any given moment has been nothing more than the product of my genetic endowment, my personal history, and the current setting. That does not mean that I can explain everything I do or have done. (Skinner, 1983, p. 400)

In what follows, we will try to feel the feelings and explore some of the meanings in Skinner's life history.

View of His Father: Aversion to Passivity

Born in 1904, in Susquehanna, Pennsylvania, Burrhus Fred Skinner was the first child of William and Grace Skinner. Family and friends called him "Fred," not Burrhus. A second child, born two-and-one-half years later, Edward James ("Ebbie") died unexpectedly years later (probably from a cerebral hemorrhage) when Fred was a freshman in college (more about this brother later).

Skinner's father was an attorney who worked as the counsel for the Hudson Coal Company. Skinner describes him as a man who was "unprepared" for each new step into the world (e.g., 1983, p. 20). He was a gentle man, with whom the young Fred had a closer relationship than with his mother. Yet for all that, Skinner pictures his father as a man doomed by his own mother (Skinner's grandmother) to struggle after levels of achievement and success for which he lacked the talent and skills. Skinner characterized his father a passive person, who lacked the capacity to see how others saw him. Skinner's father's popularity declined after he successfully defended an unpopular client named Frank, and his political aspirations to become district attorney came to an abrupt halt. Skinner suggests that, in fact, his father's life was more or less crystallized by that time, with his remaining years spent being "worn down" by life. There was nothing more to which to aspire:

> He was then about as effective, personally and professionally, as he was ever to be. At the start of his career he began to keep a 50 cent piece in his pocket. So long as he had it, "he would never be broke," and perhaps it is a proof of his success that it was in his pocket when he died. But it was by then only a thin disk of silver, wholly unmarked, with sharp edges. For more than 50 years, it had survived the perils of loss or theft, but it had been buffeted and abraded by other coins and pocketknives and had lost its character and its value.
>
> After the Frank trial my father suffered a similar fate. He had become a successful lawyer, but the minting was complete. The things that were to happen to him later would add no new details. Life was to abrade him, to wear him down. He struggled to satisfy that craving for a sense of worth with which his mother had damned him, but 40 years later he would throw himself on his bed, weeping, and cry, "I am no good, I am no good." (Skinner, 1976, p. 38)

Skinner manages to convey a wide range and depth of emotion in passages such as these. It is clear that he was disappointed by his father's passivity and failure to take charge of his life. Skinner's metaphor of the coin wearing thin is a poignant image replete with subjective significance.

View of His Mother: Aversion to Pressure and Pretentiousness

Grace Skinner, Fred's mother, was the dominant member of the family. Of her it had been said that she "made quite a man of Will Skinner" [Fred's father] (Skinner, 1976, p. 45). Skinner reports that she was not unaware of her achievement. He describes his mother as a basically critical person who pressured her husband and her sons to admire her. Skinner believes that his mother was sexually inhibited, "frigid" is the word he uses, and intensely rigid about avoiding sexual topics and behavior. She was vigilant in encouraging her family to do likewise (Skinner, 1976, p. 45).

Grace Skinner was eager for praise, just as her husband was, and she prided herself on her youthful appearance. According to Skinner, her interpersonal relationships were close, with a good deal of loyalty demanded and received by Grace Skinner. However, he also believes that his mother received such loyalty from her friends because she liked to play the role of a "bountiful Lady" who bestowed gifts and largesse on those who appreciated her.

From time to time, Skinner would be made aware by his mother that his birth had been difficult and that she had nearly died bringing him into the world (1976, p. 23). His mother had a way of portraying herself as a martyr. Skinner uncharacteristically draws an inference about his mother's thoughts:

> Perhaps she was thinking of my own difficult birth when she told me once that a boy who lived down the street "had no right to be alive" because his mother had died when he was born. (1976, p. 43)

Apparently, Skinner resented the pressures his mother placed on him, was critical of what he perceived to be her pretentiousness, and did not identify with her emotional restraint and inhibition.

View of His Brother: Disclaiming Feelings   .

Skinner reports that he felt his parents had shown more affection toward his younger brother than to him, but states that he was not too concerned with this disparity in parental love (1976, p. 210). What troubled him, he reports, was the painful loss of his brother and the fact that his own independence would be jeopardized as his family would draw him in closer as the "family boy," a role he had tried to escape by leaving for college.

Yet he was aware, as he wrote this explanation, that he was disclaiming his feelings. He helped the pathologist who performed the autopsy on his brother by describing "objectively" the brother's symptoms. Skinner's father was told that his elder son's "objectivity" had been helpful:

> With the same objectivity I had watched my parents as they reacted to the discovery that my brother was dead.
> But I was far from unmoved. I once made an arrowhead by bending the top of a tin can into a flattened cone. I fastened it to the end of an arrow, and when I shot it straight up into the air, it fell back and struck my brother in the shoulder, drawing blood. Many years later I remembered the event with a shock when I heard Laurence Olivier speaking Hamlet's lines:
>
> > . . . Let my disclaiming from a purpos'd evil
> > Free me so far in your most generous thoughts,
> > That I have shot mine arrow o'er the house,
> > And hurt my brother.
>
> (Skinner, 1976, p. 210)

It is difficult to read this description of Skinner's "external" behavior and the behavior of others without inferring that Skinner had some element of guilt in his quoting Hamlet's lines. Though he makes clear that Ebbie and he never competed, it is as if he were saying that he had to deny to himself that he felt jealousy or anger toward his brother—such feelings that emerged only in passing and to which he gave little attention until reminded by an actor's lines.

Early Interest in Religion and Writing: Troublesome Feelings

Summarizing his own experience of his family life, Skinner said that he was "taught to fear God, the police, and what people will think" (1983, p. 403). He was describing what he believed to be the inhibiting constraints that were imposed on him by his parents, especially by his mother. He recalls much of his later childhood and adolescence as attempts to escape these constraints, and he forthrightly admits that he could be an angry rebel at times. But most typically, his anger was suppressed in the service of creative ways to "escape" authority figures and demands, or, as Skinner prefers to put it, clever ways of circumventing aversive consequences (1983, pp. 403ff.).

In childhood, religion was a central issue for Skinner, who attended Bible classes and developed a certain degree of faith in the efficacy of religious belief. He was made aware early of the ethnic and religious differences among the Roman Catholics, Episcopalians, and Presbyterians, and like most children, wondered about the meaning of the strange customs of people who did not belong to his own faith. He received much of his formal training in religion in school in Miss Graves's Bible classes:

> We reached the story of Christ just when the sex urge had made itself felt in me. I was 12 or 13. . . . They were free, natural days. I was beginning to read and think and come in contact with earth. Religion and religious ideas bothered me and I thought a great deal about them. I had never associated freely with other boys and now my doubts about things and my sex shame drove me almost to solitude.
> I sensed strongly the injustice in the world. I must have been jealous and resentful. It was an uneasy age. But gradually I worked out a theory of compensation: I began to suspect that punishment or reward in afterlife brought to a balance the imbalance in this world and the

theory was practical so long as I believed it. For a year at least life was perfectly happy for me. I believed that all my trouble simply made way for compensating happiness. My jealousy was not discarded (I see this now) but was rather satisfied: the happiness of my companions which I envied, simply meant, I was sure, that they would have trouble later. (Skinner, 1976, p. 110)

Skinner tested several of his religious beliefs only to have the tests result in disappointment. For example, the maxim "Faith can move mountains" didn't quite stand up to his efforts to levitate himself from a beam scale nor did any amount of faith ever achieve his fantasy of flying around a room to impress people (1976, p. 111). Later, he decided to contribute a scholarly article to a Presbyterian magazine showing that many great composers had been of that faith. When he researched the topic, he found to his dismay that there were few, if any, Presbyterian composers, and those he admired were Catholic. Sometime in adolescence, Skinner gave up his belief in God and organized religion, and by his account, seems never to have returned to those beliefs. In response to a question by one of the authors of this text in the mid-1980s about what he was before he became a psychologist, Skinner replied, "A Presbyterian" (Skinner, 1983).

By the second semester of his senior year in college, Skinner had decided to attempt a career as a novelist. He asked for help from his father to support himself for one year while he made the attempt, and his father reluctantly agreed. He had gotten some encouragement from the poet Robert Frost, whom he met through an introduction by his creative writing teacher at college. Frost invited the young Skinner to send him some samples of his writing. Some months later Frost wrote to Skinner remarking on how Skinner's stories contained nice observations and that the writing was "clean." Frost gave the young would-be author warm support and the critical insight that Skinner had to learn to *care* for the things and people he wrote about (reproduced in Skinner, 1976, p. 248). Had Frost also detected in Skinner a reluctance to deal with feelings?

Skinner built a study for himself in the family house, where he would write. Both of his parents preferred that he prepare himself for a more reliable career than being a writer, and Skinner sensed their "shame" at having their college graduate son spend his time "doing nothing" but writing. He knew he had made a serious mistake. He felt trapped.

Skinner's Dark Year: Failure, Doubts, and Conversion to Behaviorism

By the end of that summer, it was clear to Skinner that he could not complete a novel or commercially successful stories. He decided to change his plans and "escape" writing for several years. But he had made a deal with his parents to try out this enterprise for a year, and he stuck to it. Slowly it became a "dark year" (1976, p. 265). There was little intellectual stimulation, no social support, no sign of success, and he felt pressured and criticized by his parents. He began spending long periods in the family library sitting absolutely motionless "in a kind of catatonic stupor" or making obsessive, ritualistic movements with his foot. Skinner broached the idea of seeing a psychiatrist to his father, but Will Skinner felt that it would be a waste of time and money, and the idea apparently was dropped (1976, p. 278). But the episode gives some indication of the distress in which Skinner found himself. Because he was spending more time with his father, Skinner may have realized consciously for the first time how much he did not want to become like his father, whom he viewed as a passive, helpless, and melancholy person who had not lived up to his family's expectations.

He began clearly to see that his father was depressed and had a good idea of why. Will Skinner was in the second year of his private practice as a lawyer, and already had several crises to face. He had been accused, erroneously, of lying about a fee he collected and a client threatened disbarment proceedings. Within recent years, his father had lost his younger son, Ebbie, lost an important job, moved his family to Scranton, and now watched his only son seemingly do nothing. Skinner's mother voiced her fear that her husband might commit suicide:

> "Others have done it for less," she said to me, and she was right. But other men had not believed so strongly in progress or had been so richly rewarded when they proved to their parents and friends that progress was possible. My father was too proud to kill himself; he could not confess failure that way. (Skinner, 1976, p. 278)

His father's luck changed for the better within the year, and he landed a job with the coal company, although it was not sufficiently important in his own eyes to constitute the sought-for success. The remainder of the "dark year" involved increasing loneliness, substituting writing personal observations for social contact. "I was confined to the autistic, not to say auto-erotic, satisfactions to be found in my notebook" (Skinner, 1976, pp. 279–280). He began to "look at myself as a person," although until then he had avoided self-observation. He realized that he was rarely satisfied when he had achieved a goal. He wrote this candid self-revelation in his notebook under the heading "What I Achieve I Despise":

> But why should I despise the things I attain [such as high grades, a reputation for cleverness]? Is it because I am secretly conscious of my inferiority and feel that if I achieve a "great" thing I must have been mistaken as to its greatness? I think not. I think rather that I feel that greatness is merely the result of a happy combination of trivial influences, that the great man cannot help being great, the poor man cannot help being poor. My ability to trace my own development shows this to me again and again. My only satisfaction lies in discovering that I am wrong about my "inexorable evolution"—that perhaps I have imagined it.
>
> *I* Ask of Life—
>
> 1. Pleasurable satisfaction of desire.
>
> The cardinal necessity in obtaining this is restraint. We are creatures of desire, filled with hundreds of evolved cravings, and the satisfaction of all of these is neither possible nor would it be desirable. We must make use of our knowledge and intellect to choose those desires which will give us . . . the greatest pleasure. . . . Desire may move the world but intellect may mold desire. But intellect molds desire only when desire desires to be molded. . . . (Skinner, 1976, p. 282; italics in original)

This passage was written during the dark year, when Skinner was 22. A number of features in this quotation anticipate important major themes in his later professional life and reflect his distress at that moment. First, the last lines on the nature of desire, ironically, echo Freud's views on human nature as expressed in the war between the ego and id (reason against passion), and Skinner reaches the classic Freudian conclusion that the ego (intellect) is the helpless rider of the id horse, leading the horse where it wants to go.

More important, Skinner here is giving voice to a kind of nihilism in the guise of self-effacement that is uniquely characteristic of his approach to behaviorism. He is depressed, but does not identify the depression as such. His struggle for success is stymied; he believes he has failed as a writer; he has watched his father fail and then react with despair to his own passivity; and he has lost his younger brother for what must have seemed like no reason at all. He concludes that personal effort and responsibility are unrelated to success or failure: Great men are great by chance, poor men are poor by chance. Happy circumstance produces happiness.

Characteristically, Skinner began to look at his situation from a new perspective: Had he failed as a writer, or had writing failed him as a method of studying what he was most interested in, namely, human behavior (1976, p. 291)? He concluded that writing itself, as a method, was the source of his failure. As he began to review the reasons for the misery of the "dark year," he realized that he had been interested in psychology. The stories

| BOX 14.3 | *Only Connect . . .* |

Alan Elms (1981) has interpreted Skinner's reactions during his dark year as constituting an "identity crisis" as defined by Erikson (see Chapter 8). Elms believes that the issues raised during this year were resurrected later in Skinner's life, after he had become an experimental psychologist, and his identity was again threatened with frustration. At that later point, Skinner, as a form of self-therapy, wrote his best-selling utopian novel *Walden Two* to reconcile the fragments of his identity. Elms's (1981) analysis in terms of the concept of identity crisis may be at least partially correct, if we assume that part of the identity that was crumbling for the young Skinner was his identification with his father.

The crisis was resolved, if "crisis" is the correct term, in the way that Erikson indicates many identity crises are resolved, with the adoption of an ideology that gives personal and social meaning back to the person caught up in feelings of distress (Elms, 1981, p. 471). At the time, however, Skinner reached a different conclusion expressed with his usual restrained but sardonic humor and some suppressed anger: "I see now that the only thing left for me to do in life is to justify myself for doing nothing" (1976, p. 283).

he had sent to Frost, for example, were largely psychological studies, and most of the reading he had done during the dark year was in the works of psychological authors such as Marcel Proust and Fyodor Dostoyevsky. But, abruptly, he was sidetracked by a sudden interest in the arcane and occult. He read some books on mystical phenomena (P. D. Ouspensky, for example) and began to entertain explanations that were not derived from science. Thinking about the "fourth dimension," and the subjectivity of meaning made him realize "I was floundering in a stormy sea and perilously close to drowning, but help was on the way" (1976, p. 298).

The help was in the form of *The Dial* magazine, an erudite journal that published, among others, the philosopher Bertrand Russell, who at the time was writing about the work of behaviorist John B. Watson. Skinner realized that Watson's approach to meaning and knowledge, as discussed by Russell, was quite different from the mystical or occult and from the literary approach that was failing him. Inspired by Russell, Skinner bought a copy of Watson's *Behaviorism,* and within a short time, the young Skinner was identifying himself as a scientific behaviorist, even defending Watson against critics by writing to the editors of the *Saturday Review* to criticize a book critical of behaviorism. The editors did not publish his letter, but the decision was made. Skinner decided on graduate study in psychology, and his study would be focused on the analysis of observable behaviors.

Understanding the Personal Sources of Skinner's Behaviorism

There is much more to the story of B. F. Skinner's personal evolution as a leading behaviorist. Here, we have focused on the personal origins of Skinner's particular adherence to behaviorism. We have attempted to explore the roots for three key themes to be found in Skinner's conception of human functioning:

1. Externalized human agency, so that the behaviorist looks outside the person for the basic causes of behavior.

2. Elimination or rejection of feelings as causal variables in human psychology.

3. Thought used to choose among or select environmental stimuli.

Some ironies have been noted, but note one more: Skinner's interest in psychology developed out of his failed interest in becoming a creative writer. Creative writers, such as Marcel Proust whom Skinner admired, are artists who depict the range and depth of human action and thought by explicating their characters' emotions.

Aside from the ironies, what else can we conclude from our selective survey of Skinner's personal history? To answer that question we must violate Skinner's own principles and resort to inference and educated speculation.

First, as envisioned by Skinner, behaviorism makes the concept of personality obsolete and irrelevant. In a way, humans become, to use Skinner's own self-description "nonpersons." Are "nonpersons" easier to study scientifically than "persons"?

Given the role models to whom he was exposed as a child, and the likely resentment and rebellion they triggered in him, Skinner early on adopted a kind of rationalizing style that placed blame, failure, and to be consistent, success outside personal responsibility. He was skilled at devising ways of escaping the "aversive" discipline style of his mother, but less skilled in escaping the emotional consequences of watching his mother "make quite a man of" his father. He had been taught to fear God and the police, but what he learned was to resent pressure and authority figures. Rather than confronting figures such as these directly, his adaptive strategy was to escape or to defeat them indirectly. By conceptualizing "good" and "bad" behavior, success and failure as stemming from environmental contingencies rather than from internal motives, we escape the whole issue of confrontation, responsibility, and feeling. Nonpersons do not feel. And they do not feel responsible.

Second, Skinner's insistence that feelings are only correlated with bodily states, not causes, in human action reduces emotion to a side effect. If feelings are unimportant, then we need not be concerned if our feelings momentarily hurt, or if we are momentarily threatened by emotions, or if our feelings are in painful conflict. A person can take active measures to correct or change the environment responsible for these side effects.

Skinner's book *Enjoy Old Age,* as an example of this approach, is a guide for older adults on how to cope with failing eyesight, hearing, and motor and memory skills (Skinner & Vaughn, 1983). The whole point of the book is to avoid despair and helplessness by taking an active stance to control the environment. You can't change what the ravages of old age do to your body, but you can change the environment in which you function. Skinner, perhaps in reaction to the perceived passivity and "unpreparedness" of his father, takes nothing lying down or passively.

Self-effacement or self-denial is also a major theme that Skinner relates to behaviorism, because we have to attribute our achievements to our genetic and environmental histories. The same themes, as Skinner points out, run through philosophy and particularly through Eastern mysticism: self-possession out of self-abandonment, gaining freedom by abandoning the sense of self.

Biological Limits of Conditioning

It has become increasingly clear that learning is not automatic and is not organism-free. There are several limitations on the "laws" of conditioning that appear to emerge from inside the organism.

Pavlov's discovery that arbitrary stimuli (tones, lights, vibrations) could elicit reflex behavior when paired with the natural stimulus for such responding (for example, meat powder) led to the unsurprising but erroneous conclusion that all stimuli could serve equally well (Rachlin & Logue, 1983, p. 110). It should be pointed out, however, that neither Pavlov nor Skinner made this leap of logic. Rather, the many researchers who followed in their footsteps tended to make these logical but wrong assumptions about the universal lawfulness of conditioning principles (Kling, 1971; Rescorla, 1987, 1988).

The concept of **biological preparedness** or the tendency of different animals to be more easily trained or conditioned to behavior in certain ways is a major building block of the field of evolutionary psychology, which we will explore in Chapter 18. The idea that animals and humans have instincts, and that these instincts are heritable and evolutionarily selected for their adaptive value, is a fundamental tenet of this developing approach to behavior. An empirical question is to what extent any given behavior does or does not have an instinctual component.

SOME LIMITATIONS OF BEHAVIORISM

The great scientific strength of behaviorism was its method. Both Watson's and Skinner's emphases on observable, verifiable, and controllable variables helped transform psychology into an experimental science.

For while the practitioners of radical behaviorism scientifically demonstrated the power of Pavlovian and operant conditioning, they lost sight of some of the discipline's most enduring problems. For all practical purposes, the behaviorists had removed the thinking organism from examining its thinking about its own psychology. As long as the observable and controllable stimuli and responses of the organism could be specified, a fully competent science of behavior would be developed. The principles of learned behavior became almost independent of the learner. One precise statement of this viewpoint was made by Skinner, tongue-in-cheek to be sure, but in the opening of an essay entitled "Why I Am Not a Cognitive Psychologist":

> In Pavlov's experiment a hungry dog hears a bell and is then fed. If this happens many times, the dog begins to salivate when it hears the bell. The standard mentalistic explanation is that the dog "associates" the bell with food. But it was Pavlov who associated them! (Skinner, 1978, p. 97)

Pavlovian conditioning is an associative process, but the connection is not created "inside" the dog. Watson, and to a lesser degree, Skinner, advanced the view that it is sufficient for a science of behavior to describe the relationship between observable events. Whatever the organism's view of this relationship may be, it can safely be ignored. But can it? In Chapters 15 and 16, we will explore personality theories that assign a greater role to cognitions.

EVALUATING BEHAVIORISM

As with other personality theories, we will briefly evaluate behaviorism in terms of its refutability, model of human agency, and degree of idiographic or nomothetic focus.

Refutability

Because both Watson's and Skinner's approaches were based, to differing degrees, on laboratory research, they each lend themselves to testing, each of them generates testable hypotheses, and each of them has had its share of confirmations and disconfirmations. Watson's conception of human behavior leaned heavily on the early work in Pavlovian conditioning and is based on laboratory research. B. F. Skinner also derived most of his generalizations and explanations from direct experiment. Behaviorism gets high grades in refutability. Most of the important concepts of radical behaviorism can be empirically tested, and, even though they cover a certain set of (usually animal) behaviors, they have largely been confirmed in the lab.

Behaviorism and Human Agency

Recall our discussion from Chapter 1 of the active-passive dichotomy in the history of personality theory. Both behaviorism and psychodynamic theories shared the basic assumption that reality acts upon the person.

Watson and Skinner have pictured human agency essentially as determined by external variables. In Watson's day, the person's own view of the stimuli to which he or she was exposed was considered irrelevant. Although Skinner allows for the significance of private events, such as thinking and feeling, these variables have no causal status in Skinner's account.

Skinner has developed a theoretical background for some positive human agency in his concept and methods of self-control (1953, pp. 227–241). Just as a Freudian can gain insight into his or her emotional life, Skinner indicates that a person can become aware of the stimuli controlling his or her behavior, and such awareness can lead to people promoting certain behaviors by choosing to be influenced by one or another environmental circumstance.

Idiographic Versus Nomothetic Focus

Watson's and Skinner's approaches set out to establish general laws or lawful findings about human psychology. And they have produced nomothetic research. Of the two, Watson's radical behaviorism was perhaps least successful, largely because at Watson's time in history, the methodology of conditioning was primitive and the conceptions on which it was based were primitive. By contrast, Skinner worked for years with single organisms, following an individualized approach designed to yield nomothetic data. The curves of response rates to different reinforcement schedules, based on pooled individual data, did in fact yield generalizable laws of conditioning schedules. Nonetheless, there was also an idiographic focus on the behaviors and conditioning histories of specific organisms.

SUMMARY

Watson's radical behaviorism dismissed human thought, feeling, and expectation as irrelevant to the scientific study of behavior. Watsonian behaviorism adopted the Pavlovian conditioned reflex as the fundamental "atom" of lawful behavior prediction. Watson built the behavioristic philosophy around these assumptions:

1. *Evolutionary continuity:* Animal and human behavior is not different in kind. The same laws of behavior can be used to describe and predict both animal and human behavior.

2. *Reductionism:* Watson believed that all human behavior could be viewed or *reduced to* simple instincts and subsequent conditioning. According to this view, neither conscious nor unconscious thoughts or feelings cause behavior. Thoughts are not physical, and thus, by themselves, cannot directly trigger physical events. Skinner was also reductionistic, but assigned a role to private events and covert reinforcement.

3. *Determinism:* Behavior is never random, accidental, or spontaneous. Every behavioral effect has its cause in the nature of the environment. Watson saw mental events as totally irrelevant explanations of behavior, whereas Skinner thought they played a secondary, noncausal, role.

4. *Empiricism:* The goal of psychology as a science is to predict and control behavior. In Watson's view, whatever you cannot measure, see, or manipulate is irrelevant. Skinner was also an empiricist who studied observable behavior, but he also acknowledged the existence and role of "private events" or what other psychologists would call cognitions.

Watson conceptualized psychopathology as learned maladaptive responding. Disease metaphors, unconscious processes, and subjective experience were by definition excluded from his conception of disordered behavior. And Watson's psychopathological dog was an imaginary case in point.

B. F. Skinner turned his attention to the more complex learning process introduced into psychology by Edward L. Thorndike under the label of "trial-and-error" learning. In this paradigm, complex voluntary behavior is selectively strengthened by reinforcers.

Both positive reinforcers and negative reinforcers are stimulus events that increase the probability that the response preceding them will occur again. Punishment following a response decreases the subsequent probability of that response's occurrence.

Skinner asserted, as had Watson, that key elements in psychopathology had their primary causes in the environment. Anxiety, for example, was explained as a consequence of avoidance behavior. And Freudian repression is reinterpreted as the substitution of distracting and less punishing behavior for a response that has been punished. Skinner had thus succeeded in explaining some aspects of psychopathology without resorting to internal mental agencies, unconscious processes, or to personal meanings. Skinner also assigned a role to "private events" such as thinking in choosing or selecting one or another environmental stimulus, thus providing a degree of control over one's behavior.

David Premack showed that a behavior of higher initial probability is a positive reinforcer for a behavior of initially lower probability. This phenomenon was called the Premack Principle.

In conclusion, the behavioral approaches of Skinner and Watson are based on a great deal of empirical research. These theories are refutable. Behaviorism leans, in part, in the nomothetic direction as there is an emphasis on general and universally applicable principles or laws of behavior, but there is also an idiographic focus in the sorting out of the conditioning histories and behaviors of specific individuals.

FOR FURTHER READING

A careful analysis of the meaning of empiricism and verifiability in the behavioral tradition is provided in the classic paper by Nathan Brody and P. Oppenheim: "Tensions in Psychology Between the Methods of Behaviorism and Phenomenology" (*Psychological Review,* 1966, *73,* pp. 295–305). Mary Henle and G. Baltimore's criticism of this work (*Psychological Review,* 1967, *74,* pp. 325–329), provides a critique that clarifies the Brody and Oppenheim paper with humor and cogency.

B. F. Skinner's *Science and Human Behavior* (New York: Macmillan, 1953) is his pioneering and clearly written effort to explain cognitive-emotional processes in behavioral terms and probably the closest he comes to an actual theory of personality. A fascinating article is "Selection by Consequences" (*Science,* 1931, *213,* pp. 501–504), in which Skinner indicates parallels between natural selection of species and operant conditioning. In *Beyond Freedom and Dignity* (New York: Alfred A. Knopf, 1972), Skinner indicates how the usual concepts with which people think about human behavior are ineffective in leading to desirable changes. Each volume of his three-volume autobiography was published at different times: *Particulars of My Life* (1976), *The Shaping of a Behaviorist* (1979), and *A Matter of Consequences* (1983). In part based on original source materials and interviews with Skinner, S.R. Coleman has published a series of interesting and detailed studies of Skinner's personal development and the development of his ideas. Two of them are "B.F. Skinner, 1926–1928: From Literature to Psychology." (*Behaivior Analyst,* 1985, *8,* pp. 77–92) and "Background and Change in B.F. Skinner's Metatheory from 1930 to 1938." (*Journal of Mind and Behavior,* 1984, *5,* pp. 471–500).

John B. Watson's *Behaviorism* (New York: Norton, 1930 and revised in 1957) is the landmark statement of Watson's position. But a careful reading of Watson's "founding" paper "Psychology as the Behaviorist Views It" (*Psychological Review,* 1913, *20,* pp. 158–177), is more clearly indicative of Watson's views. Kerry Buckley's biography of Watson, *Mechanical Man: John Broadus Watson and the Beginnings of Behaviorism* (New York: Guilford, 1989), is a detailed but overly critical account of Watson's life and personality. The collection of papers in James T. Todd and Edward K. Morris's (Eds.) *Modern Perspectives on John B. Watson and Classical Behaviorism* (Westport, CT: Greenwood Press, 1994) ranges, with noticeably uneven quality, from cogent historical analyses of Watson's impact on psychology to the outcome of a rare and salty, but minor interview with Watson near the end of his life.

GLOSSARY

John B. Watson

Classical conditioning: Pavlov's method of conditioning, which combines an unconditioned (unlearned) stimulus, such as food powder, that reliably elicits an unconditioned response, such as salivation, with a neutral unconditioned stimulus, such as the sound of a bell. If conditioning occurs, the neutral stimulus eventually becomes a conditioned stimulus. It then elicits a conditioned response, in this case *salivation,* similar to the original unconditioned response.

Conditioned response (CR): A learned response that is elicited by the CS in anticipation of the UCS. When the CS is paired several times with the UCS, it acquires the ability to elicit a response similar to the original unconditional response. A response is elicited by a previously neutral stimulus.

Conditioned stimulus (CS): A stimulus that has become conditioned or learned. Before conditioning or learning occurs, the stimulus is a neutral event that does not elicit a reliable response from the organism. After pairing the CS with the UCS, it loses its neutrality and can be substituted in place of the UCS to produce the same response.

Conditioning: The learning process that shapes or molds behavior through the qualities of the environment. Watson believed that any behavior, other than the simplest innate reflexes, can be acquired or changed through this process.

Determinism: The idea that behavior is an effect of prior causes. In this view, behavior is never random, accidental, or spontaneous, but rather, the product of specifiable antecedent conditions.

Empiricism: The view that only phenomena that can be measured and manipulated are fit subjects of inquiry. Only observable, measurable events can be scientifically verified. Controlled observation enables the scientist to predict and control human activity.

Evolutionary continuity: The concept that human and animal behaviors are not different in kind. According to this view, human behavior differs from animal behavior only in its degree of complexity.

Radical behaviorism: An approach that does not use inner states as explanations for behaviors and focuses on observable or measurable behaviors only. Mental states, especially unconscious ones, are irrelevant to the radical behaviorist.

Reductionism: The approach to behavior that sees it as a product of the most basic physical components. Watson thought that all behavior is understandable as the workings of glandular and nervous systems and underlying biochemical or molecular processes. In this view, behavior is "nothing but" biochemistry.

Unconditioned response (UCR): A behavior, usually a reflexive one, that is naturally and automatically elicited by the unconditional stimulus. It is an unlearned response.

Unconditioned stimulus (UCS): A stimulus or event that automatically and reliably triggers a response without prior experience with that stimulus. It elicits a natural and predictable response from an organism.

B. F. Skinner

Biological preparedness: An innate predisposition for different animals to be more easily trained or conditioned to behave in certain ways. Species-specific behaviors, and innate predispositions, thus place limitations on the effectiveness of operant conditioning.

Contingency: The idea that some event will occur if and only if another event occurs. The application of a reward or a punishment is *contingent* on the occurrence of a particular behavior.

Discrimination: The capacity to detect the difference between stimuli associated with reinforcement and those that are not. There is differential responding under different sets of circumstances.

Extinction: Elimination of a conditioned response. Pavlov's method was to present the conditioned stimulus without the unconditioned stimulus repeatedly until the conditioned stimulus no longer elicited the conditioned response. When a formerly reinforced behavior is no longer reinforced, it extinguishes.

Fixed interval schedule: This is a schedule of reinforcement in which reinforcement is provided after consistent, specified intervals. An example of this schedule would be a person being paid on an hourly or daily basis, regardless of how much work he or she might do in a given time period.

Fixed ratio schedule: Positive reinforcement is provided after a certain number of responses.

Generalization: The capacity for organisms to emit a learned behavior in environments that resemble the original learning environment. The more similar a stimulus is to the original reinforced object or event, the more likely it will elicit a similar response.

Law of Effect: A theory proposed by Thorndike that stated that a response leading to a "satisfying state of affairs" is strengthened and more likely to be repeated, whereas responses that are less satisfying or "annoying" are weakened and will occur less frequently. There is thus an observable relationship between behavior and its consequences.

Negative punishment: Removing a positive reinforcer (reward or pleasurable outcome).

Negative reinforcers: Termination of aversive stimuli as a contingency that increases the frequency of the operant behavior.

Operant behavior: Voluntary behavior, which acts or *operates* upon the environment. Such behavior can change or modify the environment in some way.

Partial reinforcement schedules: Schedules that sometimes reinforce a desired response and sometimes do not. Four types are *fixed ratio reinforcement, variable ratio reinforcement, fixed interval reinforcement,* and *variable interval reinforcement.* All such schedules of partial reinforcement are more resistant to extinction than the process of rewarding every response.

Positive punishment: Presenting a negative reinforcer (aversive or painful outcome).

Positive reinforcers: Rewards presented contingent upon a behavior, thus increasing the probability that the preceding response will recur.

Premack Principle: The principle that behavior of initially higher probability (preferred action) can be contingent on performing a behavior of initially lower probability (less preferred action). The preferred activity serves as a reinforcer.

Punishment: Operant conditioning that results in the likelihood or frequency of the prior behavior being reduced as a consequence. It can be in the form of either positive punishment or negative punishment.

Reinforcers: Contingent environmental stimuli, typically the presentation of rewards or removal of punishments, that increase the probability that the response preceding them will occur again.

Respondent behavior: Involuntary behavior, which is reflexive in nature. It is rigidly triggered or elicited by an antecedent stimulus.

Shaping: The process of teaching new behaviors incrementally by reinforcing those responses that approximate the desired one. Small behavioral components are rewarded one step at a time.

Variable interval schedule: Positive reinforcement is provided after varying intervals.

Variable ratio schedule: Positive reinforcement is provided after a varying number of responses.

Chapter 15

George A. Kelly

Personal Construct Theory

In this new way of thinking about psychology, there is no learning, *no* motivation, *no* emotion, *no* cognition, *no* stimulus, *no* response, *no* ego, *no* unconscious, *no* need, *no* reinforcement, *no* drive.

George A. Kelly, *Theory of Personality*

As a man thinketh in his heart, so he is.

King Solomon. *King James Bible*

George A. Kelly	Born: 1905	not far from Perth, Kansas
	Died: 1967	Waltham, Massachusetts

About George A. Kelly's Personal Construct Theory

Kelly emphasized the fact that persons anticipate the future on the basis of their experience. He elaborated the ways in which they try to understand events and the personalities of others. The approach to personality that emphasizes the ways people make sense of their experiences and develop new approaches to dealing with life is called constructivism. Kelly's major theory is called the personal construct theory.

A few major concepts are central to Kelly's work:

1. *It is necessary for persons to predict with some accuracy how others will behave and how events will proceed.*

2. *People maintain or revise such predictions as their experience either does or does not confirm them. They develop bipolar categories (constructs) and construct systems in order to assess and predict events and the behaviors of others.*

3. *A person's behavior and his or her own psychology can best be understood by learning about his or her own ways of categorizing people and events and making predictions.*

4. *Personality concepts such as anxiety, guilt, and ego defenses can be understood in light of this process of developing bipolar categories (constructs) and systems of categorization (construct systems) and applying them.*

UNCOVERING A PERSON'S CONSTRUCTS OF PERSONALITY

George A. Kelly thought of each individual as a theorist of human nature or as a personality scientist. In Kelly's view, each of us constructs conceptual models and tests predictions of others' behavior. In order to uncover the predictive models or constructs that people held, individuals who came to Kelly for counseling would be asked to indicate their own ways of conceptualizing others. The **Role Construct Repertory Test (REP Test)** that follows was a major method that Kelly developed for indicating and assessing such constructs. You are invited to participate in this test.

REP TEST PART A: ROLE TITLE LIST

Instructions:

Write the name of the persons indicated in the blanks provided. Do not repeat names. If any role appears to call for a duplicate name, substitute the name of another person whom the second role title suggests to you (based on Kelly, 1955).

1. Your mother or the person who has played the part of mother in your life.

   1. _____

2. Your father or the person who has played the part of a father in your life.

   2. _____

3. Your brother nearest your age. If you have no brother, the person who is most like one.

   3. _____

4. Your sister nearest your age. If you have no sister, the person who is most like one.

   4. _____

5. A teacher you liked or the teacher of a subject you liked.

   5. _____

6. A teacher you disliked or the teacher of a subject you disliked.

   6. _____

7. Your closest girl (boy) friend immediately before you started going with your wife (husband) or present closest girl (boy) friend [Ex-Flame].

   7. _____

8. Your wife (husband) or closest present girl (boy) friend.

   8. _____

9. An employer, supervisor, or officer under whom you served during a period of great stress [Boss].

10. A person with whom you have been closely associated who, for some unexplainable reason, appears to dislike you [Rejecting Person].

10. _____

11. The person whom you have met within the past six months whom you would most like to know better [Sought Person].

11. _____

12. The person whom you would most like to be of help to, or the one whom you feel most sorry for [Pitied Person].

12. _____

13. The most intelligent person whom you know personally.

13. _____

14. The most successful person whom you know personally.

14. _____

15. The most interesting person whom you know personally.

15. _____

REP TEST PART B: CONSTRUCT SORTS

Instructions:

The sets of three numbers in the following sorts refer to the numbers 1 to 15, inclusive, in Part A.

In each of the following sorts, three numbers are listed. Look at your Part A sheet and consider the three people whom you have listed for these three numbers.

In what important way are two of these three people alike and at the same time, essentially different from the third?

After you have decided what the important way is, write it in the blank opposite the sort marked CONSTRUCT.

Next encircle the numbers corresponding to the two people who are alike.

Write down what you believe to be the opposite of the construct in the blank marked CONTRAST.

NUMBERS		CONSTRUCT	CONTRAST
Sort	Part A	(EMERGENT)	(IMPLICIT)
1.	9, 11, 14	_____	_____
2.	10, 12, 13	_____	_____
3.	2, 5, 12	_____	_____
4.	1, 4, 8	_____	_____
5.	7, 8, 12	_____	_____
6.	3, 13, 6	_____	_____
7.	1, 2, 9	_____	_____
8.	3, 4, 10	_____	_____
9.	6, 7, 10	_____	_____
10.	5, 11, 14	_____	_____
11.	1, 7, 8	_____	_____
12.	2, 7, 8	_____	_____
13.	3, 6, 9	_____	_____
14.	4, 5, 10	_____	_____
15.	11, 13, 14	_____	_____

(The form of the test that appears here is a slightly modified and shortened version of an early form of the Group REP Test. Number combinations making up the 15 sorts are virtually unlimited. Subjects could be asked to repeat their constructs and contrast evaluations with a new set of sorts, depending on the judgment of the administering psychologist.)

Table 15.1   Mildred Beal's Constructs

Sort number	Similar figures	Similarity construct	Dissimilar figures	Contrasting construct
2	Rejecting Person (10) Pitied Person (12)	Very unhappy persons	Intelligent Person (13)	Contented
3	Father (2) Liked Teacher (5)	Very quiet and easygoing	Pitied Person (12)	Nervous, hypertensive
4	Mother (1) Sister (4)	Look alike Both hypercritical of people in general	Boyfriend (8)	Friendliness
11	Mother (1) Ex-Flame (7)	Socially maladjusted	Boyfriend (8)	Easygoing, self-confident
13	Disliked Teacher (6) Boss (9)	Emotionally unpredictable	Brother (3)	Even temperament

The ways in which psychologists can choose to analyze the subject's sorts are varied. They may rely on an impressionistic analysis. In this approach, they may receive assistance from a subject's answers to questions about their responses as well as spontaneous comments. Another more objective approach is to analyze the themes revealed in the construct and contrast columns more objectively. This can be done by tabulating the frequency of key phrases and combinations such as Mother-Father, Teacher-Boss, Husband-Lover.

A sample REP protocol of a pseudonymous subject identified by Kelly as "Mildred Beal" appears in Table 15.1. Only five of her sorts need be reproduced for the sake of illustration (after Kelly, 1955, pp. 242 ff.).

A number of interesting personal meanings stand out from Mildred Beal's partial protocol. For example, in sorts numbers 3 and 11, the description "easygoing" was applied by Mildred to Father, Liked Teacher, and Boyfriend. In sorts numbers 4 and 11, she described Mother as "hypercritical of other people" and "socially maladjusted." It is clear that Mildred Beal construed her sister as different from her father and boyfriend in the same way that her mother is. Analyses like these yield insights about the way Mildred construed significant people in her world and her view of their relationship patterns.

GRID FORM OF THE REP TEST: A PERSON'S OWN PERSONALITY THEORY

Mildred's responses to the role constructs of the REP test may also be analyzed mathematically. Correlation coefficients and factor analysis can be applied to a grid form of the test. In the grid version, the subject is asked to make the sorts several times, applying each of his or her constructs developed in response to particular pairs of figures successively to all 15 roles. (The full form of the REP test may include 22 figures, of which the Self is one; it has been shortened in this presentation.) The first time around, the subject is presented with the standard sort-combinations in the form of a 15″ × 15″ grid, as illustrated in Figure 15.1. He or she is instructed to indicate which two of the figures in the first sort (9, 11, 14) are similar by placing an "X" in the appropriate circles of the grid. The circles are placed in each line only in the boxes corresponding to the three figures the subject is asked to compare.

Thus, for example, in Figure 15.1, Mildred has placed an "X" in the circles of numbers 9 and 14, Employer and Successful Person, indicating that she construes these two as similar (Emergent Pole). She has left number 11 unfilled, indicating that Sought Person is,

Elements (Role Figures):

1. Mother
2. Father
3. Brother
4. Sister
5. Liked Teacher
6. Disliked Teacher
7. Ex-Flame
8. Boyfriend (Wife/Husband)
9. Employer
10. Rejecting Person
11. Sought Person
12. Pitied Person
13. Intelligent Person
14. Successful Person
15. Interesting Person

SORT NUMBER	ROLE FIGURES	EMERGENT POLE (Two as Similar)	IMPLICIT POLE (One as Different)
1	9, 11, 14	Are related to me	Unrelated
2	10, 12, 13	Very unhappy persons	Contented
3	2, 5, 12	Quiet and easygoing	Nervous, hypersensitive
4	1, 4, 8	Look alike, hypercritical	Friendliness
5	7, 8, 12	Feel inferior	Self-confident
6	3, 13, 6	Socially better than adequate	Unpleasant
7	1, 2, 9	Hypersensitive	Easygoing
8	3, 4, 10	Hypercritical	Understanding
9	6, 7, 10	Feelings of inferiority	Assured of innate worth
10	5, 11, 14	Pleasing personalities	High-powered, nervous
11	1, 7, 8	Socially maladjusted	Easygoing, self-confident
12	2, 7, 8	Relaxing	Uncomfortable to be with
13	3, 6, 9	Emotionally unpredictable	Even temperament
14	4, 5, 10	Look somewhat alike	Look unlike
15	11, 13, 14	Dynamic personalities	Weak personality

Figure 15.1 A grid analysis of Mildred Beal's role construct repertory test. Constructed after Kelly, 1955, p. 242 ff.

532

	No.	Role Figure
⊗	1	Mother
	2	Father
	3	Brother
✓	4	Sister
	5	Liked Teacher
✓	6	Disliked Teacher
⊗	7	Ex-Flame
○	8	Boyfriend (Wife/Husband)
✓	9	Employer
✓	10	Rejecting Person
	11	Sought Person
✓	12	Pitied Person
	13	Intelligent Person
	14	Successful Person
	15	Interesting Person

SORT NUMBER	ROLE FIGURES	EMERGENT POLE (Two as Similar)	IMPLICIT POLE (One as Different)
11	1, 7, 8	Socially maladjusted	Easygoing, self-confident

Figure 15.2 A single construct from Mildred Beal's grid REP analysis.
Constructed after Kelly, 1955, p. 242 ff.

in her view, different from the other two. On the first line of the emergent pole column, she then writes in her own words the way in which 9 and 14 are similar. Likewise, in the implicit pole column, she writes her ideas of what makes figure 11, Sought Person, different. Reading from Figure 15.1, Mildred regards Employer and Successful Person as similar because they are "related to me." "Sought Person" is different by being "unrelated."

The second time, after Mildred has completed all 15 sorts and listed her constructs, she is asked to make systematic comparisons of her 15 similar and different constructs to all of the remaining figures on each line. Mildred is thus instructed to start again with the constructs she listed for sort number one, namely, "related to me" versus "unrelated," and systematically consider this dichotomous construct in relation to the 12 remaining figures on line one. For each figure to which the construct of Sort 1 applies, Mildred is asked to place a check mark in that figure's box on the Sort 1 line.

Mildred proceeds down the remaining 14 constructs, repeating her search for applicable figures for each of the constructs on that line. For the sake of simplicity, Sort 11 has been abstracted from the total grid and enlarged in Figure 15.2. The first time that Mildred sorted the figures of line 11, she chose Mother and Ex-Flame as similar by placing an "X" in the circles for those roles. Now Mildred is asked to take the remaining 12 roles and to indicate whether her construct "socially maladjusted versus easygoing, self-confident" applies to any of them. For the sake of illustration, figures 4, 6, 9, 10, and 11 have been checked to indicate that Mildred feels the similarity construct "socially maladjusted" applies to them. Those she has left blank indicate that the similarity (emergent pole) construct cannot be used to describe them.

The resulting grid pattern of checks and "X's" may be converted to a series of numbered coordinates without reference to Mildred's verbal labels. All that matters is the pattern of expressed similarity and difference indicated by the check marks, not the verbal labels that led Mildred to assign these marks. The procedures employed in mathematically analyzing the data are very complex and need not concern us here.

The grid or matrix of Mildred's REP test represents her own unique personality theory, the system of personal constructs or interpretations by which she conducts her life. Kelly frequently used the term **construe** to indicate the active process of trying to explain, interpret, and give meaning to our experiences. Reading across Mildred's grid we can answer questions about the figures she construes as similar on a particular dimension of her theory. Reading down the columns, we can ask questions about how Mildred construes each person on a whole series of dimensions. To illustrate, consider what is learned about the way Mildred construes the world when columns 1 (Mother) and 12 (Pitied Person) are read downward together, as shown in Table 15.2.

KELLY: THE INVENTIVE PSYCHOLOGICAL TINKERER

Kelly's theory is an original and idiosyncratic one; it could even be labeled a "home-brewed" theory. Looking back at Kelly's development of personal construct theory, we find him in the great tradition of American tinkerers and inventors. We might include the young Wright brothers, Thomas Alva Edison, and a score of others in many fields at a time when Americans tended to be rather skeptical of traditional ways of doing things and often tried to start from scratch to solve problems that conventional wisdom proclaimed were unapproachable. Such resourceful optimism characterized George Kelly's work; it was also a keynote of the theories and methods he developed.

Writing in the 1960s, Kelly recounted his early disappointment with standard theories years earlier as a graduate student. One day his professor wrote on the blackboard an "S" with an arrow pointing to an "R." Anticipating that after several weeks of dull course

Table 15.2   Constructs Compared

(1) Mother	*(12) Pitied person*
(1) Are related to me	(1)
(2) Very unhappy person	(2) Very unhappy person
(5) Feels inferior	(5) Feels inferior
(7) Hypersensitive	(7) Hypersensitive
(8) Hypercritical	(8)
(9) Feelings of inferiority	(9) Feelings of inferiority
(11) Socially maladjusted	(11) Socially maladjusted
(13) Emotionally unpredictable	(13)
(14) Looks like sister and rejecting person	(14) Looks like sister and rejecting person

work, the crux of psychology's explanation of humans was about to be discussed, Kelly listened attentively but was disappointed: ". . . [T]he most I could make of it was that the 'S' was what you have to have in order to account for the 'R' and the 'R' was put there so the 'S' would have something to account for. I never did find out what the arrow stood for—not to this day—and I have pretty well given up trying to figure it out" (Kelly, 1963, pp. 46–47). He therefore dismissed stimulus-response psychology.

Kelly graduated from the University of Iowa in 1931 with a doctor of philosophy degree. He ran headlong into the Great Depression and spent 12 years at a small college in western Kansas, an impoverished dust bowl region. He soon discovered that his background, which was in physiological psychology and speech pathology, was useless for helping often-despairing young people. He turned to Freudian theory even though he had dismissed it as preposterous when he was a student. "Through my Freudian interpretations, judiciously offered at those moments when clients seemed ready for them, a good many unfortunate persons seemed to be profoundly helped" (Kelly, 1963, p. 51).

His Freudianisms worked most of the time. His unsophisticated clients readily accepted them. Despite his success with his quasi-Freudian approach, he was not satisfied. Kelly began to change his approach:

> . . . I began fabricating "insights." I deliberately offered "preposterous interpretations" to my clients. Some of them were about as un-Freudian as I could make them—first proposed somewhat cautiously, of course, and then, as I began to see what was happening, more boldly. My only criteria were that the explanation *account for the crucial facts as the client saw them, and that it carry implications for approaching the future in a different way.* (1963, p. 52; italics added)

Kelly might tell a client, for example, that his or her nervous stomach was "rebelling against nourishment of all kinds, "parental, educational, and nutritional." His clients felt that even these interpretations were worth applying. They often successfully changed the direction of their lives by adopting new outlooks implied in Kelly's "preposterous" suggestions. In Kelly's terminology, they had developed alternative constructions. Evidence began to mount for Kelly's developing view that patients could change if they would attempt to see things differently. When, for instance, more clients than he could handle applied to him for treatment, he began giving them a few hints about what to do while on the waiting list. Months later, when their turn came, Kelly often found that they had solved or were well on the way to resolving their difficulties. His few hints about how to look at their problems differently resulted in positive changes. He later termed this process of changing one's view or interpretation of problems and events **constructive alternativism.**

Kelly therefore began to formulate a new clinical perspective—one emphasizing present activities. "... I began to pursue the notion that one's current acts and undertakings might have as much to do with the development of his personality as did the imprint of events with which he came in contact or the insights he was able to conjure up with the help of his therapist" (1963, p. 56).

Kelly founded a statewide traveling clinic with some of his graduate students to reach more people in crisis. Visiting schools and agencies, they found that teachers and staff did not often understand problem students or clients very well. Kelly introduced a personality test, the Maller Inventory, to provide insight into how people conceptualized their experience. This test consisted of cards containing self-descriptive statements that the subject was asked to sort. It was an early version of the Q-sort technique used by Stephenson and Rogers. The results of this test aided teachers and staff to understand those they were trying to help. Kelly used the results of this test to provide information for a role-playing technique. This technique was the basis for his later development of *fixed-role therapy*.

EACH PERSON IS A SCIENTIST

According to Kelly, a major human characteristic is the need to know and to control one's own universe:

> Might not the individual man, each in his own personal way, assume more of the stature of a scientist, ever seeking to predict and control the course of events with which he is involved? Would he not have his theories, test his hypotheses, and weigh his experimental evidence? (Kelly, 1955, p. 5)

A return look at Mildred Beal's REP protocol is an example of the idea of person as scientist. Mildred created explanatory hypotheses about the significant figures in her life. She predicted their behavior with more or less accuracy on the basis of her past experiences with them; she even discerned similarities and differences among subgroups. In short, she made sense of or construed her world by attempting to anticipate the behavior of the people in it.

Early on, Kelly noted the contradiction between the self-concepts of many psychologists and their erroneous views of research subjects: "I, being a psychologist, and therefore a scientist, am performing this experiment in order to improve the prediction and control of certain human phenomena; but my subject, being merely a human organism, is obviously propelled by inexorable drives welling up within him, or else he is in gluttonous pursuit of sustenance and shelter" (1955, p. 5).[1] He noted that psychologists do not expect those whom they study to seek understanding of themselves and others.

KELLY'S FUNDAMENTAL POSTULATE AND 11 COROLLARIES

The **fundamental postulate** relates the psychological processes of a person to the way he or she understands and predicts or anticipates events:

FUNDAMENTAL POSTULATE: *A person's processes are psychologically channelized* [this term was coined by Kelly; it simply means *directed* or *determined*] *by the ways in which he anticipates events* (1955, p. 46).

---

[1] Kelly wrote his theory in an era when sensitivity to gender references in language did not prevail. In the interests of scholarly accuracy, Kelly's own words have been left unedited with respect to the use of the male pronoun and referents—even when Kelly was actually referring to *all humans*—not just males.

A key word in Kelly's fundamental postulate is *anticipates* because it is the need for prediction that Kelly sees as fundamental. Kelly presented eleven corollaries to the fundamental postulate. Together they comprise the overall framework for his theory of **personal constructs.**

FUNDAMENTAL POSTULATE

1. Construction Corollary	3. Organization Corollary
2. Individuality Corollary	4. Dichotomy Corollary

5. Choice Corollary
6. Range Corollary
7. Experience Corollary

8. Modulation Corollary	10. Commonality Corollary
9. Fragmentation Corollary	11. Sociality Corollary

CONSTRUCTION AND INDIVIDUALITY COROLLARIES: THE PERSON AS A PROCESS

Over time, the individual is able to detect recurrent themes, repetitive events, and their onset and termination. "Once events have been given their beginnings and endings, and their similarities and contrasts construed, it becomes feasible to try to predict them, just as one predicts that tomorrow will follow today" (Kelly, 1955, p. 53). Kelly therefore formulated a first corollary to the fundamental postulate:

CONSTRUCTION COROLLARY: *A person anticipates events by construing their replications* (1955, p. 50).

The next assertion follows from Kelly's emphasis on the individuality of cognitive activity. Kelly called this proposition the

INDIVIDUALITY COROLLARY: *Persons differ from each other in their constructions of events* (1955, p. 55).

HIERARCHY OF EXPERIENCE: ORGANIZATION AND DICHOTOMY COROLLARIES

Kelly believed that people impose meaning on the events they experience using bipolar constructs. The person notes the similarities among various events, and groups them together under one construct; but that same construct derives some of its meaning from those events that were excluded by contrast. Hence, the construct *introvert* not only indicates all traits the person associates with introversion but also defines what introversion is not for that person.

A person's system of constructs is not static. Their interpretations change and are modified by new experience. Contradictions and conflicts between constructs often emerge. One way to resolve any such conflicts is to organize one's constructions of events into a hierarchy in which particular constructs may subsume many other constructs in the system. When one construct subsumes another, it is called a **superordinal construct;** conversely, the construct so subsumed is termed a **subordinal construct.**

It is possible for super- and subordinal constructs to change places in the hierarchy. For example, the construct good versus bad may include the two poles of the intelligent versus stupid dimension of experience. Good subsumes intelligent, and bad subsumes stupid. Good and bad may, of course, assimilate other constructs as well. Furthermore, good and bad may change ordinal position with intelligent and stupid:

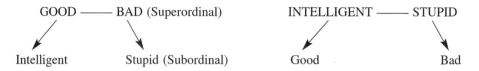

Another way in which constructs may be ordinally ranked is for one to create categories that subsume complete dimensions under one pole of a superordinal construct. For example, the good-bad construct might itself be subsumed under one pole of a broader superordinal construct: evaluative versus descriptive. Thus the pair, good bad, would be globally subsumed under evaluative, whereas other constructs like light versus dark would be subsumed under descriptive:

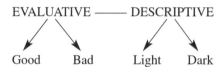

To make sense out of the world, people systematize their constructs into hierarchies for convenience in anticipating occurrences of events. This insight led to the

ORGANIZATION COROLLARY: *Each person characteristically evolves, for his convenience in anticipating events, a construction system embracing ordinal relationships between constructs* (1955, p. 56).

As we have seen, Kelly proposed that every personal construct is dichotomous and bipolar in structure. In order to derive meaning from a construct, it must indicate at least two elements as similar, and a third as contrasting. In this regard, you may recall the structure of the REP test, in which the subject is asked to find similarity between two figures and to determine how they differ from a third. Kelly's view that people think in terms of dichotomies does not accord with classical logic. In classical logic, a thing is either "A" or "not-A": masculine or not, feminine or not. But in Kelly's system, three elements are required to establish the identity of a thing: two similar and one contrasting.

To illustrate, suppose that there are three people, Alice, Betty, and Carl. Trying to find ways in which two might be similar to one another but different from the third, an individual might categorize them on the basis of the construct, "assertive-shy" Alice and Carl are viewed as similar because they are both seen as assertive, whereas Betty is shy. She is categorized under the opposite pole of this construct, assertive-shy. Kelly formulated these ideas in his fourth corollary:

DICHOTOMY COROLLARY: *A person's construction system is composed of a finite number of dichotomous constructs* (1955, p. 59).

CHOICE, RANGE, AND EXPERIENCE OF COROLLARIES: LIMITATIONS OF ANTICIPATION

People choose the pole of a dichotomized construct that provides the greater scope for secure activity and growth. Kelly formulated his fifth corollary around these ideas regarding individual choices:

CHOICE COROLLARY: *A person chooses for himself that alternative in a dichotomized construct through which he anticipates the greater possibility for extension and definition of his system* (1955, p. 64).

A sixth corollary stated the limits of constructs:

RANGE COROLLARY: *A construct is convenient for the anticipation of a finite range of events only* (1955, p. 68).

The range corollary implies that any construct is limited to a finite range of events. The limiting factor is relevance. What is outside the range of a given construct is not considered as contrasting or opposite; it is viewed as irrelevant.

One's categories and category systems are modified with changing experience:

EXPERIENCE COROLLARY: *A person as construction system varies as he successively construes the replications of events* (1955, p. 72).

When anticipations of events are violated and fail to conform to expectations, people are stimulated to modify their construct systems. They change their views and expectations. Individuals do not have to be merely inert onlookers. They are like scientists, who revise their hypotheses when they do not pan out experimentally.

> A person can be a witness to a tremendous parade of episodes and yet, if he fails to keep making something out of them, or if he waits until they have all occurred before he attempts to reconstrue them, he gains little in the way of experience from having been around when they happened. It is not what happens around him that makes a man experienced; it is the successive construing and reconstruing of what happens, as it happens, that enriches the experience of his life. (Kelly, 1955, p. 73)

Taken together, the choice, range, and experience corollaries can account for such classical psychological concepts as *motivation, anxiety,* and *learning.* Kelly did not abandon these concepts. Rather, he viewed them as inherent in the process of prediction. Motivation in Kelly's theory is related to the concept of the human need to predict; anxiety is construed as a consequence of faulty anticipations; and learning is inherent in a person's continuing process of the modification of constructs and construct systems.

MODULATION AND FRAGMENTATION COROLLARIES: VARIATION VERSUS STABILITY

People can be cognizant of the changes they make in their construction systems. Any change in construction may be placed in context and viewed in the light of its effect on the entire system. Just as scientists may use their existing theories as guides to making new observations, individuals employ their existing construction systems as guides for new constructions. And just as the scientist's theory may become a set of intellectual blinders, the individual's construction system may also be limiting.

Certain constructs are uniquely susceptible to change. Such constructs are said to be **permeable constructs.** "A construct is permeable if it will admit to its range of convenience new elements which are not yet construed within its framework" (Kelly, 1955, p. 79). Conversely, an **impermeable construct** is one that will admit of no new elements. Kelly coined the term, *range of convenience* to indicate that each construct is applicable only to a finite range of events or experiences and is not applicable to others. Kelly formulated the implications of permeable and impermeable constructs into an eighth proposition:

MODULATION COROLLARY: *The variation in a person's construction system is limited by the permeability of the constructs within whose range of convenience the variants lie* (1955, p. 77).

As a teenager, we might have divided people into the two classes of the construct "fear versus domination." There were, consequently, those whom we feared and those whom we dominated. With the passing of years, this dichotomy itself might be viewed as immature. The notion of "immaturity," itself a construct, has an opposite pole: "maturity." If this new construct, "immaturity versus maturity," is permeable, we may be able to subsume the previous construct, "fear versus domination," under "immaturity" as a rejected value. Under the pole of "maturity" we incorporate a new construct: "respect versus contempt." We are now, consequently, in a position to classify our acquaintances in what we perceive to be a more mature fashion: those whom we respect versus whose whom we hold in contempt (1955, p. 82). The permeability of the superordinal construct, "immaturity versus maturity," thus allows for this modulation or "fine-tuning" of the construct system. The respect-contempt construct can be assimilated under the permeable "maturity versus immaturity" construct. Sometimes, however, an individual may use subsystems of constructs that are not logically consistent with one another. Kelly termed this theoretical assumption, his ninth, the

> FRAGMENTATION COROLLARY: *A person may successively employ a variety of construction subsystems which are inferentially incompatible with each other* (1955, p. 83).

Kelly put the fragmentation corollary in context. He indicated that we should overlook the inconsistencies in construction subsystems to see the whole picture:

> It should make even clearer the assumed necessity for seeking out the regnant construct system [that is, the larger whole system and its dominant themes] in order to explain the behavior of men, rather than seeking merely to explain each bit of behavior as a derivative of its immediately antecedent behavior. (1955, p. 83)

COMMONALITY AND SOCIALITY COROLLARIES: SHARED EXPERIENCE

In addition to an individuality corollary, in which people see things differently, a *commonality corollary* is a logical necessity:

> COMMONALITY COROLLARY: *To the extent that one person employs a construction of experience which is similar to that employed by another, his psychological processes are similar to those of the other person* (1955, p. 90).

An example of the commonality corollary is that people with similar political views might experience an election outcome in similar ways. Kelly added some distinctions to clarify the commonality corollary:

> It is important to make clear that we have not said that if one person has experienced the same events as another he will duplicate the other's psychological processes. . . . One of the advantages of this position is that it does not require us to assume that it would take identical events in the lives of two people to make them act alike. Two people can act alike even if they have each been exposed to quite different phenomenal stimuli. It is the similarity in the construction of events that we find the basis for similar action, not in the identity of the events themselves. (1955, pp. 90–91)

Kelly's next corollary, the *sociality corollary,* deals with how people understand the construct systems of others:

> SOCIALITY COROLLARY: *To the extent that one person construes the construction processes of another, he may play a role in a social process involving the other person* (1955, p. 95).

Kelly emphasizes in this corollary that the basis of social interaction is interpersonal understanding, not simply shared experience. If one can anticipate (predict) another's behavior, one can modify one's own behavior in response.

> In order to play a constructive role in relation to another person one must not only, in some measure, see eye to eye with him but must, in some measure, have an acceptance of him and his way of seeing things. We say it in another way: the person who is to play a constructive role in a social process with another person *need not so much construe things as the other person does as he must effectively construe the other person's outlook.* (1955, p. 95; italics added)

THE MASK METAPHOR AGAIN

An important part of the sociality corollary is its use of the concept of social role. Kelly defined roles as "psychological processes based upon the role player's construction of aspects of the construction systems of those with whom he attempts to join in a social enterprise" (1955, p. 97). Kelly's definition of role is consistent with the cognitive orientation of his theory. Kelly is yet another psychologist who presents the actor-mask metaphor of personality. In his version, there is the chance of merging the actor with the role:

> It may be helpful at this point to ask ourselves a question about children at Halloween. Is the little youngster who comes to your door on the night of October 31st, all dressed up in his costume and behind a mask, piping "trick or treat, trick or treat"—is that youngster *disguising* himself or is he *revealing* himself? Is he failing to be spontaneous? Is he *not* being himself? Which is the *real* child—the child behind the mask or the barefaced child who must stand up in front of adults and say "please" and "thank you"? I suspect costumes and masks worn at Halloween time, as well as uniforms worn by officers on duty, doctoral degrees, and the other devices we employ to avoid being seen as we are, are all ways we have of extricating ourselves from predicaments. . . . *But masks have a way of sticking to our faces when worn too long.* (Kelly, 1964, p. 158; last italics added)

Kelly used the mask analogy to illustrate how individuals may be trapped into believing they are the role that they portray. Such an insight has also been verified by the classical experiments of Stanley Milgram (1974) and Philip Zimbardo (Zimbardo et al., 1974), in which experimental subjects were found to identify with their assigned roles. It has also been noted that in reality television programs such as *Survivor,* people often quickly become very attached to the roles they play.

Change Through Fixed-Role Therapy

Kelly believed that persons are free to revise their view of themselves and of their relationships to others. **Fixed-role therapy** was one of Kelly's methods to aid his clients to construe themselves deliberately differently. You may recall that fixed-role therapy involves the clinician's writing a narrative sketch for the client that represents a change from the client's present personality. The therapist says, in effect, to the client: "Here is another way of construing yourself. Pretend for two weeks or so that you are this (fictional) person. Monitor your experience."

For Kelly, fixed-role therapy was a creative process mutually shaped by client and therapist. It was not to be understood as a "repair" technique to fix wounded personalities (Kelly, 1955, p. 380). Rather, Kelly's conception of the technique is most accurately described as a kind of personal experiment.

Kelly developed some simple rules for the writing of fixed-role sketches by clinicians (1955, pp. 368 ff.):

1. It should ideally be constructed by a panel of clinicians familiar with the client.

2. The sketch should develop a major theme rather than attempt to correct minor personality faults.

3. The sketch should sharply contrast with the client's real character, for it will be easier to pretend to be a person he or she believes is totally opposite from the one he or she presently is.

4. The sketch should attempt to engage the client's own personality growth processes and mobilize his or her own resources for change.

5. Testable hypotheses that the client can immediately check in his or her own life should be part of the sketch so that it is plausible and real to the client.

6. The client should be given the full protection of "make-believe," so that he or she can experiment with the role without making a permanent commitment. Kelly called this protective screening a "protective mask" (1955, p. 373).

Writing the Fixed-Role Sketch

One basis for constructing a new fictional personality consists of clients' self-characterization sketches. In addition to explicit content, the clinician considers the way clients have organized the sketch, emphasized certain phrases, and highlighted specific themes. Clinicians also incorporate personal constructs revealed by the REP test. The actual construction of a fixed-role sketch requires both clinical skills and creativity. Table 15.3 contains, side-by-side, excerpts from the self-characterization sketch of "Ronald Barrett," the pseudonym of a patient of Kelly's, and the fixed-role sketch written for him with the fictional name of "Kenneth Norton."

This client's self-characterization and Kelly's fixed-role sketch indicate the central theme. Ronald was invited to perceive the subtle feelings of other people rather than argue with them about the literal meanings of words (Kelly, 1955, p. 375). After the period of fixed-role therapy, Ronald Barrett was able to change his way of construing himself. He began selectively to adopt aspects of "Kenneth Norton" that he found worthwhile and congenial. He found himself capable of being more open and friendly with others.

THE CPC CYCLE: CIRCUMSPECTION, PREEMPTION, AND CONTROL/CHOICE

Kelly developed a model, the **CPC cycle**—*circumspection, preemption,* and *control/choice*—for indicating how a person's constructs and construct system could accommodate new realities. The first phase, **circumspection,** involves the development of propositional thinking. In propositional thinking, a person considers alternative ways of construing experience. A **propositional construct** is one that facilitates openness to seemingly contradictory experiences. Developing propositional constructs is a flexible mode of thinking that avoids black/white pigeonholing and "nothing but" thinking. Propositional constructs are the oppositive of rigid, constellatory constructs.

The second phase, **preemption,** involves choosing the relevant elements from among various propositional alternatives. Having reduced the field to one dichotomous issue, the individual still has to make the choice between the opposing poles.

Table 15.3   Excerpts from Ronald Barrett's Self-Characterization and Fixed-Role Sketches

Self-characterization by "Ronald Barrett"	*"Kenneth Norton": Fixed-role sketch*
An overall appearance of Ronald Barrett would give one the impression that he has a rather quite [*sic*] and calm personality. Furthermore, he dislikes doing or saying anything that will draw unfavorable attention in public. . . . However, he has been known to flare up (not in public, though) very easily and often gets quite worked up or frustrated over something done or spoken by (usually not his friends or anyone with him) someone that he feels should know better. . . . He very rarely shows signs of anger toward his friends. On the other hand, he is apt to be inconsistent in that it sometimes takes a lot to get him worked up over some subject at hand, while at other times he will very easily get very worked up. . . . A feeling of guilt often comes over him if he thinks he has not been kindhearted enough. . . . His tendency to criticize and correct people, esp. in his family, on major as well as minor issues, shows some decrease outside his family, but not too much within. Proving his point, or arguing his point, and arguing against other people's points, seems to be one of his major "hobbies." . . . He has some ideas concerning girls that seem odd or just plain crazy to most people. He completely refrains from calling a girl "beautiful." She may be cute, pretty, attractive . . . but he uses the word "beautiful" only [to] describe material things that have no "feeling" as humans have. Although he listens attentively to stories or general discussion about sex, he rarely enters into the conversation. One may say that he puts too much meaning and thought into kissing a girl. . . . He is usually lost for conversation when meeting someone new, or seeing a girl he knows, but if he once "breaks the ice," he can usually talk freely.

From Kelly, 1955, pp. 326–328. | Kenneth Norton is the kind of man who, after a few minutes of conversation, somehow makes you feel that he must have known you intimately for a long time. This comes about, not by any particular questions that he asks, but by the understanding way in which he listens. It is as if he had a knack of seeing the world through your eyes. The things which you have come to see as being important he, too, soon seems to sense as similarly important. Thus, he catches not only your words but the punctuations of feeling with which they are formed and the little accents of meaning with which they are chosen.

Kenneth Norton's complete absorption in the thoughts of the people with whom he holds conversations appears to leave no place for any feelings of self-consciousness regarding himself. If indeed he has such feelings at all, they obviously run a poor second to his eagerness to see the world through other people's eyes. . . .

Girls he finds attractive for many reasons, not the least of which is the exciting opportunity they provide for his understanding the feminine point of view. Unlike some men, he does not "throw the ladies a line" but, so skillful a listener is he, soon he has them throwing him one—and he is thoroughly enjoying it. With his own parents . . . he is somewhat more expressive of his own ideas and feelings. Thus his parents are given an opportunity to share and supplement his new enthusiasms and accomplishments.

From Kelly, 1955, pp. 374–375. |

In the third phase, **control/choice,** the individual, who has already reduced the field to one dichotomous issue, finally chooses between the opposing poles.

Let us consider how these concepts would apply in a psychologically complex interpersonal scenario. Consider the predicament in which a hypothetical protagonist, young Jean-Mary, found that some of her key personal constructs had lost their usefulness. Note the process (CPC cycle) through which her thinking progressed as she dealt with a very challenging situation:

> Jean-Mary's eighth grade teacher precipitated a crisis in the relationship between Jean-Mary and her younger sister, Robin. Called to Robin's sixth-grade classroom by a note from Robin's teacher, Jean-Mary was startled to find her sister tear-stained, flushed, and trembling

BOX 15.1   *Only Connect . . .*

Had George Kelly formulated his theory in the 1970s and 1980s, instead of in the 1950s and 1960s, it would have been hailed as a cognitive theory rather than as an eclectic one. Kelly's ideas are compatible with contemporary cognitive psychology in a way that is surprising for a theory whose origins preceded psychology's current willingness to focus on what people think. There was a time in our history as a science, especially during the 1960s, when the prevailing radical behaviorism made *thinking* a dirty word in psychology. Kelly was well ahead of his time in discussing thinking, decision making, and the cognitive activity of anticipating consequences.

at the blackboard. When Jean-Mary arrived, Robin was trying to endure a tirade from the teacher. The gist of the verbal assault was an unfavorable comparison of her math abilities to the teacher's former student, Jean-Mary.

Moreover, the teacher wanted Jean-Mary to complete a problem that her sister was not able to solve correctly. Jean-Mary was caught in a conflict between obedience to an adult authority figure and compassion for and loyalty to her own sister. Unable to decide between defiance and submission, Jean-Mary initially froze. She finally relented to the teacher's pressure and solved Robin's long division problem correctly in front of the whole class. In that moment of hurt and humiliation for Robin, a wall had been built separating the two sisters in a way that neither of them could verbalize.

Jean-Mary was faced with an awful realization. Up to this time, teachers had always been objects of her respect and admiration. They were people to be obeyed without question. But clearly, as her experience had just painfully shown, a specific teacher was cruel and stupidly hurtful. Jean-Mary experienced three conflicts: She felt guilt for having participated against her own sister in a situation that required her to change her views quickly and decisively; she experienced anger at her own gullibility in having uncritically accepted teachers as paragons of virtue; she struggled against an emerging distaste for all teachers and for schoolwork in general.

Jean-Mary was belatedly able to reason that some teachers are less than perfect, and that sometimes being a teacher was no safeguard against cruelty and stupidity. Jean-Mary was even able to redefine her own self-image to admit that she had acted with less courage than her personal values had demanded. She resolved never again to be an unwitting pawn of her own preconceptions, and she apologized to her sister and re-affirmed her loyalty.

Jean-Mary's predicament and how she solved it illustrates the CPC cycle—a sequence of thought involving the revision of constructs and construct systems. Up to the time of her experience with the long division episode, her construction of teachers could be characterized as stereotypical: She thought that all teachers were necessarily good, kind, intelligent, and just. Kelly called such stereotypes **constellatory constructs** (1955, p. 155). Constellatory constructs are rigid "constellations" or configurations of qualities that are applied in an automatic manner to a person, object, or situation. Fortunately, Jean-Mary's constellatory construct of "teacher" also had the characteristic of permeability. Recall that a **permeable construct** is one that is susceptible to change through the addition of new elements to its range of convenience. Constellatory constructs, however, are not easy to modify.

When confronted with a violation of her expectancy in the form of a teacher who was capricious and hurtful, Jean-Mary was confused and anxious: "This teacher is not at all like teachers whose behaviors I thought I could anticipate." Such a discrepancy could be resolved only by eventually restructuring the construct of "teacher." It had to be changed into a more relativistic concept that admits variations to the stereotype of "good, just, and intelligent."

The series of changes in Jean-Mary's construct system involves each of the three phases—circumspection, preemption, and control/choice—of Kelly's CPC cycle.

Phase One: Circumspection

When confronted with a situation that required her to act in a way that violated several personal constructs, Jean-Mary was forced to view the elements that composed her "teacher" construct with circumspection. "A teacher is good, just, kind, and intelligent, but may sometimes also be cruel, stupid, and unjust—and a lot of other incompatible things." Unfortunately, Jean-Mary was not able, until after the fact, to enter the first phase of the CPC cycle, circumspection, and survey the situation and the persons involved for possible alternative constructions.

Phase Two: Preemption

The circumspection phase must come to an end if we are to be able to act on the propositions that have been developed. Circumspection finally enabled Jean-Mary to free herself from the rigidity of her constellatory construct of "teacher" and provided her with a more propositional version—that teachers were not necessarily considerate, kind, and intelligent. But only when Jean-Mary was able to leave the circumspection phase could she decide among the various possible options. Jean-Mary finally began thinking more preemptively. Kelly described the preemptive phase:

> The preemption of issues characterizes the "man of action." He is likely to see things in what may appear to his associates to be an oversimplified manner. He consolidates all the possible perspectives in terms of one dichotomous issue and then makes his choice between the only two alternatives he allows himself to perceive. (1955, p. 516)

Jean-Mary finally preempted the issues to one dichotomous theme: "defiance of a heretofore respected authority figure versus allegiance to my sister." Unfortunately, Jean-Mary had entered the preemption stage (and the earlier circumspection state) too late to keep from hurting her sister.

Phase Three: Control/Choice

In Jean-Mary's case, the final choice was for loyalty and trying to remedy any hurt she might have caused. Her apology and allegiance of loyalty to her sister are indicative of this choice. Unfortunately for her sister, Jean-Mary's entrance into and completion of the CPC cycle was too late to prevent harm. But real change has occurred. When confronted with similar situations in the future, Jean-Mary would not hesitate to act on her new constructions.

SOME TRADITIONAL PERSONALITY VARIABLES AS KELLY RECAST THEM

Kelly thought about some basic psychological concepts in a new way. Old concepts such as the unconscious, anxiety, hostility, and guilt were recast in his theory.

The Unconscious

The concept **unconscious** is partly subsumed under Kelly's notion of pre- and nonverbal constructs. In this sense, his idea is similar to that of Freud himself. Freud had

Only Connect . . .

What Kelly was clearly trying to do in his refor- mulations of concepts such as the unconscious, anxiety, guilt, and aggression was to create a thor- oughly cognitive psychology that would provide an alternate explanation to Freudian psychody-

namics for phenomena that Freudian theory em- phasized. Kelly wanted his cognitive approach to account for far more than simply the way in which people construed their experiences.

proposed that repression proper consisted of the preconscious system's removal of lan- guage "cathexes" from threatening ideas that have a relationship with content already pri- mally repressed into the unconscious (cf. Chapter 3). Kelly, however, suggests that lack of a word label alone is not sufficient to prevent a construct from entering awareness. For a personal construct to be truly removed from consciousness, it must be *submerged* along one of its two poles.

Recall that each construct has a *similarity pole* by which two or more elements are construed as alike, and a *contrast pole* by which at least one other element is seen as dif- ferent. One or the other pole of the construct may be submerged so that, for example, the similarity elements are kept out of awareness.

Submergence of one pole of a construct implies the *suspension* of whole categories of constructs from the total system. In contrast with some notions of repression, suspen- sion implies that the idea or element is forgotten simply because the person cannot toler- ate any structure within which the idea would have meaning. Once he or she can entertain such a structure, the idea may again become available within it (Kelly, 1955, p. 473).

Kelly has thus translated the idea of *unconscious* into the concepts of *nonverbal con- structs, submergence,* and *suspension.*

Anxiety

Constructs that compose the central anticipations by which people set their life goals and construe themselves in relation to these outcomes are called **core constructs** (Kelly, 1955, p. 482). An individual can tolerate some incompatibility between expectancy and experi- ence. As that discrepancy becomes greater, anxiety and confusion may result. Experiences that are incompatible with core constructs may threaten such constructs. According to Kelly (1955, p. 495), **anxiety** is the feeling that accompanies, *"the cognition that the events with which one is confronted lie outside the range of convenience of one's con- struct system."* Similar ideas to those of Kelly have emerged within cognitive dissonance theory (Festinger, 1957). Also, Erikson's notions of identity conflict, and his observation of the anxiety experienced from the loss of identity among combat soldiers (Chapter 8) are largely consistent with Kelly's formulations. Erikson's concept of *identity* would be considered a core construct in Kelly's theory.

Guilt

In Kelly's terms, **guilt** is defined as a *"Perception of one's apparent dislodgment from his core role structure"* (1955, p. 502). Core role structure can be thought of as one's funda- mental identity in regard to others. One might see oneself as a nurturing caretaker, for ex- ample. Parents with a core role of being such caretakers would feel guilt if they started neglecting their children to handle other competing responsibilities.

Aggressiveness

Kelly defined **aggressiveness** in a way that is clearly different from the usual usage of the term. His use of the term seems to have little to do with expressions of anger but indicates being assertive or taking initiative on the basis of one's goals and views of reality. *"Aggressiveness is the active elaboration of one's perceptual field"* (1955, p. 508). For Kelly, the individual who actively seeks to construct a greater number of alternative choices is acting "aggressively": "They are always precipitating themselves and others into situations which require decision and action" (1955, p. 508).

EVALUATING KELLY'S PERSONAL CONSTRUCT THEORY

Kelly's theories about human nature have proven quite durable over the years. His notion of personal constructs was first quite popular and led to numerous speaking engagements and visiting appointments at many universities as well as an endowed chair at Brandeis University. During the 1960s and early 1970s, his ideas were eclipsed by the behavioral movement and some less elaborate cognitive approaches. Subsequently, a number of trends have led to a renewed appreciation of Kelly's work. A constructivist movement has taken form in many disciplines as has an emphasis on individual experience and narratives. There is now an active journal devoted to constructivist psychology, the REP test has been computerized so that its scoring is simpler, books based on Kelly's ideas continue to be published, and societies devoted to personal construct psychology have sprung up in the United States and internationally.

Refutability of Kelly's Ideas

In principle, much of personal construct theory is refutable (testable). Certainly the REP test grid approach lends itself to empirical studies (Bannister & Fransella, 1971, esp. Chapters 3 and 6). Other central concepts from Kelly's theory appear to be testable:

- Repression as a kind of "refiling," "mislabeling," or "redefining" threatening ideas could certainly be tested in the laboratory with a verbal learning design or with a recognition memory design drawn from signal detection theory.

- The efficacy of Kelly's fixed-role therapeutic technique, like other psychotherapeutic techniques, is capable of being assessed with empirical studies.

- The power of expectation or anticipation has already been tested in a variety of other research paradigms in psychology that range from social psychology studies to current social learning theory research (e.g., Bandura, 1986, reviews many of these studies on what he terms, *expectancy effects*).

- Personality change in psychotherapy has been studied using Kelly's personal construct system (Martin, 1994).

Human Agency in Personal Construct Theory

Kelly developed a theory that emphasizes active human agency. In his view, it is the person who constructs meaning from reality. It is the person who tests personal hypotheses and confirms or disconfirms anticipations, much as a scientist does. The person is active in regard to challenges and to new circumstances, not reactive.

Personal Constructs Are Idiographic

Kelly's theory is idiographically focused. It is primarily concerned with understanding the personal constructs of specific individuals. Idiographic theories tend to be *ipsative,* a term drawn from psychometrics and psychological testing. Ipsative tests (and theories, and constructs) compare the individual with his or her own past and future performances, but they do not permit comparison across individuals. There is also a nomothetic aspect to Kelly's theory for the fundamental postulate and the 11 corollaries apply universally and are viewed as indicative of human nature in general.

SUMMARY

George A. Kelly's theory of personal constructs is built upon his conviction that all persons behave "as if" they were scientists. Each of us, out of the fundamental human need to understand the world, creates and tests hypotheses about the behavior of significant others. Kelly formulated a fundamental postulate to embody this concept*: "A person's processes are psychologically channelized by the ways in which he anticipates events"* (1955, p. 46).

Eleven corollaries expand this basic theme:

1. *Construction Corollary:* A person anticipates events by construing their replications.

2. *Individuality Corollary:* Persons differ from each other in their construction of events.

3. *Organization Corollary:* Each person characteristically evolves, for his or her convenience in anticipating events, a construction system embracing ordinal relationships between constructs.

4. *Dichotomy Corollary*: A person's construction system is composed of a finite number of dichotomous constructs.

5. *Choice Corollary:* A person chooses that alternative in a dichotomized construct through which he or she anticipates the greater possibility for extension and definition of his or her system.

6. *Range Corollary:* A construct is convenient for the anticipation of a finite range of events only.

7. *Experience Corollary:* A person's construction system varies as he or she successively construes the replications of events.

8. *Modulation Corollary:* The variation in a person's construction system is limited by the permeability of the constructs within whose ranges of convenience the variants lie.

9. *Fragmentation Corollary:* A person may successively employ a variety of construction subsystems that are inferentially incompatible with each other.

10. *Commonality Corollary:* To the extent that one person employs a construction of experience which is similar to that employed by another, his or her psychological processes are similar to those of the other person.

11. *Sociality Corollary:* To the extent that one person construes the construction processes of another, he or she may play a role in a social process involving the other person.

Among other innovations, Kelly developed an assessment method, the Role Construct Repertory Test (REP), and a therapeutic technique called fixed-role therapy. The REP test requires the individual to compare systematically his or her personal interpretations of the roles of significant people. Such comparisons can then be analyzed impressionistically or objectively with the tools of correlation and factor analysis. Fixed-role therapy involves the psychologist writing a personality sketch that differs in significant ways from the client's usual roles. The client is then invited to enact the role for two or more weeks. The alternative construction of events embodied in the fixed-role sketch is often sufficient to aid the client in construing life differently.

Personal constructs may be thought of as a person's means of making sense of life. Changes in a person's constructions may be necessitated by the demands of reality. The circumspection-preemption-choice/control (CPC) cycle involves the person in a restructuring of his or her construct system in three phases: (1) the circumspection phase, which involves the development of propositional constructions of events; (2) the preemption phase, during which the individual must narrow constructions to one significant dichotomous construct; and (3) the control or *choice* phase, in which the individual decides to act on one or the other pole of the dichotomous construct that was chosen in phase two.

Kelly's system has led to new ways of thinking about basic personality constructs like the unconscious, anxiety, aggression, and guilt. Each of these variables can be viewed either in terms of the individual's capacity to modify and rearrange his or her system of constructs or the emotions that result when constructs fail to predict events reliably. Kelly's theory is refutable in principle and has led to empirical studies of personality and personality change. His theory emphasizes active agency and focuses largely on uncovering the idiographic or individual aspects of personality.

Initially, Kelly's ideas were first applauded and then largely ignored by other psychologists. In the last decade or so, however, Kelly's ideas have attracted increasing interest. Today, there is much theorizing and research as well as therapeutic activity that has been inspired and influenced by Kelly's work.

FOR FURTHER READING

Kelly's influence as a personality theorist has waxed and waned and waxed again. Kelly's own comprehensive masterwork (most recent edition) is the two-volume *Psychology of Personal Constructs* (New York: Routledge, 1992). The first three chapters of Vol. 1 of this work have been published as a self-contained paperback introduction to Kelly's theory under the title *A Theory of Personality: The Psychology of Personal Constructs* (New York: Norton, 1963).

Brendan Maher has compiled and organized many of Kelly's theoretical papers into a single volume, *Clinical Psychology and Personality: Selected Papers of George Kelly* (New York: Wiley, 1969). Of particular significance among the papers in this volume are, "The Autobiography of a Theory" and the "Language of Hypothesis: Man's Psychological Instrument."

The collection of research papers contained in D. Bannister and J. M. Mair's (Eds.) *The Evaluation of Personal Constructs* (New York: Academic Press, 1968; especially Chapters 3, 4, and 10) will provide some indication of the investigations stimulated by Kelly's ideas. In a similar way, J. C. Bonarius's review, "Research in the Personal Construct Theory of George A. Kelly: Role Construct Repertory Test and Basic Theory," in Vol. 2 of B. A. Maher's (Ed.), *Progress in Experimental Personality Research* (New York: Academic Press, 1965), indicates the kinds of research questions that have been explored with Kelly's concepts.

Additional research efforts can be surveyed in D. Bannister's (Ed.) collection of papers entitled *Perspectives in Personal Construct Theory* (New York: Academic Press, 1970). Bannister and F. Fransella have put together a paperback book summarizing Kelly's theory and surveying their own and others' research efforts on its behalf: *Inquiring Man: The Theory of Personal Constructs* (Baltimore: Penguin, 1986).

J. Martin's book, *The Construction and Understanding of Psychotherapeutic Change: Conversations, Memories and Theories* (New York: Teachers College Press, 1994), utilizes Kelly's personal construct theory to investigate personality change in psychotherapy. F. Fransella's, *George Kelly* (London: Sage Publications, 1996), is a contemporary summary and evaluation of Kelly's influence on psychotherapeutic practice. Robert Neimeyer and Michael Mahoney have recently edited a comprehensive book, *Constructivism in Psychotherapy* (Washington, DC: American Psychological Association, 1999), describing a contemporary approach in a large measure based on Kelly's original theorizing and therapeutic work.

The Journal of Contructivist Psychology publishes current articles in personal construct theory and constructivist thinking as well as related empirical and applied areas in psychology.

GLOSSARY

Aggressiveness: In Kelly's eyes, actively assimilating a greater range of experiences and constructing alternative choices.

Anxiety: In Kelly's theory, the feelings of threat when confronted with experiences discrepant with one's expectations and outside of one's construct system.

Circumspection: The first stage in the CPC cycle that involves the use of propositional constructs enabling one to reason relativistically. Propositional thinking is hypothetical, tentative, and relativistic.

Constructive alternativism: The capacity of an individual to change his or her view or interpretation of problems and events. In Kelly's theory, such an ability was the key to successful adaptation.

Constellatory construct: A construct in which the elements are applied automatically and rigidly to a person, object, or situation.

Construe: An active effort to explain, interpret, and give meaning to experiences. We place interpretations on events, that is, we *construe* them.

Control/choice: The third stage of the CPC cycle, which involves deciding which pole of the dichotomous construct, selected in the preemptive phase, is most relevant to the situation.

Core constructs: Constructs, largely inflexible and resistant to change, on which we rely most heavily when explaining experience.

Corollaries: See definitions for the following as given in the chapter text.

> Construction Corollary
> Individuality Corollary
> Organization Corollary
> Dichotomy Corollary
> Choice Corollary
> Range Corollary
> Experience Corollary
> Modulation Corollary
> Fragmentation Corollary
> Commonality Corollary
> Sociality Corollary

CPC cycle: A problem-solving process in a construct system that involves three phases: *circumspection, preemption,* and *control/choice.*

Fixed-role therapy: A clinical technique that asks clients to act as if they were other people with different psychological characteristics.

Fundamental postulate: In Kelly's words, "A person's processes are psychologically channelized by the ways in which he anticipates events." This means that a person's psychological reactions are determined by the way he or she makes sense of or experiences different events.

Guilt: In Kelly's theory, feelings and thoughts that accompany a person's acting in a way that is outside or inconsistent of the person's core role or self-image.

Impermeable construct: A construct that does not admit new experiences or new elements to be included within its boundaries.

Permeable construct: A construct that assimilates new experiences within its boundaries.

Personal constructs: An individual's implicit or explicit ways of looking at, explaining, and interpreting events in the world. Personal constructs are used to give meaning to, interpret, or predict experiences and events.

Preemption: The second stage in the CPC cycle, in which a person chooses the relevant elements from among his or her propositional alternatives and chooses the one construct that seems particularly relevant.

Propositional construct: A construct in which the elements are open to modification based on new experiences.

Role Construct Repertory Test (REP Test): A test Kelly devised to identify the constructs a person uses to construe the relevant people in his or her life.

Subordinal construct: A construct that is subsumed under a broader and more general construct.

Superordinal construct: In a hierarchical construct system, a construct that subsumes others.

Unconscious: In Kelly's view, constructs with a low level of cognitive awareness.

Chapter 16

Dollard

Miller

Bandura

John Dollard & Neal E. Miller

Psychodynamic Social Learning Theory

Albert Bandura

Social Cognitive Theory

. . . trying to shape auto driving skills through operant conditioning would unshape the driver and the surrounding environment!

Albert Bandura (2001c)

The theorizing that is currently in vogue attributes behavior to multilevel subpersonal neural networks devoid of any consciousness, subjectivity or self-identity. While this line of theorizing views humans as high-level automatons, I have been emphasizing the exercise of human agency.

Albert Bandura (2001c).

An old story illustrates the limitations of conditioning and the importance of expectations as an explanation for human behavior:

A shabbily dressed person went to a fancy hotel and was treated poorly by the concierge. The concierge was surprised when this man rewarded him with a large tip. The next day he provided great service.

At the end of the day, he received no tip at all.

The concierge asked the guest, "Why did you give me a good tip when I provided poor service but no tip after I provided excellent service?

The guest replied, "Today's tip was for yesterday's service."

Anonymous

About Psychodynamic Social Learning Theory

In the 1930s through to the 1950s, a group of psychologists and social scientists studying with Clark L. Hull at Yale University began to apply the principles of conditioning to complex social behavior. Called the Yale Group, *the team was composed of such eminent scientists as Neal Miller, John Dollard, O. Hobart Mowrer, and Leonard Doob. Their contributions, both as a group and individually, have had an enduring impact on psychology.*

Dollard and Miller (1941) were interested in translating Freud's numerous psychoanalytic insights and hypotheses into the more testable formulations of stimulus-response psychology. The first such effort was The Frustration-Aggression Hypothesis *written jointly by the members of the Yale Group (Dollard, Doob, Miller, Mowrer, & Sears, 1939; Miller, 1941), in which they translated Freud's concept of the aggressive instinct into a behavioral theory stated in clear, testable terms. The book's main point, the* **frustration-aggression hypothesis,** *was that aggression is a result of blocking a person's efforts to reach a goal (Berkowitz, 1969; Dollard et al., 1939).*

The Yale Group had demonstrated that Freud's clinical formulations could be converted into testable behavioral propositions. In their work, they also found that new intervening (cognitive) variables had to be considered equal to the task of turning Freudian concepts into testable propositions.

After their work with the frustration-aggression hypothesis, Dollard and Miller continued to modify early behavioral theories to accommodate human expectations, conflict, and defense. In 1941, they published their first full account of a **psychodynamic social learning theory.** *In this theory, they added the concept of imitation learning to the existing principles of classical and instrumental conditioning. In 1950, Dollard and Miller published their major contribution,* Personality and Psychotherapy, *in which they systematically set forth behavioral formulations of Freud's main ideas about psychopathology and psychotherapy.*

John Dollard **Born: 1900** **Menasha, Wisconsin**
  Died: 1980 **New Haven, Connecticut**

Neal E. Miller **Born: 1909** **Milwaukee, Wisconsin**
  Died: 2002 **Hamden, Connecticut**

STIMULUS-RESPONSE TRANSLATION OF ANXIETY AND REPRESSION

Dollard and Miller demonstrated that there were scientifically feasible ways of testing Freud's ideas, and that the clash of behavioral and psychodynamic paradigms is not inherently irreconcilable. They endeavored to combine the strengths of behavioral methodology and psychoanalytic observations. The sample of their work that we examine concerns their reformulation of anxiety and repression, two key concepts in the Freudian model of personality.

First Step: Anxiety as a Signal of Danger

O. Hobart Mowrer and Neal Miller undertook a first step in understanding Freudian concepts using behavioral principles. Mowrer (1939) applauded Freud's formulation that emphasized anxiety as a signal of danger. Mowrer's approach used the model of Pavlovian conditioning to explain the acquisition of the signal of danger. He applied the model of operant conditioning to account for the maintenance of the resulting avoidance (defensive) behavior. For Mowrer, physical pain is an unconditioned or unlearned response (UCR) to a noxious unconditioned or unlearned stimulus (UCS). Any neutral stimuli that accompany the unlearned stimulus, UCS, will become learned or conditioned stimuli signaling the painful UCS:

> A so-called "traumatic" ("painful") stimulus (arising either from external injury, of whatever kind, or from severe organic need) impinges upon the organism and produces a more or less violent defense (striving) reaction. Furthermore, such a stimulus-response sequence is usually preceded or accompanied by originally "indifferent" stimuli, which, however, after one or more temporally contiguous associations with the traumatic stimulus, begin to be perceived as danger signals, i.e., acquire the capacity to elicit an "anxiety" reaction. (Mowrer, 1939, p. 554)

Pavlovian conditioning—stimulus substitution by association—is used in this stimulus-response (S-R) translation to explain the "signal" function of anxiety. The heart of anxiety, for both Mowrer and Freud, is the organism's capacity to anticipate painful consequences from prior experience.

A child, for example, who has been burned by a hissing steam heater eventually fears the hissing sound and uses it as a cue to avoid the hot steam heater. As Mowrer cogently pointed out, Freud suggested that once anxiety was established, certain defensive behaviors are learned to protect the organism from having ever again to experience it. In order to do so, the child must avoid stimuli similar to the ones associated with the burning incident. In order to avoid the danger signal of anxiety, not only must the child avoid a nearby heater that it hears hissing, it must also avoid being near the hissing sound itself because that signal evokes the unpleasant experience of anxiety.

To explain the continued avoidance of the anxiety associated with the burn incident, Mowrer proposed a second factor involved in anxiety learning, the factor of negative reinforcement. Any behavior that reduces the painful emotion of anxiety in anticipation of pain is functionally equivalent to the original escape from the burning heater. But note that now the escape is not from the actual burn pain; the escape is from the unpleasant emotional signal of potential pain. Avoidance of the anxiety signal (hissing steam) is being reinforced by getting away from a conditioned aversive stimulus. Avoidance of the hissing steam reduces the unpleasant experience of anxiety. As we know from reinforcement theory, any behavior that terminates or reduces aversive stimulation increases in probability. Anxiety is a negative reinforcer that maintains the avoidance behavior in the absence of the original noxious UCS. To say the same thing another way, avoidance behavior is negatively reinforced by the experience of anxiety reduction. In a similar way, a child who has negative experiences in school may feel less anxiety by playing hooky in order to avoid school altogether. Playing hooky will be reinforced by the reduction of anxiety by the fact of the youngster avoiding the anxiety-provoking situation.

In our example of the radiator burn, the avoidance response may generalize so that the child may learn not only to avoid the hissing heater, but also to stay out of the room altogether. Even contact with the aversive signal of hissing steam would thus be prevented. At a later age, the child might learn to turn the heater valve and shut it off so that both the signal (hissing) and the noxious UCS (heat) are terminated. This behavior of turning the valve off would be an instrumental response and would be reinforced.

> *In short, anxiety (fear) is the conditioned form of the pain reaction,* which has the highly useful function of motivating and reinforcing behavior that tends to avoid or prevent the recurrence of the pain-producing [unconditioned] stimulus. (Mowrer, 1939, p. 554; italics in original)

Second Step: Fear as an Acquired Drive Called Anxiety

The second step in formulating an S-R translation of Freudian theory was to convert Mowrer's model of anxiety as a learned motive into a form testable under controlled laboratory conditions. Miller (1948) did just that by showing that rats could learn a lever-pressing response to escape from a white box where they had been shocked. After learning to make the escape response to flee the pain of electric shock, the rats were never again shocked in the white box. The mere sight of the white box was sufficiently fear-arousing to provoke a rat to make the lever-pressing response that would open a door to a safer black compartment.

Thinking "outside of the box," Miller changed the procedure. He made the lever inoperative. Placed again into the white box, the rats futilely pressed the lever. The door did not drop open. After frantic scurrying, pawing, and climbing behavior, many of the rats discovered (but some did not) that turning a wheel in the wall of the box opened the door. From that point on, within five seconds of entering the white box, the rats leaped to the wheel, and scurried through the opened door into the safe black box. Figure 16.1 illustrates this experimental arrangement.

Miller had demonstrated that once fear is classically conditioned to the cue of the white box, the *learned* fear of the white color would serve as an acquired drive that motivates new escape learning. Thus, the rats developed **fear as an acquired drive,** or what Miller considered **anxiety.** None of the rats ever experienced an electric shock after the initial escape response was learned. Learning the new response of wheel turning is thus motivated by the fear of the white box, and it is reinforced, not by escaping the shock, but by reduction of anxiety associated with leaving the white box.

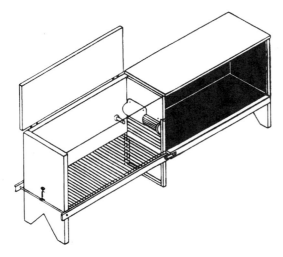

Figure 16.1 Miller's acquired fear apparatus.
Modified from Miller, 1948.

This demonstration of rats learning to escape white boxes, however elegant, is still not directly comparable to the Freudian "escape" of repression. What was now needed was a demonstration that human beings learn anxiety as a signal of danger, and that this avoidance-learning blocks conscious thought about certain subjects in the manner that Freud had described.

At this level, ideas, thoughts, and words are the appropriate stimuli and behaviors to which the experimental psychologist needed to attend. Thinking was about to be viewed through the lens of behavioral theory.

Third Step: The Functional Equivalence of Words and Thoughts

The third step was to provide experimental evidence for the proposition that anxious thoughts and anxious actions are functionally equivalent. As part of his doctoral dissertation, Miller had provided just such a demonstration.

Miller's (1950) experiment showed that anxiety-motivated avoidance behavior could be attached to abstract stimuli such as words. By generalization, the anxiety attached to the words is spread to the thoughts conveyed by the words. Not thinking the thoughts, and avoiding saying the words are two avoidance responses that come remarkably close to what Freud had called repression.

Miller's experimental design called for a subject to be shown the letter T and the number 4 in random series, with the subject required to say aloud whatever stimulus he or she was shown. Whenever the letter T appeared, the subject received a painful electric shock, but never received one when the number 4 was shown. The subject rapidly learned to respond with anticipatory anxiety to the letter T, as indicated by a subject's **galvanic skin response (GSR).** The GSR is one component of the multiple autonomic nervous system responses that can be monitored by a polygraph. During the learning phase, the subject's GSR recordings showed large peaks whenever T was followed by shock, and no large peaks in response to every appearance of the number 4.

In the next phase of Miller's study, the subject was shown a series of dots. He or she was required to *think,* not say aloud, T for the first dot, then *think* 4 for the next dot, and so on, in alternating series through 25 dots. Figure 16.2 reproduces the GSR recordings in this phase of *thinking without shock* for three blocks of five trial segments.

The tracings in Figure 16.2 show that whenever the subject was thinking T, there was a large GSR peak indicating high anxiety. Thinking of four, by contrast, evoked very little GSR change. By the 25th trial in the third block, the peaks to T were reduced by extinction (subject had not received any more shocks), but there is a residual effect for every thought of T still discernible.

The anxiety had been learned in response to the UCS of shock following presentations of T. But it clearly became generalized to thinking of T when the only overt stimulus was a dot. Miller had shown, therefore, that there is a functional equivalence between saying a word and thinking it. The behavior of thinking of specific contents was at least as effective in mediating the GSR anxiety response as the behavior of verbalizing the shocked stimulus.

To understand the full significance of Miller's demonstration, consider the plight of a small child when she is scolded for some misdeed. When she thinks about similar misbehavior in the future, the same feelings of anxiety that were attached to the scolded act return. Or, even more potently,

> Sometimes parents, with their superior intelligence and experience, can tell what a child is
> likely to do before he says or does anything obvious. Thus they may warn the child when he

GSR RESPONSES on TRIALS 1 to 5

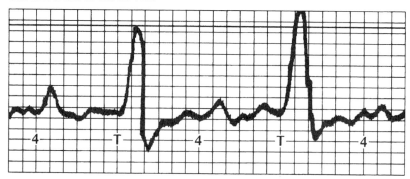

GSR RESPONSES on TRIALS 11 to 15

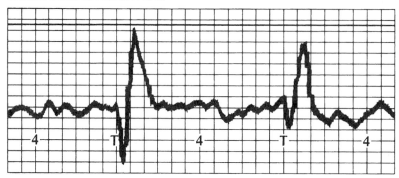

GSR RESPONSES on TRIALS 21 to 25

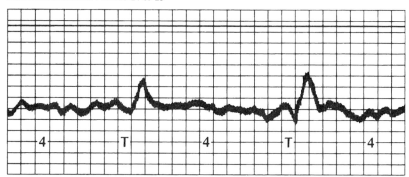

Figure 16.2 GSR responses to thought of letter previously shocked.
From Miller, 1950, p. 464.

> has an evil thought before he had made any gross overt response. Such warnings attach fear to the thought and help to break down the discrimination between thoughts on the one hand and spoken words and acts on the other. To the small child it is as if the parents could read his mind. (Dollard & Miller, 1950, p. 207)

Dollard and Miller conceptualized thinking as a behavior that, like directly observable behaviors, could be conditioned. In addition, as Freud had suggested, thinking of threatening content provokes defensive behavior designed to rid one of the thought. Miller had carried thinking as a cause of behavior into S-R theory. The next step was to describe the relationship between thinking anxiety-laden thoughts and the avoidance maneuver called "repression."

Fourth Step: Repression as "Not-Thinking"

The final step in the translation of the Freudian conception of repression into S-R terms required one further assumption: Thinking certain thoughts previously associated with "pain" is subject to the same kind of avoidance as are actual behaviors associated with punishment or pain. The "not thinking" of certain thoughts is thus functionally equivalent to avoiding certain acts. Unconscious thoughts in the Freudian framework are seen in the cognitive behavioral translation as such thoughts that one has learned "not to think."

Dollard and Miller reconceptualized the Freudian concept of repression within the framework of behavioral theory. Here are three ways in which Dollard and Miller (1950) thought that the Freudian defense of repression might be understood using behavioral concepts:

1. *Prevention of verbal labeling of a drive:* A sexually aroused person in a situation in which he would find sexual arousal aversive (such as being in the presence of a friend's wife) does not label his erotic arousal as sexual. Self-protectively, this individual might mislabel his sexual excitement as "nervousness" or even "boredom." Acknowledging the sexual nature of feelings might arouse anxiety; thinking of oneself as bored does not. Part A of Figure 16.3 illustrates this form of "repression."

2. *Prevention of responses producing a drive:* To continue the same example, the sexually aroused person detects his own arousal by noticing that he has an erection. This bodily response means "sex" and thinking about it must be avoided. His perception of his body's response increases his anxiety. He anxiously distracts his attention from his erection by declaring that he is hungry, and avidly begins preparing or eating a meal. Substitution of the eating response for the sexual one effectively

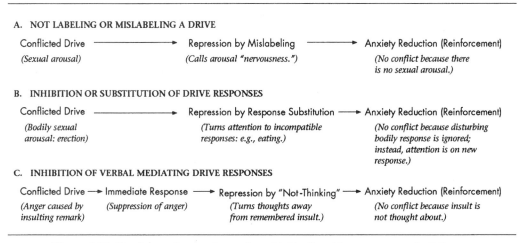

Figure 16.3 The forms of repression or "not-thinking" avoidance responses in S-R terms. Based on Dollard and Miller, 1950.

blocks further thinking about his friend's wife sexual attractiveness. Eventually, decreased anxiety results both because he no longer thinks "sex," and because, in fact, eating is an incompatible response that has reduced his sexual arousal. Part B of Figure 16.3 illustrates this form of repression.

3. *Inhibition of responses of mediating the drive:* Some people learn to be afraid of their own anger through punishments for the expression of anger during childhood. When such a person perceives some cue that ought to trigger anger (a spoken insult, for example), he or she experiences both the anger appropriate to the insult *and* the learned anxiety about expressing it. He consciously suppresses the anger for the moment. But later, *thinking* about the situation renews angry feelings as well as anxiety about them. Now the person can control anxiety by *not thinking* about the insult, for now it is not the insult itself, but the thought of it, that evokes anxiety. He or she stops thinking about the insult. "Stopping thinking" is functionally equivalent to the original suppression of the anger at the time of the actual insult, but it now occurs at the level of thought. Part C of Figure 16.3 illustrates this form of repression.

Note that all three of Dollard and Miller's explanations of repression hinge on reducing the noxious effects of anxiety that has come to be connected with particular thoughts. In each of the three instances just discussed, not thinking or thinking alternate thoughts are substituted for thinking the threatening ones. Anxiety is conceptualized as a negative drive impelling escape through the expedient of "not thinking" or by thinking of something else.

DOLLARD AND MILLER: A BRIDGE BETWEEN PSYCHODYNAMIC AND BEHAVIORAL APPROACHES

Dollard and Miller's psychodynamic social learning theory bridged the gap between psychodynamic and behavioral approaches by explaining psychoanalytic observations and S-R explanations. Dollard and Miller endeavored to combine perceptive psychoanalytic insights and the scientific need for testable hypotheses.

One strength of Dollard and Miller's approach lay in carefully conducted empirical and laboratory-based research. Starting with the frustration-aggression hypotheses, every one of their main formulations received extensive experimental or field testing. Like Freud, Dollard and Miller had to infer from conflicted behavior, from aggressive behavior, and from anxious behavior variables within the organism that could not be directly observed or manipulated. Unlike Freud's, Dollard and Miller's formulation permitted, in fact encouraged, the direct manipulation of behavior in controlled situations to assess the effects of that manipulation on thoughts and emotions.

Albert Bandura   Born: 1925   Mundare, Alberta, Canada
At present: Professor Emeritus at Stanford University

About Social Cognitive Theory

Social cognitive theory, *as proposed by Bandura, sees people as both acting on the environment and affected by their understanding of it. They are proactive and self-regulating. Cognitive processes and self-reflection are central to human behavior. People are not* *reactive organisms or conditioned by the environment; they plan and predict the consequences of their actions. In a word, they are* **agentic.**

Albert Bandura and Richard Walters, his first doctoral student (1963), took up the task of advancing our understanding of complex activities without taking on what they viewed as the limitations of psychoanalytic theory. Since Richard Walters's untimely death, Bandura and his colleagues at Stanford University have worked to develop the social cognitive theory with the methodological rigor of behaviorism, while nevertheless taking account of the human capacity to think about and to plan for experiences and to deal with the varied situations faced in daily life.

MISCONSTRUED AS A BEHAVIORIST

From the very beginning of his graduate training, Bandura was interested in approaching psychology as an empirical discipline. However, even though he was surrounded by behaviorists and in an institution known for behaviorism, he did not become a behaviorist himself. In recent correspondence, he indicated:

> At the time of my graduate training, the entire field of psychology was behaviorally oriented with an almost exclusive focus on the phenomenon of learning. But I never really fit the behavioral orthodoxy. At the time virtually all of the theorizing and research centered on learning through the effects of reinforcing outcomes. In my first major program of research, I argued against the primacy of conditioning in favor of observation learning in which people neither emit responses nor receive reinforcements during the process of learning. . . . I conceptualized observational learning as mediated through perceptual and cognitive processes. (Bandura, 2001c)

He continued,

> I rejected Miller and Dollard's view of imitation as merely a special case of instrumental [operant] conditioning. While behaviorists were plotting learning curves as a function of number of reinforced trials, I published a chapter on "No trial learning." (Bandura, 2001c)

Further, he expressed concern that he has often been mistakenly viewed as a behaviorist, even though he challenged the major tenets of behaviorism.

> In the early writings I acknowledged the phenomena encompassed under the labels of conditioning and reinforcement. But what text writers and those relying on secondary sources were missing is that I conceptualized these phenomena as operating through cognitive processes. (Bandura, 2001c)

How did this misattribution occur? One reason is that, like behaviorism, social cognitive theory largely relies on laboratory research and the results of experiments. The processes of imitation learning and vicarious reinforcement superficially seem to be behavioral processes because of the use of the words *learning* and *reinforcement.* As we shall see, however, imitation learning and vicarious reinforcement involve a cognitive change or a change in expectations that occurs as a result of observation; they are not conditioning processes involving shaping or direct reinforcement.

Bandura endeavored to study some phenomena having to do with daily behavior as well as clinically relevant behavior with empirical methods and to explain those phenomena with concepts and language drawn from the psychology of learning and cognition. The body of research literature connected with Bandura's approach is now so vast that it would require a substantial handbook merely to survey it. We cannot undertake that survey here, but we can describe the main features of the paradigm.

Imitation Learning: Dealing with the Complexities of Learning in Daily Life

Complex human learning occurs with the help of reinforcement and association, but not exclusively in those ways. We also learn by imitating others or by watching them model behavior. We attend to the details of their actions, but we also observe the consequences of their actions and can learn the principles that guide their actions. In addition, sometimes we learn through exposure to the thinking of other people, as, for instance, when we read a textbook that conveys the written ideas of others.

The novice surgeon observes many surgical procedures before attempting to participate in small ways in a supervised operation. The beginning driver observes and listens to explanations of what to do before, under careful guidance, he or she is permitted to attempt controlling a car. And the neophyte clinical psychologist observes therapy and reads extensively about the process before conducting therapy under supervision.

In short, people learn by watching other people, and by encoding all kinds of information in symbolic form. Miller and Dollard (1941) introduced the concept of learning by imitation. Bandura understood the significance of Dollard and Miller's concept of imitation learning and its improvement over a conditioning model:

> I was very attracted to Miller and Dollard's book on social learning and imitation. It seemed to provide an alternative to the somewhat prevailing theory of learning which assumed that we acquire competencies and new patterns of behavior through response consequences. At that time, it seem to me that I couldn't imagine how a culture would transmit its language, its mores and all of the complex competencies that are required to function effectively through this tedious trial and error process. *You would need three or four lifetimes to acquire even some basic functioning.* (Bandura, in Evans, 1989, italics added)

Bandura more fully developed and elaborated the concepts of modeling: Modeling is more than imitation learning or a kind of mimicry. In modeling the learner must (1) attend to the model, (2) remember what is seen and extract the essential elements, (3) reproduce symbolically what has been learned, and (4) be motivated to perform the activity. Figure 16.4 summarizes these main steps and their components. What the information in Figure 16.4 emphasizes is that the processes involved in observational learning go far beyond mere mimicry or a rote kind of imitation. They involve the observer's development and utilization of a cognitive model based on observation. The behavior described in Bandura's model thus requires more cognitive activity unlike the reinforcement of chance responses as in operant conditioning.

Bandura's research has demonstrated that a wide range of learning is possible through **modeling** and **observational learning.** All manner of novel responses may be acquired through observational learning so that the learner is able to expand his or her behavioral repertoire.

Observational learning can include response facilitation effects whereby the presence of a model performing a particular action induces the observer to make a similar response in direct imitation. Fads in hairstyles, clothing, and diet are good examples of response facilitation effects. New dance steps are often quickly adopted through the means of response facilitation that occurs when the steps are observed.

Vicarious Reinforcement

Bandura ascertained that complex behavior could be acquired by watching another's performance and the ensuing consequences. Observing another person reinforced can affect the behavior of the observer. Being so affected by such reinforcement that is not part of one's own direct experience is termed **vicarious reinforcement.** In Bandura's view, the effect of the reinforcer is on the person's *expectations* for future responding. A reinforcer,

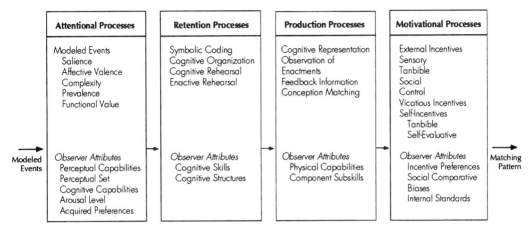

Figure 16.4 Subprocesses governing observational learning.

in his theory, provides an incentive to act; unlike the view of radical behaviorism, it is not simply a reward for past action. Reinforcement serves as a source of information to the person about his or her environment and the requirements for successful behavior. Foresight can be acquired either by direct experience or by watching what happens to another person. Figure 16.5 compares behavioral and social cognitive views of reinforcement.

It is important to emphasize that Bandura did not dismiss the importance of direct reinforcement as a powerful determinant of learning (Bandura, 1969). Rather, his social cognitive theory required the traditional view of reinforcement to be expanded to include vicarious reinforcement, in which there was actually no reinforcement provided to the learner at all.

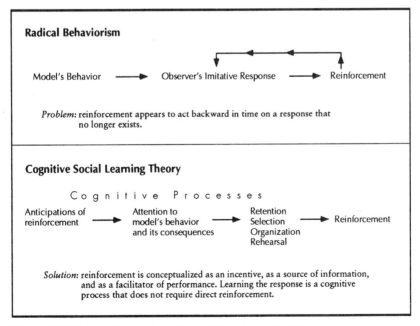

Figure 16.5 Behavioristic and social cognitive views of reinforcement.
Based on Bandura, 1977b, p. 38.

The Self-System and the Environment: Reciprocal Determinism

Bandura (1978a, 1986) proposed the existence of a cognitive-emotional set of processes regulating and regulated by environmental input. The **self-system,** as Bandura prefers to call these internal processes, is not an autonomous agent like Freud's ego. The self-system is not isolated and is not a "little person" inside the person. In Bandura's model, the self-system is a complex of processes interdependent with the person's social and physical environment (Bandura, 1977b, pp. 194ff.; 1978a, 1986, pp. 369ff.).

Bandura calls his complex interactional viewpoint **triadic reciprocal determinism,** and it is the key to the puzzle of studying private events scientifically. Human behavior is regulated in a reciprocally determined way. Bandura pictures reciprocal determinism as an interactive triad (Bandura, 1978a, p. 345). The three elements that interact are: (P) the person's awareness and thinking, (B) the person's ongoing behavior, and (E) the person's environment. In this triad, each of these three factors may both affect and in turn be affected by the other two factors. This process can continue. As the person's behavior affects his or her environment, the environment in turn affects the person's behavior, and the person's awareness and thinking about these interdependencies affects behavior, environment, and changed expectations.

A key point in the scheme in Figure 16.6 is that:

> By their actions, individuals contribute to the nature of their situations (Bandura, 1981). People are therefore at least partial *creators of their own history.* Moreover, memory representation of the past involves constructive rather than reproductive processes in which events are filtered through personal meanings and biases and cognitively transformed. People thus serve as partial authors not only of their past experiences but of their memory of them as well. (Bandura, 1982, p. 157, italics added)

There are three major classes of **self-regulatory processes in the self-system:** We will see that the common denominator connecting and underlying these processes is the theme of competence, mastery, or self-efficacy. These processes are represented in Figure 16.7.

1. The first class of self-regulatory processes involves the **self-observation of behavioral quality.** Concepts such as originality, authenticity, and ethicalness are applied as evaluative standards to one's own behavior.

2. The second set of self-regulatory processes that make up the self-system are the **judgments of excellence** and goodness of one's own behavior relative to the behavior of others and to one's own past performances.
   a. Included among these judgments is the individual style of attributing responsibility for action to self or to external causes.

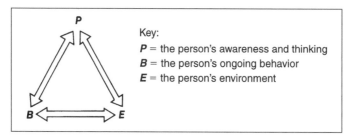

Figure 16.6 Triadic reciprocal determinism.

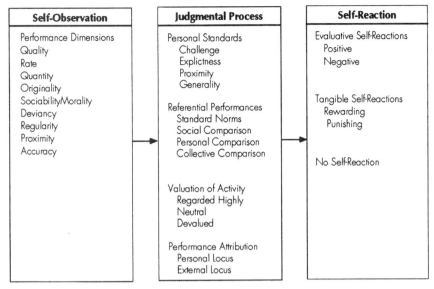

Figure 16.7 Processes involved in the self-regulation of behavior by internal standards and self-incentives.

From Bandura, 1986, p. 337.

    b. Blame for a failure attributed to self has remarkably different psychological effects from those of blame attributed to external causes.

3. The last processes in the self-system are those termed **self-reaction processes** but which would be better termed self-reward/punishment.

THE IMPORTANCE OF A SENSE OF SELF-EFFICACY

Bandura (1977a, 1982, 1997) proposed that the sense of **self-efficacy** or personal competence underlies a great many behavioral phenomena, including the effectiveness of psychotherapy (e.g., Bandura, Adams, & Beyer, 1977), persistence in the face of obstacles (Bandura & Schunk, 1981), accuracy of the self-concept (e.g., Lazarus & Launier, 1978), and depression (e.g., Abramson, Seligman, & Teasdale, 1978).

In Bandura's analysis, the experience of self-efficacy or personal competence has four sources:

1. **Enactive attainments,** or what Bandura used to refer to as **performance accomplishments** (Bandura, 1986, p. 399) are the most powerful regulators of self-efficacy. A person's own efforts either succeed or fail, and the outcome is instructive in planning future efforts.

2. Vicarious experience is derived from watching another's efforts succeed or fail. Such observations provide one with a basis of comparison by which to estimate personal competence in similar situations.

3. Verbal persuasion is the least powerful regulator of self-efficacy because being told that one can or cannot master a given task is far removed from the actual performance and does not engage the person's conviction as strongly.

4. Physiological state, or what Bandura had earlier referred to as the level of emotional arousal, is the degree of apprehension and anxiety that an individual experiences in a situation that will test his or her competence (Bandura, 1986, p. 401).

If a person concentrates on feelings of fear or anxiety, he or she may bring about the very failure that is dreaded. On the other hand, moderate degrees of arousal are likely to enhance performance. And Bandura (1986) points out that people are aware of and try to determine not only their anxiety levels, but their levels of physical fatigue and pain as well.

Bandura (1997, pp. 113 ff.) has also thought about how an individual might integrate the four components of self-efficacy—enactive attainment, vicarious experience, verbal persuasion, and physiological arousal. Each of the four sources may have different informational value for different people, who will weight various components differently. For example, one person may more heavily weight the experience of emotional arousal from past successes and failures—how good and bad such experiences felt. Another puts primary weight on past performance accomplishments. Yet another person may factor in the opinions of others.

Bandura also distinguishes between **efficacy expectations** and **outcome expectations,** an important difference for predicting effort and persistence. An efficacy expectation is an individual's belief that a given outcome can be accomplished because one possesses the requisite skills. By contrast, an outcome expectation is a person's belief that a certain course of action will result in a specific outcome, even if he or she is not the person to do it successfully.

One of the important features of Bandura's social cognitive theory is that it brought psychological concepts into understanding many complex phenomena important in daily life. In his development of the concept of self-efficacy, Bandura approaches questions that have to do with achievement, effort, goal-setting, and success and failure in daily life. Moreover, the processes that regulate our expectations are susceptible to scientific study by manipulating the variables of past performance, vicarious modeling, verbal instruction, and degree of emotional arousal.

Self-Efficacy: Its Impact in Daily Life

Bandura (1997) elevated the theoretical status of self-efficacy to the role of a nearly universal mediator of personality phenomena. His review of a wide range of research aimed to demonstrate how a person's belief in personal effectiveness and control shapes an extraordinary range of psychological phenomena extending from family interactions and general social transactions to the clinical phenomena of psychopathology. Three of the areas he considered were how a person copes with threat, how intellectual interests are developed, and the impact of self-efficacy appraisals on physical and psychological health. In all of this work, we see the further extension of his concepts to different areas of life.

BOX 16.1 *Only Connect . . .*

The personality theorist, Robert W. White (1959), also developed a theory emphasizing the importance of the development of a sense of self-efficiency or what he termed *competence*. He indicated that people are motivated by what he termed, "effectance motivation." Bandura acknowl- edged White's contribution (1997, p. 13) but also criticized it in part as not being a ". . . particularized theory from which testable deductions can be made." In other words, Bandura viewed White's theory as nonrefutable.

Coping with Threat, Revisited

Bandura maintains his earlier conception of anxiety as "a state of anticipatory apprehension over possible deleterious happenings" (1997, p. 137). A threatening perception is related to the degree of threat experienced: the more the person believes he or she can cope with a potentially noxious experience,

- the less threatening that experience will seem,
- the less likely will the person scare self with anxiously unrealistic fantasies,
- the less likely will the person dwell on unpleasant bodily arousal, and
- the more likely will the person transform the meaning of the threat into one that he or she believes they can manage.

Motivating Intellectual Interests

The process by which people develop intrinsic interests in activities at which they initially possess little or no skill is regulated by self-efficacy beliefs.

> To mountaineers, the toilsome activity of crawling over slippery rocks in foul weather is not inherently joyful. It is the self-satisfaction derived from personal triumphs over lofty peaks that provides the exhilaration. Remove the personal challenges, and crawling over rocks becomes quite boring. (Bandura, 1997, p. 219)

Personal standards and the perceived meaning of the challenge contribute to the development of interests and satisfactions in three ways:

1. Challenging personal standards enlist sustained effort and involvement in activities needed to build personal competencies. Only a long-term investment can accomplish a worthy goal.
2. Mastering a challenge yields the feeling of satisfaction, a very reinforcing subjective state that enhances interest in the activity leading to mastery.
3. Personal standards of high caliber are also highly individualized markers, and, like pencil marks on the closet door indicating spurts in height over time, such self-set appraisals permit monitoring of one's progress in mastery.

> Most academic activities present ever-rising challenges. Whatever knowledge and cognitive skills are acquired, there is always more to learn. Past accomplishments are quickly outdistanced, and self-satisfactions are sought in higher accomplishments. Thus, in the pursuit of excellence, the higher the students' efficacy beliefs, the higher the academic challenges they set for themselves and the greater their intrinsic interest in scholastic matters. . . . (Bandura, 1997, p. 220)

Biological Effects of Self-Efficacy in Health and Psychopathology

Bandura (1997, pp. 262 ff.) reviews an extensive and developing literature showing that a person's self-efficacy beliefs and self-appraisals exert significant changes in physiological status for physical and psychological "health." For example, strong and realistic self-efficacy beliefs appear to protect people from the deleterious bodily effects of prolonged stress. People who believe they are in control and can master even ordinarily unpredictable events maintain lower levels of blood pressure, heart rates, and stress hormone levels.

In the psychological arena, catecholamine secretions—neurotransmitters regulating important brain activities—were shown to fundamentally mirror self-efficacy for phobic patients in the face of threat. High self-efficacy—belief that the threat is easily managed—was associated with low levels of catecholamine activity and stress hormones. Low self-efficacy beliefs were associated with elevated levels of catecholamines. When threats were altogether removed, the levels of catecholamines and other stress hormones dropped (Bandura, 1997, p. 265).

The central point emerging from these studies is that belief in personal control shapes a person's characteristic conduct and health status across a wide variety of situations. Bandura also reviews research showing similar positive effects of high self-efficacy belief in the areas of athletic achievement, vocational goal setting, political activism and effectiveness, and several psychopathologies, including eating disorders and substance abuse. Self-efficacy, in Bandura's view, is an important mediator of behavior.

WHAT ABOUT BANDURA'S OWN LIFE?

Bandura's life and theories are, as is the case in many other theorists we have studied, all of a piece. In Bandura's case, it is precisely the limitations in his environment that provided the occasion for him to develop the agentic approach to coping that he so thoroughly formulates and demonstrates in his scientific work. He was born in a small town in northern Alberta. In a personal communication, Bandura commented on his life:

> A limited educational system in my hometown promoted many of us to become self-directed learners. This and other life experiences fostered my interest in self-directedness and the exercise of human agency, i.e. people have a hand in shaping their life course. How does a kid from a small hamlet in Northern Alberta end up with an endowed chair at Stanford University, the presidency of APA, etc? This calls for resilient agency. (Bandura, 2001a)

Bandura further stated,

> The limited resources in the small hamlet I grew up in and parental support for transcending those limitations got me on venturesome paths to the Yukon [where Bandura spent a summer after high school] and other places that provided a rich broad perspective on the human condition. (Bandura, 2001a)

In a later communication, Bandura pointed out the competitive atmosphere and the tough hardiness required in his boyhood,

> Competitive hockey is deeply ingrained in the Canadian human nature. We played it in 20 below zero in open-air rinks without any protective gear, including none for the goalie. As wee youngsters, we used the Eaton catalogues as shin pads. How's that for forging steely character? (Bandura, 2001b)

Bandura's early life history thus was an ideal background for his development of a strong personal sense of individual self-efficacy and personal agency. His own life experiences served as a background from which his theories, emphasizing just such self-efficacy and personal agency, emerged.

DEVELOPMENTAL PHASES OF SELF-EFFICACY

Bandura (1997) incorporated a developmental perspective into his theory of self-efficacy. He portrays the course of a person's life history as a series of interconnected phases, each of which requires specific types of mastery skills. Bandura (1997, p. 163) points out that people take control of their lives only in regard to the available opportunities. Occasionally even seemingly random events profoundly alter the life course. Bandura asserts that it is always the reciprocal interplay of personal qualities, such as the belief that one can control one's life, and the attributes of the social milieu that combine to launch a new life trajectory. Different kinds of interpersonal and personal competencies are required at each stage of living from birth to old age.

Infancy: Linking Action with Outcome

By observing repeatedly that events happen only when some action has been performed, infants learn that actions produce effects (Bandura, 1997). However, they must also learn to "self-observe" to make the crucial link: *my* actions produce effects. At first, effects produced by an infant have the character of pure trial and error. Infants flail about and generate all manner of outcomes, only some of which are intended and even fewer of which have desirable outcomes. Happenings unrelated to their behavior teach infants that they cannot completely control their world. If the infant's efforts appear to have little or no intended effect, the infant grows apathetic and loses interest in trying to exercise personal control. Under these overwhelming circumstances, a darker lesson is learned: There is no benefit in anticipating consequences when most things that happen in your world are unpredictable or unreliable.

Acquiring Social Competence

Competent infants, by contrast, learn that many, but not all, of their actions have intended, anticipated outcomes. Much of their earliest competency learning is linked to the physical environment during the early months because physical effects are immediate and clear. Months later, and continuing throughout childhood, the competent infant learns to produce intended effects on the important people in his or her world. Learning to control the social world and develop **social competence** is more difficult because so many intended effects are delayed or hidden from the weak attentional and discriminatory abilities of the very young child. Parents may skillfully promote mastery learning by reacting to their child's efforts. In this way, even a spontaneous game of peekaboo can be transformed into a pivotal social transaction that teaches the child that he or she can have an impact on the environment.

Recognition and Differentiation of the Self as Active Agent

Infants acquire a sense of personal agency when they realize that they are the *doers of action*. Acquisition of this sense of a personal "me as agent" is acquired through family interactions, the use of personal names, and the verbal labeling of personal possessions as "mine". By about 18 months, the typical infant has sufficient language skills to apply verbal labels to him- or herself, indicating at least a rudimentary awareness of *being* a self (Bandura, 1997, p. 167). By 20 months, children can spontaneously describe themselves as the agents or authors of intended actions, and quickly thereafter, they can describe aloud their thoughts and feelings while performing an action sequence. They are aware of personal agency at least enough to warily deny authorship of some deeds (Bart Simpson's strategic agency: "I didn't do it. No one saw me do it. You can't prove a thing"). To achieve any and all of these accomplishments, we must infer that the infant grasps the concept

---

BOX 16.2   *Only Connect . . .*

Erik Erikson's developmental theory would note the same phenomena and classify them under the areas of developing a basic sense of trust as well as initiative. Bandura's theory, like Erikson's (see Chapter 8), indicates the importance of learning that one has a reliable or trustable environment before being able to take initiative.

of self as active agent with the particular meaning of "self-as-one-who-intends-a-thing-to-happen."

Bandura emphasizes that all competency learning is possible only through the reciprocal interaction of the child and his or her environment, particularly interchanges with others. A family that enhances a child's mastery and learning is likely to be positively affected by having a bright and competent child in the family environment. A family that actively promotes the competence of younger members can usually be a family that communicates genuine enjoyment in the personal triumphs of its members (Bandura, 1997, pp. 169 ff.). As language acquisition proceeds apace, the child can use words to recall encouragement and prohibition, articulate success and failure, and actively and willfully engage the family's attention and admiration. The family's response can be supportive of the child's newfound sense of mastery or the family can discourage, humiliate, or simply ignore such efforts.

Childhood: Comparing One's Competence with Others

The earliest efficacy learning occurs almost exclusively within the family, but as the child matures, influences beyond that immediate circle take on increasing significance.

Sibling Comparisons

First born and only children are often enriched by extra attention from their parents, who initially have extra time and energy to invest in mutually satisfying mastery-enabling experiences. For second and subsequent children in larger families there is often less parental time available for parental enablement, but more time and opportunity for comparisons with siblings closest in age. Initially competition and interaction with age-close siblings are the second and middle child's most important source of self-knowledge about its capabilities compared to others like himself or herself.

Peer Comparisons and Validations

Eventually, however, peer interactions supplant the interactions of siblings as important sources of competition and comparison. The self-evaluative habits acquired in relation to brothers and sisters are extended now to comparisons with children outside the immediate family, and personal efficacy is judged against their less familiar accomplishments (Bandura, 1997, p. 170). However, children do not choose peers randomly. They tend to associate with children like themselves when they can. Thus, friendships are more likely to be formed with children of similar ages who share a child's interests, values, gender, and experiences. Such choices narrow the range of comparative experiences, but are not likely to obstruct the important avenue of learning about one's own competencies relative to others.

Beyond six years, the child's attention to comparisons becomes more focused on abstract social and psychological attributes of action and less on its immediate practical consequences. Thus, the seven- or eight-year-old child learns to compare self with similar children—sometimes preferring children who are just a *little* "better." Similarity of self to models grows increasingly important for the developing child in middle to late childhood and on into adolescence. Children are quick to imitate the admired models, quick to evaluate bluntly and loudly their own and their peers' performances, and sometimes quick to mimic dangerous performances outside the range of their current skills. Verbal instructions and evaluations, especially among a group of interactive peers, often serve as important sources of self-appraisal information.

School Age: Social Validation of Self-Efficacy

By the time the child enters school, an event that seemingly occurs earlier and earlier in our society, emphasis is placed on cognitive problem-solving skills as the chief age-appropriate competency.

Enabling Versus Discouraging Schools

The goal of attending school is to become an effective and productive member of one's culture. A child's acquired knowledge and thinking skills are tested. Institutionally sanctioned evaluations and personal comparisons with one's grademates are inherent to the educational enterprise. Schools and the classroom experiences they provide vary in the degree to which they promote self-efficacy learning or instill self-doubt and the expectation of failure.

Student Reputation

Lockstep educational programs that ignore individual differences in ability and motivation are prone to damage a child's sense of personal control and mastery. Programs that classify students into different ability groupings often communicate negative evaluations to those in the "lower" groupings, no matter how carefully the constituency of the group is disguised. Children assigned to the lowest reading level group may feel inferior to others. Classroom teaching style is also a powerful influence over the child's acquisition of realistic self-efficacy knowledge. Comparison of one child's performance with that of the others enhances only some children's sense of mastery at the inevitable motivational expense of the less successful children. Once a child's reputation among his classmates for good, average, or poor performance is established, it is difficult for the child to alter it, even when the attributes on which the reputation supposedly rests have changed. Other children's judgments, teachers' reactions and expectations, and parental evaluations all interact to solidify a child's reputation as a success or failure academically.

Social Consequences of School Efficacy Learning

The lessons the child learns about intellectual performance, competition, success, and failure are not limited to the intellectual domain as the child progresses through the grades. There are repercussions for social interaction that stem from the child's belief in his or her power to master academic challenges. A sense of poor control or cognitive inadequacy that some children acquire because of their school experience promotes aggressive acting out (Bandura, 1997, p. 176). A child who regards him- or herself as less able than peers is less likely to engage in prosocial activities, can become alienated, and is more likely to engage in antisocial behavior and substance abuse. Lack of confidence in one's cognitive abilities inhibits the child from routine learning about good health habits, grooming, exercise, nutritional eating, and disease prevention.

Adolescence: Risky but Proactive Transition to Adulthood

Adolescents are confronted with what seems to be an overwhelming number of changes. In rapid succession the adolescent experiences biological changes in the physical self at puberty, educational changes associated with the advancement to upper school grades, and the social stress of demands by parents and society for changes to behavior that is more adult-like.

Bandura points out that many of our theories of development overpredict the incidence of psychopathology under conditions of adversity. Adolescence has become a riskier developmental period in recent years because the threats loom larger and more frequently: unprotected sex, drugs, guns, fractured families, poverty, and social displacement (Bandura, 1997, p. 177).

Competence Enablement Versus Vulnerability Protection

Self-efficacy, a sense of personal control and mastery, empowers the adolescent more successfully to navigate the transition from childhood to adulthood. Bandura distinguishes the concept of "enabling competent development" from that of "protection from psychopathology." Viewed as a means to empower the developing person to construct and pursue a productive life plan, self-efficacy is the tool of an active agent rather than the "shield" of a protected victim. Enablement through self-efficacy equips adolescents:

> . . . to select and structure their environments in ways that set a successful course for their lives. This is the difference between proactive recruitment of sources of positive guidance and support and reactive adaptation to life circumstances. An agentic view of resilience also differs from the dualistic diathesis-stress model of psychopathology in which external stressors act upon personal vulnerabilities. Individuals play a proactive role in their adaptation rather than simply undergoing happenings in which environments act upon their personal endowments. The success with which the risks and challenges of adolescence are managed depends, in no small measure, on the strength of personal efficacy built up through prior mastery experiences. (Bandura, 1997, p. 178)

Biological and Social Changes at Puberty

Learning to deal with puberty often involves coping with emotionally invested partnerships. Biological maturation also has an impact on physical prowess and appearance, which in turn elicits the approval or disapproval of others. Self-efficacy is simultaneously linked to these social evaluations and is one major determinant of them.

Even the timing of pubertal changes can have an impact on the adolescent's sense of self-efficacy. In contrast to the enhanced social status usually enjoyed by early maturing boys, late-maturing boys are often the subject of peers' ridicule or deliberate indifference. Precociously developed adolescent girls may have to cope with bodily changes for which they are not ready and which may attract unwanted attention. On the whole, early maturers of both genders are more likely to be initiated prematurely by peer pressure into dating rituals, sexual conduct, drinking activities, and rule-breaking behaviors that have a negative impact on their educational and vocational progress.

Managing Adolescent Sexuality and Other High-Risk Behaviors

Teenagers are initiating sexual activity at younger ages than during previous generations. Exposure to media models and peer pressures that portray sexual conduct in the context of uncommitted relationships without consequences accelerates sexual acting out and enforces sexual ignorance, immaturity, and interpersonal blind spots. Precocious sexual activity is more closely linked with impoverished adolescents who have poor educational attainments than with middle-class, well-educated youth (Bandura, 1997, p. 179).

Bandura argues that sexual risk reduction depends on enhancing interpersonal self-efficacy to equip teenagers with the personal motivational and social skills to put protective sexual information into practice. Providing information alone is not sufficient. The adolescent should learn self-regulatory skills. Internalized standards and values play a bigger role than mere information, especially when those standards are associated with the experience of mastery that can generalize beyond sex to interpersonal relations.

In addition to sexuality, the adolescent has to learn to avoid illegal substances. Temptations range from tobacco and marijuana to alcohol, cocaine, and hallucinogens. Beginning substance abuse can lead to a vicious cycle: a weakened personal sense of control prompts further substance abuse in an effort to feel better by self-medication, and so on. Such drug involvement can often be ended by competent adult and peer guidance in concert with a network of adaptive social relationships from which the adolescent draws strength and confidence.

Adulthood: Vocation, Stable Partnerships, and Children

The demands of early adulthood bring the person face-to-face with the economic and social challenges of building a stable life.

Vocation

For those young people who pursue higher education, a structured life path usually awaits. Such continuing students often receive counseling, advice, and career information, and they may have clear-cut occupational goals that require clearly prescribed, tradition-bound steps.

Young people who do not continue their education often follow a more difficult, less structured path. According to Bandura, in addition to learning specific job-related skills, they most need preparation in self-management skills that promote adaptation to the world of work. The person's beliefs about self-capabilities are also a powerful predictor of vocational success. A high sense of personal efficacy is linked with more successful career choices, hireability, and sustained performance.

Middle Adulthood: Stability Versus Crisis

By midlife, basic economic and interpersonal issues are usually resolved, freeing the individual to pursue new interests, retrench youthful aspirations, and sometimes reluctantly scale back or exuberantly fulfill lifelong dreams.

Declining Opportunities, New Dreams

For some, midlife may represent a period of diminishing vocational opportunities. Careers that involve physical strength or prowess are most vulnerable to decline, but certainly, other occupations are sometimes in jeopardy. The needs to restructure one's life and reconstrue what might have been overambitious goals are not unique to the middle years. Efficacious people are open to new opportunities, advance to new horizons, and can envision new dreams.

Advanced Age: Reappraisals, Regrets, and Reaffirmations

Even though there have been many advances in prolonging healthy life, old age is often a time of declining physical stamina, mental capabilities, and motivation.

Cognitive Changes

Some reduction in overall intellectual functioning ordinarily does not observably affect daily performance. Indeed, the person's *expectations* may play a stronger role in diminishing performance, enthusiasm, and energy than actual biological change (Bandura, 1997, p. 199). Capacities that depend on accumulated knowledge and experience—problem solving, reasoning, forecasting—may actually improve well into advanced age. Some folks call these enhanced cognitive capacities "wisdom."

Maintaining a Sense of Control

Maintaining social connectedness is an essential aspect of adaptive advance into advanced age. A low sense of self-efficacy, as we have seen, is associated with increases in a sense of vulnerability and social withdrawal. Efficacious people are much more likely to socialize, to maintain a personal network of friends and contacts, and to feel better about each day's tasks. The stereotypical view of older adults is that they invariably become increasingly dependent and dysfunctional. Physically and psychologically healthy older adults may conduct quite masterful and satisfying lives.

Realistic Social Comparisons

Aging does not take place in a vacuum. The person advancing in years does so in the context of the larger society and its views of older people, and in the context of family expectations for its older members. Older people can sustain a high level of experiencing oneself as efficacious despite declines in physical or psychological functioning. Because of their accumulated knowledge and life experience, comparisons with younger people are often quite favorable to them. And the more those comparisons yield favorable results, the more likely the person of advanced age will be able to keep up his or her skills, continuing to use them effectively and with satisfaction.

Table 16.1 summarizes the life demands on self-efficacy through the developmental cycle.

Transitional Summary

As conceived by Bandura, self-efficacy is a central feature of personality. Bandura's analysis of the changing demands on self-efficacy with progress through the life course brings a developmental dimension to social cognitive theory. There are no startling insights in this life-course analysis that one could not encounter among other theories of personality. What typifies Bandura's approach is his consistent reliance on an active agent conception of personality functioning and his predilection for testing what are sometimes commonsense predictions with empirical data. Generally accepted psychological truisms and common sense are thus either validated or disproved. We again see in Bandura's work an expansion of cognitive behavioral concepts to a wide variety of situations and circumstances that people face in their lives.

SELECTIVE ACTIVATION OF SELF-CONTROLS

Bandura (1986, pp. 375ff.) has emphasized that self-controls are not automatic and unvarying. Theories such as Freud's that portray conscience, for example, as an "internalized" agency imply that the agency is an ever-present overseer, autonomously deciding when to act to pass judgment. Freud sometimes described the superego as if it were a "censor" ready to pounce at the first hint of a taboo wish or unacceptable impulse. Bandura, by contrast, pictures self-control as a process that the person is free to activate or deactivate. A given action will not be uniformly rewarded or punished because the circumstances may change sufficiently to deactivate or alter self-appraisal.

Table 16.1   Bandura's Developmental Analysis of Self-Efficacy

Life phase	Typical demands	Role of self-efficacy
Infancy	Learning: Actions produce effects. My actions produce effects.	Reliable link between action and outcome builds self-efficacy. Sustained caring by parents "enable" child's self-control. Self-efficacy learning is the core of infant's self.
Early childhood	Learning: Nature of family constellation Siblings' strengths and weaknesses Self-comparisons with siblings	Confidence in self permits attention to relevant models. Self-efficacious children resist risky behavior, view others' superior competence as a goal rather than as crushing competition.
School age	Knowledge and problem-solving skills Peer pressures, peer comparisons, peer competitions	Efficacious children establish "good" reputations that generalize across situations. Self-efficacy permits child to explore new interests in physical, social, and interpersonal areas without inhibition or aggression.
Adolescence	Transitions to adult-like performances in school, dating, friendships, and beginning of vocational identity explorations. Physiological changes of puberty. The temptations of risky sex, aggression, rule-breaking, and substance abuse.	Children who enter adolescence with strong self-efficacy are enabled, rather than protected, to equip themselves for a well-structured path in life. Sexual, vocational, and interpersonal issues are resolved adaptively by children who feel sufficiently in control to remain engaged in prosocial behavior.
Adulthood	Vocational identity crystallizes. Stable partnerships in world of changed families. Having and raising children.	Efficacy as "enabling," i.e., equipping adults to make realistic decisions, sustain intimate relationships, and develop good work habits, rather than as a "protector" from stress.
Advanced age	Physical, psychological, and mental capability decline; reduced vocational opportunities.	Efficacy aids person to see accumulated knowledge and skills as "wisdom" leading to favorable comparisons with others. Masterly older people seek new challenges, build new dreams.

Based on Bandura, 1997, Chapter 5.

Bandura describes this flexibility as the **selective activation of internal control,** and he describes eight cognitive strategies through which a person can disengage self from condemnation during conduct he or she would ordinarily regard as worthy of self-punishment. These eight mechanisms are largely similar to defense mechanisms, but with major differences. The strategies Bandura is describing are largely conscious—unlike most of the psychoanalytic defense mechanisms. In formulating these strategies, Bandura

---

BOX 16.3   *Only Connect . . .*

Bandura's *selective activation mechanisms* are very similar in function to Karen Horney's *secondary defenses,* which we considered in Chapter 10. Bandura's selective activation mechanisms and Horney's secondary defenses allow individuals to function relatively free of anxiety, guilt, and self-condemnation when they engage in behaviors that are damaging to others or to themselves.

---

focuses on the interaction of person and situation, not the control of internal impulses, as in Freud's defense mechanisms. The eight selective activation mechanisms are:

1. **Moral justification:** By providing what appears to be a moral explanation for conduct that would be seen by a person as reprehensible, the person may "restructure" the meaning of his or her behavior sufficiently to justify the conduct. For example, persuading soldiers that "killing the enemy" serves a higher moral purpose—such as preserving freedom—can turn reluctant recruits into skilled combatants. Moral restructuring can certainly be used for self-serving purposes, as for example when terrorists justify their random killing and maiming as serving a higher moral goal.

2. **Euphemistic labeling:** What something is called substantially affects the meaning we place upon it. Convoluted verbiage is a wonderful mask for unethical conduct. For example, when the military describes an invasion of a country with its attendant killing and destruction as an "incursion" rather than as an attack, the conduct is sanitized and euphemized. Bandura (1986, p. 378) offers the example of instructors who teach business students how to lie in competitive situations by calling it "strategic misrepresentation."

3. **Advantageous comparison:** If one chooses a sufficiently poor standard against which to compare one's own conduct, then much of the blame can be avoided. For example, if an automobile salesperson overcharges customers, he or she can justify the deception by saying that the dealer down the street overcharges even more. Bandura provides the example of the promoters of the Vietnam War who excused the killing of thousands of people as a way of stopping their enslavement by Communism. Somehow, the fact that the intended beneficiaries were being killed was obscured by the dramatic comparison with "massive Communist enslavement."

4. **Displacement of responsibility:** If the personal sense of responsibility for an action is removed from one's own shoulders, usual self-regulatory controls can be rendered ineffective. For example, soldiers might fire upon civilians or commit atrocities when so ordered. Displacement of responsibility not only weakens personal restraints, but it also lessens concern for the well-being of others (Bandura, 1986, p. 379).

5. **Diffusion of responsibility:** Similar to the displacement of responsibility, the strategy here is to confuse or "lose" a precise locus of responsibility by resorting to a kind of division of labor. Group decision making can result in inhumane treatment for others, whereas any single member of the group taken alone would not condone such conduct. A person can even go so far as to tell self that it is the other group members who are responsible.

6. **Disregarding or distorting consequences:** One can avoid facing the harm one does to others, so that the action and the outcome are disassociated. In this way,

the person can disregard consequences. For example, bomber pilots rarely see close-up the destruction and murderous effects of their efforts. The chain of command in organizations is another example. The person at the top of a very long hierarchy may be separated from observing the consequences of his or her decisions.

7. **Dehumanization:** One can disengage self-controls against mistreating people if one can find a way not to see them as people. Pejorative and stereotyping labels are one way to dehumanize another. The reverse, of course, is sometimes true. Some captors find it difficult to harm their hostages once they have gotten to know them (Bandura, 1986, p. 383).

8. **Attribution of blame:** If a person can justify mistreatment of another by saying that the person "deserved it" or was "just asking for it," then self-controls can be disengaged. This strategy is sometimes called "blaming the victim." Assaultive be-havior toward women is sometimes "justified" in this way by men who subscribe to stereotyped beliefs and myths about their victims. One can also trivialize the consequences to the victim as another way of disengaging self-condemnation. Some rapists may believe that women secretly enjoy being raped (Bandura, 1986, p. 385).

Bandura points out that none of these disengagement mechanisms by itself can turn a law-abiding or ethical person abruptly into a criminal. Rather, they tend to be cumula-tive and interactive, so that, combined and reinforced over an extended period, there can be a reduction of self-control in some people.

BANDURA'S MODEL OF ANXIETY AND REPRESSION

Bandura endeavored to fit together the signal function of anxiety, the accompanying feel-ings of helplessness, the causal status of anxious thoughts, and the resulting repressive-coping responses into a verifiable explanation.

Bandura's solution captures the clinical insight of Freud's description of the ego's helplessness and the empirical strength of behaviorism's focus on response consequences:

> . . . A painful event has two arousal components to it—discomfort produced by the aversive stimulation and the thought-produced arousal. It is the thought component—the arousal generated by repetitive perturbing ideation—that accounts for much of human distress . . . people who judge themselves inefficacious dwell on their coping deficiencies and view try-ing situations as fraught with peril. They not only magnify the severity of possible threats but worry about perils that rarely, if ever, happen. As a result, they experience a high level of cognitively generated distress. Elevated arousal, in turn, heightens preoccupation with per-sonal inefficacy and potential calamities. (Bandura, 1982, p. 137)

In Bandura's formulation, anxiety arousal and defensive behavior are co-effects rather than being causally related. The cause of defensive behavior, including repression, is not the emotional arousal of anxiety but the cause of the anxiety in the first place: expecta-tion of injury or pain (Bandura, 1977b, p. 61).

Bandura (1969, pp. 426ff.) has reviewed research that shows autonomic nervous sys-tem arousal and defensive behavior are frequently unsynchronized or even disassociated. For example, Dollard and Miller's explanation of anxiety as resulting through "not think-ing" the anxiety-arousing thought is based on the assumption that anxiety is an aversive stimulus with drive properties. Not thinking the thought associated with the anxiety stim-ulus is negatively reinforcing because it reduces the unpleasant drive state of anxiety.

A variety of research shows, however, that even when autonomic nervous system arousal is blocked chemically, defensive behavior can be triggered. In the same vein, when autonomic anxiety arousal is permitted to extinguish, defensive behavior persists (e.g., Black, 1958; see the review of much of this literature by Rescorla & Solomon, 1967).

Anxiety reduction and defensive behavior may occur together, but anxiety is not the sufficient cause of defensive behavior in the cognitive social paradigm. Rather, in Bandura's analysis, aversive events trigger avoidance behavior because they are signals of impending pain or injury; anxiety arousal is triggered simultaneously with this expectation through exposure to the threatening event. Nevertheless, it is the person's expectations of not being able to cope with the impending dangerous event that make both the event and any associated anxiety so distressing. The focus here is on the person's efficacy expectations—his or her thoughts about the meaning of anxiety stimuli and the self-evaluations of available coping skills:

> *Acquired threats activate defensive behavior because of their predictive rather than their aversive qualities.* They signal the likelihood of painful outcomes unless protective measures are taken. Defensive behavior, in turn, is maintained by its success in forestalling or reducing the occurrence of aversive events. Once established, defensive behavior is difficult to eliminate even when the hazard no longer exists. This is because consistent avoidance prevents the organism from learning that the real circumstances have changed. Hence, the failure of anticipated hazards to materialize reinforces the expectation that the defensive maneuvers forestalled them. This process of subjective confirmation is captured in the apocryphal case of a compulsive who, when asked by his therapist why he snapped his fingers ritualistically, replied that it kept ferocious lions away. When informed that obviously there were no lions in the vicinity to ward off, the compulsive replied, "See, it works!"(Bandura, 1977b, p. 62; italics added)

The defense of *repression,* in Bandura's theory, is therefore not an automatic response to anxiety. It is an avoidance response to the aversive thoughts that accompany the anxiety. Thoughts about potential failure or pain, the inability to cope with demands, and expectations that one will not meet challenges successfully can be inhibited by focusing on an incompatible thought or behavior (Bandura, 1969, p. 592).

Thus, in social cognitive theory, repression is conceptualized differently from the psychoanalytic version. Repressed ideas are not seen as having a life of their own in the unconscious; they are not held in check by an internal agency employing psychic energy; and repressed thoughts do not have independent drive properties that regulate and necessitate substitute forms of behavior to keep them perpetually restrained and out of awareness.

Rather, repressed thoughts are treated like any other behavior that lies inert until the appropriate stimulus activates it. If the person can arrange circumstances such that incompatible responses successfully compete with the inhibited ones, then those inhibited responses will not even reach the level of thought. If an anxiety-arousing thought or behavior cannot be inhibited by substitute thoughts and acts, it may emerge sufficiently strong in the person's awareness to create anxiety and conflict (Bandura, 1969, pp. 592–593).

In essence, social cognitive theory draws from the behavioristic, the cognitive, and psychodynamic formulations those elements supported by research and susceptible to laboratory testing. Anxiety is an emotional concomitant of aversive stimulation. However, the stimulation is aversive and defense-provoking because the person thinks about his or her capacities to master it. A low or inaccurate sense of self-efficacy is predictive of a person's response to threatening ideas and stimuli.

The response to repression, as in Dollard and Miller's formulation, is actually "not thinking" (or "not doing") those distressing thoughts, and/or substituting incompatible thoughts (and behaviors). The difference between Bandura's and Dollard and Miller's formulation is that Bandura does not conceptualize anxiety as a negative drive that impels the person to reduce the arousal. Instead, the person is impelled to avoid the feeling of helplessness implicit in his or her low self-efficacy expectations. It is not anxiety reduction itself that is reinforcing; it is the reduction of a sense of helplessness. Conversely, the more one can increase a person's sense of efficacy, the greater the reduction in his or her anxiety and fear (Bandura, 1982).

DOES CHANCE PLAY A ROLE IN LIFE?

In an interesting addition to the problems of synthesizing the many variables that regulate personality, Bandura (1986, p. 32) has devoted some attention to the effects of chance events on shaping a person's life. The idea is reminiscent of the existentialist's notion of destiny as circumstances that affect us but over which we have little control and even less foresight. Chance can provide an occasion for someone to enter a lifepath that he or she would not even have envisioned without the lucky accident. For example, the college student who has to meet a requirement in social science signs up for a sociology course but is placed in a psychology course when enrollments in sociology reach their ceilings. Because of the course, the student decides to become a psychology major. This opens the way toward an eventual choice of career in the counseling area.

Bandura's own life was marked by his response to chance occurrences. He recently wrote one of the authors of the present text, "The bio sketch describes the role of fortuity in my inauguration into psychology and choice of marital partner" (Bandura, 2001b).

> As an undergraduate at the University of British Columbia, I commuted to the university with a group of pre-meds and a group of engineers, who tended to be very early risers. And so, I found myself filling a gap in an early schedule by taking a psychology course that was offered at that particular time. I became fascinated with the subject matter, particularly the clinical aspects. (Bandura, in Evans, 1988)

He met his wife while they both were playing golf. Again, we see that Bandura drew on aspects of his own life experience in developing his theories.

Bandura argues that fortuitous events are not foreseeable, but, once having occurred, personal factors, talents, and personal meanings then enter into the causal chain to shape behavior. Factors such as the prior skills of the person, whether the person likes or dislikes people, personal vulnerability and emotional state all influence the degree to which a chance event can influence a person's life (Bandura, 1986, p. 35). It is to the credit of social cognitive theory that even these unpredictable events, which can have a strong impact on personality, are recognized and considered objects of study.

BANDURA'S THEORIES AND TODAY'S WORLD

The development of mass media has been a major cultural development over the latter half of the twentieth century. One of the most important aspects of Bandura's theories is their ability to help us comprehend the important impact of the media on current behavior. Modeling of behaviors and observational learning can occur quite effectively through television and the movies. In fact, one could persuasively argue that the impact of the media is of the same order of magnitude as the effect of one's family and peers and their direct influences. In fact, one's family and peers are themselves also impacted by the media.

Bandura has stated,

> I really became impressed with the growing power of the symbolic environment in shaping human thought, affect, and action. That we've had a 'communication revolution' in which television, combined with satellite transmission has greatly expanded the speed and scope of human influence, so that most of people's images of reality in which they base most of

their actions are shaped by what they see and hear rather than by their direct experience. (Bandura, as told to Evans, 1988)

Major personality theorists of the past did not account for the burgeoning effects of the media. It is Bandura's social cognitive approach that best enables us to study these contemporary phenomena.

EVALUATING THE APPROACHES OF DOLLARD AND MILLER AND BANDURA

Refutability

Both of these models were based on differing degrees on empirical findings. They each lend themselves to testing, each of them generates testable hypotheses, and each of them has had its share of confirmations and disconfirmations.

The Psychodynamic Social Learning Approach

Dollard and Miller based much of their theory on extensive experimentation. Most of the behaviorism that they incorporated came from the work of Clark Hull, but the tenor of the ideas is not altogether alien to Skinnerian behaviorism. Their work generated an astounding array of studies. It remains a highly fertile model of personality that lends itself well to testing.

Social Cognitive Theory

Bandura's model is so intimately tied to laboratory and field research; it is highly refutable, capable of generating new research ideas in many areas of life, and has been widely tested. Social cognitive theory is capable of being fine-tuned and adjusted as new data are collected. It should also be pointed out that Bandura's conception of vicarious reinforcement and observational learning give due weight to the sophistication of the human organism and the complexity of learning in real-life situations.

Human Agency

Psychodynamic Social Learning Approach

Dollard and Miller share with Freud a deterministic view of human agency. The forces that act in the world of Dollard and Miller are not restricted to the external environment, certainly, but they are deterministic forces nonetheless. Human agency in psychodynamic social learning theory is passive: We are shaped by our drives and by the consequences of our attempts to satisfy them.

Social Cognitive Theory

Bandura's model strongly emphasizes an active conception of human agency. Bandura (1989) put it this way:

> Social cognitive theory rejects the dichotomous conception of self as agent and self as object. Acting on the environment and acting on oneself entail shifting the perspective of the same agent rather than reifying different selves regulating each other or transforming the self from agent to object. In acting as agents over their environments, people draw on their knowledge and cognitive and behavioral skills to produce desired results. In acting as agents

over themselves, people monitor their actions and enlist cognitive guides and self-incentives to produce desired personal changes. They are just as much agents influencing themselves as they are influencing their environment. (Bandura, 1989, p. 1181)

It is clear that Bandura rejects any simple split between object and subject or between passive and active. The person is seen as a whole entity or agent for whom previous learning history, expectations of mastery (efficacy), and current interpretation of the world all interact to regulate behavior. Bandura's conception of reciprocal determinism is a highly sophisticated active-reactive agency viewpoint.

Idiographic Versus Nomothetic

Psychodynamic Social Learning Approach

Dollard and Miller's psychodynamic social learning approach is balanced between an idiographic and a nomothetic emphasis. What it shares with Freudian theory is idiographic, with a focus on the individual's drives, expectations, and avoidance maneuvers. But what it shares with behaviorism is nomothetic, including the conception of anxiety, the "rules" under which anxiety leads to "not thinking" or thinking about other things, and Miller's elaborate conflict theory.

Social Cognitive Theory

Again, we find that the most sophisticated approach lies with Bandura's model. Given its empirical basis, its vast research support, and its attention to the "rules" of self-control, the theory produces nomothetic (generalizable) principles. Yet, as we have seen, Bandura's principles of self-efficacy, self-monitoring or control, and his conception of triadic determinism clearly permit empirical statements about the individual. There is a genuine balance of the nomothetic and the idiographic in Bandura's model. He provides nomothetic or general principles that can be applied in individual cases.

SUMMARY

Dollard and Miller, and other members of the Yale Group, were focused on making Freud's contributions more verifiable. They succeeded in translating key Freudian ideas into stimulus-response-almost-cognitive psychology. Anxiety was treated as a subjective cognitive-emotional cause of defensive behavior. Repression was translated into a functionally equivalent response that avoids painful thoughts as rats learn to avoid cues that signal electric shock.

Bandura's approach is called the *social cognitive theory*. It emphasizes the findings of cognitive psychology and learning theory within the many contexts of daily life.

Beginning in the early 1960s, Albert Bandura and Richard Walters introduced the study of observational learning into psychology. Although Dollard and Miller had considered imitation learning as early as 1941, it was Bandura and his colleagues who drew out the implications of such learning, including:

- The internal cognitive processes of *attention, retention, reproduction,* and then *vicarious or direct reinforcement.* These have to exist for learning from a model's behavior to occur.

- The self-regulatory aspects of many behaviors, which demonstrate the person's capacity to reward and punish self for meeting or failing to meet self-standards.

- The significance of a person's efficacy expectations in regulating the process of learning and the application of self-reinforcement.

Bandura has argued cogently that even the most basic conception of reinforcement must be understood in cognitive terms. A person learns to expect, to anticipate, and to predict the consequences of his or her behavior; reinforcement does not act backward in time to stamp in a response already made. Thus reinforcement is more a matter of information and performance enhancement than it is automatic response strengthening.

Bandura developed a multicausal perspective called *reciprocal triadic determinism,* by which a person's behavior regulates and is regulated in turn by the environment, and the person's awareness of this interaction can also change the nature of the interaction. Psychopathology can be looked at through the lens of reciprocal determinism with a focus on the principles of direct and vicarious learning responsible for the acquisition of inappropriate and maladaptive behavior.

Bandura has added a welcome developmental dimension to his concept of *self-efficacy,* tracking the unique demands on personal mastery operating at the various phases of life from infancy to old age. From infancy through adolescence, successful mastery of living demands learning not only that one can be effective, but also that personal effectiveness often is linked with relationships to other people. By young adulthood, typical life demands include making vocational choices that will enhance one's sense of personal control and effectiveness and preparing for a stable intimate relationship with another to build a family. By the later years, a strong belief in personal efficacy enhances the quality of life so that the expected deterioration in cognitive and motor skills is not inevitable. The later years can also be a time of "wisdom," during which the older person passes along the wealth of experience and positive attitudes accumulated through a lifetime of efficacious living.

Our evaluation of these approaches led to the following conclusions:

- The psychodynamic social learning theory of Dollard and Miller, and the social cognitive theory of Bandura are based on a great deal of empirical research. Both of these theories are refutable, that is, they have led to numerous testable hypotheses.

- Psychodynamic social learning theory sees individuals as mostly reactive. Bandura's social cognitive theory embodies an active agent conception of the person.

- Both Dollard and Miller's ideas and the ideas of Bandura are general concepts that can be applied in individual cases. Thus, they provide some balance between nomothetic and idiographic aspects.

FOR FURTHER READING

Psychodynamic Social Learning Theory

The masterwork that spelled out the first S-R translation of Freudian ideas is to be found in John Dollard and Neal Miller's *Personality and Psychotherapy* (New York: McGraw-Hill, 1950). This book is not only interesting reading, it makes it hard to see why the Miller-Dollard theory of personality and psychopathology became more or less defunct. Paul Wachtel's *Psychoanalysis and Behavior Therapy: Toward an Integration* (New York: Basic Books, 1977) is a contemporary attempt to blend the strengths of both paradigms around an interpersonal model.

Social Cognitive Theory

Albert Bandura's *Social Learning* (Englewood Cliffs, NJ: Prentice-Hall, 1977) is a concise statement of his formulation. His more recent *Social Foundations of Thought and Action: A Social Cognitive Theory* (Englewood Cliffs, NJ: Prentice-Hall, 1986) presents the empirical findings and theoretical framework for his concepts.

As part of his series of interviews with prominent psychologists, Richard Evans has contributed *Albert Bandura, the Man and His Ideas—A Dialogue* (New York: Praeger Press, 1989). An excellent biographical web site on Bandura can be found at http://www.emory.edu/EDUCATION/mfp/bandurabio.html

Bandura's latest restatement of a major portion of his theory refocused on self-efficacy as a near-universal mediating variable can be found in *Self-Efficacy: The Exercise of Control* (New York: Freeman, 1997). In this text, Bandura presents critical arguments against many other theoretical approaches. In *Self-Efficacy in Changing Societies* (New York: Cambridge University Press, 1995), Bandura edited a companion volume of readings on self-efficacy that present a wide range of ideas and research. Chapter 3 of this book (pp. 69–113), "Developmental Analysis of Control Beliefs," by A. Flammer is particularly worthwhile reading for those interested in the parallels between object-relations theory and social cognition. Michael H. Kernis's (Ed.) *Efficacy, Agency, and Self-Esteem* (New York: Plenum, 1995) presents a broad spectrum of theoretical and research papers that extend the idea of personal competence into areas traditionally considered "self-esteem" variables.

A deep understanding of contemporary empirical work in social cognition and personality can be achieved by reading nearly any chapter in Susan T. Fiske and Shelly E. Taylor's second edition of *Social Cognition* (New York: McGraw-Hill, 1991).

GLOSSARY

John Dollard and Neal E. Miller

Anxiety: In Miller's view, anxiety is viewed as a learned signal that, in itself, has become aversive to the organism. Behavior is reinforced by the reduction of such anxiety.

Fear as an acquired drive: Once fear is classically conditioned to an aversive object or situation, the learned fear serves as an acquired drive that motivates escape learning; reduction of anxiety reinforces the escape behavior.

Frustration-aggression hypothesis: Freud believed that frustration leads to aggression. This view posits that the disruption or blocking of a goal-oriented behavior causes frustration, which in turn causes a desire to aggress the person or object that acts as a barrier to the desired goal.

Galvanic skin response (GSR): The GSR measures the skin's decrease in resistance to electrical current during sensory and emotional changes.

Psychodynamic social learning theory: Miller and Dollard's integrative theory that combined modeling with the principles of conditioning.

Albert Bandura

Advantageous comparison: Choosing a sufficiently poor standard against which to compare one's own conduct, then much of the blame can be avoided.

Agentic: A term indicating a proactive rather than a reactive approach to life. Such an approach involves active problem solving, planning, action, and, at times, innovation.

Attribution of blame: Justifying mistreatment of another by saying that the person "deserved it" or was "just asking for it;" this strategy is sometimes called "blaming the victim."

Dehumanization: Disengaging self-controls against mistreating people by finding ways not to see them as people; pejorative and stereotyping labels are one way to dehumanize another.

Diffusion of responsibility: The strategy of confusing or "losing" a precise locus of responsibility by resorting to the notion that no one in particular is accountable.

Displacement of responsibility: Hiding or distorting the relationship between a given action and its effects in order to disengage the usual self-regulatory controls; it weakens personal restraints, and lessens concern for the well-being of others.

Disregarding or distorting consequences: The strategy of dissociating the action and the outcome.

Efficacy expectations: A person's belief that given outcomes can be personally accomplished because one possesses the requisite skills.

Enactive attainments/performance accomplishments: The outcomes of a person's own efforts. A person's own efforts either succeed or fail, and the outcome can become an instructive guide to planning.

Euphemistic labeling: The idea that what something is called or labeled substantially affects the meaning we place upon it; convoluted verbiage is a wonderful mask for unethical conduct.

Judgments of excellence: Self-regulatory processes include judgments of the creativity, excellence, and goodness of one's own behavior.

Modeling: An efficient way of affecting behavior through demonstration; the steps in which a person learns through modeling are *attention, retention, symbolic reproduction* or *representation,* and finally receiving either *vicarious reinforcement* or *direct reinforcement.*

Moral justification: Providing what appears to be a moral explanation for conduct that would be seen by a person as reprehensible; a person may restructure the meaning of his or her behavior sufficiently to justify the conduct.

Observational learning: Learning by watching and imitating others engaging in behaviors. In Bandura's model, observational learning is mediated through perceptual and cognitive processes.

Outcome expectations: A person's estimate that particular outcomes will occur. They are usually based on the success or failure of similar efforts. Success is most likely to occur if the right situational and personal processes are brought to bear.

Selective activation of internal control: The processes by which a person is free to activate or deactivate self-control. They are: *moral justification, euphemistic labeling, advantageous comparison, displacement of responsibility, diffusion of responsibility, disregard or distortion of consequences, dehumanization,* and *attribution of blame.*

Self-efficacy: A person's expectancy that he or she will perform successfully in a given task or behavior, and meet the challenge competently.

Self-observation of behavioral quality: The awareness of qualities such as originality, authenticity, and ethicalness are applied as evaluative standards by the person to his or her own behavior to create incentives to act in a particular way.

Self-reaction processes: Rewards or punishments that an individual provides to his or her own behavior with feelings of competence or with feelings of self-devaluation.

Self-regulatory processes in the self-system: Processes in the self-system with the underlying themes of competence, mastery, and self-efficacy. These processes are *self-observation of behavioral quality, judgments of excellence,* and *self-reactions.*

Self-system: A complex of processes interdependent with the person's social and physical environment; the self-system is not a "little person" inside the person.

Social cognitive theory: Bandura's theory, in which cognitive processes and self-reflection are viewed as central to human behavior; people are seen as planning and predicting the consequences of their behaviors with an interpersonal context.

Social competence: The ability to have desired impacts interpersonally.

Triadic reciprocal determinism: An interactive triad that determines behavior; elements that interact are: (P) the person's awareness and thinking, (B) the person's ongoing behavior, and (E) the person's environment.

Vicarious reinforcement: A change in attitude and behavior that may ensue after a person watches another person being reinforced for engaging in a behavior; vicarious reinforcement is not actually direct reinforcement.

Chapter 17

Hans Eysenck

Biologically Based Typology

Most people of course, whatever they may say, do not in fact want a scientific account of human nature and personality at all. . . . Hence they much prefer the great story-teller, S. Freud, or the brilliant myth-creator, C. G. Jung, to those who . . . study physiological details of the nervous system, and actually carry out experiments rather than rely on interesting anecdotes, sex-ridden case histories, and ingenious speculation.

Hans Eysenck, *Psychology Is About People*

. . . our belief is finally irrelevant. What matters—all that matters—is fact.

Hans Eysenck & D. K. B. Nias,
Astrology: Science or Superstition

Hans Eysenck   Born: 1916   Berlin, Germany
Died: 1997   London, England

About Eysenck's Biologically Based Typology

Hans Eysenck constructed a multileveled model of behavior that ranges from genetics to social psychology. Eysenck's work is broad and complete. His ideas include these major points:

1. *Central nervous system activity is the source of personality functioning.*

2. *Research in learning, conditioning, perception, and drug effects shows that people can be reliably distinguished into introverts and extroverts. Introverts are considered stimulus shy, because they are acutely sensitive to incoming stimulation as if their brain arousal levels were chronically high. Extroverts are stimulus hungry because they seek and easily process intense stimulation as if their brain arousal levels were chronically low or inhibited.*

3. *Introverts—with their high arousal levels—are prone to anxiety disorders. Extroverts—with their low arousal levels—are more likely to have dramatic, acting-out disorders such as hysterical disorder and antisocial personality disorder.*

RESEARCH PSYCHOLOGIST AS SCIENTIST
AND A BIT OF A MAVERICK

When Hans Eysenck, a graduate of the University of London, obtained his first job during World War II as a research psychologist in the Mill Hill Emergency Hospital, he must have been professionally threatening to his immediate superiors. The hospital received mentally disturbed war casualties. Eysenck was not sure of the degree of reliability of the psychiatric diagnoses by which incoming airmen and soldiers were classified. If two or more physicians examined the same patient, would their diagnoses agree? Furthermore, if they did agree, would the prescribed treatments correspond? All a research psychologist had to do to find out was to collect information from a sample of cases and perform the necessary statistical calculations. Eysenck's account of what happened when he requested permission to carry out this piece of research reveals many of Eysenck's personality traits that came to typify his approach to professional issues:

> [The Superintendent] received me in a fatherly fashion, and listened patiently to my plan. Then, to my surprise, he suggested that as there were so many more interesting things that I could be doing, it would be a pity to waste my time in this fashion. After all, did not everyone know that these psychiatrists had been well trained, had medical degrees, and could therefore (almost by definition) do no wrong? When I cheerfully suggested that even such supermen might welcome definitive proof of the reliability of their judgments he became more serious. . . . [H]e told me in no uncertain terms that I was at liberty to collect these data, but I was also at liberty to look for another job. This argument seemed a winner, and I acknowledged its superior force by withdrawing from the unequal contest. I did, to be sure, collect my data but kept rather quiet about it. (1972, pp. 357–358)

Eysenck's subsequent research did show that diagnostic conclusions had very little similarity from one psychiatrist to another—even when the second diagnostician already knew of the first diagnosis. Eysenck's suspicions about the lack of reliability of the diagnostic process were confirmed.

CHILDHOOD SOURCES OF EYSENCK'S INTELLECTUAL INDEPENDENCE

In his autobiography, appropriately entitled *Rebel with a Cause,* Eysenck (1990) indicated that he was an angry, assertive person who collided early and frequently with established authority and with unexamined attitudes and beliefs, no matter how popular. He portrayed himself as a tough-minded intellectual with a tender heart. The finished autobiography also reveals that Eysenck had been a lonely child, largely ignored by his divorced parents (Eysenck, 1990).

Childhood: Neglectful Parents, Caring Grandmother

Eysenck was born during the First World War in Berlin and grew up during Germany's period of defeat and ensuing economic crisis. His mother, Ruth Werner, had been born in the late 1800s in a small town in what is now Poland. Eysenck reports that his mother's ambition was not to become a physician like her father but rather to study law. Women, however, were largely excluded from a legal career at the turn of the century, so Ruth followed her mother's advice to pursue silent film acting. By age 15, she was already regarded as quite a beauty, and her success in an acting career seemed assured. She assumed the stage name of "Helga Molander" for screen roles in the silent films of the era.

The actress, Helga Molander, met actor Anton Eduard Eysenck during her first professional engagement. She was to be a rising starlet, and he was a star of stage and operettas (Eysenck, 1990, p. 153). They fell in love, married, and Hans was born shortly thereafter. They chose "Hans Jurgen" for their son's name because, in German, it "had the connotation of a simple, honest, none-too-bright youngster, reliable and trustworthy" (Eysenck, 1990, p. 10).

> . . . that was roughly how I saw myself—a large good-natured dog, always ready to be friendly, but possibly dangerous when kicked in the teeth. I was to receive many such kicks in the course of my life—but then I suppose most people do. Rebels are particularly exposed to such extremities, of course, and a rebel I was to become, more through force of circumstances than predilection. (Eysenck, 1990, p. 10)

Although neither parent was especially religious, Eysenck's father, Anton Eysenck, had been raised in a Catholic family, whereas his mother's family was Protestant. Anton's unfaithfulness led to a quick divorce (Eysenck, 1990, p. 11). By the time Hans Jurgen was two, his parents' marriage was over (Eysenck, 1990, p. 153).

Relationship with Parents

Eysenck describes Anton Eysenck as an authoritarian man with racist views. During World War II, Anton Eysenck joined the Nazi party, a fact that Hans recalls with bitter distaste. A successful actor for many years, Anton eventually switched professions from stage and film actor to stage entertainer, stand-up comic, political commentator, and master of ceremonies who traveled from one hotel, nightclub, or convention to another. He became very successful, and as one of the few such non-Jewish entertainers in Germany, members of the Nazi regime accepted and admired him. "My own hatred of the Nazis had led me by this time to leave Germany, and my father's hobnobbing with these people did nothing to increase my love for him" (Eysenck, 1990, p. 12).

In Eysenck's account of his childhood, he recalls both parents as neglectful and unconcerned with parenting. Neither parent had an interest in children and neither communicated warmly or effectively with Hans.

> Typical perhaps of my father's method of upbringing is the occasion when he bought me a bicycle, and promised to teach me how to ride it. He took me to the top of a hill, told me that I had to sit on the saddle and pump the pedals and make the wheels go round. He then went off to release some balloons and shoot them down with the rifle he still had from the war, leaving me to learn how to ride all by myself. . . . A good training in independence, but perhaps not the behaviour of a loving father. (Eysenck, 1990, p. 12)

Of his mother, Eysenck recalls:

> I don't think nature intended her to be a mother. I saw very little of her, except occasionally on holidays, and she never managed to treat me as a child, or show much interest in what I was doing. Conversation with her was always on strictly adult lines. (1990, p. 7)

Both parents found new spouses during Hans's childhood. His mother married an important figure in the movie industry, and his father married a considerably younger woman, who was also a stage entertainer.

Eysenck's Maternal Grandmother

Eysenck's warm, accepting, loving, and actively religious maternal grandmother largely raised him. He attributes to her his rescue from what might otherwise have been a lonely and unhappy childhood (1990, p. 14). During childhood, neither parent provided Hans's grandmother with money to support him. His maternal grandmother's poverty took its toll on Hans as well as on her. She eventually died in a Nazi concentration camp.

In addition, Eysenck remembered that his parents were mean and stingy:

> If my parents were mean toward my grandmother, I felt they were equally mean toward me. I received very little pocket-money, and they seldom agreed to pay for what I considered reasonable expenses. (1990, p. 15)

He recalls how this stinginess prevented him from participating in tennis and swimming at a racquet club, where he could not pay the fees to use the facilities. In resilient and rebellious fashion, Hans found the silver lining in this cloud:

> However, all this meanness had one positive side-effect; I knew that all the girls I was friendly with loved me for myself! It couldn't have been the non-existing money that might have attracted them. . . . (1990, p. 15)

BOX 17.1   *Only Connect . . .*

Karen Horney's concepts (Chapter 10) shed light on Hans Eysenck's personality development. Eysenck was raised in a neglectful family environment with an authoritarian father. Faced with basic anxieties that come from such an upbringing, in Horney's terms, he developed the neurotic trend of consistently *moving against* others. As a youth, he repudiated his pro-Nazi father by leaving Germany to try to enroll in the Royal British Air Force. His academic career was marked by his often brilliant, persistent, iconoclastic opposition to conventional wisdom, whether it was in the form of Freudian orthodoxy or in the popular position that cigarette smoking is damaging to health. Perhaps, if Eysenck had been brought up in a more loving family, he would not have become a highly original thinker.

Eysenck characterized himself as unsatisfied with his recollection of family life, feeling unwanted and angry. In his seventies, he wrote, "I wish I had had brothers and sisters, and perhaps even a pair of loving parents; if I had, perhaps I would have been a nicer person!" (Eysenck, 1990, p. 278).

School Memories: Biting Hard and Holding on "Like a Bull Terrier"

When Eysenck was approximately eight years old, he encountered Herr Meier, the new music teacher in school. At the first class meeting, Herr Meier directed each student to sing aloud, whereupon the young Hans Jurgen informed his teacher that he could not sing a note, had no singing voice at all, and there was simply no point to it. Herr Meier insisted. Hans resisted. Meier shouted. Hans persisted in resistance. Meier responded aggressively:

> He ordered me to go up to the dais where he was sitting, grabbed my right hand with his left, and threatened to hit me with the ruler he had in his right hand. When he brought it down I drew back my hand, and he hit the table, which seemed to infuriate him even more. He again grabbed my hand, holding it very tight, and lifted the ruler, to hit my hand really hard.
>
> Without thinking I leaned forward and sank my teeth in the fleshy part of his hand, underneath his thumb. I have always been tall and strong, and I bit him very hard indeed. He dropped the ruler, blanched (I have never seen anybody's face go so white so quickly) and tried to withdraw his hand. I hung on like a bull terrier, and the class of course started erupting in a welter of shouts, screams and jumpings up and down. (Eysenck, 1990, p. 16)

Ultimately, it took the headmaster and several teachers to separate mouth from hand, or hand from mouth, depending on your viewpoint. In any event, as Eysenck recalls with relish, Herr Meier was gone from school for the next two weeks, and when he reappeared, he did not return to Hans's music class. Eysenck aptly points out the long-term, character-reflecting significance of the event:

> In many ways what I did then was prognostic of what I was to do later on, though in rather less physical fashion. You cannot let people get away with wrongdoing just because they are strong and powerful; whatever the cost, you have to stand up for yourself. (1990, p. 17)

In the episode with which we began this chapter, we noted another example of Eysenck's rebellious streak: Hans J. Eysenck, as a young experimental psychologist, doubted the psychiatric establishment at the Mill Hill Emergency Hospital, and conducted clandestine authority-defying studies of diagnostic reliability.

Eysenck's Rebellious, Iconoclastic Streak

Eysenck's autonomous mind and rebellious streak can be traced to his life history and his behavior before becoming a psychologist. As a boy and teenager, he was critical and skeptical about the tenets of Nazism. He was not swayed by the many methods the Nazis used to attract adherents. In spite of the fact that Nazi doctrines were widely held, Eysenck subjected one of them to a simple empirical test.

> On hearing that German Jews were supposed to have been cowardly during the First World War, the adolescent Eysenck promptly made his way to the public library, where he ascertained that Iron Crosses had in fact been awarded with greater relative frequency to Jewish than to non-Jewish soldiers. . . . [Later] Eysenck stood unmoved through a Hitler rally— only marveling at other's excitement and realizing that war with Britain and France must be inevitable. (Brand, 1997)

Eysenck's intellectual autonomy, rebellious streak, and personal courage were also evident when, as an 18-year-old son of a Nazi father in Hitler's Germany, he emigrated to Britain and then (unsuccessfully) attempted to join the English Royal Air Force (Brand, 1997; Eysenck, 1990).

Eysenck has frequently criticized what he considers to be nonempirical, less factual, and less scientific approaches to the study of personality. One of the chief targets of his criticism and, at times, scorn, has been Freudian psychoanalysis. He regarded psychoanalytic theory as, at worst, fictional, and at best, untestable (Eysenck, 1953a, 1957b, 1960, 1963b, 1965; Eysenck & Wilson, 1973; cf. Rachman, 1963, and Eysenck & Rachman, 1965).

Eysenck's intellectual battles often involved attacking whatever he perceived as unthinking fads or popular fallacies. Among his favorite targets, in addition to Freudian psychoanalysis, have been established psychiatry and clinical psychology, medical hierarchies, and traditional views of psychotherapy. He became a proponent of the importance of genetic and hereditary influences in personality throughout the 1960s, 1970s, and 1980s, when an emphasis on the primary importance of environmental factors prevailed in academic circles. He also criticized those who questioned the value or fairness of intelligence tests (1979). Among other targets were the prison system, the monarchy, the intellectual left, and radical feminism (Brand, 1997; Eysenck 1990). Eysenck took a fact-based, but nondebunking, attitude toward the ever-popular field of astrology (Eysenck & Nias, 1982), and encouraged an objective, empirically based approach to paranormal experiences, designed to please neither true believers nor doubters (Eysenck & Sargent, 1982).

He took the position that cigarette smoking was not proven to be a cause of lung cancer but only a correlate. He showed that both smoking and lung cancer were correlated with certain personality types, and speculated that personality type could well represent a genetic or hereditary cause of the development of such cancer (Eysenck, 1980a). He was correct in his assertion that statistical analyses of the epidemiological data regarding smoking did not (and could not) strictly prove any cause. He stuck to this position, however, in spite of increasing evidence, including physiological findings, to the contrary over the years.

EARLY DESCRIPTIVE RESEARCHES: INTROVERSION-EXTROVERSION AND NEUROTICISM

One of Eysenck's major areas of research, the description of personality types, began with his efforts empirically to assess prior typological models of personality.

Carl Jung had proposed a *typological model* of personality that included the concepts of introversion and extroversion. It will be helpful to refresh our memory of Jung's descriptions of these personality types (see also relevant sections of Chapter 4):

> The first [introvert] attitude is normally characterized by a hesitant, reflective, retiring nature that keeps to itself, shrinks from objects, is always slightly on the defensive and prefers to hide behind mistrustful scrutiny. The second [extrovert] is normally characterized by an outgoing, candid, and accommodating nature that adapts easily to a given situation, quickly forms attachments, and, setting aside any possible misgivings, will often venture forth with careless confidence into unknown situations. In the first case obviously the subject [i.e., the person himself], and in the second the object [i.e., external reality] is all-important. (1917, pp. 44–45)

It was thus Jung's opinion that extroverts focus on and are very responsive to external events and objects, and that they are very highly influenced by prevailing social opinion. **Introverts,** much to the contrary, give greatest weight to their own subjective reactions to external events; they devalue and deemphasize the significance of the objective world by focusing on their own emotions and personal reactions (Jung, 1921, p. 500). Consequently, those introverts who become neurotic are most likely to experience anxiety.

Extroverts, easily influenced by outside occurrences, are most likely to succumb to hysterical neuroses. In order to divest themselves of emotional pain they tend to repress unacceptable thoughts and to externalize or convert threatening impulses into objectified bodily symptoms. *Hysteric extroverts* often profit from the sympathy of others. The sympathy and concern of others is a positive reinforcer for the hysteric's impulsivity and demands for attention.

Partly Validating Jung's Typology

In an initial test of Jung's introversion/extraversion model (see Chapter 4), Eysenck and his colleagues selected a sample of 700 neurotically maladjusted patients at the Mill Hill Emergency Hospital for whom comprehensive case histories and clinical observational data were available. The psychiatrist in charge of each case prepared an item sheet on which the patient's familial and personal history, symptoms, diagnosis, treatment, and various social data were recorded. Eysenck selected 39 items from each of 700 such data sheets and factor-analyzed the results.

Factor analysis is a statistical method that looks at how individuals' scores on one measure correlate with their scores on other measures. Variables highly correlated with one another are highly related to a single factor. Factor analysis is therefore a method that reduces a large apparent number of original variables to fewer essential underlying variables or factors. In Eysenck's study, many correlations resulting from the data analysis yielded only two factors, each consisting of a number of traits.

Eysenck described one factor associated with a group of traits as "general **neuroticism.**" Specifically, the items in the psychiatrists' ratings that tended to be correlated on this factor included: badly organized personality, dependency, psychopathology before illness, narrow interests, dismissal from military service, parental psychopathology, unsatisfactory home, and poor muscular tone (Eysenck, 1947, p. 36).

Eysenck divided those scoring high in the general neuroticism factor into two groups. One group was neurotically maladjusted by virtue of possessing symptoms associated with high ratings on anxiety: obsessive tendencies, headache, tremor, and irritability, among others. The second group of individuals tended to have somewhat different symptoms characteristic of **hysterical disorder:** bodily symptoms with no organic basis, little energy, narrow interests, hypochondriasis, poor work history, and sexual difficulties.

In summary, Eysenck's analysis of the item sheet data thus demonstrated that a general factor or dimension of neuroticism versus normality could categorize psychologically disabled patients. Eysenck further subdivided the high neuroticism group into anxiety neurotics and hysterical neurotics.

Evidence for an Introversion-Extroversion Dimension

Starting from the premise that Jung's hypothesis of the two types of introversion and extraversion was correct, Eysenck surveyed the available experimental literature. He generally found support from a wide variety of sources that introversion was associated with anxiety, obsessive-compulsive symptoms, and reactive-depression neuroses. The extroverted personality type was associated with symptoms characteristic of hysterical neuroses (Eysenck, 1947, chapters 2 and 7).

Eysenck found direct evidence in a sample of neurotic soldiers that a dimension of extroversion-introversion could distinguish between the two groups of neurotic illnesses. Eysenck (1947, p. 37n). coined a new term, **dysthymia,** for the first group of neurotic symptoms (anxiety, phobia, depression, and obsessive-compulsive disorders). Dysthymia corresponded to Jung's concept of **psychasthenia** and to his introvert personality type label. Eysenck retained Jung's label, *hysteric,* for the second group, and he found that hysterics tended to be extroverted in accordance with Jung's hypothesis. Eysenck concluded:

> . . . (neurotic) introverts show a tendency to develop anxiety and depression symptoms . . . they are characterized by obsessional tendencies, irritability, apathy . . . their feelings are easily hurt, they are self-conscious, nervous, given to feelings of inferiority, moody, daydream easily, keep in the background on social occasions, and suffer from sleeplessness. . . . Withal, they are rather rigid, and show little interpersonal variability. (1947, pp. 246–247)

The 30 traits that cluster together into the pattern of the neurotic introvert, as stated here by Eysenck, are characteristic of his early descriptive research. More investigation into the causes underlying the clustering of traits for the neurotic introvert would eventually follow. At this stage of the research, however, Eysenck was limited to specification of descriptive traits. Thus, in contrast to the neurotic introvert, he found

> . . . (neurotic) *extraverts*[1] show a tendency to develop hysterical conversion symptoms, and a hysterical attitude to their symptoms. Furthermore, they show little energy, narrow interests, have a bad work-history, and are hypochondriacal. According to their own statement, they are troubled by stammer or stutter, are accident prone, frequently off work through illness, disgruntled, and troubled by aches and pains. . . . They are not very rigid, and show great interpersonal variability. Their aesthetic preferences are towards the colourful, modern type of picture. They appreciate jokes, and are particularly fond of sex jokes. (Eysenck, 1947, p. 247)

Neurotic introverts and extroverts share some traits, but overall their patterns of responses to Eysenck's various tests and measurements are distinguishable. The pattern of measurements for neurotic introverts and neurotic extroverts resembles the hypothesized classes of dysthymic (anxiety) neuroticism and hysterical disorder.

HISTORICAL ANTECEDENTS
OF INTROVERSION-EXTROVERSION DIMENSIONS

Eysenck went to great lengths to point out that Jung did not originate the concepts of introversion-extroversion, rather, these ideas had a 2,000-year history in philosophy, medicine, and psychology (1947, 1953a, 1967, 1970).

Two ancient Greek physicians, Hippocrates (about 460 to 377 B.C.) and Claudius Galen (about A.D. 130 to 200), devised a **temperament theory** of personality and human conduct. Galen systematized the previous notions of character types into a coherent typology. Galen related personality to four body fluids or humors: blood, black bile, yellow bile, and phlegm. He theorized that an excess of one of the four **humors** (bodily fluids) determined emotional temperament. A **sanguine temperament** (warmhearted, volatile, optimistic, easygoing) is seen to be caused by an excess of blood; a predominance of black bile results in a **melancholic temperament** (sad, depressed, anxious); yellow bile produces the **choleric temperament** (quick to action, angry, assertive); and, finally, when phlegm predominates, the resulting temperament is **phlegmatic** (slow to action, lethargic, calm) (cf. Allport, 1937; Eysenck, 1964a, 1967, 1972; R. I. Watson, 1963, p. 80).

---

[1]Eysenck uses *extravert* rather than the more conventional spelling *extrovert*.

The German philosopher, Immanuel Kant (1724–1804), amplified the classical temperament theory by proposing separate trait descriptions for each of the four temperaments. For example, Kant described the sanguine personality as one who is carefree and full of hope, good natured and sociable, but capricious and given to pranks (Eysenck & S. B. G. Eysenck, 1969, p. 12.). Kant's labels indicated how various traits were associated together in a given type of temperament. Kant's was a categorical system with four categories. He did not consider the possible overlapping of types or different degrees of temperamental expression (Figure 17.1).

Most people, however, do not fall clearly into only one compartment. Personalities generally possess some unique combination of qualities from a broader spectrum of traits than merely four. Various nineteenth-century philosophers and psychologists thus sought to revamp temperament theory. They devised a series of scales that would represent each type as a continuum. This is the dimensional approach to personality classification (Figure 17.1).

Eysenck's own work on the introversion-extroversion and neuroticism-normality dimensions produced a comparable picture of human character types. Eysenck's two dimensions agreed quite closely with the dimensions introduced into classical temperament theory by the experimental psychologist, Wilhelm Wundt. However, Wundt based his views only on descriptions and did not validate them by any research. The explanation of different types of bodily fluids or humors causing the psychological types had no empirical basis. The tasks confronting Eysenck were to subject the concept of psychological types to empirical tests and then, if the theory was validated, to explain the results. To answer the question of why a particular personality's traits cluster together, or why an introvert differs from an extrovert would require looking beneath the readily observable aspects of personality for the sources of behavior.

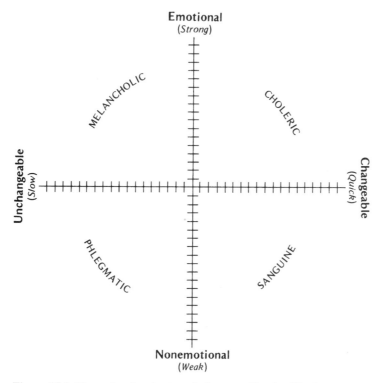

Figure 17.1 Dimensional and categorical personality classifications.
Adapted from Eysenck, 1953a, p. 17; 1967, p. 35.

Ideas that came from Pavlov's research with dogs provided the key to the explanation of personality types. In them, Eysenck discovered a possible physiological explanation for the classical temperaments. Moreover, it was not a confirmation of Galen's theory of four separate bodily fluids or humors, even though Pavlov came up with a similar typology, in which the magic number was four.

PAVLOV'S DOGS: EXCITATION-INHIBITION TEMPERAMENTS

At the start of the twentieth century, the Russian physiologist Ivan Petrovitch Pavlov (1849–1936) measured the secretion of digestive hormones in dogs in different conditions. Pavlov had the dog's salivary ducts surgically diverted so he could collect and measure the amount of saliva secreted. In addition, the upper portion of the digestive track was severed from the stomach and then rerouted to an external opening, or fistula. Food taken into the mouth, chewed and swallowed, never reached the stomachs of these dogs. Instead, it fell into a collection dish under the external opening. Pavlov could then weigh the quantity of food that the dog had temporarily ingested. He discovered that, under such conditions, gastric secretions were still produced at a rate nearly half that of normal. Pavlov concluded that some unknown brain processes were responsible for triggering digestive activity, even in the absence of food in the stomach (Pavlov, 1927, 1928).

In order to investigate this phenomenon, Pavlov devised a standard experimental setup. Dogs were isolated from distracting visual and auditory stimuli by putting them into a sound-deadened chamber. The experimenter was able to present stimuli: a ticking metronome, flashing lights of controlled intensities, and bell or buzzer sounds. The experimenter could offer meat to the dog at any time.

The first experiments consisted of a number of steps. First, the experimenter presented an unfamiliar, or what was termed a "neutral," stimulus such as the sound of a buzzer (metronome or bell) to the dog. The dog's level of salivation was measured. In this initial condition, it was very low or nonexistent and did not increase with the presentation of the unlearned or unconditioned stimulus (the meat powder.) In the next step, meat was given to the dog immediately after the neutral stimulus (the bell) was presented. The two stimuli (let's say, the sound and meat) were thus associated. The presentation of a sound came to signal the subsequent occurrence of the dog being "fed." You may recall that the food did not actually enter the dog's stomach, rather it dropped through a fistula into an outside container. During these times, the dog produced an increased level of saliva. After a suitable number of pairings of the sound and meat feedings, the experimenter began presenting the sound without providing any meat. Dogs again salivated, even though no food was given (Pavlov, 1927, Lectures II, III).

A daily life example of this type of conditioning would be a dog starting to salivate when its owner begins opening a dog food can or package. The sight of the owner taking a can or package out and beginning to open it has been paired many times with the dog's subsequent ingestion of food. People, too, will salivate when they see a can or package containing a tasty or even a not-so-tasty dish being opened.

Excitation and Inhibition Processes in the Cortex

To explain these findings, Pavlov theorized that the cortex of the brain is composed of two types of cells or neurons: those engaged in **exciting processes** and those involved in **inhibitory processes.**

When the dog's sensory receptors detect incoming stimuli, the excitation of the nerves travels to the brain, where *excitatory* cortical cells begin firing in response. This cortical process would be evoked each time the same stimulus pattern is repeated, allowing the dog to show the benefit of its experience by being able to anticipate one stimulus from the presence of the other. In short, Pavlov theorized that excitatory cell firings are the basis of positive conditioned reflexes.

Pavlov also theorized the existence of *inhibitory* cortical cells. Inhibitory centers of the cortex would function to dampen or retard the activity of the excitatory cells. In some cases, inhibitory cells would even compete with excitatory processes.

Pavlov termed one kind of inhibition *external inhibition* (1927, p. 48). Being distracted or having attention diverted would be an example of such external inhibition. A dog conditioned to salivate at the sound of a buzzer ceases to salivate if a novel stimulus like a loud bang or an unfamiliar person is suddenly introduced. Pavlov theorized the unfamiliar distracting stimulus inhibited the conditioned reflex of salivation.

Pavlov also postulated a second type of inhibition—*internal inhibition.* This cortical process involves a slow or gradual development of a tendency to withhold the response (Pavlov, 1927, Lecture IV). For example, the continual presentation of the conditioned stimulus (the bell) without the unconditioned stimulus (the meat powder) ever again being presented leads to a gradual termination of the conditioned response (salivation). In more concrete terms, the experimenter continues to press the buzzer without ever following it with meat. The dog eventually ceases to salivate at the buzzer sound. The former conditioned response is now inhibited. This process is often considered as an instance of *extinction* of a conditioned reflex. Pavlov, however, explained it in a different way as stemming from learning a new inhibitory response (Pavlov, 1927, p. 48).

Differences in Excitation and Inhibition: A Typology

Pavlov developed a typology based on the dog's level of conditionability. He based this typology on his discovery that there was a correlation between a dog's temperament and its conditionability. Dogs who were most sociable and active proved to be the worst subjects when it came to developing conditioned reflexes. Strapped into a harness in an experimental chamber, such normally active dogs soon became drowsy and often even fell asleep. By contrast, dogs that were quiet outside the experimental situation were easily conditioned (1928, p. 306).

Pavlov initially thought that, in difficult-to-condition dogs, excitatory cortical processes predominated. Pavlov assumed that the excitatory cells of such dogs would be quickly exhausted. Inhibitory processes would then take over, causing drowsiness and sleep. For such a dog, the repetition of the same constant sequence of stimuli in conditioning rapidly depletes the easily aroused excitatory cells. Pavlov also found that such dogs were good conditioning subjects if the conditioning procedure was varied so that a constant succession of novel stimuli was available (Pavlov, 1927, pp. 287ff.).

The second type of nervous temperament is predominantly inhibitory in normal behavioral activities. Outwardly, this dog appears cowardly, cringing in corners and slinking along the floor as if afraid of everything and everyone. Even though this dog is easily conditioned with repetitive experimental stimuli, its positive conditioned reflexes are easily disrupted and extinguished. Only inhibitory reflexes (e.g., learning *not* to respond to one of a pair of stimuli that is not reinforced by meat powder) are stable and strongly established (Pavlov, 1927).

Between these two extremes of excitatory and inhibitory types, Pavlov found other dogs that were equilibrated or balanced in their degree of inhibition and excitation (1928, pp. 374ff.). This *balanced type* of dog is found in two distinct varieties. In the first type, the balance between excitation and inhibition is well established so that the dog conditions well in both positive and inhibitory reflexes. This first balanced type tends to *behaviorally* resemble the extreme excitatory dog in its lively, outgoing manner. In the second balanced type of nervous system, excitatory and inhibitory processes are in a tenuous or unstable balance. The balance can easily be disrupted at the slightest provocation or distraction (Pavlov, 1928, p. 375).

Based on his experimental results, Pavlov proposed four types of nervous systems, which turned out to be the same as the classical types of temperament.

Extreme Excitatory Type:	Choleric (poor conditionability)
Extreme Inhibitory Type:	Melancholic (good inhibitory conditionability)
Balanced (Excitatory) Type:	Sanguine (good conditionability)
Balanced (Inhibitory) Type:	Phlegmatic (good, but easily distracted)

Galen and Kant would have felt vindicated by this validation of their classifications. Pavlov also ended up with the number *four* to describe the types of temperament.

Experimental Neurosis: Breakdown of the Inhibition-Excitation Balance

One of the chief distinguishing features of Pavlov's nervous system types was the degree of susceptibility to experimentally induced neurotic behavior. Pavlov could induce such a neurosis, for example, with a conditioning procedure in which both excitatory and inhibitory cortical processes are made to alternate rapidly. They are then thought to "collide" in the dog's nervous system. Whatever the explanation, each of the extreme nervous types will then succumb to a different form of what might informally be termed a "nervous breakdown."

Using a mechanical vibrator applied to the dog's skin, Pavlov conditioned an extreme excitatory dog to salivate at 30 vibrations a minute. When the vibrator was set to oscillate at only 15 vibrations per minute, no food was presented. In this way, the dog learned to discriminate between 30 and 15 vibrations. It salivated to 30 vibrations, an excitatory response, and withheld salivation to 15 vibrations, an inhibitory response. When, however, Pavlov employed 15 and 30 vibrations in close succession, dogs of the *excitatory type* suffered an extreme disorganization of behavior. Their weak inhibitory processes completely failed to keep pace with the rapid alternation between 15 and 30 vibrations. Their stronger excitatory processes assumed dominance in this collision with inhibitory processes. The animal became uncontrollably excited, straining and struggling to escape the harness and bite the experimenter. In short order, the extreme excitatory type of dog showed every sign of an anxiety attack. The effect was long-lasting, often requiring months of treatment with tranquilizers to effect a cure.

The *inhibitory type* of dog succumbed to a different type of experimentally induced neurosis when exposed to the same alternation of excitatory and inhibitory stimuli. Inhibiting all response, these dogs became rigid and drowsy. Outside the conditioning chamber, they became withdrawn and easily frightened.

Dogs of the two central or balanced types did not succumb readily, if at all, to experimentally induced neuroses (Pavlov, 1928, p. 375). They could continue to respond to both excitatory and inhibitory stimuli.

Incompleteness of Pavlov's Model

Eysenck (1957a, pp. 111ff.) noted inadequacies in Pavlov's descriptions of the four nervous types. For example, Pavlov identified the extreme excitatory nervous type as a choleric personality. Presumably, in making this classification, Pavlov was focusing his attention on the dog's behavior in the conditioning situation, where the tedious experimental procedures made the animal drowsy and difficult to condition. However, the typical dog, when it is not confined or otherwise stressed, appears to be a sanguine type— outgoing, friendly, and emotionally expressive. Yet, in Pavlov's system, this dog would have been classified as a choleric type. Under appropriate conditions, furthermore, the choleric dog succumbs to anxiety that is more characteristic of the melancholic type.

So one might wonder, which type it really is. Is it to be labeled as a sanguine type of dog because it is normally outgoing and affable? Or is it fundamentally choleric because it becomes hard to handle in the conditioning situation? Or is it melancholic because it succumbs to anxiety neurosis?

Because of such incomplete explanations, Eysenck did not accept Pavlov's classification scheme without revision. Eysenck's first step in revising the Pavlovian model was to accept Pavlov's biological strategy: that differences in the four personality types have their source in inhibition-excitation processes of the nervous system. Eysenck applied this strategy to human temperaments in a much different way in his formulation of an **arousal theory.**

For Eysenck, the essence of melancholic and phlegmatic temperaments is their withdrawal from social and physical stimulation, as described by the ancients. Because both personality types have highly aroused cortical processes, the defining property of introversion in Eysenck's model, the melancholic and phlegmatic types, should form conditioned reflexes easily and strongly. In the phlegmatic type, high cortical excitation and sensitivity lead to withdrawal behaviors designed to escape overwhelming stimulation. Yet, the phlegmatic lacks the melancholic's high emotional reactivity, and thus remains free of neurotic anxiety and despair. Eysenck therefore classified both the melancholic and the phlegmatic as **stimulus shy** introverts but only the melancholic as neurotic.

At the other extreme, the essence of the choleric and sanguine personalities in Eysenck's view is their low cortical arousal level, which leads to responsivity and rapt attention to the social and physical environment. The sanguine personality is fundamentally outgoing, sociable, and emotionally tranquil. He or she delights in a constant succession of novel experiences. The choleric personality is also **stimulus hungry** and attentive to the social environment, but finds no delight in it. He or she is more emotional, more irritable, and more prone to become irascible. The choleric may even turn mean, taking delight in manipulating or hurting others.

Eysenck thus classified the choleric and sanguine personalities as extroverts but only the choleric as neurotic. He assumed that their cortical processes were far less sensitive, far less aroused, and considerably more inhibitory than those of introverts. Strong inhibitory processes cause the extrovert types to seek constant stimulation from the social environment to provide adequate stimulation. Because both personality types have strong inhibitory processes, the defining property of extroversion in Eysenck's scheme, the sanguine and choleric personalities should, in principle, form positive conditioned reflexes poorly or weakly.

Comparisons of Pavlov's and Eysenck's explanations of temperaments are displayed in Table 17.1.

Table 17.1   Pavlov's Types and Eysenck's Dimensions Contrasted

Classical temperaments	Pavlov's types	Eysenck's dimensions	Classical temperaments
Choleric	Extreme excitatory	Extreme emotional introvert	Melancholic
Melancholic	Extreme inhibitory		Choleric emotional extrovert
Sanguine	Balanced excitatory		Phlegmatic introvert
Phlegmatic	Balanced inhibitory	Stable extrovert	Sanguine

Note reversal of classical temperaments between Eysenck's and Pavlov's schemes.
Based on Pavlov, 1928, p. 377; Pavlov, 1927, p. 286; Eysenck, 1957a.

Eysenck was aware of limitations in Pavlov's work. He eventually found in Clark Hull's theory the relevant concept that not only are external conditions important but also that the level of the drive arousal state must be taken into consideration.

HULL'S DRIVE THEORY: INDIVIDUAL DIFFERENCES IN PERFORMANCE

Clark L. Hull (1884–1952) developed a **drive theory** of learning and performance that incorporated basic concepts similar to excitation and inhibition. The advantage of Hull's formulation over Eysenck's point of view was its precision in describing the interaction of inhibition and excitation.

Hull's theory (1943, 1951, 1952) was formulated to account for a different kind of conditioning from that of Pavlov's work with dogs. Instead of involuntary reflex conditioning, Hull was more concerned with instrumental (respondent) conditioning, which deals with voluntary behavior (review the section of Chapter 14 for a description of instrumental conditioning).

The basic premise underlying Hull's formulation was that reinforcers are stimuli that reduce or satisfy an organism's biological drives. For instrumental learning to occur, an organism must first be in a state of high drive arousal, for example, very hungry. Then, those responses that the organism uses to obtain satisfaction for the drive will become associated with the stimuli connected with satisfaction of the drive. For example, if a hungry rat discovers through trial and error that turning right at a certain point in a maze brings it into contact with food, then a right turn at that point will become habitual whenever it is hungry in that maze.

To indicate the learned connection between the stimuli of the maze's choice points and the response of turning right, Hull employed a "habit" symbol: $_sH_R$. If the rat is not in a state of drive arousal (i.e., not hungry) when placed in the maze, then its habit of turning right at a particular choice point will have a low probability of being translated into actual behavior. As the hunger drive begins to mount in intensity, it will activate the previously reinforced habit of turning right at the appropriate choice point. Hull indicated this relationship between drive and habits with the following formula:

$$D \times {_sH_R} = {_sE_R}$$

In words, this formula states that observable performance ($_sE_R$), is evoked when the strength of the drive (D) is multiplied by the strength of previously learned stimulus-response connections or habits ($_sH_R$). To be accurate, this formula should be modified to take account of any additional variables that might add to or subtract from the organism's drive arousal and past habit strengths. Hull suggested two additional and competing variables: reactive inhibition (I_R) and conditioned inhibition ($_sI_R$).

Reactive and Conditioned Inhibition

Reactive inhibition (I_R) in Hull's formulation is similar to Pavlov's concept of internal inhibition. In Hull's theory, reactive inhibition is neural fatigue that develops when responses are repeated. As I_R, a negative drive state, continues to increase, it cancels the positive drive to respond. The organism suffers a general feeling of fatigue and discomfort associated with continued responding. When it finally stops responding the fatigue of this reactive inhibition state is allowed to dissipate. Dissipation of I_R is experienced as satisfying or rewarding.

But note what is now being reinforced: the act of not responding. Thus there develops a conditioned negative habit, a tendency to not respond. This second kind of inhibition is a learned inhibitory response reinforced by the reduction in I_R that rest produces. Hull referred to this kind of inhibition as learned or **conditioned inhibition** ($_SI_R$). Both of these two kinds of inhibition, internal inhibition and reactive inhibition, are subtracted from a drive's activation to obtain a net result.

Eysenck's Formulation of Drive, Habit, and Inhibition

Eysenck eventually adopted the general Hullian notion that drive multiplies habits and that inhibition reduces the effects of positive drive. Eysenck discussed the relation of performance, drive, habit, and inhibition in the activity of a person playing tennis.

> Clearly, the excellence of his [tennis] performance will depend upon two things. It will depend, in the first place, on his drive. . . . It also depends, of course, on his experience and on the amount of practice that he has previously put into the task, on the length of time he has been playing, and so on. In other words, it will depend on the system of bodily habits which he has built up during the past [$_SH_R$]. . . . His actual performance will be a function of both these variables; the stronger the drive, and the more highly developed the habits which are necessary for carrying out his task, the better his performance will be. Where does inhibition fit into this picture?
>
> The answer of course is this. If a person is carrying out a task, particularly under conditions of massed practice, then inhibition will continue to accumulate. Being a negative drive, it will subtract from the positive drive under which the organism is working. And, finally, when inhibition builds up to such an extent that it is equal to positive drive under which the person is working, he will simply cease to work altogether because now drive is equal to inhibition, and drive minus inhibition equals zero. . . . [A]nything multiplied by zero—is, of course, zero and, therefore, performance will cease. (1964a, p. 73)

The logical deduction to be made from this conceptualization of the effects of inhibition on drive is that continued performance leads ultimately to a cessation of activity. Such a cessation may be only momentary, but if the prediction is correct, the performer will experience a fleeting block to further action. A good deal of experimental evidence has verified that such blocks to performance actually do occur.

INDIVIDUAL DIFFERENCES AND EYSENCK'S TYPOLOGY

Eysenck formulated two personality postulates that would lead to a coherent, yet still tentative, experimental model of why introverts differ from extroverts. To span the distance between the theory of excitation-inhibition and personality types, Eysenck proposed the **postulate of individual differences:**

> *Human beings* differ with respect to the speed with which excitation and inhibition are produced, the strength of the excitation and inhibition produced, and the speed with which inhibition is dissipated. These differences are properties of the physical structures involved in making stimulus-response connections. (1957a, p. 114, italics added)

In this statement, Eysenck was proposing that personality psychologists and experimental psychologists join forces in investigating a variable that had often been interpreted as having interest only for the experimentalist. Excitation and inhibition were now to be conceptualized as fundamental to any understanding of personality differences.

To extend the logic of his position, Eysenck also proposed a relatively precise specification of these personality differences in relation to excitation and inhibition processes, his **typological postulate:**

> Individuals in whom excitatory potential is generated slowly and in whom excitatory potentials so generated are relatively weak, are thereby predisposed to develop extraverted patterns of behavior and to develop hysterical-psychopathic disorders in case of neurotic breakdown; individuals in whom excitatory potential is generated quickly and in whom excitatory potentials so generated are strong, are thereby predisposed to develop introverted patterns of behaviour and to develop dysthymic disorders [anxiety, phobias, obsessive-compulsive symptoms] in case of neurotic breakdown. Similarly, individuals in whom reactive inhibition is developed quickly, in whom strong reactive inhibitions are generated, and in whom reactive inhibition is dissipated slowly, are thereby predisposed to develop hysterical-psychopathic disorders in case of neurotic breakdown; conversely, individuals in whom reactive inhibition is developed slowly, in whom weak reactive inhibitions are generated, and in whom reactive inhibition is dissipated quickly, are thereby predisposed to develop introverted patterns of behaviour and to develop dysthymic disorders in case of neurotic breakdown. (1957a, p. 114)

With the typological postulate, Eysenck laid the groundwork for a model of personality based on empirical evidence as well as a concept of underlying physiological processes. Introverts were conceptualized as having stronger and more easily aroused excitatory processes, coupled with their rapid dissipation of inhibition. Extroverts, on the other hand, were conceptualized as having relatively weak excitatory processes and slow dissipation of inhibition. Taking only the extreme extrovert and the extreme introvert as models, the typological postulate can be summarized in the form of a table. When reading Table 17.2, it must be remembered that Eysenck's typology is dimensional, allowing for degrees of expression of inhibition and excitation, whereas the summary in Table 17.2 is essentially categorical.

Based on the typological postulate, a number of hypotheses can be deduced about introverts' and extroverts' performance in laboratory situations. For example, if introverts have stronger excitatory cortical processes and relatively weak inhibitory effects, they should condition more quickly than extroverts in laboratory tasks like eye-blink conditioning. Other deductions can be made along these same lines. For any task that requires strong excitatory processes and the rapid dissipation of inhibition, introverts should evidence superior performance.

Eysenck's Modifications of Pavlov's Typology

Pavlov had developed a typology that connected observable behavioral traits to underlying nervous system processes of inhibition and excitation. He then further attempted to coordinate classical temperament theory with his results.

Eysenck began with Pavlov's findings but revised his classification system. He agreed with Pavlov that observable differences between personality types are based on the

Table 17.2 Summary of Typological Postulate as Extreme Types

	Excitation	*Inhibition*	*Neurotic predisposition*
Introverts	High (rapid)	Low (slow)	Dysthymia
Extroverts	Low (slow)	High (rapid)	Hysteria-psychopathy

Based on Eysenck, 1957a.

inhibition-excitation processes of the nervous system. And he also revised Pavlov's theory. He developed a typology based on the level of cortical arousal and the level of emotional reactivity. Those with high levels of cortical arousal withdrew from external stimuli and were considered introverts. Those with low levels of cortical arousal were stimulus hungry; they sought out external stimulation. In addition, individuals could be rated as to their level of emotional reactivity.

In the melancholic type, he theorized that extreme cortical arousal is coupled with high emotional reactivity. The melancholic person thus feels intellectually and emotionally overwhelmed by even mild social and physical stimulation. He or she thus tends to retreat from his or her surroundings.

In the phlegmatic personality, this same high cortical excitation and sensitivity leads to withdrawal in the form of an apathetic attitude. The phlegmatic person lacks the melancholic's high level of emotional reactivity, and thus remains free of neurotic anxiety and despair.

Eysenck classified both types as introverts but only the melancholic as neurotic. Because both the phlegmatic and melancholic personality types have highly aroused cortical processes, the defining property of introversion in Eysenck's scheme, they should be readily conditionable.

The choleric and sanguine personalities in Eysenck's view have low levels of cortical arousal. They are both characterized by their responsivity and rapt attention to the social and physical environment. The sanguine type of person has low emotional reactivity. He or she is emotionally tranquil. The choleric personality has high emotional reactivity. He or she is thus more emotional, more irritable, and more prone to become irritated and angry.

In Eysenck's theory, the strong inhibitory processes of both the extroverted types leads them to seek constant stimulation from the social environment in order to provide cortical stimulation. Both the sanguine and choleric personalities should thus be difficult to condition. Similarities and differences between Pavlov and Eysenck's explanations of temperaments are summarized in Table 17.2.

AROUSABILITY AND THE ASCENDING
RETICULAR ACTIVATION SYSTEM (ARAS)

The clear implication of Eysenck's proposal that individuals differ in their excitation-inhibition balance is that this difference is mediated by something in the **central nervous system.** In 1967, Eysenck revised and extended his basic introversion-extroversion theory by postulating specific relationships between these personality dimensions and the **ascending reticular activating system (ARAS)** of the brain. He also rooted the dimension of normality-neuroticism in central nervous system structures. Eysenck's theory was based on earlier research. Three decades earlier, James Papez (1937) had already specified a group of subcortical structures, including the hypothalamus, the gyrus cinguli, the hippocampus, and their interconnections, as related to emotional arousal. He reviewed evidence that these structures are responsible for changes in heart rate, respiration, blood pressure, and other signs of emotional activation. Together, these structures are called the visceral brain or **limbic system.**

The relationships that Eysenck proposed can be summarized succinctly in two verbal equations:

$$\text{Introversion} - \text{Extroversion} = \text{Difference in ARAS Arousal}$$
$$\text{Normality} - \text{Neuroticism} = \text{Differences in Visceral Brain Activation}$$

ARAS and Cortical Arousal

The ARAS is a network of fibers extending from the spinal cord to the thalamus of the brain at a level below the cortex. Figure 17.2 illustrates the basic location and boundaries of the ARAS. Figure 17.2 also shows the general location of the visceral brain (VB) structures. The ascending arrows indicate the direction of influence of the ARAS on the cortex. Descending arrows, from the cortex toward the ARAS, indicate the reciprocal influence of the cortex on the ARAS. Generally, the ARAS serves to stimulate the cortex, to activate its cells to a state of excitability. The cortex may in turn provide feedback to the ARAS either to further increase its excitatory input or to dampen its activity.

Physiological interest in this arousal network or reticulum of fibers began in the 1930s when it was discovered that cutting through the brain stem at midbrain level caused cats to become almost permanently sleeping animals. The electrical activity of such cats' brains showed a characteristic sleeping wave on the **electroencephalograph (EEG).** In a normally sleeping cat, it is possible to induce an arousal EEG pattern by simply waking the animal or doing something to engage its attention. But in cats with transected brain stems it was possible to produce an arousal EEG pattern only for short periods lasting as long as the stimulus used to arouse the cat.

In 1949, Giuseppe Moruzzi and Horace W. Magoun, instead of shutting down the ARAS by cutting into the brain stem, set out to stimulate it electrically. EEG tracings from the cortex of stimulated cats showed that stimulation of the ARAS evokes cortical arousal. The ARAS seems also to be involved in states of attention and concentration. Joaquin M. Fuster (1958) was able to improve rhesus monkeys' performance on a visual discrimination task by stimulating their ARAS. Results of further studies indicated that the ARAS is responsible for cortical efficiency in learning, conditioning, wakefulness, and attention. The ARAS appears to mediate states of arousal, ranging from sleep to extreme behavioral excitation.

Another portion of the ARAS, however, seems to have an inhibitory effect on the cortex. Known as the recruiting system, this portion of the ARAS serves to damp down cortical excitation. Eysenck seems to have found the physiological causes of excitation and inhibition and, therefore, the basis of introversion-extroversion in the ARAS. He

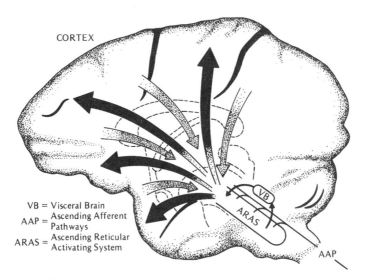

Figure 17.2 Anatomical locations of ARAS and VB.
Source: Eysenck, 1967, p. 231.

hypothesized that introverts are assumed to have higher levels of ARAS arousal (lower ARAS thresholds) than extroverts.

Visceral Brain and Emotional Activation

The second major personality dimension in Eysenck's theory is the dimension of normality-neuroticism. Eysenck assumes that this dimension consists largely of differences in emotional activation such that neurotics are more highly emotionally reactive than normal. The structures of the limbic system or visceral brain (VB) are conceptualized as the mediators of this reactivity. The hypothalamus and other parts of the VB impact the autonomic or involuntary nervous system, which in turn affects a wide range of end organs and functions. Glands, muscles, heart rate, respiration, and perspiration are among the many areas controlled, at least in part, by the **autonomic nervous system.** Individuals in whom the VB is most easily activated are thought to be most susceptible to neurotic disorder.

There is a complicating factor connected with the VB and neuroticism. In states of extreme emotional activation (e.g., intense rage, or profound sadness, or extreme fear), the normal independence of functioning between the ARAS's arousal of the cortex and the VB's emotional activation of the autonomic nervous system breaks down. (Eysenck, 1967, p. 232). Thus, although it is possible to be intellectually aroused without emotional activation, it is impossible to be emotionally activated without simultaneous intellectual or cortical arousal.

In the first case, that of cortical arousal without VB (emotional) activation, problem-solving activity dominates the individual. For example, Eysenck cites the case of a scientist who was sitting quite immobile and apparently fast asleep. But subjectively, his mind is hard at work tackling unsolved and intricate professional problems (Eysenck, 1967, p. 232). His cortex is aroused, but his emotions are not.

In cases where the level of emotional activation is intense, cortical arousal must also have occurred. Thus, in Eysenck's dimensional system, the separation of intellectual arousal from emotional activation holds only for normal individuals (Eysenck, 1967, p. 233; 1982; Eysenck & M. Eysenck, 1985). In more technical terms, the neurotic individual is reaching maximum cortical and emotional arousal nearly simultaneously because the hypothalamus and other structures in the limbic system (VB) are bombarding the ARAS with stimulation. At the same time, the ARAS is arousing the cortex.

TRANSLATION OF EXCITATION-INHIBITION INTO AROUSAL CONCEPTS

With his proposal that biological bases are responsible for the dimensions of introversion-extroversion and for normality-neuroticism, Eysenck sharpened the causal explanation in his personality theory.

To make clear the transition from Eysenck's 1957 theory of excitation-inhibition to his 1967 theory of biological functions, it is necessary to distinguish among four extreme types of personality. Individuals may be said to be normal or neurotic, introverted or extroverted, with various degrees between these absolutes. It follows that an individual may be a normal introvert or a neurotic introvert, just as he or she may be a normal extrovert or a neurotic extrovert. The hypothetical nervous system states of ARAS arousal and VB activation that correspond to these four extreme types are indicated in Table 17.3.

The emphasis in this version of Eysenck's theory is on differences in arousal level (excitation) rather than on inhibition-level differences. Experimental tests of the biological (1967) theory usually spring from hypotheses specifically about the effects of the

Table 17.3   Biological Basis of Personality

Dimensional position	Level of ARAS arousal	Level of VB activation
Normal introvert	High	Low
Normal extrovert	Low	Low
Neurotic introvert (dysthymic)	High	High
Neurotic extrovert (hysteric)	Low[a]	High

[a]Note that the neurotic extrovert's ARAS arousal is higher than the normal extrovert's ARAS arousal because of the breakdown of separation between ARAS and VB functioning in states of high (neurotic) emotion. But the extrovert's characteristic ARAS arousal level is always lower than the introvert's level and is, therefore, simply listed as "low."   Based on Eysenck, 1967.

introvert's higher cortical ARAS arousal. With this shift in theoretical emphasis came several complications. The one of immediate interest in the present context concerns a general law of motivation proposed in 1908 by Yerkes and Dodson.

The Yerkes-Dodson Law: Inverted-U Hypothesis

Robert M. Yerkes and John D. Dodson proposed a principle of motivation and performance that, with few modifications, has been widely accepted. In briefest form, *Yerkes and Dodson's law* states that motivation, or arousal, may be conceptualized as a continuum ranging from very low levels through very high levels of excitation. At the low end of the continuum, the organism is so under-aroused that it actually falls asleep. At the high end, the organism is so aroused that its behavior is disorganized, fragmented, or frenzied. Yerkes and Dodson (1908) proposed that the optimal state of arousal lies between these two extremes. In this moderate level of arousal, the individual is sufficiently motivated to perform well, but not so aroused as to be disorganized or distracted. Subsequent theorists (e.g., Broadhurst, 1959; Hebb, 1955; Lindsley, 1951; Malmo, 1959) referred to this hypothesis as the "inverted-U hypothesis." The inverted, or upside-down, U can be seen in Figure 17.3.

Figure 17.3 shows the relationship between arousal level and quality of performance. As arousal increases, performance improves until it reaches a maximum at the height of

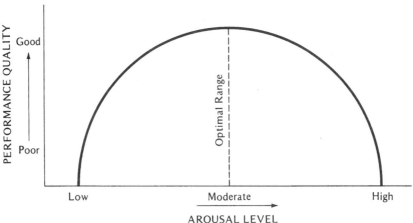

Performance is optimal at moderate levels of arousal.

Figure 17.3 Inverted-U law of motivation and performance.

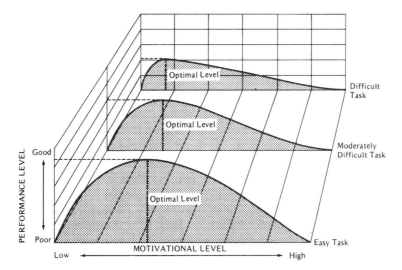

Figure 17.4 Yerkes-Dodson law for interaction of arousal level, performance, and task difficulty. As task difficulty increases, optimal level of arousal for best performance decreases.
Source: Eysenck, 1963a, p. 131.

the inverted-U curve. From that point onward, increases in arousal lead to decreases in performance.

What would happen when the task that the individual is performing varies in difficulty or complexity? Will tasks of different difficulty levels require different levels of optimal arousal? The answer is a definite "Yes." If we confine our consideration of task difficulty to three levels—low, medium, and high difficulty—then we can plot motivation-performance curves for each task level. Figure 17.4 illustrates the theoretical relationships among task-difficulty, performance, and arousal levels.

The three curves in Figure 17.4 are designed to indicate that the optimal level of arousal for best performance changes as task-difficulty level increases. For tasks of low difficulty, a somewhat higher level of arousal or motivation for tasks of moderate difficulty is optimal. Tasks of greatest difficulty require the lowest level of arousal. The general rule is: *The more difficult the task, the lower the level of optimal arousal.*

Thus, with the Yerkes-Dodson law in mind, predictions from Eysenck's biological model of personality not only can be more precise, but also can take account of the interaction between cortical arousal and emotional activation.

We are now in a position to pose an interesting question. The four extreme types of individuals (normal and neurotic introverts, and normal and neurotic extroverts) should, in principle, possess differing levels of combined cortical and emotional arousal. Presumably, neurotic introverts, in whom ARAS and VB excitation are both chronically high, should be placed at the top rank of a hierarchy of arousal. Normal extroverts, having low ARAS arousal and low VB activation, should fall at the bottom of the hierarchy of arousal. In between these extremes, normal introverts and neurotic extroverts, each having one form of high arousal, should evidence moderate degrees of excitation. The theory, however, does not specify whether the normal introvert is more highly aroused than the neurotic extrovert.

One might predict that a very neurotic extrovert would surpass a normal introvert in absolute drive level because the neurotic extrovert's emotional reactivity acts as a multiplier of habits in Hull's sense of the term. Thus, our final hypothetical hierarchy of differential combined arousal for the personality types looks like this:

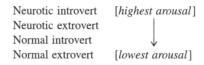

But only an empirical investigation can provide actual rankings for these personality types (cf. Eysenck, 1953b, pp. 436ff., and 1967, pp. 182ff.). To illustrate this kind of experimental test of the theory, McLaughlin and Eysenck (1967) had the four different types of criterion personalities learn lists of paired nonsense syllables. One list was difficult to learn, and the other relatively easy. Results were tabulated by the number of errors a subject made in reaching a specified criterion of learning. In addition to determining the optimum level of arousal for learning, the experiment was also designed to test a hypothesis about a phenomenon called reminiscence.

Experimental psychologists had known for a long time that memory for a learned response improves if time intervenes between the acquisition of the response and its performance. Thus, when studying for an exam in psychology, recitation of what has been learned will be better the following day when compared to immediate recitation. During the period of rest, the memory is consolidated or made more permanent. However, while the process of consolidation is in progress, performance of the learned response is impeded.

Eysenck hypothesized that the process of consolidation is most facilitated in individuals having high initial cortical arousal, that is, in introverts. Thus introverts should show poorest performance on memory tasks that require immediate performance, whereas extroverts, who have low arousal and poor consolidation, will perform best immediately after acquisition (cf. McLaughlin & Eysenck, 1967, pp. 574ff.). In the experiment conducted by McLaughlin and Eysenck (1967), tests of memory for the learned lists were performed immediately after acquisition, and thus favored extroverts. But, as we already know, the Yerkes-Dodson law also governs performance on tasks of varying difficulty. It can thus be presumed that the difficult list of paired nonsense syllables would present a task requiring a moderately low level of arousal for optimal performance. Thus, taking

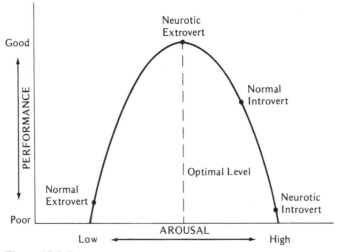

Figure 17.5 Easy list.
Based on McLaughlin & Eysenck, 1967, p. 131.

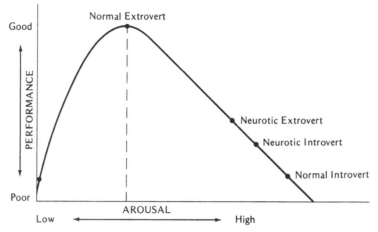

Relationship of error scores and arousal level for easy and difficult lists.

Figure 17.6 Difficult list.

Based on McLaughlin & Eysenck, 1967, p. 131.

the two effects together, the reminiscence evidence indicates that extroverts should perform better with immediate recall, whereas the Yerkes-Dodson law suggests that on the difficult list the low-arousal normal extroverts will show superior performance to neurotic extroverts, and to all highly aroused introvert personalities.

Conversely, learning the easy list should require a higher level of arousal than learning the difficult list to produce optimal performance. The prediction for the easy list thus must be that neurotic extroverts will evidence best performance because they have slightly higher arousal than normal extroverts. Neurotic introverts, having the highest level of combined ARAS and VB arousal, should, in principle, be too highly aroused to perform well on either list under conditions of immediate recall.

Figures 17.5 and 17.6 show the outcome of McLaughlin and Eysenck's investigation. The major predictions about the superiority of extroverts' performance were confirmed. Moreover, when a line is drawn through the plotted error scores for all subjects, the resulting curves resemble the inverted-U motivation-performance curve. As expected, the optimal level of arousal is shifted to the left (i.e., toward lower optimal arousal) for the difficult list.

A DIRECT TEST OF THE AROUSAL THEORY: STIMULANT AND DEPRESSANT DRUGS

If ARAS bombardment of the cortex is really the basis of the introversion-extroversion dimension of personality, then stimulant and depressant drugs should produce behavioral effects similar to those produced by excitation and inhibition. Furthermore, stimulants and depressants were hypothesized to produce different effects in introverts and extroverts. "In general, the prediction would be that stimulant drugs lead to greater arousal and hence to more introverted behavior, while depressant drugs lead to greater inhibition and hence to more extroverted behavior" (Eysenck, 1967, p. 265).

The preexisting state of arousal in a particular experimental subject would have to be taken into account to allow for the fact that introverts begin any task with a higher arousal level than extroverts. Therefore, the general hypothesis can be refined: Introverts require

BOX 17.2   *Only Connect . . .*

The relation between cortical arousal and inhibition of behavior is applied in the current use and likely overuse of Ritalin, a stimulant, for hyperactivity in youngsters (see page 647). This medication has the superficially paradoxical effect of leading to some degree of inhibition of the behavior of these children. By causing a lower threshold for cortical arousal, it promotes withdrawal from stimuli and inhibits responsivity.

less of a stimulant drug to reach a specified criterion of behavioral arousal than do extroverts. In a similar vein, it can be hypothesized that introverts require a larger dose of a depressant drug to reach a specified criterion of inhibition than do extroverts (Eysenck & M. Eysenck, 1985, p. 229).

Many research studies support these predictions (e.g., Claridge, 1967; Laverty, 1958; Shagass & Kerenyi, 1958). Such studies generally use a measurement of sedation threshold. A particular drug, for instance, a depressant, is injected intravenously at a known rate until slurred speech and specific EEG changes are noted. The amount of the drug required to reach this criterion is a measure of sedation threshold (Shagass & Kerenyi, 1958). Shagass and Kerenyi showed that subjects classified as introverts by psychiatric diagnosis and by paper-and-pencil measures had higher sedation thresholds (i.e., required a larger dosage) than extrovert subjects, thus confirming Eysenck's theory. Furthermore, subjects classified as obsessional (belonging to the dysthymic group in Eysenck's terminology) also had higher sedation thresholds than subjects classified as hysterics (see also Gupta, 1973).

ACQUISITION OF NEUROSIS: THE SOCIALIZATION OF INTROVERTS AND EXTROVERTS

Dysthymic neurotic symptoms, such as phobias, obsessions and compulsions, and intense anxiety attacks are interpreted by Eysenck (1960, 1976) as conditioned maladaptive responses acquired by neurotic introverts in coping with the demands of life. Dysthymic disorders fundamentally are learned fears. The introvert who becomes dysthymic does so precisely because his or her high cortical and high emotional arousal facilitates rapid and strong anxiety conditioning.

Some research has suggested that scores on neuroticism and extroversion/introversion are not totally uncorrelated or statistically orthogonal (Claridge, 1967; Eysenck & S. B. G. Eysenck, 1969). Introversion is more closely related to neuroticism than is extroversion. Eysenck has argued that this partial breakdown in orthogonality was a consequence of the early Maudsley Personality Inventory's overinclusion of certain biased items. To overcome the difficulty, a revision, the Eysenck Personality Inventory (Eysenck & S. B. G. Eysenck, 1968), was devised. Analysis of results with this instrument confirmed the statistical independence of the two dimensions.

Hysterical disorders result from failures to learn those anxiety-based responses that underlie normal socialization. The extrovert who becomes a hysteric (or a psychopathic personality) does so precisely because his or her cortical and emotional underarousal impedes the learning of anxiety-based self-restraint and moral or ethical inhibitions (Eysenck & Rachman, 1965, p. 40).

Some evidence suggests that extroverts may be of two types. In the first, sociability, or outgoing, stimulus-seeking behavior predominates. In the second type of extrovert, impulsivity and an inability to keep antisocial urges and behaviors in check predominate.

The first type resembles the normal personality but may succumb to hysterical disorder. Criminal or psychopathic behavior is more characteristic of the second, impulsive type (Eysenck, 1964a; Eysenck & S. B. G. Eysenck, 1969; Eysenck & Gudjonsson, 1989, pp. 118ff.). It is this second hysterical type who seems so opposite to the dysthymic personality, for the psychopath is one who has failed to acquire by conditioning the necessary socialization restraints that in the dysthymic become exaggerated into chronic anxiety symptoms (but see Sipprelle, Ascough, Detrio, & Horst, 1977).

Genetic and Environmental Interactions

Eysenck's early views stressed that dysthymic neuroses could be understood in terms of Pavlovian-like conditioning processes, just as the hysterical disorders could be thought of as failures of Pavlovian-like conditioning. Eysenck also regards differences in genetically determined central nervous system functioning as the foundation upon which life experiences lead to a healthy or unhealthy adaptation to reality. Put into its strongest form, Eysenck's theory asserts that the dimensions of normality-neuroticism and introversion-extroversion are genetically transmitted features of personality.

Eysenck has several times reviewed the evidence for the genetic basis of personality dimensions (1957a; 1967; for intelligence: 1973; 1979; for psychoticism: Eysenck & S. B. G. Eysenck, 1976; Eaves, Eysenck, & Martin, 1989). His underlying line of reasoning runs along the following lines: The introvert inherits a nervous system easily able to form conditioned responses, and if this personality type also inherits an emotionally reactive autonomic nervous system (high neuroticism), he or she will be in an ideal position to acquire strong anxiety responses. In effect, the introvert possesses a nervous system predisposition to be acutely sensitive to all forms of stimulation and therefore to become inhibited and withdrawing in the presence of a demanding social environment.

The extrovert, by contrast, inherits the type of nervous system that is not easily conditionable, not especially sensitive to stimulation, and not prone to withdrawal from a demanding environment. In fact, the extrovert is a stimulus-seeker because his or her relatively high levels of inhibitory cortical processes demand constant novel and potent input of external excitation to feed the resulting stimulus-hunger. Eysenck has summarized his position on the relative importance of biological and environmental factors in shaping personality as a **biosocial model:**

> Human behavior is rightly said to be bio-social in nature, i.e., to have both biological and social causes; it is time the pendulum started swinging back from an exclusive preoccupation with social causes to an appropriate appreciation and understanding of biological causes. . . . Biological causes act in such a way as to predispose an individual in certain ways to stimulation; this stimulation may or may not occur, depending on circumstances which are entirely under environmental control. (Eysenck, 1967, pp. 221–222)

Eysenck's theory, therefore, may be understood as an attempt to bridge two very wide gulfs: the gulf between a study of individual differences in personality and the experimental investigation of conditioning, learning, and perceptual processes, the gulf between genetic or biological differences and environmental influences on behavior.

Explaining the Neurotic Paradox

Eysenck has asserted that a cardinal feature of human neurosis is the "neurotic paradox." The neurotic person's behavior typically has consequences that are unfavorable, painful, and self-defeating. The paradox is that the neurotic person nonetheless persists in that behavior. You would think that unfavorable consequences would cause any rational person to take stock of the problem and alter his or her actions.

According to Eysenck, a strict conditioning model drawn from Pavlovian theory or even from Skinner's operant model cannot explain why neurotic symptoms endure unchanged in the face of punishing consequences. Moreover, some forms of neurotic behavior are founded on irrational fears, fears so removed from actuality that the dreaded outcome never materializes. Yet, despite the continual failure of the fear to be reinforced, the fear-based symptoms never extinguish as they should, according to conditioning theory (Solomon, Kamin, & Wynne, 1953; Solomon & Wynne, 1954). Eysenck reviews evidence that will not be presented here which suggests that, under certain circumstances, unreinforced conditioned fears may even incubate with each unreinforced presentation of the conditioned stimulus.

Eysenck hypothesizes that an adequate learning model of neurosis must include the possibility that some neurotic anxieties and fears are based on innate sensitivity to certain noxious objects or events. A similar idea first proposed by Martin Seligman (1970, 1971, 1972; see also Rachman, 1978, 1990) suggests an evolutionary mechanism through which organisms are biologically "prepared" to respond to specific stimuli with fear. Thus, for example, there certainly would be survival value in the predisposition to be fearful of darkness, of poisonous snakes and insects, or of high places. Conditioned neurotic fears built upon any of these *prepared* survival phobias would not readily obey the ordinary laws of learning, including extinction. The concept of preparedness might also explain why neurotic phobias tend to be restricted to a relatively small class of stimuli when, in contrast, conditioning theory predicts that *any* stimulus can be made fearsome by proper association with a noxious event (see the discussion of preparedness in Chapter 18).

According to this theory, neurotics persist in self-defeating behavior because the negative consequences of their symptoms and the failure of dreaded outcomes to materialize cannot suppress or extinguish fears that have roots in evolutionary survival mechanisms. Evolutionary mechanisms persist in a species because they promote environmental adaptation, but the average contemporary neurotic remains neurotic because the results of natural selection have not caught up with our civilized existence (see Chapter 18, Evolutionary Psychology).

PSYCHOTICISM: PSYCHIATRIC DIAGNOSIS REVISITED

Eysenck's work, you recall, began with a rebellious investigation of psychiatric diagnostic reliability. One of the fundamental tenets of classical diagnostic systems is the qualitative distinction between neurotic and psychotic disorders (Eysenck & S. B. G. Eysenck, 1976, pp. 5, 157).

Eysenck proposed a dimensional model of personality, which suggests that what he termed "psychoticism" is not an all-or-none phenomenon. There are gradations of psychoticism, which range from normality at one extreme to full-blown psychotic separation from reality and thought disorder at the other extreme. Thus, in principle, it is possible for a normal person to possess some degree of those traits found in extreme form in the psychotic personality, just as it is possible for the neurotic person to possess *some* normal traits or *some* psychotic traits.

Psychoticism has entered Eysenck's theory as an additional dimension of disordered personality that, like neuroticism and introversion-extroversion, is genetically based. Eysenck views psychoticism as a *polygenic* personality trait. "Polygenic" means that a trait is determined by a large number of genes, each of whose individual effect is small (Eysenck & S. B. G. Eysenck, 1976, p. 29). Another group of genes, fewer in number than the first group, determines the probability that the person will not only evidence psychotic *traits* but will also suffer a fully developed psychosis. Eysenck's model of psychoticism also allows that a person with a high psychoticism (P) score who is *not* overtly psychotic may nevertheless possess traits that make him or her different from the norm but not necessarily disadvantaged socially. Some high P personalities may in fact evidence their unusualness as genius or artistic productivity.

Characteristics of the High-P Scorer

Eysenck and S. B. G. Eysenck (1975a, 1975b, 1976) developed a questionnaire, the **Eysenck Personality Questionnaire (EPQ),** which is a measure of neuroticism and introversion-extroversion, and also assesses the level of psychoticism. Factor-analytic studies were the basis on which questions were selected to measure the psychoticism dimension. A "high-P" person is one who answers affirmatively a selected pattern of questions that paints the following personality portrait:

> A high psychoticism scorer is a loner who cares very little for the company of other people. The high-P personality shows overt hostility to others, even to close relatives and tends to disregard dangers and social conventions. Making fools of other people is an enjoyable pastime, and this trait may be carried easily to an extreme of cruelty. The high-P scorer tends to enjoy "unusual things" and stands out as "peculiar" to his acquaintances. (Eysenck & S. B. G. Eysenck, 1975b, p. 5)

A person with a high score on the P dimension is not necessarily psychotic or schizophrenic, although a schizophrenic person would be expected to have a **high P score.** A high degree of psychoticism is independent of the person's degree of introversion or extroversion, as measured by the EPQ. Some neurotics *may* happen to have elevated P scores; but there is no correlation between the two traits (Eysenck & S. B. G. Eysenck, 1976, pp. 38ff.).

A person's P score should be interpreted in terms of the other Eysenck dimensions. A high P score will have very different meanings when embodied in high and low introverted personalities, and even more varied meaning when associated with high, as contrasted with low, intelligence or with high or low neuroticism.

PSYCHOTICISM, CRIME, AND GENETICS

Recall that Eysenck argued that the basic personality dimensions have a substantial degree of genetic loading that interacts with socialization experiences. When Eysenck added the psychoticism dimension to his theory, he reaffirmed this interactionist model and created several new hypotheses about the interaction of the three dimensions of extroversion, neuroticism, and psychoticism.

Eysenck at first concluded that a person who scores high in psychoticism had inherited a vulnerability to psychotic disorder but may not in fact succumb to a diagnosable illness. Instead, a person who embodies a large number of the traits associated with psychoticism and who is also high in neuroticism and extroversion may develop a pattern of antisocial or criminal behavior. Eysenck first proposed that criminal or antisocial behavior was linked to extreme extroversion. The link, however, has always been modest or inconsistently validated in research studies (Eysenck & Gudjonsson, 1989).

Eysenck, therefore, has modified his theory to conceptualize the criminal or antisocial personality as someone who is impulsive, extroverted, high in neuroticism, and who has a high P or psychoticism level. In other words, they are impulse-laden, outgoing, full of emotional problems, and have poor-reality testing. It is not hard to see how such people could come under the jurisdiction of the criminal justice system.

Eysenck's argument incorporates his arousal hypotheses, his measurements of the factors underlying the personality dimensions, and his interactionist model of socialization. His theory has three related parts—arousal and hedonic tone, extroversion, aggression, and testosterone, and psychoticism and criminality.

Arousal and Hedonic Tone

Eysenck's own work and his review of the literature on criminality (Eaves, Eysenck, & Martin, 1989; Eysenck & Gudjonsson, 1989) suggested to him that criminal behavior is associated with underarousal because a person with a relatively nonreactive nervous system does not condition or acquire anxiety-based restraints or controls as readily as people with more highly aroused nervous systems (Eysenck & Gudjonsson, 1989, p. 119). Figure 17.7 illustrates Eysenck's basic hypothesis.

Introverts, extroverts, and **ambiverts** have different levels of optimal arousal. Optimal arousal is the level of activation produced by the person's nervous system and the current level of stimulus input. The optimal level is the point at which a given personality type is most comfortable, most pleasantly activated, and most positively motivated.

Introverts, with the highest innate arousal levels, require less stimulation to achieve the optimal level than do extroverts. By contrast, the extrovert's chronic underarousal ensures that higher levels of stimulation will be required to reach optimal levels of arousal.

The curves in Figure 17.7 indicate that the **hedonic tone** (pleasure or pain) of stimulation is a function of personality type. What is massive overstimulation and pain for the introvert is exciting or pleasant for the extrovert. The indifference level indicated in Figure 17.7 represents a kind of boredom threshold, which differs for the two extreme personality types. Extroverts reach "indifferent hedonic tone" levels at much higher levels of stimulation than do introverts. Or, said another way, what an extrovert regards as boring understimulation, the introvert would find as peaceful, undemanding stimulation.

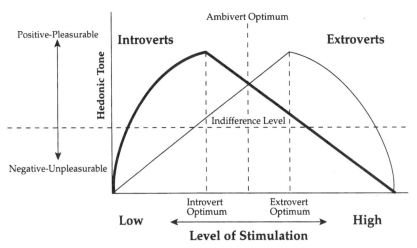

The optimal level of stimulation is higher for extroverts than for introverts both above and below the level of indifference. Eysenck predicts that levels of stimulation an introvert would find too intense would be "boring" for the extrovert. But levels of stimulation that the extrovert finds pleasurable or positively stimulating, the introvert experiences as overwhelming or painful. Most people, however, are ambiverts, and their optimal level of stimulation would fall theoretically between the optimal levels for the introvert and extrovert.

Figure 17.7 Positive and negative hedonic tone for introverts and extroverts.

Based on Eysenck & M. Eysenck, 1985, p. 249 and Eysenck & Gudjonsson, 1989, p. 118.

Eysenck suggests that the person destined to develop an antisocial personality is one whose arousal level is like that of the extreme extrovert in Figure 17.7. Specifically, the person would be excitement-seeking, easily distracted, and very resistant to levels of stimulation that would be regarded as unpleasant by others (Eysenck & Gudjonsson, 1989, p. 119).

The second link in Eysenck's argument involves the effects of hormone levels on arousal.

Extroversion, Aggression, and Testosterone

Eysenck proposed that the extroversion dimension and aggressivity were mediated by the presence of male hormones or androgens. Eysenck and Gudjonsson (1989) reviewed literature that suggests a correlation between androgens (largely testosterone) and underarousal. Some of the evidence that Eysenck reviews indicates that high androgen levels have the effect of lowering the arousal levels in the brain's reticular system (Eysenck & Gudjonsson, 1989, pp. 130ff.). Because the pattern of androgen secretion is genetically based, a person with high androgen levels inherits a predisposition to underarousal, to masculinized appearance, and, at times, to aggressive behavior. Eysenck is thus proposing that criminality is mediated, in part, by the inheritance of an underaroused nervous system, which in turn is mediated by genetically regulated androgen levels.

Psychoticism and Criminality

Eysenck's initial formulation of the relationship between the main personality dimensions and criminality pictured the extreme extrovert as prone to hysterical disorders and to psychopathy or criminal behavior (Eysenck, 1964a, 1976). But the criminal, long assumed to be an extreme extrovert and also high in neuroticism, appears with more recent evidence to fall into two different categories. The *primary psychopath* is the classical antisocial personality, who evidences little conscience, anxiety or guilt, poor judgment, and intense impulsivity. By contrast, the *secondary psychopath* may engage in antisocial behavior but is highly conflicted and anxious about his or her conduct.

Eysenck's later formulations show that criminals are high scorers on all three dimensions of extroversion, neuroticism, and psychoticism (Eysenck & M. Eysenck, 1985, pp. 330ff.). The addition of measurements for psychoticism has altered the interpretation placed on extroversion in mediating criminality. Eysenck concluded that the impulsivity component formerly associated with the extroversion dimension has to be understood as more strongly correlated to the psychoticism dimension. Thus, a person who scores highly on all three dimensions fits the role of criminal because:

1. as an extreme extrovert, the criminal is underaroused, sensation-seeking, poorly conditionable, and lacking in the restraints of conscience that are normally acquired through conditioning;

2. as a high scorer in neuroticism, the criminal evidences moody, irrational, and intensely emotional behavior;

3. as a high scorer in psychoticism, the criminal will lack empathy for other people, appear egocentric and impulsive, and act with poor judgment to gratify his or her needs.

The factors that determine whether the criminal will be a primary or secondary psychopath are to be found in the relationship between psychoticism and neuroticism. Generally, the theory predicts that the primary psychopath is one in whom the degree of psychoticism is higher than neuroticism; conversely, the secondary (anxious or guilty) criminal is a

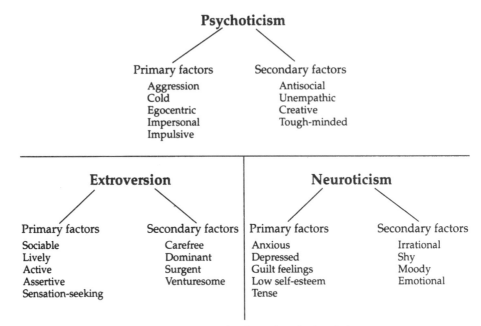

Figure 17.8 Eysenck's three main personality dimensions in descriptive terms.
Based on Eysenck & Gudjonsson, 1989, pp. 44–45.

person who scores higher on the neuroticism dimension than on the psychoticism dimension. In both types, the person is an extreme underaroused extrovert (i.e., not readily conditioned). Figure 17.8 summarizes the key qualities associated with Eysenck's three main personality dimensions.

Overview of the Psychoticism-Criminality Hypothesis

We can summarize the logic of Eysenck's **psychoticism-criminality hypothesis,** or hypotheses about psychoticism, arousal, and criminality as follows:

1. Inheritance of nervous system-associated hormonal regulators that establish chronic underarousal in the personality constitutes the predisposition to extreme extroversion and to antisocial behavior.

2. As the extreme underaroused extrovert matures socially, underarousal inhibits the acquisition of anxiety-based restraints and it promotes sensation-seeking behavior, resistance to pain, and aggressive action.

3. If the extreme extrovert also inherits a nervous system prone to neuroticism and high psychoticism, he or she is likely to develop criminal behavior. If psychoticism is higher than neuroticism, the orientation will be psychopathy or antisocial personality disorder. On the other hand, if neuroticism is stronger, the orientation is likely to be more in the direction of impulsivity.

Sensitivity to Reward and Punishment: Impulsivity and Anxiety

Jeffrey Gray (1985) reconceptualized how the limbic system and cortex of the brain function together as a kind of unified third biological system supplementing Eysenck's two systems of the visceral brain and ARAS-cortex. Gray proposed that the septum and hippocampus, and more recently, the amygdala, along with parts of the frontal cortex, constitute a *behavioral inhibition system* (BIS) that functions whenever the organism encounters one or more of three circumstances:

1. novel stimuli violating current expectations;
2. a naturally threatening stimulus engaging the organism's attention; or
3. previous experience leading the organism to expect punishment.

The BIS operates to arouse aversive states of fear that cause the organism to withdraw. Withdrawal, as Gray uses the term, consists of *inhibition* of action because particular responses provoke anxiety. Put another way, organisms differ in the sensitivity of their BIS: Some are constitutionally more prone to anxiety-inhibition and avoidance behavior than are others.

A second system proposed by Gray, the *behavioral approach system* (BAS), involves areas of the forebrain cortex, the higher cognitive centers, and complements the BIS with its own sensitivity to signals of reward and safety. The two systems work interactively in this way: The BIS works with the higher centers in "checking mode" to determine what meaning a stimulus might have. If the organism's checking registers a threatening meaning, the BIS swings into control mode and prompts withdrawal; otherwise, the BAS prompts approach, sometimes impulsively (Gray, 1985, p.7). Together, the two systems regulate much of the organism's approach and avoidance behavior and can be interpreted as one way to understand the brain's construction of the experience of anxiety.

THE "BIG FIVE": A MODEL BASED ON FACTOR ANALYSIS

A purely factor analysis approach to personality has led to five major personality traits or factors. This approach, unlike Eysenck's did not focus on trying to understand the physiological underpinnings of the factors, but simply on factoring the terms people use to describe personality. Two of the factors that emerged, *neuroticism* and *extroversion,* were very similar to Eysenck's comparable dimensions. **The Big Five** model does not have a dimension comparable to Eysenck's *psychoticism* as it is largely derived from terms used to describe the general population rather than those who manifest great psychopathology.

Raymond Cattell began the factor analytic approach to personality. He originally determined that there were 16 underlying traits. Subsequently, researchers analyzed larger and larger numbers of correlations and generally found that five major personality traits or factors emerged. An individual may be precisely described by measuring his or her location on each of the five trait dimensions. These traits are conceptualized as lying on bipolar dimensions with persons at one end of the dimension exhibiting high degrees of the trait and persons at the other end exhibiting low degrees of the trait (or its opposite).

The Big Five are:

1. *Neuroticism*
2. *Extroversion*
3. *Openness*
4. *Conscientiousness*
5. *Agreeableness*

Each of these main dimensions is composed of several secondary traits or "facets." Thus, for example, the neuroticism (versus emotional stability) dimension has been shown to embody anxiety, depression, problems with intimacy, sensitivity to stimulation, impulsiveness, and narcissism, to name just a few (e.g., Schroeder, Wormworth, & Livesley, 1994; see also the application of the Big Five to the study of borderline personality disorder in the work of Clarkin, Hull, Cantor, & Sanderson, 1993; and Eysenck & M. Eysenck [e.g., 1985]). In similar fashion, the extroversion (versus introversion) dimension embodies facets of sociability, warmth, assertiveness, and excitement-seeking, among others. Thus a score of high or low on a particular trait of the Big Five is actually a cluster of scores on the subfacets, providing for the *uniqueness* of individual combinations, a fact that would bring an I-told-you-so-smile to Gordon Allport's lips (see Chapter 11).

The working clinician planning treatment for a patient might consider, for example, that the patient's high neuroticism score includes anxiety, hopelessness, and unrealistic expectations. This same patient's low openness score reveals a preoccupation with fantasy and daydreaming along with some eccentric thinking. And the patient's high agreeableness score is associated with gullibility and indiscriminate trust of others (McCrae, 1994, p. 306). Given this kind of psychological description of personality functioning and malfunctioning using three of the Big Five dimensions as an illustration, the clinician may very well be guided not only to better understanding of the patient's personality and personality disorder but also to better avenues of providing therapeutic educational and emotional interventions.

Although there is growing agreement about the utility of the five-factor model, skeptics and critics point out that factor analysis has certain limitations and weaknesses. For one thing, a surprising degree of creativity and subjectivity enters into organizing and naming clusters of correlations as factors (Eysenck, 1993; Shadel & Cervone, 1993; but see also Watson, Clark, & Harkness, 1994). As we have seen, there is much evidence for Eysenck's physiologically based three-factor solution to factor analytic data. On the other hand, an investigator can choose a more complex solution that includes many more than five dimensions (Cattell, 1993), or even choose a multilayered, two-tier approach to the factors (Guastello, 1993).

There is also the nagging notion that what the Big Five offer in precision measurement they lack in explanation power. As Eysenck (1993) has pointed out on numerous occasions, the most productive research begins from and is guided deductively by a theory that makes predictions that can be tested. The Big Five evolved more or less the other way around, inductively collating and synthesizing sometimes unrelated measurements until they more or less coalesced into meaningful dimensions.

EVALUATING EYSENCK'S TYPOLOGY

Eysenck's strategy for constructing his theory is based on scientific method. His conception of the three dimensions of neuroticism, introversion-extroversion, and psychoticism grew from empirical studies, was altered as more studies were done, and changed again when the research suggested new directions or disconfirmed his hypotheses.

Refutability of Eysenck's Model

Eysenck's model is, and was designed to be, eminently refutable. It is a research-based conception, or set of conceptions, and one of its prime goals is to provide predictions that may be tested in the laboratory. As various hypotheses were tested, Eysenck changed basic parts of the theory that were disconfirmed, strengthened those that received support, and deduced new hypotheses that begin the cycle again.

Eysenck has subsequently fine-tuned the model, qualifying the exact conditions under which generalizations are true and when they are false (e.g., Eaves, Eysenck, &

Martin, 1989; Eysenck & Gudjonsson, 1989). However, by making many modifications to bring his theory into line with all of the exceptions it must account for, the theory runs the risk of no longer being intact or integral. It is in danger of becoming a collection of pieced-together, ad hoc explanations.

Eysenck's Conception of Human Agency

Eysenck consistently argued for a biosocial conception of humans. He thus affirmed that behavior is caused by a complex interaction between inherited nervous system predispositions and social reality. Even if a given choice may not seem predictable from the point of view of an outside observer, that choice is nonetheless lawful and determined.

Eysenck did not use the concepts of active and passive agency to describe people. But if we apply this evaluation scheme, we place Eysenck's model at the passive end of the spectrum and infer from his work that he does not view people as active agents.

The Nomothetic Nature of Eysenck's Theory

Eysenck's theory is definitely a nomothetic model of personality. It focuses on general principles. Study of the individual case is not part of Eysenck's interest or research methodology. It is possible to apply Eysenck's theory of types to specific individuals, but the vast bulk of the theory is derived from studying groups of people who are contrasted on the specific variables being studied. Eysenck commented on the question of the nomothetic versus idiographic nature of his theory:

> Modern personality theory, with its types and traits and abilities, is situated somewhere between idiographic psychology stressing *uniqueness* and experimental psychology stressing the *identity* (i.e., similarity) of human beings. What one must say, essentially, is that although human beings clearly do differ from each other, they differ along certain dimensions and their differences and similarities can therefore be quantified and measured. Measurements of traits and abilities lead us to certain *type* constructs, such as extraversion-introversion; this simply means that for certain purposes we can point to groups of people similar with respect to a given trait or ability and contrast these with groups of other people not sharing this trait or ability or showing its opposite. (Eysenck & M. Eysenck, 1985, p. 8; italics in original)

SUMMARY

Eysenck's approach to the study of personality is at one with his own personality, which was ruggedly independent, skeptical, and in which he trusted his own observations and facts more than the views of other or popular beliefs.

Eysenck's theory of personality may best be described as a hierarchical model having three major levels.

At the first observable level, personality types of introversion and extroversion are described in terms of measurable traits like sociability, shyness, impulsiveness, and activity. These traits are usually measured with paper-and-pencil instruments such as the Eysenck Personality Inventory or the Eysenck Personality Questionnaire.

At the second level of the hierarchy, performance on laboratory tasks, such as motor movements, conditioning, and vigilance, is used to define the dimensions of introversion and extroversion.

The third level is the fundamental, causal basis of the upper two divisions. Conceptualized as an excitation-inhibition balance (or ARAS arousal and inhibition of the cortex), this causal level may be classed as the genotypic basis of personality. As an inheritable dimension, excitation-inhibition (or ARAS functioning) may be thought of as the biological roots of personality. Figure 17.9 illustrates these levels of Eysenck's theory.

Eysenck's original factor analysis of personality performance and physiological data derived from a large group of subjects demonstrated that two independent dimensions could be used to describe their personalities. A dimension of introversion-extroversion and a dimension of normality-neuroticism were

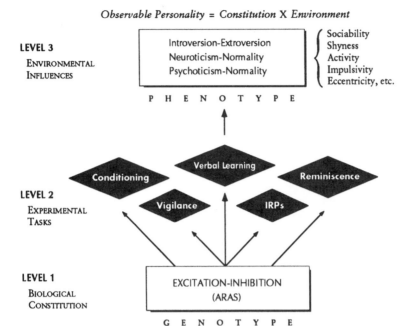

Observable Personality = Constitution X Environment

LEVEL 3
ENVIRONMENTAL
INFLUENCES

Introversion-Extroversion
Neuroticism-Normality
Psychoticism-Normality

Sociability
Shyness
Activity
Impulsivity
Eccentricity, etc.

P H E N O T Y P E

Verbal Learning

Conditioning

Reminiscence

LEVEL 2
EXPERIMENTAL
TASKS

Vigilance

IRPs

LEVEL 1
BIOLOGICAL
CONSTITUTION

EXCITATION-INHIBITION
(ARAS)

G E N O T Y P E

Figure 17.9 Three levels of Eysenck's theory.
Based on Eysenck, 1964a and 1967.

conceptualized as independent and continuous variables. The extrovert type of person likes people, and is sociable, strongly attracted to novel and exciting stimuli, easygoing, and optimistic. He or she is often fond of practical jokes and may become aggressive and impulsive, unable to inhibit or control anger. The typical introvert, by contrast, may be characterized as shy, quiet, withdrawn, and somewhat detached from the social environment. He or she is usually a planner, looking ahead to anticipate problems before they arise. He or she avoids overt and intense stimulation and excitement and usually keeps emotions under strict control (Eysenck & S. B. G. Eysenck, 1975b). The typical individual who scores high in neuroticism may be characterized as emotionally reactive, anxious, moody, and depressed.

Following Carl Jung's clinical insights that introverts succumb to dysthymic (psychasthenic) or anxiety disorders, and that extroverts succumb to hysterical neuroses, Eysenck was able to show that a long tradition stemming from Hippocrates and Galen through Pavlov and Hull had confirmed and refined Jung's hunches. Pavlov's conditioning investigations established the existence of excitation and inhibition as fundamental cortical processes underlying types of temperament.

Clark L. Hull's concepts of drive and habit, along with his notions of reactive and conditioned inhibition, provided Eysenck with key conceptual tools to begin devising a biological and causal account of the introversion-extroversion dimension. Introverts are individuals in whom the excitation-inhibition balance is tipped in the direction of excitation, giving them weak or sensitive nervous systems. Thus they condition more easily than extroverts, are more easily pained by excessive stimulation, and generally perform in a superior way on laboratory tasks requiring sustained attentiveness. Extroverts, by contrast, are individuals in whom the balance is tipped in the direction of greater inhibitory cortical functioning. For this reason, extroverts are said to have a "strong" nervous system not easily aroused by excessive stimulation, but one that is easily overcome with boredom by repetitious or monotonous tasks that rapidly build inhibition.

Eysenck provided a biological translation and refinement of his excitation-inhibition theory. The ascending reticular activating system (ARAS) has been conceptualized as the basis of cortical arousal and inhibition. In this role, the ARAS is also the basis of introversion-extroversion. Introverts have more highly aroused ARAS functioning than extroverts. The dimension of neuroticism has been conceptualized as related to the functioning of the autonomic nervous system. Subcortical brain structures of the limbic system and the hypothalamus, known collectively as the visceral brain (VB), have been postulated by Eysenck to underlie the dimension of emotionality or neuroticism. Neurotics have a higher level of chronic VB activation than do stable or normal individuals.

In terms of socialization, Eysenck has postulated that introverts are more socialized (inhibited, ethical, anxious) than extroverts because of their greater ease of conditioning. Extroverts are less socialized and may be divided into two extreme groups. Some extroverts are characterized essentially by a trait of extreme sociability, and these individuals tend to resemble the normal personality on measures of neuroticism. On the other hand, some extroverts are characterized by a trait of extreme impulsiveness and by a lack of ethical and moral inhibitions. These individuals are generally described as criminal or psychopathic personalities.

An addition to Eysenck's personality dimensions is psychoticism, represented in some personalities as inheritable traits of social withdrawal, impulsivity, hostility, and a general quality of what Eysenck termed, "peculiarity." The dimension of psychoticism, as measured by Eysenck, is not identical to the use of the term in conventional diagnosis, but his derived from his factor analysis of different traits. The psychoticism dimension, furthermore, implies that neurotic, normal, and psychotic personalities are not categorically different entities; rather, both normal and neurotic individuals may possess some degree of psychoticism without evidencing an overt psychosis.

Eysenck's theoretical strategy allows for concrete predictions and tests of its validity. Furthermore, Eysenck's theory may eventually provide the basis for more rational and scientifically precise diagnosis and treatment of disordered behavior. The possibility of altering an individual's position on the introversion-extroversion dimension by means of depressant and stimulant drugs to alter disordered behaviors may soon be feasible.

Evaluation of Eysenck's theory shows it clearly to be a highly testable, empirical, and scientific model of personality. Eysenck is fundamentally a biosocial type theorist who believes that patterns of behavior are determined by biological and psychological factors, so that human agency is essentially irrelevant. It follows that this theory is almost exclusively nomothetic.

Raymond Cattell and others, using factor analysis alone—without consideration of physiological underpinnings—arrived at five major factors of personality. These are labeled *neuroticism, extroversion, openness, conscientiousness,* and *agreeableness*. These factors have been confirmed by many empirical studies and comprise what is termed the "Big Five" model of personality. *Extroversion* and *neuroticism* are comparable to two of Eysenck's factors.

FOR FURTHER READING

Eysenck was a prolific writer with numerous empirical articles, scholarly books, and popular renditions of his theory to his credit. The development of Eysenck's continually more biological formulations may be gleaned from successive reading of three of his works: *The Scientific Study of Personality* (London: Routledge & Kegan Paul, 1952), which concerns his early descriptive measurements of introversion-extroversion; *The Dynamics of Anxiety and Hysteria* (London: Routledge & Kegan Paul, 1999), which presents his more causal inhibition theory; and *The Biological Basis of Personality* (Springfield, IL: Charles C. Thomas, 1967), which presents the definitive statement of his cortical hypotheses of arousal. Joseph LeDoux's *The Emotional Brain* (New York: Simon & Schuster [Touchstone], 1998) contains a very readable and comprehensive discussion of the limbic system and other brain structures involved in emotional arousal.

All four of the above-mentioned books are difficult reading. A reprinted key work of Eysenck is *Dimensions of Personality* (New Brunswick, NJ: Transaction Publishers, 1997). A more readable, though less comprehensive, overview of Eysenck's system is his *Crime and Personality* (London: Rout-

ledge & Kegan Paul, 1964). Related is a book he wrote with G. H. Gunderson, *The Causes and Cures of Criminality* (New York, Plenum Press 1989). At a popular level of presentation, Eysenck's *Psychology Is About People* (New York: Library Press, 1972) not only provides a short account of his introversion-extroversion concepts but also surveys some of his wartime research on humor and aesthetic preferences. Another aspect of Eysenck's theory may be observed in *The Inequality of Man* (London: Maurice Temple Smith, 1973), in which Eysenck enters the controversy surrounding the nature of IQ measurements. Eysenck's continued emphasis on genetic factors in personality reaches its strongest expression in the sophisticated arguments of *The Structure and Measurement of Intelligence* (New York: Springer, 1979). In a similar vein, Eysenck and Eysenck's *Psychoticism as a Dimension of Personality* (New York: Crane, Russak, 1976) discusses the statistical and experimental evidence in support of a genetic model of this new personality dimension. *Intelligence: A New Look* (New Brunswick, NJ: Transaction Publishers, 2000) is an updated version of Eysenck's defense of intelligence tests.

A three-volume collection of research papers connected to his theory was edited by Eysenck under the title *Readings in Extraversion-Introversion* (London: Staples, 1970–1971). Eysenck's low opinion of psychoanalytic theory and method may be sampled from his *Uses and Abuses of Psychology* (Baltimore: Penguin, 1953) and from his essay "Psychoanalysis: Myth or Science?" in Stanley Rachman's (Ed.) *Critical Essays on Psychoanalysis* (New York: Pergamon, 1960). Eysenck's controversial and largely erroneous position that lung cancer is not caused by smoking itself but rather by personality types to which smoking is correlated is presented in *Smoking, Health and Personality* (New Brunswick, NJ: Transaction Publishers, 2000).

Eysenck's position on behavior therapy for the neuroses is lucidly presented in *The Causes and Cures of Neurosis* (San Diego: Robert Knapp, 1965), which he co-authored with Stanley Rachman. Eysenck also edited a collection of research papers on the various forms of conditioning therapy, published *as Behavior Therapy and the Neuroses* (New York: Pergamon, 1960).

An interview with Eysenck, in which he discusses the implications of his work for psychotherapy and for unifying the whole of psychology, is contained in R. I. Evans's *The Making of Psychology* (New York: Knopf, 1976).

GLOSSARY

Ambivert: Someone who displays both introvert and extrovert behaviors.

Arousal theory: The theory that behavior is partially a function of the general state of arousal (excitation) or de-arousal (inhibition) of the cortex. This excitation-inhibition balance varies among individuals. People vary in how rapidly this cortical arousal occurs, and to what extent.

Ascending reticular activating system (ARAS): A system in the central nervous system that is responsible for patterns of excitation and inhibition of the cerebral cortex.

Autonomic nervous system (ANS): Part of the nervous system that governs the smooth muscles, the heart muscle, the glands, and the viscera and controls their functions, including physiological responses to emotion. It has two divisions, the sympathetic and the parasympathetic.

Biosocial model: A concept of personality that includes inherited biological tendencies and the influence of the interpersonal environment.

Central nervous system: The major part of the nervous systems, which is made up of the brain and spinal cord. It contains inhibition-excitation processes.

Choleric temperament: (Galen) Personality type said to be quick to action, angry, assertive, and irascible; thought to be caused by an excess of yellow bile, one of the four bodily fluids or humors.

Conditioned inhibition: A learned inhibitory response.

Drive theory: A theory that states that a bodily tension is a strong internal stimulus, felt as a need or an urge, that impels the individual to take action to relieve this arousal or tension.

Dysthymia: A chronic mood disorder involving mild, persistent depression, often found in disordered introverted neurotics.

Electroencephalogram (EEG): Recording of electrical activity in the cerebral cortex acquired via electrodes placed on the surface of the skull. EEG recordings assess the pattern of waves.

Excitatory processes: The processes that occur when the excitatory cells in the cortex start firing.

Extrovert: A personality type characterized by an outgoing nature that adapts easily to any given situation. Such an individual seeks social and physical stimulation.

Eysenck Personality Questionnaire (EPQ): A personality questionnaire Eysenck developed, based on factor analysis, that measured the dimensions of introversion-extroversion, psychoticism, and neuroticism.

Factor analysis: A statistical method that looks at how individuals' scores on groups of measures correlate with their scores on other measures. Particular variables often group themselves to form a factor.

Hedonic tone: Positive or negative feelings and appraisals related to different levels of arousal.

High-P scorer: A person with a high score on psychoticism on the Eysenck Personality Questionnaire.

Humors: In the view of Galen, the four vital fluids possessed by human beings: blood, phlegm, black bile, and yellow bile. The balance of these humors in each person was presumed to influence personality.

Hysterical disorder: The loss or impairment of some motor or sensory function for which there is no organic cause, often seen in disordered neurotic extroverts.

Inhibitory processes: The processes that act to dampen or retard the activation of the excitatory cortical cells. It hinders nervous system arousal.

Introvert: A personality type characterized by a hesitant, reflective, retiring nature. There is withdrawal from social and physical stimulation.

Limbic system: The visceral brain, which relates emotional feelings and expression, and influences the autonomic nervous system.

Melancholic temperament: (Galen) Personality type said to be sad, depressed, and anxious; thought to be caused by a predominance of black bile, one of the four bodily fluids or humors.

Neuroticism: A maladaptive personality pattern typified by negative emotionality. This condition includes traits of anxiety, depression, guilt, low self-esteem, and associated characteristics.

Phlegmatic temperament: (Galen) Personality type said to be slow to action, lethargic, and calm; thought to be caused by an excess of phlegm, one of the four bodily fluids or humors.

Postulate of individual differences: Human beings differ with respect to the speed with which excitation and inhibition are produced, and the speed with which inhibition is dissipated.

Psychasthenia: A disorder characterized by a lack of energy and low-level depression. This term is similar to Eysenck's concept of dysthymia.

Psychoticism: A maladaptive personality pattern characterized by traits of aggression, hostility, aloofness and egocentricity, and impulsiveness and related attributes. It is related to nonconformity or social deviance and to criminality.

Psychoticism-criminality hypothesis: Eysenck's hypothesis that the extreme extrovert is prone to hysterical disorders and to psychopathy or criminal behavior.

Reactive inhibition: (Hull) Neural fatigue that develops when responses are repeated.

Sanguine temperament: (Galen) Personality type said to be warmhearted, volatile, optimistic, and easygoing; thought to be caused by an excess of blood, one of the four bodily fluids or humors.

Stimulus hungry: Weak cortical arousal causes the extrovert to seek social and physical stimulation. This type is stimulus hungry.

Stimulus shy: Strong cortical arousal causes the introvert to avoid social and physical stimulation. This type is stimulus shy.

Temperament theory: A theory that categorizes people according to their pervasive patterns of behavior, which are presumably caused by biological factors. Some behavioral patterns considered often include level of activity, emotionality, and sociability. Hippocrates, Galen, Pavlov, and Eysenck, among others, developed temperament theories, which they based on different assumptions.

The Big Five: This model of personality is derived from factor analysis of terms used to describe personality. The five traits that emerge from this analysis are *neuroticism, extroversion, openness, conscientiousness,* and *agreeableness.*

Typological postulate: Patterns of introversion and extroversion as well as predispositions to types of psychological symptoms are based on differences in excitatory potential and reactive inhibition.

Chapter 18

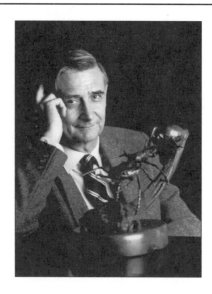

Edward O. Wilson
Evolutionary Psychology

Thinking of "Go to the ant, thou sluggard; consider her ways," *I knelt on the cobblestones to watch harvester ants carry seeds down holes to their subterranean granaries. . . . As I walked with my host back past the Temple Mount toward the Muslim Quarter, I made inner calculations of the number of ant species found within the city walls. There was a perfect logic to such eccentricity:* the million-year history of Jerusalem is at least as compelling as its past three thousand years.

Edward O. Wilson, Biophilia (emphasis added)

Grant for the moment that snake aversion does have a hereditary basis in at least some kinds of nonhuman primates. The possibility that immediately follows is that the trait evolved by natural selection.

E. O. Wilson, Biophilia

Edward O. Wilson   Born: 1929   Birmingham, Alabama
At present: Professor Emeritus, Harvard
University, Cambridge, Massachusetts

About Evolutionary Psychology

Evolutionary psychology or human sociobiology is an approach to understanding behavior that views human behaviors (including cognitions and emotions) in terms of their presumed origins in the evolutionary process. It grew out of the more inclusive field of sociobiology, which refers to "the biological basis of all forms of social behavior in all kinds of organisms, including man" (Wilson, 1978). Some of the major tenets of evolutionary psychology or human sociobiology are:

- *The process of natural selection discovered by Charles Darwin applies not only to the physical features of organisms but also to the development of instincts, or proclivities to behave in certain ways in certain circumstances.*
- *Human beings, as well as members of other species, have such instincts.*
- *Many of our current patterns of behavior, thinking, and emotion thus exist because of their adaptive significance in our evolutionary history.*
- *Evolutionary psychologists have examined a number of specific types of behavior in light of theories of evolutionary psychology. These areas include altruistic behavior, patterns of bonding, incest taboos, aggression, mate selection, and attractiveness. Numerous other areas have been explored and can be investigated using this model.*
- *One of the important mechanisms of natural selection is sexual selection, which involves both competition for mates and mate selection. Sexual selection is a major factor determining the degree to which an organism passes its genes on to the next generation.*
- *In addition to the selection of the fittest organisms through natural selection, another means of selection is inclusive fitness or kin selection, the degree to which an organism enhances the survival of relatives, who have some identical genetic material.*
- *Many of our behaviors can be understood in terms of the environment of evolutionary adaptedness (EEA) in which our hominid ancestors lived for millions of years.*
- *The concept of mental modularity, in which the brain is seen as having numerous adaptive programs, is a new area of theory and research in evolutionary psychology.*
- *Evolutionary psychology provides a new perspective for considering types of psychopathology.*

The past decade has shown a burgeoning increase of activity in this rapidly developing field, which promises to be a major integrative focus in the behavioral sciences.

The development of modern **evolutionary psychology** is best traced by following the life and thought of Edward O. Wilson. In addition, a number of other researchers and theorists have made contributions to the development of the field. These include William Hamilton, who originated the concept of inclusive fitness, Robert Trivers, who studied resource allotment and reciprocal altruism, John Tooby, Leda Cosmides, David Buss, David Barash, Randy Thornhill, and many others.

THE ROOTS OF A NATURALIST

Edward O. Wilson's parents were in the process of getting divorced when he was seven years old. They sent him, their only child, during the summer vacation to board with a family in Paradise Beach, Florida. He spent most days on the beach exploring life in the sea and on the seashore. In his autobiography, Wilson described his interactions with the natural world that summer in vivid language:

> Why do I tell you this little boy's [Wilson, himself] story of medusas, rays, and sea monsters, nearly sixty years after the fact? Because it illustrates, I think, how a naturalist is created. A child comes to the edge of deep water with a mind prepared for wonder. He is like a primitive adult of long ago . . . the experience must have been repeated countless times over thousands of generations, and it was richly rewarded. (1994, p. 11)

Sounding much like a Jungian (see Chapter 4), he continues

> The sea, the lakes, and the broad rivers . . . were impervious, it seemed, to change of any kind. The waterland was always there, timeless, invulnerable, mostly beyond reach, and inexhaustible. The child is ready to grasp this archetype, to explore and learn, but he has few words to describe his guiding emotions. Instead, he is given a compelling image that will serve in later life as a talisman, transmitting a powerful energy that directs the growth of experience and knowledge. (1994, p. 11)

He continues in the story of his life:

> Hands-on experience at the critical time, not systematic knowledge is what counts in the making of a naturalist. Better to be an untutored savage for a while, not to know the names or anatomical detail. Better to spend long stretches of time just searching and longing. (1994, pp. 11–12)

During this summer, while fishing, young Wilson pulled a small fish out of the water too fast. It flew into his face and one of its spines pierced the pupil of his right eye. He became blind in that eye as a result. His vision in his left eye was 20/10, which meant that it was more acute at close range than that of most people. In addition, he was handicapped as a naturalist by hereditary partial deafness, which made it hard for him to hear birdsongs or identify frogs by their sounds (Wilson, 1994).

In spite of these handicaps, serious deficits for a budding naturalist, the young Wilson found that his remaining senses were ideal for the study of insects. Figure 18.1 shows him pursuing this interest in a field near his home.

> I was destined to become an entomologist. . . . I would thereafter celebrate the little things of the world, the animals that can be picked up between thumb and forefinger and brought close for inspection. (Wilson, 1994, p. 15)

BOX 18.1   *Only Connect . . .*

Wilson's compensatory behavior in response to his partial blindness is consistent with Alfred Adler's (Chapter 5) early concept of organ inferiority as a motivating source of superiority strivings. In this view, the way individuals adapt to life is likely to be shaped by their reactions to their organ inferiorities. Wilson's compensatory behavior took the form of intense scientific curiosity regarding insect behavior and, eventually, a desire to understand and even protect the natural world. Whereas Adler's concept of *social interest* stressed a concern for the well-being of other people, Wilson emphasized the caring for and love of all life, *biophilia* (Wilson, 1984). His efforts to make the world a better place for generations to come is also consistent with Erik Erikson's (Chapter 8) concept of *generativity*.

Figure 18.1 Edward O. Wilson at age 13 in a field near his home in Mobile, Alabama. In this photo, young Wilson evidences his already strong level of curiosity about the insect world.

After his parents' divorce, Wilson eventually lived with his father and his new wife. He remained an only child. The family moved numerous times. Thus, young Edward had to transfer from one school to another until he finally graduated from high school in 1945. During his period of schooling, he formed a close bond with nature and the various plants and animals he found there. They provided reliable companionship. He loved nature and was fascinated by all the phenomena of life that he explored (Wilson, 1994).

Wilson majored in biology in college and received a bachelor's and a master's degree in this field. His mother offered to support him in medical school, but Edward's mind and heart were already set on becoming an entomologist. He first went to the University of Tennessee but transferred to the Harvard program, which attracted him in large part because it possessed the world's largest ant collection and had a distinguished reputation in the field of myrmecology—the study of ants (Wilson, 1994).

In 1953, as a very promising young scholar, Wilson was appointed a Junior Fellow in Harvard University's Society of Fellows. This was a three-year appointment that indicated recognition of a young scholar's promise and provided freedom and support for research. Wilson and the other young fellows stood as the initiatory statement was read to them:

> You have been selected . . . for your promise of notable contribution to knowledge and thought. That promise you must redeem with your whole intellectual and moral force. . . . You will seek not a near, but a distant, objective, and you will not be satisfied with what you have done. All that you may achieve or discover you will regard as a fragment of a larger pattern, which from his separate approach every true scholar is striving. . . . (Wilson, 1994, p. 145)

As a member of the Society of Fellows, Wilson was not only encouraged for his research as a young biologist but was able to have many discussions with leading scholars in a variety of fields. He heard the ideas of philosophers, sociologists, and leading scientists. This experience at Harvard broadened the perspectives of the young naturalist from Alabama. According to Wilson,

> The Society proceeded to transform my self-image and my career. Its greatest immediate impact was a sharp rise in my expectations. . . . I thought, I have three years to justify the confidence placed in me, the same amount of time it took to make Eagle Scout. No problem. The Society's alumni and Senior fellows were outstanding achievers; they included Nobel and Pulitzer winners, I thought. That's a reasonable standard to shoot for. (1994, p. 145)

So encouraged and stimulated, Wilson continued a career that eventually would have an impact on our thinking not only about insects but also about human behavior.

ENCOUNTERING LORENZ AND HIS IDEAS

In the fall of 1953, Niko Tinbergen and Konrad Lorenz, the founders of the field of ethology, arrived to present their work at Harvard University. Wilson attended the presentation and found himself intrigued by Lorenz and his ideas:

> He [Lorenz] was a prophet of the dais, passionate, angry, and importunate. He hammered us with phrases soon to beome famous in the behavioral sciences: imprinting, ritualization, aggressive drive. . . . He had come to proclaim a new approach to the study of behavior. Instinct has been reinstated, he said; the role of learning was grossly overestimated by B. F. Skinner and other behaviorists; we must now pass on to a new direction. (Wilson, 1994, pp. 285–286)

Lorenz subsequently explained that he saw most animal behavior as preordained. He saw the elements of behavior as **fixed action patterns.** He defined such *fixed action patterns* as:

> . . . sequences of movements programmed in the brain by heredity, which unfold through the life of an animal in response to particular signals in the natural environment. . . . (Wilson, 1994, p. 286)

Lorenz said that, when such fixed action patterns were:

> . . . triggered at the right place and time, they lead the animal through a sequence of correct steps to find food, to avoid predators, and to reproduce. The animal does not require previous experience in order to survive. It has only to obey. (Wilson, 1994, p. 286)

Wilson quickly saw the relevance of the idea of fixed action patterns for his research into the social behavior of insects:

> It occurred to me immediately that the fixed-action patterns of ants and other social insects are triggered by chemicals. . . . The idea of fixed-action patterns and releases suggested to me a way to enter this unexplored world of ant communication. The method should, I reasoned, consist of a set of straightforward steps; break ant social behavior into fixed-action patterns; then by trial and error determine which secretions contain the releaser; finally, separate and identify the active chemicals in the secretions. (Wilson, 1994, p. 288).

In the late 1950s and the early 1960s, as a member of the Harvard faculty, Wilson became increasingly interested in population biology and the related field of **evolutionary biology,** which he believed could, along with the burgeoning field of molecular biology with its newly discovered DNA, serve to unify the field of biology. Wilson wrote an article (Wilson, 1959) based on his research, which indicated the evolution of a certain species of ant toward smaller and smaller varieties. The current form of this species of ant is much smaller than that of its evolutionary ancestors.

From the early 1950s through the early1970s, Wilson, often working with other naturalists and students, made many interesting creative and theoretically important contributions to the study of ants, the workings of ant society, the evolution of species of ants and ant castes, and the use of chemical trails among ants. He even co-developed with a graduate student, Daniel Simberloff, a method called "experimental zoogeography" (Wilson, 1994, pp. 260–281) in which very small islands of the Florida Keys were stripped of life by fumigation and then species were observed and counted as they reestablished themselves on the island. Simberloff and Wilson were able to arrive at the principle that a specific number of species exists for any island, based on its size and location. Such findings eventually had great significance for the conservation movement, because they implied that only large contiguous areas would allow large numbers of species to exist.

Before proceeding further with the development of Wilson's thinking, we can review the contributions of Charles Darwin and his theory of evolution by natural selection a century before. Darwin's theory of natural selection provided a unifying view of nature that was an integral and basic part of Wilson's thinking.

DARWIN'S (AND WALLACE'S) THEORY OF NATURAL SELECTION

Charles Darwin (1809–1882) is generally credited with originating the theory of biological evolution. As is the case with most other major theories in the history of science, he did not come up with these ideas in a vacuum. Alfred Russel Wallace, another English naturalist, engaged in almost identical reasoning at about the same time. After some correspondence between the two, excerpts from Darwin and Wallace's writings were presented to the Linnaean Society in London. The date was June 30, 1858. A year later, Darwin sent Wallace a copy of *On the Origin of Species by Means of Natural Selection* (Darwin, 1859). Indicating some awareness of the revolutionary significance his ideas would have, he included a note saying, "God knows what the public will think" (Darwin as quoted in Zimmer, 2001, p. 46).

There are many similarities between the lives of Charles Darwin and Edward O. Wilson. Like Wilson a century later, Darwin was a naturalist. He too was fascinated by the natural world and wanted to learn from it. He also rejected medicine as a career in favor of becoming a naturalist. Darwin and Wilson both engaged in worldwide travels to conduct their studies and explorations. Darwin sailed to the Galapagos as a young man, Wilson traveled to the Amazon, the South Pacific, and the Florida Keys. Darwin and Wilson were independent, very logical thinkers, and excellent writers. Like Wilson, Darwin was also aware of the intellectual currents of his time in fields outside of biology. In both cases, their thinking aroused a good deal of vehement opposition and controversy that did not cause either of them to waver in their thinking.

Darwin proposed and argued for the concept of natural selection as a mechanism for biological evolution in *On the Origin of Species by Means of Natural Selection* (1859). The proposal of the mechanism of **natural selection** accompanied by the examples Darwin provided comprised a very persuasive argument for the process of biological evolution. In addition, Darwin developed a well-articulated theory of **sexual selection** (1871).

Introductory biology courses generally cover the logical rationale of Darwin's theory of natural selection:

- There is natural variation among organisms.
- There is a struggle for survival as not all organisms can survive.
- Those with characteristics that lead to greater survivability and reproductive success are likely to have more descendants.
- These descendants in turn will more likely have those qualities that have led to greater survival.

Darwin, who was familiar with the mating of domestic animals, compared this process of natural selection to the process of **artificial selection,** in which breeders of animals and plants select those with the most desirable traits to breed. Over time, the animals and plants are likely to have the traits considered desirable by the breeder. For example, one of the authors of the present text has bred guppies. Using artificial selection, he has developed a strain with long, black flowing tails and largely black bodies. They do not breed one hundred percent true but are distinctive and far more striking than the typical guppy.

The idea of evolution had been around before Darwin, but no explanation in accordance with biological science had been proposed. Jean-Baptiste de Lamarck (1744–1829), a French biological theorist, had proposed the idea that characteristics acquired during an organism's lifetime are inherited. Lamarck's explanation of how giraffes came to have long necks, for example, was that generations of ancestors each stretched their necks a little bit. Unfortunately for the viability of Lamarck's theory, no biological mechanism for such a process could be found. Darwin's theory relied simply on the idea of natural variation and the selection of the fittest, in this case giraffes with longer necks. Darwin's theory did not accept the idea of such **inheritance of acquired characteristics.** Rather, his theory focused on the notion that the taller animals would have greater survivability and thus be more likely to pass the characteristic of a long neck than their shorter-neck giraffe peers would be to pass the characteristic of a shorter neck on to the next generation. They would be more likely to survive in times of drought and the next generation would thus tend toward higher necks. The discovery of genes as the material basis for inheritance was in accordance with Darwinian rather than Lamarckian principles.

Darwin also realized that some of the selective pressure on a species was based on sexual selection: that is on the fact that some individual organisms were more able to compete with others, to attract mates and reproduce more successfully than others. Within-species reproductive competition led to the selection of certain characteristics. Some of these characteristics were those that permitted individuals to gain an advantage over others. Among mammals, direct competition among males for females has led to the development of aggressivity, larger size, sharp teeth, horns, and antlers in some species, and a variety of other behaviors and physical traits designed to help their possessor win out over other males. In many species, competitive behaviors are at least partially ritualized. In both sexes, there has been an evolution of features and behaviors designed to attract the opposite sex. Good examples of the kinds of characteristics that are selected are the bright plumage of some male birds or many of the secondary sexual characteristics of human males and females (Darwin, 1871). Mate selection strategies as well as competition between potential mates are both behaviors of interest to contemporary evolutionary psychologists.

Regarding Darwin's theory, it is fascinating to note that he had knowledge neither of genes nor of DNA. He derived his theory from commonly observed phenomena, his own exploration of the variety of species, particularly in the Galapagos, and his deep thought and reflection about the processes that might be occurring in nature. His theory of evolution was based on thousands of observations, but it did not grow out of experimental laboratory research. If there was an experimenter, it was nature herself. Darwin was an observer of the results of the experiments of nature.

Robert M. Young (1996) has reviewed the various sources of ideas leading to Darwin's theory and commented that, to a large extent, Darwin extrapolated from the competitive no-holds-barred capitalism of the eighteenth century and social doctrines compatible with such an economic system to the entire biological world. In a sense, he was reasoning from his culturally embedded understanding of human society to that of all life. It was the reverse of what the naturalist Edward O. Wilson would do a century later when, getting ahead of our story, he applied ideas drawn from biology to human society.

Darwin is often overlooked in comparison with the more modern theorists of evolutionary psychology that this chapter will consider. In part, this is because Darwin's views about the evolution of human behavior were embedded in his overall theory. In addition to the theory of natural selection itself and the idea of sexual selection, some of Darwin's contributions most relevant to the eventual development of evolutionary psychology are:

- Darwin saw the biological makeup and form of an organism, whether it is a reptile or a human, as part of a single whole, and he recognized that organisms inherit not only their biological makeup but many instincts as well—that is, proclivities to behave in certain ways.

- Also, he focused explicitly on emotional expression (Darwin, 1872) and the similarity between human emotional expression and those of other primates, thus indicating the evolutionary origins of much of human expression of emotions.

- Finally, he focused on the development of a moral sense as part of his understanding of the evolutionary legacy of mankind (Darwin, 1859).

These subjects—particularly those of an evolutionary basis for human morality and altruistic behavior—were largely ignored for a century after Darwin and did not begin to surface again until after Hamilton's contribution of the theory of kin selection in 1964.

WILSON ENCOUNTERS HAMILTON'S IDEAS

London-based evolutionary biologist, William Hamilton, then a graduate student at Oxford, published groundbreaking articles (1964a, 1964b). These papers presented a new idea, **inclusive fitness,** that would be vital in the development of neo-Darwinism and eventually of evolutionary psychology. Hamilton proposed that biological selection operated not only in choosing the most fit individual, but that individuals might be selected because they enhanced the overall fitness of related individuals. Another term that was applied to the concept was *kin selection.* It took over a century for a major addition to Darwin's ideas to be proposed, and Hamilton was the person who did it. His articles have subsequently been cited thousands of times in scientific and scholarly publications.

Wilson, a leading scholar in evolutionary theory and insect behavior, reading Hamilton's articles while traveling along the East Coast of the United States by train, quickly realized that Hamilton's ideas constituted a major paradigm shift in evolutionary theory. According to Wilson:

> What made Hamilton's idea immediately attractive was that it helped to resolve the classic problem in evolutionary theory of how self-sacrifice can become a genetically fixed trait. It might seem on first thought—without considering kin selection—that selfishness must reign complete in the living world, and that cooperation can never appear except to enhance selfish ends. But no, if an altruistic act helps relatives, it increases the survival of genes that are identical with those of the altruist, just as the case in parents and offspring, (Wilson, 1994, p. 317)

Wilson could see that Hamilton's ideas, as he proposed them, were immediately relevant to understanding the evolutionary rationale underlying the self-sacrificial behavior of the social insects. It was apparent to him that Hamilton's theory could explain such behavior in a way that Darwin's theory never could.

Hamilton's principle was **kin selection,** an inherent and inherited predisposition to act altruistically for relatives (kin or kinfolk). Most simply expressed, it works like this: an individual who is closely related to other individuals is likely to have many genes in common. That individual whose behavior enhances the survival of relatives, or *kin,* is thus likely also to promote the survival and reproduction of genes identical to those in his or her body.

Hamilton's proposal prompted a revolution in thought that led to contemporary evolutionary psychology. The switch was from focusing on differential survival of the fittest person to differential survival of the fittest gene. This gene-centered, or **selfish gene theory** (Dawkins, 1989), indicated that a gene might be selected not only if it enhanced the survivability of the individual organism in which it was found, but also if that organism acted in such a way as to enhance the survivability of other organisms with the same gene. With this shift in focus from the "fit individual" to the "selfish gene," evolutionary theory was able to accommodate not only nature "red in tooth and claw" but also the evolutionary value of prosocial and altruistic behaviors. It became a theory of much greater interest and relevance to psychologists.

Good examples of inclusive fitness, kin selection, or selfish genes can be found in an ant colony, one of Wilson's most familiar areas of study. Hamilton's theory provided a rationale for the "altruistic" behavior of a nonreproducing member of the colony such as a worker ant or, more dramatically, a soldier ant. In such cases, the activities of these ants, that do not reproduce themselves, engage in activities that enhance the survivability of the colony and, specifically the survivability of genes in the queen or males, genes which are identical to many genes in the soldier or worker ants.

David Barash drew attention to the example of a theorist, Ronald Fisher, who in the 1920s anticipated the evolutionary significance of altruism and even altruistic sacrifice. Fisher understood that a brightly colored, but bad-tasting caterpillar killed by a hungry bird would serve to make it less likely that the bird would attack other similarly colored caterpillars (Barash, 2001, p. 45). However, Fisher's ideas were that of sacrifice for the common good and did not include Hamilton's more precise and valid theory of kin selection.

A personal example of kin selection may be helpful as an illustration of the kin selection process. One of the authors' grandmothers had a sister who never married or had any children of her own. The married sister devoted much of her life to helping rear her married sister's six children, her nieces and nephews. Her genes did not directly reproduce themselves, but the family members she helped nurture in infancy and childhood had many genes identical to her own. Her altruistic maternal nature thus promoted the survival of genetic material identical to her own, even though it was passed on from her sister to her children, the aunt's nieces and nephews.

One concept that evolutionary psychologists emphasize, the meaning of the term **altruism.** In relation to the concepts of kin selection, inclusive fitness, and the selfish gene, the meaning is somewhat different and more general than the usual usage of the term. The term *altruism,* as used in ordinary discourse, usually refers to behavior that is guided by an altruistic intent. From the point of view of modern evolutionary theory, *altruism* refers to behavior or activity that may occur with or without any conscious altruistic intent.

FROM INSECT SOCIETIES TO SOCIOBIOLOGY TO HUMAN NATURE

At the beginning of the 1970s, Wilson was writing a book on the behavior of the social insects. This book, *Insect Societies* (1971), applied the principles of sociobiology, which included natural selection, sexual selection, and Hamilton's new ideas of kin selection as a unifying construct in the structure and functioning of insect society. At that time, Wilson envisaged proceeding even further in the future. He was already thinking about applying the principles of **sociobiology** to other species, even including vertebrates. He wrote:

In spite of the phylogenetic remoteness of vertebrates and insects and the basic distinction between their respective personal and impersonal systems of communication, these two groups of animals have evolved social behaviors that are similar in degree of complexity and convergent in many important details. This fact conveys a special promise that sociobiology can eventually be derived from the first principles of population and behavioral biology and developed into a single, mature science. (Wilson, 1971, p. 460)

In his next book, *Sociobiology: The New Synthesis* (1975), Wilson summarized his understanding of the principles of sociobiology to the whole array of social organisms, from colonies of bacteria, coral colonies, and social insects to social vertebrates, including the great apes. Finally, in the last chapter, he included in his analysis a sociobiological view of human behavior. He wrote that, if we were zoologists from outer space:

. . . the humanities and social science [would] shrink to specialized branches of biology—history, biography and fictions are the research protocols of human ethnology; and anthropology and sociology together constitute the sociobiology of a single primate species. (1975, p. 547)

Later, in response to criticism, Wilson said that he did not see anything wrong in including humans in *Sociobiology: The New Synthesis*. After all, he reasoned:

[Human] history did not begin 10,000 years ago. . . . It spans the 2 million years of the life of the genus *Homo*. Deep history—by which I mean biological history—made us what we are, no less than culture. (1994, p. 328)

In 1978 Wilson published *On Human Nature,* which fully focused on the relevance of sociobiology for human behavior. This book brought together many observations and areas of understanding to form a basis for a human branch of sociobiology, *human sociobiology.* Some topics that Wilson examined from the point of view of sociobiology include: aggression, altruism, bonding, child development, culture, extroversion, familial behavior, gender differences, heroism, introversion, learning, love, prepared learning, rites of passage, reciprocal altruism, sex, the soul, and warfare. As a mature scholar, Wilson still maintained his interest in ant behavior (Figure 18.2).

Sociobiology: A New Synthesis and *On Human Nature* were controversial books because they persuasively challenged prevailing environmentalist theories in psychology and the social science with new insights (Wilson, 1994, pp. 330–353). Some prominent critics incorrectly believed that Wilson's ideas were racist. Environmental determinists disagreed with the idea of a fundamental human nature and wanted to think that people could be molded to behave in radically new ways (see Watson, Chapter 14). Alcock (2001) recounts an incident illustrating the controversial nature of sociobiology in the late 1970s:

On 15 February, 1978, a young woman carefully poured a pitcher of ice water onto the head of Edward O. Wilson while he sat waiting to address an audience at the annual meeting of the American Association for the Advancement of Science. A band of accomplices joined their pitcher-pouring confederate on stage to wave placards chanting, "Wilson, you're all wet." (p. 3)

Today, much of this controversy has died down. The issue now for psychologists is to sort out the degree to which inherited behavioral proclivities play a role in our behavior and to what extent we are free to change.

Many of the ideas that Wilson put forth in *Sociobiology: A New Synthesis* and *On Human Nature* can be viewed as the presentation of the reasoning underlying a new field and the generation of ideas, many of which would be explored in the future by generations of researchers. Wilson's book has served as a basic foundation for the now burgeoning evolutionary psychology movement.

Figure 18.2 Edward O. Wilson studying ants in Costa Rica in 1984. As a middle-aged man, Wilson still had an avid interest in ant behavior.

In the last decade, the term, **evolutionary psychology,** has increasingly been used for that sub-area of sociobiology that focuses on human behavior, both individually and in groups. The term *evolutionary psychology* also emphasizes the relevance of evolutionary theory for the different fields of psychology (including abnormal psychology, cognitive psychology, developmental psychology, learning, neuropsychological personality theory, sensation and perception, and social psychology) just as the term **evolutionary medicine** indicates a field that explores diseases and their treatments from the point of view of sociobiology. The term **human sociobiology,** favored by Wilson (2001), emphasizes the connectedness of human studies with the study of other organisms.

Before considering further developments in the thinking of evolutionary psychologists, we can examine some of the evolutionary concepts in classical personality theories.

EVOLUTIONARY CONCEPTS IN CLASSICAL PERSONALITY THEORIES

Modern evolutionary psychologists are not the first to take evolutionary theory into account in their explorations of human behavior. Many of the classical personality theorists also considered the process of biological evolution as relevant to their work. They drew on various elements of evolutionary theory and applied it in different ways. Their efforts to base personality theory on evolutionary concepts were hampered, however, by their lack of expertise in evolutionary biology or by inadequacies in the theories that were available to them at the time of their theorizing. Most of them completed their theories before the development of Hamilton's concept of *inclusive fitness*.

Freud was familiar with Darwin's theory, referred to him often in his works, and had an extensive library of the writings of Darwin and related theorists (Ritvo, 1990). Freud's theorizing was very much concerned with the instinctual makeup of humans. His ideas of sexual and aggressive instincts were based as much or more on his reading of Darwin's idea of selection of the fittest as on clinical observation. Freud's *id* contained biological drives, which had evolved through the process of natural selection. He understood altruism and abstinence from behaviors hurtful to others as superego functions, which could be understood not as proclivities based on biology, but as learned forms of behavior. Today much altruistic behavior is seen as a biological proclivity based on the idea of inclusive fitness or kin selection.

In addition to Darwin's idea of natural selection, Freud referred to what he thought to be the early experiences of humanity in *Totem and Taboo* (1913b) in his derivation of many concepts (Freud, 1913b). Freud's resort to the inheritance of ancestral experiences was a throwback to discredited Lamarckian thinking, reviewed earlier in this chapter.

Does Pathology Recapitulate Phylogeny?

Freud specifically proposed that the transference and narcissistic neuroses form a chronology that parallels and recapitulates in individual development the evolutionary development of the human species **(phylogeny).** Specifically, he proposed that if the transference and narcissistic neuroses are arranged according to the developmental period in which they typically occur, a pattern emerges that parallels evolutionary development:

> . . . anxiety hysteria, almost without precondition, is the earliest [neurosis], closely followed by conversion hysteria (from about the fourth year); somewhat later in prepuberty (9–10) obsessional neurosis appears in children. The narcissistic neuroses are absent in childhood. Of these, dementia praecox [schizophrenia] in classic form is [an] illness of the puberty years, paranoia approaches the mature years, and melancholia-mania the same time period, otherwise not specifiable. (Freud, 1915d, p. 12)

Freud was wrong about the absence of what he called "the narcissistic neuroses" (especially schizophrenia) in childhood, but that was the prevailing view in his day. Nevertheless, he argued that each characteristic neurosis represents a regression to:

> . . . phases that the whole human race had to go through at some time from the beginning to the end of the Ice Age, so that at that time all human beings were the way only some of them are today, by virtue of hereditary tendency and by means of new acquisition. (Freud, 1915d, p. 13)

What can we make of Freud's speculations? They are of a piece with his speculations along evolutionary lines in such works as *Totem and Taboo* and *Beyond the Pleasure Principle*. They are fraught with biological, psychological, and anthropological errors and omissions. Nevertheless, they represent an imaginative attempt to bring order to a wealth of observations in a way that was consistent with Freud's central vision of metapsychology as the overarching theory of psychoanalysis as a science. Freud extended the biologist Ernst Haeckel's dictum ("**Ontogeny** recapitulates phylogeny"—development of the individual embryo parallels the stages of human evolution) with his own version: *pathology* recapitulates phylogeny. Today, Haeckel's concept is a historical curiosity no longer considered valid by biologists.

Jung's Lamarckian Views

Carl Jung (Chapter 4) also drew on ideas having to do with evolution in developing his theories. Jung did not believe that Darwin's ideas of selection of the fittest could adequately explain the collective unconscious and its contents. In Jung's view, all of the archetypes and their contents were derived from the repetitive experiences of our ancestors over thousands and thousands of generations. The collective unconscious was the sum total of such experiences, and the specific archetypes were, so to speak, crystallizations of experience. For example, the mother archetype was said to be the result of innumerable generations of human experiences with their mothers. Again, it should be pointed out that these Lamarckian ideas are now discredited. There is no biological mechanism to explain the inheritance of experiences.

So, Jung's view—similar to that of many contemporary evolutionary psychologists—was that humans inherit many proclivities to behave in different ways. But his idea of an explanatory mechanism was far different from that of contemporary biology or psychology. For the most part, his theories appear to be most consistent with the discredited Lamarckian view (i.e., the inheritance of acquired characteristics).

Nonetheless, many of Jung's conclusions, although without a valid biological basis, are often very similar to Wilson's views of human nature. Jung, like Wilson, wrote of deeply embedded proclivities to think, experience reality, and behave in specific ways. He spoke very clearly of the similarity of his concept of archetype with instincts in the animal world (Evans, 1964).

Adler, Erikson, and Evolutionary Theory

Alfred Adler (Chapter 5) drew conclusions based on evolutionary theory that were different from either Freud or Jung for understanding human behavior. In Adler's view, the prime motive of superiority was another way of referring to optimal adaptation. Adler believed that evolutionary factors motivated each individual to achieve maximal fitness ("superiority") in his or her environment and to overcome any inferiority feelings he or she might have. This emphasis on adaptive fitness was far different from Freud's view of our biological legacy as primarily consisting of sexual and aggressive drives.

Adler's notion of the ideal motive as an altruistic promotion of life wherever one found it is very similar to the importance of altruism in current evolutionary psychology. It did not seem to be based on any biological theory of the time.

Erik Erikson's concepts of *ritual* and *ritualization* (Chapter 8) were derived from the evolutionary views of ethologists. He thought people engaged in such patterns, as did many other vertebrates, but endowed them with human levels of meaning. This is consistent with Erikson's view of the biologically based psychosexual stages of Freud as replete with interpersonal significance.

Erikson's idea of the importance of generativity in midlife and beyond is consistent with the kin selection theory. Once a person is no longer able to reproduce, his or her evolutionary value lies only in the promotion of the viability of others. The healthy middle-aged person in Erikson's epigenetic theory moves toward helping the next generation.

Behaviorism and Evolutionary Theory

Ivan Pavlov and B. F. Skinner (Chapter 14), in their studies of conditioning, tried to demonstrate how organisms had inherited mechanisms that enabled them flexibly to adapt to a variety of conditions in which they might find themselves. In their view, the possibility of being conditioned *itself* was adaptive.

Skinner, in fact, wrote a paper in which he indicated the parallels between operant conditioning and the survival of the fittest in evolution (1981). Just as Darwin indicated that natural selection depended upon choosing the most adaptive of many variations so,

Table 18.1   Comparing Natural Selection with Operant Conditioning

	Darwin's natural selection	*Skinner's operant conditioning*
Variation in:	Individuals of a species.	Behaviors of an individual organism.
Selective mechanism:	Survival of the fittest.	Reinforcement or punishment.
Consequence:	"Fit" organisms selected.	Reinforced behaviors of a single organism persist.

in conditioning, reinforcement of adaptive behavior through rewards or punishments shaped behavior (see Table 18.1).

Pavlov and Skinner originally assumed that all neutral stimuli could serve equally well as conditioning stimuli and that different behaviors could be equally conditioned. Findings contrary to these assumptions eventually surfaced. It is noteworthy that these contrary findings are along the lines of what might be expected if organisms had behavioral predispositions or instincts to act in certain ways that were adaptive from an evolutionary point of view.

In a landmark study, John Garcia and Kurt Koelling (1966) exposed rats to specific light, noise, and taste stimuli as they licked water from a drinking tube. Following drinking, the rats were exposed to radiation of sufficient dosage to induce nausea. If Pavlovian conditioning were automatic, then each of the stimuli preceding the unconditioned stimulus (irradiation-nausea) would become an effective avoidance cue in the future. But, in fact, the rats learned to avoid only the sweet taste of the water. Sweet, but not "bright" or "noisy" water became associated with illness. A second group of rats was subjected to the same procedure, but electric shock was used in place of the radiation. This electric shock group learned to avoid the "bright" and "noisy" water, but not the sweet water. Apparently, animals are more "prepared" to associate nausea with taste cues than with auditory or visual cues. Or, more generally, rats are biologically prepared to associate specific stimuli with particular effects while selectively ignoring other stimuli (see also Garcia, McGowan, Ervin, & Koelling, 1968).

Martin Seligman (1970, 1971, 1972) and Hans Eysenck (1976) have argued that organisms evolved to learn some stimulus relationships more effectively than others. An animal that rapidly learns to make associations, for example, between taste and subsequent illness is likely to survive by avoiding poisonous foods after only one taste. However, if all stimuli impinging on the animal at the time of the first poisoning were equally conditionable, its chances of repeatedly ingesting larger doses of the same noxious food increase.

In a similar way, human phobias reflect a limited number of feared stimuli rather than all possible objects in the neurotic person's world of dangers. Phobic people fear dangerous animals such as snakes and spiders; they fear high places, cramped places, and dark places; it is very rare they have phobias of cocktail tables, stereophonic receivers, flowered wallpaper, or killer Twinkies. Our human forebears had legitimate survival needs reflected in their fears of snakes, spiders, and high and dark places, so an innate predisposition to be fearful of and to avoid certain classes of stimuli was favored by natural selection (Rachman, 1978). Such stimuli have been called "prepared" stimuli and the fears associated with them "prepared" fears on the assumption that evolution selection pressures have somehow selected nervous systems with special sensitivities (Seligman, 1970). By the same token, such "preparation" also limits the range of effective classically conditionable stimuli.

It is well to note that alternative explanations of why some stimuli are more easily conditionable than others have been offered (Bandura, 1977b, pp. 75 ff.). There is some evidence to suggest that instead of innate "preparedness" as the facilitator in some learning, it is rather the organism's capacity to discriminate selectively among stimuli and to be sensitive to the delay between the stimulus and its noxious effects (e.g., Krane & Wagner, 1975).

In the field of operant conditioning, similar biological and evolutionarily based limitations have been found. A husband and wife team of professional animal trainers, Keller and Marian Breland, reported an amusing and important set of limitations on the operant shaping techniques. Breland and Breland (1961) had, for a number of years, adopted the behavioristic spirit of the times: "If it moves, we can shape it." But they ran into trouble.

Working with a raccoon for a bank display, the Brelands tried to shape the animal to pick up coins one at a time and drop them into a container for positive reinforcement. Shaping worked well in getting the racoon to pick up two coins, but he seemed not to be able to let go of them, despite the fact that reinforcement was available only when both coins had been dropped in the "bank." As the frustrated reinforcers reported:

> He would rub [the coin] up against the inside of the container, pull it back out, clutch it firmly for several seconds. However, he would finally turn it loose and receive his food reinforcement. Then the final contingency . . . that he pick up both coins and put them in the container.
>
> Now the raccoon really had problems (and so did we). Not only could he not let go of the coins, but he spent seconds, even minutes, rubbing them together (in a most miserly fashion), and dipping them into the container. He carried on this behavior to such an extent that the practical application we had in mind—a display featuring a raccoon putting money in a piggy bank—simply was not feasible. The rubbing behavior became worse and worse as time went on, in spite of nonreinforcement. (Breland & Breland, 1961, p. 682)

The recalcitrant raccoon was merely behaving instinctually, "washing" and rubbing clean his food—or anything else that found its way into his paws. Raccoons were not the only animals whose conditioning was affected by their instinctual behavioral proclivities:

> In a similarly frustrating fashion, attempts to train a pig to pick up a silver dollar, carry it to a "piggy bank" and deposit it were blocked by the pig's increasing slowness, his constantly dropping it to root it along the ground with his nose, toss it in the air, root it, and so on. (Breland & Breland, 1961, p. 683)

Like the raccoon's, the pig's behavior could be shaped only to the point at which its instinctual repertoire of behaviors took dominance.

"Instinctual drift," as the Brelands termed it, was responsible for the human frustration in these cases of well applied but futile operant conditioning techniques:

> The general principle seems to be that whenever an animal has strong instinctive behaviors in the area of the conditioned response, after continued running the organism will drift toward the instinctive behavior even to the delay or preclusion of the reinforcement. In a very boiled-down, simplified form, it might be stated as "Learned behavior drifts toward instinctive behavior." (Breland & Breland, 1961, p. 684)

Even the most trainable animals are not the models of environmental plasticity envisioned by the early radical behaviorists. Biological limits, species-specific behaviors, and innate predispositions all place a ceiling on the effectiveness and reliability of operant conditioning (but see Skinner, 1975). It is worth mentioning in passing that in an updated account of the "misbehavior of organisms," Marian Breland-Bailey (formerly Marian Breland) and Robert Bailey (1993) have made clear that their experiences never caused them to dismiss reinforcement theory. Rather, in more sophisticated fashion, they had tried to understand the frustrating results they sometimes encountered as a window to understanding the limitations of operant theory.

FURTHER DEVELOPMENTS IN EVOLUTIONARY PSYCHOLOGICAL THINKING

We have already considered the importance of:

- the original Darwinian theory of evolution by natural selection,
- sexual selection, and
- the kin selection process

The insight that such processes have influenced the development of human as well as animal behavior has also been considered.

Some additional ideas that are central in the development of modern evolutionary psychology include: the importance of the environment of evolutionary adaptedness (EEA), reciprocal or "soft-core" altruism, the modularity of brain functioning, and the idea of the emergence of new behaviors through the process of exaptation. A timetable of developments in evolutionary psychology is presented in Table 18.2.

Why the Environment of Evolutionary Adaptedness (EEA) Is So Important

A concept of great significane to many evolutionary psychologists is called, "the **environment of evolutionary adaptedness (EEA)**." This is the presumed environment in which our ancestors lived for about seven million years. The switch to agriculture as a source of food is thought to have occurred only in the last 10,000 years. Our early ancestors were hunter-gatherers and the selective pressures of their difficult environments for millions of years have shaped much of our genetically determined behavior. Consequently, many of the genes underlying our behavior may or may not be suited to our lives in a modern, industrialized world (Tooby & DeVore, 1987, Gaulin & McBurney, 2001, pp. 88–90).

An example of the impact of the EEA is our sweet tooth and love of sugar, as well as our love of fatty meats. In the EEA—and probably for millions of years among our

Table 18.2   Evolutionary Psychology Timetable

Theorist	*Year*	*Discovery or publication*
Charles Darwin, Alfred Wallace	1859	Evolution by natural selection
Charles Darwin	1871	Sexual selection
Konrad Lorenz & Niko Tinbergen	1951	Fixed action patterns
William Hamilton	1964	Inclusive fitness, kin selection
Robert Trivers	1972	Reciprocal altruism
Numerous authors	early 1970s	Early formulations of the impact of early human, hominid environments on current human behavior
Edward O. Wilson	1975	*Sociobiology, The New Synthesis* published
Edward O. Wilson	1978	Sociobiology applied to humans
Jerry Fodor	1988	Modularity of mind
John Tooby & Leda Cosmides	1990	More modules, EEA elaborated

prehominid ancestors—a sweet tooth and a craving for sweetness were very helpful in raising the caloric intake of our ancestors. Hominids with a sweet tooth and a craving for sugary items were more likely to find leaves, stems, flowers, and plants with higher caloric value. Love of fatty meats also helped provide adequate caloric intake in the EEA.

In today's society, with its processed foods and its plentiful food supply, the proclivity to eat sugary foods and fatty meats has contributed to obesity, illness, and death. Eating sugary foods and fatty meats are risk factors for a number of life-threatening diseases including heart disease (from arterial blockages) and diabetes. Most of us are outliving our hominid ancestors, but this knowledge is not comforting to a person in his or her fifties who develops heart failure.

It has been speculated that the EEA included a very competitive, politicized, social environment. A text on evolutionary psychology, in describing social aspects of the EEA, portrays a situation not unlike a contemporary academic department or part of a large corporation.

> . . . hominids regularly associated with other members of their species. Their social groups were fairly small, consisting of fewer than one hundred individuals, and were semiclosed. As a result, hominids typically interacted with a limited set of associates whom they know as distinct individuals. (Gaulin & McBurney, 2001, p. 89)

And, perhaps more to the point:

> Within hominid groups, social interactions were complex. Members of the social group were potentially valuable allies whose favor was worth cultivating for the benefits they could provide in times of shortage or illness or when cooperative activities could increase foraging yields. However, as constant companions, other members of the groups were also often significant competitors for important resources. Gaining and keeping reliable allies without forfeiting too many key resources must have presented a constantly shifting set of social challenges. (Gaulin & McBurney, 2001, p. 89)

The more things change, the more they remain the same. We might consider human behavior to include not only altruistic behavior—as per the kin selection theory—but also tactics and strategies for dealing with others. Perhaps humans could properly be called, "the political animal."

In summary, the EEA can serve as a source of hypotheses for the genetic origins of behaviors that do not seem adaptive in the current environment.

Problems with the EEA Theory

The use of the EEA has a number of built-in problems. First, we have reason to doubt how accurate our knowledge of the EEA actually is. After all, we were not around seven million years ago to observe the behavior of our ancestors. We must extrapolate their behavior from the study of primates and from the findings of paleoanthropologists.

Also, the EEA is a rather long span of time. How do we account for the fact that our ancestors may have lived in different climatic periods, that they may have had different modes of adaptation at different times and in different eras? Are any of these periods of special importance? Any or all of these could have resulted in changes in our genomes. Perhaps, instead of EEA, we should refer to *environments* of evolutionary adaptedness, or EsEA. Different behaviors could well have had their origins in different periods of evolutionary adaptation, some occurring before our hominid ancestors existed and others more recently.

The farming-civilization period, which occurred after the EEA, may have affected our genetic inheritance. Like domesticated animals, our genetically determined behavior may have been modified to a certain extent by our ancestors not living "in the wild" but living in relatively settled communities for 10,000 or more years. This appears to be the environment in which reading first appeared as an emergent function, not in the EEA.

Reciprocal, Soft-Core Altruism

Kin selection theory indicated that organisms, including people, would act in ways to promote the survival of relatives with many genes identical to their own. Wilson termed such altruism "hard-core" altruism in that it had a specific biological mechanism. The biologist Robert Trivers (1971) proposed another type of altruism that he termed **"reciprocal altruism,"** which Wilson would later call "soft-core altruism" (Wilson, 1978, p. 157).

Gaulin & McBurney (2001, pp. 75–76) have provided an example of reciprocal altruism, in which two hunter-gatherers share food. In this example, we assume that the two hunter-gatherers are strangers and not related. When "Zug" is successful in a hunt, he gives food to "Og," who otherwise might starve to death. Later Og returns the favor. Therefore, the result is that instead of becoming two dead hunter-gatherers, both Zug and Og survive to hunt again.

But, in Trivers's analysis, the important point is that, for altruism to be beneficial to the altruist, it must be reciprocal. That is, the person who is the recipient of help must be willing to provide it in the future if the quality of altruism is to be of selective value to the giver.

So, how can hard-core and soft-core altruism be distinguished? Helping kin who share your genes and can pass them on to future generations is hard-core altruism. Helping others in cooperative ventures in which you will likely benefit also is soft-core altruism. Occasionally hard-core and soft-core altruism might overlap, as in a family business or among a tribe of related hunters.

Modularity of Mind

A relative newcomer to the theories used by evolutionary psychologists is the notion of the **modularity of mind.** The modern version of the idea of mental faculties was proposed by Jerry Fodor (1983), who proposed that the mind also consisted of general-purpose central processes. Leta Cosmides and John Tooby (2003) have reduced the emphasis of Fodor's central process and emphasized that the brain consists of many (hundreds or thousands) smaller sub-organs or modules, each of which evolved for specific purposes. They have alluded to their model as a Swiss Army knife model of the brain. Some of these modules, relatively unchanged, have an evolutionary history that is millions of years old.

We have traditionally viewed such behavioral proclivities without thinking of mental modules or neuronal wiring that underlies them. Even another way of looking at instincts

---

BOX 18.2   *Only Connect . . .*

The concept of mental modules is very similar to Gordon Allport's concept of trait. Allport's concept of trait does not, however, imply the necessary "hard-wiring" implied in the mental module concept. As indicated in Chapter 11, Allport defined trait as "a neuropsychic structure having the capacity to render many stimuli functionally equivalent and to initiate and guide equivalent (meaningfully consistent) forms of adaptive and expressive behavior (1961, p. 347). A mental module functions similarly. It, too, is a neuropsychic structure that identifies a variety of stimuli as having the same or similar meaning and leads to similar behavior. A predator detection module of a chick, for example, identifies the form of a hawk above it as a danger from which it must flee.

is to think of them as a result of inherited parts of the genome that are responsible for the development of those brain patterns leading to specified mental activities.

According to the theory of the modularity of mind, the same sense of continuity and innovation applies to the workings of our brain. In the modular view of Cosmides and Tooby (1992), our brain consists of many such modules, some of which have been passed on with little variation from our reptilian and mammalian ancestors and others of which have developed anew or from small beginnings from our hominid or early human ancestors.

According to the modular theorists, there are inherited modules for any number of functions in animals and/or humans. Many animals have a **predator detection module,** which identifies dangerous predators. There are also mate selection modules and even language modules. One proposed module in humans is the **cheater detection module,** necessary if reciprocal altruism is to work (Barkow, Cosmides, & Tooby, 1992).

Exaptation: One Means of Evolution

One facet of current evolutionary theory is the idea of how new features or behaviors may emerge. In this process, a feature or behavior that was originally not selected may emerge (Wilson, 1978, pp. 71–97). The term **exaptation** indicates that characteristics that were selected in a given environment could prove valuable in a different environment, and for novel reasons. For example, birds' feathers are thought to have arisen for purposes of insulation from cold and only millions of years later developed for the purposes of gliding and then flying (Tattersall, 1998).

Some capacities, though initially not selected for, may thus become adaptive. A human example is that the complex human brain did not originally evolve to read or to do computer programming. Reading and computer programming are exaptations or emergent functions of a nervous system that did not evolve originally in order to be able to read or to do programming.

Facultative Adaptations

Many traits are facultative, that is, their expression depends on environmental conditions. In the area of physical characteristics, a person who uses tools frequently may develop calluses. The development of calluses is a **facultative adaptation,** a genetic potential that is expressed only with use. A person who never uses his or her hands to do heavy work will never develop calluses.

Likewise, a person who goes through intensive training to engage in special combat operations is likely to demonstrate a degree of alertness and readiness to spring into action not often seen among civilians. His or her level of alertness, readiness to fight, and associated hormonal activities are different from those of a sedentary civilian. In effect, the human species can provide a "soldier human" and a "worker human." Unlike an ant colony, these types do not represent separate fixed, biologically-determined castes but are facultative adjustments to different environmental requirements.

HUMAN NATURE DOES EXIST

In his book, *On Human Nature* (1978), Wilson indicated ways in which human nature was similar to that of the great apes and many monkey species:

- Our intimate social groupings contain on the order of ten to one hundred adults, never just two, as in most birds and marmosets or up to thousands, as in many kinds of fishes and insects.

- Males are larger than females. . . . [T]he average number of females consorting with successful males closely corresponds to the size gap between males and females. . . . When the sexual size difference in human beings is plotted on the curve based on other kinds of mammals, the predicted average number of females per successful male turns out to be greater than one but less than three. The prediction is close to reality; we know we are a mildly polygynous species.

- The young are molded by a long period of social training, first by closest associations with the mother, then to an increasing degree with other children of the same age and sex.

- Social play is a strongly developed activity featuring role practice, mock aggression, sex practice, and exploration. (Wilson, 1978, pp. 20–21)

Wilson (1978) also noted commonalities among all human societies. He referred to the work of the anthropologist George Murdock (1945), who enumerated behavioral characteristics that have been noted in every culture that had been studied up to that time:

> Age grading, athletic sports, bodily adornment, calendar, cleanliness, training, community, organization, cooking, cooperative labor, cosmology, courtship, dancing, decorative art, eschatology, ethics, ethnobotany, etiquette, faith healing, family feasting, fire making, folklore, food taboos, funeral rites, games, gestures, gift giving, incest taboos, inheritance rules, joking, kin groups, kinship nomenclature, language, law, luck superstitions, magic, marriage, mealtimes, medicine, obstetrics, penal sanctions, personal names, population policy, postnatal care, pregnancy usages, property rights, propitiation of supernatural beings, puberty customs, religious ritual, residence rules, sexual restriction, soul concepts, status differentiation, surgery, tool making, trade, visiting, weaving, and weather control. (Murdock, 1945, pp. 124–142)

We could add music, dancing, and keeping rhythms.

Along the same, lines, David Barash commented,

> . . . nowhere are there people among whom men are less violent than women, who consider eighty year olds more sexually attractive than twenty year olds, or who do not favor their relative over strangers. (Barash, 2001)

Wilson proposes that such qualities are among the basics of *human* nature and states, "It is easy to imagine nonhuman societies whose members are even more intelligent and complexly organized than ourselves, yet lack a majority of the qualities just listed" (1978, p. 22). Wilson, who had been immersed for many years in the study of ants, was well aware of the differences between ant and human societies and probably did not have much trouble imagining how different a more intelligent ant society would be from the human world.

One could argue that some of these characteristics listed by Murdock may have represented cultural innovations (without a genetic basis) that spread through prehistorical human societies; nonetheless, human, by nature, had to have had the capacity to acquire and the proclivity to pass on such innovations. We might teach dogs or horses to dance in a rhythmic way, but they do not seem to continue to engage in such behaviors once outside of human influence.

The underlying ideas of sociobiology—*natural selection, sexual selection, kin selection, reciprocal altruism, exaptation, modularity of mind,* together with reference to our EEA—has led to examination of numerous behaviors and traits and could lead to the exploration of innumerable other characteristics of individuals and human groups and societies as well as interpersonal and intergroup behaviors. The purpose of this chapter is not to review all such areas but to demonstrate how the evolutionary psychological approach can proceed and to provide a number of examples.

EVOLUTIONARY PSYCHOLOGY
FROM A BROADER, MORE OBJECTIVE PERSPECTIVE

In order to gain a little more objectivity, let us take the example, not of a human infant, but of a little puppy brought home from the pet store. One level of behavior has to do with experiences the little puppy might have had before you bought him. You might wonder or even ask, "How old was he when he was weaned? Was he treated with kindness or hit by people? Was he left alone and neglected? What was his position among the rest of the litter?" Accurate information about such areas might reveal something about his physical health and (depending on your preferred psychological theory) something about his ability to form ties or to bond and his general disposition or his conditioned patterns of behavior. The last part of the story has to do with the environment you provide, in terms of both the physical environment and the human and animal environment. Also, what new behaviors does the dog learn from you and your family? What pet tricks do you teach the puppy, and so on?

The part omitted from this analysis of your dog's behavior is its actual "dogginess." As a member of the dog species, your puppy is very likely to bond with you and other family members as its wolf ancestors would have done to the wolf pack. You or another family member might become your puppy's *alpha* male or female. Your dog will be territorial and, if given the opportunity, proceed to mark his territory. He may have a tendency to chase cars, to hunt squirrels, and to pile up newspapers at the front door.

So the full understanding of your dog's behavior requires knowing, not only about his early puppy experiences and his subsequent learning, but also about his instinctive behaviors and tendencies to act in certain ways, based on his legacy as a dog. (We could even dig deeper and examine his instinctive behaviors that can be attributed to mammalian or even vertebrate legacies, which he shares with humans.) Regardless of his early and later influences, your dog is not going to behave like a cat, a ferret, a gerbil, or a pet lizard or a human. His genetic and evolutionary background is an overarching influence on his subsequent emotional development and environmental reinforcement.

Likewise, you, a human being, are shaped by your early experiences as an infant and a child, by your subsequent learning and development—as indicated by many of the theories in this text. What evolutionary psychology draws our attention to is the very fact that you are human and that it is not only your childhood and infancy that have an impact on you, but also those behaviors that evolved in your ancestors and enabled them to pass their genes on to you.

Unlike a Lamarckian or Jungian view (Chapter 4), this formulation does not indicate that your ancestors' experiences are reproduced in you or that their behaviors were in any way passed on to you. What it indicates is that, of the wide variety of humanoid beings that existed in the past, only those who had certain predispositions to behave (including thinking and feeling) in certain ways were able to continue to pass on their genes in the sequence of environments that they faced. And we current humans are *their* progeny.

An Aside: Comparing Kittens, Puppies, and Children

Concerning dog behavior, the evolutionary biologist David Barash points out a fact regarding toilet training that, using theories underlying evolutionary psychology, we can see with new eyes. He asks why it is that cats and dogs, which he terms "stupider" than humans, can be potty-trained in a few days or weeks, but human babies take years to learn the process. Answering his own question, Barash notes that the ground-dwelling ancestors of cats and dogs had to hide their fecal material or keep it away from their usual habitat in order to avoid attracting predators, while this factor was not present in tree-dwellers. But, he notes:

> By contrast [to dogs and cats], human beings, like other primates evolved in the trees. Tidy potty habits simply aren't an issue for arboreal creatures (although they can be a problem for those poor unfortunates down below!). This is almost certainly the reason why other primates, such as chimpanzees or monkeys, also resist toilet-training. It goes against a deep-seated inclination. (Barash, 2001, p. 208)

This example is a good illustration of the difference between the implications of Lamarck's theory of the inheritance of acquired characteristics and Darwin's theory of natural selection. If Lamarck's theory were correct, human infants by now would have gotten the hang of potty training because of the efforts of generations. This is clearly not the case. We might speculate that, unless facility at being toilet trained leads to a child's genes being more likely to be passed on to the next generation, human babies in the future will continue to have more trouble being toilet trained than cats and dogs.

The thinking of an evolutionary psychologist might also approach a very common phenomenon in a way different from the classical personality theories.

SOME MISCONCEPTIONS ABOUT EVOLUTIONARY PSYCHOLOGY

David M. Buss (1999) has summarized some frequent misunderstandings about evolutionary psychology. They include the following:

- Some falsely assume that evolutionary theory proposes genetic determinism without input from the environment. Buss points out that many evolutionarily determined behaviors are responses to specific environments. Such adaptations in response to specific conditions as we have noted, are termed facultative behaviors. A simple physical example of a facultative response is that calluses develop in response to use. A fight-flight response may occur in response to a physically threatening situation.

- Another false belief is that we humans cannot change our behavior, that it is entirely determined by evolution and by our genes. At the very least, our knowledge of evolutionary mechanisms can lead us to change our behavior. We might learn, for example, that we have an ingrained tendency to be afraid of closed-in places or nonvenomous snakes. We can often overcome such phobias through behavioral therapies, such as desensitization or implosion.

- A false assumption is that we have been optimally designed by evolution. Buss points to the time lag, that we in many cases are better adapted to earlier environments than to our current world. If we were better adapted to our current environment, then all of us would have as easy a time learning to read as we do to speak (cf. Cartwright, 2000, p. 40).

- Another assumption is that we are trying *consciously* to maximize our number of surviving genes in the next generation. We may exhibit genetically determined tendencies to pass on our genes to the next generation, but this is not necessarily our conscious goal.

Cartwright has added, as a false assumption, the notion of **Panglossism** (2000, p. 40). In Voltaire's classic book *Candide,* Dr. Pangloss referred to the present world as the best possible world and was such an optimist that no matter what happened, he thought it was for the best. The counterpart of Panglossism in evolutionary theory is that there must be an adaptive reason for everything, even the red color of blood. The fact is that many existing qualities and traits may have no particular adaptive significance.

In other words, unless we become clear about precisely what it is that evolutionary psychologists are saying, we can include ideas that are not part of current thinking in our view of evolutionary psychology. In many instances, people who believe that they are criticizing evolutionary psychology, are acutally criticizing their own misconceptions of its field.

Individual Identity and Evolutionary Psychology

There are some paradoxes and ironies in the viewpoint of evolutionary psychology to individuality. Evolutionary psychology is, at its base, a nomothetic discipline. It is concerned with certain general principles and how they are manifested in human behavior. However, one of the most important aspects of human nature is our strong sense of individuality. Note the similarity of this idea to Jung's concept of *persona*. A persona is individually created and molded, but each person has an innate capacity for such a psychological reality. Erikson also emphasized the importance of each person to develop a sense of individual identity.

It is not difficult to speculate about the evolutionary basis for the importance of individuality among human beings. One area where individuality is important is bonding. In forming mating bonds and family groups, we form strong bonds with individual people, not people in general. It is true that one can be "in love with love" for a certain period of life, but such generalized temporary bonding does not lead to a settled life. People usually bond with specific others. A human face is usually unmistakably identifiable as is the human voice. In addition, humans have a certain amount of personal space. This differs among cultures but remains within certain limits.

Also, the kin selection theory indicates that we are most likely to help those individuals with whom we are closely related and most likely to form the strongest bonds.

We can say with assurance that one of the main general laws of human behavior is that we have a tendency to assume individual identities and that we experience one another as different, distinguishable individuals. Much thought and effort goes into how we relate to others in our personal and professional lives. So, the paradox becomes resolved. One of the most general or nomothetic laws of human nature is that we see others and ourselves as unique individuals.

A Common Criticism of Evolutionary Psychology

Evolutionary psychology has often been criticized for the fact that it does not lead to genuine predictions, as is the case in experimental disciplines. It has thus been accused of engaging in *post hoc* **predictions.** Evolutionary psychologists cannot proceed with human evolution in a laboratory setting. They are constrained to study only the effects of evolution, and those effects are already present.

In response to a question that one of the authors of this text sent him, Wilson replied,

> . . . evolutionary psychology has considerable importance for personality studies, both as a tool to trace adaptiveness and as a heuristic device for asking new solvable questions. (Wilson, 2001)

Evolutionary psychology thus aids in understanding the causes of *currently existing* patterns of behavior. It does not lead to predictions about the future but rather can guide hypotheses about as yet unexplored or unresearched situations. It can also offer *explanations* of personality patterns in terms of their evolutionary adaptive value.

HOW MIGHT AN EVOLUTIONARY PSYCHOLOGIST PROCEED?

Let us take a common behavior that most likely would have evolutionary roots. To our knowledge, this behavior has not yet been studied from this point of view, but it provides an interesting example for us to indicate how an evolutionary psychological approach might proceed. When we see someone with a spot of food, a bug, or some unknown piece of something on his or her face, most of us experience a strong urge to let this person know about it or a desire to wipe it off ourselves. Many of us can remember times when we were very uncomfortable in the presence of someone with a glob of something on his or her face, and we were not able to mention it. Is this tendency—to be uncomfortable around a person with a speck of something on his or her face and try to get the person to remove it or to remove it ourselves—an instinct or an evolutionarily determined behavioral proclivity?

We can locate a similar pattern in primates, social grooming, which has the beneficial effect of removing insects and dirt from the hair of the one groomed. It is also important in strengthening bonds between individual animals. To determine whether such a tendency is an instinct or an evolutionary adaptation, we might also check to see how common it is in different human cultures. We might look at this behavior developmentally, to see when it first develops, and to ascertain to what extent it is a learned behavior, involving imitation learning. We could even measure the subjective intensity of the wish of one person to engage in such behavior, and look for the heritability of this trait.

Perhaps studies of identical twins, fraternal twins, and people with different degrees of relatedness could establish the degree to which this trait is heritable. Also, analyzing the genome of those with or without this trait might lead to the discovery of a gene or set of genes that contribute to the development of this human type of social grooming. Such studies might well confirm the instinctive nature of such behavior, in which case it would join the array of human behaviors that have instinctive origins.

Regarding the tendency to engage in a human version of social grooming, there is a lesser degree of *post hoc* or after-the-fact thinking, but postdiction is still present. We start by knowing about our own tendency and that of people in our culture to engage in this behavior; we also know about social grooming in primates. We need to explore empirically the cross-cultural aspects as well as the genetic basis for such behavior before coming to any conclusions about its adaptiveness or its relation to our EEA.

AN ACTUAL EXAMPLE—NOT OF POSTDICTION BUT OF PREDICTION—SORT OF

In the previous examples, the use of evolutionary psychology varies considerably from the experimental method, in which researchers predict the outcome of an experiment according to their hypotheses. In the case of toilet training, we are dealing, not with a prediction, but with a *post hoc* explanation, or what can be termed a **postdiction.** In other words, we are looking at behaviors of which we already have some knowledge, that is toilet training among humans and potty training among domestic cats and dogs, and attempting to come up with an explanation based on evolutionary theory.

The next example is a case of a prediction according to evolutionary psychological theory: starting with a theoretical premise, a prediction is made. Then empirical evidence is accumulated to see if the prediction is confirmed. In the field of evolutionary psychology, it is almost never possible to conduct an experiment in real time. Instead, what one has to do is to explore *currently existing evidence* that might be either consistent or inconsistent with the hypothesized outcomes.

Martin Daly and Margo Wilson (1985) published the unsettling results of a study they conducted. They had thought about the behavior of stepparents toward their biological children and toward stepchildren and speculated that, since the biological children contained more of their genetic material, that they would exhibit more caring toward such children. To test their hypothesis, they examined homicide data in the United States and Canada. It turned out that the percentage of children who were killed by a stepparent was about a factor of two, or one hundred times greater than the percentage of children killed by their biological parents. They did not claim that this difference was caused solely by evolutionary considerations, but certainly Daly and Wilson considered them a foundational cause. The results they studied were not really *post hoc*. The reality already existed, unlike the case in a genuine experimental model. However, the discovery of the corroborating data did occur after Daly and Wilson's generation of their hypotheses. As in a real laboratory experiment, they were not certain what their findings would be.

One does not have to look far to find a possible mechanism for the greater connectedness of biological parents and their children. One possibility is the mechanism of bonding, which occurs in the earliest part of life. Human infants and their biological parents develop strong bonds during this time. A stepparent is not often present during these early years and has less of a chance to develop such bonds.

One might argue for the presence of nonevolutionarily determined reasons for the greater danger in which stepchildren find themselves. Evolutionary psychology is open to the possibility that such nonhereditary factors may also play a role in determining such behavior. It also recognizes the fact that most stepparents do not kill or abuse their stepchildren and that many are kind and nurturing.

The Incest Taboo

One area that Wilson as well as other sociobiologists and evolutionary psychologists examined is the **incest taboo.** It is well known that, among humans, incest can lead to birth defects and reduced viability among offspring. The reasoning behind this phenomenon has to do with the fact that a defective gene often occurs twice in the chromosomes of the offspring of incestuous mating. A normal gene is not present to attenuate the phenotypic expression of the defective gene.

Over 100 years ago, the Scandinavian anthropologist Edward Westermarck (1891) ventured the hypothesis that individuals will not be interested in mating with individuals with whom they were associated as children. This phenomenon was confirmed in Israeli communes, in which children from different families spend much time together. In spite of their parents' wishes that they marry, such marriages appear to have been almost totally nonexistent. In one study, Joseph Shepher (1971) studied recorded marriages in Israel. He examined almost 2,800 marriage records and determined that not even one involved adults who were little children together before the age of six. The children reared together were like brothers and sisters and apparently experienced a type of bonding that precluded later sexual intimacy. According to Wilson, they must have experienced sexual aversion because of their proximity as children (Wilson, 1978).

To get a clear idea of how the thinking of evolutionary psychologists proceeds, it is helpful, in analyzing this example, to realize that the incest taboo occurred in spite of the fact that the children were, for the most part, *not related*. In other words, there was no increased likelihood that their offspring would have been defective. Yet they were affected by the same mechanism that human nature has provided, the purpose of which is to prevent incest. This mechanism, the product of tens of thousands of generations of evolutionary history, works against sexual involvement among children and people adjacent to them during rearing. This mechanism does not "see"; it is not able to identify kin *per se* and differentiate them from others.

Incest taboos were present before any knowledge of the biological dangers of incest was present. In other words, people do not need to make calculations about the evolutionarily most viable behavior in order to have motives in accordance with sociobiological principles.

Human culture and the law are very much in line with the biological incest taboo. The incest taboo thus stands on two legs—first, our genetic legacy, and second, cultural and legal restrictions. This should not be surprising. Both individual humans as well as human cultures of the past that did not have incest taboos were less viable than those that did. Wilson saw this phenomenon as an instance of the **leash principle,** that is, the close connection of human culture and laws with sociobiological principles. Wilson (as did Jung) thought that cultures and societies that departed too far from evolutionarily determined patterns of behavior were courting chaos and creating individual discomfort (Lumsden & Wilson, 1981). Such a thought definitely places Wilson, as well as Jung, in the position of being cultural conservatives, but evolutionary psychologists should also take into account the importance of the ability of individuals and societies to respond to change. In addition, we have inherited a brain that is capable of learning many behaviors not even imagined by our ancestors of 100 years ago.

Mate Selection

The area of sexual selection, that is the selection of mates and competition for them, as a major factor in natural selection has been well known for over a century—going back to Darwin's original theory. Evolutionary psychologists have carried out many studies in this area, as have evolutionary biologists. They have hypothesized that the purposes of sexual selection have to do with both the fertility of the mate, the number of offspring, and the likelihood that, with a specific mate, their offspring will themselves be cared for and, in turn, survive to reproduce.

All the ramifications that have to do with mate selection would take more than one volume to summarize. Here, we will touch on three areas: attractiveness in general, males' rating of the attractiveness of females, and the differential sexual choices of males and females.

Individuals with physical symmetry were found to be more attractive by both genders than others (Grammar & Thornhill, 1994). The evolutionary rationale for this behavior is that individuals with more symmetrical bodies and facial features are thought to have greater health and fewer genetic defects and thus would make better choices in the mate selection process. Subsequently, it has been found that males with the most symmetrical faces had first sexual intercourse younger than others and had more sex partners in general (Thornhill & Gangestad, 1994).

Males prefer the most physically attractive females as mates. This is a less important factor in the mate selection process of females. A survey of men from 37 countries throughout the world indicated that they emphasized physical attractiveness in mates more than their female compatriots did (Buss, 1989). Michael Wiederman (1993) actually looked at advertisements in personal sections of newspapers and found that American men were almost four times as likely as women to indicate that they were looking for a physically attractive partner.

But what features constitute attractiveness for men? A major aspect of such attractiveness, in addition to facial symmetry has turned out to be the ratio of the size of a person's waist to their hips. This is termed the waist-hip ratio. In a series of studies (Singh, 1993; Singh & Luis, 1995; Singh & Young, 1995), it was found that pictures of women with lower waist-hip ratios are rated most attractive and that, in particular, the 0.7 waist-hip ratio in women is rated as most attractive by men cross-culturally.

This ratio has been found to correspond with the highest level of fertility among young women. There is a close tie-in between physical health and the distribution of fat, as indicated by the waist-hip ratio. People at risk for diabetes, heart attack, vascular disease, and other disorders tend to have waist-hip ratios higher than 0.7 (Buss, 1999, p. 144). Thus, all other things being equal, women with the low waist-hip ratio of 0.7 are a better choice in terms of their reproductive potential and in terms of their ability to care for offspring in a vigorous manner.

Whereas men, in general, put their highest valuations on attractive women as sexual partners, the most important criterion for women is financial status and potential. This pattern reminds one of the words of reassurance to a baby in George Gershwin's "Summertime": "Your daddy's rich and your momma's good lookin." In a variety of studies, women have been found to rate financial status as twice as important as did men (Hill, 1945; McGinnis, 1958; Sprecher, Sullivan, & Hatfield, 1994). Michael Wiederman (1993) reviewed personal advertisements and found that, among heterosexuals in America, women were 11 times as likely to mention that somebody with a good financial status or prospects was desired. Buss (1989) corroborated such findings in surveying men and women in 37 countries.

Steven Gaulin and Donald McBurney have concluded that such choices did not necessarily represent a woman's lack of resources, for even well-to-do women or women with good financial prospects also were found to seek affluent men or those with excellent economic prospects (Weiderman and Allgeier, 1992). They point out, by way of explanation, that even though many women today are very well off financially, their mate-choice modules were shaped in the EEA, when women necessarily had to rely on the ability of men as hunters and providers (Gaulin & McBurney, 2001, p. 215).

EVOLUTIONARY PSYCHOLOGY AND PSYCHOPATHOLOGY

There are a number of ways of understanding psychopathology in terms of evolutionary psychology. Perhaps the simplest approach is to consider the EEA. This is clearly the case with many captive animals, particularly those with wide ranges in the wild. Kept in captive conditions, even with the best veterinary treatment, animals of many species may show signs of depression or become unable to reproduce. People in cities, which are often crowded and have high noise levels, may also show symptoms of anxiety and stress-related disorders.

In addition, some behaviors currently considered pathological might have been adaptive during the EEA. Paranoid alertness and a low threshold for arousal are two characteristics that might have been adaptive in a hunter-gatherer world, but not today. In the next section, we will look at the diagnosis of hyperactivity from this point of view.

Some traits that are adaptive when expressed to a moderate degree may be maladaptive when more extreme. In medicine, it is known that a moderate degree of the sickle cell anemia trait gives its possessor resistance to malaria. The full expression of the trait leads to an enfeebling form of anemia. An analogous process may exist in regard to the full expression of schizophrenia. It has been speculated that a more moderate expression of the schizophrenic characteristics leads to a high level of creativity. We have seen in the life history of Carl Jung (Chapter 4) the close connection between genius and psychosis.

A third area would be exemplified by dyslexia, a common disorder. In the EEA, people did not read. Individuals were not selected according to the ability to distinguish one letter from another. As indicated earlier in this chapter, the ability to read was an exaptation just as the ability to do calculus or to program computers. In other words, brain capacities that had developed for other purposes also enabled some people to be able to read. It should not be surprising, given the recent historical development of widespread literacy, that many people suffer from dyslexia.

An additional possibility is that a form of psychopathology is simply a result of an error of some sort: the psychopathology might result from a genetic defect or an environmental insult. In such cases, there might be no adaptive evolutionary basis involved.

Attention-Deficit Hyperactivity Disorder (ADHD) or Very Alert, Very Active Pattern (VAVAP)?

Attention-deficit hyperactivity disorder (ADHD) is a frequent diagnosis among school-age children in the United States. It refers to a maladaptive pattern of impulsive behavior, and difficulty paying attention, concentrating, and sitting still (APA, 2000, pp. 85–93). There is a large genetic or hereditary component to the disorder. In understanding this disorder, reference to the EEA is useful. Only in recent years have young humans been expected to devote a large portion of their day concentrating on their studies. In hominid as well as early human environments, a youngster with what today would be labeled as having ADHD might well have been as well or better adapted than a sedentary youngster. He or she might have been more alert to a predator's appearance or more likely to face a dangerous situation (Panskepp, 1998; Gaulin & McBurney, 2001). It would have thus been beneficial for the survival of groups of hominids and early humans to have some individuals with a very alert, very active pattern (VAVAP) of behavior.

From the standpoint of preevolutionary psychological theory, we might quickly draw the conclusion that an ADHD youngster's behavior is necessarily pathological. Taking the EEA into account, we can be open to the possibility that many hyperactive youngsters represent a normal, genetically determined variant, without any particular defects, family problems, or emotional issues. Along these lines, we might consider providing more physical activity in schools and more frequent breaks to accommodate the restlessness of the ADHD child who has to sit for hours on end.

Perhaps, in addition to the Axes in the *DSM-IV*, there should be one that indicates, "No emotional or situational cause for the behavior in question has been found in this case. The behavior appears to have been adaptive during the environment of evolutionary adaptedness or even more recently, but is not easily tolerated in today's society."

A FINAL WORD ON EVOLUTIONARY PSYCHOLOGY

The field of evolutionary psychology is a promising and rapidly expanding area of theory and research. New discoveries are made frequently, and many new articles and texts are being published. College and university courses on evolutionary psychology are becoming more prevalent. Evolutionary psychology is influencing thinking not only in the area of personality theory but also in other areas of psychology such as cognitive psychology, perception, sensation, social psychology, neuropsychology, and psychopathology. It is a unifying point of view that both helps explain many existing phenomena and leads to heuristic suggestions about other findings in the fields of psychology.

Because the field of evolutionary psychology is so much in the process of rapid development, it is not yet possible to predict the eventual status or to make a final evaluation of this point of view. The proponents may be overlooking or minimizing the vast cultural differences between groups of human beings or the plasticity or flexibility of individual behavior. It is not clear that a satisfactory system of ethics or morality can be based on evolutionary thinking. We can look forward, in the years ahead, to continuing dialogues between proponents of evolutionary psychology and other thoughtful advocates of a variety of different approaches to conceptualizing and understanding human behavior.

Refutability and Evolutionary Psychology

The question of refutability is an inherent problem for evolutionary psychology. One cannot conduct an experiment about events that have already happened. Given the theory as it is currently formulated, all existing behaviors must be in accordance with some evolutionary consequence, or at least *leashed* to it. If some societies have a great deal of aggression against females and rape, then there must be a reason; likewise, a reason can be found for behavior toward women that is kind and caring. Infanticide and cannibalism as well as taboos against these practices must be found to be in accordance with evolutionary psychology.

Therefore, this post hoc, after-the-fact quality of "predictions" in this field reveals that they are not predictions of the future as in experimental laboratory research. We should not, however, be too critical of the post hoc nature of much of evolutionary psychology, because such thinking is found in other areas as well. Could a behaviorist or a psychoanalyst come across evidence that counters his or her theory? Doubtful. Nor could an Adlerian ever discover a person without an inferiority complex.

One concept we might consider concerning the question of verifiability is the great variability of human behavior. If humans were like the giant panda, with a single species of bamboo that it can eat and a limited environmental range, then, perhaps predictions about our behavior would be more verifiable. What is revealed is that humans have an evolutionary history of many habitats and many conditions, many diets, and many climates. Just as we have many types of teeth to help us to eat and digest different foods, so we have an extensive repertoire of "prepared" behaviors. We are not a *tabula rasa* or blank slate but rather more like a Magic Slate, with evidence of many inherent patterns on the slate once you look beneath the surface layers. These do not represent past experiences as in Jung's theory but are our adaptive potentials, as carried in our genes and reflecting the varied environments in which our ancestors have existed, survived, and evolved.

Evolutionary Psychology and Human Agency

Evolutionary psychology can account for both human activity and passivity or, in other words, either for human choice and agency or for the idea that human behavior is determined. Some evolutionary psychologists see human behavior as a largely determined set of adaptations to situations presented in the course of evolution. Others view human agency itself as an evolutionary adaptation. Therefore, though evolutionary psychology refers human behaviors to a causal evolutionary process, it still can accommodate the model of an active, resourceful, and goal-oriented human being, at least in certain circumstances.

The Idiographic Versus Nomothetic in Evolutionary Psychology

In general, evolutionary psychology emphasizes the regularities of human behavior, not only between individuals but also between societies. From this point of view, the overwhelming similarity among individuals regarding their genetic inheritance (or what we now term their genomic makeup) is an overwhelming truth. Nonetheless, there is room in evolutionary psychology theory for an expression of individualism in every person. This apparent paradox is that our very capacity for individuality may be viewed as an evolutionarily determined quality.

SUMMARY

Evolutionary psychology is a new approach to understanding human behavior. It views patterns of behavior, thinking, and emotion in terms of their adaptive significance in our evolutionary history. Many classical personality theories included evolutionary concepts in their theories. They were handicapped, however, by using scientifically unsound ideas such as Lamarckian inheritance of acquired characteristics or unembellished Darwinian "nature red in tooth and claw" notions of evolution.

Edward O. Wilson is generally credited with spearheading the development of the modern field of evolutionary psychology, or what he prefers to call human sociobiology. His books, *Sociobiology: A New Synthesis* and *On Human Nature* have had a major impact on the creation of this field. Wilson is a leading biologist, who originally studied the social life of insects and gradually realized that some of the same factors explaining prosocial or "altruistic" behavior in insects also applied to vertebrates and, finally, to humans. He saw sociobiology as a theory that unified a wide array of findings regarding both animal and human behavior.

The development of contemporary evolutionary psychology is based on a number of contributions, starting with Charles Darwin's theory of evolution by natural selection. Darwin also proposed the importance of sexual selection and the evolution of emotional expression and a moral sense in his subsequent writings.

A necessary step in the development of modern evolutionary psychology was David Hamilton's idea of inclusive fitness or kin selection, in which he developed a broader view of the mechanism of natural selection. The kin selection theory proposed that evolution would favor behavior that increased the probability of survival of people carrying genes identical to one's own, even if these people were relatives or "kin," rather than one's own children. This development opened the way for psychologists to study the evolutionary origins of behaviors other than those merely associated with survival of the fittest and sexual selection. The idea of "the selfish gene" was a popularization of Hamilton's view and indicated that evolution proceeds, not by selection of the fittest individual, but rather by selection of the "fittest" genes.

Other ideas important in the development of evolutionary psychology are the concept of the environment of evolutionary adaptedness (EEA), the environment in which our hominid ancestors lived for millions of years. Many of our behavioral traits, ranging from our sweet tooth to fear of snakes to patterns of social behavior, can be traced to our ancestors' adaptations to this environment. Another relevant concept is the modularity of mind. This concept indicates that the mind contains many programmed or partially programmed ("hard-wired") functions that have proven useful for survival.

One area that was investigated early was that of taboos on incest. It was found that nonrelated individuals reared with others as children developed a type of bonding that precluded later sexual intimacy. Wilson proposed the *leash principle,* to indicate that behavior might not be strictly determined biologically, but that it was leashed to biology and could not depart indefinitely from the vicissitudes of evolutionary adaptation. Sexual selection has led to attractiveness being linked to fertility and health, especially in the male's perception of the female. Women seem to be more focused on their mates' financial status, again a factor promoting survival of offspring.

Psychopathology can represent an atavistic adaptation to the EEA that is no longer adaptive. This appears to be the case with attention-deficit hyperactivity disorder (ADHD). Another possibility is that pathology represents "too much" or "not enough" of a quality or trait that is adaptive in a more moderate amount. A third possibility is that what is considered pathology is the absence of a trait or ability that has not been selected by evolution. An example is this is dyslexia, or the inability to discern letters and resulting difficulty or inability to read.

FOR FURTHER READING

Wilson's writings include a prize-winning account of his work as a naturalist and his development of sociobiology and human sociobiology or what we term *evolutionary psychology*. *Sociobiology: The New Synthesis* (Cambridge, MA: Harvard University Press, 1975) is his account of the tenets of sociobiology. *On Human Nature* (Cambridge MA: Harvard University Press, 1978) is Wilson's more fully developed view of the relevance of sociobiology for understanding human behavior. *Naturalist* (Washington, DC: Island Press, 1994) is Wilson's charming autobiographical account of his life and his intellectual and personal adventures in the interrelated worlds of scientific research and academic politics and ideas. John Alcock's *The Triumph of Sociobiology* (New York: Oxford University Press, 2001) is a sympathetic view of the sociobiological theory up to the present.

For those seeking to refresh their memory about the overall theory of evolution and its current status, a wonderfully accurate, readable, and well-illustrated volume is Carl Zimmer's *Evolution: The Triumph of an Idea* (New York: Harper Collins, 2001).

Some excellent textbooks on evolutionary psychology have become available in recent years. *Psychology: An Evolutionary Approach* (Upper Saddle River: NJ: Prentice-Hall, 2001) by Steven Gaulin and Donald McBurney is a clearly written exposition that covers the main concepts of evolutionary psychology and applies them to many areas of psychology. David Buss's (1999) *Evolutionary Psychology: The New Science of the Mind.* (Needham Heights, MA: Allyn and Bacon, 1999) includes the results of many studies on a wide variety of aspects of human behavior. More textbooks on the subject can be expected in coming years.

David Barash's *Sociobiology and Behavior* (New York: Elsevier, 1977) was an early and accurate popularization of what, at that time, was the novel concept of sociobiology. More recently, in *Revolutionary Biology* (New Brunswick, NJ: Transaction, 2001), Barash has written about the rethinking about human behavior that is engendered by the new concepts of evolutionary psychology.

A little paperback full of illustrations by Dylan Evans and Oscar Zarate, *Introducing Evolutionary Psychology* (New York: Totem Books, 2000), is excellent at conveying difficult concepts in the field of evolutionary psychology, especially those having to do with the idea of the modularity of mind.

GLOSSARY

Altruism: Behavioral proclivities that benefit others, often at some cost to oneself. Altruistic behavior, in evolutionary theory, may or may not involve conscious altruistic intent.

Artificial selection: The process of selecting and breeding organisms of given species with desired characteristics.

Attention-deficit hyperactivity disorder (ADHD): A disorder characterized by poor attention span, distractibility, and impulsiveness. Some theorists have proposed that, even though no longer adaptive, it was an adaptation to the EEA.

Cheater detection module: A mental module that detects cheaters, those who benefit but do not contribute in the process of reciprocal altruism.

Environment of evolutionary adaptedness (EEA): The past environment, considered millions of years in duration, during which current human behaviors were selected. During this period, human ancestors were hunters and gatherers.

Evolutionary biology: A field that examines findings in biology through the lens of evolutionary theories. It serves as a unifying factor in the field of biology.

Evolutionary medicine: A field that considers diseases and their treatments from the point of view of their evolutionary adaptive significance.

Evolutionary psychology: The approach to understanding human psychology—including all of its basic areas such as learning, cognition, perception, personality and psychopathology—from the point of view of evolutionary theory.

Exaptation: A characteristic that evolved to serve a certain function but, once existing, was found to have other useful functions. For example, feathers are thought to have evolved to provide warmth, but later were found useful for flight.

Facultative adaptation: A trait or characteristic that is an adaptation to a specific environment. For example, calluses will develop when a person uses tools.

Fixed action patterns: Konrad Lorenz's concept of sequences of movements programmed in the brain by heredity, which unfold through the life of an animal in response to particular signals in the environment.

Human sociobiology: The application of the principles of sociobiology to all aspects of humans and their behavior. This term indicates the connectedness of human behavior with that of all organisms.

Incest taboo: The prohibition against sex with close relatives. There is a biological basis for this taboo, which is also embedded in law and culture.

Inclusive fitness: Concept that an organism's fitness is determined not only by its ability to leave descendants but also by its contribution to the overall fitness of organisms of the same species around it.

Inheritance of acquired characteristics: Lamarck's discredited idea that the acquired characteristics of an organism can be passed to its offspring. For example, a person who builds up his or her muscles will *per se* have muscular descendents.

Kin selection: William Hamilton's concept that an organism may be selected because it enhances the viability of related organisms, *kin,* with some identical genes.

Leash principle: The concept that human behavior and cultures cannot stray too far away from biologically based determinants.

Modularity of mind: The concept that the mind consists, in addition to a central processing unit, of many separate modules, each performing specific tasks.

Natural selection: Darwin's proposed means for evolution, the concept that better adapted organisms are able to pass on their genetic material to the next generation. They are thus said to be *selected* by nature.

Ontogony: The development or course of development of an individual organism, often applied to embryological levels of development.

Panglossism: The false notion that there must be an adaptive reason for every trait.

Phylogeny: The evolutionary history of an organism.

***Post hoc* predictions/postdiction:** "Predictions" that are made about conditions that already exist but of which one does not currently have knowledge. For example, one researcher "predicted" that children reared together in a kibbutz did not get married as adults. He subsequently analyzed marital records to confirm his hypothesis.

Predator detection module: A mental module that detects predators.

Reciprocal (soft-core) altruism: Robert Trivers's concept of a type of altruism involving giving and receiving help from others. He theorized that individuals demonstrating such behavior are selected for in the process of natural selection.

Selfish gene theory: A gene-focused theory of evolution proposed by Dawkins: the idea that the organism is a means of perpetuating the survival of genes. The gene is not actually selfish, but evolution proceeds as if the gene were selfishly trying to perpetuate itself.

Sexual selection: The concept that some organisms are selected as part of the natural selection process as a result of their comparative success in mating.

Sociobiology: Edward Wilson's unifying concept of viewing organisms and their behaviors through the lens of evolutionary theories. He included human beings in his analysis.

Chapter 19

Thinking about Personality Theories and Personality Theorists

Whenever we have criticized a theory or a technique it has seldom been on the grounds of validity, but rather on the grounds that some one limited point of view is falsely pretending to cover the whole of the subject.

Gordon W. Allport, *Pattern and Growth in Personality*

The heart has its reasons which reason does not know.

Blaise Pascal, *Pensées*

About the Persistence of Untestable Theories

So many of the theories presented in this book are neither testable nor have been adequately tested. This prompts us to ask two questions:

1. *Is there any reasonable way to decide which theory is right?*

2. *If psychology is a science, why does it tolerate so many unscientific theories? The answer to the first question is another question: What do we want from a theory of human nature? And can we expect to get it?*

The answer to the second question depends on how we define science and whether we are prepared to accept its findings.

Many of the theories we have reviewed share some common elements. In addition, all of the theories arrive at a small, but significant, group of human problems. Nearly all of the theorists themselves share some personality features and motives. Feelings of inferiority coupled with the sense of being unwanted by their parents shaped the personal histories of many of the theorists presented in this book. The personality theories they developed are often nested in their life histories and represent creative solutions to the issues they faced. These solutions to the difficulties the theorists have faced have proved useful to others with similar experiences—both by helping them better understand themselves and to cope more effectively with similar realities they also may have experienced.

IF THEY ARE OFTEN UNTESTABLE, WHY DO THEY SURVIVE?

In this text, it has often been necessary to point out that a particular theory is largely untestable or has not been tested empirically. With some exceptions, such as the radical behaviorisms, Hans Eysenck's biological typology, and Albert Bandura's social cognitive theory, most of the theories we have reviewed:

- make no precise or testable predictions,
- generate few, if any, laboratory studies, and
- frequently lead to disputes of opinion rather than fact.

Many theories, however, have led to the development of therapeutic approaches and to an emphasis on one or another of the many factors important in the experience of human beings.

Issues That Will Not Go Away

If the purpose of a scientific theory of personality is prediction and control, then most of the theories we have reviewed are not scientific. As the history of the development of personality theories demonstrates, we cannot assume that more empirically based and verifiable theories will replace ones that are less verifiable. The ideas of Freud and Jung, for example, continue to be attractive to many intellectuals from many disciplines, including those outside of psychology. There is no shortage of Freudians and Jungians in clinical practice. The ideas of major theorists survive and are applied in some way relevant to psychology or to professional psychological practice.

The issues these grand theories of human nature address are classical ones that have long captured the attention of thinking people. Philosophers, artists, and theologians have thought and written about themes such as justice, truth, beauty, love, hate, and destiny well before psychology became involved with the human condition. Their ideas explore core human concerns. These classical and philosophical themes generate grand theories. Many other subfields of psychology do not address such major and broad issues. Personality theories are as close as psychology gets to addressing classical questions.

Major Issues or Small Details?

Theorists such as Sigmund Freud, Abraham Maslow, Rollo May, B. F. Skinner, Albert Bandura, and Edward O. Wilson were not satisfied with answering small questions. None of these thinkers was forever satisfied with exploring discrete issues, such as neuronal thresholds (although Freud tried early on) or reinforcement schedules (although Skinner did invent the idea), dominance behavior in monkeys (although Maslow began his career with this topic), or ant behavior (Wilson's early area of research). All of these people eventually turned their thoughts to major issues: Freud tackled love and hate, life and death; May struggled with freedom, destiny, and beauty; Maslow explored truth, beauty, and the reality of peak experiences. Skinner turned his hand to the issues of societal harmony and the meaning of freedom, Bandura to human resourcefulness, and Wilson to the commonalities that tie human behavior to the rest of the living world.

In the field of personality theory, we are dealing with thinkers who pride themselves on seeing the big picture. They envision themselves as synthesizers, explorers, and creators of ideas. History shows that most of them were willing to forgo the benefits of scientific testing in favor of good, comprehensive, and compelling theories of human nature.

Humans Do Not Live by Science Alone

There are some conclusions we can draw from this persistence of largely untestable grand theories. First, and most obvious, Karl Popper's criterion of refutability is a stringent standard that makes powerful demands on theories, but it does not guarantee that psychologists and others will abide by it. Scientific theories of personality conduct business in terms of measurable, observable variables, and they generally are constructed piecemeal over long periods.

Such theories are usually neither as interesting nor as heuristic as Freudian metaphors. Freud's vivid descriptions of the seething cauldron of fury known as the id and its battles against the ego are wonderfully interesting and hypothesis-generating ways of thinking about the human conflict between reason and desire. Thresholds in the limbic system of the brain and its interaction with the brain's cortex may be more scientifically acceptable but less directly connected with experience than our hidden desires and our ways of avoiding awareness of them.

WHAT WE GET FROM THEORIES OF PERSONALITY

The life histories of the theorists we have examined suggest that they have much in common. These thinkers demonstrate intellectual independence and strong desires to excel and achieve greatness. In addition, one frequently finds that a theorist had experienced a personal crisis that he or she resolved with the creation of a grand synthesis that led to the development of a theory of personality (Ellenberger, 1970). The theories of most of the theorists are nested, to one degree or another, in their own personal life histories.

We continue to study their models of human nature because they deal with the enduring themes and problems of human existence, and they provide a kind of road map for navigating these themes and problems. None of the theories has a patent on the truth. All of them contain sufficient truths to shed light on some aspects of human experience. Personality theories are ways of understanding human behavior. Usually, these theories do not meet the strict standards of scientific acceptability, but they often address value-laden issues such as the purpose of life, meaning, and destiny.

A TREND TOWARD ACTIVE AGENCY IN THEORIES OF PERSONALITY

In the first chapter, we briefly saw that theories can be understood historically by momentarily backing away from the details of content and attending to how a theory portrays human agency. Buss (1978) indicated that all personality theories must deal with the issue of human control over the world and its people. Active human agency means that the person is portrayed as masterful, planful, resourceful, resilient, and capable of overcoming obstacles. Passive human agency means that the theory portrays people as shaped by factors over which they have little control. Feelings of powerlessness and incompetence are the result.

Early Views of Human Agency as Passive

Classical psychoanalysis and radical behaviorism are generally viewed as portraying human control as weak in the face of reality. Freud's dictum that "reality made much of us" and his use of the concept of *Ananke* (destiny) reflect a fundamental theme in classical psychoanalysis: Human reason should take charge of inner and outer reality, but it is rarely as strong as our instinctual makeup or the influence of early experience. Similarly, radical behaviorism depicts humans as largely determined by the sum total of their biology and environment, with very little room left for individual choice or the decisions of reason. Psychoanalysis and radical behaviorism picture humans as having less self-control, less self-efficacy, and less self-competence.

Modifying this standard picture, as has been noted in this text, is the fact that psychoanalysis may provide a method for a person to become aware of his or her reactions and develop new ways of dealing with drives, emotions, and reality-based problems. Behaviorism, as we have noted (Chapter 14) has also developed a theoretical background and techniques for some degree of positive human agency (Skinner, 1953, pp. 227–241).

Recent Trends Toward an Active Agency View

Many of the more recent trends in personality theory have shifted toward an active human agency view.

Ego psychology substantially changed the viewpoint of classical psychoanalysis on the issues of mastery and control. Anna Freud's concept of developmental lines of mastery emphasized the child's ability to cope with and overcome external obstacles. Erik Erikson also focused on a model of personality emphasizing, along with the importance of the environment, the activity of the individual.

Existentialism has always emphasized personal mastery and responsibility. Rollo May (1958a,b), perhaps more than any other American theorist in this tradition, has written extensively about issues of mastery and control. His concepts of destiny and will emphasize active human mastery and responsibility—all from a philosophical vantage point.

Bandura's conceptions of reciprocal determinism and active human agency place mastery motives at the core of human personality. For Bandura, people control their lives, detect external controls, react to them, and change the world they live in. Mastery motivation ("efficacy" in Bandura's language) is a central part of his theory.

Evolutionary psychology, the latest theory on the scene, is usually thought of as deterministic and thus advocating the view of human agency as passive, but it must recognize and account for the active agentic aspects of human behavior as well.

WHO BECOMES A PERSONALITY THEORIST?

The origins of various personality theories are often grounded in the life history of their respective theorists. In particular, childhood experiences appear to be the most telling. In some cases, the theorist experienced difficulties that led to a sense of inferiority. In other cases, a nonpathological view could emphasize that the theorist overcame the difficulties life presented.

Table 19.1 provides a summary of the life experience of some major theorists and their resultant ideas for nine categories of personality theory: Classical Psychoanalysis, Ego Psychology, Object Relations Theory, Neo-Freudian/Interpersonal, Humanism/Existentialism, Radical Behaviorisms, Social Cognitive Theory, Biological Basis of Personality, and Evolutionary Psychology.

The parallels between the theorists' personal sources and their resulting ideas in Table 19.1 are based on analyses of their work and lives in several editions of *Beneath the Mask*. The table entries, therefore, are restricted to those theorists for whom we have sufficiently detailed and reliable biographical information to analyze the personal origins of their intellectual creations. To understand fully the entries for a particular theorist, consult and review the relevant personal sources section of the chapter pertaining to that therapist.

Table 19.1 Theorists' Personal Sources and Resultant Ideas

CLASSICAL PSYCHOANALYSIS

Theorist	Personal sources	Resultant ideas
SIGMUND FREUD	Intense attachment to mother. Disappointment in father. Insecurity, inferiority. Sensitivity to missing family members. Strivings for personal greatness.	• Oedipus complex: child–parent sexual and aggressive attachments and conflicts. • Early (1895 "Project") attempt to make psychoanalysis scientific–with a neurological foundation. • Hunger-love, love-hate, sex-aggression, life-death drive models. • Superego as internalized parental standards, ideals, and prohibitions.

EGO PSYCHOLOGY

Theorist	Personal sources	Resultant ideas
ERIK ERIKSON	Insecurity, identity confusion. Feelings of unwantedness (father abandoned family) Inferiority feelings relative to anti-Semitism in childhood and adolescence. Feelings of not belonging.	• Ego identity. • Psychosocial moratoria. • Ego strengths through life cycle. • Crucial importance of cultural issues in ego development: ritualizations.
ANNA FREUD	Insecurity, inferiority, unwantedness. Fantasies of being beaten. Feeling responsible for father. Role reversal: parenting her parent. Special attachment to and protectiveness of father. Sigmund's "Antigone."	• Developmental lines that emphasize mastery and coping in children's ego development. • Use of psychoanalytic surrogate mothering with war orphans. • Development of methods for child analysis. • Synthesis and explanation of ego defenses, including altruistic surrender.
MARGARET MAHLER	Inferiority, unwantedness, gender dissatisfaction (father raised her as a son). Conflict with rejecting mother. Special attachment to father. Pressure from father to be totally self-sufficient.	• Importance of mother–child relationship. • Separation-individuation. • Importance of autonomy.

OBJECT RELATIONS THEORY

Theorist	Personal sources	Resultant ideas
MELANIE KLEIN	Unwantedness: Told by brother and mother that she had been an "accidental" and unwanted child. Inferiority relative to her brother.	• Maternal centrism. • View of infants as essentially aggressive and destructive. • Feminized Freud's "male" psychoanalysis with concepts of the centrality of the breast.

(continued)

Table 19.1 *(continued)*

OBJECT RELATIONS THEORY

Theorist	Personal sources	Resultant ideas
D. W. WINNICOTT	Fundamentally secure, happy childhood. Reared by multiple mothers. Absent fathering; insensitive fathering and teasing, possibly about Winnicott's maleness. Depressed mothering.	• Emphasis on positive adaptation to facilitating environment: "No such thing as a baby." • Maternal identification and emphasis on "good enough mothering." • Little attention to the role of father. • Concept of "false self" as caretaker for the the depressed mother who is "not good enough."

NEO-FREUDIAN/INTERPERSONAL

Theorist	Personal sources	Resultant ideas
ALFRED ADLER	Insecurity, inferiority. Childhood illness and resentment of physical vulnerability. Fear of death.	• Superiority strivings. • Organ inferiority. • *Gemeinschaftsgefühl* (fellow-feeling) • Safeguarding mechanisms.
KAREN HORNEY	Compliant, feeling unwanted, inferior feeling, obsessive doubting of self. Chronic depression; suicidal thoughts. Resentment of and competition with mother; competition with brother as father's favored child. Submissive to father's erratic authority.	• Basic anxiety: Lonely and helpless. • Basic hostility: Anger toward authority. • Tyranny of the "shoulds." • Coping strategies: expansive, resigned, and compliant.
CARL G. JUNG	Insecurity, lack of personal worth. Feelings of self-splitting: Belief in twin personalities inside self. Admitted need to avoid blame and responsibility. Feelings of derealization and depersonalization. Probable episodes of hallucinating. Compensatory grandiosity.	• Introversion-extroversion, and anima-animus as fundamental human dualisms. • Self-actualization: healing properties of the whole self. • "Synchronicity" as a noncausal explanation of reality. • Collective unconscious. • Enantiodromia: the tension of opposites.
HARRY S. SULLIVAN	Insecurity, inferiority, loneliness. Childhood alienation, feelings of un-wantedness. Feelings of abandon-ment by mother. Family devaluation of father. Conflicts over homosexuality.	• Interpersonal definition of personality. • Specialized treatment of schizophrenic male patients. • Interpersonal personifications.

HUMANISM/EXISTENTIALISM

Theorist	Personal sources	Resultant ideas
GORDON ALLPORT	Feelings of insecurity and inferiority . relative to brother, Floyd. Struggle for recognition of his own uniqueness relative to brother. Compensatory strivings for superiority via intellectual achievement. Belief in control over one's life, ability to transcend one's history.	• Emphasis on individuality, uniqueness. • Idiographic versus nomothetic. • Proprium or self. • Functional autonomy: Transcending personal history or distress.

(continued)

Table 19.1   *(continued)*

HUMANISM/EXISTENTIALISM

Theorist	Personal sources	Resultant ideas
ABRAHAM MASLOW	Insecure, inferior-feeling, lacking self-confidence in the extreme. Rejecting mother, psychologically absent father. Pursuit of heroes (parental substitutes?).	• Dominance-feeling in monkeys. • Studies of dominant women. • Good-specimen strategy. • Self-actualized people.
ROLLO MAY	Loneliness, feelings of helplessness, isolation, massive feelings of unwantedness and rejection leading to a substantial depressive (possibly suicidal) episode. Early exposure to discordant family life. Rebellious during adolescence. Adult confrontation with death and helplessness (tuberculosis).	• Introduction of European existential concepts to American psychology (e.g., *dasein, mitwelt, eigenwelt, umwelt*). • Psychological versions of philosophical concepts: e.g., death, will, destiny, daimonic, freedom. • Merger of selected psychoanalytic ideas (i.e., neurotic anxiety, the unconscious) with existential concepts.
CARL ROGERS	Insecurity, inferiority. Resentful of parental authority. Feelings of loneliness, isolation. Rebellious to family religious and disciplinary demands as defense against feeling superior to others. Strong needs to counter dependency feelings with autonomy strivings.	• Phenomenal self: Everyone has his or her own reality. • Empathic understanding of others without directive interventions. • Acceptance of children unconditionally to enable healthy development. • Fully functioning person: autonomous and spontaneous.

RADICAL BEHAVIORISMS

Theorist	Personal sources	Resultant ideas
JOHN B. WATSON	Angry with father and mother. Father was unpredictable and mostly absent during childhood. Rebelliousness to authority. Strong needs to be in control of self. Insecure and ambivalent about success. Strong needs to be successful, and strong fears of failure to the point of a personal breakdown in graduate school. Resentment of control by others, and their demands. Early rejection of mother's aspirations for him to have a career in the clergy. Belligerent and impulsive, pretentious, ambitious, and arrogant. Lifelong effort to escape poverty of his youth.	• Radical behaviorism: Mind and feelings are illusions. • Radical materialism, determinism, and reductionism. • Bitter criticism of psychoanalysis as mythology. • Goal: Prediction and rational control of behavior.

(continued)

Table 19.1 *(continued)*

RADICAL BEHAVIORISMS

Theorist	Personal sources	Resultant ideas
B. F. SKINNER	Rebelliousness to authority, discovery of family myth that he was a difficult birth, which caused mother great hardship: leading to unwantedness. Strong need to be in control of self. Resentment of control, demands. Disappointment with father's perceived passivity; resentment of mother's pretentiousness and tendency to pressure her husband and sons. Insecurity during adolescence. Need to control and externalize own emotions, displacing them to the outside world.	• Semiradical behaviorism: Mind and feelings are irrelevant to understanding psychological causes. • Goal: Prediction and rational control of behavior. • Semiradical determinism. • Aspiration to construct an ideal society in which control over the environment helps people want to act in their own interests. • Motivation externalized to environmental contingencies of reinforcement.

SOCIAL COGNITIVE THEORY

Theorist	Personal sources	Resultant ideas
ALBERT BANDURA	Childhood in small northern Alberta town. Growing up in a rugged, competitive environment. Experience in the Yukon after college.	• The development of research and psychological theories emphasizing individual effort, self efficacy, and resilient agency.

BIOLOGICAL BASIS OF PERSONALITY

Theorist	Personal sources	Resultant ideas
HANS EYSENCK	Unwantedness: Divorced parents had little time for or interest in their son. Described parents as mean, ungenerous, and uncaring. Inferiority and self-consciousness about being German born, especially during WW II. Confrontational attitude to established authority in psychiatry/psychology. Self-described angry, dangerous rebel.	• Critical of and rebellious to authority figures in psychiatry and the status quo in psychology. • Entire theory aimed at disconfirming established conventions in diagnosis, psychotherapy, and personality. • Harshly critical of psychodynamic theories. • Strong belief in material/biological basis of personality. • Reliance on stringent empiricism. • Extrovert as impulsive, sometimes acting-out rebel.

EVOLUTIONARY PSYCHOLOGY

Theorist	Personal sources	Resultant ideas
EDWARD O. WILSON	Poor eyesight, partial blindness from accident, partial deafness Parental divorce and frequent moves. Intense interest and curiosity about the natural world, especially the behavior of ants and other insects. Membership in the Society of Fellows at Harvard University	• Empirical studies and theories about the behavior of ants and other social insects. • Interest in evolutionary biology and its implications for the behavior of animal species and humans. • Emphasis on unifying theories of behavior and the love of life, *biophilia*.

Creative Illness or Inferiority Loves Company?

Henri Ellenberger's (1970) concept of creative illness, discussed in Chapter 1, asserts that theorists resolve a personal crisis by creating a theory that universalizes their distress. No doubt, Ellenberger's thesis has validity for some theorists. Carl Jung comes readily to mind in this context. Sigmund Freud, Karen Horney, Margaret Mahler, and Harry Stack Sullivan also universalized their personal distress in theoretical constructs that purport to describe all people. It is arguable whether these theorists were creatively ill, as we discussed in Chapter 1. Nevertheless, it is by now abundantly clear that a theorist's personal experiences, conflicts, and idiosyncratic interpretations of social reality become an experiential base in which their theories are nested. Call it a "resolution of creative illness" or call it "reliance on personal sources," either description communicates that personality theories are uniquely based in the personalities that create them.

In addition, the summaries in Table 19.1 show something else. By their own account, many of the personality theorists felt inferior during childhood. Alfred Adler (Chapter 5) proposed that we all experience feelings of inferiority that we strive to overcome. Part of the human condition, Adler thought, was an inherent striving from minus to plus, from inferiority to superiority, from incompetence to competence. If, as Adler asserted, everyone feels inferior in some way, the large percentage of our sample of theorists in whom we have noted a strong sense of inferiority is not remarkable.

Alongside nearly universal feelings of inferiority, a significant number of the theorists also had the belief that they were unwanted children. A strong case for the presence of significant feelings of unwantedness can be made for many of the theorists covered in the present text. Applying Karen Horney's concepts (Chapter 10), we might conclude that many of them faced basic anxieties having to do with a hostile environment.

But there is another way to look at it. If it were true that a large number of people have felt inferior, unwanted, or had other significant challenges to overcome, then why do many more people not create a theory of personality? Put yet another way, what is it about difficult experiences and the urge to understand them that led this group of people to create theories of human nature? What is really remarkable is that they chose to strive to overcome any early difficulties by becoming well-known intellectuals in the professions of psychiatry and psychology.

Personality theorists are not simply people who, in many cases, have experienced challenges in life or have felt inferior or unwanted. They are proselytizers who seek to impress their colleagues in the mental health professions with their insights and discoveries. They are creative intellectuals who demand answers from their science and art of the mind. The creation of a personal identity as psychologist or psychiatrist is most effective in this process of self-healing when that identity also leads to helping others and produces publicly acclaimed achievement. And what better and more pro-social way to achieve self-healing than for the psychologist or psychiatrist to create and publish an influential theory of human nature, one that has the potential to be of benefit to many people.

THE CULTURAL AND SOCIAL-HISTORICAL CONTEXTS OF PERSONALITY THEORIES

An individual's life experiences are nested in a cultural and social historical framework not unique to him or her. The personality theories and solutions that the theorists have developed speak to problems that others who face similar issues have experienced as well. Their formulations of the issues and proposals of solutions are relevant and of value to others. Personality theories are not the only means by which an individual's insights about life and solutions to important issues are provided to others.

A good example of this process outside of the field of personality theory is the "Roots" phenomenon. Alex Haley, a writer in the late twentieth century, experienced a sense of rootlessness and disconnectedness in modern society. His search for his family roots and the publication of his novel, *Roots* (1976) and the subsequent television series helped jumpstart the "roots" movement. Millions of people, who also felt disconnected from their backgrounds, began to explore their own personal and ethnic backgrounds. Thus, Haley's solution to a problem experienced by many was passed on to others in our society.

Likewise, Sigmund Freud, Carl Rogers, and Erik Erikson, for example, faced specific issues that were also experienced by many others. Freud addressed the hypocritical denial of sexual drives, Rogers the mid-century emphasis on conformity, and Erikson the factors involved in shaping a personal identity. Albert Bandura, a later theorist, proposed concepts that helped us understand the role of television and other media in influencing behavior.

How is it that so many people at specific times experience similar issues? The answer is in the process of cultural and social change. The rapid technological, demographic, and socioeconomic changes of the past century have led to changes in all facets of contemporary life. These changes require constant adjustment and readjustment on the part of new generations. Old solutions may not work for new realities, and the verities of our childhood upbringing may not help us adjust to adult conditions. The development and promulgation of personality theories and associated psychotherapeutic approaches is one means of helping people develop new ways of thinking about and coping with new realities.

A FINAL EVALUATION OF THE THEORIES

The three dimensions that we have used to compare and evaluate each theory lead to some surprising conclusions when we view theories of personality from a wider perspective than the one-theory-at-a-time approach permits. *Refutability, human agency,* and the *idiographic-nomothetic distinction* are important in themselves, but they are also important for what they tell us about the persistence of these theories in human discourse.

Refutability

When the philosopher of science, Karl Popper, proposed the criterion of refutability (1959, 1963), he had in mind the apparent universal compatibility of the theories of Alfred Adler and Sigmund Freud with any human behavior that could be observed. It seemed to Popper that these psychological theories were untestable. They could explain *everything*— a source of pride to the theorists, but a red flag to Popper.

Psychological theories can be refutable, and some are. Theories of personality, with few exceptions, are not. Some of us do not want them to be. The not-so-obvious secret is this: Theories of personality are theories of human nature. Understood in that way, it is easy to see that refutability is not likely to apply to any one of the grand theories in its entirety. One or another construct drawn from these theories may lend itself to refutation. However, for every diligent empirical psychologist who attempts to translate a grand idea into an empirical statement, there are many intellectuals who find something else of value in these ideas.

What can we learn from this resistance to scientific truth finding? Refutability is a good thing. It is even a necessary thing if psychology is to progress. However, it is not a sufficient thing. We want more of our theories of human nature than mere refutability can provide. Fortunately, we have no scarcity of unrefutable theories from which to choose.

Human Agency

The classical, or grand, theories vary when it comes to depicting human agency. Psychoanalysis and radical behaviorism fall on the side of having reality shape us. Humanism sees us as shaping reality. The social cognitive learning theory of personality has the best of both worlds: We shape and are shaped by the changes we introduce into reality. The important point is that every theory, for better or worse, has something to say about personal mastery of the world and about our perception of that mastery. George Kelly made personal control a central feature of his "man the scientist." Sigmund Freud gave coping with reality center stage instead. Alfred Adler focused on overcoming inferiority; Maslow strove for self-actualization.

Idiographic Versus Nomothetic Focus

A paradox of the idiographic-nomothetic distinction is this: Every theorist aimed to create a theory that would apply to all humans. Who would create a theory that applies to one person, at one moment in time, in one geographic place? For example, what kind of a theorist creates a theory to explain one Bronx resident, or one highlander in Scotland, or one Aboriginal person? The aspiration (literally, the hope) of every theorist is to explain and to understand the behavior of all people.

However, we find that each theorist bases his or her theory largely on some aspects of experience highlighted by his or her own life experience or by his or her own particular cultural and historical environment. Even these theorists whose aspirations are to be nomothetic nevertheless worked from individual cases—sometimes from their own case or those of some of their patients—and then sought to generalize their findings.

SUMMARY

If so many theories of personality are not refutable, why do they persist? We can suggest several answers, among them:

- Empirical research is always open to interpretation, so even when a theory is tested and refuted, some people do not accept the refutation.

- Some theorists deal with substantial issues that have enduring value in the history of humanity, and we are not very patient in waiting for scientific ways to understand these issues before we begin to deal with them.

- Most theorists pride themselves on addressing major issues rather than smaller but more empirically manageable concerns.

The issue of personal mastery, interpreted differently by different schools of thought, underlies all classical theories of personality. There has been a trend in personality theory from the view of human agency as passive to a view of it as active.

Most of the theorists share some common personality features and motives that guided their efforts to become eminent members of the mental health professions. Feelings of inferiority coupled with beliefs that they were unwanted children shaped the personal histories of many—but certainly not all—of the theorists presented in this book. The theorists' often resourceful solutions to the problems they faced were nested in their own life histories, which in turn were rooted in specific cultural and historical environments. The understanding and solutions they provided have helped other people living under similar influences to understand themselves better and to develop new means of coping with the realities they faced.

FOR FURTHER READING

Henri Ellenberger's *The Discovery of the Unconscious* (New York: Basic Books, 1970) contains a good discussion of the personal sources of theories and expounds the author's view of creative illness as the source of many psychological theories. Buss's "The Structure of Psychological Revolutions" (*Journal of the History of the Behavioral Sciences,* 1978, *14,* 57–64) is worth reading for the insight it provides into the reactivity of schools of thought to each other and the importance of human agency in psychology.

Along these same lines, Albert Bandura's "Human Agency in Social Cognitive Theory" (*American Psychologist,* 1989, *44,* 9, 1175–1184) is a thoughtful analysis of human agency in psychological theory and a rationale for cognitive social learning theory. Finally, Nevitt Sanford's "What Have We Learned About Personality?" in Sigmund Koch and David Leary (Eds.), *A Century of Psychology as a Science* (New York: McGraw-Hill, 1985) is an interesting critique of personality psychology and its various blind alleys.

Bibliography

Abramson, L. Y., Seligman, M. E. P., & Teasdale, J. (1978). Learned helplessness in humans: Critique and reformulation. *Journal of Abnormal Psychology, 87,* 32–48.

Adler, A. (1907). The study of organ inferiority and its psychical compensation. In H. L. Ansbacher & R. R. Ansbacher (Eds.), *The individual psychology of Alfred Adler.* New York: Harper, 1956.

(1908). The aggression drive in life and neurosis. In H. L. Ansbacher & R. R. Ansbacher (Eds.), *The individual psychology of Alfred Adler.* New York: Harper, 1956.

(1910). The psychology of hermaphroditism in life and in neurosis. In H. L. Ansbacher & R. R. Ansbacher (Eds.), *The individual psychology of Alfred Adler.* New York: Harper, 1956.

(1912). The neurotic character. In H. L. Ansbacher & R. R. Ansbacher (Eds.), *The individual psychology of Alfred Adler.* New York: Harper, 1956.

(1913a). Individual-psychological treatment of neurosis. In Alfred Adler, *The practice and theory of individual psychology.* Totowa, NJ: Littlefield-Adams, 1959.

(1913b). Individual-psychological treatment of neurosis. In H. L. Ansbacher & R. R. Ansbacher (Eds.), *The individual psychology of Alfred Adler.* New York: Harper, 1956.

(1913c). The function of neurotic symptoms. In H. L. Ansbacher & R. R. Ansbacher (Eds.), *The individual psychology of Alfred Adler.* New York: Harper, 1956.

(1927). *Understanding human nature.* Greenwich, CT: Fawcett.

(1929a). *The science of living.* New York: Doubleday, 1969.

(1929b). *Problems of neurosis.* Philip Mairet (Ed.). New York: Harper, 1929.

(1930a). *The problem child.* New York: Putnam, 1963.

(1930b). *The science of living.* London: Allen & Unwin, 1930.

(1930c). *The education of children.* Chicago: Henry Regnery, 1970.

(1931). *What life should mean to you.* New York: Putnam.

(1932). The structure of neurosis. In H. L. Ansbacher & R. R. Ansbacher (Eds.), *Superiority and social interest: A collection of later writings.* New York: Viking Compass, 1973.

(1933). The meaning of life. In H. L. Ansbacher & R. R. Ansbacher (Eds.), *The individual psychology of Alfred Adler.* New York: Harper, 1956.

(1935). The fundamental views of individual psychology. In H. L. Ansbacher & R. R. Ansbacher (Eds.), *The individual psychology of Alfred Adler.* New York: Harper, 1956.

(1956). *The individual psychology of Alfred Adler: A systematic presentation in selections from his writings.* H. L. Ansbacher & R. R. Ansbacher (Eds.). New York: Harper.

(1959). *The practice and theory of individual psychology.* Totowa, N.J.: Littlefield-Adams.

(1964). *Social interest: A challenge to mankind.* New York: Putnam.

(1973). *Superiority and social interest: A collection of later writings.* H. L. Ansbacher & R. R. Ansbacher (Eds.). New York: Viking Compass.

Alcock, John. (2001). *The Triumph of Sociobiology.* New York: Oxford University Press.

Allport, Floyd. (1924). *Social psychology.* Boston: Houghton Mifflin.

Allport, G. (1937). *Personality: A psychological interpretation.* New York: Henry Holt.

(1942). *The use of personal documents in psychological science.* New York: Social Science Research Council Bulletin (No. 49).

(Ed.). (1946). Letters from Jenny (published anonymously in this edition). *Journal of Abnormal and Social Psychology, 41,* 315–350 and 449–480.

(1950). *The individual and his religion.* New York: Macmillan.

(1955). *Becoming: basic considerations for a psychology of personality.* New Haven: Yale University Press.

(1960). *Personality and social encounter: Selected essays.* Boston: Beacon Press.

(1961). *Pattern and growth in personality.* New York: Holt, Rinehart and Winston.

Allport, G. (1962). "My encounters with personality theory." Recorded and edited reminiscence at the Boston University School of Theology, October 12, 1962, transcribed by Douglas, W.

——— (1963). *The person in psychology: Selected essays.* Boston: Beacon Press.

——— (1964). The fruits of eclecticism: Bitter or sweet? In G. Allport, *The person in psychology.* Boston: Beacon Press, 1968 (paper originally published in *Acta Psychological,* 1964, *23,* 27–44).

——— (Ed.). (1965). *Letters from Jenny.* New York: Harcourt, Brace & World.

——— (1966). Traits revisited. In G. Allport, *The person in psychology.* Boston: Beacon Press, 1968 (paper originally published in *American Psychologist,* 1966, *21,* 1–10).

——— (1967). Autobiography. In E. G. Boring & G. Lindzey (Eds.), *A history of psychology in autobiography,* Vol. 5. New York: Appleton.

Alsopp, J. F., & Eysenck, H. J. (1974). Personality as a determinant of paired associate learning. *Perceptual and Motor Skills, 39,* 315–324.

——— (1975). Extraversion, neuroticism and verbal reasoning ability as determinants of paired associate recall. *British Journal of Psychology, 66,* 15–24.

Ansbacher, H. L., & Ansbacher, R. R. (1956). *The individual psychology of Alfred Adler: A systematic presentation in selections from his writings.* New York: Harper.

Andreasen, N. C. (1984). *The broken brain: The biological revolution in psychiatry.* New York: Harper and Row.

Andreasen, N., & Munich, R. L. (1995). Introduction to Schizophrenia and other psychotic disorders. In G. O. Gabbard (Ed.), *Treatment of psychiatric disorders* (2nd ed., Vol. 1, pp. 943–946). Washington, DC: American Psychiatric Press.

APA. (1994). *Diagnostic and statistical manual of mental disorders [DSM-IV]* (4th ed.) Washington, DC: The American Psychiatric Association.

APA. (2000). *Diagnostic and statistical manual of mental disorders:* [DSM-IV-TRC], (4th ed., text revision). Washington, DC: The American Psychiatric Association.

Appignanesi, L., & Forrester, J. (1992). *Freud's women.* New York: Basic Books.

Aronson, E. (1969). The theory of cognitive dissonance: A current perspective. In L. Berkowitz (Ed.), *Advances in experimental social psychology,* Vol. 4. New York: Academic Press.

Atwood, G. E., & Stolorow, R. D. (1977a). The life and work of Wilhelm Reich: A case study of the subjectivity of personality theory. *The Psychoanalytic Review, 64,* 5–20.

——— (1977b). Metapsychology, reification and the representational world of C. G. Jung. *International Review of Psychoanalysis, 4,* 197–214.

Atwood, G. E., & Tomkins, S. (1976). On the subjectivity of personality theory. *Journal of the History of the Behavioral Sciences, 12,* 166–177.

Bakan, P. (1959). Extraversion-intraversion and improvement in an auditory vigilance task. In H. J. Eysenck (Ed.), *Readings in extraversion-intraversion,* vol. 3: *Bearings on basic psychological processes.* London: Staples Press, 1971 (paper originally published in *British Journal of Psychology,* 1959, *50,* 325–332).

Balmary, M. (1979). *Psychoanalyzing psychoanalysis: Freud and the hidden fault of the father.* Baltimore: Johns Hopkins Press.

Bandura, A. (1961). Psychotherapy as a learning process. *Psychological Bulletin, 58,* 143–159.

——— (1969). *Principles of behavior modification.* New York: Holt, Rinehart and Winston.

——— (1974). Behavior theory and the models of man. *American Psychologist, 29,* 859–869.

——— (1976). Conversation with Richard I. Evans. In R. I. Evans (Ed.), *The making of psychology.* New York: Knopf.

——— (1977a). Self-efficacy: Toward a unifying theory of behavioral change. *Psychological Review, 84,* 191–215.

——— (1977b). *Social learning theory.* Englewood Cliffs, NJ: Prentice-Hall.

——— (1978a). The self-system in reciprocal determinism. *American Psychologist, 33,* 344–358.

——— (1981). In search of pure unidirectional determinants. *Behavior Therapy, 12,* 30–40.

——— (1982). Self-efficacy mechanism in human agency. *American Psychologist, 37,* 122–147.

——— (1986). *Social foundations of thought and action.* Englewood Cliffs, NJ: Prentice-Hall.

——— (1989). Human agency in social cognitive theory. *American Psychologist, 44,* 9, 1175–1184.

Bandura, A. (Ed.). (1995). *Self-efficacy in changing societies.* New York: Oxford University Press.

Bandura, A. (1997). *Self-efficacy: The exercise of control.* New York: Freeman.

Bandura, A. (2001a) Personal communication. August 25, 2001.

(2001b) Personal communication. July 12, 2001.

(2001c) Personal communication. August 8, 2001.

Bandura, A., Adams, N. E., & Beyer, J. (1977). Cognitive processes mediating behavioral change. *Journal of Personality and Social Psychology, 35,* 125–139.

Bandura, A., & Schunk, D. H. (1981). Cultivating competence, self-efficacy, and intrinsic interest through proximal self-motivation. *Journal of Personality and Social Psychology, 41,* 586–598.

Bandura, A., & Walters, R. H. (1959). *Adolescent aggression.* New York: Ronald Press.

(1963). *Social learning and personality development.* New York: Holt, Rinehart and Winston.

Bannister, D., & Fransella, F. (1971). *Inquiring man. The theory of personality constructs.* New York: Penguin Books.

Barash, David P. (1977). *Sociobiology and behavior.* New York: Elsevier.

(1982). *Sociobiology and behavior.* New York: Elsevier.

(2001). *Revolutionary biology.* New Brunswick, NJ: Transaction Publishers.

Barkow, Jermone H., Cosmides, Leda & Toooby, John, ed. (1992). *The adapted mind: Evolutionary psychology and the generation of culture.* New York: Oxford University Press.

Barnes, M. & Berke, J. (1971). *Two accounts of a journey through madness.* New York: Ballantine.

Barrett, W. (1958). *Irrational man: A study in existential philosophy.* New York: Doubleday Anchor.

Basch, M. F. (1975). Perception, consciousness and Freud's "project". In *The Annual of Psychoanalysis,* Vol. 3. New York: International Universities Press, 3–19.

Berkowitz, L. (1969). The frustration-aggression hypothesis revisited. In L. Berkowitz (ed.), *Roots of aggression: A re-examination of the frustration-aggression hypothesis.* New York: Atherton.

Berman, M. (1975). Review of life history and the historical moment by Erik Erikson. In *New York Times Book Review,* March 30.

Bernstein, A. (1976). Freud and Oedipus: A new look at the Oedipus complex in the light of Freud's life. *The Psychoanalytic Review, 63,* 393–407.

Bertocci, P. A. (1950). Critique of Gordon W. Allport's theory of motivation. *Psychological Review, 47,* 501–532.

Bettelheim, B. (1967). *The empty fortress: Infantile autism and the birth of the self.* New York: Free Press.

Black, A. H. (1958). The extinction of avoidance responses under curare. *Journal of Comparative and Psychological Psychology, 51,* 519–524.

Blanck, G. & Blanck, R. (1974). *Ego psychology: Theory and practice.* New York: Columbia University Press.

Blos, Peter. (1962). *On adolescence: A psychoanalytic interpretation.* New York: Free Press.

(1970). *The young adolescent: Clinical studies.* New York: Free Press.

Bottome, Phyllis. (1957). *Alfred Adler: A portrait from life.* New York: Vanguard.

Bower, G. H., & Miller, N. (1960). Effects of amount of reward on strength of approach in an approach-avoidance conflict. *Journal of Comparative and Physiological Psychology, 53,* 59–62.

Brand, C. (1997). Obituary of Hans Eysenck. In Upstream, an Internet publication: *http://www.mugu.com/cgi-bin/Upstream/People/Eysenck/*

Breger, L., & McGaugh, J. L. (1965). Critique and reformulation of "Learning-Theory" approaches to psychotherapy and neurosis. *Psychological Bulletin, 63,* 338–358.

Breland, K., & Breland, M. (1961). The misbehavior of organisms. *American Psychologist, 16,* 681–684.

Breland-Bailey, M., & Bailey, R. E. (1993). "Misbehavior": A case history. *American Psychologist, 48,* 1157–1158.

Breuer, J., & Freud, S. (1893–1895). *Studies on hysteria,* Vol. II of *The standard edition of the complete psychological works of Sigmund Freud.* London: Hogarth Press, 1955.

(1893). On the psychical mechanism of hysterical phenomena: A preliminary communication. In J. Breuer & S. Freud, *Studies on hysteria,* Vol. II of *The standard edition of the complete psychological works of Sigmund Freud.* James Strachey (Ed.). London: Hogarth Press, 1955.

Brewster-Smith, M. (1971). Allport, Murray and Lewin on personality: Notes on a confrontation. *Journal of the History of the Behavioral Sciences, 7,* 353–362.

Broadhurst, P. L. (1959). The interaction of task difficulty and motivation: The Yerkes-Dodson law revived. *Acta Psychologica, 16,* 321–338.

Brown, Roger. (1965). *Social psychology.* New York: Free Press.

Brown, T. A., Martin, M. & Barlow, D. H. (1995). Diagnostic comorbidity in panic disorder: Effect on treatment outcome and course of comorbid diagnoses following treatment. *Journal of Consulting and Clinical Psychology, 63,* 408–418.

Bruner, J. S., Shapiro, D., & Tagiuri, R. (1958). The meaning of traits in isolation and in combination. In R. Tagiuri & L. Petrullo (Eds.), *Person perception and interpersonal behavior.* Stanford, CA: Stanford University Press.

Buckley, K. W. (1989). *Mechanical man: John Broadus Watson and the beginnings of behaviorism.* New York: Guilford.

Buckley, P. (1986). Editor's introduction. In P. Buckley (Ed.), *Essential papers on object relations.* New York: New York University Press.

Buhler, C. (1971). Basic theoretical concepts of humanistic psychology. *American Psychologist, 26,* 378–386.

Burnham, J. C. (1994). John B. Watson: Interviewee, professional figure, symbol. In J. T. Todd & E. K. Morris (Eds.), *Modern perspectives on John B. Watson and classical behaviorism.* Westport, CT: Greenwood Press.

Buss, A. R. (1978). The structure of psychological revolutions. *Journal of the History of the Behavioral Sciences, 14,* 57–64.

Buss, David M. (1989). Sex differences in human mate preferences: Evolutionary hypotheses Tested in 37 cultures. *Behavioral and Brain Science, 12,* 1–49.

(1994). *The Evolution of desire: strategies of human mating.* New York: Basic Books.

(1999). *Evolutionary psychology: The new science of the mind.* Needham Heights, MA: Allyn and Bacon.

Butler, R. A., & Harlow, H. F. (1957). Exploratory and related behavior; A new trend in animal research. *Journal of General Psychology, 57,* 257–264.

Cartwright, John (2000). *Evolution and human behavior: Darwinian perspectives on human nature.* Cambridge, MA: MIT Press.

Daly, Martin & Wilson, Margo. (1988). *Homicide.* New York: Aldine de Gruyter.

Cattell, H. E. P. (1993). Comment on Goldberg. *American Psychologist, 48,* 1302–1303.

Chapman, A. H. (1976). *Harry Stack Sullivan: The man and his work.* New York: Putnam.

Christie, R., & Geis, F. (1968). Some consequences of taking Machiavelli seriously. In E. Borgatta & W. Lambert (Eds.), *Handbook of personality theory and research.* Chicago: Rand McNally.

(1970). *Studies in Machiavellianism.* New York: Academic Press.

Claridge, G. S. (1967). *Personality and arousal.* New York: Pergamon.

Clarkin, J. F., Hull, J. W., Cantor, J., & Sanderson, C. (1993). Borderline personality disorder and personality traits: A comparison of SCID-II BPD and NEO-PI. *Psychological Assessment, 5,* 472–476.

Coon, Deborah J. (1994). "Not a creature of reason": The alleged impact of Watsonian behaviorism on advertising in the 1920s. In J. T. Todd & E. K. Morris (Eds.), *Modern perspectives on John B. Watson and classical behaviorism.* Westport, CT: Greenwood Press.

Cosmides, Leda & Tooby, John. (1992). *The adapted mind: Evolutionary psychology and the generation of culture.* New York: London: Oxford University Press.

(2002). Unraveling the enigma of human intelligence: Evolutionary psychology and the multimodular mind. In Sternberg, R.J. & Kaufman, J.C. (Eds.), *The evolution of intelligence.* Mahway, NJ: Lawrence Erlbaum Associates, 145–198.

Crain, W. C. (1992). *Theories of development: Concepts and applications,* 3rd ed. Englewood Cliffs, NJ: Prentice Hall.

Daly, M., & Wilson, M. (1985). Child abuse and other risks of not living with both parents. *Ethology and Sociology, 6,* 197–210.

(1988). *Homicide.* New York: Aldine de Gruyter.

Darwin, Charles R. (1859). *On the origin of species by means of natural selection.* London: John Murray.

(1871). *The descent of man and selection in relation to sex.* London, England: John Murray Publishers.

(1872). *The expression of emotion in man and animals.* New York: Appleton.

Dawkins, R. (1989). *The selfish gene.* New York: Oxford University Press.

Dollard, J., Doob, L., Miller, N., Mowrer, O. H. & Sears, R. (1939). *Frustration and aggression.* New Haven: Yale University Press.

Dollard, J., & Miller, N. (1950). *Personality and psychotherapy: An analysis in terms of learning, thinking and culture.* New York: McGraw-Hill.

Dyer, R. (1983). *The work of Anna Freud.* New York: Aronson.

Dymond, R. (1954). Adjustment changes over therapy from self-sorts. In C. R. Rogers & R. F. Dymond (Eds.), *Psychotherapy and personality change* (pp. 77–84). Chicago: University of Chicago Press.

Eaves, L. J., Eysenck, H. J. & Martin, N. G. (1989). *Genes, culture and personality: An empirical approach.* New York: Academic Press.

Einstein, A., & Infeld, L. (1938). *The evolution of physics: From early concepts to relativity and quanta.* New York: Simon & Schuster.

Eissler, K. R. (1971). *Talent and genius: The fictitious case of tausk contra Freud.* New York: Quadrangle Books.

(1974). On mis-statements of would-be Freud biographers, with special reference to the tausk controversy. *International Review of Psychoanalysis, 1,* Part 4, 391–414.

(1978). A challenge to Professor Roazen. *Contemporary Psychoanalysis, 14,* 330–344.

Eliade, M. (1958). *Rites and symbols of initiation.* New York: Harper (originally published as *Birth and Rebirth*).

(1961). *The sacred and the profane.* New York: Harper & Row.

Ellenberger, H. (1970). *The discovery of the unconscious.* New York: Basic Books.

(1972). The story of "Anna O.": A critical review with new data. *Journal of the History of the Behavioral Sciences, 8,* 267–279.

Elms, A. C. (1981). Skinner's dark year and *Walden Two. American Psychologist, 36, 5,* 470–479.

Erikson, E. H. (1950). *Childhood and society* (2nd ed.). New York: Norton, 1963.

(1951). Sex differences in the play configurations of preadolescents. *Journal of Orthopsychiatry, 21,* 667–692.

(1959). *Identity and the life cycle: Selected papers.* Psychological Issues, Monograph No. 1, Vol. 1. New York: International Universities Press.

(1962). *Young man Luther: A study in psychoanalysis and history.* New York: Norton.

(1963). Youth: Fidelity and diversity. In E. H. Erikson (Ed.), *The challenge of youth.* New York: Doubleday.

(1964). *Insight and responsibility.* New York: Norton.

(Ed.). (1968). *Identity: Youth and crisis.* New York: Norton.

(1969). *Gandhi's truth: On the origins of militant nonviolence.* New York: Norton.

(1974). *Dimensions of a new identity: Jefferson lectures, 1973.* New York: Norton.

(1975). *Life history and the historical moment.* New York: Norton.

(1977). *Toys and reasons.* New York: Norton.

(Ed.). (1978). *Adulthood.* New York: Norton.

(1982). *The life cycle completed.* New York: Norton.

Erikson, E. H. & Erikson, J. M. (1997). *The life cycle completed.* New York: Norton.

Evans, D., & Zarate, O. (2000). *Introducing evolutionary psychology.* New York: Totem Books.

Evans, R. I. (1964). *Conversations with Carl Jung and reactions from Ernest Jones.* New York: Van Nostrand Reinhold Co.

(1975). *Carl Rogers: The man and his ideas: A dialogue.* New York: Dutton.

(1976). *Dialogue with R. D. Laing.* New York: Praeger.

(1976a). *The making of psychology: Discussion with creative contributors.* New York: Knopf.

(1981). *Dialogues with C. G. Jung.* New York: Praeger.

(1989). *Albert Bandura, the man and his ideas— A dialogue.* New York: Praeger.

(1996). *Dialogue with Erik Erikson.* New York: Harper & Row.

Eysenck, Hans J. (1947). *Dimensions of personality.* London: Routledge & Kegan Paul.

(1952). *The scientific study of personality.* London: Routledge & Kegan Paul.

(1953a). *Uses and abuses of psychology.* Baltimore: Penguin (Pelican ed.), 1953.

(1953b). *The structure of human personality* (rev. ed.). London: Methuen, 1970.

(1957a). *The dynamics of anxiety and hysteria: An experimental application of modern learning theory to psychiatry.* London: Routledge & Kegan Paul, 1957 (American edition: Praeger).

(1957b). *Sense and nonsense in psychology.* Baltimore: Penguin, 1957.

(1960). Learning theory and behavior therapy. In H. J. Eysenck (Ed.), *Behavior therapy and the neuroses.* New York: Pergamon.

(1963a). The measurement of motivation. *Scientific American,* May 1963, 130–140.

(1963b). Psychoanalysis: Myth or science? In Stanley Rachman (Ed.), *Critical essays on psychoanalysis.* New York: Macmillan, 1963.

Eysenck, Hans J. (1964a). *Crime and personality.* London: Routledge & Kegan Paul, 1964 (American edition: Houghton Mifflin).

(1964b). Involuntary rest pauses in tapping as a function of drive and personality. In H. J. Eysenck (Ed.), *Readings in extraversion-intraversion,* vol. 3: *Bearings on basic psychological processes.* London: Staples, 1971 (paper originally published in *Perceptual and Motor Skills,* 1964, *18,* 173–174).

(1965). *Fact and fiction in psychology.* Baltimore: Penguin.

(1965a). *Fact and fiction in psychology.* Baltimore: Penguin.

(1965b). *Smoking, health and personality.* New York: Basic Books.

(1967). *The biological basis of personality.* Springfield, IL: Charles C. Thomas.

(1970). Historical introduction. In H. J. Eysenck (Ed.), *Readings in extraversion-intraversion,* vol. 1: *Theoretical and methodological issues.* London: Staples.

(1972). *Psychology is about people.* New York: The Library Press.

(1973). *The inequality of man.* London: Temple Smith (American edition: Robert R. Knapp, San Diego, CA).

(1976). The learning theory model of neurosis—a new approach. *Behavior Research and Therapy,* *14,* 251–267.

(1979). *The structure and measurement of intelligence.* New York: Springer.

(1980). Hans Jurgen Eysenck: Autobiographical essay. In G. Lindzey (Ed.), *A history of psychology in autobiography,* Vol. VII. New York: W. H. Freeman.

(1980a). *The causes and effects of smoking.* London: Maurice Temple Smith.

(1982). *Personality, genetics, and behavior: Selected papers.* New York: Praeger.

(1990). *Rebel with a cause: The autobiography of Hans Eysenck.* London: W. H. Allen.

(1993). Comment on Goldberg. *American Psychologist,* *48,* 1299–1300.

Eysenck, H. J., & Eysenck, M. (1983). *Mindwatching: Why people behave the way they do.* New York: Garden Press/Doubleday.

(1985). *Personality and individual differences: A natural science approach.* New York: Plenum Press.

Eysenck, H. J., & Eysenck, S. B. G. (1968). *The Eysenck personality inventory.* San Diego, CA: Educational and Industrial Testing Service.

(1969). *Personality structure and measurement.* San Diego, CA: Robert R. Knapp.

(1975a). *Eysenck personality questionnaire.* San Diego, CA: Educational and Industrial Testing Service, 1975.

(1975b). *The manual of the Eysenck personality questionnaire.* San Diego, CA: Educational and Industrial Testing Service, 1975.

(1976). *Psychoticism as a dimension of personality.* New York: Crane, Russak.

Eysenck, H. J. & Gudjonsson, H. G. (1989). *The causes and cures of criminality.* New York: Plenum Press.

Eysenck, H. J., & Nias, D. K. (1982). *Astrology: Science or superstition?* New York: St. Martin's Press.

Eysenck, H. J. & Rachman, S. (1965). *The causes and cures of neurosis.* London: Routledge & Kegan Paul (American edition: Robert R. Knapp, San Diego, CA).

Eysenck, H.J. & Sargent, C. (1982). *Explaining the unexplained. Mysteries of the paranormal.* London: Prion.

Eysenck, H. J., & Wilson, G. D. (1973). *The experimental study of Freudian theories.* London: Methuen (American edition: Harper & Row).

Falk, J. L. (1956). Issues distinguishing idiographic from nomothetic approaches to personality. *Psychological Review,* *63,* 53–62.

Fancher, R. (1992). *Pioneers of Psychology* (2nd ed.). New York: Norton.

Fenichel, O. (1945). *The psychoanalytic theory of neurosis.* New York: Norton.

Festinger, L. (1942). A theoretical interpretation of shifts in level of aspiration. *Psychological Review,* *49,* 235–250.

(1957). *A theory of cognitive dissonance.* New York: Row, Peterson.

Fey, W. F. (1958). Doctrine and experience: Their influence upon the psychologist. *Journal of Consulting Psychology,* *22,* 403–409.

Fiedler, F. (1950a). A comparison of therapeutic relationships in psychoanalytic, nondirective and Adlerian therapy. *Journal of Consulting Psychology,* *14,* 436–445.

(1950b). The concept of an ideal therapeutic relationship. *Journal of Consulting Psychology,* *14,* 239–245.

(1951). Factor analyses of psychoanalytic, nondirective and Adlerian therapeutic relationships. *Journal of Consulting Psychology,* *15,* 32–38.

Fingarette, H. (1974). Self-deception and the "splitting of the ego". In R. Wolheim (Ed.), *Freud: A collection of critical essays.* Garden City, NY: Doubleday.

Fischer, C. T. (1977). Historical relations of psychology as an object-science and subject-science: Toward psychology as a human science. *Journal of the History of the Behavioral Sciences, 13,* 369–378.

Fisher, S., & Greenberg, R. P. (1996). *Freud scientifically reappraised: Testing the theories and therapy.* New York: John Wiley & Sons.

Fodor, J.S. (1983). *The modularity of mind.* Cambridge, MA: MIT Press.

Frankl, V. (1959). The spiritual dimension in existential analysis and logotherapy. *Journal of Individual Psychology, 15,* 157–165.

(1963). *Man's search for meaning.* New York: Simon & Schuster (Washington Square Paperback).

(1978). *The unheard cry for meaning: Psychotherapy and humanism.* New York: Simon & Schuster.

Frazer, J. George. (1963). *The golden bough.* New York: Macmillan.

Freeman, L. (1972). *The story of Anna O.* New York: Walker Press.

French, J. D. (1972). The reticular formation. *Scientific American,* May 1957 (reprinted in R. F. Thompson [Ed.], *Physiological Psychology: Readings from Scientific American.* San Francisco: Freeman, 1972).

Freud, A. (1922). Beating fantasies and daydreams. In Vol. 1 of *The writings of Anna Freud.* New York: International Universities Press, 1974.

(1927). Four lectures on Psychoanalysis. In Vol. 1 of *The Writings of Anna Freud.* New York: International Universities Press, 1974.

(1928). The theory of child analysis. In Vol. 1 of *The Writings of Anna Freud.* New York: International Universities Press, 1974.

(1929). *Anna Freud's letters to Eva Rosenfeld.* Peter Heller (Ed.). New York: International Universities Press, 1992.

(1936). *The ego and the mechanisms of defense* (rev. ed.). In Vol. 2 of *The writings of Anna Freud.* New York: International Universities Press, 1966.

(1945). Indications for child analysis. In Vol. 4 of *The writings of Anna Freud.* New York: International Universities Press, 1968.

(1951a). The contributions of psychoanalysis to genetic psychology. In Vol. 4 of *The writings of Anna Freud.* New York: International Universities Press, 1968.

(1951b). Observations on child development. In Vol. 4 of *The writings of Anna Freud.* New York: International Universities Press, 1968.

with Dann, Sophie. (1951c). An experiment in group upbringing. In Vol. 4 of *The writings of Anna Freud.* New York: International Universities Press, 1968.

(1952). The mutual influences in the development of ego and id. In Vol. 4 of *The Writings of Anna Freud.* New York: International Universities Press, 1968.

(1952/1992). *The Harvard lectures.* J. Sandler (Ed.). Madison, CT: International Universities Press.

(1953). Instinctual drives and their bearing on human behavior. In Vol. 4 of *The writings of Anna Freud.* New York: International Universities Press, 1968.

(1958). Child observation and prediction of development: A memorial lecture in honor of Ernst Kris. In Vol. 5 of *The writings of Anna Freud.* New York: International Universities Press, 1969.

(1962). Assessment of pathology in childhood. In Vol. 5 of *The writings of Anna Freud.* New York: International Universities Press, 1969.

(1965a). Metapsychological assessment of the adult personality: The adult profile. In Vol. 5 of *The writings of Anna Freud.* New York: International Universities Press, 1969.

(1965b). *Normality and pathology in childhood.* In Vol. 6 of *The writings of Anna Freud.* New York: International Universities Press, 1965.

(1967). Doctoral award address. In Vol. 5 of *The writings of Anna Freud.* New York: International Universities Press, 1969.

(1968). Indications and contraindications of child analysis. In Vol. 7 of *The writings of Anna Freud.* New York: International Universities Press, 1971.

(1969a). Difficulties in the path of psychoanalysis: A confrontation of past with present viewpoints. In Vol. 7 of *The writings of Anna Freud.* New York: International Universities Press, 1971.

(1969b). James Strachey. In Vol. 7 of *The writings of Anna Freud.* New York: International Universities Press, 1971.

(1970a). Problems of termination in child analysis. In Vol. 7 of *The writings of Anna Freud.* New York: International Universities Press, 1971.

(1970b). The symptomatology of childhood: A preliminary attempt at classification. In Vol. 7 of

The writings of Anna Freud. New York: International Universities Press, 1971.

(1972). The widening scope of psychoanalytic child psychology, normal and abnormal. In Volume 8 of *The writings of Anna Freud.* New York: International Universities Press, 1981.

(1978). The principal task of child analysis. In Volume 8 of *The writings of Anna Freud.* New York: International Universities Press, 1981.

(1978). Inaugural lecture for the Sigmund Freud chair at the Hebrew University, Jerusalem. *International Journal of Psychoanalysis, 59,* 145–148.

Freud, A., & Burlingham, D. (1944). *Infants without families.* In Vol. 3 of *The writings of Anna Freud.* New York: International Universities Press, 1973.

Freud, A., Nagera, H., & Freud, W. E. (1965). Metapsychological assessment of the adult personality: The adult profile. *Psychoanalytic Study of the Child, 20,* 9–41.

Freud, S. (1894). The neuro-psychoses of defence. In Vol. III of *The standard edition of the complete psychological works of Sigmund Freud.* James Strachey (Ed.). London: Hogarth, 1962.

(1895). Project for a scientific psychology. In Vol. I of *The standard edition.* London: Hogarth, 1966.

(1896a). Heredity and the aetiology of the neuroses. In Vol. III of *The standard edition.* London: Hogarth, 1962.

(1896b). Further remarks on the neuro-psychoses of defence. In Vol. III of *The standard edition.* London: Hogarth, 1962.

(1896c). The aetiology of hysteria. In Vol. III of *The standard edition.* London: Hogarth, 1962.

(1897). Extracts from the Fliess papers. In Vol. I of *The standard edition.* London: Hogarth, 1966.

(1898). Sexuality in the aetiology of the neuroses. In Vol. III of *The standard edition.* London: Hogarth, 1962.

(1900). *The interpretation of dreams.* Volumes IV and V of *The standard edition.* London: Hogarth, 1953.

(1901). *The psychopathology of everyday life.* In Vol. VI of *The standard edition.* London: Hogarth, 1960.

(1905). Three essays on the theory of sexuality. In Vol. VII of *The standard edition.* London: Hogarth, 1953.

(1908a). On the sexual theories of children. In Vol. IX of *The standard edition.* London: Hogarth, 1959.

(1908b). Character and anal eroticism. In Vol. IX of *The standard edition.* London: Hogarth, 1959.

(1910a). *Five lectures on psychoanalysis.* In Vol. XI of *The standard edition.* London: Hogarth, 1957.

(1910b). The psychoanalytic view of psychogenic disturbance of vision. In Vol. XI of *The standard edition.* London: Hogarth, 1957.

(1911). Formulations of the two principles of mental functioning. In Vol. XII of *The standard edition.* London: Hogarth, 1958.

(1912). A note on the unconscious in psychoanalysis. In Vol. XII of *The standard edition.* London: Hogarth, 1958.

(1913a). On beginning the treatment. In Vol. XII of *The standard edition.* London: Hogarth, 1958.

(1913b). *Totem and taboo.* In Vol. XIII of *The standard edition.* London: Hogarth, 1958.

(1914a). On narcissism: an introduction. In Vol. XIV of *The standard edition.* London: Hogarth, 1957.

(1914b). On the history of the psychoanalytic movement. In Vol. XIV of *The standard edition.* London: Hogarth, 1957.

(1915a). Instincts and their vicissitudes. In Vol. XIV of *The standard edition.* London: Hogarth, 1957.

(1915b). Repression. In Vol. XIV of *The standard edition.* London: Hogarth, 1957.

(1915c). The unconscious. In Vol XIV of *The standard edition.* London: Hogarth, 1957.

(1915d). A phylogenetic fantasy: An overview of the transference neuroses. Cambridge, MA: Harvard University Press, 1987.

(1916). *Introductory lectures on psychoanalysis.* Volumes XV and XVI of *The standard edition.* London: Hogarth, 1961 and 1963.

(1917a). A difficulty in the path of psychoanalysis. In Vol. XVII of *The standard edition.* London: Hogarth, 1955.

(1917b). Mourning and melancholia. In Vol. XIV of *The standard edition.* London: Hogarth, 1957.

(1918). From the history of an infantile neurosis. In J. Strachey (Ed. and Trans.), *The standard edition of the complete psychological works of Sigmund Freud* (Vol. 17). London: Hogarth, 1955.

(1919). "A child is being beaten": A contribution to the study of the origin of sexual perversions. In Vol. XVII of *The standard edition.* London: Hogarth, 1955.

(1920a). *Beyond the pleasure principle.* In Vol. XVIII of *The standard edition.* London: Hogarth, 1955.

Freud, S. (1920b). A note on the prehistory of the technique of analysis. In Vol. XVIII of *The standard edition*. London: Hogarth, 1955.

(1921). *Group psychology and the analysis of the ego*. In J. Strachey (Ed. and Trans.), *The standard edition of the complete psychological works of Sigmund Freud*. (Vol. 18). London: Hogarth, 1955.

(1923a). *The ego and the id*. In Vol. XIX of *The standard edition*. London: Hogarth, 1961.

(1923b). The infantile genital organization: An interpolation into the theory of sexuality. In Vol. XIX of *The standard edition*. London: Hogarth, 1961.

(1924a). A note upon the mystic writing pad. In Vol. XIX of *The standard edition*. London: Hogarth, 1961.

(1924b). The dissolution of the Oedipal complex. In Vol. XIX of *The standard edition*. London: Hogarth, 1961.

(1924c). A short account of psychoanalysis. In Vol. XIX of *The standard edition*. London: Hogarth, 1961.

(1925a). *An autobiographical study*. In Vol. XX of *The standard edition*. London: Hogarth, 1959.

(1925b). Some psychical consequences of the anatomical distinction between the sexes. In Vol. XIX of *The standard edition*. London: Hogarth, 1961.

(1925c). Some additional notes on dream-interpretation as a whole. In Vol XIX of *The standard edition*. London: Hogarth, 1961.

(1926a). *Inhibitions, symptoms and anxiety*. In Vol. XX of *The standard edition*. London: Hogarth, 1959.

(1926b). *The question of lay analysis*. In Vol. XX of *The standard edition*. London: Hogarth, 1959.

(1927). *The future of an illusion*. In Vol. XXII of *The standard edition*. London: Hogarth, 1961.

(1930). *Civilization and its discontents*. In Vol. XXI of *The standard edition*. London: Hogarth, 1961.

(1931). Female sexuality. In Vol. XXI of *The standard edition*. London: Hogarth, 1961.

(1933). *New introductory lectures*. In Vol. XXII of *The standard edition*. London: Hogarth, 1964.

(1936). A disturbance of memory on the Acropolis. In Vol. XXII of *The standard edition*. London: Hogarth, 1964.

(1940). *An outline of psychoanalysis*. In Vol. XXIII of *The standard edition*. London: Hogarth, 1964.

(1954). *The origin of psychoanalysis: Letters to Wilhelm Fliess, drafts and notes, 1897–1902*. Marie Bonaparte, Anna Freud, & Ernst Kris (Eds.). New York: Basic Books.

(1960). *The letters of Sigmund Freud*. Ernst L. Freud (Ed.). New York: Basic Books.

Freud, S. and Jones, E. (1993). *The complete correspondence of Sigmund Freud and Ernest Jones; 1908–1939*. R. A. Paskauskas (Ed.). Cambridge, MA: Belknap-Harvard University Press.

Freud, S., & Jung, C. G. (1974). *The Freud/Jung letters*. William McGuire (Ed.). Princeton, NJ: Princeton University Press.

(1985). *The complete letters of Sigmund Freud to Wilhelm Fliess: 1894–1904*. J. M. Masson (Ed.). Cambridge, MA: Harvard University Press, 1985.

Freud, S., & Zweig, A. (1970). *The letters of Sigmund Freud and Arnold Zweig*. Ernst L. Freud (Ed.). New York: Harcourt.

Freud, W. E. (1972). The baby profile: Part II. *The Psychoanalytic Study of the Child, 26*, 172–194.

Frigon, J-Y. (1976). Extraversion, neuroticism and strength of the nervous system. *British Journal of Psychology, 67*, 467–474.

Fromm, E. (1950). *Sigmund Freud's mission: An analysis of his personality and influence*. New York: Simon & Schuster, 1962.

(1956). *The art of loving*. New York: Bantam Books (also published by Harper).

(1959). *Sigmund Freud's mission: An analysis of his personality and influence*. New York: Simon & Schuster, 1962.

(1973). *The anatomy of human destructiveness*. New York: Holt, Rinehart and Winston.

Furtmüller, C. (1973). Alfred Adler: A biographical essay. In H. L. Ansbacher & R. Ansbacher (Eds.), *Superiority and social interest*. New York: Viking.

Fuster, J. M. (1958). Effects of stimulation of brain stem on tachistoscopic perception. *Science, 127*, 150.

Garcia, J., & Koelling, R. A. (1966). The relation of cue to consequence in avoidance learning. *Psychonomic Science, 4*, 123–124.

Garcia, J., McGowan, B. K., Ervin, F. R., & Koelling, R. A. (1968). Cues: Their relative effectiveness as a function of reinforcer. *Science, 160*, 794–795.

Gaulin, S. J., & McBurney, D. (2001). *Psychology: An evolutionary approach*. Upper Saddle River, NJ: Prentice Hall.

Gay, P. (1987). *A godless Jew: Freud, atheism and the making of psychoanalysis*. New Haven, CT: Yale University Press.

Gay, P. (1988). *Freud: A life for our time.* New York: Norton.

Gedo, J. E. (1976). Freud's self-analysis and his scientific ideas. In J. E. Gedo & G. H. Pollock (Eds.), *Freud: The fusion of science and humanism. Psychological Issues,* Monograph Nos. 34/35. New York: International Universities Press.

Gendlin, E. T. (1964). A theory of personality change. In P. Worschel & D. Byrne (Eds.), *Personality change.* New York: Wiley.

(1966). Research in psychotherapy with schizophrenic patients and the nature of that illness. In J. T. Hart & T. M. Tomlinson (Eds.), *New directions in client-centered therapy.* Boston: Houghton Mifflin, 1970 (paper originally published in *American Journal of Psychotherapy,* 1966, *20,* 4–16).

(1968). Focusing ability in psychotherapy, personality, and creativity. In J. M. Shlien (Ed.), *Research in psychotherapy,* vol. III. Washington, DC: American Psychological Association.

(1970). Existentialism and experiential psychotherapy. In J. T. Hart & T. M. Tomlinson (Eds.), *New directions in client-centered therapy.* Boston: Houghton Mifflin.

Gill, M. (1977). Psychic energy reconsidered. *Journal of the American Psychoanalytic Association, 25,* 581–597.

Goble, F. (1970). *The third force: The psychology of Abraham Maslow.* New York: Grossman.

Goldfried, M. R. (1980). Toward the delineation of therapeutic change principles. *American Psychologist, 35,* 991–999.

Goldstein, K. (1939). *The organism.* New York: American Book Co. (Van Nostrand).

Goldman, D. (1993). *In search of the real: The origins and originality of D. W. Winnicott.* New York: Jason Aronson.

Grammar, K. & Thornhill, R. (1994). Human (Homo sapiens) facial attractiveness and sexual selection: The role of symmetry and averageness. *Journal of Comparative Psychology, 108,* 233–242.

Gray, J. A. (1964). Strength of the nervous system as a dimension of personality in man. In J. A. Gray (Ed. and Trans.), *Pavlov's typology.* New York: Macmillan.

(1981). A critique of Eysenck's theory of personality. In H. J. Eysenck (Ed.), *A model for personality.* New York: Springer-Verlag.

(1985). Issues in the neuropsychology of anxiety. In A. H. Tuma & Jack D. Masser (Eds.), *Anxiety and the anxiety disorders,* pp. 5–26. Hillsdale, NJ: Lawrence Erlbaum Associates.

Grigg, K. A. (1973). "All roads lead to Rome": The role of the nursemaid in Freud's dreams. *American Journal of Psychoanalysis, 21,* 108–126.

Groddeck, Georg (1922). *The book of the it.* New York: New American Library, 1961.

Grosskurth, P. (1986). *Melanie Klein: Her world and her work.* Cambridge, MA: Harvard University Press.

Grubrich-Simitis, Ilse. (1987). Preface to *A phylogenetic fantasy.* In S. Freud, *A phylogenetic fantasy: An overview of the transference neuroses.* Cambridge, MA: Harvard University Press.

Guastello, S. J. (1993). A two (and a half) tiered trait taxonomy. *American Psychologist, 48,* 1298.

Gupta, B. S. (1973). The effects of stimulant and depressant drugs on verbal conditioning. *British Journal of Psychology, 64,* 553–557.

Haley, A. (1976). *Roots.* Garden City, NY: Doubleday.

Hall, M. H. (1968). A conversation with Abraham Maslow, In R. E. Schell (Ed.), *Readings in Developmental Psychology Today.* New York: CRM Books, 1977 (first published in *Psychology Today,* July, 1968).

Hamachek, D. E. (1988). Evaluating self-concept and ego development within Erikson's psychosocial framework: A formulation. *Journal of Counseling and Development, 66,* 354–360.

Hamilton, William D. (1964a). The genetical evolution of social behavior. I. *Journal of Theoretical Biology, 7,* 1–16.

(1964b). The genetical evolution of social behavior. II. *Journal of Theoretical Biology, 7,* 17–52.

Hart, J. (1970). The development of client-centered therapy. In J. T. Hart & T. M. Tomlinson (Eds.), *New directions in client-centered therapy.* Boston: Houghton Mifflin.

Hart, J. T., & T. M. Tomlinson (Eds.). (1970). *New directions in client-centered therapy.* Boston: Houghton Mifflin.

Hartmann, H. (1939). *Ego psychology and the problem of adaptation.* New York: International Universities Press, 1958.

(1947). On rational and irrational action. In H. Hartmann, *Essays on ego psychology.* New York: International Universities Press, 1964.

(1964). *Papers on psychoanalytic psychology. Psychological Issues,* Monograph No. 14. New York: International Universities Press.

Hebb, D. O. (1955). Drives and the C. N. S. (conceptual nervous system). *Psychological Review, 62,* 243–254.

Heinrichs, R. W. (1993). Schizophrenia and the brain: Conditions for a neuropsychology of madness. *American Psychologist, 48,* 221–233.

Hill, R. (1945). Campus values in mate selection. *Journal of Home Economics, 37,* 554–558.

Hoffer, A., & Hoffer, P. T. (1987). Foreword to *A phylogenetic fantasy.* In S. Freud, *A phylogenetic fantasy: An overview of the transference neuroses.* Cambridge, MA: Harvard University Press.

Hoffman, Edward. (1988). *The right to be human: The biography of Abraham Maslow.* Los Angeles, CA: J. P. Tarcher, Inc.

Hofstadter, D. R. (1979). *Gödel, Escher, Bach: An eternal golden braid.* New York: Vintage/Random House.

Holt, R. R. (1962). Individuality and generalization in the psychology of personality. *Journal of Personality, 30,* 377–402.

(1963). Two influences on Freud's scientific thought. In R. W. White (Ed.), *The study of lives* (pp. 365–387). New York: Atherton.

Horney, K. (1937). *The neurotic personality of our time.* New York: Norton.

(1939). *New ways in psychoanalysis.* New York: Norton.

(1942). *Self-analysis.* New York: Norton.

(1945). *Our inner conflicts.* New York: Norton.

(1946). *Are you considering psychoanalysis?* New York: Norton.

(1950). *Neurosis and human growth.* New York: Norton.

(1967). *Feminine psychology.* New York: Norton.

(1980). *The adolescent diaries of Karen Horney.* New York: Basic Books.

Howard, K. I., & Orlinsky, D. E. (1970). Therapist orientation and patient experience in psychotherapy. *Journal of Consulting Psychology, 17,* 263–270.

Hughes, J. M. (1989). *Reshaping the psychoanalytic domain: The work of Melanie Klein, W. R. D. Fairbairn, and D. W. Winnicott.* Berkeley, CA: University of California Press.

Hull, C. L. (1943). *Principles of behavior.* New York: Appleton.

(1951). *Essentials of behavior.* New Haven, CT: Yale University Press.

(1952). *A behavior system.* New Haven, CT: Yale University Press.

Jacobs, M. (1995). *D. W. Winnicott.* London, Great Britain: Sage.

Jaffé, A. (1971). *From the life and work of C. G. Jung.* New York: Harper & Row.

(1979). *C. G. Jung: Word and image.* Princeton, NJ: Princeton University Press.

James, W. (1902). *The varieties of religious experience.* New York: Modern Library.

(1963). *Principles of psychology.* Greenwich, CT: Fawcett, 1963.

Jones, Ernest. (1953). *The life and work of Sigmund Freud: The formative years and the great discoveries,* vol. 1. New York: Basic Books.

(1955). *The life and work of Sigmund Freud: Years of maturity,* vol. 2. New York: Basic Books.

(1957). *The life and work of Sigmund Freud: The last phase,* vol. 3. New York: Basic Books.

Jourard, S. M. (1971a). *The transparent self* (rev. ed.). New York: Van Nostrand.

(1971b). *Self-disclosure: An experimental analysis of the transparent self.* New York: Wiley.

Jucknat, M. (1937). Performance, level of aspiration and self-consciousness. *Psychologische Forschung, 22,* 89–179.

Jung, C. G. (1905). The reaction time ratio in the association experiment. In Vol. 2 of *The collected works of C. G. Jung.* R. F. C. Hull (Trans.). Princeton, NJ: Princeton University Press, 1973.

(1907). *The psychology of dementia praecox.* In Vol. 3 of *The collected works of C. G. Jung.* Princeton, NJ: Princeton University Press, 1960.

(1908). The content of the psychoses. In Vol. 3 of *The collected works of C. G. Jung.* Princeton, NJ: Princeton University Press, 1960.

(1909a). The psychological diagnosis of evidence. In Vol. 2 of *The collected works of C. G. Jung.* Princeton, NJ: Princeton University Press, 1973.

(1909b). The psychological diagnosis of evidence. In Vol. 2 of *The collected works of C. G. Jung.* Princeton, NJ: Princeton University Press, 1973.

(1912). Symbols of transformation (2nd ed.) In Vol. 5 of *The collected works of C. G. Jung.* Princeton, NJ: Princeton University Press, 1956.

(1913). On the doctrine of complexes. In Vol. 2 of *The collected works of C. G. Jung.* Princeton, NJ: Princeton University Press, 1973.

(1914). On psychological understanding. In Vol. 3 of *The collected works of C. G. Jung.* Princeton, NJ: Princeton University Press, 1960.

Jung, C. G. (1916). General aspects of dream psychology. In Vol. 8 of *The collected works of C. G. Jung.* Princeton, NJ: Princeton University Press, 1969.

(1917). Two essays on analytical psychology. In Vol. 7 of *The Collected Works of C. G. Jung.* Princeton, NJ: Princeton University Press, 1953 and 1966.

(1921). Psychological types. In Vol. 6 of *The collected works of C. G. Jung.* Princeton, NJ: Princeton University Press, 1971.

(1931). The Structure of the psyche. In Vol. 8 of *The collected works of C. G. Jung.* Princeton, NJ: Princeton University Press, 1969.

(1936). The archetypes and the collective unconscious. In Vol. 9i of *The collected works of C. G. Jung.* Princeton, NJ: Princeton University Press, 1959 and 1969.

(1938). Psychological aspects of the mother archetype. In Vol. 9i of *The collected works of C. G. Jung.* Princeton, NJ: Princeton University Press, 1959 and 1969.

(1939). Conscious, unconscious and individuation. In Vol. 9i of *The collected works of C. G. Jung.* Princeton, NJ: Princeton University Press, 1959 and 1969.

(1940). The psychology of the child archetype. In Vol. 9i of *The collected works of C. G. Jung.* Princeton, NJ: Princeton University Press, 1959 and 1969.

(1948). On psychic energy. In Vol. 8 of *The collected works of C. G. Jung.* Princeton, NJ: Princeton University Press, 1959.

(1950a). On mandalas. In Vol. 9i of *The collected works of C. G. Jung.* Princeton, NJ: Princeton University Press, 1959 and 1969.

(1950b). Aion: Researches into the phenomenology of the self. Volume 9ii of *The collected works of C. G. Jung.* Princeton, NJ: Princeton University Press, 1959 and 1969.

(1952). Synchronicity: An acausal connecting principle. In Vol. 8 of *The collected works of C. G. Jung.* Princeton, NJ: Princeton University Press, 1969.

(1954). On the psychology of the trickster figure. In Vol. 9i of *The collected works of C. G. Jung.* Princeton, NJ: Princeton University Press, 1959 and 1969.

(1957). The undiscovered self: Present and future. In Vol. 10 of *The collected works of C. G. Jung.* Princeton, NJ: Princeton University Press, 1970.

(1959). Televised interview with John Freeman: *Face to Face: Carl Gustav Jung.* British Broadcasting Corporation, October 22, 1959.

(1961). *Memories, dreams, reflections.* A. Jaffé (Ed.). New York: Pantheon.

(1968). *Analytical psychology: Its theory and practice.* (The Tavistock Lectures.) New York: Pantheon.

Kagan, J., & Berkun, M. (1954). The reward value of running activity. *Journal of Comparative and Physiological Psychology, 47,* 108.

Kahr, B. (1996). *D. W. Winnicott: A biographical portrait.* New York: International Universities Press.

Kanner, L. (1942). Autistic disturbances of affective contact. *Nervous Child, 2,* 217–250.

(1944). Early infantile autism. *Pediatrics, 25,* 211–217.

Kelly, G. A. (1955). *The psychology of personal constructs,* vols. 1 and 2. New York: Norton.

(1958a). Man's construction of his alternatives. In B. Maher (Ed.), *Clinical psychology and personality: Selected papers of George Kelly.* New York: Wiley, 1969 (paper originally published: Gardner Lindzey (Ed.), *The Assessment of Human Motives.* New York: Holt, Rinehart and Winston, 1958).

(1958b). Personal construct theory and the psychotherapeutic interview. In B. Maher (Ed.), *Clinical Psychology and Personality: Selected Papers of George Kelly.* New York: Wiley, 1969.

(1963). The autobiography of a theory. In B. Maher (Ed.), *Clinical psychology and personality: Selected papers of George Kelly.* New York: Wiley, 1969.

(1964). The language of hypothesis: Man's psychological instrument. In B. Maher (Ed.), *Clinical psychology and personality: Selected papers of George Kelly.* New York: Wiley, 1969 (paper originally published: *Journal of Individual Psychology,* 1964, *20,* 137–152).

(1966). Ontological acceleration. In B. Maher (Ed.), *Clinical psychology and personality: Selected papers of George Kelly.* New York: Wiley, 1969.

Kernberg, O. F. (1976). *Object relations theory and clinical psychoanalysis.* New York: Jason Aronson.

(1986). *Severe personality disorders. Psychotherapeutic strategies.* New Haven: Yale University Press.

Kernberg, O. F. (1992). *Aggression in personality disorders and perversions.* New Haven: Yale University Press.

Khan, M. (1975/1992). Introduction. In D. W. Winnicott, *Through paediatrics to psycho-analysis. Collected papers.* New York: Bruner-Mazel (Originally published: New York: Basic Books, 1958).

Klein, M. (1921/1975a). Development of a child. In R. E. Money-Kyrle (Ed.), *The writings of Melanie Klein* (Vol I, 1–53). New York: The Free Press (Macmillan).

(1926/1975a). The psychological principles of early analysis. In R. E. Money-Kyrle (Ed.), *The writings of Melanie Klein* (Vol I, 128–138). New York: The Free Press (Macmillan).

(1927/1975a). Symposium on child-analysis. In R. E. Money-Kyrle (Ed.), *The writings of Melanie Klein* (Vol I, 139–169). New York: The Free Press (Macmillan).

(1928/1975a). Early stages of the Oedipus conflict. In R. E. Money-Kyrle (Ed.), *The writings of Melanie Klein* (Vol I, 210–218). New York: The Free Press (Macmillan).

(1929/1975a). Infantile anxiety-situations reflected in a work of art and in the creative impulse. In R. E. Money-Kyrle (Ed.), *The writings of Melanie Klein* (Vol I, 210–218). New York: The Free Press.

(1931/1975a). A contribution to the theory of intellectual inhibition. In R. E. Money-Kyrle (Ed.), *The writings of Melanie Klein* (Vol I, 236–247). New York: The Free Press.

(1932). *The psychoanalysis of children.* London: Hogarth (reissued by Delacorte Press, 1975).

(1932/1975b). *The psycho-analysis of children.* In H. A. Thorner (Ed.) and Alix Strachey (Trans.), *The writings of Melanie Klein* (Vol II). New York: The Free Press (Macmillan).

(1933/1975a). The early development of conscience in the child. In R. E. Money-Kyrle (Ed.), *The writings of Melanie Klein* (Vol I, 248–257). New York: The Free Press (Macmillan).

(1935/1975a) A contribution to the psychogenesis of manic-depressive states. In R. E. Money-Kyrle (Ed.), *The writings of Melanie Klein* (Vol. I, 262–289). New York: The Free Press (Macmillan).

(1936/1975a). Weaning. In R. E. Money-Kyrle (Ed.), *The writings of Melanie Klein* (Vol. I, 290–305). New York: The Free Press (Macmillan).

(1937/1975a). Love, guilt and reparation. In R. E. Money-Kyrle (Ed.), *The writings of Melanie Klein* (Vol I, 306–343). New York: The Free Press (Macmillan).

(1940/1975a). Mourning and its relation to manic-depressive states. In R. E. Money-Kyrle (Ed.), *The writings of Melanie Klein* (Vol. I, 344–359). New York: The Free Press (Macmillan).

(1945/1975a). The Oedipus complex in the light of early anxieties. In R. E. Money-Kyrle (Ed.), *The writings of Melanie Klein* (Vol. I, 370–419). New York: The Free Press (Macmillan).

(1946/1975c). Notes on some schizoid mechanisms. In Roger Money-Kyrle (Ed.), *The writings of Melanie Klein* (Vol III, 1–24). New York: The Free Press (Macmillan).

(1952/1975c). *The emotional life of the infant.* In Roger Money-Kyrle (Ed.), *The writings of Melanie Klein* (Vol. III, 61–93). New York: The Free Press (Macmillan).

(1957/1975c). *Envy and gratitude.* In Roger Money-Kyrle (Ed.), *The writings of Melanie Klein* (Vol III, 176–235). New York: The Free Press (Macmillan).

(1958/1975c). On the development of mental functioning. In Roger Money-Kyrle (Ed.), *The writings of Melanie Klein* (Vol III, 236–246). New York: The Free Press (Macmillan).

(1961). *Narrative of a child analysis.* In Eliott Jacques (Ed.), *The writings of Melanie Klein* (Vol IV). New York: The Free Press (Macmillan).

Klein, M. & Riviere, J. (1964). *Love, hate and reparation.* New York: Norton.

Kline, P. (1972). *Fact and fantasy in Freudian theory.* London: Methuen, 1972 (American edition published by Harper & Row).

Kling, J. W. (1971). Learning. In J. W. Kling & L. A. Riggs (Eds.), *Woodworth and Schlosberg's experimental psychology* (pp. 551–614). (3d ed.). New York: Holt, Rinehart and Winston.

Koffka, K. (1935). *Principles of Gestalt psychology.* New York: Harcourt, Brace.

Kohut, H. (1971). *The analysis of the self.* New York: International Universities Press.

(1977). *The restoration of the self.* New York: International Universities Press.

(1984). *How does analysis cure?* Chicago: University of Chicago Press.

Kohut, H., & Wolff, E. (1978). The disorders of the self and their treatment: An outline. *The International Journal of Psychoanalysis, 59,* 413–425.

Kraeplin, E. (1905). *Lectures on clinical psychiatry* (2d, rev. ed.) London: Baillere, Tindall and Cox, 1905 (as cited by R. D. Laing, 1959).

Krane, R. V., & Wagner, A. R. (1975). Taste aversion learning with a delayed shock US: implications for the generality of the laws of learning. *Journal of Comparative and Physiological Psychology, 88,* 882–889.

Kris, E. (1954). Editor's introduction. In M. Bonaparte, E. Kris, & A. Freud (Eds.), *The origins of psychoanalysis: Letters of Sigmund Freud to Wilhelm Fliess, drafts and notes, 1897–1902.* New York, Basic Books.

Lamarck, J. B. (1809). *Zoological philosophy,* trans., Hugo Elliot. New York: Hafner, 1963.

Langs, R. (1973). *The technique of psychoanalytic psychotherapy,* vol. 1. New York: Jason Aronson.

Laufer, M. (1965). Assessment of adolescent disturbances: The application of Anna Freud's diagnostic profile. *The Psychoanalytic Study of the Child, 20,* 99–123.

Laverty, S. G. (1958). Sodium amytal and extraversion. In H. J. Eysenck (Ed.), *Readings in extraversion-intraversion,* vol. 3: *Bearings on basic psychological processes.* London: Staples, 1971 (paper originally published in *Journal of Neurology and Neurosurgery and Psychiatry, 1958, 21,* 50–54).

Lazarus, R. S., & Launier, R. (1978). Stress-related transactions between person and environment. In L. A. Pervin & M. Lewis (Eds.), *Perspectives in interactional psychology.* New York: Plenum.

LeDoux, J. (1996). *The emotional brain.* New York: Touchstone (Simon and Shuster).

Leites, N. (1971). *The new age: Pitfalls in current thinking about patients in psychoanalysis.* New York: Science House.

Lindsley, D. B. (1951). Emotion. In S. S. Stevens (Ed.), *Handbook of experimental psychology* (pp. 473–516). New York: Wiley.

Little, M. I. (1990). *Psychotic anxieties and containment: A personal record of an analysis with Winnicott.* New York: Jason Aronson.

Lumsden, C. J., & Wilson, E. O. (1981). *Genes, mind, and culture, the coevolutionary process.* Cambridge, MA: Harvard University Press.

Lynn, R., Ed. (1981). *Dimensions of personality: Papers in honour of H.J. Eysenck.* New York: Pergamon Press.

Macleod, R. B. (1964). Phenomenology: A challenge to experimental psychology. In T. W. Wann (Ed.), *Behaviorism and phenomenology: Contrasting bases for modern psychology.* Chicago: University of Chicago Press.

Mahler, M. S. (1968). *On human symbiosis and the vicissitudes of individuation: Infantile psychosis.* New York: International Universities Press.

(1988). *The memoirs of Margaret S. Mahler.* Paul E. Stepansky, (Ed.) New York: The Free Press.

Mahler, M. S., Pine, F., & Bergman, A. (1975). *The psychological birth of the human infant.* New York: Basic Books.

Malmo, R. B. (1959). A neurophysiological dimension. *Psychological Review, 66,* 367–386.

Marcia, J. (1966). Development and validation of ego-identity status. *Journal of Personality and Social Psychology, 3,* 551–558.

(1993). The ego identity status approach to ego identity. In J. E. Marcia, A. S. Waterman, D. R. Matteson, S. L. Archer, & J. L. Orlofsky (Eds.), *Ego identity: A handbook for psychosocial research.* New York: Springer-Verlag.

Marcia, J., & Friedman, M. L. (1970). "Ego identity status in college women," *Journal of Personality, 38,* 249–263.

Martin, J. (1994). *The construction and understanding of psychotherapeutic change.* New York: Teachers College Press.

Martindale, C. (1981). *Cognition and consciousness.* Homewood, IL: Dorsey.

Masling, J. (1983). *Empirical studies of psychoanalytical theories* (vol. 1). Hillsdale, NJ: The Analytic Press.

Maslow, A. H. (1936a). The role of dominance in the social and sexual behavior of infra-human primates: I. Observations at Vilas Park Zoo. In R. J. Lowry (Ed.), *Dominance, self-esteem, self-actualization: Germinal papers of A. H. Maslow.* Monterey, CA: Brooks-Cole, 1973 (paper originally published in *Journal of Genetic Psychology,* 1936, *48,* 261–277).

(1936b). The role of dominance in the social and sexual behavior of infra-human primates: II. An experimental determination of the behavior syndrome of dominance. In R. J. Lowry (Ed.), *Dominance, self-esteem, self-actualization: Germinal papers of A. H. Maslow.* Monterey, CA: Brooks-Cole, 1973 (paper originally published in *Journal of Genetic Psychology,* 1936, *48,* 278–309).

(1937). Dominance-feeling, behavior and status. In R. J. Lowry (Ed.), *Dominance, self-esteem, self-actualization: Germinal papers of A. H. Maslow.* Monterey, CA: Brooks-Cole, 1973 (paper originally published in *Psychological Review,* 1937, *44,* 404–429).

Maslow, A. H. (1939). Dominance, personality and social behavior in women. In R. J. Lowry (Ed.), *Dominance, self-esteem, self-actualization: Germinal papers of A. H. Maslow.* Monterey, CA: Brooks-Cole, 1973 (paper originally published in *Journal of Social Psychology,* 1939, *10,* 3–39).

(1942). Self-esteem (dominance-feeling) and sexuality in women. In R. J. Lowry (Ed.), *Dominance, self-esteem, self-actualization: Germinal papers of A. H. Maslow.* Monterey, CA: Brooks-Cole, 1973 (paper originally published in *Journal of Social Psychology,* 1942, *16,* 259–294).

(1943). A theory of human motivation. In R. J. Lowry (Ed.), *Dominance, self-esteem, self-actualization Germinal papers of A. H. Maslow.* Monterey, CA: Brooks-Cole, 1973 (paper originally published in *Psychological Review,* 1943, *50,* 370–396).

(1962). *Toward a psychology of being.* New York: Van Nostrand.

(1964). *Religions, values and peak-experiences.* New York: Viking.

(1966). *The psychology of science: A reconnaissance.* New York: Harper & Row.

(1970). *Motivation and personality* (2nd ed.). New York: Harper & Row.

(1971). *The farther reaches of human nature.* New York: Viking.

(1979). *The journals of Abraham Maslow.* R. J. Lowry (Ed.). Lexington, MA: Lewis Publishing, 1982 (originally published as a two-volume work by Brooks-Cole Publishing, Monterey, CA, 1979).

Maslow, A., & Chiang, Hung-Min. (1977). Laboratory in self-knowledge: A verbatim report of the workshop with Abraham Maslow. In Abraham Maslow and Hung-Min Chiang (Eds.), *The healthy personality: Readings* (pp. 240–258). (2nd ed.). New York: Van Nostrand.

Masson, J. M. (1984a). Freud and the seduction theory. *The Atlantic Monthly,* February, 33–60.

(1984b). *The assault on truth: Freud's suppression of the seduction theory.* New York: Farrar, Straus & Giroux.

(Ed.). (1985). *The complete letters of Sigmund Freud to Wilhelm Fliess: 1887–1904.* Cambridge, MA: Harvard University Press.

Masterson, J. F., Tolpin, M., & Sifneos, P. E. (1991). *Comparing psychoanalytic psychotherapies.* New York: Brunner Mazel.

May, Rollo (1939/1967). *The art of counseling.* New York: Abingdon Press.

(1950/1970). *The meaning of anxiety.* New York: Ronald Press (paperback reissue) New York, Washington Square Press.

(1953). *Man's search for himself.* New York: Norton.

(1958a). "The origins and significance of the existential movement in psychology." In R. May, E. Angel, and H. F. Ellenberger (Eds.), *Existence: A new dimension in psychiatry and psychology.* New York: Basic Books.

(1958b). "Contributions of existential psychotherapy." In R. May, E. Angel, and H. F. Ellenberger (Eds.), *Existence: A new dimension in psychiatry and psychology.* New York: Basic Books.

(1960/1965). "Existential bases of psychotherapy." In Ohmer Milton (Ed.) *Behavior disorders: Perspectives and trends.* New York: Lippincott (originally published: *Journal of OrthoPsychiatry,* 1960, *30,* 685–695; also anthologized in R. May [Ed.], *Existential psychology.* New York: Random House, 1961; see also May, 1983, Ch. 2).

(1961). "The emergence of existential psychology." In R. May (Ed.), *Existential psychology.* New York: Random House.

(1967/1979). *Psychology and the human dilemma.* New York: Norton.

(1969). *Love and will.* New York: Norton (paperback: New York, Delta Books, 1969).

(1972). *Power and innocence: A search for the sources of violence.* New York: Norton.

(1973). *Paulus: A personal portrait of Paul Tillich.* New York: Harper & Row.

(1975). "The courage to create." In M. Richler, A. Fortier, and R. May (Eds.), *Creativity and the university: The 1972 Gerstein Lectures at York University.* Toronto: York University.

(1981). *Freedom and destiny.* New York: Norton.

(1983). *The discovery of being: Writings in existential psychology.* New York: Norton.

(1985). *My quest for beauty.* Dallas, TX: Saybrook Publishing.

(1986a). "The destiny of America." In *Politics and innocence.* Dallas, TX: Saybrook.

(1986b). "The problem of evil." In *Politics and innocence.* Dallas, TX: Saybrook.

(1989). "Rollo May: A man of meaning and myth." Interview with F. E. Rabinowitz, Glenn Good, and Liza Cozad. *Journal of Counseling and Development, 67,* 436–441.

McCarley, R. W., & Hobson, J. A. (1977). The neurobiological origins of psychoanalytic dream theory. *American Journal of Psychiatry, 134,* 1211–1221.

McCrae, R. R. (1994). A reformulation of Axis II: Personality and personality-related problems. In P. T. Costa, & T. A. Widiger (Eds.), *Personality disorders and the five-factor model of personality.* Washington, DC: American Psychological Association.

McGinnis, R. (1958). Campus values in mate selection. *Social Forces, 35,* 368–373.

McLaughlin, R. J., & Eysenck, H. J. (1967). Extraversion, neuroticism and paired-associate learning. In H. J. Eysenck (Ed.), *Readings in extraversion-intraversion,* vol. 3: *Bearings on basic psychological processes.* London: Staples, 1971 (paper originally published in *Journal of Experimental Research in Personality,* 1967, *2,* 128–132).

McLeary, R. A., & Lazarus, R. S. (1949). Autonomic discrimination without awareness. *Journal of Personality, 18,* 171–179.

McLynn, F. (1997). *Carl Gustav Jung.* New York: St. Martin's Press.

Menninger, K., Mayman, M., & Pruyser, P. (1963). *The vital balance: The life process in mental health and illness.* New York: Viking Press.

Milgram, S. (1974). *Obedience to authority.* New York: Harper & Row.

Miller, L. (1991). *Freud's brain: Neuropsychodynamic foundations of psychoanalysis.* New York: Guilford.

Miller, N. (1941). The frustration-aggression hypothesis. *Psychological Review, 48,* 337–342.

(1948). Studies of fear as an acquirable drive: I. Fear as motivation and fear reduction as reinforcement in the learning of new responses. *Journal of Experimental Psychology, 38,* 89–101.

(1950). Learnable drives and rewards. In S. S. Stevens (Ed.), *Handbook of experimental psychology* (pp. 435–472). New York: Wiley.

Miller, N., & Dollard, J. (1941). *Social learning and imitation.* New Haven, CT: Yale University Press.

Millon, T. (1981). *Disorders of personality: DSM III: Axis II.* New York: Wiley-Interscience.

(1994). Personality disorders: Conceptual distinctions and classification issues. In P. T. Costa, & T. A. Widiger, (Eds.), *Personality disorders and the five-factor model of personality.* Washington, DC: American Psychological Association.

Mitchell, Juliet (Ed.), (1986). *The selected Melanie Klein.* New York: The Free Press (Macmillan).

Monte, C. F. (1975). *Psychology's scientific endeavor.* New York: Praeger.

(1993). *Still, Life: Clinical portraits in psychopathology.* Englewood Cliffs, NJ: Prentice-Hall.

(1995). *Beneath the mask: An introduction to theories of personality.* (5th ed.). New York: Harcourt, Brace.

(1999). *Beneath the mask: An introduction to theories of personality.* (6th ed.). New York: Harcourt, Brace.

Moruzzi, G., and Magoun, H. W. (1949/1964). Brain stem reticular formation and activation of the EEG. In R. L. Isaacson (Ed.), *Basic readings in neuropsychology.* New York: Harper & Row. (paper originally published: *Electroencephalography and Clinical Neurophysiology,* 1949, *1,* 455–473).

Mosak, H. H. (1958). Early recollections as a projective technique. *Journal of Projective Techniques, 22,* 302–311.

Mosak, H. H., & Kopp, R. R. (1973). The early recollections of Adler, Freud, and Jung. *Journal of Individual Psychology, 29,* 157–166.

Mosak, H. M. & Maniacci, M. (1999). *A primer of Adlerian psychology: The analytic-behavioral-cognitive psychology of Alfred Adler.* Philadelphia: Brunner-Routledge.

Moustakas, C. E. (Ed.). (1956). *The self: Explorations in personal growth.* New York: Harper.

Mowrer, O. H. (1939). A stimulus-response analysis of anxiety and its role as a reinforcing agent, *Psychological Review, 46,* 553–565.

(1950). Identification: A link between learning theory and psychotherapy. In O. H. Mowrer, *Learning theory and personality dynamics* (pp. 69–94). New York: Ronald Press.

Murphy, G., & Kovach, J. K. (1972). *Historical introduction to modern psychology* (3d ed.). New York: Harcourt.

Murray, H. A. (1938). *Explorations in personality.* New York: Oxford University Press.

Myers, I. B. (1972). *Myers-Briggs type indicator manual.* Palo Alto, CA: Consulting Psychologists Press.

Nisbett, R., & Wilson, T. (1977). Telling more than we can know: Verbal reports on mental processes. *Psychological Review, 84,* 231–259.

Orgler, H. (1963). *Alfred Adler: The man and his work.* New York: Capricorn (Putnam).

Panskepp, J. (1988) Attention deficit hyperactivity disorders, psychostimulants and intolerance of childhood playfulness: A tragedy in the making? *Current Directions in Psychological Science. 7,* 91–98.

Papez, J. W. (1937). A proposed mechanism of emotion. *Archives of Neurology and Psychiatry, 38,* 725–744.

Parisi, T. (1987). Why Freud failed. *American Psychologist, 42*(3), 235–245.

——— (1988). Freud's stance and mine. *American Psychologist, 43*(8), 663–664.

Pavlov, I. P. (1927). *Conditioned reflexes: An investigation into the physiological activity of the cortex.* G. V. Anrep (Trans.). New York: Dover.

——— (1928). *Lectures on conditioned reflexes,* vol. 1. W. Horsely Gantt (Trans.). New York: International Publishers.

Peele, S. (1981). Reductionism in the psychology of the eighties. *American Psychologist, 36,* 807–818.

Perry, W. G. (1970). *Forms of intellectual and ethical development in the college years: A scheme.* Fort Worth, TX: Harcourt, Brace Jovanovich.

Pettigrew, T. (1999). Gordon Willard Allport: A tribute. *Journal of Social Issues, 55, 3.* 415–427.

Phillips, A. (1988). *Winnicott.* Cambridge, MA: Harvard University Press.

Piaget, J. (1954). *The construction of reality in the child.* Margaret Cook (Trans.). New York: Basic Books.

Pinker, S. (1997). How the mind works. New York: Norton.

Pollock, G. H. (1968). The possible significance of childhood object loss in the Josef Breuer-Bertha Pappenheim (Anna O.)-Sigmund Freud relationship. I. Josef Breuer. *Journal of the American Psychoanalytic Association, 16,* 711–739.

——— (1972). Bertha Pappenheim's pathological mourning: Possible effects of childhood sibling loss. *Journal of the American Psychoanalytic Association, 20,* 478–493.

——— (1973). Bertha Pappenheim: Addenda to her case history. *American Journal of Psychoanalysis, 21,* 328–332.

Popper, K. (1959). *The logic of scientific discovery.* New York: Basic Books.

——— (1963). *Conjectures and refutations.* New York: Basic Books.

——— (1965). *Conjectures and refutations* (rev. ed). London: Routledge and Kegan Paul.

Postman, L. (1962). *Psychology in the making.* New York: Knopf.

Premack, D. (1965). Reinforcement theory. In M. R. Jones (Ed.), *Nebraska symposium on motivation: 1965.* Lincoln, NE: University of Nebraska Press.

Quinn, S. (1987). *A mind of her own: The life of Karen Horney.* New York: Summit Books (Simon & Schuster).

Rabinowitz, F. E., Good, G., & Cozad, L. (1989). Rollo May: A man of meaning and myth. *Journal of Counseling and Development,* 1989, *67,* 436–441.

Rachlin, H., & Logue, A. W. (1983). Learning. In M. Hersen, A. Kazdin, & A. Bellack (Eds.), *The clinical psychology handbook* (pp. 107–121). New York: Pergamon.

Rachman, S. (Ed.). (1963). *Critical essays on psychoanalysis.* New York: Macmillan.

——— (1978). *Fear and courage.* San Francisco: Freeman.

——— (1990). *Fear and courage* (2nd ed.) San Francisco: Freeman.

Rank. O. (1929). *The trauma of birth.* New York: Harper & Row, 1973.

——— (1932). *The myth of the birth of the hero.* New York: Vintage, 1959.

——— (1941). *Beyond psychology.* New York: Dover.

Redlich, F., & Kellert, S. R. (1978). Trends in American mental health. *American Journal of Psychiatry, 135,* 22–28.

Rescorla, R. A. (1987). A Pavlovian analysis of goal-directed behavior. *American Psychologist, 42*(2), 119–129.

——— (1988). Pavlovian conditioning: It's not what you think it is. *American Psychologist, 43*(3), 151–160.

Rescorla, R. A., & Solomon, R. (1967). Two-process learning theory: Relationships between Pavlovian conditioning and instrumental learning. *Psychological Review, 74,* 151–182.

Ritvo, Lucille B. (1990). *Darwin's influence on Freud: A tale of two sciences.* New Haven: Yale University Press.

Roazen, P. (1968). *Freud: Political and social thought.* New York: Knopf.

——— (1969). *Brother animal: The story of Freud and Tausk.* New York: Knopf.

——— (1971). *Freud and his followers.* New York: Meridian Books.

——— (1977). Orthodoxy on Freud: The case of Tausk. *Contemporary Psychoanalysis, 13,* 102–115.

——— (1978). Reading, writing, and memory in Dr. K. R. Eissler's thinking. *Contemporary Psychoanalysis, 14,* 345–353.

Rogers, C. R. (1942). *Counseling and psychotherapy.* Boston: Houghton Mifflin.

Rogers, C. R. (1951). *Client-centered therapy.* Boston: Houghton Mifflin.

——— (1954). The case of Mrs. Oak: A research analysis. In C. R. Rogers & R. F. Dymond (Eds.), *Psychotherapy and personality change* (pp. 259–348). Chicago: University of Chicago Press.

——— (1957). The necessary and sufficient conditions of therapeutic personality change. *Journal of Consulting Psychology, 21,* 95–103.

——— (1958). A tentative scale for the measurement of process in psychotherapy. In A. Rubenstein & M. B. Parloff (Eds.), *Research in psychotherapy,* vol. 1. Washington, DC: American Psychological Association, 1962.

——— (1959). A theory of therapy, personality and interpersonal relationships as developed in the client-centered framework. In S. Koch (Ed.), *Psychology: A study of a science,* Vol. III, *Formulations of the person in the social context.* New York: McGraw-Hill.

——— (1961). *On becoming a person.* Boston: Houghton Mifflin.

——— (1964). The concept of the fully functioning person. *Psychotherapy: Theory, Research and Practice, 1,* 17–26.

——— (Ed.) (1967a). *The therapeutic relationship and its impact: A study of psychotherapy with schizophrenics.* Madison: University of Wisconsin Press.

——— (1967b). Autobiography. In E. G. Boring & G. Lindzey (Eds.), *A history of psychology in autobiography,* vol. 5. New York: Appleton, 1967.

——— (1969). *Freedom to learn,* Columbus, OH: Charles E. Merrill, esp. chap. 14.

——— (1974a). In retrospect: forty-six years. *American Psychologist, 29*(2), 115–123.

——— (1974b). The emerging person: A new revolution. Mimeograph paper for private circulation. La Jolla, CA: Center for Studies of the Person (also published: Richard I. Evans, *Carl Rogers: The man and his ideas: A dialogue.* New York: Dutton, 1975).

——— (1974c). Remarks on the future of client-centered therapy. In D. A. Wexler & L. North Rice (Eds.), *Innovations in client-centered therapy.* New York: Wiley.

Rogers, C. R., & R. F. Dymond. (1954). *Psychotherapy and personality change.* Chicago: University of Chicago Press.

Rogers, C. R., (1978). Personal communication, July 10, 1978. Sollod record, Archives of the History of American Psychology. University of Akron, Akron, OH.

Rowe, I., & Marcia, J. (1980). Ego identity status, formal operations, and moral development. *Journal of Youth and Adolescence, 9,* 87–99.

Rubins, J. L. (1978). *Karen Horney: Gentle rebel of psychoanalysis.* New York: Dial.

Rudnytsky, P. L. (1991). *The psychoanalytic vocation: Rank, Winnicott and the legacy of Freud.* New Haven: Yale University Press.

Ruesch, J. (1961). *Therapeutic communication.* New York: Norton.

Sandler, J. & Freud, A. (1985). *The analysis of defense: The ego and the mechanisms of defense revisited.* New York: International Universities Press.

Sanford, N. (1985). What have we learned about personality? In S. Koch & D. Leary (Eds.), *A century of psychology as a science.* New York: McGraw-Hill.

Sayers, J. (1991). *Mothers of psychoanalysis.* New York: Norton.

Schafer, R. (1976). *A new language for psychoanalysis.* New Haven, CT: Yale University Press.

——— (1983). *The analytic attitude.* New York: Basic Books.

Schneider, S. M., Morris, Edward K. (1987). A history of the term *radical behaviorism:* From Watson to Skinner. Behavior Analyst Vol 10, *1,* 1987 p. 27–39.

Schorske, C. E. (1975). Politics and patricide. In *The annual of psychoanalysis,* vol. 2. New York: International Universities Press.

Schroeder, M. L., Wormworth, J. A., & Livesley, W. J. (1994). Dimensions of personality disorder and the five-factor model of personality. In P. T. Costa & T. A. Widiger (Eds), *Personality disorders and the five-factor model of personality.* Washington, DC: American Psychological Association.

Schulz, C. G. (1978). Sullivan's clinical contributions during the Sheppard Pratt era: 1923–1930. *Psychiatry, 41,* 117–128.

Schur, M. (1972). *Freud, living and dying.* New York: International Universities Press.

Segal, J. (1992). *Melanie Klein.* London: Sage Publications.

Seligman, M. E. (1970). On the generality of the laws of learning. *Psychological Review, 37,* 406–418.

Seligman, M. E. (1971). Phobias and preparedness. *Behavior Therapy, 2,* 307–320.

(1972). *Biological boundaries of learning.* New York: Appleton-Century.

Shadel, W. G., & Cervone, D. (1993). Comment on Goldberg: The big five versus nobody? *American Psychologist, 48,* 1300–1302.

Shagass, C., & Kerenyi, A. B. (1958). Neurophysiological studies of personality. In H. J. Eysenck (Ed.), *Reading in extraversion-intraversion,* vol. 3: *Bearings on basic psychological processes.* London: Staples, 1971 (paper originally published in *Journal of Nervous and Mental Diseases,* 1958, *126,* 141–147).

Shepher, J. (1971). Mate selection among second generation kibbutz adolescents and adults: Incest avoidance and negative imprinting. *Archives of Sexual Behavior, 1,* 293–307.

Shevrin, H., & Dickman, S. (1980). The psychological unconscious: A necessary assumption for all psychological theory? *American Psychologist, 35,* 421–434. New York: The Analytic Press (Lawrence Erlbaum).

Siegal, Nancy L. (1999). *Entwined lives: Twins and what they tell us about human behavior.* New York: Dutton.

Singh, D. (1993). Adaptive significance of waist-to-hip ration and female physical attractiveness. *Journal of Personality and Social Psychology, 65,* 293–307.

Singh, D. & Luis, S. (1995). Ethnic and gender consensus for the effect of waist-to-hip ratio on judgments of women's attractiveness. *Human Nature, 6,* 51–65.

Singh, D. & Young, R.K. (1995). Body weight, waist-to-hip ratio, breasts, and hips: Role in judgments of female attractiveness and desirability for relationships. *Ethology and Sociobiology, 16,* 483–507.

Silverstein, B. (1984). Psychoanalyzing psychoanalysis: Freud and the hidden fault of the father: A book review. *Review of Psychoanalytic Books, 3,* 333–343.

(1985). Freud's psychology and its organic foundation: Sexuality and mind-body interactionism. *The Psychoanalytic Review, 72,* 204–228.

(1988). Will the real Freud stand up, please? *American Psychologist, 43*(8), 662–664.

(1989a). Oedipal politics and scientific creativity: Freud's 1915 phylogenetic fantasy. *The Psychoanalytic Review, 76*(3), 403–424.

(1989b). Contributions to the history of psychology: LVIII. Freud's dualistic mind-body interactionism: Implications for the development of his psychology. *Psychological Reports, 64,* 1091–1097.

Sipprelle, C. R., Ascough, J. C., Detrio, D. M., & Horst, P. A. (1977). "Neuroticism, extroversion, and response to stress." *Behavior Research and Therapy, 15,* 411–418.

Skinner, B. F. (1938). *The behavior of organisms.* New York: Appleton Century Crofts, 1966.

(1950). Are theories of learning necessary? *Psychological Review, 57,* 193–216.

(1953). *Science and human behavior.* New York: Free Press.

(1968). Conversation with R. I. Evans. In R. I. Evans, *B. F. Skinner: The man and his ideas.* New York: Dutton.

(1971). *Beyond freedom and dignity.* New York: Knopf.

(1974). *About behaviorism.* New York: Knopf.

(1975). The steep and thorny way to a science of behavior. *American Psychologist, 30,* 42–49.

(1976). *Particulars of my life.* New York: Knopf.

(1978). *Reflections on behaviorism and society.* Englewood Cliffs, NJ: Prentice-Hall.

(1979). *The shaping of a behaviorist.* New York: Knopf.

(1981). Selection by consequences. *Science, 213,* 501–504.

(1983). *A matter of consequences.* New York: Knopf.

(1983a). *Personal telephone communication with Sollod, R.*

(1987a). What is wrong with daily life in the western world? *American Psychologist, 41*(5), 568–574.

(1987b). Whatever happened to psychology as the science of behavior? *American Psychologist, 42*(8), 780–786.

(1989). The origins of cognitive thought. *American Psychologist, 44*(1), 13–18.

Skinner, B. F., & Vaughn, M. E. (1983). *Enjoy old age: Living fully in your later years.* New York: Warner Books (W. W. Norton).

Sollod, R.N. (1978). Carl Rogers and the origins of client-centered therapy. *Professional Psychology,* 93–104.

Solomon, R. L., & Wynne, L. C. (1954). Traumatic avoidance learning: The principles of anxiety conservation and partial irreversibility. *Psychological Review, 61,* 353–385.

Solomon, R. L., Kamin, L. J., Wynne, L. C. (1953). Traumatic avoidance learning: The outcomes of several extinction procedures with dogs. *Journal of Abnormal and Social Psychology, 48,* 291–302.

Solomon, R. C. (1974). Freud's neurological theory of mind. In R. Wolheim (Ed.), *Freud: A collection of critical essays.* Garden City, NY: Doubleday.

Sprecher, S. Sullivan, Q., & Hatfield, E. (1994). Mate selection preferences: Gender differences examined in a national sample. *Journal of Personality and Social Psychology, 66,* 1074–1080.

Stepansky, P. E. (1983). *In Freud's shadow: Adler in context.* Hillsdale, NJ: The Analytic Press (Lawrence Erlbaum Associates).

(Ed.). (1988). Introduction in M. S. Mahler, *The memoirs of Margaret S. Mahler.* New York: The Free Press.

Stephenson, W. (1953). *The study of behavior: Q-technique and its methodology.* Chicago: University of Chicago Press.

Stern, D. N. (1985). *The interpersonal world of the infant: A view from psychoanalysis and developmental psychology.* New York: Basic Books.

Stern, Paul J. (1976). *C. G. Jung: The haunted prophet.* New York: Braziller.

Stolorow, R. D., & Atwood, G. E. (1976). An ego-psychological analysis of the work and life of Otto Rank in the light of modern conceptions of narcissism. *The International Review of Psychoanalysis, 3,* 441–459.

(1978). A defensive-restitutive function of Freud's theory of psychosexual development. *The Psychoanalytic Review, 65,* 217–238.

(1979). *Faces in a cloud: Subjectivity in personality theory.* New York: Aronson.

Storr, A. (1984). Did Freud have clay feet? *New York Times Book Review,* February 1984, 3 and 35.

Sullivan, H. S. (1953a). *Conceptions of modern psychiatry.* New York: Norton.

(1953b). *The interpersonal theory of psychiatry.* New York: Norton.

(1956). *Clinical studies in psychiatry.* New York: Norton.

(1962). *Schizophrenia as a human process.* New York: Norton.

(1964). *The fusion of psychiatry and social science.* New York: Norton.

(1972). *Personal psychopathology.* New York: Norton.

Sulloway, F. J. (1979). *Freud: Biologist of the mind.* New York: Basic Books.

Summers, F. (1994). *Object relations theories and psychopathology.* Hillsdale, NJ: The Analytic Press.

Sutton, N. (1996). *Bettelheim: A life and a legacy.* New York: Basic Books.

Swick-Perry, Helen. (1962). Editor's introduction to H. S. Sullivan, *Schizophrenia as a human process.* New York: Norton.

(1982). *Psychiatrist of America: The life of Harry Stack Sullivan.* Cambridge, MA: Belknap Press of Harvard University.

Taft, J. (1951). *The dynamics of therapy in a controlled relationship.* New York: Harper.

Tattersall, I. (1998). *Becoming human: Evolution and human uniqueness.* New York: Harcourt Brace.

Thompson, C. (1962). Harry Stack Sullivan, the man. In H. S. Sullivan, *Schizophrenia as a human process.* New York: Norton (first published in *Psychiatry,* 1949, *12,* 435–437).

Thorndike, E. L. (1911). *Animal intelligence.* New York: Macmillan.

Thornhill, R. & Gangestad, S (1994). Human fluctuating symmetry and sexual behavior. *Psychological Science, 5,* pp. 297–302.

Tillich, P. (1952). *The courage to be.* New Haven, CT: Yale University Press.

Tooby, J. & DeVore, I. (1987). The reconstruction of hominid behavioral evolution through strategic modeling. In W. Kinzey, (Ed.) *Primate models of the origin of human behavior* (pp. 183–237). New York: SUNY Press

Torrey, F., E., Bowler, A. E., Taylor, E. H., & Gottesman, I. I. (1994). *Schizophrenia and manic-depressive disorder.* New York: Basic Books.

Trivers, R.L. (1971). The evolution of reciprocal altruism. *Quarterly Review of Biology, 46,* pp. 35–37.

Vaihinger, H. (1911). *The philosophy of "as if."* New York: Harcourt, Brace and World, 1925.

Vaillant, G. E. (1994). Ego mechanisms of defense and personality psychopathology. *Journal of Abnormal Psychology, 103,* 44–50.

Van den Berg, J.H. (1961). *The changing nature of man.* New York: Pantheon.

Van der Post, L. (1975). *Jung and the story of our time.* New York: Pantheon.

Vaugan, F., & Walsh, R. (2000). Transpersonal psychology. A. E. Kazdin (Ed.), *Encyclopedia of psychology, 8,* 111–114.

Vitz, Paul (1977). *Psychology as religion: The cult of self worship.* Grand Rapids, MI: Eerdmans.

(1988). *Sigmund Freud's Christian unconscious.* New York: Guilford Press.

Wallace, E. R. (1976). Thanatos—A reevaluation. *Psychiatry, 39,* 386–393.

(1977). The psychodynamic determinants of *Moses and Monotheism. Psychiatry, 40,* 79–87.

(1978). Freud's father conflict: The history of a dynamic. *Psychiatry, 41,* 33–56.

Wallach, M. & Wallach, L. (1983). *Psychology's sanction for selfishness: The error of egoism in theory and therapy.* San Francisco, CA: W.H. Freeman.

Watson, D., Clark, L. A., & Harkness, A. R. (1994). Structures of personality and their relevance to psychopathology. *Journal of Abnormal Psychology, 103,* 18–31.

Watson, G. (1940). Areas of agreement in psychotherapy. *American Journal of Orthopsychiatry, 10,* 698–710.

Watson, J. B. (1913). Psychology as the behaviorist views it. *Psychological Review, 20,* 158–177.

(1914). *Behavior: An introduction to comparative psychology.* New York: Holt, Rinehart and Winston, 1967.

(1924/1930). *Behaviorism.* New York: Norton.

(1936). Autobiography. In C. Murchison (Ed.), *A history of psychology in autobiography,* vol. III. Worcester, MA: Clark University Press.

Watson, J. B., & Rayner, R. (1920). Conditioned emotional reactions. *Journal of Experimental Psychology, 3,* 1–14.

(1928). *Psychological care of infant and child.* New York: Norton.

Watson, R. I. (1963). *The great psychologists.* Philadelphia: Lippincott.

(1978). *The great psychologists* (4th ed.). Philadelphia: Lippincott.

Westermarck, E. A. (1891). *The history of human marriage.* London: MacMillan.

White, M. J. (1977). Sullivan and treatment. *Contemporary Psychoanalysis, 13,* 317–346.

White, R. S. (1960). Competence and the psychosexual stages of development. In S. R. Maddi (Ed.), *Perspectives on personality.* Boston: Little Brown, 1971 (Originally published in M. R.

Jones (Ed.), *Nebraska symposium on motivation.* Lincoln: University of Nebraska Press, 1960).

White, R. W. (1959). Motivation reconsidered: The concept of competence. *Psychological Review, 66,* 297–333.

(1960). Competence and the psychosexual stages of development. In S. R. Maddi (Ed.), *Perspectives on personality.* Boston: Little Brown, 1971 (Originally published in M. R. Jones (Ed.), *Nebraska symposium on motivation.* Lincoln: University of Nebraska Press, 1960).

(1981). Exploring personality the long way: The study of lives. In A. I. Rabin, J. Aronoff, A. M. Barclay, & R. A. Zucker (Eds.). *Further explorations in personality.* New York: Wiley-Interscience.

Wiederman, M. (1993). Evolved gender differences in mate selection: Evidence from personal advertisements. *Ethology and Sociology, 14,* 331–352.

Wiederman, M. & Allgeier, E. (1992). Gender differences in mate selection criteria: Sociobiological or socioeconomic explanations? *Ethology and Sociobiology, 13,* 115–124.

Wilson, C. (1972). *New pathways in psychology.* New York: Taplinger Publishing Co.

Wilson, Edward O. (1959). Adaptive shift and dispersal in a tropical ant fauna, *Evolution 13*(1), pp. 122–144.

(1971). *The insect societies.* Cambridge MA: Harvard University Press.

(1975). *Sociobiology: The new synthesis.* Cambridge, MA: Harvard University Press.

(1978). *On human nature.* Cambridge, MA: Harvard University Press.

(1984). *Biophilia.* Cambridge, MA: Harvard University Press.

(1994). *Naturalist.* Washington, DC: Island Press.

(2001). Personal communication. May 25, 2001.

Windelband, W. (1894). *History and natural science.* Strassburg, Germany: Heitz.

Winnicott, C. (1978). D. W. W.: A reflection. In S. A. Grolnick & L. Barkin (Eds.), *Between reality and fantasy: Transitional objects and phenomena* (15–33). New York: Jason Aronson.

(1983/1991). Interview with M. Neve. In P. L. Rudnytsky, *The psychoanalytic vocation: Rank, Winnicott and the legacy of Freud* (181–193). New Haven: Yale University Press.

(1989). D. W. W.: A reflection. In C. Winnicott, R. Shepherd, & M. Davis, *Psychoanalytic explorations.* Cambridge, MA: Harvard University

Press. (For an earlier version, see C. Winnicott, 1978).

Winnicott, D. W. (1931a/1992). A note on normality and anxiety. In D. W. Winnicott, *Through paediatrics to psycho-analysis. Collected papers.* (3–21). New York: Bruner-Mazel.

(1931b/1992). Fidgetiness. In D. W. Winnicott, *Through paediatrics to psycho-analysis. Collected papers* (22–30). New York: Bruner-Mazel.

(1935/1992). The manic defence. In *Through paediatrics to psycho-analysis. Collected papers* (129–144). New York: Bruner-Mazel.

(1936/1992). Appetite and emotional disorder. In D. W. Winnicott, *Through paediatrics to psychoanalysis. Collected papers* (33–51). New York: Bruner-Mazel.

(1941/1992). The observation of infants in a set situation. In D. W. Winnicott, *Through paediatrics to psycho-analysis. Collected papers* (52–69). New York: Bruner-Mazel.

(1944/1992). Ocular psychoneuroses of childhood. In D. W. Winnicott, *Through paediatrics to psycho-analysis. Collected papers* (85–90). New York: Bruner-Mazel.

(1945a). Primitive emotional development. In *Through paediatrics to psycho-analysis. Collected papers* (145–156). New York: Bruner-Mazel (Collection originally published: New York: Basic Books, 1958).

(1945b/1996) Towards an objective study of human nature. In D. W. Winnicott, *Thinking about children* (3–12). R. Shepherd, J. Johns, & H. T. Robinson (Eds.). Reading, MA: Addison-Wesley.

(1948a/1996). Primary introduction to external reality: The early stages. In D. W. Winnicott, *Thinking about children* (21–28). R. Shepherd, J. Johns, & H. T. Robinson (Eds.). Reading, MA: Addison-Wesley.

(1948b/1996). Environmental needs; the early stages; total dependence and essential independence. In D. W. Winnicott, *Thinking about children* (29–36). R. Shepherd, J. Johns, & H. T. Robinson (Eds.). Reading, MA: Addison-Wesley.

(1948c/1992). Paediatrics and psychiatry. In D. W. Winnicott, *Through paediatrics to psychoanalysis. Collected papers* (157–173). New York: Bruner-Mazel.

(1948d/1992). Reparation in respect of mother's organized defence against depression. In D. W. Winnicott, *Through paediatrics to psychoanalysis. Collected papers.* (91–96). New York: Bruner-Mazel.

(1951/1992). Transitional objects and transitional phenomena. In D. W. Winnicott, *Through paediatrics to psycho-analysis. Collected papers.* (229–242). New York: Bruner-Mazel.

(1952). Anxiety associated with insecurity. In D. W. Winnicott, *Through paediatrics to psychoanalysis. Collected papers.* (97–100). New York: Bruner-Mazel.

(1954–55/1992). The depressive position in normal emotional development. In *Through paediatrics to psycho-analysis. Collected papers* (262–277). New York: Bruner-Mazel.

(1955/1989). Private practice. In D. W. Winnicott, R. Shepherd, and M. Davis (Eds.), *Psychoanalytic explorations* (291–298). Cambridge, Mass: Harvard University Press.

(1956/1992). Primary maternal preoccupations. In *Through paediatrics to psychoanalysis. Collected papers* (300–305). New York: Bruner-Mazel (Collection originally published: New York: Basic Books, 1958).

(1957/1965c) Advising parents. In D. W. Winnicott, *The family and individual development* (114–120). Great Britain: Tavistock.

(1958/1965c) Theoretical statement of the field of child psychiatry. In D. W. Winnicott, *The family and individual development* (97–105). Great Britain: Tavistock.

(1959/1989). The fate of the transitional object. In *Psychoanalytic explorations* (53–58). C. Winnicott, R. Shepherd, & M. Davis (Eds.). Cambridge, Mass: Harvard University Press.

(1960a/1965a). String: A technique of communication. In D. W. Winnicott, *The maturational processes and the facilitating environment. Studies in the theory of emotional development* (153–157). New York: International Universities Press (Originally published: *Journal of Child Psychology and Psychiatry,* 1960, *1,* 49–52).

(1960b/1965a). Ego integration in child development. In D. W. Winnicott, *The maturational processes and the facilitating environment. Studies in the theory of emotional development* (56–63). New York: International Universities Press.

(1960c/1965a). Ego distortion in terms of true and false self. In D. W. Winnicott, *The maturational processes and the facilitating environment. Studies in the theory of emotional development* (140–152). New York: International Universities Press.

(1961a/1989). Psycho-neurosis in childhood. In *Psychoanalytic explorations* (64–72). C. Winnicott, R. Shepherd, & M. Davis (Eds.). Cambridge, Mass: Harvard University Press.

(1961b/1990). Varieties of psychotherapy. In D. W. Winnicott, *Deprivation and delinquency* (232–240). C. Winnicott, R. Shepherd, & M. Davis (Eds.). Great Britain: Tavistock/Routledge.

(1962a/1965a). The aims of psychoanalytical treatment. In D. W. Winnicott, *The maturational processes and the facilitating environment. Studies in the theory of emotional development* (166–170). New York: International Universities Press.

(1962b/1965a). A personal view of the Kleinian contribution. In D. W. Winnicott, *The maturational processes and the facilitating environment. Studies in the theory of emotional development* (171–178). New York: International Universities Press.

(1962c/1965a). Ego integration in child development. In D. W. Winnicott, *The maturational processes and the facilitating environment. Studies in the theory of emotional development.* pp. 56–63. New York: International Universities Press.

(1963a/1965a). Training for child psychiatry. In D. W. Winnicott. *The maturational processes and the facilitating environment. Studies in the theory of emotional development* (193–202). New York: International Universities Press. (Originally published: *Journal of Child Psychology and Psychiatry,* 1963, *4,* 85–89).

(1963b/1989) D. W. W.'s dream related to reviewing Jung. In *Psychoanalytic explorations* (228–230)). C. Winnicott, R. Shepherd, & M. Davis (Eds.). Cambridge, Mass: Harvard University Press.

(1964a). *The child, the family, and the outside world.* Reading MA: Addison-Wesley (alternate edition: Pelican Books, 1964).

(1964b/1989). The squiggle game. In *Psychoanalytic explorations* (299–317). C. Winnicott, R. Shepherd, and M. Davis (Eds.). Cambridge, Mass: Harvard University Press.

(1964c/1987). The newborn and his mother. In D. W. Winnicott, (1987). *Babies and their mothers* (35–50). C. Winnicott, R. Shepherd, & M. Davis (Eds.). Reading, MA: Addison-Wesley.

(1964d/1986). The concept of the false self. In D. W. Winnicott, *Home is where we start from.* C. W. Winnicott, R. Shepherd, & M. Davis (Eds.). New York: Norton.

(1965a). *The maturational processes and the facilitating environment. Studies in the theory of emotional development.* New York: International Universities Press.

(1965b/1989). A child psychiatry case illustrating delayed reaction to loss. In C. Winnicott, R. Shepherd, & M. Davis (Eds.), *Psychoanalytic explorations* (341–368). Cambridge, MA: Harvard University Press.

(1965c/1989). Notes made on the train, part 2. In C. Winnicott, R. Shepherd, & M. Davis (Eds.), *Psychoanalytic explorations* (231–233). Cambridge, MA: Harvard University Press.

(1966a/1987). The beginning of the individual. In Winnicott, D. W. *Babies and their mothers* (51–58). C. Winnicott, R. Shepherd, & M. Davis (Eds.). Reading, MA: Addison-Wesley.

(1966b/1996). Autism. In D. W. Winnicott, *Thinking about children* (197–217). R. Shepherd, J. Johns, & H. T. Robinson (Eds.). Reading, MA: Addison-Wesley.

(1966c/1987). The ordinary devoted mother. In D. W. Winnicott, *Babies and their mothers* (3–14). C. Winnicott, R. Shepherd, M. Davis (Eds.). Reading, MA: Addison-Wesley.

(1967/1996). The aetiology of infantile schizophrenia in terms of adaptive failure. In D. W. Winnicott, *Thinking about children* (218–223). R. Shepherd, J. Johns, & H. T. Robinson (Eds.). Reading, MA: Addison-Wesley.

(1968a/1987). Communication between infant and mother, and mother and infant, compared and contrasted. In Winnicott, D. W. (1987). *Babies and their mothers* (89–103). C. Winnicott, R. Shepherd, & M. Davis (Eds.). Reading, MA: Addison-Wesley.

(1968b/1989). The use of an object and relating through identifications. In *Psychoanalytic explorations* (218–227). C. Winnicott, R. Shepherd, & M. Davis (Eds.). Cambridge, Mass: Harvard University Press.

(1969a/1986). The pill and the moon. In D. W. Winnicott, *Home is where we start from* (195–209). New York: Norton.

(1969b/1989). The use of an object in the context of *Moses and Monotheism.* In *Psychoanalytic explorations* (240–246). C. Winnicott, R. Shepherd, & M. Davis (Eds.). Cambridge, Mass: Harvard University Press.

(1969c/1989). Development of the theme of the mother's unconscious as discovered in psychoanalytic practice. In C. Winnicott, R. Shepherd,

& M. Davis (Eds.), *Psychoanalytic explorations* (247–250). Cambridge, MA: Harvard University Press.

(1969d/1989). The mother-infant experience of mutuality. In C. Winnicott, R. Shepherd, & M. Davis (Eds.), *Psychoanalytic explorations* (251–260). Cambridge, MA: Harvard University Press.

(1971). *Playing and reality.* Great Britain: Penguin Books.

(1972/1986). *Holding and interpretation: Fragment of an analysis.* New York: Grove Press.

(1989). *Psychoanalytic explorations.* C. Winnicott, R. Shepherd, and M. Davis (Eds.). Cambridge, MA: Harvard University Press.

(1992). *Through paediatrics to psycho-analysis. Collected papers.* New York: Bruner-Mazel (Originally published: New York: Basic Books, 1958).

(1993). *Talking to parents.* Reading MA: Addison-Wesley.

(1996a/1996). The niffle. In D. W. Winnicott, *Thinking about children* (104–109). R. Shepherd, J. Johns, & H. T. Robinson (Eds.). Reading, MA: Addison-Wesley.

Woodworth, R. S., & Schlosberg, H. (1954). *Experimental psychology* (rev. ed.). New York: Holt, Rinehart and Winston.

Yankelovich, D., & Barrett, W. (1970). *Ego and instinct.* New York: Vintage.

Yerkes, R. M., & Dodson, J. D. (1908). The relation of strength of stimulus to rapidity of habit formation. *Journal of Comparative and Physiological Psychology, 18,* 459–482.

Young-Bruehl, E. (1988). *Anna Freud: A biography.* New York: Summit Books (Simon and Schuster).

Young, Robert M. (1996). Evolution, biology and psychology from a Marxist point of view. In Parker, I., & Spears, R. Eds. *Psychology and society: Radical theory and practice.* Chicago: Pluto Press, pp. 35–49.

Zeigarnik, B. (1927). On finished and unfinished tasks. In W. D. Ellis (Ed.), *A source book of Gestalt psychology.* New York: Humanities Press, 1967.

Zilboorg, G. (1941). *A history of medical psychology.* New York: Norton.

Zimbardo, P. G., Haney, C., Banks, W. C., & Jaffe, D. (1974). The psychology of imprisonment: Privation, power and pathology. In Z. Rubin (Ed.), *Doing unto others: Explorations in social behavior.* Englewood Cliffs, NJ: Prentice-Hall. 61–73.

Zimmer, C. (2001). *Evolution: The triumph of an idea.* New York: Harper Collins.

Photo Credits

CHAPTER 1

Opener: Corbis Digital Stock.

CHAPTER 2

Opener: Hulton-Deutsch Collection/CORBIS. Page 25: Sigmund Freud Copyrights. Pages 26 & 29: Freud Museum, London/A.W. Freud, et al. Page 52: Sigmund Freud Copyrights. Page 61: General Research Division, The New York Public Library, Astor, Lenox and Tilden Foundations.

CHAPTER 3

Opener: Corbis-Bettmann. Page 96: Library of Congress.

CHAPTER 4

Opener: National Library of Medicine. Page 123: Library of Congress. Page 149: Jung (1950b) "Concerning Mandala Symbolism." Pages 150–152: Jung (1950a).

CHAPTER 5

Opener: Corbis-Bettmann. Page 179: Erich Salomon/Magnum Photos, Inc.

CHAPTER 6

Opener *(left):* Corbis-Bettmann. Opener *(right):* Courtesy Margaret Mahler Research Foundation. www.margaretmahler.org. Page 194: © Hulton/Archive/Getty Images. Page 201: Corbis-Bettmann. Page 203: Freud Museum, London/A.W. Freud, et al.

CHAPTER 7

Opener *(left & center):* © The Wellcome Trust Medical Photographic Library, London. Opener *(right):* Courtesy of McLean Library's

Franz/Alexander Archives of Psychoanalytic History. Page 244: anonymous. Pages 246–248 & 250: Reprinted with the permission of The Free Press, a Division of Simon & Schuster from *The Writings of Melanie Klein, Volume IV: Narrative of A Child Analysis,* by Melanie Klein. © 1961 by The Melanie Klein Trust. Page 275: © The Wellcome Trust Medical Photographic Library, London. Page 278: Reprinted from *Drives, Affects, Behavior,* by Max Schur (ed.) by permission of International Universities Press, Inc. © 1965 by International Universities Press, Inc.

CHAPTER 8

Opener: Corbis-Bettmann.

CHAPTER 9

Opener: Stock Montage. Page 352: © James Inscoe Sullivan.

CHAPTER 10

Opener: Corbis-Bettmann.

CHAPTER 11

Opener: Corbis-Bettmann.

CHAPTER 12

Opener: Photo by Bernard Gotfryd. Page 423: From Rollo May, 1985, used by permission.

CHAPTER 13

Openers (left & right): Corbis-Bettmann. Page 455: © 1960 by Saul Steinberg. From the book, The Labyrinth. Harper Row. Originally published in *The New Yorker Magazine.*

CHAPTER 14

Opener *(left):* Archives of the History of American Psychology. Opener *(right):* Photo by Kathy Bendo.

CHAPTER 15

Opener: Courtesy Ralph Norman.

CHAPTER 16

Opener *(left):* Courtesy Yale University. Opener *(center):* Stella Kupferberg. Opener *(right):* Courtesy Albert Bandura.

CHAPTER 17

Opener: Stock Montage.

CHAPTER 18

Opener, pages 623 & 630: Courtesy E.O. Wilson.

Subject Index

Page references followed by italic *n* indicate material in footnotes. All mentions of Freud refer to Sigmund Freud unless written as "Anna Freud." Readers can look up names of the primary personologists in the Subject Index for a reminder of their respective personality theories. So, for example, if a person looked up Adler, he or she would find: "Adler's individual psychology, *See* Individual psychology," or "Jung's analytical psychology, *See* Analytical psychology."

A

Abnormal psychology, 7–8
Abreaction, 33
Absolute euphoria, 348, 367
Absolute narcissism, 302–303, 313
Absolute tension, 348, 367
Accusation, 176, 177, 188
Acropolis episode (Freud), 72–74
Active human agency, 10, 16. *See also* Human agency dimension
  recognition of self as active agent, 567–568
  trend toward in personality theories, 654–655
Active imagination, 147, 157
Actual self, 381, 392
Adaptive viewpoint, 86, 114
Adler's individual psychology, *See* Individual psychology
Adolescents. *See also* Genital stage; Psychosexual development; Psychosexual stages
  developmental epochs, 363–364
  emergence of self, 412
  humanistic trait and self theory on, 412, 413
  psychosocial stages (Erikson), 322, 330–332, 335
  self-efficacy development, 569–571, 573
Adults
  danger situations, 106
  humanistic trait and self theory on, 412, 413
  modes of experience (Sullivan), 344–345
  psychosocial stages (Erikson), 332–336

self-efficacy development, 571, 573
Advantageous comparison, 574, 581
Affiliative ritualization, 333, 341
Agapé, 435–436, 438, 446
Agentic approach, 559, 581
Aggression
  and conscience, 102
  and death instinct (Freud), 97
  and death instinct (Klein), 239–240, 253
  and infantile amnesia, 80, 81
  Kelly's views on, 547, 549
  and testosterone, 611
Aggression drive, 167–169, 178, 187, 188
  Lorenz on, 624
Aggressive strategies, 175–177, 188
Aggressive type, 370, 384, 393
Agreeableness, Big Five dimension, 613–614
Aim, of instincts, 88, 114
Albert B. conditioning (Watson), 495, 496–498
Allport's humanistic trait and self theory, *See* Humanistic trait and self theory
Altruism, 628, 632, 650
  reciprocal, 637, 638, 651
Altruistic surrender, 176
  as classic defense, 214, 233
Ambiverts, 610, 618
Amygdala, and impulsivity, 613
Anal-erotic personality, 60–61, 109
Anal frustration, 241–242, 311
Anal-retentive personality, 109
Anal sadism, 255–256
Anal stage, 54, 57–58, 59

and anxiety, 105, 106
Erikson's views on, 324
and Not-Me personification, 357
Analytical psychology (Jung), 14, 16, 117–118. *See also* Archetypes; Extrovert types; Introvert types
  attitude types, 141–142
  brief summary, 155
  collective unconscious, 125, 131, 133, 134–135, 156
  complexes, 119–120, 156
  development of self, 148–153
  evaluating, 153–154
  Eysenck's research into introversion-extroversion, 588–592
  individuation, 147–148, 155, 157
  Jung and Freud, 117–118, 132
  Jungian aspects of interpersonal theory, 346–348
  Jung's boyhood, themes from, 127–131
  Jung's concept of libido, 122–124, 155, 157
  Jung's Lamarckian views, 135, 631–632
  Jung's mystical experiences, 126–131
  Jung's perceptions of death, 160–161
  Jung's unlikely sources of insight, 124–127
  Jung's views on Freud's and Adler's clinical perspectives, 140–141
  mandalas, 149–153, 157
  personal experiences and resultant ideas summarized, 657

principles of equivalence and entropy, 123–124, 157
psyche functions, 142–144
psyche structure, 132–134, 157
word association studies, 118–122, 157
Androgens, and arousal, 611
Angst, 430–431, 446
Anima archetype, 137–138, 147, 156
Animus archetype, 137–138, 147, 156
Annihilation, 262
Anorexia, Frau Emmy von N., 32
Anticathexis, 83, 86, 114
Anti-Semitism
  and Bertha Pappenheim, 24
  and persecution of Freud, 96
  Jung's apparent anti-Semitism, 132
  and Margaret Mahler, 227–228
  and Melanie Klein in Hungary, 275
  and Erik Erikson's childhood, 317
  Eysenck's youthful questioning of, 587–588
Ant societies, Wilson's research into, 628–630
Anxiety
  Bandura's views on, 564–565, 575–578
  basic anxiety (Horney), 371–379, 390, 392
  equivalence of anxious words and thoughts, 555–557
  and helplessness, 513–514
  and impulsivity, 612–613
  and introversion, 589
  Kelly's views on, 546, 549

691

Name Index

Page references followed by italic *n* indicate names in footnotes.